T0189571

Lecture Notes in Computer Science   12384

Founding Editors

Gerhard Goos
Karlsruhe Institute of Technology, Karlsruhe, Germany
Juris Hartmanis
Cornell University, Ithaca, NY, USA

Editorial Board Members

Elisa Bertino
Purdue University, West Lafayette, IN, USA
Wen Gao
Peking University, Beijing, China
Bernhard Steffen 🆔
TU Dortmund University, Dortmund, Germany
Gerhard Woeginger 🆔
RWTH Aachen, Aachen, Germany
Moti Yung
Columbia University, New York, NY, USA

More information about this series at http://www.springer.com/series/7407

Dongxiao Yu · Falko Dressler ·
Jiguo Yu (Eds.)

Wireless Algorithms, Systems, and Applications

15th International Conference, WASA 2020
Qingdao, China, September 13–15, 2020
Proceedings, Part I

 Springer

Editors
Dongxiao Yu
Shandong University
Qingdao, China

Jiguo Yu
Qilu University of Technology
Jinan, China

Falko Dressler
TU Berlin
Berlin, Germany

ISSN 0302-9743 ISSN 1611-3349 (electronic)
Lecture Notes in Computer Science
ISBN 978-3-030-59015-4 ISBN 978-3-030-59016-1 (eBook)
https://doi.org/10.1007/978-3-030-59016-1

LNCS Sublibrary: SL1 – Theoretical Computer Science and General Issues

© Springer Nature Switzerland AG 2020
This work is subject to copyright. All rights are reserved by the Publisher, whether the whole or part of the material is concerned, specifically the rights of translation, reprinting, reuse of illustrations, recitation, broadcasting, reproduction on microfilms or in any other physical way, and transmission or information storage and retrieval, electronic adaptation, computer software, or by similar or dissimilar methodology now known or hereafter developed.
The use of general descriptive names, registered names, trademarks, service marks, etc. in this publication does not imply, even in the absence of a specific statement, that such names are exempt from the relevant protective laws and regulations and therefore free for general use.
The publisher, the authors and the editors are safe to assume that the advice and information in this book are believed to be true and accurate at the date of publication. Neither the publisher nor the authors or the editors give a warranty, expressed or implied, with respect to the material contained herein or for any errors or omissions that may have been made. The publisher remains neutral with regard to jurisdictional claims in published maps and institutional affiliations.

This Springer imprint is published by the registered company Springer Nature Switzerland AG
The registered company address is: Gewerbestrasse 11, 6330 Cham, Switzerland

Preface

The 15th International Conference on Wireless Algorithms, Systems, and Applications (WASA 2020) was held virtually during September 13–15, 2020. The conference focused on new ideas and recent advances in computer systems, wireless networks, distributed applications, and advanced algorithms that are pushing forward the new technologies for better information sharing, computer communication, and universal connected devices in various environments, especially in wireless networks. WASA has become a broad forum for computer theoreticians, system and application developers, and other professionals in networking related areas to present their ideas, solutions, and understandings of emerging technologies and challenges in computer systems, wireless networks, and advanced applications.

The technical program of WASA 2020 consisted of 67 regular papers and 14 short papers, selected by the Program Committee from 216 full submissions in response to the call for papers. All submissions were reviewed by the Program Committee members. These submissions cover many hot research topics, including machine learning algorithms for wireless systems and applications, Internet of Things (IoTs) and related wireless solutions, wireless networking for cyber-physical systems (CPSs), security and privacy solutions for wireless applications, blockchain solutions for mobile applications, mobile edge computing, wireless sensor networks, distributed and localized algorithm design and analysis, wireless crowdsourcing, mobile cloud computing, vehicular networks, wireless solutions for smart cities, wireless algorithms for smart grids, mobile social networks, mobile system security, storage systems for mobile applications, etc. First, we would like to thank all Program Committee members for their hard work in reviewing all submissions. Furthermore, we would like to extend our special thanks to the WASA Steering Committee for their consistent leadership and guidance; we also would like to thank the the local chairs (Prof. Feng Li and Prof. Jianbo Li), the publication chairs (Prof. Wei Li, Prof. Yi Liang, and Prof. Xiao Zhang), the publicity chair (Prof. Yanwei Zheng) and the Web chairs (Dr. Cheng Zhang, Dr. Qi Luo, and Dr. Jinfeng Dou) for their hard work in making WASA 2020 a success. In particular, we would like to thank all the authors for submitting and presenting their exciting ideas and solutions at the conference.

August 2020

Xiuzhen Cheng
Yinglong Wang
Dongxiao Yu
Falko Dressler
Jiguo Yu

Organization

Steering Committee Members

Xiuzhen Susan Cheng (Co-chair) The George Washington University, USA
Zhipeng Cai (Co-chair) Georgia State University, USA
Jiannong Cao Hong Kong Polytechnic University, Hong Kong, China
Ness Shroff The Ohio State University, USA
Wei Zhao University of Macau, Macau, China
PengJun Wan Illinois Institute of Technology, USA
Ty Znati University of Pittsburgh, USA
Xinbing Wang Shanghai Jiao Tong University, China

General Co-chairs

Yinglong Wang Qilu University of Technology, China
Xiuzhen Cheng Shandong University, China

Program Co-chairs

Dongxiao Yu Shandong University, China
Falko Dressler University of Paderborn, Germany
Jiguo Yu Qilu University of Technology, China

Publicity Co-chair

Yanwei Zheng Shandong University, China

Publication Co-chairs

Wei Li Georgia State University, USA
Yi Liang Georgia State University, USA
Xiao Zhang Shandong University, China

Local Co-chairs

Feng Li Shandong University, China
Jianbo Li Qingdao University, China

Web Co-chairs

Cheng Zhang   The George Washington University, USA
Qi Luo   Shandong University, China
Jinfeng Dou   Shandong University, China

Program Committee

Ashwin Ashok   Georgia State University, USA
Yu Bai   California State University Fullerton, USA
Ran Bi   Dalian University of Technology, China
Edoardo Biagioni   University of Hawaii at Manoa, USA
Salim Bitam   University of Biskra, Algeria
Azzedine Boukerche   SITE, Canada
Zhipeng Cai   Georgia State University, USA
Sriram Chellappan   University of South Florida, USA
Changlong Chen   Microsoft, USA
Fei Chen   Shenzhen University, China
Quan Chen   Guangdong University of Technology, China
Songqing Chen   George Mason University, USA
Xianfu Chen   VTT Technical Research Centre of Finland, Finland
Yingwen Chen   National University of Defense Technology, China
Siyao Cheng   Harbin Institute of Technology, China
Soufiene Djahel   Manchester Metropolitan University, UK
Yingfei Dong   University of Hawaii, USA
Zhuojun Duan   James Madison University, USA
Luca Foschini   University of Bologna, Italy
Jing Gao   Dalian University of Technology, China
Xiaofeng Gao   Shanghai Jiao Tong University, China
Sukhpal Singh Gill   Queen Mary University of London, UK
Daniel Graham   University of Virginia, USA
Meng Han   Kennesaw State University, USA
Zaobo He   Miami University, USA
Pengfei Hu   VMWare Inc., USA
Qiang-Sheng Hua   Huazhong University of Science and Technology,
                         China
Baohua Huang   Guangxi University, China
Yan Huang   Kennesaw State University, USA
Yan Huo   Beijing Jiaotong University, China
Holger Karl   University of Paderborn, Germany
Donghyun Kim   Georgia State University, USA
Hwangnam Kim   Korea University, South Korea
Abderrahmane Lakas   UAE University, UAE
Sanghwan Lee   Kookmin University, South Korea
Feng Li   IUPUI, USA
Feng Li   Shandong University, China

Fuliang Li	Northeastern University, USA
Peng Li	The University of Aizu, Japan
Ruinian Li	Bowling Green State University, USA
Wei Li	Georgia State University, USA
Yingshu Li	Georgia State University, USA
Zhenhua Li	Tsinghua University, China
Yi Liang	Georgia State University, USA
Yaguang Lin	Shaanxi Normal University, China
Bin Liu	Ocean University of China, China
Weimo Liu	The George Washington University, USA
Jun Luo	Nanyang Technological University, Singapore
Liran Ma	Texas Christian University, USA
Jian Mao	Beihang University, China
Bo Mei	Texas Christian University, USA
Hung Nguyen	Princeton University, USA
Li Ning	Shenzhen Institutes of Advanced Technology, China
Linwei Niu	West Virginia State University, USA
Pasquale Pace	University of Calabria, Italy
Claudio Palazzi	University of Padova, Italy
Junjie Pang	Qingdao University, China
Javier Parra-Arnau	Universitat Rovira i Virgili, Spain
Lianyong Qi	Qufu Normal University, China
Tie Qiu	Tianjin University, China
Ruben Rios	University of Malaga, Spain
Kazuya Sakai	Tokyo Metropolitan University, Japan
Bharath Kumar Samanthula	Montclair State University, USA
Oubbati-Omar Sami	University of Laghouat, Algeria
Kewei Sha	University of Houston-Clear Lake, USA
Zhaoyan Shen	Shandong University, China
Hao Sheng	Beihang University, China
Tuo Shi	Harbin Institute of Technology, China
Junggab Son	Kennesaw State University, USA
Riccardo Spolaor	University of Oxford, UK
Violet Syrotiuk	Arizona State University, USA
Guoming Tang	National University of Defense Technology, China
Srinivas Chakravarthi Thandu	Amazon, USA
Luis Urquiza	Universitat Politècnica de Catalunya, Spain
Chao Wang	North China University of Technology, China
Chaokun Wang	Tsinghua University, China
Tian Wang	Huaqiao University, China
Yawei Wang	The George Washington University, USA
Yingjie Wang	Yantai University, China
Zhibo Wang	Wuhan University, China
Alexander Wijesinha	Towson University, USA
Mike Wittie	Montana State University, USA

Hui Xia	Qingdao University, China
Yang Xiao	The University of Alabama, USA
Yinhao Xiao	The George Washington University, USA
Kaiqi Xiong	University of South Florida, USA
Kuai Xu	Arizona State University, USA
Wen Xu	Texas Woman's University, USA
Zhicheng Yang	PingAn Tech, US Research Lab, USA
Dongxiao Yu	Shandong University, China
Wei Yu	Towson University, USA
Sherali Zeadally	University of Kentucky, USA
Bowu Zhang	Marist College, USA
Cheng Zhang	The George Washington University, USA
Xiao Zhang	Shandong University, China
Yang Zhang	Wuhan University of Technology, China
Yong Zhang	Shenzhen Institutes of Advanced Technology, Chinese Academy of Sciences, China
Xu Zheng	University of Science and Technology of China, China
Yanwei Zheng	Shandong University, China
Jindan Zhu	Amazon, USA
Tongxin Zhu	Harbin Institute of Technology, China
Yifei Zou	The Hong Kong University, Hong Kong, China

Contents – Part I

Contents – Part II

Full Papers

Full Papers

Reinforcement Learning Based Group Event Invitation Algorithm

Chunyu Ai[1](✉), Wei Zhong[1], and Longjiang Guo[2,3]

[1] Division of Math and Computer Science, University of South Carolina Upstate, Spartanburg, SC 29303, USA
aic@uscupstate.edu
[2] Engineering Laboratory of Teaching Information Technology of Shaanxi Province, Xi'an 710119, China
[3] School of Computer Science, Shaanxi Normal University, Xi'an 710119, China

Abstract. Nowadays, we rely increasingly on mobile applications and social networking websites to organize group events and/or search events to participate. Most existing services and platforms focus on distributing event invitations based on user profiles thus neglecting the fact that event attendees can significantly affect each other's degree of satisfaction. To address this issue, we propose a reinforcement learning based group event invitation algorithm that can track relationships of users and use response rate and post-event reviews as feedback to guide invitation receiver selection process. Experimental results indicate that our proposed algorithm achieves better performance in term of satisfaction and connectivity of users when k-core algorithm and greedy search algorithm are compared.

Keywords: Group event · Event invitation distribution · Reinforcement learning · Q-Learning

1 Introduction

Popular social networks tend to have a large number of users and/or strong user engagement, and the usage of social network is highly diverse. Facebook, the first social network, has more than 1 billion monthly active users. There are 2 billion Internet users using social networks approximately. Due to increasingly use of smartphones and mobile social network applications, these figures are expected grow rapidly [2]. In the world there are 3.5 billion smartphone users based on Statista's statistical data in 2020; in other words, 45.04% population of the world owns a smartphone [1]. In addition, smart devices such as iWatch, Fitbit, and GPS watch are widely used by people who likes exercising and outdoor activities to track their performance. The collected information by smartphones and smart devices are valuable for learning users' habits and activity level. Due to a constant presence in our lives, social networks and smart devices have a strong social impact. Nowadays, social networks have emerged into our daily lives in every possible form [11, 13, 14, 17, 20].

© Springer Nature Switzerland AG 2020
D. Yu et al. (Eds.): WASA 2020, LNCS 12384, pp. 3–14, 2020.
https://doi.org/10.1007/978-3-030-59016-1_1

Social networks are valuable for users to search information, events, and activities and increase connections with others to attend virtual and offline activities together. More and more users use social network applications to organize and find online and offline events and activities to attend since using social network sites/apps to organize group activities and events is more efficient. Meetup, Plancast, Yahoo! Upcoming and Eventbrite are popular platforms for organizing events. Also, there are many regional club websites for organizing events and activities regionally. On these social networks, online or offline social events such as conferences, riding bikes, group yoga, and online gaming can be posted. Due to COVID-19 pandemic, more and more people attend various virtual activities. These platforms usually have very simple event invitation distribution mechanism. Most platforms distribute invitations according to user's subscription choices and their profiles. Obviously, the simple subscription and distribution approaches don't consider the satisfaction levels of users. Users have to spend tremendous time to find an event they really can enjoy from many invitations they received. If this is not improved, it is hard to keep current customers be active and attract more users.

The k-core method proposed in [3] was the first work to use historical data to select candidates to receive event invitations. Since the system guarantee that every invitation receiver has at least k friends invited as well, it effectively solves the common cold start issue of other platforms have. Also, it can improve response rate since users know their friends are invited as well. However, the satisfaction degrees of attendees cannot be guaranteed since not every invited friend will attend the event.

In this paper, we proposed a Reinforcement learning based Group event Invitation algorithm (RGI) to select invitation receivers step by step and use response results and post-event reviews as feedback to guide the system to make better choices. Moreover, we also addressed cold start, less active members, and low response rate issues. Most importantly, our proposed algorithm can efficiently improve degree of satisfaction of event attendees.

The main contributions of our work are as follows:

1. Define optimization goals for the group event invitation distribution system.
2. Design an efficient reward mechanism to guide the algorithm to make better selection iteratively.
3. Propose a reinforcement learning based algorithm to select invitation receivers.
4. Handle the low response rate or no response issue as early as possible during the step by step selection process.

The rest of the paper is organized as follows. The proposed reinforcement base group invitation algorithm is introduced in Sect. 2. Section 3 shows the simulation results. Section 4 reviews related work. Section 5 concludes our work.

2 Reinforcement Learning Based Invitation Algorithm

In this section, we introduce our proposed Reinforcement learning based Group event Invitation algorithm (RGI). A user can post an event, and of course the user who posts the event is the organizer of the event. The organizer of an event may invite other users as co-organizers or assistants. The event description includes all details of the event and also requirements of attendees. Our proposed RGI algorithm only chooses eligible users to send event invitations. The optimization goal of our algorithm is to maximize satisfaction levels of all event attendees.

2.1 Collecting and Recording Data

Whether a user enjoys participating in an event or not is heavily affected by other attendees as well. In order to improve the degrees of satisfaction of event attendees, the system collects and summarizes history data of smart devices of users and information of previous attending events. If a user uses a smart device such as smart phone, apple watch, and Fitbit to record their activities, history data of these smart devices can be utilized to create an activity profile for the user. In general, time, duration, and location of these solo activities or attended group events are recorded. Other than these general information, the criteria and details of different activities can be varied. For instance, for hiking, running, and cycling, the criteria of evaluating difficulty levels include pace and distance. However, for online video games, year of experience, level/rank, and favorite roles are necessary information to have an enjoyable team play. Also, the system can use the historical data of smart devices to learn daily schedule and frequent locations of users. After a user participates in a group event, he/she can rate the event, organizers and other attendees. Moreover, a user can rate another user as *dislike*, that means never willing to see that person again.

Possibly, a user never used any smart device to track activities or is not willing to share these historical data. Therefore, the system also gives users an option to fill their own profiles including interests, activities they like to attend, usual free time and acceptable event location ranges. Once these kind of users attend an event, their profiles are updated accordingly.

2.2 Problem Definition

After an event organizer posts an event with all necessary details such as time, location, minimal and maximal attendees, activity type and description, and requirements for attendees, the system needs to decide the list of users who receive event invitations. Most of event organizing applications either distribute event invitations according to users' subscribing filtering conditions or sending to all users. Primary disadvantages of these methods include 1) attractive invitations are swallowed up by tons of invitations, 2) cold start since users have no idea their friends or dislike users attending or not, and 3) don't consider attendees can affect each other's satisfaction at all.

To address the common issues of most event invitation methods, we define invitation distribution optimization goal of a group event E as follows:

$$maximize \sum_{i=1}^{n} S_i \qquad (1)$$

where n is the number of attendees of E and S_i is the satisfaction degree of Attendee A_i for event E. The event organizers play significant role. The system can set constraints for who can be an event organizer in order to guarantee satisfaction of most users. Only users attended some events already can post a new event and to be an organizer. For these organizers who receive too many negative reviews, the system will not allow them to post an event again until their rating is improved by co-organizing events with other organizers. Moreover, for each user, other attendees of the same event can affect the satisfaction degree significantly as well. So how to choose who will receive the event invitation becomes the key of the invitation distribution algorithm. After analyzing event reviews, we found out that usually a user rates an event with a higher score if their *friends* also attend it and there is no dislike attendee in the event. Specifically, *friends* can be real life friends or users attending the same event and giving each other positive reviews. This fact is very important for designing an effective algorithm of invitation distribution. The framework in [3] can guarantee that for each event invitation receiver there are at least k friends are invited as well. It seems like this method perfectly solves the problem. However, not every user will attend the event after receiving the invitation. For any user, it is possible that all their friends don't respond to the invitation; therefore, this approach cannot achieve the optimization goal. To solve this problem, instead of calculating the invitation list only once, our designed algorithm gradually discovers users to receive the invitation according to the respond result of sent invitations; thus, we can guarantee that every user has friends attending the event as well.

In this paper, $G = (V, E)$ represents a graph with a node set $V = V(G)$ and a directed edge set $E = E(G)$. A node $v \in V$ represents a user. V is a set of all users of the system. The system can use a user's profile to judge whether satisfying an event's requirements or not. Only users satisfy all event requirements can be invited. Invited users need to match activity difficulty level, be free during event scheduled time slot, and the event location should be within user's activity location range. Directed edge $e(u, v) \in E$ connecting node u and v indicates u and v attended same events before and w_{uv} is the weight of edge $e(u, v)$ which is the most recent rate user u received from user v. The rating value is -1 (dislike) or in the range $(0, 1]$, and negative value -1 means dislike and never willing to attend any event with that user again. If user u and v did attend events together, but user v did not rate user u, we set weight w_{uv} to 0.5.

With very high probability a user will rate another user similar as he/she did last time. Therefore, we can use history event rating results to guide how to choose invitation receivers in order to achieve the optimization goal.

Problem Definition. For given event E and graph $G = (V, E)$, discover a subgraph $G'(V', E')$ of G to

$$
\begin{aligned}
maximize \quad &\sum_{e(u,v)\in E'} w_{uv} \\
subject\ to \quad &E_{min} \leq |V'| \leq E_{max} \\
&O_E \in V'
\end{aligned}
\tag{2}
$$

where E_{min} and E_{max} are the minimum and maximum number of attendees of the event E respectively and O_E is the organizer of event E.

The system can control to choose which users to receive an event invitation but not who will respond and attend the event. Thus, the k-core method in [3] cannot achieve the optimization goal defined in Eq. 2. Our designed idea is to start discovering friends of organizers, then according to who respond to the invitation to continue to approach more users step by step until enough event invitation receivers respond to attend the event.

2.3 Reinforcement Learning Based Group Event Invitation Algorithm

Reinforcement learning is a popular method in machine learning domains and it is widely used for an environment with feedback to train an agent to learn without supervision. Agents choose actions based on a policy which can balance between exploration and exploitation [8]. Usually, traditional reinforcement learning problems have the following common characteristics:

1. Different actions lead to different rewards;
2. Rewards have delay;
3. The reward of an action relies on the current state.

These features match the event invitation problem. A user is considered as a state. Different selections of invitation receivers can be regarded as different actions. An invitation receiver's different responses (attend, don't attend, or no response) are feedback. The feedback is significant for making next step decisions.

Q-learning [19] is a temporal difference technique of reinforcement learning. The strength of Q-learning is able to find the optimal policy without requiring model of the environment. Therefore, we use the Q-Learning theory to model and analyze the group event invitation problem. The model includes an agent, state set S and a set of actions per state A. Each user is a state, and a user invites another user to attend an event is an action. Via applying an action $a \in A$, the agent can transfer from one to another state. A reward r is provided to the agent for performing an action. Table 1 shows the details of reward values for different types of feedback. Negative reward value defines a punishment decision since these behaviors can reduce the system performance and overall satisfaction of event attendees. The reward strategy has delay since the current event rewards can only be evaluated after the decisions of who are invited has been made. However, the rewards are helpful feedback for the agent to make better selections

Table 1. Parameter settings.

Parameter	Value
Reward of receiving a dislike	-1
Reward of giving a dislike	-1
Reward of canceling an event	-1
Reward of receiving a positive review	$score/max\_score$
Reward of one user accepting the invitation	1
Reward of response time	As shown in Eq. 3
Learning Rate α	0.2
Discount Factor γ	0.8
Exploration Probability ε	0.05
k	4

for the future events since users have habits and behaviors to follow a certain pattern.

Since the response of invited users is necessary for choosing who else are invited, the response time plays significant role for decision making. If a user never responds to an event invitation before the scheduled event time, the reward is 0. Otherwise, no matter the response is attending or not, the response time reward is calculated as in Eq. 3.

$$R_{response} = 1 - \frac{r_{time} - s_{time}}{e_{time} - s_{time}} \tag{3}$$

where e_{time} is the scheduled event time, s_{time} is the sending time of the invitation, and r_{time} is the user's response time. The earlier a user responds to an invitation, the higher the reward is.

$$Q = \begin{array}{c} \\ State \\ 0 \\ 1 \\ 2 \\ \vdots \\ n \end{array} \begin{array}{c} Action \\ 0 \ 1 \ 2 \ \cdots \ n \\ \left[\begin{array}{ccccc} -1 & & & \cdots & \\ & -1 & & \cdots & \\ & & -1 & \cdots & \\ \vdots & \vdots & \vdots & \ddots & \vdots \\ & & & \cdots & -1 \end{array} \right] \end{array} \tag{4}$$

The matrix as shown in Eq. 4 is used to store the quality values for each state and its actions. As we mentioned early, each state represents a user, and an action v from a state u means user u invites v to attend the event. Values on the diagonal are initialized to -1 because users don't invite themselves. The rest of values of the matrix are initialized randomly within range $[1, 10]$. The quality value of each action under each state is updated according to Eq. 5. α $(0 < \alpha \leq 1)$ is the learning rate defining how important the history data are. γ $(0 < \gamma \leq 1)$

is the discount factor which determines the importance of future rewards. r_t is the reward received after execution of action a_t at the state s_t. $\max\limits_{a} Q(s_{t+1}, a)$ is the possible max Q value of the next state.

$$Q^{new}(s_t, a_t) = (1 - \alpha)Q(s_t, a_t) + \alpha \times (r_t + \gamma \times \max\limits_{a} Q(s_{t+1}, a)) \qquad (5)$$

Algorithm 1. RGI Algorithm

1: Initialize Q-Value Matrix randomly
2: **for** each new posted event $E(u_{organizer}, Max, Min, Requirements, e_{time})$ **do**
3:     Find all eligible users $u \in V$ which satisfies all event requirements and add to set V'
4:     empty set C and A (C is candidate set and A is attendee set)
5:     Add $u_{organizer}$ to set C and A
6:     **if** $u_{organizer}$ invites other users as co-organizers or assistants **then**
7:         Add co-organizers and assistants to C and send event invitations to them.
8:     **end if**
9:     Applying the ε-greedy policy, $U_{organizer}$'s agent selects k users from V' to add to C and sends the invitation
10:    **while** $|A| < Max$ **do**
11:        **if** Receive an attending response from u **then**
12:            Add u to A
13:            User u's agent to select top k users from V' to add to C and send the invitation according to the ε-greedy policy
14:        **end if**
15:    **end while**
16:    **for** each user in C **do**
17:        obtain rewards and update Q matrix after the event
18:    **end for**
19: **end for**

The RGI algorithm is described in Algorithm 1. Max and Min are the maximum and minimum number of event attendees respectively. For each new posted event, all eligible users are discovered and added to set V'. When the agent searches users to receive the invitation, the ε-greedy policy is applied. In other words, the selection strategy is that each state has the probability of ε to explore (select an action randomly) and $(1 - \varepsilon)$ to develop (select an action with the largest Q-value). This policy can prevent a user always inviting same friends thus losing opportunities to meet new friends. The event organizer, $U_{organizer}$'s agent applies ε-greedy policy to find k users to receive the invitation. The value of k is determined by the system designer according to the number of users in the system and statistical information of events. If any invited user decides to attend the event, the system continues to use that user's agent and ε-greedy policy to invite k users to receive the invitation. This process continues until there are Max number of users attending the event or running out the time. It is very possible that a user is invited by more than one user, and this can actually increase the possibility of the user accepting the invitation.

2.4   Solving the Cold Start

If the first few invited users don't reply, the system does not even have a chance to invite more users. In order to solve this issue, from the time of posting a new event to the scheduled event time, the time duration is divided to M time slots evenly. We set a checkpoint at the end of each time slot, if $|A| < (Max/M) *$ $the\_number\_of\_current\_time\_slot$, that means the number of attending users is behind. So, for each user in A, if there is no invited user respond, the agent applies ε-greedy policy to invite another user. After the half number of time slots passed, if the response rate is still low, ε is doubled since the low response rate is caused by low connectivity quality of organizers and invited users. Increasing the probability of exploring can approach more users with better quality of connectivity.

3   Simulation

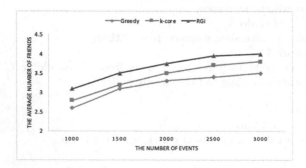

Fig. 1. The average number of friends with different number of events.

A general event invitation environment is simulated to test RGI performance. We create 3000 members with different free time schedules, interests, and activity levels. There are five difficulty levels. Higher level qualified members can attend lower level events, but not vice versa. Half amount of events don't define difficult levels. The activity location of each member is generated randomly within 200 mile diameter. For each member, a random response rate r (range $[0.1, 0.9]$) is generated. When a member receives an invitation, a random number r_e within $(0, 1)$ is generated. If $r_e < r$, the member responds to the invitation; otherwise, there will be no response. 70% of response is attending and 30% is not attending. Each invitation response has a random delay within the randomly generated range specifically for that user. Moreover, if the number of respondents is greater than the maximum group size, first come first serve principal is applied. We set 5% as the average rate that a member dislikes another member. In the post-event review, -1 is for dislike and positiver review scale is within $[1, 5]$.

First, we generate 1000 events to train the system. Then, we create 2000 events to test the performance of our proposed algorithm, RGI. The average number of friends and the minimum number of friends among event attendees are criteria to evaluate the efficiency of the proposed algorithms. All simulation results are the average of 10 runs. We compare our proposed RGI algorithm with the k-core and greedy search methods proposed in [3].

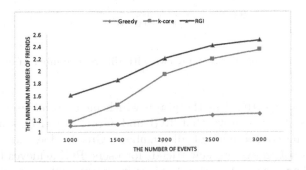

Fig. 2. The minimum number of friends with different number of events.

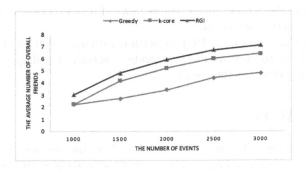

Fig. 3. The overall connectivity.

The average and the minimum number of friends with different number of events are shown in Fig. 1 and Fig. 2 respectively. The results indicate that the performance gets better and better after more and more events applied for all three methods. This is because the more events a member attended, he/she made more friends; thus, the connectivity of the graph is improved gradually. Our proposed RGI performs better than k-core algorithm due to its choosing process considers the feedback of response rate of users and post-event reviews. Both RGI and k-core algorithms are obviously better than Greedy search method because both of them can build connections among disconnected subgraphs but the greedy algorithm cannot.

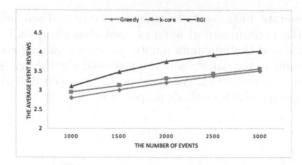

Fig. 4. The average event reviews with different number of events.

The overall connectivity of the graph which includes all users is shown in Fig. 3. The results also prove that RGI and k-core algorithms are beneficial to increasing the connectivity of all members. Greedy does not perform well since it prefers not to explore new friends for users. RGI achieves better overall connectivity than k-core algorithm because it always explores new friends with ε probability.

The user satisfaction degree is evaluated based on their post-event reviews. Figure 4 shows comparison results. Obviously, RGI achieves significant better user satisfaction degrees than k-core and Greedy methods. This is because when a user's agent decides who to invite, the reviews of past events play an important role for making better decisions.

In summary, the proposed RGI algorithm performs well in choosing event invitation receivers to improve event attendees' satisfaction degree and increase the overall connectivity of the society.

4 Related Work

Many websites and mobile applications such as Eventbrite(www.eventbrite.com) and Meetup provide event organizing services. The event invitation method of these websites and applications is very simple. Users can browse and search events and subscribe events in chosen categories. Event-based social networks are addressed in [15] and heavy-tailed degree distributions and strong locality of social interactions are discovered via analyzing data collected from Meetup. Moreover, event recommendation problems are studied. User response rate is evaluated in the simulation results. However, satisfaction of users to events is not considered. Partner matching problem is studied in [4,5], and the optimization goal of partner matching algorithm is to maximize stable partnerships. In this work, feedback of users is taken into account. Influence maximization problem of social events are studied in [6,9,10]. Both online social networks and physical world or environment are considered when the proposed propagation model was designed.

k-core and Greedy searching algorithms for choosing event invitation receivers are proposed in [3]. This was the first work which considers satisfaction of users. We compared our proposed algorithm with k-core and Greedy searching algorithms in Sect. 3. A reinforcement learning based expert search algorithm in social networks is studied in [16]. The proposed algorithm exploits Q-Learning to discover experts. It achieves better performance than simple search and referral algorithms.

A smart privacy protection framework for an event invitation system is proposed in [18]. A deception policy is studied to preserve privacy of smartphone owners in [21]. In [7,12] a data sanitization method is proposed to protect against inference attacks for gaining social relationship privacy of users. The approach can preserve both data benefits and social structure to achieve optimal latent-data privacy.

5   Conclusion

In this paper, the optimization goal of an event invitation system is defined, and we proposed a reinforcement learning based group event invitation distribution algorithm. The main contribution of this work is designing an effective rewarding mechanism to guide the agent to make better choices. The simulation results show that our proposed RGI algorithm performs well in all different aspects compared to existing methods.

Acknowledgement. This work is partially supported by the National Natural Science Foundation of China under Grant No.61977044, the Key R&D Program of Shaanxi Province under grant No.2020GY-221, 2020ZDLGY10-05, the Natural Science Basis Research Plan in Shaanxi Province of China under Grant No.2020JM-303, 2020JM-302), the Fundamental Research Funds for the Central Universities of China under Grant No.GK201903090.

References

1. How many smartphones are in the world (2020). https://www.bankmycell.com/blog/how-many-phones-are-in-the-world
2. Most popular social networks worldwide as of April 2020, ranked by number of active users (2020). https://www.statista.com/statistics/272014/global-social-networks-ranked-by-number-of-users/
3. Ai, C., Han, M., Wang, J., Yan, M.: An efficient social event invitation framework based on historical data of smart devices. In: 2016 IEEE International Conferences on Big Data and Cloud Computing (BDCloud), Social Computing and Networking (SocialCom), Sustainable Computing and Communications (SustainCom) (BDCloud-SocialCom-SustainCom), pp. 229–236 (2016)
4. Ai, C., Zhong, W., Yan, M., Gu, F.: Partner matching applications of social networks. In: Cai, Z., Zelikovsky, A., Bourgeois, A. (eds.) COCOON 2014. LNCS, vol. 8591, pp. 647–656. Springer, Cham (2014). https://doi.org/10.1007/978-3-319-08783-2_56

5. Ai, C., Zhong, W., Yan, M., Gu, F.: A partner-matching framework for social activity communities. Comput. Soc. Netw. **1**(1), 1–12 (2014). https://doi.org/10.1186/s40649-014-0005-0
6. Cai, J.L.Z., Yan, M., Li, Y.: Using crowdsourced data in location-based social networks to explore influence maximization. In: The 35th Annual IEEE International Conference on Computer Communications (INFOCOM 2016) (2016)
7. Cai, Z., He, Z., Guan, X., Li, Y.: Collective data-sanitization for preventing sensitive information inference attacks in social networks. IEEE Trans. Dependable Secur. Comput. **15**(4), 577–590 (2018)
8. Derhami, V., Majd, V.J., Ahmadabadi, M.N.: Exploration and exploitation balance management in fuzzy reinforcement learning. Fuzzy Sets Syst. **161**(4), 578–595 (2010). http://www.sciencedirect.com/science/article/pii/S0165011409002450, theme: Forecasting, Classification, and Learning
9. Han, M., Yan, M., Cai, Z., Li, Y.: An exploration of broader influence maximization in timeliness networks with opportunistic selection. J. Netw. Comput. Appl. **63**, 39–49 (2016)
10. Han, M., Yan, M., Cai, Z., Li, Y., Cai, X., Yu, J.: Influence maximization by probing partial communities in dynamic online social networks. Trans. Emerg. Telecommun. Technol. pp. n/a-n/a (2016). ett.3054
11. He, Z., Cai, Z., Wang, X.: Modeling propagation dynamics and developing optimized countermeasures for rumor spreading in online social networks. In: 2015 IEEE 35th International Conference on Distributed Computing Systems (ICDCS), pp. 205–214, June 2015
12. He, Z., Cai, Z., Yu, J.: Latent-data privacy preserving with customized data utility for social network data. IEEE Trans. Veh. Technol. **67**(1), 665–673 (2018)
13. He, Z., Cai, Z., Yu, J., Wang, X., Sun, Y., Li, Y.: Cost-efficient strategies for restraining rumor spreading in mobile social networks. IEEE Trans. Veh. Technol. **PP**(99), 1–1 (2016)
14. Kumar, R., Novak, J., Tomkins, A.: Structure and evolution of online social networks. In: Yu, P.S., Han, J., Faloutsos, C. (eds.) Link Mining: Models, Algorithms, and Applications, pp. 337–357. Springer, New York (2010). https://doi.org/10.1007/978-1-4419-6515-8_13
15. Liu, X., He, Q., Tian, Y., Lee, W.C., Mcpherson, J., Han, J.: Event-Based Social Networks: Linking the Online and Offline Social Worlds (2012)
16. Peyravi, F., Derhami, V., Latif, A.: Reinforcement learning based search (RLS) algorithm in social networks. In: 2015 The International Symposium on Artificial Intelligence and Signal Processing (AISP), pp. 206–210 (2015)
17. Szell, M., Lambiotte, R., Thurner, S.: Multirelational organization of large-scale social networks in an online world. Proc. Natl. Acad. Sci. **107**(31), 13636–13641 (2010)
18. Tong, W., Buglass, S., Li, J., Chen, L., Ai, C.: Smart and private social activity invitation framework based on historical data from smart devices. In: EAI, December 2017. https://doi.org/10.4108/eai.13-7-2017.2270271
19. Watkins, C.J., Dayan, P.: Q-learning. Mach. Learn. **8**(3–4), 279–292 (1992)
20. Xiang, R., Neville, J., Rogati, M.: Modeling relationship strength in online social networks. In: Proceedings of the 19th International Conference on World Wide Web, WWW 2010, pp. 981–990. ACM, New York (2010)
21. Zhang, L., Cai, Z., Wang, X.: Fakemask: a novel privacy preserving approach for smartphones. IEEE Trans. Netw. Serv. Manage. **13**(2), 335–348 (2016)

OSCD: An Online Charging Scheduling Algorithm to Optimize Cost and Smoothness

Yanhua Cao[1], Shiyou Qian[1(✉)], Qiushi Wang[1], Hanwen Hu[1], Weidong Zhu[2], Jian Cao[1], Guangtao Xue[1], Yanmin Zhu[1], and Minglu Li[3]

[1] Shanghai Jiao Tong University, Shanghai, China
{buttons,qshiyou,windows,shanghaijiaoda609,cao-jian,gt_xue,
yzhu}@sjtu.edu.cn
[2] Xuzhou University of Technology, Xuzhou, Jiangsu, China
zweidong@xzit.edu.cn
[3] Zhejiang Normal University, Jinhua, Zhejiang, China
mlli@sjtu.edu.cn

Abstract. A large number of electric vehicles (EVs) operating in cities result in huge charging demands. For a charging station, it is important to balance between the immediate charging cost and the future maintenance cost. In this paper, we model the two optimization objectives and employ the efficiency coefficient method to transform the two optimization objectives into a single one. In addition, we propose a heuristic algorithm called OSCD (Online Smooth Charging Decision) to coordinate the charging rate of EVs. To evaluate the effectiveness of OSCD, a series of simulations are conducted based on a real-world charging dataset of EVs. The results show that OSCD achieves a nice trade-off between cost and smoothness, while keeping the ratio of service rejection near zero.

Keywords: Electric vehicles · Online charging schedule · Cost · Smoothness

1 Introduction

Electric vehicles (EVs) have been attracting increasing attention in the transportation sector. To satisfy the huge charging demands of a large number of EVs, thousands of charging stations have been constructed, which are geographically distributed in the city [4]. For a charging station, it is important to balance between the immediate charging cost and the future maintenance cost under the premise of satisfying the charging demands of as many EVs as possible. However, due to the different charging demands of EVs and varying electricity prices, developing an online charging scheduling algorithm is challenging in practice.

To address this problem, many charging scheduling algorithms have been proposed [2,6,9,11,12,15]. For example, Tang et al. [12] propose an online charging algorithm that minimizes the charging cost without considering the smoothness of the charging rate of EVs at the charging period. However, most existing algorithms only optimize one goal, either minimizing the charging cost or maximizing the stability of the charging load.

© Springer Nature Switzerland AG 2020
D. Yu et al. (Eds.): WASA 2020, LNCS 12384, pp. 15–27, 2020.
https://doi.org/10.1007/978-3-030-59016-1_2

In this paper, we model the online charging schedule of EVs as a bi-objective optimization problem that minimizes the charging cost and maximizes the charging smoothness simultaneously. The goal is to stabilize the charging rate under the charging cost minimum. To solve this bi-objective optimization problem, we employ the efficiency coefficient method to transform the two optimization objectives into a single one. We also propose an online smooth charging decision (OSCD) algorithm to coordinate the charging rates of EVs at a charging station, which guarantees that the charging demands of EVs can be satisfied at a high ratio while maintaining a smooth charging rate with a low cost.

To evaluate the effectiveness and performance of our proposed algorithm, a series of simulations is conducted based on a real-world charging dataset of EVs collected in Shanghai, China. In the simulations, we consider three different scenarios, a light, moderate and heavy charging burden. We compare *OSCD* with three existing algorithms, namely MCT, ORCHARD [12] and CCR [2]. The simulation results demonstrate that OSCD can guarantee workload stability at a lower cost by making a nice trade-off between the charging cost and the smoothness of the charging rate.

The main contributions of this paper are summarized as follows. 1) We model the online charging schedule of EVs at a station as a bi-objective optimization problem. 2) We propose an online smooth charging decision algorithm to coordinate the charging of EVs. 3) We evaluate the effectiveness of OSCD by conducting a series of simulations on the real-world charging records of EVs.

2   Related Work

Most existing works aim at either minimizing the charging costs or maximizing the stability of the total charging load of the charging station.

2.1   Minimizing Charging Cost

Tang *et al.* [12] propose an efficient online charging decision algorithm called ORCHARD to minimize the energy cost. The work in [5] considers scheduling the charging and discharging of EVs in a small geographic area and proposes an online charging algorithm based on an assumption that no future EVs will arrive when a charging schedule is made. Valogianni *et al.* [14] present a coordination mechanism for variable-rate electric vehicle charging that allows independent decisions by self-interested EV agents. Turker *et al.* [13] deal with the problem of EV charging cost in the housing sector and propose three smart unidirectional and three smart bidirectional charging algorithms. The work in [8] proposes an online model-free mechanism that accommodates EVs with heterogeneous and flexible charging speeds per period, and the work in [10] presents a per-commitment mechanism to charge EVs by their reported departure time. However, these two works that analyze the performance of the algorithm do not provide a theoretical analysis. Malhotra *et al.* [7] propose a novel distributed algorithm to coordinate EV charging and eliminate the need for a central aggregator.

2.2   Stabilizing Charging Load

In order to balance the charging load, Bilh *et al.* [2] propose a novel charging algorithm which deals with stochastic fluctuations and uses the flexibility of EV loads to adjust the overall load to get a more desirable load profile. Cao *et al.* [3] propose an optimized EV charging model considering time of use price and state of charge (SOC) curve, which employs time-of-use pricing as an incentive to EV owners to shift the charging time of EVs to off-peak periods. One shortcoming of this approach is the possibility of forming a new peak at the beginning of the off-peak period when many EVs are likely to start charging simultaneously. Zhao *et al.* [15] present a peak-minimizing online EV charging decision algorithm which models the objective of the aggregator as minimizing the peak consumption from the grid under the constraints that all EVs must be charged before their deadlines. However, it ignores the smoothness of the charging rate of EVs.

In summary, most of existing algorithms consider only one goal. In this paper, we model the scheduling problem of EV charging at a station as a bi-objective optimization that minimizes the charging cost and maximizes the stability of the total load of the station at the same time under the premise of meeting the charging demands of as many EVs as possible.

3   Optimization Model

3.1   Problem Formulation

Let $d_i = [t_i^a, t_i^d, Q_i]$ represent the charging demand of EV i that arrives at the charging station at t_i^a, departs the station at t_i^d, and has the charging quantity Q_i in the unit of kWh. We define r_{it} as the charging rate of EV i at time t. Due to the battery constraint, EV i can be charged at a rate $r_{it} \in [0, \beta_i]$, where β_i is the maximum charging rate. We assume that R is the allowable maximum charging rate of the station, and let $\mathbb{I}(t)$ be the set of EVs being charged at time t. We define R_t as the total charging rate of the station at time t, $(0 \leq R_t \leq R)$ which is

$$R_t = \sum_{i \in \mathbb{I}(t)} r_{it}. \tag{1}$$

3.2   Optimizing Charging Cost

In this paper, we assume that the charging station pays a wholesale electricity cost in terms of the time-of-use price [3]. The price function with time is denoted by $\lambda(t)$ and λ^{min} denotes the minimum price. The optimization objective of minimizing the total charging cost is then formulated as

$$\min_{r_{it}} \int_{t=0}^{T} \lambda(t) R_t \, dt \tag{2}$$

s.t.

$$R_t \leq R, \quad t \in [0, T] \tag{3}$$

$$r_{it} \in [0, \beta_i], \quad i \in \mathbb{I}(t), t \in [0, T] \tag{4}$$

$$\int_{t_i^c}^{t_i^d} r_{it}\, dt = Q_i, \quad i \in \mathbb{I}(t). \tag{5}$$

$$|\mathbb{I}(t)| \leq N, \quad t \in [0, T] \tag{6}$$

where t_i^c is the time when EV i starts to charge and N is the total number of charging ports at the station. Equation (2) represents the total charging cost of the station until time T, which is determined as

$$T = max\{t_1^d, t_2^d, \cdots, t_{|\mathbb{I}(t)|}^d\}. \tag{7}$$

Constraint (3) restricts the total charging rate of the station to be below the maximum charging capacity R. Constraint (4) gives the definition of the decision variables. Constraint (5) guarantees that all the charging demands of EVs will be fulfilled. Constraint (6) restricts the number of charging vehicles to be below the total number of charging ports at the station.

3.3   Optimizing the Smoothness of Charging Station

We characterize the smoothness of the charging rate of the station as follows:

$$\int_{t=0}^{T} (R_t - \overline{R})^2\, dt, \tag{8}$$

where $\overline{R}$ is the average charging rate of the station and is calculated based on the historical charging data of the station. We define the objective of optimizing the smoothness of the charging station as follows:

$$\min_{r_{it}} \int_{t=0}^{T} (R_t - \overline{R})^2\, dt \tag{9}$$

s.t. (3), (4), (5), (6).

3.4   Transformation of Optimization Objectives

Since Eq. (2) and Eq. (9) have the same constraints, to optimize the two objectives simultaneously, we must find a suitable solution in the constraint domain. So, the two optimization objectives are defined as follows:

$$\min_{r_{it}} \int_{t=0}^{T} \lambda(t) R_t\, dt;$$
$$\min_{r_{it}} \int_{t=0}^{T} (R_t - \overline{R})^2\, dt \tag{10}$$

s.t. (3), (4), (5), (6).

Model Discretization. A close look at the two optimization objectives in Eq. (10) suggests that there are infinite values for variables r_{it} because time t is continuous. We realize the discretization by taking care of events such as the arrival or departure of EVs, the occurrence of electricity price change, or the expiration of the scanning period. When these kinds of events occur, the charging rate of EVs may need to be adjusted in order to optimize cost and smoothness. As the events occur in a sequential order, the time interval between two adjacent events is defined as a time slot. In each time slot, the charging rate of EVs remains constant, as utilized in [12].

Let r_{ik} denote the charging rate of EV i in time slot k which is initiated by an event occurring at time t, and $\lambda(k)$ be the electricity price in time slot k, so the total charging rate of the station in time slot k is

$$R_k = \sum_{i \in \mathbb{I}(t)} r_{ik}. \tag{11}$$

Therefore, we can equivalently transform the continuous optimization objectives expressed in Eq. (10) to the following form that has finitely many variables:

$$\min_{r_{ik}} \sum_{k \in \mathbb{S}} \lambda(k) R_k \delta_k;$$
$$\min_{r_{ik}} \sum_{k \in \mathbb{S}} (R_k - \overline{R})^2 \tag{12}$$

s.t.

$$R_k \leq R, \quad k \in \mathbb{S}, \tag{13}$$

$$r_{ik} \in [0, \beta_i], \quad i \in \mathbb{I}(k), k \in \mathbb{S}, \tag{14}$$

$$\sum_{k \in \mathbb{S}} r_{ik} \delta_k = Q_i, \quad i \in \mathbb{I}(k). \tag{15}$$

$$|\mathbb{I}(k)| \leq N, \quad k \in \mathbb{S} \tag{16}$$

where $\mathbb{S}$ is the set of time slots, $\mathbb{I}(k)$ denotes the set of charging EVs in slot k, and δ_k is the duration of time slot k.

We can see that the objectives and the constraints in the bi-objective optimization problem are all decoupled in different time slots, so it is equivalent to optimizing the two sub-problems for any time slot k:

$$f_1 : \min_{r_{ik}} \lambda(k) R_k;$$
$$f_2 : \min_{r_{ik}} (R_k - \overline{R})^2; \tag{17}$$

s.t. (13), (14), (16), (18).

$$\sum_{k \in \mathbb{S}(t, t_i^d)} r_{ik} \delta_k = RQ_{ik}, \quad i \in \mathbb{I}(k). \tag{18}$$

where RQ_{ik} denotes the residual quantity to be satisfied for EV i at the beginning of time slot k, and $\mathbb{S}(t, t_i^d)$ denotes the set of time slots from t to t_i^d.

Transformation from Two Objectives to a Single Objective. In the bi-objective optimization problem, if all the sub-objectives reach the optimal solution at the same time, this is called the absolute optimal solution. However, it is difficult to get the absolute optimal solution, so it is meaningful to find non-inferior solutions of the bi-objective optimization problem. In this paper, we employ the efficiency coefficient method to transform the bi-objective optimization problem into a single-objective optimization.

Definition 1. *The efficiency coefficient function p_i of f_i is*

$$p_i(x) = \frac{f_i^{max} - f_i(x)}{f_i^{max} - f_i^{min}},$$

and $p_i(x) \in [0, 1]$.

For the convenience of explanation, here we let

$$h_1(x) = \lambda(k)R_k;$$
$$h_2(x) = (R_k - \overline{R})^2.$$

Then, the two optimization objectives defined in Eq. (17) can be transformed to:

$$\min_{r_{ik}} h_1(x);$$
$$\min_{r_{ik}} h_2(x) \tag{19}$$

s.t. (13), (14), (16), (18).

For the two transformed objectives given in Eq. (19), based on Definition 1, we can get $p_1(x)$ and $p_2(x)$.

$$p_1(x) = \frac{h_1^{max} - h_1(x)}{h_1^{max} - h_1^{min}}, \tag{20}$$

$$p_2(x) = \frac{h_2^{max} - h_2(x)}{h_2^{max} - h_2^{min}}. \tag{21}$$

Let α be the weight of cost which is a super parameter. We define an evaluation function $COSM(x)$ as,

$$COSM(x) = \alpha p_1(x) + (1 - \alpha)p_2(x). \tag{22}$$

Therefore, we get a single-objective optimization problem as follows:

$$\max_{x_{ik}}(COSM(x)) \tag{23}$$

s.t. (13), (14), (16), (18).

4   Design of *OSCD*

4.1   Lower-Bound Charging Rate of EVs

Due to the limited charging capacity at the station, it is inevitable that some EVs need to wait in queue q during the peak charging periods. Whether charging or waiting, we define the Lower-Bound Charging Rate, $LBCR_{ik}$, of each EV i in time slot k that is initiated by an event occurring at time t as

$$LBCR_{ik} = \frac{RQ_{ik}}{t_i^d - t} \tag{24}$$

where RQ_{ik} is the residual charging quantity of EV i in time slot k and t_i^d is the departure time of EV i. $LBCR$ is used to compute the charging rate of EVs being charged and used as the criterion to reject some waiting EVs. Specifically, for any charging EV i, to meet its charging demand, its charging rate should not be smaller than $LBCR_{ik}$ in each time slot k, thus satisfying constraint (16). For any waiting EV i, when $LBCR_{ik} \geq \beta_i$ in time slot k, where β_i is the allowable maximum charging rate of EV i, the charging demand of EV i cannot be fulfilled.

4.2   OSCD Algorithm

The procedure of OSCD consists of four steps: updating parameters, computing the charging rates of charging EVs, selecting some waiting EVs from q, and preparing for some urgent waiting EVs. The pseudo code of OSCD is shown in Algorithm 1.

Updating Parameters. At the beginning of each time slot k, OSCD updates the following parameters: (1) the set of charging EVs $\mathbb{I}(k)$ as some charging EVs may depart from the station; (2) the current total charging rate R_k of all charging EVs in $\mathbb{I}(k)$; (3) the $LBCR_{ik}$ of all EVs, including both charging and waiting EVs; (4) the electricity price $\lambda(k)$ in time slot k.

Determining Charging Rates. For each charging EV i in $\mathbb{I}(k)$, OSCD computes its charging rate in time slot k based on the following formula,

$$r_{ik} = max(LBCR_{ik}, \frac{\lambda^{min}\beta_i}{\lambda(k)}), \quad i \in \mathbb{I}(k), \tag{25}$$

where λ^{min} is the minimum electricity price. To minimize the charging cost, OSCD recommends EV i to charge at the maximum charging rate β_i when time slot k lies in periods with the lowest price; otherwise, the charging rate decreases in proportion to $\frac{\lambda^{min}}{\lambda(k)}$ when time slot k is in other periods with a higher price. To optimize smoothness, the charging rate of EV i is lower-bounded at the rate $LBCR_{ik}$, upper-bounded by β_i and keeps constant in each time slot, avoiding frequent fluctuation.

Algorithm 1. OSCD

Require: New and finished charging requests, and changed electricity price
Ensure: r_{ik} for each charging EV i
1: At the beginning of each time slot k, update parameters.
2: Compute the charging rate r_{ik} of each EV i in $\mathbb{I}(k)$ according to Eq. (25).
3: **if** $R_k < R$ and $|\mathbb{I}(k)| < N$ **then**
4:     Select top M waiting EVs from q satisfying the constraint defined in Eq. (26).
5:     **if** There is enough charging capacity **then**
6:        Compute the charging rate of the M EVs according to Eq. (25)
7:     **else**
8:        Compute the charging rate of the top $M - 1$ EVs according to Eq. (25) and the charging rate of the Mth EV is $(R - R_k - \sum_{j=1}^{M-1} r_{jk})$.
9:     **end if**
10: **end if**
11: **for** Each urgent EV u in q satisfying Eq. (27) **do**
12:     **if** There exists a charging EV v satisfying Eq. (28) or (29) **then**
13:        Increase the charging rate of EV v to β_v and adjust the charging rate of other charging EVs in $\mathbb{I}(k)$.
14:     **else**
15:        Reject the charging request of EV u
16:     **end if**
17: **end for**

Selecting Waiting EVs from q. At the beginning of time slot k, given the charging rate of all charging EVs, we can get the total charging rate of station R_k. In a case where some charging EVs depart from the station, such that $R_k < R$ and $|\mathbb{I}(k)| < N$ where N is the total number of charging ports at the station, the top $M \le (N - |\mathbb{I}(k)|)$ waiting EVs are selected from q while satisfying the constraint

$$\sum_{j=1}^{M} r_{jk} \le R - R_k \tag{26}$$

If there is enough capacity for the M EVs, their charging rates are determined according to Eq. (25). Otherwise, the charging rates of the top $M - 1$ EVs are computed according to Eq. (25), and the charging rate of the Mth EV is $(R - R_k - \sum_{j=1}^{M-1} r_{jk})$.

Preparing for Urgently Waiting EVs in Advance. In peak periods, OSCD makes a trade-off between the number of EVs charged and the percentage of charging quantities fulfilled by a threshold ρ. We consider partially satisfying the charging quantity of EVs and set ρ $(0 \le \rho \le 1)$ as the ratio of an unsatisfying charging quantity in order to let some charging EVs leave the station earlier to vacate some charging ports for urgently waiting EVs.

When there are some EVs waiting in q, we need to consider each urgently waiting EV u such that it must start to charge in the next scanning period in order to satisfy even its partial charging quantity $(1 - \rho)Q_u$. Let ω be the

Table 1. Charging burden of a light (Sc.1), moderate (Sc.2) and heavy (Sc.3) scenario

Time	Sc.1	Sc.2	Sc.3	MPT (hour)	Charging quantity (kWh)
08:00–10:00	5	7	7	2.6	68.5
10:00–14:00	3	3	3	2.5	55.0
14:00–16:00	30	48	62	3.2	75.9
16:00–20:00	5	5	7	2.0	40.5
20:00–22:00	27	45	60	3.8	92.6
22:00–08:00	3	3	3	3.1	68.0

duration of scanning periods, the $LBCR$ of an urgently waiting EV u in the next scanning period satisfies the constraint

$$LBCR_u = \frac{(1-\rho)Q_u}{t_u^d - t - \omega} > \beta_u. \tag{27}$$

For each urgently waiting EV u, we select an EV v from the set of charging EVs satisfying the constraint

$$RQ_{vk} \leq \omega\beta_v \tag{28}$$

which means EV v can leave the charging station in the next scanning period when it is charged at the maximum rate β_v. If $\sum_{i\in\mathbb{I}(k)} r_{ik} = R$ and r_{vk} is increased to β_v, the charging rate of other charging EVs is updated to $r_{ik} = r_{ik} - \frac{\beta_v - r_{vk}}{|\mathbb{I}(k)|-1}$. If no EV v satisfies (28) in $\mathbb{I}(k)$, the OSCD algorithm searches for any EV v with less than ρ of residual charging quantity unsatisfied in the next scanning period,

$$RQ_{vk} - \rho Q_v \leq \omega\beta_v \tag{29}$$

For any EV v found, we expect it to leave the charging station in the next scanning period when it is charged at β_v, partially satisfying its charging quantity. If no charging EV v satisfies (28) or (29) in $\mathbb{I}(k)$, OSCD has to reject the charging request of the urgently waiting EV u immediately.

5 Performance Evaluation

5.1 Evaluation Settings

In the simulations, we use the charging records collected in September 2017 in Shanghai, China. Each record includes the start of the charging time of EVs, the completion time, the charging quantity and the charging cost. We consider three different scenarios that have different mean arrival, parking duration and charging quantity, as listed in Table 1, where the 2nd to 4th columns indicate the arrival rate of EVs (EVs/hour) and the MPT column denotes the mean

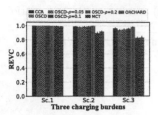

Fig. 1. Ratio of EVs charged.

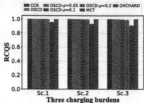

Fig. 2. Ratio of charging quantity satisfied

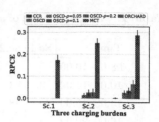

Fig. 3. Ratio of partially charged EVs

parking time (hours). Sc.1–3 represent a light, moderate and heavy charging burden, respectively. The time-of-use price is from the Shanghai Electric Power Company [1].

We compare OSCD using different ρ values with MCT, ORCHARD [12] and CCR [2]. MCT is a baseline method for minimizing charging cost. ORCHARD is an online coordinated charging decision algorithm which minimizes the energy cost without knowing the future information. CCR considers keeping the charging rate constant at β_i for each EV to optimize stability. Our proposed method has four variants in the simulations, namely OSCD, OSCD-$\rho = 0.05$, OSCD-$\rho = 0.1$ and OSCD-$\rho = 0.2$. By default, the number of charging ports in the station is set to $N = 35$. The maximum charging rate of each EV i is set to 70 kW, namely $\beta_i = 70$ kW. We set the maximum charging rate of the station $R = 70 * 35 = 2450$ kW. The duration of the scanning periods is set to $\omega = 18$ min.

We use five metrics to evaluate the performance of the scheduling algorithms: 1) ratio of EVs charged ($REVC$); 2) ratio of charging quantity satisfied ($RCQS$); 3) ratio of partially charged EVs ($RPCE$); 4) average charging cost per kWh; 5) workload variance.

5.2   Evaluation Results

Figure 1 shows the ratio of EVs charged at the station. All the seven algorithms work well under a light burden, but differences appear when the charging burden increases. Under a heavy burden, CCR can serve more than 96.6% of the EVs. As for MCT and ORCHARD, this figure is about 83%. When partial charging is not enabled, OSCD can serve 94.2% of the EVs. When $\rho = 0.2$, more than 98.7% of the EVs are served by OSCD, which is better than CCR.

As OSCD can terminate the charging of some EVs to vacate charging ports for urgent EVs, we analyze the average ratio of charging quantity satisfied for EVs in Fig. 2. For CCR, ORCHARD and OSCD, the charging electricity quantity of EVs is completely met. For MCT, the ratio is 90.8% on average. When $\rho > 0$, the variants of OSCD can meet more than 98% of the charging quantity of EVs on the whole, even when ρ is set to 0.2.

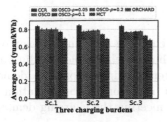

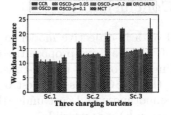

Fig. 4. Average charging cost per kWh   **Fig. 5.** Workload variance of station

We also count the ratio of partially charged EVs for each algorithm and the results are shown in Fig. 3. Under a heavy burden, the ratio of partially charged EVs is about 6.5% for OSCD when $\rho = 0.2$, which contributes to the high ratio of the charging quantity being satisfied, whereas the ratio of partially charged EVs reaches 28.7% for MCT, which explains why the ratio of charging quantity satisfied is the lowest, at 90.8%.

We analyze the average charging cost per kWh for the seven algorithms, as shown in Fig. 4. Of the seven algorithms, CCR has the highest cost while ORCHARD has the lowest. Compared with ORCHARD, OSCD costs about 12% more on average, but OSCD can serve about 15% more EVs than ORCHARD, as shown in Fig. 1.

The workload variance for the seven algorithms is shown in Fig. 5. MCT is the most stable and OSCD is the second, while CCR and ORCHARD have a variance over 21, therefore performing the worst. Under a heavy burden, OSCD improves smoothness by 36.9% over ORCHARD.

Table 2. The $COSM$ values defined in Eq. (22) of the seven algorithms

α	CCR	OSCD	OSCD-$\rho = 0.05$	OSCD-$\rho = 0.1$	OSCD-$\rho = 0.2$	MCT	ORCHARD
0.3	0.69	0.73	0.77	0.83	**0.90**	0.27	0.09
0.4	0.62	0.72	0.75	0.80	**0.85**	0.36	0.16
0.5	0.54	0.69	0.71	0.76	**0.79**	0.42	0.25
0.6	0.45	0.66	0.68	0.71	**0.73**	0.49	0.36
0.7	0.35	0.62	0.63	**0.66**	0.65	0.55	0.48

From the above analysis, we identify three attractive features of OSCD. 1) Strong service capability: When $\rho = 0.2$, OSCD can serve 98.7% of the EVs under a heavy burden and satisfy 98% of the charging quantity on the whole. 2) Nice trade-off between cost and smoothness: In terms of the $COSM$ values (defined in Eq. (22)) listed in Table 2, OSCD makes a nice trade-off between cost and smoothness. 3) Execution efficiency: The execution of OSCD is very efficient, taking only 0.85 ms on average.

6   Conclusion

Based on a bi-objective model to optimize the charging cost and the smoothness of workload, we propose the OSCD algorithm which is able to adjust the charging rate of EVs in real-time. Through extensive simulations, we demonstrate that OSCD has the best overall strength, realizing the optimization on both smoothness and cost under the premise of meeting the charging demands of as many EVs as possible.

Acknowledgments. This work was supported by National Key R&D Program of China (2018YFB2101100), the National Science Foundation of China (61772334, 61702151), and the Joint Key Project of the National Natural Science Foundation of China (U1736207).

References

1. Shanghai state grid electric power company (2018). http://www.sh.sgcc.com.cn
2. Bilh, A., Naik, K., El-Shatshat, R.: A novel online charging algorithm for electric vehicles under stochastic net-load. IEEE Trans. Smart Grid **9**(3), 1787–1799 (2016)
3. Cao, Y., et al.: An optimized EV charging model considering TOU price and SOC curve. IEEE Trans. Smart Grid **3**(1), 388–393 (2011)
4. Du, B., Tong, Y., Zhou, Z., Tao, Q., Zhou, W.: Demand-aware charger planning for electric vehicle sharing. In: Proceedings of the 24th ACM SIGKDD International Conference on Knowledge Discovery & Data Mining, pp. 1330–1338 (2018)
5. He, Y., Venkatesh, B., Guan, L.: Optimal scheduling for charging and discharging of electric vehicles. IEEE Trans. Smart Grid **3**(3), 1095–1105 (2012)
6. Kong, F., Liu, X., Sun, Z., Wang, Q.: Smart rate control and demand balancing for electric vehicle charging. In: 2016 ACM/IEEE 7th International Conference on Cyber-Physical Systems (ICCPS), pp. 1–10. IEEE (2016)
7. Malhotra, A., Binetti, G., Davoudi, A., Schizas, I.D.: Distributed power profile tracking for heterogeneous charging of electric vehicles. IEEE Trans. Smart Grid **8**(5), 2090–2099 (2016)
8. Robu, V., Stein, S., Gerding, E.H., Parkes, D.C., Rogers, A., Jennings, N.R.: An online mechanism for multi-speed electric vehicle charging. In: Coles, P., Das, S., Lahaie, S., Szymanski, B. (eds.) AMMA 2011. LNICST, vol. 80, pp. 100–112. Springer, Heidelberg (2012). https://doi.org/10.1007/978-3-642-30913-7_22
9. Savari, G.F., Krishnasamy, V., Sugavanam, V., Vakesan, K.: Optimal charging scheduling of electric vehicles in micro grids using priority algorithms and particle swarm optimization. Mobile Netw. Appl. **24**(6), 1835–1847 (2019)
10. Stein, S., Gerding, E., Robu, V., Jennings, N.R.: A model-based online mechanism with pre-commitment and its application to electric vehicle charging. In: International Conference on Autonomous Agents and Multiagent Systems, pp. 669–676 (2012)
11. Tang, Q., Xie, M., Yang, K., Luo, Y., Zhou, D., Song, Y.: A decision function based smart charging and discharging strategy for electric vehicle in smart grid. Mobile Netw. Appl. **24**(5), 1722–1731 (2018). https://doi.org/10.1007/s11036-018-1049-4
12. Tang, W., Bi, S., Zhang, Y.J.A.: Online coordinated charging decision algorithm for electric vehicles without future information. IEEE Trans. Smart Grid **5**(6), 2810–2824 (2014)

13. Turker, H., Bacha, S.: Optimal minimization of plug-in electric vehicle charging cost with vehicle-to-home and vehicle-to-grid concepts. IEEE Trans. Veh. Technol. **67**(11), 10281–10292 (2018)
14. Valogianni, K., Ketter, W., Collins, J.: A multiagent approach to variable-rate electric vehicle charging coordination. In: Proceedings of the 2015 International Conference on Autonomous Agents and Multiagent Systems, pp. 1131–1139 (2015)
15. Zhao, S., Lin, X., Chen, M.: Peak-minimizing online EV charging: price-of-uncertainty and algorithm robustification. In: 2015 IEEE Conference on Computer Communications (INFOCOM), pp. 2335–2343. IEEE (2015)

Maximizing the Expected Influence in Face of the Non-progressive Adversary

T.-H. Hubert Chan[1], Li Ning[2]($\boxtimes$), and Yong Zhang[2]

[1] Department of Computer Science, The University of Hong Kong, Hong Kong, China
hubert@cs.hku.hk
[2] Shenzhen Institutes of Advanced Technology, CAS, Shenzhen, China
{li.ning,zhangyong}@siat.ac.cn

Abstract. In [5], the problem of influence maximization under non-progressive linear threshold model has been considered, and it has been shown that unless the underlying network is acyclic, the direct extension of the classic *linear threshold model* [16] does not preserve the submodularity of the objective function that measures the influence effect. In this paper, we introduce a new feature called *activation score* to the threshold model, and relax the constraint of the threshold selection to allow the thresholds drawn independently from a distribution whose pdf is non-increasing. We proved that the influence objective function under the proposed model is monotone and submodular for any given information network. Consequently, the advertiser can achieve $\frac{1}{2}$-approximation on maximizing the average number of active nodes over a certain period of time, and $(1 - \frac{1}{e})$-approximation in expectation with a randomized algorithm. Furthermore, we also consider the extension of the non-progressive threshold model in the two-agents case, in which the similar approximation results can be achieved.

Keywords: Influence maximization · Non-progressive influence · Multi-agent competition

1 Introduction

In the typical instances of the social network, it often requires much less cost to spread the influence (e.g. to promote the innovations and the products). Inspired by this exciting feature, a lot of effort has been devoted to discover the more efficient advertising strategy to make further use of the power of the networks. In the idea of *viral marketing* [8], the advertiser can convince only a subset of users to use the new product, perhaps by giving out a limited number of free samples with a limited budget. Then the popularity of the product is spread by word-of-mouth, i.e., through the existing connections between users in the underlying social network. The behavior that transmit information in a network is known as

T.-H. Hubert Chan was partially supported by the Hong Kong RGC under the project 17200418.

© Springer Nature Switzerland AG 2020
D. Yu et al. (Eds.): WASA 2020, LNCS 12384, pp. 28–39, 2020.
https://doi.org/10.1007/978-3-030-59016-1_3

information cascading and have been modeled using the *information networks* [8,12,15,16] which is a directed edge-weighted graph. A node in the network represents a user, whose behavior is influenced by its (outgoing) neighbors, and the weight of an edge reflects how influential the corresponding neighbor is. A node adopting the new behavior becomes *active* and is otherwise *inactive*. In [16], the authors studied the *threshold model* in which the resistance of a node v to adopt the new behavior is represented by a random threshold θ_v (higher value means higher resistance). Then the new behavior is spread in the information network in discrete time steps. An inactive node changes its state to active if the weighted influence from the active neighbors in the previous time step reaches its threshold.

Most of the study of the threshold model focus on the progressive case, in which once a user became active, it is forced to be active forever. In [5], the authors extended the classic linear threshold model [16] to allow the non-progressive behavior (i.e. the nodes can become inactive again after being activated) and they proved that unless the underlying network is acyclic, the expected influence, which is the objective function defined under their model, is not always submodular.

1.1   Our Contribution

In this paper, we introduce another non-progressive threshold model, which can be proved NP-Hard and has the following features

- *Choosing thresholds with non-increasing probability density function (pdf).* In most of the existing threshold model, including the classical one and the non-progressive one introduced in [5], it is assumed that the thresholds are chosen from $(0, 1)$ uniformly at random. However, recall that the threshold reflects the resistance level of a user, and we argue that the uniform selection is too restrictive. In our proposed non-progressive threshold model for one agent case, we allow the thresholds to be drawn independently from a distribution whose pdf is non-increasing, i.e., smaller thresholds are at least as likely to be chosen as larger thresholds. Because of this relaxed constraint, the non-progressive threshold mode is no longer called *linear*.
- *Influence with Activation Scores.* In previous models, users can only observe whether their neighbors are active or inactive. However, in practice, users can also express their opinions on a product, for instance by giving ratings or leaving comments. In our model, the opinion of a user is represented by an *activation score*, which for example can reflect how much a user likes a product. A user is activated if his current activation score is at least his threshold and inactivated otherwise. In our model, cascading behavior is modeled as modifying a user's activation score based on observing his neighbors' activation scores. This reflects the situation that it is usually a user's opinion that affects the others, but not necessarily whether he has bought a product or not.

– **Efficient evaluation of the objective function.** Given an initial active set, even computing the exact value of the objective function can be hard in some models [7]. In such case, the only known method for estimating the objective function given some initial active set is through random sampling, which can be expensive as multiple accesses to the objective function is required in some submodular function maximization algorithms [3,11]. Our model does not have this issue, i.e., given initial transient and permanent active sets, the expected influence can be evaluated in polynomial time.

In this paper, we use the expected influence introduced by [5] to measure the effect of the information spread. Briefly speaking, the expected influence is the average number of active nodes over the considered period. (The formal definition of expected influence is described in Definition 2.) For the proposed non-progressive threshold model, we showed that the problem of influence maximization is NP-Hard and a $\frac{1}{2}$-approximation (and $(1 - \frac{1}{e})$-approximation by randomized algorithm) of the optimal can be achieved since the expected influence is proved monotone and submodular (Sect. 2, Theorems 2 and 3).

Furthermore, we consider the non-progressive threshold model for the situation with two agents. For both of the disjoint-active-set case and the general-active-set case, we have proved the submodularity of the expected influence respectively. Consequently, the constant approximation can also be achieved under the two agents model (Sect. 3, Theorem 6). In the full version of this work, our conclusions about the non-progressive threshold model were applied to give a theoretical support to explain the efficiency of the often used *maximum degree heuristic.*

Due to the page limit, some of the proofs are moved to the appendices.

1.2 Related Works

The progressive cascading behavior in information networks was first studied in the computer science community by Kempe, Kleinberg and Tardos [16]. In the same paper, a non-progressive case in which for every time step the threshold of each node is re-drawn independently. Kempe et al. [15,16] also proved that the influence maximization problem under their models are NP-hard. In [5], the authors introduced a more general non-progressive linear threshold model in which the thresholds are not changing once they are initially selected.

In a common approach to approximate the optimal, at first show one should show that the objective functions in question are submodular, and then applying a standard greedy algorithm (*hill climbing*) analyzed by Nemhauser and Fisher et al. [11,18] will give the $\frac{1}{2}$-approximation. Calinescu et al. [3] introduced a randomized algorithm that achieves $(1 - \frac{1}{e})$-approximation in expectation for the monotone and submodular function.

Chen et al. [6] considered how *positive* and *negative* opinions spread in the same network, which can be interpreted as the influence process involving two agents. The influence maximization problem considering multiple competing agents in an information network has also been studied in [2,4,9]. We follow a similar setting in which a new comer can observe the strategies of existing agents, and stategizes accordingly to maximize his influence in the network.

Mossel and Roch [17] have shown that under more general submodular threshold functions (as opposed to linear threshold functions), the objective function is still submodular and hence the same maximization framework can still be applied. The relationship between influence spreading and random walks has been investigated by Asavathiratham et al. [1], and Even-Dar and Shapira [10] in other information network models.

In [13,14], He et al. considered restraining rumor spreading in the social networks, and proposed the strategy to optimize the countermeasures; Recently, Tang et al. introduced a second-order diffusion model for social influence [19].

2   One Agent Model

The preliminaries are omitted due to the page limit. One can refer to [5] or the full version of this paper for the formal definition of *the information network*, as well as the notation of monotonicity and submodularity.

Next, we describe the non-progressive threshold model for the one agent case, which keeps an interesting feature of the model introduced in [5]: an initially active node can be either *transient* or *permanent*.

Model 1 (Non-progressive Threshold Model (NT)). *Consider an information network $G = (V, E, b)$. Each node in V is associated with a threshold θ_v, which is chosen independently from the interval $(0, 1)$ according to some distribution with **non-increasing probability density function**, i.e., smaller thresholds are at least as likely to be sampled as larger thresholds.*

At any time step $t \geq 0$, each node v has an activation score $x_v^t \in [0, 1]$, *with a value closer to 1 meaning that it is more likely to be activated. Node v is* inactive $(\mathcal{N})$ *at time t if $x_v^t < \theta_v$, and* active $(\mathcal{A})$ *otherwise. We use A_t to denote the set of active nodes at time t. Given a transient initial set $A \subseteq V$, a permanent initial set $\widehat{A} \subseteq V$ (where $A \cap \widehat{A} = \emptyset$), and a configuration of thresholds $\theta = \{\theta_v\}_{v \in V}$, the* Influence Process *is defined as follows.*

1. *At time $t = 0$, $A_0 := A \cup \widehat{A}$. For node v, $x_v^0 = 1$ if $v \in A \cup \widehat{A}$ and $x_v^0 = 0$ otherwise.*
2. *At time $t > 0$,*
   - *for node $v \in \widehat{A}$, $x_v^t = 1$;*
   - *for node $v \in V \setminus \widehat{A}$, $x_v^t := \sum_{u \in \Gamma(v)} b_{vu} \cdot x_u^{t-1}$.*
   Then, $A_t := \{v \in V \mid x_v^t \geq \theta_v\}$.

Remark 1. Observe that activation score $x_v^t := x_v^t(A, \widehat{A})$ is a (deterministic) function of A and $\widehat{A}$. To simplify the notation, we write $x_v^t(A)$ when $\widehat{A} = \emptyset$.

We can consider the update in each time step as consisting of two phases. In the first phase, each node v calculates its activation score x_v^t. In the second phase, each node v compares its activation score with the threshold θ_v and determines if it is activated.

Definition 1 (Indicator Variable). *In an information network G, given a transient initial set A and a permanent initial set $\widehat{A}$, a node v and a time t, let $X_v^t(A, \widehat{A})$ be the indicator random variable that takes value 1 if node v is active at time t, and 0 otherwise. When $\widehat{A} = \emptyset$, we sometimes write $X_v^t(A) := X_v^t(A, \emptyset)$.*

Recall that the indicator variable's usefulness is based on the following equality:

$$\overline{\sigma}(A, \widehat{A}) = \mathbb{E}[\frac{1}{T} \sum_{t=1}^{T} \mid A_t \mid] = \frac{1}{T} \sum_{t=1}^{T} \sum_{v \in V} \mathbb{E}[X_v^t(A, \widehat{A})].$$

Hence, if the function $(A, \widehat{A}) \mapsto \mathbb{E}[X_v^t(A, \widehat{A})]$ is submodular and monotone, then so is $\overline{\sigma}$.

Without loss of generality, we can assume $A \cap \widehat{A} = \emptyset$, otherwise we can use $A \setminus \widehat{A}$ as the transient initial set instead. Given a transient initial set A and a permanent initial set $\widehat{A}$, we measure the influence of the agent by the average number of active nodes over T time steps, where T is some pre-specified time scope in which the process evolves. Observe that once the initial sets and the configuration of the thresholds are given, the active sets A_t's are totally determined. Next, we define the influence function and expected influence in the same way introduced in [5].

Definition 2 (Influence Function and Expected Influence). *Given an information network G, a transient initial set A, a permanent initial set $\widehat{A}$, a configuration θ of thresholds, and the number T of time steps for consideration, the average influence over time is defined as $\sigma_\theta(A, \widehat{A}) := \frac{1}{T} \sum_{t=1}^{T} \mid A_t \mid$. We define the expected influence $\overline{\sigma}$ as the expectation of $\sigma_\theta(A, \widehat{A})$ over the random choice of θ, i.e., $\overline{\sigma}(A, \widehat{A}) := \mathbb{E}_\theta[\sigma_\theta(A, \widehat{A})]$.*

Definition 3 (Influence Maximization Problem). *In an information network G, suppose the advertising cost of a transient initial node is c and that of a permanent initial node is $\widehat{c}$, where the costs are uniform over the nodes. Given a budget K, the goal is to find a transient initial set A and a permanent initial set $\widehat{A}$ with total cost $c \cdot |A| + \widehat{c} \cdot |\widehat{A}|$ at most K such that $\overline{\sigma}(A, \widehat{A})$ is maximized.*

Theorem 1. *The influence maximization problem under the* **NT** *Model is NP-hard when all the initially active nodes are permanent.*

Proof. It should be noticed that for the case $T = 1$, the **NT** Model performs exactly the same action with the non-progressive linear threshold model (**NLT**) introduced in [5]. Hence, the hardness proof given in [5] also works for Theorem 1. Briefly speaking, the hardness is shown using a reduction from vertex cover similar to that in [15, 16]. $\qquad\square$

In the remaining part of this section, we prove that the expected influence is submodular on both initial sets (A and $\widehat{A}$). To prove this, the following lemma concludes that it is sufficient to prove the submodularity of x_v^t for each time point t and each node v.

Lemma 1. *Consider the* **NT** *Model. If for any* $0 \leq t \leq T$, *and node* $v \in V$, $x_v^t(A, \widehat{A})$ *is monotone and submodular on both initial sets, then the expected influence is monotone and submodular on both initial sets.*

Then in the remaining part, we focus on the proof of the submodularity of x_v^t. To show this fact, we apply an approach similar to the one used in [5], which introduced a random walk process as the auxiliary.

Model 2 (Random Walk Process (RW). [5]) *Consider an information network* G. *For any given node* $v \in V$, *we define the Random Walk Process as follows.*

1. *At time* $t = 0$, *the walk starts at node* v.
2. *Suppose at some time* t, *the current node is* u. *A node* $w \in \Gamma(u)$ *is chosen with probability* b_{uw}. *The walk moves to node* w *at time* $t + 1$.[1]

Definition 4 (Reaching Event). *Let* G *be an information network. For any node* v, *subset* $C \subseteq V$ *and* $t \geq 0$, *we use* $R_v^t(C)$ *to denote the event that a Random Walk Process on* G *starting from* v *would be at a node in* C *at precisely time* t.

Definition 5 (Passing-Through Event). *Let* G *be an information network. For any node* v, *subset* $C \subseteq V$ *and* $t \geq 0$, *we use* $S_v^t(C)$ *to denote the event that a Random Walk Process on* G *starting from* v *would reach a node in* C *at time* t *or before.*

Lemma 2 (Connection between the NT Model and the RW Model). *Consider an information network* G, *and let* $v \in V$ *be a non-void node, and* $1 \leq t \leq T$. *On the same network* G, *consider the Non-progressive Threshold Model with a transient initial set* A *(the permanent initial set is empty) and the Random Walk Process starting at node* v. *Then* $x_v^t(A) = Pr[R_v^t(A)]$.

Remark 2. **(Computing** $\mathbb{E}[X_v^t(A)]$). The Random Walk Process can be expressed as a Markov Chain. Suppose M is the transition matrix, where $M(v, u) := b_{vu}$ if $(v, u) \in E$ and $M(v, u) := 0$ otherwise. Then, $Pr[R_v^t(\{u\})] = M^t(v, u)$, and $x_v^t(A) = Pr[R_v^t(A)] = \sum_{u \in A} M^t(v, u)$. Let $F(x)$ be the cumulative distribution function used for choosing θ's. Then, $\mathbb{E}[X_v^t(A)] = F(x_v^t(A))$.

Next, we consider the case where the permanent initial set $\widehat{A}$ is non-empty. Similar to the argument in [5], we show that this general case can be reduced to the case where only transient initial set A is non-empty.

Lemma 3. *Suppose we are given an instance on information network* G, *with transient initial set* A *and permanent initial set* $\widehat{A}$. *Let* v *be any non-void node in* G *and* $0 \leq t \leq T$. *Suppose in the transformed network* $\overline{G}(\widehat{A})$, *for any subset*

---

[1] Observe that if w is the void node, then the walk remains at w.

C of nodes in G, $\overline{R}_v^t(C)$ is the event that starting at v, the **RW** Model on $\overline{G}$ for t steps ends at a node in C. Then,

$$x_v^t(A, \widehat{A}) = \sum_{u \in A} Pr[\overline{R}_v^t(\{u\})] + \sum_{y \in \widehat{A}} \sum_{i=0}^{t} Pr[\overline{R}_v^i(\{y\})].$$

Lemma 4 (General Connection). *Suppose G is an information network, and let v be a non-void node, and $1 \leq t \leq T$. On the same network G, consider the Non-progressive Threshold Model with transient initial set A and permanent initial set $\widehat{A}$, and the Random Walk Process starting at v. Then, $x_v^t(A, \widehat{A}) = Pr[R_v^t(A) \cup S_v^t(\widehat{A})]$.*

Remark 3. (**Computing** $\mathbb{E}[X_v^t(A, \widehat{A})]$). Given an information network, we can use the modified transition matrix $\overline{M}$ such that each node in $\widehat{A}$ corresponds to an absorbing state. Then, $x_v^t(A, \widehat{A}) = \sum_{u \in A \cup \widehat{A}} \overline{M}^t(v, u)$, and $\mathbb{E}[X_v^t(A, \widehat{A})] = Pr[x^t(A, \widehat{A}) \geq \theta_v] = F(x_v^t(A, \widehat{A}))$, where $F(x)$ is the cumulative distribution function from which θ's are selected.

Theorem 2. (Submodularity and Monotonicity of $x_v^t(A, \widehat{A})$). *Consider the **NT** Model on an information network G with transient initial set A and permanent initial set $\widehat{A}$. Then, the function $(A, \widehat{A}) \mapsto x_v^t(A, \widehat{A})$ is submodular and monotone.*

Proof. For notational convenience, we drop the superscript t and the subscript v, and write for instance $x(A, \widehat{A}) := x_v^t(A, \widehat{A})$. For the reaching and the passing-through events associated with the Random Walk Process in G, we write $R(A) := R_v^t(A)$ and $S(A) := S_v^t(A)$

It is sufficient to prove that, for any $A \subseteq B \subseteq V$, $\widehat{A} \subseteq \widehat{B} \subseteq V$, and node $w \notin (B \cup \widehat{B})$, the following inequalities hold:

$$x(A \cup \{w\}, \widehat{A}) - x(A, \widehat{A}) \geq x(B \cup \{w\}, \widehat{B}) - x(B, \widehat{B}); \tag{1}$$
$$x(A, \widehat{A} \cup \{w\}) - x(A, \widehat{A}) \geq x(B, \widehat{B} \cup \{w\}) - x(B, \widehat{B}). \tag{2}$$

By Lemma 4, for any subsets C and $\widehat{C}$ such that $w \notin (C \cup \widehat{C})$, $x(C \cup \{w\}, \widehat{C}) - x(C, \widehat{C}) = Pr[R(C \cup \{w\}) \cup S(\widehat{C})] - Pr[R(C) \cup S(\widehat{C})] = Pr[R(\{w\}) \setminus S(\widehat{C})]$, where the last equality follows from definitions of reaching and passing-through events. Hence, inequality (1) follows because $\widehat{A} \subseteq \widehat{B}$ implies that $R(\{w\}) \setminus S(\widehat{A}) \supseteq R(\{w\}) \setminus S(\widehat{B})$.

Similarly, $x(C, \widehat{C} \cup \{w\}) - x(C, \widehat{C}) = Pr[S(\{w\}) \setminus (R(C) \cup S(\widehat{C}))]$. Hence, inequality (2) follows because $R(A) \cup S(\widehat{A}) \subseteq R(B) \cup S(\widehat{B})$. ☐

Corollary 1 (Objective Function is Submodular and Monotone). *With the same hypothesis as in Theorem 2, the function $(A, \widehat{A}) \mapsto \overline{\sigma}(A, \widehat{A})$ is submodular and monotone.*

Finally we have the main result of the one agent model, that is formally presented in Theorem 3.

Theorem 3. *Given an information network, a time period $[1, T]$, a budget K and advertising costs (transient or permanent) that are uniform over the nodes, an advertiser can use a standard greedy algorithm (hill climbing) to compute a transient initial set A and a permanent initial set $\widehat{A}$ with total cost at most K in polynomial time such that $\overline{\sigma}(A, \widehat{A})$ is at least $\frac{1}{2}$ of the optimal value. Moreover, there is a randomized algorithm that outputs A and $\widehat{A}$ such that the expected value (over the randomness of the randomized algorithm) of $\overline{\sigma}(A, \widehat{A})$ is at least $1 - \frac{1}{e}$ of the optimal value, where e is the natural number.*

The proof of Theorem 3 is not novel and hence is omitted here.

3   Two Agents Model

We extend our influence model to the case with two agents $\mathcal{A}$ and $\mathcal{B}$. In the two agents case, we restrict the thresholds to be selected from $(0, 1)$ uniformly at random, and a node can be inactive $\mathcal{N}$, or active with a label $\mathcal{A}$ or $\mathcal{B}$, depending on which agent has influence on it. Again, each agent can choose a transient initial set and a permanent initial set. Suppose Agent $\mathcal{A}$ has already chosen his sets A and $\widehat{A}$. Agent $\mathcal{B}$ is the new comer and she has to find good choices of initial sets B and $\widehat{B}$.

3.1   Disjoint Initial Sets

We first consider the case where $A \cup \widehat{A}$ and $B \cup \widehat{B}$ are disjoint. Next (in Sect. 3.2), we consider the case where Agent $\mathcal{B}$'s initial sets could intersect with Agent $\mathcal{A}$'s initial sets.

Model 3 (Non-progressive Threshold Model with Two Agents). *Consider an information network $G = (V, E, b)$. Each node $v \in V$ is associated with a threshold θ_v, which is chosen from the interval $(0, 1)$ uniformly at random.*

At any time step $t \geq 0$, each node $v \in V$ has two activation scores $x_v^t, y_v^t \in [0, 1]$. Node v can be inactive $(\mathcal{N})$ at time t, or active with $\mathcal{A}$, or active with $\mathcal{B}$. We use A_t to denote the set of nodes active with $\mathcal{A}$, and B_t to denote the set of nodes active with $\mathcal{B}$, at time t. Given two transient initial sets $A, B \subseteq V$, two permanent initial sets $\widehat{A}, \widehat{B} \subseteq V$ (for Agent $\mathcal{A}$ and Agent $\mathcal{B}$ respectively) such that $(A \cup \widehat{A}) \cap (B \cup \widehat{B}) = \emptyset$, and a configuration of thresholds $\theta = \{\theta_v\}_{v \in V}$, the Multiple Influence Process is defined as follows.

1. *At time $t = 0$, $A_0 := A \cup \widehat{A}$ and $B_0 := B \cup \widehat{B}$. For any node v, $x_v^0 = 1$ if $v \in A_0$ and $x_v^0 = 0$ otherwise. Similarly, $y_v^0 = 1$ if $v \in B_0$ and $y_v^0 = 0$ otherwise.*
2. *At time $t > 0$,*
   - *for node $v \in \widehat{A}$, let $x_v^t = 1$ and $y_v^t = 0$;*

- *for node $u \in \widehat{B}$, let $y_v^t = 1$ and $x_v^t = 0$;*
- *for each node $v \in V \setminus (\widehat{A} \cup \widehat{B})$, let $x_v^t = \sum_{u \in \Gamma(v)} b_{uv} \cdot x_u^{t-1}$, and $y_v^t = \sum_{u \in \Gamma(v)} b_{uv} \cdot y_u^{t-1}$.*

For each node $v \in V$ satisfying $x_v^t + y_v^t \geq \theta_v$, it makes a choice between $\mathcal{A}$ and $\mathcal{B}$ with probabilities $\frac{x_v^t}{x_v^t + y_v^t}$ and $\frac{y_v^t}{x_v^t + y_v^t}$, respectively.

Then, $A_t := \{v \in V : x_v^t + y_v^t \geq \theta_v \text{ and } v \text{ chooses } \mathcal{A}\}$ and $B_t := \{v \in V : x_v^t + y_v^t \geq \theta_v \text{ and } v \text{ chooses } \mathcal{B}\}$.

Remark 4. In the Multiple Influence Process, the randomness comes from two sources. One is the uniformly random choices of the thresholds. The other is the nodes' choices between $\mathcal{A}$ and $\mathcal{B}$. Denote the random sample space as Ω, then a point $\omega \in \Omega$ is a configuration of all random choices involved in Model 3.

Definition 6 (Indicator Variable). *In an information network G, let v be a node and t be a time step. Given Agent $\mathcal{A}$'s initial sets A and $\widehat{A}$, and Agent $\mathcal{B}$'s initial sets B and $\widehat{B}$, consider the Multiple Influence Process on these initial sets. Define $Y_v^t(B, \widehat{B} \mid A, \widehat{A})$ to be the indicator random variable that takes value 1 if node v is active with $\mathcal{B}$ at time step t, and 0 otherwise.*

Remark 5. From the description of the Multiple Influence Process, it holds that

$$\mathbb{E}[Y_v^t(B, \widehat{B} \mid A, \widehat{A})] = y_v^t(A, \widehat{A}, B, \widehat{B}),$$

for all $0 < t \leq T$ and non-void node v.

Definition 7 (Influence Function and Expected Influence). *Given an information network G, two transient initial sets A, B, two permanent initial sets $\widehat{A}, \widehat{B}$, the average influence for $\mathcal{B}$ given $\mathcal{A}$ over the first T time steps is defined as*

$$\sigma_\omega(B, \widehat{B} \mid A, \widehat{A}) = \frac{1}{T} \sum_{t=1}^{T} \mid B_t \mid.$$

Then, we define the expected influence $\overline{\sigma}$ as

$$\overline{\sigma}(B, \widehat{B} \mid A, \widehat{A}) = \mathbb{E}_\omega[\sigma_\omega(B, \widehat{B} \mid A, \widehat{A})],$$

where the expectation is over the random choices involved in Model 3.

Definition 8 (Multiple Influence Maximization Problem). *In an information network $G = (V, E, b)$, suppose the cost of a transient initial node is c and that of a permanent initial node is $\widehat{c}$. Given a transient initial set A, a permanent initial set $\widehat{A}$, and a budget K, the goal is to find a transient initial set B and a permanent initial set $\widehat{B}$, such that $(A \cup \widehat{A}) \cap (B \cup \widehat{B}) = \emptyset$, $c|B| + \widehat{c}|\widehat{B}| \leq K$, and $\overline{\sigma}(B, \widehat{B}, \mid A, \widehat{A})$ is maximized.*

Using similar techniques as before, we conclude (in Theorem 4) an important relation between the two agents model and the one agent model with thresholds chosen from $(0, 1)$ uniformly at random. Recall the indicator variable $X_v^t(A, \widehat{A})$ for the one agent model. In the case that the thresholds are chosen from $(0, 1)$ uniformly at random, it holds that $\mathbb{E}[X_v^t(A, \widehat{A})] = Pr[x_v^t(A, \widehat{A}) \geq \theta_v] = x_v^t(A, \widehat{A})$.

Theorem 4. *Suppose G is an information network, with Agent $\mathcal{A}$'s transient initial set A and permanent initial set $\widehat{A}$, and Agent $\mathcal{B}$'s transient initial set B and permanent initial set $\widehat{B}$. The thresholds are chosen from $(0, 1)$ uniformly at random. Let v be a non-void node and $t > 0$ be a time step. Consider running the one agent model with the uniformly chosen thresholds, the initial sets B and $\widehat{B}$ on the transformed network $\overline{G}[\widehat{A}]$, and recall the corresponding indicator variable $\overline{X}_v^t(B, \widehat{B})$. Then, $\mathbb{E}[Y_v^t(B, \widehat{B} \mid A, \widehat{A})] = \mathbb{E}[\overline{X}_v^t(B, \widehat{B})]$.*

Remark 6. Note that $\overline{X}_v^t(B, \widehat{B})$ is an indicator variable defined with network $\overline{G}(\widehat{A})$. Since the transient initial set A and permanent initial set $\widehat{A}$ are always fixed when we seek to maximize Agent $\mathcal{B}$'s influence, then we do not include the script $\widehat{A}$ in $\overline{X}_v^t(B, \widehat{B})$.

Corollary 2. *Consider the Non-progressive Threshold Model with two agents. Then, the function $(B, \widehat{B}) \mapsto \overline{\sigma}(B, \widehat{B} \mid A, \widehat{A})$ (with domain $2^{V \setminus (A \cup \widehat{A})} \times 2^{V \setminus (A \cup \widehat{A})}$) is submodular and monotone.*

3.2   Intersecting Initial Sets

We consider the case where $(A \cup \widehat{A}) \cap (B \cup \widehat{B}) \neq \emptyset$. When a node is chosen by both agents as initially active, we have a (randomized) tie breaking procedure to decide whether that node is activated with $\mathcal{A}$ or $\mathcal{B}$. After that, the Influence Process for disjoint initial sets can be applied. The tie breaking procedure can be summarized as follows.

- If a node is chosen as permanent by one agent and transient by another, the former agent will prevail and that node will be permanent for that agent.
- If a node is chosen as permanent by both agents or transient by both agents, the node will be activated with one of the agents according to his preference distribution.

Definition 9 (Preference Distribution). *For any node v in an information network G, its* preference distribution *is a pair of non-negative real numbers $(p_v^{\mathcal{A}}, p_v^{\mathcal{B}})$ such that $p_v^{\mathcal{A}} + p_v^{\mathcal{B}} = 1$.*

Given an information network with two transient initial sets A, B and two permanent initial sets $\widehat{A}, \widehat{B}$ (without loss of generality, we can assume $A \cap \widehat{A} = \emptyset$ and $B \cap \widehat{B} = \emptyset$), the influence process consists of two stages:

Stage I. Breaking Ties. In this stage, according to the following rules, we construct the initial sets A', $\widehat{A}'$, B', and $\widehat{B}'$ such that $A' \cap \widehat{A}' = \emptyset$, $B' \cap \widehat{B}' = \emptyset$ and $(A' \cup \widehat{A}') \cap (B' \cup \widehat{B}') = \emptyset$.

- **Case: permanent set has priority.** For a node $v \in \widehat{A} \setminus \widehat{B}$, it is selected to $\widehat{A}'$. For a node $v \in \widehat{B} \setminus \widehat{A}$, it is selected to $\widehat{B}'$.
- **Case: only in one transient set.** For a node $v \in A \setminus (B \cup \widehat{B})$, it is selected to A'. For a node $v \in B \setminus (A \cup \widehat{A})$, it is selected to B'.

- **Case: the nodes chosen by two transient sets.** For a node $v \in A \cap B$, it selects Agent $\mathcal{A}$ and is put into A' with probability $p_x^{\mathcal{A}}$ and it selects Agent $\mathcal{B}$ and is put into B' with probability $p_x^{\mathcal{B}}$.
- **Case: the nodes chosen by two permanent sets.** For a node $v \in \widehat{A} \cap \widehat{B}$, it selects Agent $\mathcal{A}$ and is put into $\widehat{A}'$ with probability $p_x^{\mathcal{A}}$ and selects Agent $\mathcal{B}$ and is put into $\widehat{B}'$ with probability $p_x^{\mathcal{B}}$.

When all nodes finish the stage of breaking ties, we get sets A' and $\widehat{A}'$ (or B' and $\widehat{B}'$) as Agent $\mathcal{A}$'s (or $\mathcal{B}$'s) new initial sets.

Stage II. Multiple Influence Process with Disjoint Initial Sets. Run the Multiple Influence Process of Model 3 with the initial sets A', $\widehat{A}'$, B' and $\widehat{B}'$.

We use indicator random variable $Z_v^t(B, \widehat{B} \mid A, \widehat{A})$ to indicate in the influence process of Stages I and II, whether v is active with $\mathcal{B}$ at time t, given the transient initial sets A, B and the permanent initial sets $\widehat{A}, \widehat{B}$. Observe that we use $Y_v^t(\cdot)$ to denote the same quantity when the initial sets are disjoint.

Accordingly, we can extend concept **Expected Influence** $\overline{\sigma}(B, \widehat{B}|A, \widehat{A})$ to be over all the random choices involved in Stages I and II. Furthermore, the **Maximization Problem** can be defined as to find initial sets B and $\widehat{B}$, for Agent $\mathcal{B}$ subject to a budget K, given Agent $\mathcal{A}$'s choices of initial sets A and $\widehat{A}$, such that $\overline{\sigma}(B, \widehat{B}|A, \widehat{A})$ is maximized.

Theorem 5. *Consider an information network G, where Agent $\mathcal{A}$ has chosen transient initial set A and permanent initial set $\widehat{A}$. Suppose Agent $\mathcal{B}$ chooses transient initial set B and permanent initial set $\widehat{B}$. Then, the function $(B, \widehat{B}) \mapsto \mathbb{E}[Z_v^t(B, \widehat{B} \mid A, \widehat{A})]$ is submodular and monotone.*

Finally, we get the following result on our model with two agents.

Theorem 6. *Suppose in an information network an adversary (Agent $\mathcal{A}$) has made his choice of initial set A and permanent set $\widehat{A}$ in advance. Then, given a time period $[1, T]$, a budget K and advertising costs (transient or permanent) that are uniform over the nodes, an advertiser (Agent $\mathcal{B}$) can compute a transient initial set B and a permanent initial set $\widehat{B}$ with total cost at most K in polynomial time such that $\overline{\sigma}(B, \widehat{B}|A, \widehat{A})$ is at least $\frac{1}{2}$ of the optimal value. Moreover, there is a randomized algorithm that outputs B and $\widehat{B}$ such that the expected value of $\overline{\sigma}(B, \widehat{B}|A, \widehat{A})$ is at least $1 - \frac{1}{e}$ of the optimal value, where e is the natural number.*

References

1. Asavathiratham, C., Roy, S., Lesieutre, B., Verghese, G.: The influence model. IEEE Contr. Syst. Mag. **21**(6), 52–64 (2001)
2. Bharathi, S., Kempe, D., Salek, M.: Competitive influence maximization in social networks. In: Proceedings of the 3rd International Conference on Internet and Network Economics. pp. 306–311 (2007)

3. Călinescu, G., Chekuri, C., Pál, M., Vondrák, J.: Maximizing a monotone submodular function subject to a matroid constraint. SIAM J. Comput. **40**(6), 1740–1766 (2011)
4. Carnes, T., Nagarajan, C., Wild, S.M., van Zuylen, A.: Maximizing influence in a competitive social network: a follower's perspective. In: Proceedings of the 9th International Conference on Electronic Commerce. pp. 351–360 (2007)
5. Chan, T.H.H., Ning, L., Zhang, Y.: Influence maximization under the nonprogressive linear threshold model. In: Proceedings of the 14th International Frontiers of Algorithmics Workshop (2020)
6. Chen, W., et al.: Influence maximization in social networks when negative opinions may emerge and propagate. In: SDM. pp. 379–390 (2011)
7. Chen, W., Yuan, Y., Zhang, L.: Scalable influence maximization in social networks under the linear threshold model. In: Proceedings of the 2010 IEEE International Conference on Data Mining. pp. 88–97 (2010)
8. Domingos, P., Richardson, M.: Mining the network value of customers. In: Proceedings of the 7th ACM SIGKDD International Conference on Knowledge Discovery and Data Mining. pp. 57–66 (2001)
9. Dubey, P., Garg, R., Meyer, B.D.: Competing for customers in a social network. Department of Economics Working Papers 06–01 (2006)
10. Even-Dar, E., Shapira, A.: A note on maximizing the spread of influence in social networks. In: Deng, X., Graham, F.C. (eds.) WINE 2007. LNCS, vol. 4858, pp. 281–286. Springer, Heidelberg (2007). https://doi.org/10.1007/978-3-540-77105-0_27
11. Fisher, M.L., Nemhauser, G.L., Wolsey, L.A.: An analysis of approximations for maximizing submodular set functions. II. Math. Programming Stud. pp. 73–87(1978)
12. Goldenberg, J., Libai, B.: Muller: using complex systems analysis to advance marketing theory development. Acad. Mark. Sci. Rev. **3**, 1–18 (2001)
13. He, Z., Cai, Z., Wang, X.: Modeling propagation dynamics and developing optimized countermeasures for rumor spreading in online social networks. In: 2015 IEEE 35Th International Conference on Distributed Computing Systems. pp. 205–214. IEEE (2015)
14. He, Z., Cai, Z., Yu, J., Wang, X., Sun, Y., Li, Y.: Cost-efficient strategies for restraining rumor spreading in mobile social networks. IEEE Trans. Veh.Technol. **66**(3), 2789–2800 (2016)
15. Kempe, D., Kleinberg, J., Tardos, E.: Influential nodes in a diffusion model for social networks. In: Proceedings of the 32nd International Colloquium on Automata, Languages and Programming. pp. 1127–1138 (2005)
16. Kempe, D., Kleinberg, J., Tardos, É.: Maximizing the spread of influence through a social network. In: Proceedings of the Ninth ACM SIGKDD International Conference on Knowledge Discovery and Data Mining. pp. 137–146. ACM (2003)
17. Mossel, E., Roch, S.: On the submodularity of influence in social networks. In: Proceedings of the 39th Annual ACM Symposium on Theory of Computing. pp. 128–134 (2007)
18. Nemhauser, G.L., Wolsey, L.A., Fisher, M.L.: An analysis of approximations for maximizing submodular set (functions i). Math. Program. **14**(1), 265–294 (1978)
19. Tang, W., Luo, G., Wu, Y., Tian, L., Zheng, X., Cai, Z.: A second-order diffusion model for influence maximization in social networks. IEEE Trans. Computat. Social Syst. **6**(4), 702–714 (2019)

A Novel Anti-attack Revenue Optimization Algorithm in the Proof-of-Work Based Blockchain

Hao Chen[1], Yourong Chen[1,2]($\boxtimes$), Meng Han[3], Banteng Liu[1,2], Qiuxia Chen[2], and Zhenghua Ma[1]

[1] School of Information Science and Engineering, Changzhou University,
Changzhou, China
Jack_chenyr@163.com
[2] College of Information Science and Technology, Zhejiang Shuren University,
Hangzhou, China
[3] College of Computing and Software Engineering, Kennesaw State University,
Marietta, USA

Abstract. To improve the revenues of both the attack mining pools and miners under block withholding attack, this paper proposes a novel anti-attack mining revenue optimization algorithm (MROA) in the Proof-of-work (PoW) based blockchain. MROA considers the situation that the miners have the flexibility to select an attack mining pool to join and carry out honest mining or attack on other mining pools. The proposed approach achieved the revenue optimization on each attack mining pool, and maintained high group efficiency of the mining pools under block withholding attack by utilizing a modified artificial bee colony algorithm based on Pareto to solve the models. Furthermore, MROA could obtain a composition scheme of each attack mining pool and work scheme of each miner under block withholding attack. The comprehensive evaluation demonstrates that MROA can always identify the optimized miner work scheme for each attack mining pool with any miner population. Our test result of MROA also outperforms the state-of-arts such as ABC, NSGA2 and MOPSO with reduces miner revenue variance and spacing value of solution set.

Keywords: Mining revenue · Attack mining pool · Miner · Blockchain pow

1 Introduction

With the widespread application of new technologies such as cloud computing, big data, and artificial intelligence, the resulting information security issues have become increasingly prominent [1–4]. In the blockchain, all of the nodes follow the same accounting transaction rules and reach a consensus in the consensus mechanism. Thus blockchain technology has the characteristics of decentralization, collective maintenance and non-tamperability, the wide usage in medical care, intelligent transportation and other fields [5,8,19] have attracted heavy attention in

© Springer Nature Switzerland AG 2020
D. Yu et al. (Eds.): WASA 2020, LNCS 12384, pp. 40–50, 2020.
https://doi.org/10.1007/978-3-030-59016-1_4

recent years. Proof of Work (PoW) consensus mechanism as one of the signature implementation in Bitcoin has been broadly used in many blockchain systems [14]. Most of miners in the network cannot obtain stable revenue, so miners join the mining pool to improve mining efficiency through cooperative mining. However, there are block withholding attacks and other attacks against the mining pool in the actual process [11]. Block withholding attack is the situation that malicious miner always chooses to send part work certificate to the mining pool manager, and discards the full work certificate directly when it generates full work certificate [7]. The behavior of malicious miner does not produce any effective help to the attacked mining pool and obtains part revenue of attacked mining pool.

Rosenfeld M. firstly proposed the concept of block withholding attack in 2011 [13]. Then more and more scholars study the block withholding attacks. Currently, some scholars focus on block withholding attacks between two mining pools. For example, the authors of [6] calculate the revenue of cooperation strategy and the revenue of betrayal strategy and propose an adaptive zero row strategy. Reference [12] proposes an evolutionary mining algorithm with the mathematical formulas of mining probability, average time and revenue. Reference [17] establishes an iterative prisoner's dilemma model solved by indefinite value strategy. References [6,12,17] solve the game problem between two mining pools. But in the actual process, there is often a game problem among multiple mining pools. Therefore, some scholars focus on the block withholding attack methods among multiple mining pools. For example, reference [9] proposes an evolutionary game theory based on the blockchain network to analyze the miner revenue. Reference [16] regards the game process as an iterative prisoner's dilemma model, and uses a gradient algorithm of deep reinforcement learning to solve the game problem among multiple mining pools. But references [9,16] do not consider mining cost and miner strategy choice, and only analyzes the revenue from the perspective of the mining pool.

In conclusion, several scholars have studied game strategies between mining pools. But they have neither considered mining cost of honest mining and block withholding attack, nor considered dynamic game problems among multiple mining pools. At the same time, the above references only study the mining pool revenue, and has not considered miner strategy choice. Therefore, we propose a novel anti-attack mining revenue optimization algorithm (MROA) in the PoW based blockchain. Briefly, our contributions are as follows:

1. We establish a revenue optimization model of each attack mining pool and revenue optimization model of entire mining attack pools under block withholding attack.
2. We use a modified artificial bee colony algorithm based on Pareto to solve the model, and obtain the composition scheme of each attack mining pool and work scheme of each miner under block withholding attack. The algorithm improves the group revenue of attack mining pools, and improves the revenues of each attack mining pool and its miners.

The rest of the paper is organized as follows. In Sect. 2, we describe our algorithm principles which include model establishment and model solution.

In Sect. 3, we present the simulation results. Finally, we conclude the paper in Sect. 4.

2 Algorithm Principles

To illustrate our algorithm principles, we have the assumption as follows:

1. The attack mining pools and honest mining pools exist in the same network. The attack mining pools carry out block withholding attack and honest mining. Honest mining pools only carry out honest mining.
2. Many miners exist in the network. The miners can choose to exit or join an attack mining pool according to the current information.
3. In an attack mining pool, miners can carry out honest mining by himself to help the mining pool obtain mining revenue. Or according to the task of attacking other pool, miners carry out block withholding attack on other pools to help its mining pool obtain the revenue of block withholding attack.

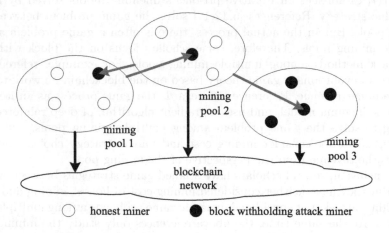

Fig. 1. Schematic diagram of miner attacking each other.

As shown in Fig. 1, miners in the blockchain network join an attack mining pool to carry out honest mining or block withholding attack on another mining pool according to current information such as computing power and miner revenue. Then they obtain mining revenue or block withholding attack revenue and reduces the revenue of the attacked mining pool.

2.1 Model Establishment

Let x_{ijk} represent the correlation between miner i and mining pool k after miner i joins attack mining pool j. If $x_{ijk} = 1$ and $j = k$, miner i is related to attack mining pool j, and carries out honest mining in attacking mining pool j. If $x_{ijk} = 1$ and $j \neq k$, according to the assignment of attack mining pool j, miner i carries out block withholding attack on mining pool k. If $x_{ijk} = 0$, there is no correlation. So the correlation should meet the following condition.

$$\sum_j \sum_k x_{ijk} = 1, \forall i \tag{1}$$

Let w_{ij} represents indicator whether miner i carries out honest mining in attack mining pool j. It is

$$w_{ij} = \begin{cases} 1 & j = k \\ 0 & others \end{cases} \tag{2}$$

Let s_{ijk} represents indicator whether miner i carries out block withholding attack on mining pool k according to the assignment of attacking mining pool j. It is

$$s_{ijk} = \begin{cases} 1 & j \neq k \ and \ x_{ijk} = 1 \\ 0 & others \end{cases} \tag{3}$$

Then the effective computing power of each attack mining pool is

$$y_j = \sum_i c_i w_{ij} \tag{4}$$

Where y_j represents the total computing power of honest mining in attack mining pool j. c_i represents computing power of miner i. The computing power of block withholding attack in each attack mining pool j and the computing power of block withholding attack assigned by attack mining pool j are

$$a_j = \sum_k \sum_i c_i s_{ikj}, v_j = \sum_k \sum_i c_i s_{ijk} \tag{5}$$

Where a_j represents the total computing power of block withholding attack in the mining pool j assigned by other mining pools. v_j represents the total computing power of block withholding attack in other mining pools assigned by attack mining pool j. In the mining pool j, part of its honest mining revenue is allocated to the computing power of block withholding attack a_j against the mining pool j. Therefore, real honest mining revenue R_j^H is

$$R_j^H = \frac{y_j}{\sum_j y_j + y_H} \times \frac{y_j + v_j}{y_j + a_j + v_j} \tag{6}$$

Where y_H represents the computing power of the mining pool that only carries out honest mining in the network. Then the real block withholding attack revenue R_j^W of mining pool j is the block withholding attack revenue allocated by its computing power v_j. So R_j^W is

$$R_j^W = \sum_k \left(\frac{y_k}{\sum_j y_j + y_H} \times \frac{\gamma_{jk}}{y_k + a_k + v_k} \right) \tag{7}$$

Where γ_{jk} represents the computing power of block withholding attack on mining pool k assigned by attack mining pool j.

When miners in the mining pool carry out honest mining or block withholding attack, they need to consume power, equipment damage and other resources. Therefore, the honest mining cost which per unit of computing power consumes is C_H. The block withholding attack cost which per unit of computing power consumes is C_P. Then total revenue R_j of mining pool j is

$$R_j = R_j^W + R_j^H - y_j C_H - v_j C_P \tag{8}$$

Considering that miner revenue in the mining pool is allocated according to the provided computing power, that is, revenue R_i^c of miner i, which provides part of computing power in y_j and v_j to mining pool j, is defined as

$$R_i^c = R_j \frac{c_i}{y_j + v_j} \tag{9}$$

Because of the fixed computing power of miner and average revenue allocation method, the miner revenue optimization model converts into the revenue optimization model of the attack mining pool. So we establish a revenue optimization model of each attack mining pool j.

$$\max(R_j)$$
$$s.t. formulas(1) - (8), \forall i, k \tag{10}$$
$$x_{ijk} \in \{0, 1\}, \forall i, k$$

On the other hand, as the maintainer of attack mining pool group, it hopes that every miner in each attack mining pool can improve his revenue, and try to make the unit computing power revenue of all miners have little difference. Therefore, we establish a group efficiency optimization model of mining pools under block withholding attack.

$$\max(R_m^{av} R_m^{\min} / \text{var}_m)$$
$$s.t. formulas(1) - (9), \forall i, j, k \tag{11}$$
$$x_{ijk} \in \{0, 1\}, \forall i, j, k$$

Where R_m^{av} represents average miner revenue, R_m^{min} represents minimum miner revenue, var_m represents miner revenue variance, that is, represents revenue balance state.

2.2   Model Solution

Population Initialization. The current number of miners is N_w, while the number of attack mining pools is N_c. The number of food sources is SN. MROA initializes the food source as $N_w * 2$ array. The first column represents the mining pool's serial number which the miner belongs to, and the second column represents the mining pool's serial number where the miner is currently located.

If two serial numbers in the same row are the same, it means that the miner is honest mining in the mining pool. Otherwise, it means that the miner is assigned by the first mining pool to carry out block withholding attack on the second mining pool.

Employed Bee Operation. According to the food source in the population, MROA calculates the evaluation value of each food source according to formula (12), and regards the food source with the highest evaluation value as optimal food source x_{sta}.

$$f_m = R_m^{av} R_m^{min} / \mathrm{var}_m \tag{12}$$

Where f_m represents evaluation value of the mth food source. Combining with formula (13), the selection probability of food source is as follows.

$$P_m^{se} = f_m / \sum_{m=1}^{SN} f_m \tag{13}$$

Where P_m^{se} represents the selection probability of food source.

After obtaining the evaluation value and selection probability of each food source, MROA selects optimal food source x_{sta}, and determines another crossover food source x_{alt} by the selection probability and roulette method. Then it crosses the rows of food sources for N_w times. Next, MROA uses mutation operation of each row of the food source for N_w times to ensure that the revenue gap among mining pools is not large.

Then the Pareto dominance method implements through formula (14). That is, MROA compares the revenue of each attack mining pool in any two food sources. If the revenue of every attack mining pool in one food source is larger than or equal to that of same attack mining pool in another food source, and there is at least one attack mining pool whose revenue is larger than that of the same attack mining pool in another food source, it means that the food source dominates another food source. Then it deletes another food source. Finally, MROA obtains the non-dominated solution set QF_1.

$$R_i(\kappa) \geq R_i(\lambda) \ and \ \exists R_\varepsilon(\kappa) > R_\varepsilon(\lambda), i = 1, \ldots \varepsilon \ldots, N_c \tag{14}$$

Where κ and λ represent two food sources, $R_i()$ represents the revenue of attack mining pool i in food source.

Onlooker Bee Operation. MROA calculates the revenue of each attack mining pool in each food source of set QF_1, and sorts the food sources according to the revenue of each attack mining pool. According to the sort of all food sources based on the revenue of each attack mining pool, MROA finds the adjacent food sources in the sort and obtains the corresponding attack mining pool revenue $R_j(\mathbf{x}_{m+1})$ and $R_j(\mathbf{x}_{m-1})$. The crowding degree of each food source in the non-dominated solution set QF_1 is as follows.

$$d_i = \begin{cases} \infty & , i = 1 \ and \ s_{QF_1} \\ \sum_{j=1}^{M} \frac{|R_j(\mathbf{x}_{m+1}) - R_j(\mathbf{x}_{m-1})|}{R_j^{\max} - R_j^{\min}}, 1 < i < s_{QF_1} \end{cases} \tag{15}$$

Where d_i represents crowding degree of food source i, s_{QF_1} represents numbers of food sources in the non-dominated solution set QF_1, $R_j^{\max}$ represents maximum revenue of attack mining pool j in the food source, $R_j^{\min}$ represents minimum revenue of attack mining pool j in the food source.

In each onlooker bee, according to the crowding degree of each food source in the non-dominated solution set QF_1, MROA determines the food source $\mathbf{x}_\psi$ and carries out neighborhood crossover and mutation operations which are consistent with those of employed bee. Then the new food source is into the non-dominated solution set QF_1 and the non-dominated solution set QF_2 is obtained by Pareto domination method. The food source with the largest evaluation value is an effective solution in the solution set.

Scout Bee Operation. During each iteration, MROA records the number of times ς_i of food source i that no new food source can be generated in the food source i. If $\varsigma_i > \varsigma_{thr}$, then it deletes the food source i from the set, and generates a new food source into the set QF_2 and $\varsigma_i = 0$.

3 Algorithm Simulation

3.1 Simulation Parameters and Performance Parameters

To verify the performance of MROA, we select simulation parameters in Table 1 through parameter simulation. Because NSGA2 (Non-dominated Sorting Genetic Algorithm II) [18], MOPSO (Multiple Objective Particle Swarm Optimization) [15] and ABC (Artificial Bee Colony) [10] both can find the miner allocation scheme for each attack mining pool under the block withholding attack. So we select them as comparison algorithms and calculate the minimum miner

Table 1. Simulation Parameter.

Parameter name	Value	Parameter name	Value
Number of honest mining pool N_v	1	Initial computing power c_i	0.1
Number of attack mining pool N_c	6	Number of onlooker bees	10
Maximum number of iterations θ	50	Crossover factor threshold η_{1thr}	0.05
Block withholding attack cost C_P	0.02	Revenue value in each iteration	1000
Number of food sources SN	20	Honest mining cost C_H	0.05

revenue, miner revenue variance, spacing value and the evaluation value of optimal solution when the number of miners changes. The miner revenue is defined as the minimum revenue of miners in the output solution. The miner revenue variance is defined as the revenue variance of all miners in the output solution. The spacing value is defined as the minimum standard deviation from each solution to other solutions in the non-dominated solution set. The spacing value measures the uniformity of the non-dominated solution set, which is expressed as

$$S_P = \sqrt{\frac{1}{|P|} \sum_{i=1}^{|P|} (\bar{z} - z_i)^2} \qquad (16)$$

Where P represents non-dominated solution set, $|P|$ represents the number of solutions in set, z_i represents the minimum euclidean distance from the ith solution to other solutions in set P, $\bar{z}$ represents the mean value of z_i.

3.2   Analysis of Simulation Results

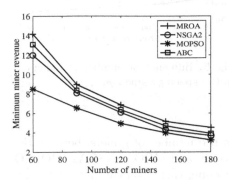

Fig. 2. Influence of number of miners on the minimum miner revenue.

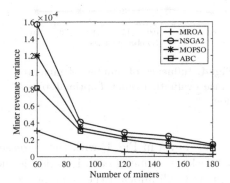

Fig. 3. Influence of number of miners on the miner revenue variance.

As shown in Fig. 2, with the increase in the number of miners, in order to improve the revenues of their mining pools and reduce the influence of block withholding attack from other mining pools to their mining pools, the mining pools tend to put more computing power into block withholding attack, resulting in the decline of minimum miner revenues in MROA, NSGA2 and MOPSO. MROA takes minimum miner revenue as one of the evaluation parameters of the food source. And through the improved crossover and mutation operations, Pareto domination calculation and crowding degree calculation, the food source with higher minimum miner revenue is selected to the next generation of the food source, so as to improve the minimum miner revenue. Therefore, the minimum miner revenue in MROA is higher than those in NSGA2, MOPSO and ABC.

As shown in Fig. 3, with the increase in the number of miners, the disposable computing power in single mining pool increases, so each mining pool has sufficient computing power to allocate and improve its revenue, resulting in the gradual decline of miner revenue variance in each algorithm. MROA takes miner revenue variance as one of the food source's evaluation parameters, and improves the traditional crossover operation and elite retention strategy to eliminate the food source with poor evaluation value. At the same time, it uses Pareto domination method to ensure the revenue balance of mining pools, and keeps the miner revenue gap among mining pools in a certain range. Therefore, the miner revenue variance in MROA is lower than those in NSGA2, MOPSO and ABC.

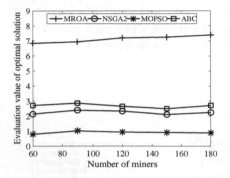

Fig. 4. Influence of number of miners on the evaluation value of optimal solution.

Fig. 5. Influence of number of miners on the spacing value S_P.

As shown in Fig. 4, with the increase in the number of miners, because the network's revenue of each iteration is the same, and MROA, NSGA2, MOPSO and ABC all allocate the same network revenue, their average miner revenues gradually decrease. At the same time, their miner revenue variances and minimum miner revenues decrease, resulting in that the evaluation values of the optimal solution in MROA, NSGA2, MOPSO and ABC basically do not change. With the same number of miners, MROA improves the minimum and average miner revenue, and reduces miner revenue variance. Therefore, the evaluation value of the optimal solution in MROA is higher than those in NSGA2, MOPSO and ABC.

As shown in Fig. 5, with the increase in the number of miners, the disposable computing power in a single mining pool increases significantly, which makes the computing power allocation of algorithms in food source approximately similar. The solution difference in the non-dominated solutions sets shrinks, resulting in that the spacing values of MROA, NSGA2, MOPSO and ABC gradually decrease. MROA keeps the current optimal solution scheme with elite retention, and better determines the search direction of the optimal solution with mutation operation. It also expands the range of solution set with crossover operation, and searches for the non-dominated solution set with balanced distribution in multi-dimensional space as much as possible by onlooker bee operation such as crowding degree calculation and Pareto domination calculation. Therefore, spacing value S_P in MROA is lower than those in NSGA2, MOPSO and ABC.

4 Conclusion

We propose a mining revenue optimal algorithm (MROA) in the PoW based blockchain. First, we establish a revenue optimization model of each attack mining pool and group efficiency optimization model of mining pools under block withholding attack. Secondly, in order to maximize the self-revenue optimization model and group revenue optimization model of mining pools, we use a modified artificial bee colony algorithm based on Pareto. The simulation results show that no matter how the numbers of miners change, MROA can find a reasonable miner allocation scheme for each attack mining pool, so as to improves minimum miner revenue and evaluation value of the optimal solution, and reduces miner revenue variance and spacing value of solution set.

Acknowledgments. This work was supported by the Natural Science Foundation of Zhejiang Province of China under Grants No. LQ18F030006 and Y21F020114, and Zhejiang Shuren University Basic Scientific Research Special Funds under Grant No. 2020XZ009.

References

1. Cai, Z., He, Z.: Trading private range counting over big IoT data. In: 2019 IEEE 39th International Conference on Distributed Computing Systems (ICDCS). pp. 144–153. IEEE (2019)
2. Cai, Z., He, Z., Guan, X., Li, Y.: Collective data-sanitization for preventing sensitive information inference attacks in social networks. IEEE Trans. Depend. Secure. Comput. 15(4), 577–590 (2018)
3. Cai, Z., Zheng, X.: A private and efficient mechanism for data uploading in smart cyber-physical systems. IEEE Trans. Netw. Sci. Eng. 7(2), 766–775 (2020)
4. Cai, Z., Zheng, X., Yu, J.: A differential-private framework for urban traffic flows estimation via taxi companies. IEEE Trans. Ind. Inf. 15(12), 6492–6499 (2019)
5. Cao, S., Cong, L.W., Han, M., Hou, Q., Yang, B.: Blockchain architecture for auditing automation and trust building in public markets. Computer 53(7), 20–28 (2020)
6. Fan, L., Zheng, H., Huang, J., Li, Z., Jiang, Y.: Cooperative evolution method for blockchain mining pool based on adaptive zero-determinant strategy. J. Comput. Appl. 39(03), 918–923 (2019)
7. Han, J., Zou, J., Jiang, H., Xu, Q.: Research on mining attacks in bitcoin. J. Cryptol. Res. 5(05), 470–483 (2018)
8. Joshi, A.P., Han, M., Wang, Y.: A survey on security and privacy issues of blockchain technology. Math. Found. Comput. 1(2), 121–147 (2018)
9. Kim, S., Hahn, S.: Mining pool manipulation in blockchain network over evolutionary block withholding attack. IEEE Access 7, 144230–144244 (2019)

10. Li, G., Cui, L., Fu, X., Wen, Z., Lu, N., Lu, J.: Artificial bee colony algorithm with gene recombination for numerical function optimization. Appl. Soft Comput. **52**, 146–159 (2017)
11. Ling, X., Wu, C., Ji, S., Han, M.: Http/2 dos: an application-layer dos attack towards http/2 protocol. In: International Conference on Security and Privacy in Communication Systems. pp. 550–570 (2017)
12. Liu, X., Wang, W., Niyato, D., Zhao, N., Wang, P.: Evolutionary game for mining pool selection in blockchain networks. IEEE Wirel. Commun. Lett. **7**(5), 760–763 (2018)
13. Rosenfeld, M.: Analysis of bitcoin pooled mining system (2011), https://arxiv.org/pdf/1112.4980.pdf
14. Singh, A., Parizi, R.M., Han, M., Dehghantanha, A., Karimipour, H., Choo, K.-K.R.: Public blockchains scalability: an examination of sharding and segregated witness. In: Choo, K.-K.R., Dehghantanha, A., Parizi, R.M. (eds.) Blockchain Cybersecurity, Trust and Privacy. AIS, vol. 79, pp. 203–232. Springer, Cham (2020). https://doi.org/10.1007/978-3-030-38181-3_11
15. Sivaranjani, R., Roomi, S.M.M., Senthilarasi, M.: Speckle noise removal in sar images using multi-objective pso (mopso) algorithm. Appl. Soft Comput. **76**, 671–681 (2019)
16. Wang, T., Yu, S., Baomin, X.: Research on proof of work mining dilemma based on policy gradient algorithm. J. Comput. Appl. **39**(05), 1336–1342 (2019)
17. Yang, T., Xue, Z.: Game theory among mining pools in blockchain system. Commun. Technol. **52**(05), 1189–1195 (2019)
18. Zhao, B., Xue, Y., Xu, B., Ma, T., Liu, J.: Multi-objective classification based on nsga-ii. Int. J. Comput. Math. **9**(6), 539–546 (2018)
19. Zhu, S., Cai, Z., Hu, H., Li, Y., Li, W.: Zkcrowd: a hybrid blockchain-based crowdsourcing platform. IEEE Trans. Ind. Inf. **16**(6), 4196–4205 (2020)

Can the Max-Min Fair Allocation Be Trustful in a Centralized Resource System?

Zheng Chen[1], Zhaoquan Gu[2(✉)], and Yuexuan Wang[1]

[1] College of Computer Science and Technology, Zhejiang University,
Hangzhou, China
{21721122,amywang}@zju.edu.cn
[2] Cyberspace Institute of Advanced Technology, Guangzhou University,
Guangzhou, China
zqgu@gzhu.edu.cn

Abstract. Resource allocation draws much attention from various areas and it is a hot topic to explore trustful allocation mechanisms. In this paper, we study the problem in a centralized resource system where a controller allocates appropriate resources to other nodes according to their demands. **The max-min fair allocation** enables fairness among the nodes and we explore whether the allocation is trustful when a node behaves strategically. We first introduce a simple but efficient algorithm to generate the max-min fair allocation, and then we analyze how the allocated resources vary when a new node is added to the system. To discuss about the trustfulness of the allocation, we propose two strategic behaviors: *misreporting strategy* which the new node misreports its resource demand and *spitting strategy* which the node misrepresents itself by creating several fictitious nodes but keeps the sum of their resource demands the same. Surprisingly, we show that the allocation is trustful against the misreporting strategy while it is not trustful against the spitting strategy. Specifically, we present some illustrative examples to verify the results, and we show that a node can achieve 1.83 times resource if it misrepresents itself as two nodes.

Keywords: Max-min fairness · Trustfulness · Mechanism design · Centralized resource system

1 Introduction

Resource allocation has been widely studied in various areas when facing with limited resources such as fossil fuels, clean water and network resources. In early 1940s, the method to ensure n participants receive at least $1/n$ of each

This work was supported in part by the National Natural Science Foundation of China under Grant No. U1636215, the Guangdong Province Key Research and Development Plan under Grant No. 2019B010136003, and the National Key Research and Development Program of China 2018YFB1004003.

© Springer Nature Switzerland AG 2020
D. Yu et al. (Eds.): WASA 2020, LNCS 12384, pp. 51–64, 2020.
https://doi.org/10.1007/978-3-030-59016-1_5

participant's own value is proposed in [27] and the notion of "envy-freenes", which participants prefer to keep their own allocation is proposed in [16]. Since then, research concerning resource allocation in a centralized system has aroused widespread concern and has been applied to solve many important real-world problems [5,10,22]. However it is still an open problem to design a trustful allocation in a centralized resource system.

Motivated by sharing economy concepts [28], nodes in a resource system may take strategic behaviors to gain more resources. In [19], it proves that designing a trustful mechanism that guarantees a market equilibrium outcome in general is impossible when a node has the incentive to misreport its information (such as its resource amount or demand). Some extant works also show that the trustfulness of resource allocating mechanisms cannot hold for a cheating node [1,8]. However, the impossibility theorem proposed in [19] is not correct for some restricted settings. For example, the proportional sharing mechanism is proved to be robust to nodes' cheating in [12,13].

In this paper, we explore whether the max-min fair allocation is trustful in a centralized resource system. In the system, a central controller holds the resources; each node reports its resource demand and the controller allocates appropriate resources according to the demands. For example, computers in a cluster of data center require network resources but the central controller have to design a fair allocation mechanism regarding all the computers' demands. To evaluate the fairness of a resource allocation, we use the concept of *max-min fair allocation*, which is widely adopted in networks, such as window flow central protocols [18], packer-switched networks [6], and data networks [14].

A max-min fair allocation is unique in a centralized resource system and we present a simple but efficient algorithm to compute it. In order to explore the trustfulness of the allocation, we first assume a new node is added to the system and we analyze how the allocated resources vary. Then we introduce two strategic behaviors, *misreporting strategy* assumes the new node may misreport its resource demand and *spitting strategy* [11] assumes the node may misrepresent itself by creating several fictitious nodes but keep the sum of reported resource demands unchanged. In this paper, we prove that the new node cannot gain more resources by the misreporting strategy but it could gain more by the spitting strategy. Specifically, if a node is split into two nodes, it can achieve about two times resource compared to the allocation that it is honest. We also present some numerical examples to illustrate these results which the spitting strategy could indeed help a node gain about 1.83 times resource if it misrepresents itself as two nodes (as shown in Table 3). Therefore the max-min fair allocation in a centralized resource system is not trustful against the spitting strategy.

The rest of the paper is organized as follows. The next section lists some related works about trustfulness of resource allocation mechanisms. The preliminaries are introduced in Sect. 3. We present the efficient algorithm that generates the max-min fair allocation in Sect. 4. When a new node is added to the system, we analyze the change of the allocation in Sect. 5. The trustfulness of the allocation against the misreporting strategy and the spitting strategy are discussed in Sect. 6 and Sect. 7 respectively. Finally, we present some numerical examples in Sect. 8 and conclude the paper in Sect. 9.

2 Related Work

Resource allocation in a centralized system has drawn much attention from various areas. Cake cutting problem is a relevant one, which divides a birthday cake for several children with fairness. The problem is initiated in [27] and a large number of allocating mechanisms have emerged in [22, 25, 26]. Max-min fairness is a simple but well-recognized approach to define a fair allocation in resource allocation systems [7, 20, 21, 23], and it has been widely adopted in economics [2, 11], load balancing in cloud systems[17], and image classification [4].

In a resource allocation system, nodes may be strategic, which means it may take strategic behaviors to gain more resources. Therefore, studying the trustfulness of the allocation mechanisms has been of paramount importance. In order to gain more resources, a node may misreport its true information, which may affect the market equilibrium. In [19], it proves that it is impossible to design a truthful mechanism that guarantees a market equilibrium outcome in general. In a Fisher market game with linear utility, nodes can unilaterally deviate and get a better payoff [1]. More specifically, nodes may double their benefit by strategic behaviors [8]. However, some extant works show that a trustful allocation may exist in some restricted settings [12, 13]. Therefore, we intend to explore whether the max-min fair allocation is trustful in a centralized resource system.

Generally, we consider two types of strategic behaviors: a node may misreport its own information (such as resource amount or demand) and a node may cheat on its connectivity with the rest of the network. By cheating on the connectivity, such as a missing edge or splitting a node into multiple nodes may affect the resource allocation mechanism. In [15], it examines the incentive problem in mechanism design in internet applications or peer-to-peer systems when a node misrepresents itself by creating several fictitious agents. In [9], it measures how a node gains if it deviates from its trustful behavior. In [24], it shows that nodes' selfish behavior may contribute to the loss of social efficiency in Nash equilibrium in comparison to social optimality. In this paper, we analyze the max-min fair allocation against these two strategies.

3 Preliminaries

Consider a centralized resource system $G = (V, E)$ where a central node c holds the resources W_c that can be allocated to other nodes $E \setminus \{c\} = \{v_1, v_2, \ldots, v_n\}$. For any node $v_i, i \in [1, n]$, denote its resource demand as m_i and we assume it cannot gain more resource than m_i in reality. Considering a resource allocation R, denote the allocation vector as $\overrightarrow{X}_{cv} = \{x_{cv_1}, x_{cv_2}, \ldots, x_{cv_n}\}$, where $x_{cv_i} \leq m_i$ represents the received resource of node v_i. Since resources may decay during the transferring process (such as fossil fuels and clean water), denote $t_i \geq 1$ as the transfer rate and the central node allocates $x_{cv_i} \cdot t_i$ resources to node v_i in reality. Some resource allocation mechanisms [11,13] do not consider the loss during the transmission, we can set $t_i = 1$.

In this paper, we study max-min fair allocation and explore whether the allocation is trustful against different strategic behaviors. Max-min fairness is a common adopted concept and we introduce max-min fair vector [3] briefly.

Definition 1. *A vector $\vec{x}$ is a max-min fair vector on set χ if and only if for all $\vec{y} \in \chi$, if there exists $s \in \{1, 2, \ldots, n\}$ such that $y_s > x_s$, there must exist $t \in \{1, 2, \ldots, n\}$ such that $y_t < x_t < x_s$.*

The definition reveals that increasing some element of a max-min fair vector $\vec{x}$ must be at the expense of decreasing some smaller (or equal) element of the vector. The uniqueness of the max-min fair vector is suggested in [3]. We would present an efficient algorithm to compute the allocation and discuss about the trustfulness when a new node is added.

4   The Max-Min Fair Allocation Algorithm

We present the algorithm to generate the max-min fair allocation in Algorithm 1. Denote the resource demands of all nodes as $\vec{m} = \{m_1, m_2, \ldots, m_n\}$ and the transfer rates as $\vec{t} = \{t_1, t_2, \ldots, t_n\}$. The algorithm is to generate the max-min fair vector $\vec{X}_{cv} = \{x_{cv_1}, x_{cv_2}, \ldots, x_{cv_n}\}$.

Algorithm 1. The Max-Min Fair Allocation Algorithm

1: Input $\vec{m} = \{m_1, m_2, ..., m_n\}$, $\vec{t} = \{t_1, t_2, ..., t_n\}$
2: Output $\vec{U} = \{u_1, u_2, \ldots, u_n\}$
3: Sort $\vec{m}$ by increasing order as $\vec{m}' = \{m_1', m_2', \ldots, m_n'\}$ where $m_i' \leq m_j', \forall i < j$; denote the corresponding nodes as $\{v_{1'}, v_{2'}, \ldots, v_{n'}\}$;
4: **for** $i \leftarrow 1$ to n **do**
5:     **if** $\sum_{j=1}^{i-1} t_{j'} \cdot m_j' + m_i' \sum_{j=i}^{n} t_{j'} \leq W_c$ **then**
6:         $x_{cv_{i'}} = m_i'$
7:     **else**
8:         **for** $k \leftarrow i$ to n **do**
9:             $x_{cv_{k'}} = \frac{W_c - \sum_{j=1}^{i-1} t_{j'} \cdot m_j'}{\sum_{j=i}^{n} t_{j'}}$;
10:        **end for**
11:    **end if**
12: **end for**

As depicted in Algorithm 1, $\vec{m}$ is sorted by increasing order (line 3) and denote the corresponding nodes as $\{v_{1'}, v_{2'}, \ldots, v_{n'}\}$ where $m_i' \leq m_j'$ for any $i < j$. The resources are allocated to nodes from $v_{1'}$ to $v_{n'}$ according to lines 5–9. There are two situations: if the resources are adequate enough (line 5), node $v_{i'}$ can receive the resources that are up to its demand m_i' (line 6); or it is set as line 8. We show the correctness of the algorithm by verifying the allocation vector $\overrightarrow{X}_{cv} = \{x_{cv_1}, \dots, x_{cv_n}\}$ is the max-min fair vector.

Theorem 1. *Algorithm 1 generates the max-min fair allocation vector.*

Proof. For simplicity, we assume the input vector $\overrightarrow{m}$ is already ordered such that $v_{i'} = v_i$. We prove the theorem from two situations.

For the first case, suppose $W_c \geq \sum_{j=1}^{n} t_j m_j$, which implies the central node has enough resources to ensure all nodes' resource demands be satisfied. Thus, $\overrightarrow{X_{c_v}} = \{m_1, m_2, \dots, m_n\}$. According to the definition of the max-min fair vector, any element of the $\overrightarrow{X_{c_v}}$ can not be larger, hence $\overrightarrow{X_{c_v}}$ is the max-min fair vector.

For the second case, suppose $W_c < \sum_{j=1}^{n} t_j m_j$; there must exist $i \in [1, n]$ such that $\forall j < i$, $x_{cv_j} = m_j$ and $x_{cv_i} = \frac{W_c - \sum_{j=1}^{i-1} t_j m_j}{\sum_{j=i}^{n} t_j} < m_j$ since Algorithm 1 computes x_{cv_i} sequentially from $i = 1$ to $i = n$. Then, we derive the output of Algorithm 1 as

$$\overrightarrow{X}_{cv} = \{m_1, \dots, m_{i-1}, \frac{W_c - \sum_{j=1}^{i-1} t_j m_j}{\sum_{j=i}^{n} t_j}, \dots, \frac{W_c - \sum_{j=1}^{i-1} t_j m_j}{\sum_{j=i}^{n} t_j}\}.$$

For any other allocation vector $\overrightarrow{X}_{cv}^* = \{x_{cv_1}^*, \dots, x_{cv_n}^*\}$, if there exists $s \in [1, n]$ such that $x_{cv_s}^* > x_{cv_s}$, for any $t \in [1, n]$ satisfying $x_{cv_t} < x_{cv_s}$, suppose $x_{cv_t}^* \geq x_{cv_t}$; then we have: $x_{cv_1}^* t_1 + \dots + x_{cv_n}^* t_n > x_{cv_1} t_1 + \dots + x_{cv_n} t_n = W_c$, which leads to a contradiction since the allocation exceeds the amount of all resources W_c. Therefore, there exists $t \in [1, n]$ such that $x_{cv_t}^* < x_{cv_t} < x_{cv_s}$. By Definition 1, $\overrightarrow{X}_{cv}$ is the max-min fair vector. Combining the two cases, the theorem holds. $\blacksquare$

We analyze the complexity of Algorithm 1 briefly. The complexity of sorting on line 3 is $O(n \log n)$, and the complexity of computing each x_{cv_i} in each step (line 5–9) is $O(1)$. Thus, the complexity of the algorithm is $O(n \log n + n) = O(n \log n)$ and it works efficiently. In the following parts, we adopt the algorithm to find out the max-min allocation when a new node is added or it behaviors strategically.

5   Resource Allocation Varies for a New Node

In a centralized resource system $G = (V, E)$ with the max-min fair allocation vector $\overrightarrow{X_{cv}^*} = \{x_{cv_1}^*, x_{cv_2}^*, \dots, x_{cv_n}^*\}$, we analyze how the allocation varies if a new node v_δ is added. Denote the new node's demand as m_δ, transfer rate as t_δ, and the max-min fair allocation vector of the new system as $\overrightarrow{X_{cv}} = \{x_{cv_1}, x_{cv_2}, \dots, x_{cv_n}, x_{cv_\delta}\}$. We analyze the relationship between $\overrightarrow{X_{cv}^*}$ and $\overrightarrow{X_{cv}}$.

Let R be the spare resources under the original allocation $\overrightarrow{X_{cv}^*}$, and it can be formulated as $R = W_c - \sum_{j=1}^{n} x_{cv_j} t_j$. For simplicity, suppose the nodes' demands satisfy $m_1 \leq m_2 \leq \ldots \leq m_n$. We analyze how the allocation varies when node v_δ is added from two cases: **Case 1:** $R \geq t_\delta m_\delta$; **Case 2:** $0 \leq R < t_\delta m_\delta$. We first introduce a property of the max-min fair allocation:

Property 1. In the max-min allocation, if there exists $k \in [1, n]$ such that $x_{cv_k} = m_k$, for all $i \in [1, k)$, $x_{cv_i} = m_i$.

The property reveals that nodes with less received resources remain the same if a node with more resources does not change in the new allocation.

Proof. Suppose there exists $v_i \in [1, k)$ satisfying $x_{cv_i} < m_i$; according to the allocation algorithm (Algorithm 1), since $i < k$, we can derive:

$$\sum_{j=1}^{k-1} t_j m_j + m_k \sum_{j=k}^{n} t_j \geq \sum_{j=1}^{i-1} t_j m_j + m_i \sum_{j=i}^{n} t_j > W_c; \qquad (1)$$

hence $x_{vu_k} < m_k$, which makes a contradiction.

We analyze how the max-min fair allocation varies for the first case.

Theorem 2. *If $R \geq t_\delta m_\delta$, the new allocation holds $x_{cv_\delta} = m_\delta$ and $x_{cv_i} = m_i$ does not change when the new node v_δ is added.*

The proof for the theorem is obvious and we omit the details. The overall resources are enough for all nodes to receive the resources up to their demands.

When $0 \leq R < t_\delta m_\delta$, we analyze how the max-min fair allocation varies. We find out a threshold r such that the nodes with resources less than r do not change (Lemma 1). Considering nodes who received resources larger than r, we analyze them from two cases: $m_\delta > r$ (Lemma 2) and $m_\delta \leq r$ (Lemma 3). Finally, we compute the allocated resources of the new node v_δ (Lemma 4).

Lemma 1. *If $R < t_\delta m_\delta$, there exists $r = \frac{W_c - \sum_{j=1}^{i-1} t_j m_j}{\sum_{j=i}^{n} t_j + t_\delta}$ such that node $v_i, i \in [1, n]$ remains $x_{cv_i} = m_i$ if it satisfies $m_i \leq r$.*

Proof. Suppose $m_1 \leq m_2 \leq \ldots \leq m_{i-1} \leq r \leq m_i \leq \ldots \leq m_n$, we derive

$$\sum_{j=1}^{i-2} t_j m_j + m_{i-1} \sum_{j=i-1}^{n} t_j + t_\delta m_{i-1} \leq W_c \Rightarrow m_{i-1} \leq \frac{W_c - \sum_{j=1}^{i-2} t_j m_j}{t_\delta + \sum_{j=i-1}^{n} t_j}.$$

Then we find the largest integer $i - 1$ satisfying the above inequality and derive

$$r(\sum_{j=i}^{n} t_j + t_\delta) = W_c - \sum_{j=1}^{i-1} t_j m_j \Rightarrow r = \frac{W_c - \sum_{j=1}^{i-1} t_j m_j}{\sum_{j=i}^{n} t_j + t_\delta}.$$

Since $x_{cv_{i-1}} = m_{i-1}$, for any node v_k with $m_k \leq m_{i-1} \leq r$, $x_{cv_k} = m_k$ by Property 1. The lemma holds.

It is easy to check that the node v_k with $m_k \leq r$ received resources $x^*_{cv_k} = m_k$ in the original allocation vector before the new node is added. Finding out the threshold value r, these nodes do not change the received resources. Considering nodes v_k satisfying $m_k < r$, we analyze them from two cases: $m_\delta > r$ and $m_\delta \leq r$.

Lemma 2. *If $R < t_\delta m_\delta$, $m_\delta > r = \frac{W_c - \sum_{j=1}^{i-1} t_j m_j}{\sum_{j=i}^{n} t_j + t_\delta}$, node $v_i, i \in [1, n]$ satisfying $m_i > r$ receives less resources $x_{cv_i} < x^*_{cv_i} \leq m_i$ under the new allocation.*

Proof. First, we show that $x_{cv_i} < m_i$ under the new max-min fair allocation for any node v_i satisfying $m_i > r$. This means the threshold r divides the nodes into two subsets; one subset contains nodes that receive resources up to their demands as Lemma 1, while the other subset consists of nodes that cannot receive resources up to their demands even though their demands are larger than r.

Suppose there exists a node v_k such that $m_k > r$ and $x_{cv_k} = m_k$. According to Property 1, node v_i ($v \in [1, k-1]$) receives resources $x_{cv_i} = m_i$. There are two cases: $m_k \geq m_\delta$ and $m_k < m_\delta$. For the first case that $m_k \geq m_\delta$, we drive

$$\sum_{j=1}^{k-1} t_j m_j + m_\delta t_\delta + m_k \sum_{j=k}^{n} t_j > \sum_{j=1}^{k-1} t_j m_j + r t_\delta + r \sum_{j=k}^{n} t_j = W_c,$$

which is a contradiction. When $m_\delta > m_k$, we can deduce a contradiction similarly. Therefore, $x_{cv_i} < m_i$ for node v_i with $m_i > r$.

Then, we show that node v_i with $m_i > r$ receive less resources compared to the original max-min fair allocation; that is $x_{cv_i} < x^*_{cv_i}$. Denote $x^*_{cv_i} = \alpha$, suppose $x_{cv_i} \geq x^*_{cv_i} = \alpha$, we can derive

$$\sum_{j=1}^{i-1} t_j m_j + m_\alpha t_\delta + \alpha \sum_{j=i}^{n} t_j > \sum_{j=1}^{i-1} t_j m_j + \alpha \sum_{j=i}^{n} t_j > W_c,$$

which is a contradiction. Combining the two sides, $x_{cv_i} < x^*_{cv_i} \leq m_i$ holds.

Lemma 2 implies that if the new node's demand is large $m_\delta > r$, all nodes with large demands ($m_i > r$) have to reduce their received resources. If $m_\delta \leq r$, fewer nodes have to reduce their resources and we show it in the next lemma.

Lemma 3. *If $R < t_\delta m_\delta$, $m_\delta \leq r = \frac{W_c - \sum_{j=1}^{i-1} t_j m_j}{\sum_{j=i}^{n} t_j + t_\delta}$, there exists $r_1 \geq r$ such that the following two results hold:*

1) If node v_i satisfies $m_i > r_1$, $x_{cv_i} < x^*_{cv_i} \leq m_i$;
2) If node v_i satisfies $m_i \leq r_1$, $x_{cv_i} = x^*_{cv_i} = m_i$.

Proof. If $m_\delta \leq r$, there exists $i_1 \leq i_2$ such that $m_1 \leq m_2 \leq \ldots \leq m_{i_1-1} \leq m_\delta \leq \ldots \leq m_{i_2-1} \leq r \leq m_{i_2} \leq \ldots \leq m_n$, we have:

$$\sum_{j=1}^{i_2-1} t_j m_j + m_\delta t_\delta + m_{i_2-1} \sum_{j=i_2}^{n} t_j \leq \sum_{j=1}^{i_2-1} t_j m_j + r(t_\delta + \sum_{j=i_2}^{n} t_j) \leq W_c;$$

thus $x_{cv_{i_2-1}} = m_{i_2-1}$. According to Property 1, $x_{cv_k} = m_k$ if $k \leq i_2 - 1$, which implies $x_{cv_\delta} = m_\delta$. Since $R < t_\delta m_\delta$, nodes with more resources would reduce its resources and there must exist $r_1 \geq m_{i_2-1}$ such that $x_{cv_k} = x^*_{cv_k} = m_k$ if $m_k \leq r_1$ (nodes do not change their resources), and $x_{cv_k} < x^*_{cv_k} \leq m_k$ if $m_k > r_1$ (nodes reduce their resources).

Next we show that the value $r_1 \geq r$. It is clear that if $r_1 \geq m_{i_2}$, $r_1 > r$. Suppose $m_{i_2-1} \leq r_1 < m_{i_2}$, we derive

$$r_1 \sum_{j=i_2}^{n} t_j + m_\delta t_\delta = W_c - \sum_{j=1}^{i_2-1} t_j m_j; \Rightarrow (r_1 - r) \sum_{j=i_2}^{n} t_j = (r - m_\delta)t_\delta \geq 0. \quad (2)$$

Thus $r_1 \geq r$ holds. It is easy to check that the node v_k with $m_k \leq r_1$ receives resources $x^*_{cv_k} = m_k$ in the original allocation. Finding out the threshold value r_1, these nodes' received resources do not change. Under the new max-min fair allocation, v_k with $m_k > r_1$ receives resources $x_{cv_k} < x^*_{cv_k} \leq m_k$ and the proof is similar to that of Lemma 2.

We compute the received resource of the new node v_δ as the next lemma. Due to page limits, we omit the details of the proof.

Lemma 4. *If $R < t_\delta m_\delta$, there exists $r = \frac{W_c - \sum_{j=1}^{i-1} t_j m_j}{\sum_{j=i}^{n} t_j + t_\delta}$ such that $x_{cv_\delta} = m_\delta$ if $m_\delta \leq r$, and $x_{cv_\delta} < m_\delta$ if $m_\delta > r$.*

Combining Lemmas 1–4, we conclude the situation when the spare resources are inadequate $0 \leq R < t_\delta m_\delta$ as Theorem 3.

Theorem 3. *If $0 \leq R < t_\delta m_\delta$, there exist two thresholds r, r_1 as Lemma 1 and Lemma 3. If $m_\delta > r$, the nodes satisfy:*

$$\begin{cases} x_{cv_i} = x^*_{cv_i} & \text{if } m_i \leq r \\ x_{cv_i} < x^*_{cv_i} \leq m_i & \text{if } m_i > r \\ x_{cv_\delta} < m_\delta; \end{cases}$$

If $m_\delta \leq r$, the nodes satisfy:

$$\begin{cases} x_{cv_i} = x^*_{cv_i} & \text{if } m_i \leq r_1 \\ x_{cv_i} < x^*_{cv_i} \leq m_i & \text{if } m_i > r_1 \\ x_{cv_\delta} = m_\delta. \end{cases}$$

6   Trustfulness Against the Misreporting Strategy

In this section, we analyze the trustfulness against the misreporting strategy of the new node. Denote $\overrightarrow{X}_{cv} = (x_{cv_1}, x_{cv_2}, \ldots, x_{cv_{i-1}}, x_{cv_\delta}, x_{cv_i}, x_{cv_n})$ as the allocation vector after v_δ is added. Denote $\overrightarrow{M} = \{m_1, m_2, \ldots, m_{i-1}, m_\delta, m_i, \ldots, m_n\}$ as the resource demands where the new node's demand suits $m_{i-1} \leq m_\delta \leq m_i$. Denote $\overrightarrow{M}_{-u} = \{m_1, m_2, \ldots, m_n\}$ as the vector before v_δ is added.

As shown in the previous section, the allocated resources x_{cv_δ} of the new node v_δ can be regarded as a function of m_δ when $\overrightarrow{M}_{-u}$ is fixed. Suppose the new node misreports its resource demand as m_{nt}; we analyze the effect from two situations $R \geq t_\delta m_\delta$ (the spare resources are adequate, refer to Lemma 5) or $R < t_\delta m_\delta$ (refer to Lemma 6).

Lemma 5. *When $R \geq t_\delta m_\delta$, the node v_δ cannot gain more resources by the misreporting strategy.*

Proof. According to Theorem 2, $x_{cv_\delta} = m_{nt}$ for any $m_{nt} \in (0, m_\delta]$ under the max-min fair allocation; this implies the node would receive less resources if it reports less. However, if the node reports more resources than its demand, from Lemma 1, the largest amount of resources the new node could receive is $r = \frac{W_c - \sum_{j=1}^{i-1} t_j m_j}{\sum_i^n t_j + t_\delta}$; it is larger than the amount of resources the new node could receive if it reports its true demand. Therefore, the lemma holds.

Lemma 6. *When $R < t_\delta m_\delta$, there exists a real number r_2 satisfying the following conditions:*

- *If $m_\delta \leq r_2$, the node may receive more resources than its real demand;*
- *If $m_\delta > r_2$, the node cannot receive more resources.*

Proof. To begin with, we derive the value of r_2 by the following three cases:

1) If $R \geq t_\delta m_n$, $r_2 = \frac{R}{t_\delta}$;
2) If $m_1(\sum_{j=1}^n t_j + t_\delta) \geq W_c$, $r_2 = \frac{W_c}{\sum_{j=1}^n t_j + t_\delta}$;
3) If $R < t_\delta m_n$ and $m_1(\sum_{j=1}^n t_j + t_\delta) < W_c$, from Lemma 1 to derive $r_2 = \frac{W_c - \sum_{j=1}^{i-1} t_j m_j}{\sum_{j=i}^n t_j + t_\delta}$.

For simplicity, we only show the proof sketch of the third case. According to Theorem 3, if $m_\delta \leq r_2$, for any $m_{nt} \in [m_\delta, +\infty]$, $x_{cv_\delta} > m_\delta$, which means the new node can increase its received resources if it misreports its demand. However, the received resource exceeds its demand which would cause waste, while the node can also receive m_δ resources if it reports its real demand. The received resources (in reality) do not change by the strategy. Similarly, when $m_\delta > r_2$, it is easy to show that the new node cannot increase its received resources by misreporting its demand. Combining these cases, the lemma holds.

Combining the lemmas, we regard the allocation mechanism as trustful under the misreporting strategy.

7   Trustfulness Against the Spitting Strategy

We introduce *spitting strategy* that may help node v_δ gain more resources. Suppose its demand is m_δ, but it reports to the central node that two nodes are added and the sum of their demands is m_δ. This implies the node is assumed to be split into two fictitious nodes with resource demands m_{np_1}, m_{np_2} and $m_{np_1} + m_{np_2} = m_\delta$. We analyze when the new node could gain more resources.

There are three cases according to the values of m_δ (the resource demand of the new node), m_n (the largest resource demand of the original nodes), R (the spare resources before the new node is added):

- Case 1: $R \geq t_\delta m_\delta$;
- Case 2: $R < t_\delta m_\delta$ and $R \geq 2t_\delta m_n$;
- Case 3: $R < t_\delta m_\delta$ and $R < 2t_\delta m_n$;

We show that the new node cannot gain more resources for the first two cases (Lemmas 7, 8), while it could gain more resources for Cases 3 (Lemma 9). Denote the two virtual nodes as v_{np_1}, v_{np_2} and the received resources as $x_{cv_{np_1}}, x_{cv_{np_2}}$ respectively. Denote the received resources of node v_δ as x_{cv_δ} if it reports honestly. We show the following lemmas:

Lemma 7. *If $R \geq t_\delta m_\delta$, the new node cannot gain more resources by the spitting strategy, i.e. $x_{cv_{np_1}} + x_{cv_{np_2}} = x_{cv_\delta}$.*

It is obvious that the overall resource is enough to satisfy all nodes' demands. Thus, the lemma holds.

Lemma 8. *If $R < t_\delta m_\delta$ and $R \geq 2t_\delta m_n$, the new node cannot gain more resources by the spitting strategy, i.e. $x_{cv_{np_1}} + x_{cv_{np_2}} = x_{cv_\delta}$.*

Proof. Since $2t_\delta m_n \leq R < t_\delta m_\delta$, we derive $t_\delta m_\delta > 2t_\delta m_n$, which implies $m_\delta > 2m_n$. Without loss of generality, suppose $m_{np_1} \leq m_{np_2}$, there are two cases:

1) $m_{np_1} \leq m_n < m_{np_2}$ and $m_{np_1} + m_{np_2} = m_\delta > 2m_n$;
2) $m_n < m_{np_1} \leq m_{np_2}$ and $m_{np_1} + m_{np_2} = m_\delta > 2m_n$.

Considering the first case, suppose $m_1 \leq m_2 \leq \ldots \leq m_{i-1} \leq m_{np_1} \leq m_i \leq \ldots \leq m_n < m_{np_2}$; notice that

$$(m_{np_1} + x_{cv_{np_2}} - 2m_*)t_\delta \leq \left(\sum_{j=1}^{i-1} t_j m_j + m_* \sum_{j=i}^{n} t_j\right) - \left(\sum_{j=1}^{i_2} t_j m_j + x_{cv_{np_2}} \sum_{j=i_2+1}^{n} t_j\right) \leq 0.$$

When node v_{np_1} is added, $x_{cv_{np_1}} = m_{np_1}$. When node v_{np_2} is added, from $t_\delta m_\delta > W_c - \sum_{j=1}^{n} m_j t_j$, we have

$$t_\delta m_{np_2} > W_c - t_\delta m_{np_1} - \sum_{j=1}^{n} t_j m_j \Rightarrow x_{cv_{np_2}} = \frac{W_c - t_\delta m_{np_1} - \sum_{j=1}^{n} t_j m_j}{t_\delta}.$$

Combining two nodes' resources, we derive

$$x_{cv_{np_1}} + x_{cv_{np_2}} = m_{np_1} + \frac{W_c - t_\delta m_{np_1} - \sum_{j=1}^{n} t_j m_j}{t_\delta} = \frac{W_c - \sum_{j=1}^{n} t_j m_j}{t_\delta} = x_{cv_\delta}.$$

Considering the second case, notice that after the two nodes are added, for any node $v_i, i \in [1, n]$, $x_{cv_i} = m_i$. If $W_c - \sum_{j=1}^{n} t_j m_j \geq 2t_\delta m_{np_1}$, we derive

$$x_{cv_{np_1}} = m_{np_1}; x_{cv_{np_2}} = \frac{W_c - \sum_{j=1}^{n} t_j m_j - t_\delta m_{np_1}}{t_\delta}$$

Therefore, $x_{cv_{np_1}} + x_{cv_{np_2}} = \frac{W_c - \sum_{j=1}^{n} t_j m_j}{t_\delta} = x_{cv_\delta}$. If $W_c - \sum_{j=1}^{n} t_j m_j \leq 2t_\delta m_{np_1}$, we derive $x_{cv_{np_1}} = x_{cv_{np_2}} = \frac{W_c - \sum_{j=1}^{n} t_j m_j}{2t_\delta}$, thus $x_{cv_{np_1}} + x_{cv_{np_2}} = \frac{W_c - \sum_{j=1}^{n} t_j m_j}{t_\delta} = x_{cv_\delta}$. Combining these cases, the lemma holds.

The allocation is trustful against the first two situations. However, we show that it is not trustful for the following situation.

Lemma 9. *If $R < t_\delta m_\delta$ and $R < 2t_\delta m_n$, the new node can gain more resources through the spitting strategy. For some special situations, the received resources could be about two times, i.e. $x_{cv_{np_1}} + x_{cv_{np_2}} \approx 2x_{cv_\delta}$.*

Proof. If $R < t_\delta m_\delta$ and $R < 2t_\delta m_n$, there exists m_* such that the largest amount of resources two nodes can receive is $2m_*$. Suppose $m_1 \leq m_2 \leq \ldots \leq m_{i-1} \leq m_* \leq m_i \leq \ldots \leq m_n$; similar as Lemma 1, we derive

$$\sum_{j=1}^{i-2} t_j m_j + m_{i-1} \sum_{j=i-1}^{n} t_j + 2t_\delta m_{i-1} \leq W_c.$$

Thus, $m_{i-1} \leq \frac{W_c - \sum_{j=1}^{i-2} t_j m_j}{2t_\delta + \sum_{j=i-1}^{n} t_j}$ and we find the largest value $i-1$ such that $m_{i-1} \leq m_*$ and $m_i \geq m_*$. Since $\sum_{j=1}^{i-1} t_j m_j + m_* \sum_{j=i}^{n} t_j + 2t_\delta m_* = W_c$, we derive

$$m_* = \frac{W_c - \sum_{j=1}^{i-1} t_j m_j}{2t_\delta + \sum_{j=i}^{n} t_j}. \tag{3}$$

According to Algorithm 1, if $m_* \leq m_{np_1} \leq m_{np_2}$, $x_{cv_{np_1}} = x_{cv_{np_2}} = m_*$. If $m_{np_1} \leq m_* \leq m_{np_2}$, we show that the sum of two nodes' resources is no more than $2m_*$.

Suppose $m_1 \leq m_2 \leq \ldots \leq m_{i_1} \leq m_{np_1} \leq \ldots \leq m_* \leq \ldots \leq m_{i_2} \leq m_{np_2} \leq \ldots \leq m_n$, it is easy to get $x_{cv_{np_1}} = m_{np_1}$ and $x_{cv_{np_2}} \geq m_*$. We analyze the maximum value $x_{cv_{np_2}}$ can achieve. Combining the inequality $\sum_{j=1}^{i_1} t_j m_j + t_\delta m_{np_1} + \sum_{j=i_1+1}^{i_2} t_j m_j + x_{cv_{np_2}} t_\delta + x_{cv_{np_2}} \sum_{j=i_2+1}^{n} t_j \leq W_c$ and the equation $\sum_{j=1}^{i-1} t_j m_j + m_* \sum_{j=i}^{n} t_j + 2t_\delta m_* = W_c$, we derive

$$(m_{np_1} + x_{cv_{np_2}} - 2m_*)t_\delta \leq (\sum_{j=1}^{i-1} t_j m_j + m_* \sum_{j=i}^{n} t_j) - (\sum_{j=1}^{i_2} t_j m_j + x_{cv_{np_2}} \sum_{j=i_2+1}^{n} t_j) \leq 0.$$

Hence, $x_{cv_{np_1}} + x_{cv_{np_2}} \leq m_{np_1} + x_{cv_{np_2}} \leq 2m_*$. More specifically, if $t_\delta << \sum_{j=1}^{n} t_j$, the node can receive about 2 times resources compared to the original allocation (we omit the details). Therefore, the lemma holds.

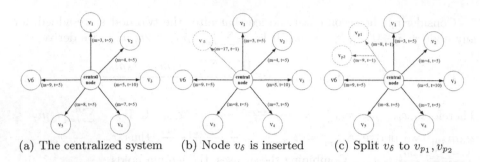

(a) The centralized system   (b) Node v_δ is inserted   (c) Split v_δ to v_{p_1}, v_{p_2}

Fig. 1. A centralized resource system: six nodes are connected to the central node; a new node v_δ is added with $m_\delta = 17, t_\delta = 1$; the node is split into two nodes v_{p_1}, v_{p_2} with $m_{p_1} = 8, m_{p_2} = 9$.

From the lemma, we know that the new node can achieve more resources by the splitting strategy. For some special situations, the node can gain appropriate two times resources compared to a honest node. Combining Lemmas 7–9, we conclude the theorem as follows:

Theorem 4. *If the spare resources are adequate ($R \geq t_\delta m_\delta$) or inadequate ($R < t_\delta m_\delta$) but suits $R \geq 2t_\delta m_n$, the max-min fair allocation is trustful against the splitting strategy. If the spare resources suit $R < t_\delta m_\delta$ and $R < 2t_\delta m_n$, the allocation is not trustful against the strategy.*

8   Numerical Examples

In this section, we present some numerical examples to illustrate these results. As shown in Fig. 1(a), six nodes are connected to the central node in the system and (m, t) (resource demand, transfer rate) are depicted on each edge. For example, node v_1 has $m_1 = 3, t_1 = 5$. Assume the amount of all resources the central node holds is $W_c = 205$.

By Algorithm 1, the max-min allocation is listed in Table 1 where x_{cv_i} is the received resource of the node and $x_{cv_i} \cdot t_i$ is the resource the central node allocates. There is no spare resource since $R = W_c - \sum_{i=1}^{6} x_{cv_i} t_i = 0$. As shown in Fig. 1(b), if a new node v_δ is added with $m_\delta = 17, t_\delta = 1$, the max-min allocation is presented as Table 2. Nodes v_5, v_6 receive less resources since their resources are allocated to the new node. If the node misreports its demand m_δ, it cannot gain more resources.

In order to gain more resources, the new node splits itself into two nodes v_{p_1}, v_{p_2} such that $m_{p_1} = 8, m_{p_2} = 9$ ($m_{p_1} + m_{p_2} = m_\delta = 17$) (as shown in Fig. 1(c)). The max-min allocation is presented in Table 3; nodes v_5, v_6 receive less resources and nodes v_{p_1}, v_{p_2} both receive $\frac{85}{12}$ resources. Therefore, with the splitting strategy, the new node receives resources $x_{cv_{p_1}} + x_{cv_{p_2}} = \frac{85}{6} \approx 14.166$. Compared to the received resources in Table 2, the splitting strategy achieves $\frac{14.166}{7.727} \approx 1.83$ times that of the original allocation.

Table 1. Before v_δ is added

Node i	m_i	t_i	x_{cv_i}	$x_{cv_i} \cdot t_i$	u_i
v_1	3	5	3	15	3
v_2	4	5	4	20	4
v_3	5	10	5	50	5
v_4	7	5	7	35	7
v_5	8	5	8	40	8
v_6	9	5	9	45	9

Table 2. After v_δ is added

Node i	m_i	t_i	x_{cv_i}	$x_{cv_i} \cdot t_i$	u_i
v_1	3	5	3	15	3
v_2	4	5	4	20	4
v_3	5	10	5	50	5
v_4	7	5	7	35	7
v_5	8	5	$\frac{85}{11} \approx 7.727$	$\frac{425}{11}$	$\frac{85}{11}$
v_6	9	5	$\frac{85}{11} \approx 7.727$	$\frac{425}{11}$	$\frac{85}{11}$
v_δ	17	1	$\frac{85}{11} \approx 7.727$	$\frac{85}{11}$	$\frac{85}{11}$

Table 3. After v_δ is Split

Node i	m_i	t_i	x_{cv_i}	$x_{cv_i} \cdot t_i$	u_i
v_1	3	5	3	15	3
v_2	4	5	4	20	4
v_3	5	10	5	50	5
v_4	7	5	7	35	7
v_5	8	5	$\frac{85}{12} \approx 7.083$	$\frac{425}{12}$	$\frac{85}{12}$
v_6	9	5	$\frac{85}{12} \approx 7.083$	$\frac{425}{12}$	$\frac{85}{12}$
v_{p_1}	8	1	$\frac{85}{12} \approx 7.083$	$\frac{85}{12}$	$\frac{85}{12}$
v_{p_2}	9	1	$\frac{85}{12} \approx 7.083$	$\frac{85}{12}$	$\frac{85}{12}$

9 Conclusion

In this paper, we study the trustfulness of the max-min fair allocation in a centralized resource system. Max-min fairness is a common adopted concept in evaluating an allocation mechanism. We propose a simple but efficient algorithm to find out the allocation. On the foundation of the algorithm, we analyze how the allocation varies when a new node is added to the system. Furthermore, we explore whether the allocation is trustful against two strategic behaviors. The misreporting strategy cannot affect the allocation while the new node can gain more resources by the splitting strategy. Hence, the max-min allocation mechanism is not trustful especially against the splitting strategy. It is still an open problem to design a fair and trustful allocation mechanism in a centralized resource system.

References

1. Adsul, B., Babu, C.S., Garg, J., Mehta, R., Sohoni, M.: Nash equilibria in fisher market. In: Kontogiannis, S., Koutsoupias, E., Spirakis, P.G. (eds.) SAGT 2010. LNCS, vol. 6386, pp. 30–41. Springer, Heidelberg (2010). https://doi.org/10.1007/978-3-642-16170-4_4
2. Aloui, C., Hkiri, B., Hammoudeh, S., Shahbaz, M.: A multiple and partial wavelet analysis of the oil price, inflation, exchange rate, and economic growth nexus in Saudi Arabia. Emerg. Mark. Finance Trade **54**(4), 935–956 (2018)
3. Bertsekas, D., Gallager, R.: Data Networks, 2nd edn. Prentice-Hall Inc., Upper Saddle River (1992)
4. Blot, M., Cord, M., Thome, N.: Max-min convolutional neural networks for image classification. In: IEEE International Conference on Image Processing, pp. 3678–3682 (2016)
5. Brams, S.J., Taylor, A.D.: Fair division: from cake-cutting to dispute resolution. Soc. Justice Res. **12**(2), 149–162 (1999)
6. Charny, A.: An algorithm for rate allocation in a packet. Massachusetts Institute of Technology (1994)
7. Chen, L., Liu, S., Li, B., Li, B.: Scheduling jobs across geo-distributed datacenters with max-min fairness. In: INFOCOM 2017 - IEEE Conference on Computer Communications, pp. 1–9. IEEE (2017)

8. Chen, N., Deng, X., Zhang, H., Zhang, J.: Incentive ratios of fisher markets. In: Czumaj, A., Mehlhorn, K., Pitts, A., Wattenhofer, R. (eds.) ICALP 2012. LNCS, vol. 7392, pp. 464–475. Springer, Heidelberg (2012). https://doi.org/10.1007/978-3-642-31585-5_42

9. Chen, N., Deng, X., Zhang, J.: How profitable are strategic behaviors in a market? In: Demetrescu, C., Halldórsson, M.M. (eds.) ESA 2011. LNCS, vol. 6942, pp. 106–118. Springer, Heidelberg (2011). https://doi.org/10.1007/978-3-642-23719-5_10

10. Chen, Y., Lai, J.K., Parkes, D.C., Procaccia, A.D.: Truth, justice, and cake cutting. Games Econ. Behav. **77**(1), 284–297 (2013)

11. Chen, Z., Cheng, Y., Deng, X., Qi, Q., Yan, X.: Agent incentives of strategic behavior in resource exchange. In: International Symposium on Algorithmic Game Theory, pp. 227–239 (2017)

12. Cheng, Y., Deng, X., Pi, Y., Yan, X.: Can bandwidth sharing be truthful? In: Hoefer, M. (ed.) SAGT 2015. LNCS, vol. 9347, pp. 190–202. Springer, Heidelberg (2015). https://doi.org/10.1007/978-3-662-48433-3_15

13. Cheng, Y., Deng, X., Qi, Q., Yan, X.: Truthfulness of a proportional sharing mechanism in resource exchange. In: International Joint Conference on Artificial Intelligence (IJCAI), pp. 187–193 (2016)

14. Cretch, P., Michielsens, J., Taeymans, J.: Data network (2002)

15. Feldman, M., Lai, K., Stoica, I., Chuang, J.: Robust incentive techniques for peer-to-peer networks. In: ACM Conference on Electronic Commerce, pp. 102–111 (2004)

16. Gamow, G., Stern, M.: Puzzle-Math. The Viking Press, New York (1958)

17. Ghumman, N.S., Kaur, R.: Dynamic combination of improved max-min and ant colony algorithm for load balancing in cloud system. In: International Conference on Computing, Communication and NETWORKING Technologies, pp. 1–5 (2016)

18. Hahne, E.L.: Round-robin scheduling for max-min fairness in data networks. IEEE J. Sel. Areas Commun. **9**(7), 1024–1039 (1991)

19. Hurwicz, L.: On Informationally Decentralized Systems (1972)

20. Jia, Y., Zhao, M., Zhou, W.: Joint user association and eICIC for max-min fairness in HetNets. IEEE Commun. Lett. **20**(3), 546–549 (2016)

21. Khamse-Ashari, J., Kesidis, G., Lambadaris, I., Urgaonkar, B., Zhao, Y.: Constrained max-min fair scheduling of variable-length packet-flows to multiple servers. Ann. Telecommun. **73**(3–4), 219–237 (2018)

22. Menon, V., Larson, K., Menon, V., Larson, K., Menon, V., Larson, K.: Deterministic, strategyproof, and fair cake cutting (2017)

23. Pham, T.V., Pham, A.T.: Max-min fairness and sum-rate maximization of MU-VLC local networks. In: IEEE GLOBECOM Workshops, pp. 1–6 (2016)

24. Roughgarden, T., Tardos, E.: How bad is selfish routing? J. ACM (JACM) **49**(2), 236–259 (2002)

25. Segal-Halevi, E.: Cutting a cake with both good and bad parts (2017)

26. Segal-Halevi, E., Nitzan, S.: Envy-free cake-cutting among families (2016)

27. Steinhaus, H.: The problem of fair division. Econometrica **16**, 101–104 (1948)

28. Wahlen, S., Laamanen, M.: Collaborative consumption and sharing economies (2017)

A Novel Blockchain Network Structure Based on Logical Nodes

Jiancheng Chi, Tie Qiu$^{(\boxtimes)}$, Chaokun Zhang, and Laiping Zhao

College of Intelligence and Computing, Tianjin University, Tianjin 300350, China
{chijiancheng,qiutie,zhangchaokun,laiping}@tju.edu.cn

Abstract. With the continuous maturity and evolution of blockchain, applying blockchain to edge computing has increasingly become a trend, and also brings many great challenges. For the traditional blockchain structure, each peer node of blockchain network stores exactly the same content, which leads to strong data redundancy and excessive storage capacity is wasted. In this paper, we propose a novel blockchain network structure to reduce the storage occupation for blockchain node, which combine multiple physical nodes into one logical node and try to ensure that the storage capacity between the logical nodes is similar. The experimental simulation results show that the proposed new blockchain network structure can effectively reduce the storage usage of physical nodes and decrease the difficulty to deploy blockchain to the edge network.

Keywords: Blockchain · Edge computing · Logical node · Physical nodes division · Physical master node election

1 Introduction

As one of the underlying technologies of bitcoin, blockchain has attracted increasing attentions. Blockchain is a comprehensive application mode of distributed data storage, point-to-point transmission, consensus mechanism, encryption algorithm and other technologies [11]. It is essentially a decentralized distributed database, with decentralized, tamper-proof, open and transparent features. Therefore, blockchain can guarantee the security and tamper-proof of stored data, and guarantee the trust and consistency of multi-party collaboration [2].

All the nodes in the blockchain are peers with similar capabilities. When a transaction occurs during the blockchain operation, each node has the right to process this transaction. The node finished the transaction processing first will send the result to the other nodes for confirmation [14]. When the result is confirmed by most of the nodes in the network, the transaction takes effect and is recorded by all the blockchain nodes. This approach has an important advantage. The data is recorded by all nodes, so it is difficult to tamper with the data. At the same time, all nodes store the same data, which can be regarded as backup data between nodes.

© Springer Nature Switzerland AG 2020
D. Yu et al. (Eds.): WASA 2020, LNCS 12384, pp. 65–76, 2020.
https://doi.org/10.1007/978-3-030-59016-1_6

In recent years, applying blockchain to edge computing has gradually become a trend [15]. Generally, each edge node will become a blockchain node to complete the functions of the blockchain network. However, for edge nodes, storage capacity and scalability are relatively poor. If the blockchain networking structure mentioned above is applied to edge computing without modification, the performance of edge network will be greatly affected [16]. Although data stored in this blockchain networking structure is difficult to lose and tamper with, the cost is excessive redundancy of backups and excessive storage occupation. In addition, excessive data backup is not necessary, even the number of important data backup is limited. Therefore, it is necessary to improve the blockchain network structure to solve the serious problems of excessive data backup and storage redundancy.

In this paper, we propose a new blockchain network structure (NBNS) based on logical nodes. In NBNS, we combine multiple physical nodes into one logical node, and take the storage capacity of the logical node as the evaluation index to establish the logical node. All the logical nodes constitute the novel blockchain network together. Each logical node implements the functions of the original blockchain node. Within the logical node, the physical master node is generated by random and polling from all the physical nodes. The physical master node is responsible for collecting and distributing information internally, and communicating and reaching consensus externally.

The main contributions of this paper are as follows:

1. In blockchain network, we proposed the concept of logical node, which is consist of several physical nodes.
2. A novel blockchain network structure based on logical nodes in edge computing is proposed to reduce the storage occupation of each blockchain node.
3. The physical nodes division algorithm and physical master node selection algorithm are designed to build logical nodes and select the physical master node from each logical node.

The remainder of this paper is structured as follows. Section 2 discusses related works done. Section 3 introduces the logical nodes-based novel blockchain network structure. Section 4 illustrates the physical nodes division and physical master node selection in detail. The simulation results are discussed in Sect. 5, and the concluding remarks of this study are provided in Sect. 6.

2   Related Work

With the maturity of blockchain technology, some works about the improvements of blockchain structures have been emerging. The traditional structure of blockchain is a chain structure that starts from the creation block and connects the heads and ends of each block. Each block is generated in the order of transactions and has the same structure and size. Recently, some researches attempt to change the block type to improve the performance of the blockchain. For instance, Eyal et al. [3] proposed a new blockchain structure called bitcoin-NG by changing the block type. The bitcoin-NG introduced two types of block, namely Keyblocks and Microblocks. The Keyblock only saves the authentication information of the proof-of-work and no transaction information is contained. Each time the keyblock is generated, the miner is selected as the leader to generate the Microblock. The transaction records are only stored in the Microblocks, so the transactions can be processed in batches to improve the throughput. Vizier et al. [13] proposed the concept of Community Blockchain, which is called ComChain in their researches. ComChain introduced new block type, namely configuration block. Each configuration block contains a collection of nodes that make up the consensus committee. Consensus committees are chosen in turn, and new consensus committees are created through consultation with the old consensus committees.

Some researches attempt to change the structure of blockchain to improve the performance of blockchain. Hanke et al. [4] proposed the concept of Beacon Chain. Beacon chain is currently being studied for practical use in Ethereum, which manages the PoS protocol (Casper) and all shard chains. The work done by the beacon chain includes managing the verifiers and their stakes; specifying the block proposer for each shard; organizing verifiers to enter the committee to vote on the proposed block; applying the consensus rule; rewarding and punishing the verifiers; registering shard status to facilitate cross-shard transactions. Kokoris-Kogias et al. [5] proposed a new blockchain structure called ByzCoin. ByzCoin separates transactions from blocks and improves the throughput of blockchain transactions by processing transactions separately. In ByzCoin, transactions and blocks are stored on two separate chains, which store their information in parallel. One chain stores transactions and the other chain stores blocks. In the process of creating a KeyBlock, the blockchain nodes form a consensus committee. The MicroBlocks are generated by agreement between the consensus committee nodes and are added to the chain of MicroBlocks. Similar to the core idea of ByzCoin, Fruitchain [7] is a new blockchain structure that separates transactions from blocks. In the Fruitchain, transactions are packaged into a single package called Fruit instead packaged into a block with data directly. The fruit is then attached to a chain of data blocks. The fruit connected to the data block must be close to its related blocks. The Fruitchain will enable the entire blockchain system to provide faster transaction processing speed without affecting security. Recently, a new blockchain structure called Tangle [8] has gradually received attention. Unlike the traditional blockchain structure, Tangle stores each transaction as a vertex of a graph structure, instead of packaging the transaction into data blocks and storing it in a chain. Each transaction will refer to the past two transaction records Hash, so that the previous transaction will prove the legitimacy of the past two transactions, and indirectly prove the legitimacy of all previous transactions.

In addition, there are some related works to study how to lighten the structure or process of the blockchain to improve the performance of the blockchain system. For instance, Tuli et al. [12] proposed a framework called FogBus that uses blockchain and identity verification and encryption technology to avoid the leakage of private data. The FogBus provides independent interfaces for IoT applications and is easy to deploy and expand. Liu [6] et al. proposed a lightweight blockchain system LightChain. LightChain encourages different devices to collaborate with each other through a consensus mechanism called collaborative multiple proofs, and simplifies the message content of collaboration and dissemination between different devices through a lightweight data structure called LightBlock.

3   Logical Nodes-Based Blockchain Network Structure

In order to deploy the blockchain in the edge computing environment and overcome the long-term impact of the limited storage performance of edge nodes on the performance of the blockchain, this section proposes a novel blockchain network structure based on logical nodes as shown in the Fig. 1. In this novel blockchain structure, there are three types of nodes, namely logical node, physical master node and physical slave node.

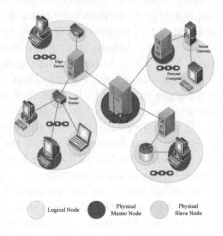

Fig. 1. A novel blockchain network structure based on logical nodes

Logical Node: In the blockchain network structure proposed in this paper, a logical node is composed of multiple physical nodes and the physical nodes in a logical node can be divided into two types: physical master nodes and physical slave nodes. All logical nodes are connected to each other to form a blockchain network. A logical node in the proposed novel blockchain network structure is functionally the same as a single blockchain node in a traditional blockchain network structure. A logical node stores all data of the blockchain which are stored dispersedly on different physical nodes within the logical node. The logical nodes cooperate with each other to jointly complete the consensus on all transactions in the blockchain network.

Physical Master Node: The physical master node in a logical node is the brain of this logical node. It is responsible for external communication, synchronization and consensus with other logical nodes, internally responsible for communicating with physical slave nodes and distributing blockchain data among different physical nodes. In a logical node, the physical master node is not static, but constantly changes through periodic elections. The advantage of the constantly changing master node is that the physical nodes participating in consensus in the new blockchain network are random, so it is difficult for the blockchain network to launch an attack by mastering more than 51% of the computing resources of the entire network.

Physical Slave Node: The main role of the physical slave node is to assist the physical master node to complete the distributed storage of blockchain data on different physical nodes within the same logical node. In addition, physical slave nodes are also candidates for physical master node. In the process of changing the physical master node, the physical slave nodes inside the logical node have a probability of being elected as the physical master node and take over the work of the previous physical master node.

In order to ensure the long-term smooth operation of the system under this blockchain network structure, there are some main issues need to be taken into consideration:

1. Balanced storage capability among logical nodes. In the environment of edge computing, edge physical nodes usually have greatly different physical storage performance. Since a logical node is composed of multiple physical nodes, in the initial stage of the system, the existing physical nodes in the system need to be divided into clusters, and each cluster is a logical node. The basic requirement for logical node division is that the sum of storage resources of physical nodes in each logical node is approximately equal.
2. The physical master nodes within the logical nodes are elected in turn. The communication and consensus process between logical nodes are performed by the only physical master node within the logical nodes. Therefore, the computing and communication resources of the physical master node are used more frequently. In order to avoid the long-term use of a single physical master node may cause node failure, it is necessary to periodically replace the physical master node by random polling. Another advantage of randomly replacing the physical master node is that it can prevent the physical master node from being mastered by a few malicious users for a long time, and then launch a malicious attack on the system.

In order to solve the above problems and make the system based on the novel blockchain network structure stable for a long time, we discuss the physical nodes division and physical master node election related issues in the logical nodes in Sect. 4 of this paper.

4   Physical Nodes Division and Physical Master Node Election

As mentioned in the previous section, in order to make the system based on the proposed blockchain network structure stable for a long period of time, physical nodes division, physical master node election must be considered. In this section, we propose corresponding strategies to the above problems.

4.1   Physical Nodes Division

Before initializing the system, which physical nodes can be divided together to form a logical node need to be determined. Therefore, given a set of physical nodes, a strategy to divide the physical nodes into multiple logical nodes is necessary [1]. Since each logical node needs to completely store all the data of the blockchain, the storage performance of each logical node should be approximately equal. The problem then can be formulated that the storage capacity of the m physical nodes PN_i is known as $C_i, i = 1, 2..., m$, how to divide m physical nodes into n groups $LN_j, j = 1, 2, ..., n$ (each group is a logical node), and $\sum_{i=1}^{N_j} C_{ij}$ for each group LN_j should be as equal as possible, where C_{ij} is the storage capacity of ith physical node belonging to group LN_j. The objection is to find a G with minimized S shown in (1).

$$S = \frac{1}{n} \sum_{j=1}^{n} (\sum_{i=1}^{N_j} C_{ij} - \frac{1}{n} \sum_{j=1}^{n} \sum_{i=1}^{N_j} C_{ij})^2 \tag{1}$$

An effective method to solve this problem is the dynamic programming method. The steps of the dynamic programming method to solve this problem are shown in Algorithm 1. Given the storage capacity list L of physical nodes and the number of logical nodes N, the purpose is to output a division result G of physical nodes to satisfy the average of the storage capacity of N groups. First, calculate the average storage capacity C_{avg} of n all logical nodes. Then, Sort the physical nodes in list L in descending order according to the storage capacity of each physical node.

Starting with the physical node PN_i with the largest storage capacity in the list L'(i.e. the first node). If $C_i \geq C_{avg}$, then directly divide C_i into a separate group sg_j; otherwise, put C_i into a group g_k, and calculate δ by

$$\delta = C_{avg} - \sum_{k=1}^{N_j} C_k \tag{2}$$

where C_k is the storage capacity of physical nodes in group g_k. Determine whether there are new physical node can be added to g_k through δ. When δ is greater than 0, the loop selects the C_i by (3) from the remaining C_i in L' to incorporate into g_k, and updates δ.

$$C_i = arg \min(C_i - \delta)^2 \tag{3}$$

Algorithm 1. Physical Nodes Division Algorithm

Input: L, N
Output: G
1: /*Calculate the average storage capacity C_{avg} of all logical nodes*/
2: $C_{avg} = \frac{1}{n} \sum\limits_{i=1}^{m} C_i$
3: /*Sort the physical nodes in list L by descending order of the storage capacity*/
4: $L' = Sort(L)$
5: **for** $C_i \in L'; i = 0; i++$ **do**
6: 　 **if** $C_i > C_{avg}$ **then**
7: 　　 Put C_i into a separate group sg_j and remove C_i from L'
8: 　 **end if**
9: 　 Put C_i into a group g_k and remove C_i from L'
10: 　 /*Calculate the difference δ between the sum storage capacity of g_k, C_{avg} */
11: 　 $\delta = C_{avg} - \sum\limits_{k=1}^{N_j} C_k$
12: 　 **while** $\delta > 0$ **do**
13: 　　 **for** $C_l \in L'; l = 0; l++$ **do**
14: 　　　 $C_l = arg\min(C_l - \delta)^2$
15: 　　　 Put C_l into group g_k
16: 　　 **end for**
17: 　　 update δ
18: 　 **end while**
19: **end for**
20: $G = \text{Merge}(g, sg)$
21:
22: **return** G

When δ is less than 0, the composition of group g_k ends. Continue to repeat the above steps from the remaining physical nodes in the list L' until all physical nodes in L' are allocated. Finally, merge g and sg to get the result of dividing physical nodes into logical nodes.

4.2　Physical Master Node Election

When all physical nodes are divided into logical nodes, the physical master node needs to be elected within the logical nodes. In order to avoid a single physical master node failure due to running too long and affecting the operation of the logical node, the physical master node should be changed periodically [9,10]. In addition, in order to prevent the laws of physical master node changes from being leaked, the physical master node changes should be done in a random manner. A significant advantage of the physical master node randomly changing is that it is difficult to launch attacks on the blockchain system by controlling most physical master nodes.

The election of the physical master node can be conducted by random polling. Given a physical node list S within a logical node, the goal is to periodically and randomly select the physical nodes in S as the physical master node of the logical node. The election is conducted in rounds, and a round is defined as from a new physical node is elected as physical master node to the next new physical node is elected. In each round of elections, those who have been elected as physical master nodes will not be re-elected and the un-elected nodes will be recorded in list R. In each round, the next elected physical master node is determined by the threshold $T(r)$, which is defined by (4).

$$T(r) = \frac{1}{n_R - r \ mod \ n} \tag{4}$$

where r is the number of rounds; n is the number of all physical nodes in the logical node; n_R is the number of physical nodes in the un-elected nodes list G in round r.

The specific steps of the physical master node election algorithm are shown as Algorithm 2. First, a list S of all physical nodes in the logical node is given and the physical master node PMN_r need to be determined. The number of rounds r is initialized to 0. At the beginning of the first round of the algorithm, all physical nodes are recorded into the un-elected physical node list R, and a random number m_i is randomly generated for each physical node between 0 and 1, and sequentially recorded into the list N. Calculate the threshold $T(r)$ according to Eq. (4), and compare the random number corresponding to each physical node in the list N with the threshold $T(r)$. Select all the physical nodes corresponding to the random number less than the threshold, select the physical node with the smallest random value as the master node, and remove it from the list R. Set a master node replacement time threshold t_c. When the commitment time of the physical master node exceeds t_c, continue to use (4) to calculate the new threshold $T(r)$, repeat the selection steps, and select the next physical master node from the list R. Increase the number of rounds r by one, and perform the next round of physical master node election until the list R is empty. Then, reset the un-elected physical node list R by recording all physical nodes and execute next round of algorithm.

5   Experimental Simulation

In this section, we evaluate the performance of the new blockchain network structure proposed in this paper based on simulation experiments. The performance evaluation mainly includes three parts, which are the performance evaluation of the physical nodes division algorithm, the storage occupation of a single physical node and the ability of the new blockchain structure to resist 51% attacks compared with other blockchain structures.

We first evaluate the performance of the physical node division algorithm. The goal of the physical node division algorithm is to divide multiple physical nodes with large differences in storage capacity into multiple logical nodes, and

---

Algorithm 2. Physical Master Node Election Algorithm

Input: S
Output: PMN_r
1: $r = 0$
2: **while** True **do**
3:     $R = S$
4:     /*Generate a random number $m_i \in (0,1)$ for each physical node in R, write sequentially in list N*/
5:     $N = \{m_i | m_i = rand(0,1), i = 1, 2, ..., n\}$
6:     $timer = t_c$
7:     **while** $R \neq \emptyset$ **do**
8:         **while** $timer < t_c$ **do**
9:             Check $timer$
10:         **end while**
11:         /*Calculate the threshold $T(r)$ */
12:         $T(r) = \frac{1}{n_{R-r \mod n}}$
13:         $L_{tmp} = \emptyset$
14:         **for** $m_i \in N; i < length(N); i++$ **do**
15:             **if** $m_i < T(r)$ **then**
16:                 $L_{tmp} = m_i \bigcup L_{tmp}$
17:             **end if**
18:         **end for**
19:         Select physical node PN_i as PMN_r whose $m_j = arg\min(T(r) - m_j), m_j \in L_{tmp}$
20:         Set $timer = 0$ and start $timer$
21:         Remove PN_i from R
22:         $r += 1$
23:
24:         **return** PMN_r
25:     **end while**
26: **end while**

---

ensure that the sum of the storage capacities of the physical nodes contained in each logical node is approximately equal. The division effect is evaluated by S defined by (1). In addition, the running speed of the partitioning algorithm should also be evaluated. To reflect the large difference in storage capacity between physical nodes, we set the range of storage capacity of physical nodes between 10G and 100G, and randomly generate a list L of the storage capacity of 200 physical nodes. Physical node division is performed on the randomly generated list L using a physical node division algorithm. The range of the number N of logical nodes is set to 10–60, and the interval is 10. For each number N of logical node, a random generation list and physical node division are repeated 50 times, and the average time-cost and S defined by (1) are calculated.

As shown in the Fig. 2, with the number of logical nodes increasing, the average value of S is increasing, and the maximum value does not exceed 80. It shows that the effect of the physical node division algorithm is relatively good, and the storage capacity among the logical nodes in the division result is relatively balanced. In addition, as the number of logical nodes increases, the algorithm execution time has a gentle downward trend. However, for the number of logical nodes in the experiment, the time cost of the algorithm does not exceed 3 s, so the execution rate of the algorithm is relatively reasonable.

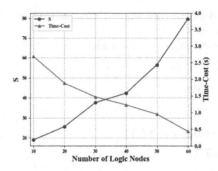

Fig. 2. The S and time-cost with the change of the number of logical nodes.

Compared with the existing structure, we also conducted an experimental evaluation on the improvement of the storage capacity of the NBNS. In this experiment, due to the difference of blockchain network structures, the data volume stored by a single physical node will be very different if the data volume of the blockchain is fixed. Therefore, we use the average data storage volume of a single physical node as a measurement index and compare it with the blockchain network structure of LightChain [6] and Fruitchain [7]. In our scheme, the number of logical nodes is 60. As shown in the Fig. 3, the average data storage volume (AvgD) of a single physical node (SPN) in our scheme is apparently much lower than other schemes.

A 51% attack means that someone who has controlled more than 51% of the computing power of the entire blockchain network can preemptively complete a longer chain of counterfeit transactions. If the attack is successful, this chain is synchronized by all nodes in the blockchain network, and the blockchain has been tampered with maliciously. We simulated the probability of blockchain failure for different solutions when different numbers of nodes were attacked and mastered maliciously. In this experiment, the number of physical nodes is set to 200, and the number of logical nodes is set to 60. After the number of different physical nodes is controlled, the probability of the blockchain network failure is calculated. As shown in the Fig. 4, compared with the blockchain network structure of LightChain [6] and Fruitchain [7], the NBNS has better resistance to 51% attacks. In the blockchain network structure of LightChain [6] and Fruitchain [7], when the number of physical nodes being attacked exceeds 100, the probability of blockchain network failure probability is already 1. In the NBNS, when the number of attacked nodes reaches 120, the failure probability of the blockchain network is close to 1.

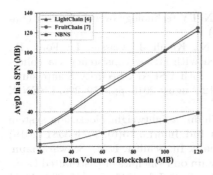

Fig. 3. The AvgD of a SPN.

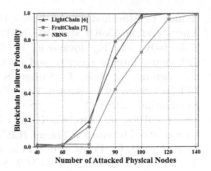

Fig. 4. Failure probability of 51% attack.

6 Conclusion

In this paper, we propose a novel blockchain network structure. This structure reorganizes the physical nodes in the blockchain network into multiple logical nodes. Each logical node contains several physical nodes, thus sharing the data originally stored on one physical node to multiple logical nodes Storage on physical nodes reduces the storage pressure of a single physical machine. In order to ensure the normal operation of the function of the logical node, we design the election algorithm of the physical master node in the logical node. The election algorithm selects a physical master node from multiple physical nodes of the logical node, and the physical master node is responsible for the consensus and synchronization process of the blockchain system. Experimental simulation results show that the proposed new blockchain network structure can effectively reduce the storage occupation of a single physical node and reduce the difficulty of deploying the blockchain to the edge network. Meanwhile, the novel blockchain network structure can significantly resist 51% attack.

Acknowledgements. This work is supported by the National Key R&D Program of China (No. 2019YFB1703601), National Natural Science Foundation of China (No. 61672131), and the new Generation of Artificial Intelligence Science and Technology Major Project of Tianjin (No. 19ZXZNGX00010).

References

1. Chen, N., Qiu, T., Zhou, X., Li, K., Atiquzzaman, M.: An intelligent robust networking mechanism for the Internet of Things. IEEE Commun. Mag. **57**(11), 91–95 (2019)
2. Conti, M., Sandeep Kumar, E., Lal, C., Ruj, S.: A survey on security and privacy issues of bitcoin. IEEE Commun. Surv. Tutor. **20**(4), 3416–3452 (2018)
3. Eyal, I., Gencer, A.E., Sirer, E.G., Renesse, R.V.: Bitcoin-NG: a scalable blockchain protocol. In: 13th USENIX Symposium on Networked Systems Design and Implementation (NSDI 2016), pp. 45–59. USENIX Association, Santa Clara, CA, March 2016

4. Hanke, T., Movahedi, M., Williams, D.: DFINITY technology overview series, consensus system. CoRR abs/1805.04548 (2018)
5. Kokoris-Kogias, E., Jovanovic, P., Gailly, N., Khoffi, I., Gasser, L., Ford, B.: Enhancing bitcoin security and performance with strong consistency via collective signing. In: Holz, T., Savage, S. (eds.) 25th USENIX Security Symposium, USENIX Security 16, Austin, TX, USA, 10–12 August 2016, pp. 279–296. USENIX Association (2016)
6. Liu, Y., Wang, K., Lin, Y., Xu, W.: LightChain: a lightweight blockchain system for industrial Internet of Things. IEEE Trans. Ind. Inform. 15(6), 3571–3581 (2019)
7. Pass, R., Shi, E.: FruitChains: a fair blockchain. In: Schiller, E.M., Schwarzmann, A.A. (eds.) Proceedings of the ACM Symposium on Principles of Distributed Computing (PODC 2017), Washington, DC, USA, 25–27 July 2017, pp. 315–324. ACM (2017)
8. Popov, S.: The tangle, April 2018. https://iota.org/IOTA_Whitepaper.pdf
9. Qiu, T., Li, B., Qu, W., Ahmed, E., Wang, X.: TOSG: a topology optimization scheme with global small world for industrial heterogeneous Internet of Things. IEEE Trans. Ind. Inform. 15(6), 3174–3184 (2019)
10. Qiu, T., Liu, J., Si, W., Wu, D.O.: Robustness optimization scheme with multi-population co-evolution for scale-free wireless sensor networks. IEEE/ACM Trans. Netw. 27(3), 1028–1042 (2019)
11. Tschorsch, F., Scheuermann, B.: Bitcoin and beyond: a technical survey on decentralized digital currencies. IEEE Commun. Surv. Tutor. 18(3), 2084–2123 (2016)
12. Tuli, S., Mahmud, R., Tuli, S., Buyya, R.: FogBus: a blockchain-based lightweight framework for edge and fog computing. J. Syst. Softw. 154, 22–36 (2019)
13. Vizier, G., Gramoli, V.: ComChain: bridging the gap between public and consortium blockchains. In: 2018 IEEE International Conference on Internet of Things (iThings) and IEEE Green Computing and Communications (GreenCom) and IEEE Cyber, Physical and Social Computing (CPSCom) and IEEE Smart Data (SmartData), pp. 1469–1474 (2018)
14. Zheng, Z., Xie, S., Dai, H., Chen, X., Wang, H.: An overview of blockchain technology: architecture, consensus, and future trends. In: 2017 IEEE International Congress on Big Data (BigData Congress), pp. 557–564 (2017)
15. Zhu, S., Cai, Z., Hu, H., Li, Y., Li, W.: zkCrowd: a hybrid blockchain-based crowdsourcing platform. IEEE Trans. Ind. Inform. 16(6), 4196–4205 (2020)
16. Zhu, S., Li, W., Li, H., Tian, L., Luo, G., Cai, Z.: Coin hopping attack in blockchain-based IoT. IEEE IoT J. 6(3), 4614–4626 (2019)

Dynamic Distribution Routing Algorithm Based on Probability for Maritime Delay Tolerant Networks

Xuerong Cui[1]([envelope]), Tong Xu[1]([envelope]), Juan Li[2]([envelope]), Meiqi Ji[2], Qiqi Qi[2], and Shibao Li[1]

[1] College of Oceanography and Space Informatics,
China University of Petroleum (East China), Qingdao, China
{cxr,lishibao}@upc.edu.cn, 370284518@qq.com
[2] College of Computer Science and Technology,
China University of Petroleum (East China), Qingdao, China
lij@upc.edu.cn, 506353930@qq.com, 577101053@qq.com

Abstract. The characteristics of marine environment restricts the deployment of base station. When seaborne ships are far away from the shore base, the quality of communication between ships will rapidly decline. Compared with the high cost of using satellite communication, this paper applies Delay Tolerant Networks (DTNs) to ship communication and proposes a Dynamic Distribution Routing Algorithm Based on Probability (DDPR), which selects the appropriate next hop for the message according to the historical encounter probability between ships, and uses the strategy of multiple copies to realize the dynamic distribution of the message. Simulation results show that DDPR has good performance in terms of delivery rate and transmission overhead.

Keywords: Delay tolerant networks · Routing protocol · Ship communications

1 Introduction

DTNs are characterized by their lack of connectivity due to node mobility and typical sparse topologies, very long and variable propagation delay, and high error rate of the communication channels [1, 2]. Recently, DTNs has been used in many fields, such as Vehicular Ad-hoc Network (VANET) [3], Cognitive Wireless Network (CWN). The "Store-Carry-Forward" routing mode is adopted in DTNs to relay messages. That is, after the source node generates a message, it will carry the message until it encounters a more suitable relay node or destination node.

Compared with the current development status of onshore communications, the development of maritime communication systems is relatively slow. Due to the constraints of the marine geographical environment, it is not practical to build fixed long-term infrastructure at ocean. Satellite communication is regarded as one of the optimal ways of message transmission by ocean-going ships. However, when the size of the data packet being transmitted is large, this method will lead to expensive communication costs and occupy precious satellite resources for a long time. Therefore, we hold that it is a feasible way to apply DTNs to offshore communication.

© Springer Nature Switzerland AG 2020
D. Yu et al. (Eds.): WASA 2020, LNCS 12384, pp. 77–84, 2020.
https://doi.org/10.1007/978-3-030-59016-1_7

An efficient routing algorithm is a prerequisite for data transmission [4]. In DTNs, the contacts are completely opportunistic, that is neither the meeting schedule nor the contact period of the nodes in the network is known in advance [5]. Early DTNs routing algorithms were mostly based on single copy strategies, such as Direct Delivery (DD) algorithm and First Contact (FC) algorithm, which are suitable for small networks but perform poorly in real and complex environments. In order to solve the said problems, researchers have proposed algorithms based on flooding and fixed copies strategy. Epidemic Routing is a kind of algorithm that is entirely based on flooding, which attempts to flood the messages to all the nodes in the communication range. The way that the Epidemic algorithm floods the network, however, is unrestricted and unconstrained, which will cause huge routing overhead. Several algorithms based on the fixed copies strategy have been proposed to further reduce network overhead, such as Spray and Wait [6] (hereinafter "SaW"), Binary Spray and Wait [6] (hereinafter "B-SaW"), TBR [5], etc. Moreover, in PROPHET-TC [7], nodes only forward messages to those nodes with higher transmission capacity. In EDR [8], nodes use the number of encounters and the distance as a relay criterion. However, maintaining global information requires a lot of network resources. LanePost [9] constructs the lane graph through a brute-force search for ships and boats, and then finds the chance of encounter. But this search method increases the complexity of algorithm and the difficulty of routing decisions.

Considerable research and surveys indicate that human movement actually follows a regular pattern [10, 11]. That is, the future motion track can be predicted based on the previous track. There is evidence that the reliability of this prediction can reach 93% [12], which provides a reference for the design of the routing algorithm. Moreover, we improve the delivery rate of messages by allowing each message to generate multiple copies. It is necessary to minimize the total cost of sending data to the destination node [13]. DDPR incorporates the idea of dynamically distributing copies into a probability mechanism, which aims to improve the message delivery rate and reduce the network routing overhead.

The rest of the paper is organized as follows. System model and the detailed design of DDPR are described in Sect. 2. The performance of DDPR is analyzed in Sect. 3. At last, conclusions are stated in Sect. 4.

2   Algorithm

2.1   System Model and Probability Update

If the entire network is represented by the symbol N, and a total of m nodes are active in the network, then any node is in the following set:

$$N = \{n_r | 0 \leq r \leq m\} \tag{1}$$

where n_r indicates the r-th node in the network. N can be represented as the set of all nodes in the network. We consider that each node is equipped with an omnidirectional antenna with a transmission range R_r. The necessary and sufficient conditions for node n_A and n_B to establish a communication connection successfully are as follows:

$$d(n_A, n_B) \leq min(R_A, R_B) \tag{2}$$

where $d(n_A, n_B)$ denotes Euclidean distance between n_A and n_B.

In addition, the buffer resources of each node are limited. When the remaining buffer size of node is not big enough to receive a new message, the oldest received message will be deleted. Any node in the network can generate messages, which will be attached with the address of the destination node, the size of the message (denoted as M_s), initial Time To Live (TTL), number of copies (denoted as L), and other properties. Considering the transmission speed between the two nodes is T_s KBps, then the message is successfully forwarded only when the following formula holds:

$$t_{down}^{(A,B)} - t_{up}^{(A,B)} \geq M_s/T_s \tag{3}$$

where $t_{up}^{(A,B)}$ represents the time when two nodes establish a communication connection. Similarly, $t_{down}^{(A,B)}$ is deemed as the time of disconnection. Within the scope of our system model, message fragmentation will not be considered.

In terms of the node probability update mechanism, we use the method in PRO-PHET [14]. Each node has a prediction variable for each destination, which indicates the probability of the successful delivery of the message to the destination [15]. When nodes encounter, their probability value increases according to the following formula:

$$P_{AB} = P_{AB(old)} + \left(1 - P_{AB(old)}\right) * P_{init} \tag{4}$$

where P_{AB} denotes the successful delivery probability between n_A and n_B. P_{init} stands for the initialization constant. $P_{AB(old)}$ represents the updated probability result of the last encounter. If two nodes lose contact with each other for a long time, the probability between them will decrease as follows:

$$P_{AB} = P_{AB(old)} * \gamma^k \tag{5}$$

where γ refers to the aging constant. k is the number of time units that have elapsed since the last metric update. Besides, the algorithm defines the transitive property of probability. If n_A often encounters n_B and n_B often encounters n_C, then n_C may be a suitable relay node for n_A. P_{AC} can be updated according to the following formula:

$$P_{AC} = P_{AC(old)} + \left(1 - P_{AC(old)}\right) * P_{AB} * P_{BC} * \beta \tag{6}$$

where β represents the weight factor, and it takes a value between [0, 1].

2.2 DDPR Algorithm

Message Forwarding Strategy. When two nodes contact, whether or not to forward messages depends on the comparison results of the probability of contacting two nodes. An encounter table is defined in each node, which maintains many key-value pairs. The key here is the ID of the encountered node and the value denotes the corresponding success probability in delivering message to the encountered node. In the beginning, the encounter table of each node does not contain any information. When two nodes encounter for the first time, a key-value pair with the ID of the encountered node and a probability success equal to P_{init} is created. In subsequent encounters, nodes will update the probability values using the method in Sect. 2.1. After a node determines the other end of its communication connection as the relay node of the message, it will calculate the number of message copies needed to forward according to the following formula,

$$L_{AB} = \frac{P_{BD}}{P_{AD} + P_{BD}} * L \tag{7}$$

where P_{AD} is the successful delivery probability between n_A and n_D, and n_D is assumed to be the destination node of the message. Through this copies allocation method, those nodes that contact with the destination node more regularly can get more copies of messages, thus improving the reliability of delivery. After the message is successfully relayed (Eq. (3) holds), the number of message copies of the sending node n_A will be updated by Eq. (8),

$$L_A' = L_A - L_{AB} \tag{8}$$

where L_A' represents the number of remaining copies of n_A. L_A is the total number of message copies before sending it. When L_A' decreases to 1, the node will no longer forward this message until it encounters the destination node of the message.

Buffer Management Strategy. In real scenarios, the buffer resources of maritime mobile nodes are not unlimited. In order to utilize the buffer efficiently, each node maintains another list besides the messages list to record the delivered messages. The delivered messages list is only used to record the ID of the delivered messages instead of the content of the message, so it is simple for the node to maintain. After the two nodes establish a communication connection, they will first exchange lists with each other, and then relay messages. Each node will take the first ID in the received list and browse its own message list to determine whether it contains the ID. If it indeed does contain, the message represented by this ID will be removed from the messages list, and this ID will be added to its list of delivered messages. Otherwise, the ID of the message is added directly to its list of delivered messages.

Moreover, the TTL value of each message decreases over time. When this value of a message reaches zero, all the nodes that contain this message in their buffer will delete this message.

In DDPR, if the node encounters the destination node of the message in the process of moving, it will directly deliver all copies of the message to the destination node. Then, the node will delete the message and mark it as delivered.

3 Performance

3.1 Simulation Settings

As shown in Table 1, we use simulation parameters to map the real scene. A preliminary simulation was done and we found that 63% of the nodes had a contact time of less than 100 s. In other words, about 48 messages can be sent in one communication. Due to the sparse distribution of ships in the marine environment, we deployed 70 ship nodes in the sea area of 2200 km × 1040 km.

Table 1. Parameters and mapping

Parameters	Simulation value	Real value
Simulation time	12 h	24 days
Simulation area	5500 m × 2600 m	2200 km × 1040 km
Transmission distance (R_r)	50 m	20 km
Node speed	0.8–1.2 m/s	12–20 min/h
Time-to-live (*TTL*)	300 min	10 days
Message generation interval	20–25 s	16–20 min
Message size (M_s)	1 MB	500 MB
Buffer size	100 MB	50,000 MB
Transmission speed (T_s)	480 kBps	5 MB/S
Movement model	MapRouteMovement	MapRouteMovement

3.2 Results

Figures 1, 2, and 3 show how different numbers of copies of messages (*L*), different TTL, and different buffer sizes impact the result.

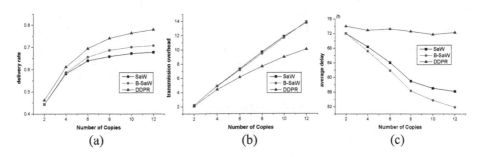

(a)   (b)   (c)

Fig. 1. Varying number of message copies

As the number of copies increases in Fig. 1(a) and (b), the number of relayed messages increases correspondingly, resulting in a greater probability of successful message delivery. Therefore, the delivery rate and the overhead show an upward trend. In Fig. 1(c), however, DDPR's simulation results are inferior to the other two. Because in the same time period, the probability mechanism makes the number of messages forwarded inferior to SaW and B-SaW.

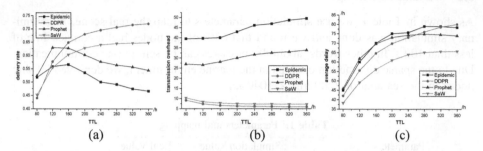

(a)   (b)   (c)

Fig. 2. Varying TTL value

When the buffer space is sufficient, properly increasing the TTL will increase the chance of messages being successfully forwarded, so the delivery rate of all of the algorithms will initially show an upward trend, as shown in Fig. 2(a). However, the flooding mechanism will cause the node to delete messages and therefore reduce the delivery rate. In Fig. 2(b), for PROPHET and Epidemic, the number of relay messages increases while the number of messages delivered decreases due to messages deletion, so the overhead increases gradually. For SaW and DDPR, the growth rate of the number of delivered messages is higher than that of relay number, so the overhead is gradually reduced. In Fig. 2(c), a larger TTL means that the number of messages that need to wait longer to be delivered increases, ergo the delay gradually increases.

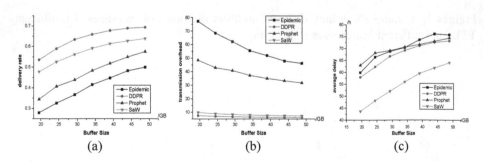

(a)   (b)   (c)

Fig. 3. Varying Buffer size

In Fig. 3(a), the larger buffer size represents the improvement of the storage capacity of the node, so the delivery rate increases. Meanwhile, the proportion of messages that are delivered increases, so the overhead decreases in Fig. 3(b). As far as delay is concerned, which is presented in Fig. 3(c), the larger buffer size keeps messages that would otherwise be deleted. Therefore, the delayed delivery of these messages makes the average delay larger.

4 Conclusion

In this paper, we purpose a routing algorithm suitable for ship-to-ship communication, which is called DDPR. The algorithm combines the idea of dynamic copies allocation with probability mechanism. We evaluated the algorithm by setting appropriate simulation parameters and establishing mapping. Simulation results show that the algorithm has better comprehensive performance. In future work, we will focus on optimizing the performance of DDPR in terms of delay and node energy consumption.

Acknowledgments. This work was supported by National Natural Science Foundation of China (No. 61671482, 61902431, 91938204 and 61972417), the Key Research and Development Program of Shandong Province with No. 2019GGX101048 and Fundamental Research Funds for the Central Universities (No.19CX05003A-9, 19CX05003A-4 and 18CX02136A).

References

1. Rahim, M. S., Casari, P., Guerra, F., et al.: On the performance of delay-tolerant routing protocols in underwater networks. In: OCEANS, pp. 1–7. IEEE, Spain (2011)
2. Zhang, L., Cai, Z., Lu, J., Wang, X.: Mobility-aware routing in delay tolerant networks. Pers. Ubiquit. Comput. **19**(7), 1111–1123 (2015). https://doi.org/10.1007/s00779-015-0880-x
3. Zhou, J., Dong, X., Cao, Z., et al.: Secure and privacy preserving protocol for cloud-based vehicular DTNs. IEEE Trans. Inf. Forensics Secur. **10**(6), 1299–1314 (2015)
4. Cai, Z., Goebel, R., Lin, G.: Size-constrained tree partitioning: a story on approximation algorithm design for the multicast k-tree routing problem. In: Du, D.-Z., Hu, X., Pardalos, P. M. (eds.) COCOA 2009. LNCS, vol. 5573, pp. 363–374. Springer, Heidelberg (2009). https://doi.org/10.1007/978-3-642-02026-1_34
5. Prodhan, A.T., Das, R., Kabir, H., et al.: TTL based routing in opportunistic networks. J. Netw. Comput. Appl. **34**(5), 1660–1670 (2011)
6. Spyropoulos, T., Psounis, K., Raghavendra, C.S.: Spray and wait: an efficient routing scheme for intermittently connected mobile networks. In: Proceedings of the 2005 ACM SIGCOMM workshop on Delay-tolerant networking, pp. 252–259. ACM (2005)
7. Wang, G., Zheng, L., Yan, L., et al.: Probabilistic routing algorithm based on transmission capability of nodes in DTN. In: 11th IEEE International Conference on Anti-counterfeiting, Security, and Identification, pp. 146–149. IEEE, China (2017)
8. Dhurandher, S.K., Borah, S., Woungang, I., et al.: EDR: an encounter and distance based routing protocol for opportunistic networks. In: 30th International Conference on Advanced Information Networking and Applications, pp. 297–302. IEEE (2016)
9. Geng, X., Wang, Y., Feng, H., et al.: LanePost: lane-based optimal routing protocol for delay-tolerant maritime networks. China Commun. **14**(002), 65–78 (2017)

10. Zeng, S., Wang, H., Li, Y., et al.: Predictability and prediction of human mobility based on application-collected location data. In: 14th International Conference on Mobile Ad Hoc and Sensor Systems, pp. 28–36. IEEE (2017)

11. Li, A., Lv, Q., Qiao, Y., et al.: Improving mobility prediction performance with state based prediction method when the user departs from routine. In: 2016 IEEE International Conference on Big Data Analysis, pp. 1–7. IEEE (2016)

12. Song, C., Qu, Z., Blumm, N., et al.: Limits of predictability in human mobility. Science **327**(5968), 1018–1021 (2010)

13. Cai, Z., Randy, G., Lin, G.: Size-constrained tree partitioning: approximating the multicast k-tree routing problem. Theoret. Comput. Sci. **412**(3), 240–245 (2011)

14. Lindgren, A., Doria, A., Schelén, O.: Probabilistic routing in intermittently connected networks. In: ACM SIGMOBILE mobile computing and communications review, pp. 19–20. ACM (2003)

15. Derakhshanfard, N., Sabaei, M., Rahmani, A.M.: Sharing spray and wait routing algorithm in opportunistic networks. Wireless Netw. **22**(7), 2403–2414 (2015). https://doi.org/10.1007/s11276-015-1105-y

Learning-Aided Mobile Charging for Rechargeable Sensor Networks

Xinpeng Duan[1], Feng Li[1(✉)], Dongxiao Yu[1(✉)], Huan Yang[2], and Hao Sheng[3]

[1] School of Computer Science and Technology, Shandong University, Qingdao, China
201814810@mail.sdu.edu.cn
{fli,dxyu}@sdu.edu.cn
[2] College of Computer Science and Technology, Qingdao University, Qingdao, China
cathy_huanyang@hotmail.com
[3] School of Computer Science and Engineering, Beihang University, Beihang, China
shenghao@buaa.edu.cn

Abstract. Recent years have witnessed the advancement of *Rechargeable Wireless Sensor Networks* (RWSNs) for permanent environment monitoring or survey, while one fundamental problem is to find out the optimal cycle in a RWSN on the basis of *Traveling Salesman Problem* (TSP), to drive a *Mobile Charger* (MC) to periodically visit and charge the rechargeable sensor nodes. In this paper, by taking into account the uncertainties of the travel costs among the rechargeable sensor nodes, we investigate the so-called *Sequential Mobile Charging* (SMC) problem, where the MC sequentially travels along the cycles, towards the minimization of the resulting expected cumulative travel cost without being aware of the travel cost assignment. By leveraging a *Multi-Armed Bandit* (MAB) framework, we propose a learning-aided mobile charger scheduling algorithm, namely "BanditCharger", which induces a regret growing logarithmically with respect to the number of the sequential cycles. The efficacy of BanditCharger also can be verified by extensive simulations

Keywords: Mobile charging · Rechargeable wireless sensor networks · Multi-Armed Bandit

1 Introduction

One barrier to the pervasive deployment of *Wireless Sensor Networks* (WSNs) is their constrained energy supplies, since sensor nodes are usually powered by batteries with limited capacity. Although we can let the sensor nodes harvest energy from surrounding environments (e.g., in [7,11–13,15]), the power sources

This work is partially supported by National Key R&D Program of China (Grant No. 2019YFB2102600), NSFC (Grant No. 61702304, 61971269, 61832012), Shandong Provincial Natural Science Foundation (Grant No. ZR2017QF005), and Industrial Internet Innovation and Development Project in 2019 of China.

© Springer Nature Switzerland AG 2020
D. Yu et al. (Eds.): WASA 2020, LNCS 12384, pp. 85–96, 2020.
https://doi.org/10.1007/978-3-030-59016-1_8

may not always be available, while we may also suffer from the low efficiency of energy harvesting. Fortunately, recent years have witnessed the advancement of *Wireless Power Transfer* (WPT) [5,6], by which we can recharge the sensor nodes, to enable the so-called *Rechargeable Wireless Sensor Networks* (RWSNs) to work permanently.

Nevertheless, the WPT techniques are still constrained by their effective ranges, such that wireless chargers have to be placed very close to the sensor nodes which we intend to charge. Hence, static deployment of wireless chargers is not feasible, especially for large-scale deployment of sensor nodes. An alternative is to employ a mobile charger (e.g., a vehicle equipped with WPT devices) to visit the individual rechargeable sensor nodes. This mobile charger-based solution has been adopted in many recent proposals (e.g., [9,10,16,18,24]). To improve the efficiency of the mobile charging, the mobile charger should be properly scheduled. One fundamental problem in the mobile charger scheduling is how to find the shortest cycle in a RWSN, towards the minimization of the mobile charger's cost for traveling (e.g., in terms of energy consumption or time overhead). In fact, most of existing proposals, e.g. [14,20–22], follow this thread and establish their models based on the *Traveling Salesman Problem* (TSP). Specifically, given a set of rechargeable sensor nodes, previous proposals assume the cost for traveling between any two of the sensor nodes is known. Such an assumption actually is adopted by most of the existing proposals. However, since the sensor nodes are usually deployed in unknown environment, it may not be always allowed to carefully profile the cost assignment. Additionally, the traveling cost between the sensor nodes may be time-varying, e.g., due to the behaviors of the operators of the mobile chargers or the traffic conditions.

To this end, we investigate *Sequential Mobile Charging* (SMC) problem in this paper, where we sequentially schedule a mobile charger to visit the rechargeable sensor nodes periodically by traveling in cycles under an *unknown* travel cost assignment, and our aim is at minimizing the cumulative total travel cost of the mobile charger. To server this goal, we leverage the *Multi-Armed Bandit* (MAB) framework such that the feasible cycles are exploited to gain immediate decrease in travel cost and explored to reduce the travel cost in a long run. Moreover, since directly applying the state-of-the-art MAB algorithm (e.g., the *Upper Confidence Bound* (UCB) algorithm) results in considerable storage and computation overhead, we innovate in fully exploiting the overlaps among different feasible cycles so as to design an efficient UCB-based algorithm with polynomial storage complexity. The efficacy of our algorithm can be verified by theoretical analysis and extensive simulations. It is shown that our algorithm delivers a regret which is polynomial with respect to the number of the sensor nodes and grows logarithmically in time.

The rest of this paper is organized as follow. We first introduce the system model and formulate our SMC problem in Sect. 2. We then present our algorithm design and the theoretical analysis in Sect. 3 and Sect. 4, respectively. We also give a short discussion in Sect. 5. We perform extensive simulations to evaluate our proposed algorithm in Sect. 6. We finally survey the closely related proposals in Sect. 7 and conclude this paper in Sect. 8.

2 System Model and Problem Formulation

2.1 System Model

We consider a RWSN consisting of N rechargeable sensor nodes $\mathcal{N} = \{n_i\}_{i=1,\cdots,N}$. We suppose there is a mobile charger (MC) which periodically starts from service station n_0, charges the sensor nodes sequentially and returns back to n_0. We denote by $\mathcal{P}$ the set of all the possible *simple* cycles (i.e., the paths starting from n_0, going through each sensor node n_i only once and finally ending at n_0). We define an *epoch* as a time interval within which the MC travels along any $p \in \mathcal{P}$. Specifically, a new epoch begins when the MC starts from the service station n_0, and terminates when the MC returns back to n_0. We denote by p_t the cycle adopted in the t-th epoch.

For each pair of n_i and n_j (where $i, j \in \{0, 1, \cdots, N\}$ and $i \neq j$), we define an edge $(i, j) \in \mathcal{E}$ representing the path along which the MC travel between n_i and n_j. Hence, the size of $\mathcal{E}$, denoted by E, is $N(N+1)/2$. In the t-th epoch, we define a cost assignment $c_{i,j}(t)$ for $\forall (i, j) \in \mathcal{E}$, which represents the cost for the MC traveling between n_i and n_j. We assume that $c_{i,j}(t)$ is *independently and identically distributed* (i.i.d.) across t, obeying a probability distribution with the mean being $\mu_{i,j}$. Without loss of generality, we assume that $\mu = \{\mu_{i,j}\}_{(i,j)\in\mathcal{E}}$ is an Euclidean metric satisfying the triangle inequality. Especially, $\mu_{i,j} = \infty$ implies n_j (resp. n_i) is not reachable from n_i (resp. n_j).

2.2 Problem Formulation

For the cycle p_t, its cost can be defined by $c(p_t) = \sum_{(i,j)\in p_t} c_{i,j}(t)$. Considering T epochs, we aim at designing a policy to sequentially select a cycle for the MC in each epoch, such that the resulting *expected cumulative cost* can be minimized. Formally, the above *Sequential Mobile Charging* (SMC) problem can be formulated as

$$\min_{\{p_t\}_{t=1,\cdots,T}} f_\mu(\{p_t\}_{t=1,\cdots,T}) := \sum_{t=1}^{T} \mathbb{E}_\mu[c(p_t)] = \sum_{t=1}^{T} \sum_{(i,j)\in p_t} \mu_{i,j} \qquad (1)$$

When the cost assignment μ is known, the above SMC problem is degenerated such that the MC repeatedly travels along the "shortest" cycle calculated by the state-of-the-art TSP solvers under the cost assignment μ. However, as mentioned in Sect. 1, such a knowledge may not always be available; while it is highly non-trivial to address the SMC problem with the uncertainty of μ.

3   Learning-Aided Mobile Charger Scheduling

In this section, we leverage the MAB approach to design a learning-aided mobile charger scheduling algorithm to address the SMC problem with uncertain cost assignment. We first introduce an intuitive application of the MAB in Sect. 3.1, and then present in Sect. 3.2 our BanditCharger algorithm which fully exploits the correlations among the cycles.

3.1   An Intuitive Solution Based on Multi-Armed Bandit

We consider a bandit with all the possible cycles as the arms. Our aim is then transformed into selecting a sequence of cycles such that the resulting expected cumulative cost approaches the minimum one of the optimal cycle as closely as possible. To serve this goal, one choice is to adopt the UCB method. Particularly, in the t-th epoch, we define an UCB index $u_p(t)$ for each cycle $p \in \mathcal{P}$ as follows

$$u_p(t) = \bar{c}_p(t-1) - \sqrt{\frac{2\ln t}{m_p(t-1)}} \tag{2}$$

where $\bar{c}_p(t-1)$ represents the average cost of cycle p up to the $(t-1)$-th epoch and $m_p(t-1)$ denotes the number of times cycle p is selected up to the $(t-1)$-th epoch. We then select the cycle with the minimum UCB index, i.e.,

$$p_t = \arg\min_{p \in \mathcal{P}} u_p(t) \tag{3}$$

According to [1], the above method results in an upper-bound for the regret function as follows

$$\left[8 \sum_{p:\mu_p > \mu^*} \left(\frac{\ln t}{\Delta_p} \right) \right] + \left(1 + \frac{\pi^2}{3} \right) \sum_{p \in \mathcal{P}} \Delta_p \tag{4}$$

where

$$\mu_p = \sum_{(i,j) \in p} \mu_{i,j}, \quad \mu^* = \min_{p \in \mathcal{P}} \mu_p \text{ and } \Delta_p = \mu_p - \mu^* \tag{5}$$

Unfortunately, the above intuitive application of the UCB method entails considerable storage and computation overheads, as the set of the possible cycles $\mathcal{P}$ has an exponentially large size and we have to maintain the two variables $\bar{c}_p(t)$ and $m_p(t)$ for each cycle $p \in \mathcal{P}$. One observation is that, different cycles may share the same edge, inspired by which, it is promising to improve the efficiency of the mobile charger scheduling algorithm in storage and computations, by fully exploiting such correlations among different cycles.

3.2   BanditCharger

To this end, we hereby present our BandiCharger algorithm in Algorithm 1. The algorithm proceeds relying on two variables $\bar{c}_{i,j}(t)$ and $m_{i,j}(t)$ for $\forall(i,j) \in \mathcal{E}$. Specifically, $\bar{c}_{i,j}(t-1)$ denotes the average cost spent by the MC on traveling between i and j up to the $(t-1)$-th epoch, and $m_{i,j}(t-1)$ is the number of times the MC travels between i and j up to the $(t-1)$-th epoch. Our algorithm is initialized by $m_{i,j}(0) = 1$ for each $\forall(i,j) \in \mathcal{E}$ and letting the MC travel along each $(i,j) \in \mathcal{E}$ so as to set the initial value of $c_{i,j}(0)$ and thus the one of $\bar{c}_{i,j}(0)$ (see Lines 1–5). In the t-th epoch (with $t = 1, \cdots, T$), as demonstrated in Line 7, we first compute the UCB index for $\forall(i,j) \in \mathcal{E}$ as follows

$$u_{i,j}(t) = \bar{c}_{i,j}(t-1) - \sqrt{\frac{3 \ln t}{2 m_{i,j}(t-1)}} \qquad (6)$$

The above UCB indices actually specify a weight assignment for $\forall(i,j) \in \mathcal{E}$, based on which, we then compute the "shortest" cycle p_t through TSP solvers, e.g., the *Dynamic Programming* (DP) method[1] (see Line 8). Let the MC travel along the cycle p_t to charge the rechargeable sensor nodes, and we can observe

---

Algorithm 1: BanditCharger.

Input: A rechargeable sensor network $\mathcal{N} \bigcup \{n_0\}$.
Output: A sequence of cycles $p_1, p_2, \cdots, p_T \in \mathcal{P}$ for charging

1 **Initialization**
2     $m_{i,j}(0) = 1$ for $\forall i,j \in \{0, 1, \cdots, N\}$;
3   Let the MC travel along each $(i,j) \in \mathcal{E}$ and observe $c_{i,j}(0)$;
4   Let $\bar{c}_{i,j}(0) = c_{i,j}(0)$;
5 **end**
6 **foreach** *epoch* $t = 1, \cdots, T$ **do**
7   Compute $u_{i,j}(t) = \bar{c}_{i,j}(t-1) - \sqrt{\frac{3 \ln t}{2 m_{i,j}(t-1)}}$ for $\forall i,j \in \tilde{\mathcal{N}}$;
8     $p_t = \mathsf{DP}\left(\mathcal{N} \bigcup \{n_0\}, \{u_{i,j}(t)\}_{i,j \in \{0,1,\cdots,N\}}\right)$;
9   Let the MC travel along p_t and observe $c_{i,j}(t)$ for $\forall(i,j) \in p_t$;
10   **foreach** $i,j \in \tilde{\mathcal{N}}$ **do**
11   **if** $(i,j) \in p_t$ **then**
12          $\bar{c}_{i,j}(t) = \frac{c_{i,j}(t-1) \cdot m_{i,j}(t-1) + c_{i,j}(t)}{m_{i,j}(t-1)+1}$;
13          $m_{i,j}(t) = m_{i,j}(t-1) + 1$;
14   **else**
15          $\bar{c}_{i,j}(t) = \bar{c}_{i,j}(t-1)$;
16          $m_{i,j}(t) = m_{i,j}(t-1)$;
17   **end**
18   **end**
19 **end**

---

[1] We will discuss the choices of the TSP solvers later in Sect. 5.

$c_{i,j}(t)$ for $\forall (i,j) \in p_t$ (see Lines 9). The algorithm finally updates $\bar{c}_{i,j}(t)$ and $m_{i,j}(t)$ for $\forall i,j \in \mathcal{E}$ (see Lines 10–18) and proceeds to the next epoch.

4   Analysis

In this section, we analyze the performance our BanditCharger algorithm by showing the upper-bound of the following regret function

$$\text{Regret}(\{p_t\}_{t=1,2,\cdots,T}) = \sum_{t=1}^{T} f_\mu(\{p_t\}_{t=1,2,\cdots,T}) - T \cdot \sum_{(i,j)\in p^*} \mu_{i,j}$$

$$= \sum_{t=1}^{T} \sum_{(i,j)\in p_t} \mu_{i,j} - T \cdot \sum_{(i,j)\in p^*} \mu_{i,j} \qquad (7)$$

where p^* denotes the optimal cycle (with the minimum cost under the cost assignment $\{\mu_{i,j}\}_{(i,j)\in\mathcal{E}}$) calculated by some TSP solver (e.g., the DP method as shown in Algorithm 1). In fact, the above regret function measures the gap between the expected performance of our scheduling policy and the one of the (off-line) optimal solution.

Before diving into the details of our analysis, we first introduce a few notations which will be used in our later analysis. We assume that, a cycle $p \in \mathcal{P}$ is said to be "bad", if $\mu_p > \mu^*$ (see (5)). Let $\mathcal{Q} = \{p \in \mathcal{P} \mid \mu_p > \mu^*\}$ be the set of all the bad cycles, and suppose

$$\Delta_{min} = \min_{p\in\mathcal{Q}} \mu_p - \mu^* \text{ and } \Delta_{max} = \max_{p\in\mathcal{Q}} \mu_p - \mu^* \qquad (8)$$

For the t-th each epoch (where $t = 1, \cdots, T$), we define event $\text{Event}_1(t)$ as

$$\text{Event}_1(t) = \{p_t \in \mathcal{Q} \text{ and } m_{i,j}(t-1) > h(t) \text{ for } \forall (i,j) \in p_t\} \qquad (9)$$

where

$$h(t) = \frac{6(N+1)^2 \ln t}{\Delta_{min}^2} \qquad (10)$$

Additionally, event $\text{Event}_2(t)$ is defined as

$$\text{Event}_2(t) = \left\{ |\mu_{i,j} - \bar{c}_{i,j}(t-1)| \le \sqrt{\frac{3\ln t}{2m_{i,j}(t-1)}}, \text{ for } \forall i,j \in \tilde{\mathcal{N}} \right\} \qquad (11)$$

In the t-th epoch t, if $\text{Event}_1(t)$ holds, we have

$$\Delta_{min} > 2(N+1)\sqrt{\frac{3\ln t}{2m_{i,j}(t-1)}} \qquad (12)$$

for $\forall i,j \in \tilde{\mathcal{N}}$, while the the following inequality holds

$$u_{i,j}(t) \le \mu_{i,j} \le u_{i,j}(t) + 2\sqrt{\frac{3\ln t}{2m_{i,j}(t-1)}} \qquad (13)$$

if both $\text{Event}_1(t)$ and $\text{Event}_2(t)$ holds.

Lemma 1. *For each epoch $t = 1, 2, \cdot, T$, we have*

$$\mathbb{P}[\mathsf{Event}_1(t)] \leq N(N+1)t^{-2} \tag{14}$$

Proof. In the t-th epoch, if $\mathsf{Event}_1(t)$ and $\mathsf{Event}_2(t)$ both holds,

$$f_\mu(p_t) - \Delta_{min} = \sum_{(i,j)\in p_t} \left(\mu_{i,j} - \frac{\Delta_{min}}{N+1} \right) < \sum_{(i,j)\in p_t} \left(\mu_{i,j} - 2\sqrt{\frac{3\ln t}{2m_{i,j}(t-1)}} \right)$$

$$\leq \sum_{(i,j)\in p_t} u_{i,j}(t) \leq \sum_{(i,j)\in p^*} u_{i,j}(t) \leq \sum_{(i,j)\in p^*} \mu_{i,j} \tag{15}$$

Note that we have the first and the second inequalities hold according to (12) and (13), respectively; we have the third inequality based on the fact that our algorithm can output the optimal cycle p_t under the weight assignment $\{u_{i,j}(t)\}_{(i,j)\in\mathcal{E}}$; the forth inequality is due to (13) again. It is apparent that the above inequality (15) is a contradiction to the definition of Δ_{min} (see (8)). Therefore, neither $\mathsf{Event}_1(t)$ nor $\mathsf{Event}_2(t)$ holds in each epoch, i.e.,

$$\mathbb{P}\left[\mathsf{Event}_1(t) \wedge \mathsf{Event}_2(t)\right] = 0 \tag{16}$$

for $\forall t = 1, \cdots, T$. In each epoch, according to the Chernoff-Hoeffding bound,

$$\mathbb{P}\left[|\bar{c}_{i,j}(t) - \mu_{i,j}| \geq \sqrt{\frac{3\ln t}{2m_{i,j}(t-1)}}\right] \leq \sum_{t'=1}^{t-1} 2t^{\frac{-3t'}{m_{i,j}(t')}} \leq 2t^{-2} \tag{17}$$

for $\forall (i,j) \in \mathcal{E}$, based on which, the probability of the negative of $\mathsf{Event}_2(t)$ can be written as

$$\mathbb{P}[\neg\mathsf{Event}_2(t)] = \mathbb{P}\left[\left\{\exists(i,j) \in \mathcal{E}, |\mu_{i,j} - \bar{c}_{i,j}(t-1)| > \sqrt{\frac{3\ln t}{2m_{i,j}(t-1)}}\right\}\right]$$

$$\leq \sum_{(i,j)\in\mathcal{E}} \mathbb{P}\left[|\mu_{i,j} - \bar{c}_{i,j}(t-1)| > \sqrt{\frac{3\ln t}{2m_{i,j}(t-1)}}\right]$$

$$\leq \sum_{(i,j)\in\mathcal{E}} \mathbb{P}\left[|\mu_{i,j} - \bar{c}_{i,j}(t-1)| \geq \sqrt{\frac{3\ln t}{2m_{i,j}(t-1)}}\right]$$

$$\leq 2Et^{-2} = N(N+1)t^{-2} \tag{18}$$

Hence, the lemma can be concluded by

$$\mathbb{P}[\mathsf{Event}_1(t)] = \mathbb{P}[\mathsf{Event}_2(t) \wedge \mathsf{Event}_1(t)] + \mathbb{P}[\neg\mathsf{Event}_2(t) \wedge \mathsf{Event}_1(t)]$$

$$= \mathbb{P}[\neg\mathsf{Event}_2(t) \wedge \mathsf{Event}_1(t)] \leq \mathbb{P}[\neg\mathsf{Event}_2(t)] \leq N(N+1)t^{-2}$$

Theorem 1. *The regret of BanditCharger across T epochs is upper-bounded by*

$$N(N+1)\Delta_{max} \left(\frac{1}{2} + \frac{\pi^2}{6} + \frac{3(N+1)^2 \ln T}{\Delta_{min}^2} \right) \tag{19}$$

Proof. We define a variable $Y_{i,j}(t)$ for $\forall i, j \in \mathcal{E}$ in each epoch t. $Y_{i,j}(t)$ evolves across the epochs as follows

$$Y_{i,j}(t) = \begin{cases} Y_{i,j}(t-1) + 1, & \text{if } (i,j) = \arg\min_{(i',j') \in p_t} Y_{i,j}(t-1) \text{ and } p_{t-1} \in \mathcal{Q} \\ Y_{i,j}(t), & \text{otherwise} \end{cases}$$

(20)

Initially, let $Y_{i,j}(0) = 1$ for each $(i,j) \in \mathcal{E}$. Note that in any epoch t, if $p_t \in \mathcal{Q}$, there exists exactly one (i,j)-tuple having its $Y_{i,j}(t)$ increased by 1, while there is no $Y_{i,j}(t)$ increased if $p_t \notin \mathcal{Q}$. Therefore, assuming $\mathbb{I}: \{True, False\} \to \{0,1\}$ denotes an indicator function, we have

$$\sum_{(i,j) \in \mathcal{E}} Y_{i,j}(T) - E \cdot h(T)$$

$$= \sum_{t=1}^{T} \sum_{(i,j) \in \mathcal{E}} \mathbb{I}(p_t \in \mathcal{Q}, Y_{i,j}(t) > Y_{i,j}(t-1)) - E \cdot h(T)$$

$$\leq \sum_{t=1}^{T} \sum_{(i,j) \in \mathcal{E}} \mathbb{I}(p_t \in \mathcal{Q}, Y_{i,j}(t) > Y_{i,j}(t-1), Y_{i,j}(t-1) > h(T))$$

$$\leq \sum_{t=1}^{T} \sum_{(i,j) \in \mathcal{E}} \mathbb{I}(p_t \in \mathcal{Q}, Y_{i,j}(t) > Y_{i,j}(t-1), Y_{i,j}(t-1) > h(t))$$

$$\leq \sum_{t=1}^{T} \mathbb{I}(p_t \in \mathcal{Q}, m_{i,j}(t-1) > h(t), \forall (i,j) \in p_t) = \sum_{t=1}^{T} \mathbb{I}(\mathsf{Event}_1(t))$$

(21)

According to the linearity of expectations, we have

$$\sum_{(i,j) \in \mathcal{E}} \mathbb{E}[Y_{i,j}(T)] \leq \sum_{t=1}^{T} \mathbb{P}[\mathsf{Event}_1(t)] + E \cdot h(T)$$

$$\leq \sum_{t=1}^{T} N(N+1)t^{-2} + \frac{3N(N+1)^3 \ln T}{\Delta_{min}^2}$$

$$\leq N(N+1)\left(\frac{1}{2} + \frac{\pi^2}{6} + \frac{3(N+1)^2 \ln T}{\Delta_{min}^2}\right)$$

(22)

where the second inequality is due to (14) shown in Lemma 1. We finally conclude this theorem by substituting (22) into the following inequality

$$\mathsf{Regret}(\{p_t\}_{t=1,2,\cdots,T}) = \sum_{t=1}^{T} \sum_{(i,j) \in p_t} \mu_{i,j} - T \cdot \sum_{(i,j) \in p^*} \mu_{i,j}$$

$$= \sum_{t=1}^{T} \left(\sum_{(i,j) \in p_t} \mu_{i,j} - \sum_{(i,j) \in p^*} \mu_{i,j}\right) \leq \sum_{(i,j) \in \mathcal{E}} \mathbb{E}[Y_{i,j}(T)] \cdot \Delta_{max}$$

(23)

5   Discussion

As shown in Sect. 3.2, we calculate a cycle under the cost assignment specified by $\{u_{i,j}(t)\}_{(i,j)\in\mathcal{E}}$. Nevertheless, according to the definition of $u_{i,j}(t)$ (see (6)), it may not satisfy the triangle inequality and also may be negative. To accommodate the above properties of $u_{i,j}(t)$, we adopt dynamic programing method to compute the optimal cycle (with the minimum cost) under the cost assignment $\{u_{i,j}(t)\}_{(i,j)\in\mathcal{E}}$. Unfortunately, it is well known that, the dynamic programming method usually entails computation overhead, especially when dealing with large-scale RWSNs. In this case, one choice is to adopt other TSP solvers (e.g. *Ant Colony Optimization* (ACO) method), which induces light-weight computations with a slight compromise in the optimality in each epoch. As shown in Sect. 6 later, the ACO-based BanditCharger is of much higher efficiency in handling (relatively) large-scale RWSNs with comparable performance.

6   Simulations

In this section, we evaluate the performance of our BanditCharger algorithm by extensive numerical simulations.

We first compare the BanditCharger algorithm with another variation (so-called "ϵ-greedy algorithm") where we make the "exploitation-exploration" trade-off in a greed manner. Specifically, the trade-off is realized by a probability ϵ such that with probability ϵ, we uniformly construct a cycle (by assigning identical weight to the edges) for the exploration purpose, while with probability $1 - \epsilon$, we calculate the cycle in each epoch t by adopting $\bar{c}_{i,j}(t-1)$ as the weight assignment, to exploit the empirical knowledge. For any two of the sensor nodes (say n_i and n_j) in a given RWSN instance, we take the Euclidean distance between them as the mean of the cost $\mu_{i,j}$. We suppose that, in each epoch t, $c_{i,j}(t) = \mu_{i,j} + \tau_{i,j}(t)$ where $\tau_{i,j}(t)$ denotes an i.i.d. random noise (across t) with its mean being zero. We also assume that $\tau_{i,j}(t)$ is bounded so that we can normalize $c_{i,j}(t)$ into $[0, 1]$ for $t = 1, \cdots, T$ to facilitate the illustration of our simulation results. The comparison results (in terms of both regret and average regret) are illustrated in Fig. 1. It is shown that, although our BanditCharger may results in higher regret value than the ϵ-greedy algorithm, its UCB-based exploitation-exploration trade-off is able to produce much lower regret value in a long run as well as higher convergence rate.

We also verify the efficacy of our algorithm under different deployment densities by varying the number of the rechargeable sensor nodes from 20 to 100 in a 1×1 km^2. Since the DB method is constrained by it high complexity, we hereby adopt ACO method to calculated the nearly optimal cycle for the mobile charger in each epoch. It is implied by the results shown in Fig. 2, the convergence of our BanditCharger algorithm still can be ensured even with the compromise in the optimality of the "shortest" cycle calculation. Since the increasing number of the rechargeable sensor nodes implies higher searching space for calculating the nearly optimal cycles in each epoch, increasing the number of the sensor nodes

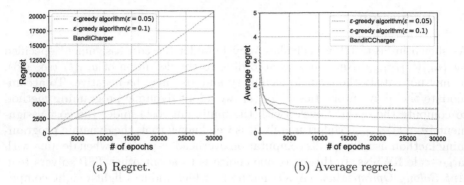

(a) Regret.   (b) Average regret.

Fig. 1. A Comparison between BanditCharger and ε-greedy algorithm.

results in higher regret values, which is also consistent with what we have shown in Theorem 1.

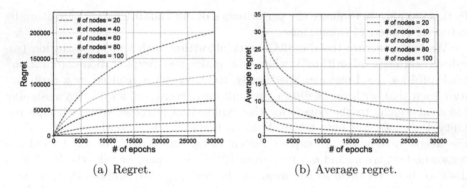

(a) Regret.   (b) Average regret.

Fig. 2. The performance of BanditCharger with different numbers of rechargeable sensor nodes.

7   Relate Work

There have been a vast body of studies on the mobile charging problem in RWSNs. Most of these proposals are on the basis of TSP. For example, in [14], a mobile charger visits each sensor node along a so-called "renewable energy cycle" which is actually defined as the optimal Hamiltonian cycle. By taking into account the energy consumption diversity of the sensor nodes, [4] proposes a scheme to synchronize the energy supply of sensor nodes based on a set of nested TSP tours. [9,16] leverage the framework of *Dynamic Traveling Salesman Problem* (DTSP) to investigate the on-demand mobile charging problem. [3,10,18] design algorithms for periodic mobile charging, by assuming a mobile charger can charge multiple sensor nodes simultaneously. By carefully controlling the moving speed on the charging cycle and the sojourn time at each charging spot, [2] proposes a scheduling algorithm to fully exploit the charging opportunities. By utilizing the redundancy of a densely deployed sensor network, [24] allows a mobile charger partially visit the sensor nodes for power charging, while retaining the coverage of the sensor nodes. Different from the above proposals where a single mobile charger is employed, [17,19,23] considers a RWSN with multiple mobile chargers and investigate the investigate their coordination. Nevertheless, none of these proposals takes into account the uncertainty of mobile charger's travel cost. Inspired by the application of MAB in wide spectrum (e.g. [8]), we present a MAB-based framework, by which the mobile charger can learn such an uncertainty in an on-line manner with bounded regret in travel cost.

8 Conclusion

In this paper, we have leveraged the MAB framework to design a learning-aided scheduling algorithm, namely "BanditCharger", for mobile charging. Specifically, by a carefully designed UCB-based indexing mechanism, the mobile charger periodically visits the sensor nodes along the "shortest" cycle calculated according to the UCB indices. According to our theoretical analysis, the regret (i.e., the performance gap between the sequential cycles outputted by our algorithm and the optimal one) grows polynomially to the number of the sensor nodes and logarithmically to the number of the sequential cycles.

References

1. Auer, P., Cesa-Bianchi, N., Fischer, P.: Finite-time analysis of the multiarmed bandit problem. Mach. Learn. **47**(2–3), 235–256 (2002). https://doi.org/10.1023/A:1013689704352
2. Chen, F., et al.: Speed control of mobile chargers serving wireless rechargeable networks. Future Gener. Comput. Syst. **80**, 242–249 (2018)
3. Chen, F., Zhao, Z., Min, G., Wu, Y.: A novel approach for path plan of mobile chargers in wireless rechargeable sensor networks. In: Proceeding of the 12th MSN, pp. 63–68 (2016)
4. He, L., et al.: Esync: an energy synchronized charging protocol for rechargeable wireless sensor networks. In: Proceedings of the 15th ACM MobiHoc, pp. 247–256 (2014)
5. Kurs, A., Karalis, A., Moffatt, R., Joannopoulos, J., Fisher, P., Soljačić, M.: Wireless power transfer via strongly coupled magnetic resonances. Science **317**(5834), 83–86 (2007)
6. Kurs, A., Moffatt, R., Soljačić, M.: Simultaneous mid-range power transfer to multiple devices. Appl. Phys Lett. **96**(4), 044102 (2010)
7. Li, F., Yang, Y., Chi, Z., Zhao, L., Yang, Y., Luo, J.: Trinity: enabling self-sustaining WSNS indoors with energy free sensing and networking. ACM Trans Embedded Comput. Syst. **17**(2), 57:1–57:27 (2018)
8. Li, F., Yu, D., Yang, H., Yu, J., Karl, H., Cheng, X.: Multi-armed-bandit-based spectrum scheduling algorithms in wireless networks: a survey. IEEE Wireless Commun. **27**(1), 24–30 (2020)

9. Lin, C., Han, D., Deng, J., Wu, G.: P^{2}S: a primary and passer-by scheduling algorithm for on-demand charging architecture in wireless rechargeable sensor networks. IEEE Trans. Veh. Technol. **66**(9), 8047–8058 (2017)
10. Ma, Y., Liang, W., Xu, W.: Charging utility maximization in wireless rechargeable sensor networks by charging multiple sensors simultaneously. IEEE/ACM Trans Network. **26**(4), 1591–1604 (2018)
11. Martin, P., Charbiwala, Z., Srivastava, M.: DoubleDip: leveraging thermoelectric harvesting for low power monitoring of sporadic water use. In: Proceedings of the 10th ACM SenSys, pp. 225–238 (2012)
12. Shi, T., Cheng, S., Li, J., Gao, H., Cai, Z.: Dominating sets construction in RF-based battery-free sensor networks with full coverage guarantee. ACM Trans Sensor Netw **15**(4), 43:1–43:29 (2019)
13. Shi, T., Li, J., Gao, H., Cai, Z.: Coverage in Battery-Free Wireless Sensor Networks. In: Proceedings of IEEE INFOCOM, pp. 108–116 (2018)
14. Shi, Y., Xie, L., Hou, Y., Sherali, H.: On renewable sensor networks with wireless energy transfer. In: Proceedings of IEEE INFOCOM, pp. 1350–1358 (2011)
15. Talla, V., Kellogg, B., Ransford, B., Naderiparizi, S., Gollakota, S.: Powering the Next Billion Devices with WiFi. In: Proceedings of the 11th ACM CoNEXT, pp. 1–13 (2015)
16. Tomar, A., Muduli, L., Jana, P.K.: An efficient scheduling scheme for on-demand mobile charging in wireless rechargeable sensor networks. Pervasive Mob. Comput. **59**, 101074 (2019)
17. Wang, C., Li, J., Ye, F., Yang, Y.: NETWRAP: an NDN based real-time wireless recharging framework for wireless sensor networks. IEEE Trans. Mobile Comput. **13**(6), 1283–1297 (2014)
18. Wang, N., Wu, J., Dai, H.: Bundle charging: wireless charging energy minimization in dense wireless sensor networks. In: Proceedings of the 39th IEEE ICDCS, pp. 810–820 (2019)
19. Wei, Z., Li, M., Zhao, Q., Lyu, Z., Zhu, S., Wei, Z.: Multi-MC charging schedule algorithm with time windows in wireless rechargeable sensor networks. IEEE Access **7**, 156217–156227 (2019)
20. Xie, L., Shi, Y., Hou, Y., Lou, W., Sherali, H., Midkiff, S.: On renewable sensor networks with wireless energy transfer: the multi-node case. In: Proceedings of the 9th IEEE SECON, pp. 10–18 (2012)
21. Xie, L., Shi, Y., Hou, Y.T., Lou, W., Sherali, H.D.: On traveling path and related problems for a mobile station in a rechargeable sensor network. In: Proceedings of the 13th ACM MobiHoc, pp. 109–118 (2013)
22. Xie, L., Shi, Y., Hou, Y.T., Lou, W., Sherali, H.D., Midkiff, S.F.: Bundling mobile base station and wireless energy transfer: modeling and optimization. In: Proceedings of IEEE INFOCOM, pp. 1636–1644 (2013)
23. Xu, W., Liang, W., Lin, X., Mao, G., Ren, X.: Towards perpetual sensor networks via deploying multiple mobile wireless chargers. In: Proceedings of the 43rd ICPP, pp. 80–89 (2014)
24. Zhou, P., Wang, C., Yang, Y.: Static and mobile target k-coverage in wireless rechargeable sensor networks. IEEE Trans. Mobile Comput. **18**(10), 2430–2445 (2019)

A Social Relationship Enabled Cooperative Jamming Scheme for Wireless Communications

Jingjing Fan, Yan Huo$^{(\boxtimes)}$, Qinghe Gao, and Tao Jing

School of Electronics and Information Engineering, Beijing Jiaotong University, Beijing, China
yhuo@bjtu.edu.cn

Abstract. With the massive growth of mobile devices and data traffic, it is important to ensure wireless security. Physical layer security utilizing properties of wireless transmission is regarded as a common and promising technology. As a typical physical layer security technology, cooperative jamming is usually affected by social relationships between devices. Devices with excellent social relationships are willing to provide friendly cooperative jamming. Some researchers start to study cooperative jamming using social relationship. In the paper, we propose a social relationship enabled cooperative jamming scheme to achieve secure communications by combining both physical and social information. In particular, we utilize a novel approach to quantify the social relationship metric according to physical locations and effective contact duration between devices. Then, density of legitimate devices as cooperative jammers can be obtained through social relationships. In our scheme, we theoretically analyze the connection outage probability and the secrecy outage probability. Finally, comprehensive numerical results are presented to validate both connection and secrecy performance of cooperative jamming with social relationship.

Keywords: Physical layer security · Cooperative jamming · Social relationship · Connection outage probability · Secrecy outage probability

1 Introduction

The development of future mobile communications will make explosive growth of mobile devices and data traffic [1]. Due to the openness nature of broadcast communications and ubiquitous malicious users, it is a critical issue to achieve data transmission security between devices. Eavesdropping and interception attacks on data availability, confidentiality and integrity by these malicious users may reveal legitimate data [2,3]. Although cryptography based approaches are introduced directly to cope with these threats, there are still some new issues. The most critical issue is the security and adaptability of encryption algorithms based

© Springer Nature Switzerland AG 2020
D. Yu et al. (Eds.): WASA 2020, LNCS 12384, pp. 97–108, 2020.
https://doi.org/10.1007/978-3-030-59016-1_9

on computational complexity and secret key management for a heterogeneous wireless network [4,5]. Consequently, as an effective complement of traditional encryption, physical layer security (PLS) utilizing the randomness of wireless channels is considered to be very promising [6,7].

A common PLS technology to achieve secure communications of wireless devices is cooperative jamming [8]. Different from traditional cryptography-based security methods [9,10], existing cooperative jamming solutions mainly focus on design of precoding schemes [11,12], power constraint based optimization [13,14], resource allocation and scheduling [15,16], interference control [17,18], and jammer selection [19,20], so as to broadcast artificial noise to degrade signal reception of an eavesdropper.

In these works, the authors exploit features of physical layer in wireless links, including channel state information (CSI), signal power and phase, and antenna transmission parameters to achieve physical layer security. However, they ignore a basic problem, i.e., why a jammer is willing to selflessly transmit artificial noise to achieve secure data transmission for legitimate users. In general, it is possible to provide friendly cooperative jamming between nodes with excellent social relationship. Social relationships play an important role to enhance the performance of cooperative jamming and have drawn wide attention in recent years [21–24]. As a result, design of cooperative jamming schemes needs to consider the integrated social relationship attributes between nodes.

Some researchers utilize social relationship among devices when designing cooperative communication schemes. In [25], Zhang et al. evaluated the reliability of link establishment through the physical domain and the social domain and then proposed a social-based relay selection scheme. [26] designed a social-aware distributed algorithm based on resource allocation and achieved the Nash equilibrium to maximize the utility of the social group. A noticeable challenge in the above researches is that there is no specific description of social relationship measurement. In [27], the authors formulated a social relationship model with similar interests, qualified encounter duration, and adjacent locations, and then proposed an information caching strategy utilizing features of two layers. In addition, the authors of [18] exploited Bayesian nonparametric learning to obtain the social relationship, and designed an iterative matching algorithm with respect to power control and pairing scheduling. To the best of our knowledge, there is no research to explore the security performance of a cooperative jamming scheme from the aspect of social relationships.

In the paper, we propose a social relationship enabled cooperative jamming scheme. In the scheme, the spatial distribution of legitimate devices is modeled as homogeneous Poisson point process (PPP). Using social relationships, we can obtain the density of the reserved legitimate devices by refining the parent homogeneous PPP. To be specific, we define the social relationship metric with physical locations and qualified contact duration between devices. According to the social relationship analysis, we theoretically study the connection outage probability (COP) and the secrecy outage probability (SOP) for the considered network scenario. Finally, simulations are demonstrated subsequently to evaluate the connection and secrecy performance of the proposed scheme.

The rest of the paper is organized as follows. In Sect. 2, we present the system model, signal transmission model and social relationship model. Next, we formulate and analyze the connection outage probability and the secrecy outage probability of a cooperative jamming system considering social relationship in Sect. 3. Finally, numerical simulations and a conclusion are drawn in Sect. 4 and Sect. 5, respectively.

2 System Model

2.1 Network Model

In the paper, we consider a typical wireless communication system as depicted in Fig. 1. In the physical layer of the system, there exist a transmitter (Tr), a receiver (Re), an eavesdropper (Eve), and several legitimate devices. Each entity in the system is equipped with a single omnidirectional antenna. When the transmitter sends a private message to its receiver through a quasi-static Rayleigh fading link, the eavesdropper attempts to intercept the message due to the broadcast nature of the wireless medium. In this case, the transmitter intends that the legitimate devices can transmit artificial noise to degrade the receiving performance of the eavesdropper while do not interfere with the reception of the receiver.

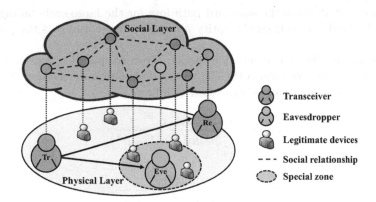

Fig. 1. A typical wireless communication system with social relationship.

The system exists several legitimate devices that can be considered as candidate jammers in the physical layer. We assume that the spatial distribution of these legitimate devices follows a homogeneous Poisson point process Φ with intensity λ. An intuitive issue is to analyze the security performance achieved by these jammers through the wireless link. Note that there is a social relationship between entities. For example, with the better channel state and frequent connection with transceivers, a series of devices are more effective as jammers. This idea inspires us to combine a social layer with a physical layer to design a cooperative jamming scheme. Next, we will present the transmission model on the physical layer and the corresponding social relationship model between entities.

2.2   Signal Transmission Model

Within the physical layer, a transmitter with one omnidirectional antenna sends signals s_t to its receiver, while an eavesdropper wiretaps the signals at the same time. The corresponding received signals of the receiver and the eavesdropper, y_{tr} and y_{te}, are written as follows.

$$y_{tr} = h_{tr} r_{tr}^{-\frac{\alpha}{2}} s_t + \sum_{k \in \Phi} h_{kr} r_{kr}^{-\frac{\alpha}{2}} s_k + n_r, \tag{1}$$

$$y_{te} = h_{te} r_{te}^{-\frac{\alpha}{2}} s_t + \sum_{k \in \Phi} h_{ke} r_{ke}^{-\frac{\alpha}{2}} s_k + n_e, \tag{2}$$

where s_k is a signal transmitted by the kth legitimate devices. n_r and n_e are the additive white Gaussian noise (AWGN) over each transmission link at the destination device and the corresponding eavesdropper. The AWGN are known to have complex normal distributions $\mathcal{CN}(0, \sigma^2)$. Here, we adopt a quasi-static channel model that comprises the small-scale Rayleigh fading and large-scale fading. In particular, $h_{uv}, u, v \in \{t, r, e, k\}$ represents the small-scale Rayleigh fading and $r_{uv}^{-\frac{\alpha}{2}}$ denotes the standard path loss for the large-scale fading. Note that r_{uv} is the distance from the entity u to the entity v and α is the path loss factor.

Based on the signal transmission model, the corresponding received signal-to-interference-plus-noise-ratio (SINR) at the destination device and the corresponding eavesdropper can be expressed as follows.

$$\gamma_{tr} = \frac{p_t |h_{tr}|^2 r_{tr}^{-\alpha}}{\sum_{k \in \Phi} p_k |h_{kr}|^2 r_{kr}^{-\alpha} + \sigma^2}, \tag{3}$$

$$\gamma_{te} = \frac{p_t |h_{te}|^2 r_{te}^{-\alpha}}{\sum_{k \in \Phi} p_k |h_{ke}|^2 r_{ke}^{-\alpha} + \sigma^2}, \tag{4}$$

where $p_t = |s_t|^2$ and $p_k = |s_k|^2$ refer to the transmission power of the transmitter and legitimate devices. The small-scale Rayleigh fading follows an exponential distribution with unit mean, i.e., $|h_{uv}|^2 \sim \exp(1)$.

2.3   Social Relationship Model

We consider that the social relationship metric includes two parts. The first part, Pr_c, is the probability of qualified contact duration. It means that the total contact duration needs to be higher than the threshold $T_{\min}$. When we assume that the number of contacts between devices follows a Poisson process with rate μ, i.e.,

$$P(N = k) = \frac{e^{-\mu}\mu^k}{k!}, \tag{5}$$

And the nth contact duration, denoted as T_n, follows the negative exponential distribution with parameter $\frac{1}{\kappa}$. Thus, the total contact duration $T = \sum_{n=1}^{N} T_n$ follows the Erlang distribution and its probability density function (PDF) can be expressed as follows.

$$f_T(x, N, \kappa) = \frac{x^{N-1}e^{-\kappa x}\kappa^N}{\Gamma(N)}, \tag{6}$$

where $\Gamma(\cdot)$ is the gamma function. As a result, Pr_c is calculated as

$$Pr_c = P(T > T_{\min}) = \sum_{n=1}^{\infty} \frac{e^{-\mu}\mu^n}{n!} \int_{T_{\min}}^{\infty} \frac{x^{n-1}e^{-\kappa x}\kappa^n}{\Gamma(n)} dx. \tag{7}$$

The other metric, Pr_d, represents the probability that the distance between devices meet certain requirements. We believe that legitimate devices can provide enough secure requirements based on cooperative jamming if the distance between an eavesdropper and legitimate devices is smaller than a predefined distance threshold R_1. Otherwise, the cooperative jamming capability of legitimate devices decreases along with the increase of the distance between an eavesdropper and legitimate devices [28]. In detail, Pr_d related to physical locations of legitimate devices can be expressed as follows.

$$Pr_d(r) = \begin{cases} 1, & \text{when } 0 < r \leq R_1 \\ \frac{R_1^2}{r^2}, & \text{when } r > R_1 \end{cases} \tag{8}$$

Here, Pr_d is set to be the maximum factor, 1, when a legitimate user is in the special zone as shown in Fig. 1. Otherwise, Pr_d is defined as a factor less than 1 when a legitimate device is far from an eavesdropper. Using the above two metrics, we present our social relationship metric, $Pr_s = Pr_c Pr_d$. Next, we intend to explore the impact of social relationships on physical layer security.

3 Analysis of Cooperative Jamming with Social Relationship

In this section, we analyze the connection outage probability (COP) and the secrecy outage probability (SOP) for the above wireless communication system. In order to achieve secure transmission in our network, we assume that the transmitter encodes its secret messages using the Wyner's encoding scheme. Thus, the transmitter needs to satisfy a successful connection without secrecy outage.

3.1   Connection Outage Probability

In order to analyze the connection performance of a wireless link, we analyze the COP considering the proposed social relationship model. In general, a connection outage occurs when a receiver cannot decode signals transmitted from a transmitter. It means that the transmit rate of the transmitter is below the target transmission rate R_t. Here, we define that the COP is $p_{co} = \Pr(\log(1 + \gamma_{tr}) < R_t) = 1 - \Pr(\gamma_{tr} > T)$, where $T \triangleq 2^{R_t} - 1$ is the given target SINR's threshold. Thus, the connection cumulative probability can be calculated as follows.

$$\Pr(\gamma_{tr} > T) = P\left(|h_{tr}|^2 > \frac{r_{tr}^\alpha T}{p_t} \left(\sum_{k \in \Phi} p_k |h_{kr}|^2 r_{kr}^{-\alpha} + \sigma^2 \right) \right)$$
$$= \exp\left(-\frac{r_{tr}^\alpha T \sigma^2}{p_t} \right) \mathcal{L}^B\left(\frac{r_{tr}^\alpha T}{p_t} \right),$$

$$(9)$$

where $\mathcal{L}^B(s) = E_\Phi\left[e^{-s \sum_{k \in \Phi} p_k |h_{kr}|^2 r_{kr}^{-\alpha}} \right]$ denotes the Laplacian transform of random variable s. It can be computed as follows.

$$\mathcal{L}^B(s) \overset{(a)}{=} \exp\left\{ -\lambda \int_{R^2} Pr_s \left(1 - E_h \left[e^{-s p_k |h_{kr}|^2 r_{kr}^{-\alpha}} \right] \right) dr_{kr} d\theta \right\}$$
$$\overset{(b)}{=} \exp\left\{ -\lambda Pr_c \int_{R^2} Pr_d(r_{ke}) \frac{s p_k r_{kr}}{s p_k + r_{kr}^\alpha} dr_{kr} d\theta \right\}$$
$$= \exp\left\{ -\lambda Pr_c \left(\int_{\mathcal{D}_1} \frac{s p_k r_{kr} dr_{kr} d\theta}{s p_k + r_{kr}^\alpha} + \int_{\mathcal{D}_2} \frac{s p_k R_1^2 r_{kr} dr_{kr} d\theta}{(s p_k + r_{kr}^\alpha) r_{ke}^2} \right) \right\}$$
$$= \mathcal{L}_d^1(s) \mathcal{L}_d^2(s),$$

$$(10)$$

where (a) is obtained from the independence in the homogeneous Poisson point process [29] and (b) follows from channel characteristics. $\mathcal{D}_1$ and $\mathcal{D}_2$ correspond to the regions for two cases of (8) respectively. $\mathcal{D}_1$ is the circular region centered on the eavesdropper with radius R_1 and $\mathcal{D}_2$ is the portion of the whole region minus the region $\mathcal{D}_1$. Note that we have two Laplacian transform equations in (10), i.e., $\mathcal{L}_d^1(s) = \exp\left\{ -\lambda Pr_c \int_{\mathcal{D}_1} \frac{s p_k r_{kr}}{s p_k + r_{kr}^\alpha} dr_{kr} d\theta \right\}$ and $\mathcal{L}_d^2(s) = \exp\left\{ -\lambda Pr_c \int_{\mathcal{D}_2} \frac{s p_k R_1^2 r_{kr}}{(s p_k + r_{kr}^\alpha) r_{ke}^2} dr_{kr} d\theta \right\}$. By using the flabellate annulus approximation method [30] to complete our calculations, we can obtain following two equations.

$$\mathcal{L}_d^1(s) = \exp\left\{ -\theta_m \lambda Pr_c (\eta(r_{re} + R_1) - \eta(r_{re} - R_1)) \right\}.$$

$$(11)$$

where $\theta_m = \arcsin \frac{R_1}{r_{re}}$, $\eta(r) = r^2 \cdot {}_2F_1(1, \frac{2}{\alpha}; 1 + \frac{2}{\alpha}; -\frac{r^\alpha}{s p_k})$, and ${}_2F_1(a; b; c; z)$ is the hypergeometric series function.

$$\mathcal{L}_d^2(s) = \exp\left\{-\lambda Pr_c \int_{\mathcal{D}_2} \frac{sp_k R_1^2 r_{kr} \mathrm{d}r_{kr}\mathrm{d}\theta}{(sp_k + r_{kr}^\alpha)(r_{kr}^2 + r_{re}^2 - 2r_{re}r_{kr}\cos\theta)}\right\}$$

$$= \exp\left\{-\lambda Pr_c \int_{\mathcal{D}_a + \mathcal{D}_b + \mathcal{D}_c} \frac{sp_k R_1^2 r_{kr}\mathrm{d}r_{kr}\mathrm{d}\theta}{(sp_k + r_{kr}^\alpha)(r_{kr}^2 + r_{re}^2 - 2r_{re}r_{kr}\cos\theta)}\right\} \quad (12)$$

$$= \mathcal{L}_d^a(s)\mathcal{L}_d^b(s)\mathcal{L}_d^c(s),$$

where $\mathcal{L}_d^m(s) = \exp\left\{-\lambda Pr_c \int_{\mathcal{D}_m} \frac{sp_k R_1^2 r_{kr}}{(sp_k + r_{kr}^\alpha)(r_{kr}^2 + r_{re}^2 - 2r_{re}r_{kr}\cos\theta)}\mathrm{d}r_{kr}\mathrm{d}\theta\right\}$, $m \in \{a, b, c\}$. Here, $\mathcal{D}_a$ is the inner circular region centered on the receiver with radius $r_{re} - R_1$ adjacent to the region $\mathcal{D}_1$, $\mathcal{D}_b$ is the outer annulus region of the region $\mathcal{D}_1$, and $\mathcal{D}_c$ is the portion of the other annulus region centered on the receiver with radius $2R_1$ minus the region $\mathcal{D}_1$. In particular, considering the path loss factor α is generally set to be 4 in existing studies, $\mathcal{L}_d^m(s)$, $m \in \{a, b, c\}$ can be simplified as below.

$$\mathcal{L}_d^a(s) = \exp\left\{-\int_0^\pi \int_0^{r_{re}-R_1} \frac{2\lambda Pr_c sp_k R_1^2 r_{kr}\mathrm{d}r_{kr}\mathrm{d}\theta}{(sp_k + r_{kr}^4)(r_{kr}^2 + r_{re}^2 - 2r_{re}r_{kr}\cos\theta)}\right\}$$

$$= \exp\left\{-Q(g(r_{re} - R_1) + h(r_{re} - R_1) + \ln\frac{r_{re}^4}{sp_k})\right\}, \quad (13)$$

$$\mathcal{L}_d^b(s) = \exp\left\{-\int_0^\pi \int_{r_{re}+R_1}^\infty \frac{2\lambda Pr_c sp_k R_1^2 r_{kr}\mathrm{d}r_{kr}\mathrm{d}\theta}{(sp_k + r_{kr}^4)(r_{kr}^2 + r_{re}^2 - 2r_{re}r_{kr}\cos\theta)}\right\}$$

$$= \exp\left\{-Q(g(r_{re} + R_1) + h(r_{re} + R_1) - \frac{\pi r_{re}^2}{\sqrt{sp_k}})\right\}, \quad (14)$$

and

$$\mathcal{L}_d^c(s) = \exp\left\{-2\lambda sp_k R_1^2 Pr_c \int_{\theta_m}^\pi \int_{r_{re}-R_1}^{r_{re}+R_1} \frac{r_{kr}\mathrm{d}r_{kr}\mathrm{d}\theta}{(sp_k + r_{kr}^4)(r_{kr}^2 + r_{re}^2 - 2r_{re}r_{kr}\cos\theta)}\right\}$$

$$\overset{(a)}{=} \exp\left\{-4\lambda sp_k R_1^2 Pr_c \int_{r_{re}-R_1}^{r_{re}+R_1} \frac{r_{kr}\arctan\frac{|r_{kr}-r_{re}|}{(r_{kr}+r_{re})\tan\frac{\theta_m}{2}}\mathrm{d}r_{kr}}{(sp_k + r_{kr}^4)|r_{kr}^2 - r_{re}^2|}\right\}$$

$$\overset{(b)}{\approx} \exp\left\{-\frac{4\lambda sp_k R_1^2 Pr_c}{\tan\frac{\theta_m}{2}} \int_{r_{re}-R_1}^{r_{re}+R_1} \frac{r_{kr}\mathrm{d}r_{kr}}{(sp_k + r_{kr}^4)(r_{kr} + r_{re})^2}\right\}$$

$$= \exp\left\{-W(\frac{-2R_1 r_{re}}{(sp_k + r_{re}^4)(4r_{re}^2 - R_1^2)} + \frac{A + B + 2\sqrt{sp_k}r_{re}(C + D)}{4sp_k(sp_k + r_{re}^4)^2})\right\}. \quad (15)$$

where $g(t) = \frac{2r_{re}^2}{\sqrt{sp_k}}\arctan\frac{t^2}{\sqrt{sp_k}}$, $h(t) = \ln\frac{sp_k + t^4}{R_1^2(r_{re}+t)^2}$, and $Q = \frac{\pi\lambda sp_k R_1^2 Pr_c}{2(sp_k + r_{kr}^4)}$. (a) follows from applying to simplify the double integral formula to the single definite integral [31], and (b) is obtained from substituting the infinite small replacement formula to approximate the arctangent function. In addition, a series of coefficients in (15) is as follows.

$$W = \frac{4\lambda sp_k R_1^2 Pr_c}{\tan\frac{\theta_m}{2}},$$

$$A = sp_k(sp_k - 3r_{re}^4)\ln\frac{(sp_k + (r_{re} - R_1)^4)(2r_{re} + R_1)^4}{(sp_k + (r_{re} + R_1)^4)(2r_{re} - R_1)^4},$$

$$B = \sqrt{2}r_{re}(sp_k)^{\frac{3}{4}}(r_{re}^4 + 2\sqrt{sp_k}r_{re}^2 - sp_k)$$

$$\cdot \ln\frac{sp_k + 2\sqrt{2}(sp_k)^{\frac{3}{4}}R_1 + 4\sqrt{sp_k}R_1^2 - 2\sqrt{2}(sp_k)^{\frac{1}{4}}R_1(r_{re}^2 - R_1^2) + (r_{re}^2 - R_1^2)^2}{sp_k - 2\sqrt{2}(sp_k)^{\frac{3}{4}}R_1 + 4\sqrt{sp_k}R_1^2 + 2\sqrt{2}(sp_k)^{\frac{1}{4}}R_1(r_{re}^2 - R_1^2) + (r_{re}^2 - R_1^2)^2},$$

$$C = (\sqrt{2}(sp_k)^{\frac{5}{4}} + 3sp_k r_{re} + 2\sqrt{2}(sp_k)^{\frac{3}{4}}r_{re}^2 - \sqrt{2}(sp_k)^{\frac{1}{4}}r_{re}^4 - r_{re}^5)$$

$$\cdot (\arctan(1 + \frac{\sqrt{2}(r_{re} + R_1)}{(sp_k)^{\frac{1}{4}}}) - \arctan(1 + \frac{\sqrt{2}(r_{re} - R_1)}{(sp_k)^{\frac{1}{4}}})),$$

$$D = (\sqrt{2}(sp_k)^{\frac{5}{4}} - 3sp_k r_{re} + 2\sqrt{2}(sp_k)^{\frac{3}{4}}r_{re}^2 - \sqrt{2}(sp_k)^{\frac{1}{4}}r_{re}^4 + r_{re}^5)$$

$$\cdot (\arctan(1 - \frac{\sqrt{2}(r_{re} - R_1)}{(sp_k)^{\frac{1}{4}}}) - \arctan(1 - \frac{\sqrt{2}(r_{re} + R_1)}{(sp_k)^{\frac{1}{4}}})).$$

3.2   Secrecy Outage Probability

The SOP is defined as the probability that the achievable secrecy rate $\log(1 + \gamma_{tr}) - \log(1 + \gamma_{te})$ is lower than the target secrecy rate R_s. Note that we will discuss secure transmission when satisfying the connection requirement. This can be expressed as $\log(1 + \gamma_{te}) > R_t - R_s$. Concretely, the SOP is defined as $p_{so} = \Pr(\log(1 + \gamma_{te}) > R_t - R_s) = \Pr(\gamma_{te} > M)$. We set the SINR's threshold as $M = 2^{R_t - R_s} - 1$ and the SOP can be expressed as follows.

$$\Pr(\gamma_{te} > M) = \exp\left(-\frac{r_{te}^\alpha M}{p_t}\left(\sum_{k\in\Phi} p_k |h_{ke}|^2 r_{ke}^{-\alpha} + \sigma^2\right)\right)$$

$$= \exp\left(-\frac{r_{te}^\alpha M\sigma^2}{p_t}\right)\mathcal{L}^E\left(\frac{r_{te}^\alpha M}{p_t}\right), \tag{16}$$

where $\mathcal{L}^E(s) = E_\Phi\left[e^{-s\sum_{k\in\Phi} p_k |h_{ke}|^2 r_{ke}^{-\alpha}}\right]$ denotes the Laplacian transform of random variable s, which can be calculated as follows.

$$\mathcal{L}^E(s) = \exp\left\{-\lambda Pr_c\left(\int_{\mathcal{D}_1}\frac{sp_k r_{ke}}{sp_k + r_{ke}^\alpha}dr_{ke}d\theta + \int_{\mathcal{D}_2}\frac{sp_k R_1^2}{(sp_k + r_{ke}^\alpha)r_{ke}}dr_{ke}d\theta\right)\right\}$$

$$\overset{(a)}{=} \exp\left\{-2\pi\lambda Pr_c\left(\int_0^{R_1}\frac{sp_k r_{ke}}{sp_k + r_{ke}^\alpha}dr_{ke} + \int_{R_1}^\infty\frac{sp_k R_1^2}{(sp_k + r_{ke}^\alpha)r_{ke}}dr_{ke}\right)\right\}$$

$$= \exp\left\{-\pi\lambda Pr_c\left(\eta(R_1) + \frac{2R_1^2}{\alpha}\ln\left(1 + \frac{sp_k}{R_1^\alpha}\right)\right)\right\}, \tag{17}$$

where (a) is obtained according to the double integral in polar coordinates. As a result, the SOP can be derived as follows.

$$p_{so} = \exp\left\{-\frac{r_{te}^\alpha M\sigma^2}{p_t} - \pi\lambda Pr_c\left(\eta(R_1) + \frac{2R_1^2}{\alpha}\ln\left(1 + \frac{r_{te}^\alpha Mp_k}{R_1^\alpha p_t}\right)\right)\right\}. \quad (18)$$

4 Numerical Simulation

In this section, we present numerical results to analyze the connection outage probability and the secrecy outage probability in a typical wireless communication system with social relationship. Here, we assume that the target transmission rate R_t is 4 bps/Hz and the target secrecy rate R_s is 2 bps/Hz. The path loss factor α is set to be 4 and the power of AWGN σ^2 is set to be 10^{-10} W. In addition, we define ν as the ratio of the distance R_1 to r_{re}.

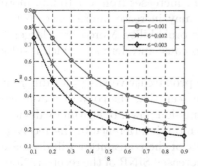 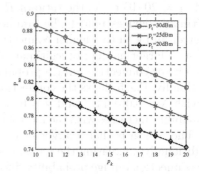

Fig. 2. P_{so} v.s. ν.   **Fig. 3.** P_{so} v.s. p_k.

First, we assume that transmission power of a transmitter and legitimate devices is set to be $p_t = 30$ dBm and $p_k = 20$ dBm. Figure 2 illustrates the impact of ν on the secrecy outage probability for different intensity of legitimate devices λ. We can observe that a larger ν is equivalent to a larger R_1. This results in a larger regional scope where legitimate devices tend to be jammers. In this case, interference to the eavesdropper is enhanced and the secrecy outage probability is reduced. In addition, we also observe that the secrecy outage probability decreases with the increase of λ. This is because that the eavesdropper interfered by more legitimate devices in the network.

Next, Fig. 3 analyzes the impact of p_k on the secrecy outage probability for different transmission power of a transmitter, p_t, with $\lambda = 0.001$ m^{-2} and $\nu = 0.4$. Note that, the growth of p_k will increase interference to the eavesdropper. This should decrease the secrecy outage probability. Besides, when the transmission power p_t increases from 20 dBm to 30 dBm, the SINR of the eavesdropper increases. This also lead to a larger secrecy outage probability as well.

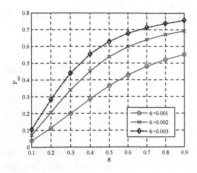
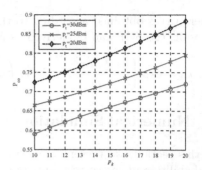

Fig. 4. P_{co} *v.s.* ν.   **Fig. 5.** P_{co} *v.s.* p_k.

In Fig. 4, we demonstrate the relationship between ν and the connection outage probability for different intensity of legitimate devices λ with $p_t = 30$ dBm and $p_k = 20$ dBm. As the ratio of R_1 to r_{re}, ν, increases from 0.1 to 0.9, more legitimate devices tend to be jammers. This may increase interference to the receiver and lead to a higher connection outage probability. Moreover, a larger λ means a larger number of legitimate devices to cause interference, which results in a higher connection outage probability.

Finally, Fig. 5 shows the connection outage probability versus p_k for different p_t with $\lambda = 0.001$ m^{-2} and $\nu = 0.4$. It can be seen that the connection outage probability increases with the increasing transmission power of legitimate devices p_k. The reason is that a larger p_k can lead to more interference to the receiver. Additionally, increasing the transmission power of the transmitter will decrease the connection outage probability due to the increased SINR of the receiver. Note that a legitimate device acted as a jammer can cause interference to the receiver. This means that the data transmission rate and the security issue cannot be guaranteed at the same time. In the future, we will study how to set the relevant configuration parameters so as to achieve the balance between the connection outage probability and the secrecy outage probability.

5   Conclusion and Future Work

In this paper, we exploit social relationship to study secure performance of wireless communications from the aspect of the physical layer, and propose a cross layer cooperative jamming scheme. In the scheme, we first analyze and quantify the social relationship metric according to physical locations and effective contact duration between devices. Secondly, we use social relationships to filter legitimate devices to obtain the density of cooperative jammers. Finally, we theoretically derive expressions of the connection outage probability and the secrecy outage probability. Numerical simulation results demonstrate both connection and secrecy performance in the theoretical analysis. In the future, we are going to study more practical solutions to equilibrate the connection outage probability and the secrecy outage probability.

Acknowledgments. This work was supported by the National Natural Science Foundation of China (Grant No. 61871023 and 61931001)and Beijing Natural Science Foundation (Grant No. 4202054).

References

1. Cai, Z., He, Z.: Trading private range counting over big IoT data. In: 2019 IEEE 39th International Conference on Distributed Computing Systems (ICDCS), pp. 144–153 (2019)
2. Zheng, X., Cai, Z.: Privacy-preserved data sharing towards multiple parties in industrial IoTs. IEEE J. Sel. Areas Commun. **38**(5), 968–979 (2020)
3. Liang, Y., Cai, Z., Yu, J., Han, Q., Li, Y.: Deep learning based inference of private information using embedded sensors in smart devices. IEEE Netw. **32**(4), 8–14 (2018)
4. Zheng, X., Cai, Z., Li, Y.: Data linkage in smart internet of things systems: a consideration from a privacy perspective. IEEE Commun. Mag. **56**(9), 55–61 (2018)
5. Cai, Z., Zheng, X.: A private and efficient mechanism for data uploading in smart cyber-physical systems. IEEE Trans. Netw. Sci. Eng. **7**(2), 766–775 (2020)
6. Huo, Y., Fan, X., Ma, L., Cheng, X., Tian, Z., Chen, D.: Secure communications in tiered 5G wireless networks with cooperative jamming. IEEE Trans. Wirel. Commun. **18**(6), 3265–3280 (2019)
7. Cai, Z., Zheng, X., Yu, J.: A differential-private framework for urban traffic flows estimation via taxi companies. IEEE Trans. Ind. Inf. **15**(12), 6492–6499 (2019)
8. Huo, Y., Tian, Y., Ma, L., Cheng, X., Jing, T.: Jamming strategies for physical layer security. IEEE Wirel. Commun. **25**(1), 148–153 (2018)
9. Wang, J., Cai, Z., Yu, J.: Achieving personalized k-anonymity-based content privacy for autonomous vehicles in CPS. IEEE Trans. Ind. Inf. **16**(6), 4242–4251 (2020)
10. Zheng, X., Cai, Z., Li, J., Gao, H.: Location-privacy-aware review publication mechanism for local business service systems. In: IEEE INFOCOM 2017 - IEEE Conference on Computer Communications, pp. 1–9 (2017)
11. Sadeghzadeh, M., Maleki, M., Salehi, M.: Large-scale analysis of regularized block diagonalization precoding for physical layer security of multi-user MIMO wireless networks. IEEE Trans. Veh. Technol. **68**(6), 5820–5834 (2019)
12. Xu, J., Xu, W., Ng, D.W.K., Swindlehurst, A.L.: Secure communication for spatially sparse millimeter-wave massive MIMO channels via hybrid precoding. IEEE Trans. Commun. **68**(2), 887–901 (2020)
13. Gao, Q., Huo, Y., Jing, T., Ma, L., Wen, Y., Xing, X.: An intermittent cooperative jamming strategy for securing energy-constrained networks. IEEE Trans. Commun. **67**(11), 7715–7726 (2019)
14. Choi, Y., Lee, J.H.: A new cooperative jamming technique for a two-hop amplify-and-forward relay network with an eavesdropper. IEEE Trans. Veh. Technol. **67**(12), 12447–12451 (2018)
15. Huo, Y., Xu, M., Fan, X., Jing, T.: A novel secure relay selection strategy for energy-harvesting-enabled internet of things. EURASIP J. Wirel. Commun. Netw. **2018**, 1–18 (2018)
16. Wang, J., Huang, Y., Jin, S., Schober, R., You, X., Zhao, C.: Resource management for device-to-device communication: a physical layer security perspective. IEEE J. Sel. Areas Commun. **36**(4), 946–960 (2018)

17. Huang, L., Fan, X., Huo, Y., Hu, C., Tian, Y., Qian, J.: A novel cooperative jamming scheme for wireless social networks without known CSI. IEEE Access 5, 26476–26486 (2017)
18. Zhou, Z., Gao, C., Xu, C., Zhang, Y., Mumtaz, S., Rodriguez, J.: Social big-data-based content dissemination in internet of vehicles. IEEE Trans. Ind. Inf. 14(2), 768–777 (2018)
19. Wen, Y., Huo, Y., Ma, L., Jing, T., Gao, Q.: A scheme for trustworthy friendly jammer selection in cooperative cognitive radio networks. IEEE Trans. Veh. Technol. 68(4), 3500–3512 (2019)
20. Zhou, H., He, D., Wang, H.: Joint relay and jammer selection for secure cooperative networks with a full-duplex active eavesdropper. IET Commun. 14(6), 1043–1055 (2020)
21. Zhou, Y., Yu, F.R., Chen, J., Kuo, Y.: Cyber-physical-social systems: a state-of-the-art survey, challenges and opportunities. IEEE Commun. Surv. Tutor. 22(1), 389–425 (2020)
22. Zhang, L., Cai, Z., Wang, X.: Fakemask: a novel privacy preserving approach for smartphones. IEEE Trans. Netw. Serv. Manag. 13(2), 335–348 (2016)
23. Cai, Z., He, Z., Guan, X., Li, Y.: Collective data-sanitization for preventing sensitive information inference attacks in social networks. IEEE Trans. Dependable Secure Comput. 15(4), 577–590 (2018)
24. He, Z., Cai, Z., Yu, J.: Latent-data privacy preserving with customized data utility for social network data. IEEE Trans. Veh. Technol. 67(1), 665–673 (2018)
25. Zhang, Z., Zhang, P., Liu, D., Sun, S.: SRSM-based adaptive relay selection for D2D communications. IEEE Internet Things J. 5(4), 2323–2332 (2018)
26. Zhao, Y., Li, Y., Cao, Y., Jiang, T., Ge, N.: Social-aware resource allocation for device-to-device communications underlaying cellular networks. IEEE Trans. Wireless Commun. 14(12), 6621–6634 (2015)
27. Zhang, X., et al.: Information caching strategy for cyber social computing based wireless networks. IEEE Trans. Emerging Top. Comput. 5(3), 391–402 (2017)
28. Ma, C., et al.: Socially aware caching strategy in device-to-device communication networks. IEEE Trans. Veh. Technol. 67(5), 4615–4629 (2018)
29. Mustafa, H.A., Shakir, M.Z., Imran, M.A., Tafazolli, R.: Distance based cooperation region for D2D pair. In: 2015 IEEE 81st Vehicular Technology Conference (VTC Spring), pp. 1–6, May 2015
30. Wang, H., Xu, Y., Huang, K., Han, Z., Tsiftsis, T.A.: Cooperative secure transmission by exploiting social ties in random networks. IEEE Trans. Commun. 66(8), 3610–3622 (2018)
31. Gradshteyn, I.S., Ryzhik, I.M.: Table of integrals, series and products, vol. 20, no. 96, pp. 1157–1160 (2007)

Multi-job Associated Task Scheduling Based on Task Duplication and Insertion for Cloud Computing

Yuqi Fan$^{(\boxtimes)}$, Lunfei Wang, Jie Chen, Zhifeng Jin, Lei Shi, and Juan Xu

School of Computer Science and Information Engineering,
Anhui Province Key Laboratory of Industry Safety and Emergency Technology,
Hefei University of Technology, Hefei 230601, Anhui, China
{yuqi.fan,2019170960,shilei,xujuan}@hfut.edu.cn,
{cxwlf,jie.chen}@mail.hfut.edu.cn

Abstract. The jobs processed in cloud computing systems may consist of multiple associated tasks which need to be executed under ordering constraints. The tasks of each job are run on different nodes, and communication is required to transfer data between nodes. The processing and communication capacities of different components have great heterogeneity. For multiple jobs, simple task scheduling policies cannot fully utilize cloud resources and hence may degrade the performance of job processing. Therefore, careful multi-job task scheduling is critical to achieve efficient job processing. The performance of existing research on associated task scheduling for multiple jobs needs to be improved. In this paper, we tackle the problem of associated task scheduling of multiple jobs with the aim to minimize jobs' makespan. We propose a task Duplication and Insertion based List Scheduling algorithm (DILS) which incorporates dynamic finish time prediction, task replication, and task insertion. The algorithm dynamically schedules the tasks based on the finish time of scheduled tasks, replicates some of the tasks on different nodes, and inserts the tasks into idle time slots to expedite successive task execution. We finally conduct experiments through simulations. Experimental results demonstrate that the proposed algorithm can effectively reduce the jobs' makespan.

Keywords: Task scheduling · Associated tasks · Job priority · Makespan

1 Introduction

Cloud computing is an increasingly essential platform for various applications, since cloud computing can achieve scalability and economy of scale. In order

This work was partly supported by the National Key Research Development Plan of China under Grant 2018YFB2000505 and the Key Research and Development Project in Anhui Province under Grant 201904a06020024.

© Springer Nature Switzerland AG 2020
D. Yu et al. (Eds.): WASA 2020, LNCS 12384, pp. 109–120, 2020.
https://doi.org/10.1007/978-3-030-59016-1_10

to enable on-demand resource provisioning and allocation, cloud platform is built on various hardware, i.e. computing and network components, which show great heterogeneity. Users submit jobs to the cloud platform for execution. Each job processed by the cloud is split into multiple tasks which are assigned to multiple servers to execute in a parallel and distributed manner, and hence communication is required to transfer the data between the servers so that the tasks can get the required input data.

The tasks of a job may need to be executed under ordering constraints, and the associated tasks of a job are represented by a directed acyclic graph (DAG), where each node is a task and each directed arc is the ordering constraint between two consecutive tasks [1,2]. The DAG-based jobs are widely found in some real applications such as DNA detection in genetic engineering, image recognition, climate prediction, geological exploration, etc. [3].

Extensive research has been conducted on associated task scheduling. A heuristic algorithm based on genetic algorithms and task duplication was proposed in [4]. A task duplication based scheduling algorithm was introduced in [5]. A heterogeneous scheduling algorithm with improved task priority (HISP) which calculates task priority based on standard deviation with improved magnitude as computation weight and communication weight was proposed; the algorithm adopts an entry task duplication selection policy and an idle time slots insertion-based optimizing policy [6]. A list-based scheduling algorithm called Predict Earliest Finish Time (PEFT) was proposed to introduce an optimistic cost table (OCT), which was used for task ranking and processor selection [7]. The joint problem of task assignment and scheduling considering multidimensional task diversity was modeled as a reverse auction with task owners being auctioneers; four auction schemes were designed to satisfy different application requirements [8,9]. A solution was proposed to detect and remove both short-term and long-term traffic redundancy through a two-layer redundancy elimination design [10]. A stochastic load balancing scheme was designed to provide probabilistic guarantee against the resource overloading with virtual machine migration, while minimizing the total migration overhead [11]. An algorithm was proposed to schedule tasks by calculating the priority of each task; the algorithm first processes the tasks with higher priority to meet the deadline [12]. A Heterogeneous Earliest-Finish-Time (HEFT) algorithm was proposed to select the task with the highest upward rank value at each step and assign the selected task to the processor, which minimizes earliest finish time of the task with an insertion-based approach [13]. A task scheduling mechanism based on two levels of load balance was proposed to meet the dynamic task requirements of users and improve the utilization of resources [14]. A performance effective task scheduling (PETS) algorithm was proposed to calculate the priority of each task based on task communication cost and average computation cost and select the processor with the minimum earliest finish time for each task [15].

During the execution of each job, there may be some idle time slots on the processors. For multiple jobs, simple task scheduling policies cannot fully utilize the idle resources, such that the performance of job processing may be degraded.

Therefore, careful multi-job task scheduling is critical for achieving high performance of cloud computing systems. The performance of existing research on associated task scheduling for multiple jobs needs to be improved. In this paper, we deal with the multi-priority associated task scheduling problem with the objective of minimizing the jobs' makespan, when the underlying computing and communication components of the cloud computing platform have great diversity.

The main contributions of this paper are as follows. We formulate the problem of prioritized associated task scheduling with the aim to minimize the jobs' makespan. We then propose a task Duplication and Insertion based List Scheduling (DILS) algorithm which incorporates dynamic finish time prediction, task replication, and task insertion. The algorithm dynamically predicts the remaining execution time for each task according to the scheduling of previously scheduled tasks, replicates some of the tasks on different nodes, and inserts the tasks into idle time slots to expedite task execution. We also conduct experiments through simulations. Experimental results demonstrate that the proposed algorithm can effectively reduce the jobs' makespan.

The rest of the paper is organized as follows. The problem is defined in Sect. 2. We present the proposed algorithm in Sect. 3. The performance evaluation of the proposed algorithm is given in Sect. 4. Finally, Sect. 5 concludes the paper.

2   Prioritized Associated Task Scheduling Model

Assume the finite set of jobs with different priorities to be processed is $J = \{J_1, ..., J_k, ...\}$, where J_k is the k-th DAG-based job consisting of multiple associated tasks. Job J_k is represented by a tuple $J_k =< T_k, E_k >$, where T_k is the task set of job J_k and E_k is the directed arc set $\{e_{i,j}^k | t_i^k, t_j^k \in T_k\}$. Each arc $e_{i,j}^k \in E_k$ signifies the ordering constraint of task t_i^k and task t_j^k, where t_i^k and t_j^k are the i-th task and the j-th task of job J_k, respectively. To be specific, arc $e_{i,j}^k$ signifies that task t_j^k cannot be executed until the execution of task t_i^k is completed, i.e. task t_j^k is the successive task of task t_i^k and task t_i^k is the preceding task of task t_j^k. Arc $e_{i,j}^k$ also indicates that task t_j^k requires the data generated by task t_i^k, and the data need to be transmitted to the server executing task t_j. The weight $c(t_i^k, t_j^k)$ of arc $e_{i,j}^k$ is the time for data transmission from the server running task t_i^k to the server executing task t_j^k. When the two tasks are scheduled on the same server, $c(t_i^k, t_j^k) = 0$; that is, the communication within a single server is negligible.

A DAG-based job example is shown in Fig. 1. In the DAG, task set $T_k = \{t_1^k, ..., t_i^k, ..., t_{10}^k\}$ consists of 10 tasks. The directed arc from node t_2^k to node t_8^k indicates task t_2^k is the preceding task of task t_8^k, and the weight of the directed arc specifies that the communication time from task t_2^k to task t_8^k is 3, if the two tasks are assigned on different servers.

The execution time of a task may be different on different servers due to the diversity of servers' computing capacities. Assuming $P = \{p_1, ..., p_s...\}$ is the set of servers which will run the jobs, we use an execution time matrix

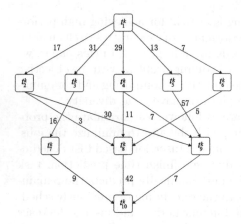

Fig. 1. DAG-based job example.

Table 1. Execution time matrix example

	p_1	p_2	p_3
t_1^k	22	21	36
t_2^k	22	18	18
t_3^k	32	27	43
t_4^k	7	10	4
t_5^k	29	27	35
t_6^k	26	17	24
t_7^k	14	25	30
t_8^k	29	23	36
t_9^k	15	21	8
t_{10}^k	13	16	33

$W_k = T_k \times P$ to list all the possible mapping between task t_i^k and server p_s. Each element $w(t_i^k, p_s)$ in matrix W_k is the execution time of server p_s running task t_i^k. An execution time matrix example for the DAG shown in Fig. 1 is described in Table 1. Assuming the server set $P = \{p_1, p_2, p_3\}$ consists of 3 servers, the element of mapping task t_2^k and server p_2 indicates that the execution time of task t_2^k on server p_2 is 18.

Definition 1. *In DAG-based job J_k, ingress task t_{in}^k is the task without any preceding tasks, and egress task t_{out}^k is the task without any successive tasks.*

For the DAG-based job shown in Fig. 1, the ingress task and egress task are tasks t_1^k and t_{10}^k, respectively. If a job includes more than one ingress task, we add a virtual task node with zero computation cost as the virtual ingress task, and add a directed arc from the virtual ingress task to each of the original ingress task nodes with zero weight.

Definition 2. *$EST(t_i^k, p_s)$, the earliest start time (EST) that task t_i^k can be executed on server p_s, is defined via Eq. (1), where $EAT(p_s)$ is the earliest time that server p_s is available, $pre(t_i^k)$ is the set of the preceding tasks of task t_i^k, and $AFT(t_j^k)$ is the actual finish time of task t_j^k.*

$$EST(t_i^k, p_s) = max\{ EAT(p_s), max_{t_j^k \in pre(t_i^k)}\{AFT(t_j^k) \\ +c(t_j^k, t_i^k)\}\}, \forall t_i^k \in T_k, \forall p_s \in P. \tag{1}$$

Definition 3. *$EFT(t_i^k, p_s)$, the earliest finish time (EFT) that server p_s can complete the execution of task t_i^k, is calculated via Eq. (2).*

$$EFT(t_i^k, p_s) = EST(t_i^k, p_s) + w(t_i^k, p_s), \forall t_i^k \in T, \forall p_s \in P. \tag{2}$$

Definition 4. *For job set J in which the jobs have different priorities, the makespan of job set J, $\Gamma(J)$, is the completion time of all the jobs and can be calculated via Eq. (3).*

$$\Gamma(J) = \max_{J_k \in J} AFT(t_{out}^k). \tag{3}$$

Given job set J, the DAG of each job, server set P, and the execution time of each job on each server, we need to schedule the jobs in J on the servers in P, so as to minimize $\Gamma(J)$, i.e. the makespan of job set J.

3 Multi-job Task Scheduling Algorithm

It is known that the single-job associated task scheduling problem with the aim to minimize the makespan is an NP-hard problem. Obviously, the multi-job associated task scheduling problem is also NP-hard [16].

In this section, we propose a task Duplication and Insertion based List Scheduling (DILS) algorithm which incorporates dynamic finish time prediction, task replication, and task insertion. The algorithm dynamically predicts the remaining execution time for each task according to the scheduling of previously scheduled tasks. The algorithm then schedules the task with the latest remaining time on the server which can minimize the remaining time. After each task is scheduled, the algorithm adopts task duplication and task insertion to advance the start time of this task. The remaining execution time of each to-be-scheduled task is updated upon the scheduling of a task. Algorithm DILS shown in Algorithm 1 consists of five components: task remaining time calculation, selection of the task to be scheduled, server allocation for the task to be scheduled, task duplication, and task insertion.

Algorithm 1. *Algorithm DILS*

Input: Server set P, job set J with each job's DAG, and execution time matrices
Output: Makespan of the jobs
1: **for** each job $J_k \in J$ **do**
2:     Calculate the predicted remaining time of each task via Eq. (6) and create the Prediction of Remaining Time (PRT) table;
3:     Create an empty ready task list and add the ingress task to the list;
4:     **while** ready task list is not empty **do**
5:         **for** each task t_i^k in ready task list **do**
6:             Compute the average path length of task t_i via Eq. (8);
7:         **end for**
8:         Select the task with the maximum average path length with Eq. (9);
9:         Assign the server leading to the minimum estimated path length via Eq. (10) to the task;
10:        Task duplication and task insertion;
11:        Update the ready task list;
12:     **end while**
13: **end for**
14: **return** the completion time of the last scheduled task.

3.1 Task Remaining Time Calculation

Each task is assigned a weight which is the total computation and communication time of all the subsequent tasks. The weights of all the tasks are maintained in a Predicted Remaining Time (PRT) table, and each element $PRT(t_i^k, p_s)$ in table PRT is the predicted remaining time required for executing all the subsequent tasks of task t_i^k ($1 \leq i \leq N$), if it is allocated to server $p_s \in P$. The weight of task t_i^k is closely related to its successive tasks and the number of servers, and we let

$$A_{i,s}^k = max_{t_j^k \in suc(t_i^k)}\{min_{p_t \in P}\{ PRT(t_j^k, p_t) + w(t_j^k, p_t) \\ +c(t_i^k, t_j^k)\}\}, \tag{4}$$

where $suc(t_i^k)$ is the set of successive task of task t_i^k, and let

$$B_i^k = \frac{\sum_{t_j^k \in suc(t_i^k)} \frac{\sum_{p_t \in P} PRT(t_j^k, p_t)}{M}}{M}. \tag{5}$$

Note that the weight of the egress task of each job is 0, no matter which server runs the egress task. That is, for any $p_t \in P$, $PRT(t_{out}^k, p_t) = 0$.

$$PRT(t_i^k, p_s) = max\{A_{i,s}^k, B_i^k\}, \forall t_i^k \in T, \forall p_s \in P. \tag{6}$$

The weight of task t_i^k is calculated via Eq. 6. Starting from the egress task to the ingress task in each DAG, algorithm DILS recursively calculates backwards the weight of each task on each server, and obtains the PRT table.

3.2 Selection of the Task to Be Scheduled

We call task t_i^k is *ready*, when all the preceding tasks of task t_i^k are scheduled. We create a ready task list (RTL) to maintain all the tasks which are ready. Initially, only the ingress task of each DAG-based job is ready, and hence the ready task list contains only one task, t_{in}^k. We calculate the EST of each task which is in the ready task list. The EST of task t_i^k on server p_s, $EST(t_i^k, p_s)$, is calculated via Eq. (1). The estimated path length (EPL) when task t_i^k is assigned to server p_s, $EPL(t_i^k, p_s)$, can be calculated via Eq. (7).

$$EPL(t_i^k, p_s) = EST(t_i^k, p_s) + w(t_i^k, p_s) \\ +PRT(t_i^k, p_s), \forall t_i^k \in T_k, \forall p_s \in P. \tag{7}$$

Each task may be placed on each $p_s \in P$. For task t_i^k which is ready, $APL(t_i^k)$, the average path length (APL) of task t_i^k, is calculated with Eq. (8).

$$APL(t_i^k) = \frac{\sum_{p_s \in P} EPL(t_i^k, p_s)}{M}, \forall t_i^k \in T_k. \tag{8}$$

We select task t_i^k which is ready and has the maximum average path length as the task to be scheduled by considering the difference of the task execution time on different paths; that is,

$$t_i^k = argmax_{t_j^k \in RTL}\{APL(t_j^k)\}. \tag{9}$$

The selection is related to the task's EST which dynamically changes with the previous scheduling result. Therefore, the selection of to-be-scheduled task is dynamically changed during the associated task scheduling process.

3.3   Allocation of the Server for the Task to Be Scheduled

We allocate to-be-scheduled task t_i^k to server p_s which leads to the minimum estimated path length to reduce the makespan, i.e.

$$p_s = argmin_{p_t \in P}\{EPL(t_i^k, p_t)\}. \tag{10}$$

If multiple servers achieve the same minimum estimated path length for task t_i^k, we randomly assign task t_i^k to one of the servers. The actual start time of task t_i^k is calculated by Eq. (2). After the server allocation for the task to be scheduled is completed, some other tasks may be ready to scheduled, and hence we update the ready task list.

3.4   Task Duplication

Task duplication makes multiple copies of task t_i^k and assigns the task copies on different processors to reduce the data transmission time between tasks. In this way, the direct successive tasks of task t_i^k can be started right after the execution of t_i^k, without waiting for the data generated by task t_i^k to be transmitted through network. Task duplication works as follows.

(1) Assign each task t_j^k in $pre(t_i^k)$ a time weight τ_j^k which is the time when the data generated by the preceding task of task t_i^k are sent to processor p_s where task t_i^k is to be executed.

(2) Sort all the preceding tasks in $pre(t_i^k)$ according to non-ascending order of the time weights.

(3) Process each of the preceding tasks in $pre(t_i^k)$ iteratively. Schedule a copy of task $t_j^k \in pre(t_i^k)$ in the earliest idle time slot (ITS) on processor p_s, if the following conditions are satisfied: (I) $\tau_j^k > EAT(p_s)$, that is, τ_j^k is greater than the earliest available time of processor p_s; (II) there is an idle time slot for the copy of t_j^k; (III) task t_i^k can start earlier by duplicating t_j^k.

3.5   Task Insertion

Task insertion inserts a task into an idle time slot on a processor which is occupied by some tasks after the time slot. Task insertion works as follows.

1) When task t_i^k is to be scheduled on processor p_s, we search all idle time slots on processor p_s, and the idle time slot chosen to insert task t_i^k meets the following conditions: (I) $EST(t_i^k, p_s)$, the earliest start time of task t_i^k, is no ealier than the start time of the idle time slot; (II) $EFT(t_i^k, p_s)$, the earliest finish time of task t_i^k on processor p_s, is no later than the end time of the idle time slot;

2) When multiple idle time slots meet the conditions above, we select the ITS with the smallest difference between the length of the ITS and the execution time of task t_i^k.

4   Simulation

In this section, we evaluate the performance of the proposed algorithm DILS against two state-of-the-art algorithms PEFT [7] and HSIP [6]. We also investigate the impact of important parameters on the performance of algorithm DILS.

The scheduling results of the three algorithms for job set $J_s = <J_1, J_2>$ are illustrated in Fig. 2, where DAGs J_1 and J_2 are the same as the DAG shown in Fig. 1 and Table 1. The gray shadowed block represents the task that algorithms DILS and HSIP choose to replicate. We can see that algorithm DILS achieves better results than algorithms HSIP and PEFT in this example.

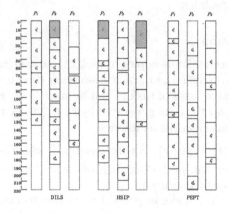

Fig. 2. The example of scheduling result

4.1   Simulation Setup

In this paper, we evaluate the performance of the three algorithms in terms of Schedule Length Ratio (SLR) which is the ratio of the scheduling length to the minimum scheduling length by ignoring the communication time as defined via Eq. (11).

$$SLR = \frac{\sum_{J_k \in J} makespan}{\sum_{J_k \in J} \sum_{t_i^k \in CP_{MIN}} min_{p_s \in P} \left\{ w \left(t_i^k, p_s \right) \right\}} \tag{11}$$

where CP_{MIN} is the minimum length of the critical path in the DAG-based job after ignoring the communication time between tasks, and the critical path of a DAG-based job is the longest path from its ingress task to its egress task.

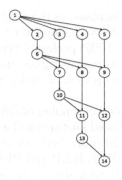 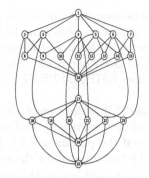 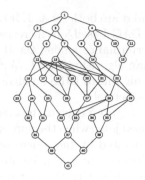

(a) Gaussian Elimination.   (b) Montage Workflow.   (c) Molecular Dynamics.

Fig. 3. Real-world DAGs

We use both DAG-based jobs randomly generated by a DAG generator and real-world DAG-based jobs in the simulations, where the parameters used by the generator are consistent with those in [17,18]. The DAG topology parameters are as follows:

(1) DAG average calculation time $\overline{c_{DAG}}$: indicating the average execution time of the tasks in the DAG, which is randomly set during the simulation.
(2) Communication Calculation Ratio CCR: the ratio of the average communication time and the average execution time; the larger the value, the more communication-intensive the DAG-based job; the smaller the value, the more computation-intensive the DAG-based job.
(3) Heterogeneous parameter α: representing the task execution time range on different processors; the larger the value, the more heterogeneous the processors.

We select three classic DAG-based jobs from the real-world applications in the simulations.

(1) Gaussian Elimination: it is used in linear algebraic programming for solving linear equations as shown in Fig. 3(a). The number of nodes is $N = \frac{\beta^2+\beta-2}{2}$ according to matrix parameter β.
(2) Montage Workflow: it is applied to construct astronomical image mosaic. An example of Montage Workflow is shown in Fig. 3(b).
(3) Molecular Dynamics Code: it is an algorithm to implement the atomic and the molecular physical motion. An example of Molecular Dynamics Code is depicted in Fig. 3(c).

4.2   Performance of Algorithm DILS and Impact of Parameters

Figure 4 shows the makespan performance of the three algorithms by varying the number of DAG-based jobs, when the number of processors is set as 4, the DAG-based jobs are randomly generated by the generator, and the parameters CCR

and α are both set as 1. It can be seen that the makespan increases as the number of DAG-based jobs increases. In general, algorithm DILS always achieves the best performance among the three algorithms, and algorithm HSIP performs better than algorithm PEFT. With 10 DAG-based jobs, the performance improvement of algorithm DILS on algorithms HSIP and PEFT reaches up to 4.5% and 7.9%, respectively.

Figure 5 depicts the average SLR performance with different number of DAG-based jobs, when the number of processors is 8, the DAG-based jobs are randomly generated by the generator, and the parameters CCR and α are both set as 1. The average SLR generated by the three algorithms of DILS, HSIP and PEFT decreases with the increase of the number of DAG-based jobs, since more idle time slots are utilized. Algorithm DILS leads to the least average SLR among the three algorithms since algorithm DILS can make the best use of idle time slots. Algorithm DILS outperforms algorithms HSIP and PEFT from 16.3% to 17.6% and from 17.9% to 25.0%, respectively, when the number of DAG-based jobs increases from 2 to 10.

Figure 6 illustrates the average SLR performance versus different matrix size parameter β for the Gaussian Elimination jobs when the number of processors is 2. It can be observed that the average SLR of the three algorithms increases with the increase of β. There are more tasks in the jobs with a larger β than that with a smaller β, which requires more computation and communication time to execute all the associated tasks. The performance improvement of algorithm DILS on algorithms HSIP and PEFT is up to 11.9% and 12.1%, respectively.

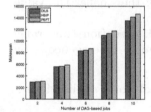 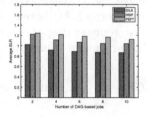 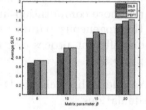

Fig. 4. The makespan with the different number of DAG-based jobs

Fig. 5. The average SLR with the different number of DAG-based jobs

Fig. 6. The average SLR with the different matrix parameter β

Table 2 describes the average SLR for Montage Workflow and Molecular Dynamics Code. Parameter α varies in $\{01, 0.5, 1, 2\}$, when parameter $CCR = 1$ and the numbers of DAG-based jobs and processors are 5 and 4, respectively. Parameter CCR increases from 0.2 to 10, when $\alpha = 1$ and the number of DAG-based jobs and processors is 5 and 8, respectively. The average SLR increases with the increase of CCR, since the communication between tasks consumes more time as parameter CCR increases. Algorithm DILS always achieves the best performance in all the three algorithms.

Table 2. Average SLR with Montage Workflow and Molecular Dynamics Code

DAG type	Algorithm	Parameter α				Parameter CCR					
		0.1	0.5	1	2	0.2	0.5	1	2	5	10
Montage Workflow	DILS	1.00	1.04	1.12	1.15	0.53	0.58	0.61	0.62	0.67	0.93
	HSIP	1.22	1.33	1.43	1.50	0.74	0.75	0.84	0.87	0.92	1.13
	PEFT	1.25	1.36	1.38	1.48	0.73	0.75	0.83	0.84	0.98	1.22
Molecular Dynamics Code	DILS	1.25	1.36	1.46	1.53	0.66	0.70	0.75	0.80	0.87	1.01
	HSIP	1.31	1.45	1.56	1.67	0.73	0.79	0.87	1.03	1.21	1.33
	PEFT	1.29	1.44	1.62	1.61	0.74	0.76	0.92	1.06	1.31	1.58

5   Conclusion

Careful multi-job task scheduling is critical to achieve efficient job processing. In this paper, we studied the problem of associated task scheduling of multiple jobs with the aim to minimize jobs' makespan. We proposed a task Duplication and Insertion based List Scheduling algorithm (DILS) which incorporates dynamic finish time prediction, task replication, and task insertion. The algorithm dynamically schedules the tasks based on the finish time of scheduled tasks, replicates some of the tasks on different nodes, and inserts the tasks into idle time slots to expedite successive task execution. The simulation results demonstrate that the proposed algorithm can effectively reduce the jobs' makespan.

References

1. Chen, W., Xie, G., Li, R., Bai, Y., Fan, C., Li, K.: Efficient task scheduling for budget constrained parallel applications on heterogeneous cloud computing systems. Future Gener. Comput. Syst. **74**(C), 1–11 (2017)
2. Arabnejad, H., Barbosa, J.: Fairness resource sharing for dynamic workflow scheduling on heterogeneous systems. In: 2012 IEEE 10th International Symposium on Parallel and Distributed Processing with Applications (ISPA), Leganes, Spain, 10–13 July 2012, pp. 633–639 (2012)
3. Panda, S.K., Jana, P.K.: Efficient task scheduling algorithms for heterogeneous multi-cloud environment. J. Supercomput. **71**(4), 1505–1533 (2015). https://doi.org/10.1007/s11227-014-1376-6
4. Tsuchiya, T., Osada, T., Kikuno, T.: A new heuristic algorithm based on GAs for multiprocessor scheduling with task duplication. In: Proceedings of 3rd International Conference on Algorithms and Architectures for Parallel Processing, pp. 295–308. IEEE (1997)
5. Bajaj, R., Agrawal, D.P.: Improving scheduling of tasks in a heterogeneous environment. IEEE Trans. Parallel Distrib. Syst. **15**(2), 107–118 (2004)
6. Wang, G., Wang, Y., Liu, H., Guo, H.: HSIP: a novel task scheduling algorithm for heterogeneous computing. Sci. Programm. **2016**, 1–11 (2016)
7. Hamid, A., Barbosa, J.G.: List scheduling algorithm for heterogeneous systems by an optimistic cost table. IEEE Trans. Parallel Distrib. Syst. **25**(3), 682–694 (2014)
8. Duan, Z., Li, W., Cai, Z.: Distributed auctions for task assignment and scheduling in mobile crowdsensing systems. In: 2017 IEEE 37th International Conference on Distributed Computing Systems (ICDCS), pp. 635–644 (2017)

9. Cai, Z., Duan, Z., Li, W.: Exploiting multi-dimensional task diversity in distributed auctions for mobile crowdsensing. IEEE Trans. Mob. Comput. (2020)
10. Yu, L., Shen, H., Sapra, K., Ye, L., Cai, Z.: CoRE: cooperative end-to-end traffic redundancy elimination for reducing cloud bandwidth cost. IEEE Trans. Parallel Distrib. Syst. **28**(2), 446–461 (2017)
11. Yu, L., Chen, L., Cai, Z., Shen, H., Liang, Y., Pan, Y.: Stochastic load balancing for virtual resource management in datacenters. IEEE Trans. Cloud Comput. **8**(2), 459–472 (2020)
12. Choudhari, T., Moh, M., Moh, T.-S.: Prioritized task scheduling in fog computing. In: Proceedings of the ACMSE 2018 Conference, pp. 1–8 (2018)
13. Topcuoglu, H., Hariri, S., Wu, M.-Y.: Performance-effective and low-complexity task scheduling for heterogeneous computing. IEEE Trans. Parallel Distrib. Syst. **13**(3), 260–274 (2002)
14. Fang, Y., Wang, F., Ge, J.: A task scheduling algorithm based on load balancing in cloud computing. In: Wang, F.L., Gong, Z., Luo, X., Lei, J. (eds.) WISM 2010. LNCS, vol. 6318, pp. 271–277. Springer, Heidelberg (2010). https://doi.org/10.1007/978-3-642-16515-3_34
15. Ilavarasan, E., Thambidurai, P., Mahilmannan, R.: Performance effective task scheduling algorithm for heterogeneous computing system. In: 4th International Symposium on Parallel and Distributed Computing (ISPDC 2005), Lille, France, 4–6 July 2005, pp. 28–38 (2005)
16. Ullman, J.D.: NP-complete scheduling problems. J. Comput. Syst. Sci. **10**(6), 384–393 (1975)
17. Cordeiro, D., Mounié, G., Swann, P., Trystram, D., Vincent, J.-M., Wagner, F.: Random graph generation for scheduling simulations. In: Proceedings of the 3rd International ICST Conference on Simulation Tools and Techniques (SIMUTools 2010), Torremolinos, Malaga, Spain, 15–19 March 2010 (2010)
18. Fan, Y., Tao, L., Chen, J.: Associated task scheduling based on dynamic finish time prediction for cloud computing. In: The 39th IEEE International Conference on Distributed Computing Systems (ICDCS 2019), Dallas, Texas, USA, 7–10 July 2019 (2019)

Communication-Efficient and Privacy-Preserving Protocol for Computing Over-Threshold Set-Union

Xuhui Gong, Qiang-sheng Hua$^{(\boxtimes)}$, and Hai Jin

National Engineering Research Center for Big Data Technology and System,
Services Computing Technology and System Lab, Cluster and Grid Computing Lab,
School of Computer Science and Technology, Huazhong University of Science
and Technology, Wuhan 430074, China
{xuhuigong,qshua,hjin}@hust.edu.cn

Abstract. In a variety of applications, the data items of multiple participants are collected and analyzed, and meanwhile the participants' privacy needs to be protected. This paper studies an over-threshold data aggregation problem, i.e., over-threshold set-union. In our model, we assume there are n participants, an untrusted data aggregator and a proxy, and each participant has a sensitive data item. The over-threshold set-union is normally defined as follows: given a threshold t, the aggregator only learns the data items which appear at least t times in the union of data items of all participants without learning anything else. Existing solutions either suffer from high communication cost or leak the multiplicity information of data items. In order to handle this defect, we present an efficient protocol in the honest-but-curious model by leveraging threshold secret sharing and dual pairing vector spaces. We prove that the proposed protocol not only has $O(n \log^2 n)$ communication complexity which nearly matches the lower bound $\Omega(n/\log n)$ but also protects the data privacy.

Keywords: Over-threshold set-union · Data aggregation · Secure multi-party computation · Privacy

1 Introduction

The privacy-preserving data aggregation problem is of particular interest in many important applications. Most applications need to collect participants' data and compute some algebraic statistics. However, the data items of participants usually include sensitive information and the participants are reluctant to leak the data privacy to anyone. For example [1], in privacy-preserving distributed network monitoring, every node monitors local behavior and a service provider is responsible for a global anomalous monitoring task, and when the number of local anomalous behaviors exceeds a predetermined system threshold, the service provider identifies the anomaly.

© Springer Nature Switzerland AG 2020
D. Yu et al. (Eds.): WASA 2020, LNCS 12384, pp. 121–133, 2020.
https://doi.org/10.1007/978-3-030-59016-1_11

There are two major challenges for the privacy-preserving data aggregation problem. One is communication efficiency. In many practical systems, monitoring nodes usually have tight resource constraints. Thus, minimizing communication overhead is a pursued goal of related researchers for designing the protocol. Another issue is privacy-preserving. After a protocol has been executed, the result of the computation is leaked and no adversary can learn more extra information than what can be inferred from the result.

Many types of research have been proposed on the privacy-preserving data aggregation problem. For example, linear aggregation function-SUM [2], and non-linear aggregation functions [2–7]. In this paper, we study a particular privacy-preserving data aggregation problem, i.e., the over-threshold set-union. This problem can be used in many application scenarios, such as the privacy-preserving distributed network monitoring [1]. As far as we know, there are some works [1,3,8–10] that discuss the over-threshold set-union. In [1,10] the authors present a probabilistic protocol based on polynomial representation of sets and additively homomorphic encryption. In [3], a closely related work is proposed by using secure multi-party computation. But the techniques used in their protocols can lead to high communication complexity $(O(n^2))$. In [8,9], the authors show cryptographic methodologies to compute the over-threshold set-union. Although their protocols have lower communication complexity, their schemes can reveal the multiplicity of data.

Thus, a natural question is: can we design a protocol which has lower communication complexity and can protect data privacy including the multiplicity of data. A positive answer is presented in this paper. We propose a new probabilistic protocol for this problem. Our protocol can ensure that the data aggregator obtains accurate results with high probability(a probability with at least $1-1/n^\epsilon$, where $\epsilon \geq 1$). Our protocol has nearly linear communication complexity regarding the number of participants while protecting the privacy of participants. We summarize the comparison results in Table 1.

Table 1. Complexity comparisons

Communication	Method	Lower bound	Multiplicity privacy
$O(n^2)$	[1]	$\Omega(n/\log n)^*$[11]	√
$O(n^2)$	[3]		√
$O(n^2)$	[10]		√
$O(n)$	[8]		×
$O(n)$	[9]		×
$O(n\log^2 n)$	our		√

* The lower bound on communication complexity does not consider data privacy and security

Our main contributions in this paper are summarized as follows:

- The proposed protocol can precisely calculate the over-threshold set-union with high probability.
- The proposed protocol not only has $O(n \log^2 n)$ communication complexity which nearly matches the lower bound $\Omega(n/\log n)$ but also protects the data privacy.

The remainder of this paper is organized as follows. We introduce our system model, problem definition, the adversary model, and cryptographic background in Sect. 2. In Sect. 3, we describe our efficient protocol for the over-threshold set-union problem. We show the detailed analysis for our protocol in terms of correctness, security, and complexity in Sect. 4. Finally, we conclude this paper in Sect. 5.

2 PRELIMINARIES

2.1 System Model

In this paper, we adopt the PDA system architecture [8] (see Fig. 1), which is composed of three parts: an untrusted data aggregator $\mathcal{A}_{gg}$, a proxy $\mathcal{P}$ and n participants $\{p_1, ..., p_n\}$. Each participant p_i holds a private data item $x_i \in [1, M]$. The data aggregator has a powerful computational and storage capacity and is responsible for computing some aggregate functions (over-threshold set-union in this paper). Let S denote the multiset $\{x_1, ..., x_n\}$, and $[[x_i]]$ denote the number of times of data item x_i which appears in the multiset S. For any set A, let $x \xleftarrow{U} A$ denote that x is sampled uniformly at random from A. We denote by $|A|$ the number of elements in the set A.

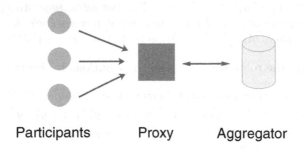

Participants   Proxy   Aggregator

Fig. 1. PDA system architecture

2.2 Problem Definition

In the paper, we mainly investigate the over-threshold set-union problem. Informally speaking, this problem is as follows: the aggregator only learns the data items which appear at least t times in the union of private data items of all participants without obtaining extra knowledge about other data items. The formal definition states as follows.

Definition 1 (Over-Threshold Set-Union) *In our system model, each participant p_i has a data item x_i, and let $S = \{x_1, ..., x_n\}$. Given a threshold t, the aggregator wants to compute the set $\mathcal{U} = \{x'_1, ..., x'_{l'}\}$ without obtaining extra knowledge, where $x'_j \in S, [[x'_j]] \geq t$ for any $j \in \{1, ..., l'\}$.*

2.3 Adversary Model

Like most other related work [1,8,9], we consider the honest-but-curious adversaries model. In this model, each party faithfully executes the prescribed actions of the protocol and meanwhile is curious about the private information of other nodes. Moreover, we assume that the participants, proxy and data aggregator do not collude with each other.

2.4 Cryptographic Background

Asymmetric Bilinear Pairing Groups. Let us denote the asymmetric bilinear pairing groups by $(q, \mathbb{G}_1, \mathbb{G}_2, \mathbb{G}_T, e)$ which is produced by $\mathcal{G}(1^\lambda)$, where q is a prime, λ is a security parameter, $\mathbb{G}_1$, $\mathbb{G}_2$ and $\mathbb{G}_T$ are cyclic groups of order q, and $e: \mathbb{G}_1 \times \mathbb{G}_2 \longrightarrow \mathbb{G}_T$. Let g_1 and g_2 be generators of $\mathbb{G}_1$ and $\mathbb{G}_2$, respectively. The bilinear map e has the following properties:

1. Bilinearity: $\forall a, b \in \mathbb{Z}_q$, $e(g_1{}^a, g_2{}^b) = e(g_1, g_2)^{ab}$;
2. Non-degeneracy: $e(g_1, g_2) \neq 1$.

Definition 2 *(Symmetric External Diffie-Hellman: SXDH Assumption [12]). Given the following distributions $((q, \mathbb{G}_1, \mathbb{G}_2, \mathbb{G}_T, e) \leftarrow \mathcal{G}(1^\lambda), g_1, g_2, g_1^a, g_1^b, Y_\sigma)$, where $Y_0 = g_1^{ab}$, $Y_1 = g_1^{ab+r}$, $a, b, r \xleftarrow{U} \mathbb{Z}_p$, the advantage $\boldsymbol{Adv}_A^{\mathrm{SXDH}}$ that any probabilistic polynomial time (PPT) adversary determines whether $\sigma = 0$ or 1 is negligible in λ, where $\boldsymbol{Adv}_A^{\mathrm{SXDH}} = |\Pr[\mathcal{A}(1^\lambda, Y_0) \longrightarrow 1] - \Pr[\mathcal{A}(1^\lambda, Y_1) \longrightarrow 1]|$.*

If $\mathbb{G}_1, \mathbb{G}_2$ reverse the roles, the analogous distributions is also true.

Definition 3 *(External Decisional Linear Assumption: XDLIN [13]). Given $P_a = ((q, \mathbb{G}_1, \mathbb{G}_2, \mathbb{G}_T, e) \leftarrow \mathcal{G}(1^\lambda), g_1^\xi, g_1^\kappa, g_1^{\delta\xi}, g_1^{\sigma\kappa}, g_2^\xi, g_2^\kappa, g_2^{\delta\xi}, g_2^{\sigma\kappa}, Y_a)$ for $b \in \{1, 2\}$, where $Y_0 = g_b^{\delta+\sigma}$, $Y_1 = g_b^{\delta+\sigma+\rho}$, $\delta, \kappa, \sigma, \rho \xleftarrow{U} \mathbb{Z}_p$, the advantage $\boldsymbol{Adv}_A^{\mathrm{XDLIN}}$ that any PPT adversary determines whether $a = 0$ or 1 is negligible in λ, where $\boldsymbol{Adv}_A^{\mathrm{XDLIN}} = |\Pr[\mathcal{A}(1^\lambda, Y_0) \longrightarrow 1] - \Pr[\mathcal{A}(1^\lambda, Y_1) \longrightarrow 1]|$.*

Definition 4 (Dual Pairing Vector Spaces [14,15]). *Dual Pairing Vector Spaces are defined by the tuple $(q, \mathbb{V}, \mathbb{V}^*, \mathbb{G}_T, \mathbb{A}, \mathbb{A}^*)$ and can be constructed by $\mathcal{G}(1^\lambda)$. $\mathbb{V} = \mathbb{G}_1^m$ and $\mathbb{V}^* = \mathbb{G}_2^m$ are n dimensional vector spaces and $\mathbb{V} = (\boldsymbol{a}_1, ..., \boldsymbol{a}_m)$ and $\mathbb{V}^* = (\boldsymbol{a}_1^*, ..., \boldsymbol{a}_m^*)$ are canonical bases of $\mathbb{V}$ and $\mathbb{V}^*$, respectively, where $\boldsymbol{a}_i = (0^{i-1}, G_1, 0^{m-i})$, $\boldsymbol{a}_i^* = (0^{i-1}, G_2, 0^{m-i})$, 0^j represents a line of j zeros, e.g., $(0^4, 0) = (0, 0, 0, 0, 0)$. $\tilde{e} : \mathbb{V} \times \mathbb{V}^* \longrightarrow \mathbb{G}_T$ is pairing and is defined by $\tilde{e} = (\boldsymbol{x}, \boldsymbol{y}) = \prod_{i=1}^m e(X_i, Y_i) \in \mathbb{G}_T$, where $\boldsymbol{x} = (X_1, ..., X_m) \in \mathbb{V}$ and $\boldsymbol{y} = (Y_1, ..., Y_m) \in \mathbb{V}^*$.*

Then, given $(q, \mathbb{V}, \mathbb{V}^*, \mathbb{G}_T, \mathbb{A}, \mathbb{A}^*, \widetilde{e})$, we present random dual orthonormal bases $\mathcal{G}_{ob}(1^\lambda, m)$ as follows:

$$\psi \xleftarrow{U} Z_p^*, \mathbf{B} = (\chi_{i,j}) \leftarrow GL(m, Z_q), (\phi_{i,j}) \leftarrow \psi(\mathbf{B}^T)^{-1}, \mathbf{b}_i = \sum_{j=1}^m \chi_{i,j} \mathbf{a}_j, \mathbf{b}_i^* = \sum_{j=1}^m \phi_{i,j} \mathbf{a}_j^*, (i = 1, ..., m), \mathbb{B} = (\mathbf{b}_1, ..., \mathbf{b}_m), \mathbb{B}^* = (\mathbf{b}_1^*, ..., \mathbf{b}_m^*), g_T = e(G_1, G_2)^\psi, \text{output}(\mathbb{B}, \mathbb{B}^*),$$

where $GL(m, Z_q)$ denotes the general linear group of degree m over Z_p.

For $\mathbf{x} = (X_1, ..., X_m)^T$ and $\mathbb{B} = (\mathbf{b}_1, ..., \mathbf{b}_m)$,, we use $(\mathbf{x})_{\mathbb{B}}$ to denote $\sum_{i=1}^m X_i \mathbf{b}_i$. So we have $\widetilde{e}(((\mathbf{x})_{\mathbb{A}}, (\mathbf{y})_{\mathbb{A}^*}) = \prod_{i=1}^m e(X_i G_1, Y_i G_2) = e(G_1, G_2)^{\sum_{i=1}^m X_i Y_i}$ and $\widetilde{e}((\mathbf{x})_{\mathbb{B}}, (\mathbf{y})_{\mathbb{B}^*}) = \widetilde{e}((\mathbf{Bx})_{\mathbb{A}}, (\psi(\mathbf{B}^T)^{-1}\mathbf{y})_{\mathbb{A}^*}) = e(G_1, G_2)^{\psi \mathbf{Bx} \cdot \mathbf{B}^{-1} \mathbf{y}} = g_T^{\sum_{i=1}^m X_i Y_i}$.

Threshold Secret Sharing. In this paper, we use an (n, t)-threshold secret sharing scheme, i.e., Shamir's secret sharing technique [16]. The secret sharing scheme is that a secret s is split and distributed to n participants, and only t or more than t participants which work together can reconstruct the secret s. For the secret s, it constructs polynomial $h(x) = s + s_1 x + s_2 x^2 + \cdots + s_{t-1} x^{t-1}$, where $s_1, ..., s_{t-1} \xleftarrow{U} Z_q$. Then, it randomly chooses n distinct elements $\alpha_1, ..., \alpha_n$ from Z_q and computes $h(\alpha_1), ..., h(\alpha_n)$ and sends $(\alpha_i, h(\alpha_i))$ to participant p_i for any $i \in [n]$. For any set $B = \{\alpha_{i_1}, ..., \alpha_{i_t}\}$ of size t, the secret s can be recovered as followings: $s = \sum_{j=1}^t \Delta_{\alpha_{i_j}, B}(0) h(\alpha_{i_j})$, where $\Delta_{\alpha_{i_j}, B}(0) = \prod_{r \in B, r \neq \alpha_{i_j}} \frac{-r}{\alpha_{i_j} - r}$.

Moreover, we introduce the distributed ElGamal cryptosystem [17] in a threshold manner, which will be adopted in our paper. A simplified description of the cryptosystem between the proxy $\mathcal{P}$ and data aggregator $\mathcal{A}_{gg}$ is described as follows. Let $\mathbb{G}$ be a multiplicative cyclic group of prime order q and g is one of its generators. $\mathcal{P}$ and $\mathcal{A}_{gg}$ choose private keys sk_1 and sk_2 from Z_q, respectively. Then, they publish $y_1 = g^{sk_1}$ and $y_2 = g^{sk_2}$, and compute the public key $pu = y_1 y_2 = g^{sk_1 + sk_2}$. In order to encrypt a message m, any participant chooses $r \xleftarrow{U} Z_q$ and outputs a ciphertext $\mathbf{E}_{pu}[m] = (A, B) = (g^r, m y^r)$. To decrypt the ciphertext (A, B), $\mathcal{A}_{gg}$ needs to send A to $\mathcal{P}$. Then, $\mathcal{P}$ computes $A_1 = A^{sk_1}$ and sends $A_1 = A^{sk_1}$ to $\mathcal{A}_{gg}$, and $\mathcal{A}_{gg}$ can obtain the message m by computing $B/(A_1 A^{sk_2})$ (it is not difficult to see that $B/(A_1 A^{sk_2}) = m y^r/(g^{r sk_1} g^{r sk_2}) = m y^r/g^{(sk_1 + sk_2)r} = m y^r/y^r = m$). The distributed ElGamal cryptosystem has an improtant property: re-encryption. That is, given $\mathbf{E}_{pu}[m] = (A, B)$, the proxy can compute another encryption of m: $(A g^{r'}, B y^{r'})$, where $r' \xleftarrow{U} Z_q$, which is still denoted as $\mathbf{E}_{pu}[m]$ for convenience.

3 Efficient Protocol for Threshold-Over Set-Union

3.1 Overview

In the previous schemes [1,3,8–10] they process the data items directly. And yet we use the binary bits of data items to compute the over-threshold set-union. The main idea for our protocol is that only t or more than t ciphertexts which are generated by using the same data item can be decrypted. To achieve the design goal and reduce the communication complexity, we propose a novel protocol based on the threshold secret sharing and dual pairing vector spaces. Our protocol is composed of the four phases as follows: the **System Setup**, **Ciphertext Generation**, **Blind Ciphertext** and **Ciphertext Aggregation**.

3.2 Basic Protocol

We first introduce a basic protocol which can exactly compute the over-threshold set-union with high probability.

System Setup. A trusted authority produces some private keys and distributes to the participants, and the data aggregator and proxy generate their own secret keys. Specifically, it selects $(q, \mathbb{G}_1, \mathbb{G}_2, \mathbb{G}_T, e) \leftarrow \mathcal{G}(1^\lambda)$ and generates $(q, \mathbb{V}, \mathbb{V}^*, \mathbb{G}_T, \mathbb{A}, \mathbb{A}^*, \tilde{e})$, $\{(\mathbb{B}_j, \mathbb{B}_j^*), (\mathbb{C}_j, \mathbb{C}_j^*)\}_{j=1}^3$ from $\mathcal{G}_{ob}(1^\lambda, m)$, where $\mathbb{B}_j = (\mathbf{b}_{j,1}, ..., \mathbf{b}_{j,9}), \mathbb{B}_j^* = (\mathbf{b}_{j,1}^*, ..., \mathbf{b}_{j,9}^*)$ for $j = 1, 2$, $\mathbb{B}_3 = (\mathbf{b}_{3,1}, ..., \mathbf{b}_{3,6l+11}), \mathbb{B}_3^* = (\mathbf{b}_{3,1}^*, ..., \mathbf{b}_{3,6l+11}^*)$, $\mathbb{C}_j = (\mathbf{c}_{j,1}, ..., \mathbf{c}_{j,6l+9}), \mathbb{C}_j^* = (\mathbf{c}_{j,1}^*, ..., \mathbf{c}_{j,6l+9}^*)$ for $j = 1, 2$, $\mathbb{C}_3 = (\mathbf{c}_{3,1}, ..., \mathbf{c}_{3,6l+11}), \mathbb{C}_3^* = (\mathbf{c}_{3,1}^*, ..., \mathbf{c}_{3,6l+11}^*)$. Then it computes $\{(\alpha_{i,j}, h_{i,j}), (\alpha_{i,j}, \overline{h}_{i,j})\}$ for secrets $\{\beta_j, \gamma_j\}$ by using the Shamir's protocol and samples $\{a_1, b_1\}$ from $\{0,1\}^\lambda$ (to be used in pseudorandom function (PRF)), where $i \in [n], j \in [2] = \{1, 2\}$. It sends $(q, \mathbb{G}_1, \mathbb{G}_2, \mathbb{G}_T, e), \{(\mathbb{B}_j, \mathbb{B}_j^*), (\mathbb{C}_j, \mathbb{C}_j^*)\}_{j=1}^3, \{a_1, b_1\}, \{(\alpha_{i,j}, h_{i,j}), (\alpha_{i,j}, \overline{h}_{i,j})\}_{j=1}^2$ to participant p_i for any $i \in [n]$ and $(q, \mathbb{G}_1, \mathbb{G}_2, \mathbb{G}_T, e)$ to the data aggregator and proxy.

The data aggregator together with proxy compute secret key sk_1 and sk_2, respectively, and they publish common public key pu by running the distributed ElGamal cryptosystem.

Ciphertext Generation. In this phase, each participant p_i encrypts its own data item x_i by using private keys.

Specifically, participant p_i first converts x_i into binary vector $\mathbf{v}_i = (x_{i,l-1}, ..., x_{i,0})$, where $l = \lceil \log M \rceil$. Let $\mathbf{X}_{i,1}$ and $\mathbf{X}_{i,2}$ denote the vectors $(\mathbf{v}_i, 1, \mathbf{v}_i)$ and $(1, \mathbf{v}_i, -2\mathbf{v}_i)$, respectively, where $\mathbf{1} = (1, 1, ..., 1)$ which has l elements. $f_{a_1}(\cdot)$ $(f_{b_1}(\cdot))$ is a pseudorandom function of the PRF family $\mathcal{F}_\lambda = \{f_s : \{0,1\}^\lambda \to \{0,1\}^\lambda\}_{s \in \{0,1\}^\lambda}$ that uses a_1 (b_1) as parameter [18]. Then it computes the ciphertexts $\overline{C}_i = \{C_{i,1}, ..., C_{i,6}, C_i\}$ as follows:

$$C_{i,1} = (r_{i,1}, h_{i,1}, 0^2, r_{i,2}, r_{i,3}, 0, 0, 0)_{\mathbb{B}_1}, C_{i,2} = (r_{i,4}, r_{i,5}, 0^2, 0, 0, r_{i,6}, r_{i,7}, 0)_{\mathbb{B}_1^*},$$

$$C_{i,3} = (r_{i,4}, \overline{h}_{i,1}, 0^2, \hat{r}_{i,1}, \hat{r}_{i,2}, 0, 0, 0)_{\mathbb{B}_2}, C_{i,4} = (r_{i,1}, \hat{r}_{i,3}, 0^2, 0, 0, \hat{r}_{i,4}, \hat{r}_{i,5}, 0)_{\mathbb{B}_2^*},$$

$$C_{i,5} = (\overline{r}_{i,1} f_{a_1}(r) \cdot \mathbf{X}_{i,1}, r_{i,5}, \hat{r}_{i,3}, 1, 0^{3l+3}, \overline{r}_{i,2}, \overline{r}_{i,3}, 0, 0, 0)_{\mathbb{B}_3},$$

$$C_{i,6} = (f_{b_1}(r) \cdot \mathbf{X}_{i,2}, h_{i,1}, \overline{h}_{i,1}, \overline{r}_{i,4}, 0^{3l+3}, 0, 0, \overline{r}_{i,5}, \overline{r}_{i,6}, 0)_{\mathbb{B}_3^*},$$

$$C_i = e(G_1, G_2)^{\beta_1 r_{i,5} + \gamma_1 \hat{r}_{i,3} + \overline{r}_{i,4}},$$

where $\{r_{i,j}\}_{j=1}^{7}, \{\hat{r}_{i,j}\}_{j=1}^{5}, \{\overline{r}_{i,j}\}_{j=2}^{6} \xleftarrow{U} Z_q, \overline{r}_{i,1} \xleftarrow{U} Z_{q'}$ $(q' < q/tl)$, and r is a nonce about the message, and $f_{a_1}(r)f_{b_1}(r) \neq 0$.. Similarly, it computes the following ciphertexts $\overline{D}_i = \{\{D_{i,j}\}_{j=1}^{6}, D_i\}$:.

$$D_{i,1} = (s_{i,1} \cdot \boldsymbol{X}_{i,1}, s_{i,2}, h_{i,2}, 0^{3l+2}, s_{i,3}, s_{i,4}, 0, 0, 0)_{C_1},$$
$$D_{i,2} = (s_{i,5} \cdot \boldsymbol{X}_{i,2}, s_{i,6}, s_{i,7}, 0^{3l+2}, 0, 0, s_{i,8}, s_{i,9}, 0)_{C_1^*},$$
$$D_{i,3} = (\hat{s}_{i,1} \cdot \boldsymbol{X}_{i,1}, s_{i,6}, \overline{h}_{i,2}, 0^{3l+2}, \hat{s}_{i,2}, \hat{s}_{i,3}, 0, 0, 0)_{C_2},$$
$$D_{i,4} = (\hat{s}_{i,4} \cdot \boldsymbol{X}_{i,2}, s_{i,2}, \hat{s}_{i,5}, 0^{3l+2}, 0, 0, \hat{s}_{i,6}, \hat{s}_{i,7}, 0)_{C_2^*},$$
$$D_{i,5} = (\overline{s}_{i,1} \cdot \boldsymbol{X}_{i,1}, s_{i,7}, \hat{s}_{i,5}, 1, 0^{3l+3}, \overline{s}_{i,2}, \overline{s}_{i,3}, 0, 0, 0)_{C_3},$$
$$D_{i,6} = (\overline{s}_{i,4} \cdot \boldsymbol{X}_{i,2}, h_{i,2}, \overline{h}_{i,2}, \hat{s}_{i,5}, 0^{3l+3}, 0, 0, \overline{s}_{i,6}, \overline{s}_{i,7}, 0)_{C_3^*},$$
$$D_i = e(G_1, G_2)^{x_i + \beta_2 s_{i,7} + \gamma_2 \hat{s}_{i,5} + \overline{s}_{i,5}},$$

where $\{s_{i,j}\}_{j=1}^{9}, \{\hat{s}_{i,j}, \overline{s}_{i,j}\}_{j=1}^{7} \xleftarrow{U} Z_q$.

Then, p_i handles $\overline{C}_i$ and $\overline{D}_i$ by using pu according to the distributed ElGamal cryptosystem, and obtains $E_i = (\mathbf{E}_{pu}[C_i], \{\mathbf{E}_{pu}[C_{i,j}]\}_{j=1}^{6}, \mathbf{E}_{pu}[\alpha_{i,1}])$ and $E_i' = (\mathbf{E}_{pu}[D_i], \{\mathbf{E}_{pu}[D_{i,j}]\}_{j=1}^{6}, \mathbf{E}_{pu}[\alpha_{i,2}])$.

Finally, p_i sends $\{E_i, E_i'\}$ to the proxy.

Note that although $C_{i,j}$ and $D_{i,j}$ are similar to the secret keys and ciphertexts defined in [15], we do not need to assume the restriction of queries (full-hiding security) used in the paper.

Blind Ciphertext. In this phase, the proxy needs to blind the ciphertexts such that the data aggregator does not learn knowledge about the source of ciphertexts. In fact, communication is very expensive and the participants drop out at any time in many important applications. Thus, denote the index i of the participants p_i that the proxy receives messages by active set $\mathcal{A}$. After receiving messages from $\mathcal{A}$, the proxy performs the blind operation as follows.

It first performs two shuffle operations for the ciphertext $\{E_i\}_{i \in \mathcal{A}}$ and $\{E_i'\}_{i \in \mathcal{A}}$. Specifically, the proxy picks two random permutations π and π' from the set $\mathcal{A}$, and re-encrypts $E = \{E_{\pi(i)}\}_{i \in \mathcal{A}}$ and $E' = \{E_{\pi(i)'}'\}_{i \in \mathcal{A}}$ by using the re-encryption property of distributed ElGamal cryptosystem.

Finally, it sends $\{E, E'\}$ to the data aggregator.

Ciphertext Aggregation. In this phase, $\mathcal{A}_{gg}$ computes the over-threshold set-union by using decryption operation. The detailed decryption operation is summarized in Algorithm 1.

More specifically, with the help of the proxy, $\mathcal{A}_{gg}$ decrypts the ciphertexts E and E' and obtains $\{\overline{C}_j, \alpha_{j,1}\}_{j \in \mathcal{A}}$, $\{\overline{D}_j, \alpha_{j,2}\}_{j \in \mathcal{A}}$ (line 1). Next, if $|\mathcal{A}| < t$, the participants' data items do not contain the over-threshold set-union and the data aggregator outputs an empty set ϕ (lines 2-3). Otherwise, they may contain the over-threshold set-union. Any t participants' data items could be the same. $\mathcal{A}_{gg}$ needs to traverse all possible combination of t participants' ciphertexts. Thus, it computes a family of sets $\mathcal{U}_1$ whose elements are all subsets of size t of $\mathcal{A}$ (line 5). Obviously, $|\mathcal{U}_1| = \binom{|\mathcal{A}|}{t}$. Then it randomly chooses an element $\mathcal{E} = \{e_1, ..., e_t\}$ from $\mathcal{A}$ and removes $\mathcal{E}$ from $\mathcal{A}$ and computes B, B' (line 8). Next, $\mathcal{A}_{gg}$ computes $H, F_{i,1}, F_{i,2}, \hat{F}_{i,1}, \hat{F}_{i,2}$ and $\overline{F}_i$ (lines 9). Then, it calculates $\prod_{i \in \mathcal{E}} \left(\frac{F_{i,1} \hat{F}_{i,1} \overline{F}_i}{F_{i,2} \hat{F}_{i,2}} \right)^{\Delta_{\alpha_{i,1}, B}(0)}$ and H, and decides whether

$$\prod_{i \in \mathcal{E}} \left(\frac{F_{i,1} \hat{F}_{i,1} \overline{F}_i}{F_{i,2} \hat{F}_{i,2}} \right)^{\Delta_{\alpha_{i,1}, B}(0)} = H \text{ (line 10)}.$$

If the above equation holds, the data aggregator continues to compute $K, J_{i,1}, J_{i,2}, \hat{J}_{i,1}, \hat{J}_{i,2}$ and $\hat{U}$ (lines 11–12). To recover U, it needs to compute the discrete logarithm of $\hat{U}$ to the base $e(G_1, G_2)$. By using the Pollard's lambda algorithm [19], this takes expected time $O(\sqrt{M})$ since $x_i \in [1, M]$. Note that if the above equation (line 10) holds, then it means the t ciphertexts contain the same data item which belongs to over-threshold set-union (see Theorem 1). We can obtain the data item by using the above operations.

Finally, to obtain over-threshold set-union, the data aggregator requires at most $\binom{n}{t}$ times of the above computation (lines 6–13), because $\mathcal{U}_1$ contains at most $\binom{n}{t}$ elements when $|\mathcal{A}| = n$.

Algorithm 1: Ciphertext Aggregation: $\mathcal{A}_{gg}$

Input: $\{E_i, \overline{E}_i\}_{i \in \mathcal{A}}, \mathcal{U} \leftarrow \phi$
Output: Over-Threshold Set-Union $\mathcal{U}$

1 with the help of the proxy, $\mathcal{A}_{gg}$ decrypts $\{E_i, \overline{E}_i\}_{i \in \mathcal{A}}$ based on the distributed ElGamal cryptosystem and obtains $\{\overline{C}_j, \alpha_{j,1}\}_{j \in \mathcal{A}}, \{\overline{D}_j, \alpha_{j,2}\}_{j \in \mathcal{A}}$;

2 **if** $|\mathcal{A}| < t$ **then**

3 $\quad \lfloor \; \mathcal{A}_{gg}$ outputs an empty set ϕ;

4 **else**

5 $\quad \mathcal{A}_{gg}$ computes a family of sets $\mathcal{U}_1$ whose elements are all subsets of size t of $\mathcal{A}$, where $|\mathcal{U}_1| = \binom{|\mathcal{A}|}{t}$;

6 $\quad$ **while** $|\mathcal{U}_1| > 0$ **do**

7 $\quad\quad \mathcal{A}_{gg}$ randomly chooses an element $\mathcal{E} = \{e_1, ..., e_t\}$ from $\mathcal{U}_1$;

8 $\quad\quad \mathcal{U}_1 \leftarrow \mathcal{U}_1 - \{\mathcal{E}\}, B \leftarrow \{\alpha_{i,1} | i \in \mathcal{E}\}, B' \leftarrow \{\alpha_{i,2} | i \in \mathcal{E}\}$;

9 $\quad\quad \mathcal{A}_{gg}$ computes $H = \prod_{j \in \mathcal{E}} C_j$, $F_{i,1} = \prod_{j \in \mathcal{E}} e(C_{i,1}, C_{j,2})$,
$\quad\quad F_{i,2} = \prod_{j \in \mathcal{E}} e(C_{i,4}, C_{j,3})$, $\hat{F}_{i,1} = \prod_{j \in \mathcal{E}} e(C_{i,3}, C_{j,4})$,
$\quad\quad \hat{F}_{i,2} = \prod_{j \in \mathcal{E}} e(C_{i,2}, C_{j,1})$, $\overline{F}_i = \prod_{j \in \mathcal{E}} e(C_{i,5}, C_{j,6})$;

10 $\quad\quad$ **if** $\prod_{i \in \mathcal{E}} \left(\frac{F_{i,1} \hat{F}_{i,1} \overline{F}_i}{F_{i,2} \hat{F}_{i,2}} \right)^{\Delta_{\alpha_{i,1}, B}(0)} == H$ **then**

11 $\quad\quad\quad \mathcal{A}_{gg}$ computea $K = \prod_{j \in \mathcal{E}} D_j$, $J_{i,1} = \prod_{j \in \mathcal{E}} e(D_{i,1}, D_{j,2})$,
$\quad\quad\quad J_{i,2} = \prod_{j \in \mathcal{E}} e(D_{i,4}, D_{j,3})$, $\hat{J}_{i,1} = \prod_{j \in \mathcal{E}} e(D_{i,3}, D_{j,4})$,
$\quad\quad\quad \hat{J}_{i,2} = \prod_{j \in \mathcal{E}} e(D_{i,2}, D_{j,1})$, $\overline{J}_i = \prod_{j \in \mathcal{E}} e(D_{i,5}, D_{j,6})$;

12 $\quad\quad\quad \hat{U} = \left(\prod_{i \in \mathcal{E}} K_i \left(\frac{J_{i,2} \hat{J}_{i,2}}{J_{i,1} \hat{J}_{i,1} \overline{J}_i} \right)^{\Delta_{\alpha_{i,2}, B'}(0)} \right)^{\frac{1}{t}}$, $U = \log \hat{U}$;

13 $\quad\quad\quad \mathcal{U} \leftarrow \mathcal{U} \bigcup U$;

14 **return** $\mathcal{U}$

3.3   Further Improvement

In fact, each p_i generates a new private data item in a certain time interval. If participants use the basic protocol to encrypt their data items in each time interval, the data aggregator may learn more information than the over-threshold set-union. For example, suppose that p_1 produces the same data item in t time intervals and encrypts it by using the basic protocol, and if the data item does not belong to over-threshold set-union in the t time intervals, the data aggregator can obtain the data item by using the decryption operation. Thus, the basic protocol cannot be applied to this scenario.

To resolve this drawback, we propose our improved algorithm in this section. The main idea is that the ciphertexts can be decrypted only if they are at the same time interval. Specifically, since ciphertexts $C_{i,j}$ and $D_{i,j}$ are computed by using some vectors and random dual orthonormal bases in each time interval, we can use different vectors in different time interval. An efficient method is that we can rearrange the order of the elements in the vectors. For example, $D_{i,1}$ is computed by using vector $(s_{i,1} \cdot X_{i,1}, s_{i,2}, h_{i,2}, 0^{3l+2}, s_{i,3}, s_{i,4}, 0, 0, 0)$, and we use a new vector whose elements are randomly arranged to compute ciphertexts in each time interval. Although the scheme is feasible, there is a disadvantage to this approach. Because the number of elements in vectors is limited. Thus, the number of random permutations is limited. To overcome the weakness, we can add some elements to vectors. In the following, we will illustrate our improved algorithm in detail.

We again run the **System Setup** phase for the trusted authority, but we make the following modifications.

- Add: samples $c_i, d_{i,j} \leftarrow \{0,1\}^\lambda$ $(i = 1, ..., 6, j = 1, ..., 4)$ and sends to all participants;
- Replace $\{(\mathbb{B}_i, \mathbb{B}_i^*), (\mathbb{C}_i, \mathbb{C}_i^*)\}_{i=1}^3$ by $\{(\overline{\mathbb{B}}_i, \overline{\mathbb{B}}_i^*), (\overline{\mathbb{C}}_i, \overline{\mathbb{C}}_i^*)\}_{i=1}^3$: Samples $\{(\overline{\mathbb{B}}_i, \overline{\mathbb{B}}_i^*), (\overline{\mathbb{C}}_i, \overline{\mathbb{C}}_i^*)\}_{i=1}^3 \leftarrow \mathcal{G}_{ob}(1^\lambda, m)$, where $m = 6l + 11 + c_\eta \log n + c_u$;

To rearrange the order of the elements in the vectors in different time intervals, we use a pseudorandom permutation and the Luby-Rackoff construction [20]. Let $\overline{f}_{s_1, s_2, s_3, s_4}()$ be a pseudorandom permutation indexed by s_1, s_2, s_3, s_4 (because it uses four pseudorandom functions), where $\overline{f}_{s_1, s_2, s_3, s_4}()$: $\{0,1\}^{6l+11+c_\eta \log n + c_u} \times \{0,1\}^\lambda \longrightarrow \{0,1\}^{6l+11+c_\eta \log n + c_u}$, and c_η and c_u are large constants. For a vector (x_1, x_2, x_3), we use positive integers $1, 2, 3$ to label the positions of the elements x_1, x_2, x_3 in the vector from left to right and let $R(x_1, x_2, x_3)$ denote them, i.e., $R(x_1, x_2, x_3) = (1, 2, 3)$. Let $\overline{f}_{s_1, s_2, s_3, s_4}(R(x_1, x_2, x_3))$ denote $\overline{f}_{s_1, s_2, s_3, s_4}(R(x_1, x_2, x_3)) = \overline{f}_{s_1, s_2, s_3, s_4}(1, 2, 3) = (\overline{f}_{s_1, s_2, s_3, s_4}(1), \overline{f}_{s_1, s_2, s_3, s_4}(2), \overline{f}_{s_1, s_2, s_3, s_4}(3))) = (y_1, y_2, y_3))$. Let $\overline{R}(y_1, y_2, y_3)$ denote a new vector which consists of x_1, x_2, x_3 and rearranges the positions of x_1, x_2, x_3 according to y_1, y_2, y_3, respectively. For example, when $(y_1, y_2, y_3) = (3, 2, 1)$, we have $\overline{R}(y_1, y_2, y_3) = (x_3, x_2, x_1)$. For convenience, we use $< k_i(r) >$ to denote $f_{d_{i,1}}(r), f_{d_{i,2}}(r), f_{d_{i,3}}(r), f_{d_{i,4}}(r)$ for $i = 1, ..., 6$.

We again run the **Ciphertext Generation** phase for p_i $(i \in [n])$, but we make the following modifications.

- Replace $\{\{C_{i,j}\}_{j=1}^6, C_i\}$ by $\{\{\widetilde{C}_{i,j}\}_{j=1}^6, \widetilde{C}_i\}$:

$$\widetilde{C}_{i,1} = \overline{R}\Big(\overline{f}_{<k_1(r)>}\big(R(r_{i,1}, h_{i,1}, 0^2, r_{i,2}, r_{i,3}, 0, 0, 0, f_{c_1}(1), ..., f_{c_1}(t'))\big)\Big)_{\overline{\mathbb{B}}_1},$$

$$\widetilde{C}_{i,2} = \overline{R}\Big(\overline{f}_{<k_1(r)>}\big(R(r_{i,4}, r_{i,5}, 0^2, 0, 0, r_{i,6}, r_{i,7}, 0, u_{i,1}, ..., u_{i,t'})\big)\Big)_{\overline{\mathbb{B}}_1^*},$$

$$\widetilde{C}_{i,3} = \overline{R}\Big(\overline{f}_{<k_2(r)>}\big(R(r_{i,4}, \overline{h}_{i,1}, 0^2, \hat{r}_{i,1}, \hat{r}_{i,2}, 0, 0, 0, f_{c_2}(1), ..., f_{c_2}(t'))\big)\Big)_{\overline{\mathbb{B}}_2},$$

$$\widetilde{C}_{i,4} = \overline{R}(\overline{f}_{<k_2(r)>}\big(R(r_{i,1}, \hat{r}_{i,3}, 0^2, 0, 0, \hat{r}_{i,4}, \hat{r}_{i,5}, 0, \hat{u}_{i,1}, ..., \hat{u}_{i,t'})\big)\Big)_{\overline{\mathbb{B}}_2^*},$$

$$\widetilde{C}_{i,5} = \overline{R}\Big(\overline{f}_{<k_3(r)>}\big(R(\overline{r}_{i,1} f_{a_1}(r)\cdot \boldsymbol{X}_{i,1}, r_{i,5}, \hat{r}_{i,3}, 1, 0^{3l+3}, \overline{r}_{i,2}, \overline{r}_{i,3}, 0, 0, 0,$$
$$f_{c_3}(1), ..., f_{c_3}(t''))\big)\Big)_{\overline{\mathbb{B}}_3},$$

$$\widetilde{C}_{i,6} = \overline{R}\Big(\overline{f}_{<k_3(r)>}\big(R(f_{b_1}(r)\cdot \boldsymbol{X}_{i,2}, h_{i,1}, \overline{h}_{i,1}, \overline{r}_{i,4}, 0^{3l+3}, 0, 0, \overline{r}_{i,5}, \overline{r}_{i,6}, 0, \overline{u}_{i,1},$$
$$..., \overline{u}_{i,t''})\big)\Big)_{\overline{\mathbb{B}}_3^*},$$

$$\widetilde{C}_i = e(G_1, G_2)^{\beta_1 r_{i,5} + \gamma_1 \hat{r}_{i,3} + \overline{r}_{i,4}}$$

where $t' = 6l + 2 + c_\eta \log n + c_u$, $t'' = c_\eta \log n + c_u$, and $u_{i,j}$ $\hat{u}_{i,j}$, $\overline{u}_{i,j'} \leftarrow Z_q$ for $j = 1, ..., t' - 1$ and $j' = 1, ..., t'' - 1$, and $\sum_{j=1}^{t'} f_{c_1}(j)u_{i,j} = 0$, $\sum_{j=1}^{t'} f_{c_2}(j)\hat{u}_{i,j} = 0$, $\sum_{j'=1}^{t''} f_{c_3}(j')\overline{u}_{i,j'} = 0$

- Replace $\{\{D_{i,j}\}_{j=1}^6, D_i\}$ by $\{\{\widetilde{D}_{i,j}\}_{j=1}^6, \widetilde{D}_i\}$:

$$\widetilde{D}_{i,1} = \overline{R}\Big(\overline{f}_{<k_4(r)>}\big(R(s_{i,1}\cdot \boldsymbol{X}_{i,1}, s_{i,2}, h_{i,2}, 0^{3l+2}, s_{i,3}, s_{i,4}, 0, 0, 0, f_{c_4}(1), ..., f_{c_4}$$
$$(\hat{t}'))\big)\Big)_{\overline{\mathbb{C}}_1},$$

$$\widetilde{D}_{i,2} = \overline{R}\Big(\overline{f}_{<k_4(r)>}\big(R(s_{i,5}\cdot \boldsymbol{X}_{i,2}, s_{i,6}, s_{i,7}, 0^{3l+2}, 0, 0, s_{i,8}, s_{i,9}, 0, j_{i,1}, ...,$$
$$j_{i,\hat{t}'})\big)\Big)_{\overline{\mathbb{C}}_1^*},$$

$$\widetilde{D}_{i,3} = \overline{R}\Big(\overline{f}_{f_{<k_5(r)>}}\big(R(\hat{s}_{i,1}\cdot \boldsymbol{X}_{i,1}, s_{i,6}, \overline{h}_{i,2}, 0^{3l+2}, \hat{s}_{i,2}, \hat{s}_{i,3}, 0, 0, 0, f_{c_5}(1), ..., f_{c_5}$$
$$(\hat{t}'))\big)\Big)_{\overline{\mathbb{C}}_2},$$

$$\widetilde{D}_{i,4} = \overline{R}\Big(\overline{f}_{<k_5(r)>}\big(R(\hat{s}_{i,4}\cdot \boldsymbol{X}_{i,2}, s_{i,2}, \hat{s}_{i,5}, 0^{3l+2}, 0, 0, \hat{s}_{i,6}, \hat{s}_{i,7}, 0, \hat{j}_{i,1}, ...,$$
$$\hat{j}_{i,\hat{t}'})\big)\Big)_{\overline{\mathbb{C}}_2^*},$$

$$\widetilde{D}_{i,5} = \overline{R}\Big(\overline{f}_{f_{<k_6(r)>}}\big(R(\overline{s}_{i,1}\cdot \boldsymbol{X}_{i,1}, s_{i,7}, \hat{s}_{i,5}, 1, 0^{3l+3}, \overline{s}_{i,2}, \overline{s}_{i,3}, 0, 0, 0, f_{c_6}(1), ...,$$
$$f_{c_6}(\hat{t}''))\big)\Big)_{\overline{\mathbb{C}}_3},$$

$$\widetilde{D}_{i,6} = \overline{R}\Big(\overline{f}_{<k_6(r)>}\big(R(\overline{s}_{i,4}\cdot \boldsymbol{X}_{i,2}, h_{i,2}, \overline{h}_{i,2}, \overline{s}_{i,5}, 0^{3l+3}, 0, 0, \overline{s}_{i,6}, \overline{s}_{i,7}, 0, \overline{j}_{i,1}, ...,$$
$$\overline{j}_{i,\hat{t}''})\big)\Big)_{\overline{\mathbb{C}}_3^*},$$

$$\widetilde{D}_i = e(G_1, G_2)^{x_i + \beta_2 s_{i,7} + \gamma_2 \hat{s}_{i,5} + \overline{s}_{i,5}},$$

where $\hat{t}' = 2 + c_\eta \log n + c_u$ and $\hat{t}'' = c_\eta \log n + c_u$, and $j_{i,k}$ $\hat{j}_{i,k}$, $\overline{j}_{i,k'} \leftarrow Z_q$ for $k = 1, ..., \hat{t}' - 1$ and $k' = 1, ..., \hat{t}'' - 1$, and $\sum_{k=1}^{\hat{t}'} f_{c_4}(k)j_{i,k} = 0$, $\sum_{k=1}^{\hat{t}'} f_{c_5}(k)\hat{j}_{i,k} = 0$, $\sum_{k'=1}^{\hat{t}''} f_{c_6}(k')\overline{j}_{i,k'} = 0$.

Note that we add some elements to the vectors used to compute cipher-texts such that the vectors have the same number of elements. Moreover, the added elements do not affect the result of executed protocol. For $O(\log n)$ elements, we have that the number of different permutations is $O((\log n)!)$. By using Stirling's approximation, we have $O((\log n)!) \sim O(\sqrt{2\pi \log n}(\frac{\log n}{e})^{\log n})$. On the other hand, $O((\log n)^{\log n}) = O(e^{\log n \log \log n})$. Thus, we have $O((c_\eta \log n)!) = O(e^{(\log \log n - 1)c_\eta \log n}) = O(n^{c_\eta \log \log n})$.

Finally, the proxy and data aggregator again run the **Blind Ciphertext** and **Ciphertext Aggregation** phases to decrypt ciphertexts and do not make any modifications.

4 Protocol Analysis

4.1 Correctness

Theorem 1. *In our protocol, the data aggregator can accurately obtain the over-threshold set-union.*

Proof. We omit here due to limited space. A detailed proof can be found in [21]. ∎

4.2 Privacy

Theorem 2. *Our protocol is secure under the SXDH and XDLIN assumptions.*

Proof. We omit here due to limited space. A detailed proof can be found in [21]. ∎

4.3 Complexity

It is not difficult to see that the communication complexity of **System Setup**, **Ciphertext Generation** and **Blind Ciphertext** of our protocol are $O(n \log^2 n)$, $O(n \log n \log p)$ and $O(n \log n \log p)$, respectively. Thus, the total communication complexity of our protocol is $O(n \log^2 n)$.

5 Conclusions

In this paper, we propose a novel communication-efficient and privacy-preserving protocol for the over-threshold set-union problem. Compared with previous schemes, our protocol has nearly optimal communication complexity and meanwhile can protect data privacy.

Acknowledgements. This work is supported in part by the National Natural Science Foundation of China Grant No. 61972447.

References

1. Kissner, L., Song, D.: Privacy-preserving set operations. In: Shoup, V. (ed.) CRYPTO 2005. LNCS, vol. 3621, pp. 241–257. Springer, Heidelberg (2005). https://doi.org/10.1007/11535218_15
2. Qinghua, L., Guohong, C.: Efficient and privacy-preserving data aggregation in mobile sensing. In: ICNP, pp. 1–10. IEEE, 2012
3. Martin, B., Xenofontas, D.: Fast privacy-preserving top-k queries using secret sharing. In: ICCCN, pp. 1–7. IEEE, 2010
4. Cai, Z., Zheng, X., Yu, J.: A differential-private framework for urban traffic flows estimation via taxi companies. IEEE Trans. Ind. Inform. **15**(12), 6492–6499 (2019)
5. Cai, Z., Zheng, X.: A private and efficient mechanism for data uploading in smart cyber-physical systems. IEEE Trans. Netw. Sci. Eng., 2018
6. Zhipeng, C., Zaobo, H.: Trading private range counting over big IoT data. In: ICDCS, pp. 144–153. IEEE, 2019
7. Zheng, X., Cai, Z.: Privacy-preserved data sharing towards multiple parties in industrial iots. IEEE J. Sel. Areas Commun. **38**(5), 968–979 (2020)
8. Applebaum, B., Ringberg, H., Freedman, M.J., Caesar, M., Rexford, J.: Collaborative, privacy-preserving data aggregation at scale. In: Atallah, M.J., Hopper, N.J. (eds.) PETS 2010. LNCS, vol. 6205, pp. 56–74. Springer, Heidelberg (2010). https://doi.org/10.1007/978-3-642-14527-8_4
9. Myungsun, K., Aziz, M., Jung, H.C., Yongdae, K.: Private over-threshold aggregation protocols over distributed datasets. IEEE Trans. Knowl. Data Eng. **28**(9), 2467–2479 (2016)
10. Ji, Y.C., Dong, H.L., Ik, R.J.: Privacy-preserving range set union for rare cases in healthcare data. IET Commun. **6**(18), 3288–3293 (2012)
11. Woodruff, D.P., Zhang, Q.: When distributed computation is communication expensive. Distributed Comput. **30**(5), 309–323 (2014). https://doi.org/10.1007/s00446-014-0218-3
12. Bishop, A., Jain, A., Kowalczyk, L.: Function-hiding inner product encryption. In: Iwata, T., Cheon, J.H. (eds.) ASIACRYPT 2015. LNCS, vol. 9452, pp. 470–491. Springer, Heidelberg (2015). https://doi.org/10.1007/978-3-662-48797-6_20
13. Abe, M., Chase, M., David, B., Kohlweiss, M., Nishimaki, R., Ohkubo, M.: Constant-size structure-preserving signatures: Generic constructions and simple assumptions. J. Cryptol. **29**(4), 833–878 (2016)
14. Okamoto, T., Takashima, K.: Fully secure functional encryption with general relations from the decisional linear assumption. In: Rabin, T. (ed.) CRYPTO 2010. LNCS, vol. 6223, pp. 191–208. Springer, Heidelberg (2010). https://doi.org/10.1007/978-3-642-14623-7_11
15. Tomida, J., Abe, M., Okamoto, T.: Efficient functional encryption for inner-product values with full-hiding security. In: Bishop, M., Nascimento, A.C.A. (eds.) ISC 2016. LNCS, vol. 9866, pp. 408–425. Springer, Cham (2016). https://doi.org/10.1007/978-3-319-45871-7_24
16. Shamir, A.: How to share a secret. Commun. ACM **22**(11), 612–613 (1979)
17. Gennaro, R., Jarecki, S., Krawczyk, H., Rabin, T.: Secure distributed key generation for discrete-log based cryptosystems. J. Cryptol. **20**(1), 51–83 (2007)
18. Castelluccia, C., Chan, A.C.F., Mykletun, E., Tsudik, G.: Efficient and provably secure aggregation of encrypted data in wireless sensor networks. ACM TOSN **5**(3), 1–36 (2009)

19. Menezes, A.J., Katz, J., Van Oorschot, P.C., Vanstone, S.A.: Handbook of applied cryptography. CRC Press, United States (1996)
20. Luby, M., Rackoff, C.: How to construct pseudorandom permutations from pseudorandom functions. SIAM J. Comput. **17**(2), 373–386 (1988)
21. Xuhui, G., Qiang-Sheng, H., Hai, J.: Communication-efficient and privacy-preserving protocol for computing over-threshold set-union. https:// qiangshenghua.github.io/papers/otsu-full.pdf

Approximation Algorithm for the Offloading Problem in Edge Computing

Xinxin Han[1,2], Guichen Gao[1,2], Li Ning[1], Yang Wang[1], and Yong Zhang[1(✉)]

[1] Shenzhen Institutes of Advanced Technology,
Chinese Academy of Sciences, Shenzhen, China
{xx.han,gc.gao,li.ning,yang.wang1,zhangyong}@siat.ac.cn
[2] University of Chinese Academy of Sciences, Beijing, China

Abstract. In the edge-cloud environment, offloading technique decides the task to be executed either at the cloud or at the edge. Offloading can improve the quality of service and the efficiency of the system. In most previous works on the offloading problem, the communication costs between tasks on both cloud side or the edge side are often ignored. We consider a general offloading model where the communication costs between any two tasks is non-zero and asymmetric. Moreover, due to the resource limitation on the edge side, we assume that the number of tasks executed on the edge side is bounded by a fixed constant k. This generalized offloading problem is NP-hard in minimizing the total cost with cardinality constraint. Based on semidefinite program, we give an approximation algorithm with the performance guarantee of $2/\pi$.

Keywords: Offloading · Edge computing · Approximation algorithm · Semidefinite program.

1 Introduction

Cloud computing is actually an internet-based computing method that treats all computing resources, storage resources and network resources as one kind of infrastructure. Big data generated from devices such as mobile phones, laptops, sensors, digital cameras and Internet-connected devices of vehicles over times. Since local devices often has insufficient computing power, weak CPU, small memory and low efficiency, such tasks can be executed and data can be analyzed at the cloud, where user requests on demand by 'pay-as-you-go'.

Unfortunately, as the distance between the cloud and the user increases, so does the latency ch12LX2014, which is critical in some application. For example, in the automatic driving, a 10ms increase in speed may prevent a traffic accident. Some task is better to be executed in the local server. Thus, edge computing become an effective way to bridge the distance between the cloud and the user which is

Supported by National Key R&D Program of China (No. 2018YFB0204005), Shenzhen grants (KQJSCX20180330170311901, JCYJ20180305180840138 and GGFW-2017073114031767).

© Springer Nature Switzerland AG 2020
D. Yu et al. (Eds.): WASA 2020, LNCS 12384, pp. 134–144, 2020.
https://doi.org/10.1007/978-3-030-59016-1_12

conducive to offloading some of the workload from the cloud server. It may speed up the generation of many applications requiring low latency, such as automatic driving, intelligent security front end, mobile data analysis and so on.

On the other hand, the emergence of edge computing eases the pressure of cloud center and saves bandwidth [15], so the expansion from cloud to edge has many applications in reality. Edge computing can provide more real-time, faster processing power and lower cost. With the advance of 5G networks, it is promising to become a spotlight in the next wave of the cloud research [8].

The advantages of edge computing can be seen in the computation offloading. When resources are scarce, the client device can maximize its computational efficiency by using the available resources from the remote server with the minimal power consumption or memory costs [9,10]. There are different objectives studied in distributed computing, especially in the mobile cloud computing [6,11,12,19,21,22]. Besides, some works related to the quality of service and balance the performance and the cost have been studied in [7,13,20]. In these papers, the structure of such applications can be modeled as weighted directed graphs, in which the node represents the computing task to be offloaded, while the edge indicates the data communication between tasks. Node weight and edge weight represent computing cost and communication cost respectively. In edge computing, the underlying graph will be partitioned into two disjoint parts in corresponding to the cloud side and the edge side respectively.

In traditional cloud computing, we usually only consider offloading between a single mobile device and a single remote proxy server. The communication cost between any two tasks in the same sides is often ignored. The network bandwidth of the communication between the device and the server remains a fixed value. So the communication cost between two tasks in different sides is considered to be symmetric. Such assumptions are well adopted in many offloading models [3,16–18]. But in many real applications, the communication between tasks in the same side cannot be ignored, and the bandwidth of upload and download is unbalanced. The above assumptions are not comprehensive enough when considering the offloading problem in the edge-cloud environment. Therefore, a generalized offloading model was introduced in [5], in which they consider that (1) the communication cost is non-zero between tasks in the same side and (2) the communication cost between different sides is asymmetric. They are the first to take these facts into account. They design an algorithm and obtain a sub-optimal solution in the heterogeneous case, and transform it into a min-cut problem when the model is homogeneous.

In this paper, we consider a similar model of the offloading problem. Due to the resource limitation, the edge side cannot afford too many tasks. Thus, we consider the offloading model with cardinality constraints, i.e., the number of executed tasks in the edge side is upper bounded by a fixed constant k. In addition, we analyze the model from the theoretical point of view and with the help of semidefinite program, we design an approximation algorithm with the performance ratio of $2/\pi$.

In the following part, we first introduce the offloading model under the cardinality constraint. The original problem will be simplified by some preprocessing and transformed to be a quadratic program form. We then relax it to a vector program which is equivalent to the semidefinite program. With the randomized rounding by choosing a random hyperplane, a $2/\pi$-approximation algorithm can be achieved.

2   Problem Statement

In this section we state the offloading model in the edge-cloud environment under the cardinality constraint, that is, tasks executed at the edge are no more than k.

We consider the offloading problem depended on a computation model and a cost model, which is different from traditional model. And its applications are much richer than simple models. Our computation model can be described as a weighted graph $G = (V, E)$ with nodes set $V = \{v_1, v_2, \cdots, v_n\}$ and edge weight for each $e(v_i, v_j) \in E$. We need to find a partition for V such that $V_C \cup V_E = V$ and $V_C \cap V_E = \emptyset$ to minimize the total cost.

Nodes in our computation model represent tasks or databases, and each task having a weight $w_i = (w_i^E, w_i^C)$ can be executed at the edge or at the cloud, where w_i^E and w_i^C are the execution cost of task v_i at the edge and the cloud respectively, that is, the value of w_i depends on which side task v_i is executed on. For w_i, if $w_i^E = +\infty$, the task has to be executed at the cloud. Otherwise when $w_i^C = +\infty$ the task is computed at the edge. Thus the total computation cost is denoted as:

$$C_{comp}(G) = \sum_{i=1}^{n} \left(w_i^E x_i + w_i^C \bar{x}_i \right),$$

where $x_i \in \{0, 1\}$ is decision variable, $\bar{x}_i$ is the opposite value of x_i. Let $x_i = 1$ if task v_i is executed at the edge and $x_i = 0$ otherwise.

The communication cost is involved with weight of edge. Edge $e(v_i, v_j) \in E$ indicates the communication from task v_i to task v_j, and w_{ij} is the communication cost. There are four possible values for the edge weight w_{ij}, since nodes can be offloaded to different sides in the edge-cloud environment. Therefore we define

$$w_{ij} = (w_{ij}^1, w_{ij}^2, w_{ij}^3, w_{ij}^4),$$

where $w_{ij}^1 = w(e(v_i^E, v_j^E))$, $w_{ij}^2 = w(e(v_i^E, v_j^C))$, $w_{ij}^3 = w(e(v_i^C, v_j^E))$, $w_{ij}^4 = w(e(v_i^C, v_j^C))$. v_i^E and v_i^C represent vertic v_i located at the edge and the cloud respectively. w_{ij}^1 and w_{ij}^4 always be assumed as 0 in the traditional offloading model. That means there is no communication cost between tasks in the same side. Obviously, it's not true when a cluster of servers at each side are involved in distributed systems. So it makes sense to assume $w_{ij}^1 \geq 0$ and $w_{ij}^4 \geq 0$. Moreover, $w_{ij}^2 \neq w_{ij}^3$ because of the network configurations, and this assumption generalize the offloading model. So in our offloading model the total communication cost is

$$C_{comm}(G) = \sum_{i,j}^{n} \left(w_{ij}^1 x_i x_j + w_{ij}^2 x_i \bar{x}_j + w_{ij}^3 \bar{x}_i x_j + w_{ij}^4 \bar{x}_i \bar{x}_j \right).$$

In addition, the cost is also essential when task v_i is transferred from the cloud to the edge,

$$C_{tran}(G) = \sum_{i=1}^{n} m_i x_i.$$

Based on the above computation model and cost model, we consider the total cost for our offloading problem as:

$$
\begin{aligned}
C_{total}(G) &= C_{comp}(G) + C_{comm}(G) + C_{tran}(G) \\
&= \sum_{i,j}^{n} (w_{ij}^1 x_i x_j + w_{ij}^2 x_i \bar{x}_j + w_{ij}^3 \bar{x}_i x_j + w_{ij}^4 \bar{x}_i \bar{x}_j) + \sum_{i=1}^{n} ((w_i^E + m_i)x_i + w_i^C \bar{x}_i)
\end{aligned}
\tag{1}
$$

For some reasons, the number of tasks executed at the edge system is limited. Supposed that the numbers are no more than k. Therefore the offloading model with cardinality constraint to minimize the total cost by the above Eq. (1) can be simplifyed as

$$\min\{\sum_{i,j}^{n} (w_{ij}^1 x_i x_j + w_{ij}^2 x_i \bar{x}_j + w_{ij}^3 \bar{x}_i x_j + w_{ij}^4 \bar{x}_i \bar{x}_j) + \sum_{i=1}^{n} (w_i^E x_i + w_i^C \bar{x}_i)\} \tag{2}$$

$$s.t: \quad x_i, x_j \in \{0,1\} \quad \forall i,j = 1,2,\cdots,n;$$

$$\sum_{i=1}^{n} x_i \le k. \tag{3}$$

Given a example of our offloading model in Fig. 1. There are seven nodes in the task graph. The node weight is the computation cost, and the edge weight is the communication cost. Moreover, assume that $k = 3$, we show a partition results in Fig. 2. In the result graph, the values of computation cost and communication cost can be known.

3   Model Analysis

We have known the unconstrained offloading problem is NP-hard, which was proved by reduction from Weighted MAX-2SAT [5]. Therefore, the NP-hardness of offloading under cardinality constraint is obvious. In this section, first, we make preprocessing for the offloading problem. Then we introduce the laplacian matrix to gain the equivalent form for the unnormalized quadratic, and relax the equivalent form to the vector program, which can be solved in polynomial time. Besides, we prove an approximation algorithm for the quadratic program by randomized rounding of semidefinite program.

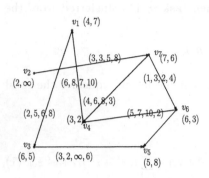

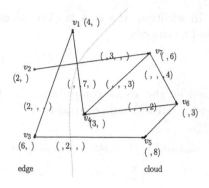

Fig. 1. A 7-node graph model.

Fig. 2. A partition result for the above model.

3.1 Model Preprocessing

Note that some tasks will have to be executed at the edge or the cloud for certain reasons, then they computation costs are $+\infty$ at the other side. If we substitute $+\infty$ directly into Eq. (2), the value of minimizing target function may be negative infinitesimal, which affects the final partition. In this case we do preprocessing for the offloading problem. When $w_i^E, w_i^C, w_{ij}^2, w_{ij}^3$ is $+\infty$, we preprocess the offloading model by Algorithm 1.

Algorithm 1: Offloading Preprocessing

---

1 **Input:** $G = (V, E)$; and all $w_i = (w_i^E, w_i^C)$, $w_{ij} = (w_{ij}^1, w_{ij}^2, w_{ij}^3, w_{ij}^4)$ for
    $i \in [1, n]$, $j \in [1, n]$;
2 **Output:** sets: V, V_E, V_C;
3 **Initialize:** $V_E \leftarrow \emptyset$, $V_C \leftarrow \emptyset$;
4 **for** *each $i = 1$ to n* **do**
5   **if** $w_i^E = +\infty$ *or* $w_{ij}^2 = +\infty$ **then**
6         $V_C \leftarrow V_c \cup \{v_i\}$;
7         $V \leftarrow V \setminus \{v_i\}$;
8         $x_i \leftarrow 0$;
9   **else if** $w_i^C = +\infty$ *or* $w_{ij}^3 = +\infty$ **then**
10        $V_E \leftarrow V_E \cup \{v_i\}$;
11        $V \leftarrow V \setminus \{v_i\}$;
12        $x_i \leftarrow 1$;

    return V, V_E, V_C;

Preprocessing does not affect calculation of the offloading problem. We assume that the last $n - m$ points are fixed at the edge or the cloud. The total cost of our offloading problem can be simplified as:

$$\sum_{i,j}^{n} (w_{ij}^1 x_i x_j + w_{ij}^2 x_i \bar{x}_j + w_{ij}^3 \bar{x}_i x_j + w_{ij}^4 \bar{x}_i \bar{x}_j) + \sum_{i=1}^{n} (w_i^E x_i + w_i^C \bar{x}_i)$$

$$= \sum_{i,j}^{m} (w_{ij}^1 x_i x_j + w_{ij}^2 x_i \bar{x}_j + w_{ij}^3 \bar{x}_i x_j + w_{ij}^4 \bar{x}_i \bar{x}_j) + \sum_{i=1}^{m} (w_i^E x_i + w_i^C \bar{x}_i)$$

$$+ \sum_{j=1, i \in V_E}^{m} (w_{ij}^1 x_j + w_{ij}^2 \bar{x}_j + w_i^E) + \sum_{j=1, i \in V_C}^{m} (w_{ij}^3 x_j + w_{ij}^4 \bar{x}_j + w_i^C) \quad (4)$$

$$= \sum_{i,j}^{m} (w_{ij}^1 - w_{ij}^2 - w_{ij}^3 + w_{ij}^4) x_i x_j + \sum_{ij}^{m} (w_{ij}^2 x_i + w_{ij}^3 x_j - w_{ij}^4 x_j - w_{ij}^4 x_i)$$

$$+ \sum_{i=1}^{m} (w_i^E - w_i^C) x_i + \sum_{j=1, i \in V_E}^{m} (w_{ij}^1 - w_{ij}^2) x_j + \sum_{j=1, i \in V_C}^{m} (w_{ij}^3 - w_{ij}^4) x_j + C_1$$

$$= \sum_{i=1}^{m} [\sum_{j=1}^{m} (w_{ij}^2 - w_{ij}^4 + w_{ji}^3 - w_{ji}^4) + (w_i^E - w_i^C) + \sum_{j \in V_E} (w_{ij}^1 - w_{ij}^2) + \sum_{j \in V_C} (w_{ij}^3 - w_{ij}^4)] x_i$$

$$+ \sum_{i,j}^{m} (w_{ij}^1 - w_{ij}^2 - w_{ij}^3 + w_{ij}^4) x_i x_j + C_1$$

$$= \sum_{i,j}^{m} w_{ij} x_i x_j + \sum_{i=1}^{m} w_i x_i + C_1 \quad (5)$$

where C_1 is a constant, $w_i = \sum_{j=1}^{m} (w_{ij}^2 - w_{ij}^4 + w_{ji}^3 - w_{ji}^4) + (w_i^E - w_i^C) + \sum_{j \in V_E} (w_{ij}^1 - w_{ij}^2) + \sum_{j \in V_C} (w_{ij}^3 - w_{ij}^4)$, $w_{ij} = w_{ij}^1 - w_{ij}^2 - w_{ij}^3 + w_{ij}^4$. Equation (5) is obtained from Eq. (4) by replacing $\bar{x}_i$ with $1 - x_i$. Given a matrix $\mathbf{W} = (w_{ij})_{m \times m}$ of order m and an m-dimensional vector $\mathbf{c} = (w_i)_{m \times 1}$. So our objective function is equivalent to the following problem of quadratic $0 - 1$ minimization:

$$(QP_{(0-1)}) \quad min \quad \mathbf{x}^T \mathbf{W} \mathbf{x} + \mathbf{c}^T \mathbf{x}$$

$$s.t : \quad \mathbf{x} \in \{0, 1\}^m,$$

$$\sum_{i=1}^{m} x_i \leq k. \quad (6)$$

For the cardinality constraint Eq. (3) in the original offloading model, we do not need to deal with it here, but change it to Eq. (6).

3.2   Model Analysis

Claim 1. $(QP_{(0-1)})$ *is equivalent to a problem of quadratic maximization problem* $\max\{\mathbf{z}^T \mathbf{L} \mathbf{z} : \mathbf{L}$ *is positive semidefinite,* $\mathbf{z} \in \{0, 1\}^m\}$.

The proof is involved in reference [14] and [1], we state it here briefly. In order to achieve the above result, we introduce the Laplacian matrix. Let $G = (V, E)$

be an undirected graph of $n = |V|$ vertices and $m = |E|$ edges with edge weights a_{ij} for $(i, j) \in E$. And the weighted adjacency matrix $\mathbf{A} = (a_{ij})$. Then the Laplacian matrix $\mathbf{L}$ associated with $\mathbf{A}$ is denoted as $\mathbf{L} = diag(\mathbf{Ae}) - \mathbf{A}$. Where $\mathbf{e}$ denotes the vector of all ones and $diag(\mathbf{u})$ is the operator that maps a n-dimensional vector $\mathbf{u}$ into the n-dimensional matrix $\mathbf{M}$, where $M_{ii} = u_i$ and all the off-diagonal components are zero.

Proof. Set

$$\mathbf{M} = \begin{pmatrix} 0 & -(\mathbf{We} + \mathbf{c})^{\mathrm{T}} \\ -(\mathbf{We} + \mathbf{c}) & \mathbf{W} \end{pmatrix}$$

to be the weighted adjacency matrix of a graph with $m + 1$ nodes($v = \{0, 1, \cdots, m\}$) and $x_0 = 1$, $x_i = 2z_i - 1$ for all $1 \leq i \leq m$.

Inversely, we assume the laplacian matrix

$$\mathbf{L} = \begin{pmatrix} l_{11} & \mathbf{L_{12}}^{\mathrm{T}} \\ \mathbf{L_{12}} & \mathbf{L_{22}} \end{pmatrix}$$

definite $\mathbf{W} = -\mathbf{L_{22}}$, $\mathbf{c} = \mathbf{L_{12}} + \mathbf{L_{22}e}$, $z_1 = 1$, $z_i = \frac{1}{2}(1 + x_i)$ for all $1 \leq i \leq m$.∎

By the Claim 1, we have the following equivalent quadratic program:

$$(QP_k) \quad max \quad \sum_{1 \leq i,j \leq m} l_{ij} z_i z_j$$

$$s.t: \quad z_i \in \{-1, 1\}, \quad \forall i = 1, \cdots, m,$$

$$\sum_{i=1}^{m} z_i \leq 2k - m.$$

Further, the vector programming relaxation can be obtained as following:

$$(VP_k) \quad max \quad \sum_{1 \leq i,j \leq m} l_{ij} \mathbf{v_i} \mathbf{v_j}$$

$$s.t: \quad \mathbf{v_i} \cdot \mathbf{v_i} = 1, \forall i = 1, \cdots, m,$$

$$\mathbf{v_i} \in \Re^m, \forall i = 1, \cdots, m,$$

$$\mathbf{e}^{\mathrm{T}} \sum_{i=1}^{m} \mathbf{v_i} \leq 2k - m.$$

The above program is a relaxation of (QP_k), since we can get a feasible solution of (VP_k) by setting $\mathbf{v_i} = (z_i, 0, \cdots, 0)$ for any feasible solution $\mathbf{z}$ to QP_k. And then relax $\mathbf{v_i}$ to the vector on the unit sphere, where every element is in $[-1, 1]$. Let $O_{(VP_k)}$ be the value of an optimal solution for the above vector program, OPT is the optimal value of (QP_k), it must be $O_{(VP_k)} \geq OPT$.

3.3 Approximation Analysis of (QP_k)

The problem of (VP_k) can be solved in polynomial time. We wish to obtain an approximate solution to (QP_k). If there is no cardinality constraint for the (VP_k), it's similar to the maximum cut problem solved by semidefinite programming, all vector lie on the unit sphere, We choose a random hyperplane with normal $\mathbf{r}$, and let $z_i = 1$ if $\mathbf{r} \cdot \mathbf{v_i} \geq 0$ and $z_i = -1$ otherwise. Details in [2,4]. However, the cardinality constraint changes the feasible region from a unit sphere to a unit hemisphere. Next, we analyze an approximation algorithm on the unit hemisphere.

As shown in the Fig. 3, since $\mathbf{v_i}$ and $\mathbf{v_j}$ are both on the unit hemisphere, assume the angle formed by $\mathbf{v_i}$ and $\mathbf{v_j}$ is θ, $\mathbf{v_i} \cdot \mathbf{v_j} = -1$ when the value range of a normal is in $\widehat{AB}$ and $\widehat{CD}$, then the probability that edge (i, j) is divided into different partition is $\frac{\theta}{\pi}$, where $\theta = \arccos(\mathbf{v_i} \cdot \mathbf{v_j})$.

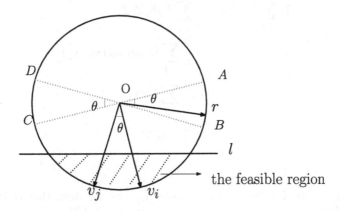

Fig. 3. The probability of edge (i, j) is divided into different partition.

Corollary 1. *For matrices* $\mathbf{A} = (a_{ij})$ *and* $\mathbf{B} = (b_{ij})$, *define* $\mathbf{A} \bullet \mathbf{B} = (a_{ij}b_{ij})$. $\mathbf{A} \bullet \mathbf{B}$ *is positive semidifinite when* $\mathbf{A}$ *and* $\mathbf{B}$ *are both positive semidifinite* [2].

Lemma 1. $\arcsin(\mathbf{v_i} \cdot \mathbf{v_j}) - (\mathbf{v_i} \cdot \mathbf{v_j})$ *is positive semidifinite.*

Proof. Let $x_{ij} = (\mathbf{v_i} \cdot \mathbf{v_j})$, Since $\mathbf{v_i} \cdot \mathbf{v_j} = |\mathbf{v_i}| \cdot |\mathbf{v_j}| \cdot \cos\theta = \cos\theta \in [-1, 1]$, $|x_{ij}| \leq 1$. Set $\mathbf{V} = (\mathbf{v_1}, \mathbf{v_2}, \cdots, \mathbf{v_m})$, then the matrix $\mathbf{X} = (x_{ij}) = \mathbf{V}^T\mathbf{V}$ is positive semidifinite as a conclusion. The details of proof can be seen in [4]. We recall the Taylor series expansion for $\arcsin x$ around $x = 0$ is

$$\arcsin x = x + \frac{1}{2 \cdot 3}x^3 + \frac{1 \cdot 3}{2 \cdot 4 \cdot 5}x^5 + \cdots + \frac{1 \cdot 3 \cdots (2n + 1)}{2 \cdot 4 \cdots 2n \cdot (2n + 1)}x^{2n+1} + \cdots,$$

let $z_{ij} = \arcsin x_{ij} - x_{ij}$, $\mathbf{Z} = (z_{ij})$, we write it as

$$\mathbf{Z} = \frac{1}{2 \cdot 3}(\mathbf{X} \bullet \mathbf{X} \bullet \mathbf{X}) + \frac{1 \cdot 3}{2 \cdot 4 \cdot 5}(\mathbf{X} \bullet \mathbf{X} \bullet \mathbf{X} \bullet \mathbf{X} \bullet \mathbf{X}) + \cdots,$$

$\mathbf{X}$ is positive semidifinite, then $\mathbf{Z}$ is also positive semidifinite as their sum. ∎

Theorem 1. *Rounding based on choosing a random hyperplane is a $\frac{2}{\pi}$ approximation algorithm for (QP_k).*

Proof.

$$\mathbf{E}[Z_i Z_j] = \mathbf{Pr}[Z_i Z_j = 1] - \mathbf{Pr}[Z_i Z_j = -1]$$
$$= (1 - \frac{1}{\pi} \arccos{(\mathbf{v_i} \cdot \mathbf{v_j})}) - (\frac{1}{\pi} \arccos{(\mathbf{v_i} \cdot \mathbf{v_j})})$$
$$= (1 - \frac{2}{\pi} \arccos{(\mathbf{v_i} \cdot \mathbf{v_j})})$$
$$= \frac{2}{\pi} \arcsin{(\mathbf{v_i} \cdot \mathbf{v_j})}$$

By Lemma 1, so the expected value of the solution for (QP_k) is

$$\mathbf{E}[\sum_{i,j} l_{ij} Z_i Z_j] = \sum_{i,j} l_{ij} \mathbf{E}[Z_i Z_j]$$

$$= \frac{2}{\pi} \sum_{i,j} l_{ij} \arcsin{(\mathbf{v_i} \cdot \mathbf{v_j})} \tag{7}$$

$$\geq \frac{2}{\pi} \sum_{i,j} l_{ij}(\mathbf{v_i} \cdot \mathbf{v_j}) \tag{8}$$

$$\geq \frac{2}{\pi} \cdot OPT$$

■

From Eq. (7) to Eq. (8), if we consider l_{ij} one by one, this is false when $l_{ij} < 0$. In this case, we consider the inequality by a global analysis, rather than a term-by-term analysis. Globally, $\mathbf{L}$ and $\mathbf{Z}$ are positive semidefinite. Then, the offloading problem can be solved by Algorithm 2.

According to the objective function, we find that the offloading model is a non-standard quadratic form. We use Laplacian matrix to transform the problem into a standard quadratic program to solve it. Further, we relax the problem to vector programming, because it can be solved in polynomial time. Finally, obtain the solution to quadratic program by choosing a random hyperplane on the unit sphere, which provides a new way to solve the offloading problem. And this algorithm guarantees the quality of the solution to a certain extent.

At fact, we can claim $k \leq \lfloor \frac{m}{2} \rfloor$ in the problem of (QP_k). Otherwise the number of $z_i = -1$ is $m - k$ which is no more than $\lfloor \frac{m}{2} \rfloor$, we can make a change between 1 and -1. This has no effect on the result because the matrix $\mathbf{L}$ is symmetric.

Algorithm 2: Algorithm for the Offloading under Cardinality Constraint

---

1 **Input:** $G = (V, E)$; and all $w_i = (w_i^E, w_i^C)$, $w_{ij} = (w_{ij}^1, w_{ij}^2, w_{ij}^3, w_{ij}^4)$ for
   $\quad i \in [1, n], j \in [1, n]$;
2 **Output:** sets: V_E, V_C;
3 **Initialize:** $V_E \leftarrow \emptyset$, $V_C \leftarrow \emptyset$;
4 Offloading Preprocessing;
5 **if** $|V_E| = k$ **then**
6 $\quad \lfloor$ break;
7 **else if** $|V_E| < k$ **then**
8 $\quad \lfloor$ run $(VP_{k-|V_E|})$;

$\quad$ **return** V_E, V_C;

---

4 Conclusion

We studied the offloading model in the edge-cloud environment to minimize the total cost under cardinality constraint. As a conclusion, the hardness of our model is obvious since we know the same unconstrained offloading problem is NP-hard. The quadratic form by processing the offloading model is equivalent to a normalised positive semidefinite quadratic program. Then relax it to a vector program which can be solved in polynomial time, we can obtain an approximate solution by rounding the optimal solution of the vector program. We get a $\frac{2}{\pi}$ approximate algorithm by choosing a random hyperplane. Furthermore, the offloading model can be considered between multi-systems by adding the fog computing and the local system.

References

1. Barahona, F., Jnger, M., Reinelt, G.: Experiments in quadratic 0–1 programming. Math. Program. **44**(1), 127–137 (1989)
2. Williamson, D., Shmoys, D.: The Design of Approximation Algorithms. Cambridge University Press, Cambridge (2011)
3. Dong, L., Wang, F., Shan, J.: Computation offloading for mobile-edge computing with maximum flow minimum cut. In: Proceedings of the 2nd International Conference on Computer Science and Application Engineering, Article no. 57 (2018)
4. Du, D., Ko, K., Hu, X.D.: Design and Analysis of Approximation Algorithms. Springer, New York (2012). https://doi.org/10.1007/978-1-4614-1701-9
5. Du, M., Wang, Y., Ye, K., Xu, C.: Algorithmics of cost-driven computation offloading in the edge-cloud environment. IEEE Trans. Comput. **PP**, 1 (2020)
6. Fang, X., et al.: Job scheduling to minimize total completion time on multiple edge servers. IEEE Trans. Netw. Sci. Eng. (Accepted)
7. Gao, B., Zhou, Z., Liu, F., Xu, F.: Winning at the starting line: joint network selection and service placement for mobile edge computing. In: Proceedings of the Conference on Computer Communications, pp. 1459–1467 (2019)

8. Hu, Y.C., Patel, M., Sabella, D., Sprecher, N., Young, V.: Mobile edge computing-a key technology towards 5G. ETSI White Paper **11**(11), 1–16 (2015)
9. Hua, Q., et al.: Faster parallel core maintenance algorithms in dynamic graphs. IEEE Trans. Parallel Distrib. Syst. **31**(6), 1287–1300 (2020). https://doi.org/10. 1109/TPDS.2019.2960226
10. Kumar, K., Liu, J., Lu, Y., Bhargava, B.: A survey of computation offloading for mobile systems. Mob. Netw. Appl. **18**(1), 129–140 (2013)
11. Li, F., Yu, D., Yang, H., Yu, J., Holger, K., Cheng, X.: Multi-armed-bandit-based spectrum scheduling algorithms in wireless networks: a survey. IEEE Wirel. Commun. **27**(1), 24–30 (2020)
12. Meng, J., Tan, H., Xu, C., Cao, W., Liu, L., Li, B.: Dedas: online task dispatching and scheduling with bandwidth constraint in edge computing. In: Proceedings of the Conference on Computer Communications, pp. 2287–2295 (2019)
13. Ouyang, T., Li, R., Chen, X., Zhou, Z., Tang, X.: Adaptive user-managed service placement for mobile edge computing: an online learning approach. In: Proceedings Conference on Computer Communications, pp. 1468–1476 (2019)
14. Rendl, F., Rinaldi, G., Wiegele, A.: Solving max-cut to optimality by intersecting semidefinite and polyhedral relaxations. Math. Program. **121**(2), 307–335 (2010)
15. Shi, W., Cao, J., Zhang, Q., Li, Y., Xu, L.: Edge computing: vision and challenges. IEEE Internet Things J. **3**(5), 637–646 (2016)
16. Wang, W., Zhou, W.: Computational offloading with delay and capacity constraints in mobile edge. In: Proceedings of the IEEE International Conference on Communications, pp. 1–6 (2017)
17. Wang, Y., He, S., Fan, X., Xu, C., Sun, X.: On cost-driven collaborative data caching: a new model approach. IEEE Trans. Parallel Distrib. Syst. **30**(3), 662–676 (2019)
18. Wu, H., Knottenbelt, W., Wolter, K., Sun, Y.: An optimal offloading partitioning algorithm in mobile cloud computing. In: Proceedings of the International Conference on Quantitative Evaluation Systems, pp. 3110–328 (2016)
19. Xiao, Y., Jia, Y., Liu, C., Cheng, X., Yu, J., Lv, W.: Edge computing security: state of the art and challenges. Proc. IEEE **99**, 1–24 (2019)
20. Yu, D., et al.: Implementing abstract MAC layer in dynamic networks. IEEE Trans. Mob. Comput. **PP**(99), 1 (2020)
21. Zhu, T., Li, J., Cai, Z., Li, Y., Gao, H.: Computation scheduling for wireless powered mobile edge computing networks. In: The 39th Annual IEEE International Conference on Computer Communications. INFOCOM (2020)
22. Zhu, T., Shi, T., Li, .J., Cai, Z., Zhou, X.: Task scheduling in deadline-aware mobile edge computing systems. IEEE Internet Things J. **6**(3), 4854–4866 (2019)

Quality of Service Optimization in Mobile Edge Computing Networks via Deep Reinforcement Learning

Li-Tse Hsieh[1], Hang Liu[1(✉)], Yang Guo[2], and Robert Gazda[3]

[1] The Catholic University of America, Washington, DC 20064, USA
liuh@cua.edu
[2] National Institute of Standards and Technology,
Gaithersburg, MD 20878, USA
[3] InterDigital Communications, Inc., Conshohocken, PA 19428, USA

Abstract. Mobile edge computing (MEC) is an emerging paradigm that integrates computing resources in wireless access networks to process computational tasks in close proximity to mobile users with low latency. In this paper, we propose an online double deep Q networks (DDQN) based learning scheme for task assignment in dynamic MEC networks, which enables multiple distributed edge nodes and a cloud data center to jointly process user tasks to achieve optimal long-term quality of service (QoS). The proposed scheme captures a wide range of dynamic network parameters including non-stationary node computing capabilities, network delay statistics, and task arrivals. It learns the optimal task assignment policy with no assumption on the knowledge of the underlying dynamics. In addition, the proposed algorithm accounts for both performance and complexity, and addresses the state and action space explosion problem in conventional Q learning. The evaluation results show that the proposed DDQN-based task assignment scheme significantly improves the QoS performance, compared to the existing schemes that do not consider the effects of network dynamics on the expected long-term rewards, while scaling reasonably well as the network size increases.

Keywords: Mobile edge computing (MEC) · Task assignment · Double deep Q networks (DDQN)

1 Introduction

The rapid development of Internet of Things (IoT) has generated a huge volume of data at the edge of the network. This requires a large amount of computing resources for big data analysis and processing, the capability of real-time remote control over both real and virtual objects, as well as physical haptic experiences. Cloud computing has been

This work is partially supported by the National Science Foundation under Grants CNS-1910348 and CNS-1822087, and InterDigital Communications, Inc.

© Springer Nature Switzerland AG 2020
D. Yu et al. (Eds.): WASA 2020, LNCS 12384, pp. 145–157, 2020.
https://doi.org/10.1007/978-3-030-59016-1_13

proposed as a promising solution to meet the fast-growing demand for IoT applications and services. However, centralized cloud data centers are often far from the IoT devices and users. How to provide high quality of service (QoS) to the interactive IoT applications, especially at the edge of the network, is still an open problem. This motivates a new paradigm referred to as mobile edge commuting (MEC), also called multi-access edge computing or fog computing, which extends cloud computing to the network edge [1, 2]. Edge nodes or edge devices provide computing services and carry out computationally intensive application and data processing tasks at the edge of the network between end users and cloud data centers. They can be computing servers or micro data centers deployed with routers, gateways, and access points in wireless access networks, and can also correspond to portable devices such as mobile phones, drones, robots, and vehicles with excessive computing resources that can be utilized to offer services to others. MEC can reduce transmission latency and alleviate network congestion. It also allows network operators to provide value-added real-time services and enhance QoS to end users.

A resource demand estimation and provisioning scheme for an edge micro data center is presented in [3] to maximize resource utilization. In [4], the authors proposed a hierarchical game framework to model the interactions where the edge nodes help the cloud data center operators process delay-sensitive tasks from mobile users and to determine the edge node resource allocation, service price, and pairing of edge nodes and data center operators with Stackelberg game and matching theory. These works focus on the interaction between edge nodes and cloud data centers to better serve the users, but they either abstract the MEC layer as a single edge server or assume that the edge nodes are independent of each other without consideration of their cooperation in processing tasks. The authors in [5] proposed an offloading scheme that allows a MEC edge node to forward its tasks to its neighboring edge nodes for execution to balance the workload fluctuations on different nodes and reduce the service delay. However, the paper made many idealized assumptions in assigning the tasks to the edge nodes, such as a fixed task arrival rate at each edge node as well as pre-known queuing delay of each node and transmission delay between the nodes. Their task assignment algorithm utilizes the classical model-based techniques that relies on these idealized assumptions to minimize service delay for one-shot optimization under a given deterministic MEC network state. Such an approach fails to capture the broad range of network parameters and ignores the impacts of dynamic network situations and heterogeneous nodes to the network performance.

On the other hand, reinforcement learning techniques can capture a wide range of control parameters and learn the optimal action, i.e. the policy for task assignments, with no or minimal assumptions on the underlying network dynamics. The conventional Q-learning algorithm is based on a tabular setting with high memory usage and computation requirements and is known to overestimate action values under certain conditions [6]. Recently, double deep Q networks (double DQN or DDQN) were introduced to address the problems of conventional Q-learning, which combines double Q-learning with two deep neural networks [7]. DDQN can provide large-scale function approximation with a low error and reduces the overestimations.

In this paper, we propose an online DDQN-based algorithm for task assignment in dynamic MEC networks, which accounts for both performance and complexity.

The proposed algorithm takes into consideration the cooperation among the edge nodes as well as the cooperation between the edge nodes and a cloud data center. It performs sequential task assignment decisions in a series of control epochs to enable the nodes to help each other process user tasks and optimize a long-term expected QoS reward in terms of the service delay and task drop rate. The algorithm is designed to operate under stochastic and time-varying task arrivals, node processing capabilities, and network communication delays without a prior knowledge of these underlying dynamics. A decomposition technique is also introduced to reduce computational complexity in DDQN learning.

The remainder of the paper is organized as follows: Sect. 2 describes the problem formulation. In Sect. 3, we derive the online DDQN-learning based cooperative MEC task assignment algorithm in detail. In Sect. 4, we provide the numerical experimental results. Finally, the conclusions are given in Sect. 5.

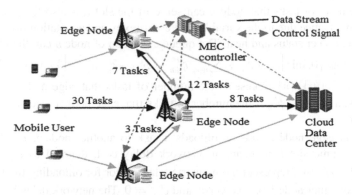

Fig. 1. An example MEC system model.

2   Problem Formulation

Figure 1 illustrates an example MEC system model for consideration in this paper. A set of N edge nodes, $\mathcal{N} = \{1, \ldots, N\}$, with computing, storage, and communication resources are co-located or integrated with cellular base stations (BSs) or WiFi access points (APs) in a wireless access network. IoT devices or mobile users connect to nearby edge nodes through their cellular or WiFi radios and send their computation-intensive tasks to the edge nodes to be processed. When an edge node receives tasks from its associated users, it either processes them locally, or forwards part or all of its unprocessed tasks to other edge nodes or to a remote cloud data center for processing if the node does not have sufficient resources to complete all the tasks. The remote cloud data center, n_c is modeled as a special node that is equipped with powerful computing capability but incurs a high network delay due to the distant location.

We assume that the system operates over discrete scheduling slots of equal time duration. At the beginning of a time slot t, a controller in the MEC network collects the network conditions and determines a task assignment matrix, $\mathbf{\Phi}^t = [\phi_{n,j}^t : n, j \in \mathcal{N} \cup n_c]$. It informs the edge nodes to offload or receive computing tasks to/from the other nodes depending on the task assignment, where $\boldsymbol{\phi}_n^t = [\phi_{n,j}^t, \phi_{j,n}^t : j \in \mathcal{N} \cup n_c]$ represents the task assignment vector regarding edge node n. $\phi_{n,j}^t$ specifies the number of tasks that edge node n will send to node j for processing in the time slot t, and $\phi_{n,n}^t$ is the number of tasks that are processed locally by edge node n. We assume that the data center n_c will process all the received tasks by itself without offloading them to the edge nodes, i.e. $\phi_{n_c,j}^t = 0, j \in \mathcal{N}$.

We first formulate the problem of stochastic task assignment optimization and then explore the methods to solve the optimization problem. Each edge node maintains a queue buffering the tasks received from its users, and q_n^t represents the queue length of node n at the beginning of time slot t. The queue size is bounded as $q_n^{(max)}$. It is assumed that the number of computational tasks arrived at edge node n in time slot t, A_n^t, is random and its distribution is unknown in advance. We denote $A^t = \{A_n^t : n \in \mathcal{N}\}$. The task processing capability of node n in time slot t, denoted as s_n^t, which is the maximal number of tasks that node n can serve in the slot t, is also time-varying and unknown in advance due to the variable task complexity and adaptation of CPU cycles based on the power status and heat. The queue evolution of node n can then be written as $q_n^{t+1} = \max\{0, \min\left[q_n^t + A_n^t + \sum_{i \in e_n} \phi_{i,n}^t - \phi_{n,i}^t - s_n^t, q_n^{(max)}\right]\}$, where $\sum_{i \in e_n} \phi_{n,i}^t$ with $e_n = \{\mathcal{N} \cup n_c\} \backslash \{n\}$ represents the number of tasks that edge node n offloads to other nodes, and $\sum_{i \in e_n} \phi_{i,n}^t$ is the number of tasks that edge node n receives from other nodes in slot t.

When an edge node n, $n \in \mathcal{N}$ offloads a task to another node j, $j \in \mathcal{N} \cup n_c$ for execution at time slot t, it incurs an network delay cost, denoted as $c_{n,j}^t$. Let $\boldsymbol{c}_n^t = (c_{n,j}^t, c_{j,n}^t : j \in \mathcal{N} \cup n_c)$ represent the network delay vector for offloading the tasks from node n to any other node j, or vice versa, and $c_{n,n}^t = 0$. The network delay between two nodes is also time-varying and unknown in advance due to dynamic network conditions, traffic load, and many other uncertain factors. For a node n, $n \in \mathcal{N} \cup n_c$, at the beginning of time slot t, we characterize its state by its queue size q_n^t, its task processing capability s_n^t, and the delay cost to offload a task to other nodes $\boldsymbol{c}_n^t$, thus $\boldsymbol{\chi}_n^t = \left(q_n^t, s_n^t, \boldsymbol{c}_n^t\right)$. The global state of the MEC network at the beginning of scheduling slot t can be expressed as $\boldsymbol{\chi}^t = (\boldsymbol{\chi}_n^t : n \in \mathcal{N} \cup n_c) = (\boldsymbol{q}^t, \boldsymbol{s}^t, \boldsymbol{c}^t) \in X$, where $\boldsymbol{q}^t = \{q_n^t : n \in \mathcal{N} \cup n_c\}$, $\boldsymbol{s}^t = \{s_n^t : n \in \mathcal{N} \cup n_c\}$, $\boldsymbol{c}^t = \{\boldsymbol{c}_n^t : n \in \mathcal{N} \cup n_c\}$, and X represents the whole MEC system state space.

We consider real-time interactive IoT applications and employ the task service delay and task drop rate to measure the system QoS. The task service delay, d_n^t, is defined as the duration from the time a task arrives at an edge node to the time it is served, and the task drop rate, o_n^t, is defined as the number of dropped tasks per unit of time. Given the MEC network state, $\boldsymbol{\chi}^t = (\boldsymbol{q}^t, \boldsymbol{s}^t, \boldsymbol{c}^t)$ at the beginning of a time slot t, a task assignment $\boldsymbol{\Phi}^t = \boldsymbol{\Phi}(\boldsymbol{\chi}^t) = [\phi_{n,j}(\boldsymbol{\chi}^t) : n, j \in \mathcal{N} \cup n_c]$ is performed, which results in an instantaneous QoS reward. We define the instantaneous QoS reward at time slot t as

$$U(\chi^t, \Phi(\chi^t)) = \sum\nolimits_{n \in \mathcal{N}} [w_d U_n^{(d)}(\chi^t, \Phi(\chi^t)) + w_o U_n^{(o)}(\chi^t, \Phi(\chi^t))], \tag{1}$$

where $U_n^{(d)}(.)$ and $U_n^{(o)}(.)$ measure the satisfaction of the service delay and task drop rate, respectively. w_d and w_o are the weight factors indicating the importance of delay and task drop in the reward function of the MEC system, respectively.

As mentioned before, the task arrivals and network states are non-deterministic and vary over time. We therefore want to cast the task assignment as a dynamic stochastic optimization problem, which maximizes the expected long-term QoS reward of an MEC network while ensuring the service delay and task drop rate are within their respective acceptable thresholds. More specifically, we define $V(\chi, \Phi) = \mathrm{E}\big[(1 - \gamma) \sum_{t=1}^{\infty} \gamma^{t-1} U(\chi^t, \Phi(\chi^t)) | \chi^1\big]$ as the discounted expected value of the long-term QoS reward of an MEC network, where $\gamma \in [0, 1)$ is a discount factor that discounts the QoS rewards received in the future, and $(\gamma)^{t-1}$ denotes the discount to the $(t - 1)$-th power. χ^1 is the initial network state. $V(\chi, \Phi)$ is also termed as the state value function of the MEC network in state χ under task assignment policy Φ. Therefore, the objective is to design an optimal task assignment control policy Φ^* that maximizes the expected discounted long-term QoS reward, that is,

$$\Phi^* = \arg \max_{\Phi}(V(\chi, \Phi))$$
$$\text{subject to } d_n^t \le d^{(\max)}, o_n^t \le o^{(\max)}, \forall : n \in \mathcal{N} \cup n_c \tag{2}$$

where $d^{(\max)}$ and $o^{(\max)}$ are the maximal tolerance thresholds for the service delay and the task drop rate, respectively. $V^*(\chi) = V(\chi, \Phi^*)$ is the optimal state value function. We assume that the probability of a network state in the subsequent slot depends only on the state attained in the present slot and the control policy, i.e. the MEC network state χ^t follows a controlled Markov process across the time slots. The task assignment problem can then be formulated as a Markov decision process (MDP) with the discounted reward criterion, and the optimal task assignment control policy can be obtained by solving the following Bellman's optimality equation [8],

$$V^*(\chi) = \max_{\Phi}\Big\{(1 - \gamma)U(\chi, \Phi(\chi)) + \gamma \sum\nolimits_{\chi'} \Pr\{\chi'|\chi, \Phi(\chi)\}V^*(\chi')\Big\}, \tag{3}$$

where $\chi' = \{q', s', c'\}$ is the subsequent MEC network state, and $\Pr\{\chi'|\chi, \Phi(\chi)\}$ represents the state transition probability to the next state χ' if the task assignment $\Phi(\chi)$ is performed in state χ. $q' = \{q_n' : n \in \mathcal{N} \cup n_c\}$, $s' = \{s_n' : n \in \mathcal{N} \cup n_c\}$, and $c' = \{c_n' : n \in \mathcal{N} \cup n_c\}$ are the queue, task processing capability, and network delay states in the subsequent time slot.

The traditional solutions to (3) are based on value iteration, policy iteration, and dynamic programming [9, 10], but these methods require a full knowledge of the network state transition probabilities and task arrival statistics that are unknown beforehand in our dynamic network case. Thus, we seek the online reinforcement learning approach which does not have such a requirement. In previous research, we introduced an algorithm based on conventional Q-learning [6], which defines an evaluation function, called Q function,

$Q(\boldsymbol{\chi}, \boldsymbol{\Phi}) = (1 - \gamma)U(\boldsymbol{\chi}, \boldsymbol{\Phi}) + \gamma \sum_{\chi'} \Pr\{\chi'|\boldsymbol{\chi}, \boldsymbol{\Phi}\}Q(\chi', \boldsymbol{\Phi})$ and learns an optimal state-action value table in a recursive way to decide the optimal task assignment control policy for each time slot. However, for the cooperative MEC network, the task assignment decision-making for a node depends on not only its own resource availability and queue state, but also is affected by the resource availabilities and queue states of other nodes. The system state space and control action space grows rapidly as the number of involved nodes increases. The conventional tabular-based Q-learning process will search and update a large state-action value table, which incurs high memory usage and computation complexity.

3 Optimal Task Assignment Scheme Based on DDQN

In this section, we focus on developing an efficient algorithm to approach the optimal task assignment policy based on recent advances in deep reinforcement learning, which combines Q-learning and deep neural networks to address the state and action space explosion issue of the conventional Q learning with no requirement for a prior statistical knowledge of network state transitions and user task arrivals. Specifically, we design a DDQN-based algorithm to approximate the optimal state value function. In addition, it can be observed that the QoS reward function is of an additive structure, which motivates us to linearly decompose the state value function, and incorporate the decomposition technique into the deep reinforcement learning algorithm to lower its complexity.

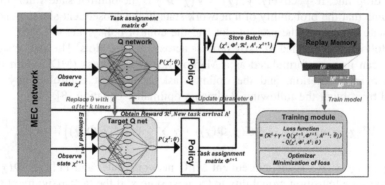

Fig. 2. DDQN-based cooperative MEC task assignment.

Figure 2 illustrates the DDQN-based reinforcement learning scheme for the collaborative MEC task assignment. DDQN replaces the tabular setting of conventional Q-learning with two neural networks, Q evaluation network and Q target network, to learn and approach the optimal state value function and decide the optimal action [7]. The Q evaluation network (Q-eval) is used to select the task assignment matrix $\boldsymbol{\Phi}^t(\boldsymbol{\chi}^t; \theta)$ based on the collected network states $\boldsymbol{\chi}^t$ at the time slot t, and the Q target network (Q-tar) is used to select the task assignment matrix $\boldsymbol{\Phi}^{t+1}(\boldsymbol{\chi}^{t+1}; \overline{\theta})$ at the following time slot

$t + 1$. The parameters θ and $\overline{\theta}$ can be learned and updated iteratively. The standard DDQN algorithm outputs the state-action values and select the action with the maximum Q value. Unfortunately, the traditional DDQN approach in [7] cannot be directly applied to solve our problem because we do not know the number of the new task arrivals in a time slot at the beginning of that time slot. To solve the problem, we modified the Q-eval and Q-tar networks in the standard DDQN to output a probability matrix, which indicates the probability to forward a task from one edge node to another edge node in the slot.

The modified DDQN is used to approximate the optimal state value function in (3) and select the best action. We redefine the state value function (3) as

$$V^t(\chi^t) = \max_{\Phi}\{(1 - \gamma^t)U(\chi^t, \Phi^t(\chi^t, P(\chi^t; \theta^t)))$$
$$+ \gamma^t\Big[\Pr\{\chi^{t+1}|\chi^t, \Phi^t(\chi^t, P(\chi^t; \theta^t))\}U\Big(\chi^{t+1}, \Phi^{t+1}\Big(\chi^{t+1}, P'\Big(\chi^{t+1}; \overline{\theta}^t\Big)\Big)\Big)\Big]\}' \tag{4}$$

where $P(\chi^t; \theta^t)$ and $P'\Big(\chi^{t+1}; \overline{\theta}^t\Big)$ are the probability matrices calculated by Q evaluation and Q target networks, respectively. In the standard DDQN algorithm, the state value will be updated in each time slot and used to determine the optimal action. To simplify the updates, in our implementation, the state value obtained from (4) is stored in a replay memory for training and updating θ and $\overline{\theta}$ in the learning process so that the Q-eval and Q-tar can select the optimal task assignment matrices directly and accurately. The loss function for updating the parameters θ of Q-eval can be defined as

$$\mathbb{L}(\theta) = E\Big[\big((1 - \gamma)U(\chi, \Phi(\chi, P(\chi; \theta))) + \gamma U(\chi', \Phi'(\chi', P'(\chi'; \overline{\theta}))) - V(\chi)\big)^2\Big], \tag{5}$$

and the parameters $\overline{\theta}$ will be updated by copying θ after a predefined number of steps.

At the beginning of each time slot t, the MEC controller determines the task assignment matrix $\Phi^t(\chi^t)$ based on the collected network states and informs the edge nodes of the task assignment decision. The task assignment matrix $\Phi^t = [\phi^t_{n,j} : n,j \in \mathcal{N} \cup n_c\}$ at the beginning of scheduling slot t is determined as,

$$\Phi^t = P^t(\chi^t; \theta^t) \tag{6}$$

An edge node then offloads the tasks to other nodes or receives tasks from other nodes and processes these tasks based on the task assignment decision. The new task arrivals A^t will be counted at the end of time slot t and the new network state is collected and updated to χ^{t+1} by the controller. The MEC network receives a QoS reward $U^t = U(\chi^t, \Phi^t(\chi^t, P(\chi^t; \theta^t)))$ by performing the task processing. The Q-tar network is used to calculate Φ^{t+1}. As mentioned before, the DDQN includes a replay memory that is used to store a pool of the most recent M transition experiences, $\Omega^t = \{m^{t-M+1}, ..., m^t\}$, where each experience $m^t = (\chi^t, \Phi^t, U^t, \chi^{t+1}, \Phi^{t+1})$ is occurred at the transition of two consecutive slots t and $t + 1$ during the learning process. At each slot t, the k previous experiences are randomly sampled as a batch from the memory pool Ω^t to train the DDQN online. The learning process will calculate the approximated overall state value for each experience in the batch and update the parameters θ with an goal to minimize the loss function (5). Once the state value function is converged, we can obtain the optimal parameters θ^* for Q-eval. The optimal policy will be

$$\Phi^* = \mathcal{P}^*(\chi; \theta^*) \tag{7}$$

The MEC network QoS reward in (1) is the summation of the service delay and task drop rate satisfactions of the edge nodes, and the task arrival statistics and task processing capabilities of the edge nodes are independent each other. We can then decompose (4) into per node QoS reward and separate the satisfactions regarding the service delay and the task drops [11]. We first rewrite (6) as

$$\Phi^t = \Phi^t(\chi^t) = \{\phi_n^t(\chi_n^t) : n \in \mathcal{N}\}. \tag{8}$$

n agents $n \in \mathcal{N}$ can be employed and each agent learns the respective optimal state value function through a per node sub-DDQN. An optimal joint task assignment control decision is thus made to maximize the aggregated state value function from all the agents. The task assignment related to node n can be expressed as

$$\phi_n^t(\chi_n^t) = \mathcal{P}_n^t(\chi_n^t; \theta_n^t), \tag{9}$$

where $\mathcal{P}_n(.)$ is the task assignment probability obtained through DDQN n. The state value function in (4) can be decomposed and expressed as in (10) and (11)

$$V^t(\chi^t) = \sum_{n \in \mathcal{N}} V_n^t(q_n^t, s_n^t, c_n^t), \tag{10}$$

$$V_n^t(\chi_n^t) = (1 - \gamma^t)U(\chi_n^t, \Phi^t(\chi_n^t, \mathcal{P}_n(\chi_n^t; \theta_n^t))) + \gamma^t\left[\Pr\{\chi_n^{t+1}|\chi_n^t, \Phi^t(\chi_n^t, \mathcal{P}_n(\chi_n^t; \theta_n^t))\}U\left(\chi_n^{t+1}, \Phi^{t+1}\left(\chi_n^{t+1}, \mathcal{P}_n'\left(\chi_n^{t+1}; \overline{\theta}_n^t\right)\right)\right)\right] \tag{11}$$

With the linear decomposition, the problem to solve a complex Bellman's optimality Eq. (4) is broken into simpler MDPs and the computation complexity is lowered. In order to derive a task assignment policy based on the global MEC network state, $\chi = (\chi_n : n \in \mathcal{N} \cup n_c)$ with $\chi_n = (q_n, s_n, c_n)$ and $c_n = (c_{n,j}, c_{j,n} : j \in \mathcal{N} \cup n_c)$, at least $\prod_{n \in \mathcal{N} \cup n_c} \prod_{j \in \mathcal{N} \cup n_c} (|q_n||s_n||c_{n,j}||c_{j,n}|)$ states should be trained. Using linear decomposition, only $(N+1)|q_n||s_n|\prod_{j \in \mathcal{N} \cup n_c}(|c_{n,j}||c_{j,n}|)$ states need to be trained, resulting in much simplified task assignment decision makings and significantly reducing training time. The online DDQN-based algorithm to estimate the optimal state value function and determine the optimal task assignment policy is summarized in Algorithm 1.

	Algorithm 1. Online DDQN-based Cooperative MEC Task Assignment
1.	Initialize the Q-eval and the Q-tar with two sets of θ^t and $\bar{\theta}^t$ random parameters for $t = 1$; the replay memory M^t with a finite size of M for experience replay.
2.	At the beginning of scheduling slot t, the MEC controller observes the network state, $\chi^t = \{\chi_n^t : n \in \mathcal{N}\}$ with $\chi_n^t = (q_n^t, s_n^t, c_n^t)$, and the Q-eval with parameters θ^t determines the task assignment matrix, $\Phi^t = [\phi_n^t : n \in \mathcal{N}]$ according to (8) and (9).
3.	After offloading and processing the tasks according to the above task assignment decision, the edge nodes will receive new tasks $A^t = \{A_n^t : n \in \mathcal{N}\}$ at the end of slot t.
4.	The controller determines the QoS reward U^t after new task arrivals and calculates the state value V^t according to (10) and (11)
5.	The network state transits to $\chi^{t+1} = \{\chi_n^{t+1} : n \in \mathcal{N}\}$ where $\chi_n^{t+1} = (q_n^t + A_n^t, s_n^{t+1}, c_n^{t+1})$, which is taken as input to the target DQN with parameter $\bar{\theta}^t$ to select task assignment matrix $\Phi^{t+1} = \{\phi_n^{t+1}, n \in \mathcal{N}\}$ at the following scheduling slot $t+1$.
6.	The replay memory M^t is updated with most recent transition $m^t(\chi^t, \phi^t, U^t, \phi^{t+1}, \chi^{t+1})$.
7.	Once the memory replay collect $\bar{M}$ transitions, the controller updates the Q-eval parameter θ^t with a randomly sampled batch of transitions to minimize (5)
8.	The target DQN parameters $\bar{\theta}^t$ are reset every k time slots, and otherwise $\bar{\theta}^t = \bar{\theta}^{t-1}$
9.	The scheduling slot index is updated by $t \leftarrow t + 1$.
10.	Repeat from step 2 to 9.

4 Numerical Experiments

In this section, we evaluate the cooperative MEC task assignment performance achieved by our derived online DDQN-based algorithm. Throughout the simulation experiments, we assume that the processing capability s_n^t, $\forall n \in \mathcal{N}$ of different edge nodes are independent of each other and evolve according to a Markov chain model, each modeled with three states characterizing the high, medium, and low with $\{4, 2, 1\}$ tasks per slot. We simulated multiple MEC network scenarios with different system parameters. Due to the page limit, we present the results for several typical settings. The slot duration is set to be 30 ms. The network delay between two edge nodes, c_{nj}^t, $\forall n, j \in \mathcal{N}$, is also modeled as a Markov chain with three states, $\{1, 0.5, 0.2\}$ slots. Edge nodes communicate with a cloud data center through the Internet. The network delay between the edge node and the cloud data center $c_{nn_c}^t$, $\forall n \in \mathcal{N}$ is assumed to be 10 slots. $U_n^{(d)}$ and $U_n^{(o)}$ in the QoS reward function are chosen to be the exponential functions [12] with $U_n^{(d)} = \exp\left(-d_n^t/d^{(\max)}\right)$ and $U_n^{(o)} = \exp\left(-o_n^t/o^{(\max)}\right)$.

The neural networks used for Q-tar and Q-eval have a single hidden layer with 15 neurons. We use ELU (Exponential Linear Unit) as the activation function for the hidden layer and Softmax for the output layer to output the probability matrices for the action selection. The optimizer is based on RMSProp [7]. The number of iterations for updating parameters of Q-tar is set to be 30, and the memory replay size and the batch size are also set to be 30. The training process will be triggered when the system collects enough samples and it will pull out all samples to train. There are other sampling optimization techniques, e.g. prioritized experience replay, which will be included in our future work.

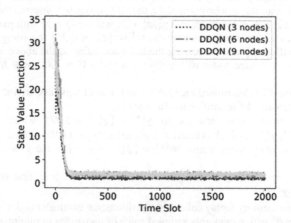

Fig. 3. Convergence of the proposed DDQN-based learning process.

We first investigate the convergence performance of the proposed online DDQN-based cooperative MEC task assignment algorithm under dynamic stochastic MEC network environments with different number of MEC edge nodes. As shown in Fig. 3, we can observe that the proposed algorithm spends a short time period to learn and then converges to the global optimal solution at a reasonable time period which is less than 150 slots. In addition, the network size does not have noticeable effects on the convergence time of the algorithm.

Next, we evaluate the QoS performance of the proposed online DDQN-based cooperative task assignment scheme. For the purpose of comparison, we simulate four baselines as well, namely,

1) No Cooperation: An edge node processes all the tasks it receives from its associated users by itself. There is no task offloading.
2) Cloud Execution: An edge node offloads all its received tasks to the cloud data center for execution.
3) One-shot Optimization: Like the scheme in [5], at each scheduling slot, the task assignment is performed with the aim of minimizing the immediate task service delay. Note that the power efficiency constraint is not considered here because we assume the edge nodes have sufficient power supply.
4) Q-Learning: Task assignment optimization based on conventional Q-learning.

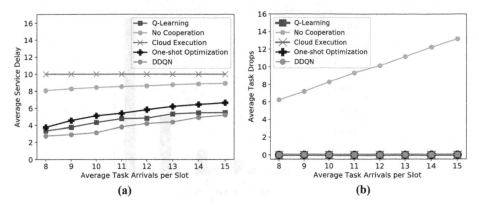

Fig. 4. (a) the average task service delay and (b) the average number of dropped tasks per slot versus the average task arrivals per slot for different algorithms.

Figures 4 (a) and (b) show the average task service delay and the average number of dropped tasks per slot, respectively, for the proposed scheme and baselines, with three edge nodes and one cloud data center as the task arrivals per slot at the edge nodes follow independent Poisson arrival process. The delay is measured in the unit of the time slot duration. We can observe that the DDQN-based and conventional Q-learning based task assignment schemes perform better than the other baselines such as No Cooperation, Cloud Execution, and One-shot Optimization schemes. This is because they not only consider the current task processing performance but also take into account the QoS performance in the future when determining the optimal task assignment matrix under time-varying stochastic task arrivals and network states. Their task drops are zero because the algorithms tend to minimize the task drops, and the edge nodes will forward the tasks to the cloud data center when their buffers are full. For the No Cooperation scheme, an edge node does not send the unprocessed tasks to the cloud and other edge nodes, so that there are tasks drops when the node's buffer becomes overflow. For the Cloud Execution scheme, a large network delay is always incurred to ship the tasks to the cloud data center for processing over the Internet. The One-Shot Optimization scheme performs relatively well. However, it makes task assignment decisions to minimize the immediate task service delay in a slot and may cause shipping many tasks to the cloud data center for processing under fluctuating task arrivals and non-stationary node process capabilities, with such tasks incurring a large network delay.

Figure 5 shows the memory usage of DDQN- and Q-learning task assignment schemes. The traditional tabular Q-learning consumes much higher system resources than the DDQN scheme and cannot scale well due to the explosion in state and action spaces, making the solution unviable. On the other hand, the memory usage by the DDQN-based task assignment scheme scales well as the number of edge nodes in the network increases.

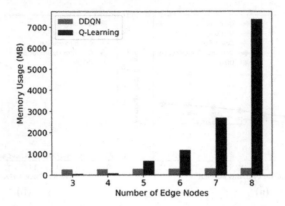

Fig. 5. The memory usage of DDQN and Q-learning task assignment schemes.

5 Conclusions

In this paper, we have investigated the task assignment problem for cooperative MEC networks, which enables horizontal cooperation between geographically distributed heterogeneous edge nodes and vertical cooperation between MEC edge nodes and remote cloud data centers to jointly process user computational tasks. We have formulated the optimal task assignment problem as a dynamic Markov decision process (MDP), and then proposed an online double deep Q-network based algorithm to obtain the optimal task assignment matrix. A function decomposition technique is also proposed to simplify the problem in DDQN learning. The proposed online DDQN algorithm does not require for a statistical knowledge of task arrivals and network state transitions. The evaluation results validate the convergence of the proposed algorithm and demonstrate that it outperforms the traditional schemes that optimize the immediate task service delay with no consideration of the impacts of network dynamics to the expected long-term QoS rewards. In addition, the proposed DDQN scheme can scale reasonably well, and requires much less memory than the conventional Q-learning based algorithm.

Acknowledgements. Certain commercial equipment, instruments, or materials are identified in this paper in order to specify the experimental procedure adequately. Such identification is not intended to imply recommendation or endorsement by the National Institute of Standards and Technology, nor is it intended to imply that the materials or equipment identified are necessarily the best available for the purpose.

References

1. Patel, M., Naughton, B., Chan, C., Sprecher, N., Abeta, S., Neal, A., et al.: Mobile-edge computing introductory technical white paper. White Paper, Mobile-Edge Computing (MEC) Industry Initiative (2014)
2. Liu, H., Eldarrat, F., Alqahtani, H., Reznik, A., de Foy, X., Zhang, Y.: Mobile edge cloud system: architectures, challenges, and approaches. IEEE Syst. J. **12**(3), 2495–2508 (2018)
3. Aazam, M., Huh, E.-N.: Dynamic resource provisioning through fog micro datacenter. In: Proceedings of IEEE PerCom Workshops, St. Louis, MO, pp. 105–110, March 2015
4. Zhang, H., Xiao, Y., Bu, S., Niyato, D., Yu, F.R., Han, Z.: Computing resource allocation in three-tier IoT fog networks: a joint optimization approach combining stackelberg game and matching. IEEE Internet Things J. **4**(5), 1204–1215 (2017)
5. Xiao, Y., Krunz, M.: QoE and power efficiency tradeoff for fog computing networks with fog node cooperation. In: Proceedings of IEEE INFOCOM 2017, Atlanta, GA, May 2017
6. Sutton, R.S., Barto, A.G.: Reinforcement Learning: An Introduction. MIT Press, Cambridge (1998)
7. van Hasselt, H., Guez, A., Silver, D.: Deep reinforcement learning with double Q-learning. In: Proceedings of the Thirtieth AAAI Conference on Artificial Intelligence (AAAI 2016), pp. 2094–2100, February 2016
8. Bertsekas, D.P.: Dynamic Programming and Optimal Control. Athena Scientific, Belmont (1995)
9. Puterman, M.L., Shin, M.C.: Modified policy iteration algorithms for discounted Markov decision problems. Manag. Sci. **24**(11), 1127–1137 (1978)
10. Howard, R.: Dynamic Programming and Markov Processes. MIT Press, Cambridge (1960)
11. Tsitsiklis, J.N., van Roy, B.: Feature-based methods for large scale dynamic programming. Mach. Learn. **22**(1–3), 59–94 (1996)
12. Chen, X., et al.: Multi-tenant cross-slice resource orchestration: a deep reinforcement learning approach. IEEE J. Selected Areas Commun. (JSAC) **37**(10), 2377–2392 (2019)

Camera Style Guided Feature Generation for Person Re-identification

Hantao Hu[1,3], Yang Liu[1,3], Kai Lv[1,3], Yanwei Zheng[4], Wei Zhang[5], Wei Ke[5], and Hao Sheng[1,2,3(✉)]

[1] State Key Laboratory of Software Development Environment,
School of Computer Science and Engineering, Beihang University,
Beijing 100191, People's Republic of China
{zy1806602,liu.yang,lvkai,shenghao}@buaa.edu.cn
[2] Beijing Advanced Innovation Center for Big Data and Brain Computing,
Beihang University, Beijing 100191, People's Republic of China
[3] Beihang Hangzhou Institute for Innovation at Yuhang, Beihang University,
Hangzhou 311121, People's Republic of China
[4] School of Computer Science and Technology, Shandong University,
Qingdao 266237, People's Republic of China
zhengyw@sdu.edu.cn
[5] School of Applied Sciences, Macao Polytechnic Institute,
Macau, People's Republic of China
{wei.zhang,wke}@ipm.edu.mo

Abstract. Camera variance has always been a troublesome matter in person re-identification (re-ID). Recently, more and more interests have grown in alleviating the camera variance problem by data augmentation through generative models. However, these methods, mostly based on image-level generative adversarial networks (GANs), require huge computational power during the training process of generative models. In this paper, we propose to solve the person re-ID problem by adopting a feature level camera-style guided GAN, which can serve as an intra-class augmentation method to enhance the model robustness against camera variance. Specifically, the proposed method makes camera-style transfer on input features while preserving the corresponding identity information. Moreover, the training process can be directly injected into the re-ID task in an end-to-end manner, which means we can deploy our methods with much less time and space costs. Experiments show the validity of the generative model and its benefits towards re-ID performance on Market-1501 and DukeMTMC-reID datasets.

Keywords: Person re-identification · Camera-style guided · Feature generation · Generative adversarial networks · Adaptive batch normalization

1 Introduction

Person re-ID [1–7] aims to match a same person appeared in different camera views. In the test phase, given a query image, re-ID model seeks to retrieve

© Springer Nature Switzerland AG 2020
D. Yu et al. (Eds.): WASA 2020, LNCS 12384, pp. 158–169, 2020.
https://doi.org/10.1007/978-3-030-59016-1_14

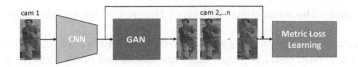

Fig. 1. Conceptual illustration of our method. Given a feature from encoded from an image, this GAN model shall translate it into arbitrary camera styles without changing its identity information. Then these generated features can play as an auxiliary role in the training process.

images with the same identity from non-overlapping cameras. Due to the camera variance in surveillance system, images of a same pedestrian often show significant differences in pose, illumination and background, which increase the intra-class variations in the model and injure its retrieval performance. Current state-of-the-art methods often treat this matter as deep metric learning problem [8–10], or use reformed classification losses to enhance model robustness against intra-class variations [11, 12].

Some other methods [13, 14] use generative models to make image-level data augmentation. Benefiting from the augmented dataset, re-ID model can directly perceive these variations. With the recent rapid progress of the GAN theory [15–18], many GAN-based practices have been proved as a reliable alliance in the re-ID tasks [13, 14, 19–21]. However, they are all coupled with off-the-backbone generative networks which consume high space and time in the training process. Taking Zhun Zhong [14]'s work as an example, the training time of the person re-ID model on the extended dataset only cost about one hour. However, the training time of the generative model, indicated as a bunch of CycleGANs [22] in this task, require another couple of days.

One intuitive solution is to make augmentation in the feature space directly. Several approaches have been presented to explore the feature-level generation. Dixit *et al.* [23] learns a mapping function based on attribute information. Gao and Yin *et al.* [24, 25] introduces a feature-level GAN to explicitly transfer the long-tail distribution occurs in the regular distribution to overcome the limits of low-shot learning.

Based on the above observation, we propose an augmentation method by directly placing style transfer GANs into feature-level, which is deployed after neural networks of the re-ID model, as shown in Fig. 1. For a feature vector extracted from a pedestrian image, multiple samples that remain their identity information but vary their camera-style codes can be obtained through this generative model. Specifically, following the practice of [20, 26], adaptive batch normalization blocks in the generator are designed to overcome the semantic confusion brought by the simple feature concatenation. Finally, we present a light framework, which combines person re-ID model and generative model together. Note that the entire network is deployed in an end-to-end manner.

In summary, the main contributions of this paper are as following:

- To overcome camera variations, a feature-level camera-style guided generative model for person re-ID is proposed. This model can make identity-preserving camera-style transformation in the feature-level, act as data augmentation approach which benefits re-ID model training.
- To alleviate the semantic confusions caused by feature concatenation, Adaptive Batch Normalization (ABN) layer is proposed to make more accurate style transfer through linear affine parts of generative model.
- To optimize system's overall performance in time and space, a lightweight framework is proposed to train generative model and re-ID model in an end-to-end manner.

2   Camera-Style Guided Feature Generation

In this section, we first introduce our GAN-based feature-level generative model, which can make accurate camera-sytle transformation assist by adaptive normalization blocks. Then, a lightweight framework is designed to combine the training process of generative model and re-ID model together, realizing the entire pipeline in an end-to-end manner.

2.1   Generative Model

The generative model aims to make camera-style transformation towards input features while preserving their identity information. Hence, these generated features can work as data augmentation and benefit re-ID model training later on. We first define the input and output of the generative model. To ensure the generation quality of the model, GAN-based losses and camera-style classification loss are introduced into it. Besides, adaptive batch normalization (ABN) blocks are designed to make more precise camera-style injection.

Inputs and Outputs. The entire system takes a pair of images $(x_i|y_i, x_j|c_j)$ as input, where x_i, x_j represent two arbitrary images in the dataset, y_i denotes identity label of x_i and c_j denotes camera label of x_j. Firstly, two separated encoders E_I, E_C (details in Sect. 2.2) are used to extract identity feature f_i^I from x_i and camera-style feature f_j^C from x_j. Then, the generator in the generative model G takes (f_i^I, f_j^C) as input and generates feature f' conditioned on identity label y_i from f_i^I and camera label c_j from f_j^C. The whole process of generative model can be expressed as:

$$f_i^I|y_i = E_I(x_i|y_i) \tag{1}$$
$$f_j^C|c_j = E_C(x_j|c_j) \tag{2}$$
$$f'|y_i, c_j = G(f_i^I, f_j^C) \tag{3}$$

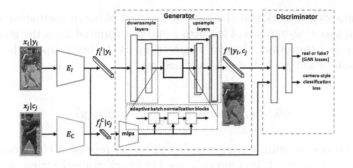

Fig. 2. A schematic representation of the generative model.

GAN Losses. To ensure the reliability of the generated features, an additional discriminator D is introduced into the generative model to fulfil the role of minmax game:

$$\min_{\theta_G} \max_{\theta_D} L_{adv} = \mathbb{E}_{f' \sim P_G}[\log(1 - D_{adv}(f'|y_i, c_j))]$$
$$+ \mathbb{E}_{f_i^I \sim P_I}[\log D_{adv}(f_i^I|y_i, c_i)] \tag{4}$$

where θ_G and θ_D indicates the parameters of G and D respectively. We refer to the loss function in [15,17] as base adversarial training objective function due to its stable performance in the generation process. Therefore, a gradient penalty loss is added to confirm the lipschitz constraint of D:

$$L_{gp} = \mathbb{E}_{\hat{f} \sim P_{\hat{f}}}[(||\nabla_{\hat{f}} D(\hat{f})||_2 - 1)^2] \tag{5}$$

Camera-Style Classification Loss. The generated features ought to be camera-discriminative. To achieve this, an auxiliary classifier is added into the discriminator D to perform camera label classification loss when optimizing G and D:

$$L_{cls}^f = \mathbb{E}[-\log D_{cls}(f'|c_j)] \tag{6}$$
$$L_{cls}^r = \mathbb{E}[-\log D_{cls}(f_i^I|c_i)] \tag{7}$$

Overall Objective Function. Finally, the objective loss functions for G and D can be expressed as:

$$L_D = -L_{adv} + \lambda_{cls}^{cam} L_{cls}^r + \lambda_{cls}^{cam} L_{cls}^f + \lambda_{gp} L_{gp} \tag{8}$$
$$L_G = L_{adv} + \lambda_{cls}^{cam} L_{cls}^f + \lambda_{gp} L_{gp} \tag{9}$$

where λ_{cls}^{cam} and λ_{gp} control the relative importance of camera classification loss and gradient penalty.

Adaptive Batch Normalization. To avoid the semantic confusion caused by feature concatenation, we present adaptive batch normalization (ABN) layers which make camera style injection at the linear affine part of batch normalization layers in G. Given two mini-batches of features x and y originated from the identity feature branch and the camera branch respectively as the layer input, the adaptive batch normalization process can be defined as:

$$ABN(x, y) = m_1(y)\frac{x - \mu(x)}{\sigma(x)} + m_2(y) \tag{10}$$

where N denotes the minibatch size, $\mu(x)$ and $\sigma(x)$ represent the mean and the standard deviation which is commonly used in batch normalization. m_1 and m_2 are both mapping functions which map f_c to the proper dimension.

Other Network Details. The schematic architecture of G is illustrated in Fig. 2. All transition layers in G and D are fully-connected (FC) layers. For G, a U-Net [27] based architecture is used as the network backbone, all normalization layers in the middle transition layers are replaced by adaptive batch normalization layers. Three-layers MLP are used to play the roles of m_1 and m_2. For D, inputs' dimension are reduced gradually from 2048 to 64 in five FC layers. A camera classifier is branched out at the third layers of D to calculate L_{cls}^{cam}. We use leaky ReLU of slope 0.1, and only batch normalization layers in G.

2.2 Overall Framework

To further improve the performance of the entire system in time and space cost, An end-to-end framework is designed to combine the training process of re-ID model and generative model together. The whole training process can be divided into three steps: baseline pretraining, generative model training and joint training, corresponding to Fig. 3(a), Fig. 3(b), Fig. 3(c) respectively.

Baseline Encoders. ResNet50 [28] and ResNet18 pretrained on ImageNet is chosen as the backbone networks for E_i and E_c. For both E_i and E_c, the last FC layer in the ResNet is replaced by a batch normalization layer with the corresponding dimension.

Baseline Pretraining. In this stage, encoders are pretrained as two separated classification problems: A pair of classifiers C_I and C_C are introduced to calculate corresponding classification losses for E_i and E_c:

$$L_{cls}^{id} = \mathbb{E}[-\log C_I \circ E_I(x_i|y_i)] \tag{11}$$

$$L_{cls}^{cam} = \mathbb{E}[-\log C_C \circ E_C(x_j|c_j)] \tag{12}$$

To achieve a higher performance in the identity branch, triplet loss [8] is also computed based on $f^I = E_I(x_i|y_i)$ to enhance the effectiveness of the pretrained model:

$$L_{trip}^{id} = [d_p - d_n + m]_+ \tag{13}$$

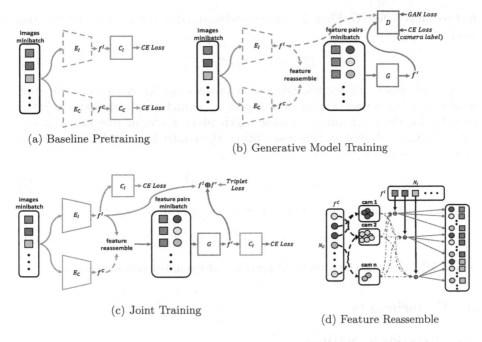

(a) Baseline Pretraining

(b) Generative Model Training

(c) Joint Training

(d) Feature Reassemble

Fig. 3. Overview of the training pipelines of our network. Blocks and arrows represents models and the flow of tensors respectively. Solid lines indicate the model is being trained or the gradient flows unimpeded in the tensor, dashed lines indicate the model is freezed or the gradient flow is truncated in the tensor.

where d_p and d_n denotes the distance measurement of feature pairs sampled in f^I. The 2048-dim feature vector in E_I before the final batch normalization layer is chosen to calculate the triplet loss.

Generative Model Training. All parameters in E_I and E_C are frozen from update since they both act as data providers in this stage. Meanwhile, the generative model with generator G and discriminator D are introduced into the framework. A reformulation method is designed to reassemble identity features and camera-style features in f^I and f^C, as shown in Fig. 3(d). Obviously, f^I and f^C share the same batch size, denoted as N. f^C can be classified into M categories by their camera labels. Then, for each identity feature f_i^I in this batch,one camera-style feature f_j^C is selected from each category to form a feature pair (f_i^I, f_j^C). Therefore, the augmented feature pairs with batch size $N \times M$ are obtained. In this formulation scheme, G and D are fed with augmented feature pairs with the training objective functions mentioned in Sect. 2.1.

Joint Training. The re-ID model and the generator are trained jointly in this stage. All parameters in the system are unfrozen, so the generative model and encoders can update synchronously. Besides the constraint functions mentioned in generative model training stage, the same assemble strategy is used to form feature pairs to feed G. First, f' can be used to enhance the identity classification loss:

$$L_{cls}^{gen} = \mathbb{E}[-\log C_I \circ f'] \tag{14}$$

Second, since this feature generation process can be regarded as feature-level intra-class augmentation, it can provide abundant positive and negative samples for the hard sample mining which plays a crucial role in the triplet loss calculation. Based on this assumption, the triplet loss can be enhanced by augmented features $f^I \oplus f'$:

$$L_{trip}^{gen\&id} = [d_p - d_n + m]_+ \tag{15}$$

Finally, the full objective function in this stage can be expressed as:

$$L = L_{cls}^{id} + \lambda_{cls}^{gen} L_{cls}^{gen} + L_{trip}^{id\&gen} \tag{16}$$

where λ_{cls}^{gen} controls the relative importance of extended classification loss.

3   Experiments

3.1   Experiment Settings

We implement our method on Pytorch Framework. Input images are resized to $256 \times 128 \times 3$. we use random horizontal flip and random erasing (with probabilities 0.5) to preprocess images and set batch size to be 64. The proposed architecture is optimized within 450 epochs (0–60 for baseline pretraining, 60–360 for generative model training and 360–450 for joint training). We adopt Adam optimizer for all networks. For G and D, the learning rate starts with 0.001 and it divides by 10 every 100 epochs. For E_I and E_C, we set initial learning rate 0.00035, and it will decay in 360, 400 epochs with the same decay rate 0.1.

We evaluate the performance of our method on Market-1501 [29] and DukeMTMC-reID [30]. **Market-1501** contains 32668 labeled images with 1501 identities from 6 camera views. The training set has 12936 images with 751 identities. In the inference stage, 3368 images from the rest 750 identities are used as query images to retrieve the matching persons in gallery of size 15913. **DukeMTMC-reID** is collected from 8 cameras with 702 identities for both training and test sets. Similar to Market-1501, it consists of 16522 images in training set, 2228 images in query and 17661 images in gallery. We use CMC curves and mean average precision (mAP) as evaluation protocol for both datasets.

3.2   Evaluation Results

Experiment results are shown in Table 1. Despite a high baseline we adopt in experiment, our methods still achieve remarkable improvement over the previous

Table 1. The performance comparison between our methods and camstyle on Market1501 and DukeMTMC datasets. Results of our methods are marked in bold.

	Market1501				DukeMTMC			
	mAP	Rank-1	Rank-5	Rank-10	mAP	Rank-1	Rank-5	Rank-10
SVDNet [31]	62.1	82.3	92.3	95.2	56.8	76.7	86.4	89.9
IDE [2]	68.5	85.3	94.0	96.3	52.8	73.2	84.0	87.6
KPM [32]	75.3	90.1	96.7	97.9	63.2	80.3	89.5	91.9
PCB [11]	77.4	92.3	97.2	98.2	66.1	81.7	89.7	91.9
HA-CNN [33]	75.7	91.2	–	–	63.8	80.5	–	–
MLFN [34]	74.3	90.0	–	–	62.8	81.0	–	—
LRSO [30]	66.1	84.0	–	–	47.1	67.7	–	–
Camstyle [14]	71.6	89.5	–	–	78.3	57.6	–	–
PN-GAN [35]	72.6	89.4	–	–	53.2	73.6	–	–
FD-GAN [36]	77.7	90.5	–	–	64.5	80.0	–	–
L_{cls}^{id} (Baseline)	75.0	89.1	96.4	97.9	65.0	79.1	90.1	93.8
Baseline+L_{cls}^{gen}	**78.9**	**91.3**	**97.4**	**98.5**	**69.8**	**83.6**	**92.9**	**94.9**
Baseline+L_{trip}^{id}	79.8	91.6	97.0	98.1	70.6	84.6	93.0	95.3
Baseline+L_{cls}^{gen}+$L_{trip}^{id\&gen}$	**82.3**	**92.8**	**97.6**	**98.7**	**74.0**	**86.6**	**93.9**	**95.9**

works. Compared to our baseline, the insertion of classification loss on generated features obtains +3.9% and +4.8% improvement in mAP and +2.2% and +4.5% improvement in rank-1 accuracy on Market1501 and DukeMTMC respectively. In addition, we evaluate the effectiveness of our augmented triplet loss. Even the combination of our baseline and triplet loss already reaches a relative high level, our method still reaches +2.5% and +3.4% improvement in mAP on Market1501 and DukeMTMC. We speculate this by the effectiveness of generation in feature space, the expansion of intra-class sample space restricts feature extractor to reduce intra-class variations.

Table 2. performance between different camera-style injection strategies. 'Onehot' means the identity feature f_i is concated with one-hot camera label as the input of G. 'Concat' means G takes the concatenation of the identity feature f_i and camera feature f_j as input. 'ABN' means adaptive normaliztion block.

	Market1501				DukeMTMC			
	mAP	Rank-1	Rank-5	Rank-10	mAP	Rank-1	Rank-5	Rank-10
Onehot	77.1	90.9	96.7	98.3	67.1	83.8	92.4	94.6
Concat	76.9	91.2	97.1	98.3	66.0	82.9	91.9	94.3
ABN (Ours)	**78.9**	**91.3**	**97.4**	**98.5**	**69.8**	**83.6**	**92.9**	**94.9**

3.3   Ablation Studies

Effectiveness of the ABN Blocks. We compare the performance between simple concatenation strategies and ABN blocks in Table 2. It is observed that the simple concatenation strategies confuse the generator since it cannot figure out which part of the input comes from identity branch and which part comes from camera-style branch. The ABN block, however, can alleviate this problem by shifting the style injection part from the entrance of the generator to the linear affine part inside it.

Influence of Hyper-parameters. We analyze the sensitivities of hyper-parameters in Fig. 4, *i.e.*, the weight of camera classification loss λ_{cls}^{cam} and gradient penalty λ_{gp} which both control the reality of generated features, the weight of extended classification loss λ_{cls}^{gen} which controls the relative importance of generated data. When $\lambda_{cls}^{cam} = 0.3$ and $\lambda_{gp} = 1.0$, our model reaches best score. It is worth mentioning that the camera-style information is not identity-related, so too much pressure on the generation quality objective function result in counterproductive outcomes. We can obtain best performance when $\lambda_{cls}^{gen} = 0.5$. Assigning a too large value λ_{cls}^{gen} reduce the result. This suggests our generative model can act as an effective data augmentation scheme in the appropriate range.

Convenience of the Generative Model. We compare the time and space cost between methods using generative model and not using generative model, as shown in Table 3. Compared to those image-level GAN-based methods which require extra days for the training of the generator, our generative model only introduces limited additional GPU memory cost ($\approx +100$MB) and acceptable training time ($\approx +48$min), proving the convenience and feasibility of our approach.

Table 3. Computational cost analysis of the our generative model.

Method	Market1501		
	mAP	Time (mins)	Memory (MB)
Ours w/o generator	65.0	≈ 42.0	≈ 6500
Ours w/ generator	69.8	≈ 90.0	≈ 6600

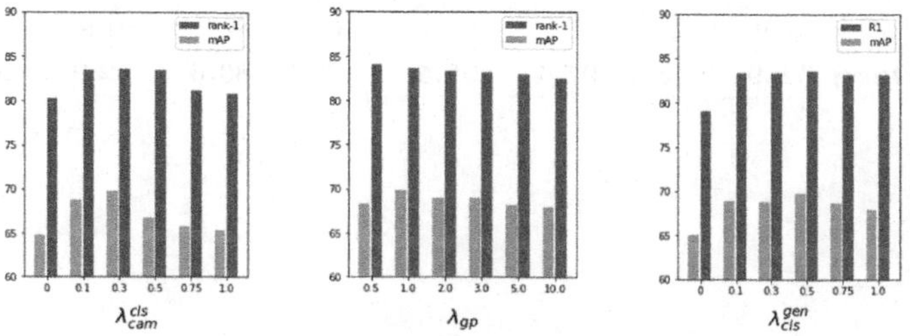

Fig. 4. Evaluations with different values of hyper-parameters.

4   Conclusion

In this paper, we propose feature-level GAN guided by camera-style in person re-ID. Adaptive batch normalization layers are introduced into the system to achieve precise camera-style code injection. Moreover, we design a lightweight framework which fuse re-ID model and generative model together. Experiments have shown these generated features can be used as auxiliary information in the calculation of classification loss and triplet loss, proving the effectiveness and feasibility of feature-level generation as augmentation methods in person re-ID theory.

Acknowledgement. This study is partially supported by the National Key R&D Program of China (No. 2019YFB2101600), the National Natural Science Foundation of China (No. 61861166002, 61872025, 61635002) , the Science and Technology Development Fund, Macau SAR (File no. 0001/2018/AFJ), the Fundamental Research Funds for the Central Universities and the Open Fund of the State Key Laboratory of Software Development Environment (No. SKLSDE2019ZX-04). Thank you for the support from HAWKEYE Group.

References

1. Sheng, H., et al.: Mining hard samples globally and efficiently for person re-identification. IEEE Internet Things J. (2020)
2. Zheng, L., Yang, Y., Hauptmann, A.G.: Person re-identification: past, present and future. arXiv preprint arXiv:1610.02984 (2016)
3. Cheng, S., Cai, Z., Li, J., Fang, X.: Drawing dominant dataset from big sensory data in wireless sensor networks, pp. 531–539 (2015)
4. He, Z., Cai, Z., Cheng, S., Wang, X.: Approximate aggregation for tracking quantiles and range countings in wireless sensor networks. Theoret. Comput. Sci. **607**, 381–390 (2015)
5. Cheng, S., Cai, Z., Li, J.: Curve query processing in wireless sensor networks. IEEE Trans. Veh. Technol. **64**(11), 5198–5209 (2015)
6. Shi, T., Cheng, S., Li, J., Gao, H., Cai, Z.: Dominating sets construction in RF-based battery-free sensor networks with full coverage guarantee. ACM Trans. Sens. Netw. **15**(4), 1–29 (2019)
7. Shi, T., Li, J., Gao, H., Cai, Z.: Coverage in battery-free wireless sensor networks, pp. 108–116 (2018)
8. Hermans, A., Beyer, L., Leibe, B.: In defense of the triplet loss for person re-identification. arXiv preprint arXiv:1703.07737 (2017)
9. Zheng, Z., Zheng, L., Yang, Y.: A discriminatively learned CNN embedding for person reidentification. ACM Trans. Multimed. Comput. Commun. Appl. (TOMM) **14**(1), 1–20 (2017)
10. Lv, K., et al.: Vehicle re-identification with location and time stamps. In: Proceedings of the IEEE Conference on Computer Vision and Pattern Recognition Workshops, pp. 399–406 (2019)
11. Sun, Y., Zheng, L., Yang, Y., Tian, Q., Wang, S.: Beyond part models: person retrieval with refined part pooling (and a strong convolutional bascline). In: Proceedings of the European Conference on Computer Vision (ECCV), pp. 480–496 (2018)

12. Wang, F., Cheng, J., Liu, W., Liu, H.: Additive margin softmax for face verification. IEEE Signal Process. Lett. **25**(7), 926–930 (2018)
13. Zhong, Z., Zheng, L., Luo, Z., Li, S., Yang, Y.: Invariance matters: Exemplar memory for domain adaptive person re-identification. In: Proceedings of the IEEE Conference on Computer Vision and Pattern Recognition, pp. 598–607 (2019)
14. Zhong, Z., Zheng, L., Zheng, Z., Li, S., Yang, Y.: Camera style adaptation for person re-identification. In: Proceedings of the IEEE Conference on Computer Vision and Pattern Recognition, pp. 5157–5166 (2018)
15. Arjovsky, M., Chintala, S., Bottou, L.: Wasserstein GAN. arXiv preprint arXiv:1701.07875 (2017)
16. Goodfellow, I., et al.: Generative adversarial nets. In: Advances in Neural Information Processing Systems, pp. 2672–2680 (2014)
17. Gulrajani, I., Ahmed, F., Arjovsky, M., Dumoulin, V., Courville, A.C.: Improved training of wasserstein GANs. In: Advances in Neural Information Processing Systems, pp. 5767–5777 (2017)
18. Lv, K., Sheng, H., Xiong, Z., Li, W., Zheng, L.: Pose-based view synthesis for vehicles: a perspective aware method. IEEE Trans. Image Process. **29**, 5163–5174 (2020)
19. Deng, W., Zheng, L., Ye, Q., Kang, G., Yang, Y., Jiao, J.: Image-image domain adaptation with preserved self-similarity and domain-dissimilarity for person re-identification. In: Proceedings of the IEEE Conference on Computer Vision and Pattern Recognition, pp. 994–1003 (2018)
20. Huang, X., Liu, M.-Y., Belongie, S., Kautz, J.: Multimodal unsupervised image-to-image translation. In: Proceedings of the European Conference on Computer Vision (ECCV), pp. 172–189 (2018)
21. Wei, L., Zhang, S., Gao, W., Tian, Q.: Person transfer GAN to bridge domain gap for person re-identification. In: Proceedings of the IEEE Conference on Computer Vision and Pattern Recognition, pp. 79–88 (2018)
22. Zhu, J.-Y., Park, T., Isola, P., Efros, A.A.: Unpaired image-to-image translation using cycle-consistent adversarial networks. In: Proceedings of the IEEE International Conference on Computer Vision, pp. 2223–2232 (2017)
23. Dixit, M., Kwitt, R., Niethammer, M., Vasconcelos, N.: AGA: attribute-guided augmentation. In: Proceedings of the IEEE Conference on Computer Vision and Pattern Recognition, pp. 7455–7463 (2017)
24. Gao, H., Shou, Z., Zareian, A., Zhang, H., Chang, S.-F.: Low-shot learning via covariance-preserving adversarial augmentation networks. In: Advances in Neural Information Processing Systems, pp. 975–985 (2018)
25. Yin, X., Yu, X., Sohn, K., Liu, X., Chandraker, M.: Feature transfer learning for deep face recognition with long-tail data. arXiv preprint arXiv:1803.09014 (2018)
26. Huang, X., Belongie, S.: Arbitrary style transfer in real-time with adaptive instance normalization. In: Proceedings of the IEEE International Conference on Computer Vision, pp. 1501–1510 (2017)
27. Isola, P., Zhu, J.-Y., Zhou, T., Efros, A.A.: Image-to-image translation with conditional adversarial networks. In: Proceedings of the IEEE Conference on Computer Vision and Pattern Recognition, pp. 1125–1134 (2017)
28. He, K., Zhang, X., Ren, S., Sun, J.: Deep residual learning for image recognition. In: Proceedings of the IEEE conference on Computer Vision and Pattern Recognition, pp. 770–778 (2016)
29. Zheng, L., Shen, L., Tian, L., Wang, S., Wang, J., Tian, Q.: Scalable person re-identification: a benchmark. In: Proceedings of the IEEE International Conference on Computer Vision, pp. 1116–1124 (2015)

30. Zheng, Z., Zheng, L., Yang, Y.: Unlabeled samples generated by GAN improve the person re-identification baseline in vitro. In: Proceedings of the IEEE International Conference on Computer Vision, pp. 3754–3762 (2017)

31. Sun, Y., Zheng, L., Deng, W., Wang, S.: SVDNet for pedestrian retrieval. In: Proceedings of the IEEE International Conference on Computer Vision, pp. 3800–3808 (2017)

32. Shen, Y., Xiao, T., Li, H., Yi, S., Wang, X.: End-to-end deep kronecker-product matching for person re-identification. In: Proceedings of the IEEE Conference on Computer Vision and Pattern Recognition, pp. 6886–6895 (2018)

33. Li, W., Zhu, X., Gong, S.: Harmonious attention network for person re-identification. In: Proceedings of the IEEE Conference on Computer Vision and Pattern Recognition, pp. 2285–2294 (2018)

34. Chang, X., Hospedales, T.M., Xiang, T.: Multi-level factorisation net for person re-identification. In: Proceedings of the IEEE Conference on Computer Vision and Pattern Recognition, pp. 2109–2118 (2018)

35. Qian, X., et al.: Pose-normalized image generation for person re-identification. In Proceedings of the European Conference on Computer Vision (ECCV), pp. 650–667 (2018)

36. Ge, Y., et al. FD-GAN: pose-guided feature distilling GAN for robust person re-identification. In Advances in Neural Information Processing Systems, pp. 1222–1233 (2018)

Sync or Fork: Node-Level Synchronization Analysis of Blockchain

Qin Hu[1], Minghui Xu[2], Shengling Wang[3(✉)], and Shaoyong Guo[4]

[1] Indiana University - Purdue University Indianapolis, Indianapolis, USA
qinhu@iu.edu
[2] The George Washington University, Washington, D.C., USA
mhxu@gwu.edu
[3] Beijing Normal University, Beijing, China
wangshengling@bnu.edu.cn
[4] Beijing University of Posts and Telecommunications, Beijing, China
syguo@bupt.edu.cn

Abstract. As the cornerstone of blockchain, block synchronization plays a vital role in maintaining the security. Without full blockchain synchronization, unexpected forks will emerge and thus providing a breeding ground for various malicious attacks. The state-of-the-art works mainly study the relationship between the propagation time and blockchain security at the systematic level, neglecting the fine-grained impact of peering nodes in blockchain networks. To conduct a node-level synchronization analysis, we take advantage of the large deviation theory and game theory to study the pull-based propagation from a microscopic perspective. We examine the blockchain synchronization in a bidirectional manner via investigating the impact of full nodes as responders and that of partial nodes as requesters. Based on that, we further reveal the most efficient path to speed up synchronization from full nodes and design the best synchronization request scheme based on the concept of correlated equilibrium for partial nodes. Extensive experimental results demonstrate the effectiveness of our analysis.

Keywords: Block synchronization · Large deviation theory · Game theory · Correlated equilibrium

1 Introduction

Since the appearance of Bitcoin [1], cryptocurrency as the killer application of blockchain piques substantial attention from the whole society to the underlying distributed ledger technology. Research on blockchain from all walks of life indicates its great potential and versatility. It is reported that the blockchain market size over the globe reaches $3 billion in 2020 and is expected to surge to $39.7 billion by 2025 [2].

As the infrastructure of blockchain systems, the peer-to-peer network consisting of peering nodes supports the most important operations of information dissemination and exchange, including both control and data messages.

© Springer Nature Switzerland AG 2020
D. Yu et al. (Eds.): WASA 2020, LNCS 12384, pp. 170–181, 2020.
https://doi.org/10.1007/978-3-030-59016-1_15

To maintain the consistent recognition of the main chain, the synchronization of newly generated blocks among all nodes becomes extremely important. Otherwise, unexpected forks will emerge, which might be exploited by malicious clients to achieve various attacks, such as double spending and selfish mining, and can even lead to the breakdown of a blockchain system.

To enable the synchronization of blockchain, there exist five types of block propagation mechanisms [3], i.e., advertisement, header sending, unsolicited push, relay network, and push-advertisement hybrid. Focusing on the behaviors of nodes propagating block information, we can summarize them as pull-based and push-based. In the pull-based propagation, nodes with timely information of the blockchain, termed as full nodes, respond to the requests of updating block information from neighboring nodes, named as partial nodes, which can achieve block synchronization cost-efficiently in an on-demand manner. While in the push-based one, any node receiving the newly generated block automatically pushes this piece of information to neighbors, which can synchronize the blockchain network quickly but will cause unnecessary communication among nodes. Other works about blockchain synchronization mainly study the relationship between the propagation time and blockchain security at the systematic level [4–7], neglecting the fine-grained impact of peering nodes in blockchain networks.

In this paper, we study the blockchain synchronization in pull-based propagation from a microscopic perspective, using the large deviation theory and game theory to investigate different roles of peering nodes in synchronizing block information. This suggests the feature of *node-level* analysis of this work. Besides, our research is *bidirectional*, which captures the feature of impacts on block synchronization from two main types of nodes in the blockchain, i.e., the full node as the responder and the partial node as the requester. Specifically, we reveal clues about three critical questions: *How will the full node's response capability affect the synchronization? How to efficiently reduce its negative effect on synchronization? And how should the partial node to actively achieve the synchronization?*

In summary, our contributions in this work include the following three aspects:

- The impact of full nodes on synchronization is quantitatively characterized by the concept of response failure rate, which straightforwardly uncovers the synchronization probability of connected partial nodes.
- The negative impact of full nodes on synchronization can be fast eliminated via increasing the decay speed of the response failure rate, and the derived expression of the decay speed indicates that enlarging the response capacity related parameter is more efficiently than improving the response rate. This paves a clear path to facilitate synchronization from full nodes.
- The optimal synchronization scheme for the partial node is established based on the concept of correlated equilibrium, where a Node Synchronization (NS) problem is formulated to guarantee that the partial node can get synchronized without unnecessary cost or redundant response from full nodes.

The remaining of this paper is organized as follows. In Sect. 2, we investigate the most related work on blockchain synchronization. Then we introduce the node-level synchronization model for both the full node and the partial node in Sect. 3, where the full node's response capability is further analyzed in Sect. 4 while the best synchronization request mechanism for the partial node is presented in Sect. 5. All theoretical analysis are evaluated in Sect. 6. And finally, we conclude the whole paper in Sect. 7.

2   Related Work

Similar to traditional distributed systems, there are three levels of synchrony of blockchain networks, namely synchronous, partially synchronous, and asynchronous. As the representative blockchain application, Bitcoin whitepaper [1] provides an initial analysis on its security against forks and double-spending attacks with an oversimplified model. Since 2015, Bitcoin consensus algorithm has been thoroughly investigated considering three levels of synchrony [8,9]. Garay et al. [8] formalize the Bitcoin consensus within a fully synchronous network. Persistence and liveliness are proved to be guaranteed hinging on the synchronous setting. Pass et al. [9] show that Bitcoin consensus satisfies consistency and liveliness in a partially synchronous network, but consistency cannot be satisfied in an asynchronous network.

As the most critical factor affecting blockchain synchronization, the propagation time of control messages and data messages is investigated to reveal how it affects blockchain security against various attacks, such as forks, double spending, and selfish mining, and how to mitigate the corresponding vulnerabilities. The propagation time is shown as the primary cause for blockchain forks [4]. In response, researchers propose three methods to speed up propagation: minimizing verification, pipelining block propagation, and increasing connectivity. Sompolinsky and Zohar [5] study the relation between higher transaction rate and the vulnerability to double-spending attacks, which shows that increasing block size and block generation rate can improve the throughput, but will increase the propagation time so that even weaker attackers can launch double-spending attacks. Besides, the selfish mining is investigated in a realistic setting where propagation time is taken into account [6], indicating that it becomes easier with increasing propagation delay. For PoS-based consensus, Kang et al. [7] propose a Stackelberg game based incentive mechanism to encourage miners to propagate blocks, enabling lower propagation delay and higher security level.

For the propagation mechanism in blockchain networks, five popular categories are summarized in [3], including advertisement, header sending, unsolicited push, relay network, and push-advertisement hybrid. Early on, the advertisement-based propagation is adopted by Bitcoin, which has a two-round message exchange procedure. Afterward, Bitcoin resorts to the header propagation to avoid using *inv* messages. In unsolicited push propagation, miners directly broadcast newly-mined blocks. The relay network, adopted by FIBRE [10], BloXroute [11], and Geeqchain [12], is to distribute relay nodes globally to which miners can connect to and exchange information at a high speed. However, relay nodes are criticized for introducing centralization to blockchain. Ethereum adopts push and advertisement hybrid propagation by which a node can automatically push messages to $\sqrt{n}$ nodes and advertises messages to neighboring nodes simultaneously [13].

In summary, existing works about blockchain synchronization focus on macroscopically investigating blockchain protocol to figure out the relationship between propagation time and security or propose new propagation mechanisms. However, in this paper, we study the blockchain synchronization from a microscopic and node-level perspective, using the large deviation theory and game theory to depict blockchain nodes precisely and investigate how nodes' capability affect synchronization.

3   System Model

In this paper, we assume that full nodes are homogeneous in terms of information request and response performance. Thus, we can shed light on the synchronization status of the whole blockchain system via studying the response capability of any specific full node. And all partial nodes are also assumed to be similar in terms of interacting with full nodes to get synchronized. As full nodes and partial nodes play different roles in blockchain synchronization, we introduce their models separately in the following.

3.1   Response Model of the Full Node

Considering that the requests of updating block information from partial nodes arrive at the full node randomly, we assume that this stochastic event is a Poisson process with arrival rate λ, which is inspired by the typical model of packet arrival process in communication networks [14]. It usually takes some time for the full node to respond and send out the latest block information since the node might be busy on handling other tasks, which can also be assumed as a Poisson process with response rate μ. To guarantee that the full node can finish responding to the requests from partial nodes most of the time, we assume $\mu > \lambda$. However, even with this condition, there might still exist some cases where the full node fails to respond.

To investigate this issue, we define the number of synchronization requests arrived at the full node and that the node can respond during time period $(t-1, t)$ as a_t and r_t, respectively, where $t \in \mathbb{N}^*$. Then we can describe the request queue at the full node as

$$Q_t = (Q_{t-1} + a_t - r_t)^+,$$

where $(\cdot)^+$ denotes the positive part of the inside expression.

Next, we focus on the cumulative arrival and response process, denoted as $A_t = a_1 + \cdots + a_t$ and $R_t = r_1 + \cdots + r_t$, respectively. Thus, the length of the request queue until time t at the full node, defined as L_t, will be

$$L_t = A_t - R_t. \tag{1}$$

Generally speaking, since $\mu > \lambda$, one may expect that L_t would be negative, making it pointless with the definition of queue length. However, due to the randomness of the arrival and response process, the queue length can become positive, which may even overwhelm the response capability of the full node, leading to the failure of responding synchronization requests. To prepare for the worst case of response failure in blockchain, we focus on the maximum possible queue length at the full node when $t \to \infty$, which is defined as $\mathcal{L} = \sup_{t>0} L_t$, and further investigate the possibility of the request queue being over-length, i.e., $\mathcal{L} > \Gamma$, where Γ is defined as follows:

Definition 1 (Response capacity). *The response capacity Γ of the full node is the longest queue of synchronization requests that it can process without any failure.*

According to Definition 1, we can know that if $\mathcal{L} \leq \Gamma$, the fulll node can handle all synchronization requests successfully. But if $\mathcal{L} > \Gamma$, the request queue is too long for the full node to handle, which will make the partial nodes sending block synchronization requests fail to achieve the distributed consistency. To analyze this important event, we introduce the following definition:

Definition 2 (Response failure rate). *The response failure rate is the probability that the longest synchronization request queue arrived at the full node, i.e., $\mathcal{L}$, exceeds its response capacity Γ, denoted as $P(\mathcal{L} > \Gamma)$.*

With the help of $P(\mathcal{L} > \Gamma)$, we can capture the full node's failure of responding to block synchronization requests in a quantitative manner, which provides us a more straightforward clue about the synchronization status of the neighboring partial nodes. Based on this index, we can make adjustment or countermeasure in time to avoid unpredictable loss brought by the asynchronous blockchain information among partial nodes, which will be analyzed in Sect. 4.

3.2 Synchronization Model of the Partial Node

We assume that the number of partial nodes in a blockchain network is N, and each of them has direct access to multiple full nodes to obtain block synchronization information. Specifically, for any partial node, we denote the set of full nodes it has direct connections as $\mathcal{M} = \{M_i\}$, $i \in \{1, \cdots, m\}$, where $m \in \mathbb{N}^*$ is the number of full nodes. And the above-defined response failure rate of these full nodes can be denoted as P_i, $i \in \{1, \cdots, m\}$.

For a cautious partial node, it may send the synchronization request to all connected full nodes so as to obtain a higher successful synchronization probability. Thus, the synchronization failure event can only happen to this partial node when all full nodes failed to respond with the latest block information, which means that the synchronization failure probability is $\prod_{i=1}^{m} P_i$. And accordingly, the successful synchronization probability of this partial node is $1 - \prod_{i=1}^{m} P_i$.

While in a more general case, a normal partial node might need to seriously consider where to send the synchronization request. First, sending the request costs communication resource, and thus generously sending the request to all available full nodes can bring too much burden on the resource consumption for the partial node. What's more, with the assumption that all full nodes have the same new information of the blockchain, it would be enough for the partial node to receive at least one response and thus other redundant responses become a waste. With this in mind, we can see that wisely sending the synchronization request is vital for the partial node, which will be elaborated in Sect. 5.

4   Response Failure Analysis

In this section, we analyze the response failure rate $P(\mathcal{L} > \Gamma)$ in detail. We first focus on the derivation of its decay speed $I(x)$, based on which two critical factors impacting the systematic response are discussed.

We first let $\Gamma = lx$ with $x > 0$. Then according to the Cramér's theorem [15], for large l, there exists $P(\mathcal{L} > \Gamma) = P(\mathcal{L} > lx) \approx exp(-lI(x))$, which indicates that the probability of $\mathcal{L} > lx$ will decay exponentially with the rate $I(x)$ when $l \to \infty$. In detail, we have

$$\lim_{l \to \infty} \frac{1}{l} \log P(\mathcal{L} > lx) = -I(x), \tag{2}$$

where $I(x)$ is the rate function with the following expression

$$I(x) = \inf_{t>0} t\Phi^*(\frac{x}{t}). \tag{3}$$

According to the large deviation theory and the calculation process in [16], we can have the expression of $I(x)$ as:

$$I(x) = x \ln \frac{\mu}{\lambda}. \tag{4}$$

As we mentioned earlier, $I(x)$ reveals the decay speed of response failure rate $P(\mathcal{L} > \Gamma)$. In other words, the larger $I(x)$, the sharper decrease of $P(\mathcal{L} > \Gamma)$, and thus the more successful the block synchronization for the requested partial nodes. With this in mind, we desire to enlarge $I(x)$ as much as possible. On one hand, from the above expression of $I(x)$, one can tell that it is linearly increasing with the response capacity related parameter x when the ratio of the response rate μ to the arrival rate λ is fixed. On the other hand, if x is given, we can see $I(x)$ is logarithmically correlated to $\frac{\mu}{\lambda}$. Therefore, theoretically speaking, increasing x is more effective to improve $I(x)$ than increasing μ/λ, which will be numerically analyzed in Sect. 6.

Considering that x and $\frac{\mu}{\lambda}$ are two main factors impacting the value of $I(x)$, we study them further in the following. As x is based on the response capacity Γ

and the arrival rate λ is a system-wide parameter which cannot be adjusted, we mainly focus on Γ and μ since they are more controllable from the perspective of the full node. In the following, we investigate how to set Γ and μ to meet some specific system-performance requirements on response failure rate. To this end, we first denote a *response failure tolerance degree* as $\epsilon \in (0, 1]$, which acts as the constraint for the failure rate $P(\mathcal{L} > \Gamma)$. And then we introduce the following two definitions.

Definition 3 (Effective response capacity). *The effective response capacity $\Gamma^*(\epsilon)$ is the minimum capacity that the full node needs to provide to enforce that the response failure rate will never greater than ϵ, i.e.,*

$$\Gamma^*(\epsilon) = \min\{\Gamma : P(\mathcal{L} > \Gamma) \leq \epsilon\}.$$

Definition 4 (Effective response rate). *The effective response rate $\mu^*(\epsilon)$ is the minimum response rate requirement for the full node to guarantee that the response failure rate will never greater than ϵ, i.e.,*

$$\mu^*(\epsilon) = \min\{\mu : P(\mathcal{L} > \Gamma) \leq \epsilon\}.$$

Further, we have the following theorems to present the specific results of $\Gamma^*(\epsilon)$ and $\mu^*(\epsilon)$.

Theorem 1. *For $\epsilon \in (0, 1]$ and $\mu > \lambda$, we can calculate $\Gamma^*(\epsilon)$ as:*

$$\Gamma^*(\epsilon) = -\frac{\ln \epsilon}{\ln \frac{\mu}{\lambda}}.$$

Proof. As we mentioned at the beginning of this section, for $l \to \infty$, we have $P(\mathcal{L} > \Gamma) \approx e^{-lI(x)}$. Then it comes to $e^{-lI(x)} \leq \epsilon$ according to Definition 3. Besides, based on (4) and $\Gamma = lx$, we can prove that the value of $\Gamma^*(\epsilon)$ is $-\frac{\ln \epsilon}{\ln \frac{\mu}{\lambda}}$.

Theorem 2. *For $\epsilon \in (0, 1]$ and $\mu > \lambda$, we can calculate $\mu^*(\epsilon)$ as:*

$$\mu^*(\epsilon) = \lambda e^{-\frac{\ln \epsilon}{\Gamma}}.$$

Proof. Similar to the proof of Theorem 1, due to $P(\mathcal{L} > \Gamma) \approx e^{-lI(x)} \leq \epsilon$, we can have $lx \ln \frac{\mu}{\lambda} \geq -\ln \epsilon$, which leads to the result of $\mu^*(\epsilon)$.

5   Correlated Equilibrium Based Node Synchronization Mechanism

As mentioned earlier, the synchronization of one certain partial node is collectively completed by the surrounding full nodes, which heavily depends on how many of them the partial node requests. In fact, each full node has a particular response capability with respect to the synchronization request, which is well captured by the response failure tolerance degree introduced in the above section, and it takes some cost for the partial node to send the synchronization request to a specific full node. For a reasonable and intelligent partial node, it is essential to work out an efficient and effective strategy to select the subset of full nodes as synchronization request targets. In other words, *given different ϵ_i ($i \in \{1, \cdots, m\}$) of all connected full nodes, how should the partial node make decisions on whether to send the blockchain synchronization request to each of them?*

To solve this problem, we first define that the decision strategy of the partial node is $\mathbf{p} = (p_1, \cdots, p_m)$ with $p_i \in \{0, 1\}$, where 0 (or 1) denotes not sending (or sending) the synchronization request to the full node M_i. From the perspective of the partial node, the ultimate goal of this decision is to guarantee that it can obtain the up-to-date information of the main chain from at least one full node. Thus, the profit of deciding whether to send the request to one specific full node M_i is jointly affected by the decisions of sending to other full nodes, which can be defined as

$$\phi_i(\mathbf{p}) = \frac{p_i(1 - \epsilon_i)}{\sum_{j=1}^{m} p_j(1 - \epsilon_i)}.$$

Note that in the case of $\mathbf{p} = \mathbf{0}$, we define $\phi_i(\mathbf{p}) = 0$.

With C_i denoting the cost of sending the request to M_i, we can define the utility of this decision as

$$U_i(\mathbf{p}) = \alpha_i \phi_i(\mathbf{p}) - p_i C_i, \tag{5}$$

where $\alpha_i > 0$ is a scalar parameter.

On one hand, as a utility-driven decision maker, the partial node desires to obtain an optimal utility for each individual decision about one specific full node, which is collectively affected by the decision vector $\mathbf{p}$ about all full nodes and can be described by the following game-theoretic concept named *correlated equilibrium*.

Definition 5 (Correlated equilibrium). *Denote the strategy space as $\mathcal{V} = \{0, 1\}$ with the size of $V = 2$ and a probability distribution over the space $\mathcal{V}^m$ as $G(\mathbf{p})$. Then $G(\mathbf{p})$ is a correlated equilibrium if and only if $G(\mathbf{p})$ makes that for any decision $p_i, p_i' \in \mathcal{V}$, there exists*

$$\sum_{\mathbf{p}_{-i} \in \mathcal{V}^{m-1}} G(p_i, \mathbf{p}_{-i}) \Big(U_i(p_i, \mathbf{p}_{-i}) - U_i(p_i', \mathbf{p}_{-i}) \Big) \geq 0,$$

where $\mathbf{p}_{-i} = (p_1, \cdots, p_{i-1}, p_{i+1}, \cdots, p_n)$ denotes other decisions except for p_i.

The above definition implies that under the correlated equilibrium $G(\mathbf{p})$, there is no motivation for the partial node to deviate from the strategy p_i about sending the request to M_i given other strategies $\mathbf{p}_{-i}$. In other words, the partial node can only obtain the maximized utility with respect to the individual decision via selecting p_i according to the decision vector $\mathbf{p}$ sampled from the correlated equilibrium $G(\mathbf{p})$. It is obvious that there may exist various correlated equilibria meeting the above-defined constraint.

On the other hand, the partial node cares about the overall utility of all decisions about all surrounding full nodes since it reflects the general synchronization status of this partial node, which can be calculated as $\sum_{\mathbf{p}\in\mathcal{V}^m} G(\mathbf{p}) \sum_{i=1}^{m} U_i(\mathbf{p})$. Therefore, we can obtain the best correlated equilibrium for the partial node considering the global optimization goal, which is summarized as the following Node Synchronization (NS) problem.

NS Problem:

$$\max : \sum_{\mathbf{p}\in\mathcal{V}^m} G(\mathbf{p}) \sum_{i=1}^{m} U_i(\mathbf{p}) \tag{6}$$

$$\text{s.t.} : G(\mathbf{p}) \geq 0, \ \forall \mathbf{p} \in \mathcal{V}^m, \tag{7}$$

$$\sum_{\mathbf{p}\in\mathcal{V}^m} G(\mathbf{p}) = 1, \tag{8}$$

$$\sum_{\mathbf{p}_{-i}\in\mathcal{V}^{m-1}} G(p_i, \mathbf{p}_{-i})\Big(U_i(p_i, \mathbf{p}_{-i}) - U_i(p_i', \mathbf{p}_{-i})\Big) \geq 0, \forall p_i, p_i' \in \mathcal{V}. \tag{9}$$

Obviously, the above NS problem is an optimization problem with respect to the variable $G(\mathbf{p})$, where the optimization object (6) is to maximize the overall expected utility for all decisions, constraint (7) is a natural requirement for the probability distribution, constraint (8) refers to that the sum of all probability distribution is 1, and the last one (9) is directly obtained from the definition of correlated equilibrium to achieve individual utility maximization. Besides, via scrutinizing the NS problem, one can find that it is exactly a linear programming problem with respect to the probability distribution $G(\mathbf{p})$. In fact, there exist a lot of efficient algorithms to solve the linear programming problem with polynomial time complexity, such as interior point and simplex-based algorithms.

6   Experimental Evaluation

In this section, we first numerically analyze the key factor impacting the response failure rate $P(\mathcal{L} > \Gamma)$, i.e., the decay speed $I(x)$. Further, the proposed correlated equilibrium based node synchronization mechanism is validated to demonstrate its effectiveness. Specifically, all experiments are carried out using a laptop running with 2.7 GHz Dual-Core Intel Core i5 processor and 8 GB memory. And for the sake of statistical confidence, we report average values of all experimental results via repeating each experiment for 20 times.

6.1   Numerical Analysis of Response Failure Rate

We first plot $I(x)$ changing with the response capacity related parameter x and the response rate μ in Fig. 1. In particular, we use the difference between μ and λ, i.e., $\mu - \lambda$, to capture the impact of $\frac{\mu}{\lambda}$ in (4) on $I(x)$ for easy understanding. Specifically, we set $x \in [0, 1]$, $\lambda = 3$ and $\mu - \lambda \in [0, 10]$.

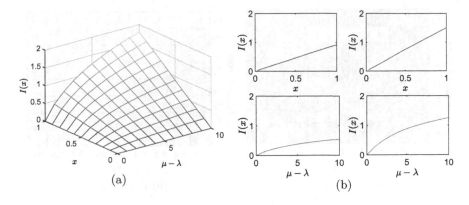

Fig. 1. Decay speed of the synchronization failure rate.

It can be seen that $I(x)$ increases with the larger x and $\mu - \lambda$, which means that we can achieve a higher decay speed for the response failure rate via either improving the response capacity $\Gamma = lx$ or enhancing the full node's response rate μ given a specific arrival rate λ. Besides, via comparing the first and second lines of subfigures in Fig. 1(b), one can tell that the decay speed has different changing trends with respect to x and $\mu - \lambda$, where the increasing x can lead to linear change while the increase of $\mu - \lambda$ can only bring logarithmic variation. Thus, we can conclude that raising the response capacity can achieve a lower response failure rate more efficiently.

6.2 Evaluation of Node Synchronization Mechanism

Next, we explore the effectiveness of our proposed node synchronization mechanism in Sect. 5. In detail, we take the case of $m = 8$ as an example and focus on the decision of sending the synchronization request to the full node M_1 who has a varying response failure tolerance degree $\epsilon_1 \in (0, 1)$ with an interval of 0.1. Other parameters are set as $\alpha_i = 10, C_i = 5$. The request sending decisions are reported in Fig. 2 with two representative cases, where the response failure tolerance degrees of all other full nodes, i.e., M_2 to M_m, are the same and fixed as $\epsilon_{-1} = 0.2$ and 0.8. It is obvious that the request decision vectors in two cases are very different. In the case of $\epsilon_{-1} = 0.2$ in Fig. 2(a), p_1 is 1 until ϵ_1 is larger than others, which means that sending the request to M_i is a good choice until its response failure rate is higher than others. And similarly, when $\epsilon_{-1} = 0.8$ as shown in Fig. 2(b), p_1 keeps to be 1 except for $\epsilon_1 = 0.9$ which is larger than response failure rates of other full nodes.

Finally, we examine the maximized total utility in the NS problem and evaluate its performance under the impacts of the scalar parameter α_i and the cost C_i. Here the number of full nodes is still set to $m = 8$. The experimental results are reported in Fig. 3. From Fig. 3(a), one can see that the maximized total utility keeps the same as zero until $\alpha_i = 5$, which is because we set $C_i = 5$ in this experiment and the profit $\phi_i \in [0, 1]$. This means that only when the profit parameter

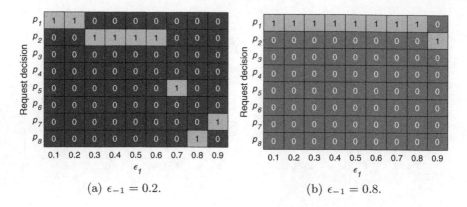

(a) $\epsilon_{-1} = 0.2$.   (b) $\epsilon_{-1} = 0.8$.

Fig. 2. Synchronization request decision of the partial node.

α_i is larger than the cost, can the partial node obtain a positive overall utility. While within Fig. 3(b), it is shown that the maximized utility first increases with C_i and then decreases when C_i is too large. This is because with a lower C_i, the partial node can still obtain a better utility via strategically making the request decision; while when the cost is too high, even the best decision cannot compensate the high resource consumption in request sending process.

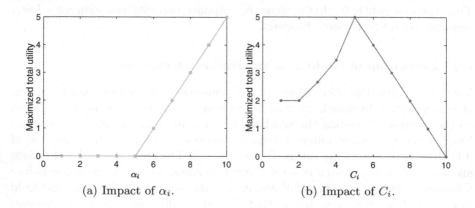

(a) Impact of α_i.   (b) Impact of C_i.

Fig. 3. Maximized total utility of the partial node changing with α_i and C_i.

7   Conclusion

In this paper, we take advantage of the large deviation theory and game theory to study the blockchain synchronization in the pull-based propagation from a microscopic perspective. To be specific, we investigate the fine-grained impacts of peering nodes in synchronizing block information at the node level. On one hand, the full node as the synchronization responder is analyzed based on the queuing model, which reveals the most efficient path to speed up synchronization via increasing the response capacity. On the other hand, the partial node is inspected as the requester, where the best synchronization request scheme is designed using the concept of correlated equilibrium. Extensive experiments are conducted to demonstrate the effectiveness of our analysis.

References

1. Nakamoto, S.: Bitcoin: a peer-to-peer electronic cash system. Technical report, Manubot (2019)
2. Blockchain market. https://www.marketsandmarkets.com/Market-Reports/blockchain-technology-market-90100890.html. Accessed 30 May 2020
3. Gervais, A., Karame, G.O., Wüst, K., Glykantzis, V., Ritzdorf, H., Capkun, S.: On the security and performance of proof of work blockchains. In: Proceedings of the 2016 ACM SIGSAC Conference on Computer and Communications Security, pp. 3–16 (2016)
4. Decker, C., Wattenhofer, R.: Information propagation in the bitcoin network. In: IEEE P2P 2013 Proceedings, pp. 1–10. IEEE (2013)
5. Sompolinsky, Y., Zohar, A.: Secure high-rate transaction processing in bitcoin. In: Böhme, R., Okamoto, T. (eds.) FC 2015. LNCS, vol. 8975, pp. 507–527. Springer, Heidelberg (2015). https://doi.org/10.1007/978-3-662-47854-7_32
6. Göbel, J., Keeler, H.P., Krzesinski, A.E., Taylor, P.G.: Bitcoin blockchain dynamics: the selfish-mine strategy in the presence of propagation delay. Perform. Eval. **104**, 23–41 (2016)
7. Kang, J., Xiong, Z., Niyato, D., Wang, P., Ye, D., Kim, D.I.: Incentivizing consensus propagation in proof-of-stake based consortium blockchain networks. IEEE Wirel. Commun. Lett. **8**(1), 157–160 (2018)
8. Garay, J., Kiayias, A., Leonardos, N.: The bitcoin backbone protocol: analysis and applications. In: Oswald, E., Fischlin, M. (eds.) EUROCRYPT 2015. LNCS, vol. 9057, pp. 281–310. Springer, Heidelberg (2015). https://doi.org/10.1007/978-3-662-46803-6_10
9. Pass, R., Seeman, L., Shelat, A.: Analysis of the blockchain protocol in asynchronous networks. In: Coron, J.-S., Nielsen, J.B. (eds.) EUROCRYPT 2017. LNCS, vol. 10211, pp. 643–673. Springer, Cham (2017). https://doi.org/10.1007/978-3-319-56614-6_22
10. Bicoin relay network. https://github.com/bitcoinfibre/bitcoinfibre. Accessed 30 May 2020
11. Klarman, U., Basu, S., Kuzmanovic, A., Sirer, E.G.: bloXroute: a scalable trustless blockchain distribution network whitepaper. IEEE Internet Things J. (2018)
12. Conley, J.P.: The Geeq project white paper (2018)
13. Wüst, K., Gervais, A.: Ethereum eclipse attacks. Technical report, ETH Zurich (2016)
14. Cao, J., Cleveland, W., Lin, D., Sun, D.: Internet traffic tends to poisson and independent as the load increases. Technical report, Technical report, Bell Labs (2001)
15. Ganesh, A.J., O'Connell, N., Wischik, D.J.: Big Queues. Springer, Heidelberg (2004). https://doi.org/10.1007/978-3-540-39889-9
16. Wang, S., Wang, C., Hu, Q.: Corking by forking: Vulnerability analysis of blockchain. In: IEEE INFOCOM 2019-IEEE Conference on Computer Communications, pp. 829–837. IEEE (2019)

Multi-user Cooperative Computation Offloading in Mobile Edge Computing

Wei Jiang, Molin Li, Xiaobo Zhou$^{(\boxtimes)}$, Wenyu Qu, and Tie Qiu

Tianjin Key Laboratory of Advanced Networking, College of Intelligence
and Computing, Tianjin University, Tianjin 300350, China
{jiangw,molinchn,xiaobo.zhou,wenyu.qu,qiutie}@tju.edu.cn

Abstract. Mobile edge computing (MEC) is a promising technique to
reduce users' response latency by deploying computation and storage
resources at the network edge. In a multi-user MEC system, the MEC
server may not be able to process the tasks offloaded from all users in its
coverage area since it has limited computation resources as compared to
the remote cloud. Device-to-device (D2D) assisted computation offloading may help to relieve the pressure on the MEC server, however, D2D
communication is not always possible due to its short communication
range. To overcome the limitation of D2D-assisted computation offloading, in this paper, we study the computation offloading of computation-
intensive tasks in a single base station multi-user MEC system and propose a cooperative computation offloading scheme to fully utilize the
computation resources of the idle devices. The key idea is that the busy
devices partially offload tasks to the MEC server, and the server can further offload tasks that cannot be accommodated to the idle devices. We
model the computation offloading process as a sequential game and prove
that the process can reach Nash equilibrium. Thus, each busy device can
obtain the optimal decision for task offloading. A multi-user cooperative offloading algorithm is also proposed to solve the problem. Through
extensive simulations, we verify the effectiveness of the proposed scheme
and demonstrate that the proposed scheme can reduce the average task
execution delay, as compared with other three schemes where cooperative
computation offloading is not allowed.

Keywords: Mobile edge computing · Computation offloading scheme ·
Game theory

1 Introduction

With the rapid development of 5G technology, computer vision (CV) and artificial intelligence (AI), new applications, e.g., face recognition, augment reality,
and interactive online gaming, are emerging and changing our daily lives. Due to
their computation-intensive and latency-sensitive characteristics, executing such
applications takes up a mass of computation resources and consumes energy
highly, while the mobile devices are usually limited by energy and computation

© Springer Nature Switzerland AG 2020
D. Yu et al. (Eds.): WASA 2020, LNCS 12384, pp. 182–193, 2020.
https://doi.org/10.1007/978-3-030-59016-1_16

capacity [1]. Resource-limited devices have struggled to meet the users' growing demand for resource-hungry applications, posing a significant challenge to the current cellular and Internet of Things (IoT) networks [2,3].

As a promising technology, mobile edge computing (MEC) has drawn considerable attention from both industry and academia in recent years. The MEC server is located at the edge of the cellular network, which is close to mobile users. In a MEC system, the tasks can be executed on the devices locally, or offloaded to MEC servers with more computing capacities and resources. While offloading can greatly relieve the computation burden at the mobile devices and reduce the task response latency, it should be noted that data is transmitted via the wireless channel to the MEC servers, resulting in additional transmission delay and energy [4]. Therefore, a critical and fundamental problem of MEC systems is how to design efficient and effective offloading algorithms to optimize the system performance [5].

Note in a single-user MEC system, the mobile device can offload tasks to the MEC server as long as the task execution delay and/or the energy consumption is reduced, since the resources of the MEC server are always available. However, in a multi-user MEC system, more sophisticated offloading schemes are required [6]. According to [7], the limited computation resource is not always adequate to support all mobile devices in the coverage of the MEC server. Since the MEC server is "shared" by all mobile devices, it may be overwhelmed by the offloaded tasks if the single-user offloading strategy is adopted at each mobile device independently. In other words, the MEC server can not accommodate the offloading demands of all the mobile devices due to its computation capacity constraint.

A great number of work has been done to alleviate this problem, which can be classified into three categories: (i) The mobile devices make the offloading decisions independently, and the MEC server offload tasks to the remote cloud or other MEC servers once its computing resource utilization exceeds a certain threshold such as [8]. Although the mobile devices can save energy by offloading to other servers or even to the cloud platform, the task execution delay may be increased due to the transmission delay of the backbone network. (ii) The mobile devices make the offloading decisions jointly where the computation capacity constraint of the MEC server is taken into account, such as [9]. In this case, only a part of the mobile devices can enjoy the benefit of computation offloading. (iii) Device-to-device (D2D) assisted task offloading, where the mobile devices can offload tasks to the MEC server, as well as to its neighbor nodes via D2D links such as [10,11]. However, D2D communication is not always possible due to its short communication range.

Due to task arrival rate variation, the mobile devices within the coverage area of the MEC server can be divided into busy devices and idle devices. The computing resources of the idle devices can be utilized to facilitate the task execution on the busy devices, which is ignored in the previous works. To overcome this weakness, in this paper, we propose an efficient cooperative computation offloading scheme for multiple users to further reduce the average task execution delay. The key idea is to fully utilize the computing resources of the idle devices by enabling further offloading from the MEC server to the idle devices. More specifically, the tasks from the busy devices can be executed on local devices, offloaded to the MEC server, or offloaded to idle devices for execution. In order to minimize the task execution delay, task offloading decisions of busy devices are made in a collaborative way. The main contributions of this paper are generalized as follows:

- We propose a novel and efficient cooperative computation offloading scheme for multi-user system to fully utilize the computing resources within the system's coverage area, with the aim of further reducing the average task execution delay. In our scheme, the MEC server is allowed to split tasks and offload them to multiple idle devices separately. Therefore, the busy devices can execute its tasks by themselves, offload to the MEC server, or offload to other idle devices for parallel execution.
- We formulate the task offloading of all busy devices in a time period as a sequential game, and show that the Nash equilibrium is reached when certain conditions are met, based on which the optimal offloading decisions can be obtained. We also propose a multi-user cooperative computing algorithm to solve the formulated problem.
- The performance of the proposed scheme is evaluated by extensive simulations. The simulation results prove that the proposed offloading algorithm can relieve the pressure of the MEC server and obviously reduce the average execution delay compared with other offloading methods.

The rest of this paper is organized as follows. We describe the system model in Sect. 2. The problem formulation and the proposed multi-user cooperative offloading algorithm are presented in Sect. 3. Simulation results and analysis are shown in Sect. 4. Finally, Sect. 5 draws the conclusions.

2 System Model

In the section, we present the overview of the multi-user MEC system considered in this paper, as well as the communication and computation models of the tasks executed locally, offloaded to the MEC server, and offloaded to the idle devices, respectively.

2.1 System Overview

As depicted in Fig. 1, there are one base station (BS) and multiple mobile devices in the communication range of the BS. The MEC server is in the same location as the BS. We discrete the system and divide the total time into T time slots with slot duration τ. We use t, $t = 1, 2, \cdots, T$ to index the time slots. For each mobile device, the tasks arrive at each slot with the arrival rate follows the Poisson distribution. According to the task arrival rate of each device, mobile

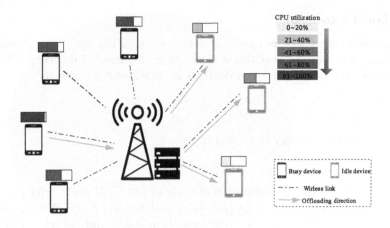

Fig. 1. The overview of the cooperative computation offloading system.

devices are divided into: (1) J busy devices with high task arrival rate, and (2) K idle devices with low task arrival rate. Both the busy and idle devices communicate with the MEC server via the unstable wireless channels.

We consider a quasi-static scenario in which the number and location of mobile devices remain constant during the task execution period. As mentioned above, the idle devices can help to relieve the pressure on the server by allowing the MEC server to offload to the idle devices, therefore, each busy device can execute the tasks locally, or offload the tasks to the MEC server, or offload to the idle devices. We refer to these offloading execution as *local execution, MEC offloaded execution,* and *idle device offloaded execution,* respectively. We assume that tasks can be executed in chunks and partial offloading strategy is adopted by the busy devices, i.e., the busy device will offload a part of its tasks to the MEC server or the idle devices once the offloading decision is made.

Let $I_{t,j}$ denote the size of the input data of the arrived tasks for device j, $j = 1, 2, \cdots, J$ in time slot t. Let $S_{t,j}$ denote the total CPU cycles required to process $I_{t,j}$. According to [12], we have $S_{t,j} = \alpha I_{t,j}$, where α ($\alpha > 0$) is a coefficient that is related to computational complexity of the task.

Since all the devices communicate with the MEC server, it is possible for the MEC server to collect all the relevant information, such as the channel gains and the input data sizes of the devices, to deal with the offloading decisions of the busy devices. Let $D_{t,j} \in \{0, 1, 2\}$ denote the offloading decision of busy device j in time slot t. More specifically, $D_{t,j} = 0$ indicates the tasks are executed locally, $D_{t,j} = 1$ indicates the tasks are offloaded to and executed at the MEC server, and $D_{t,j} = 2$ indicates the tasks are offloaded to the idle devices via the MEC server.

2.2　Local Execution

Let C_j denote the CPU frequency of device j, i.e., CPU cycles per second, and $\beta_{t,j}$ denote the ratio of available computation resources of device j. The delay of executing the tasks locally on device j in time slot t is given by

$$T_{t,j}^L = \frac{S_{t,j}}{\beta_{t,j}C_j}. \tag{1}$$

The corresponding energy consumption is

$$E_{t,j}^L = S_{t,j}e_{t,j}, \tag{2}$$

where $e_{t,j}$ is the energy consumption of device j per CPU cycle, which is defined as $e_{t,j} = \eta \cdot (C_j)^2$ according to [13]. Here η depends on the chip architecture of task execution devices. Since task execution delay and energy consumption are two key performance indicators of task execution, we define the overhead of local execution as

$$V_{t,j}^L = \lambda_j^T T_{t,j}^L + \lambda_j^E E_{t,j}^L, \tag{3}$$

where $0 < \lambda_j^T, \lambda_j^E < 1$ are weighting factors that satisfy $\lambda_j^T + \lambda_j^E = 1$ [11].

2.3　MEC Offloaded Execution

When the tasks are offloaded to the MEC server, busy device j needs to transfer the input data to the server and receive the computation results returned from the server. Since the size of the results is negligible, we do not consider the energy and time consumption of returning the results to busy device j [14].

Because the tasks are partially offloaded to the MEC server, we have to consider (1) devices j transfers the input data to the MEC server, (2) devices j executes the rest of tasks locally, and (3) the MEC server executes the queuing tasks. Let $R_{t,j}$ be the data transmission rate of the wireless channel between the MEC server and busy device j in time slot t, which can be expressed as

$$R_{t,j} = B \log_2 \left(1 + \frac{G_{t,j}P}{N_0}\right), \tag{4}$$

where P denotes the transmission power of busy device j, N_0 denotes the noise power, and B denotes the channel bandwidth. The channel power gain $G_{t,j}$ is exponentially distributed with mean $g_0(d_0/d_n)^4$, where g_0 is the path-loss constant, and d is the distance between busy device j and the MEC server [13].

Thus, the transmission time between busy device j and the MEC server is

$$T_{t,j}^{tran} = \frac{\omega I_{t,j}}{R_{t,j}}, \tag{5}$$

where ω $(0 \leq \omega \leq 1)$ is the proportion of partial offloading. The time that the rest of the tasks executed by device j is

$$T_{t,j}^{local} = \frac{(1-\omega)S_{t,j}}{\beta_{t,j}C_j}. \tag{6}$$

Let C_m denote the CPU frequency of the MEC server and $\beta_t \in [0.7,1]$ be the ratio of available computation resources. The tasks that offloaded from multiple busy devices will be kept in a First Input First Output (FIFO) queue and executed by the MEC server sequentially. We denote the length of the queue when the data from device j arrives in time slot t as $Q_{t,j}$. It is easily to obtain

$$Q_{t+1,j} = \max \left\{ 0, Q_{t,j} + \sum_{i=1}^{J}(\omega g_{t,i}S_{t,i}) - \tau C_m \beta_t \right\}, \tag{7}$$

where $g_{t,i} \in \{0,1\}$ indicates whether it is MEC offloaded execution or not, i.e., $g_{t,i} = 1$ means the tasks generated on busy device j are partially offloaded to the MEC server in time slot t, and $g_{t,i} = 0$ otherwise. Thus, the delay of MEC offloaded execution is

$$T_{t,j}^M = \max \left\{ T_{t,j}^{local}, T_{t,j}^{tran} + \frac{Q_{t,j} + \omega S_{t,j}}{\beta_t C_m} \right\}. \tag{8}$$

Note that mobile devices are powered by batteries with limited energy, while edge servers are usually not subject to power restrictions, so we ignore the energy consumed by the MEC server and only focus on the energy consumed by mobile devices. Therefore, the corresponding energy consumption is expressed as

$$E_{t,j}^M = P \cdot T_{t,j}^{tran} + (1 - \omega)S_{t,j}e_{t,j}. \tag{9}$$

The overhead of MEC offloaded execution is

$$V_{t,j}^M = \lambda_j^T T_{t,j}^M + \lambda_j^E E_{t,j}^M. \tag{10}$$

2.4   Idle Device Offloaded Execution

In idle device offloaded execution, the tasks of busy device j are offloaded to K idle devices via the MEC server. We define $\boldsymbol{\theta}_t = [\theta_{t,1}, \theta_{t,2}, \cdots, \theta_{t,K}]$, where $\theta_{t,k}$ denote the ratio of the tasks that offloaded to idle device k in time slot t. Obviously, we have $\sum_{k=1}^{K} \theta_{t,k} = 1$. During the execution process, we have to consider (1) input data is transferred from the device j to the MEC server, (2) the server distributes tasks to k idle devices, (3) devices j executes part of the tasks locally, and (4) devices k executes other parts of the tasks in parallel. The transmission delay between the MEC server and idle device k is

$$T_{t,k}^{tran} = \frac{\omega \theta_{t,k} I_{t,j}}{R_{t,k}}, \tag{11}$$

where $R_{t,k}$ be the data rate of the channel between the MEC server and idle device k and the execution time on idle device k is

$$T_{t,k}^{idle} = \frac{\omega \theta_{t,k} S_{t,j}}{\beta_{t,k} C_k}, \tag{12}$$

where $\beta_{t,k}$ is the ratio of available computation resources of idle device k, and C_k is the CPU frequency of idle device k. Therefore, the delay of idle device offloaded execution can be obtained as

$$T_{t,j}^{ID} = \max\left\{T_{t,j}^{local}, T_{t,j}^{tran} + \max_k\left\{T_{t,k}^{tran} + T_{t,k}^{idle}\right\}\right\}. \tag{13}$$

The corresponding energy consumption is

$$E_{t,k}^{ID} = P \cdot T_{t,j}^{tran} + (1-\omega)S_{t,j}e_{t,j} + \sum_{k=1}^{K}\omega\theta_{t,k}S_{t,j}e_{t,k}. \tag{14}$$

where $e_{t,k}$ denotes the energy consumption of idle device k per CPU cycle. The overhead of idle device offloaded execution is

$$V_{t,j}^{ID} = \lambda_j^T T_{t,k}^{ID} + \lambda_j^E E_{t,k}^{ID}. \tag{15}$$

3   Multi-user Cooperative Computation Offloading Algorithm

In this section, first we formulate the offloading process as a optimization problem to minimize the task execution overhead. Next we propose an efficient multi-user cooperative computation offloading algorithm that based on game theory to solve the problem formulated.

3.1   Problem Formulation

Recall that tasks on busy devices j can choose local execution, MEC offloaded execution, and idle device offloaded execution. Let $D_{t,-j} \cong (D_{t,1}, ..., D_{t,j-1}, D_{t,j+1}, ..., D_{t,J})$ denote offloading decisions by all other busy devices except device j in time slot t. Because the MEC server can broadcast messages such as offloading decisions, busy device j has perfect knowledge of $D_{t,-j}$, based on which device j can make a decision $D_{t,j}$ to minimize the task execution overhead in time slot t, that is

$$\min_{\theta_{t,k}, D_{t,j}} O_{t,j}(D_{t,j}, D_{t,-j}), \ \forall j \in J, \tag{16}$$

where

$$O_{t,j}(D_{t,j}, D_{t,-j}) = \begin{cases} V_{t,j}^L, & \text{if } D_{t,j} = 0, \\ V_{t,j}^M, & \text{if } D_{t,j} = 1, \\ V_{t,j}^{ID}, & \text{if } D_{t,j} = 2. \end{cases} \tag{17}$$

To solve this optimization problem and get a lower overhead on the whole system, we first choose the optimal $\theta_{t,k}$ which is equivalent to

$$\min_{\theta_{t,k}}\left\{\max_k\left\{T_{t,k}^{tran} + T_{t,k}^{idle}\right\}\right\}. \tag{18}$$

Intuitively, to solve (18), we have to ensure the summation of $T_{t,k}^{tran}$ and $T_{t,k}^{idle}$ of all idle devices are basically equal, this can be done through utilizing the water-filling algorithm.

3.2   Multi-user Cooperative Computation Offloading Algorithm

As can be seen from the problem formulation, the offloading decisions of the busy devices are mutually dependent. We model the offloading decisions of all busy devices as a sequential game $G = \langle J, D, (O_{t,j})_{j \in J} \rangle$, where J is the set of busy devices, D is the offloading strategy set of all busy devices, and $O_{t,j}$ is the payoff function, i.e., the overhead function.

Definition 1. When the multi-user cooperative offloading game reaches the Nash equilibrium, the optimal strategy set $D_{t,j}^*$ satisfies the following properties:

$$O_{t,j}(D_{t,j}^*, D_{t,-j}^*) \leq O_{t,j}(D_{t,j}, D_{t,-j}^*), \forall j \in J, \forall D_{t,j} \in D. \tag{19}$$

$D_{t,j}^*$ is the optimal offloading decision for busy device j, which means that device j achieves the lowest system overhead with $D_{t,j}^*$. This also indicates that the Nash equilibrium of the game can be achieved by making the optimal decision for each busy device [15]. Next, we show the specific conditions to achieve the optimal decision of busy device j in detail.

1) If $D_{t,j}^* = 2$ is the optimal offloading decision for busy device j, we have that

$$O_{t,j}(2, D_{t,-j}^*) \leq O_{t,j}(i, D_{t,-j}^*) \quad \text{for} \quad i = 0, 1. \tag{20}$$

For $O_{t,j}(2, D_{t,-j}^*) \leq O_{t,j}(0, D_{t,-j}^*)$, we can obtain from (3) and (15) that

$$\frac{a}{R_{t,j}} + \frac{b}{R_{t,k}} \leq \frac{\lambda_j^T S_{t,j}}{\beta_{t,j} C_j} - \frac{c}{\beta_{t,k} C_k} + d - f, \tag{21}$$

where

$$a = \omega I_{t,j}(\lambda_j^T + \lambda_j^E P), b = \omega \theta_{t,k} S_{t,j}(\lambda_j^T + \lambda_j^E P),$$
$$c = \omega \lambda_j^T \theta_{t,k} S_{t,j}, d = \omega \lambda_j^T S_{t,j} e_{t,j},$$
$$e = \lambda_j^T(Q_{t,j} + \omega S_{t,j}), f = \omega \lambda_j^E \theta_{t,k} S_{t,j} e_{t,k}.$$

For $O_{t,j}(2, D_{t,-j}^*) \leq O_{t,j}(1, D_{t,-j}^*)$, we can obtain from (10) and (15) that

$$\frac{b}{R_{t,k}} \leq \frac{e}{\beta_t C_m} - \frac{c}{\beta_{t,k} C_k} - f. \tag{22}$$

2) If $D_{t,j}^* = 1$, similarly the conditions can be obtained as

$$\frac{a}{R_{t,j}} \leq \frac{\lambda_j^T S_{t,j}}{\beta_{t,j} C_j} - \frac{e}{\beta_t C_m} + d, \tag{23}$$

and

$$\frac{b}{R_{t,k}} > \frac{e}{\beta_t C_m} - \frac{c}{\beta_{t,k} C_k} - f. \tag{24}$$

Therefore, the optimal offloading decision is

$$D_{t,j}^* = \begin{cases} 2, & \text{if (21) and (22) hold,} \\ 1, & \text{if (23) and (24) hold,} \\ 0, & \text{otherwise.} \end{cases} \tag{25}$$

Algorithm 1. Multi-User Cooperative Computation Offloading Algorithm

---

Input:
    Task $I_{t,j}$, α, N_0, λ_j^T ;
    Parameters: C_j, C_m, η, P, ω, g_0, β_t, d_0, d.
Output:
    The offloading decision: $D_{t,j}^*$;
  1: Initialize decision $D_{t,j} = 0$ for each busy device j.
  2: **for** $j = 1$ to J **do**
  3:    Obtain $\theta_{t,k}$ by solving (18);
  4:    Calculate $R_{t,j}$, $R_{t,k}$ according to (4);
  5:    Calculate $T_{t,j}$, $E_{t,j}$ and $V_{t,j}$;
  6:    Select the best strategy $D_{t,j}^*$ according to (25);
  7:    **if** $D_{t,j} \neq D_{t,j}^*$ **then**
  8:      Update decision $D_{t,j} = D_{t,j}^*$.
  9:    **end if**
10: **end for**
11: **return** $D_{t,j}^*$;

In summary, in each slot t, a busy device selects the optimal decision according to (25). Other busy devices will be updated with this decision via the help of the MEC server, and select their own optimal decision in the same way sequentially. When all the busy devices have selected its optimal decision, the convergence state of the system, i.e., the Nash equilibrium, is achieved. At this moment, busy devices execute tasks according to D^*. The proposed multi-user cooperative computation offloading algorithm is detailed in Algorithm 1.

4   Simulation Results

In the section, the proposed computation offloading scheme is evaluated by simulations. We simulate a region of $200\,\mathrm{m} \times 200\,\mathrm{m}$, where the BS and the MEC server is located in the center and 50 mobile devices are randomly distributed. An example of the device distribution is shown in Fig. 2. The other simulation parameters are listed in the Table 1.

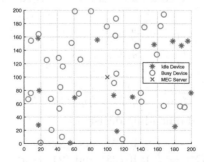

Fig. 2. An example of mobile device distribution with $J = 35$, $K = 15$.

Table 1. Simulation parameters

Parameter	Default value
Transmission power P	200 mw
Channel bandwidth B	10 MHz
Noise power N_0	10^{-10} mW
Input data size $I_{t,j}$	[100, 500] Kb
Factor of CPU cycle α	[1000, 2000] cycles/bit
CPU frequency C_j, C_k	1.5 GHz
CPU frequency C_m	10 GHz
Factor of energy consumption η	10^{-28}
The path-loss constant g_0	-40 dB

We compare the proposed scheme with the following three offloading schemes.

Local: All busy devices execute computation tasks locally.

Local-MEC: Busy devices can execute tasks locally or choose to offload tasks partially to the MEC server.

D2D-MEC [11]**:** The devices can select to offload computation tasks to the MEC server, or to offload to its neighbor device via D2D communication. We limit the D2D communication range to 20 m. As can be observed from Fig. 2, not all the busy devices can have a D2D device.

The average task execution delay curves of the four schemes are shown in Fig. 3, where the number of busy devices varies from 5 to 50. The curve of "Local" is the highest among the four schemes, which is due to the poor computation capacity of the mobile devices. By allowing computation offloading from the busy devices to the MEC server, the average delay of "Local-MEC" is much lower than that of "Local". As J increases, the delay of "Local-MEC" also increases. This is because more and more busy devices choose to execute the tasks locally if the MEC server is occupied. Moreover, as J approaches 50, the curve increases slowly. The average task execution delay curve of "D2D-MEC" exhibits the same trend with that of "Local-MEC". However, the curve of "D2D-MEC" is lower than that of "Local-MEC", this is because the D2D devices can help the MEC server execute some tasks. It is surprisingly to find that, by exploiting the computing resources of the idle devices, the delay curve of the proposed scheme is much lower than other three schemes. As J exceeds 45, the average delay of the proposed scheme increases sharply. Note in the case J = 50, there is no idle device in the cell, the average task execution delay of "Local-MEC", "D2D-MEC" and the proposed scheme should be the same, which is also verified in the figure.

Figure 4 illustrates the average system energy consumption of the four schemes, where the number of idle devices changes from 5 to 50. As can be seen from the figure, the average system energy consumption of "Local" is the

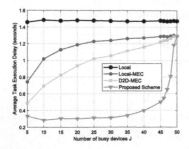
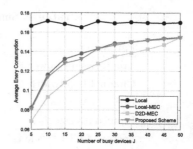

Fig. 3. The average task execution delay.

Fig. 4. The average energy consumption.

highest among the four schemes, since all the tasks are executed locally. On the contrary, the average system energy consumption of "D2D-MEC" is the lowest. The average energy consumption of "Local-MEC" and the proposed scheme are quite close to each other, which is lower than that of "Local" but higher than that of "D2D-MEC". This shows that the proposed scheme is energy-efficient.

5   Conclusion

In this paper, we proposed an efficient multi-user cooperative offloading scheme by allowing the busy devices with latency-sensitive tasks to offload to both MEC server and other idle devices. We modeled the offloading process as a sequential game, and showed how to achieve its Nash equilibrium. Accordingly, a multi-user cooperative computation offloading algorithm is also proposed. Simulation results showed that the proposed scheme can fully utilize the computing resources of the idle devices to reduce the average execution delay of tasks, providing users with better quality of user experience. It is also shown that the increase of the average energy consumption of the proposed scheme is not so significant. In the proposed scheme, we simply assume all the idle devices are willing to participate in the cooperative offloading process which is too optimistic, an efficient incentive mechanism to encourage the idle devices to be involved in the cooperative offloading process is left as a future study.

Acknowledgement. This work is supported in part by National Key R&D Program of China under Grant 2019YFB2102404, in part by NSFC-Guangdong Joint Funds under Grant U1701263, in part by the National Natural Science Foundation of China under Grant No. 61702365 and 61672379, and also in part by the Natural Science Foundation of Tianjin under Grant No. 18ZXZNGX00040 and 18ZXJMTG00290.

References

1. Zhu, T., Shi, T., Li, J., Cai, Z., Zhou, X.: Task scheduling in deadline-aware mobile edge computing systems. IEEE Internet Things J. **6**(3), 4854–4866 (2019)

2. Xiao, Y., Krunz, M.: QoE and power efficiency tradeoff for fog computing networks with fog node cooperation. In: The 36th Annual IEEE International Conference on Computer Communications, INFOCOM, Atlanta, GA, USA, 1–4 May, pp. 1–9 (2017)
3. Qiu, T., Li, B., Qu, W., Ahmed, E., Wang, X.: TOSG: a topology optimization scheme with global small world for industrial heterogeneous Internet of Things. IEEE Trans. Ind. Inf. **15**(6), 3174–3184 (2019)
4. You, C., Huang, K., Chae, H., Kim, B.: Energy-efficient resource allocation for mobile-edge computation offloading. IEEE Trans. Wireless Commun. **16**(3), 1397–1411 (2017)
5. Zhu, T., Li, J., Cai, Z., Li, Y., Gao, H.: Computation scheduling for wireless powered mobile edge computing networks. In: The 39th Annual IEEE International Conference on Computer Communications, INFOCOM, Beijing, China, 27–30 April, pp. 1–9 (2020)
6. Qiu, T., Li, B., Zhou, X., Song, H., Lee, I., Lloret, J.: A novel shortcut addition algorithm with particle swarm for multi-sink Internet of Things. IEEE Trans. Ind. Inf. **16**(5), 3566–3577 (2020)
7. Guo, S., Xiao, B., Yang, Y., Yang, Y.: Energy-efficient dynamic offloading and resource scheduling in mobile cloud computing. In: The 35th Annual IEEE International Conference on Computer Communications, INFOCOM, San Francisco, CA, USA, 10–15 April, pp. 1–9 (2016)
8. Fang, X., et al.: Job scheduling to minimize total completion time on multiple edge servers. IEEE Trans. Netw. Sci. Eng., 1 (2019)
9. Xiao, M., Shan, Z., Li, W., Zhang, P., Shen, X.: Cost-efficient workload scheduling in cloud assisted mobile edge computing. In: IEEE/ACM 25th International Symposium on Quality of Service, IWQoS, Barcelona, Spain, 14–16 June, pp. 1–10 (2017)
10. Yu, S., Langar, R., Wang, X.: A D2D-multicast based computation offloading framework for interactive applications. In: IEEE Global Communications Conference, GLOBECOM, Washington, DC USA, 4–8 December, pp. 1–6 (2016)
11. Hu, G., Jia, Y., Chen, Z.: Multi-user computation offloading with D2D for mobile edge computing. In: IEEE Global Communications Conference, GLOBECOM, Abu Dhabi, United Arab Emirates, 9–13 December, pp. 1–6 (2018)
12. Wang, Y., Sheng, M., Wang, X., Wang, L., Li, J.: Mobile-edge computing: partial computation offloading using dynamic voltage scaling. IEEE Trans. Commun. **64**(10), 4268–4282 (2016)
13. Mao, Y., Zhang, J., Letaief, K.B.: Dynamic computation offloading for mobile edge computing with energy harvesting devices. IEEE J. Sel. Areas Commun. **34**(12), 3590–3605 (2016)
14. Chen, X.: Decentralized computation offloading game for mobile cloud computing. IEEE Trans. Parallel Distrib. Syst. **26**(4), 974–983 (2015)
15. Zhang, F., Zhou, M., Qi, L., Du, Y., Sun, H.: A game theoretic approach for distributed and coordinated channel access control in cooperative vehicle safety systems. IEEE Trans. Intell. Transp. Syst. **21**(6), 2297–2309 (2020)

SDTCNs: A Symmetric Double Temporal Convolutional Network for Chinese NER

Wei Jiang, Yuan Wang, and Yan Tang[✉]

School of Computer and Information Science, Southwest University,
No. 2, Tiansheng Road, Chongqing, China
jw2312@email.swu.edu.cn,645763395@qq.com,ytang@swu.edu.cn

Abstract. Chinese NER is a basic task of Chinese natural language processing. Most current models for Chinese NER can be roughly divided into two categories: character-based models and word-based models. Character-based models cannot effectively utilize the inherent information of a word. Word-based models cannot effectively disambiguate words under different word segmentation norms. In this paper, we propose a symmetric double temporal convolutional network for Chinese NER: SDTCNs. SDTCNs is built on the BERT model and is composed of two symmetric temporal convolutional networks, where one is used to learn the location features of named entities and the other is used to learn the class features of named entities. Finally, a fusion algorithm proposed in this paper is used to fuse location features and class features to obtain the final named entity. Experiments on various datasets show that SDTCNs outperforms multiple state-of-the-art models for Chinese NER, achieving the best results.

Keywords: Artificial intelligence · Natural language processing · Chinese NER · Temporal convolutional network · BERT

1 Introduction

Named entity recognition (NER) is a basic task of natural language processing. It solves the problem of information overload by extracting key information with special meaning in the sentence. The key information is also called named entity. Chinese is different from other letter-based languages. Chinese NER needs to consider its inherent characteristics.

The earliest paper about NER was published by Rau in 1991 [17]. In 1996, Grishman and Sundheim, first time formally proposed the term—"named entity", and defined the task of NER [8]. In 2003, Hammerton tried to use an LSTM network to build an NER model [10] that was the first attempt to use a neural network model to solve the NER task. In 2011, Collobert proposed an NER model combining the CRF model and the CNN model that the model achieved similar performance with the best machine learning model at the time [4]. Since Collobert, with the rapid development of the deep learning,

© Springer Nature Switzerland AG 2020
D. Yu et al. (Eds.): WASA 2020, LNCS 12384, pp. 194–205, 2020.
https://doi.org/10.1007/978-3-030-59016-1_17

Character-based: 张 重 庆 在 重 庆 吃 火 锅
Norm 1: 张重庆 在 重庆 吃 火锅
Norm 2: 张 重庆 在 重庆 吃火锅
Meaning: Chongqing Zhang eats hot pot in Chongqing

Fig. 1. Examples of segmentation of the sentence by different word segmentation norms.

a growing number of researchers have applied deep learning methods to build NER models.

Most Chinese NER models based on deep learning models can be roughly divided into two categories according to the choice of the basic unit of language processing: character-based models and word-based models. The character-based model cannot effectively exploit the rich information contained in words. Dong proposed a character-based Chinese NER model based on the BiLSTM-CRF model [7]. The word-based model cannot effectively disambiguate words under different word segmentation norms. He and Sun proposed a Bi-LSTM NER model with a maximum distance neural network [11]. As shown in Fig. 1, the character-based model divides a sentence inputting to the model into a sequence of characters. The word-based model divides a sentence into a sequence of words while different word segmentation norms result in different word sequences. In the Norm 1, "张重庆" is a word representing a person's name, while in the Norm 2, "张 重庆" is two words, which does not mean a whole meaning. Different word sequences will produce different results of named entities. How to effectively use the information of words and effectively eliminate the ambiguity of words under different word segmentation norms has become an important problem in the research of Chinese NER.

Faced with this problem, scholars have begun to explore some new methods to solve this problem. Zhang and Yang proposed a lattice LSTM model to gain Chinese named entities [22]. Liu proposed a WC-LSTM model based on the lattice LSTM model [14]. Gui proposed a faster Chinese NER model based the CNN [9].

In this paper, we propose a double temporal convolutional network for Chinese NER: SDTCNs. SDTCNs uses character as the basic unit of language processing. It is built on the BERT model that converts the characters of the input sentence into pre-trained embedding vectors. SDTCNs is composed of two symmetric temporal convolutional networks, where one is used to learn the location features of named entities and the other is used to learn the class features of named entities. The location feature is the related position information of all characters or words of a named entity in the input sentence. The location feature can help to eliminate the ambiguity of words under different word segmentation norms. The class feature is the relevant class information that represents which key information class that a named entity belongs to. The class feature can help to identify which key information class that the named entity belongs to. Finally, a fusion algorithm proposed in this paper is used to fuse location features and class features to obtain the final named entity. Experiments on multiple datasets show that SDTCNs outperforms multiple state-of-the-art Chinese NER models and achieves the best results.

2   Related Work

BERT Pre-training Fine-tuning Model: BERT (Bidirectional Encoder Representations from Transformers) is a pre-trained fine-tuning model proposed by Devlin in 2018 [6]. BERT pre-trains on a corpus containing billions of words to generate a unique dictionary of pre-trained embedding vectors. A vector in the dictionary represents a word. For a Chinese corpus, a vector in the dictionary represents a word or character. The vector in the dictionary is not static, it is fine-tuned according to the needs of the natural language processing task to make the task achieve the best result. On the General Language Understanding Evaluation (GLUE) benchmark dataset, BERT and its derivative models have achieved the best results at present.

$$Attention(Q, K, V) = softmax(\frac{Q \cdot K^T}{\sqrt{d_k}}) \cdot V \tag{1}$$

The BERT model is based on the Transformer model proposed by Vaswani who proposed a multi-headed self-attention mechanism based on the point-multiplied self-attention mechanism [18]. The point-multiplied self-attention mechanism is shown in Formula 1. The mechanism converts the sentence inputting to the Transformer model into three 2-dimensional matrices Q, K, V, and the first dimension of K is the length of the sentence and the second dimension of K is the dimensions d of the embedding vector. The multi-head attention mechanism divides the second dimension of K into multiple parts, where each part is called a head. Each head calculates its respective point-multiplied attention score. Finally, obtain the output of the Transformer model by concatenation of the attention scores of all the heads.

Generic Temporal Convolutional Network: Generic temporal convolutional network (GTCN) is a convolutional network model proposed by Bai for processing sequence structure data [1]. The sequence structure data includes data such as natural language sentence sequences, audio sequences, and video frame sequences. GTCN uses a left-to-right convolution sliding strategy, which only slides one step to the right at a time, adding zero-padding blocks to the left to ensure alignment.

3   SDTCNs

A sentence inputting to SDTCNs can be described as $\{x_1, x_2, \ldots, x_m\}$, where x_i is the i-th character in the sentence, and m is the length of the sentence. The NER task needs to find the named entities in the input sentence. Generally speaking, the NER task needs to gain the named entity identification sequence

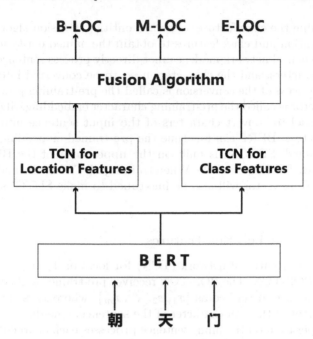

Fig. 2. The architecture of SDTCNs. For example, a sentence "朝天门" is inputted to SDTCNs, which is one of the seventeen ancient city gates in Chongqing. BERT converts the characters into embedding vectors, and the vectors are sent to the temporal convolutional network (TCN) for location features and the TCN for class features. Finally, the outputs of the two networks are fused by the fusion algorithm to obtain the named entity identification sequence.

$\{y_1, y_2, \ldots, y_m\}$ corresponding to characters of the input sentence. A named entity identifier consists of two parts: location identifier and class identifier. The location identifier is used to indicate the starting, middle and ending positions of characters of the named entity. BIOES or BMOES strategies are generally applied to the location identifier. B indicates the starting position of the named entity. E indicates the ending position of the named entity. I and M indicate the middle position of the named entity. S indicates that the named entity is a separate character. O indicates the unnamed entity. The class identifier is used to indicate which class of the key information that the named entity belongs to. For example, a simple three-class NER task can define three named entity classes as person name (PER), organization name (ORG), location name (LOC), and other (O) that indicates unnamed entity. An input sentence is "朝天门在重庆", which means "Chaotianmen in Chongqing". According to the definition of the three classes, the named entity identification sequence corresponding to characters of the sentence is {B-LOC, M-LOC, E-LOC, O, B-LOC, E-LOC}.

As shown in Fig. 2, SDTCNs is built on the upper layer of the BERT model and is composed of two symmetrical temporal convolutional networks, one for learning the location features of named entities of the input sentence, and the other for learning the class features of named entities. A fusion algorithm is used to fuse the location and class features to obtain the named entity identification sequence. The neural network model cannot directly process sentences composed of original characters, and the characters need to be converted into embedding vectors. The process of the conversion is called the pre-training process, and the embedding vector is called the pre-training character embedding. SDTCNs apply the BERT model to convert characters of the input sentence into pre-trained embedding vectors. BERT can fine-tune the pre-trained embedding vector that has been obtained. SDTCNs is built on the upper layer of the BERT model. SDTCNs and BERT form a whole. When training SDTCNs, the underlying pre-trained embedding vector will also be fine-tuned to make SDTCNs achieve the best result.

3.1   The TCN for Location Features

The temporal convolutional network (TCN) for location features hereinafter is referred to as POS-TCN. The POS-TCN receives pre-trained embedding vectors of an input sentence, described as $\{x_1, x_2, \ldots, x_m\}$, where x_t is the pre-trained embedding vector of the t-th character of the sentence. One-dimensional dilated convolution operation on the input sentence processes each character of the sentence in order from left to right. The output of x_t after performing 1-dimensional dilated convolution is h_t, $h_t = \{c_1, c_2, \ldots, c_n\}$. The c_j is the calculation result of the j-th convolution kernel, and the c_j is described as Formula 2.

$$c_j = w_j^T \cdot x_{t:t+d\cdot(k-1)} + b_j \tag{2}$$

In Formula 2, the w_j is the weight of the j-th convolution kernel, $w_j \in R^{k \times n}$, and k is the size of the convolution window, and n is the dimension of the pre-trained embedding vector. The b_j is the deviation of the j-th convolution kernel, $b_j \in R^1$. The $x_{t:t+d\cdot(k-1)}$ are k embedding vectors corresponding to k characters that are selected from left to right to perform the convolution operation starting from x_t. The selection of every two characters is spaced by d characters, which is called dilated convolution, d indicating the dilation factor. The dilated convolution is described as $x_{t+d\cdot i}$. The $x_{t+d\cdot i}$ is the i-th embedding vector of the $x_{t:t+d\cdot(k-1)}$, $0 \leq i \leq k-1$. To ensure that the dimensions of h_t and x_t are equal, the number of convolution kernels is set to n.

As shown in Fig. 3, the POS-TCN converts pre-trained embedding vectors into the Hidden 1 and the Hidden 2 in order. The output of the Hidden is the result after performing the residual connection on the result of the 1-dimensional dilated convolution. The residual connection operation for the t-th character is defined as Formula 3.

$$o_t = GeLU(x_t + h_t) \tag{3}$$

The o_t is the vector of the Hidden corresponding to the t-th character of input sentence. $GeLU$ is a high-performance neural network activation function [12]. GeLU is described as Formula 4.

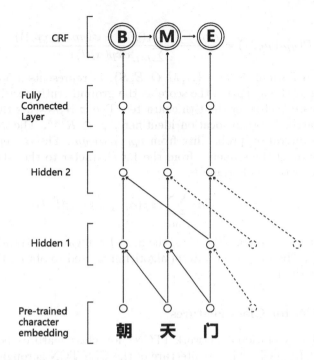

Fig. 3. The temporal convolutional network for location features. Solid circles represent the real pre-trained embedding vectors. Dotted circles indicate padding blocks. The padding block is a zero vector.

$$GeLU(x) = 0.5x(1 + tanh[\sqrt{\frac{2}{\pi}}(x + 0.044715x^3)]) \qquad (4)$$

The POS-TCN is used to gain the location features of the input sentence. The location features are location identifiers of named entities of the sentence. The POS-TCN adopts the BMOES as an identification strategy. The sequence of location identifiers is described as $\{yp_1, yp_2, \ldots, yp_m\}$. As shown in Fig. 3, the POS-TCN transmits the result of the Hidden 2 to the fully-connected layer. The fully-connected layer is responsible for converting o_t into a 5-dimensional score vector. Each dimension of the 5-dimensional vector represents the score of an identifier in BMOES. This 5-dimensional vector is transmitted to the CRF layer, and the CRF layer obtains a sequence of location identifiers.

The Conditional Random Fields (CRF) is generally used to process sequence data, such as natural language data, where the data elements have dependencies. For example, "朝天门" is a named entity representing a toponym, and its sequence of location identifiers is {B, M, E}. There is a dependency relationship between B and M and a dependency between M and E. In general, at the CRF layer, the probability of yp_t is described as Formula 5.

$$P(yp_t|yp_{t-1}) = \frac{exp(\sum_{t=1}^{m}(s_t(\overline{yp_t}) + \varphi(yp_{t-1}, yp_t)))}{\sum_{l \in L} exp(\alpha_t(l))} \tag{5}$$

As shown in Formula 5, $L = \{B, M, O, E, S\}$, s_t represents a 5-dimensional score vector, and the $s_t(\overline{yp_t})$ is the score at the ground-truth position of the 5-dimensional score vector for the t-th character. The φ represents the transition probability matrix between location identifiers, $\varphi \in R^{5 \times 5}$. The $\varphi(yp_{t-1}, yp_t)$ represents the migration probability from yp_{t-1} to yp_t. The α_t represents the total score vector of the sequence from the 1st character to the t-th character, and $\alpha_t(l)$ is described as Formula 6.

$$\alpha_t(l) = s_t(l) + log \sum_{l' in L} exp(\alpha_{t-1}(l') + \varphi(l', l)) \tag{6}$$

After supervised training SDTCNs, the model will gain the transition probability matrix φ. The first-order Viterbi algorithm is used to obtain the sequence of location identifiers.

3.2 The TCN for Class Features

The temporal convolutional network (TCN) for class features hereinafter is referred to as CLS-TCN. The architecture of the CLS-TCN is roughly the same as that of the POS-TCN. However, there are adopted different methods to gain the sequence of identifiers. The POS-TCN uses the first-order Viterbi algorithm to obtain the sequence of location identifiers. The CLS-TCN directly takes the class identifier corresponding to the maximum score in the class identifier score vector from the fully connected layer output. There are no strong dependencies between the classes of named entities of the input sentence. In order to obtain the class identifier, the class identifier with the largest score is generally taken.

3.3 Fusion Algorithm

Generally, it can be spliced one-to-one between the sequence of position identifiers obtained by POS-TCN and the sequence of class identifiers obtained by CLS-TCN to obtain the named entity identification sequence. The one-to-one stitching strategy makes SDTCNs a pure character-based model, which cannot effectively utilize the rich information of a named entity. The fusion algorithm uses the sequence of location identifiers obtained by the POS-TCN to obtain the starting and ending positions of a named entity, and then finds the classes between the starting and ending positions of the named entity in the sequence of class identifiers obtained by CLS-TCN. The class with the most occurrence of the classes is set as the prediction class for the named entity.

The basic idea of the fusion algorithm: 1. It obtains the span between the start and end positions of the named entity according to the named entity position identification sequence obtained by the POS-TCN; 2. It finds the named entity class identifications in the span of the class identification sequence obtained by the CLS-TCN; 3. It selects the class with the most occurrences among these class identifications as the class of this named entity.

4 Experiments

In order to verify the performance of SDTCNs, we experiment on three currently popular Chinese NER datasets and the Boson dataset. Experimental results show that SDTCNs outperforms multiple advanced Chinese NER models and achieves the best results.

4.1 Datasets

We experiment on four Chinese NER datasets that the four datasets are OntoNotes [5], MSRA [13], Weibo NER [15], and Boson[1]. The OntoNotes and Weibo NER datasets have four non-empty entities: GPE (indicating a geographic name in a political sense, usually used to indicate a country, city, state, etc.), ORG (organization name), PER (person name), LOC (indicating a geographic name that the GPE cannot indicate, such as mountains, water systems, etc.). The MSRA dataset has three non-empty entities: ORG, PER, LOC that the LOC represents all geographic names. The Boson dataset has six non-empty entities: COMP (company or business name), PROD (product name), TIME (time), ORG, PER, LOC that the LOC represents all geographic names. All datasets use O for empty entities. The OntoNotes and Weibo NER datasets are divided into three parts: training set (Train), development set (Dev), and test set (Test). The MSRA and Boson datasets are divided into two parts: training set (Train) and test set (Test).

4.2 Experiment Environment and Evaluation Criteria

The experiment environment has an Intel Core i7-8700K 3.7 GHz CPU, 16 GB of memory, and an Nvidia GeForce RTX 2080 GPU with 8G video memory. In order to evaluate the performance of the NER model, we apply the F1-index to measure the performance of the NER model. The F1-index can be referred to as the F1-score, and it consists of two parts: Precision (P) and Recall (R). The higher the F1-score, the better the performance of the NER model.

4.3 Final Results

The SDTCNs model is trained on the training sets of the four datasets respectively to obtain the best parameters. Recently, the advanced Chinese NER models are the Lattice model proposed by Zhang and Yang [22], and the WC-LSTM model proposed by Liu [14], and the LR-CNN model proposed by Gui [9]. Compared with these models, SDTCNs outperforms them and achieves the best results.

---

[1] https://bosonnlp.com/resources/BosonNLP_NER_6C.zip.

OntoNotes: Table 1 shows the experimental results on OntoNote4 dataset. The "Input" column shows the representation of an input sentence, where "Gold seg" means a sequence of words with gold-standard segmentation, and "No seg" means a sequence of characters without any segmentation. As shown in Table 1, the "Gold seg" models achieve good performance by using gold-standard segmentation and external labeled data. However, SDTCNs is a character-based model and achieves a better performance than the "Gold seg" models. The WC-LSTM is an optimization model based on the Lattice model, whose performance is improved by 0.55% than the Lattice model. Compared with the Lattice, SDTCNs improves by 5.67% in F1-score. Compared with the WC-LSTM, SDTCNs improves by 5.12% in F1-score. Compared with the LR-CNN, SDTCNs improves by 5.1% in F1-score. Compared with the LR-CNN, SDTCNs improves by 5.1% in F1-score. Compared with the model proposed by Yang[20], SDTCNs improves by 3.15% in F1-score.

Table 1. Results on OntoNotes.

Input	Model	P	R	F1
Gold seg	Wang *et al.* 2013 [19]	76.43	72.32	74.32
	Che *et al.* 2013 [3]	77.71	72.51	75.02
	Yang *et al.* 2016 [20]	72.98	80.15	**76.40**
No seg	Lattice [22]	76.35	71.56	73.88
	WC-LSTM [14]	76.09	72.85	74.43
	LR-CNN [9]	76.40	72.60	74.45
	SDTCNs	**79.44**	**79.67**	**79.55**

Weibo NER: Table 2 shows the experimental results on Weibo NER dataset. As shown in Table 2, the F1-score of the LR-CNN on the Weibo NER dataset is 59.92%. Compared with the WC-LSTM, SDTCNs improves by **10.15%** in F1-score. Compared with the LR-CNN, SDTCNs improves by **10.07%** in F1-score.

MSRA: Table 3 shows the experimental results on MSRA dataset. As shown in Table 3, the F1-score of the WC-LSTM on the MSRA dataset is 93.74%. Compared with the WC-LSTM, SDTCNs improves by 1.34% in F1-score. Compared with the LR-CNN, SDTCNs improves by 1.37% in F1-score.

Boson: Table 4 shows the experimental result of SDTCNs on Boson dataset. The Boson dataset contains 2000 sentences, where the most are long sentences. Experimental results on the Boson dataset can show the ability of the NER model to handle long sentences.

Table 2. Results on Weibo NER.

Model	F1
Peng and Dredze 2015 [15]	56.05
Peng and Dredze 2016 [16]	58.99
He and Sun 2017 [11]	54.23
Cao *et al.* 2018 [2]	58.70
Lattice [22]	58.79
WC-LSTM [14]	59.84
LR-CNN [9]	**59.92**
SDTCNs	**69.99**

Table 3. Results on MSRA.

Model	P	R	F1
Zhang *et al.* 2006 [21]	92.20	90.18	91.18
Zhou *et al.* 2013 [23]	91.86	88.75	90.28
Dong *et al.* 2016 [7]	91.28	90.62	90.95
Cao *et al.* 2018 [2]	91.73	89.58	90.64
Lattice [22]	93.57	92.79	93.18
LR-CNN [9]	94.50	92.93	93.71
WC-LSTM [14]	94.58	92.91	**93.74**
SDTCNs	**95.51**	**94.64**	**95.08**

Table 4. Results on Boson.

Model	P	R	F1
SDTCNs	**80.38**	**79.82**	**80.10**

Table 5. Result of the sentence containing ambiguous words.

Sentence	中 国 内 陆 大 省 四 川
Ground-truth	B E O O O O B E (GPE)
Lattice [22]	B M M M M E B E (GPE)
SDTCNs	**B E O O O O B E (GPE)**

4.4 Experiment for Sentences Containing Ambiguous Words

In order to test the performance of SDTCNs in processing sentences containing ambiguity segmentation words. We select "中国内陆大省四川" as the experimental sentence, which means "Sichuan, a large inland province of China". According to different word segmentation criteria, the sentence can be divided into different word sequences such as "中国,内陆,大省,四川" and "中国,内陆大省,四川". As shown in Table 5, SDTCNs can handle the sentence well and get the correct sequence of named entity identifiers.

5 Conclusion

In this paper, we propose an SDTCNs model built on the BERT model for Chinese named entity recognition. The SDTCNs uses the character as the basic unit of language processing. It consists of two symmetrical temporal convolutional networks, one for learning the location features of named entities of the input sentence, and the other for learning the class features of named entities. Finally, a fusion algorithm is used to fuse the location and class features to obtain the named entity identification sequence. Experiments on multiple Chinese NER datasets show that SDTCNs outperforms multiple state-of-the-art Chinese NER models and achieves the best results.

References

1. Bai, S., Kolter, J.Z., Koltun, V.: An empirical evaluation of generic convolutional and recurrent networks for sequence modeling. arXiv preprint arXiv:1803.01271 (2018)
2. Cao, P., Chen, Y., Liu, K., Zhao, J., Liu, S.: Adversarial transfer learning for Chinese named entity recognition with self-attention mechanism. In: Proceedings of the 2018 Conference on Empirical Methods in Natural Language Processing, pp. 182–192 (2018)
3. Che, W., Wang, M., Manning, C.D., Liu, T.: Named entity recognition with bilingual constraints. In: Proceedings of the 2013 Conference of the North American Chapter of the Association for Computational Linguistics: Human Language Technologies, pp. 52–62 (2013)
4. Collobert, R., Weston, J., Bottou, L., Karlen, M., Kavukcuoglu, K., Kuksa, P.: Natural language processing (almost) from scratch. J. Mach. Learn. Res. **12**(Aug), 2493–2537 (2011)
5. Consortium, L.D., et al.: Ontonotes release 4.0 (2011). https://catalog.ldc.upenn.edu/LDC2011T03
6. Devlin, J., Chang, M.W., Lee, K., Toutanova, K.: Bert: pre-training of deep bidirectional transformers for language understanding. arXiv preprint arXiv:1810.04805 (2018)
7. Dong, Chuanhai., Zhang, Jiajun., Zong, Chengqing., Hattori, Masanori, Di, Hui: Character-based LSTM-CRF with radical-level features for Chinese named entity recognition. In: Lin, Chin-Yew, Xue, Nianwen, Zhao, Dongyan, Huang, Xuanjing, Feng, Yansong (eds.) ICCPOL/NLPCC -2016. LNCS (LNAI), vol. 10102, pp. 239–250. Springer, Cham (2016). https://doi.org/10.1007/978-3-319-50496-4_20
8. Grishman, R., Sundheim, B.: Message understanding conference-6: a brief history. In: COLING 1996 Volume 1: The 16th International Conference on Computational Linguistics (1996)
9. Gui, T., Ma, R., Zhang, Q., Zhao, L., Jiang, Y.G., Huang, X.: CNN-based Chinese NER with lexicon rethinking. In: Proceedings of the Twenty-Eighth International Joint Conference on Artificial Intelligence, IJCAI-19, pp. 4982–4988. International Joint Conferences on Artificial Intelligence Organization, July 2019. https://doi.org/10.24963/ijcai.2019/692

10. Hammerton, J.: Named entity recognition with long short-term memory. In: Proceedings of the Seventh Conference on Natural Language Learning at HLT-NAACL 2003, vol. 4, pp. 172–175. Association for Computational Linguistics (2003)
11. He, H., Sun, X.: F-score driven max margin neural network for named entity recognition in Chinese social media. In: EACL 2017, p. 713 (2017)
12. Hendrycks, D., Gimpel, K.: Gaussian error linear units (GELUs). arXiv preprint arXiv:1606.08415 (2016)
13. Levow, G.A.: The third international Chinese language processing bakeoff: word segmentation and named entity recognition. In: Proceedings of the Fifth SIGHAN Workshop on Chinese Language Processing, pp. 108–117 (2006)
14. Liu, W., Xu, T., Xu, Q., Song, J., Zu, Y.: An encoding strategy based word-character LSTM for Chinese NER. In: Proceedings of the 2019 Conference of the North American Chapter of the Association for Computational Linguistics: Human Language Technologies, (Long and Short Papers), vol. 1, pp. 2379–2389 (2019)
15. Peng, N., Dredze, M.: Named entity recognition for Chinese social media with jointly trained embeddings. In: Proceedings of the 2015 Conference on Empirical Methods in Natural Language Processing, pp. 548–554 (2015)
16. Peng, N., Dredze, M.: Improving named entity recognition for Chinese social media with word segmentation representation learning. In: Proceedings of the 54th Annual Meeting of the Association for Computational Linguistics (Short Papers), vol. 2, pp. 149–155 (2016)
17. Rau, L.F.: Extracting company names from text. In: [1991] Proceedings of the Seventh IEEE Conference on Artificial Intelligence Application, vol. 1, pp. 29–32. IEEE (1991)
18. Vaswani, A., et al.: Attention is all you need. In: Advances in Neural Information Processing Systems, pp. 5998–6008 (2017)
19. Wang, M., Che, W., Manning, C.D.: Effective bilingual constraints for semi-supervised learning of named entity recognizers. In: Twenty-Seventh AAAI Conference on Artificial Intelligence (2013)
20. Yang, Jie., Teng, Zhiyang., Zhang, Meishan, Zhang, Yue: Combining discrete and neural features for sequence labeling. In: Gelbukh, Alexander (ed.) CICLing 2016. LNCS, vol. 9623, pp. 140–154. Springer, Cham (2018). https://doi.org/10.1007/978-3-319-75477-2_9
21. Zhang, S., Qin, Y., Hou, W.J., Wang, X.: Word segmentation and named entity recognition for SIGHAN bakeoff3. In: Proceedings of the Fifth SIGHAN Workshop on Chinese Language Processing, pp. 158–161 (2006)
22. Zhang, Y., Yang, J.: Chinese NER using lattice LSTM. In: Proceedings of the 56th Annual Meeting of the Association for Computational Linguistics (Long Papers), vol. 1, pp. 1554–1564 (2018)
23. Zhou, J., Qu, W., Zhang, F.: Chinese named entity recognition via joint identification and categorization. Chin. J. Electron. 22(2), 225–230 (2013)

Verifiable Encrypted Search with Forward Secure Updates for Blockchain-Based System

Han Li[1], Hongliang Zhou[1], Hejiao Huang[1], and Xiaohua Jia[1,2(✉)]

[1] Department of Computer Science and Technology, Harbin Institute of Technology,
Shenzhen, China
linyuhan32@gmail.com, {hlzhou,huanghejiao}@hit.edu.cn
[2] Department of Computer Science, City University of Hong Kong,
Hong Kong, China
csjia@cityu.edu.hk

Abstract. Enabling secure and reliable search over encrypted data is essential for data owners to protect their sensitive data from a compromised server. Recent advances in cloud computing are further pushing forward the development of this technique, known as searchable encryption. However, existing encrypted search schemes mainly consider a centralized setting, where a search is conducted in a traditional client-server model. How to apply searchable encryption schemes to an untrusted distributed setting like the blockchain environment remains to be explored. Meanwhile, the advanced security property like forward security is posing new challenges that traditional technologies are no longer sufficient to cope with. In this work, we explore the potential of blockchain technique and propose a novel dual index structure for forward-secure encrypted search with dynamic file updates. We show how to synthesize this design strategy in the context of blockchain-based storage systems and achieve both optimal search and update complexity. We also propose a verification scheme to verify the correctness of search results and customize an encrypted on-chain checklist to achieve strong data protection and lower the blockchain overhead. We implement the prototype on a Redis cluster and conduct performance evaluations on Amazon Cloud. Extensive experiments demonstrate the security and efficiency of the design.

Keywords: Encrypted search · Forward security · Blockchain system

1 Introduction

The advancement of cloud storage vigorously pushes forward the innovation of secure data outsourcing technologies. Among which, searchable symmetric encryption (SSE) [1–3] is a widely adopted security scheme for encrypted search. Specifically, it allows a storage server to search encrypted keyword indexes without decryption. Despite extensive research on search over encrypted data, most of SSE schemes work only in a traditional centralized setting. They fail to address the needs demanded by the blockchain-based storage systems [4–6] such as ensuring the integrity of search results and using distributed computing paradigms.

© Springer Nature Switzerland AG 2020
D. Yu et al. (Eds.): WASA 2020, LNCS 12384, pp. 206–217, 2020.
https://doi.org/10.1007/978-3-030-59016-1_18

As the increasing development of blockchain-based applications, there is an urgent need to develop new solutions for this new paradigm to meet security and utility requirements.

To fill the gap, two research directions are recently explored. The first is to store the entire encrypted keyword indexes in the blockchain and conduct search queries on the blockchain [7]. Since the blockchain is an append-only structure and the data stored in the chain cannot be changed, it would incur a high cost to store indexes in the blockchain and is difficult for file update. The other direction is to store encrypted indexes together with the files at storage servers, making the blockchain light-weight [8]. This approach can be viewed as a starting point in the design, but achieve secure file updates and verifiable search remain to be the unsolved issues. Intuitively, the efficiency of search operations often conflicts with the efficiency of update operations. The existing design of index structure for encrypted search either requires the rebuild of the indexes for each update to make search efficient, or sacrifices the search efficiency to trade for the flexibility of updates. Moreover, it is a challenging task to rely on either storage servers or data owners to verify search results in a blockchain environment. Storage servers may not return complete or accurate search results for saving computational cost or other reasons. Vice versa, some users may mis-accuse the honest storage servers in order to deny the payment.

Motivated by the observations above, our objectives are to address the following two challenges. First, an efficient index structure needs to be carefully designed to balance search and update operations, and further integrated into the aforementioned blockchain-based systems. The proposed design should also preserve forward-security for update operations. That is, the storage server cannot learn whether the newly added files match the previous search result. Second, the verification scheme should be highly customized to meet security and efficiency requirements in the blockchain network.

In this paper, we first devise a new dual chain index structure that can support dynamic file updates and yet achieve efficient search operations. Technically, duplicates of encrypted file IDs and corresponding keywords are mapped to two related chain indexes, where the address of each index entry is derived from the unique keyword-file pair. With this dual index structure, both keyword search and file update operations can be done in sub-linear complexity.

For forward-secure updates, we note that only those keywords that already queried in the indexes may cause the forward-secure problem. Therefore, we propose to exploit the append-only property of blockchain and store all previous search results in the blockchain. Then, we use a fresh random mask to generate each newly added index and leverage chain-based index structure to link it to the header of the previous index chain. For searching a keyword that is associated with the newly added file, the user can use the new trapdoor to obtain the result from the storage server and fetch the previous results from the blockchain. As a result, the storage server cannot learn whether the newly added entry matches previous search results without querying it.

To make results easily verifiable, we develop an efficient on-chain checklist for encrypted search results. Here, we leverage the incremental set hash technique [9] to design a compressed checklist for reducing the on-chain storage cost. But, directly storing the encrypted keyword-files checklist can still reveal auxiliary information, such as result distribution of different keywords. To address this issue, we further embed a unique nonce into each result set. Thus, an attacker who can steal and dump encrypted checklists will not derive any useful information. For practical considerations, we further propose a batch update protocol to avoid unnecessary checklist updates.

In summary, our contributions are listed as follows:

- We design an index structure that supports dynamic file updates and efficient search in blockchain-based systems. The proposed design enables parallel query processing and preserves forward-security for update operations.
- We develop a practical verification scheme to verify the correctness and integrity of search results. The customization offers guaranteed security with lightweight on-chain storage.
- We implement our system prototype and deploy it on amazon web service. The result confirms that our design is applicable to a blockchain-based system that is secure, verifiable, and efficient.

2 Related Work

2.1 Blockchain Systems

Decentralized cryptocurrencies, such as Bitcoin [10], Ethereum [11], have gained great popularity. The blockchain, as the underlying technology, has attracted a lot of attention. Specifically, a blockchain can be considered as a cryptographic and distributed database that stores the data records in an ordered manner. Once a record is written, it cannot be altered. With advances in blockchain technology, many well-known decentralized storage platforms have been developed [4–6,12]. These systems leverage blockchain to tie cryptocurrencies to data outsourcing service and ensure the integrity of data. For example, IPFS uses Filecoin [6] as a fundamental layer to motivate storage peers to provide storage and retrieval services. Datacoin [13] uses the blockchain as a data store for file storage. For security consideration, Storj [4] and Sia [5] employ end-to-end encryption and store cryptographic hash fingerprints of files on the blockchain to enable the file integrity check. However, none of these blockchain storage systems support search functions over the encrypted data, where a file can only be located via its identifier.

2.2 Searchable Symmetric Encryption

Searchable symmetric encryption (SSE) [1–3] is a cryptographic primitive that allows a server to search directly over encrypted data. A line of work [14–19] has been made to realize various SSE schemes with tradeoffs between efficiency, expressiveness, and security. To enable update operations over encrypted data, the notion of dynamic SSE was first introduced in [2]. However, data update in most existing dynamic SSE schemes leaks more information than search. Specifically, data addition reveals relations between newly added data and previous search result. To improve security, Stefanov et al. [20] further introduced the notion of forward-security. In [15], Bost et al. formally defined forward-security and designed an insertion-only SSE scheme based on asymmetric cryptography (i.e., trapdoor permutations). However, this construction requires heavy public key encryption operations, which leads to performance degradation. For data deletion, most of existing schemes require the server to maintain a revocation list for deleted data, which imposes a performance penalty for each search. Recent work [16] introduced an index structure to achieve optimal search and update complexity. However, its counter-based design incurs heavy state management, which is not suitable for result verification after update operations. Moreover, the above works on encrypted search are mostly designed for centralized systems. They are not applicable to blockchain-based systems that require lightweight storage and efficient verification on the chain.

3   Overview

3.1   System Model

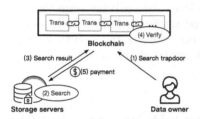

Fig. 1. Overview of system framework

Figure 1 shows the overview of blockchain-based system framework, containing two main parties: the data owners and a set of storage servers. Storage servers are the individuals that lease out their computing resources (i.e., storage and computation), while data owners are users that outsource their data to the storage servers and make search queries about their data. The binding between a data owner and a storage server can be done via other platforms, such as [4], which is beyond the scope of this work.

To make operations immutable and non-repudiable, all operations are in the form of transactions in this blockchain network, so that other peers can verify the faithful execution of the search requests and enforce the payment for the services. From a high-level point of view, the procedures of this storage framework are as followings. The data owner first builds the encrypted indexes and uploads the indexes to the contracted server. A storage contract, signed by both the server and the user, is then broadcast to the blockchain network as a transaction and is recorded in the blockchain for later result verifications. When a user submits a search query, it generates a search trapdoor, containing encrypted keywords and broadcasts it as a transaction to the blockchain network. Upon receiving the search trapdoor, the contracted server will perform the search operation on the indexes to produce the search result and broadcast it to the blockchain network for result verification. Once the result verified by the blockchain peers turns out to be correct, the contracted server can acquire the payment from its search service. Finally, the user can retrieve the verified search result from the blockchain, and later use the result (i.e., file IDs) to fetch the outsourced files. In order to focus on our targeted issues, operations on the encrypted files are not shown in the work, since the user could easily outsource encrypted files to any decentralized storage network like IPFS, and later download the file with its ID. Meantime, we always use the fresh key to generate the newly added index and add it to the beginning of the encrypted index chain to guarantee the forward security of our design.

3.2   Threat Model

In light with the property of blockchain, we consider a powerful adversary. Specifically, we assume three potential threats come from the blockchain network and storage servers. (1) a storage server might intend to learn the sensitive information from its local storage; (2) a malicious storage server could provide unfaithful query execution intentionally, thereby returning incorrect or incomplete query results; (3) other blockchain peers might try to learn data privacy from the on-chain checklists. All peers can monitor encrypted traffic, including both search trapdoors and encrypted result. Finally, we do not consider the case that users expose the keys to others, and keys are securely stored at the client.

3.3   Cryptographic Primitives

Searchable Symmetric Encryption: A searchable symmetric encryption scheme is a set of three polynomial time algorithms $\Pi = (\mathsf{KGen}, \mathsf{Enc}, \mathsf{Dec})$: The key generation algorithm KGen takes a security parameter k as input and outputs a secret key K; The encryption algorithm Enc takes a key K and a value $v \in \{0,1\}^*$ as inputs and outputs a ciphertext $v^* \in \{0,1\}^*$; The decryption algorithm Dec takes a key K and a ciphertext v^* as inputs and returns v.

Multiset Hash Function: A multiset hash function is probabilistic polynomial algorithms $(\mathbf{H}, \equiv_{\mathbf{H}}, +_{\mathbf{H}}, -_{\mathbf{H}})$ that can map multisets of arbitrary finite size to strings of fixed length, and for all $S \subset \mathbb{S}$,

- $\mathbf{H}(S) \equiv_{\mathbf{H}} \mathbf{H}(S)$.
- $\forall x \in \mathbb{S} \backslash S, \mathbf{H}(S \cup \{x\}) \equiv_{\mathbf{H}} \mathbf{H}(S) +_{\mathbf{H}} \mathbf{H}(\{x\})$.
- $\forall x \in S, \mathbf{H}(S \backslash \{x\}) \equiv_{\mathbf{H}} \mathbf{H}(S) -_{\mathbf{H}} \mathbf{H}(\{x\})$.

where multiset hash function $\mathbf{H}$ is collision-resistant.

Pseudo-random Function: Define pseudo-random function $F : \mathcal{K} \times X \to R$, if for all probabilistic polynomial-time distinguishers Y, $|Pr[Y^{F(k,\cdot)} = 1 | k \leftarrow \mathcal{K}] - Pr[Y^g = 1 | g \leftarrow \{\mathsf{Func} : X \to R\}]| < negl(k)$, where $negl(k)$ is a negligible function in k.

4   The proposed Design

This section presents the design of our encrypted dual indexes in detail, based on our enhanced dynamic SSE schemes with forward security. We show that our design is compatible with the blockchain-based system setting, and further introduce secure search protocols for security and practical considerations. Features such as dynamic operations and result verification are also presented here.

4.1   Design Rationale

To improve the security strength while simultaneously maintaining service efficiency, our observation lies in the following two aspects. First, the desired index design should have an efficient structure for forward-secure dynamic search operations. Second, it is possible to mitigate the aforementioned leakage, i.e., the result distribution of on-chain checklist. For efficient file updates with forward security, we propose a novel dual index structure for off-chain data storage. The core idea of our dual index is to utilize one-time trapdoor to generate encrypted file and keyword index chains simultaneously, and always add newly encrypted entries at the beginning of the chain. Thus, the server cannot learn whether the newly added entry contains a keyword used in a previous search trapdoor. To ensure the correctness of results and public verifiability, we introduce a highly customized on-chain checklist. In particular, we protect the result distribution via embedding a random nonce for each result set, where the nonce is hidden at the last entry of the index chain. As a result, only the honest storage server can unmask the nonce by querying the entire index chain and later pass the result verification accordingly.

4.2   Encrypted Index Design

The detailed algorithm to index file IDs $\{f_1,..,f_n\}$ for a given keyword w_i is shown in Algorithm 1. This procedure is executed at the user side. Firstly, the data owner derives the keys $K_{w_i}, K^1_{w_i}, K^2_{w_i}$ from the private key K, update state $u1, u2$ and search times s, where K_{w_i} is the query trapdoor, $K^1_{w_i}$ is the encryption key, $K^2_{w_i}$ is the keyword label for the checklist and $u1, u2$ record the update state of $K_{w_i}, K^2_{w_i}$. Given a keyword-file pair (w_i, f_j), the user computes the address $id^{f_j}_{w_i}$ of it, and embeds the next keyword index address $id^{f_{j+1}}_{w_i}$ with the query trapdoor K_{w_i}, i.e, $H_1(K_{w_i}, id^{f_j}_{w_i}) \oplus id^{f_{j+1}}_{w_i}$. Note that we mask the random nonce α_{w_i} to the last index entry, and later use it to generate the encrypted checklist. Similar to the keyword index I_{w_i}, the user leverages the file trapdoor K_{f_j} to generate the file index I_{f_j}. After that, the user adds $\{id^{f_j}_{w_i}, I_{w_i}, I_{f_j}\}$, and encrypted data $F(K^1_{w_i}, f_j)$ to the dual index. Finally, the user aggregates results set with the nonce via multiset hash H, and stores the keyword/file state locally.

Algorithm 1. Build encrypted dual index chain

Input: Private key K; secure PRFs $\{G_w, G_f, F\}$; (mulit)hash functions $\{H_1, H_2, H\}$; index addresses id; update state $u1, u2$; search times s; keywords set $\{w_i\}$, $i \in \{1, m\}$; file IDs $\{f_j\}$, $j \in \{1, n\}$.

Output: Encrypted index I, checklist L, state table S.

1: Initialize a hash table S to maintain state;
2: **for** $w_i \in \{w_1, .., w_m\}$ **do**
3:     Generate a nonce α_{w_i}, $u1, u2, s \leftarrow 0$;
4:     $K_{w_i}^1, K_{w_i}, K_{w_i}^2 \leftarrow G_w(K, w_i || (\bot, u1, u2))$;
5:     $id_{w_i}^{f_n} \leftarrow \alpha_{w_i}$; //last entry of I_{w_i} index
6:     **for** $f_j \in DB(w_i)$ **do**
7:         $K_{f_j} \leftarrow G_f(K, f_j)$, $id_{w_i}^{f_j} \leftarrow H_1(w_i, f_j)$; // current index I address
8:         $id_{w_i}^{f_{j+1}} \leftarrow H_1(w_i, f_{j+1})$; // next I_{w_i} address
9:         $id_{w_{i+1}}^{f_j} \leftarrow H_2(w_{i+1}, f_j)$; // next I_{f_j} address
10:         $I_{w_i} \leftarrow H_1(K_{w_i}, id_{w_i}^{f_j}) \oplus id_{w_i}^{f_{j+1}}$, $I_{f_j} \leftarrow H_2(K_{f_j}, id_{w_i}^{f_j}) \oplus id_{w_{i+1}}^{f_j}$;
11:         $I_{w_i}^{f_j} \leftarrow F(K_{w_i}^1, f_j)$; // encrypted data
12:         PUT $[id_{w_i}^{f_j} : I_{w_i}, I_{f_j}, I_{w_i}^{f_j}]$ to index I;
13:         PUT $[f_j : id_{w_1}^{f_j}]$ to table S, $j + +$;
14:     **end for**
15:     PUT $[K_{w_i}^2 : H(I_{w_i}^{f_1})+, .., H(I_{w_i}^{f_n}) + H(\alpha_{w_i})]$ to L;
16:     PUT $[w_i : id_{w_i}^{f_1}, u1, u2, s]$ to table S, $i + +$;
17: **end for**
18: Upload the signed checklist L to the blockchain;
19: Send the encrypted index I to the contracted server;

Algorithm 2. Secure query protocol

Input: Private key K; secure PRFs $\{G_w, F\}$; hash functions $\{H_1, H_2, H\}$; query keyword w; state table S; checklist L.

Output: Matched results $\{f_1, .., f_n\}$.

User.Token

1: $id_w^{f_1}, u1, u2, s \leftarrow S[w]$, $K_w^1, K_w, K_w^2 \leftarrow G_w(K, w || (\bot, u1, u2))$, $s + +$;
2: Upload $\{K_w, K_w^2, id_w^{f_1}\}$ to blockchain network;

Server.Query

1: **for** $j \in \{1, n\}$ **do**
2:     $I_w, I_w^{f_j} \leftarrow I[id_w^{f_j}]$, $id_w^{f_{j+1}} \leftarrow H_1(K_w, id_w^{f_j}) \oplus I_w$, Return $I_w^{f_j}$, $j + +$;
3: **end for**
4: Broadcast $\{I_w^{f_1}, .., I_w^{f_n}, \alpha\}$ to blockchain nodes;

Node.Verify

1: **while** $L[K_w^2] == H(I_w^{f_1})+, .., +H(I_w^{f_n}) + H(\alpha)$ **do**
2:     Upload $\{I_w^{f_1}, .., I_w^{f_n}\}$ to blockchain;
3: **end while**
4: User decrypts $\{I_w^{f_1}, .., I_w^{f_n}\}$ using K_w^1;

Algorithm 3. Secure file insertion protocol

Input: Private key K; secure PRFs $\{G_w, G_f, F\}$; (mulit)hash functions $\{H_1, H_2, H\}$; state table S; checklist L; new file f.
Output: Updated index I_{upt}, checklist L, updated state table S_{upt}.
1: $K_f \leftarrow G_f(K, f)$;
2: **for** $w_i \in DB(f)$ **do**
3:    $id_{w_i}^{f_1}, u1, u2, s \leftarrow S[w_i]$; //start address of w_i's index
4:    $u2++$; // update $K_{w_i}^2$
5:    **while** $s! = 0$ **do** // w_i has been searched
6:       $u1++, s = 0$; // update K_{w_i} and reset s
7:    **end while**
8:    $K_{w_i}^1, K_{w_i}, K_{w_i}^2 \leftarrow G_w(K, w_i||(\bot, u1, u2))$, $id_{w_i}^f \leftarrow H_1(w_i, f)$;
9:    $I_{w_i} \leftarrow H_1(K_{w_i}, id_{w_i}^f) \oplus id_{w_i}^{f_1}$, $I_f \leftarrow H_2(K_f, id_{w_i}^f) \oplus id_{w_{i+1}}^f$;
10:   $I_{w_i}^f \leftarrow F(K_{w_i}^1, f)$;
11:   PUT $[id_{w_i}^f : I_{w_i}, I_f, I_{w_i}^f]$ to index I_{upt};
12:   UPDATE $[w_i : id_{w_i}^f, u1, u2, s]$ at table S_{upt};
13:   $L[w_i] + = H(I_{w_i}^f)$, $i++$;
14: **end for**
15: PUT $[f : id_{w_1}^f]$ to table S_{upt};
16: Upload the newly updated checklist L to the blockchain;
17: Send the updated index I_{upt} to the contracted server;

4.3 Secure Query Protocol

Based on the index construction, we present a secure query protocol in details in Algorithm 2. Given a query keyword w, the user wants to find all files IDs containing the keyword. Firstly, the user generates the keyword trapdoor K_w, corresponding checklist label K_w^2, and finds the start address of this keyword $id_w^{f_1}$ from the table S. After receiving the trapdoor K_w from the blockchain, the contracted server can retrieve all matched results from the key index I_w via computing $H_1(K_w, id_w^{f_j}) \oplus I_w$. Then, the other node can verify the search result with the checklist L and multiset hash value of results. Once passing the verification, the contracted server can receive service fees from the blockchain network. Finally, the client can also obtain the result from the blockchain and get the IDs $\{f_1, .., f_n\}$ via decryption. Since all previous search queries and results are permanently recorded in the blockchain, the user can always retrieve the results by using the old trapdoor, which is similar as the Algorithm 2.

4.4 Secure Update Protocol

To enable update files with forward security that requires the newly added files shall not have any link to the previous search results, we always use the fresh key to generate the newly added index and add it to the beginning of the encrypted index chain. Algorithm 3 presents the details of the insertion protocol. Given the newly added file ID f containing keywords w_i, firstly the user obtains the latest state from table S, and uses it to build the newly added index entry. Then the user puts $\{f : id_{w_1}^f\}$ to table S_{upt}, uploads the updated checklist L to the

Algorithm 4. Secure file deletion protocol

Input: Private key K; secure PRFs G_f; hash function H_2; state table S; revocation tag "$-$"; delete file ID f.

Output: Updated index I_{upt}.

User.Token

1: $id^f_{w_1} \leftarrow S[f]$; // start address of f's index
2: $K_f \leftarrow G_f(K, f)$, Send $\{K_f, id^f_{w_1}\}$ to server;

Server.Delete

1: **for** $i \in \{1, m\}$ **do**
2:     $I_{w_i}, I_f, I^f_{w_i} \leftarrow I[id^f_{w_i}]$, $id^f_{w_{i+1}} \leftarrow H_2(K_f, id^f_{w_i}) \oplus I_f$;
3:     UPDATE $I[id^f_{w_i}]$ with tag "$-$"; //mark deleted entries
4:     $i + +$;
5: **end for**
6: Delete "$-$" entries after w_i has been searched;

---

blockchain and the updated index I_{upt} to the contracted server. As for file deletion, the user first generates the trapdoor K_f, and uploads it to the blockchain. Then, the server uses it to locate all matched indexes, and marks these entries with a tag "$-$" representing file revocation, as shown in Algorithm 4. In our design, all matched indexes are deleted by directly retrieving I_f without traversing the whole index. Moreover, These revoked entries are removed after they have been retrieved, there is no need to update the checklist after each file deletion, and the previous on-chain checklist is still valid. Hence, our construction can greatly reduce computation overhead and achieve optimized update efficiency.

4.5 Security Analysis

The proposed index construction holds the security notion of SSE. Only the index size is known to the storage server. Without querying, no other information about the underlying content is learned. Due to the blockchain verification, the user can always receive correct search results with assurance. For dynamic operations, each newly added index is generated from the latest state and a fresh key. This approach can effectively hide the association between the previously searched keywords and the newly added files (forward-secure). In terms of the on-chain checklist, we note that the inference attack utilizes the result distribution to map each result set to the element of the plaintext space with the same distribution. By encoding the result set into a random mask, it is infeasible to determine the correlations among different result set. The formal proof is omitted from this version of the paper to save space and will be discussed in extension version.

5 Experimental Evaluation

5.1 Prototype Implementation

We implement the proposed system prototype in C++ and execute the performance evaluation on Amazon Web Services. We create the AWS "C5.xlarge"

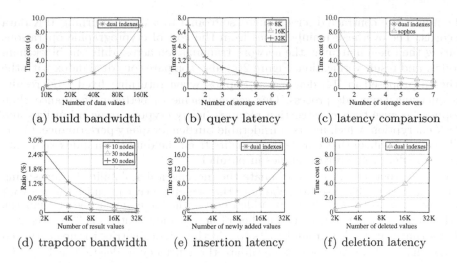

Fig. 2. Performance evaluation

instances with 4 vcores (3 GHz Intel Xeon® Platinum 8124M), and 8 GB RAM. In this experiment, we generate a Redis (v3.2.0) server that consists of 9 AWS "C5.xlarge" instances to simulate the blockchain nodes and one AWS "C5.xlarge" instances as the storage server. All of these instances are installed on Ubuntu server 14.04. Our system uses Apache Thrift (v0.9.2) to implement the remote procedure call (RPC). For cryptographic primitives, we use OpenSSL (v1.01f) to implement the symmetric encryption via AES-128 and the pseudo-random function via HMAC-256.

5.2   Performance Evaluation

Index Evaluation: We first assess the space consumption of our dual index. Here, we use HMAC-256 algorithm to generate building blocks. Since each index contains the file and keyword entries, the size of each index entry $\langle I_w, I_f \rangle$ is 256×2 bits. Therefore, our design imposes modest overhead on space cost. Figure 2(a) presents the time cost of building the encrypted indexes at the client side. Specifically, it only takes less than 9.0s to finish the building procedure when encrypting 160K index entries.

Query Evaluation: To assess the system efficiency and security overhead, we measure the processing latency under different workload, the time cost of data insertion and deletion, and the bandwidth overhead. To evaluate the performance of our design, Fig. 2(b) first evaluates the query latency for keyword-match operation. It is worth to note that our dual index chain can map duplicates to single chain reference and locates them all in a scan. When the number of data set is 8K, the query latency with 3 storage servers is around 0.6 s, which is almost one-third of the latency with 32K data set. Besides, since the local indexes are stored together with the data files at storage servers, it can process the user's request in parallel. Specifically, the query latency decreases from about 3.6 s to 1.2 s as the number of contracted servers increase from 1 to 4 when returning 16K data records. The overhead mainly comes from the cost of cryptographic operations during the token matching, the network transmission across different blockchain nodes, and result verification. Figure 2(c) also compares our dual index with the scheme proposed in [14] denoted as Sophos when returning fixed $16K$ results in querying keywords process. Our scheme achieves better performance than Sophos because their construction requires heavy cryptographic primitives and RSA encryption, which incurs considerable burden for query performance. Overall, we can confirm that our design benefits from the dual chain index structure and can effectively process queries in parallel.

In this experiment, we also evaluate the incremental scalability by measuring the time cost for file insertion. We note that the time cost includes the network transmission cost for each newly added entry, thus it is much higher than the index building time. When the number of newly added entries is 32K, Fig. 2(e) shows that it just takes around 13.2 s to add these index entries to the encrypted index chain. Meanwhile, we also evaluate the efficiency of deletion in Fig. 2(f). As mentioned in Sect. 4.4, the process of delete operations is exactly the same as the search operation. Specifically, it only takes 7.4 s to delete 32K records.

Recall that the distributed blockchain network requires the client to broadcast query trapdoors to each blockchain node. To understand the bandwidth overhead, Fig. 2(d) shows the ratio between the query token size and result size. The result indicates that the bandwidth ratio of search trapdoor decreases gradually with the increased size of results. When there are 50 nodes at the blockchain network, the bandwidth ratio drops from about 2.50% to approximately 0.16% when the number of retrieved result values rises from 2K to 32K. Nevertheless, the bandwidth overhead is still negligible to the size of results.

6 Conclusion

In this paper, we present a completely new index structure enabling forward security and reliable search in blockchain-based storage systems. To enable verification within the blockchain, an efficient on-chain checklist accordingly is provided, which can also protect partial information of underlying results. Extensive experiments show that it preserves advantages in existing decentralized systems. Overall, our design can be viewed as complementary components to be integrated with existing blockchain systems that support secure and reliable queries for more comprehensive file outsourcing services.

References

1. Curtmola, R., Garay, J., Kamara, S., Ostrovsky, R.: Searchable symmetric encryption: improved definitions and efficient constructions. J. Comput. Secur. **19**(5), 895–934 (2011)
2. Kamara, S., Papamanthou, C., Roeder, T.: Dynamic searchable symmetric encryption. In: Proceedings of the 2012 ACM Conference on Computer and Communications Security, pp. 965–976 (2012)

3. Cash, D., et al.: Dynamic searchable encryption in very-large databases: data structures and implementation. In: NDSS, vol. 14, pp. 23–26. Citeseer (2014)
4. Wilkinson, S., Boshevski, T., Brandoff, J., Buterin, V.: Storj a peer-to-peer cloud storage network (2014)
5. Przydatek, B., Song, D., Perrig, A.: SIA: secure information aggregation in sensor networks. In: Proceedings of the 1st International Conference on Embedded Networked Sensor Systems, pp. 255–265 (2003)
6. Benet, J., Greco, N.: Filecoin: A decentralized storage network. Protoc, Labs (2018)
7. Hu, S., Cai, C., Wang, Q., Wang, C., Luo, X., Ren, K.: Searching an encrypted cloud meets blockchain: a decentralized, reliable and fair realization. In: IEEE INFOCOM 2018-IEEE Conference on Computer Communications, pp. 792–800. IEEE (2018)
8. Cai, C., Weng, J., Yuan, X., et al.: Enabling reliable keyword search in encrypted decentralized storage with fairness. IEEE Trans. Depend. Secure Comput. 1 (2018)
9. Clarke, D., Devadas, S., van Dijk, M., Gassend, B., Suh, G.E.: Incremental multiset hash functions and their application to memory integrity checking. In: Laih, C.-S. (ed.) ASIACRYPT 2003. LNCS, vol. 2894, pp. 188–207. Springer, Heidelberg (2003). https://doi.org/10.1007/978-3-540-40061-5_12
10. Nakamoto, S.: Bitcoin: a peer-to-peer electronic cash system. Technical report, Manubot (2019)
11. Wood, G., et al.: Ethereum: A secure decentralised generalised transaction ledger. Ethereum project yellow paper, vol. 151, no. 2014, pp. 1–32 (2014)
12. Yao, J., et al.: A privacy-preserving system for targeted coupon service. IEEE ACCESS **7**, 120817–120830 (2019)
13. Wilkinson, S., Lowry, J., Boshevski, T.: Metadisk a blockchain-based decentralized file storage application. Technical report (2014)
14. Bost, R.: Sophos: forward secure searchable encryption. In: Proceedings of the 2016 ACM SIGSAC Conference on Computer and Communications Security, pp. 1143–1154 (2016)
15. Bost, R., Minaud, B., Ohrimenko, O.: Forward and backward private searchable encryption from constrained cryptographic primitives. In: Proceedings of the 2017 ACM SIGSAC Conference on Computer and Communications Security, pp. 1465–1482 (2017)
16. Kim, K.S., Kim, M., Lee, D., Park, J.H., Kim, W.-H.: Forward secure dynamic searchable symmetric encryption with efficient updates. In: Proceedings of the 2017 ACM SIGSAC Conference on Computer and Communications Security, pp. 1449–1463 (2017)
17. Guo, Y., Yuan, X., Wang, X., Wang, C., Li, B., Jia, X.: Enabling encrypted rich queries in distributed key-value stores. IEEE TPDS **30**(7), 1283–1297 (2018)
18. Wang, Q., Guo, Y., Huang, H., Jia, X.: Multi-user forward secure dynamic searchable symmetric encryption. In: Proceedings of NSS (2018)
19. Guo, Y., Wang, C., Yuan, X., Jia, X.: Enabling privacy-preserving header matching for outsourced middleboxes. In: Proceedings of IEEE IWQoS (2018)
20. Stefanov, E., Papamanthou, C., Shi, E.: Practical dynamic searchable encryption with small leakage. In: NDSS, vol. 71, pp. 72–75 (2014)

Capacity Analysis of Ambient Backscatter System with Bernoulli Distributed Excitation

Pengfei Li, Xin He$^{(\boxtimes)}$, Nikolaos M. Freris, and PanLong Yang$^{(\boxtimes)}$

LINKE Lab, School of Computer Science and Technology,
University of Science and Technology of China, Hefei, China
lpf96314@mail.ustc.edu.cn
{xhe076,nfr,plyang}@ustc.edu.cn

Abstract. In recent years, building Internet of Things (IoT) systems through backscatter communication techniques has gained rapid popularity. Backscatter communication relying on passive reflections of the existing RF signals enables low-power and low-complexity communication, which exactly meets the requirements of many emerging IoT applications. However, the performance of the backscatter communication systems severely degrades due to the fact that the real-life radio-frequency excitation signals such as WiFi transmissions have dynamic property. To examine how the dynamic property affects the performance of backscatter systems, it is of great significance to theoretically analyze the capacity and data rate. We can then use these analyses to optimize the backscatter systems. In this paper, we investigate the capacity and the achievable data rate of the ambient backscatter with the dynamic excitation. In particular, we model the dynamic source as a Bernoulli distribution and derive the corresponding channel capacity. We then use the maximum a posteriori criterion to build the optimal signal detection algorithm. The numerical results verify our theoretical analysis and prove that the effect of dynamic property is significant. Moreover, we find that the random excitation has much more influence on the system performance than other impact factors, like the signal-to-noise ratio.

Keywords: Ambient backscatter · Dynamic excitation · Capacity · Achievable rate

1 Introduction

The Internet of things (IoT) is gaining momentum which will connect ten billions of devices in the near future. The big challenge is how to power these huge number of devices and achieve ubiquitous communications with them. It is hard to fully rely on the existing communication techniques with batteries. Recently, a backscatter communication technique [1–4] has been recognized as a promising solution for enabling large scale IoT. With the backscatter communication, the

© Springer Nature Switzerland AG 2020
D. Yu et al. (Eds.): WASA 2020, LNCS 12384, pp. 218–230, 2020.
https://doi.org/10.1007/978-3-030-59016-1_19

IoT devices could work without batteries and deliver their sensing data to a gateway with a very low communication cost.

In a backscatter communication system, the IoT device (hereafter it is referred as "tag") modulates its data on carrier signals which are not generated by itself. The power consumption of the communication at the tag is thus significantly low. The excitation source which generates the carrier signal can be particularly deployed or the existing radio-frequency (RF) infrastructures, like TV [1], WiFi [5], Bluetooth [6], etc. The backscatter system operates in the latter mode is referred as *ambient* backscatter which shows its great potentials. The major advantage of an ambient backscatter system is the ubiquitous nature of the excitation sources, which enables an easy-to-deploy backscatter system.

The tag in an ambient backscatter system can simply transmit the data using the on-off signalling, for example, it delivers the bit "1" by reflecting the incoming excitation signal from an ambient source to a receiver, and the bit "0" by not reflecting the signal. The receiver decodes the data from the tag by some specific signal detection techniques. The data rate of the ambient backscatter is restricted due to the reason that it is extremely difficult to implement sophisticated signal processing and communication algorithms at the tag with simple structures. In the BackFi system, the achievable data rate is 5 Mbps [2] in a field study. It is of great importance to answer the question what is the limit on the data rate of an ambient backscatter system. The reason is twofold. First, like the regular communication systems, we have a criterion (theoretical limit on the data rate) to determine how well a designed backscatter system is. Second, from the analysis of the achievable data rate, it is able to optimize the system design in practice using theoertical results. To this end, from the theoretical perspective, the capacity and achievable data rate have been analyzed in [7,8] for ambient backscatter systems. Furthermore, a series of detection algorithms have been proposed in the theoretical analysis framework [9–11]. However, as stated in [12], the data rate significantly drops if the excitation source is dynamic, i.e., the RF signals from the excitation sources are occupied (available) occasionally. For example, the WiFi excitation is in a burst manner and the ambient backscatter cannot work if the excitation is off. Such dynamic property of the excitation brings new challenges on designing the backscatter system. However, the existing theoretical work rarely consider the impact of the dynamic excitation. This motivates us to work on the theoretical analysis of the ambient backscatter system with a dynamic excitation.

The address the dynamic characteristics of the excitation source, we introduce a random distribution in the capacity analysis and derives a signal detection based on the *maximum a posteriori* (MAP) criterion. Through the capacity analysis, we find that the dynamic property, specifically, the random on/off nature of the excitation source has a greater impact on the system performance than other factors. Our capacity analysis has shed the light on building the optimization framework of the practical design and the signal processing algorithms of the ambient backscatter with the dynamic excitation. In particular, our contributions are summarized as follow.

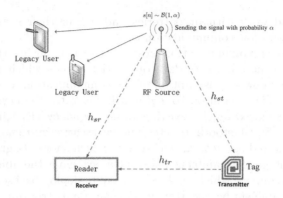

Fig. 1. A communication system utilizing ambient backscatter.

- We generalize the dynamic property of the excitation source as a Bernoulli distribution. Using different parameters of the Bernoulli distribution to describe the random on/off states, we analyze the impact of the dynamic property on the achievable data rate.
- An optimal detection algorithm for the dynamic ambient backscatter system is designed based on MAP criterion. The detection can be used in practice for improving the system performance.
- We analyze the capacity of the proposed system and evaluate the capacity performance with different parameters. The results verify that the system performance is significantly affected by the dynamic property of the excitation.

In the rest of the paper, we describe our system model of the dynamic ambient backscatter in Sect. 2. We derive the detection algorithm in Sect. 3. In Sect. 4, the capacity of the backscatter system is derived based on the mutual information. The results is presented in Sect. 5, followed by the discussion on the results in Sect. 6. Finally, we conclude this paper in Sect. 7.

2   System Model

As shown in Fig. 1, we consider a representative ambient backscatter communication system which includes an ambient source, a reader and a batteryless tag [1]. The reader and the tag can receive the RF signals simultaneously. An environment source sends over signals to its legacy users such as televisions, mobile phones or other devices. Specifically, the tag will backscatter or absorb the received signal by switch its antenna load coefficients. Accordingly, the reader's receiving end can detect two conditions: backscatter and non-backscatter, the former can represent bit "1" and the latter represents bit "0".

Let h_{st}, h_{sr} and h_{tr} respectively denote the channel coefficients between the ambient source and the tag, between the ambient source and the reader, and between the reader and the tag. The channel coefficients h_{st}, h_{sr} and h_{tr} are assumed as zero-mean Gaussian random with different variances, slow-fading meanwhile remain unchanged during at least one consecutive interval.

The received signal at the tag can be then expressed as

$$x[n] = h_{st}s[n] + w_t[n] \tag{1}$$

The RF signal from the ambient source $s[n]$ is generally assumed to be Bernoulli distribution, i.e., $s[n] \sim \mathcal{B}(1, \alpha)$. If the excitation source $s[n]$ takes the value 1, then the excitation is available. Otherwise, the excitation is absent and the backscatter system cannot work. $w_t[n]$ is the tag internal noise which can be ignored because the tag is a passive component and only takes few signal processing operations [10].

As described earlier, the tag receives the RF signal $s[n]$ from the source and transmit its own binary message through backscattering the signal $s[n]$ or not. Specifically a part of the ambient signal $x[n]$ is harvested to support the operation of the circuit of the tag [7].

Then we can obtain the signal transmitted by the tag as

$$x_b[n] = \eta dx[n] \quad d = 0, 1 \tag{2}$$

where η is a coefficient representing complex attenuation of the backscattered signals relative to the received signal $s[n]$. Let d denote the binary transmitter symbols of the tag.

Noting that the data rate of the legacy signal $s[n]$ is much higher than transmitting data of tag, so we can assume tag's symbol remains unchanged for N consecutive $s[n]$'s.

Finally, the reader receives the signal

$$y[n] = (h_{sr} + \eta h_{st}h_{tr}d)s[n] + w[n] \tag{3}$$

where $w[n]$ is the zero-mean additive white Gaussian noise (AWGN) term at the reader with noise power σ_w^2, i.e., $s[n] \sim \mathcal{N}(0, \sigma_w^2)$. Next, the reader aims to recover the tag signals d from the received signals $y[n]$.

3   Detection Algorithm and Performance Analysis

We introduce our presented detection algorithm and analyze its bit error rate (BER) performance in this section. In particular, we derive the theoretical bit error rate with a closed-form expression and prove the existence of lower bound on the bit error rate.

3.1   Detector Design

Now we start to describe the principle of the decoding process of the symbol d at the receiver. Denote $h_0 = h_{st}$, $h_1 = h_{sr} + \eta h_{st}h_{tr}$ and H_i is assuming that $d = i$ is transmitted by the tag. There is

$$y[n] = \begin{cases} \sqrt{P_s}h_0 s[n] + w[n], & case H_0 : d = 0 \\ \sqrt{P_s}h_1 s[n] + w[n], & case H_1 : d = 1 \end{cases} \tag{4}$$

We in general assume that the binary input distribution of d is $P_{d=0} = p$, $P_{d=1} = 1 - p$ and $p/(1-p) = \lambda$. Notice that if $p = 0.5$, then our derived MAP detector reduces to a maximum likelihood detector.

Next, the receiver in the reader calculates the average power of the N samples about $y[n]$ corresponding to one single backscattered bit, as

$$\Gamma_l = \frac{1}{N} \sum_{n=(l-1)N+1}^{lN} y[n], \quad 1 < l < L. \tag{5}$$

Assume h_0 and h_1 are known to the reader. The term $\sum_{n=(l-1)N+1}^{lN} s[n]$ is approximated to a Gaussian distribution $\mathcal{N}(N\alpha, N\alpha(1-\alpha))$ when N is large enough [11] according to the central limit theorem. Therefore, we obtain the following results

$$\Gamma_l = \begin{cases} \Gamma_0 \sim \mathcal{N}(\sqrt{P_s}h_0\alpha, \frac{1}{N}(P_s h_0^2 \alpha(1-\alpha) + \sigma_w^2)) & d = 0 \\ \Gamma_1 \sim \mathcal{N}(\sqrt{P_s}h_1\alpha, \frac{1}{N}(P_s h_1^2 \alpha(1-\alpha) + \sigma_w^2)) & d = 1 \end{cases} \tag{6}$$

when $d = i$, of which the probability density function (PDF) is given by

$$P(\Gamma_k|H_i) = \frac{1}{\sqrt{2\pi}\sigma_i} exp\left(\frac{-(x-\mu_i)^2}{2\sigma_i^2}\right) \tag{7}$$

with means and variances:

$$\mu_0 = \sqrt{P_s}h_0\alpha, \qquad \mu_1 = \sqrt{P_s}h_1\alpha \tag{8}$$

$$\sigma_0^2 = \frac{1}{N}(P_s h_0^2 \alpha(1-\alpha) + \sigma_w^2), \qquad \sigma_1^2 = \frac{1}{N}(P_s h_1^2 \alpha(1-\alpha) + \sigma_w^2) \tag{9}$$

Moreover, we can derive the posteriori probability as

$$P(H_i|\Gamma_k) = \frac{P(\Gamma_k|H_i)P(H_i)}{P(\Gamma_k)} \tag{10}$$

The likelihood ratio related to the optimal MAP [9] detection is

$$\Lambda(\Gamma_l) = \frac{P(\Gamma_l|H_0)}{P(\Gamma_l|H_1)} = \frac{\sigma_1}{\sigma_0} \exp\left(\frac{(x-\mu_1)^2}{2\sigma_1^2} - \frac{(x-\mu_0)^2}{2\sigma_0^2}\right) = \frac{1}{\lambda} \tag{11}$$

The solutions of (11) is derived as (12) and (13)

$$T_a = \frac{(2\sigma_0^2\mu_1 - 2\sigma_1^2\mu_0) + \sqrt{(2\sigma_0^2\mu_1 - 2\sigma_1^2\mu_0)^2 - 4(\sigma_0^2 - \sigma_1^2)(\sigma_0^2\mu_1^2 - \sigma_1^2\mu_0^2 - 2\sigma_0^2\sigma_1^2 ln\frac{\sigma_0}{\lambda\sigma_1})}}{2(\sigma_0^2 - \sigma_1^2)} \tag{12}$$

$$T_b = \frac{(2\sigma_0^2\mu_1 - 2\sigma_1^2\mu_0) - \sqrt{(2\sigma_0^2\mu_1 - 2\sigma_1^2\mu_0)^2 - 4(\sigma_0^2 - \sigma_1^2)(\sigma_0^2\mu_1^2 - \sigma_1^2\mu_0^2 - 2\sigma_0^2\sigma_1^2 ln\frac{\sigma_0}{\lambda\sigma_1})}}{2(\sigma_0^2 - \sigma_1^2)} \tag{13}$$

The MAP threshold based on (11) is set as

$$T_{map} = \begin{cases} T_a, & |T_a - \mu_0| < |T_b - \mu_0| \\ T_b, & |T_a - \mu_0| \geq |T_b - \mu_0| \end{cases} \tag{14}$$

At last, the relevant detection rules are summarized as follows

In the case of $h_{st}h_{tr} > 0$

$$\widehat{H} = \begin{cases} H_0, & if \ \Gamma_k < T_{map} \\ H_1, & if \ \Gamma_k \geq T_{map} \end{cases} \tag{15}$$

In the case of $h_{st}h_{tr} < 0$

$$\widehat{H} = \begin{cases} H_0, & if \ \Gamma_k \geq T_{map} \\ H_1, & if \ \Gamma_k < T_{map} \end{cases} \tag{16}$$

3.2   BER Performance Analysis

The transition probability matrix $\boldsymbol{P}$ of the backscatter system is given by

$$\boldsymbol{P} = \begin{pmatrix} P_{0|0} & P_{1|0} \\ P_{0|1} & P_{1|1} \end{pmatrix} \tag{17}$$

where $P_{j|i}$ denotes the conditional probability that the input i gets the output j.
The error probability related to our detector is given by

$$P_e = p * P_{1|0} + (1 - p) * P_{0|1} \tag{18}$$

where

$$P_{1|0} = P(\Gamma_k > T_{map}|H_0) = Q(\frac{T_{map} - \mu_0}{\sigma_0}) \tag{19}$$

$$P_{0|1} = P(\Gamma_k < T_{map}|H_1) = 1 - Q(\frac{T_{map} - \mu_1}{\sigma_1}) \tag{20}$$

with $Q(x)$ denoting the Gaussian Q-function and being

$$Q(x) = \int_x^\infty e^{-\frac{t^2}{2}} \, dt \tag{21}$$

Furthermore, we can get the BER expression as

$$P_e = pQ(\frac{T_{map} - \mu_0}{\sigma_0}) + (1 - p)Q(\frac{\mu_1 - T_{map}}{\sigma_1}) \tag{22}$$

3.3   Performance Analysis at High SNR

Define $\gamma = \frac{P_s}{\sigma_w^2}$ as the SNR at the receiver side. Now we turn to investigate the asymptotic error probability performance when $\gamma \to +\infty$, i.e., $\lim\limits_{\gamma \to +\infty} P_e$. For the simplicity of our discussion, we only consider the situation when $T_{map} = T_a$.

At the high SNR regime, we have $P_s \gg \sigma_w^2$. Thus, we obtain the following approximation

$$\sigma_0^2 = \frac{1}{N}(P_s h_0^2 \alpha (1 - \alpha)), \qquad \sigma_1^2 = \frac{1}{N}(P_s h_1^2 \alpha (1 - \alpha)) \tag{23}$$

However, in reality, the variation on the received SNR is caused by both the change on P_s and σ_w^2. Therefore we cannot just make P_s very large and keep σ_w^2 the same, or assume P_s a constant and let σ_w^2 go to zero to make SNR go to infinity. Instead, we assume that the received SNR γ goes to infinity to analyze the performance for the high SNR regime.

Thus, when assuming high SNR, we obtain for the first term of (19) that

$$\lim_{\gamma \to +\infty} P_{1|0} = \lim_{\gamma \to +\infty} Q(\frac{T_{map} - \sqrt{P_s} h_0 \alpha}{\sqrt{\frac{1}{N}(P_s h_0^2 \alpha (1 - \alpha) + \sigma_w^2)}}) \tag{24}$$

$$= Q(\frac{\lim\limits_{\gamma \to +\infty} \frac{T_{map}}{\sqrt{P_s}} - h_0 \alpha}{\sqrt{\frac{1}{N} h_0^2 \alpha (1 - \alpha)}})$$

And it can be readily checked that

$$\lim_{\gamma \to +\infty} \frac{T_{map}}{\sqrt{P_s}} = \frac{h_0 h_1 (\alpha + \sqrt{\alpha^2 + \alpha(1 - \alpha) \frac{2}{N} \frac{h_0 + h_1}{h_0 - h_1} ln \frac{h_0}{\lambda h_1}})}{h_0 + h_1} \tag{25}$$

The reference [13] gives a good and simple approximation for $Q(x)$ as

$$Q(x) \approx \frac{1}{12} e^{-\frac{x^2}{2}} + \frac{1}{4} e^{-\frac{2x^2}{3}} \tag{26}$$

Finally, we can obtain $\lim\limits_{\gamma \to +\infty} P_e$ through equations (18), (24), (25) and (26).

4   Capaciy Analysis

4.1   Mutual Information

We basically focus on the binary input case for the ambient backscattering system to evaluate the capacity [14]. Thus, the Shannon capacity with Gaussian input cannot be used to the derivation to the capacity of the ambient backscattering system.

The channel output is in the form of a binary discrete random variable, denoted as Y that possible values may be $\hat{d} = 0$ or $\hat{d} = 1$. For the binary input and binary output channel with input X and output Y, the mutual information expression is

$$I(X;Y) = \sum_{i=0,1} P(d=i)I(d=i;Y) = pI(d=0;Y) + (1-p)I(d=1;Y) \quad (27)$$

with $I(d=i;Y)$ being the mutual information between the input X and the output Y, as

$$I(d=i;Y) = \sum_{j=0}^{1} P(\hat{d}=j|d=i) \times log\frac{P(\hat{d}=j|d=i)}{\sum_{k=0}^{1} P(d=k)P(\hat{d}=j|d=k)} \quad (28)$$

$$= \sum_{j=0}^{1} P_{j|i} \times log\frac{P_{j|i}}{pP_{j|0} + (1-p)P_{j|1}}$$

4.2   Capacity-Achieving

We know that the independent variable of the mutual information function is p, so we define the capacity as a funciton of p, as

$$C = \max I(X;Y) = C(p) \quad (29)$$

And then the way we get the optimal p is by solving the following optimization problem

$$p^* = \arg\max C(p) \quad (30)$$

The optimal input distribution should be achieved when $\frac{\partial C(p)}{\partial p} = 0$ holds which a closed-form expression is unfortunately difficult to acquire. However,since the function $C(p)$ has only one single variable p, we could simply apply a one-dimensional searching in $\frac{\partial C(p)}{\partial p} = 0$ to get the optimal value under a certain signal-to-noise ratio.

4.3   Capacity-Ceiling

As stated in Sect. 3 that when the SNR is infinite, the BER of symbol detection in ambient backscatter communication system based on the MAP criterion reachs a lower bound. Therefore, it is reasonable to know that when the SNR goes to infinity, the channel capacity also reachs an upper bound, which is called the capacity-ceiling.

Because our method for calculating the mutual information of the channel capacity is composed of the conditional probability $P_{i|j}$ in the transition probability matrix P in ambient backscatter communication system. In the previous section, we have derived the expression of conditional probability q under a high SNR. Therefore, the expression can be directly substituted into the mutual information equation to obtain the mutual information expression under a high SNR. Finally, the channel capacity is obtained according to the method in the previous section.

5   Numerical Results

Next, we conduct a numerical analysis of our derived capacity and MAP detection in this section. We first set the ambient noise variance in the system as a unit quantity, i.e., $\sigma_w^2 = 1$. As we mentioned previously, the channel coefficients h_{st}, h_{sr} and h_{tr} are all subject to Gaussian random variables with the mean value of 0, but the variances of the channel coefficients is different due to different communication distances. In reality, in the environmental backscatter communication system we studied, the distance between the tag and the reader is usually very close, but the distance between the tag and the RF source, or between the reader and the RF source, is much longer than the distance between the tag and the reader. In view of this, we set variables of channel h_{st} and h_{sr} as unit variance, and set the variance of channel variable as 5.

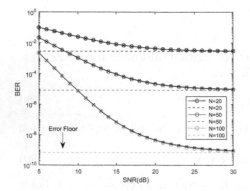

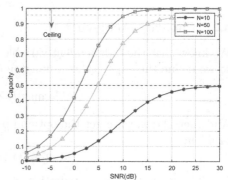

Fig. 2. SNR versus BER under three different sampling numbers.

Fig. 3. Channel capacity versus transmit SNR of a specific channel realization.

In most actual channel transmissions, the information bits "0" and "1" are equally likely to transmit [15].

Here we set $\eta = 0.7$, $p = 0.5$, and increase SNR from 0 dB to $30 dB$. We detect the BER for each given signal-to-noise ratio evaluated at the reader. For each given SNR, we repeated the simulation 10^5 times to get the average BER. We set the number of samples to be 20, 50 and 100 respectively. With the change of SNR, the performance of BER is shown in the Fig. 2. As we can be seen from the figure, the error between the BER obtained by simulation and the theoretical BER is almost negligible. Moreover, with the increase of SNR, the BER also decreases, and the drop speed is from fast to slow, and finally approach 0. At this time, the BER decreases to the lower bound at the high SNR region, which also verifies our inference.

In Fig. 3, we show the relationship between the channel capacity and the SNR under several different sampling numbers. We can clearly see from the figure that, with the increase of SNR, the channel capacity first increases slowly, then grows faster gradually, and then slows down nearly unchanged. When the

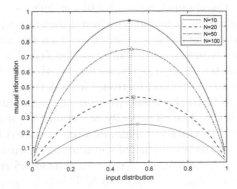

Fig. 4. Mutual information $I(X;Y)$ versus input distribution p under four different sampling numbers.

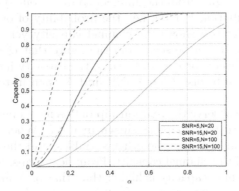

Fig. 5. Channel capacity versus excitation probability α of a specific channel realization.

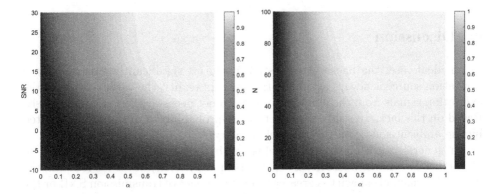

Fig. 6. The heat map of the influence of SNR, N and the probability α of excitation signal on channel capacity.

SNR is large enough, the channel capacity will not increase, which corresponds to the capacity ceiling region. It can also be found that the capacity performance almost keeps at a certain value when N increases to a certain value.

Figure 4 shows the change of mutual information $I(X; Y)$ as the input distribution p increases from 0 to 1. Obviously, we can see that as the input increases, the mutual information $I(X; Y)$ first increases from 0, then becomes a downward trend and falls back to 0. In the whole process, the maximum value of mutual information $I(X; Y)$ is the channel capacity we require. To make the value clear, we use a special marker to mark the maximum and a dotted line to connect the corresponding inputs to the maximum of the mutual information $I(X; Y)$. Further, we can observe that the maximum value of mutual information is not when the input distribution p is exactly equal to 0.5. This is because after the receiver of the reader detects the signal, the decoded signal will not always be correct, and the wrong decoding will result in the input distribution p that maximizes the mutual information $I(X; Y)$ being shifted from 0.5 to one side.

The unknown RF signal from the ambient source in our system is assumed to be a Bernoulli distribution $\mathcal{B}(1, \alpha)$, i.e., the probability of our excitation signal producing 1 is α. Figure 5 shows the channel capacity versus α under several different parameters. It can be seen from the figure that channel capacity and α are generally positively correlated. Clearly, the capacity increases over α at a much greater speed in terms of large SNR and N than in terms of small SNR and N.

In order to better observe the relationship between channel capacity and each variable, we made two heat maps as shown in Fig. 6. Where we take α as one of the variables, N and SNR as the other variables, and the depth of the color represents the size of the channel capacity. From heat maps, we can see that the influence of α on channel capacity is higher than that of N and SNR. When the value of α is greater than 0.25, a good result is usually achieved, except in a very bad environment such as when the SNR is less than 0 dB. On the other hand, when α is small, the performance remains unchanged no matter how much we increase N or SNR.

6   Discussion

In an ideal case, the backscatter system performs significantly superior if the excitation source is always available. However, in reality, the various types of the excitation signals from the ambient sources do not necessarily exist continuously. Based on this fact, we study the effect of the probability α of the signal emitted by the ambient source on the channel capacity.

In general, we come to the conclusion that probability α is obviously an important factor which affects the channel capacity. When its value is small, the impact on channel capacity is greater than the impact of transmission SNR or the number of samples on channel capacity. Particularly, if α exceeds a small value, such as 0.25, the SNR and the sampling number have a significant impact on the performance of the channel capacity. Moreover, when both SNR and sampling number are large enough, the channel capacity basically reachs the best. On the contrary, when α is very small, the performance of the channel capacity is very poor, even if the signal-to-noise ratio or the number of samples is increased.

However, our limitation is that the environmental excitation signals in the reality does not follow an identical random distribution, and the signals emitted by the signal source in different environments may have a certain pattern, which is worth further exploration.

7 Conclusion

Ambient backscatter has a great potential of which the theoretical analysis is valuable. In this paper, we investigated the detection problem of the ambient backscattering system with a dynamic ambient sources. The detection threshold based on the MAP criterion was derived and the closed expression of channel capacity was analyzed from the viewpoint of the information theory. We also derive the expression of the BER and its lower bound, and the upper bound on the capacity when the SNR is relatively large. Finally, the simulation results verified the correctness of the theoretical analyses. Meanwhile, we observed that α has a significant influence on the channel capacity, which also provide some inspirations for our future study.

Acknowledgement. This research is in part supported by National key research and development plan 2018YFB2100302, and in part by PCL Future Greater-Bay Area Network Facilities for Large-scale Experiments and Applications (LZC0019) and Education Department Fundamental Research Project WK2150110010, and by the NSF China under Grants No. 61702011, 61772546, 61625205, 61632010, 61751211, 61190114, 61232018, PAPD, CICAEET and NSF of Jiangsu For Distinguished Young Scientist: BK20150030, and in part supported by the Anhui Provincial Natural Science Foundation: 1808085QF191, 1908085QF296, and in part supported by the University Synergy Innovation Program of Anhui Province under Grant No. GXXT-2019-024. Corresponding authors are Panlong Yang and Xin He.

References

1. Liu, V., Parks, A., Talla, V., Gollakota, S., Wetherall, D., Smith, J.R.: Ambient backscatter: wireless communication out of thin air. In: Proceedings of ACM SIGCOMM, New York, NY, USA. ACM (2013)
2. Bharadia, D., Joshi, K.R., Kotaru, M., Katti, S.: BackFi: high throughput wifi backscatter. In: Proceedings of ACM SIGCOMM, New York, NY, USA, pp. 283–296. ACM (2015)
3. Chen, G., Li, Z.: Peer-to-Peer Network: Structure, Application and Design. Tsinghua University Press, Beijing (2007)
4. Mi, N., et al.: Cbma: Coded-backscatter multiple access. In: 2019 IEEE 39th International Conference on Distributed Computing Systems (ICDCS), pp. 799–809 (2019)

5. Zhang, P., Bharadia, D., Joshi, K., Katti, S.: HitchHike: Practical backscatter using commodity wifi. In: Proceedings of ACM SenSys, New York, NY, USA. ACM (2016)
6. Zhang, P., Josephson, C., Bharadia, D., Katti, S.: FreeRider: backscatter communication using commodity radios. In: Proceedings of CoNEXT, New York, NY, USA. ACM (2017)
7. Qian, J., Zhu, Y., He, C., Gao, F., Jin, S.: Achievable rate and capacity analysis for ambient backscatter communications. IEEE Trans. Commun. **67**(9), 6299–6310 (2019)
8. Zhao, W., Wang, G., Gao, F., Zou, Y., Atapattu, S.: Channel capacity and lower bound for ambient backscatter communication systems. In: 2017 9th International Conference on Wireless Communications and Signal Processing (WCSP) (2017)
9. Wang, G., Gao, F., Fan, R., Tellambura, C.: Ambient backscatter communication systems: Detection and performance analysis. IEEE Trans. Commun. **64**(11), 4836–4846 (2016)
10. Qian, J., Gao, F.: Semi-coherent detector of ambient backscatter communication for the internet of things. In: 2017 IEEE 18th International Workshop on Signal Processing Advances in Wireless Communications (SPAWC), pp. 1–5 (2017)
11. Liu, Y., Wang, G., Dou, Z., Zhong, Z.: Coding and detection schemes for ambient backscatter communication systems. IEEE Access **5**, 4947–4953 (2017)
12. He, X., Jiang, W., Cheng, M., Zhou, X., Yang, P., Kurkoski, B.: Guardrider: reliable WiFi backscatter using reed-Solomon codes with QoS guarantee. In: Proceedings IEEE/ACM IWQoS, Hangzhou, China, June 2020
13. Chiani, M., Dardari, D., Simon, M.K.: New exponential bounds and approximations for the computation of error probability in fading channels. IEEE Trans. Wireless Commun. **2**(4), 840–845 (2003)
14. Moskowitz, I.S.: Approximations for the capacity of binary input discrete memoryless channels. In: 2010 44th Annual Conference on Information Sciences and Systems (CISS), pp. 1–5 (2010)
15. Chen, W.: Cao-sir: channel aware ordered successive relaying. IEEE Trans. Wireless Commun. **13**(12), 6513–6527 (2014)

Multiset Synchronization with Counting Cuckoo Filters

Shangsen Li[1], Lailong Luo[1(✉)], Deke Guo[1(✉)], and Yawei Zhao[2]

[1] Science and Technology on Information Systems Engineering Laboratory,
Changsha, People's Republic of China
{luolailong09,dekeguo}@nudt.edu.cn
[2] School of Computer Science and Technology, National University of Defense
Technology, Changsha 410073, Hunan, People's Republic of China

Abstract. Set synchronization, which targets at identifying and then exchanging the different elements between two given sets, is a fundamental task in distributed applications and implementations. Existing methods that synchronize simple sets are mainly based on compact data structures such as Bloom filter and its variants. However, these methods are infeasible to synchronize a pair of multisets that allow an element to appear multiple times. To this end, in this paper, we propose to leverage the counting cuckoo filter (CCF), a novel variant of cuckoo filter, to represent and, after that, synchronize a pair of multisets. The cuckoo filter (CF) is a minimized hash table that uses cuckoo hashing to resolve collisions. CF has an array of buckets, each of which has multiple slots to store element fingerprints. Based on CF, CCF extends each slot as two fields, the fingerprint field, and the counter field. The fingerprint field records the fingerprint of element which is stored by this slot; while the counter field counts the multiplicity of the stored element. With such a design, CCF is competent to represent any multiset. After generating and exchanging the respective CCFs which represent the local multisets, we propose a query-based and decoding-based methods to identify the different elements between the given multisets. The comprehensive evaluation results indicate that CCF outperforms its same kind in terms of both synchronization accuracy and the space-efficiency, at the cost of a little higher time-consumption.

Keywords: Multiset synchronization · Cuckoo filter · Bloom filter

1 Introduction

Consider a couple of hosts $host_A$ and $host_B$ with set A and B respectively, set synchronization means to derive out the elements in $(A \cup B) - (A \cap B)$ and then exchange them, such that eventually $A = B = A \cup B$. Set synchronization is a fundamental task in distributed applications and implementations. For example, in Vehicular Network [23], before two vehicles (nodes) communicate useful information, they need to determine the trustfulness among them while

© Springer Nature Switzerland AG 2020
D. Yu et al. (Eds.): WASA 2020, LNCS 12384, pp. 231–243, 2020.
https://doi.org/10.1007/978-3-030-59016-1_20

preserving their privacy. In wireless sensor networks [12], two hosts need to get a union of their sets, which could be file blocks or link-state packets. In cloud storage systems [3], the data synchronization among personal digital devices, such as smartphones, PC, and tablets, is implemented as multiple two-party set synchronization tasks. And sensitive data sharing through cloud storage environments have brought various and flexible demands. In Internet of Things (IoT)[1], data acquisition is a fundamental problem. Sensor nodes are distributed over a region of interests, and the data is collected at a specified time interval. In distributed file systems [22], data consistency must be guaranteed during asynchronous updates between the heterogeneous or homogeneous storage systems.

Nowadays, more and more applications rely on the multiset abstraction [16] rather than the previous simple set abstraction. In a multiset, an element can have multiple replicas; by contrast, a simple set element only allows one element instance. For example, in network monitoring, the flows are modeled as multiset elements whose contents are the source and destination IP addresses, and multiplicities are the respective number of packets contained by the flows. In online shopping, to evaluate the popularity of commodities, customer behaviors are formed as multiset elements whose element content is the commodity ID, and the multiplicity is the user' visiting frequency of this article. In Wi-Fi networks [11], it is a ubiquitous phenomenon that users roam between different access points (APs), institutions, regions, and countries. To enhance the network security and management, users should be authenticated before connecting to the network. Moreover, the users' information should be synchronized on a distributed consensus mechanism. In the blockchain, efficient set synchronization protocols are applied to synchronize newly-authored transactions and newly mined blocks of validated transactions [18]. Such protocols upgrade critical performance and reduce bandwidth consumption significantly in the blockchain context.

Existing methods that synchronize simple sets are mainly based on the compact data structures. The insight is to employ Bloom filter (BF) [2] and its variants to provide a content summarization of the local set. After exchanging and comparing these data structures, the different elements can be determined accordingly. Specifically, the counting Bloom filter (CBF) [6], compressed Bloom filter [17], invertible Bloom filter (IBF) [4] and invertible Bloom lookup table (IBLT) [7] represent all elements in a set with a vector of cells, each of which can be one single bit or a field with multiple bits. After exchanging these data structures, the different elements are determined by either a query-based (BF and CBF) or a decoding-based (IBLT and IBF) mechanism. Consequently, it is not necessary to transfer the common elements.

However, the above simple set synchronization methods are not feasible for multisets. First, they may fail to represent the multiplicity information of multiset members. The original BF bit vector definitely cannot record elements whose multiplicities are larger than 1. The XOR operations in IBF and IBLT, however, disable the representation of multiset elements since the elements with even multiplicities will be eliminated from the multiset. Second, these methods may fail to distinguish the different elements caused by distinct content (d_E) from the different elements due to unequal multiplicities (d_M). For example, CBF represents multiset elements with its counters in its cell vector naturally. However, the query-based mechanism cannot distinguish d_E from d_M. Generally, only the elements in d_E are required to be transferred, while the elements in d_M are synchronized via generating a dedicated number of replicas. Consequently, distinguishing them is quite essential for bandwidth-scarce scenarios.

In this paper, we leverage a novel design of cuckoo filter [5,14], namely the counting cuckoo filter (CCF), to represent and synchronize multisets.

After receiving CCF from the other host, the local host compares the received CCF with its own and determines the elements in d_E and d_M, respectively. By traversing the elements in the root set, local host query the multiplicity information of elements in the received CCF. By jointly considering the existence and multiplicity information, the local host can effectively distinguish d_E from d_M. The host can also directly compare two CCFs and eliminate common elements. By decoding the labeled slots in the decoded CCF, local host can correctly identify the corresponding elements' content and classify the different elements into d_E and d_M, respectively. The elements in d_M can be replicated locally for synchronization. Only the elements in d_E will be transmitted to the other host.

2   Preliminaries

2.1   Cuckoo Filter

A Cuckoo filter (CF) is a hash table with b buckets, and each bucket has w slots to accommodate at most w elements. When inserting a key, the hash table applies two perfectly random hash functions to determine two possible bucket entries where the key can be inserted [20]. Unlike the traditional cuckoo hashing table, which stores the element content directly, Fan $et\ al.$[5] represent the elements by recording their fingerprints instead in cuckoo filter. Cuckoo filter further applies the partial-key strategy to determine the candidate buckets during the insertion phase and locate the alternative candidate bucket during the reallocation phase. Specifically, for an element x with fingerprint η_x, the partial-key hashing mechanism calculates the index of two candidate buckets as follows:

$$h_1 = hash\,(x)$$
$$h_2 = h_1 \oplus hash\,(\eta_x) \tag{1}$$

CF is elegant to represent simple set, but is inefficient to represent multiset. The reason is that representing each element replicas separately with a CF slot aggressively occupies the space. As plotted in Fig. 1, a CCF consists of b buckets, each of which has w slots to accommodate at most w element fingerprints. Besides, each slot contains two fields, i.e., the fingerprint field η and the *counter* field. The fingerprint field is responsible for recording the fingerprint of element which are stored into this slot; while the *counter* field identifies the multiplicity

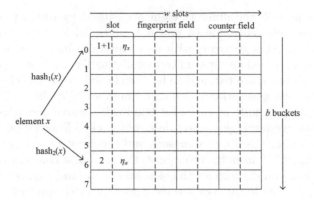

Fig. 1. Structure of counting Cuckoo filter

of that element. With such a design, CCF can naturally represent multiset with the insertion, deletion and query operations.

2.2 Counting Bloom Filter

CBF [6] is a known variant of Bloom filter [2], which leverages the k bits in a vector to represent the existence of an element in a set. Bloom filter cannot support deletion. As stated in [15], it is possible to realize multiset synchronization with CBF. However, this method incurs unacceptable synchronization accuracy. To achieve higher synchronization accuracy, the CBFs should be lengthened. The space overhead can be tremendous to achieve expected synchronization accuracy. Besides, one counter may be increased by the insertion of multiple elements, so that it can overflow easily. To avoid this overflow, CBF needs to augment more bits to the counter field, which further leads to more space overhead [21].

3   Multiset Synchronization with CCF

3.1 The Synchronization Framework

As shown in Fig. 2, to synchronize a pair of multisets, there are two rounds of interactions in the synchronization process between two hosts. In the first round of interaction, the hosts exchange their local CCFs; while the second round of interaction is to transmit the discovered different elements in d_E. The details of the synchronization framework are specified as follows.

First of all, $host_A$ and $host_B$ represent their local multisets with the CCF data structure as CCF_A and CCF_B, respectively. After that, $host_A$ sends its CCF_A to $host_B$ and vice versa. After such an interaction, both $host_A$ and $host_B$ acquire the information of the other multiset.

Then the task is to deduce the different elements at each host. Let d_{E_A} and d_{E_B} denote the elements that only contained in the multiset A and B, respectively. Let $m_A(x)$ and $m_B(x)$ represent the queried multiplicity of element x in

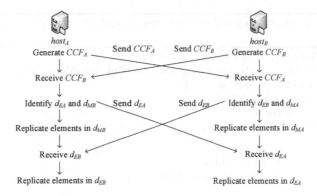

Fig. 2. The framework of multiset synchronization

CCF_A and CCF_B, respectively. Pair-wisely, let d_{M_B} and d_{M_A} denote the set of elements such that $m_B(x) > m_A(x)$ and $m_A(x) > m_B(x)$, respectively. Then $host_A$ should identify the elements in both d_{E_A} and d_{M_B}, such that the elements in d_{E_A} will be thereafter sent to $host_B$ and the elements in d_{M_B} will be replicated locally for the synchronization purpose. Note that, the number of further generated replicas of elements in d_{M_B} is $m_B(x) - m_A(x)$ at $host_A$. Similarly, $host_B$ needs to identify the elements in d_{E_B} and d_{M_A}. Then the elements in d_{E_B} will be transferred to $host_A$ while the elements in d_{M_A} will be replicated locally such that $m_A(x) = m_B(x)$ eventually. After receiving d_{E_B} from $host_B$, $host_A$ generates dedicated number of replicas according to the multiplicity information and $host_A$ also does the same thing to complete the synchronization process.

According to the above framework, the core problem of multiset synchronization with CCF is how to deduce the different elements, in both d_E and d_M. In this paper, we state that the CCF data structure enables both the query-based method and the decoding-based method to identify different elements between multisets A and B. The details are given as follows.

3.2   Identify the Different Elements via Querying

After receiving CCF_B from $host_B$, $host_A$ can deduce the different elements by simply querying its local elements in its set A^* (with no replicas) against CCF_B. CCF responds the query by returning either 0 to indicate that the queried element is not stored by this CCF or the exact multiplicity of queried element. Therefore, the joint consideration of the query result and the local element information will tell whether the queried element is a different element or not.

With the above insight, Algorithm 1 details our query-based method. Note that, this query-based method is capable of distinguishing elements in d_E from those in d_M. If the query result is zero, x is not a member of multiset B and should be added into d_{E_A} for later transmission (Line 3 to 4). On the other hand, if the query result is more than zero, it means that x is also a member of multiset B and the $m_B(x)$ equals to the returned value. Especially, if $m_A(x)$

Algorithm 1: Identifying different elements with the query-based method at $host_A$

Input   : Root set A^* of multiset A, CCF_B
Output : Elements in d_{E_A} and d_{M_B} with multiplicity information
1 **for** each element x in root set A^* **do**
2     $m_B(x) = query(x, CCF_B)$
3   **if** $m_B(x) = 0$ **then**
4   add x and $m_A(x)$ into d_{E_A}
5   **else**
6   **if** $m_A(x) < m_B(x)$ **then**
7   add x and $m_B(x) - m_A(x)$ into d_{M_B}

---

is equal to $m_B(x)$, it implies that the element x shares the same multiplicity in both multisets, no further action is triggered. On the contrary, if $m_B(x)$ is larger than $m_A(x)$, element x is identified as a member of d_{M_B} (Line 6 to 7). According to the framework presented above, additional $m_B(x) - m_A(x)$ replicas of x will be generated at $host_A$ such that eventually $m_B(x) = m_A(x)$.

Pair-wisely, $host_B$ queries the elements in its local root set B^* against the received CCF_A. The query result derives elements in d_{E_B} and d_{M_A} respectively.

3.3   Identify the Different Elements via Decoding

In this subsection, we specify how the decoding-based method eliminate the common elements and determine the different elements in d_E and d_M.

After receiving CCF_B from $host_B$, $host_A$ decodes the different elements in d_{E_A} and d_{M_B} with two main steps. The first step is to eliminate the common elements from CCF_A and label slots which hold the different elements. The second step is to determine the exact element content of the labeled slots in CCF_A. To this end, one more bit, i.e., the flag bit, is added into each slot in CCF. As specified in Algorithm 2 for each non-empty slot in CCF_A, we try to search out the stored fingerprint in the two corresponding buckets in CCF_B (Line 4 to 11). If we fortunately find this fingerprint in the *slot* of CCF_B and *slot.count* is larger than $CCF_A[i][j].count$, the flag bit in $CCF_A[i][j]$ is set to 1 to explicitly indicate that this fingerprint corresponds to an element in d_{M_B} (Line 6 to 7). On the other hand, if *slot.count* is not larger than $CCF_A[i][j].count$, we empty the $CCF_A[i][j]$ slot (Line 9). Unfortunately, if the fingerprint $CCF_A[i][j].\eta$ can be found in neither of the two candidate buckets of CCF_B, we set $CCF_A[i][j].flag$ value as 0 to signify that this element belongs to d_{E_A} (Line 11). After the above elimination and labeling process, CCF_A only stores the fingerprints corresponding to elements in d_{E_A} and d_{M_B}. Then Algorithm 2 can easily decode them out by traversing the CCF vector and the local multiset (Line 12 to 17). Similarly, $host_B$ also performs the same algorithm to decide the elements in d_{E_B} and d_{M_A}.

Algorithm 2: Identifying different elements with the decoding-based method at $host_A$

Input   : Root set A^* of multiset A, CCF_A, CCF_B
Output : Elements in d_{E_A} and d_{M_B} with multiplicity information

1 **for** $i<b$ **do**
2   **for** $j<w$ **do**
3   **if** $CCF_A[i][j].\eta$ is not empty **then**
4   **if** $CCF_A[i][j].\eta$ in $slot$ of CCF_B **then**
5                  $count=CCF_A[i][j].count$
6   **if** $count<slot.count$ **then**
7                      $CCF_A[i][j].flag=1$, $CCF_A[i][j].count=slot.count-count$
8   **else**
9   clear the slot $CCF_A[i][j]$
10   **else**
11                  $CCF_A[i][j].flag = 0$

12 **for** each element x in root set A^* **do**
13   **if** $m_A(x)>0$ and $flag=0$ **then**
14   add x and $m_A(x)$ into d_{E_A}
15   **else**
16   **if** $m_A(x)>0$ and $flag=1$ **then**
17   add x and $m_A(x)$ into d_{M_B}

---

4 Performance Analysis

In this section, we conduct a theoretical analysis of CCF and the proposed synchronization methods by using CBF as a reference.

BF leverages $\frac{m}{n} \ln 2$ bits [13] for each element to achieve high space efficiency. To realize the target false positive rate ϵ, the parameters, *i.e.*, the length of BF bits array m, the number of employed hash functions k, and the number of elements in simple set n, need to be carefully designed. Theoretically, the minimum false positive rate $\epsilon \approx 0.5^k \approx 0.6185^{m/n}$. Therefore, to get false positive rate decreased by 38.15%, extra n counters are introduced.

In contrast, CCF randomly generates a tuple $(h_{1_x}, h_{2_x}, \eta_x)$ for any inserted element x, including the index of two candidate buckets and the fingerprint η_x. We observe that there are two kinds of hash collisions in CCF. The first kind of collision is caused by the complete collision of two tuples, i.e., the three items contained in the tuples for two distinct elements are equal. For example, for element x, y in multiset X, the tuples of elements are $(h_{1_x}, h_{2_x}, \eta_x)$ and $(h_{1_y}, h_{2_y}, \eta_y)$, respectively. If $h_{1_x} = h_{1_y}, \eta_x = \eta_y$, and $h_{2_x} = h_{2_y}$. Another kind of collision is caused by the order of bucket indexes, i.e., $h_{1_x} = h_{2_y}, \eta_x, = \eta_y$ and $h_{2_x} = h_{1_y}$.

Then, we discuss the detail of the false positive rate when a multiset is represented by the CCF data structure. Let N represent the cardinality of a multiset. A default assumption of the following analysis is that all the multiset elements are inserted successfully into CCFs. The total number of possible tuples can be estimated as $b \times 2^f$. Suppose a CF represents $j - 1$ elements without collisions among these elements. The ratio of tuples which have been mapped by these $j - 1$ elements is $\frac{j-1}{b \times 2^f}$. When we insert the jth element into CCF, the ratio of tuples that are available and incur no collision with the existing $j - 1$ elements is estimated as $1 - 2 \times \frac{j-1}{b \times 2^f} = 1 - \frac{j-1}{b \times 2^{f-1}}$. Thus the probability that the jth element won't collide with other elements can be calculated as $1 - \frac{j-1}{b \times 2^{f-1}}$. Thus the false positive rate is estimated as follows:

$$\epsilon \approx 1 - \prod_{j=2}^{N} \left(1 - \frac{j-1}{b \times 2^{f-1}} \right) \tag{2}$$

Considering the complexity of Eq. 2, we propose an approximation to get a lower bound as follows. We note that the probability that the jth ($j \geqslant 2$) element doesn't collide with the former $j - 1$ elements is less than or equal to the fixed value $1 - \frac{2}{b \times 2^f}$. Then we reason the lower bound of false positive rate as follows:

$$\epsilon \geqslant 1 - \left(1 - \frac{2}{b \times 2^f} \right)^{N-1} \approx \frac{2(N-1)}{b \times 2^f} \approx \frac{2b \times w}{b \times 2^f} = \frac{w}{2^{f-1}} \tag{3}$$

In Eq. 3, we assume that the number of inserted elements equals to the number of slots in the CCF. In other words, we assume that all the elements are inserted successfully into the CCF ideally.

Combine with the conclusions derived from [5], which get the upper bound of the total probability of a false positive hit is:

$$\epsilon \leqslant 1 - \left(1 - 1/2^f \right)^{2w} \approx \frac{w}{2^{f-1}} \tag{4}$$

we can form the relationship between fingerprint field length f and the target false positive rate ϵ as follows:

$$f \approx \log_2 w + \log_2 \frac{1}{\epsilon} + 1 \tag{5}$$

We can also estimate the upper bound of collided elements when a CCF represents the multiset, as $N \times \frac{w}{2^{f-1}} = b \times w \times \frac{w}{2^{f-1}}$.

Conclusively, to get the false positive rate decreased by 38.15%, CBF needs to add one more counter for each distinct element in the multiset. By contrast, CCF can get the false positive rate decreased by 50% by only augmenting one more bit to each fingerprint. Compare with CBF, to obtain the targeted ϵ, CCF is more space-efficient and communication-friendly for multiset synchronization.

Furthermore, as reported in [8] and our later implementation, the value calculated by $\epsilon \approx 0.6185^{m/n}$ is lower than the practice of CBF. In contrast, the value estimated by the Eq. 3 is a precise estimation of the false positive rate for CCF.

5   Evaluation

In this section, we implement both CBF-based and CCF-based methods to compare their synchronization accuracy and time-consumption. The synchronization accuracy is defined as the percentage of common elements after synchronization. We also quantify the respective time-consumption of element insertion and different elements identify in both CCF and CBF.

5.1   Experiment Methodology

A testbed with 2.24 GHz CPU and 8GB RAM is employed as a host. All the multiset elements are 32-bit integers derived out by a random number generator. For the CBF-based method [9,15], we borrow the CBF implementation from one of the prior work [10]. The independent k hash functions for a CBF with m cells are generated as follows:

$$h_i(x) = (g_1(x) + i \times g_2(x)) \bmod m \tag{6}$$

where $g_1(x)$ and $g_2(x)$ are two random and independent integers ranging from 1 to m. The integer i belongs to the range $[0, k-1]$. As for CCF, we need two independent hash functions, one for the fingerprint generation and another for the candidate bucket selection. We let the threshold of reallocation times max equal to bucket number b instead of fixed 500 in [5]. The number of slots in each bucket w is fixed as 4. As for hash functions, we choose CityHash [19] for each element to generate the random candidate buckets index and the fingerprint.

5.2   Comparing CCF with CBF

In this subsection, we compare the performance of CCF and CBF in terms of space-efficiency, time-consumption, and synchronization accuracy.

We vary bits per element (bpe) in CCF from 16 to 80. For CCF, more bits are used to augment fingerprint η; for CBF, the added bits are used to lengthen the CBF vector to represent the elements' content and multiplicity information. And we maintain the number of elements in each root set as fixed 64000. The cardinality of each multiset is fixed as 640000, which is 10 times as many as the number of elements in the root set. As illustrated in Fig. 3(a), with the change of bits per element, the performance of CCF-based methods are more robust than the CBF-based method. For CBF, when more counters are added into the vector, the stored multiplicity information is more precise. For CCF, the more bits are used in fingerprints, the less false positive errors will occur. As demonstrated in Fig. 3(b), with much fewer bits per element, CCF-based methods can achieve

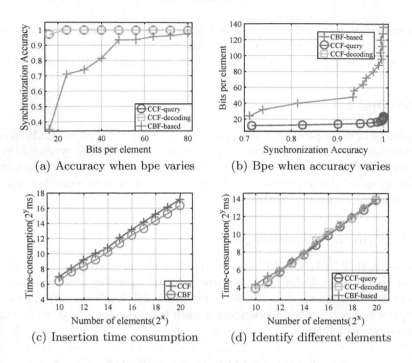

Fig. 3. Performance comparison between CCF and CBF

the same synchronization accuracy as the CBF-based method. And the increased bits per element for the CCF-based methods is only 7 bits, compared with 96 bits for the CBF-based method, when the synchronization accuracy increases from 0.7 to 0.9999. Therefore, compared to the CBF-based method, given the same bpe, our CCF-based method achieves much higher synchronization accuracy; for the same synchronization accuracy, our CCF-based method needs much less bpe.

In our multiset synchronization framework, the hosts need to insert their local elements into the CCFs. The query-based method has to query each local element to distinguish the different elements from the common ones. The decoding-based method needs to delete common elements from the CCF vector. Therefore, we further compare the time-consumption that caused by element insertion, and different element uncovering. Certainly, the transmission of employed data structures and the different elements in d_E also consumes some time. However, this kind of time-consumption is beyond the scope of our consideration. In our experiments, we vary the number of elements in the multiset from 500×2^1 to 500×2^{11} and record the two kinds of time-consumption in Fig. 3(c), and Fig. 3(d) respectively.

As illustrated in Fig. 3(c) and Fig. 3(d), CCF causes comparable (actually a little bit more) time-consumption as CBF. Note that both CCF and CBF need to calculate two hash values when inserting an element. Specifically, CBF has to calculate two random value $g_1(x)$ and $g_2(x)$ to generate the k hash values.

The CCF calculates the index of the two candidate buckets for each element during element insertion, query, and deletion. Besides, CCF maps the original element content to an integer in $[0, 2^f - 1]$ to generate the fingerprint of each element. This explains why CCF results in a bit more time-consumption than CBF. Moreover, for element insertion, the reallocation process may be triggered in CCF, when the two candidate buckets are both occupied. This reallocation process surely increases the time-consumption of CCF insertion.

Moreover, we quantify the time-consumption of identifying the different elements with CCF and CBF. During a membership query, CBF needs to checks the k corresponding counters; while CCF may access the number of slots from 1 to $2w$ randomly. Usually, $2w$ is larger than the value of k. The results are given in Fig. 3(d). We consider both the query-based and the decoding-based methods enabled by CCF. Notice that, CBF performs better than the CCF-decoding to some extent, but slightly worse than the CCF-query. The reason is that the decoding-based method consumes more time to query the corresponding different elements after the elimination phase.

According to the above results, we conclude that CCF achieves much better synchronization accuracy than CBF, with a little compromise of time-consumption.

6   Conclusion

In this paper, we propose to leverage counting cuckoo filter to represent and thereafter synchronize multisets. CCF extends each slot as two fields, the fingerprint field and the counter field. With such a design, CCF is competent to represent multisets. After exchanging the respective CCFs which represent the local multisets, the hosts determine the different elements with either the query-based or the decoding-based method. CCF can distinguish the different elements in d_M from d_E, so that the elements in d_M can be synchronized by generating the dedicated number of local replicas. Only the different elements in d_E need to be transmitted to the other host with multiplicity information. This property decreases the communication overhead significantly. The comprehensive evaluation results indicate that CCF outperforms CBF in terms of synchronization accuracy and space-efficiency, at the cost of a little higher time-consumption.

Acknowledgment. This work is partially supported by the National Key Research and Development Program of China under Grant No. 2018YFB1800203 and 2018YFE0207600, and the National Natural Science Foundation of China under Grant Nos. U19B2024 and 61772544.

References

1. Bi, R., Ren, J., Wang, H., Liu, Q., Huang, S.: Model based adaptive data acquisition for Internet of Things. In: Biagioni, E.S., Zheng, Y., Cheng, S. (eds.) WASA 2019. LNCS, vol. 11604, pp. 16–28. Springer, Cham (2019). https://doi.org/10.1007/978-3-030-23597-0_2

2. Bloom, B.H.: Space/time trade-offs in hash coding with allowable errors. Commun. ACM **13**(7), 422–426 (1970)
3. Deng, N., Deng, S., Hu, C., Lei, K.: An efficient revocable attribute-based signcryption scheme with outsourced designcryption in cloud computing. In: Proceedings of WASA, Honolulu, HI, USA, 24–26 June, pp. 84–97 (2019)
4. Eppstein, D., Goodrich, M.T., Uyeda, F., Varghese, G.: What's the difference? efficient set reconciliation without prior context. In: Proceedings of the SIGCOMM, Toronto, ON, Canada, August 15–19, pp. 218–229 (2011)
5. Fan, B., Andersen, D.G., Kaminsky, M., Mitzenmacher, M.D.: Cuckoo filter: practically better than bloom. In: Proceedings of ACM, CoNEXT, pp. 75–88 (2014)
6. Fan, L., Cao, P., Almeida, J., Broder, A.Z.: Summary cache: a scalable wide-area web cache sharing protocol. IEEE/ACM Trans. Netw. **8**(3), 281–293 (2000)
7. Goodrich, M.T., Mitzenmacher, M.: Invertible bloom lookup tables. In: Proceedings of the Allerton, Montice, vol. 28–30, 792–799, September 2011
8. Gremillion, L.L.: Designing a bloom filter for differential file access. Commun. ACM **25**(9), 600–604 (1982)
9. Guo, D., Li, M.: Set reconciliation via counting bloom filters. IEEE Trans. Knowl. Data Eng. **25**(10), 2367–2380 (2013)
10. Kirsch, A., Mitzenmacher, M.: Less hashing, same performance: Building a better bloom filter. Random Struct. Algorithms **33**(2), 187–218 (2008). https://doi.org/10.1007/11841036_42
11. Li, C., Wu, Q., Li, H., Liu, J.: Trustroam: a novel blockchain-based cross-domain authentication scheme for Wi-Fi access. In: Biagioni, E.S., Zheng, Y., Cheng, S. (eds.) WASA 2019. LNCS, vol. 11604, pp. 149–161. Springer, Cham (2019). https://doi.org/10.1007/978-3-030-23597-0_12
12. Li, F., Yang, H., Zou, Y., Yu, D., Yu, J.: Joint optimization of routing and storage node deployment in heterogeneous wireless sensor networks towards reliable data storage. In: Biagioni, E.S., Zheng, Y., Cheng, S. (eds.) WASA 2019. LNCS, vol. 11604, pp. 162–174. Springer, Cham (2019). https://doi.org/10.1007/978-3-030-23597-0_13
13. Luo, L., Guo, D., Ma, R.T.B., Rottenstreich, O., Luo, X.: Optimizing bloom filter: Challenges, solutions, and comparisons. IEEE Commun. Surv. Tutorials **21**(2), 1912–1949 (2019). https://doi.org/10.1109/COMST.2018.2889329
14. Luo, L., Guo, D., Rottenstreich, O., Ma, R.T.B., Luo, X.: Set reconciliation with cuckoo filters. In: Proceedings of CIKM, Beijing, China, 3–7 November 2019, pp. 2465–2468 (2019)
15. Luo, L., Guo, D., Wu, J., Rottenstreich, O., He, Q., Qin, Y., Luo, X.: Efficient multiset synchronization. IEEE/ACM Trans. Netw. **25**(2), 1190–1205 (2017)
16. Luo, L., Guo, D., Zhao, X., Wu, J., Rottenstreich, O., Luo, X.: Near-accurate multiset reconciliation (extended abstract). In: Proceedings of ICDE, Macao, China, 8–11 April 2019, pp. 2153–2154 (2019)
17. Mitzenmacher, M.: Compressed bloom filters. In: Proceedings of PODC, Newport, Rhode Island, USA, 26–29 August, pp. 144–150 (2001)
18. Ozisik, A.P., Andresen, G., Levine, B.N., Tapp, D., Bissias, G., Katkuri, S.: Graphene: efficient interactive set reconciliation applied to blockchain propagation. In: Proceedings of SIGCOMM, Beijing, China, 19–23 August, pp. 303–317 (2019)
19. Pike, G., Alakuijala, J.: Introducing cityhash, 02 March 2015. http://googleopensouree.blogspot.com/2011/04/introducing-CityHash/. Accessed 11 Oct 2019

20. Richa, A.W., Mitzenmacher, M., Sitaraman, R.: The power of two random choices: a survey of techniques and results. Comb. Optim. **9**, 255–304 (2001)
21. Rottenstreich, O., Kanizo, Y., Keslassy, I.: The variable-increment counting bloom filter. IEEE/ACM Trans. Netw. **22**(4), 1092–1105 (2014)
22. Xie, J., Guo, D., Shi, X., Cai, H., Qian, C., Chen, H.: A fast hybrid data sharing framework for hierarchical mobile edge computing. In: Proceedings of INFOCOM (2020)
23. Zou, P., Qingge, L., Yang, Q., Zhu, B.: Trajectory comparison in a vehicular network i: computing a consensus trajectory. In: Biagioni, E.S., Zheng, Y., Cheng, S. (eds.) WASA 2019. LNCS, vol. 11604, pp. 533–544. Springer, Cham (2019). https://doi.org/10.1007/978-3-030-23597-0_43

Privacy-Aware Online Task Offloading for Mobile-Edge Computing

Ting Li[1,2], Haitao Liu[1,2], Jie Liang[1,2], Hangsheng Zhang[1,2], Liru Geng[1],
and Yinlong Liu[1,2(✉)]

[1] Institute of Information Engineering, Chinese Academy of Sciences, Beijing, China
{liting0715,liuhaitao,liangjie,zhanghangsheng,gengliru,
liuyinlong}@iie.ac.cn
[2] School of Cyber Security, University of Chinese Academy of Sciences,
Beijing, China

Abstract. Mobile-edge computing (MEC) has great advantages in reducing latency and energy consumption, where mobile devices (MDs) can offload their computation-demanding and latency-critical tasks. However, privacy leakage may occur during the tasks offloading process, and most existing works ignored these issues or just investigated the system-level solution for MEC. Privacy-aware and device-level task offloading optimization problems receive much less attention. In order to tackle these challenges, a privacy-preserving and device-managed task offloading scheme is proposed in this paper for MEC to achieve a delay and energy sub-optimal solution while protecting the location privacy and usage pattern privacy of users. Firstly, we formulate the joint optimization problem of task offloading and privacy preservation as a semi-parametric contextual Multi-armed Bandit (MAB) problem, which has a relaxed reward model. Then, we propose a Privacy-Aware Online Task Offloading (PAOTO) algorithm based on the transformed Thompson-Sampling (TS) architecture, through which we can: 1) receive the best possible delay and energy consumption performance; 2) achieve the goal of preserving privacy; and 3) obtain an online device-managed task offloading policy without requiring any system-level information. Simulation results demonstrate that the proposed scheme outperforms the existing methods in terms of minimizing the system cost and preserving the privacy of users.

Keywords: Mobile-edge computing · Task offloading · Privacy preservation · Multi-armed bandit · Online learning

1 Introduction

With the emergence of new applications, such as augmented reality (AR), virtual reality (VR), and connected cars [1], the resource-limited mobile devices (MDs) become unable to meet the stringent requirements of these applications which are computing-demanding and latency-sensitive. To get rid of such limitations,

© Springer Nature Switzerland AG 2020
D. Yu et al. (Eds.): WASA 2020, LNCS 12384, pp. 244–255, 2020.
https://doi.org/10.1007/978-3-030-59016-1_21

a novel paradigm of mobile-edge computing (MEC) is proposed to push computing and storage resources to the network edges [2]. In such computing paradigm, computation tasks can be offloaded to nearby MEC servers via wireless channels by MDs, which can receive ultra-low latency and improve the Quality of Service.

Despite the benefits, MEC still has shortcomings in terms of security and privacy leakage. In this work, we investigate the location privacy and usage pattern privacy problem [3], which are related to the MEC task offloading feature. Intuitively, when MD want to obtain optimal offloading performance, it tends to offload all its tasks to the MEC server. Accordingly, an honest-but-curious MEC server can infer the location privacy and usage pattern privacy of users who are privacy-sensitive, which may prevent these users from accessing the MEC system if not properly addressed. Although these two privacy issues have been extensively studied in other fields, one challenge still needs to be addressed in MEC systems, which is how to protect both the location privacy and usage pattern privacy while minimizing the delay and energy consumption cost.

The most related works that studied the optimization of delay and energy consumption cost while considering both location privacy and usage pattern privacy, probably are [3] and [4]. The former scheme formulates this problem as a constrained Markov decision process (CMDP) and the latter one applies a Dyan-Q architecture based on the CMDP to achieve a better privacy-aware offloading policy. However, both of them rely on the assumption of the wireless channel power gain that is formulated as a Markov chain model, in which some system-level information should be known in advance.

In order to minimize system cost (e.g.., latency and energy consumption) and protect user's privacy without requiring any system-level information as a prior knowledge, we propose a device-level and privacy-preserving task offloading scheme for MEC system. The location privacy and usage pattern privacy of users will be preserved in this paper. And an online-learning algorithm will be proposed to make adaptive task offloading decisions under dynamic network environment. The contributions can be summarized as follows:

- We study a joint optimization problem of task offloading and privacy preservation in MEC system. And then this problem is transformed as a semi-parametric contextual Multi-armed Bandit (MAB) problem to overcome the challenge of unknown network dynamics.
- We propose an online learning algorithm, called PAOTO (Privacy-Aware Online Task Offloading), to make device-managed task offloading decisions while protecting user's location privacy and usage pattern privacy.
- We carry out simulations to demonstrate the effectiveness of the proposed algorithm. The results show that the PAOTO algorithm performs close-to-optimal and far better than the newly-proposed Dyna-Q algorithm in [4].

The remaining parts of this paper are organized as follows. In Sect. 2, we discuss the related works. We will formally describe the system model in Sect. 3. Next, we present algorithm design and simulation evaluation in Sect. 4 and 5, respectively. Finally, we draw some conclusions and highlight the direction for future work in Sect. 6.

2   Related Work

In recent years, designing an optimal offloading strategy for MEC has attracted significant attention [5–7]. For example, J. Xu et al. proposed an online algorithm based on Lyapunov optimization for MEC to jointly optimize dynamic service caching and task offloading [5]. B. Dab et al. proposed a joint computation offloading and resource allocation algorithm in edge cloud to minimize the energy consumption cost under the latency constraint [7]. However, none of them considered user's privacy issues.

There are a few works considering both task offloading and privacy preservation. For example, X. He et al. developed an offloading strategy for MEC-Enabled IoT, which can learn a good offloading strategy while protect the devices' location privacy [8]. In [9], H. Zhang et al. proposed a strategy that can achieve an efficient task scheduling policy on edge while ensuring privacy. In [10], a privacy-preserving and contextual online learning algorithm was proposed at the cloud layer to perform tasks allocation. Besides, X. He et al. [3] and P. Zhou et al. [4] both proposed privacy-aware offloading schemes for MEC. Nevertheless, these works mentioned above were implemented at the system level. They all need to explore system-level information in advance, which is difficult to obtain and may cause additional system cost.

In general, none of the aforementioned works consider both tasks offloading and privacy protection problem at the user level. To conquer this challenge, we propose a novel privacy-aware task offloading scheme based on an online learning algorithm that just requires device-level information, and it can achieve the best possible system performance while protecting the user's privacy.

3   System Model

As illustrated in Fig. 1, we consider a scenario in which the mobile user/device communicates with MEC server through access point (e.g.., 5G base station) via the wireless channel[1]. For arriving tasks, the MD has three ways to process them, i.e., computing in the local processing unit, offloading to the MEC server through the transmission unit and queuing in the buffer for processing in the next time slot. We assume that the system organizes in time slots $t \in \{1, 2, ..., T\}$ of equal duration. At each t, the mobile user will newly generate N^t computation tasks to the MD, denoted by a set of $N^t \in \{1, 2, ..., N^t_{max}\}$ (N^t_{max} is the maximum possible number of generated tasks). And the $b^t \in \mathcal{B} = \{0, 2, ..., b_{max}\}$ (with the maximum buffer size b_{max}) can be denoted as the number of tasks in the buffer. A two-parameters model [11] can be used to describe each task $n \in \mathcal{N}^t = \{0, 2, ..., (N^t + b^t)\}$. It consists of input data size λ_n (bits) and computation intensity δ_n (CPU cycles/bit). Whereupon, the computation demand is $m_n = \lambda_n * \delta_n$(CPU cycles). Besides, we assume that all the $(N^t + b^t)$ tasks can be executed during each time slot t.

---

[1] For ease of exposition, the bandwidth constraint of wireless channel is not considered in this paper, and we will consider it in the next work.

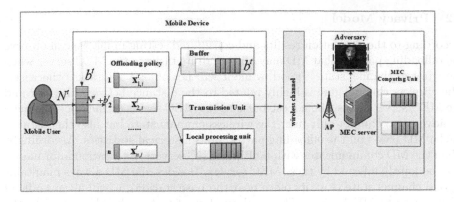

Fig. 1. An illustration of task offloading in MEC system.

3.1   Task Offloading Model

At each t, the tasks can be dynamically offloaded to the three different execution platforms $i \in \mathcal{I} = \{l, s, b\}$ by MD (called operator), where the l, s and b represent the local processing unit, MEC server and the buffer, respectively. Then, a binary indicator $x_{n,i}^t \in \{0, 1\}$ is designed to denote the dynamic task offloading decision variable, let $x_{n,i}^t = 1$ if the task n is offloaded to platform i, and $x_{n,i}^t = 0$ otherwise. Given a t, each task n can be offloaded to only one platform (l, s or b). Hence, we have $x_{n,l}^t + x_{n,s}^t + x_{n,b}^t = 1$.

Processing Latency: for ease of exposition, we assume that the buffer can be treated as a micro processor, and the queuing delay can be converted to computing delay. Hence, the total processing latency in this paper is consisted of different parts, i.e., queuing delay in buffer, computing delay in either local processing unit or MEC server. To illustrate, we use the $d_{n,i}^t$ to denote the processing delay of each task n and the γ_i is the available computing capability (i.e., CPU cycles per second). Therefore, the total processing latency can be expressed as:

$$D^t = \sum_{n=0}^{N^t+b^t} \sum_{i \in \mathcal{I}} d_{n,i}^t x_{n,i}^t = \sum_{n=0}^{N^t+b^t} \sum_{i \in \mathcal{I}} \frac{m_n^t}{\gamma_i} x_{n,i}^t \tag{1}$$

Energy Consumption: in this paper, the energy consumption cost of the MD may include the CPU cycles, transmitting energy and electric energy. In particular, we use the $e_{n,i}^t$ to denote the energy consumption for offloading task n to platform i. Thus, the overall energy consumption can be expressed as:

$$E^t = \sum_{n=0}^{N^t+b^t} \sum_{i \in \mathcal{I}} e_{n,i}^t x_{n,i}^t \tag{2}$$

3.2   Privacy Model

According to the simulation results and considered setting in [3], we can observe the offloading pattern that MD may offload all its tasks to the MEC server when the wireless channel state is good, while it will not offload any tasks otherwise[2]. The wireless channel gain is highly related to the distance between the user and the MEC server. Thus, the honest-but-curious MEC server (it may be controlled by adversary) can not only infer the wireless channel state but also the distance to the MD based on the offloading pattern and historical statistics. Accordingly, when the MD communicates with multiple MEC servers, its location information may be jointly inferred by these MEC servers. Besides, if a MD always maintains a good channel state (e.g.. its office near the base station), it will always offload all its tasks to MEC server. The total number of tasks is highly related to the user's usage pattern (i.e., user's app running if a certain pattern exists in the number of tasks generated by the app), which may be very important for the privacy-sensitive users. Hence, the MEC server may be able to infer personal information of user through monitoring the total number of offloading tasks and analyzing the historical statistics.

Accordingly, the privacy metric P^t will be discussed, which jointly quantify the location privacy and usage pattern privacy. Specifically, we use the q^t to denote the total number of tasks offloaded to the MEC server and the Δ^t to indicate the difference between N^t and q^t. Hence, we have:

$$P^t = \mathbb{I}(\Delta^t = 0) \cdot K + \mathbb{I}(\Delta^t \neq 0) \cdot \left[\mathbb{I}(q^t = 0) \cdot \xi + \mathbb{I}(q^t \neq 0) \cdot \frac{\hat{\xi}}{\Delta^t} \right] \quad (3)$$

where the $\mathbb{I}$ is an indicator function; the $K \in [1, N^t]$ is a metric of usage pattern privacy, which is the number of dummy tasks[3]; the ξ and $\hat{\xi}$ are the weighting factors reflecting the importance of the location privacy over the usage pattern privacy in different situations. The first term of (3) represents that if the MD offloaded all its tasks to the MEC server ($\Delta^t = 0$), in order to protect the usage pattern privacy, it will continue to offload K dummy tasks to the MEC server to confuse the adversary. As such, the adversary cannot pinpoint the number of tasks actually generated by the user. According to the second term of (3), there are two situations correspond to the $\Delta^t \neq 0$. In the first situation, the $q^t = 0$ denotes that the tasks either queued or processed locally. To protect the location privacy, the MD need to offload ξ tasks (which queuing in the buffer, $0 \leq \xi \leq b^t$) to MEC server for preventing the adversary from inferring wireless channel status. In the second situation of $\Delta^t \neq 0$, some tasks are offloaded to MEC server ($q^t \neq 0$), and the privacy level can be achieved by $\frac{\hat{\xi}}{\Delta^t}$, which increases as the Δ^t decreases.

---

[2] For simplicity, it is assumed that the wireless channel states are only good and bad in this work. It can be extended to the multi-state case.

[3] The dummy tasks may sacrifice some system performance, but will increase the privacy level, and the proposed algorithm will balance them.

3.3   Objective Function

In order to strike a balance between system cost (i.e., computing delay and energy consumption) and user's privacy level, the weights ω_{delay}^t, ω_{energy}^t and $\omega_{privacy}^t$ will be designed to indicate the different preference of MD. These weights also can convert privacy level and system cost into the same dimension. Thus, given a finite time horizon T, the objective function can be formulated as [12]:

$$\min \sum_{t=1}^{T} \omega_{delay}^t D^t + \omega_{energy}^t E^t + \omega_{privacy}^t \frac{1}{Pt} \tag{4}$$

From the MD perspective, it is difficult for them to explore the system-wide information (e.g., the wireless channel states and resource availability) in advance. Therefore, devising a device-managed and privacy-preserving task offloading policy is highly desirable, in which the future system-level information will not be needed.

4   Algorithm Design

4.1   Problem Transformation

In order to learn the network dynamics and take the privacy protection into consideration, the problem in this paper can be transformed as a semi-parametric contextual MAB problem [13], which can address the exploration/exploitation trade-offs inherent in the sequential decision problem and has a relaxed, semi-parametric reward model. This model can be described as:

$$\mathbb{E}(\sum_{n \in \mathcal{N}^t} r_{n,i}(t) | \mathcal{F}^{t-1}) = \nu(t) + \sum_{n \in \mathcal{N}^t} b(t)^\top \bar{\mu}_{n,i}(t) \tag{5}$$

where the $r_{n,i}(t)$ is the received cost of offloading task n to platform i; $\nu(t)$ is a non-parametric component; $b(t)$ is a current contextual feature vector; $\bar{\mu}_{n,i}(t)$ is a fixed but unknown underlying expectations of the feature vector $\mu_{n,i}(t)$; the $\mathcal{F}^{t-1}$ is the union of historical information and $b(t)$.

According to the system cost (including processing latency and energy consumption cost) defined in Sect. 3, we transform them as a feature vector $\mu_{n,i}(t) = [\frac{1}{\gamma_i^t}, e_{n,i}^t] \in \mathbb{R}^{(2(N_{max}^t + b_{max}))}$ to better learn the network uncertainty and resource availability, which is related to $\bar{\mu}_{n,i}(t)$. In addition, the current user-level state information can be described as a contextual feature vector $b(t) = [\omega_{delay}^t \mathbb{M}^t, \omega_{energy}^t \mathbb{S}^t] \in \mathbb{R}^{(2(N_{max}^t + b_{max}))}$. More specifically, $\mathbb{M}^t \in \mathbb{R}^{(N_{max}^t + b_{max})}$ denotes computation demand vector of tasks. The first $N^t + b^t$ values of $\mathbb{M}^t$ are corresponding computation demand m_n^t of each task n, and the remaining values are 0; $\mathbb{S}^t \in \mathbb{R}^{(N_{max}^t + b_{max})}$ is a transition vector, which denotes the number of tasks in time slot t. The first $N^t + b^t$ values of $\mathbb{S}^t$ are 1, and the remainder are 0. Besides, the privacy level in this task offloading policy will be formulated as the aggregated non-parametric component $\nu(t) = \omega_{privacy}^t \frac{1}{P^t}$, and we assume that it can be calculated when all task decisions are completed at the end of t.

Hereinafter, we define $\mathcal{H}^{t-1} = \{\mathcal{A}(\tau), r_{\mathcal{A}(\tau)}(\tau), b(\tau)\}$, $\tau = \{1, 2, ..., t-1\}$ as the historical observations until $t - 1$, where $\mathcal{A}(\tau)$ represents the set of actions for all tasks at time τ, and $r_{\mathcal{A}(\tau)}(\tau)$ denotes the aggregated received cost at τ. Given $\mathcal{F}^{t-1}$, the expectation of the aggregated received cost $r_{\mathcal{A}(t)}(t)$ can be expressed as:

$$\mathbb{E}(r_{\mathcal{A}(t)}(t)) = \mathbb{E}(\sum_{n=0}^{N^t+b^t} r_{n,i}(t) | \mathcal{F}^{t-1}) = \omega_{privacy}^t \frac{1}{P^t} + \sum_{n=0}^{N^t+b^t} b(t)^\top \bar{\mu}_{n,i}(t) \qquad (6)$$

Since the non-parametric component $\nu(t)$ depends on time and historical information, but not on the current action [13], the optimal received cost $r_{n,i}(t)$ of each task can obtained by minimum $b(t)^\top \bar{\mu}_{n,i}(t)$. Therefore, we can achieve the optimal offloading decision of each task by $a_n^*(t) = argmin_i b(t)^\top \bar{\mu}_{n,i}(t)$. Indeed, the privacy level $\nu(t)$ will have an impact on the aggregated received cost of all tasks at the end of time slot t, and this aggregated received cost will be used to update the contextual feature vector for the next interval t.

4.2   Privacy-Aware Online Task Offloading Algorithm

In this subsection, an online PAOTO algorithm is proposed, which keeps the framework of Thompson Sampling [14] with a semi-parameter reward model. According to the MAB transformation of our problem, it is known that the optimal offloading decision and the received cost $r_{n,i}(t)$ of each task mainly depend on the current contextual feature vector $b(t)$ and the feature vector $\bar{\mu}_{n,i}(t)$. Through the previous trial and error, the underlying relationship between the feature vectors and received cost will be learned by MD. Hence, it can estimate the feature vector, and hence decide how to offload the tasks can obtain the minimum cost. The estimate of feature vector $\hat{\mu}_{n,i}(t)$ and the cumulative contextual vector $B_i(t)$ can be denoted as:

$$\hat{\mu}_{n,i}(t) = (I_d + \hat{\Sigma}_t + \Sigma_t)^{-1} \sum_{\tau=1}^{t-1} 2X_\tau r_{\mathcal{A}(\tau)}(\tau)$$

$$(7)$$

$$B_i(t) = I_d + \hat{\Sigma}_t + \Sigma_t = I_d + \sum_{\tau=1}^{t-1} X_\tau X_\tau^\top + \sum_{\tau=1}^{t-1} \mathbb{E}(X_\tau X_\tau^\top | \mathcal{F}_{\tau-1})$$

where $X_\tau = b(\tau) - \mathbb{E}(b(\tau) | \mathcal{F}_{\tau-1})$; I is a $d = 2(N_{max}^t + b_{max})$ dimensional identity matrix. Moreover, we use the $\bar{b}(\tau)$ to denoted the $\mathbb{E}(b(\tau) | \mathcal{F}_{\tau-1})$, it has $\bar{b}(\tau) = \sum_{n=1}^{N^t+b^t} \sum_{i=1}^{3} \pi_{n,i}(\tau) b(\tau)$, and the $\pi_{n,i}(\tau)$ is the probability of offloading task n to the i-th platform at time τ. Accordingly, we can calculate the covariance by $\mathbb{E}(X_\tau X_\tau^\top | \mathcal{F}_{\tau-1}) = \sum_{n=1}^{N^t+b^t} \sum_{i=1}^{3} \pi_{n,i}(\tau) (b(\tau) - \bar{b}(\tau)) (b(\tau) - \bar{b}(\tau))^\top$.

In proposed algorithm, which is based on Thomson sampling [14], the received cost $r_{n,i}(t)$ will be sampled by the Gaussian distribution. For the Gaussian distribution, the expectation is $b(t)^\top \hat{\mu}_{n,i}(t)$, and the standard deviation is

$\sqrt{b(t)^\top B_i(t)^{-1} b(t)}$ [12]. Therefore, the Gaussian distribution can be represented as $\mathcal{N}\left(b(t)^\top \hat{\mu}_{n,i}(t), v^2 b(t)^\top B_i(t)^{-1} b(t)\right)$, where the $v = (2R + 6)\sqrt{6d \log(T/\delta)}$ is a control parameter. Hence, guided by the problem transformation and key vectors mentioned above, we introduce the PAOTO algorithm in Algorithm 1.

Algorithm 1. Privacy-Aware Online Task Offloading (PAOTO) Algorithm

---

Input: N^t, N_{max}^t, b^t, b_{max}, m_n^t, $i \in \mathcal{I}$;

Output: aggregated received cost $r_{\mathcal{A}(t)}(t)$;

1: **Initialization:** Initialize the cumulative contextual vector $B_i = I_d$, where I_d is a $2(N_{max}^t + b_{max})$ dimensional identity matrix, the cumulative contextual system cost $y_i = 0_d$, and a control parameter $v = (2R + 6)\sqrt{6d \log(T/\delta)}, \delta \in (0, 1)$;

2: **End initialization**

3: **for** $t = 1, 2, ..., T$ **do**

4:     **for** $n = 1, 2, ..., N^t + b^t$ **do**

5:         **for** $i = 1, 2, 3$ **do**

6:             **Compute** the estimated feature vector $\hat{\mu}_{n,i}(t) = B_i^{-1} y_i$;

7:             **Sample** the cost $r_{n,i}(t)$ independently for each task n and each execution platform i from the Gaussian distribution $\mathcal{N}\left(b(t)^\top \hat{\mu}_{n,i}(t), v^2 b(t)^\top B_i(t)^{-1} b(t)\right)$;

8:             **Compute** the probability of offloading task n to the i-th execution platform $\pi_{n,i}(t) = \mathbb{P}\left(a_n(t) = i | \mathcal{F}_{t-1}\right)$;

9:         **end for**

10:         **Select** the offloading execution platform $a_n(t) = \arg\min_i r_{n,i}(t)$;

11:         **Record** the selection $a_n(t)$ into offloading decisions vector $\mathcal{A}(t)$;

12:     **end for**

13:     **Compute** the privacy level $\nu(t)$;

14:     **Compute** the aggregated received cost $r_{\mathcal{A}(t)}(t)$ according to $r_{n,i}(t)$ of all tasks and privacy level $\nu(t)$;

15:     **Update** B: $B_{\mathcal{A}(t)} \leftarrow B_{\mathcal{A}(t)} + \left(b(t) - \bar{b}(t)\right)\left(b(t) - \bar{b}(t)\right)^\top + \sum_{n=1}^{N^t + b^t} \sum_{i=1}^{i=3} \pi_{n,i}(t)\left(b(t) - \bar{b}(t)\right)\left(b(t) - \bar{b}(t)\right)^\top$

16:     **Update** y using $r_{\mathcal{A}(t)}(t)$: $y_{\mathcal{A}(t)} \leftarrow y_{\mathcal{A}(t)} + 2\left(b(t) - \bar{b}(t)\right) r_{\mathcal{A}(t)}(t)$;

17: **end for**

Algorithm 1 gives the details of exploring the optimal task offloading decisions and preserving the privacy of users. It estimates the cost $r_{n,i}(t)$ of each task based on context information $b(t)$ and performance feature vector $\mu_{n,i}(t)$, and selects the best offloading decision based on the minimum estimated cost $r_{n,i}(t)$. Then, the privacy level $\nu(t)$ and the aggregated received cost $r_{\mathcal{A}(t)}(t)$ are calculated after all tasks are scheduled. At the end, it utilizes aggregated received cost $r_{\mathcal{A}(t)}(t)$ to update cumulative contextual vector B and cumulative system cost y corresponding to the decisions vector $\mathcal{A}(t)$ of all tasks at every time slot t.

5 Simulation Results

5.1 Simulation Settings

We consider a MEC offloading scenario where the N_{max}^t varies from 10 to 60 over different offloading periods t. The maximum buffer capacity b_{max} of the MD can be set to 10. The length of each time slot is 1s. Moreover, we assume that the computation capacity of MEC server γ_s is uniformly distributed in $[10, 15]$ GHz, the γ_l is $[1, 3]$ GHz, and the γ_b is $[0.1, 0.15]$ GHz. Based on [15], the data size of each task λ_n is determined randomly from 300 Kbits to 800 Kbits, and the computation intensity δ_n is taken randomly within $[250, 1000]$ CPU cycles/bit. Besides, the energy consumption for transmitting one task to the MEC server is uniformly distributed in $[0.1, 0.5]$ J, and the MD consumes 0.8 8 J to 3 3 J to locally compute one task and 0.5 5 J to 1 1 J to buffer one task. The weights ω_{delay}^t, ω_{energy}^t and $\omega_{privacy}^t$ can be dynamically set by the users according to the user's preferences. In our simulation, we set them to 1, 1 and 10. The control parameter v of PAOTO algorithm is usually set to 1.

In addition, two typical benchmarks are implemented to manifest the effectiveness of the proposed algorithm, which are the *random offloading algorithm* and *Dyna-Q algorithm* [4]. The former will arrange the offloading in a random way, and the latter is a reinforcement learning (RL)-based privacy-aware offloading scheme. The implementation details of *Dyna-Q algorithm* in our simulation may be slightly different from the [4], but the main framework are the same.

5.2 Numerical Results

In this section, the numerical results are presented to evaluate the effectiveness of the proposed algorithm.

In the first set of simulations, the N^t is taken randomly within $[5, 30]$, where the N_{max}^t is 30. The simulation results are averaged for each task to smooth out the fluctuations that occur with different N^t per round. The results of average weighted sum-cost, privacy level, computing delay and energy consumption cost are reported in Fig. 2, and the results is plotted at every 100 time slot. It can be seen in Fig. 2(a), Fig. 2(c) and Fig. 2(d) that the PAOTO algorithm can obtain lower weighted sum-cost, computing delay and energy consumption with about 23.0%, 22.5% and 25.4% reduction comparing to the Dyna-Q algorithm, and about 50.1%, 43.6%, 51% to the random offloading algorithm at the 1000th time slot. However, compared to another scenario that the privacy is not considered, the proposed PAOTO algorithm has a higher system cost. This shows that the PAOTA algorithm has compromised the cost in order to protect privacy, which obtains the sub-optimal solution. Besides, according to Fig. 2(b), we can see that the proposed algorithm achieves a better privacy-preserving level comparing to the random offloading and Dyna-Q algorithm. Given these facts, it can be observed that PAOTO algorithm outperforms the other two benchmarks, and it obtains sub-optimal task offloading performance while protecting user's privacy.

In the second set of simulations, as shown in Fig. 3, we investigate the performance evaluations with different N_{max}^t, which are ranged from 10 to 60. These simulation results in the second set are averaged over the first 2000 time slots. As shown in Fig. 3(a), PAOTO algorithm can get a lower average weighted sum-cost than the other two benchmarks. And the improvements of these performance (histogram difference) increase as the N_{max}^t increases from 10 to 60. The reason is that as the total number of tasks increases, the Dyna-Q algorithm requires

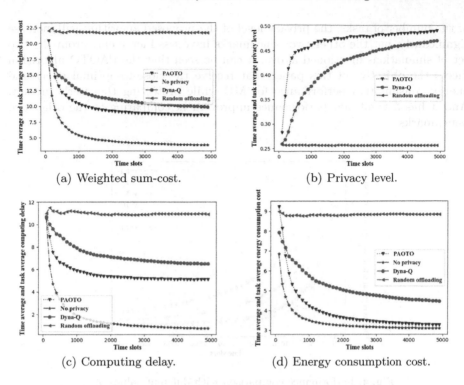

(a) Weighted sum-cost.

(b) Privacy level.

(c) Computing delay.

(d) Energy consumption cost.

Fig. 2. The first set of simulations: simulation results comparison of time average and task average weighted sum-cost, privacy level, computing delay and energy consumption cost for PAOTO algorithm, random offloading algorithm and Dyna-Q algorithm.

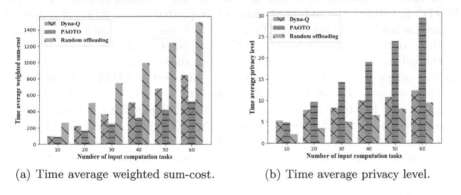

(a) Time average weighted sum-cost.

(b) Time average privacy level.

Fig. 3. The second set of simulations: simulation results comparison of time average weighted sum-cost and privacy level for PAOTO algorithm, random offloading algorithm and Dyna-Q algorithm under different number of input computation tasks.

more time to learn and the random offloading do not have any performance optimization effects, but the proposed algorithm has stable processing efficiency to obtain a lower cost. Additionally, as shown in the Fig. 3(b), with the increment of the number of tasks, the privacy level of the proposed algorithm will increase significantly, but the other two benchmarks have less increment. From the two set of simulations mentioned above, it can be seen that the PAOTO algorithm meets the objective of this paper that receive the close-to-optimal delay and energy consumption performance for MD while protecting the user's privacy. And it has a significant performance improvement comparing to the other two benchmarks.

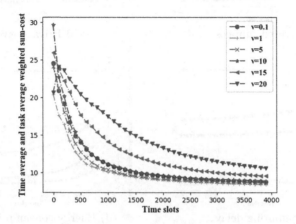

Fig. 4. Performance comparison with different values of v.

In order to analyze the effect of different key parameters (i.e., δ) on the PAOTO algorithm, the weighted sum-cost is plotted under different values of v. The parameter v in the PAOTO algorithm is associated with the standard deviation of the sampling, where $v = (2R+6)\sqrt{6d\log(T/\delta)}, \delta \in (0,1)$. Thus, we set the values of v as 0.1, 1, 5, 10, 15, 20. As shown in Fig. 4, we can observe that the values of v and the average weighted sum-cost of PAOTO algorithm are positively correlated when $v \geq 1$, such as the curves $v = 1$, $v = 5$ and $v = 10$. As the value of v is larger, the convergence of PAOTO algorithm becomes worse. However, when $v < 1$, the average cost of PAOTO algorithm will increase with the decrease of v, such as the curves $v = 1$ and $v = 0.1$. The reason is that the cost trade-off in the theoretical bound, and there are different effects before and after reaching the bound.

6   Conclusion

In this paper, we investigate the joint task offloading and privacy preservation problem for the small-size and low-power MDs without any system-level network information in the MEC system. The objective is to minimize a weighted sum of computing delay, energy consumption cost and the privacy level. In particular, the joint optimization problem has been formulated as a contextual MAB problem with a semi-parametric reward model to accommodate network dynamics, in which privacy metric is taken into account. Subsequently, a PAOTO algorithm is proposed to explore the balance between optimal system performance and the privacy level. The simulation results show that the proposed algorithm can provide near-optimal solutions in a short computing time. In the future, we will take the bandwidth constraint and multiple MEC servers scenario into account.

Acknowledgement. This work was supported by the Strategic Priority Research Program of Chinese Academy of Sciences, Grant No. XDC02040300.

References

1. Yang, T., Wolff, F., Papachristou, C.: Connected car networking. In: National Aerospace and Electronics Conference, pp. 60–64 (2018)
2. Nasrin, W., Xie, J.: A joint handoff and offloading decision algorithm for mobile edge computing (MEC). In: Global Communications Conference, pp. 1–6 (2019)
3. He, X., Liu, R., Dai, H.: Privacy-aware offloading in mobile-edge computing. In: Global Communications Conference, pp. 1–6 (2017)
4. Min, M., Wan, X.: Learning-based privacy-aware offloading for healthcare IoT with energy harvesting. Internet Things J. **6**(3), 4307–4316 (2018)
5. Xu, J., Chen, L., Zhou, P.: Joint service caching and task offloading for mobile edge computing in dense networks. In: IEEE International Conference on Computer Communications, pp. 207–215 (2018)
6. Wei, F., Chen, S., Zou, W.: A greedy algorithm for task offloading in mobile edge computing system. China Commun. **15**(11), 149–157 (2018)
7. Dab, B., Aitsaadi, N., Langar, R.: Q-learning algorithm for joint computation offloading and resource allocation in edge cloud. In: Symposium on Integrated Network and Service Management (IM), pp. 45–52 (2019)
8. He, X., Jin, R., Dai, H.: Deep PDS-learning for privacy-aware offloading in MEC-enabled IoT. Internet Things J. **6**(3), 4547–4555 (2019)
9. Zhang, H., Zeng, K.: Pairwise Markov chain: a task scheduling strategy for privacy-preserving SIFT on edge. In: IEEE International Conference on Computer Communications, pp. 1432–1440 (2019)
10. Zhou, P., Chen, W., Ji, S., Jiang, H.: Privacy-preserving online task allocation in edge-computing-enabled massive crowdsensing. Internet Things J. **6**(5), 7773–7787 (2019)
11. Yu, X., Guan, M., Liao, M., Fan, X.: Pre-migration of vehicle to network services based on priority in mobile edge computing. IEEE Access **7**, 3722–3730 (2019)
12. Ouyang, T., Li, R., Chen, X., Zhou, Z., Tang, X.: Adaptive user-managed service placement for mobile edge computing: an online learning approach. In: IEEE International Conference on Computer Communications, pp. 1468–1476 (2019)
13. Kim, G. S., Paik, M. C.: Contextual Multi-armed Bandit Algorithm for Semiparametric Reward Model (2019)
14. Agrawal, S., Goyal, N.: Thompson sampling for contextual bandits with linear payoffs. In: International Conference on Machine Learning, pp. 127–135 (2013)
15. Kwak, J., Kim, Y., Lee, J.: Dream: dynamic resource and task allocation for energy minimization in mobile cloud systems. IEEE J. Sel. Areas Commun. **33**(12), 2510–2523 (2015)

A Class Incremental Temporal-Spatial Model Based on Wireless Sensor Networks for Activity Recognition

Xue Li[⊠], Lanshun Nie, Xiandong Si, and Dechen Zhan

Harbin Institute of Technology, Harbin, China
lixuecs@hit.edu.cn

Abstract. With the development of Internet of Things (IoT), all kinds of sensors appear everywhere in our lives. Sensor-based Human Activity recognition (HAR) as the most common application of IoT system, has attracted attentions from both academia and industry due to the popularity of IoT. In most real-life scenarios, HAR is dynamic. For instance, in the process of classifying the activities, a new class is often encountered. To effectively recognize new activities, we propose a three-stage class incremental temporal-spatial model based on wireless sensor networks for activity recognition. In the first stage, when the new class arrives, rather than using the traditional method to train all the old class data, we design a method based on the recognition score to select part of the old class data as a sample for training, which represents the data distribution of the old class data. In the second stage, we analyze the temporal and spatial characteristics of activity data in combination with physical knowledge, the model extract temporal-spatial features, which further enhances the recognition effect. In the third stage, we avoid the phenomenon of 'catastrophic forgetting' of a network by finetuning distillation loss and classification loss. To demonstrate the effectiveness of our proposed model, we conducted comparative experiments using different models on different public datasets. The results showed our proposed model can not only recognize new classes, but also maintain the recognition ability of old classes.

Keywords: Class incremental · Sensor-based activity recognition · Temporal-spatial model

1 Introduction

Human activity recognition (HAR) is gaining increasing attention in Internet of Things (IoT) and pattern recognition. Sensor-based HAR is collecting activity data by wireless sensor networks. It is an important and promising application for IoT System. Moreover, sensors have become the main data collection devices for HAR because they are user-friendly and non-invasive. Common sensors include accelerometer, gyroscope, magnetometer, acoustic sensor, etc. In addition to being ubiquitous, smart phones integrate all kinds of sensors, including the aforementioned sensors. Therefore, mobile phones are now the most direct and popular data collection device [1, 2]. The commonly used activity recognition methods are machine learning and deep learning

© Springer Nature Switzerland AG 2020
D. Yu et al. (Eds.): WASA 2020, LNCS 12384, pp. 256–271, 2020.
https://doi.org/10.1007/978-3-030-59016-1_22

algorithms. Deep learning is more prominent with HAR [3, 4], because deep learning algorithms require no shallow feature extraction, thus directly learning the data and eliminating the limitation of domain knowledge in feature extraction [5]. Moreover, deep learning has achieved significant performance in several fields, such as image, text, and activity recognition, with excellent recognition performance [6, 7].

Most previous studies have focused on sensor modality and deep model, and there are still several aspects to explore in the application of HAR in industry. The popular deep learning model requires a large amount of data in the static environment for batch learning. Once the training is completed, the model will not be updated. However, the process of HAR is dynamic, which generates some new requirements, such as the change of sample, class and feature. Therefore, it is expected that the model can be automatically updated to meet the new requirements (i.e., automatically recognize more activity categories). To learn a new activity class, the traditional batch learning method faces the following problems. (i) It needs to collect a large quantity of new activity data; thus, combining all the old classes to learn from scratch. (ii) Meanwhile, the increase in the categories learned by the model will significantly increase the data, which will consume considerable computing time and resources. (iii) Additionally, if the model is updated with new class data, the new model will lose the ability to recognize the old activity data.

To address these problems, this paper proposes a three-stage class incremental temporal-spatial (CITS) model based on deep learning for activity recognition. We designed a method to select example data based on the score of the recognition sample data. This strategy ensures that when a new activity class is generated in the process of HAR, the network is trained using the new class data and part of old class data (which can represent the data distribution of all old class data), thus saving the calculation time and resources. Further, we combine the analysis of the temporal and spatial characteristics of the activity data with physical knowledge to extract temporal-spatial features, which further enhances the recognition effect. Finally, we propose a novel class incremental learning method—CITS model, which can both recognize the new activity class and maintain the ability of recognizing the old class.

The rest of this paper is organized as follows. Section 2 mainly examines the related work on class incremental learning, and Sect. 3 describes our proposed method. Section 4 evaluate the performance and presents comparisons with other approaches on three public datasets. Finally, Sect. 5 concludes the paper and high-lights scope for future work.

2 Related Work

The research on wireless sensor networks mainly focuses on wireless algorithm [8, 9], system [10, 11] and application [12, 13]. Sensor based-HAR is an important application for wireless sensor networks. Transfer learning and incremental learning are two extreme methods of learning and recognizing new classes. Transfer learning refers to using the knowledge learned from a task to learn new tasks. Hence, it can effectively avoid learning new classes from scratch.

An efficient training methodology and incrementally growing deep convolutional neural network (CNN) have been proposed [14] to learn new tasks while sharing part of the base network. Several studies [15, 16] share the network structure to complete a new task. This makes it possible for the network to learn new tasks one after the other without any performance loss in old tasks. By introducing attribute-based classification, By introducing attribute-based classification, researchers [17] have achieved zero-shot learning (learning a new class from zero-labeled samples). Li et al. [18] first proposed the one-shot learning concept, which makes it possible to learn a new category from a single sample. One-shot learning and zero-shot learning are two extreme forms of transfer learning. Incremental learning means that a learning system can learn new knowledge from new samples consistently and can remember most of the learned knowledge. An incremental learning of new samples has been realized [19] by adding new branches to the CNN's improved model. Additionally, an automatic learning mechanism [20] based on a hidden Markov model has been proposed, which can detect the occurrence of new activities and accordingly update the dictionary. Chen et al. [21] designed an incremental learning method based on an online sequential extreme learning machine for continuously sensing new categories from Bluetooth data. Through these works, it is clear that the biggest difference between incremental learning and transfer learning is how they handle the old knowledge. Incremental learning needs to remember the old knowledge as much as possible while learning the new knowledge, whereas transfer learning only uses the old knowledge to learn the new knowledge. After learning, it only focuses on the performance of the new class and disregards the performance of the old data.

In the process of HAR, the amount of data increases with time, and the appearance of new class is probable. Subsequently, the classification model that is trained based on historical data may be unsuitable to some new data. Therefore, it is necessary for an incremental learning system that is application-oriented to achieve automated classification and dynamic updates to ensure that the ever-changing data can be correctly classified. One method is to train the classification model with all the old and new data, but the method requires high computational cost. Another method is to use the new data to fine-tune the training model. Although this method learns new information, it forgets the previously learned information, which is called the catastrophic forgetting problem. In [22], the new data and the corresponding small samples in the old data are used to fine-tune the neural network to incrementally learn new class. SupportNet [23] is presented, which combines the strength of deep learning and support vector machine (SVM); here, SVM is used to identify the support data from the old data, which are fed to the deep learning model together with the new data for further training. This enables the model to review the essential information of the old data when learning the new information. To overcome catastrophic forgetting, Lee et al. [24] proposed a global distillation to distill the knowledge of how to distinguish classes across different tasks to avoid overfitting in the most recent task. A study [25] has showed that it is possible to overcome this limitation and train networks that can maintain expertise on tasks that they have not experienced for a long time. The method proposed in the study remembers old tasks by selectively slowing down learning on the weights important for those tasks. In addition, other studies [26, 27] have been conducted to overcome the problem of catastrophic forgetting.

There are few works on incremental learning for activity recognition. Automatic activity recognition is of great significance because it can provide important information for in various fields, such as environmental intelligence and pervasive computing. Authors have proposed an effective class incremental learning method, named class incremental random forests (CIRF), to enable existing activity recognition models to identify new activities [28]. Likewise, a hybrid user-assisted incremental model adaptation was proposed to recognize interleaved and concurrent activities in a dynamic smart-home scenario [29]. Wang et al. [30] proposed an incremental activity recognition classifier based on probabilistic neural networks (PNN) and adjustable fuzzy clustering (AFC). AFC is used to divide training instances into clusters and endow PNN with incremental learning ability.

3 Methods

3.1 CITS Architecture

Given the training activity dataset $S = X_1 \cup \ldots \cup X_i \ldots \cup X_k$, where k refers to the number of activity classes, and $X_i = \{x_{ij}\}_{j=1}^{n_i}$ denotes the sub-set of the i-th class, which contains n_i samples represented by x_{ij}. Correspondingly, the class label of each sample is denoted as $y_{ij} \in \{1, 2, \ldots, k\}$. Using these data for training, we can learn the CNN based discriminative classifier $f(\theta_2; \varphi(x_{ij}; \theta_1))$, where $\varphi(x_{ij}; \theta_1)$ represents the extracted deep features parameterized by θ_1, and θ_2 can be regarded as the learnable parameters for classification. Supposing that, a new class (k + 1) is encountered. Then, we can achieve the corresponding training set X_{k+1} for the (k + 1)-th class. Our goal is to learn a CNN based discriminative classifier $g(\theta_2'; \varphi'(x_{ij}; \theta_1'))$, $x_{ij} \in S \cup X_{k+1}$ with significant performance on the new class, but without catastrophic forgetting problem.

Figure 1 illustrates the proposed CITS architecture. First, we select examples randomly from X_{k+1} and S as the input of CNN. More details are provided in Sect. 3.2. Then, we aim to learn the temporal-spatial features $\varphi'(\cdot; \theta_1')$. Particularly, we analyze the temporal and spatial characteristics of activity data combined with physical knowledge. The learned deep feature enhances the feature representation of activity data, and further benefits to the recognition performance. More details will be explained in Sect. 3.3. Finally, we use the distillation loss L_{diss} and classification loss L_{class} to finetune the network and achieve the CNN based classifier $g(\theta_2'; \varphi'(\cdot; \theta_1'))$.

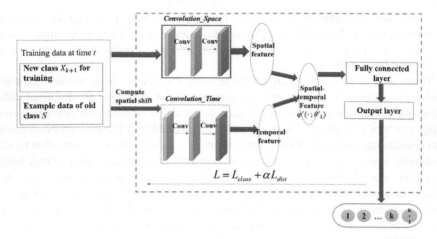

Fig. 1. CITS architecture

3.2   Example Data Selection

Traditional methods adopted when performing on samples from new classes are basically illustrated in Fig. 2. Only applying the new data on existing model shown as in Fig. 2(a) will lead to the catastrophic forgetting problem. However, combination with all existing data brings large amounts of computation and storage cost with the increasing of data. On the contrary, in this paper, we present a method to select example data based on the difficulty score of data sample recognition.

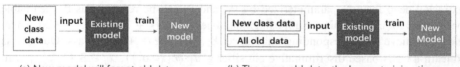

(a) New model will forget old data   (b) The more old data, the longer training time

Fig. 2. The most commonly methods for recognizing new classes.

Supposing that we have n_{k+1} samples in the new class X_{k+1}. Here, we first construct a new example data set Z_{k+1}, which has N samples and consists of two parts. One part is the N/2 pieces of data selected at random from X_{k+1}, and the other part is the N/2 pieces of data are selected from Z_{k+1}, which are difficult to recognize. These unrecognizable data represent the data that are easily confused between this class and other classes in the feature space. In the process of training the model, these unrecognizable data are used as example data to update the model, which is helpful to improve the recognition performance and avoid catastrophic forgetting. A crucial question is how to select $\frac{N}{2}$ pieces of data that are difficult to recognize. In this paper, we define a fraction F for each data, which is the difficulty of the data to be recognized. The larger F is, the easier the recognition will be. For new tasks, the loss encourages predictions $\hat{Y}_{k+1}$ to be consistent with the ground truth Y_{k+1}. The score F is given by

$$F = F^{softmax} - F^{loss} \tag{1}$$

$$F^{softmax} = e^{X_i} / \sum e^{X_{k+1}} \tag{2}$$

$$F^{loss} = -\sum Y_{k+1} \log(\hat{Y}_{k+1}) \tag{3}$$

3.3 Spatial-Temporal Feature Extraction

The sensors commonly used in HAR include accelerometers, gyroscopes, and magnetometers, and sensor-based activity data are time series and contain the internal activity mechanism. As shown in Fig. 3(a), the data collected by the sensor changes with the occurrence of the activity, and the laws of acceleration data change are different for different activities. Thus, we analyzed the activity data according to domain and physical knowledge. As the original data collected by a sensor contains considerable noises, it is difficult to analyze the original data directly. However, we can analyze these physical quantities because we can use the physical knowledge to transform and obtain the physical quantities that can represent the activity state.

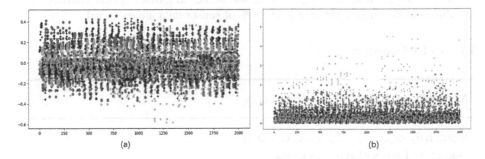

Fig. 3. The data collected by the sensor changes with the occurrence of the activity

The acceleration collects data in the X, Y and Z axes in the space, which are represented by Ax, Ay, and Az respectively. If the initial velocity at a particular time is V_1, the acceleration value of the X axis is A_{x_1}, and each sampling time is T, then the displacement S_1 can be calculated by

$$S_1 = V_1 * T + 1/2 * A_{x_1} * T^2 \tag{4}$$

The displacement difference S_x between S_1 and S_2 at the next moment is

$$S_x = 1/2 * A_{x_1} * T^2 + 1/2 * A_{x2} * T^2 \tag{5.}$$

S is the sum of displacement interpolation in three directions

$$S = \sqrt{S_x^2 + S_y^2 + S_z^2} \qquad (6.)$$

The larger S is, the larger the displacement changes and the more intense the activity is. Therefore, we can use the physical knowledge contained in the sensor data itself to extract the temporal feature.

After the above physical conversion, the collected acceleration value is converted into a displacement that can better represent the activity state. The displacement difference of the three activities obtained after the conversion is shown in Fig. 3(b). In the above experiment, after the acceleration value collected in the activity is converted into displacement, the original three-dimensional features are converted into one-dimensional features which is temporal features.

For the spatial feature of sensor-based activity data, as only the acceleration and angular velocity information about the object motion are obtained when using sensors (e.g., accelerometer and gyroscope) to collect the activity data, we arrange the sensor data in a two-dimensional matrix form, in which each column represents a certain axis in the sensor, and each row represents the sensor collected at a certain time. Consequently, the sensor data is two-dimensional, which is also similar to two-dimensional images. Finally, similar to using convolution kernel to extract spatial features from two-dimensional images, the spatial features of sensor data are extracted.

3.4   CITS Algorithm

Algorithm 1   *CITS algorithm*

Input: $f(\theta_2; \varphi(x_{ij}; \theta_1)), X_{k+1}, Z_1 \cup ... \cup Z_k$
Output: k+1 types of activity classes
1: At time t, T_t:
2:    Compute S_m which is input to softmax layer on M of training $Z_1 \cup ... \cup Z_k$
3:    Train X_{k+1} and $Z_1 \cup ... \cup Z_k$
4:    Extract Spatial feature
5:    Extract Temporal feature
6:    Combine Spatial feature and Temporal feature
7:    Compute Distillation Loss: $L_{dist} = -\sum S_m log(S_{m'})$
8:    Compute Classification Loss: $L_{class} = -\frac{1}{N}\sum_{n=1}^{N} Y_{k+1} \log(\widehat{Y_{k+1}})$
9:    Compute Loss $L_{loss} = L_{class} + \alpha * L_{dist}$
10:    Compute gradient: $\Delta\omega = -\eta \frac{\partial L_{loss}}{\partial \omega}$
11:    Update weight: $\omega \leftarrow \omega + \Delta\omega$
12:    Compute score of X_{k+1}:   F
13:    Select example data Z_{k+1}
14:    Update old class dataset: $T_t^{example} = Z_1 \cup ... \cup Z_k \cup Z_{k+1}$
15:    End of task T_t

---

4 Experiments

4.1 Experimental Setup

We performed all the experiments on a machine with Ubuntu 16.04, two GPUs (NVidia GTX 1080 Ti), 32 GB memory, and 512 GB SSD. We adopted two deep learning development frameworks: Keras 2.0.6 and TensorFlow 1.2.1. Further, we evaluated our proposed method with different models and datasets, as well as three public datasets, namely the UCI human activity recognition using smartphones dataset (UCIHAR) [1], UniMiB SHAR (USHAR) [2], and WISDM [3]. The comparison methods/models are shown in Table 1, and the differences from our model are marked in yellow.

Table 1. Description of seven comparison methods/models

Model/Model	Description
CNN	Convolution model with 3 convolution layers
CITS	Stage1: Select some of the old class data as example data based on the recognition score F
	Stage2: Extract spatial-temporal features using CNN
	Stage3: Finetune model with distillation loss and classification loss
TScnn	Stage1: Extract spatial-temporal features using CNN
cnn_F	Stage1: Select some of the old class data as example data based on the recognition score F
	Stage2: Extract temporal features using CNN
	Stage3: Finetune model with distillation loss and classification loss
cnn_SVM	Paper[25]
TScnn_svm	Stage1: Select some of the old class data as example data based on SVM
	Stage2: Extract spatial-temporal features using CNN
	Stage3: Finetune model with distillation loss and classification loss
CITS_Alldata	Stage1: Use all the old data to train model
	Stage2: Extract spatial-temporal features using CNN
	Stage3: Finetune model with distillation loss and classification loss

4.2 Correctness and Effectiveness

We used the public dataset UCIHAR, which has an average of 1200 of each activity class; however, in this experiment we only use 300 pieces of data as example data. We add new one class at a time in the following order as Table 6 in Section Appendix. The comparison results with other methods are shown in Table 2, which show that our method can retain the memory of the old class. And the recognition performance is better than other methods. Meanwhile, it can be observed that these methods can keep the memory of the old class. According to previous paper [31], it is difficult to distinguish sitting and standing activities in UCIHAR. Hence, the overall recognition accuracy of the model will decrease when the model recognizes these two activities. Therefore, in Task2–Task4, the fluctuation of recognition accuracy of all methods is very small, whereas, in Task5, the model is required to classify sitting and standing after learning new classes; thus, the recognition accuracy of all methods decline. However, in Task5, the recognition accuracy based on score F (including cnn_F and CITS) is higher than that of SVM (including cnn_SVM and TScnn_SVM). This is because the method based on score F select the example data of sitting in Task3, and those data that are easy to be confused. Therefore, in Task5, the data that are easy to be confused in sitting and standing will be used to update the parameters of the model. After Task5, the model has a better recognition performance on sitting and standing.

Table 2. Accuracy of different model on Task1-Task5

Model	Task1	Task2	Task3	Task4	Task5
cnn_svm	98.13%	95.89%	95.84%	94.86%	84.35%
cnn_F	98.13%	94.52%	97.71%	**98.96%**	92.39%
TScnn_svm	98.34%	92.79%	96.43%	93.37%	78.01%
CITS	**98.34%**	**97.26%**	**98.13%**	98.38%	**94.60%**

To explore the effect of model recognition under different activity orders, we changed the order of learning new classes (Table 7 in Section Appendix) to prove that our method is still effective, and the accuracy in Table 3. In the process of incremental learning of new classes, for the same model, the performance of the model learning new classes also depends on the difficulty of recognizing the activity classes themselves. Additionally, the overall recognition accuracy depends on the recognition difficulty of each activity class. If the new class learned by the model is easily confused with an old class, the overall recognition accuracy of all activity classes after learning the new class will decrease. In addition, we recognize the easily confused sitting and standing activities in Task2'. From the experimental results, it can be seen that in Task2', after learning the standing activities, the recognition accuracy of all the three methods decreased.

Table 3. Accuracy of different model on Task1'-Task5'

Model	Task1'	Task2'	Task3'	Task4'	Task5'
cnn_svm	1	77.24%	83.75%	79.34%	80.55%
cnn_F	1	85.06%	89.29%	90.46%	89.24%
TScnn_svm	1	71.92%	74.85%	72.10%	70.37%
CITS	1	**93.65%**	**94.11%**	**94.57%**	**94.43%**

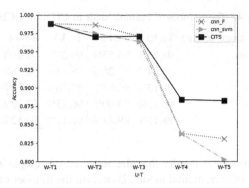

Fig. 4. Accuracies of different models on WISDM. The order of learning new classes is shown as Table 8 in Section Appendix.

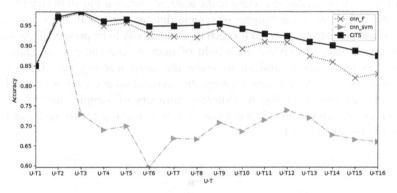

Fig. 5. Accuracies of different models on USHAR. The order of learning new classes is shown as Table 9 in Section Appendix.

In addition, we performed the same experiments on the other two datasets, namely WISDM and USHAR, and the results are shown in the Fig. 4 and 5. The result shows our method is the best.

4.3   The Number of Example Data

To verify the number of example data and show the validity of the selection method more clearly, we selected 300, 200, 100 and 50 in UCIHAR as the number of sample data to observe the impact of the number on the recognition effect. We defined result of the CITS_Alldata as the upper limit. The results are shown in Table 4. The more number selected, the more data can be remembered in the old class, and the better the recognition result.

Table 4. The number of example data in CITS on UCIHAR

Number of example data	Task1	Task2	Task3	Task4	Task5
CITS_Alldata	98.13%	98.55%	99.20%	99.29%	95.18%
CITS (300)	98.34%	97.26%	98.13%	98.38%	94.60%
CITS (200)	98.13%	96.03%	97.76%	98.13%	91.00%
CITS (100)	98.13%	93.00%	96.43%	97.22%	90.70%
CITS (50)	98.13%	89.47%	92.17%	95.52%	90.05%

It can be seen from the results that the number of sample data will affect the recognition accuracy of incremental model. Based on the number of sample data, it can be roughly divided into three intervals: (1) when the number of sample data is very large, it is equivalent to using all data; (2) when the number of sample data is equivalent to approximately one-fifth of all the data of this activity, the recognition accuracy after model updating is close to the accuracy when using all the data to update the model; and (3) when the number of sample data is very small. For example, only dozens of sample data are selected for each type of activity to be preserved. As the deep learning model needs to update the weight of neurons according to the data during training, too little data is difficult to make the deep learning model learn better recognition results. After the new learning, the recognition accuracy is relatively low. The results are shown in Fig. 6. Different numbers of sample data in CITS on UCI HAR are shown in Table 5, and it can be seen that 200 pieces of data can achieve at least 300 pieces of effect.

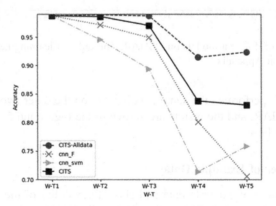

Fig. 6. Accuracy of different model on WISDM using 100 pieces of example data

Table 5. The number of example data in CITS on WISDM

Number of example data	W-T1	W-T2	W-T3	W-T4	W-T5
CITS_Alldata	98.77%	98.93%	98.74%	91.44%	92.35%
CITS (300)	98.77%	96.98%	97.05%	88.37%	88.25%
CITS (200)	98.77%	98.63%	97.05%	83.77%	83.06%

5 Conclusions

Owing to the dynamic nature of HAR, precisely, the process of class incremental learning, we propose a novel CITS method based on deep learning. When a new activity class arrives, CITS recognizes the new class and maintains the ability of recognizing the old classes. CITS comprises three stages: 1) a method based on the recognition score F is used to select part of the old class data as a sample for training, 2) the model extracts temporal-spatial features, and 3) finetunes the network with distillation loss and classification loss. Experimental results on three public activity datasets showed that our method is an effective solution to recognize new classes in activity recognition. For the test accuracy, CITS can achieve better recognition performance using sample data, which is one-fifth of all the data. In a future work, we will improve our model to recognize multiclass activities.

Foundation. This work was supported by the National Key R&D Program of China under Grant 2018YFB1703403.

Appendix

Table 6. The order of learning new classes in UCIHAR

Task	New class	Model can recognize classes after learning a new class
1	Walking, Going upstairs	Walking, Going upstairs
2	Going downstairs	Walking, Going upstairs, Going downstairs
3	Sitting	Walking, Going upstairs, Going downstairs, Sitting
4	Lying	Walking, Going upstairs, Going downstairs, Sitting, Lying
5	Standing	Walking, Going upstairs, Going downstairs, Sitting, Lying, Standing

Table 7. The order of learning new classes in UCIHAR

Task	New class	Model can recognize classes after learning a new class
1'	Sitting, Lying	Sitting, Lying
2'	Standing	Sitting, Lying, Standing
3'	Walking	Sitting, Lying, Standing, Walking
4'	Going downstairs	Sitting, Lying, Standing, Walking, Going downstairs
5'	Going upstairs	Sitting, Lying, Standing, Walking, Going downstairs, Going upstairs

Table 8. The order of learning new classes in WISDM

Task	New class	Model can recognize classes after learning a new class
W-T1	Walking, Jogging	Walking, Jogging
W-T2	Going upstairs	Walking, Jogging, Going upstairs
W-T3	Going downstairs	Walking, Jogging, Going upstairs, Going downstairs
W-T4	Sitting	Walking, Jogging, Going upstairs, Going downstairs, Sitting
W-T5	Standing	Walking, Jogging, Going upstairs, Going downstairs, Sitting, Standing

Table 9. The order of learning new classes in USHAR

Task	New class	Model can recognize classes after learning a new class
U-T1	Going upstairs (GoingUpS, Going downstairs) (GoingDownS)	GoingUpS, GoingDownS
U-T2	Walking	GoingUpS, GoingDownS, Walking
U-T3	Running	GoingUpS, GoingDownS, Walking, Running
U-T4	Jumping	GoingUpS, GoingDownS, Walking, Running, Jumping
U-T5	SittingDown	GoingUpS, GoingDownS, Walking, Running, Jumping, SittingDown
U-T6	Standing up from sitting (StandingUpFS)	GoingUpS, GoingDownS, Walking, Running, Jumping, SittingDown, StandingUpFS
U-T7	Lying down from standing (LyingDownFS)	GoingUpS, GoingDownS, Walking, Running, Jumping, SittingDown, StandingUpFS, LyingDownFS
U-T8	Standing up from laying (StandingUpFL)	GoingUpS, GoingDownS, Walking, Running, Jumping, SittingDown, StandingUpFS, LyingDownFS, StandingUpFL
U-T9	Falling with protection strategies (FallingWithPS)	GoingUpS, GoingDownS, Walking, Running, Jumping, SittingDown, StandingUpFS, LyingDownFS, StandingUpFL, FallingWithPS
U-T10	FallingLeft(FL)	GoingUpS, GoingDownS, Walking, Running, Jumping, SittingDown, StandingUpFS, LyingDownFS, StandingUpFL, FallingWithPS, FL
U-T11	FallingRightward(FR)	GoingUpS, GoingDownS, Walking, Running, Jumping, SittingDown, StandingUpFS, LyingDownFS, StandingUpFL, FallingWithPS, FL, FR

(continued)

Table 9. (*continued*)

Task	New class	Model can recognize classes after learning a new class
U-T12	FallingBackward(FB)	GoingUpS, GoingDownS, Walking, Running, Jumping, SittingDown, StandingUpFS, LyingDownFS, StandingUpFL, FallingWithPS, FL, FR, FB
U-T13	Falling backward-sitting-chair (FallingBackSC)	GoingUpS, GoingDownS, Walking, Running, Jumping, SittingDown, StandingUpFS, LyingDownFS, StandingUpFL, FallingWithPS, FL, FR, FB, FallingBackSC
U-T14	Syncope	GoingUpS, GoingDownS, Walking, Running, Jumping, SittingDown, StandingUpFS, LyingDownFS, StandingUpFL, FallingWithPS, FL, FR, FB, FallingBackSC, Syncope
U-T15	HittingObstacle	GoingUpS, GoingDownS, Walking, Running, Jumping, SittingDown, StandingUpFS, LyingDownFS, StandingUpFL, FallingWithPS, FL, FR, FB, FallingBackSC, Syncope, HittingObstacle

References

1. Anguita, D., Ghio, A., Oneto, L., Parra, X., Reyes-Ortiz, J.L.: A public domain dataset for human activity recognition using smartphones. In: 21th European Symposium on Artificial Neural Networks, Computational Intelligence and Machine Learning, ESANN 2013, 24–26 April 2013, Bruges, Belgium (2013)
2. Wannenburg, J., Malekian, R.: Physical activity recognition from smartphone accelerometer data for user context awareness sensing. Syst. Man Cybern. **47**(12), 3142–3149 (2017)
3. Wang, J., Chen, Y., Hao, S., et al.: Deep learning for sensor-based activity recognition: a survey. Pattern Recogn. Lett. **119**, 3–11 (2018). S016786551830045X
4. Plotz, T., Guan, Y.: Deep learning for human activity recognition in mobile computing. Computer **51**(5), 50–59 (2018)
5. Ploetz, T., Hammerla, N., Olivier, P.: Feature learning for activity recognition in ubiquitous computing. In: Proceedings 22nd International Joint Conference Artificial Intelligence (IJCAI 2011), pp. 1729–1734 (2011)
6. Yang, Q.: Activity recognition: linking low-level sensors to high-level intelligence. In: IJCAI, pp. 20–25 (2009)
7. Krizhevsky, A., Sutskever, L., Hinton, G.E.: Imagenet classification with deep convolutional neural networks. In: Neural Information Processing Systems (2012)
8. Cai, Z., Duan, Z., Li, W.: Exploiting multi-dimensional task diversity in distributed auctions for mobile crowdsensing. IEEE Trans. Mobile Comput. 1 (2020)

9. Yu, L., Chen, L., Cai, Z., et al.: Stochastic load balancing for virtual resource management in datacenters. IEEE Trans. Cloud Comput. **8**, 1, (2016)
10. Duan, Z., Li, W., Cai, Z.: Distributed auctions for task assignment and scheduling in mobile crowdsensing systems. In: 2017 IEEE 37th International Conference on Distributed Computing Systems (ICDCS). IEEE (2017)
11. Cheng, S., Li, Y., Tian, Z., et al.: A model for integrating heterogeneous sensory data in IoT systems. Comput. Netw. **150**, 1–14 (2019)
12. Cheng, S., Cai, Z., Li, J., et al. Drawing dominant dataset from big sensory data in wireless sensor networks. In: 2015 IEEE Conference on Computer Communications (INFOCOM). IEEE (2015)
13. Cheng, S., Cai, Z., Li, J., et al.: Extracting kernel dataset from big sensory data in wireless sensor networks. IEEE Trans. Knowl. Data Eng. **29**, 1 (2017)
14. Sarwar, S.S., Ankit, A., Roy, K., et al.: Incremental learning in deep convolutional neural networks using partial network sharing. arXiv: Computer Vision and Pattern Recognition (2017)
15. Rosenfeld, A.: Incremental learning through deep adaptation. IEEE Trans. Pattern Anal. Mach. Intell. **42**, 1 (2018)
16. Lampert, C.H., Nickisch, H., Harmeling, S., et al.: Learning to detect unseen object classes by between-class attribute transfer. In: Computer Vision and Pattern Recognition, pp. 951–958 (2009)
17. Feifei, L., Fergus, R., Perona, P., et al.: One-shot learning of object categories. IEEE Trans. Pattern Anal. Mach. Intell. **28**(4), 594–611 (2006)
18. Luo, J., Wu, J., Lin, W., et al.: ThiNet: a filter level pruning method for deep neural network compression. In: International Conference on Computer Vision, pp. 5068–5076 (2017)
19. Liu, Z., Li, J., Shen, Z., et al.: Learning efficient convolutional networks through network slimming. In: International Conference on Computer Vision, pp. 2755–2763 (2017)
20. Chen, Z., Chen, Y., Hu, L., et al.: ContextSense: unobtrusive discovery of incremental social context using dynamic bluetooth data. In: Ubiquitous Computing, pp. 23–26 (2014)
21. Castro, F.M., Marinjimenez, M.J., Guil, N., et al.: End-to-end incremental learning. In: European Conference on Computer Vision, pp. 241–257 (2018)
22. Li, Y., Li, Z., Ding, L., et al.: SupportNet: solving catastrophic forgetting in class incremental learning with support data. arXiv: Neural and Evolutionary Computing (2018)
23. Lee, K., Lee, K., Shin, J., et al.: Incremental learning with unlabeled data in the wild. arXiv: Computer Vision and Pattern Recognition (2019)
24. Kirkpatrick, J., Pascanu, R., Rabinowitz, N.C., et al.: Overcoming catastrophic forgetting in neural networks. Proc. Natl. Acad. Sci. U.S.A. **114**(13), 3521–3526 (2017)
25. Aljundi, R., Babiloni, F., Elhoseiny, M., et al.: Memory aware synapses: learning what (not) to forget. In: European Conference on Computer Vision, pp. 144–161 (2018)
26. Rebuffi, S., Kolesnikov, A., Sperl, G., et al.: iCaRL: incremental classifier and representation learning. In: Computer Vision and Pattern Recognition, pp. 5533–5542 (2017)
27. Hu, C., Chen, Y., Peng, X., et al.: A novel feature incremental learning method for sensor-based activity recognition. IEEE Trans. Knowl. Data Eng. **31**(6), 1038–1050 (2019)
28. Chinghu, L., Yuchen, H., Yihan, C., Lichen, F.: Hybrid user-assisted incremental model adaptation for activity recognition in a dynamic smart-home environment. IEEE Trans. Hum. Mach. Syst. **43**(5), 421–436 (2013)

29. Zhelong, W., Ming, J., Yaohua, H., Hongyi, L.: An incremental learning method based on probabilistic neural networks and adjustable fuzzy clustering for human activity recognition by using wearable sensors. IEEE Trans. Inf. Technol. Biomed. Publ. IEEE Eng. Med. Biol. Soc. **16**(4) 691–699 (2012)
30. Li, Y., Li, Z., Ding, L., et al.: SupportNet: solving catastrophic forgetting in class incremental learning with support data. In: Neural and Evolutionary Computing (2018)
31. Li, X., et al.: Understanding and improving deep neural network for activity recognition. In: MOBIMEDIA (2018)

Sensor Deployment for Composite Event Monitoring in Battery-Free Sensor Networks

Ke Lin and Jianzhong Li[✉]

The School of Computer Science and Tech, Harbin Institute of Technology,
Harbin, China
{linke,lijzh}@hit.edu.cn

Abstract. Composite event monitoring, which focuses on detecting complicated events from multi-model sensory data, is an important application of heterogeneous sensor networks. Before carrying out such tasks, the deployment of heterogeneous sensors is indispensable, and is vital to the quality of event monitoring. Existing works discussing sensor deployment for composite event coverage are primarily on traditional sensor networks. Recently, a novel network architecture, namely Battery-free Sensor Networks (BF-WSNs) are proposed. Unlike the traditional ones, the BF-WSNs harvest ambient energy and have unlimited lifetime. Considering the difference in characteristics of networks, novel deploying strategies for heterogeneous BF-WSNs are eagerly demanded for better quality in composite event monitoring. In this paper, we address the problem of Sensor Deployment for Composite Event Monitoring in Battery-free Sensor Networks (BF-SDCEM). It is formalized and proved to be NP-hard. Then, the approximate solution is proposed to optimize the quality of coverage and maintain network connectivity. Simulations are carried out to evaluate the performance of the proposed method under different network parameters and to show their effectiveness.

Keywords: Battery-free sensor networks · Wireless sensor networks · Heterogeneous networks

1 Introduction

In the era of Internet of Things, the Wireless Sensor Networks (WSNs) find wide applications in medical care, scientific research, environment monitoring, industry, and agriculture, *etc.* The event detection, which is one of major duties of WSNs, has attracted much attention in the past decades [1,2]. Nowadays, some of the events in the practical applications become so complicated that homogeneous sensor networks are hard to ensure [3]. For example, temperature, smoke density, and light intensity are all important in detecting a fire. Thus, heterogeneous sensor networks with multiple types of sensor nodes play an important role in complex event detection. Such networks can obtain multi-model data from the

© Springer Nature Switzerland AG 2020
D. Yu et al. (Eds.): WASA 2020, LNCS 12384, pp. 272–284, 2020.
https://doi.org/10.1007/978-3-030-59016-1_23

physical world. In this paper, we refer to the complex events as composite events [3] which consists of several atomic events. The atomic event are those can be detected from single-model data.

Meanwhile, the widely-used battery-powered sensor networks for event monitoring have obvious shortcomings. The lifetime of a sensor node is limited by the battery, and it's almost impossible to replace the batteries of a large-scale sensor network. The whole sensor network becomes dead if some critical nodes has insufficient energy. Therefore, the battery-free sensor networks, which are not equipped with batteries and harvest the ambient energy like RF energy, luminous energy, and mechanical energy, are proposed in recent years [4–6]. They have unlimited lifetime since the infinite energy that can be harvested from the environment.

Before performing monitoring tasks, sensor deployment is an indispensable step for WSNs. A well-designed deployment scheme brings noticeable growth in monitoring quality. However, existing works discussing sensor deployment for heterogeneous sensor networks primarily focus on traditional networks. And the sensor deployment addressing the energy harvesting networks doesn't consider the composite event monitoring problem and heterogeneous networks. The sensor deployment for composite event monitoring in heterogeneous battery-free sensor networks requires novel strategies because it asks for comprehensive consideration on all the following points. (1) *The coverage of composite events.* The coverage of each atomic event by the heterogeneous sensor nodes has to be considered according to their contribution to the detection of the composite event. (2) *The feasibility of deploying.* Unlike in many previous works, in practical, not all the locations in the monitoring area are feasible or reachable to deploy nodes due to the terrain or other reasons. (3) *The heterogeneous ambient energy and harvesters.* The heterogeneous sensor nodes can harvest different kinds of ambient energy. Deploying a node at different locations, or deploying different type of node at the same location can have different energy harvested and performance. We also permit that some of the nodes may have multiple energy harvesters [7–9]. (4) *The connectivity of network.* The connectivity of network has to be guaranteed to exchange event messages. (5) *The budget.* The deployment has a budget limit so that we cannot deploy unlimited number of sensors.

Therefore, we address the Sensor Deployment for Composite Event Monitoring in Heterogeneous Battery-free Sensor Networks (BF-SDCEM) in this paper. The contributions of this paper are summarized as follows,

1) The BF-SDCEM problem is formalized and is proved to be NP-hard. To the best of our knowledge, this paper is the first work that addresses this problem.
2) The approximate algorithm is proposed to solve the battery-free sensor deployment for composite event monitoring in polynomial time complexity.
3) The approximate algorithm to guarantee network connectivity of the heterogeneous battery-free sensor deployment is also designed.
4) Simulations are carried out to evaluate the performance of our proposed methods under different network parameters.

2 Related Works

The composite event coverage in traditional networks was studied in [3,10–12]. Gao et al. discussed the stochastic sensor deployment for composite event coverage in traditional sensor networks in [3]. Yang et al. discussed the scheduling problem for composite event coverage in traditional sensor networks to promote the network lifetime in [11]. Li et al. studied the coverage problem to detect composite event in battery-powered sensor networks to optimize the energy efficiency in [10]. The re-deploying problem of traditional mobile sensor networks was solved in [12]. Those papers didn't consider the battery-free sensors that harvest ambient energy.

The deployment problem in traditional heterogeneous wireless sensor networks was addressed in [13–15]. Deploying directional nodes in city-scale 3D real world was studied in [13]. Li et al. studied deploying storage nodes to form a heterogeneous networks for better reliability on data storage and routing in [14]. The heterogeneous sensor deployment towards hybrid point and barrier coverage was discussed in [15]. Although those works studied the deployment problem in heterogeneous WSNs, but they only considered the traditional battery-powered networks.

There were a few studies discussing the deployment problem in energy harvesting/rechargeable networks [16–18]. The deploying problem in energy harvesting sensor networks based on energy transferring was studied in [16]. Hsu et al. studied the deploying energy harvesting sensor networks in reconstructing a spatial Gaussian random field in [17]. Liu et al. discussed the node deployment in homogeneous energy harvesting networks in [18]. Those papers primarily addressed the homogeneous networks instead of heterogeneous networks or composite event monitoring.

Moreover, some recent works on battery-free networks [4–6] did not discuss the sensor deployment.

To Summarize, none of the papers address the sensor deployment problem for composite event monitoring in heterogeneous batter-free sensor networks.

3 Problem Formulation

3.1 Event Model

The event model consists of the composite event and the atomic events [3]. An atomic event is described as a triple $e = \langle condition, time, location \rangle$. The *condition* could be ensured either satisfied or unsatisfied by the sensory data from one type of sensing module or a single attribute. The *time* and *location* indicate when and where the *condtion* is satisfied. A composite event, $E = \langle e_1 \wedge e_2 \wedge \cdots \wedge e_i, time, location \rangle$ is a conjunction of multiple atomic events. It means the *condition* in each e_i are satisfied at same time and location.

Each atomic event e_i has a confidence ξ_i in detecting the composite event E. Such confidence is the conditional probability of E's happening when e_i happens, i.e $\xi_i = p(E|e_i)$. ξ_i can be calculated from the prior knowledge and historical statistics. Furthermore, such confidence must satisfy $\sum_{i=1}^{|S|} \xi_i = 1$.

3.2   Candidate Nodes

There are a set of candidate sensor nodes to be deployed, noted as $N = \{n_j\}$, where j is the type of the node. Each type of node n_j is equipped with a sensing module, labeled as $s(n_j) = s_i$. Different nodes may have the same type of sensing module. The sensing module s_i has the sensing range r_i. The node n_j consumes λ_j in a time slot to collect sensory data and detect events. A node is equipped with one or more energy harvesters, noted as $h(n_j) = \{h_1, h_2, ..., h_q\}$, that can harvest different types of energy. Each node is equipped with a communication module. It is generally assumed that the communication range R is twice or larger than the sensing range of each sensing module [19]. Moreover, the cost of node n_j is v_j.

3.3   Monitoring Area Model

The monitoring area is a convex polygon on an Euclidean plane. In the monitoring area, there's a set of targets to be monitored $O = \{o_1, o_2, \ldots, o_k\}$. Meanwhile, there are candidate sites $C = \{c_1, c_2, \ldots, c_l\}$ for the candidate nodes. At each candidate site c_l, the ambient energy of each type that can be harvested in a monitoring duration T is noted as $\epsilon_{m,l}$. The geographical location of the the targets and candidate sites can be represented by a 2-D coordinate system, i.e. $\mathcal{G}_{c_l} = (x, y)$ and $\mathcal{G}_{o_k} = (x, y)$.

3.4   The Objective Function

In this section, we provide the objective function to measure the quality of a certain deployment. At first, we provide the deployment scheme by Definition 1 to describe how the sensor nodes are deployed.

Definition 1 (Deployment Scheme).   A Deployment Scheme is a matrix $\mathcal{D}_{|N| \times |C|}$, where each element $x_{j,l} \in \{0, 1\}$. $x_{j,l} = 1$ means deploying a node with the type n_j at the candidate site c_l.

Here we assume that at most one sensor node can be deployed at a certain site c_l, i.e. $\left\| \boldsymbol{x}_l^T \right\|_1 \in \{0, 1\}$, where $\boldsymbol{x}_l^T$ is a column vector in $\mathcal{D}$. $\left\| \boldsymbol{x}_l^T \right\|_1 = 0$ means no sensor node is deployed at c_l. Meanwhile, with the definition of deployment scheme, the total cost of a deployment scheme can be represented as follows,

$$V(\mathcal{D}) = \sum_{j=1}^{|N|} v_j \cdot \left\| \boldsymbol{x}_j \right\|_1 \tag{1}$$

where each $\boldsymbol{x}_j$ is a row vector in $\mathcal{D}$.

Definition 2 (Monitoring Scheme).   The Monitoring Scheme is a matrix $\mathcal{M}_{|O| \times |S|}$, where $\mathcal{M}_{k,i}$ is the number of time slots that the target o_k can be monitored by sensor type s_i in a monitoring duration T.

According to Definition 2, with a finite $\mathcal{T}$ with length $|\mathcal{T}|$, we have $\mathcal{M}_{k,i} \in [0, |\mathcal{T}|]$.

Definition 3 (Quality of Coverage). Given a deployment scheme $\mathcal{D}$. The quality of coverage is described by Eq. 2.

$$Q(\mathcal{D}) = \frac{\sum_{k=1}^{|O|} \sum_{i=1}^{|S|} \xi_i \cdot \mathcal{M}_{k,i}}{|O| \cdot |\mathcal{T}|} \tag{2}$$

The $Q(\mathcal{D})$ is the weighted average of the attribute coverage ratio on each target in a monitoring duration, where each attribute is to monitor/detect an atomic event. We use $Q(\mathcal{D})$ as the objective function, and to measure the quality of a certain deployment.

3.5   Problem Definition

The Sensor Deployment for Composite Event Monitoring in Battery-free Sensor Networks (BF-SDCEM) problem is formulated as follows,

Input:

1. $O = \{o_1, o_2, \ldots, o_k\}$: The target set to monitor,
2. $C = \{c_1, c_2, \ldots, c_l\}$: The candidate location set for deployment,
3. $N = \{n_1, n_2, \ldots, n_j\}$: The set of candidate nodes,
4. $\mathcal{G}$: The coordinate for O and C,
5. $\mathcal{T}$: The monitoring duration.
6. λ_j: The power consumption in a time slot of each type of node,
7. $s(n_j)$: The type of sensing module of n_j,
8. $h(n_j) \subset H$: The set of energy harvesters that n_j is equipped,
9. $\epsilon_{m,l}$: The ambient energy of type m that can be harvested at c_l in $\mathcal{T}$,
10. v_j: the cost of each type of node and,
11. V: The total budget of the deployment.

Output:

1. A Deployment Scheme $\mathcal{D}$ such that the cost of $\mathcal{D}$, i.e. $V(\mathcal{D}) \leq V$, and the $Q(\mathcal{D})$ is maximized.

Theorem 1. *The BF-SDCEM problem is at least NP-hard.*

Due to the page limit, the proof of Theorem 1 is given in our supplementary material in [20].

4   Solution

Considering the complexity of the BF-SDCEM problem, we propose an approximate solution in this section. Our solution to solve BF-SDCEM problem includes the following three phases,

- *Phase 1* Initialization and Pruning.
- *Phase 2* Sensor Deployment for Composite Event Monitoring.
- *Phase 3* Sensor Deployment for Connectivity (optional, see Sect. 4.3).

We will present the details of those phases in the following sections.

4.1   Initialization and Pruning

The Algorithm for Initialization and Pruning is formalized in Algorithm 1. It has the following two aims. (1) Calculating the energy that can be harvested at a certain site. Since in the BF-WSNs, there are different type of energy harvesters, a candidate site that is not suitable for node n_1 may be suitable for n_2. Thus, it's necessary to calculate the amount of energy harvested for each type of node. Then, the (j, l) pairs where the c_l has too low energy for n_j are pruned. (2) Building an extended adjective matrix for each c_l, o_k and n_j according to the geographical relationship. If a node deployed at a site cannot monitor any target, it's pruned and not considered in deployment for monitoring. Notice that even though a node at a certain site cannot monitor any target, the it might still be useful in maintaining network connectivity. Thus, we use different labels to note them.

Algorithm 1: The Initialization and Pruning Algorithm

Input: $C, N, O, \mathcal{G}, h(n_j) \subset H$
Output: $\mathcal{D}, \mu$ (the energy matrix for each j and l), z (the number of zero's in $\mathcal{D}$)

1 **for** $l \leftarrow 1$ *to* $|C|$ **do**
2   **for** $j \leftarrow 1$ *to* $|N|$ **do**
3   **for** $m \leftarrow 1$ *to* $|H|$ **do**
4   **if** $h_m \in h(n_j)$ **then**
5              $\mu_{j,l} \leftarrow \mu_{j,l} + \epsilon_{m,l}$
6   **if** $\mu_{j,l} < \lambda_j$ **then**
7           $\mathcal{D}_{j,l} \leftarrow -2$
8   continue
9        $\gamma \leftarrow false$
10   **for** $k \leftarrow 1$ *to* $|O|$ **do**
11   **if** $d(\mathcal{G}_{o_k}, \mathcal{G}_{c_l}) \leq r_{s(j)}$ **then**
12             $\mathcal{A}_{k,j,l} \leftarrow 1$
13             $\gamma \leftarrow true$
14   **else**
15             $\mathcal{A}_{k,j,l} \leftarrow 0$
16   **if** *not* γ **then**
17          $\mathcal{D}_{j,l} \leftarrow -1$
18   **else**
19          $\mathcal{D}_{j,l} \leftarrow 0$; $z \leftarrow z + 1$
20 **return** $\mathcal{D}, \mu, z$

Theorem 2. *The complexity of Algorithm 1 is* $O(|C| \cdot |N| \cdot (|O| + |H|))$.

The proof of Theorem 2 is presented in our supplementary material [20] due to the page limit.

4.2   The Sensor Deployment for Event Monitoring

After the Initialization and Pruning Algorithm, we provide the Sensor Deployment for Event Monitoring Algorithm (Algorithm 2) to deploy sensor nodes to monitor the composite event. The algorithm includes the following steps,

Step 1 (line 1–3). When there are still remaining budget and feasible candidate sites to deploy nodes, execute Step 2 contentiously.

Step 2 (line 4–12). For each candidate site and candidate node pair $x(n_j, c_l)$, generate a temporary monitoring scheme $\mathcal{M}'$ with deploying n_j to c_l. Then with the new temporary for each target o_k that lies in the sensing range of n_j at c_l, update their temporary monitoring scheme of them and incrementally calculate the value of u' as an estimation of Q. Then run Step 3.

Step 3 (line 13–14). If such (n_j, c_l) brings larger growth in quality ratio Δ than ever before. Record it as a and keep the related monitoring scheme, quality and deployment scheme.

Step 4 (line 15–21). After the loop in Step 2. Update the monitoring scheme, quality and deployment scheme according to a. Here we keep a record, i.e L,

---

Algorithm 2: The Sensor Deployment for Event Monitoring

Input: $C, N, O, \mu, \mathcal{A}, \mathcal{T}, V, v_j$

Output: $\mathcal{D}, L, V_r$ (The remaining budget after deployment)

1 $V_r \leftarrow V$; $u \leftarrow 0$
2 $L \leftarrow$ an empty queue
3 **while** $V_r - \min v(N_0) > 0$ *and* $z > 0$ **do**
4 $\quad$ $a \leftarrow (0,0)$; $\Delta \leftarrow 0$; $\mathcal{M}^a \leftarrow \mathcal{M}$
5 $\quad$ **foreach** (j, l) *where* $\mathcal{D}_{l,j} = 0$ **do**
6 $\quad\quad$ **if** $V_r < v_j$ **then**
7 $\quad\quad\quad$ continue
8 $\quad\quad$ $\mathcal{M}' \leftarrow \mathcal{M}$; $u' \leftarrow u$
9 $\quad\quad$ **for** $k \leftarrow 1$ *to* $|O|$ **do**
10 $\quad\quad\quad$ **if** $\mathcal{A}_{k,j,l} = 1$ **then**
11 $\quad\quad\quad\quad$ $\mathcal{M}'_{o,i} \leftarrow \min(|\mathcal{T}|, \mathcal{M}_{o,i} + \frac{h}{\lambda_i})$
12 $\quad\quad\quad\quad$ $u' \leftarrow u' + \xi_i \cdot (\mathcal{M}'_{o,i} - \mathcal{M}_{o,i})$
13 $\quad\quad$ **if** $(u' - u)/v_j > \Delta$ **then**
14 $\quad\quad\quad$ $\Delta \leftarrow (u' - u)/v_j$; $a \leftarrow (j, l)$; $\mathcal{M}^a \leftarrow \mathcal{M}'$
15 $\quad$ **if** $\Delta = 0$ **then**
16 $\quad\quad$ break
17 $\quad$ $u \leftarrow u + \Delta \cdot v_{a.j}$
18 $\quad$ $\mathcal{D}_a \leftarrow 1$; $z \leftarrow z - 1$
19 $\quad$ $\mathcal{M} \leftarrow \mathcal{M}^a$
20 $\quad$ $L.enqueue(a)$
21 $\quad$ $V_r \leftarrow V_r - v_{a.j}$
22 **return** $\mathcal{D}, L, V_r$

which is the sequential list of all a's chosen in each Step 3. It will be used in next section.

Theorem 3. *The time complexity of Algorithm 2 is* $O(|C|^2 \cdot |N|^2 \cdot |O| \cdot |S|)$.

The proof of Theorem 3 can be found in our supplementary material [20].

4.3   The Sensor Deployment for Connectivity

Besides the coverage of the composite event, the connectivity of the deployed nodes to guarantee their communication with each other is also important. In some of the networks that satisfy diameter of the deploying area is smaller than the communication range R, the further steps for connectivity is not necessary. That condition can be achieved by small deploying area or long range communication, for example, some types of sensor nodes can be equipped with a narrow-band and long-range communication module (like LoRa, NB-IoT, Sigfox) *etc.* However, we cannot guarantee that all type of nodes are equipped with the above-mentioned modules, especially the battery-free ones. Therefore, we still provide an algorithm to ensure connectivity for the nodes that does not require the above-mentioned condition.

Our Algorithm to fix network connectivity of is formalized in Algorithm 3. The algorithm includes the following steps.

Algorithm 3: The Sensor Deployment for Connectivity

Input: $\mathcal{D}, C, \mathcal{G}, V_r, L, v_j$
Output: $\mathcal{D}$

1 Create a communication network G_c from C and $\mathcal{D}$ (where the weight of each edge is 1)
2 **if** G_c *is connected* **then**
3 $\quad$ **return** G_c
4 Generate a Network Steiner Tree Tr_c from G_c
5 Reduce a sub-graph G'_c from G_c with the nodes from Tr_c
6 $V_c = \min(v_j) \cdot (|Tr_c| - |L|)$
7 **foreach** $l \in Tr_c - L$ **do**
8 $\quad$ $b \leftarrow (\arg\min_j v_j, l)$
9 $\quad$ $D_b \leftarrow 1$
10 $v \leftarrow V_r$
11 **while** $v < V_c$ *and* $|L| > 0$ **do**
12 $\quad$ $a = L.\text{pop\_back}()$
13 $\quad$ **if** $G'_c - a.l$ *is connected* **then**
14 $\quad\quad$ $G'_c \leftarrow G'_c - a.l$
15 $\quad\quad$ $v \leftarrow v + v_{a.j}$
16 $\quad\quad$ $D_a \leftarrow 0$
17 **return** $\mathcal{D}$

Step 1 (line 1–3). Generate a communication graph based on existing deployment scheme and candidate sites. The weight of each edge is 1. If the deployed nodes are connected, return.

Step 2 (line 4–5). Generate a Network Steiner Tree T_c from G_c, where the terminal vertexes are the deployed nodes. Then, generate a sub-graph G_c' of G_c where the nodes are the nodes in T_c.

Step 3 (line 6–9). Deploy the cheapest type of nodes on the Steiner vertexes.

Step 4 (line 10–16). If there is lacking of budget for doing Step 3, we remove the deployed nodes that provide the least contribution for event monitoring and doesn't affect the connectivity of the remaining networks until the budget is enough.

Theorem 4. *The time complexity of Algorithm 3 is $O(f_{st}(|C|)+|C| \cdot f_{con}(|C|))$, the f_{st} is the complexity of generating a Network Steiner Tree. The f_{con} is the complexity of checking the connectivity of the networks.*

The complexity of connectivity checking is related to its storage structure, thus it is represented by a function. The proof of Theorem 4 is also given in our supplementary material [20].

5   Evaluation

5.1   Simulation Settings

In this section, we carry out simulations to evaluate the performance under different network parameters. Without special notification, we use the following fundamental simulation settings. The event to be monitored is the conjunction of three atomic events. Their confidences ξ_i are 0.25, 0.35, 0.4 respectively. The monitoring area is a $50\,\mathrm{m} \times 50\,\mathrm{m}$ plane. Two types of ambient energy can be harvested in the area, they are different at each location. The energy 1 is randomly $0.8 - 1.8$ unit per time slot while the energy 2 is randomly $1 - 2$ unit per time slot. There are 6 type of candidate nodes noted n_1-n_6. The characteristics of the nodes are summarized by Table 1. We consider two types of networks, type L is equipped with long-ranged communication modules, where fixing connectivity of the networks is not needed. The type S has limited communication range $R = 10$. Notice that the results for type L also indicates the quality of coverage before the adjustment for connectivity for type S.

5.2   The Quality of Coverage Under Different Network Parameters

1) The total budget. Firstly, we carried out a set of simulations to study the quality of coverage with different total budget. The candidate sites and targets are randomly generated, The number of sites $|C| = 1000$, and the number of targets $|O| = 10$ in this group of simulation. The budget range is 900–1500. Figure 1 illustrates the coverage of coverage under different total budget.

Table 1. Candidate nodes

Type	n_1	n_2	n_3	n_4	n_5	n_6
Sensing module type	s_1	s_1	s_2	s_2	s_3	s_3
Energy consumption	2	2	3	3	4	4
Sensing range	5					
Communication range	10					
Energy harvester	h_1	h_2	h_1	h_1,h_2	h_1	h_2
Cost	10	15	12	20	25	30

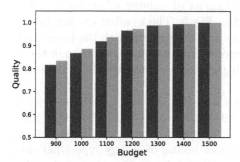

Fig. 1. The quality of coverage under different total deployment budget

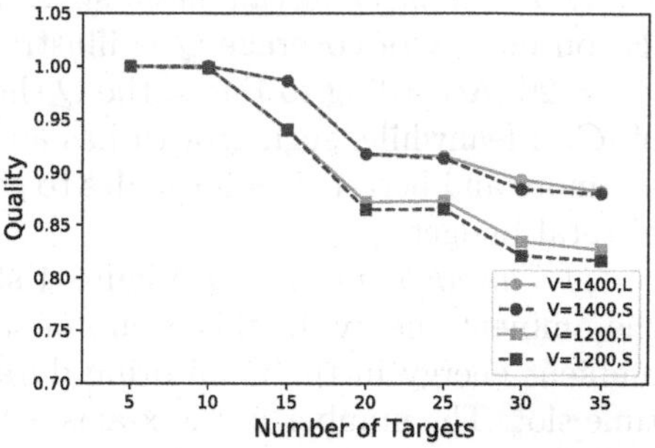

Fig. 2. The quality of coverage under different number of targets

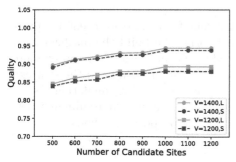

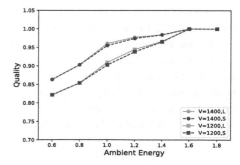

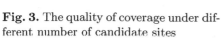

Fig. 3. The quality of coverage under different number of candidate sites

Fig. 4. The quality of coverage under different ambient energy

The red bar is type L and the blue bar is type S. The result indicates three facts. (a) The quality of coverage increases with the total budget because the density of nodes becomes higher, and the growth becomes slower with the increasing of budget. (b) $Q_L \geq Q_S$, because some of the nodes has to be redeployed to fix the connectivity and cannot monitor any targets in network type S. (c) The difference of Q_L and Q_S becomes less when the budget is higher. That's because dense networks are naturally easier to get connected so that less nodes has to be redistributed for connectivity.

2) The number of targets. Figure 2 presents the relationship between quality of coverage Q and number of targets $|O|$. We set two groups of simulation with the total budget $V = 1400$ and $V = 1200$. The number of candidate sites $|C| = 1000$. From the figure we can infer that with a same total budget, the quality of deployment gets lower with the growth of $|O|$. The reason is that more targets are harder to be covered by the nodes purchased with the same budget. The decrease is more intensive when the total budget is lower.

3) The number of candidate sites. The impact of number of candidate sites $|C|$ on quality of coverage Q is illustrated in Fig. 3. The number of targets are $|O| = 20$. According to Fig. 3, the Q shows a smooth growth with the increasing of $|C|$. Meanwhile, such growth has an upper bound because even though there are more and better sites for nodes to get better performance, there's still a limit of total budget.

4) The ambient energy. Figure 4 shows how the Q_L and Q_S changes with the ambient energy. In this group of simulation, $|O| = 20$ and $|C| = 1000$. The ambient energy in the monitoring duration is randomly generated time slot by time slot. The number in the x-axis is the lower bound of energy type 1 per slot and the range is 1. The scale of energy type 2 is 0.2 larger than type 1, i.e. the 0.6 in x-axis means type 1 is (0.6, 1.6) per slot, and type 2 is (0.8, 1.8) per slot. As shown in Fig. 4, the Q is positively related to the amount of ambient energy and the impact is more intensive in the deploying with smaller budget.

6   Conclusion

In this paper, we studied the sensor deployment for composite event monitoring in heterogeneous battery-free sensor networks. We build the mathematical model and formalized the problem and proved its NP-hardness. The approximate solution for sensor deployment in composite event monitoring and the strategy to maintain connectivity are proposed and analyzed. Finally, simulation results indicates the quality of coverage of our deployment strategy under different network parameters and show the effectiveness of the proposed methods.

References

1. Wang, M., Xue, A., Xia, H.: Abnormal event detection in wireless sensor networks based on multiattribute correlation. J. Electr. Comput. Eng. **2017**, 2587948:1–2587948:8 (2017)
2. Shirvanimoghaddam, M., Li, Y., Vucetic, B.: Sparse event detection in wireless sensor networks using analog fountain codes. In: IEEE Global Communications Conference, GLOBECOM 2014, pp. 3520–3525 (2014)
3. Gao, J., Li, J., Cai, Z., Gao, H.: Composite event coverage in wireless sensor networks with heterogeneous sensors. In: 2015 IEEE Conference on Computer Communications, INFOCOM 2015, pp. 217–225 (2015)
4. Shi, T., Li, J., Gao, H., Cai, Z.: Coverage in battery-free wireless sensor networks. In: 2018 IEEE Conference on Computer Communications, INFOCOM 2018, pp. 108–116 (2018)
5. Chen, K., Gao, H., Cai, Z., Chen, Q., Li, J.: Distributed energy-adaptive aggregation scheduling with coverage guarantee for battery-free wireless sensor networks. In: 2019 IEEE Conference on Computer Communications, INFOCOM 2019, pp. 1018–1026 (2019)
6. Shi, T., Cheng, S., Li, J., Cai, Z.: Constructing connected dominating sets in battery-free networks. In: 2017 IEEE Conference on Computer Communications, INFOCOM 2017, pp. 1–9 (2017)
7. Park, C., Chou, P.H.: AmbiMax: autonomous energy harvesting platform for multi-supply wireless sensor nodes. In: Proceedings of SECON 2006, pp. 168–177 (2006)
8. Carli, D., Brunelli, D., Benini, L., Ruggeri, M.: An effective multi-source energy harvester for low power applications. DATE **2011**, 836–841 (2011)
9. Boscaino, V., Ferraro, V., Miceli, R., Cavallaro, C., Raciti, A.: Performance evaluation of a multisource renewable power converter prototype. In: 2014 16th International Power Electronics and Motion Control Conference and Exposition, pp. 1318–1323. IEEE (2014)
10. Yang, Y., Ambrose, A., Cardei, M.: Coverage for composite event detection in wireless sensor networks. Wirel. Commun. Mob. Comput. **11**(8), 1168–1181 (2011)
11. Li, Y., Ai, C., Vu, C.T., Pan, Y., Beyah, R.A.: Delay-bounded and energy-efficient composite event monitoring in heterogeneous wireless sensor networks. IEEE Trans. Parallel Distrib. Syst. **21**(9), 1373–1385 (2010)
12. Yang, Y., Cardei, M.: Sensor deployment for composite event detection in mobile WSNs. In: Li, Y., Huynh, D.T., Das, S.K., Du, D.-Z. (eds.) WASA 2008. LNCS, vol. 5258, pp. 249–260. Springer, Heidelberg (2008). https://doi.org/10.1007/978-3-540-88582-5_25
13. Cao, B., Zhao, J., Yang, P., Yang, P., Liu, X., Zhang, Y.: 3-d deployment optimization for heterogeneous wireless directional sensor networks on smart city. IEEE Trans. Ind. Inf. **15**(3), 1798–1808 (2019)
14. Li, F., Yang, H., Zou, Y., Yu, D., Yu, J.: Joint optimization of routing and storage node deployment in heterogeneous wireless sensor networks towards reliable data storage. In: Biagioni, E.S., Zheng, Y., Cheng, S. (eds.) WASA 2019. LNCS, vol. 11604, pp. 162–174. Springer, Cham (2019). https://doi.org/10.1007/978-3-030-23597-0_13
15. Karatas, M.: Optimal deployment of heterogeneous sensor networks for a hybrid point and barrier coverage application. Comput. Netw. **132**, 129–144 (2018)

16. Hajikhani, M.J., Labeau, F.: Deploying autonomous sensors in a substation area using energy harvesting and wireless transfer of energy. In: 2016 IEEE International Conference on Communication Systems, ICCS 2016, Shenzhen, China, 14–16 December 2016, pp. 1–6 (2016)
17. Hsu, T.-C., Hong, Y.-W.P., Wang, T.-Y.: Optimized random deployment of energy harvesting sensors for field reconstruction in analog and digital forwarding systems. IEEE Trans. Signal Process. **63**(19), 5194–5209 (2015)
18. Liu, Y., Chin, K.-W., Yang, C., He, T.: Nodes deployment for coverage in rechargeable wireless sensor networks. IEEE Trans. Veh. Technol. **68**(6), 6064–6073 (2019)
19. Zhang, H., Hou, J.C.: Maintaining sensing coverage and connectivity in large sensor networks. Ad Hoc Sens. Wirel. Netw. **1**(1–2), 89–124 (2005)
20. http://note.youdao.com/noteshare?id=d2def349925440a23b5144b10748a414

Optimizing Motion Estimation with an ReRAM-Based PIM Architecture

Bing Liu, Zhaoyan Shen, Zhiping Jia, and Xiaojun Cai[✉]

Shandong University, Binhai Road No. 72, Qingdao, China
xj_cai@sdu.edu.cn

Abstract. Motion estimation (ME) is an HEVC process for determining motion vectors that describe the blocks transformation direction from one frame to a future adjacent frame in a video sequence. ME is a memory and computationally intensive process which consumes more than 50% of the total running time of HEVC. To remedy the memory and computation challenges, in this paper, we present ReME, a highly paralleled Processing-In-Memory accelerator for ME based on ReRAM.

In ReME, the space of ReRAM is separated into storage engine and ME processing engine. The storage engine acts as the conventional memory to store video frames and intermediate data while the processing engine is for ME computation. Each ME processing engine in ReME consists of a SAD (Sum of Absolute Differences) model, an interpolation model, and a SATD (Sum of Absolute Transformed Difference) model that transfer ME functions into ReRAM-based logic analog computation units. ReME further cooperates these basic computation units to perform ME processes in a highly parallel manner. Simulation results show that the proposed ReME accelerator significantly outperforms other implementations with time consuming and energy saving.

Keywords: Processing-in-Memory · Motion estimation · ReRAM

1 Introduction

HEVC (High Efficiency Video Coding, or H.265) [15] is a new video compression standard that has been widely deployed. HEVC achieves a much higher coding efficiency compared with its predecessors, H.264/AVC [11]. Meanwhile, it also brings 40% more computation time and $2\times$ more memory accesses due to higher demand for storage and transmission operations [12,18,19]. Thus, these extra computations and memory overheads make HEVC quite energy consuming [12] and do not suitable for resources or energy limited devices.

ME usually consists of a SAD module, an interpolation (IPOL) module, and a SATD module. All the three modules involve a large scale of position search operations and similarity computations between different frame blocks, which makes ME a both memory and computation intensive process. Therefore, SAD, IPOL and SATD take the major part of the whole encoding complexity

© Springer Nature Switzerland AG 2020
D. Yu et al. (Eds.): WASA 2020, LNCS 12384, pp. 285–297, 2020.
https://doi.org/10.1007/978-3-030-59016-1_24

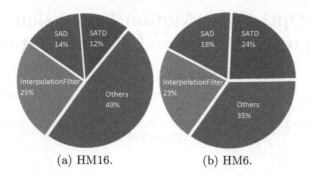

(a) HM16.   (b) HM6.

Fig. 1. Running time distribution of HEVC encoder.

(57%–68%) [16]. Hence, the acceleration for them has a huge impact on the overall encoding complexity. Furthermore, as for memory, fetching the reference frames from external memory and its on-chip storage leads to a significant energy consumption (>92% of the ME energy) [21].

We have conducted several preliminary experiments to explore the cost of ME in HEVC, as shown in Fig. 1. The coding platform is HEVC test Model (HM) [1] version 16 and 6 (the hardware configuration is shown in Table 1). The results show that ME consumes around 51% to 65% of the total encoding time.

Processing-in-memory (PIM) technique is a promising approach for alleviating computing and memory bottlenecks by integrating the computation logic within or near memory [2]. ReRAM (Resistive Random Access Memory) [8] is a kind of emerging non-volatile memory that can perform in-place matrix-vector multiplication operation with its crossbar structure. Designing PIM accelerators for applications, such as neural network [4,9,13,20,22], graph computing [14], and Blockchain designs [17], has been widely explored. And the integration of applications and ReRAM-based in-memory computing have shown great potential in improving applications performance.

Although ReRAM shows great advantages in computation and energy efficiency, applying it to the ME process is still challenging: (1) The ME working process is not the standard matrix-vector multiplication process. How to transfer the ME process to basic ReRAM crossbar calculate modules is still unsolved. (2) The mapping of video sequences to ReRAM crossbar-based modules should be carefully designed. (3) How to efficiently explore the parallelism potentials between the ME algorithm and ReRAM crossbar design is a tough task.

In this paper, we aims to expand ReRAM crossbars to support these basic operations and map the ME working process on ReRAM crossbars to eliminate the memory movement and mitigate the system computation overhead. We propose an ReRAM-based PIM architecture, named ReME, to accelerate the ME process of the HEVC algorithm. We first analyze the computation process of ME, and divide the process into a series of basic operations, such as SUB, SUM, absolute and Multiply-add operation. Then, we extend the design of the peripheral circuits of ReRAM crossbars to implement these operations through mapping video frame data to ReRAM cells carefully. ReME is designed as a multifunctional computing unit, each computing unit performs SAD, IPOL and SATD calculations in parallel. Simulation results indicate that ReME outperforms 165× and 6.8× in terms of performance compared with CPU-based and GPU-based implementations, respectively. Moreover, ReME consumes 25.2× and 3.8× less energy. The contributions of this paper are summarized as follows.

- We design an ME accelerator based on ReRAM, which implements three different calculation tasks of SAD, IPOL and SATD efficiently in the same calculation unit.
- We mapped the Prediction Unit (PU) pixels to ReRAM crossbars. Based on the in-memory computation capability of ReRAM, we achieve a highly paralleled calculation of pixels in the PU block.
- We evaluated the designed system. The ReME system can efficiently accelerate the calculation of ME and save energy consumption.

2 Background

2.1 ReRAM Basics

ReRAM is an emerging non-volatile memory that can perform in-memory computations [7]. ReRAM cells are usually organized into the crossbar array structure for area-efficiency [13]. ReRAM cells in a crossbar are connected by wordlines (WLs) and bitlines (bLs). By applying an external voltage across an ReRAM cell W_{ij}, its internal resistance (G_{ij}) changes with "low" and "high" status, which can be utilized to represent '1' and '0'. By selecting a WL_i with voltage v_i and sensing the current i_j at the end of the bL_j, we can get $i_j = v_i \times G_{ij}$. By applying input voltage to all rows (i.e. WLs) of a crossbar, a current will be obtained on each bL, which is the sum of the product of the conductance of each cell in the column and its corresponding WL voltage.

A sample and hold (S/H) circuit receives the current and feeds it to a shared ADC unit. By adding a rectifier and a zero-crossing comparator at the Sense Amplifier (SA) front end, the positive or negative current on bL will be sensed and the current polarity will be obtained. When using multiple cells to represent an integer, and computing the matrix multiply-add calculation (MAC) results of each column Pixel value, the ADC results of each bL need to be shifted and summed by shift and adder (S&A) to get the final result.

2.2 ME Process

To adapt to different image characteristics, HEVC divides a video frame into coding tree units (CTUs) of 16 × 16 to 64 × 64 size. Each CTU is divided into coding units (CUs) of different sizes for encoding. Each CU is further divided into

PUs as prediction units. PU is the basic unit for both intra and inter prediction modules.

ME in the inter prediction module is to find the location of the best matching block in a reference frame for the block in the current frame. The inputs of ME include the encoded reference frame and PU of the coding current frame. The output of ME is a Motion Vector (MV) that is obtained after the integer pixel ME (IME), interpolation, and fractional pixel ME (FME) process.

ME can be separated into three parts: searching for integer pixels (integer-pel) ME with SAD as the matching criterion to complete the IME (integer-pel ME), performing interpolation to generate fractional sample positions, and matching the fractional pixels (frac-pel) MV to complete FME with SATD.

3   ReME Architecture

In this section, we first present an overview of the ReME design, and then give the detailed descriptions for each of its function modules.

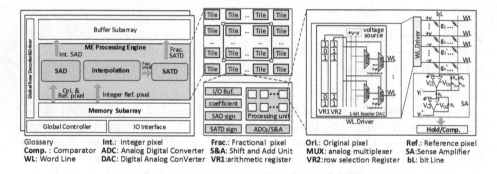

Glossary	Int.: integer pixel	Frac.: Fractional pixel	Ori.: Original pixel	Ref.: Reference pixel
Comp. : Comparator	ADC: Analog Digital Converter	S&A: Shift and Add Unit	MUX: analog multiplexer	SA:Sense Amplifier
WL: Word Line	DAC: Digital Analog ConVerter	VR1:arithmetic register	VR2:row selection Register	bL: bit Line

Fig. 2. Architecture overview of ReME.

3.1   Architecture Overview of ReME

Figure 2 illustrates the architecture overview of ReME. The whole ReRAM bank consists of a global IO interface, a controller, a global row decoder and driver, buffer subarrays, memory subarrays, and ME processing engines. The global IO interface is an input/output interface for data exchange between memory and storage. The controller decodes instructions and provides control signals for all units. The global row decoder and driver are responsible for providing working voltage for the WLs of ReRAM crossbars. The buffer array is mainly used to store intermediate data. The memory array stores the input video sequences and the ME processing engine (PE) is used to perform computation operations. Each PE has a few crossbar arrays, S/H, and ADCs, connected with a shared bus. The PE has input/output registers and S&A units. Each ME processing engine can perform SAD, interpolation and SATD operations. In the following subsections, we will provide more details about the core designs of ReME.

3.2   SAD Acceleration

SAD operations are composed of basic subtraction, absolute value, and summation operations, as shown in Eq. (1). We use the efficient summation feature of ReRAM to explore the parallel operation of SAD operations. To make ReRAM corssbar support the absolute value calculation, we adopt the WL dual power supply scheme [6] to support subtraction preset and absolute value preprocessing.

$$SAD\,(i,j) = \sum_{s=1}^{M} \sum_{t=1}^{N} |R_{ef}\,(i+s,j+t) - O_{ri}\,(s,t)| \tag{1}$$

Here R_{ef} is the reference block pixel value in the reference frame, O_{ri} is the pixels in the current PU block. The block size is M × N. i, j is the offset position of the reference block.

- **Subtraction preset.** Positive and negative power are provided to WL for subtraction and sum operation on the same bL, respectively. As shown in Fig. 2, through configuring the conductance of each memristor cell of the crossbar as g, input +v voltage to the first n rows of WL, and input −v voltage to the next n rows. We can get y_- and y_+ through bL SA, as shown in Eq. (3) and Eq. (3).

$$y_j{}^- = -R_r \left(\sum_{i=1}^{n} v \cdot g_i - v \cdot g_i{}' \right) \tag{2}$$

$$y_j{}^+ = -\frac{R_f}{R_f} y_j{}^- = -y_j{}^- \tag{3}$$

In ReME crossbar, the subtraction operation is to write the subtrahend (the current PU block pixel) and the minuend (the reference block pixel) into the same bL of the crossbar. By operating the WL of the minuend and subtrahend (applying +v voltage to WL corresponding to minuend, applying −v voltage to WL corresponding to subtrahend), we can get the sum of the differences from bL. To complete the SAD calculation in the crossbar, we write the pixels in the current PU block and the reference block into the ReRAM Crossbar, and activate the pixels column by column, then inputting voltage to corresponding WL.

In practice, a memristor cannot accurately represent a pixel value. Considering the actual accuracy [3], when we map pixels to crossbar, we use 8 memristors to represent 1 pixel value (pixels with 8-bit depth), as shown in Fig. 3(a). If +v voltage is applied to the WL of the current PU block pixel and −v voltage is applied to the WL of the reference PU block, the bL value obtained from each column of each pixel will be shifted and summed to obtain the sum of the difference values of the pixels in the column.

The WL positive or negative voltage drive signal is provided by a 1-bit bipolar DAC consisting of a 2:1 multiplexer and a voltage source. As shown in Fig. 2,

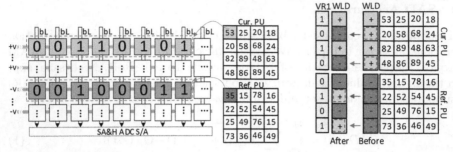

(a) Pixel block mapping in ReRAM Crossbar.   (b) Absolute value preprocessing.

Fig. 3. Pixel mapping and absolute value preprocessing.

VR1 is an arithmetic register, and its value (1 or 0) correspond to the positive and negative arithmetic signs of the pixels, respectively. VR2 is used as a preset register, which is always preset to 1 in SAD operations. When the value of VR1 is 1, the fore-stage multiplexer outputs +v. When it is 0, the output is −v. When VR2 is preset to a post-stage, multiplexer outputs the same as the previous stage. We change the value of the VR1 register to achieve the switching of WL positive and negative voltages, and map the pixel operator to VR1.

We input 0 and 1 to the corresponding VR1 bits of the pixel pair to implement the subtraction operation of the pixel pairs. The result of the subtraction operation will be obtained from the corresponding bL. Note that we do not need to calculate the subtraction result separately. We only need to preset +v to the WL of the current block pixel, −v to the WL of the reference block pixel, and preset VR2 to 1 to prepare for absolute value preprocessing.

- **Absolute value preprocessing.** Absolute value preprocessing is used for calculating the absolute values during SAD operation. We first compare the two pixel values in the pixel pair and modify the sign of each pixel in the pixel pair (input value of WL), to ensure that the difference is always positive.

As shown in Fig. 3(b), on the basis of subtraction preprocessing, we activate pixel pairs row by row to perform a subtraction operation on each pixel pair in the row. According to the result, the sign of the larger pixel value is recorded as positive and the smaller one is recorded as negative. The sign of each pixel is recorded in the sign register (SR). The absolute value preprocessing of each pixel in the same row can be performed in parallel at crossbar. Through absolute value preprocessing, we adjusted the relationship between the minuend and the subtrahend of each pixel pair to achieve the absolute operation.

- **Sum operation.** We use the crossbar in-place summation feature to calculate the sum of the pixel residual values in each column, and then sum the results of each column through the accumulator to get the SAD value. To guarantee the accuracy of the calculation, we perform sum with a smaller operating unit (OU). Based on the absolute value preprocessing, we use the controller to input the sign values corresponding to the activated column pixels into the VR1. We activate pixel by column, using 8 columns (8 bit represents a pixel) as a group. When activate 64×8 Crossbar, the calculation result of 32 pixel pairs SAD value is obtained.

3.3 Interpolation Acceleration

As shown in Eq. (4), the interpolation operation is used to calculate the sum of the product of the tap coefficient and the corresponding integer pixel. The calculation consists of multiplication, addition, and subtraction. ReRAM-based Crossbar natively supports this kind of operation. One naive way to calculation interpolation is to calculate the positive and negative coefficients separately, and then complete the subtraction operation through a subtraction circuit.

$$b_{0,0} = \left(\sum_{i=-3}^{4} A_{i,0} \cdot hfilter[i] \right) \gg (B - 8), \tag{4}$$

Here $A_{i,0}$ is the integer-pel value and B is the depth of pixel (8 bits in this paper). $hfilter[i]$ is the 8-tap filter coefficient. When calculating the quarter pixel positions, the 8-tap filter $hfilter[i]$ in Eq. (4) will be replaced by the 7-tap filter $qfilter[i]$.

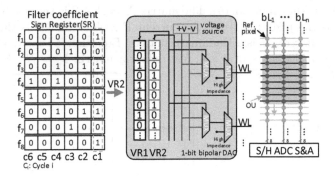

Fig. 4. 1/2 position filter coefficient vector generation process.

To further optimize the computation, we propose a scheme to perform sum and subtract together. We implement positive and negative filter coefficients as the input of WL, integer pixels are written into Crossbar, and the multiply-add operation is completed by Crossbar's multiply-add feature. The number of WLs activated in the crossbar is the same as the number of filter coefficients.

The filter coefficients (represented by 6 bits) for interpolation calculation are outputted to WL bit by bit, through a 1-bit bipolar DAC. The DAC conversion is different from SAD. As shown in Fig. 4, where VR1 is used to preset the positive and negative polarities of the WL. VR2 is used to accept the input of the coefficient vector. When VR1 is preset to 1, the fore-stage multiplexer outputs $+v$ (when preset is 0, the output is $-v$). The filter coefficient generates a column vector and outputs it to VR2. As shown in Fig. 4, f1–f8 are the filter coefficients of the fraction pixels at $1/2$ position. At the ith period ci, the vector in VR2 is composed of b_{i-1} of each filter coefficient, and the interpolation operation is completed after the period c1-c6. When VR2 is 1, the output of the post-stage multiplexer is the voltage value of the fore-stage, and when it is 0, the output is a high-impedance (HI) state (the WL is not calculated and is represented by 0).

Through the DAC conversion, we map 0, 1 of each bit of positive and negative coefficients to high-impedance 0, $+v$ and high-impedance 0, $-v$, respectively, and output to WL to achieve the addition and subtraction on the same bL. After that, the bL value is shifted and accumulated to obtain the interpolation operation result.

3.4   SATD Acceleration

In this subsection, we propose a computation scheme based on transformed sign vectors to simplify the SATD calculations.

$$SATD = \sum_{i=1}^{m} \sum_{j=1}^{m} |HXH| \tag{5}$$

- **The principle of SATD calculation based on ReRAM.** The SATD calculation is shown in Eq. (5). The matrix $X = A - B$ is the residual matrix, where A is the pixel matrix of the current PU block and B is the reference block pixel matrix. H is a Hadamard matrix. Equation (6) shows an example of a Hadamard matrix of 4×4. We define a matrix $Y = H \cdot X$, a matrix $Z = Y \cdot H$, and $SATD = \sum \sum |Z|$.

$$H_{4\times4} = \frac{1}{2} \begin{bmatrix} 1 & 1 & 1 & 1 \\ 1 & -1 & 1 & -1 \\ 1 & 1 & -1 & -1 \\ 1 & -1 & -1 & 1 \end{bmatrix}_{4\times4} \tag{6}$$

For simplicity, we show the SATD calculation process with the 4×4 matrix. The matrix Y is shown in Eq. (7), and its elements are the product of the row vector of the Hadamard matrix and the corresponding column vector of the X matrix. The Z matrix is calculated according to $Z = Y \cdot H$, and the Eq. (8) is an expanded form of the z_{11} element calculation process of the Z matrix. Here, h_{ij} is the element of the Hadamard matrix, H_{*i} is the row vector of the Hadamard matrix, and X_{j*} is the column vector of the residual matrix.

$$Y = \begin{bmatrix} H_{1i}X_{j1} & H_{1i}X_{j2} & H_{1i}X_{j3} & H_{1i}X_{j4} \\ H_{2i}X_{j1} & H_{2i}X_{j2} & H_{2i}X_{j3} & H_{2i}X_{j4} \\ H_{3i}X_{j1} & H_{3i}X_{j2} & H_{3i}X_{j3} & H_{3i}X_{j4} \\ H_{4i}X_{j1} & H_{4i}X_{j2} & H_{4i}X_{j3} & H_{4i}X_{j4} \end{bmatrix} \tag{7}$$

$$z_{11} = h_{11}H_{1i}X_{j1} + h_{21}H_{1i}X_{j2} + h_{31}H_{1i}X_{j3} + h_{41}H_{1i}X_{j4} \tag{8}$$

Equation (8) is consist of the sum of the inner product of four pairs of vectors. The inner product calculation and sum operation of vectors are very suitable for multiplication and addition operations based on ReRAM-based Crossbar.

The Eq. (8) can be transformed into $z_{11} = S_{11} \cdot X_{11}$ (where $X_{11} = [X_{j1}\ X_{j2}\ X_{j3}\ X_{j4}]^T$, $S_{11} = [h_{11}H_{1i}\ h_{21}H_{1i}\ h_{31}H_{1i}\ h_{41}H_{1i}]$). To perform summation on ReRAM, we use S_{11} as the input of WL, and the residual pixels X_{11} are stored in the cell of the crossbar. In the 1-bit bipolar DAC shown in Fig. 5, storing 0 in VR1 can output -1 to WL, and S_{11} is input to VR1, and z_{11} can be obtained by multiplying, adding, and summing analog operation characteristics of bL.

We combine the residual calculation with the vector product in one step. Since the residual matrix column vector X_i can be decomposed into the sum of the column vector A_i of the source pixel and the column vector $-B_i$ of the corresponding reference pixel, that is, $X_i = A_i + (-1) * B_i$. Equation (8) expands to $z_{ij} = \sum [S_i \cdot A_i ((-1) \cdot S_i) \cdot B_i]^T$. The mapping in our crossbar is: $V_{11} = [S_{11}\ {-S_{11}}]^T$, as the input of WLs. X_{11}, as shown in Eq. (9), is written to the cell corresponding to the crossbar. A bipolar 1-bit DAC converts 0 or 1 of V_{11} to $+v$ or $-v$ and outputs it to WL for parallel operation.

$$X_{11} = [A_1\ A_2\ A_3\ A_4\ B_1\ B_2\ B_3\ B_4]^T \tag{9}$$

- **ReRAM-based SATD calculation process.** According to the above analysis, for the SATD operation of different PU blocks, the operator vector is fixed, and WL only needs to input a predetermined operator vector. We write the source pixel matrix and the reference pixel matrix into ReRAM crossbar with the order of the new vectors generated, and complete the calculation of the Z matrix elements through crossbar's analog arithmetic operations, and then accumulate the element values to obtain the SATD value.

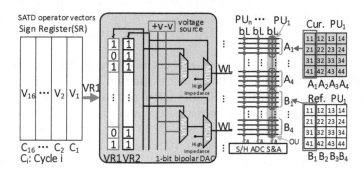

Fig. 5. Mapping relationship of SATD (4×4) operation based on ReRAM crossbar.

Taking the SATD calculation of a 4×4 PU block as an example, our calculation is divided into two steps. As shown in Fig. 5, the current block vector and

Table 1. Hardware configuration of the CPU&GPU platform.

CPU	Intel i7-5820k Processor, 6 cores 3.3 GHz, $(32 \times 6 + 32 \times 6$ KB) L1 Cache, 256 × 6 KB L2 Cache, 15 MB L3 Cache, Memory 64 GB, Storage 1 TB
GPU	GeForce GTX 1070, CUDA Cores 1920, Base Clock 1.5 GHz, Graphic Memory 8 GB GDDR5, Memory Bandwidth 256 GB/s, CUDA version 10.1

the reference block vector are written into crossbar in the order of the generated new vector. Then, the V_i operator vectors are input to the corresponding WL to activate an OU in crossbar. Each bL of the crossbar obtains the absolute value of the bL current through SA, and then obtains the value of 1 element of the Z matrix through S/H, ADC and S&A. Each element is accumulated by an adder to obtain a SATD value.

4   Evaluation

In this section, we first present the experimental setup and then show the evaluation results of the proposed ReME architecture.

4.1   Experimental Setup

We implement a prototype of ReME based on a behavior level simulation platform NVSIM [5]. The component parameters of our processing unit are the same as ISAAC [13]. We use 8192 processing units divided into 683 processing engine blocks, and each processing unit contains eight 64 × 256 crossbars. We set the HRS/LRS resistances as 25 MΩ/50 KΩ, the read voltage (V_r) and write voltage (V_w) as 0.7 V and 2 V, and the current of LRS/HRS as 40 uA and 2 uA respectively. The latency and energy cost of read/write operations are set as 29.31 ns/50.88 ns, 1.08 pJ/3.91 nJ, respectively [10]. The main circuit parameters of the PE engine are shown in Table 2. The capacity of ReRAM is set as 8 GB (same as GPU memory), and 128 MB of which are adopted as computation engine.

In our experiments, we compare the performance of ReME with a CPU baseline platform and a GPU platform in aspect of latency and energy consumption. Specifications of the CPU and GPU platforms are shown in Table 1. The CPU energy consumption is estimated by Intel Product Specifications with Intel Power Gadget application. Meanwhile, the GPU energy consumption estimation is measured by NVIDIA System Management Interface (NVIDIA-SMI). Both the processing latency of CPU and GPU platforms are evaluated in the computing framework.

For the evaluation result, we have excluded the disk I/O time from the execution time of all the three platforms.

Table 2. ReME Processing unit configurations.

Component	Params	Spec	Power	Area (mm^2)
Memristor Array	Size	64×256	2.4 mW	0.0002
	Bits per cell	1		
	Num	8		
ADC	Resolution	6 bits	5.14 mW	0.0094
	Frequency	1.28 GSps		
Hold	Num	8×256	20 uW	0.00008
S&A	Num	1	0.02 uW	0.000001
Reg	Size	1 kB	0.62 mW	0.0011

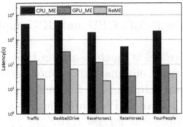

(a) ME performance comparison.

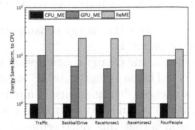

(b) Energy saving comparison.

Fig. 6. Performance and energy comparison.

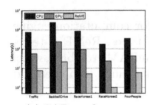

(a) SAD performance.

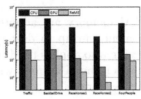

(b) Interpolation performance.

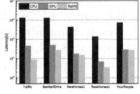

(c) SATD performance.

Fig. 7. Performance comparison of SAD, Interpolation, and SATD modules, separately.

4.2 Performance Comparison

Figure 6(a) presents the performance comparison of ReME, CPU, and GPU implementations in terms of ME execution time. Generally, ReME has the lowest execution time across the board. On average, the performance improvement of ReME over CPU and GPU implementations is of 101× and 5×, respectively. The performance improvement mainly comes from the elimination of video data movement between memory and the highly parallelism of ReRAM crossbar structure. With the video sequence Traffic, ReME achieves the highest improvement over CPU and GPU, which are 165× and 5.4×.

We further dig into the evaluation result and analyze the performance improvement of SAD, interpolation, and SATD modules separately. Figure 7 shows the performance comparison of these three modules in terms of ME execution time. Similarly, for both these three modules, ReME is far more efficient than CPU and GPU implementations for all the video sequences. On average, the SAD, interpolation, and SATD process of ReME are 123×, 244×, 58× better than CPU, and 13×, 4×, 2× better than GPU, respectively. Moreover, with the video sequence RaceHorses2, SAD of ReME achieves the highest improvement over CPU and GPU, which are 173× and 23×. Interpolation of ReME achieves the highest improvement over CPU and GPU, which are 395× and 7.5×. With the video sequence Traffic, SATD of ReME achieves the highest improvement over CPU and GPU, which are 149× and 5×.

4.3   Energy Consumption Analysis

Figure 6(b) shows the energy consumption of ReME, CPU and GPU implementations, respectively.

As shown, the energy consumption of ReME is much less than that of CPU and GPU. This is because ReME significantly eliminate data movements and perform energy efficient in-situ computations. On average, the energy saving of ReME are 25.2× and 3.8× compared with CPU and GPU platforms, respectively. The reason is that this video sequence involves the largest frame data and also the most computations.

4.4   Overhead Analysis

In this paper, 1.5% of ReRAM memory are adopted for computation engine, but the performance improvement can up to dozens of times. ReME is tested with SLC ReRAM, but our design also applies to MLC ReRAM crossbars, which requires more modification for peripheral circuits without much area overhead. We will discuss this in our future work.

5   Conclusion

In this paper, we propose an ReRAM-based PIM accelerator, ReME. To transfer pixel matching process of ME to ReRAM matrix-vector multiplication operations, ReME is designed to consist a SAD module, a interpolation module, and a SATD module. We extend the design of the peripheral circuits of ReRAM crossbars to implement these modules through carefully mapping video frame data to ReRAM cells.

Simulation results show that ReME outperforms 165× and 6.8× in terms of performance when compared with CPU-based and GPU-based implementations, respectively. Moreover, ReME consumes 25.2× and 3.8× less energy.

References

1. JCT-VC, HEVC Test Model HM (2018)
2. Ahn, J.: A scalable processing-in-memory accelerator for parallel graph processing. In: ACM SIGARCH Computer Architecture News (2016)
3. Chen, W.H.: A 65nm 1mb nonvolatile computing-in-memory ReRAM macro with sub-16ns multiply-and-accumulate for binary DNN AI edge processors. In: ISSCC (2018)
4. Chi, P.: PRIME: a novel processing-in-memory architecture for neural network computation in ReRAM-based main memory. In: ACM SIGARCH Computer Architecture News (2016)
5. Dong, X.: NVSim: a circuit-level performance, energy, and area model for emerging nonvolatile memory. TCAD **31**(7), 994–1007 (2012)
6. Yakopcic, C., et al.: Extremely parallel memristor crossbar architecture for convolutional neural network implementation. In: IJCNN (2017)
7. Han, L.: A novel ReRAM-based processing-in-memory architecture for graph traversal. TOS **14**(1), 1–26 (2018)
8. Hu, M.: Dot-product engine for neuromorphic computing: programming 1T1M crossbar to accelerate matrix-vector multiplication. In: DAC (2016)
9. Liang, Y.: Deep learning based inference of private information using embedded sensors in smart devices. IEEE Netw. **32**(4), 8–14 (2018)
10. Niu, D: Design of cross-point metal-oxide ReRAM emphasizing reliability and cost. In: ICCAD (2013)
11. Ohm, J.R.: Comparison of the coding efficiency of video coding standards-including high efficiency video coding HEVC. TCSVT **22**(12), 1669–1684 (2012)
12. Sampaio, F.: dSVM: energy-efficient distributed scratchpad video memory architecture for the next-generation high efficiency video coding. In: DATE (2014)
13. Shafiee, A.: ISAAC: a convolutional neural network accelerator with in-situ analog arithmetic in crossbars. In: ACM SIGARCH Computer Architecture News (2016)
14. Song, L.: GraphR: accelerating graph processing using ReRAM (2018)
15. Sze, V.: High efficiency video coding HEVC. In: Integrated circuit and systems, algorithms and architectures (2014)
16. Vanne, J.: Comparative rate-distortion-complexity analysis of HEVC and AVC video codecs. TCSVT **22**(12), 1885–1898 (2012)
17. Wang, F.: ReRAM-based processing-in-memory architecture for blockchain platforms. In: ASP-DAC (2019)
18. Yu, D.: Stable local broadcast in multihop wireless networks under SINR. IEEE/ACM Trans. Netw. **26**(3), 1278–1291 (2018)
19. Yu, D.: Implementing abstract MAC layer in dynamic networks. IEEE Trans. Mobile Comput. (2020)
20. Yu, J.: Efficient link scheduling in wireless networks under Rayleigh-fading and multiuser interference. IEEE Trans. Wirel. Commun. (2020)
21. Zatt, B.: Run-time adaptive energy-aware motion and disparity estimation in multiview video coding. In: DAC (2011)
22. Zheng, X.: Data linkage in smart Internet of Things systems: a consideration from a privacy perspective. IEEE Commun. Mag. (2018)

Trajectory-Based Data Delivery Algorithm in Maritime Vessel Networks Based on Bi-LSTM

Chao Liu, Yingbin Li, Ruobing Jiang$^{(\boxtimes)}$, Qian Lu, and Zhongwen Guo

Department of Computer Science and Engineering, Ocean University of China,
Qingdao 266100, China
jrb@ouc.edu.cn

Abstract. An efficient and low-cost communication system has great significance in the field of maritime communication, but it faces great challenges because of high communication cost, incomplete communication infrastructure, and inefficient data delivery algorithms. In this paper, we develop a long-term accurate trajectory prediction model by Bidirectional Long-Short Term Memory (Bi-LSTM) model. Based on predicted trajectories, we propose a data delivery algorithm based on predicted results to achieve efficient communication performance. Finally, we carry out simulation experiments with extensive real data. Compared with existing algorithms, the simulation results show that our algorithm can achieve higher delivery ratio with lower transmission delay.

Keywords: Delay tolerant vessel networks · Routing algorithm · Maritime communication · Bi-LSTM · Trajectory prediction

1 Introduction

As the core technology of smart ocean, a low cost and efficient maritime communication system has great significance on daily communication and information sharing [1]. Many maritime activities, such as environment monitoring, fishery operating, information sharing and so on, need to be supported by efficient and low-cost communication systems [2–5]. Existing maritime communication systems, which include satellite-based, sea-based and shored based, have severe shortages in terms of high volume cost, low network coverage and infrastructure absence. Existing communication can not meet the requirements of low-cost large-scale data transmission in ocean areas [6].

With increasing activities in marine, the mobile vessel plays an important role in ocean because of its storage and communication abilities. Recent works mainly focus on modeling the mobile regularity by setting up default movement model and mining social relationship [7–13]. Those works most focus on coarse-grained attributes, which is not enough to describe precise mobility patterns.

C. Liu, Y. Li—Equal Contributor.

© Springer Nature Switzerland AG 2020
D. Yu et al. (Eds.): WASA 2020, LNCS 12384, pp. 298–308, 2020.
https://doi.org/10.1007/978-3-030-59016-1_25

Future trajectory is one of the most important factors to build an efficient delay tolerant network system [14].

To solve the above problems, we should design a trajectory prediction algorithm to get the long-term accurate predicted trajectory. In addition, the evaluation results of predicted trajectory should be given to design the routing algorithm. In this paper, we propose a data delivery algorithm based on long-term predicted trajectory. Firstly, we design our Bi-LSTM trajectory predict model with great cross-regional extendibility to model the mobile regularity. Then, confident degree of each predicted step calculation method is designed by utilizing prediction model's performance on test set. Finally, a data delivery algorithm based on predicted trajectory is designed.

We have made the following intellectual contributions in this paper:

1. We design a long-term accurate trajectory prediction model based on Bi-LSTM to model vessels' mobility pattern, which can realize more than 3-h accurate prediction.
2. A novel evaluation method on trajectory regression results is designed to solve the problem of regression model evaluation.
3. We propose the routing algorithm based on predicted trajectory to solve the optimal data delivery problem. Simulation in extensive real trajectory data set, including 5123 vessels in 3 years, shows that our routing algorithm can achieve a higher delivery ratio than other routing strategies with lower cost and delay.

The rest of the paper is organized as follows. System model and problem formulation are given in Sect. 2. The structure of our trajectory prediction model is proposed Sect. 3. Routing algorithm based on trajectory prediction is presented in Sect. 4. Section 5 shows the performance of our algorithm. Section 6 reviews related works. This paper is concluded in Sect. 7.

2 System Model and Problem Formulation

In this section, system model of this paper is introduced. Then, we describe the optimal target of system, *expected delivery probability*, and system evaluation metrics including, *delivery delay* and *delivery ratio*.

2.1 System Model

All vessels in maritime networks are treated as a set of nodes, which is represented by S. The trajectory of node s in S is defined as a sequence of states in a period of time (t_1, t_n)

$$T_s = \{c_{s,t_1}, c_{s,t_2}, ..., c_{s,t_n}\}, s \in S. \tag{1}$$

In T_s, each state $c_{s,t}$ has its information, including latitude, longitude, speed and direction. For nodes s_i and s_j in S, we use $Dis(s_i, s_j)$ to denote the distance between them and utilize r_{s_i}, r_{s_j} to represent their communication radius.

Therefore, s_i and s_j can form a communication link when $Dis(s_i, s_j)$ is smaller than $min(r_{s_i}, r_{s_j})$. The whole set S can form a link set at time t, which can be given by

$$L_t = \{(s_i, s_j) | s_i, s_j \in S\}, Dis(p_{s_i,t}, p_{s_j,t}) < min(r_{s_i}, r_{s_j}). \tag{2}$$

For a packet p, we use $\delta(p)$ and $\zeta(p)$ denote its source and destination. The p could be copied for transfer to the node when they have links between them. Then, the packet set P_n of size n is defined as

$$P_n = \{p_i(\delta(p_i), \zeta(p_i)) | \delta(p), \zeta(p) \in S\}, i = 1, 2, ..., n. \tag{3}$$

We also set TTL (Time-To-Live) for the packet's remaining living time, TTL_{max} for the maximum living time, H for remaining hops and H_{max} for maximum hops. Packet delivery will fail if p_i does not get to its destination under the situation that TTL or H is equal to 0.

We next give the formal definitions of two system evaluation metrics *delivery delay* and *delivery ratio*.

Definition 1 (Delivery Delay). *To measure the delivery time of p from source $\delta(p)$ to destination $\zeta(p)$, $\chi(p)$ is denoted as the delivery delay of p. $t(\delta(p))$ is defined as the timestamp of p at the source node. So is $t(\zeta(p))$ at the destination node. Delivery delay of p can be defined as $\chi(p) = t(\zeta(p)) - t(\delta(p))$. The system delivery delay is the average delay of P_n, which can be given by*

$$\chi(P_n) = \frac{1}{n} \sum_{p_i \in P_n} \chi(p_i) \tag{4}$$

Definition 2 (Delivery Ratio). *Delivery ratio is defined as the proportion of the packets successfully delivered to total packets number n. The delivery ratio can be given as $(|p_{success}|/n)$.*

2.2   Problem Formulation

The target of the system is to respectively deliver all packets from sources to destinations. Our system's objective is to maximize *system expected delivery probability*. Several definitions are given as follows.

Definition 3 (Packet Expected Delivery Probability). *Given a packet p with its source $\delta(p)$ and destination $\zeta(p)$, the packet expected delivery probability ϱ_p is the expected delivery probability of p, which can be calculated by a function $f()$. ϱ_p can be given by*

$$\varrho_p = f(\delta(p), \zeta(p)), \ \delta(p), \zeta(p) \in S. \tag{5}$$

ϱ_p can be a fixed value if all the future trajectory T can be obtained. Additionally, it can be changed with node's different predicted future trajectories over time.

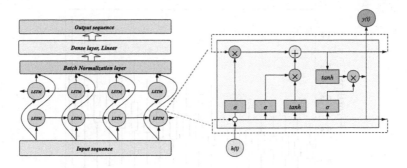

Fig. 1. The structure of trajectory predict model and Bi-LSTM

Definition 4 (System Expected Delivery Probability). *Each packet p in P_n can get ϱ_p at current time, the system expected delivery probability would be defined as $\sum_{p \in P_n} \varrho_p$.*

The goal of our system is to maximize system expected delivery probability. In conclusion, the whole optimal target of the system can be given by

$$max \sum_{p \in P_n} \varrho_p \tag{6}$$

3 Trajectory Prediction Model

In this section, our trajectory prediction model based on Bi-LSTM is presented.

The raw data in our dataset is the vessel's state each 3 min in 3 years, including time, ship ID, latitude, longitude, speed and heading. To train the neural network, we first need to get the training sample by transferring the time series to the supervised learning problem. It means we require to get the input state sequence and output sequence from the original series of state. So, we first assume the length proportion between input and output sequence is m, and the length of the predicted sequence is $\Im$. For the state sequence $\{c_1, c_2, ..., c_n\}$ and $1 \leq i \leq n - (\Im + 1)m$, the set of sample is:

$$Sample = \{< c_i, ..., c_{i+m\Im-1} >, < c_{i+m\Im}, ..., c_{i+(\Im+1)m} >\} \tag{7}$$

where $1 \leq i \leq n - (\Im + 1)m$. In this paper, we set $m = 3$ in our model, which means the model utilizes 3-h historical information to predict the future 1-h information. In addition to the location, our model also gives the prediction results of speed and direction. Therefore, if TTL is more than 1 h, we can utilize the sliding window for long-term trajectory prediction. We shuffle the sample set and split the training, validation and test sets according to the ratio of 7:2:1. Our model applies normalization to avoid the negative effect of feature range in learning process.

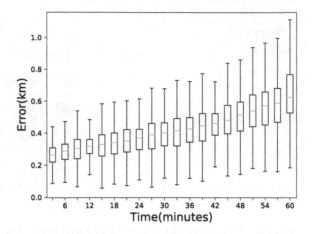

Fig. 2. Average error of Bi-LSTM model

Figure 1 illustrates our model structure. We use 1D convolution with $stride =$ 4 as the first feature extractor to get the information, which will be utilized by the next layer. Then, we apply 4-layer Bi-LSTM with 128 cells in the middle of our model to learn the patterns from the previous layer. Between the Bi-LSTM layer and the output layer, we add a *Dense* layer with 240 cells and use *linear* activation function for linear mapping. $Huber()$, which has great robustness to outlier point, is adopted as the loss function of the network. We use *tanh* as the activation function in our model, except for the output layer. *tanh* usually has higher performance than *sigmoid* because of its origin-symmetric character. In our learning process, *Adam* is applied to optimize the learning process according to gradient. In order to solve vanishing gradient and exploding gradient problems, *BNlayer* (Batch Normalization layer) is added between Bi-LSTM layers. We add *Dropoutlayer* after the last Bi-LSTM layer to avoid overfitting. It can solve overfitting problem by randomly abandoning some cells. Hence, the structure of the network could be different in every iterative learning process. Then, we set the early stop value to terminate the training process when the loss does not reduce in several epochs. Finally, we use $L2$ as metrics to regularize the kernel parameters in our model.

The initialize of parameters in the network is also important to improve the model's efficiency and performance. So, we use *he_normal* to initialize the kernel parameters. This strategy initializes the distribution of parameters according to the connected unit number. The model trains all samples in 2000 epochs with the limitation of the early stop.

Figure 2 illustrates the average error on the test set. We can notice that our model can predict future trajectory in 1 h with an average error of less than 600 m. To further verify the performance of our model, we use the sliding window for 3-h trajectory prediction. The result shows that our model can realize 3-h trajectory prediction with average error of less than 1.46 km.

4   Routing Algorithm

In this section, we design the routing algorithm for vessel networks with global knowledge. Similar to traditional delay tolerant networks, vessels with large expected encounter probability are more likely to meet in the future. When two vessels are within their communication range, packets should be copied and forwarded to vessel with larger expected delivery probability in H hops. Therefore, the expected delivery probability calculation is the key issue of this algorithm. The process of expected delivery probability calculation is introduced in Sect. 4.1 and 4.2. Section 4.3 will give a detailed description of the routing algorithm.

4.1   Confident Degree of Predicted Trajectory

Definition 5 (Confident Degree of Predicted Trajectory). *Confident degree of predicted trajectory approximately represents the probability that the vessel is on its predicted location.*

Because regression results of Bi-LSTM model do not contain such metrics, in order to evaluate the results of predicted trajectories, the confident degree calculation method based on model's performance on the test set is proposed.

The mean error μ_n and standard deviation σ_n on each prediction step n on test set can be obtained, after the model training process. μ_n and σ_n can reflect the model's performance on historical data, which is helpful to evaluate the predicted results. For all prior assume distribution, if we have the mean and standard deviation, the normal distribution has the maximum entropy, which means it has maximum adaptability. So we choose normal distribution to fit the error of each predicted step.

The $error_n$, which is the errors of step n, is denoted as the random variable. We could assume that $error_n \sim \mathcal{N}(\mu_n, \sigma_n^2)$. The Probability Density Function (PDF) with μ_n and σ_n can be given by

$$f_n(error_n) = \frac{1}{\sqrt{2\pi}\sigma_n} e^{-\frac{(error_n - \mu_n)^2}{2\mu_n^2}}. \tag{8}$$

Then, $\mathcal{N}(\mu_n', \sigma_n'^2)$ can be fitted according to the results of Eq. (8).

Therefore, the probability of $error_n$ less than $(\mu_n' + 3\sigma_n')$ is 99.87%. However, in routing scenarios, the predicted error can be tolerated when communication radius R is very large. So the confident degree of predicted trajectory should not only relate to μ_n' and σ_n', but also relate to R. Considering vessels are moving in 2D space, so, in this paper, the confident degree of predicted trajectory on step n can be given by

$$E_{v,n} = 99.87\% \frac{(R - (\mu_n' + 3\sigma_n'))^2}{R^2}, (\mu_n' + 3\sigma_n') \le R. \tag{9}$$

where v is the identifier of vessel v. When $(\mu_n' + 3\sigma_n') \ge R$, we define $E_{v,n} = 0$, because the error is too large to guarantee communication. The $E_{v,n}$ could also

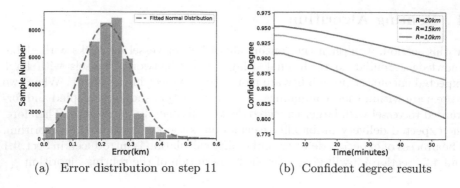

(a)   Error distribution on step 11   (b)   Confident degree results

Fig. 3. Confident degree of vessel 'Zhe31828'

be denoted as $E_{v,t}$ where t is the timestamp of step n. $E_{v,t}$ can be approximately treated as the probability of vessel appeared on the predicted location based on empirical error and communication radius.

Figure 3(a) shows the error distribution on 11 step of vessel 'Zhe31828' and its fitted distribution. We can see that the error distribution is fitted to normal distribution. Confident degree results are shown in Fig. 3(b). We can observe that confident degree changes with different communication radius. The confident degree decreases in long-term prediction. The vessel with smaller communication radius has a lower confident degree, because of its tolerance for error.

4.2   Calculation of Packet Delivery Probability Within N Hops

For each vessel v at time t, the confident degree of the predicted trajectory $E_{v,t}$ can be obtained. We use v and τ to denote two nodes in the ocean. $\varrho_{v,\tau}^{n}(t_{start}, t_{end})$ stands for expected delivery probability in time period $[t_{start}, t_{end}]$ from v to τ at just n hops, which means $\varrho_{v,\tau}^{n}(t_{start}, t_{end})$ does not include the situation that packet is delivered in less than n hops.

When v and τ are expected to meet (within their communication range) at time t, the one-hop delivery probability is $E_{v,t} \times E_{\tau,t}$. So, the one-hop delivery probability can be given by

$$\varrho_{v,\tau}^{1}(t_{start}, t_{end}) = 1 - \prod_{t \in [t_{start}, t_{end}]} (1 - E_{v,t} \times E_{\tau,t}). \qquad (10)$$

Where t is the start time of expected contacts. The accompany time is not considered in this equation to avoid repeated calculation. The meaning of t is the same in following derivation procedures in this subsection.

The condition of two-hop delivery can be treated as two one-hop delivery procedures with the time constraint. The delivery probability of two-hops can be calculated as follows

$$\varrho_{v,\tau}^{2}(t_{start}, t_{end}) = 1 - \prod_{t_{start} \leq t \leq t_{end}} (1 - \varrho_{v,m}^{1}(t_{start}, t) \times \varrho_{m,\tau}^{1}(t, t_{end})). \qquad (11)$$

Then, three-hop delivery probability can be divide into one one-hop delivery procedure and one two-hop delivery. The three-hops delivery probability can be derived by

$$\varrho_{v,\tau}^3(t_{start}, t_{end}) = 1 - \prod_{t_{start} \leq t \leq t_{end}} (1 - \varrho_{v,m}^1(t_{start}, t) \times \varrho_{m,\tau}^2(t, t_{end})) \quad (12)$$

Therefore, the delivery probability of n-hops is given by

$$\varrho_{v,\tau}^n(t_{start}, t_{end}) = 1 - \prod_{t_{start} \leq t \leq t_{end}} (1 - \varrho_{v,m}^1(t_{start}, t) \times \varrho_{m,\tau}^{n-1}(t, t_{end})) \quad (13)$$

Consider the routing in vessel networks, a vessel has a packet p that needs to be delivered to $\zeta(p)$ with its remaining hops H and time-to-live TTL. When the vessel meets its neighbour v at time t_c, neighbour's delivery probability within $(H - 1)$ hops needs to be calculated. The equation can be given by

$$\psi_{v,\zeta(p)}^{H-1}(t_c, t_c + TTL) = 1 - \prod_{i=1}^{H-1} (1 - \varrho_{v,\zeta(p)}^i(t_c, t_c + TTL)) \quad (14)$$

4.3   Algorithm Description

The routing algorithm based on long-term trajectory prediction is described as follows. We assume that each vessel can get recent historical information and trajectory prediction model of other vessels, and vessels sharing the same channel resource set need to compete for limited useful links.

For packet list P in vessel v, the source vessel first calculates $\psi_{v,\zeta(p)}^{H-1}(t_c, t_c + TTL)$ of each p in P on v's neighbours. The algorithm selects the relay node with the largest delivery probability. If links in the area are over link limitation, the algorithm will transfer the packet by probability rank to avoid channel collision.

When the packet p is copied and transferred, system will update the information of copied packet. The algorithm would renew $H_{p_{copy}}$. The packet would be abandoned if its TTL becomes 0. The packet p will stop forwarding when H is 0. So, the distributed algorithm will repeatedly find best relays for packets until packets in P are all delivered.

5   Performance Evaluation

We first give the methodology for performance evaluation, introduce compared algorithms and finally show simulation results.

Trajectory-driven simulations are performed to show the performance of our algorithm compared with Epidemic.

We use a total of 5123 vessels that had appeared from May 2015 to May 2018. Trajectory prediction models are trained by the first 24 months' data in default. For each packet, we randomly select its source and destination pairs which have

Table 1. Default system parameters

Parameter	Default value
Number of vessels	5123
Communication range	20 km
H_{max}	20
TTL_{max}	6 h
Number of packets	200, 600, 1000, 1400, 1800

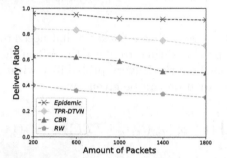
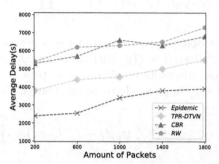

(a) Delivery ratio versus number of pack- (b) Average delay versus number of packets   ets

Fig. 4. Comparative results

at least one contact before, because vessels that hadn't met each other barely have communication requirements. The number of packets is varied from 200 to 1800. 5 simulations are performed on 5 different fishing months (Oct 2017, Nov 2017, Dec 2017, Jan 2018, Feb 2018) to get average results. The default system parameters are listed in Table 1.

We compare the performance of different routing algorithms by the delivery ratio and delay. We vary packets number from 200 to 1800 to simulation different network overhead. Figure 4(a) and Fig. 4(b) show the two algorithms in terms of delivery ratio and average delay. Epidemic has the best performance in both metrics as expected. We could notice that our algorithm performs better, because we utilize historical information. Our algorithm's probability calculation process is with the limitation of TTL, which leads to more accurate results.

6   Relate Works

Some researches applying fixed mobility models or encounter models to design routing algorithms in Maritime Networks. These algorithms are often appropriate for vessels which have stable mobility behaviour, such as cargo ship, cruise ship and waste-dumping vessel. Raj et al. assume that all vessels following Gaussian-Markov mobility model [7]. Forwarding metrics based on this assumption are calculated for routing. Lanepost [15] and Mar-DTN [16] are typical graph based optimal routing algorithms. These algorithms construct an opportunistic routing graph based on fixed expected routes of each vessel and use the graph for forwarding decisions. Liu et al. [17] and Qin et al. [18] study delay tolerant routing problem in the seaway model, which all vessels are moving in fixed seaways. Vessels predict the speed and arrival time based on proper models and utilize them for decisions.

7 Conclusion

In this paper, we have presented a routing algorithm for efficient data delivery in vessel networks. It employs a forwarding metric which characterizes the expected delivery probability of relay nodes. To solve the challenge of long-term trajectory prediction, we design a Bi-LSTM based trajectory predict model and an evaluation method to get practicable predicted trajectory. Then, We evaluate expected delivery probability based on future contacts of pairwise vessels with predicted information. Extensive trace-driven simulations show that our algorithms can achieve a higher delivery ratio with lower transmission delay.

Acknowledgements. C. Liu and Y. Li contributed equally to this work and should be regarded as co-first authors. This research was supported by the National Natural Science Foundation of China Grant Nos. 61902367 and 41976185, the Natural Science Foundation of Shandong Grant No. ZR2018BF006, the National Key R&D Program 2016YFC1401900, and the Qingdao National Labor for Marine Science and Technology Open Research Project QNLM2016ORP0405.

References

1. Metcalfe, K., et al.: Using satellite AIS to improve our understanding of shipping and fill gaps in ocean observation data to support marine spatial planning. J. Appl. Ecol. **55**(4), 1834–1845 (2018)
2. Carnie, P., et al.: Global marine trends 2030: implications for naval ship technology. In: Pacific 2013 International Maritime Conference: The Commercial Maritime and Naval Defence Showcase for the Asia Pacific, p. 241. Engineers Australia (2013)
3. Tu, E., Zhang, G., Rachmawati, L., Rajabally, E., Huang, G.B.: Exploiting AIS data for intelligent maritime navigation: a comprehensive survey. IEEE Trans. Intell. Transp. Syst. **PP**(99), 1–24 (2016)
4. Yu, J., Yu, K., Yu, D., Lv, W., Cheng, W.: Efficient link scheduling in wireless networks under Rayleigh-fading and multiuser interference. IEEE Trans. Wirel. Commun. **PP**(99), 1 (2020)
5. Cai, Z., Goebel, R., Lin, G.: Size-constrained tree partitioning: approximating the multicast k-tree routing problem. Theor. Comput. Sci. **412**(3), 240–245 (2011)
6. Liu, C., Li, Y., Jiang, R., Hong, F., Guo, Z.: OceanNet: a low-cost large-scale maritime communication architecture based on D2D communication technology. In: Proceedings of the ACM Turing Celebration Conference-China, pp. 1–6 (2019)

7. Raj, D., Ramesh, M.V., Duttagupta, S.: Delay tolerant routing protocol for heterogeneous marine vehicular mobile ad-hoc network. In: 2017 IEEE International Conference on Pervasive Computing and Communications Workshops (PerCom Workshops), pp. 461–466. IEEE (2017)
8. Mohsin, R.J., Woods, J., Shawkat, M.Q.: Density and mobility impact on MANET routing protocols in a maritime environment. In: 2015 Science and Information Conference (SAI), pp. 1046–1051. IEEE (2015)
9. Bing, Q., Jiang, R., Hong, F.: Exploiting social network characteristics for efficient routing in ocean vessel ad hoc networks. In: 2019 IEEE 38th International Performance Computing and Communications Conference (IPCCC), pp. 1–8. IEEE (2019)
10. Liu, C., Sun, Z., Liu, J., Huang, H., Guo, Z., Feng, Y.: VSTP: vessel spatio-temporal contact pattern detection based on MapReduce. EURASIP J. Wirel. Commun. Network. **2017**(1), 1–11 (2017). https://doi.org/10.1186/s13638-017-0960-x
11. Yu, D., Zou, Y., Yu, J., Zhang, Y., Lau, F.C.: Implementing abstract MAC layer in dynamic networks. IEEE Trans. Mobile Comput. **PP**(99), 1 (2020)
12. Cai, Z., Chen, Z., Lin, G.: A 3.4713-approximation algorithm for the capacitated multicast tree routing problem. Theor. Comput. Sci. **410**(52), 5415–5424 (2009)
13. Yuan, Y., et al.: Fast fault-tolerant sampling via random walk in dynamic networks. In: 2019 IEEE 39th International Conference on Distributed Computing Systems (ICDCS), pp. 536–544 (2019)
14. Zhu, Y., Wu, Y., Li, B.: Trajectory improves data delivery in urban vehicular networks. IEEE Trans. Parallel Distrib. Syst. **25**(4), 1089–1100 (2013)
15. Geng, X., Wang, Y., Feng, H., Zhang, L.: Lanepost: lane-based optimal routing protocol for delay-tolerant maritime networks. China Commun. **14**(2), 65–78 (2017)
16. Kolios, P., Lambrinos, L.: Optimising file delivery in a maritime environment through inter-vessel connectivity predictions. In: 2012 IEEE 8th International Conference on Wireless and Mobile Computing, Networking and Communications (WiMob), pp. 777–783. IEEE (2012)
17. Liu, C., Guo, Z., Hong, F., Wu, K.: DCEP: data collection strategy with the estimated paths in ocean delay tolerant network. Int. J. Distrib. Sens. Netw. **10**(3), 518439 (2014)
18. Qin, S., Feng, G., Qin, W., Ge, Y., Pathmasuntharam, J.S.: Performance evaluation of data transmission in maritime delay-tolerant-networks. IEICE Trans. Commun. **96**(6), 1435–1443 (2013)

Cold Start and Learning Resource Recommendation Mechanism Based on Opportunistic Network in the Context of Campus Collaborative Learning

Hong Liu[1,2,3], Peng Li[1,2,3(✉)], Yuanru Cui[1,3], Qian Liu[1,3],
Lichen Zhang[1,2,3], Longjiang Guo[1,2,3], Xiaojun Wu[1,2,3],
and Xiaoming Wang[1,2,3]

[1] School of Computer Science, Shaanxi Normal University,
Xi'an 710119, China
lipeng@snnu.edu.cn
[2] Key Laboratory of Modern Teaching Technology, Ministry of Education,
Xi'an 710062, China
[3] Engineering Laboratory of Teaching Information Technology of Shaanxi
Province, Xi'an 710119, China

Abstract. The mainstream cold start scheme in social network mainly deals with the problems of information overload and the accuracy and efficiency of recommendation. However, the problem of information overload is quite different from the problem of information transmission delay caused by insufficient contact of nodes in the mobile Opportunistic network. And in the campus collaborative learning environment, learner nodes often have a lack of awareness of their own needs of learning resources and lack of search ability for learning resources, in order to solve the above problems, this paper for the mobile social network cold start stage definition and stage division, On this basis, the paper provides solutions to the file transfer strategies in the cold start-up stage and the community operation stage of the nodes respectively, And according to the high degree of activity nodes can often be contact more information, the higher intimacy between nodes means that the nodes are more familiar and higher transmission success rate characteristics, In this paper, a learning resource recommendation mechanism based on node activity and social intimacy is proposed, and the algorithm has been tested and verified to have high accuracy for the recommendation mechanism based on message attributes.

Keywords: Opportunistic network · Collaborative learning · Cold start · Recommendation mechanism

1 Background and Related Research

In the social network, the cold start service refers to the use of a large number of new creation services [1], which have no use records and are constantly released. The cold start problem can be divided into new project cold start and new user cold start [2]; In the mobile social network, cold start problem refers to the Opportunistic network in the

© Springer Nature Switzerland AG 2020
D. Yu et al. (Eds.): WASA 2020, LNCS 12384, pp. 309–321, 2020.
https://doi.org/10.1007/978-3-030-59016-1_26

early stage, because each node for the link connection situation is not sufficient, as well as for each node and parameters to obtain the slow, resulting in the interaction between nodes and the proliferation of data there is a certain blindness.

In order to solve the problem of cold start in social networks, LC et al. Proposed a social recommendation method [3, 4]. Based on the consideration of the results of social network analysis (SNS), this method constructs the social relationship network between users according to the social relationship information between users, and recommends the new user through the user who has direct or indirect relationship with the new user. Huang et al. Based on the modeling of service relationship and the prediction of potential cooperative relationship among users, realize the relevant recommendation mechanism [5], Linqi et al. Based on the consideration of user context information (emotion, location, time, etc.), realize the personalized demand of new users for information [6], Zhang et al. Based on LDA (latent Dirichlet allocation) model and keyword information The user's demand information is analyzed to improve the accuracy of recommendation [7]. In the social network, the above and mainstream cold start solutions are mainly aimed at providing customers with commodity information and suggestions [8], and dealing with the problems of information overload and accuracy and efficiency of recommendation. However, there is a big difference between the problem of information overload and the problem of information transmission delay caused by insufficient contact of nodes in the mobile Opportunistic network, Therefore, the above schemes are not applicable in the mobile social network.

Because of the characteristics of more intensive nodes and more complex social relations between individuals and communities in the campus collaborative learning environment, the link between nodes is often more complicated. Therefore, how to select the correct transfer node is particularly important. In the Opportunistic network, when the learner node forms a new learning community or the unfamiliar learner node joins the network learning community. Because the link conditions of other nodes and the characteristics of mobile and communication can not be mastered, it is easy to lead to low message delivery, redundant messages, and waste of transmission opportunities. Therefore, it is necessary to consider the cold start situation under campus collaborative learning, accurately grasp the contact utility and characteristics between any nodes, and promote the efficient and fast transmission of the information of the nodes in the new collaborative environment.

2   The Division of the Cold Start Phase

On campus, the population is dense, the routine has obvious regularity and shows obvious characteristics of group activities, so the community between the learner nodes is more obvious. Therefore, the stage division of a single node can be based on the establishment of a single node's communication community. It can be considered that when the community of a learner's node is in a stable state, its cold start-up phase will end. How to measure the stability of any node's communication community, we consider the following mechanisms. Suppose in the mobile social network, there is a network $G = (V, E)$, where V is the set of nodes, and a contact of any two nodes is regarded as adding one to the weight value of the undirected edge between the two nodes, and E is used to represent the set of all edges. For any node St_i, its own signal initial value $Sig_i = n - 1$ (n is the number of learner nodes), initial queue, additional queue, initialization matrix and other parameter types are maintained, as shown in Table 1:

Table 1. Node initialization information table

Meaning	Symbol
Node ID	$i(0 \leq i \leq n)$
Signal value	Sig_i
Initial queue	$Init\_i\{ St^i_{x1}, \ldots, St^i_{xp}\} \{0 \leq x_1 \leq x_p \leq n\}$
Additional queue	$Init\_i'\{ St^i_{y1}, \ldots, St^i_{yq}\} \{0 \leq y_1 \leq y_p \leq n\}$
Initialization matrix	A_i

ST^i_x is the initial constant value of the node i for the node x, The evolution strategy of initialization phase is as follows:

A. When any node p's own signal value is greater than 0 and meets with node q, and the initial signal value of q node is greater than 0, p and q nodes subtract one from their own signal value respectively, and add one to the signal value of the other node in the signal queue.

B. When the initial signal value of any node p is less than or equal to 0, it meets with node q and the initial signal value of node q is greater than 0:

1) If node q is not in the initial queue of the p node, then the p node's own signal value remains unchanged, and the q node is incorporated into the additional queue of the p node, and the signal value is added one. The q node will also incorporate the p node into its own initial queue, and the signal value is added one. The signal value of node p's own minus two.

2) If node q is in the initial queue of node p, then node p adds one to node q's signal value, node q itself subtracts two, and node q adds one to node p's signal value.

C. When the signal value of any node p is less than or equal to 0 and the signal value of node q is less than or equal to 0. No longer change the value of its own signal, signal queue and additional queue.

In the initialization stage, when any node contacts, it will perfects its initialization matrix, which is described as follows:

$$A_{St_i} = \begin{bmatrix} & St_i & St_{x_1} & St_{x_2} & St_{x_{...}} & St_{x_{p-1}} & St_{x_p} \\ St_i & 0 & St_{x_1}^i & St_{x_2}^i & St_{x_{...}}^i & St_{x_{p-1}}^i & St_{x_p}^i \\ St_{x_1} & St_i^{x_1} & 0 & St_{x_2}^{x_1} & St_{x_{...}}^{x_1} & St_{x_{p-1}}^{x_1} & St_{x_p}^{x_1} \\ St_{x_2} & St_i^{x_2} & St_{x_1}^{x_2} & 0 & St_{x_{...}}^{x_2} & St_{x_{p-1}}^{x_2} & St_{x_p}^{x_2} \\ St_{x_{...}} & St_i^{x_{...}} & St_{x_1}^{x_{...}} & St_{x_2}^{x_{...}} & 0 & St_{x_{p-1}}^{x_{...}} & St_{x_p}^{x_{...}} \\ St_{x_{p-1}} & St_i^{x_{p-1}} & St_{x_1}^{x_{p-1}} & St_{x_2}^{x_{p-1}} & St_{x_{...}}^{x_{p-1}} & 0 & St_{x_p}^{x_{p-1}} \\ St_{x_p} & St_i^{x_p} & St_{x_1}^{x_p} & St_{x_2}^{x_p} & St_{x_{...}}^{x_p} & St_{x_{p-1}}^{x_p} & 0 \end{bmatrix}$$

In this paper, module degree [9, 10] is used to evaluate the community perfection degree of nodes. The basic idea of modularity is that if the connection rate of nodes in any community is higher than that of nodes in random case, the community structure is stable. The expression of community modular Q is as follows:

$$Q = \frac{1}{2m} \sum_{vw} \left(A_{vw} - \frac{k_v k_w}{2m} \right) \delta(c_v, c_w) \tag{1}$$

Where m is the total number of sides in the network, k_v and k_w respectively represent the degree of node v and node w. A_{vw} represents the connection weight between v node and w node, if there is no connection between nodes v, w, A_{vw} value is 0, otherwise, it is equal to the number of communication. C_v represents the community of node v, C_w represents the community of node w, if node v and node w are in the same community, $\delta(C_v, C_w)$ value is 1, otherwise, it is 0;

In this scenario, the community of C_v and C_w is unknown, so it can be judged according to the connection with nodes with higher degree of center. For example, in the initial community A_{St_i} of node St_i, the center degree of St_i node is higher. If the number of connections between v node and w node is greater than the average number of connections between St_i node and all initial nodes, it indicates that v, w node is in the same community.

Therefore, the module degree is defined as follows:

$$Q' = \frac{1}{2m} \sum_{vw} \left(A_{vw} - \frac{k_v k_w}{2m} \right) \cdot R_{vw} \tag{2}$$

R_{vw} indicates whether nodes v, w are in the same community. and if the number of connections between v, w is greater than the average number of connections between the St_i nodes and all the initial nodes, the R_{vw} value is 1, otherwise it is 0;

As shown in Fig. 1, assuming that the number of connections A_{vw} between node w and node v is 5, and the average number of connections between node St_i and all initial nodes is 2, it is clear that the node v, w is in the same community. But using this method will form overlapping communities among different communities.

In the actual social network analysis, Q value generally exists between 0.1–0.7, and it is generally believed that when Q value is greater than 0.3 [11, 12], there is a relatively stable network community in the social network.

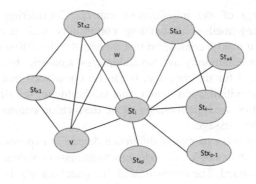

Fig. 1. Community diagram of node initialization network connectivity

According to the above initialization mechanism, it can be considered that:

When the initial queue value of any node is greater than n, the community evolution of the node is faster, that is, the activity of the node is higher.

When there is a signal value in the additional queue of any node, it indicates that the node contacts a wide range of communities with a high degree.

3   Cold Start Mechanism of Node

In the early stage of the mobile Opportunistic network learning community, because no node contains or only contains less communication characteristic information of other nodes. When any node needs to carry out message transmission, the transport node cannot be selected correctly based on the node information table it contains, so it will cause a lot of waste of contact opportunities, message redundancy and the transmission delay will be greatly increased.

For the cold start node to select the node when transmitting messages, we consider selecting the next-hop node by using node activeness and node community difference. Relevant scholars have carried out a series of explorations on node activity and node similarity. For example, Han et al. [13] calculated the node activeness according to the area of the node moving track and the average dwell time of the node. Feng et al. [14] made a back-off selection based on the busy state of the network in the previous period, and chose to transmit to the nodes whose network conditions were idle in the previous period. Fu et al. Considered the link similarity of nodes based on their link conditions within k hops. The LFM algorithm proposed by Shen et al. is based on the similarity between the feature nodes in contact with the nodes. In the cold start phase of Opportunistic Network, due to the lack of initial information of the node, it is unable to make effective statistics on the link state of a period of time and the characteristics of other nodes, and the above algorithms are not applicable to the cold start phase of the node.

In this paper, we consider using the initial queue signal value and the additional queue signal value to characterize the relative activity between nodes, and calculate the difference of the initial community of any two nodes according to the community difference (similarity) of the initialization matrix. Considering that collaborative learning is a learning method of building community with interest and common learning objectives, it can be considered that the smaller the difference of initialization matrix, the higher the community overlap and interest similarity between nodes, that is, the higher the demand for the message. It can be considered that the lower the difference degree of the initialization matrix, that is, the higher the similarity degree, the easier it is to spread or send the message to the destination community or destination node interested in the message.

The calculation process of matrix difference degree is expressed as follows:

Taking Fig. 2 as an example, set node a as transmission node and d and f nodes be the nodes to be transmitted. The matrix A_a and The matching matrix $A_{f\&a}$ for node f and node a is expressed as follows:

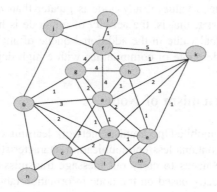

Fig. 2. Social network community structure diagram

$$A_a = \begin{array}{c|ccccccccc} & a & b & c & d & e & f & g & h & k \\ \hline a & 0 & 3 & 1 & 1 & 2 & 4 & 2 & 1 & 2 \\ b & 3 & 0 & 0 & 2 & 0 & 0 & 1 & 0 & 0 \\ c & 1 & 0 & 0 & 2 & 0 & 0 & 0 & 0 & 0 \\ d & 1 & 2 & 2 & 0 & 1 & 0 & 1 & 0 & 3 \\ e & 2 & 0 & 0 & 1 & 0 & 0 & 0 & 1 & 1 \\ f & 4 & 0 & 0 & 0 & 0 & 0 & 4 & 1 & 5 \\ g & 2 & 1 & 0 & 1 & 0 & 4 & 0 & 0 & 0 \\ h & 1 & 0 & 0 & 0 & 1 & 1 & 0 & 0 & 1 \\ k & 2 & 0 & 0 & 3 & 1 & 5 & 0 & 1 & 0 \end{array}, \quad A_{f\&a} = \begin{bmatrix} 0 & 0 & 0 & 0 & 0 & 4 & 2 & 1 & 2 \\ 0 & 0 & 0 & 0 & 0 & 0 & 0 & 0 & 0 \\ 0 & 0 & 0 & 0 & 0 & 0 & 0 & 0 & 0 \\ 0 & 0 & 0 & 0 & 0 & 0 & 0 & 0 & 0 \\ 0 & 0 & 0 & 0 & 0 & 0 & 0 & 0 & 0 \\ 4 & 0 & 0 & 0 & 0 & 0 & 4 & 1 & 5 \\ 2 & 0 & 0 & 0 & 0 & 4 & 0 & 0 & 0 \\ 1 & 0 & 0 & 0 & 0 & 1 & 0 & 0 & 1 \\ 2 & 0 & 0 & 0 & 0 & 5 & 0 & 1 & 0 \end{bmatrix}$$

The difference degree of the initial matrix between node a and node f is calculated as follows:

$$|A_{a-f\&a}| = A_a - A_{f\&a}$$

$$= \begin{bmatrix} 0 & 3 & 1 & 1 & 2 & 4 & 2 & 1 & 2 \\ 3 & 0 & 0 & 2 & 0 & 0 & 1 & 0 & 0 \\ 1 & 0 & 0 & 2 & 0 & 0 & 0 & 0 & 0 \\ 1 & 2 & 2 & 0 & 1 & 0 & 1 & 0 & 3 \\ 2 & 0 & 0 & 1 & 0 & 0 & 0 & 1 & 1 \\ 4 & 0 & 0 & 0 & 0 & 0 & 4 & 1 & 5 \\ 2 & 1 & 0 & 1 & 0 & 4 & 0 & 0 & 0 \\ 1 & 0 & 0 & 0 & 1 & 1 & 0 & 0 & 1 \\ 2 & 0 & 0 & 3 & 1 & 5 & 0 & 1 & 0 \end{bmatrix} - \begin{bmatrix} 0 & 0 & 0 & 0 & 0 & 4 & 2 & 1 & 2 \\ 0 & 0 & 0 & 0 & 0 & 0 & 0 & 0 & 0 \\ 0 & 0 & 0 & 0 & 0 & 0 & 0 & 0 & 0 \\ 0 & 0 & 0 & 0 & 0 & 0 & 0 & 0 & 0 \\ 0 & 0 & 0 & 0 & 0 & 0 & 0 & 0 & 0 \\ 4 & 0 & 0 & 0 & 0 & 0 & 4 & 1 & 5 \\ 2 & 0 & 0 & 0 & 0 & 4 & 0 & 0 & 0 \\ 1 & 0 & 0 & 0 & 0 & 1 & 0 & 0 & 1 \\ 2 & 0 & 0 & 0 & 0 & 5 & 0 & 1 & 0 \end{bmatrix}$$

$$= \sqrt{\sum_{x,y}\left(a_{x,y}^2 - f_\& a_{x,y}^2\right)} = \sqrt{74}$$

In the same way, the difference degree of the initial matrix between node a and node d is calculated as follows:

$$|A_{a-d\&a}| = A_a - A_{d\&a}$$

$$= \begin{bmatrix} 0 & 3 & 1 & 1 & 2 & 4 & 2 & 1 & 2 \\ 3 & 0 & 0 & 2 & 0 & 0 & 1 & 0 & 0 \\ 1 & 0 & 0 & 2 & 0 & 0 & 0 & 0 & 0 \\ 1 & 2 & 2 & 0 & 1 & 0 & 1 & 0 & 3 \\ 2 & 0 & 0 & 1 & 0 & 0 & 0 & 1 & 1 \\ 4 & 0 & 0 & 0 & 0 & 0 & 4 & 1 & 5 \\ 2 & 1 & 0 & 1 & 0 & 4 & 0 & 0 & 0 \\ 1 & 0 & 0 & 0 & 1 & 1 & 0 & 0 & 1 \\ 2 & 0 & 0 & 3 & 1 & 5 & 0 & 1 & 0 \end{bmatrix} - \begin{bmatrix} 0 & 3 & 1 & 1 & 2 & 0 & 2 & 0 & 2 \\ 3 & 0 & 0 & 2 & 0 & 0 & 1 & 0 & 0 \\ 1 & 0 & 0 & 2 & 0 & 0 & 0 & 0 & 0 \\ 1 & 2 & 2 & 0 & 1 & 0 & 1 & 0 & 3 \\ 2 & 0 & 0 & 1 & 0 & 0 & 0 & 0 & 1 \\ 0 & 0 & 0 & 0 & 0 & 0 & 0 & 0 & 0 \\ 2 & 1 & 0 & 1 & 0 & 0 & 0 & 0 & 0 \\ 0 & 0 & 0 & 0 & 0 & 0 & 0 & 0 & 0 \\ 2 & 0 & 0 & 3 & 1 & 0 & 0 & 0 & 0 \end{bmatrix}$$

$$= \frac{1}{\sqrt{\sum_{x,y}\left(a_{x,y}^2 - d_\& a_{x,y}^2\right)}} = \sqrt{122}$$

It can be seen that, although d node and a node have more common neighbor nodes, the community difference between a node and f node is smaller due to the different weights of contact times.

Therefore, on the basis of considering the relative activity degree of nodes, the transport nodes are selected according to the community difference degree of nodes, in which the nodes with small community difference degree are given priority in transmission, The above cold start mechanism is named ONCSRouter (Opportunistic Network - Cold Start Router) algorithm.

4 Learning Resource Recommendation Mechanism

In the campus collaborative learning environment, learners' nodes often have insufficient knowledge cognition of their own needs and lack of searching for learning resources. The lack of knowledge cognition of their own needs is mainly reflected in that learners' nodes often do not know what kind of learning resources they need, for example, students often need teachers to recommend relevant books or courses to themselves The students with poor learning often recommend the students who need to learn excellent knowledge due to their fuzzy knowledge points; however, the phenomenon of weak search for learning resources is mainly reflected in the learners' nodes do not know how to find or where to find the learning resources they need. Therefore, we introduce learning resources to push in the campus collaborative learning environment based on Opportunistic network Recommendation mechanism.

Considering that the nodes with higher activity can often access more information, and the higher intimacy between nodes means that the nodes are more familiar with each other and have higher transmission success rate [15, 16], in this paper, the recommendation ability of nodes relative to other nodes is calculated by the activity and intimacy of nodes.

A recommendable coefficient Rec is established for each node pair, which is asymmetric, that is [17, 18], the Rec values of each node pair are not equal to each other. When any multiple nodes meet, the recommendable nodes are sorted according to the recommendable coefficient;

$$Rec_{ij} = \alpha \cdot C_j + \beta \cdot Sm_{ij} \tag{3}$$

Rec_{ij} is the recommended coefficient of node j for node i, C_j is the comprehensive activity of node j, Sm_{ij} is the social intimacy of node i and node j. α, β are the weight coefficients set by the node according to the different needs of the recommended message, and the node influence and the social intimacy between nodes are discussed below.

4.1 Node Influence Model

For node influence C, consider the following:

It can be considered that the activity of a node not only depends on the link of the node in the community, but also is closely related to the link of the node with the external community [19]. Therefore, we comprehensively consider the community activity of any node Coa (Community activity) and the community external activity Cea (Community external activity) to calculate the comprehensive activity of the node. In the calculation, we will The activity in the community can be divided into two parts: the activity of Coa_dir which can be contacted directly and the activity of Coa_rel which can be contacted indirectly;

Assume that the total activity value of any node i is 100%, that is:

$$\begin{cases} Coa_i + Cea_i = C_i; \\ Coa\_dir_i + Coa\_rel_i = Coa_i; \end{cases} \tag{4}$$

As shown in Table 1, each activity value of node St_i is calculated as follows according to node initialization.

$$Coa\_dir = \sum_{j=St_{x_1}^i}^{St_{x_p}^i} j, \quad Coa\_rel = \sum_{j=St_{x_1}^i}^{St_{x_p}^i} \left(\frac{|j\_Asb| \cdot j}{\sum\limits_{St_k^j \in j\_Asb} St_k^j} \right), \quad Cea = \sum_{m=St_{y_1}^i}^{St_{y_q}^i} m \tag{5}$$

Where j_Asb is the initial community direct node set of node j, and $|j\_Asb|$ is the module of node j set, that is, the number of nodes in set j_Asb, $C = Act'$.

4.2 Social Intimacy

In this paper, we use the common neighbor node to calculate the social intimacy between nodes, assuming that there is node i and node j to be transmitted, and the node intimacy of the two nodes is calculated as follows;

$$Sm_{ij} = Sh_{ij} \cdot Sc_{ij} \tag{6}$$

Sm_{ij} is the social intimacy of nodes i and j, Sh_{ij} is the proportion of common neighbors of nodes i and j in all nodes contacted by nodes i and j, and Sc_{ij} is the contribution of common neighbors of nodes i and j to the links of nodes i and j. Define a node to edge strength K_{ij}, which is the ratio of the weight of two node edges to the sum of the weights of i, j nodes and their neighbors. It can be considered that the larger the ratio is, the higher the contribution of all the neighbors to the links of i and j nodes is, $S_{(i)}$ is the sum of the weights of all the edges connected with node i, W_{ij} is the weight value of the edges between node i and node j. The calculation of Sh_{ij}, Sc_{ij} and K_{ij} is as follows respectively:

$$Sh_{ij} = \frac{i\_Asb \cap j\_Asb}{i\_Asb \cup j\_Asb}, K_{ij} = \frac{W_{ij}}{S_{(i)} + S_{(j)}}, Sc_{ij} = \sum_{c \in i\_Asb \cap j\_Asb} |A_{c\&i,j}| \cdot K_{ij} \tag{7}$$

Where c is the node in the set of i and j neighbor nodes, i_Asb is the direct node set of i nodes, $A_{c\&i,j}$ is the matching matrix of c for i and j nodes.

5   Simulation Experiment and Result Analysis

In order to evaluate the performance of the algorithm described in this paper, ONE (Opportunistic Network Environment) simulator is used for experimental simulation. In this paper, the real data set haggle6-infocom6 is used for simulation experiment, and the main experimental parameters are set as shown in Table 2:

Table 2. Simulation parameter settings

Parameter type	Value
Data set	haggle6-infocom6
Simulation duration/s	92000
Transfer file size/kB	50 k, 5000 k
Message generation interval/s	300, 5000
Number of nodes	98
Number of message copies from SprayAndWait	20
SprayAndWaitRouter.binaryMode	True

When other main parameters of the simulation environment are set to *initialenergy* = 50000, *buffersize* = 100 MB, and *transmitspeed* = 150 KB/s, the impact of msgTtl on ONCSRouter is tested. The simulation results are as shown in Fig. 3:

It can be seen from Fig. 3 that when TTL is less than 400 min, the impact on each route is large, and when TTL is greater than 400 min, the performance of each route is gradually stable. Among them, the impact of TTL on ONCSrouter and Epidemic router is relatively small.

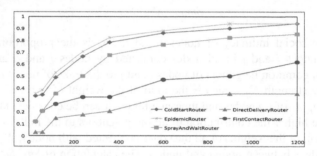

Fig. 3. Schematic diagram of the effect of msgTtl on routing

When other main parameters of the simulation environment are set to *initialenergy* = 50000, *buffersize* = 100 MB and *msgttl* = 900 min, the impact of transmitspeed on ONCSrouter is tested. The simulation results are as shown in Fig. 4:

From Fig. 4, it can be seen that when the transmitspeed is less than 50 KB\s, the impact on ONCSRouter, EpidemicRouter, FirstContactRoute, SprayAndWait- Router, etc. is greater than that on DirectdeliveryRouter. When the transmitspeed is greater than 50 KB\s, the performance of each route gradually stabilizes.

When other main parameters of the simulation environment are set to *initialenergy* = 50000, *transmitspeed* = 150 KB/s and *msgTtl* = 900 min, the impact of buffersize on oncsrouter is tested. The simulation results are as shown in Fig. 5.

From Fig. 5, it can be seen that buffersize has a greater impact on oncsrouter, epicrouter sprayand waitorouter, but a smaller impact on epicrouter and firstcontactroute. Among them, it has the greatest impact on epicrouter routing, mainly because the nodes using epicrouter routing will transmit all messages to all the nodes in contact, resulting in a higher message redundancy And the waste of node storage space.

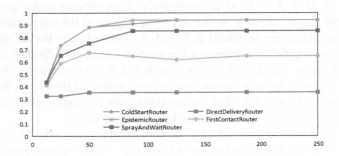

Fig. 4. Schematic diagram of transmitspeed impact on routing results

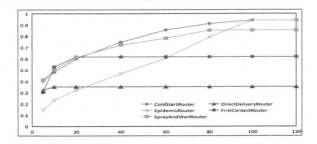

Fig. 5. Schematic diagram of buffersize impact on routing results

When other main parameters of the simulation environment are set to *buffer-size* = 100 MB, *transmitspeed* = 150 Kb/s and *msgttl* = 900 min, the impact of initialenergy on ONCSRouter is tested. The simulation results are as shown in Fig. 6:

It can be seen from Fig. 6 that when the *initialenergy* is less than 20000, it has a great impact on all routes. When the *initialenergy* is greater than 20000, the performance of each route is gradually stable. Among them, when the *initialenergy* is low, it has a great impact on the epidemic router.

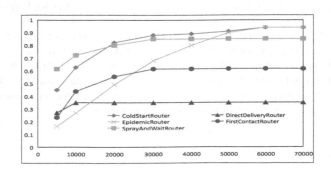

Fig. 6. Schematic diagram of initial energy impact on routing results

In order to evaluate the learning resource recommendation mechanism, this paper divides 98 nodes of infocom 6 dataset into 14 groups according to the initialization community after the simulation of infocom 6 dataset, and marks the group ID as *A, B, C, D, E, F, G, H, I, J, K, L, M, N* respectively; Each group's nodes determine five intimate communities according to the difference degree of the initial matrix, and the intimate communities can be labeled as 5, 4, 3, 2, 1 according to the difference degree of the initial matrix; then the generated messages are randomly divided into 14 categories, which are labeled as *a, b, c, d, e, f, g, h, i, j, k, l, m, n* respectively.

Each group is labeled with its own interest type, which is called the original interest type. Each node selects 1–7 original interest types from the nodes outside the group as its own additional interest type according to social intimacy.

For the matching degree between the recommended message and the recommended node, if the message type exists in the interest type of the recommended node, the matching value of the message and the recommended node is the corresponding interest type level of the node, otherwise the matching value is 0;

The simulation results of the recommendation mechanism are as shown in Fig. 7:

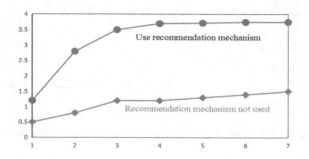

Fig. 7. Sketch map of average matching value of recommendation mechanism

It can be seen from Fig. 7 that the matching value between nodes and messages pushed by recommendation mechanism for messages is much higher than that obtained by random recommendation, that is, the recommendation mechanism has a good application effect in opportunistic network environment.

Acknowledgement. This work was supported by the National Natural Science Foundation of China under Grant No. 61877037, 61872228, 61977044, the National Key R&D Program of China under grant No. 2017YFB1402102, the Key R & D Program of Shaanxi Province under grant No. 2020GY-221, 2019ZDLSF07-01, 2020ZDLGY10-05, the Natural Science Basis Research Plan in Shaanxi Province of China under Grant No. 2020JM-303, 2020JM-302, 2017JM6060, the S&T Plan of Xi'an City of China under Grant No. 2019216914GXRC005CG006-GXYD5.1, the Fundamental Research Funds for the Central Universities of China under Grant No. GK201903090, GK201801004,the Shaanxi Normal University Foundational Education Course Research Center of Ministry of Education of China under Grant No. 2019-JCJY009.

References

1. Hao, Y.: Mining and prediction of service cooperation relationship of cold start in service system. J. Tsinghua Univ. (Nat. Sci. Ed.) **59**(11), 917–924 (2019)
2. Yu, H.: A recommended algorithm to solve the cold start problem of new projects. J. Softw. **26**(06), 1395–1408 (2015)
3. Wang, L.C.: Context-aware recommender systems: a survey of the state-of-the-art and possible extensions. J. Softw. **23**(1), 1–20 (2012)
4. Tang, J., Wang, K.: Personalized top-N sequential recommendation via convolutional sequence embedding. In: WSDM 2018, pp. 565–573. ACM, Marina Del Rey (2018)
5. Huang, K.: Recommendation in an evolving service ecosystem based on network prediction. IEEE Trans. Autom. Sci. Eng. **11**(3), 906–920 (2014)
6. Song, L.: Online learning in large-scale contextual recommender systems. IEEE Trans. Serv. Comput. **9**(3), 433–445 (2017)
7. Zhang, Y.: A service recommendation algorithm based on modeling of implicit demands. In: ICWS 2016, pp. 17–24. IEEE Computer Society, San Francisco (2016)
8. Resnick, P.: Recommender systems. Commun. ACM **40**(3), 56–58 (1997)
9. Rabbany, R.: Relative validity criteria for community mining algorithms. In: Advances in Social Networks Analysis and Mining (ASONAM), pp. 258–265. IEEE Computer Society, Istanbul (2012)
10. Li, S.: Detecting community structure via synchronous label propagation. Neurocomputing **151**, 1063–1075 (2015)
11. Wang, L.: Dynamic community discovery and evolution of online social networks. J. Comput. Sci. **38**(02), 219–237 (2015)
12. Han, Z.: Discovery algorithm of important nodes in weighted social networks. Comput. Appl. **33**(06), 1553–1562 (2013)
13. Feng, J.: An adaptive backoff algorithm based on neighbor activity in ad hoc networks. J. Syst. Simul. 2008(05), 1348–1352 (2008)
14. Fu, R.: Overlapping community discovery algorithm based on node importance and similarity. Comput. Eng. **44**(09), 192–198 (2018)
15. Yu, L., Chen, L., Cai, Z., Shen, H., Liang, Y., Pan, Y.: Stochastic load balancing for virtual resource management in datacenters. IEEE Trans. Cloud Comput. **8**(2), 459–472 (2020)
16. Wang, Y., Yin, G., Cai, Z., Dong, Y., Dong, H.: A trust-based probabilistic recommendation model for social networks. J. Netw. Comput. Appl. **55**, 59–67 (2015)
17. Liang, Y., Cai, Z., Yu, J., Han, Q., Li, Y.: Deep learning based inference of private information using embedded sensors in smart devices. IEEE Netw. Mag. **32**(4), 8–14 (2018)
18. Pang, J., Huang, Y., Xie, Z., Han, Q., Cai, Z.: Realizing the heterogeneity: a self-organized federated learning framework for IoT. IEEE Internet Things J. https://doi.org/10.1109/jiot.2020.3007662
19. Zhang, L., Cai, Z., Wang, X.: FakeMask: a novel privacy preserving approach for smartphones. IEEE Trans. Netw. Serv. Manag. **13**(2), 335–348 (2016)

Outsourced Multi-authority ABE with White-Box Traceability for Cloud-IoT

Suhui Liu[1], Jiguo Yu[2($\boxtimes$)], Chunqiang Hu[3($\boxtimes$)], and Mengmeng Li[1]

[1] School of Information Science and Engineering, Qufu Normal University, Rizhao, Shandong, China
suhliu@126.com, 1143075608@qq.com
[2] School of Computer Science and Technology, Qilu University of Technology (Shandong Academy of Sciences), Shandong Computer Science Center (National Supercomputer Center in Jinan), Shandong Laboratory of Computer Network, Jinan, Shandong, People's Republic of China
jiguoyu@sina.com
[3] School of Big Data and Software Engineering, Chongqing University, Chongqing, China
chu@cqu.edu.cn

Abstract. Some unsettled security issues, such as illegal data access and secret key leakage, dramatically impact the popularity of cloud-assisted Internet of Things (Cloud-IoT). The attribute-based encryption (ABE) achieves data confidentiality and one-to-many data sharing simultaneously, yet it consumes too much to decrypt. In this paper, a multi-authority ABE scheme with verifiable outsourced decryption and white-box traceability is proposed, which greatly lightens the burden on IoT devices. Moreover fully hidden policy and user traceability are realized and replayable chosen ciphertext security is proved.

Keywords: Cloud-IoT · Attribute-based encryption · Verifiable outsourced decryption · White-box traceability · Fully hidden policy

1 Introduction

Cloud-assisted Internet of things (Cloud-IoT) is a new paradigm which can handle the huge amount of data produced by IoT devices more efficiently [10,16,22]. However, there are several security issue of outsourced storage [19,24], such as illegal access. The attribute-based encryption (ABE) [17,18] not only ensures the confidentiality of the cloud-stored data, it also achieves fine-grained access control and one-to-many data sharing. Traditional single-authority CP_ABE schemes do not adequately address the needs of the ubiquitous IoT devices. In [7], Chase *et al.* achieved a truly decentralized multi-authority ABE without a trusted central authority. Lewko *et al.* [12] proposed a distributed ABE scheme which uses the dual system encryption methodology to prove the security. In [8],

© Springer Nature Switzerland AG 2020
D. Yu et al. (Eds.): WASA 2020, LNCS 12384, pp. 322–332, 2020.
https://doi.org/10.1007/978-3-030-59016-1_27

Green *et al.* proposed an outsourced ABE scheme which minimizes the computational overhead of equipments by outsourcing the computational cost to the cloud.

In this paper, we propose a multi-authority attribute-based encryption scheme with verifiable outsourced decryption and white-box traceability for cloud-IoT. The main constrictions are summarized here:

- Considering the large number of devices in cloud-IoT, the attributes in our scheme are controlled by multiple authorities independently.
- Our scheme allows the access policy to be expressed as any monotone access structures. And the fully hidden access policy is supported to satisfy the privacy protection of IoT users.
- To meet the needs of resource-constrained IoT devices, our scheme realizes verifiable outsourced decryption.
- The white-box trace method is used to solve the private key leaking problem.

The rest of this paper is organized as follows: Sect. 2 reports the most related works and Sect. 3 introduces some preliminaries and the system model of our scheme. In Sect. 4, we propose the concrete construction of our scheme. Sect. 5 outlines the security theories of our scheme. The performance analysis is discussed in Sect. 6. We conclude in Sect. 7.

2   Related Work

Many advanced ABE papers have been proposed. Belguith *et al.* [2] proposed an private preserving ABE scheme which partially hides the access policy. In [5], Božović *et al.* proposed a multi-authority attribute-based encryption (MAABE) to manage the large amount of attributes more efficiently. Recently, Liu et al. proposed a searchable ABE scheme [15] which harnesses a coalition blochchain to manage user keys and control the user revocation efficiently. Hu *et al.* [11] proposed a fuzzy attribute-based signcryption scheme for the body area network. In [20], Yu et al. proposed an lightweight signcryption scheme with hybrid policy where most designcryption work are outsourced to the cloud server.

Table 1. Function comparison.

Scheme	MA	Access policy	Hidden policy	OutDecryption	Security	Traceability
[3]	Yes	LSSS	No	Yes	Selective RCPA	No
[14]	No	LSSS	No	Yes	Selective CPA	Yes
[21]	Yes	LSSS	No	No	Static security	Yes
Ours	Yes	LSSS	Fully	Verifiable	Selective RCCA	Yes

Abbreviation: MA: multiple authorities, RCPA: replayable chosen-plaintext attack security, CCA: chosen-ciphertext attack security.

The expensive pairing computations involved in the ABE decryption are obviously unacceptable for resource-constrained IoT devices. Green *et al.* [8]

proposed an outsourced attribute-based encryption scheme which uses a third-part server to pre-decrypt for users. Recently Li *et al.* [13] proposed an improved ABE scheme, which achieves verifiable outsourced decryption while reducing the computational burden greatly.

Another issue hinders the ABE for application is the leakage of decryption keys. Hinek *et al.* [9] considered the identity tracking solution to achieve white-box traceability by using the Boneh-Boyen signature [4]. Li *et al.* [14] proposed an outsourced ABE scheme in eHealth cloud, while they did not consider the privacy of access policies which might include sensitive information of users.

The comparison with some ABE schemes is in Table 1. As we can see, our scheme fulfills the basic security requirement and provides more comprehensive functions, such as fully-hidden policy, outsourced decryption and traceability.

3   Preliminaries and System Model

One-Way Anonymous Key Agreement [23]. We adopt a one-way anonymous key agreement [23] scheme to guarantee anonymity of our access structure. Assume there are two users Alice (ID_A) and Bob (ID_B) in this scheme. The KGC (key generation center) whose master secret is s. When Alice wants to keep her anonymity with Bob, the procedure of key agreement is listed as follows:

1) Alice calculates $Q_B = H(ID_B)$. She randomly chooses a number $r_a \in \mathbb{Z}_p^*$ to generate the pseudonym $P_A = Q_A^{r_a}$ and computes the session key $K_{A,B} = e(d_A, Q_B)^{r_a} = e(Q_A, Q_B)^{s \cdot r_a}$. Finally, she sends her pseudonyms P_A to Bob.
2) Bob calculates the session key $K_{A,B} = e(P_A, d_B) = e(Q_A, Q_B)^{s \cdot r_a}$ using his secret key d_B where $d_i = H(ID_i)^s \in \mathbb{G}$ is his private key for $i \in \{A, B\}$ and $H : \{0, 1\}^* \to \mathbb{G}$ is a strong collision-resistant hash function.

Strong Diffie Hellman Problem (q-SDH) [21]. Let $\mathbb{G}$ be a multiplicative cyclic group of order p with a generator g. Given a random $x \in \mathbb{Z}_p^*$ and a $q+1$ tuple $(g, g^x, g^{x^2}, ..., g^{x^q})$, the problem of computing a pair $(c, g^{\frac{1}{x+c}})$, where $c \in \mathbb{Z}_p^*$, is called the q-strong Diffie Hellman problem.

System Model. In this section, we present the system model in Fig. 1, which includes five entities as follows. 1) The central trusted authority (CTA) is only used to generate the public parameter. 2)Each attribute authority (AA) controls a set of attributes independently which can trace who leaks the private decryption key by recovering the global identity of a user from its key. 3) The cloud storage service provider (CS) is responsible for storing the ciphertext and outdecrypting for users. 4) The data owners (DO) are responsible for encrypting and uploading the ciphertext to the CS. 5) The data users (DU) denote someone who want to decrypt and use the data.

The proposed scheme consists of eight random algorithms, defined as follows:

1) *Setup*(λ) $\to PP$: The CTA runs this algorithm to generate the global parameters PP where λ is a security parameter.

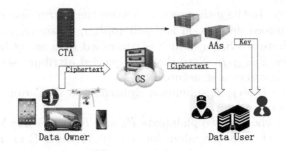

Fig. 1. System Model.

2) $Setup_{auth}(PP) \rightarrow (sk_{AAj}, pk_{AAj})$: Each AA runs this algorithm to generate their own pair of private key and public key.
3) $Encrypt(PP, \{pk_{AAj}\}, MSG, (\mathbb{M}, \rho)) \rightarrow CT$: The DO runs this algorithm to encrypt MSG then uploads the ciphertext to the cloud server.
4) $Keygen(PP, \{sk_{AAj}, pk_{AAj}\}, GID, S_{GID,j}) \rightarrow sk_{GID,j}$: Each related AA runs this algorithm independently and then sends the results to the user.
5) $Keygen_{out}(PP, sk_{GID}, (\mathbb{M}, \rho), CT) \rightarrow ok_{GID}$: The user runs this algorithm to generate his/her outsourced decryption key.
6) $Decrypt_{out}(PP, opk_{GID}, (\mathbb{M}, \rho), CT) \rightarrow CT'$: The CS runs this algorithm to partially decrypt the ciphertext.
7) $Decrypt(CT', osk_{GID}) \rightarrow MSG$: The user runs this algorithm to get the plaintext.
8) $Trace(PP, sk_{GID}, \{pk_{AAj}\}) \rightarrow GID$: First each AA_j verify the format of the decryption key needed to be traced, and then it runs the tracing algorithm to output the global identity (GID) of the guilty user.

Security Models - Confidentiality. Confidentiality is used against malicious data users. Our scheme adopts the replayable chosen-ciphertext security, which is proposed by Canetti *et al.* [6]. In our security model, we assume that the adversary can query any decryption key that cannot be used to decrypt the challenge ciphertext. In addition, we use the assumption in Lewko *et al.* [12], in which the adversary can only corrupt the authority statically. Let S_{AA} be the universe set of attribute authorities, S'_{AA} be the set of corrupted authorities. The details of the Exp^{Conf} security experiment defined between an adversary $\mathbb{A}$ and a challenger $\mathbb{C}$ are presented as follows.

1) **Initialization:** The adversary $\mathbb{A}$ chooses a challenge access structure $\Psi^* = (\mathbb{M}^*, \rho^*)$ and sends it to the challenger $\mathbb{C}$.
2) **Set Up:** $\mathbb{C}$ runs the $Setup(\lambda)$ algorithm to generate the global parameter PP. $\mathbb{A}$ chooses a set of corrupted attribute authorities: $S'_{AA} \subset S_{AA}$, then $\mathbb{A}$ runs the $Setup_{auth}$ algorithm to get corrupted AAs' pairs of private keys and public keys. And $\mathbb{C}$ runs the $Setup_{auth}$ algorithm to get pairs of private keys and public keys of honest attribute authorities then publishes the public keys.
3) **Query Phase 1:** $\mathbb{A}$ can repeatedly make any of the following queries:

a) Key Query: In the q-th query, $\mathbb{A}$ queries the decryption key sk_{GID_q} and the outsourced decryption key pair $(opk_{GID_q}, osk_{GID_q})$ associated with the attribute set S_{GID_q} which is controlled by a set of honest attribute authorities $S_{AA,GID}$. Note that the queried attribute set cannot satisfy the challenge access structure.

b) Decryption Query: $\mathbb{A}$ submits a ciphertext to $\mathbb{C}$. $\mathbb{C}$ runs the decryption algorithm to answer.

4) **Challenge:** $\mathbb{A}$ chooses two plaintexts R_0 and R_1 with same length and send them to $\mathbb{C}$. $\mathbb{C}$ chooses a random bit $b \in \{0, 1\}$, then $\mathbb{C}$ encrypts R_b under $(\mathbb{M}^*, \rho^*)$. Finally $\mathbb{C}$ returns the ciphertext CT_b to $\mathbb{A}$.

5) **Query Phase 2:** After receiving CT_b, $\mathbb{A}$ still can query a polynomially bounded number of queries as in Query Phase 1. Note that the response of the decryption query cannot be neither R_0 or R_1

6) **Guess:** $\mathbb{A}$ tries to guess b based on CT_b. The advantage of the adversary to win the experiment is defined as: $Adv_{\mathbb{A}}[Exp^{Conf}(1^{\xi})] = |Pr[b = b'] - \frac{1}{2}|$.

Definition 1. *An outsourced ABE scheme is RCCA-Secure against static corruption of the attribute authorities if $Adv_{\mathbb{A}}[Exp^{Conf}(1^{\xi})]$ is negligible for all PPT adversaries.*

4   Construction

Assume that there are n authorities in our scheme and each authority controls an attribute set denoted as S_{A,AA_j}. Assume that the number of attributes included in each S_{A,AA_j} is unequal and we define that each attribute is associated with an unique AA, such that $S_{A,AA_i} \cap S_{A,AA_j} = \emptyset$ for $\forall i, j$, and $\bigcup S_{A,AA_j} = S_A$.

Phase I: System Set Up. First, the CTA defines two multiplicative group $\mathbb{G}, \mathbb{G}_T$ of prime order p, and a symmetric bilinear map $e : \mathbb{G} \times \mathbb{G} \to \mathbb{G}_T$, where g is a generator of $\mathbb{G}$. Then the CTA defines three collusion resistant hash functions: $H : \{0.1\}^* \to \mathbb{G}, H_1 : \{0, 1\}^* \to \mathbb{Z}_p^*, H_2 : \{0, 1\}^* \to \{0, 1\}^k$ where k is the length of the symmetric key. Finally it outputs the global parameter:

$$PP = \{\mathbb{G}, \mathbb{G}_T, p, e, g, H, H_1, H_2\}$$

Phase II: Authority Set Up. First, the AA_j chooses two random numbers $\alpha_i, \beta_i \in \mathbb{Z}_p^*$ for each attribute $i \in S_{A,AA_j}$. Then it chooses three random numbers $h_j, a_j, b_j \in \mathbb{Z}_p^*$. Finally, it generates its pair of private key and public key:

$$sk_{AAj} = (\{\alpha_i, \beta_i\}_{i \in S_{AAj}}, h_j, a_j, b_j), \quad pk_{AAj} = (\{g^{\alpha_i}, g^{\beta_i}\}_{i \in S_{AAj}}, \ g^{h_j}, g^{a_j}, g^{b_j})$$

Phase III: Encryption. We assume the DO encrypts a message MSG with an access structure Ψ. Let S_Ψ be the attribute set which contains all attributes in the access structure Ψ. This phase contains three steps:

(1) Chooses a random number $a \in \mathbb{Z}_p^*$ and then computes $h = g^a$ and $q_i = e((g^{h_j})^a, H(i))$ where $i \in S_\Psi$. In order to fully hide the access policy, the DO replaces each attribute with the corresponding q_i. Then it converts the access policy to a LSSS access matrix $(\mathbb{M}_{l \times n}, \rho)$.

(2) Chooses a random element $R \in \mathbb{G}_T$ to calculate $s = H_1(R, MSG)$ and the symmetric key $Ksym = H_2(R)$. It computes $C_0 = Re(g, g)^s$. Then it selects a $p_i \in \mathbb{Z}_p$ for each row $\mathbb{M}_i$ of $\mathbb{M}$ and two random vectors $\boldsymbol{v} = [s, v_1, ..., v_n] \in \mathbb{Z}_p^n, \boldsymbol{w} = [0, w_1, ..., w_n] \in \mathbb{Z}_p^n$ to computer $\lambda_i = \mathbb{M}_i \times \boldsymbol{v}$ and $w_i = \mathbb{M}_i \times \boldsymbol{w}$. It computes:

$$C_{1,i} = g^{\lambda_i} g^{\alpha_{\rho(i)} p_i}, C_{2,i} = g^{p_i}, C_{3,i} = g^{w_i} g^{\beta_{\rho(i)} p_i}, C_{4,i} = g^{a_j p_i}, C_{5,i} = g^{b_j p_i}$$

It outputs the tuple $CT_{ABE} = (h, (\mathbb{M}_{l \times n}, \rho), C_0, \{C_{1,i}, C_{2,i}, C_{3,i}, C_{4,i}, C_{5,i}\}_{i \in [1,l]})$ where i presents a matrix row corresponding to an attribute.

(3) Uses K_{sym} to encrypts the message MSG by using a symmetric encryption algorithm. Denote the result as $CT_{sym} = Enc_{sym}(K_{sym}, MSG)$. Finally it uploads $CT = \{CT_{ABE}, CT_{sym}\}$ to the CS.

Phase IV: Decryption Key Generation. Each user holds an unique identity $GID \in \mathbb{Z}_p^*$ and an attribute set S_{GID} where each attribute is associated with a different attribute authority. Let $S_{AA,GID}$ be the set of related attribute authorities. According to $S_{AA,GID}$, we divide S_{GID} into $\{S_{GID,j}\}_{j \in S_{AA,GID}}$. When the user queries its decryption key, each related AA runs this algorithm as follows. First, the AA_j chooses a random number $r \in \mathbb{Z}_p^* \setminus \{-\frac{a_j + GID}{b_j}\}$ for each $i \in S_{GID,j}$, then it computes and returns the decryption key $sk_{GID,j} = \{K_{1,i}, K_{2,i}, K_{3,i}\}_{i \in S_{GID,j}}$ where:

$$K_{1,i} = g^{\frac{\alpha_j}{a_j + GID + b_j r}} H(GID)^{\frac{\beta_j}{a_j + GID + b_j r}}, \quad K_{2,i} = H(i)^{h_j}, \quad K_{3,i} = r$$

Finally the user can get its decryption key as $sk_{GID} = (\{sk_{GID,j}\}_{j \in S_{AA,GID}}, GID) = (\{K_{1,i}, K_{2,i}, K_{3,i}\}_{i \in S_{GID}}, GID)$.

Phase V: Outsourced Decryption Key Generation. The user runs this algorithm to get its outsourced decryption key and sends this key and the ciphertext to the CS. This phase contains the following two steps:

(1) Computes $q_i' = e(h, H(i)^{h_j}) = e(g^a, H(i)^{h_j}), \forall i \in S_{GID}$. Then it uses q_i' to replace the attribute i to get the attribute set S_{GID}'. The user gains the access structure $(\mathbb{M}_{l \times n}, \rho)$ from CT. Finally, the user identifies the set of attributes $L' = \{i : (\rho(i) \cap S_{GID}')_{i \in [l]}\}$ required for the decryption.

(2) Chooses a random number $z \in \mathbb{Z}_p^*$ as its $osk_{GID} = z$. It computes the outsourced decryption key $\{ok_{GID}\} = (\{opk_{GID}\}, osk_{GID})$ where:

$$opk_{GID} = (GID, \{K_{1,i}^{\frac{1}{z}}, K_{3,i}\}_{i \in L'}, g^{\frac{1}{z}}, H(GID)^{\frac{1}{z}})$$

Phase VI: Outsourced Decryption. First for each matrix row corresponding to an attribute i, the CS computes :

$$Q = \frac{e(g^{1/z}, C_{1,i}) e(H(GID)^{1/z}, C_{3,i})}{(K_{1,i}^{\frac{1}{z}}, C_{2,i}^{GID} C_{4,i} C_{5,i}^{K_{3,i}})} = e(g, g)^{\lambda_i/z} e(g, H(GID))^{w_i/z}$$

Then, the CS chooses a set of constants $\{c_i\}_{i \in [1,l]} \in \mathbb{Z}_p$ such that $\sum_i c_i \mathbb{M}_i = [1, 0, ..., 0]$ and computes the following equation, where $\lambda_i = \mathbb{M}_i \boldsymbol{v}$ and $w_i = \mathbb{M}_i \boldsymbol{w}$, so $\sum_{i=1}^{l} \lambda_i c_i = \sum_{i=1}^{l} M_i \boldsymbol{v} c_i = \boldsymbol{v}[1, 0, ..., 0] = s$ and $\sum_{i=1}^{l} w_i c_i = \sum_{i=1}^{l} M_i \boldsymbol{w} c_i = \boldsymbol{w}[1, 0, ..., 0] = 0$.

$$CT' = \prod_{i=1}^{l} Q^{c_i} = \prod_{i=1}^{l} e(g,g)^{c_i \lambda_{\rho(i)}/z} e(g, H(GID))^{c_i w_i/z} = e(g,g)^{s/z}$$

Finally the CS returns CT' to the user.

Phase VII: User Decryption. This phase contains the following two steps:

(1) Recovers the message: (Note that this step requires one exponentiation only and no pairing performance.)

$$R = \frac{C_0}{(CT')^{osk}} = \frac{C_0}{(e(g,g)^{s/z})^z} = \frac{C_0}{e(g,g)^s}$$

(2) Computes $K_{sym} = H_2(R)$, $MSG = Decrypt_{sym}(K_{sym}, CT_{sym})$ and $s = H_1(R, MSG)$. Judge if $CT' = e(g,g)^{s/z}$. If no, outputs $\perp$. Else, the user gains the right MSG.

Phase VIII: Trace. The traceability of our scheme is realized by the $Trace(PP, sk_{GID}, \{pk_{AAj}\})$ algorithm. Given a private key $sk_{GID} = (\{sk_{GID,j}\}_{j \in S'_{AA}}, GID) = (\{K_{1,i}, K_{2,i}, K_{3,i}\}_{i \in S_{GID}}, GID)$, this algorithm first checks the form of the key. If the key satisfies the form, then each authority runs the trace algorithm to find if: $\exists i \in S_{GID}$, s.t.

$$K_{1,i}, K_{2,i} \in \mathbb{G}, \qquad K_{3,i}, GID \in \mathbb{Z}_p^*,$$

$$e(K_{1,i}, g^{a_j} \cdot g^{(b_j)^{K_{3,i}}} \cdot g^{GID}) = e(g,g)^{\alpha_i} e(H(GID), g^{\beta_i}).$$

If so, the algorithm outputs the global identity GID of the guilty user.

5   Security Analysis

Theorem 1. *If Lewko et al. decentralized CP-ABE [12] is CPA-Secure, then our scheme is selectively RCCA-Secure according to Definition 1 such that $Adv_A[Exp^{Conf}] < Adv_A[Exp^{Lewko}]$.*

The main idea of this proof is that the advantage of a PPT adversary to break our scheme is smaller than the advantage to break scheme [12]. Details are omitted due to the space limitation.

Theorem 2. *If the q-SDH problem is hard in $\mathbb{G}$, our scheme is fully traceable.*

The main idea of this proof is that the advantage of a PPT adversary to break our scheme is equal to the advantage to break the Boneh-Boyen signature [4] which is proved to be secure based on the q-SDH assumption. Details are omitted due to the space limitation.

6   Performance Analysis

In Table 2 and Table 3, we compare our scheme with some ABE schemes in storage cost and computational cost. (Results do not include the computational and storage costs of the symmetric cryptography including hash operations.)

From Table 2, the length of the decryption key of all schemes are associated with the number of attributes in user attribute sets. The length of the outsourced decryption key of scheme [3] and ours are related to N_d. While the decryption key length of scheme [14] is related to N_u. The length of the ciphertext of all four schemes are associated with N_e. From Table 3, in [21], a user needs to operate $4N_d$ exponentiations in group $\mathbb{G}_T$ and $3N_d$ pairings to decrypt in which is too heavy for resource-limited devices. While a user only need one exponentiation in group $\mathbb{G}_T$ to decrypt in [3]. The cloud server performs N_d exponentiations in group $\mathbb{G}_T$ and $3N_d + 1$ pairings to semi-decrypt in [14], hence a user only needs three exponentiations in group $\mathbb{G}_T$ to decrypt.

Table 2. Storage cost.

Scheme	Decryption Key Length	OutDec Key Length	Ciphertext Length
[3]	$2N_u\|\mathbb{G}\|$	$(N_d+2)\|\mathbb{G}\|+\|\mathbb{Z}_p^*\|$	$(3N_e+1)\|\mathbb{G}\|+1\|\mathbb{G}_T\|$
[14]	$(2N_u+3)\|\mathbb{G}\|+2\|\mathbb{Z}_p\|$	$(2N_u+2)\|\mathbb{G}\|$	$(3N_e+2)\|\mathbb{G}\|+1\|\mathbb{G}_T\|$
[21]	$3N_u\|\mathbb{G}\|+N_u\|\mathbb{Z}_p^*\|+\|\mathbb{Z}_p\|$	–	$5N_e\|\mathbb{G}\|+(N_e+1)\|\mathbb{G}_T\|$
Ours	$2N_u\|\mathbb{G}\|+N_u\|\mathbb{Z}_p\|$	$(N_d+2)\|\mathbb{G}\|+\|\mathbb{Z}_p^*\|$	$(5N_e+1)\|\mathbb{G}\|+1\|\mathbb{G}_T\|$

Table 3. Computational cost.

Scheme	Key Gen	Encryption	OutDecryption	User decryption
[3]	$3N_u E$	$(N_u+5N_e+1)E+1E_T+N_u P_e$	$N_d E_T+3N_d P_e$	$1E_T$
[14]	$(4N_u+4)E$	$(5N_e+2)E+1E_T$	$N_d E_T+(3N_d+1)P_e$	$3E_T$
[21]	$5N_u E$	$(2N_e+1)E_T+6N_e E$	–	$4N_d E_T+3N_d P_e$
Ours	$3N_u E$	$(N_u+7N_e+1)E+1E_T+N_u P_e$	$3N_d E_T+3N_d P_e$	$1E_T$

Abbreviation: E: one exponentiation in $\mathbb{G}$, E_T: one exponentiation in $\mathbb{G}_T$, P_e: one pairing operation of the function e, N_e: the number of rows of the encryption LSSS access matrix, N_u: the number of attributes contained in the user attribute set, N_d: the number of attributes used in decryption, N_a: the number of attributes in the attribute universe.

Our scheme realizes verifiable outsourced decryption. The cloud costs $3N_d$ exponentiations in group $\mathbb{G}_T$ and $3N_d$ pairings to pre-decrypt. Thus, IoT devices only require one exponentiation in group $\mathbb{G}_T$ to decrypt in our scheme which significantly reduces the computational burden of resource-limited devices. More importantly, the verification cost of our verifiable outsourced decryption is one hash operation only. Moreover our scheme realises the additional trace function with little computational cost. The trace cost is $N_a(2E+H+3P)$ which is linear of the size of the universe set of attribute. However, because each attribute authority controls a specific attribute set and any two authority attribute set are disjoint in our scheme, the computational cost of this algorithm for each AA is linear of the size of its own attribute set.

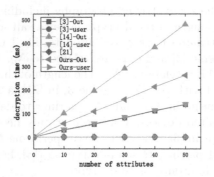

Fig. 2. Decryption Cost. (Color figure online)

The simulation is performed in a Ubuntu 16.4 desktop system with 3.0-GHz Intel Core(TM) i5-7400 CPU and 2-GB RAM by using Charm (version 0.50) [1], a Python-based rapid prototyping framework for cryptographic schemes. The results of decryption time cost are illustrated in Fig. 2. From that, we can see that most decryption work of our scheme is done in the outsourced decryption phase (the orange line) while the user overhead is super low (the green line) and nonlinear with the number of attributes, about 0.1 ms.

7   Conclusion

In this paper, we propose an outsourced attribute-based encryption scheme with white-box traceability which protects the privacy of the encryptor and the decryptor by fully hiding the access policy. Meanwhile the key leakage problem in ABE is solved by the user traceability algorithm to improve the security and applicability of our scheme. More importantly, our scheme outsources the decryption operation to an honest-but-curiouts third party, a resource-rich cloud server, which makes our scheme suitable for resource-constrained IoT devices.

Acknowledgment. This work was partially supported by National Key R&D Program of China with grant No. 2019YFB2102600, the NNSF of China under Grants 61832012, 61672321, 61771289, 61373027, 61702062 and 61932006, the Fundamental Research Funds for the Central Universities (2019CDQYRJ006), Chongqing Research Program of Basic Research and Frontier Technology (Grant cstc2018jcyjAX0334), Key Project of Technology Innovation and Application Development of Chongqing (CSTC2019jscx-mbdxX0044), and Overseas Returnees Innovation and Entrepreneurship Support Program of Chongqing (cx2018015).

References

1. Akinyele, J.A., et al.: Charm: a framework for rapidly prototyping cryptosystems. J. Cryptogr. Eng. **3**(2), 111–128 (2013). https://doi.org/10.1007/s13389-013-0057-3
2. Belguith, S., Kaaniche, N., Jemai, A., Laurent, M., Attia, R.: PAbAC: a privacy preserving attribute based framework for fine grained access control in clouds (2016)
3. Belguith, S., Kaaniche, N., Laurent, M., Jemai, A., Attia, R.: Phoabe: securely outsourcing multi-authority attribute based encryption with policy hidden for cloud assisted IoT. Comput. Netw. **133**, 141–156 (2018)
4. Boneh, D., Boyen, X.: Short signatures without random Oracles. In: Cachin, C., Camenisch, J.L. (eds.) EUROCRYPT 2004. LNCS, vol. 3027, pp. 56–73. Springer, Heidelberg (2004). https://doi.org/10.1007/978-3-540-24676-3_4
5. Božović, V., Socek, D., Steinwandt, R., Villányi, V.I.: Multi-authority attribute-based encryption with honest-but-curious central authority. Int. J. Comput. Math. **89**(3), 268–283 (2012)
6. Canetti, R., Krawczyk, H., Nielsen, J.B.: Relaxing chosen-ciphertext security. In: Boneh, D. (ed.) CRYPTO 2003. LNCS, vol. 2729, pp. 565–582. Springer, Heidelberg (2003). https://doi.org/10.1007/978-3-540-45146-4_33
7. Chase, M., Chow, S.S.: Improving privacy and security in multi-authority attribute-based encryption. In: Proceedings of the 16th ACM Conference on Computer and Communications Security, pp. 121–130 (2009)
8. Green, M., Hohenberger, S., Waters, B., et al.: Outsourcing the decryption of abe ciphertexts. In: USENIX Security Symposium, vol. 2011 (2011)
9. Hinek, M.J., Jiang, S., Safavi-Naini, R., Shahandashti, S.F.: Attribute-based encryption without key cloning. Int. J. Appl. Cryptogr. **2**(3), 250–270 (2012)
10. Hu, C., Pu, Y., Yang, F., Zhao, R., Alrawais, A., Xiang, T.: Secure and efficient data collection and storage of IoT in smart ocean. IEEE Internet Things J. 1 (2020). https://doi.org/10.1109/JIOT.2020.2988733
11. Hu, C., Zhang, N., Li, H., Cheng, X., Liao, X.: Body area network security: a fuzzy attribute-based signcryption scheme. IEEE J. Sel. Areas Commun. **31**(9), 37–46 (2013)
12. Lewko, A., Waters, B.: Decentralizing attribute-based encryption. In: Paterson, K.G. (ed.) EUROCRYPT 2011. LNCS, vol. 6632, pp. 568–588. Springer, Heidelberg (2011). https://doi.org/10.1007/978-3-642-20465-4_31
13. Li, J., Sha, F., Zhang, Y., Huang, X., Shen, J.: Verifiable outsourced decryption of attribute-based encryption with constant ciphertext length. Secur. Commun. Netw. **2017** (2017)
14. Li, Q., Zhu, H., Ying, Z., Zhang, T.: Traceable ciphertext-policy attribute-based encryption with verifiable outsourced decryption in ehealth cloud. Wirel. Commun. Mobile Comput. **2018** (2018)
15. Liu, S., Yu, J., Xiao, Y., Wan, Z., Wang, S., Yan, B.: BC-SABE: blockchain-aided searchable attribute-based encryption for cloud-IoT. IEEE Internet Things J. (2020). https://doi.org/10.1109/JIOT.2020.2993231
16. Pu, Y., Hu, C., Deng, S., Alrawais, A.: R^{2}PEDS: a recoverable and revocable privacy-preserving edge data sharing scheme. IEEE Internet Things J. 1 (2020)
17. Wang, X., Yu, H.: How to break MD5 and other hash functions. In: Cramer, R. (ed.) EUROCRYPT 2005. LNCS, vol. 3494, pp. 19–35. Springer, Heidelberg (2005). https://doi.org/10.1007/11426639_2

18. Waters, B.: Ciphertext-policy attribute-based encryption: an expressive, efficient, and provably secure realization. In: Catalano, D., Fazio, N., Gennaro, R., Nicolosi, A. (eds.) PKC 2011. LNCS, vol. 6571, pp. 53–70. Springer, Heidelberg (2011). https://doi.org/10.1007/978-3-642-19379-8_4

19. Xiao, Y., Jia, Y., Liu, C., Cheng, X., Yu, J., Lv, W.: Edge computing security: state of the art and challenges. Proc. IEEE **107**(8), 1608–1631 (2019)

20. Yu, J., Liu, S., Wang, S., Xiao, Y., Yan, B.: LH-ABSC: a lightweight hybrid attribute-based signcryption scheme for cloud-fog assisted IoT. IEEE Internet Things J. (2020). https://doi.org/10.1109/JIOT.2020.2988733

21. Zhang, K., Li, H., Ma, J., Liu, X.: Efficient large-universe multi-authority ciphertext-policy attribute-based encryption with white-box traceability. Sci. China Inf. Sci. **61**(3), 1–13 (2017). https://doi.org/10.1007/s11432-016-9019-8

22. Zheng, X., Cai, Z.: Privacy-preserved data sharing towards multiple parties in industrial IoTs. IEEE J. Sel. Commun. **38**(5), 968–979 (2020)

23. Zhong, H., Zhu, W., Xu, Y., Cui, J.: Multi-authority attribute-based encryption access control scheme with policy hidden for cloud storage. Soft Comput. **22**(1), 243–251 (2016). https://doi.org/10.1007/s00500-016-2330-8

24. Zhu, S., Li, W., Li, H., Tian, L., Luo, G., Cai, Z.: Coin hopping attack in blockchain-based IoT. IEEE Internet Things J. **6**(3), 4614–4626 (2018)

Deep Learning Enabled Reliable Identity Verification and Spoofing Detection

Yongxin Liu, Jian Wang, Shuteng Niu, and Houbing Song[(✉)]

Embry-Riddle Aeronautical University, Daytona Beach, FL 32114, USA
{liuy11,wangj14,shutengn}@my.erau.edu,
songh4@erau.edu

Abstract. Identity spoofing is one of the severe threats in Cyber-Physical Systems (CPS). These attacks can cause hazardous issues if they occur in Air Traffic Control (ATC) or other safety-critical systems. For example, a malicious UAV (Unmanned Aerial Vehicle) could easily impersonate a legitimate aircraft's identifier to trespass controlled airspace or broadcast falsified information to disable the airspace operation. In this paper, we propose a joint solution of identity verification and spoofing detection in ATC with assured performances. First, we use an enhanced Deep Neural Network with a zero-bias dense layer with an interpretable mechanism. Second, based on the enhanced Deep Neural Network, we reliably verify airborne targets' identity with the capability of detecting spoofing attacks. Third, we provide a continual learning paradigm to enable the dynamic evolution of the Deep Neural Network. Our approaches are validated using real Automatic dependent surveillance–broadcast (ADS–B) signals and can be generalized to secure other safety-critical CPS.

Keywords: Quickest detection · Deep learning · Continual learning

1 Introduction

The Internet of Things (IoT), the networking infrastructure for Cyber-Physical Systems (CPS), support a wide variety of next-generation applications and services [11]. And big data analytics enables the move from IoT to real-time control [18,23]. However, the open nature of IoT raises concerns in information security and public safety [1,2,4,5,17]. One example is the Air Traffic Control (ATC) system, which provides real-time tracking information of commercial flights. The compromise in such systems can cause catastrophic accidents. Currently, commercial aircraft can broadcast their positions, velocities, headings, and other essential information automatically to control towers and aircraft nearby. The most widely used protocol is the Automatic Dependent Surveillance-Broadcast (ADS–B) with the 1090ES data link [22].

ADS-B is the foundation of Next Generation Air Transportation System, or NextGen. However, from the perspective of IoT, the ADS-B protocol is not yet

© Springer Nature Switzerland AG 2020
D. Yu et al. (Eds.): WASA 2020, LNCS 12384, pp. 333–345, 2020.
https://doi.org/10.1007/978-3-030-59016-1_28

ready for global deployment, in which unmanned aircraft and manned aircraft have to co-exist. Currently, ADS-B messages are sent in plain text and do not contain cryptographic authentication features. The only way to know the sender of a message is by decoding the ICAO ID [22], which can be intercepted and forged easily. As a result, it is vulnerable to the identity spoofing attacks [7]. For example, a malicious unmanned aircraft system (UAS) or rogue aircraft can listen to the broadcasting channel and fetc.h legitimate ICAO IDs and trespass the controlled airspace with one or more fake identities. Therefore, it is of great significance for ATC to provide identity verification features.

Various efforts have been made to introduce cryptographic features to enhance ADS-B protocols [25–27]. However, these solutions have to modify millions of functioning devices. In contrast, non-cryptographic solutions are preferred to guarantee trustworthiness and maintain transparent compatibility with existing systems. Moreover, non-cryptographic can provide an extra layer of security when cryptographic mechanisms are compromised [3].

From a broader perspective of wireless communication, non-cryptographic verification of ADS-B falls within the topic of Specific Emitter Identification (SEI) [9]. In this context, to verify that a message signal is from a known source, traditional approaches require manual selection of distinctive features and apply the nearest neighbor matching [12]. In contrast, newer approaches directly apply Deep Neural Networks (DNN) to bypass the hardship of manual feature selection [6,20]. Even though DNNs provide promising results, their unclear internal mechanism causes concerns in safety-critical systems such as ADS-B in ATC. Moreover, continually inserting and deleting memories in DNNs require retraining from scratch and remain a time-consuming task.

In this paper, we provide a novel framework based on DNNs to achieve reliable non-cryptographic identify verification and identity spoofing detection with assured performances. The contributions of this paper are as follows:

- We propose an enhanced last layer to DNN classifiers, which provides interpretable behaviors and equivalent accuracy. To our best knowledge, this is one of the first works to reveal the close relationship between Deep Neural Networks and Nearest Neighbor Algorithm.
- We propose an enhanced continual learning strategy that shows less catastrophic forgetting.
- We use massive real ADS-B signals to verify the novelty and usability of our solutions.

The remainder of this paper is organized as follows: A literature review of identity verification is presented in Sect. 2. We formulate our problem in Sect. 3. Our proposed methodology is presented in Sect. 4. Performance evaluation is presented in Sect. 5. We conclude our paper in Sect. 6.

2 Related Works

Non-cryptographic identity verification have been investigated in ADS-B systems. Existing approaches can be classified into two categories: kinetic feature-based and radiometric feature-based.

2.1 Kinetic Feature-Based Approaches

Kinetic feature-based approaches aim to verify that a message is transmitted from an airborne platform with a known moving pattern. To verify that an ADS-B message is from a known aircraft, one can assume that the fake transmitters have different locations and velocities compared with real ones. On one hand, to verify locations, in [19], a practical reliability classifier of ADS-B broadcasts based on wide-area multilateration is presented, and they show that the error probabilities of GPS devices and the noises on the time of arrival has to be handled. A drawback of the multilateration methods is that receivers' timestamps need to be aligned in posterior processing. To eliminate the time synchronization, in [16], the authors propose to use the RSSI and Time of Arrival (ToA) feature map within the surveillance area to estimate the location of an aircraft roughly. On the other hand, the relative velocity of a transmitter can be measured by Doppler frequency shifting. For Doppler frequency spread based methods, in [8] and [21], frequency discrepancies are employed to verify the received location and velocity of ADS-B transponders. Their method increases the difficulty of ground-based static spoofing attacks. However, a malicious may control the center frequency of a transmitter to mimic a real transponder pattern.

2.2 Radiometric Feature-Based Approaches

Radiometric feature-based approaches aim to verify that a known transmitter transmits a message with identifiable signal features [15]. The imperfectness of wireless transmitters causes these features during manufacturing. Authors in [13] uses a statistical learning method to show that signal phrase features are useful to distinguish various ADS-B transponders. In [14], the authors only use the instantaneous phrase varying pattern of the intermediate frequency signal to feed in a simple two-layer neural network. The results of radiometric feature-based approaches indicate that statistical learning relies highly on the manual feature selection. To automate the process, in [28], the authors extract phase of each sample in each ADS-B packet and use the DNN to identify spoofing messages. In [6], the authors propose a deep CNN based classifier with residual-reception structure. They use raw ADS-B signals to distinguish the RF transmitters. Their work indicates that the deep neural network pre-trained using 50 labeled planes is capable of being transfer-trained to recognize with more than 100 aircraft. In general, Kinetic feature-based approaches require synchronized receivers or precise knowledge of the airspace, while the radiometric approaches only require general-purpose Software-Defined receivers with comparable performances. However, the behavior uncertainty, time-inefficiency, and flexibility of black-box algorithms such as DNN cause concerns on their applicability to safety-critical and latency-constrained wireless communication systems.

3   Problem Definition

The key idea of non-cryptographic radiometric identity verification in ADS-B is to exploit RF transmitters' unique signal patterns from received messages. We access the baseband signals of each message on the receiver side through Software-Defined Radio (SDR) receivers (e.g., USRP B210 or BladeRF2). At the receiver side, let's define that the rational message signal is $m[k]$ while the transmitted signal from transmitter i is $T_i(m[k])$, where $T_i(\cdot)$ represents the characteristics of transmitters. At the receiver side, signals are represented as:

$$\hat{r}_j[k] = R_{ij}(T_i(m[k])) + \delta[k] \tag{1}$$

where $R_{ij}(\cdot)$ and $\delta[k]$ denotes the receiver j's channel characteristics and channel noise, respectively. In the digital baseband, $R_{ij}(\cdot)$ is automatically removed and we actually have:

$$r_j[k] = T_i(m[k]) + R_{ij}^{-1}(\delta[k]) \tag{2}$$

Therefore, the goal of non-cryptographic identification of wireless transmitters is to estimate the joint features of function $T_i(\cdot)$, which discloses uniquely distinctive information of wireless transmitters. This process can be approximate by designing a classifier using Deep Neural Networks. The problem then converts into two questions:

1. How to design a DNN enabled classifier with assured performance and interpretable behaviors.
2. How to learn new transmitter continuously within the DNN in real-time without time-consuming re-training.

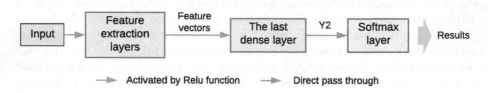

Fig. 1. Typical data flow of deep neural network

4   Methodology

4.1   Interpretable Zero-Bias Neural Network with Assured Performance

A typical architecture of conventional DNN is depicted in Fig. 1: input data are passed through a various convolutional layers for feature extraction and derive the final classification results in the last fully-connected layer (a.k.a, dense layer) with *Softmax* function. In the last dense layer, suppose that we have m-dimension input vectors with batch size k, we need to convert the input into k n-dimension outputs. A linear calculation is performed:

$$Y_1 = W_1 X + b_1 \tag{3}$$

where X denotes the input data, which is a m by k matrix. W_1 denotes the weights, which is an n by m matrix. Finally, b_1 denotes an n-dimension bias vector. We break the regular dense layer into two consecutive parts, depicted in Fig. 2, a regular dense layer denoted by L_1 and a dense layer with not bias neurons, L_2, respectively. Then, the function applied to input data becomes:

$$Y_2 = W_2 Y_1 = W_2 W_1 X + W_2 b_1 \tag{4}$$

where W_1 and b_1 belong to L_1 and W_2 belongs to L_2, respectively. Note that Eq. (4) and (3) are performing equivalent transforms to X and should not degrade the network performance.

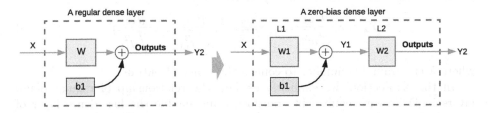

Fig. 2. Equavilent conversion of regular dense layer

In L_2, we can rewrite the matrix calculation into vectors:

$$Y_2 = [w_{21}, w_{22}, ..., w_{2n}]^T [y_{11}, y_{12}, ..., y_{1k}] \tag{5}$$

where $w_{21}, ..., w_{2n}$ are row vectors corresponding to n output classes; $y_{11}, ..., y_{1k}$ are k column vectors corresponding to the batch size. Each column vector denotes latent features. For specific vector y_{1k}, its corresponding output at L_2 is:

$$Y_2[y_{1k}] = [w_{21} \cdot y_{1k}, w_{22} \cdot y_{1k}, ..., w_{2n} \cdot y_{1k}] \tag{6}$$

where y_{1k} are feature vectors. If the output is followed by a *Softmax* layer, the position of the largest element in $Y_2[y_{1k}]$ is picked up as classification output. Equation (6) can be rewritten using *Cosine Similarity*:

$$w_{2n} \cdot y_{1k} = ||w_{2n}|| \cdot ||y_{1k}|| \cdot cos(w_{2n}, y_{1k}) \tag{7}$$

If we take $w_{21}, ..., w_{2n}$ as fingerprints of classes 1 to n, we conclude that the zero-bias dense layer L_2 actually calculates a scaled version of cosine similarities among input against fingerprints of target classes.

Although the magnitude of an input feature vector $\|\boldsymbol{y_{1k}}\|$ seems to take effect as in Eq. (7), but in the consecutive Softmax layer, the magnitude $\|\boldsymbol{y_{1k}}\|$ only contributes to a common base number as in Eq. (8):

$$Softmax(L_2) = \frac{(\exp \|\boldsymbol{y_{1k}}\| \cdot \|\boldsymbol{w_{2n}}\|)^{cos(\boldsymbol{w_{2n}},\boldsymbol{y_{1k}})}}{\sum_n (\exp \|\boldsymbol{y_{1k}}\| \cdot \|\boldsymbol{w_{2n}}\|)^{cos(\boldsymbol{w_{2n}},\boldsymbol{y_{1k}})}} \tag{8}$$

Where $\exp \|\boldsymbol{y_{1k}}\|$ is the common base number and controls the steepness of the monotonic Softmax curve. However, the non-uniform magnitudes of fingerprints $\boldsymbol{w_{21}}, ..., \boldsymbol{w_{2n}}$ could cause unnecessary decision bias or partiality. For alleviation, we can replace Eq. (5) with Eq. (9):

$$\boldsymbol{Y_2} = [\frac{\boldsymbol{w_{21}}}{\sqrt{\boldsymbol{w_{21}^2}}}, ..., \frac{\boldsymbol{w_{2n}}}{\sqrt{\boldsymbol{w_{2n}^2}}}]^T [\boldsymbol{y_{11}}, ..., \boldsymbol{y_{1k}}] \tag{9}$$

Noted that, Eq. (9) is still a linear operation as long as network weights are fixed after training. In practical scenarios, we can further eliminate the magnitude of feature vectors as in Eq. (10). Our experiments show that there's no significant influence to the network performance.

$$\boldsymbol{Y_2} = \lambda[\frac{\boldsymbol{w_{21}}}{\sqrt{\boldsymbol{w_{21}^2}}}, ..., \frac{\boldsymbol{w_{2n}}}{\sqrt{\boldsymbol{w_{2n}^2}}}]^T [\frac{\boldsymbol{y_{11}}}{\sqrt{\boldsymbol{y_{11}^2}}}, ..., \frac{\boldsymbol{y_{1k}}}{\sqrt{\boldsymbol{y_{1k}^2}}}] \tag{10}$$

where λ is a trainable number to control the range of output.

In this subsection, we explicitly explain the relationship of regular dense layers in DNN with equivalent transforms and enable the last dense layer of any DNN to perform zero-bias nearest neighbor matching. We provide two close remarks of dense layers for arbitrary neural networks:

Remark 1 (Property of dense layers). If outputs of a dense layer represent the degrees of confidence of corresponding class/position against an input, then each confidence degree is jointly controlled by the magnitude of the class/position-related fingerprint, the fingerprint's cosine similarity to the input, and the bias neuron of this class.

Remark 2 (Zero-bias enhancement). We replace the last dense layer of any DNN with a serialized structure consisting of a regular dense layer (L_1) and a zero-bias similarity comparing layer (L_2). Moreover, this replacement would not degrade the networks' performance after training.

4.2   Zero-Bias Neural Network-Enabled Identity Verification of ADS-B Transmitters

Signal Feature Extraction: Pulse Position Modulation (PPM) is used in ADS-B. The modulation scheme is equivalent to the Binary Amplitude Shift Keying. Therefore, a transmitter's characteristic function $T_i(\cdot)$ can be expressed as:

$$T_i(m[k]) = m[k] + \Phi_i(m[k]) \tag{11}$$

where $\Phi(m[k])$ denotes the nonlinear effects. Therefore, from the perspective of signal processing we can first remove the rational part $m[k]$ from raw based bands. The rational signal is reconstructed from decoded bit streams:

$$\hat{m}[k] = Amp_m \cdot Intp(B[p]) \tag{12}$$

where Amp_m is the amplitude of received digital baseband signal $r_j[k]$ and $Intp(\cdot)$ is the interpolation function which transform binary bits into amplitude pulses. Combine with Eq. (2), We estimate $\Phi_i(m[k])$ as:

$$\hat{\Phi}_i(m[k]) \approx r_j[k] - \hat{m}[k] \tag{13}$$

Hereon, we denote $\hat{\Phi}_i(m[k])$ as time domain residuals. The time domain residual does not contain message related information and can prevent learning algorithms from converging onto trivial features.

In ADS-B system, frequency shift may occur due to the Doppler effects, therefore, we further derive the frequency domain residuals as:

$$R_f(\omega) = FFT(r_j[k]) - FFT(\hat{m}[k]) \tag{14}$$

where $FFT(\cdot)$ represents the 1024 point Fast Fourier Transform. Noted that we can not mathematically combine the two Fourier transforms since $r_j[k]$ can be complex-valued while $\hat{m}[k]$ is in real numbers. We convert it into a magnitude sequence ($\|R_f(\omega)\|$), namely Mag.-Freq. residual, and a phase sequence ($\angle R_f(\omega)$), namely Phase-Freq. residual, respectively.

Reliable Identity Verification: We use similar architecture as in ResNet [24] as depicted in Fig. 3.

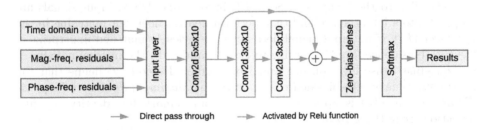

Fig. 3. Zero-bias deep neural network for ADS-B transponder verification

Signal features are fed into a zero-bias dense layer enabled DNN. The convolutional layers are used to extract latent features, and the final zero-bias dense layer is employed to perform the nearest neighbor matching in the latent space. We combine the automatic latent feature extraction of DNN with the explainable behavior of nearest neighbor matching in equivalent performances.

Continual Learning in Zero-Bias Deep Neural Network. Continual learning requires that a neural network can learn to classify new novel targets without needing to re-training all samples from scratch. In Eq. (7), we show that in the zero-bias dense layer, each class (transponder) is automatically associated with a unique fingerprint vector $w_{21}, ..., w_{2n}$. Therefore, we can propose a continual learning scheme:

Remark 3 (Continual learning using the zero-bias dense layer). To enable a neural network to recognize a new class, we only need to insert its representative fingerprint in the nearest neighbor matching layer (L_2).

Given a pre-trained neural network (DNN_1) with the zero-bias dense layer, continual learning on a new task is performed as follows:

Step 1: Generate initial fingerprint of each new class by averaging their feature vectors, that are generated from the training set of a new task.

Step 2: Concatenate initial fingerprints into the last dense layer.

Step 3: Lock the weights of previous layers and old fingerprints in the zero-bias dense layer. The newly concatenated fingerprints are allowed to change freely. Noted that at this stage, the network is partially locked.

Step 4: Use training set of Task-2 to perform network training.

Notably, we do not need to retrain old training data to learn a new task. This advantage is critical for device identification in latency-constrained scenarios.

Identity Spoofing Detection: In the context of identity spoofing attack, we define that an adversary has collected various legitimate ICAO IDs within controlled airspace passively, and it can transmit falsified ADS-B message with arbitrary legitimate ICAO IDs. We also assume that the fingerprint of an adversary's transponder does not exist zero-bias layer of the surveillance DNN.

According to the analysis in Sect. 4.1, in zero-bias DNN, input signals are mapped into a latent space and then perform nearest neighbor matching in the last layer (L_2). If an input signal does not find a closely matched fingerprint in the zero-bias dense layer, according to Eq. (9) and (10), the maximum value of the zero-bias dense layer output would be smaller. Hereon, we define that the maximum value of zero-bias dense layer output as *Maximum Similarity Response (MSR)*. If Eq. (10) is applied, we come to our remark for identity spoofing detection using the zero-bias dense layer:

Remark 4. The Maximum Similarities Response (MSR) of known inputs would distribute close to positive λ while the maximum confidences of abnormal inputs are smaller and would be distributed relatively closer to negative λ.

In this way, we can use threshold methods to securely separate known (legitimate) and unknown (unauthorized) transponder signals.

5   Evaluation and Discussions

5.1   Data Collection

In the data collection pipeline (in Fig. 4), we used a modified *gr-adsb* library to decode ADS-B messages and store raw baseband digital signals. We collected the ADS-B signal from more than 140 aircraft at Daytona Beach international airport (ICAO: DAB) for 24 24 h (Jan 4th, 2020) using a Software-Defined Radio receiver (USRP B210). Our receiver is configured with a sample rate of 8 8 MHz. During this period, more than 30,000 ADS-B messages are collected with signal-to-noise ratio depicted in Fig. 5.

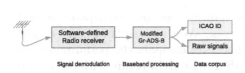

Fig. 4. Collection pipeline of ADS-B signals.

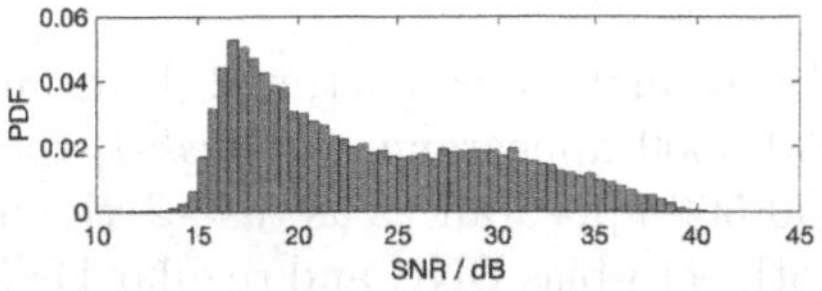

Fig. 5. SNR distribution of received signals.

5.2   Identity Verification and Spoofing Attack Detection

We compare the training performance of proposed zero-bias layer and regular dense layer, on the same dataset is given in Fig. 6. They can reach almost identical performance in terms of validation accuracy. However, the zero-bias layer requires more training iterations. The results indicate that the zero-bias DNN can clearly verify known transponders. We further compare the maximum similarity response of DNNs with our zero-bias dense layer. We randomly pick ADS-B signals from 30 aircraft to train the neural network and use signals from the remaining 120 aircraft as unseen novel devices' signals. The results are given in Fig. 8. As depicted, the maximum similarity response of known and unknown signals forms two statistically distinctive distributions. Even if we do not know the distribution of maximum similarity response of unknown wireless transponders with a fake identity, we can still safely assume that their similarity response is statistically different from known (legitimate) ones (Fig. 8).

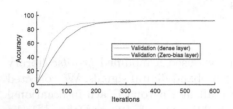

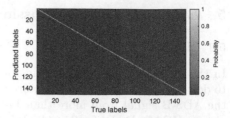

Fig. 6. Comparison of training performance.

Fig. 7. Confusion matrix of known transponder verification.

5.3   Continual Learning of New Wireless Transmitters

To evaluate our continual learning mechanism, we use transponders with 500 5000 appearances as *task-1*, the old task. We then use transponders with 250 500 appearances as *task-2*, the new task. We compare the performances on both zero-bias DNN and regular DNN with similar architecture with our continual learning strategy and Elastic Weight Consolidation (EWC) [10]. The neural networks are initially trained on *task-1* and use continual learning mechanisms to learn *task-2*. We compare their performances in terms of catastrophic forgetting (loss of old task after training on new class). As depicted in Fig. 9, the proposed zero-bias dense layer enabled DNN is less likely to forget than regular DNN. Moreover, the elastic weight consolidation don't seem to be a good solution since dramatic severe forgetting is observed. This phenomenon indicates that DNN with zero-bias dense layer needs better protection on critical connections.

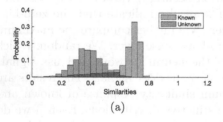

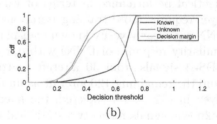

(a)

(b)

Fig. 8. Performance of maximum similarity response of spoofing detection in deep neural networks

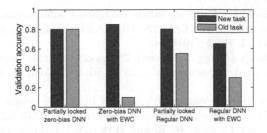

Fig. 9. Comparison of continual learning

6 Conclusion

In this paper, we provide a novel and reliable deep learning framework for reliable identity verification and spoofing detection. Unlike existing works, we focus on how to enable deep learning to be dependable in real-world safety-critical scenarios. It's highlighted that we thoroughly analyze the essence of deep neural networks and provide an enhanced solution, the zero-bias layer for better interpretability and reliability in ADS-B signal classification. Accordingly, we design our own continual learning and identity spoofing detection mechanisms. Experiments using real ADS-B signals demonstrate promising results, which convinces us that our solution is adaptable to practice.

Acknowledgement. This research was partially supported through Embry-Riddle Aeronautical University's Faculty Innovative Research in Science and Technology (FIRST) Program and the National Science Foundation under Grant No. 1956193.

References

1. Butun, I., Österberg, P., Song, H.: Security of the Internet of Things: vulnerabilities, attacks, and countermeasures. IEEE Commun. Surv. Tutorials **22**(1), 616–644 (2020)
2. Cai, Z., He, Z.: Trading private range counting over big IoT data. In: IEEE 39th International Conference on Distributed Computing Systems (ICDCS), pp. 144–153. IEEE (2019)
3. Cai, Z., He, Z., Guan, X., Li, Y.: Collective data-sanitization for preventing sensitive information inference attacks in social networks. IEEE Trans. Dependable Secure Comput. **15**(4), 577–590 (2016)
4. Cai, Z., Zheng, X.: A private and efficient mechanism for data uploading in smart cyber-physical systems. IEEE Trans. Network Sci. Eng. **7**, 766–775 (2018)
5. Cai, Z., Zheng, X., Yu, J.: A differential-private framework for urban traffic flows estimation via taxi companies. IEEE Trans. Ind. Inf. **15**(12), 6492–6499 (2019)
6. Chen, S., Zheng, S., Yang, L., Yang, X.: Deep learning for large-scale real-world ACARS and ADS-B radio signal classification. arXiv preprint arXiv:1904.09425 (2019)
7. Costin, A., Francillon, A.: Ghost in the air (traffic): on insecurity of ADS-B protocol and practical attacks on ADS-B devices. Black Hat, USA, pp. 1–12 (2012)

8. Ghose, N., Lazos, L.: Verifying ads-b navigation information through doppler shift measurements. In: IEEE/AIAA 34th Digital Avionics Systems Conference (DASC), pp. 4A2-1. IEEE (2015)

9. Huang, G., Yuan, Y., Wang, X., Huang, Z.: Specific emitter identification based on nonlinear dynamical characteristics. Can. J. Electri. Comput. Eng. **39**(1), 34–41 (2016)

10. Huszár, F.: Note on the quadratic penalties in elastic weight consolidation. In: Proceedings of the National Academy of Sciences, p. 201717042 (2018)

11. Jeschke, S., Brecher, C., Song, H., Rawat, D.B. (eds.): Industrial Internet of Things. SSWT. Springer, Cham (2017). https://doi.org/10.1007/978-3-319-42559-7

12. Leonardi, M.: ADS-B anomalies and intrusions detection by sensor clocks tracking. IEEE Trans. Aerosp. Electron. Syst. **55**(5), 2370–2381 (2018)

13. Leonardi, M., Di Fausto, D.: ADS-B signal signature extraction for intrusion detection in the air traffic surveillance system. In: 2018 26th European Signal Processing Conference (EUSIPCO), pp. 2564–2568. IEEE (2018)

14. Leonardi, M., Di Gregorio, L., Di Fausto, D.: Air traffic security: aircraft classification using ADS-B message's phase-pattern. Aerospace **4**(4), 51 (2017)

15. Liang, Y., Cai, Z., Yu, J., Han, Q., Li, Y.: Deep learning based inference of private information using embedded sensors in smart devices. IEEE Netw. **32**(4), 8–14 (2018)

16. Liu, G., Zhang, R., Wang, C., Liu, L.: Synchronization-free gps spoofing detection with crowdsourced air traffic control data. In: 2019 20th IEEE International Conference on Mobile Data Management (MDM), pp. 260–268. IEEE (2019)

17. Liu, Y., Wang, J., Song, H., Li, J., Yuan, J.: Blockchain-based secure routing strategy for airborne mesh networks. In: 2019 IEEE International Conference on Industrial Internet (ICII), pp. 56–61. IEEE (2019)

18. Lv, Z., Song, H., Basanta-Val, P., Steed, A., Jo, M.: Next-generation big data analytics: state of the art, challenges, and future research topics. IEEE Trans. Ind. Inf. **13**(4), 1891–1899 (2017)

19. Monteiro, M., Barreto, A., Kacem, T., Carvalho, J., Wijesekera, D., Costa, P.: Detecting malicious ADS-B broadcasts using wide area multilateration. In: 2015 IEEE/AIAA 34th Digital Avionics Systems Conference (DASC), pp. 4A3-1. IEEE (2015)

20. Pang, J., Huang, Y., Xie, Z., Han, Q., Cai, Z.: Realizing the heterogeneity: a self-organized federated learning framework for IoT. IEEE Internet Things J. 1 (2020). https://doi.org/10.1109/JIOT.2020.3007662

21. Schäfer, M., Leu, P., Lenders, V., Schmitt, J.: Secure motion verification using the doppler effect. In: Proceedings of the 9th ACM Conference on Security & Privacy in Wireless and Mobile Networks, pp. 135–145. ACM (2016)

22. Sun, J.: An open-access book about decoding mode-s and ADS-B data, May 2017. https://mode-s.org/

23. Sun, Y., Song, H., Jara, A.J., Bie, R.: Internet of things and big data analytics for smart and connected communities. IEEE Access **4**, 766–773 (2016)

24. Szegedy, C., Ioffe, S., Vanhoucke, V., Alemi, A.A.: Inception-v4, inception-resnet and the impact of residual connections on learning. In: Thirty-first AAAI Conference on Artificial Intelligence (2017)

25. Wang, J., et al.: Fountain code enabled ads-b for aviation security and safety enhancement. In: 2018 IEEE 37th International Performance Computing and Communications Conference (IPCCC), pp. 1–7. IEEE (2018)

26. Yang, A., Tan, X., Baek, J., Wong, D.S.: A new ADS-B authentication framework based on efficient hierarchical identity-based signature with batch verification. IEEE Trans. Serv. Comput. **10**(2), 165–175 (2015)
27. Yang, H., Zhou, Q., Yao, M., Lu, R., Li, H., Zhang, X.: A practical and compatible cryptographic solution to ADS-B security. IEEE Internet Things J. **6**(2), 3322–3334 (2018)
28. Ying, X., Mazer, J., Bernieri, G., Conti, M., Bushnell, L., Poovendran, R.: Detecting ADS-B spoofing attacks using deep neural networks. arXiv preprint arXiv:1904.09969 (2019)

On-Line Learning-Based Allocation
of Base Stations and Channels in
Cognitive Radio Networks

Zhengyang Liu[1], Feng Li[1(✉)], Dongxiao Yu[1(✉)], Holger Karl[2], and Hao Sheng[3]

[1] School of Computer Science and Technology, Shandong University, Qingdao, China
2018148240mail.sdu.edu.cn,
{fli,dxyu}@sdu.edu.cn
[2] Department of Computer Science, Paderborn University, Paderborn, Germany
holger.karl@upb.de
[3] School of Computer Science and Engineering, Beihang University, Beijing, China
shenghao@buaa.edu.cn

Abstract. We consider the following fundamental problem of dynamic spectrum scheduling in cognitive radio networks. There are N secondary users, each of which gets access to a set of K channels through a collection of M base stations for data communications. Our aim is at addressing the so-called *Joint Optimization of Base Station and Channel Allocation* (JOBC) towards maximizing the total throughput of the users with the diverse uncertainties of the channels across different base stations and users. To serve this goal, we first investigate a simplified off-line version of the problem where we propose a greedy $1/M$-approximation algorithm with the qualities of the channels assumed to be known. By taking the greedy off-line algorithm as a subroutine, we then propose an on-line learning-based algorithm by leveraging a combinatorial multi-armed bandit, which entails polynomial storage overhead and results in a regret (with respect to its off-line counterpart) logarithmic in time.

Keywords: Cognitive radio networks · Multi-armed bandits · Channel allocation

1 Introduction

Cognitive radio techniques have stimulated considerable interests in improving spectrum utilization by dynamic spectrum access. Since spectrum is usually of dynamic quality due to intermittent primary users' channel use, while a careful

This work is partially supported by National Key R&D Program of China (Grant No. 2019YFB2102600), NSFC (Grant No. 61702304, 61971269, 61832012), Shandong Provincial Natural Science Foundation (Grant No. ZR2017QF005), Industrial Internet Innovation and Development Project in 2019 of China, the DFG Priority Programme Cyber-Physical Networking (SPP 1914), and German Research Foundation grant (NICCI).

© Springer Nature Switzerland AG 2020
D. Yu et al. (Eds.): WASA 2020, LNCS 12384, pp. 346–358, 2020.
https://doi.org/10.1007/978-3-030-59016-1_29

prior measurement of the spectrum is not always available. It is quite challenging to improve the utilization of the spectrum with such uncertainties.

In this paper, we consider a typical cognitive radio system where a group of secondary users have access to a set of channels through a collection of base stations for data communications. The goal is to dynamically allocate M base stations and K channels to the N secondary users to improve the data rate summed over all these users. On one hand, since the base stations and the users are usually geographically dispersed, the transmission links (from the secondary users to the base stations) may be in proximity of different primary users such that each channel has its quality varying across different links; on other hand, the base stations usually have limited capacities to serve the secondary users, so as to ensure the qualities of the services offered to the connected ones. Therefore, although prior proposals utilized machine learning techniques (e.g., multi-armed bandit approaches in [5,9,15]) to address the uncertainties of the channels, they usually only matched channels and users, while extending the existing channel allocation approaches to this scenario is highly non-trivial.

To this end, we investigate the problem of *Joint Optimization of Base station and Channel allocations* (JOBC) towards maximizing expected network throughput with the diverse uncertainties of the channels. We first investigate a simplified off-line version of our JOBC problem to inspire our on-line learning-based algorithm design. In particular, we prove its NP-hardness and propose a $1/M$-approximation algorithm. We then leverage the multi-armed bandit approach to design an on-line, learning-based algorithm where we fully exploit the correlation across different allocation configurations to guarantee polynomial storage overhead. With the help of the trade-off between exploitation and exploration enabled by *Upper Confidence Bound* (UCB) indexing, the regret between our algorithm and its off-line counterpart can be polynomial in M, N and K, and logarithmic in time.

2   System Model and Problem Formulation

Consider a cognitive radio network with N secondary users (which are termed as "users" in the following without inducing any ambiguity), M base stations (BSes) and K channels where $N \geq M$ and $K \geq M$. We suppose the network is well synchronized such that time can be divided into a sequence of slots $t = 1, 2, \cdots, T$ where T denotes the time horizon. We assume each BS $j \in [M]$ [1] has a capacity $\tau_j \geq 1$ which indicates the maximum number of the users it serves simultaneously with one of the channels in a time slot. Let $\tau = \{\tau_j\}_{j \in [M]}$ and $\tau_{max} = \max\{\tau_1, \cdots, \tau_M\}$. Without loss of generality, we assume that $\sum_{j=1}^{M} \tau_j \geq N$. Let $r_{i,j,k}(t)$ denote the stochastic throughput (reward) of user i accessing channel k through BS j in slot t when there is no primary user occupying the channel. For $\forall i \in [N], j \in [M], k \in [K]$, we assume $r_{i,j,k}(t)$ is normalized into $[0, 1]$ and follows a probability distribution independently and identically across

---

[1] In this paper, let $[M] = \{1, 2, \cdots, M\}$ where M is a positive integer.

time t. We also suppose the probability has an *unknown* mean $\mu_{i,j,k}$, and denote by μ the set of all these means.

A configuration in slot t is defined by $x_u(t) = \{(i, b_i(t), c_i(t))\}_{i \in [N]}$ where $b_i(t) \in [M]$ and $c_i(t) \in [K]$ are the BS and channel assigned to user i in slot t, respectively. In any slot t, the configuration $x_u(t)$ is said to be *feasible* if the following constraints are respected in each time slot t: i) a BS works with at most one channel; ii) to avoid interference, each channel is assigned to at most one BS; iii) for each BS, the number of the connected users cannot exceed its capacity; iv) each user is connected to at most one BS. In each slot t, the expected total reward yielded by adopting the configuration $x_u(t)$ is defined by

$$R_\mu(x_u(t)) = \sum_{(i,j,k) \in x_u(t)} \mathbb{E}[r_{i,j,k}(t)] = \sum_{(i,j,k) \in x_u(t)} \mu_{i,j,k} \qquad (1)$$

Assuming $\mathcal{X}$ denote the set of all feasible configurations, our JOBC problem can be formulated as

$$\max_{x_u(t) \in \mathcal{X}} \mathbb{R}_\mu(T) = \sum_{t=1}^{T} \mathbb{E}[R_\mu(x_u(t))] \qquad (2)$$

In particular, we are interested in designing sequential configurations $\{x(t)\}_{t \in [T]}$ such that the expected cumulative reward $\mathbb{R}_\mu(T)$ within the time horizon T can be maximized with $\mu_{i,j,k}$ unknown for $\forall(i, j, k) \in \mathcal{D}$ (where $\mathcal{D} = [N] \times [M] \times [K]$). Note that, the randomness of $R_\mu(x_u(t))$ stems from the randomized sequential configurations $x_u(t)$.

3   An Off-Line Greedy Algorithm

To inspire our on-line learning-based algorithm design, we start with a simplified off-line version of our JOBC problem where we assume $\mu_{i,j,k}$ is known for $\forall(i, j, k) \in \mathcal{D}$ and our goal is to find the optimal off-line configuration x_μ such that the expected total throughput of the users can be maximized as follows

$$\max_{x \in \mathcal{X}} \ R_\mu(x) = \sum_{(i,j,k) \in x} \mu_{i,j,k} \qquad (3)$$

To this end, we propose a greedy algorithm as shown in Algorithm 1. We initialize $\mathcal{N} = [N]$, $\mathcal{M} = [M]$ $\mathcal{K} = [K]$, and repeat the following steps until $\mathcal{N} = \emptyset$. In each iteration, for $\forall(j, k) \in \mathcal{M} \times \mathcal{K}$, we first assume $\ell = \min\{|\mathcal{N}|, \tau_j\}$ and compute the top-ℓ users

$$\mathcal{N}_{j,k} = \{i \in \mathcal{N} \mid \mu_{i,j,k} \geq \mu_{i',j,k}, \text{for } \forall i' \notin \mathcal{N}_{j,k}\}, \qquad (4)$$

with $|\mathcal{N}_{j,k}| = \ell$ (see Lines 3–6). By letting the users in $\mathcal{N}_{j,k}$ access channel k through BS j, the yielded expected total reward can be calculated as $\sum_{i \in \mathcal{N}_{j,k}} \mu_{i,j,k}$. We select $(\hat{j}, \hat{k}) \in \mathcal{M} \times \mathcal{K}$ such that

$$(\hat{j}, \hat{k}) = \arg \max_{(j,k) \in \mathcal{M} \times \mathcal{K}} \sum_{i \in \mathcal{N}_{j,k}} \mu_{i,j,k} \qquad (5)$$

and allocate the users in $\mathcal{N}_{\hat{j},\hat{k}}$ and channel $\hat{k}$ to the BS $\hat{j}$ (see Lines 7–10). We terminate the iteration by removing the BS $\hat{j}$ from $\mathcal{M}$, the channel k from $\mathcal{K}$ and the users $\mathcal{N}_{\hat{j},\hat{k}}$ from $\mathcal{N}$ (as shown by Lines 11–13).

Algorithm 1: An off-line greedy algorithm Greedy_μ.

Input: A problem instance $([N], [M], [K], \tau, \mu)$
Output: A (nearly) optimal configuration $x_\mu^* \in \mathcal{X}$
1 Initialization: $\mathcal{N} = [N]$, $\mathcal{M} = [M]$, $\mathcal{K} = [K]$ and $x_\mu^* = \emptyset$;
2 **while** $\mathcal{N} \neq \emptyset$ **do**
3   **foreach** $(j, k) \in \mathcal{M} \times \mathcal{K}$ **do**
4        $\ell = \min\{|\mathcal{N}|, \tau_j\}$;
5   Compute the set of the top-ℓ users $\mathcal{N}_{j,k}$;
6   **end**
7     $(\hat{j}, \hat{k}) = \arg\max_{(j,k)\in\mathcal{M}\times\mathcal{K}} \sum_{i\in\mathcal{N}_{j,k}} \mu_{i,j,k}$;
8   **foreach** $i \in \mathcal{N}_{\hat{j},\hat{k}}$ **do**
9        $x_\mu^* \leftarrow x_\mu^* \cup \{(i, \hat{j}, \hat{k})\}$;
10   **end**
11    $\mathcal{N} \leftarrow \mathcal{N}/\mathcal{N}_{\hat{j},\hat{k}}$;
12    $\mathcal{M} \leftarrow \mathcal{M}/\{\hat{j}\}$;
13    $\mathcal{K} \leftarrow \mathcal{K}/\{\hat{k}\}$;
14 **end**

Theorem 1. *The off-line version of our JOBC problem is NP-hard, and the approximation ratio of Algorithm 1 is $\frac{1}{M}$.*

Proof. We hereby construct a conflict graph $\mathcal{G} = (\mathcal{V}, \mathcal{E})$ to facilitate the analysis of our algorithm. Each vertex $v \in \mathcal{V}$ represents a three-tuple, i.e, $v = (\mathcal{I}, j, k)$ with $\mathcal{I} \subseteq [N]$ being any subset of the users which the BS j can serve with channel k. The vertex v is associated with a weight $\mu_v = \sum_{i\in\mathcal{I}} \mu_{i,j,k}$. The edges in $\mathcal{E}$ represent the conflict relationship between the vertices. Specifically, for $\forall v = (i, j, k), v' = (i', j', k') \in \mathcal{V}$, there exists an edge $(v, v') \in \mathcal{E}$ between them if either of the following two conditions is satisfied: i) the two vertices share the same BS, i.e., $j = j'$, since one BS cannot neither serve different sets of users nor works with different channels; ii) if $j \neq j$, either the vertices have their user sets overlapped (i.e., $\mathcal{I} \cap \mathcal{I}' \neq \emptyset$) or they share the same channel (i.e., $k = k'$), since a user cannot be connected to different base stations and one channel cannot be allocated to different base stations. Our off-line JOBC problem is then transformed into the *Maximum Weight Independent Set* (MWIS) problem in the conflict graph $\mathcal{G}$. Therefore, our problem is of NP-hardness.

As shown in Algorithm 1, our off-line greedy algorithm in each iteration is to select the vertex with the maximum weight in the current residual graph, from which we then remove the vertices and edges adjacent to the selected vertex.

Specifically, suppose $\mathcal{S}_\mu^*$ denotes the MWIS in graph $\mathcal{G}$ and $\mathcal{S}_\mu$ is the output of our greedy algorithm.

Fact 1. *$\mathcal{S}_\mu$ can be divided into two disjoint groups: $\mathcal{S}_\mu/\mathcal{S}_\mu^*$ and $\mathcal{S}_\mu \cap \mathcal{S}_\mu^*$. For $\forall v \in \mathcal{S}_\mu \cap \mathcal{S}_\mu^*$, it has no neighbors in $\mathcal{S}_\mu^*$ and $\mathcal{S}_\mu$, since v and its neighborhood $\mathcal{V}_v = \{v' \in \mathcal{V} \mid (v, v') \in \mathcal{E}\}$ cannot be in the same independent set.*

Fact 2. *For $\forall v \in \mathcal{S}_\mu/\mathcal{S}_\mu^*$, it has at most M neighbors in $\mathcal{S}_\mu^*/\mathcal{S}_\mu$, since the MWIS in our problem has at most M vertices. Therefore, we have $\sum_{v' \in \mathcal{V}_v \cap (\mathcal{S}_\mu^*/\mathcal{S}_\mu)} \mu_{v'} \leq M\mu_v$, as we always select the maximally weighted vertex in each iteration of our greedy algorithm.*

Fact 3. *For $\forall v \in \mathcal{S}_\mu^*/\mathcal{S}_\mu$, it must have at least one neighbor (say $v' \in \mathcal{S}_\mu/\mathcal{S}_\mu^*$) in $\mathcal{S}_\mu/\mathcal{S}_\mu^*$; otherwise, it would be selected into $\mathcal{S}_\mu$. Therefore, it is in either $\mathcal{S}_\mu^* \cap \mathcal{S}_\mu$ or $(\mathcal{S}_\mu^*/\mathcal{S}_\mu) \cap \mathcal{V}_v'$ for some $v' \in \mathcal{S}_\mu/\mathcal{S}_\mu^*$.*

According to the above three facts, we have

$$\sum_{v \in \mathcal{S}_\mu} \mu_v = \sum_{v \in \mathcal{S}_\mu^* \cap \mathcal{S}_\mu} \mu_v + \sum_{v \in \mathcal{S}_\mu/\mathcal{S}_\mu^*} \mu_v \geq \sum_{v \in \mathcal{S}_\mu^* \cap \mathcal{S}_\mu} \mu_v + \frac{1}{M} \sum_{v \in \mathcal{S}_\mu/\mathcal{S}_\mu^*} \sum_{v' \in (\mathcal{S}_\mu^*/\mathcal{S}_\mu) \cap \mathcal{V}_v} \mu_{v'}$$

$$\geq \frac{1}{M} \left(\sum_{v \in \mathcal{S}_\mu^* \cap \mathcal{S}_\mu} \mu_v + \sum_{v \in \mathcal{S}_\mu/\mathcal{S}_\mu^*} \sum_{v' \in (\mathcal{S}_\mu^*/\mathcal{S}_\mu) \cap \mathcal{V}_v} \mu_{v'} \right) \geq \frac{1}{M} \sum_{v \in \mathcal{S}_\mu^*} \mu_v$$

and thus conclude that our greedy algorithm has an approximation ratio of $1/M$.

4   An On-Line Learning-Based Algorithm

In this section, we leverage the MAB framework to learn the rewards we can get by allocating the bases stations and channels to the users. One intuitive choice is to take all possible configurations $\mathcal{X}$ as the arms of the bandit, and sequentially try these arms out to learn their performances. For example, in *Upper Confidence Bound* (UCB) method, we maintain an UCB index for each feasible configuration and select the one with the largest UCB index in each time slot. However, since there are a very large number of feasible configurations, such a method entails significant computation and storage overheads. Fortunately, we observe that each feasible configuration consists of N "user-BS-channel" combinations and one combination may occur in different feasible configuration. Therefore, in this paper, we design an efficient algorithm by fully exploiting the correlations between different feasible configurations. In the following, we first introduce the details of our algorithm in Sect. 4.1 and then analyze the algorithm in Sect. 4.2.

4.1   Algorithm

We maintain two variables $\bar{r}_{i,j,k}(t)$ and $\gamma_{i,j,k}(t)$ for $\forall (i, j, k) \in \mathcal{D}$ in each slot $t = 1, \cdots, T$. $\bar{r}_{i,j,k}(t)$ denotes the average reward which user i obtains by accessing

---

Algorithm 2: An on-line learning-based algorithm.

Input: A problem instance $([N], [M], [K], \tau, \mu)$

Output: An on-line configuration $x_u(t) \in \mathcal{X}$ for $\forall t = 1, 2 \cdots, T$

1 **Initialization**

2     $\gamma_{i,j,k}(0) = 1$, $\bar{r}_{i,j,k}(0) = r_{i,j,k}(0) = 0$, for $\forall (i, j, k) \in \mathcal{D}$;

3   Activate each $(i, j, k) \in \mathcal{D}$ and update $r_{i,j,k}(0)$ and $\bar{r}_{i,j,k}(0)$;

4 **end**

5 **foreach** $t = 1, \cdots, T$ **do**

6   Compute $u_{i,j,k}(t) = \bar{r}_{i,j,k}(t-1) + \sqrt{\frac{3\ln t}{2\gamma_{i,j,k}(t-1)}}$ for $\forall (i, j, k) \in \mathcal{D}$;

7     $x_u(t) = \mathsf{Greedy}_u([N], [M], [K], \tau, \{u_{i,j,k}(t)\}_{(i,j,k)\in\mathcal{D}})$;

8   Implement $x(t)$ and observe $r_{i,j,k}(t)$ for $\forall (i, j, k) \in x(t)$;

9   **foreach** $(i, j, k) \in x(t)$ **do**

10        $\bar{r}_{i,j,k}(t) = \frac{\bar{r}_{i,j,k}(t-1)\cdot\gamma_{i,j,k}(t-1)+r_{i,j,k}(t)}{\gamma_{i,j,k}(t-1)+1}$;

11        $\gamma_{i,j,k}(t) = \gamma_{i,j,k}(t-1) + 1$;

12   **end**

13   **foreach** $(i, j, k) \in \mathcal{D}/x(t)$ **do**

14        $\bar{r}_{i,j,k}(t) = \bar{r}_{i,j,k}(t-1)$;

15        $\gamma_{i,j,k}(t) = \gamma_{i,j,k}(t-1)$;

16   **end**

17 **end**

---

channel k through BS j up to slot t, and $\gamma_{i,j,k}(t)$ represents the number of times user i accesses channel k through BS j up to slot t. The algorithm starts with an initialization stage where we try each $(i, j, k) \in \mathcal{D}$ and let $r_{i,j,k}(t) = 0$ and $\gamma_{i,j,k}(t) = 1$ (with $t = 0$) respectively (see Lines 1–4). In each time slot t, we first compute a weight $u_{i,j,k}(t)$ for each $(i, j, k) \in \mathcal{D}$ according to

$$u_{i,j,k}(t) = \bar{r}_{i,j,k}(t-1) + \sqrt{3\ln t/(2\gamma_{i,j,k}(t-1))} \tag{6}$$

as shown in Line 6. We then perform the greedy algorithm (as shown in Algorithm 1) as a subroutine with the weight assignment $u(t) = \{u_{i,j,k}(t)\}_{(i,j,k)\in\mathcal{D}}$, and $r_{i,j,k}(t)$ (for $\forall (i, j, k) \in x(t)$) can be observed by implementing the resulting configuration $x_u(t)$ (see Lines 7–8). We finally update $\bar{r}_{i,j,k}(t)$ and $\gamma_{i,j,k}(t)$ for $\forall (i, j, k) \in \mathcal{D}$, according to Lines 9–16.

4.2 Analysis

We hereby evaluate the performance of the on-line algorithm by comparing it to the off-line one. Specifically, we are interested in investigating the upper-bound of the following regret function

$$\mathsf{Regret}\left(\{x_u(t)\}_{t\in[T]}\right) = \sum_{t=1}^{T}\left(R_\mu^* - \mathbb{E}[R_\mu(x_u(t))]\right) \tag{7}$$

where $R_\mu^* = \sum_{(i,j,k) \in x_\mu^*} \mu_{i,j,k}$ is the expected total reward yielded by our off-line approximation algorithm. Letting $\widetilde{\mathcal{X}} = \{x \in \mathcal{X} \mid R_\mu(x) < R_\mu^*\}$ be the set of the feasible configurations $x \in \mathcal{X}$ such that $R_\mu(x) < R_\mu^*$, we first define some (constant) notations used in the following analysis [2]

$$\Delta_{max}^{(i,j,k)} = R_\mu^* - \min_{x \in \widetilde{\mathcal{X}} \mid (i,j,k) \in x} \{R_\mu(x)\}, \ \Delta_{min}^{(i,j,k)} = R_\mu^* - \max_{x \in \widetilde{\mathcal{X}} \mid (i,j,k) \in x} \{R_\mu(x)\}$$

$$\Delta_{max} = \max_{(i,j,k) \in \mathcal{D}} \{\Delta_{max}^{(i,j,k)}\}, \ \Delta_{min} = \min_{(i,j,k) \in \mathcal{D}} \{\Delta_{min}^{(i,j,k)}\}$$

$$\bar{\Delta}_{min} = \min\{|\mu_v - \mu_{v'}| \mid \forall v, v' \in \mathcal{V}\}, \ \widetilde{\Delta}_{min} = \min_{(i,j,k) \in \mathcal{D}} \left\{\Delta_{min}, \frac{\bar{\Delta}_{min}}{\tau_{max}}\right\}$$

We also define two events for $\forall t \in [T]$ as

$$E_1(t) = \left\{x(t) \in \widetilde{\mathcal{X}}, \gamma_{i,j,k}(t-1) > \frac{6 \ln t}{\widetilde{\Delta}_{min}^2}, \text{for } \forall (i,j,k) \in x(t)\right\} \quad (8)$$

and

$$E_2(t) = \left\{|\bar{r}_{i,j,k}(t-1) - \mu_{i,j,k}| \le \sqrt{\frac{3 \ln t}{2\gamma_{i,j,k}(t-1)}}, \text{for } \forall (i,j,k) \in \mathcal{D}\right\} \quad (9)$$

Lemma 1. *In any slot $t \in [T]$ where $E_1(t)$ holds, for $\forall (i,j,k) \in \mathcal{D}$, we have*

$$\widetilde{\Delta}_{min} > 2 \cdot \max_{(i,j,k) \in x(t)} \left\{\sqrt{3 \ln t / (2\gamma_{i,j,k}(t-1))}\right\} \quad (10)$$

This lemma can be straightforwardly proved by substituting the inequality condition in $E_1(t)$ into $\sqrt{3 \ln t / (2\gamma_{i,j,k}(t-1))}$. By substituting the definition of $u_{i,j,k}(t)$ (see Eq. (6)) into the inequality condition in $E_2(t)$, we have

Lemma 2. *In any slot $t \in [T]$ with $E_2(t)$ holding, for $\forall (i,j,k) \in \mathcal{D}$, we have*

$$u_{i,j,k}(t) - 2\sqrt{3 \ln t / (2\gamma_{i,j,k}(t-1))} \le \mu_{i,j,k} \le u_{i,j,k}(t) \quad (11)$$

Lemma 3. *In any slot $t \in [T]$ where $E_1(t)$ and $E_2(t)$ both hold, we have*

$$\sum_{(i,j,k) \in x_u(t)} u_{i,j,k}(t) \ge \sum_{(i,j,k) \in x_\mu^*} \mu_{i,j,k} \quad (12)$$

Proof. We hereby borrow the conflict graph shown in Theorem 1 to facilitate our analysis. As demonstrated in Algorithm 2, our on-line learning-based algorithm adopts the greedy algorithm (see Algorithm 1) as a subroutine to produce a

---

[2] For simplicity, we assume that $\mu_v \ne \mu_{v'}$ for $\forall v, v' \in \mathcal{V}$ such that $\bar{\Delta}_{min}$ (and thus $\widetilde{\Delta}_{min}$) is non-zero without compromising the practical rationality of our later theoretical analysis.

configuration by taking $u(t)$ as the weight assignment in slot t. Therefore, we consider two algorithm instance $\mathsf{Greedy}_{u(t)}$ and Greedy_{μ} working on the same conflict graph $\mathcal{G} = (\mathcal{V}, \mathcal{E})$ but with different weight assignments $u(t)$ and μ. In another word, each vertex $v = (\mathcal{I}, j, k) \in \mathcal{V}$ is associated with two weights defined by $u_v(t) = \sum_{i \in \mathcal{I}} u_{i,j,k}(t)$ and $\mu_v = \sum_{i \in \mathcal{I}} \mu_{i,j,k}$, respectively. We first show that, for $\forall v = (\mathcal{I}', j, k), v' = (\mathcal{I}', j', k') \in \mathcal{V}$, if $\mu_v > \mu_{v'}$, we then have $u_v > u_{v'}$ as follows

$$u_{v'} \leq \sum_{i' \in \mathcal{I}'} \left(\mu_{i',j',k'} + 2\sqrt{3 \ln t / (2\gamma_{i',j',k'}(t))} \right) < \sum_{i \in \mathcal{I}'} \mu_{i,j',k'} + |\mathcal{I}'| \widetilde{\Delta}_{min}$$

$$\leq \mu_{v'} + \tau_{max} \cdot \frac{\bar{\Delta}_{min}}{\tau_{max}} \leq \mu_v \leq u_v \tag{13}$$

The first two inequalities are due to (11) and (10) respectively; we get the third and forth inequalities according to the definition of $\widetilde{\Delta}_{min}$ and the one of $\bar{\Delta}_{min}$; we apply (11) again in the fifth inequality.

Suppose the outputs of Greedy_{μ} and Greedy_u are denoted by $\mathcal{S}_{\mu} \subset \mathcal{V}$ and $\mathcal{S}_u \subset \mathcal{V}$ respectively, and let $s_{\mu}^{[\beta]} \in \mathcal{S}_{\mu}$ and $s_u^{[\beta]} \in \mathcal{S}_u$ be the outputs of Greedy_{μ} and Greedy_u in the β-th iteration respectively. If Greedy_{μ} and Greedy_u proceed in the first η steps such that $s_{\mu}^{[\beta]} = s_u^{[\beta]}$ for $\forall \beta = 1, \cdots, \eta$, we have $s_{\mu}^{[\eta+1]} = s_u^{[\eta+1]}$, since Greedy_{μ} and Greedy_u work with the same residual conflict graph $\mathcal{G}$, and the vertex with the highest weight assignment by μ is also assigned by u with the highest weight according to (13). Moreover, since Greedy_{μ} and Greedy_u have the same output in the first step (according to (13) again) and they have the same terminating condition, we get $\mathcal{S}_{\mu} = \mathcal{S}_u$ and thus $x_u(t) = x_{\mu}^*$. Therefore, the proof can be completed by applying the inequality (11).

Theorem 2. *The regret of our on-line learning-based algorithm (see Algorithm 2) is upper-bounded by*

$$\mathsf{Regret}(T) \leq NMK \cdot \Delta_{max} \cdot \left(1 + \pi^2/3 + 6 \ln T / \widetilde{\Delta}_{min}^2 \right) \tag{14}$$

Proof. We associate a variable $\Gamma_{i,j,k}(t)$ with each $(i, j, k) \in \mathcal{D}$ in each slot t. In any slot $t \in [T]$, if $x(t) \in \widetilde{\mathcal{X}}$, $\Gamma_{i,j,k}(t)$ evolves as

$$\Gamma_{i,j,k}(t) = \begin{cases} \Gamma_{i,j,k}(t-1) + 1, & \text{if } (i,j,k) = \underset{(i,j,k) \in x_u(t)}{\arg\min} \Gamma_{i,j,k}(t-1) \\ \Gamma_{i,j,k}(t-1), & \text{otherwise} \end{cases} \tag{15}$$

otherwise, $\Gamma_{i,j,k}(t) = \Gamma_{i,j,k}(t-1)$ for $\forall (i, j, k) \in \mathcal{D}$. Initially, let $\Gamma_{i,j,k}(0) = 1$ for $(i, j, k) \in \mathcal{D}$. It is worthy to being noted that, in any slot t such that $x(t) \in \widetilde{\mathcal{X}}$, exactly one (i, j, k)-tuple has its $\Gamma_{i,j,k}(t)$ increased by 1; while there is no $\Gamma_{i,j,k}(t)$ increased if $x(t) \notin \widetilde{\mathcal{X}}$. Therefore

$$\mathsf{Regret}(T) = \sum_{t \in [T]} \left(R_{\mu}^* - \mathbb{E}[R_{\mu}(x_u(t))] \right) \leq \sum_{(i,j,k) \in \mathcal{D}} \mathbb{E}[\Gamma_{i,j,k}(T)] \cdot \Delta_{max} \tag{16}$$

We suppose $h(t) = 6\ln t/\widetilde{\Delta}_{min}^2$ and $\mathbb{I}(\cdot)$ is an indicator function, and thus have

$$
\sum_{(i,j,k)\in\mathcal{D}} \Gamma_{i,j,k}(T) - NMK \cdot h(T)
$$

$$
= \sum_{t=1}^{T} \sum_{(i,j,k)\in\mathcal{D}} \mathbb{I}\left(x_u(t) \in \widetilde{\mathcal{X}}, \Gamma_{i,j,k}(t) > \Gamma_{i,j,k}(t-1)\right) - NMK \cdot h(T)
$$

$$
\leq \sum_{t=1}^{T} \sum_{(i,j,k)\in\mathcal{D}} \mathbb{I}\left(x_u(t) \in \widetilde{\mathcal{X}}, \Gamma_{i,j,k}(t) > \Gamma_{i,j,k}(t-1), \Gamma_{i,j,k}(t-1) > h(T)\right)
$$

$$
\leq \sum_{t=1}^{T} \sum_{(i,j,k)\in\mathcal{D}} \mathbb{I}\left(x_u(t) \in \widetilde{\mathcal{X}}, \Gamma_{i,j,k}(t) > \Gamma_{i,j,k}(t-1), \Gamma_{i,j,k}(t-1) > h(t)\right)
$$

$$
\leq \sum_{t=1}^{T} \mathbb{I}\left(x_u(t) \in \widetilde{\mathcal{X}}, \gamma_{i,j,k}(t-1) > h(t), \forall (i,j,k) \in x(t)\right) = \sum_{t=1}^{T} \mathbb{I}(\mathsf{E}_1(t)) \quad (17)
$$

Taking the expected values on the both sides of (17), we have

$$
\sum_{(i,j,k)\in\mathcal{D}} \mathbb{E}[\Gamma_{i,j,k}(T)] \leq \sum_{t=1}^{T} \mathbb{P}[\mathsf{E}_1(t)] + NMK \cdot \frac{6\ln T}{\widetilde{\Delta}_{min}^2} \quad (18)
$$

For $\forall(i,j,k) \in \mathcal{D}$ and $\forall t \in [T]$, according to the Chernoff-Hoeffding bound,

$$
\mathbb{P}\left[|\bar{r}_{i,j,k}(t-1) - \mu_{i,j,k}| \geq \sqrt{3\ln t/(2\gamma_{i,j,k}(t-1))}\right] \leq \sum_{t'=1}^{t-1} 2(t^{-3})^{\frac{t'}{\gamma_{i,j,k}(t')}} \leq \frac{2}{t^2}
$$

and the probability of the negative of event E_2 can be upper-bounded by $\mathbb{P}[\mathsf{E}_2^-(t)] \leq 2NMK/t^2$ according to the union bound. In any slot t, if $\mathsf{E}_1(t)$ and $\mathsf{E}_2(t)$ holds,

$$
\sum_{(i,j,k)\in x_u(t)} \mu_{i,j,k} + \widetilde{\Delta}_{min} \geq \sum_{(i,j,k)\in x_u(t)} u_{i,j,k}(t) \geq \sum_{(i,j,k)\in x_\mu^*} \mu_{i,j,k} = R_\mu^* \quad (19)
$$

which contradicts the definition of $\widetilde{\Delta}_{min}$. Note that, we apply (10) and (11) (see Lemmas 1 and 2, respectively) in the first inequality; while the third one is due to the inequality (12) shown in Lemma 3. Therefore, the contradiction implies $\mathbb{P}[\{\mathsf{E}_1(t), \mathsf{E}_2(t)\}] = 0$. It follows that $\mathbb{P}[\mathsf{E}_1(t)] \leq 1 - \mathbb{P}[\mathsf{E}_2(t)] = \mathbb{P}[\mathsf{E}_2^-(t)] \leq 2NMKt^{-2}$, by substituting which into (18), we have

$$
\sum_{(i,j,k)\in\mathcal{D}} \mathbb{E}[\Gamma_{i,j,k}(T)] \leq \sum_{t=1}^{T} 2NMKt^{-2} + NMK \cdot \frac{6\ln T}{\widetilde{\Delta}_{min}^2}
$$

$$
\leq NMK\left(2\sum_{t=1}^{T} t^{-2} + 6\ln T/\widetilde{\Delta}_{min}^2\right) \leq NMK\left(1 + \pi^2/3 + 6\ln T/\widetilde{\Delta}_{min}^2\right)
$$

We finally accomplish the proof by substituting the above inequality into (16).

5   Experiments

We evaluate our on-line learning based algorithm in this section, mainly in terms of regret. We assume that, for $\forall (i, j, k) \in \mathcal{D}$, the throughput reward $r_{i,j,k}(t)$ follows a Bernoulli distribution parameterized by $p_{i,j,k}$ and is i.i.d. across time slots. In another word, the mean of the Bernoulli random variable $\mu_{i,j,k} = p_{i,j,k}$. We choose a value for each $p_{i,j,k}$ uniformly from the range $(0, 1)$. We also randomly set the capacities of the BSes such that $\sum_{j=1}^{M} \tau_j \geq N$. The default setting is $(N = 50, M = 5, K = 8)$.

We first compare our algorithm with the MLPS algorithm [15] and the ε-greedy algorithm [1]. The former approach defines the UCB index for each $(i, j, k) \in \mathcal{D}$ by $\min\{\gamma_{i',j',k'}(t-1), \forall (i', j', k') \in x_u(t-1)\}$ (instead of $\gamma_{i,j,k}(t-1)$), while the latter one greedily leverages the trade-off between the exploitation and exploration through a probability ε, i.e., with probability ε, we randomly choose a configuration, and with probability $1 - \varepsilon$, we employ our off-line greedy algorithm (with weight $\bar{r}_{i,j,k}(t - 1)$ in slot t) to choose the one empirically yielding the highest average throughput reward. The regrets of the three algorithms are shown in Fig. 1. It is demonstrated that both our algorithm and the MLPS algorithm have lower regrets than the ε-greedy algorithm, since they take into account the confidence intervals for the average through rewards to explore more "promising" configurations, while the exploration in the ε-greedy algorithm is randomly performed. Moreover, although the regret of our algorithm is slightly higher than the one of the MLPS algorithm in the first 16000 rounds, it thereafter "converges" to a better configuration with a much smaller regret.

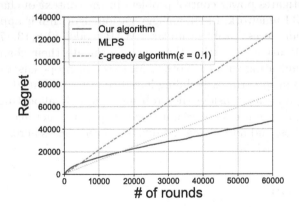

Fig. 1. The regrets of the three algorithms.

We then verify the efficacy of our algorithm under different system settings. We vary the numbers of the users, channels and BSes and report the results in Fig. 2(a), (b) and (c), respectively. It is demonstrated that, increasing the number of users (or channels or BSes) results in larger regret values, which consists with what we have shown in Theorem 2.

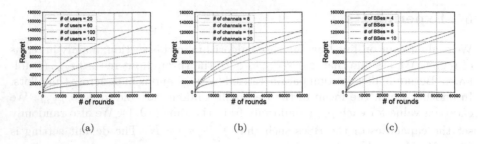

Fig. 2. The performances of our algorithm under different settings.

6 Related Work

There have been a vast body of studies on dynamic channel allocation problem where a set of given channels is allocated to a group of users, since it could serve as a foundation for routing (e.g. [6]), data collection (e.g. [7]) etc. The on-line learning techniques are usually employed to address the uncertainties of the channels, e.g., Markov decision process in [3,14], deep reinforcement learning in [11,16], and MAB-based approaches which we are interested in. For example, [15] formulates the channel allocation problem as a maximum weight matching problem in a bipartite graph where each edge is with an uncertain weight, while [9] then decreases the complexity but with a sacrifice in regret bound. [5] propose an MAB-based on-line learning framework such that the rewards gained by the users can be maximized with the utilization of the channels also guaranteed. [12] investigates power control problem in the context of channel selection under the MAB framework. In [4], an aggregation algorithm is applied to opportunistic spectrum access problem under a MAB model. [2,8,13,17] decentralize the channel allocation by letting the users coordinate their channel selections through communicating with each other. More recent proposals about the applications of MAB in spectrum scheduling have been surveyed in [10]. Nevertheless, these existing proposals consider the problem of directly allocating the channels to the users, while the users are assumed in this paper to get access to the channels through BSes, and addressing the diverse uncertainties across the BSes and users is highly non-trivial.

7 Conclusion

In this paper, we have investigated the so-called JOBC problem in cognitive radio networks where we aim at allocating BSes and channels to users, by taking into account the limited capacity of the BSes and the diverse uncertainty of the channels across the BSes and users. Inspired by a simplified off-line version of the problem for which we have proposed an approximation algorithm, we have leveraged a combinatorial MAB to design an on-line algorithm, which entails polynomial storage overhead and results in a regret logarithmic in time.

References

1. Auer, P., Cesa-Bianchi, N., Fischer, P.: Finite-time analysis of the multiarmed bandit problem. Mach. Learn. **47**(2–3), 235–256 (2002). https://doi.org/10.1023/A:1013689704352
2. Avner, O., Mannor, S.: Multi-user lax communications: a multi-armed bandit approach. In: Proceedings of the 35th IEEE INFOCOM, pp. 1–9 (2016)
3. Avrachenkov, K., Cottatellucci, L., Maggi, L.: Dynamic rate allocation in Markovian quasi-static multiple access channels: a game theoretic approach. In: Proceedings of the 11th WiOpt, pp. 162–169 (2013)
4. Besson, L., Kaufmann, E., Moy, C.: Aggregation of multi-armed bandits learning algorithms for opportunistic spectrum access. In: Proceedings of IEEE WCNC, pp. 1–6 (2018)
5. Cai, K., Liu, X., Chen, Y., Lui, J.C.S.: An online learning approach to network application optimization with guarantee. In: Proceedings of IEEE INFOCOM, pp. 2006–2014 (2018)
6. Cai, Z., Duan, Y., Bourgeois, A.: Delay efficient opportunistic routing in asynchronous multi-channel cognitive radio networks. J. Comb. Optim. **29**(4), 815–835 (2015)
7. Chen, Q., Cai, Z., Cheng, L., Gao, H.: Low-latency data aggregation scheduling for cognitive radio networks with non-predetermined structure. IEEE Trans. Mobile Comput. (2020). https://doi.org/10.1109/TMC.2020.2979710
8. Gai, Y., Krishnamachari, B.: Decentralized online learning algorithms for opportunistic spectrum access. In: Processing of IEEE GLOBECOM, pp. 1–6 (2011)
9. Kang, S., Joo, C.: Low-complexity learning for dynamic spectrum access in multi-user multi-channel networks. In: Proceedings of The 37th IEEE INFOCOM, pp. 1–9 (2018)
10. Li, F., Yu, D., Yang, H., Yu, J., Holger, K., Cheng, X.: Multi-armed-bandit-based spectrum scheduling algorithms in wireless networks: a survey. IEEE Wirel Commun. **27**(1), 24–30 (2020)
11. Liu, J., Zhao, B., Xin, Q., Liu, H.: Dynamic channel allocation for satellite internet of things via deep reinforcement learning. In: Proceedings of ICOIN, pp. 465–470 (2020)
12. Maghsudi, S., Stanczak, S.: Joint channel selection and power control in infrastructureless wireless networks: a multiplayer multiarmed bandit framework. IEEE Trans. Veh. Technol. **64**(10), 4565–4578 (2015)
13. Stahlbuhk, T., Shrader, B., Modiano, E.: Learning algorithms for scheduling in wireless networks with unknown channel statistics. Ad Hoc Netw. **85**, 131–144 (2019)
14. Teotia, V., Dhurandher, S., Woungang, I., Obaidat, S.: Markovian model based channel allocation in cognitive radio networks. In: Proceedings of IEEE International Conference on Data Science and Data Intensive Systems, pp. 478–482 (2015)
15. Gai, Y., Krishnamachari, B., Jain, R.: Learning multiuser channel allocations in cognitive radio networks: a combinatorial multi-armed bandit formulation. In: Proceedings of IEEE DySPAN, pp. 1–9 (2010)

16. Zheng, W., Wu, G., Qie, W., Zhang, Y.: Deep reinforcement learning for joint channel selection and power allocation in cognitive internet of things. In: Milošević, D., Tang, Y., Zu, Q. (eds.) HCC 2019. LNCS, vol. 11956, pp. 683–692. Springer, Cham (2019). https://doi.org/10.1007/978-3-030-37429-7_69
17. Zhou, Y., Li, X., Li, F., Liu, M., Li, Z., Yin, Z.: Almost optimal channel access in multi-hop networks with unknown channel variables. In: Proceedings of the 34th IEEE ICDCS, pp. 461–470 (2014)

A Deep Spatial-Temporal Network for Vehicle Trajectory Prediction

Zhiqiang Lv, Jianbo Li$^{(\boxtimes)}$, Chuanhao Dong, and Wei Zhao

College of Computer Science and Technology, Qingdao University,
Qingdao 266071, China
lvzq7614@163.com, lijianbo@188.com

Abstract. To plan travel routes reasonably and alleviate traffic congestion effectively, trajectory prediction of vehicles plays an important and necessary role in intelligent transportation. This paper presents a deep spatial-temporal network for long-term trajectory prediction of vehicles. Our network mainly includes the spatial layer, the temporal layer and local-global estimation layer. The spatial layer uses dilated convolution to build a long distance location convolution that functions as calculating the spatial features of trajectories. In the temporal layer, temporal prediction employs the Temporal Convolutional Network (TCN) for the first time to calculate deep spatial-temporal features in the process of prediction. The traditional linear method is replaced by special global-local estimation layer in order to improve accuracy of prediction. The NGSIM US-101 and GeoLife data sets are used for training and evaluation of experiments which contain 17,621 trajectories with a total distance of more than 1.2 million km. As results show, compared with other existing prediction network models, our network can produce almost the same short-term prediction results and has higher accuracy in long-term trajectory prediction.

Keywords: Intelligent transportation · Vehicle trajectory · Deep learning · Spatial-temporal network

1 Introduction

With the rapid development of the transportation and automobile industry, vehicle trajectory prediction has become a focus in the field of transportation big data. It helps people plan better driving routes, as well as saving more manpower and material resources. More importantly, the public basic resources are allocated more precisely with the help of trajectory prediction.

Vehicle velocity is an important factor influencing the change of trajectory. The acceleration motion model combined with the Constant Yaw Rate realized a mechanism of maneuver recognition [1]. The lateral velocity and potential feature of vehicle

This research was supported in part by National Key Research and Development Plan Key Special Projects under Grant No. 2018YFB2100303, Key Research and Development Plan Project of Shandong Province under Grant No. 2016GGX101032 and Program for Innovative Postdoctoral Talents in Shandong Province under Grant No. 40618030001.

© Springer Nature Switzerland AG 2020
D. Yu et al. (Eds.): WASA 2020, LNCS 12384, pp. 359–369, 2020.
https://doi.org/10.1007/978-3-030-59016-1_30

were used to estimate driver's intention and predict the change of lane [2]. The turning of a vehicle is very different from the linear motion and it should be expressed by a special implicit method. Curve radius and acceleration status were expressed implicitly by the quaternion-based rotationally invariant longest common subsequence metric and radial basis function [3]. Wang [4] build the trajectory model of vehicle motion on the basis of Gause theorem, thus predictive trajectories were obtained through the statistical distribution characteristics of trajectories. In the previous studies of vehicle prediction, the traditional model only focuses on the calculation of short-term spatial relation. However, the data mining [5] and machine learning [6] prove that temporal relation calculations can realize the long-term trajectory perdition. In recent years, the deep learning has made huge development in the field of vehicle trajectory prediction. Recurrent neural networks such as Long Short Term Memory (LSTM) [7] and Gate Recurrent Unit (GRU) [8] have become the main choices of temporal trajectory prediction [9]. Kim [10] divided lanes into grid matrices and added the spatial features of vehicles to the LSTM. The shortcut connections [11] was added to the LSTM in order to solve the problem of gradient disappearance. The LSTM combined with the encoder-decoder architecture makes trajectory prediction have a better linkage mechanism. The encoder-decoder employed beam search technique so that the mode generated most likely candidate targets of trajectory on the occupancy grid map [12], and the convolutional social pooling [13] can also increase the robustness of the model. Multi-modal vehicle trajectory and lane structure were applied to the encoder-decoder to predict multi-modal trajectory of future motions [14]. Donggi [15] employed the Deep Neural Network (DNN) in order to realize long-term prediction of vehicle trajectories. However, DNN has a very large-scale parameter network to connect samples, which easily leads to over-fitting and local optimum. So, the problem of parameter expansion is prone to occur during the training process.

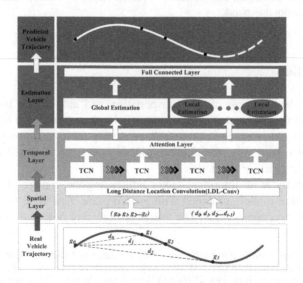

Fig. 1. DeepVTP model framework

This paper presents a deep spatial-temporal network called Deep Vehicle Trajectory Prediction (DeepVTP) (see Fig. 1). DeepVTP completes long-term prediction of the vehicle trajectory based on the GPS points in the vehicle trajectory. The main creative points of this network are: firstly, the Long Distance Location Convolution (LDL-Conv) employs dilated convolution to extract the features of real GPS points. We associate GPS features with the distance sequence $\{d\}$ which represents the distance between the first node and the non-first node. LDL-Conv can calculate deeper trajectory spatial features that temporal network layer needs through the above methods. Secondly, Temporal Convolutional Network [16] (TCN) is applied to the field of trajectory prediction for the first time. According to the results of simulation, TCN has higher accuracy and higher training speed [17] compared with other recurrent neural networks such as LSTM, GRU, etc. The output of the temporal layer is input to the Attention [18] Layer to enhance the weight of non-linear trajectories. Finally, special global-local estimation layer [19] replaces traditional linear methods in order to improve the accuracy of prediction.

2 Model Framework

2.1 Spatial Layer

The driving process of vehicles is complex and diverse. Although the prediction of straight lines is simple, it is often the case that the traveling route becomes a complex curve due to the influence of turns and traffic congestion [23]. This makes it particularly important to study the spatial relationship of vehicle positions in the feature extraction process of trajectory prediction. Therefore, it is necessary to perform another round of extraction of feature from the trajectory and strengthen the weight of the local curve of the trajectory before making temporal predictions, instead of using standardized GPS data directly. First of all, the latitude and longitude data are compressed to calculate the feature of spatial dependencies in the process of LDL-Conv, as shown in the formula (1).

$$l_i = active\left(cat\left[\sigma^{lng_k} \times lng_i + \mu^{lng_k}, \sigma^{lat_k} \times lat_i + \mu^{lat_k}\right]\right) \tag{1}$$

The latitude and longitude of the i-th point is calculated with the standard deviation σ and mean μ of the k-th trajectory sequence, which represents standardization of GPS data. The result of cat which fuses the latitude and longitude into the same dimension is closer to the real result compared to the result of processing latitude or longitude matrix separately. We choose the active function $tanh$ that is convenient for derivation. It can compress the data and ensure that the range of the data is not abnormal. Capturing multi-scale context information is important in the process of feature extraction, which determines the strength of the model's spatial dependence on the trajectory nodes. Generally, traditional convolution achieves the process of capturing information by down-sampling which can expand the range of receptive field, however, there must be a loss of information in the above process. We build two layers of dilated convolution [28] to achieve the process of capturing multi-scale context information (see Fig. 2). Filter kernels are depicted in square with grid pattern in each layer, The blue cells in dilated kernel represent valid weights. The dilation factor of the three-layer dilation convolutional network changes by 2^2, 2^1, and 2^0. Traditional prediction networks usually integrate multi-scale context information through continuous pooling or other down-sampling layers, which will lose feature information. For dense prediction tasks, not only multi-scale context information is required, but also a large enough receptive field. The biggest advantage of dilation convolutional network is that it can expand the receptive field exponentially without losing feature information. $\{d\}$ is the distance features of the first and the non-first nodes of every trajectory.

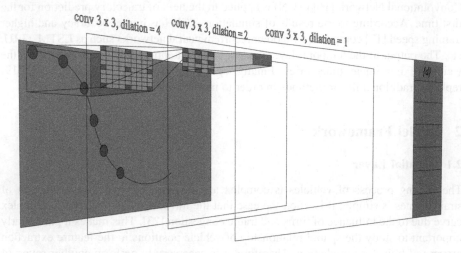

Fig. 2. Dilation convolution process

We combine the O^{conv} and data which are distance of the i-th node and the first node of the k-th trajectory after the activation of the $ReLu$ function in order to strengthen the spatial dependence of features. The formula is as (2).

$$O = cat\left[O^{conv}, \sigma^{D_k} \times d_i + \mu^{D_k}\right] \tag{2}$$

2.2   Temporal Layer

Recurrent neural network plays an important role in the study of temporal data prediction. As the researches of deep leaning develop, researchers have found that LSTM and GRU are not effective in saving and capturing longer historical information. TCN not only retains longer history information based on the principle of causal convolution, but also has a unique residual architecture that has obvious advantages in the speed and accuracy of training [17]. Based on this characteristic of TCN, we build a TCN network with 7 hidden layers to process the spatial feature of the LDL-Conv layer. The number of neurons in every hidden layer should be the same according to the requirements of causal convolution and number is 128 in this experiment. Every hidden layer has one dilation factor and every factor is exponential growth for 2. The temporal prediction sequence $\{h_0, h_1, \ldots, h_k\}$ is the output of TCN (see Fig. 3).

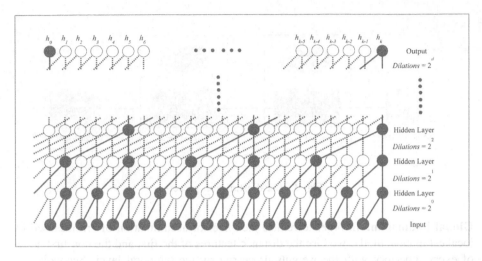

Fig. 3. TCN architecture

2.3 Estimation Layer

We designed a network layer for local-global estimation of traffic trajectories in order to improve the accuracy of trajectory prediction. The original intention of the layer design is extracting features from the next position which is relative to the current position in each trajectory and the features are added to the network training as an influence factor, thus the layer design needs a process of local estimation of each node. Although the local estimation calculates the matrix features which are processed by the temporal layer, it does not consider the temporal and spatial dependence and just estimates the nodes within a short distance in a trajectory. When local estimates are made multiple times, multiple local errors will occur. The accumulation of these local errors has a huge impact on the accuracy of the data prediction. Therefore, we have designed a global estimation process that can not only reduce local errors but also predict future nodes of the entire trajectory, which can achieve better accuracy.

Local Estimation. Multi-dimensional [22] matrix is obtained through the temporal layer, which is the temporal and spatial feature of each trajectory. In the process of local estimation, the initial 128 dimensions of each h_k which is from the sequence {h_0, h_1,....., h_k} is linearly transformed into 64 dimensions, and then it is transformed into 32 dimensions in the second linear process. Finally, matrix becomes 1 dimension. An activation function should be performed after each linear transformation. Here we take the *Leaky ReLU* [21] function that has the advantage of a negative saturation region to make the data more inclined to be saturated in the negative region rather than completely return to zero (see Fig. 4).

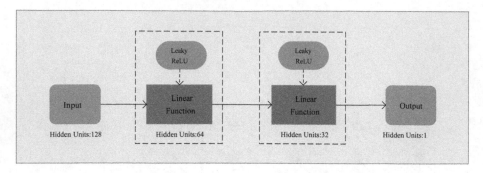

Fig. 4. Local estimation process

Global Estimation. In order to reduce the effect of accumulation of error caused by local estimation, firstly, we fuse the distance features of the first and the non-first nodes of every trajectory with the weights processed by the temporal layer. Secondly, we build a 3-layers residual network [24] that is constructed by the jump layer connection. The formula is as (3).

$$h_i = active(h_{i-1} + re(i)) \tag{3}$$

The *re(i)* is the *i-th* residual process and the h_{i-1} is the result of the previous residual process. The input of the residual unit is directly combined with the output of the residual unit. Experiments show that multi-level residual network solves the problem of degradation of deep neural network and this structure makes the convergence process take less time. Finally, we use fully connected layers [27] to calculate the weighted sums of the features of the local estimates and residual network. The global estimation layer calculates the weight of the specified number of nodes and number of these points represents the number of nodes for each trajectory we need to predict.

3 Experiment

3.1 Data Set Preparation

We choose the NGSIM US-101 [25] and GeoLife [26] as the experimental data sets after comprehensively considering the amount of data and real time interval of GPS nodes. These two data sets have dense trajectories and these time nodes are 2 s–10 s. We randomly select 80% of the data set for training and evaluation, and the remaining 20% is used for testing. In addition, We make the following process on the data set:

- The number of node in every trajectory is fixed at 21, which can be adjusted according to the requirements and specific size of the data set.
- We calculate and keep the distance between the first node and the non-first node.
- Trajectories over 20 km are considered abnormal data. Abnormal length and repeated trajectories are not used in the data set used for experimental training.

3.2 Training and Evaluation

The training in experiment uses 4 NVIDIA Tesla V100, and the experimental results are the average value after 20 epochs of training under the premise of consistent data sets. The optimization algorithm selects the Adam algorithm, because learning rate of each iteration has a certain range after bias correction of the Adam algorithm, which makes the parameters relatively stable. We have designed the corresponding method of error calculation considering the particularity of the data set used (see Fig. 5). $\{t_1, t_2, \ldots t_n\}$ is the sequence of distance which is from real GPS points and $\{p_1, p_2, \ldots p_n\}$ is the sequence of distance which is between n-th predicted points and $(n-1) - th$ real points. We calculate the errors of these two sequences.

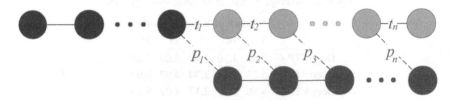

Fig. 5. Error calculation process

We have built three different temporal model architectures: DeepVTP-G, DeepVTP-L, and DeepVTP-T, which respectively represent GRU, LSTM and TCN selected in the temporal layer. These different models are trained by the same parameters and same data size. In order to increase the scientificity of the experimental results, we use the data set and evaluation index values from the paper proposing the CS-LSTM. We add the baseline experiment according to the method described in other papers. RMSE is used to measure the deviation between the predicted value and true value and it can reflect precision of the measurement. The comparison of RMSE error is shown in Table 1. DeepVTP can basically achieve the effect of CS-LSTM for short-term prediction and DeepVTP-T has higher accuracy for long-term prediction (see Table 1).

Table 1. RMSE error comparison results.

Horizon (s)	C-VGMM [20]	CS-LSTM [13]	ST-LSTM [12]	LS-LSTM [11]	DNN [15]	DeepVTP-G	DeepVTP-L	DeepVTP-T
1	0.66	**0.61**	0.87	0.76	0.69	0.73	0.64	0.62
2	1.56	1.27	1.93	1.86	1.78	1.71	1.26	**1.24**
3	2.75	2.09	3.12	3.65	3.21	2.81	2.19	**2.01**
4	4.24	3.10	4.32	4.01	3.96	4.12	3.21	**2.96**
5	5.99	4.37	5.83	5.79	5.78	5.62	4.41	**4.02**

In this experiment, we set the length of each trajectory to 21 GPS points, and we verified the advantages of 21 points, as shown in Table 2. The data in Table 2 is the average of 5 predicted values. From the experimental results, we can know that the prediction result of the model is the best when the length of trajectory is 21 points. When the trajectory length is short, the spatial-temporal features extracted by the model are insufficient. As the number of trajectory points increases, the features calculated by the model will gradually close to true features. However, too long trajectories have more complex environmental impact factors. It is greatly affected by the intention of driver and distribution of road. So, too long trajectories are beyond the computing power range of the model.

Table 2. Average RMSE error comparison results.

Models	Number of trajectory nodes				
	7	14	21	28	35
DeepVTP-G	5.42	4.36	**3.00**	5.09	7.39
DeepVTP-L	5.23	3.71	**2.34**	4.97	6.94
DeepVTP-T	4.86	3.21	**2.17**	4.02	5.84

As mentioned earlier, TCN can achieve large-scale parallel processing by virtue of the special dilated structure [17]. Faster training and verification process of network can shorten the phrase of feedback. We set up three kinds of recurrent neural networks for training during the temporal prediction stage in this experiment and distribute the average loss in training based on time (see Fig. 6). The experimental results prove that the convergence speed of DeepVTP-T training is faster in the temporal prediction stage. It is about 34.5% higher than DeepVTP-L and about 15.1% higher than DeepVTP-G. The average loss of DeepVTP-T is the lowest after model convergence.

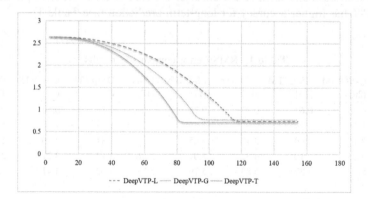

Fig. 6. Time-Loss curve. The abscissa represents the number of epochs for model training and ordinate represents the value of loss.

We mainly describe the prediction results of the next five points from the straight and curved trajectories. The time difference between two adjacent nodes is 1 s (see Fig. 7). DeepVTP-T has the best prediction results for three types of trajectory prediction. The comparison results of DeepVTP-G, DeepVTP-L and DeepVTP-T prove that TCN has played a role in improving accuracy in the model. The experimental results prove the network model make better predictions for trajectories that are approximate straight-lines, especially for the nodes within the first 3 s. Although the errors in the results of predication of curve trajectory are relatively large compared to that of straight trajectory, the network model can achieve the basic predication of curve trajectory.

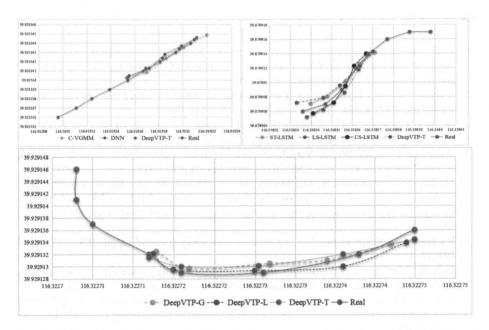

Fig. 7. Real and predicted trajectories. The abscissa represents the longitude of the location and the abscissa represents the latitude of the location.

4   Conclusion

In this paper, we propose a deep spatial-temporal network for long-term vehicle trajectory prediction. This network consists of three parts: the spatial layer which is used to calculate deep spatial features, the temporal layer being used to calculate the recursive relationship of trajectories in time and local-global estimation layer which is used for the linearization process of features. We build the LDL-Conv consisting of dilated convolutions to solve the problem that the feature space dependence of traditional convolution calculations is insufficient in spatial layer. The temporal layer uses TCN which is applied to the field of temporal trajectory prediction for the first time. The local-global estimation layer replaces the traditional linearization method that does not fit well with non-linear data and reduces the error caused by local prediction. The experimental results show that our network can not only achieve short-term prediction, but also attain higher accuracy in long-term prediction. However, there are some limitations that should be addressed. The road distribution should be considered in the process of prediction in the urban area when the longer-term prediction is conducted. In addition, adding changes in vehicle velocity should be taken into account since velocity determines the distance of vehicles trajectory within a fixed period of time. Future research will not only focus on resolving the above problems but will investigate the impact of other indirect factors on the trajectory including weather, holidays, and so on.

References

1. Houenou, A., Bonnifait, P., Cherfaoui, V., et al.: Vehicle trajectory prediction based on motion model and maneuver recognition. In: International Conference on Intelligent Robots and Systems 2013, pp. 4363–4369. IEEE (2013)
2. Woo, H., Ji, Y., Kono, H., et al.: Lane-change detection based on vehicle-trajectory prediction. IEEE Robot. Autom. Lett. **2**(2), 1109–1116 (2017)
3. Hermes, C., Wohler, C., Schenk, K., et al.: Long-term vehicle motion prediction. In: Intelligent Vehicles Symposium 2009, pp. 652–657. IEEE (2009)
4. Wang, L., Chen, Z., Wu, J.: Vehicle trajectory prediction algorithm in vehicular network. Wireless Netw. **25**(4), 2143–2156 (2018). https://doi.org/10.1007/s11276-018-1803-3
5. De Leege, A., van Paassen, M., Mulder, M.: A machine learning approach to trajectory prediction. In: Guidance, Navigation, and Control Conference 2013, p. 4782. AIAA (2013)
6. Zheng, Y.: Trajectory data mining: an overview. Trans. Intell. Syst. Technol. **6**(3), 1–41 (2015)
7. Hochreiter, S., Schmidhuber, J.: Long short-term memory. Neural Comput. **9**(8), 1735–1780 (1997)
8. Cho, K., Van Merriënboer, B., Gulcehre, C., et al.: Learning phrase representations using RNN encoder-decoder for statistical machine translation. arXiv1406.1078 (2014)
9. Jiang, H., Chang, L., Li, Q., et al.: Trajectory prediction of vehicles based on deep learning. In: International Conference on Intelligent Transportation Engineering 2019, pp. 190–195. IEEE (2019)
10. Kim, B., Kang, C.M., Kim, J., et al.: Probabilistic vehicle trajectory prediction over occupancy grid map via recurrent neural network. In: Intelligent Transportation Systems 2017, pp. 399–404. IEEE (2017)
11. Dai, S., Li, L., Li, Z.: Modeling vehicle interactions via modified LSTM models for trajectory prediction. IEEE Access **7**, 38287–38296 (2019)
12. Park, S.H., Kim, B., Kang, C.M., et al.: Sequence-to-sequence prediction of vehicle trajectory via LSTM encoder-decoder architecture. In: Intelligent Vehicles Symposium 2018, pp. 1672–1678. IEEE (2018)
13. Deo, N., Trivedi, M.M.: Convolutional social pooling for vehicle trajectory prediction. In: Computer Vision and Pattern Recognition Workshops 2018, pp. 1468–1476. IEEE (2018)
14. Deo, N., Trivedi, M.M.: Multi-modal trajectory prediction of surrounding vehicles with maneuver based lstms. In: Intelligent Vehicles Symposium 2018, pp. 1179–1184. IEEE (2018)

15. Jeong, D., Baek, M., Lee, S.S.: Long-term prediction of vehicle trajectory based on a deep neural network. In: Information and Communication Technology Convergence 2017, pp. 725–727. IEEE (2017)
16. Lea, C., Flynn, M.D., Vidal, R., et al.: Temporal convolutional networks for action segmentation and detection. In: Computer Vision and Pattern Recognition 2017, pp. 156–165. IEEE (2017)
17. Bai, S., Kolter, J.Z., Koltun, V.: An empirical evaluation of generic convolutional and recurrent networks for sequence modeling. arXiv1803.01271 (2018)
18. Mnih, V., Heess, N., Graves, A.: Recurrent models of visual attention. In: Neural Information Processing Systems 2014, pp. 2204–2212. NIPS (2014)
19. Wang, D., Zhang, J., Cao, W., et al.: When will you arrive? estimating travel time based on deep neural networks. In: Thirty-Second AAAI Conference on Artificial Intelligence 2018, pp. 2500–2507. AAAI (2018)
20. Deo, N., Rangesh, A., Trivedi, M.M.: How would surround vehicles move? A unified framework for maneuver classification and motion prediction. IEEE Trans. Intell. Veh. 3(2), 129–140 (2018)
21. Stöckl, C., Maass, W.: Classifying images with few spikes per Neuron. arXiv2002.00860 (2020)
22. Bremer, J., Pang, Q., Yang, H.: Fast algorithms for the multi-dimensional Jacobi polynomial transform. Applied and Computational Harmonic Analysis, arXiv1901.07275v3 (2020)
23. Yang, J., Purevjav, A.O., Li, S.: The marginal cost of traffic congestion and road pricing: evidence from a natural experiment in Beijing. Am. Econ. J. Econ. Policy 12(1), 418–453 (2020)
24. Günther, S., Ruthotto, L., Schroder, J.B., et al.: Layer-parallel training of deep residual neural networks. SIAM J. Math. Data Sci. 2(1), 1–23 (2020)
25. Colyar, J., Halkias, J.: US Highway 101 dataset. federal highway administration. Technical report FHWA-HRT-07-030 (2007)
26. Zheng, Y., Xie, X., Ma, W.Y.: GeoLife: a collaborative social networking service among user, location and trajectory. IEEE Data Eng. 33(2), 32–39 (2010)
27. Huang, F., Zhang, J., Zhou, C., Wang, Y., Huang, J., Zhu, L.: A deep learning algorithm using a fully connected sparse autoencoder neural network for landslide susceptibility prediction. Landslides 17(1), 217–229 (2019). https://doi.org/10.1007/s10346-019-01274-9
28. Hamaguchi, R., Fujita, A., Nemoto, K., et al.: Effective use of dilated convolutions for segmenting small object instances in remote sensing imagery. In: Winter Conference on Applications of Computer Vision 2018, pp. 1442–1450. IEEE (2018)

Beamforming for MISO Cognitive Radio Networks Based on Successive Convex Approximation

Ruina Mao[1], Anming Dong[2(✉)] , and Jiguo Yu[1,2,3]

[1] School of Information Science and Engineering, Qufu Normal University, Rizhao 276826, China
[2] School of Computer Science and Technology, Qilu University of Technology (Shandong Academy of Sciences), Jinan 250353, China
anmingdong@qlu.edu.cn
[3] Shandong Provincial Key Laboratory of Computer Networks, Shandong Computer Science Center (National Supercomputer Center in Jinan), Qilu University of Technology (Shandong Academy of Sciences), Jinan 250014, China
jiguoyu@sina.com

Abstract. This paper presents a novel beamforming optimization method for downlink underlying multiple-input single-output (MISO) cognitive radio (CR) networks. We formulate a beamforming optimization problem to maximize the sum rate of a CR network with one primary user (PU) pair and multiple secondary user (SU) pairs, subject to the quality of service requirement of the PU given the transmit power budgets at the base stations (BSs). To find the solution of the nonconvex problem, an iterative solving algorithm is proposed based on successive convex approximation (SCA). In developing the algorithm, we first reformulate the original nonconvex objective function as the difference of two concave functions. A concave substitute function is then derived using the one-order Taylor expansion. Based on this concave substitute, a convex semidefinite programming (SDP) is derived and solved. The new solution is then utilized to construct a new substitute. This process is repeated until a smooth point is reached. Simulation results show the effectiveness of the proposed SCA-based beamforming algorithm to achieve spectrum sharing.

Keywords: Beamforming · Cognitive radio network · Multiple-input single-output (MISO) · Semidefinite programming · Successive convex approximation

---

This work was partially supported by the National Natural Science Foundation of China (NSFC) under Grants 61701269, 61672321, 61832012, 61771289 and 61373027, the Key Research and Development Program of Shandong Province under Grants 2019JZZY010313 and 2019JZZY020124, the Natural Science Foundation of Shandong Province under Grant ZR2017BF012, the Joint Research Fund for Young Scholars in Qilu University (Shandong Academy of Sciences) under Grant 2017BSHZ005.

© Springer Nature Switzerland AG 2020
D. Yu et al. (Eds.): WASA 2020, LNCS 12384, pp. 370–380, 2020.
https://doi.org/10.1007/978-3-030-59016-1_31

1   Introduction

Cognitive radio (CR) is recognized as a promising technology that can improve the spectrum efficiency and alleviate the spectrum resource scarcity by allowing a secondary network to dynamically access the spectrum of the primary network [1–3]. The underlay mode is a basic strategy to achieve the spectrum sharing in CR networks [4–6], in which the PUs and SUs access the same spectrum simultaneously.

Interference management is crucial in an underlying CR network, since spectrum reusing among multiple users may deteriorate the quality of received signals at both PUs and SUs [7–10]. Beamforming is an effective interference management technique that improves the signal-to-interference-plus-noise ratio (SINR) by exploiting multiple antennas to steer the direction of the transmitted signal towards the desired users [11–16]. Consequently, beamformer design for CR networks has drawn great research interests in the past decade.

Although there have been a huge number of works on the beamforming of CR networks in the literature, many problems are still open. Even in the simplest scenario of a two-user network, the sum rate maximization has been proven to be NP-hard in [17]. The main difficulty in the beamforming designs originates the non-convexity of the optimization problems, which are usually caused by the inter-user interference. Due to such non-convexity property, maximize the total throughput or sum rate in response to various quality of service (QoS) demands remains challenging [12].

In this work, we focus on the transmit beamforming to maximize the sum rate subject to an SINR QoS requirement of the PU in the multiple-input single-output (MISO) CR network. We successfully circumvent the non-convexity barrier using the method of successive convex approximation (SCA) [18]. Specifically, we formulate a beamforming optimization problem to maximize the sum rate for a CR network that consists of a primary network with one MISO PU pair and a secondary network with multiple MISO secondary user (SU) pairs. To maintain the QoS of the PU, we consider the minimum SINR requirement for the PU in the beamforming design problem. The non-convexity of the problem originates two folds, i.e., the objective and the SINR constraint. For the objective, we derive a concave substitute by first reforming it as an equivalent difference of concave (D.C.) and then approximating it using the first-order Taylor expansion. To deal with the non-convexity of the SINR constraint of the PU, we rely on the technique of semidefinite programming relaxation (SDR). The solution is finally obtained by successively solving the relaxed convex semidefinite programming (SDP) problems. The key contributions of this paper are listed as follows:

- A sum rate maximization problem subject to PU SINR constraint is formulated for the MISO CR network with multiple SU pairs. The considered scenario is a MISO CR interference channel, the sum rate maximization problem of which is still challenging to date.
- A convex approximation method is proposed to substitute the original non-convex sum rate function. It is novel to apply the SCA technique to relax the

nonconvex sum rate objective as a concave one in the scenario of MISO CR networks.
- An effective iterative algorithm is devised by combining the convex approximating with SDR. There is no similar work in the literature as far as we know.
- The behavior of the algorithm is interesting. It is observed that the proposed SCA-based beamforming algorithm is capable of guaranteeing the QoS demand of the PU.

Notations: $\mathcal{C}$ denotes the complex field. Bold uppercase and lowercase letters represent matrix and column vectors, respectively. Non-bold italic letters represent scalar values. $\mathbf{A}^H$ and $\mathbf{A}^{-1}$ represent the Hermitian transpose and inverse of $\mathbf{A}$, respectively. $\mathrm{Tr}(\mathbf{A})$ is the trace of matrix $\mathbf{A}$. $\mathbb{E}[\cdot]$ denotes the statistical expectation. $\|\cdot\|_F$ denotes the Frobenius-norm. $\mathbf{A} \succeq \mathbf{0}$ means $\mathbf{A}$ is semidefinite, i.e., $\mathbf{x}^H \mathbf{A} \mathbf{x} \geq 0$. $\mathbf{x} \sim \mathcal{CN}(\mathbf{m}, \mathbf{C})$ denotes $\mathbf{x}$ is a complex Gaussian vector variable with mean vector $\mathbf{m}$ and covariance matrix $\mathbf{C}$.

2   System Model and Problem Formulation

In this section, we first present the system model of the considered MISO CR network, and then formulate the sum rate maximization problem.

2.1   MISO Cognitive Radio Network Model

We consider a MISO cognitive radio network, consisting of a primary base station (PBS) and K secondary base stations (SBSs). Assume each BS serves one user, i.e., there are one primary user (PU) and K secondary users (SUs). We assume all the BSs in the CR network are equipped with M antennas. We consider the downlink scenario and each BS transmits one data symbol to a single-antenna receiver at one channel use. The CR network works on the underlay model, i.e., all the SUs share the same frequency resource of the PU, i.e., they are allowed to transmit simultaneously.

In such a network, the signal emitted by one transmitter constitutes interference at the receivers of other users. We denote the set of users in the CR network as $\mathcal{K} = \{0, 1, 2, \ldots, K\}$, with 0 denote the PU. The received signal at the receiver of user k is then written as

$$y_k = \mathbf{h}_{kk}^H \mathbf{v}_k s_k + \sum_{j=0, j \neq k}^{K} \mathbf{h}_{kj}^H \mathbf{v}_j s_j + n_k , \forall k \in \mathcal{K} , \tag{1}$$

where $\mathbf{h}_{kj} \in \mathbb{C}^{M \times 1}$ denotes the complex channel matrix between the j-th transmitter to the k-th receiver, $s_k \in \mathcal{C}$ is the data symbol sent by user k with $\mathbb{E}[|s_k|^2] = 1$, $\mathbf{v}_k \in \mathcal{C}^{M \times 1}$ is the beamformer of user k, and $n_k \sim \mathcal{CN}(0, \sigma_k^2)$ is the additive white Gaussian noise (AWGN). The achievable rate of user k is then written as

$$R_k = \log(1 + \mathrm{SINR}_k), \forall k \in \mathcal{K} , \tag{2}$$

with

$$\text{SINR}_k = \frac{|\mathbf{h}_{kk}^H \mathbf{v}_k|^2}{\sum_{j=0, j \neq k}^{K} |\mathbf{h}_{kj}^H \mathbf{v}_j|^2 + \sigma_k^2}. \tag{3}$$

2.2 Problem Formulation

In this work, our goal is to find the beamforming vectors that maximize the throughput of the CR after satisfying the SINR demand of PU when a power budget is given at individual BS. The problem is mathematically written as

$$\max_{\{\mathbf{v}_k, \forall k \in \mathcal{K}\}} \sum_{k=0}^{K} R_k \tag{4a}$$

$$s.t. : \quad \text{SINR}_0 \geq \gamma_0^{min}, \tag{4b}$$

$$\|\mathbf{v}_k\|_F^2 \leq P_k, \forall k \in \mathcal{K}. \tag{4c}$$

where $P_k > 0$ denotes the power budget of user k. The constraint (4b) guarantees the minimum rate requirement of the PU. The power budgets are embodied by the constraint (4c).

Problem (4) is well known nonconvex due to the existence of interference. It is generally NP-hard and thus difficult to solve. In the following, we develop an iterative algorithm to solve this problem based on the method of SCA.

3 Proposed SCA-Based Algorithm

In this section, we propose an iterative algorithm to solve the formulated sum rate maximization beamforming problem for the considered MISO CR network. The key ingredient of the proposed algorithm is the idea of SCA. Specifically, we first reformulate the objective of the problem (4) as a D.C. function. Then, we substitute the second term of the D.C. function as a linear function, which is the first-order Taylor expansion near a given point. The objective is thus substituted by the newly constructed concave function. Finally, we obtain a solution for this concave function thorough SDR. A new Taylor expansion is then applied at this new point, and a new solution can be obtained. We successively update the solution, until a stable point is reached.

3.1 Problem Reformulation

Based on the basic property of logarithmic function, problem (4) can be equivalently written as

$$\max_{\{\mathbf{v}_k, \forall k\}} \quad \phi - \varphi \tag{5a}$$

$$s.t. : \quad \text{SINR}_0 \geq \gamma_0^{min}, \tag{5b}$$

$$\text{Tr}(\mathbf{v}_k \mathbf{v}_k^H) \leq P_k, \forall k \in \mathcal{K}, \tag{5c}$$

where the concave function ϕ is defined as

$$\phi = \sum_{k=0}^{K} \log_2(\sum_{j=0}^{K} |\mathbf{h}_{kj}\mathbf{v}_j|^2 + \sigma_k^2) , \tag{6}$$

and the concave function φ is defined as

$$\varphi = \sum_{k=0}^{K} \log_2(\sum_{j=0,j\neq k}^{K} |\mathbf{h}_{kj}^H \mathbf{v}_j|^2 + \sigma_k^2) . \tag{7}$$

In its current form, the objective of problem (5) is a D.C. function and problem (5) is thus a D.C. programming. The D.C. programming is not convex nor concave. We want to find a concave substitute to it to relax the nonconvex problem as a convex one. In the following, a convex approximation function to the D.C. function is presented.

3.2   Convex Approximation to the D.C. Function

Equation (7) can be equivalently written as

$$\varphi(\mathbf{Q}) = \sum_{k=0}^{K} \log_2 \Big(\sum_{j=0,j\neq k}^{K} \mathbf{h}_{kj}^H \mathbf{Q}_j \mathbf{h}_{kj} + \sigma_k^2 \Big) , \tag{8}$$

where $\mathbf{Q}_j \triangleq \mathbf{v}_j \mathbf{v}_j^H$ and φ is now a function of $\{\mathbf{Q}_j, \forall j \in \mathcal{K}\}$. For the convenience of expression, we denote $\mathbf{Q}$ as the shorthand notation of $\{\mathbf{Q}_k, \forall k \in \mathcal{K}\}$ in the following.

Given a feasible point $\{\tilde{\mathbf{Q}}_k, \forall k\}$, the first-order Taylor approximation of $\varphi(\mathbf{Q})$ can be derived from the principle of matrix differentiation

$$\bar{\varphi}(\mathbf{Q}) = \varphi(\tilde{\mathbf{Q}}) + \frac{1}{\ln 2} \sum_{k=0}^{K} tr[\tilde{\mathbf{D}}_k(\mathbf{Q}_k - \tilde{\mathbf{Q}}_k)] , \tag{9}$$

where $\tilde{\mathbf{D}}_k \triangleq \sum_{j=0,j\neq k}^{K} \mathbf{h}_{jk} z_j^{-1}(\tilde{\mathbf{Q}})\mathbf{h}_{jk}^H$ and $z_j(\tilde{\mathbf{Q}}) = \sum_{i=0,i\neq j}^{K} \mathbf{h}_{ji}^H \tilde{\mathbf{Q}}_i \mathbf{h}_{ji} + \sigma_j^2$. Since $\varphi(\mathbf{Q})$ is concave, the following inequalities hold $\varphi(\mathbf{Q}) \leq \bar{\varphi}(\mathbf{Q})$, and thus

$$\phi(\mathbf{Q}) - \bar{\varphi}(\mathbf{Q}) \leq \phi(\mathbf{Q}) - \varphi(\mathbf{Q}) . \tag{10}$$

This reveals that the substitute function $\phi(\mathbf{Q}) - \bar{\varphi}(\mathbf{Q})$ is a lower bound of $\phi(\mathbf{Q}) - \varphi(\mathbf{Q})$, and they are tangent at the point $\tilde{\mathbf{Q}}$.

3.3   Convex Approximating Problem

By substituting the function φ in (5) as (9) and discarding the constant terms, problem (5) is approximated by

$$\max_{\mathbf{Q}_k, \forall k} \quad \phi(\mathbf{Q}) - \frac{1}{\ln 2} \sum_{k=0}^{K} tr[\tilde{\mathbf{D}}_k \mathbf{Q}_k] \tag{11a}$$

$$s.t.: \quad \text{SINR}_0 \geq \gamma_0^{min} , \tag{11b}$$

$$\text{Tr}(\mathbf{Q}_k) \leq P_k , \tag{11c}$$

$$\mathbf{Q}_k \succeq \mathbf{0}, \tag{11d}$$

$$\text{rank}(\mathbf{Q}_k) = 1, \forall k \in \mathcal{K} . \tag{11e}$$

Problem (11) is a SDP with rank constraints shown by (11e). The rank constraints result to noconvex. To solve it, we discard the rank constraint, and obtain the following relaxed problem

$$\min_{\mathbf{Q}_k, \forall k} \quad -\left(\phi(\mathbf{Q}) - \frac{1}{\ln 2} \sum_{k=0}^{K} \text{Tr}[\tilde{\mathbf{D}}_k \mathbf{Q}_k]\right) \tag{12a}$$

$$s.t.: \quad \frac{\text{Tr}(\mathbf{h}_{00}\mathbf{h}_{00}^H \mathbf{Q}_0)}{\gamma_0^{min}} \geq \sum_{j=1}^{K} \text{Tr}(\mathbf{h}_{0j}\mathbf{h}_{0j}^H \mathbf{Q}_j) + \sigma_0^2 , \tag{12b}$$

$$\text{Tr}(\mathbf{Q}_k) \leq P_k , \tag{12c}$$

$$\mathbf{Q}_k \succeq \mathbf{0}, \forall k \in \mathcal{K} . \tag{12d}$$

This SDP relaxation (SDR) problem (12) is now convex, which can be solved effectively using CVX.

3.4   Recover Beamformers from the Solution of SDR

Denote $\{\mathbf{Q}_k^*, \forall k\}$ as the solution of the SDP relaxation (SDR) problem (12), the beamformers $\{\mathbf{v}_k, \forall k \in \mathcal{K}\}$ can be recovered from the SDR solution. Specifically, after applying the singular value decomposition (SVD), $\mathbf{Q}_k^*$ is decomposed as $\mathbf{Q}_k^* = \mathbf{A}_k \mathbf{\Lambda}_k \mathbf{A}_k^H$, where $\mathbf{A}_k = [\mathbf{a}_1, \mathbf{a}_2, \ldots, \mathbf{a}_M]$ is the eigen-matrix and $\mathbf{\Lambda}_k = \text{diag}(\lambda_1, \lambda_2, \ldots, \lambda_M)$ is a diagonal matrix with the diagonal elements being the descending-ordered singular values. The beamforming vector is then recovered by the eigenvector corresponding the maximum singular value, i.e.,

$$\mathbf{v}_k = \sqrt{\lambda_1}\mathbf{a}_1 . \tag{13}$$

We note that if the ranks of $\mathbf{Q}_k^*, \forall k$ are equal to one, the SDR solution is the optimal solution to the problem (11), and the recovered vectors $\mathbf{v}_k, \forall k$ are also optimal for the original problem (4). In our simulations, we find that the ranks of the solutions are always one after several iterating.

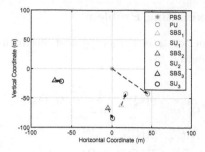

Fig. 1. An instance of the distribution of user pairs for the considered MISO CR network with one PU pair and $K = 3$ SU pairs.

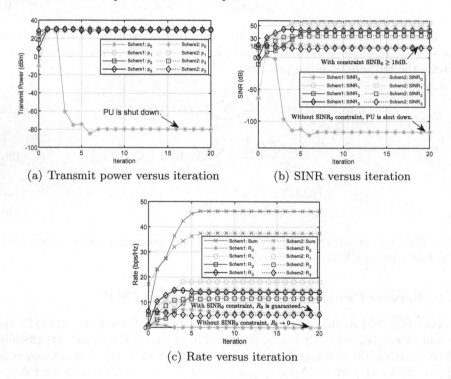

(a) Transmit power versus iteration

(b) SINR versus iteration

(c) Rate versus iteration

Fig. 2. Convergence of the SCA-based algorithm respect to achieved rate for a MISO CR network with $K = 3$, $M = 3$. The Scheme 1 represents that the minimum requirement of $SINR_0$ for the PU is not added in the simulation, and the Scheme 2 sets $\gamma_0^{min} = 18$ dB.

3.5   SCA-Based Algorithm

The solution $\mathbf{Q}^*$ obtained at the current step can be used as the reference point for the next iteration, near which a new substitute function can be constructed to start the next round of optimization. In such a successive appropriating process, we can finally obtain a solution when a smooth point is reached. Such an SCA-based iterative beamforming method for the MISO CR network is summarized as Algorithm 1.

Algorithm 1: SCA-Based Beamforming Algorithm for MISO CR Networks

---

1 **Given:** The channel matrices $\{\mathbf{H}_{kj}, \forall j, k \in \mathcal{K}\}$, the power budgets $\{P_k, \forall k \in \mathcal{K}\}$, the SINR requirement of PU γ_0^{min}, and the maximum iterating number $N_{\max}$;
2 **Initialize:** $\{\tilde{\mathbf{Q}}_k, \forall k\}$, $n = 0$;
3 **while** $n < N_{\max}$ **do**
4      $n = n + 1$;
5      $z_k(\tilde{\mathbf{Q}}) = \sum_{i=0, i \neq k}^{K} \mathbf{h}_{ki}^H \tilde{\mathbf{Q}}_i \mathbf{h}_{ki} + \sigma_k^2, \forall k \in \mathcal{K}$;
6      $\tilde{\mathbf{D}}_k = \sum_{j=0, j \neq k}^{K} \mathbf{h}_{jk} z_j^{-1}(\tilde{\mathbf{Q}}) \mathbf{h}_{jk}^H, \forall k \in \mathcal{K}$;
7   Solve the SDR problem (12), obtain the solution $\{\mathbf{Q}_k^*, \forall k\}$;
8   Recover $\mathbf{v}_k, \forall k \in \mathcal{K}$ following (13);
9   Update $\tilde{\mathbf{Q}}_k = \mathbf{v}_k \mathbf{v}_k^H, \forall k \in \mathcal{K}$;
10 **end**

---

4   Simulations and Discussions

In this section, we carry out simulations to validate the performance of the proposed SCA-based transmit beamforming algorithm for solving the sum rate maximization problem of MISO CR networks with PU quality of service guarantee as well as fairness consideration.

In the simulations, we consider a MISO CR network with one PU pair and $K = 3$ SU pairs. Thus there are 4 pairs of transceivers in total, and each transmitter has 3 antennas. In such a case, no transmitter has enough space dimension to completely suppressing the interference from the other 3 users, except one of them is powered off (shut down). We are interested in *how the SCA-based algorithm behaves when the number of transmit antennas is not sufficiently large to provide interference-free space for all signals in the CR networks, and whether the SINR requirement of the PU can be guaranteed.*

We assume all the transceiver pairs are located in an area of $200\,\mathrm{m} \times 200\,\mathrm{m}$, with the PBS located at the origin. The receivers are distributed randomly around their BSs. We assume the channels follow a Rayleigh fading model with large-scale path loss. The large-scale path loss factor is calculated as $G_{kj} = 1/(1 + D_{kj}^2)$, where D_{kj} denotes the distance between the jth transmitter to the kth receiver. The small-scale factors are generated following the i.i.d. complexity Gaussian distribution with zero mean and unit variance. By combining the large-scale and small scale factors, the channel vector $\mathbf{h}_{kj} \sim \mathcal{CN}(\mathbf{0}, G_{kj}\mathbf{I}_M)$. A randomly generated distribution of users are shown in Fig. 1, based on which we test the performance of the proposed algorithm. We note that although any randomly generated instance can be used to test our algorithm, we provide the instance shown by Fig. 1, since the interference to the PU is severe and the signal is relatively weak. This is reflected by the distributing of the users, where the SBS_1 is near the PU and the distance between the PBS to the PU is relatively far. Without loss of generality, the transmit power budget of all the transmitters in the network are equally set as $P_k = 30\,\text{dBm}\ \forall k$, and the power of noise are also equally set as $\sigma_k^2 = \sigma^2 = 10^{-6}, \forall k$.

The convergence performance of the algorithm is shown in Fig. 2. Two schemes of the proposed algorithm are simulated. For the *Scheme 1*, we inactive the SINR constraint for the PU, i.e., the constraint (4b) is removed. In such case, the problem degenerates into a sum rate maximization problem subject to power constraints. For the *Scheme 2*, we set the minimum required SINR value of the PU as $\gamma_0^{min} = 18\,\text{dB}$ and the constraint (4b) is considered in the algorithm. In the simulations, the algorithm initiates the transmitters by randomly generated vectors. It can be observed from the curves that the algorithm converges after several iterations.

In Fig. 2(a), the curves of transmit power versus iteration are demonstrated, with the power at BS k calculated as $p_k = \|\mathbf{v}_k\|_F^2$. It is observed that the PBS is shut down ($p_0 \approx -80\,\text{dBm}$) for the Scheme 1. The effects of shut-down of transmit power at PBS are also reflected in Fig. 2(b) and Fig. 2(c), where the $SINR_0$ and R_0 are tend to zero for the Scheme 1.

Why the PU is shut down? Recall that the number of user pairs in the considered CR network is 4, while the space degree of freedom (DoF) of the network is restricted by the number of transmit antenna $M = 3$. Then, the capacity of the CR network is interference limited if all the users are activated simultaneously. If the sum rate of the whole network is optimized, the weakest user will be shut down by the proposed algorithm if no special consideration is taken to the PU.

In Fig. 2(b), we can observe that the $SINR_0$ tends to $18\,\text{dB}$ for Scheme 2. Accordingly, the achievable rate of the PU is guaranteed as shown in Fig. 2(c). As a trade-off to guarantee the data rate of the PU, the sum rate of the whole

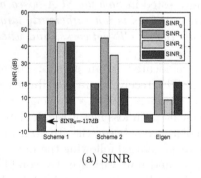

(a) SINR

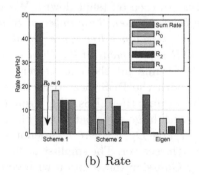

(b) Rate

Fig. 3. Comparison of achieved SINR and Rate values over different schemes for all the user in the CR network with $K = 3$, $M = 3$.

network is sacrificed, which is shown by Fig. 2(c) that the sum rate of the Scheme 2 is lower than that of the Scheme 1.

To better demonstrate the performance of the proposed SCA-based scheme, we compare the optimized SINR values in Fig. 3(a) using the bar figure. The *eigen-transmission* (Eigen) scheme is also provided as a performance benchmark. For the Eigen scheme, the beamformer at each BS k is designed as $\mathbf{v}_k^{eigen} = \sqrt{P_k}\mathbf{h}_{kk}/\|\mathbf{h}_{kk}\|_F$. It is observed that the SINR of PU is much lower than that of the SUs for either the Scheme 1 or the Eigen scheme. While Scheme 2 guarantees the minimum required SINR for the PU, i.e., $\text{SINR}_0 = 18\,\text{dB}$. This reflects the effectiveness of the proposed SCA-based algorithm in guaranteeing the QoS of the PU.

As the final performance indicator, the achieved rates of the users are compared in Fig. 3(b). It is observed again that the sum rate achieved by the Scheme 1 is better than the Scheme 2, but the PU is shut down in the Scheme 1, while the data rate of PU is guaranteed in the Scheme 2. It is also demonstrated that the proposed SCA-based schemes are superior to the Eigen transmission scheme. This is because the proposed SCA-based scheme suppressed the inter-user interference, while the Eigen scheme ignores the interference.

5 Conclusion

We studied a beamforming method for sum rate maximization in MISO CR networks. We formulated a sum rate maximization problem subject to the SINR requirement constraint of the PU given the power budget of each transmitter. Since the objective is nonconvex, we developed an iterative solving algorithm based on successive convex approximation. We verified the performance of the proposed SCA-based algorithm through simulations, which showed that the SINR of the PU can be guaranteed. This work provided some new insights into the beamforming design for MISO CR networks.

References

1. Mitola, J., Maguire, G.Q.: Cognitive radio: making software radios more personal. IEEE Pers. Commun. **6**(4), 13–18 (1999)
2. Haykin, S.: Cognitive radio: brain-empowered wireless communications. IEEE J. Sel. Areas Commun. **23**(2), 201–220 (2005)
3. Cai, Z., Ji, S., He, J., Bourgeois, A.G.: Optimal distributed data collection for asynchronous cognitive radio networks. In: 2012 IEEE 32nd International Conference on Distributed Computing Systems. IEEE (2012)
4. Tuan, P.V., Duy, T.T., Koo, I.: Multiuser miso beamforming design for balancing the received powers in secure cognitive radio networks. In: 2018 IEEE Seventh International Conference on Communications and Electronics (ICCE), pp. 39–43. IEEE (2018)
5. Zhang, R., Liang, Y.-C., Cui, S.: Dynamic resource allocation in cognitive radio networks. IEEE Sig. Process. Mag. **27**(3), 102–114 (2010)

6. Cai, Z., Ji, S., He, J., Wei, L., Bourgeois, A.G.: Distributed and asynchronous data collection in cognitive radio networks with fairness consideration. IEEE Trans. Parallel Distrib. Syst. **25**(8), 2020–2029 (2014)

7. Pang, J.-S., Scutari, G., Palomar, D.P., Facchinei, F.: Design of cognitive radio systems under temperature-interference constraints: a variational inequality approach. IEEE Trans. Sig. Process. **58**(6), 3251–3271 (2010)

8. Huang, S., Liu, X., Ding, Z.: Decentralized cognitive radio control based on inference from primary link control information. IEEE J. Sel. Areas Commun. **29**(2), 394–406 (2011)

9. Dadallage, S., Yi, C., Cai, J.: Joint beamforming, power, and channel allocation in multiuser and multichannel underlay miso cognitive radio networks. IEEE Trans. Veh. Technol. **65**(5), 3349–3359 (2015)

10. Wang, W., et al.: Joint precoding optimization for secure SWIPT in UAV-aided NOMA networks. IEEE Trans. Commun. **68**(8), 5028–5040 (2020)

11. Zhao, N., et al.: Secure transmission via joint precoding optimization for downlink MISO NOMA. IEEE Trans. Veh. Technol. **68**(8), 7603–7615 (2019)

12. Lai, I.-W., Zheng, L., Lee, C.-H., Tan, C.W.: Beamforming duality and algorithms for weighted sum rate maximization in cognitive radio networks. IEEE J. Sel. Areas Commun. **33**(5), 832–847 (2014)

13. Du, H., Ratnarajah, T., Pesavento, M., Papadias, C.B.: Joint transceiver beamforming in MIMO cognitive radio network via second-order cone programming. IEEE Trans. Sig. Process. **60**(2), 781–792 (2011)

14. Yao, R., Liu, Y., Lu, L., Li, G.Y., Maaref, A.: Cooperative precoding for cognitive transmission in two-tier networks. IEEE Trans. Commun. **64**(4), 1423–1436 (2016)

15. Dong, A., Zhang, H., Yuan, D., Zhou, X.: Interference alignment transceiver design by minimizing the maximum mean square error for MIMO interfering broadcast channel. IEEE Trans. Veh. Technol. **65**(8), 6024–6037 (2016)

16. Zhang, H., Dong, A., Jin, S., Yuan, D.: Joint transceiver and power splitting optimization for multiuser MIMO SWIPT under MSE QoS constraints. IEEE Trans. Veh. Technol. **66**(8), 7123–7135 (2017)

17. Luo, Z.-Q., Zhang, S.: Dynamic spectrum management: complexity and duality. IEEE J. Sel. Top. Sign. Process. **2**(1), 57–73 (2008)

18. Razaviyayn, M., Sanjabi, M., Luo, Z.-Q.: A stochastic successive minimization method for nonsmooth nonconvex optimization with applications to transceiver design in wireless communication networks. Math. Program. **157**(2), 515–545 (2016)

K-Anonymous Privacy Preserving Scheme Based on Bilinear Pairings over Medical Data

Linghang Meng[1], Xueshu Hong[1], Yingwen Chen[1(✉)], Yuke Ding[2], and Chengzhuo Zhang[1]

[1] College of Computer, National University of Defense Technology, Changsha, China
lhmeng,hongxueshu,ywch,zhangchengzhuo18}@nudt.edu.cn
[2] School of Humanities and Social Science,
North China Electric Power University, Baoding, China
yukeding@ncepu.edu.cn

Abstract. Recent years have witnessed the advent of technologies such as the Internet of Things, cloud computing, and big data. Also, the analysis and research of data have attracted more and more attention from researchers. For example, the analysis of medical data can help government agencies do right decisions in public health services, or assist medical research institutes in conducting medical research. But it is followed by the privacy preserving of patient medical data in a cloud environment. Our paper proposes a problem-solving scheme that is a k-anonymous privacy preserving scheme based on bilinear pairings (KPSBP) which combines k-anonymity and secure searchable encryption to ensure the patient data privacy is not compromised and the medical data is well shared.

Keywords: Privacy preserving · K-anonymity · Bilinear pairings · Medical data

1 Introduction

The storage of medical data has transformed from traditional paper storage to electronic storage. And the format of data is diverse, including structured data, semi-structured data, unstructured data, and various video, audio and image data. In addition to being a record of the therapeutic process, the tremendous amount of medical data can also be used to conduct medical big data analysis and research. Furthermore, with the continuous elevating of data analysis and mining technology, the trouble of user data security and privacy is more and more attract researchers' attention.

Data security and privacy contain two aspects. One is data security, which means that data is guaranteed to be complete, consistent, and not falsified during transmission. The other is data privacy that means data can only be viewed by specific authorized persons [16,19]. In a cloud computing environment, once the data owner uploads the data to cloud service providers (CSPs), this process involves data security issues [10]. However, whether CSPs use data correctly

© Springer Nature Switzerland AG 2020
D. Yu et al. (Eds.): WASA 2020, LNCS 12384, pp. 381–393, 2020.
https://doi.org/10.1007/978-3-030-59016-1_32

and reasonably involves data privacy issues. In the traditional cloud computing environment, the data in cloud storage is not directly controlled by data owners. So, improper utilization of data by CSPs may jeopardize the privacy and interests of data owners [20].

If those issues cannot be resolved, medical institutions will be unwilling to share their data [15]. In the state of art of research, they mainly concentrate on how to locate a specific data owner in the cloud environment and get the data of the corresponding data owner. However, exposing the search results may also reveal the data owner's privacy. For example, the search results are obtained by data users through keywords search. Then, the keyword in the search process exposes the specific characteristics to the data users of the data owners. Also, there is a problem that cloud servers are "honest but curious" [3].

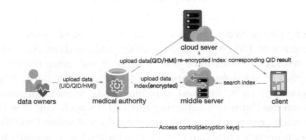

Fig. 1. System architecture.

In this paper, we propose KPSBP that adopts the k-anonymity method and public key searchable encryption. KPSBP can solve the above problems extensively in the medical field. Thus, this scheme can ensure both data privacy and security.

The main contributions of our work are listed as the following items:

- Define a medical privacy preserving ciphertext keyword searching model.
- Proposed an implementation method of using k-anonymity combined with searchable encryption to protect user privacy.
- Describe the algorithmic procedure of ciphertext search with keywords.
- Conducted practical experiments on the corresponding algorithms, including processing time and hitting accuracy, etc.

The contents of each section are as follows. In Sect. 1, we introduce the content of the paper in general. Section 2 presents questions of this paper, i.e., system models, threat model, design goals, and notion definitions. Section 3 carries out assumptions and related techniques introductions. Section 4 mainly introduces the system model in detail. In Sect. 5, we formulate security analysis about this scheme. Section 6 does the relevant system experiments. Related work is discussed in Sect. 7. In the end, in Sect. 8, the article is summarized.

2   Problem Formulation

2.1   System Model

As shown in Fig. 1, the system has five main components: patients, medical institutions, cloud server, middle server, and data users. The patients share their personal information ID (SID, QID), medical data D and keyword W. Then D and W are encrypted by the medical institutions. The medical institutions then upload the QID and the encrypted data and keywords to the cloud server, upload the encrypted keywords to the middle server, respectively. Later, the middle server re-encrypts the keywords and delivers the re-encrypted keywords to the cloud server. If the data users want to initiate a keyword search from the client side, they can input the keyword to the application on mobile phone or other wireless devices. The corresponding keyword trapdoor is first calculated and submitted to the middle server, and the middle server re-encrypts the trapdoor to the cloud server. After receiving the trapdoor, the cloud server searches the patients' medical data keyword and then returns the corresponding patients' QID and encrypted medical data to the data users. Once data users get the QID and encrypted medical data, they obtain authorization from the corresponding medical institutions to attain relevant medical data for further medical research.

2.2   Threat Model

In this article, we assume that the middle server is absolutely trustworthy to the entire system [20]. The middle server can be any trusted third party entity, e.g., the certificate authority in public-key infrastructure (PKI) [12] or the third party auditor [9]. Medical institutions and data users can rely on middle servers to communicate with them without worrying about the leakage of privacy. However, in our scheme, the cloud server is not completely reliable, that is, the cloud server is "honest but curious" [3]. Cloud server usually completely follows the instructions of the system, but the cloud can gradually find out the information after many query requests.

2.3   Design Goals

Under our scheme, we assume that patients, medical institutions, cloud servers, middle servers, and data users are independent to each other. And, medical institutions are absolutely reliable to patients, and medical institutions will not reveal patient privacy for profit or other reasons. In order to achieve the goal that privacy will not be compromised when patients' medical records are shared on the cloud. Our system design should simultaneously satisfy the following functions.

- Scheme Scaleability This architecture allows patients and data users to freely join in a cloud computing environment, i.e., a plug-and-play model.

- Medical Data Security Medical data will be encrypted before uploading it to the cloud. Therefore, as long as the encryption algorithm is not compromised, the medical will not be breached as well.
- Keywords Secrecy We use searchable encryption mechanisms based on bilinear pairing. It can be proved that the adversary can not breach keywords with a probabilistic polynomial time.
- Trapdoors Unlinkability Trapdoors are generated before the search is initiated. In our scheme, where every time we construct trapdoors we will generate a random number. Accordingly, the cloud cannot acquire valid information from trapdoors.
- Patient Identity Leakage In our proposed scheme, the search result represents k patients at least. This can stave off the link attacks. Also, patients' identity leakage can be avoided.

2.4 Notions

- SID: the patient identifier, denoted as one specific patient, could be Social Security Number.
- QID: quasi-identifier, e.g., zip code, address, age, gender, birthday, etc.
- M: the medical institution collection, denoted as a set of m medical institutions $M = (M_1, M_2, \ldots, M_m)$.
- D_i: the plain medical data text of M_i, denoted as a set of n data $D_i = (D_{i,1}, D_{i,2}, \ldots, D_{i,n})$.
- C_i: the ciphertext of medical data, medical data can be encrypted by medical institution, denoted as $C_i = (C_{i,1}, C_{i,2}, \ldots, C_{i,n})$.
- W: the keywords of medical data, that can represent a medical data, denoted as a set of u keywords $W = (w_1, w_2, \ldots, w_u)$.
- $\widehat{W}$: encrypted keyword of W, medical institutions' encrypted keywords collection, denoted as $\widehat{W} = (\hat{w}_1, \hat{w}_2, \ldots, \hat{w}_u)$.
- $\widetilde{W}$: represent the queried keywords, the subset of the keywords W, denoted as a set of q keywords $\widetilde{W} = (w_1, w_2, \ldots, w_q)$.
- T: the trapdoor for $\widetilde{W}$, denoted as $T = (T_{w_1}, T_{w_2}, \ldots, T_{w_q})$.

3 Preliminaries

Before we describe the system in detail, in this section, we should briefly introduce the crucial techniques needed for the scheme proposed in the article.

3.1 K-Anonymity

First, several definitions of k-anonymity are explained below.

Definition 1. *Quasi-Identifier Attribute Set A quasi-identifier is a minimal set of attributes in table S that can be combined with external information records to re-identify personal information. This paper assumes that quasi-identifiers are known based on empirical and epistemology.*

Definition 2. *Quasi-Identifier Attribute Set A quasi-identifier is a minimal set of attributes in table S that can be combined with external information records to re-identify personal information. This paper assumes that quasi-identifiers are known based on empirical and epistemology.*

Definition 3. *Equivalent Class A table S contains multiple tuples, and the equivalent class in S indicates that each tuple is the same as several other tuples.*

Definition 4. *K-Anonymity Property Table S is a set of determined values of the attribute group in K that is anonymized to appear at least k times in S, i.e., each of the equivalent classes is at least k in size.*

Mondrian [8] Multidimensional Partitioning is a k-anonymous multidimensional partitioning algorithm with k-anonymous processing in two steps. In the first step, the multidimensional regions covering all the domain space attributes are defined, that is, the partition stage constructs kd-trees [7]. The second step is to construct recoding functions for data recoding.

Algorithm 1. Mondrian partitioning algorithm

Input: Table S to be partitioned.
Output: Partitioning result.
 1: Anonymize(partition)
 2: **if** (no allowable multidimensional cut for partition) **then**
 3:     return ϕ : partition $\rightarrow$ summary
 4: **else**
 5:     dim $\leftarrow$ choose_dimension()
 6:     fs $\leftarrow$ frequencySet(partition, dim)
 7:     splitVal $\leftarrow$ find.median(fs)
 8:     lhs $\leftarrow$ t $\in$ partition : t.dim $\leq$ splitVal
 9:     rhs $\leftarrow$ t $\in$ partition : t.dim $>$ splitVal
10:     return Anonymize(rhs) $\cup$ Anonymize(lhs)
11: **end if**

The partitioning algorithm is described in the Algorithm 1. In the algorithm, each dimension selects the dimension and the value of the partition. In the literature of kd-trees, one approach is to use the median as the value of the partition. The partition is completed to get k-groups. and each k-group spontaneously includes at least k records. Each k-group is then generalized. Thereby, the QID of each group is the same.

3.2 Blinear Pairings

Blinear Map. Let G_1 and G_2 denote two cyclic group with a prime order p. We additional denote g_1 and g_2 as the generator of G_1 and G_2, repspectively. Let $\hat{e}$ be a bilinear map $\hat{e}$: $G \times G$, and then the following three properties are satisfied:

a) Bilinearity: $\forall a, b \in \mathbb{Z}_p^*$, $\hat{e}(g^a, g^b) = \hat{e}(g, g)^{ab}$.
b) Non-degeneracy: $\hat{e}(g, g) \neq 1$.
c) Computability: $\hat{e}$ can be efficiently computed in polynomial time.

Decisional Bilinear Diffie-Hellman (DBDH) Assumption. Suppose a adversary choose random a, b, c, $z \in \mathcal{Z}_p$, the DBDH assumption [13] means that there is no probabilistic polynomial time adversary, anyone can distinguish the tuple ($A = g^a$, $B = g^b$, $C = g^c$, $Z = e(g, g)^{abc}$) from the tuple ($A = g^a$, $B = g^b$, $C = g^c$, $Z = e(g, g)^z$), with a non-neligible advantage.

4 System Overview

4.1 Initialization

In the beginning, medical institutions were responsible for collecting patient data (i.e., SID, QID, medical data) and stored it in a place similar to a relational database. Subsequently, the medical institutions extracted the keywords for medical data. At the same time, each medical institution generates its own secret key. After that, medical institutions upload QID and encrypted keywords to the middle server and upload encrypted keywords and encrypted medical data to the cloud server.

Before uploading the encrypted medical data to the cloud server and the middle server, there is a k-anonymity processing procedure of the medical institution, which is elaborated in detail below.

4.2 K-Anonymity Phase

Before Processing. For example, as shown in Table 1, suppose the patient data structure is shown in the table, QID includes age, sex, zip code. These attributes that appear in private personal data may also appear in public datasets. If the two sets of data are linked together, the patient's private data may be leaked. Therefore, these attributes need to be k-anonymized to avoid privacy leakage.

Table 1. Patient data.

Age	Sex	Zipcode	Diease
25	Male	53711	Flu
25	Female	53712	Hepatitis
26	Male	53711	Brochitis
27	Male	53710	Broken Arm
27	Female	53712	AIDS
28	Male	53711	Hang Nail

Table 2. A 2-anonymity example.

Age	Sex	Zipcode	Diease
[25−26]	Male	53711	Flu
[25−27]	Female	53712	Hepatitis
[25−26]	Male	53711	Brochitis
[27−28]	Male	[53710−53711]	Broken Arm
[25−27]	Female	53712	AIDS
[27−28]	Male	[53710−53711]	Hang Nail

After Process. The multidimensional anonymization of patients is shown in Table 2. It can be seen that under the condition of 2-anonymity, each record has one another record that is exactly the same in the QID attributes.

4.3   Searchable Encryption

Here, we use an example to illustrate the details of searchable encryption. Medical institution i, i.e., M_i, needs to encrypt D_i into C_i with its own key before sharing medical data D_i. At the same time, in order for the data user to be able to perform search, the medical institution needs to extract the keyword $w_{i,h}$ from the document and send the encrypted keyword $\hat{w}_{i,h} = (E_{a'}, E_0)$ to the middle server. The middle server is further encrypted $E_{a'}$ to E_a and obtains $\hat{w}_{i,h} = (E_a, E_0)$, then the result is sent to the cloud server. Next, assume data user U want to search for a document related to the keyword $w_{h'}$. Basically, he needs to generate a trapdoor $T'_{w_{h'}}$ and upload it to the middle server. The middle server then re-encrypts the trapdoor $T'_{w_{h'}}$ to obtain $T_{w_{h'}}$, while generating secret data S_a. Then, $T_{w_{h'}}$ and S_a are upload to the cloud server. The cloud server finally calculates $\hat{e}(E_0, T_3) = \hat{e}(E_0, T_1) \cdot \hat{e}(S_a, T_2)$ for keyword search.

Encryption Construction. The construction is based on a bilinear map. Let g be the generators of the cyclic groups G_1 and G_2, and order is p. $\hat{e}$ is a bilinear map $\hat{e} : G_1 \times G_1 \to G_2$. In the process of encryption construction, the random key generation algorithm generates different keys for different inputs. $k_{m1} \in \mathbb{Z}_p^+$, $k_{m2} \in \mathbb{Z}_p^+$, $k_{i,w} \in \mathbb{Z}_p^+$, $k_{i,d} \in \mathbb{Z}_p^+ \leftarrow (0,1)^*$. k_{m1} and k_{m2} are the private keys of the middle server, $k_{i,w}$ and $k_{i,d}$ are the private keys used to encrypt keywords and data of medical institution M_i, respectively. $H(\cdot)$, locates in $\mathbb{Z}_p^+$, is a hash function.

Keyword Encryption. The keys of different medical institutions are different in this system, and the ciphertext generated each time for the same keyword is different. For the hth keyword of the medical institution M_i, i.e., $w_{i,h}$. the encryption calculation is as follows.

$$\hat{w}_{i,h} = (g^{k_{i,w} \cdot r_o \cdot H(w_{i,h})}, g^{k_{i,w} \cdot r_o}). \tag{1}$$

Where r_o is a random number generated randomly each time. Noted as $E'_a = g^{k_{i,w} \cdot r_o \cdot H(w_{i,h})}$ and $E_o = g^{k_{i,w} \cdot r_o}$.

The medical institution submits $\hat{w}_{i,h} = (E'_a, E_o)$ to the middle server, and the middle server re-encrypts E'_a with its own key k_{m1}, k_{m2} to obtain E_a, as follows.

$$E_a = (E'_a \cdot g^{k_{m1}})^{k_{m2}}. \tag{2}$$

Finally, the middle server submits the $\hat{w}_{i,h} = (E_a, E_o)$ to the cloud server. In this process, the middle server is always unable to know the specific value of the keyword.

Trapdoor Generation. Data users do not need to know the key of the medical institution, and the trapdoors generated for the same keyword each time are different. The trapdoor is generated in two steps. First, the data user generates a trapdoor based on the search key and the random number, and then submits the trapdoor to the middle server. Second, the middle server re-encrypts the trapdoor. Here we assume that the data user wants to search for the keyword $w_{h'}$, and the encryption is calculated as follows.

$$T'_{w_{h'}} = (g^{H(w_{h'}) \cdot r_u}, g^{r_u}). \tag{3}$$

Where r_u is a random number generated randomly each time. After receiving the $T'_{w_{h'}}$, the middle server generates a random number r_m and re-encrypts $T'_{w_{h'}}$ as follows.

$$T_{w_{h'}} = (g^{H(w_{h'}) \cdot r_u \cdot k_{m1} \cdot k_{m2} \cdot r_m}, g^{r_u \cdot k_{m1}}, g^{r_u \cdot k_{m1} \cdot r_m}). \tag{4}$$

Let's make $T_1 = g^{H(w_{h'}) \cdot r_u \cdot k_{m1} \cdot k_{m2} \cdot r_m}$, $T_2 = g^{r_u \cdot k_{m1}}$, $T_3 = g^{r_u \cdot k_{m1} \cdot r_m}$, i.e., $T_{w_{h'}} = (T_1, T_2, T_3)$. Finally, the middle server submits $T_{w_{h'}}$ to the cloud server.

Keywords Matching. The cloud server stores encrypted data and keywords for all medical institutions. The middle server saves a secret data $S_a = g^{k_{m1} \cdot k_{m2} \cdot r_m}$ to the cloud server. After receiving the search request, the cloud server performs a global search to match all stored keywords on the cloud to obtain corresponding medical data. The search process is described here. After getting trapdoors $T_{w_{h'}}$ and (E_a, E_o), first of all, the cloud server performs the following calculations.

$$
\begin{aligned}
\hat{e}(S_a, T_2) \\
&= \hat{e}(g^{k_{m1} \cdot k_{m2} \cdot r_m}, g^{r_u \cdot k_{m1} \cdot r_m}) \\
&= \hat{e}(g, g)^{r_m \cdot k_{m1} \cdot k_{m2} \cdot r_u \cdot k_{m1}}.
\end{aligned}
\tag{5}
$$

Then the cloud server judges whether $w_h = w_{h'}$ according to the following equation.

$$
\begin{aligned}
\hat{e}(E_a, T_3) \\
&= \hat{e}((g^{k_{i,w} \cdot r_o \cdot H(w_{i,h})} \cdot g_{k_{m1}})^{k_{km2}}, g^{r_u \cdot k_{m1} \cdot r_m}) \\
&= \hat{e}(g, g)^{(k_{i,w} \cdot r_o \cdot H(w_{i,h}) + k_{m1}) \cdot r_u \cdot k_{m1} \cdot r_m} \\
&= \hat{e}(g, g)^{k_{i,w} \cdot r_o \cdot H(w_{i,h}) \cdot r_u \cdot k_{m1} \cdot r_m} \cdot \hat{e}(S_a, T_2) \\
&= \hat{e}(g^{k_{i,w} \cdot r_o}, g^{H(w_{i,h}) \cdot r_u \cdot k_{m1} \cdot r_m}) \cdot \hat{e}(S_a, T_2) \\
&= \hat{e}(E_o, T_1) \cdot \hat{e}(S_a, T_2).
\end{aligned}
\tag{6}
$$

4.4   Data Authorization

Following the previous step, the search results were QID and medical data. When the data user gets the search results, he will initiate a request to the middle server by QID, and the middle server returns the medical institution to which QID belongs. Then, the data user initiates a data authorization request to the medical institution. Thereby, the plain text of medical data is acquired by the data users.

5   Security Analysis

In this section, we perform detailed security analysis. We demonstrate security requirements have been satisfied.

- Scheme Scaleability In this system, data owners and data users can freely join and leave the system in the cloud computing environment. By the way, the data user need authorization to join the system.
- Medical Data Security In the system initialization phase, medical data is encrypted before uploading to the cloud. Therefore, as long as the encryption algorithm is not compromised, the medical data is secure and there will be no privacy leakage.
- Keywords Secrecy With a probabilistic polynomial time, adversary $\mathcal{A}$ inquires the challenger $\mathcal{B}$ for the ciphertext of his queried keywords. Later, $\mathcal{B}$ stochastically selects a keyword w^+, encrypts it to $\hat{w}^+$, and send it to adversary $\mathcal{A}$. Then, $\mathcal{A}$ performs guessing w' for w^+. And if $w' = w^+$, adversary $\mathcal{A}$ will win. We define the probability of keywords leakage as $Adv = Pr[w' = w^+]$, i.e., $Adv = \frac{1}{a-t} + \varepsilon$, which is a negligible parameter, a denotes the size of keywords dictionary, t is the size of keywords that $\mathcal{A}$ knows.
- Trapdoors Unlinkability In our proposed scheme, a random number parameter is conflated when generating trapdoors. Therefore, even if the keywords are the same when generating trapdoors, the trapdoor results generated each time will not be the same. Consequently, the cloud server cannot obtain valid keyword information from the trapdoor.
- Patient Identity Leakage We all know that one of the possibilities of k-anonymity that may leak user privacy is link attacks [21]. In our scheme, the search results are a set of k-anonymous attributes, and there are k eligible patients. This avoids the leakage of the patient's identity through the keywords due to the keyword searched by the data users.

6   Experiment

We perform relevant experiments based on a real dataset about the architecture presented in this article. Using the Mondrian algorithm in k-anonymity, we utilize Python programming language and Adults database from the UC Irvine Machine Learning Repository [1] for experimental performance and privacy preserving analysis.

There exists a systematic evaluation parameter, i.e., hitting accuracy. Since we use the k-anonymity technique, we take privacy issues into account. As Fig. 2 shows, this has the advantage that it can better protect the privacy of patient data. But, it will loss some information. Thus, we need to determine a suitable k to ensure privacy and improve the hitting accuracy. The hitting accuracy may be slightly lower, but it does not affect much. Each medical institution is uniformly authorized. Therefore, medical institutions can handle the efficiency of searching accuracy to patients well.

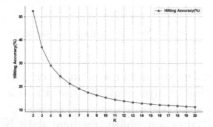 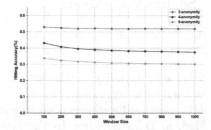

Fig. 2. For the different value k, the hitting accuracy by the search.

Fig. 3. For the different value window size, the hitting accuracy by the search.

Window size is another factor that affects hitting accuracy. In Fig. 3, we assume a uniform distribution of the 10 kinds of disease. Taking 2-anonymity, 4-anonymity, 6-anonymity as examples, we can know that the larger the window size, the lower the hitting accuracy.

7 Related Work

7.1 K-Anonymity

K-anonymity has been proposed as a privacy preserving model for data sharing, and there are various algorithm variants. When the data is published, the identifiers (e.g., name, SSN) of the private attributes are removed. In addition, it should be noticed that some user attributes may be combined with external data containing the user's unique identifier to reveal the user's identity [18].

The original privacy preserving model was based primarily on user-defined value generalization hierarchies [4,17]. Later, partitioning models were proposed, partitioning models include two types that are single-dimensional and multi-dimensional.

7.2 Searchable Encryption

Recently, searchable encryption [6] has been developed as a fundamental approach to ensure secure search over encrypted cloud data.

Song et al. [14] first defined the searchable encryption method and proposed a technique for keyword searches on encrypted data. A searchable encryption method has been further developed. For instance, [2] proposed a searchable encryption architecture. Data owners use asymmetric encryption to encrypt uploaded text and index. They use the method k-nearest neighbors and inner product similarity in their paper. The method searches for the index, and obtains the encrypted data, then requests the data authorization to attain the data. [20] improved the architecture. The difference is that multiple data owners are involved. And the data owner encrypts the text and index, then uploads them to the cloud server and the administrator server respectively.

7.3   Medical Data Privacy Preserving

Medical data has a variety of identity information and medical data that contains private data. Once these data are lost or leaked, it can lead to some serious privacy disclosure events.

Chen et al. [5] proposed a medical data privacy preserving framework, which uses a multi-path asymmetric encryption fragment transmission mechanism, storage protection using distributed symmetric encryption cloud storage scheme and access control with identity authentication and dynamic access authorization. Combining privacy preserving policies, different desensitization schemes [11] are formulated for users of different trust levels, and different desensitization methods are invoked to achieve personalized for patient privacy preserving of medical data.

8   Conclusion

We are concerned about data privacy issues in the medical field and have proposed an improved scheme, i.e. KPSBP, that is applicable to the medical field. First, we use k-anonymity to process the patient QID attributes, and then apply public key searchable encryption method to provide encryption and search. Our architecture supports secure search over multiple medical institutions to share data. At the same time, the difference from previous work is that the search results of our scheme are not targeted to a specific patient. The benefit of our scheme is that the patient's identity will not be leaked through the keywords searched by the data user. Furthermore, we carry out relevant related experiments. Our further work will consider the combination of differential privacy to provide privacy preserving of medical data.

Acknowledgements. This work is supported by National Key Research and Development Program of China (No. 2018YFB0204301).

References

1. Blake, C., Merz, C.: UCI repository of machine learning databases (1998)
2. Cao, N., Wang, C., Li, M., Ren, K., Lou, W.: Privacy-preserving multi-keyword ranked search over encrypted cloud data. IEEE Trans. Parallel and Distrib. Syst. **25**(1), 222–233 (2013)
3. Chai, Q., Gong, G.: Verifiable symmetric searchable encryption for semi-honest-but-curious cloud servers. In: 2012 IEEE International Conference on Communications (ICC), pp. 917–922. IEEE (2012)
4. Chawla, S., Dwork, C., McSherry, F., Smith, A., Wee, H.: Toward privacy in public databases. In: Kilian, J. (ed.) TCC 2005. LNCS, vol. 3378, pp. 363–385. Springer, Heidelberg (2005). https://doi.org/10.1007/978-3-540-30576-7_20
5. Chen, F., et al.: An infrastructure framework for privacy protection of community medical Internet of Things. World Wide Web **21**(1), 33–57 (2017). https://doi.org/10.1007/s11280-017-0455-z
6. Cui, J., Zhou, H., Zhong, H., Xu, Y.: AKSER: attribute-based keyword search with efficient revocation in cloud computing. Inf. Sci. **423**, 343–352 (2018)
7. Friedman, J.H., Bentley, J.L., Finkel, R.A.: An algorithm for finding best matches in logarithmic time. ACM Trans. Math. Softw. **3**, 209–226 (1976). (SLAC-PUB-1549-REV. 2)
8. LeFevre, K., DeWitt, D.J., Ramakrishnan, R., et al.: Mondrian multidimensional k-anonymity. In: ICDE, vol. 6, p. 25 (2006)
9. Mahdavi-Hezavehi, S., Alimardani, Y., Rahmani, R.: An efficient framework for a third party auditor in cloud computing environments. Comput. J. (2019)
10. Rong, H., Wang, H.M., Liu, J., Xian, M.: Privacy-preserving k-nearest neighbor computation in multiple cloud environments. IEEE Access **4**, 9589–9603 (2016)
11. Ronglei, H., Yanqiong, H., Ping, Z., Xiaohong, F.: Design and implementation of medical privacy protection scheme in big data environment. Netinfo Secur. (2018)
12. Seidl, R., Goetze, N., Bauer-Hermann, M.: Certificate authority, US Patent 9,979,716, 22 May 2018
13. Shi, E., Bethencourt, J., Chan, T.H., Song, D., Perrig, A.: Multi-dimensional range query over encrypted data. In: 2007 IEEE Symposium on Security and Privacy (SP 2007), pp. 350–364. IEEE (2007)
14. Song, D.X., Wagner, D., Perrig, A.: Practical techniques for searches on encrypted data. In: Proceeding 2000 IEEE Symposium on Security and Privacy. S&P 2000, pp. 44–55. IEEE (2000)
15. Steinberg, M.J., Rubin, E.R.: The HIPAA privacy rule: Lacks patient benefit, impedes research growth. Association of Academic Health Centers (2009)
16. Sun, W., Cai, Z., Li, Y., Liu, F., Fang, S., Wang, G.: Security and privacy in the medical internet of things: a review. Secur. Commun. Netw. **2018** (2018)
17. Sweeney, L.: Achieving k-anonymity privacy protection using generalization and suppression. Int. J. Uncertainty Fuzziness Knowl.-Based Syst. **10**(05), 571–588 (2002)
18. Sweeney, L.: k-anonymity: a model for protecting privacy. Int. J. Uncertainty Fuzziness Knowl.-Based Sys. **10**(05), 557–570 (2002)

19. Tang, J., Liu, A., Zhao, M., Wang, T.: An aggregate signature based trust routing for data gathering in sensor networks. Secur. Commun. Netw. **2018** (2018)
20. Zhang, W., Lin, Y., Xiao, S., Wu, J., Zhou, S.: Privacy preserving ranked multi-keyword search for multiple data owners in cloud computing. IEEE Trans. Comput. **65**(5), 1566–1577 (2015)
21. Zhu, X.L., Chen, T.G.: Research on privacy preserving based on k-anonymity. In: He, X., Hua, E., Lin, Y., Liu, X. (eds.) Computer, Informatics, Cybernetics and Applications, pp. 915–923. Springer, Netherlands (2012). https://doi.org/10.1007/978-94-007-1839-5_99

Incentive Mechanism for Socially-Aware Mobile Crowdsensing: A Bayesian Stackelberg Game

Jiangtian Nie[1,2], Jun Luo[2], Zehui Xiong[2(✉)], Dusit Niyato[2], Ping Wang[3], and Yang Zhang[4(✉)]

[1] ERI@N, Interdisciplinary Graduate Programme, Nanyang Technological University, Singapore, Singapore
jnie001@e.ntu.edu.sg

[2] School of Computer Science and Engineering, Nanyang Technological University, Singapore, Singapore
{junluo,zxiong002,dniyato}@ntu.edu.sg

[3] Department of Electrical Engineering and Computer Science, York University, Toronto, Canada
ping.wang@lassonde.yorku.ca

[4] Hubei Key Laboratory of Transportation Internet of Things, School of Computer Science and Technology, Wuhan University of Technology, Wuhan, China
yangzhang@whut.edu.cn

Abstract. Incentive mechanisms are pivotal in encouraging mobile users to participate to contribute their sensing information. However, most studies on incentive mechanisms merely considered individual behaviors of the users rather than their interdependency. The interdependent behaviors of the users are common as they originate from the social network effects that exist in the underlying mobile social domain. For example, a user from a crowdsensing-based traffic condition application can obtain a more accurate traffic mapping if other users share their road traffic information. Moreover, the incomplete information problem is also a critical but open issue in the real-life applications of crowdsensing. To address these issues, we propose a novel incentive mechanism considering both the social network effects and the incomplete information situation. In particular, we develop a Bayesian Stackelberg game, and study the participation strategies of users as well as the incentive mechanism through backward induction method. We then analytically prove that the Bayesian Stackelberg equilibrium is uniquely determined. Moreover, the numerical results are provided to evaluate the proposed socially-aware incentive mechanisms.

Keywords: Socially-aware · Mobile crowdsensing · Bayesian game · Uncertainty · Incomplete information

© Springer Nature Switzerland AG 2020
D. Yu et al. (Eds.): WASA 2020, LNCS 12384, pp. 394–406, 2020.
https://doi.org/10.1007/978-3-030-59016-1_33

1   Introduction

The rapid proliferation of smart devices that are equipped with a richness of embedded sensors have drastically boosted the process of gathering environmental data. These improvements greatly stimulate the development of mobile sensing applications and technologies, which hence leads the mobile crowdsensing being one of the most prevalent yet efficient sensing paradigm. Basically, the crowdsensing platform is composed of a cloud system and a group of crowdsensing Mobile Users (MUs). In crowdsensing, the cloud manager, i.e., the Crowdsensing Service Provider (CSP) is able to publish a series of sensing tasks, and MUs are proactively engaged to execute the tasks. In view of the promising business opportunities, many crowdsensing-based applications have been adopted in the real-life scenario. For example, OpenSignal [1] is proposed to report the wireless coverage mapping, and Waze [2] is dedicated to collect road information for traffic evaluation, e.g., GPS.

Due to the limited resources of MUs such as battery or computing power for performing the tasks, it is not sustainable for the voluntary participation in the crowdsensing platform. In other words, the crowdsensing MUs are not willing to collect or share their sensing information without sufficient benefits to compensate their cost. Therefore, it is necessary for the CSP to offer a reward as a monetary incentive to motivate the crowd to participate. As such, the incentive mechanisms in crowdsensing have been investigated by a large number of researchers with different methods in the last a few years [4,9,10,15,22]. For example, the authors in [4] investigated a sealed crowdsensing market, where the MUs cannot perfectly observe the behaviors of other MUs. The iterative game-theoretic framework is presented and the optimal incentive mechanism is investigated through the best response dynamics. In [9], the authors studied a quality-aware Bayesian incentive problem for robust crowdsensing, aiming to minimize the expected payment. In [22], the bargaining game is formulated to capture the long-term interplay between the CSP and MUs. Therein, the authors proposed the distributed algorithm to guarantee the MUs' privacy as well as to reduce the CSP's computing load.

However, most of the previous studies lack the consideration on fighting against interdependent behaviors of self-interested users, which is mainly caused by the network effects. Conventionally, *network effect* refers to the case that public goods and services have higher valuations if they are consumed by more users. Network effect has been studied in various situations [18,20,21]. In the scenario of crowdsensing, the existence of network effects indicate that the crowdsensing users are more inclined to participate if more other users join and contribute [14]. For example, in an crowdsensing-based traffic condition application, more accurate and timely traffic reports can be predicted if many other users participate and share the sensed road information. As a result, interdependency of user behaviors makes the incentive mechanism design much more complicated in the crowdsensing platform. As one of the key factor to stimulate the diffusion in crowds, the network effects that exist in close-connected social networks are well worth our great attention. Similar works have been conducted as in [5,16], where the authors designed the incentive mechanism while taking the network effects that stimulate the overall participation into account. However, the authors studied a complete information scenario where the information of social structure is perfectly observed by the CSP and MUs. This is not practically applied in the real-life mobile crowdsensing.

In this work, a Bayesian game-theoretic model to investigate the socially-aware incentive mechanism is presented. In the model, the social network effects are utilized to engage more MUs in crowdsensing. Specifically, a Bayesian Stackelberg game is developed to analyze the interplay between the CSP and MUs, taking the uncertainty of social structure into account. The key contributions of this work are listed in the following:

- Incentive mechanisms for mobile crowdsensing are studied, taking the incomplete information of social network effects into consideration. Therein, the impacts of social network effects that utilize the structural properties of the social domain and characterize the heterogeneity of MUs are explored;
- The interactions among the CSP and MUs is formulated as a Bayesian Stackelberg game. The unique Bayesian Nash equilibrium among all the MUs is firstly derived. Through backward induction method, the existence as well as uniqueness of the Bayesian Stackelberg equilibrium are then validated;
- Numerical results are provided to confirm the effectiveness of the proposed incentive mechanisms, and to show some game equilibrium properties. For example, the social network effects largely enhance the higher overall participation and the greater revenue. Moreover, the grasp of social structure information leads to the greater revenue.

The rest of this work is structured as follows. In Sect. 2, we describe the system model and formulate a Bayesian Stackelberg game with the consideration of uncertain social network effects. In Sect. 3, we present the game equilibrium analysis. Section 4 presents the numerical results, and Sect. 5 concludes the paper.

2   System Model

A Bayesian Stackelberg game [6] is developed to formulate the interactions among the CSP and the socially-aware MUs. The MUs' actions are to decide on their individual participation level and the CSP determines how much reward to offer to stimulate the MUs. To fit the game model into the real-life crowdsensing applications, an incomplete information scenario is considered, where the social structure information (the social network effects) is uncertain, i.e., not perfectly observed by the CSP and MUs. Thereafter, the expected payoff, i.e., the utilities and the revenue of MUs and the CSP are defined, respectively.

2.1   Utilities of Mobile Users

We consider N MUs in the mobile network, the set of which is denoted as $\mathcal{N} \triangleq \{1, \dots, N\}$. The decision of each MU $i \in \mathcal{N}$ is the individual participation level denoted by $x_i \in (0, +\infty)$, which is known as the effort level of participation (e.g., sensing data transmission frequency). $\mathbf{x} \triangleq (x_1, \ldots, x_N)$ and $\mathbf{x}_{-i}$ denote the participation levels of all MUs and all other MUs except the MU i, respectively. The reward per effort unit offered to the MUs is denoted as: $\mathbf{r} = [r_1, \ldots r_i, \ldots, r_N]^{\mathsf{T}}$. Therefore, the utility of MU i is formulated as:

$$u_i(x_i, \mathbf{x}_{-i}) = f_i(x_i) + \Phi(x_i, \mathbf{x}_{-i}) + r(x_i) - c(x_i). \tag{1}$$

The internal benefits of MU i obtained from the participation is denoted as $f_i(x_i) = a_i x_i - b_i x_i^2$, where $a_i, b_i > 0$ are the coefficients capturing the intrinsic participation value to heterogeneous MUs [3,19]. For example, in a crowdsensing-based traffic condition application, the accuracy of traffic prediction on a particular location is higher provided that there is a user reporting information on that location more frequently [2], i.e., larger x_i. The linear-quadratic function is adopted to model the properties of diminishing marginal returns from participation. For the sake of focusing on the networking structure uncertainty only, $a_i = 1$ and $b_i = 1/2$ are set in the following analysis. $\Phi(x_i, \mathbf{x}_{-i})$ represents the additional benefits obtained from the network effects. From the social domain point of view, external benefits obtained by an MU come from the information contributed by other MUs [7]. Considering the structural properties of the social domain, we define an adjacency matrix $G = [g_{ij}]_{i,j \in \mathcal{N}}$ to facilitate the analysis, in which g_{ij} represents the influence of MU j on MU i. Specifically, we denote $\sum_{j \in \mathcal{N}_i} g_{ij} x_i x_j$ as the additional benefits because of the network effects, as per in [3,19], where $\mathcal{N}_i$ represents the socially-connected neighbors of the MU i.

Lastly, $r(x_i) = r_i x_i$ is denoted as the reward offered by the CSP to MU i. $c(x_i)$ represents the associated cost of the MU from the participation, e.g., energy consumption. Without loss of generality, we consider that the cost $c(x_i)$ is equal to $c x_i$, where c is the MU's unit cost.

It is worth noting that the important social structure information is uncertain in the real-life scenario, i.e., not perfectly observed by the decision makers including the CSP and MUs. As such, we develop the Bayesian game where the Bayesian analysis is employed to study the game solutions. Specifically, the social degree of each MU is treated as the private information (the type of MUs) and only its probability distribution is common knowledge. As discussed, the mobile social networking structure can be represented by the adjacency matrix G. As the adjacency matrix G is common knowledge, the utility of MU i is given as follows:

$$u_i(x_i, \mathbf{x}_{-i}, \mathbf{r}) = x_i - \frac{1}{2}x_i^2 + \sum_{j \in \mathcal{N}_i} g_{ij} x_i x_j + r_i x_i - c x_i. \tag{2}$$

In addition, we consider that, w.l.o.g., for all the socially-connected neighbors of the MU i, i.e., $j \in \mathcal{N}_i$, $g_{ij} = \gamma > 0$, where γ is a given social network effect coefficient. Thus, Eq. (2) is given as follows:

$$u_i(x_i, \mathbf{x}_{-i}, \mathbf{r}) = x_i - \frac{1}{2}x_i^2 + \gamma x_i \sum_{j \in \mathcal{N}_i} x_j + r_i x_i - c x_i. \tag{3}$$

The expected utility can be therefore expressed as follows:

$$U_i(x_i, \mathbf{x}_{-i}, \mathbf{r}) = E\left[u_i(x_i, \mathbf{x}_{-i}, \mathbf{r})\right] = x_i - \frac{1}{2}x_i{}^2 + \gamma x_i E\left[\sum_{j \in \mathcal{N}_i} x_j\right] + r_i x_i - c x_i. \tag{4}$$

Different values of in-degree and out-degree of each MU are determined by the social structure, where the in-degree indicates the number of other MUs that the MU influences, and the out-degree indicates the number of other MUs influencing the MU. As such, the in-degree represents the influence and the out-degree represents the susceptibility. The distributions of in-degree and out-degree imply the network interaction patterns with social network effects [3]. We denote the in-degree $l \in D$ and the out-degree $k \in D$, where $D = \{0, 1, \ldots, k^{max}\}$ and k^{max} are the maximum possible degree value. We define $P : D \to [0, 1]$ and $H : D \to [0, 1]$ as the probability distributions of out-degree and in-degree, respectively, and we have $\sum_{k \in D} P(k) = \sum_{l \in D} H(l) = 1$. Furthermore, we assume that two probability distributions are independent with two variance $\sigma_k{}^2$ and $\sigma_l{}^2$. From the consistency theory, $\sum_{k \in D} P(k)k = \overline{k} = \sum_{l \in D} H(l)l$, and thus $\overline{k}$ is referred to as the average level of social network effects. We have $\mathbb{E}\left[\sum_{j \in \mathcal{N}_i} x_j\right] = k_i \times \mathrm{Avg}(\mathbf{x}_{-i})$, where $\mathrm{Avg}(\mathbf{x}_{-i}) = \mathbb{E}\left[x_j | j \in \mathcal{N}_i\right]$ denotes the average participation level of socially-connected neighbors of MU i.

We observe that the participation level of MU i depends only on the reward and its out-degree k, given $\mathrm{Avg}(\mathbf{x}_{-i})$. In particular, we denote the participation level of the MU with out-degree k and in-degree l as $x(k, l)$, and hence we have

$$\mathrm{Avg}(\mathbf{x}_{-i}) = \sum_{l \in D}\left(\overline{H}(l)\left(\sum_{k \in D} P(k)x(k, l)\right)\right), \tag{5}$$

where $\overline{H}(l) = \frac{H(l)l}{\sum_{l' \in D} H(l')l'}$. Therefore, the expected utility of MU i is written as follows:

$$U_i(x_i, \mathbf{x}_{-i}, \mathbf{r}, k_i) = (1 + r_i - c)x_i - \frac{1}{2}x_i{}^2 + \gamma k_i x_i \mathrm{Avg}(\mathbf{x}_{-i}), \tag{6}$$

and the type of the MU denoted as (l, k) is its in-degree and out-degree.

2.2   Revenue of the Crowdsensing Service Provider

The revenue formulation of the CSP is the profit derived from the total participation of all the MUs minus the reward offered to all MUs:

$$\mathcal{R} = \mu \sum_{i \in \mathcal{N}} (s x_i - t x_i{}^2) - \sum_{i \in \mathcal{N}} r_i x_i. \tag{7}$$

The linear-quadratic function [16,19] is adopted to transform the participation from MUs to the monetary revenue of the CSP, which features the law of decreasing marginal return due to data redundancy. μ is an adjustable parameter representing the equivalent monetary worth of MUs' participation level, and $s, t > 0$ are coefficients that capture the concavity of the function.

As the CSP only knows distribution information of the in-degree and out-degree, instead of maximizing its revenue as defined in Eq. (7), the CSP aims to maximize its expected revenue, which is formulated as follows:

$$\Pi = \sum_{l \in D} \left(\sum_{k \in D} H(l)P(k)\big((\mu s - r(k,l))x(k,l) - \mu t x^2(k,l)\big) \right), \quad (8)$$

where $r(k,l)$ denotes the offered reward to the MU with out-degree k and in-degree l.

3   Bayesian Game Equilibrium Analysis

In this section, we analyze the formulated Bayesian Stackelberg game with incomplete information through backward induction method. In particular, we analyze the follower game and leader game sequentially.

3.1   Follower Game

In the follower game, each MU simultaneously and competitively decides the individual participation level to maximize the expected utility. Given the reward offered from the CSP, the Bayesian Nash equilibrium [12,17] is first investigated in the follower game. Accordingly, we have the following theorem.

Theorem 1. *The Bayesian Nash equilibrium in follower game are uniquely determined, provided that the condition* $\gamma k^{\max} < 1$ *holds.*

Proof. **The existence of Bayesian Nash equilibrium:** To prove that there exists at least one Bayesian Nash equilibrium in the follower game (Proposition 1 in [8]), the following condition needs to be satisfied

$$\frac{\partial U_i(\overline{x}, \mathbf{x}_{-i}, \mathbf{r}, k_i)}{\partial x_i} \leq 0, k \in Z^+, r \in \mathbb{R}^+, \exists \overline{x} \geq 0, \forall x \leq \overline{x}, \quad (9)$$

where $\overline{x} = \mathrm{Avg}(\mathbf{x}_{-i})$. As we have $\frac{\partial U_i(\overline{x}, \mathbf{x}_{-i}, \mathbf{r}, k_i)}{\partial x_i} = (1+r_i-c)-\overline{x}+\gamma k_i \mathrm{Avg}(\mathbf{x}_{-i}) \leq (1 + r_i - c) - \overline{x} + \gamma k^{\max}\overline{x} = 1 + r_i - c + (\gamma k^{\max} - 1)\overline{x}$, and hence the condition in Eq. (9) holds if $\gamma k^{\max} < 1$ is satisfied.

The uniqueness of Bayesian Nash equilibrium: The proof of the uniqueness of the pure Bayesian Nash equilibrium can be derived from [8]. Specifically, the sufficient condition that implies there exists at most one Bayesian Nash equilibrium is provided as follows (Proposition 3 in [8]):

$$\left| \frac{\partial^2 U_i(\overline{x}, \mathbf{x}_{-i}, \mathbf{r}, k_i)}{\partial x_i \partial \mathrm{Avg}(\mathbf{x}_{-i})} \middle/ \frac{\partial^2 U_i(\overline{x}, \mathbf{x}_{-i}, \mathbf{r}, k_i)}{\partial x_i \partial x_i} \right| < 1, \forall i \in \mathcal{N}. \quad (10)$$

With minor steps, we have $\left| \frac{\partial^2 U_i(\overline{x}, \mathbf{x}_{-i}, \mathbf{r}, k_i)}{\partial x_i \partial \mathrm{Avg}(\mathbf{x}_{-i})} \middle/ \frac{\partial^2 U_i(\overline{x}, \mathbf{x}_{-i}, \mathbf{r}, k_i)}{\partial x_i \partial x_i} \right| = |\gamma k_i| \leq |\gamma k^{\max}|$. Thus, if $\gamma k^{\max} < 1$ holds, the condition given in Eq. (10) is ensured. The proof is then completed.

In order to derive the closed-form expression for the unique Bayesian Nash equilibrium, we first derive the first-order derivative of the expected utility that is given in Eq. (6), i.e., $\frac{\partial U_i(\bar{x}, \mathbf{x}_{-i}, \mathbf{r}, k_i)}{\partial x_i} = 0$, as shown as follows: $x_i^* = 1 + r_i - c + \gamma k_i \mathbb{E}\left[x_j | j \in \mathcal{N}_i\right]$. Thus, we have

$$x(k, l) = 1 + r(k, l) - c + \gamma k \mathbb{E}\left[x(k, l) | (k, l) \in D^2\right]. \tag{11}$$

From Eq. (5), we have the expression of $\mathbb{E}\left[x(k', l') | (k', l') \in D^2\right]$, as shown in

$$
\begin{aligned}
\mathbb{E}\left[x(k', l') | (k', l') \in D^2\right] &= \sum_{l' \in D} \overline{H}(l') \sum_{k' \in D} P(k') x(k', l') \\
&= \sum_{l' \in D} \left(\overline{H}(l') \sum_{k' \in D} \left(P(k') \left(1 + r(k', l') - c + \gamma k' \mathbb{E}\left[x(k'', l'') | (k'', l'') \in D^2\right]\right)\right)\right) \\
&= 1 + \overline{r} - c + \gamma \overline{k} \mathbb{E}\left[x(k'', l'') | (k'', l'') \in D^2\right],
\end{aligned}
\tag{12}
$$

where $\overline{r} = \sum_{l \in D} \overline{H}(l) \sum_{k \in D} P(k) r(k, l)$ and $\overline{k} = \sum_{l \in D} \overline{H}(l) \sum_{k \in D} P(k) k = \sum_{k \in D} P(k) k$. Since we also have $\mathbb{E}\left[x(k', l') | (k', l') \in D^2\right] = \mathbb{E}\left[x(k'', l'') | (k'', l'') \in D^2\right]$, it can be concluded from Eq. (12) with the following expression

$$\text{Avg}(\mathbf{x}_{-i}) = \mathbb{E}\left[x_j | j \in \mathcal{N}_i\right] = \frac{1 + \overline{r} - c}{1 - \gamma \overline{k}}. \tag{13}$$

Therefore, we derive the closed-form expression for the optimal strategy of the MU with the type (k, l) in the Bayesian follower game, which is

$$x^*(k, l) = 1 + r(k, l) - c + \gamma k \frac{1 + \overline{r} - c}{1 - \gamma \overline{k}}. \tag{14}$$

3.2   Leader Game

It is worth noting that the CSP has the information on the degree distributions of the MUs instead of the information on types of the MU. Therefore, only a uniform reward can be offered, i.e., $r(k, l) = r$ for all the MUs. Through backward induction, the optimal incentive mechanism can be characterized by the following theorem:

Theorem 2. *The optimal reward offered by the CSP in the Bayesian Stackelberg game is uniquely determined, which is given as follows:*

$$r^* = c - 1 + \frac{(\mu s + 1 - c)\left(1 - \gamma \overline{k}\right)}{2\left(1 - \gamma \overline{k} + \mu t + \mu t \gamma^2 \sigma_k^2\right)}. \tag{15}$$

Proof. We first plug the Bayesian Nash equilibrium in Eq. (14) into the objective function in Eq. (8). As the unique participation level of the MU depends only on its out-degree k as per Eq. (14), i.e., $x^*(k, l) = x^*(k)$, the expected revenue of the CSP in (8) is then formulated as

$$\Pi = \sum_{k \in D} P(k)\left((\mu s - r)x^*(k) - \mu t(x^*(k))^2\right). \tag{16}$$

In particular, we have the expression for the revenue of the CSP, as presented in

$$
\Pi = (\mu s - r)\left(1 + r - c + \gamma\overline{k}\frac{1 + r - c}{1 - \gamma\overline{k}}\right)
$$

$$
- \mu t \sum\nolimits_{k \in D} P(k)\left(1 + r - c + \gamma\overline{k}\frac{1 + r - c}{1 - \gamma\overline{k}}\right)^2
$$

$$
= (\mu s + 1 - c)\frac{1 + r - c}{1 - \gamma\overline{k}} - \left(1 - \gamma\overline{k} + \mu t + \mu t \gamma^2 \sigma_k{}^2\right)\left(\frac{1 + r - c}{1 - \gamma\overline{k}}\right)^2. \quad (17)
$$

Then, we evaluate its first-order optimality condition with respect to the reward, and we have $\frac{\partial \Pi}{\partial r} = \frac{\partial \Pi}{\partial \frac{1+r-c}{1-\gamma\overline{k}}}\frac{\partial \frac{1+r-c}{1-\gamma\overline{k}}}{\partial r}$, which yields

$$
\left((\mu s + 1 - c) - 2\left(1 - \gamma\overline{k} + \mu t + \mu t \gamma^2 \sigma_k{}^2\right)\left(\frac{1 + r^* - c}{1 - \gamma\overline{k}}\right)\right)\frac{1}{1 - \gamma\overline{k}} = 0.
$$

As such, we can conclude that $1 + r^* - c = \frac{(\mu s + 1 - c)(1 - \gamma\overline{k})}{2(1 - \gamma\overline{k} + \mu t + \mu t \gamma^2 \sigma_k{}^2)}$. Therefore, the optimal uniform incentive under Bayesian formulation is uniquely determined, which is written as follows: $r^* = c - 1 + \frac{(\mu s + 1 - c)(1 - \gamma\overline{k})}{2(1 - \gamma\overline{k} + \mu t + \mu t \gamma^2 \sigma_k{}^2)}$. For the detailed steps, the readers are referred to [13]. The proof is then completed.

As a comparison, we study the benchmark case where the CSP knows both the in-degree and out-degree of any individual follower. In such a case, the CSP can offer the discriminatory reward, $r(k,l)$ for the MU with out-degree k and in-degree l. In particular, we have the following theorem.

Theorem 3. *If the CSP clearly knows the type of each individual MU, the optimal discriminatory reward $r(k,l)$ offered to the MU with out-degree k and in-degree l, is uniquely determined.*

Proof. The CSP decides $r(k,l)$ for the MU with out-degree k and in-degree l to maximize its expected profit. The derivation of the optimal reward follows the similar steps discussed in the last case. We have the expected revenue of the CSP, which is formulated as follows: $\Pi =$

$$
\sum\nolimits_{l \in D}\left(\sum\nolimits_{k \in D} H(l)P(k)\left((\mu s - r(k,l))\left(1 + r(k,l) - c + \gamma k\frac{1 + \overline{r} - c}{1 - \gamma\overline{k}}\right) - \mu t\left(1 + \right.\right.\right.
$$

$$
\left.\left.\left. r(k,l) - c + \gamma k\frac{1 + \overline{r} - c}{1 - \gamma\overline{k}}\right)^2\right)\right).
$$
Taking the first-order derivative of $r(m,n)$ with respect to any out-degree $k \in D$ and in-degree $l \in D$, and with $\frac{\partial \Pi}{\partial r(m,n)} = 0$, we can conclude that

$$H(n)P(m)\left(-\left(1+r(m,n)-c+\gamma m\frac{1+\overline{r}-c}{1-\gamma\overline{k}}\right)+\mu s-r(m,n)\right.$$

$$-2\mu t\left(1+r(m,n)-c+\gamma m\frac{1+\overline{r}-c}{1-\gamma\overline{k}}\right)\bigg)+\gamma\frac{\overline{H}(n)P(m)}{1-\gamma\overline{k}}\sum_{l\in D}\sum_{k\in D}H(l)P(k)k$$

$$\times\left(\mu s-r(k,l)-2\mu t\left(1+r(k,l)-c+\gamma k\frac{1+\overline{r}-c}{1-\gamma\overline{k}}\right)\right)=0. \qquad (18)$$

With simple steps, we obtain the expression of $r^*(m,n)$. Moreover, we have $\overline{r}=\sum_{m\in D}\sum_{n\in D}\overline{H}(n)P(m)r(m,n)$ based on the definition of $\overline{r}$. Thus, we can obtain the final expression of $\overline{r}$.

We can then derive the closed-form expression for both $\overline{r}$ and ψ [11]. Consequently, $r(m,n)$ can also be derived, which hence is unique. For the detailed steps, the readers are referred to [13]. The proof is then completed.

4   Performance Evaluation

In this section, the performance of the Bayesian Stackelberg game based incentive mechanisms in socially-aware crowdsensing is evaluated. We also investigate the impacts of different parameters in mobile networks on the performance. We consider a mobile crowdsensing network with N MUs, the in-degree and out-degree of them follow the normal distribution $\mathcal{N}(\overline{k},\sigma_k^2)$ and $\mathcal{N}(\overline{k},\sigma_l^2)$, respectively. Unless otherwise specified, the default parameters are shown as follows: $\gamma=0.01$, $\overline{k}=20$, $\sigma_k^2=\sigma_l^2=10$, $\mu=10$, $s=20$, $t=0.05$, $c=15$, and $N=100$.

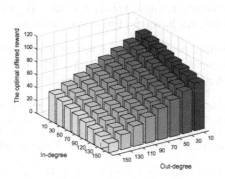

Fig. 1. The depiction of the optimal offered reward when in-degrees and out-degrees change.

Firstly, we examine the optimal offered reward when in-degrees and out-degrees change, as depicted in Fig. 1. It is observed that the optimal offered reward increases as in-degree increases or the out-degree decreases. As aforementioned, the in-degree and out-degree represent the influence and susceptibility of the MU, respectively. When the in-degree of one MU increases, such MU can attract more other MUs because of the underlying social network effects. In a crowdsensing-based traffic condition application, the drivers in critical central paths can be treated as the higher in-degree MUs. The road traffic information shared by these drivers plays an important role, since the participation of these drivers can significantly encourage the participation of others. Consequently, in consideration of the network effects, the CSP inclines to provide more reward to the MUs which have the higher in-degree.

The impacts of underlying network effects on the system performance are also studied, as shown in Fig. 2. As expected, it is observed that the optimal offered reward decreases with the increase of the mean level of social network effects. This is because as the mean level of social network effects increases, the MUs can encourage each other to contribute more sensing information, i.e., have the higher participation level because of the interdependent behaviors. As such, the total utilities of MUs increase, and hence the CSP inclines to offer the fewer reward in order to economize the cost. As a results, the CSP achieves the greater revenue. Moreover, we observe that as the equivalent monetary worth of MUs' participation level, i.e., μ increases, the CSP inclines to offer more reward. This is because the CSP is more willing to stimulate the enthusiasms of MUs when the CSP can efficiently transform the equivalent participation from MUs to more monetary revenue. Thus, the CSP offers more reward so as to extract more surplus and hence achieves the greater revenue.

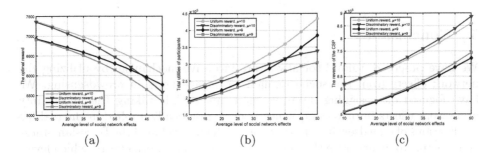

Fig. 2. The system performance when the average level of network effects changes.

The impacts of the distribution variance of social network effects on the system performance are shown in Fig. 3. As the variance decreases, the revenue obtained from the uniform incentive mechanism closely approaches that from the discriminatory incentive mechanism. This is because the heterogeneity of MUs decreases with the decrease of the variance value. By contrast, when the variance value increases, the attained revenue under the discriminatory incentive mechanism increases. This due to the fact that the discriminatory incentive mechanism allows the CSP to exploit the different preferences of each MU. This hence results in the decrease of total utilities of MUs and the increases of revenue. Moreover, with the increase of the participation cost of MUs, the total utilities of MUs decrease. As such, the CSP inclines to compensate the participation cost by offering more reward.

Finally, both Figs. 2 and 3 validate the fact that the discriminatory incentive mechanism has the better performance in terms of the attained revenue. The reason is that the CSP is able to provide different reward for various MUs given with the complete social structure information, as demonstrated by the Fig. 1. Therefore, the CSP can largely promote the greater participation from MUs, which hence leads to the greater revenue.

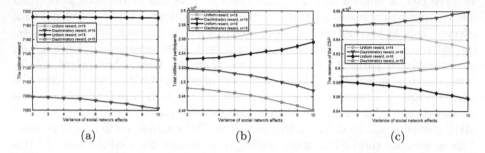

(a)   (b)   (c)

Fig. 3. The system performance when the distribution variance of network effects changes.

5   Conclusion

We have proposed a novel socially-aware incentive mechanism by utilizing the network effects from the social domain to engage users in crowdsensing. We have focused on designing incentive mechanism while taking the uncertainty of network effects into account, which is more practically applied in the real-life applications of crowdsensing. To that end, we have developed the Bayesian Stackelberg game to incorporate the impacts of uncertain network effects, which leverages the structural characteristics from the social domain. The unique Bayesian Stackelberg equilibrium has been considered as the optimal solution. Performance evaluation of this game model has shown the impressive impacts of network effects on socially-aware crowdsensing incentivizing.

Acknowledgement. This work is supported by the National Research Foundation (NRF), Singapore, under Singapore Energy Market Authority (EMA), Energy Resilience, NRF2017EWT-EP003-041, Singapore NRF2015-NRF-ISF001-2277, Singapore NRF National Satellite of Excellence, Design Science and Technology for Secure Critical Infrastructure NSoE DeST-SCI2019-0007, A*STAR-NTU-SUTD Joint Research Grant on Artificial Intelligence for the Future of Manufacturing RGANS1906, Wallenberg AI, Autonomous Systems and Software Program and Nanyang Technological University (WASP/NTU) under grant M4082187 (4080). This work is also supported in part by National Natural Science Foundation of China (Grant No. 51806157).

References

1. Opensignal. https://www.opensignal.com/
2. Waze. https://www.waze.com/
3. Candogan, O., Bimpikis, K., Ozdaglar, A.: Optimal pricing in networks with externalities. Oper. Res. **60**(4), 883–905 (2012)
4. Chakeri, A., Jaimes, L.G.: An iterative incentive mechanism design for crowd sensing using best response dynamics. In: IEEE Conference on Communications (ICC). Paris, France, May 2017
5. Cheung, M.H., Hou, F., Huang, J.: Make a difference: diversity-driven social mobile crowdsensing. In: IEEE Conference on Computer Communications (INFOCOM). Atlanta, GA, USA, May 2017
6. Duong, N.D., Madhukumar, A., Niyato, D.: Stackelberg Bayesian game for power allocation in two-tier networks. IEEE Trans. Veh. Technol. **65**(4), 2341–2354 (2016)
7. Easley, D., Kleinberg, J.: Networks, Crowds, and Markets: Reasoning about a Highly Connected World. Cambridge University Press, Cambridge (2010)
8. Glaeser, E.L., Scheinkman, J.: Non-market interactions. Technical report, National Bureau of Economic Research (2000)
9. Han, K., Huang, H., Luo, J.: Posted pricing for robust crowdsensing. In: Proceedings of ACM MobiHoc. Paderborn, Germany, July 2016
10. Han, K., Zhang, C., Luo, J., Hu, M., Veeravalli, B.: Truthful scheduling mechanisms for powering mobile crowdsensing. IEEE Trans. Comput. **65**(1), 294–307 (2016)
11. Kailath, T.: Linear Systems, vol. 156. Prentice-Hall, Englewood Cliffs (1980)
12. Myerson, R.B.: Game Theory. Harvard university press (2013)
13. Nie, J., Luo, J., Xiong, Z., Niyato, D., Wang, P.: A Stackelberg game approach towards socially-aware incentive mechanisms for mobile crowdsensing (online report). arXiv preprint arXiv:1807.08412 (2018)
14. Nie, J., Luo, J., Xiong, Z., Niyato, D., Wang, P., Guizani, M.: An incentive mechanism design for socially aware crowdsensing services with incomplete information. IEEE Commun. Mag. **57**(4), 74–80 (2019)
15. Nie, J., Xiong, Z., Niyato, D., Wang, P., Luo, J.: A socially-aware incentive mechanism for mobile crowdsensing service market. In: 2018 IEEE Global Communications Conference (GLOBECOM), pp. 1–7. IEEE (2018)
16. Nie, J., Xiong, Z., Niyato, D., Wang, P., Luo, J.: A socially-aware incentive mechanism for mobile crowdsensing service market. In: IEEE Global Communications Conference (GLOBECOM). Abu Dhabi, UAE, December 2018
17. Osborne, M.J., Rubinstein, A.: A Course in Game Theory. MIT Press, Cambridge (1994)
18. Xiong, Z., Feng, S., Niyato, D., Wang, P., Zhang, Y.: Economic analysis of network effects on sponsored content: a hierarchical game theoretic approach. In: GLOBECOM 2017–2017 IEEE Global Communications Conference, pp. 1–6. IEEE (2017)
19. Xiong, Z., Feng, S., Niyato, D., Wang, P., Zhang, Y.: Economic analysis of network effects on sponsored content: a hierarchical game theoretic approach. In: IEEE Global Communications Conference (GLOBECOM). Singapore, December 2017
20. Xiong, Z., Feng, S., Niyato, D., Wang, P., Zhang, Y., Lin, B.: A Stackelberg game approach for sponsored content management in mobile data market with network effects. IEEE Internet Things J. (2020)

21. Xiong, Z., Niyato, D., Wang, P., Han, Z., Zhang, Y.: Dynamic pricing for revenue maximization in mobile social data market with network effects. IEEE Trans. Wirel. Commun. **19**(3), 1722–1737 (2019)
22. Zhan, Y., Xia, Y., Zhang, J.: Incentive mechanism in platform-centric mobile crowdsensing: a one-to-many bargaining approach. Comput. Netw. **132**, 40–52 (2018)

Adaptive Task Scheduling via End-Edge-Cloud Cooperation in Vehicular Networks

Hualing Ren[1], Kai Liu[1(✉)], Penglin Dai[2], Yantao Li[1], Ruitao Xie[3], and Songtao Guo[1]

[1] College of Computer Science, Chongqing University, Chongqing, China
{renharlin,liukai0807,liyantao,guosongtao}@cqu.edu.cn
[2] College of Information Science and Technology, Southwest Jiaotong University, Chengdu, China
penglindai@swjtu.edu.cn
[3] College of Computer Science and Software Engineering, Shenzhen University, Shenzhen, China
drtxie@gmail.com

Abstract. Service latency is one of the most crucial factors to be considered in vehicular networks, especially for safety-critical applications with complex tasks. This paper presents a three-layer service architecture in vehicular networks, including the cloud layer, the edge layer and the terminal layer, and the nodes on different layers have different capacities on task processing. Specifically, vehicles may generate a set of tasks, and each task may be composed of multiple subtasks, which may require different amount of computation and memory resources for processing, and the task is served only when all of its subtasks are completed. On this basis, we formulate an adaptive task scheduling (ATS) problem, with the objective of minimizing the overall service latency by best cooperating those heterogeneous nodes on the cloud, edge and terminal layers. Further, we propose a genetic algorithm GA_ATS to solve the problem. In particular, we design a real number vector representation for encoding solutions, a fitness function for solution evaluation, a set of crossover and mutation operations for offspring generation and a balanced greedy algorithm for fixing infeasible solutions. Finally, we build the simulation model and conduct a comprehensive performance evaluation. The result shows that our proposed algorithm can effectively improve the system performance in terms of minimizing service latency.

Keywords: Task scheduling · End-Edge-Cloud cooperation · Genetic algorithm · Vehicular networks

1 Introduction

With the rapid development of wireless communication as well as artificial intelligence technologies, a variety of intelligent applications emerge in vehicular

© Springer Nature Switzerland AG 2020
D. Yu et al. (Eds.): WASA 2020, LNCS 12384, pp. 407–419, 2020.
https://doi.org/10.1007/978-3-030-59016-1_34

networks, such as autonomous driving [1], intersection control [2] and road-way management [3]. Common features of these applications, among others, include complex task processing and low service latency requirements. Dedicated Short-Range Communication (DSRC) is regarded as one of the communication technologies in IoV, which enables both vehicle-to-vehicle (V2V) and vehicle-to-infrastructure (V2I) communications. Besides, with the development of Long-Term Evolution (LTE), vehicle-to-cloud (V2C) communication is becoming another prominent solution.

In previous research, great effort has been paid on scheduling tasks in vehicular network. Software-Defined Networking (SDN), as a new technology that can separate the control plane and data plane, has been widely combined with cloud to make decisions for task scheduling [4–6]. Besides, since edge nodes are more accessible for vehicles, edge computing is expected to benefit from the advantages of geo-distribution and fast response of edge nodes. A few studies have considered edge nodes as task offload nodes, and proposed different task scheduling strategies [7–9]. However, existing edge computing based solutions cannot completely exploit the computation and communication resources of terminal vehicles. In view of this, vehicular fog computing was widely adopted to better coordinate heterogeneous resources of both edge nodes and terminal nodes on task processing [10–12]. Nevertheless, due to intrinsic characteristics of vehicular networks including highly dynamic workloads, high mobility of vehicles, and diverse application requirements, etc., it is imperative to best coordinate the heterogenous resources of both the cloud, the edge and the terminal nodes [13].

With above motivation, in this work, we present a three-layer framework to explore the cooperation among the cloud, the edges and the terminals for efficient task processing in vehicular networks. Particularly, we consider latency sensitive service with complex tasks, which can be further decomposed into a set of subtasks. Each subtask may require different resources including computation, communication and memory. A task is served only when all of its subtasks are completed.

The main contributions of this work are outlined as follows:

- We make the first effort on considering complex task processing in vehicular networks. The tasks are submitted from vehicles to the cloud for making scheduling decisions. Different subtasks can be offloaded to different nodes, but a task is served only when all of its subtasks are processed.
- We formulate an adaptive task scheduling (ATS) problem, aiming at minimizing the overall service latency via the cooperation of the cloud, edge and terminal nodes in vehicular networks. The task service time is modeled based on task sizes, required resources, and available resources of different nodes. Meanwhile, vehicle mobility is also considered when offloading tasks.
- We propose a genetic algorithm GA_ATS to solve ATS. Specifically, a real number vector is designed for encoding solutions. Then, a fitness function is designed based on the objective of ATS. On this basis, we design corresponding crossover and mutation operations, which facilitate the GA_ATS to

search global optimal solution. Finally, a repair operation is designed to fix infeasible solutions.

- We build the simulation model based on the presented service architecture and adopt real vehicle trajectories for performance evaluation. The simulation results demonstrate the superiority of GA_ATS on reducing service latency for complex tasks in vehicular networks.

The rest of this paper is organized as follows. The system framework is presented in Sect. 2. Section 3 formulates the ATS problem. Section 4 proposes a genetic algorithm GA_ATS. Section 5 builds the simulation model and evaluates algorithm performance. Finally, we conclude this work in Sect. 6.

2   System Model

Figure 1 presents a three-layer service architecture in vehicular networks, including the terminal layer, the edge layer and the cloud layer. Specifically, in the terminal layer, vehicles can communicate with each other via V2V communication. Vehicles may submit tasks, which are composed of multiple subtasks. For example, a task generated by AR-based driving assistance may consist of two subtasks including video streaming and object recognition. Each subtask requires certain resources (i.e. computation, communication, and memory) and subtasks can be offloaded to different nodes for processing. A task is served only when all of its subtasks are completely processed. Meanwhile, each vehicle also possesses certain computation and memory capacities, so that tasks/subtasks could be processed locally or in peer vehicles within the communication range.

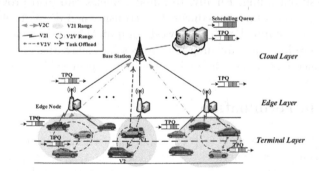

Fig. 1. End-Edge-Cloud cooperation on task scheduling in vehicular networks.

In the edge layer, service infrastructures such as road-side units (RSUs) are deployed along the road as edge nodes, which are physically closer to terminals (i.e. vehicles) compared with the cloud. Vehicles can communicate with an edge node via V2I communication when they are in its radio coverage. Edge nodes typically possess higher communication, computation and memory capacities than that of terminal nodes. Note that due to high mobility of vehicles, even though a vehicle can offload its task/subtask to an edge node when passing by, it may have already left the coverage when the task/subtask is processed. Consequently, the processing result has to be transferred to the cloud or certain peer edge node where the vehicle is dwelling, and then it is delivered to the vehicle. Apparently, such a case will cause extra service delay.

In the cloud layer, the cloud node is connected with cellular base station via the backbone network, while vehicles can communicate with it via V2C communication. Meanwhile, the cloud node can retrieve global information including the submitted tasks, available resources of the edge and terminal nodes, as well as status of vehicles (i.e. GPS coordinates, velocities, driving directions and neighborhood nodes, etc.). With such information, the cloud node maintains a scheduling queue and makes scheduling decisions by offloading tasks/subtasks to certain nodes. Each node assigned with tasks will maintain its own task pending queue (TPQ), where tasks/subtasks are waiting for being processed [14].

With above illustration, the system characteristics are analyzed as follows. First, both terminal and edge nodes have to update their status mentioned above to the cloud node periodically. We assume that the cloud node can communicate with all the vehicles in the system. Nevertheless, it would cause excessive transmission delay if all tasks were submitted to the cloud due to the limited V2C bandwidth and the huge amount of data volume required to be transmitted. On the other hand, although offloading tasks to the distributed edge node can alleviate the workload of the cloud to certain extent, and it may also reduce the transmission delay, the constraints of memory and computation capacities of edge nodes is one of the major hurdles of such a policy. Moreover, the limited radio coverage of the edge node and high mobility of vehicles make it more challenging on task offloading. Finally, terminal vehicles can also provide help for task processing, which further reduces data transmission delay. However, terminals are typically equipped with the lowest computation and memory capacities, which may cause long task queuing and processing delay. Besides, the intermittent V2V connections makes the task offloading to peer vehicles non-trivial.

3   Problem Formulation

Denote the set of vehicles as $V = \{v_1, v_2, ..., v_{|V|}\}$, where $|V|$ is the total number of vehicles. Each vehicle generates a set of tasks. The task set required by $v_j \in V$ is denoted by $T_j = \{t_{j,1}, t_{j,2}, ..., t_{j,|T_j|}\}$, where $|T_j|$ is the total number of tasks submitted by v_j. A task is composed of one or more subtasks, represented as $t_{j,i} = \{t_{j,i,1}, t_{j,i,2}, ..., t_{j,i,|t_{j,i}|}\}$ where $|t_{j,i}|$ is the total number of subtasks of $t_{j,i}$. Each $t_{j,i,k} \in t_{j,i}$ is associated with four-tuple $(d_{j,i,k}, l_{j,i,k}, m_{j,i,k}, d_{j,i,k}{}^*)$, where $d_{j,i,k}$ represents the input data size of $t_{j,i,k}$, $d_{j,i,k}{}^*$ represents the output data size after being processed; $m_{j,i,k}$ and $l_{j,i,k}$ represent required memory and computation resources, respectively.

The set of nodes in the system is denoted by $B = \{b_1, b_2, ..., b_{|B|}\}$, where $|B|$ is the total number of nodes, including cloud node C, edge node E and terminal node V. Each node $\beta \in B$ is related with five attributes, represented by $\left(R^{\beta}_{upload}, R^{\beta}_{download}, L^{\beta}, M^{\beta}, D^{\beta} \right)$, where R^{β}_{upload} denotes uploading rate and $R^{\beta}_{download}$ denotes the downloading rate. L^{β} represents the computation capability (i.e. the number of CPU cycles per second), and M^{β} represents the memory capability. The radius coverage of the node is denoted by D^{β}. Then, the neighboring set of the requested vehicle $v_j \in V$ is computed as $N_{v_j} = \{\beta | d_{v_j, \beta} \leq D^{\beta}, \forall \beta \in B\}$, which is the set of nodes whose distance to vehicle v_j is within D^{β}, where $d_{v_j, \beta}$ is the distance between vehicle v_j and node β.

Then, we analyze the service time of a subtask, which consists of four parts, including uploading time, waiting time, processing time and downloading time.

Definition 1. *Uploading time. It refers to the time duration by transmitting data required by subtask $t_{j,i,k}$ to the scheduled node β. which is computed by*

$$
e^{\beta}_{j,i,k}{}^{upload} = \begin{cases} 0 & \beta = v_j \\ \frac{\min(n, x - p \cdot n) \cdot d_{j,i,k}}{R^{\beta}_{upload}} + \sum_{m=1}^{p} X_m & \\ & \forall \beta \in N_{v_j} \cap (C \cup E) \\ \frac{\min(n, x - y - p \cdot n) \cdot d_{j,i,k}}{R^{\beta}_{upload}} + \sum_{m=1}^{p} X_m & \\ & \forall \beta \in N_{v_j} \cap V \end{cases} \tag{1}
$$

where x is the total number of subtasks scheduled to node β simultaneously. Suppose each node owns n channels for task transmission and each channel has the same transmission rate. y represent the number of subtasks that processed locally. Regard the transmission of n subtasks as a cycle, p is the number of cycles has been uploaded. X_m denotes the uploading time of the mth cycle.

Definition 2. *Waiting time. It refers to the time duration of the subtask pended in the TPQ of the scheduled node until it is being processed, which is denoted by $e^{\beta}_{j,i,k}{}^{wait}$.*

Definition 3. *Processing time. Given the scheduled node β, the processing time for subtask $t_{j,i,k}$ is the time duration that it is being processed, which is computed by*

$$
e^{\beta}_{j,i,k}{}^{process} = \frac{l_{j,i,k}}{L^{\beta}} \quad \forall \beta \in N_{v_j} \tag{2}
$$

Definition 4. *Downloading time. Given the scheduled node β and the subtask $t_{j,i,k}$, the downloading time is the duration that node β returns the processed result to v_j, which is computed by*

$$
e^{\beta}_{j,i,k}{}^{download} = \begin{cases} 0 & \beta = v_j \\ \frac{x \cdot d^*_{j,i,k}}{R^{\beta}_{download}} + \tau & \forall \beta \in N_{v_j} \cap (C \cup E) \\ \frac{(x - y) \cdot d_{j,i,k}}{R^{\beta}_{download}} + \tau & \forall \beta \in N_{v_j} \cap V \end{cases} \tag{3}
$$

As the downloading data size usually smaller than the uploading data size, we suppose the downloading rate are divided equally among subtasks. Since vehicles move fast and the network topology changes rapidly, we set a penalty value τ to denote the delay cost for v_j moves out of the communication range. Specially, τ is set to 0 if v_j keeps communication with β.

With above knowledge, the service time of a subtask is computed by

$$e_{j,i,k}^\beta = e_{j,i,k}^{\beta\ upload} + e_{j,i,k}^{\beta\ wait} + e_{j,i,k}^{\beta\ process} + e_{j,i,k}^{\beta\ download} \tag{4}$$

Then, the service time of task $t_{j,i}$ is the maximum latency among all its subtasks. Since the task needs to stay in the scheduling queue to wait for processing, there's also a queuing time $e_{j,i}^{queue}$, which is time duration from $t_{j,i}$ is generated to finally be scheduled. The response time of $t_{j,i}$ is computed by

$$e_{j,i} = \max_{\beta_1,\beta_s \in N_{v_j}, t_{j,i,1}, t_{j,i,|t_{j,i}|} \in t_{j,i}} \left\{ e_{j,i,1}^{\beta_1}, ..., e_{j,i,|t_{j,i}|}^{\beta_s} \right\} + e_{j,i}^{queue} \tag{5}$$

where β_1, β_s are the nodes to which $t_{j,i,1}$ and $t_{j,i,|t_{j,i}|}$ are scheduled respectively.

Now, the adaptive task scheduling (ATS) problem to schedule each subtask to a node to minimize average service delay while satisfying processing, memory and communication constraints is represented by

$$\min \frac{\sum_{j=1}^{|V|} \sum_{i=1}^{|T_j|} e_{j,i}}{\sum_{j=1}^{|V|} |T_j|} \tag{6}$$

s.t.

$$\sum_{\beta=1}^{|B|} \chi_{j,i,k}^\beta \leq 1, \forall v_j \in V, \forall t_{j,i} \in T_j, \forall t_{j,i,k} \in t_{j,i} \tag{7}$$

$$\chi_{j,i,k}^\beta \in \{0,1\} \tag{8}$$

$$\sum_{j=1}^{|V|} \sum_{i=1}^{|T_j|} \sum_{k=1}^{|t_{j,i}|} \chi_{j,i,k}^\beta \cdot m_{j,i,k} \leq M^\beta, \forall \beta \in B \tag{9}$$

$$\chi_{j,i,k}^\beta = 0, if\ \beta \notin N_{v_j} \tag{10}$$

where $\chi_{j,i,k}^\beta$ indicates whether the subtask $t_{j,i,k}$ is scheduled to node β. Constraints (7) and (8) guarantee each subtask $t_{j,i,k}$ can be allocated to at most one node in B. Constraint (9) ensures the allocation will not exceed the node's memory capacity. Constraint (10) ensures request vehicle v_j and the scheduled node β are in the communication range.

4   Algorithm Design

In this section, we propose a genetic algorithm GA_ATS to solve the ATS.

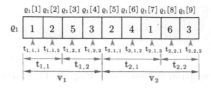

Fig. 2. An example of a chromosome.

Encoding for Scheduling Decision: The real number coding chromosome [15] is applied to represent a scheduling solution. Specifically, the element in a chromosome is represented by an integer $\theta \in \{1, 2, ..., |B|\}$, and the index of the element implies a corresponding subtask in condition that all the subtasks have been ordered according to their indexes. Given the total vehicles number $|V|$, the number of tasks requested per vehicle and the number of subtasks compose a task, the dimension of each solution is $Y = \sum_{j=1}^{|V|} \sum_{i=1}^{|T_j|} |t_{j,i}|$. For easy understanding, a chromosome is shown in Fig. 2, where ϱ_m means the m-th solution in the population and $\varrho_1[1] = 1$ means subtask $t_{1,1,1}$ is scheduled on node 1 for processing. Then, the population initialization is completed by randomly generating M feasible solutions, denoted by $\xi_0 = \{\varrho_1, \varrho_2, ..., \varrho_M\}$.

Fitness Function and Parent Chromosome Selection: Fitness function is used to control the population evolution towards optimal results. In this paper, we adopt the objective function as defined in (6) as the fitness function. First, we select $\frac{M}{4}$ pairs of parents through a tournament selection strategy; then after crossover, mutation and repair operations, $\frac{M}{2}$ offsprings are generated; further, among the parent and children solutions, there are $\frac{3}{2} \times M$ chromosomes in total. To maintain the population size, M chromosomes with higher fitness value are selected for next generation. In particular, the basic idea of tournament selection strategy is to select the best two solutions ϱ_1 and ϱ_n with highest fitness value from k individuals, which are randomly selected from previous generation population ξ_s.

Crossover Operation: The designed crossover policy to ATS is related with the crossover possibility p_c, which is described as follows. Regarding the selected chromosome ϱ_1 and ϱ_n as parents, crossover operation is performed based on the units of subtasks generated by the same vehicle v_j. Supposing K_j subtasks are requested by v_j, two random numbers μ, ν in range $[1, K_j]$ are generated, we can then get the exchange range as $\left[\sum_{y=1}^{j-1} K_y + \min(\mu, \nu), \sum_{y=1}^{j-1} K_y + \max(\mu, \nu)\right]$. Finally, generate a random number r and compare r with p_c: if $r \leq p_c$, it exchanges the gene segment between ϱ_1 and ϱ_n to generate two new chromosomes ϱ_1' and ϱ_n'; otherwise, it performs the mutation operation directly. Supposing two random numbers r_1, r_2 of v_1, v_2 are less than p_c, a crossover operation is described as Fig. 3, which first randomly generates two gene indexes a, b and c, d of v_1, v_2, respectively and then exchanges the gene segment between $[a, b]$ and $[c, d]$.

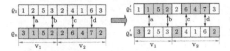

Fig. 3. The crossover operation of two chromosomes.

Fig. 4. The rollover mutation of chromosome.

Mutation Operation: In order to increase the solution search space as well as make full use of the superiority of self-chromosome, two mutation strategies are designed, one is traditional mutation strategy, the other is rolling-over mutation. The traditional mutation operation is applied to all dimensions in each offspring solution with a predefined mutation probability p_m. The chromosome after traditional mutation is denoted as ϱ_n''.

Rolling-over mutation is decided by rollover probability p_f. Given an individual ϱ_n'', regarding the genes belongs to the same vehicle as a mutation unit, a random number $r \in (0,1)$ is generated for each unit. If $r < p_f$, the reversal operation is triggered and two genes belonging to the same unit are selected randomly, and reverse the order between the selected two genes to generate a new chromosome. The rollover mutation is shown in Fig. 4.

Repair Operation: Obviously, infeasible solutions may be generated during the operations of crossover and mutation. In view of this, a repair operation combined with a balanced greedy algorithm is designed. First, it traverses all the nodes in the system and records their resource consumption. The nodes can be divided into non-overloaded nodes and overloaded nodes: for non-overloaded nodes, the remaining memories are recorded, and for overloaded nodes, the overloaded size and the corresponding subtasks are recorded. Second, after crossover and mutation, compute the average computation time and transmission time of all subtasks based on each offspring's chromosome. If the transmission time is larger than the computation time, the subtasks which cause node overload are offloaded to other neighborhood vehicles until none of them has enough memory resources, and the rest of tasks are offloaded to the edge node until all edge node's memory constraint is violated. Finally, the remaining tasks are scheduled to the cloud node. Otherwise, if the average transmission time is less than computation time, the overloaded subtasks would offload to cloud node directly; so that the differences between diverse layers are fully utilized.

Finally, the stopping criterion is defined as the condition that the predefined maximum number of generations is reached.

5   Performance Evaluation

5.1   Simulation Model

The simulation model is implemented based on the system architecture presented in section II. Specially, the real-world map, as shown in Fig. 5, extracted from area of $1.5\,km \times 1.5\,km$ Chengdu downtown is used in our experiment, which contains 300s taxi trajectories on August 20, 2014.

Fig. 5. $2.25\,km^2$ areas of Chengdu downtown.

In the default setting, there are 4 RSUs in the area, which act as edge nodes and install at fixed locations (as shown in Fig. 5). 100 vehicles are randomly selected as terminal nodes. For the cloud node, the transmission rate is set to 60 Mbps [16]. Assume it has unlimited running memory. The computation capability of cloud node is set to 1.5×10^{11} cycle/s [17]. For edge nodes, the transmission rate, computation capability and the running memory are in range of [22,27] Mbps, [25,50] $\times 10^9$ cycle/s and [600,800] GB, respectively [17]. Besides, the default radius of communication coverage of the edge node is set as 375 m. For terminal nodes, the transmission rate, computation capability, memory are in the range of [10,15] Mbps, [5,10] $\times 10^9$ cycle/s, [200,250] GB, respectively, and the radius of communication coverage is set as 250 m. The task requested interval of each vehicle follows exponential distribution with parameter $1/\lambda$ and each vehicle randomly generates [2,12] tasks at a time. Each task is composed of [3,4] subtasks. The required running memory of subtask is uniformly distributed in [10,200] MB, the upload size is randomly generated in [0.5,1.5] MB, and the number of required CPU cycles are uniformly generated in the range of [1,10] $\times 10^9$ cycle/s. Since the result size of tasks is typically much smaller than the data size (such as the result of face recognition), we ignore the download time in this evaluation. The penalty time τ is set to 0.3 s. The number of subtasks that can be uploaded simultaneously is set to 100.

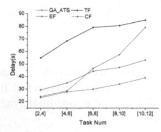

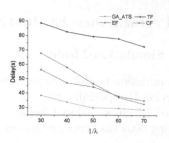

Fig. 6. Average service time under different number of tasks.

Fig. 7. Average service time under different task arrival interval.

For performance evaluation, we implemented three greedy algorithms: *1) Terminal-First (TF)*: it always prefers to offload tasks to the terminal vehicles. Only when it exceeds the memory constraint of vehicles, the task would be offloaded to the edge node. The task would be scheduled to cloud node when it exceeds the memory capacity of the edge node. *2) Edge-First (EF)*: it always prefers to offload tasks to the edge node. Only when the constraint on memory is violated, the tasks will be scheduled to the cloud. *3) Cloud-First (CF)*: it offloads all tasks to the cloud node. For GA_ATS, by default, the population size is set to 100; the maximum evolution generation is set to 150; the crossover probability p_c is set to 0.95; the traditional mutation probability p_m is set to 0.03; and the rollover probability p_f is set to 0.5.

5.2 Experimental Results

1) Effect of task number: The first set of experiments evaluate the algorithm performance under different number of tasks. The x-axis represents the number of tasks requested per vehicle each time. The more tasks requested by vehicles represents the higher system workload. Specifically, Fig. 6 compares the average service time of the four algorithms. As noted, GA_ATS achieves the lowest average service time, which can be explained with the observations from Fig. 8 and 10, where the service time composition and process ratio of each layer among the four algorithms are compared. Figure 8(a) shows that with the increase of the task requested number, the average uploading time of the tasks increases for all algorithms, because the transmission capability of each subtask decreases as the number of tasks increases. Nevertheless, GA_ATS always has the lowest uploading time. Meanwhile, the similar trend can be found in Fig. 8(b), in which GA_ATS has shorter waiting time than other algorithms. The computating time of different algorithms are shown in Fig. 8(c). As noted, the computation time is closely related to the proportion of tasks offloaded to the cloud. Finally, the percentage of subtasks completed at each layer is shown in Fig. 10.

2) Effect of Task Arrival Interval: As shown in Fig. 7, the service time of the four algorithms decrease with the increasing of the task arrival interval, since the larger request arrival interval gives lower system workloads. Obviously, GA_ATS has the lowest service time. The time composition is shown in Fig. 9. Figure 9(a)

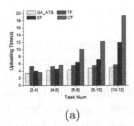
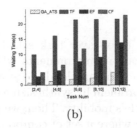
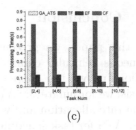

(a)   (b)   (c)

Fig. 8. (a) Average uploading time under different number of tasks; (b) Average waiting time under different number of tasks; (c) Average processing time under different number of tasks.

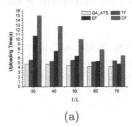
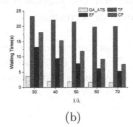
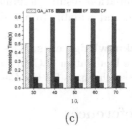

(a)   (b)   (c)

Fig. 9. (a) Average uploading time under different task arrival interval; (b) Average waiting time under different task arrival interval; (c) Average processing time under different task arrival interval.

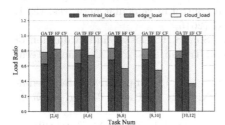

Fig. 10. The percentage of subtasks on each layer under different number of tasks.

Fig. 11. The percentage of subtasks on each layer under different task arrival interval.

is the average uploading time of four algorithms under different task arrival interval. With the increasing of the interval, the uploading time decreases, whereas GA_ATS constantly outperforms other algorithms in all ranges. Figure 9(b) compares the average waiting time. As shown, the waiting time also decreases with larger task arrival interval, and is slightly less than other algorithms. Figure 9(c) shows the average computation time. As shown, the computing time of GA_ATS is lower than TF, which demonstrates that GA_ATS can adaptively schedule subtasks to appropriate node. Finally, the percentage of subtask allocated to each layer under different task arrival interval is shown in Fig. 11.

6 Conclusion

In this paper, we present a three-layer task scheduling framework in heterogeneous vehicular communication environments which supports adaptive task offloading via the cooperation among cloud, edge and terminal layer. On this basis, we formulate the ATS problem by synthesizing task composition, transmission rate allocation and vehicle's mobility. Then, we propose a genetic algorithm GA_ATS for task scheduling, where a set of components are designed, including a real number encoding, a new crossover operation, two mutation operations, a repair operation based on a balanced greedy algorithm. Finally, we build the simulation model and conducted a comprehensive performance evaluation. The simulation results demonstrate that the proposed scheduling algorithm is effective and scalable in a wide range of scenarios.

Acknowledgments. This work was supported in part by the National Natural Science Foundation of China under Grant No. 61872049, and in part by the Fundamental Research Funds for the Central Universities under Project No. 2020CDCGJ004.

References

1. Feng, J., Liu, Z., Wu, C., Ji, Y.: AVE: autonomous vehicular edge computing framework with ACO-based scheduling. IEEE Trans. Veh. Technol. **66**(12), 10660–10675 (2017)
2. Dai, P., Liu, K., Zhuge, Q., Sha, E.H.M., Lee, V.C.S., Son, S.H.: Quality-of-experience-oriented autonomous intersection control in vehicular networks. IEEE Trans. Intell. Transp. Syst. **17**(7), 1956–1967 (2016)
3. Liu, K., Chan, E., Lee, V., Kapitanova, K., Son, S.H.: Design and evaluation of token-based reservation for a roadway system. Transp. Res. Part C: Emerg. Technol. **26**, 184–202 (2013)
4. Liu, K., Ng, J.K., Lee, V.C., Son, S.H., Stojmenovic, I.: Cooperative data scheduling in hybrid vehicular ad hoc networks: VANET as a software defined network. IEEE/ACM Trans. Netw. **24**(3), 1759–1773 (2015)
5. Aujla, G.S., Chaudhary, R., Kumar, N., Rodrigues, J.J., Vinel, A.: Data offloading in 5G-enabled software-defined vehicular networks: a Stackelberg-game-based approach. IEEE Commun. Mag. **55**(8), 100–108 (2017)
6. Baron, B., Spathis, P., Rivano, H., de Amorim, M.D., Viniotis, Y., Ammar, M.H.: Centrally controlled mass data offloading using vehicular traffic. IEEE Trans. Netw. Serv. Manage. **14**(2), 401–415 (2017)
7. Chen, X., Jiao, L., Li, W., Fu, X.: Efficient multi-user computation offloading for mobile-edge cloud computing. IEEE/ACM Trans. Netw. **24**(5), 2795–2808 (2015)
8. Zhang, K., Zhu, Y., Leng, S., He, Y., Maharjan, S., Zhang, Y.: Deep learning empowered task offloading for mobile edge computing in urban informatics. IEEE Internet Things J. **6**(5), 7635–7647 (2019)
9. Ning, Z., Huang, J., Wang, X., Rodrigues, J.J., Guo, L.: Mobile edge computing-enabled internet of vehicles: toward energy-efficient scheduling. IEEE Netw. **33**(5), 198–205 (2019)
10. Wang, X., Sui, Y., Wang, J., Yuen, C., Wu, W.: A distributed truthful auction mechanism for task allocation in mobile cloud computing. IEEE Trans. Serv. Comput. (2018)

11. Feng, J., Liu, Z., Wu, C., Ji, Y.: Mobile edge computing for the internet of vehicles: offloading framework and job scheduling. IEEE Veh. Technol. Mag. **14**(1), 28–36 (2018)

12. Fan, X., Cui, T., Cao, C., Chen, Q., Kwak, K.S.: Minimum-cost offloading for collaborative task execution of MEC-assisted platooning. Sensors **19**(4), 847 (2019)

13. Liu, K., Xu, X., Chen, M., Liu, B., Wu, L., Lee, V.C.: A hierarchical architecture for the future internet of vehicles. IEEE Commun. Mag. **57**(7), 41–47 (2019)

14. Li, Z., Dai, Y., Chen, G., Liu, Y.: Content Distribution for Mobile Internet: A Cloud-Based Approach. Springer, Singapore (2016). https://doi.org/10.1007/978-981-10-1463-5

15. Ono, I., Kita, H., Kobayashi, S.: A real-coded genetic algorithm using the unimodal normal distribution crossover. In: Ghosh, A., Tsutsui, S. (eds.) Advances in Evolutionary Computing. Natural Computing Series, pp. 213–237. Springer, Heidelberg (2003). https://doi.org/10.1007/978-3-642-18965-4_8

16. Wang, J., Liu, T., Liu, K., Kim, B., Xie, J., Han, Z.: Computation offloading over fog and cloud using multi-dimensional multiple knapsack problem. In: 2018 IEEE Global Communications Conference (GLOBECOM), pp. 1–7. IEEE (2018)

17. Du, J., Zhao, L., Feng, J., Chu, X.: Computation offloading and resource allocation in mixed fog/cloud computing systems with min-max fairness guarantee. IEEE Trans. Commun. **66**(4), 1594–1608 (2018)

An Improved Parallel Network Traffic Anomaly Detection Method Based on Bagging and GRU

Xiaoling Tao[1,2,3], Yang Peng[1(✉)], Feng Zhao[1], SuFang Wang[1], and Ziyi Liu[1]

[1] Guangxi Colleges and Universities Key Laboratory of Cloud Computing and Complex Systems, Guilin University of Electronic Technology, Guilin, China
1471463183@qq.com
[2] Guangxi Cooperative Innovation Center of Cloud Computing and Big Data, Guilin University of Electronic Technology, Guilin, China
[3] State Key Laboratory of Integrated Service Networks (ISN), Xidian University, Xi'an, China

Abstract. In the current large-scale and complex network environment, the types of networks are gradually diversified and the scale is constantly expanding. The network traffic has increased dramatically, and has the characteristics of the high-dimensional multivariable structure, which makes network traffic anomaly detection more and more difficult. Therefore, the paper proposes an improved parallel network traffic anomaly detection method based on Bagging and GRU (PB-GRU). This method uses GRU deep neural network to perform efficient hierarchical feature representation and learn the time-dependent characteristics of network traffic data to achieve more accurate detection. Then use Spark technology to process the training and testing of GRU detector in parallel to improve the overall performance. In order to reduce the individual differences between parallel detectors and improve the generalization error, and Bagging algorithm is used to improve the training process of GRU detector, so that the combined GRU detector has better detection performance. Experimental results show that the proposed method achieves a detection accuracy of 99.6%, and the error rate is only 0.0036%. In addition, after parallel processing with Spark, the overall efficiency and scalability have been improved.

Keywords: Network traffic anomaly detection · Deep neural networks · GRU · Spark · Bagging

1 Introduction

In recent years, network technology has achieved unprecedented development, which has brought great convenience to people's lives. However, with the development of the network, it also brings many challenges to the supervision of network security. With the explosive growth of Internet services and the number

© Springer Nature Switzerland AG 2020
D. Yu et al. (Eds.): WASA 2020, LNCS 12384, pp. 420–431, 2020.
https://doi.org/10.1007/978-3-030-59016-1_35

of users, network traffic data has also shown an exponential growth trend [1], and also caused problems in resource management of cloud networks [2]. Therefore, accurate and efficient anomaly detection of massive traffic data is one of the important means to maintain network security. Network traffic anomaly detection technology as one of the most popular research branches in the field of network security, it can detect abnormal behaviors such as suspicious hosts, sudden traffic changes, and vulnerability attacks.

Essentially, network traffic can be seen as a superposition of the Origin-Destination (OD) flows and whole-network traffic analysis is a difficult objective [3]. The principal challenge for OD flows' anomaly detection is that OD flows form a high-dimensional multivariable structure and massive data volume. These problems will cause a large consumption of computer resources and time resources. In addition, the attack behavior in modern networks is no longer an independent model, and generally exhibits many characteristics such as large-scale, collaborative and multi-stage [4]. Moreover, with the complication of network types, many unknown network attack methods are gradually increasing. Many existing network traffic anomaly detection technologies cannot find the time correlation between different attacks, so they cannot identify some unknown, planned, and long-term continuous attacks.

In summary, efficient feature representation and time-dependent pattern learning of network traffic data are particularly necessary to accurately and efficiently perform network traffic anomaly detection.

1.1 Contributions

The main contributions of this paper are summarized as follows.

(1) GRU deep neural network is used for efficient feature representation and time-dependent pattern learning of network traffic data.
(2) Spark is used to realize parallel training and testing of detection models, and improve overall detection efficiency.
(3) Bagging algorithm is joined into the training process of the GRU detectors, to reduce the individual differences between the parallel detectors, and improve the generalization error.

1.2 Related Work

Network traffic anomaly detection is a technology that analyzes the difference between normal traffic data and abnormal traffic data to find abnormal traffic in a given network traffic data that does not conform to the established normal behavior pattern [5]. Current mainstream network traffic anomaly detection methods can be summarized into the following categories: methods based on statistical analysis, methods based on time series, methods based on Sketch data structures, and methods based on machine learning.

The first three methods are essentially unsupervised methods, which need to rely on the manual rule base for exception discrimination. Gu et al. [6] developed a method that uses maximum entropy estimation and relative entropy to compare current network traffic and baseline distribution to detect network anomalies. This method can effectively detect different types of SYN attacks and port scanning anomalies. Zaidi et al. [7] developed an anomaly recognition scheme based on PCA (Principal Components Analysis, PCA), which can automatically distinguish between false alarms and real anomalies, and can accurately locate the perpetrators under real fault or threat situations. Song et al. [8] proposed a Storm-based dynamic k-NN cumulative distance anomaly detection method. They used time-domain change point detection to determine whether the flow was abnormal.

In recent years, some researchers have studied the detection method based on the transform domain [9], which converts the flow signal in the time domain into a frequency domain signal or a wavelet domain signal, and then detects anomalies based on the converted characteristics. Han and Zhang [10] proposed a new method for detecting abnormal activity on the Internet using weighted self-similarity parameters. They perform real-time EMD (Empirical Mode Decomposition, EMD) on network traffic, and then calculate weighted self-similarity parameters based on the first intrinsic mode function to analyze and detect suspicious activities in the network. Ye et al. [11] introduced an anomaly detection method based on Fractional Fourier Transform (FRFT) and Hurst parameter estimation algorithm, which is not affected by non-fixed time series and has good estimation performance. Pukkawanna et al. [12] use a summary structure to divide the IP service flow into sub-flows, and detect anomalies in the sub-flow based on time-frequency analysis of the entropy of the sub-flows. And literature [13] and [14] have designed a system that combines an overview data structure and an improved-MSPCA (Multi-scale Principal Element Analysis, MSPCA) algorithm for anomaly detection, which can detect anomalous source IP addresses. Although these methods can perform well in certain situations, but they are always limited to a fixed rule base and cannot be applied to scenarios with large amounts of data.

Machine learning technology can quickly process large-scale data through self-learning, and can automatically improve the performance of algorithms through experience. It can remedy the shortcomings of traditional rule-based methods. Therefore, machine learning methods have been widely used in network traffic anomaly detection. Huang et al. [15] used Growing Hierarchical Self-Organizing Maps to analyze the network traffic data and used SVM to classify the network traffic data into predefined categories, then perform anomaly detection. Kim and Cho [16] proposed a C-LSTM architecture for network traffic anomaly detection, which combined convolutional neural network, long and short term memory network and deep neural network to extract more complex features, and achieved nearly perfect anomaly detection performance for Web traffic data. In addition, Lu et al. [17] proposed a deep learning-based method, which combined CNN and LSTM. This method uses CNN to extract the higher-dimensional features of the input data, and then uses LSTM to understand the temporal characteristics of network traffic.

However, physical statistical methods and rule-based methods cannot well show the characteristics of real traffic, so the accuracy and efficiency of anomaly detection are not very high. Moreover, the traditional network traffic anomaly detection scheme cannot efficiently deal with large-scale network traffic data, nor solve online, real-time detection and other problems. Therefore, it is necessary to study the intelligent and efficient method of parallel networks traffic anomaly detection.

1.3 Organization

The remainder of this paper is organized as follows. In Sect. 1.2, we review the related work, and give some preliminaries in Sect. 2. Then, we propose the improved parallel network traffic anomaly detection method based on Bagging and GRU in Sect. 3. In Sect. 4, we briefly introduce the experimental environment and data we used, and the experimental results are analyzed in detail. Finally, we conclude the paper in Sect. 5.

2 Preliminaries

2.1 Gated Recurrent Unit (GRU)

As a part of Recurrent Neural Network, GRU [18,19] is a variant of LSTM network. It simplifies the gate structure in the network based on LSTM, and

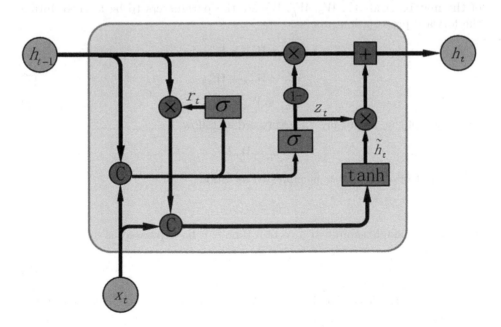

Fig. 1. GRU network structure.

combines the input gate and forgetting gate in LSTM into a single update gate. Therefore, GRU has fewer parameters and is more likely to converge, while the two are comparable in performance. There are three kinds of gate structures in LSTM: input gate, forgetting gate and output gate, which control the input value, memory value and output value in the network respectively; while there are only two kinds of gate structures in GRU model: update gate and reset gate, as shown in Fig. 1.

Z_t and r_t in Fig. 1 represent update gate and reset gate, where Z_t is used to control how much state information of the previous time can be brought into the current state. The larger the value is, the more it will be brought in. r_t is responsible for controlling the degree to which the information of the previous state is written to the current candidate set $\tilde{h}_t$, The lower the value, the less written. According to Fig. 1, the forward propagation formula of GRU network can be expressed as follows:

$$r_t = \sigma(W_r \cdot [h_{t-1}, x_t]) \tag{1}$$

$$Z_t = \sigma(W_z \cdot [h_{t-1}, x_t]) \tag{2}$$

$$\tilde{h}_t = \tanh(W_{\tilde{h}} \cdot [r_t * h_{t-1}, x_t]) \tag{3}$$

$$h_t = (1 - z_t) * h_{t-1} + z_t * \tilde{h}_t \tag{4}$$

$$y_t = \sigma(W_o \cdot h_t) \tag{5}$$

Among them, [] means that two vectors are connected, and * means the product of the matrix. And W_r, W_z, $W_{\tilde{h}}$, W_o are the parameters to be learned during the forward propagation process.

$$W_r = W_{rx} + W_{rh} \tag{6}$$

$$W_z = W_{zx} + W_{zh} \tag{7}$$

$$W_{\tilde{h}x} = W_{\tilde{h}} + W_{\tilde{h}h} \tag{8}$$

The input of the output layer is expressed as follow.

$$y_t^i = W_o h \tag{9}$$

The output of output layer is expressed as follow.

$$y_t^o = \sigma(y_t^i) \tag{10}$$

The loss of a single sample at a certain time can be expressed as follow.

$$E_t = \frac{(y_t - y_t^o)^2}{2} \tag{11}$$

The accumulated loss of a single sample at all times can be calculated by the following formula.

$$E = \sum_{t=1}^{T} E_t \tag{12}$$

After the forward propagation process is completed, the backward error propagation algorithm is used to learn and update the parameters of the entire network, and then iteration is carried out until the loss value converges.

Generally speaking, LSTM and GRU both retain important characteristics through various gate functions to ensure that they will not be lost in the long-term propagation process. However, compared with LSTM, GRU has one less gate function, so the number of parameter is obviously less than LSTM, and the training speed is faster than LSTM, and both of them are equally effective in accuracy.

2.2 Bagging

In the field of machine learning, in order to get a stable and comprehensive model, supervised learning algorithms are often used to achieve this goal. However, the performance of the learning model may not be perfect. Instead, it only obtains multiple weakly supervised models with preferences. These models only perform well in some aspects, but not in others. In order to solve this problem, integrated learning emerged. Its purpose is to average or integrate multiple weakly supervised models according to a certain strategy, in order to expect a better and more comprehensive strong supervised model.

Bagging algorithm (Bootstrap aggregating) is one of the most basic group learning algorithms in the field of machine learning. When the Bagging algorithm is combined with the anomaly detection algorithm, the parallel fitting and model averaging method can be used to reduce the mean square error value of the integrated detector and reduce the generalization error, so as to improve the detection accuracy and reduce the false recognition rate. There is no dependency between the weak learners of the Bagging algorithm, and each learner is trained by parallel fitting, and finally, a strong learner is obtained by integrating through a certain strategy. Therefore, the Bagging algorithm is more suitable for parallel processing.

2.3 Spark

Apache Spark is a unified analytics engine for large-scale data processing. It uses the most advanced DAG (Database Availability Group, DAG) scheduler, query optimizer, and physical execution engine to provide high performance for batch data and stream data processing. Spark has obvious advantages in big data processing and is loved by scholars at home and abroad.

In recent years, the ecosystem with Spark as the core has gradually improved and its functions have become more and more complete. The Spark ecosystem has many components. Spark Core is the core component of the Spark ecosystem, which not only can realize the reading of data, but also the analysis and processing of applications. In addition, Spark Streaming provides streaming real-time big data processing services, Spark Submit and Spark Shell provide batch interactive services, SparkSQL provides instant query services, Machine Learning Library (Machine Learning Library, MLlib) provides machine learning algorithm services, GraphX provides image processing services, and SparkR provides data analysis and calculation services. Among them, various components can be seamlessly combined and coordinated with each other, which can be applied to most of today's task scenarios.

3   Proposed Model

3.1   System Structure

Due to the high-dimensional multivariable structure and massive characteristics of modern network traffic data, existing methods have been unable to achieve efficient detection, nor can they learn the time dependence of traffic data, so the detection accuracy will be reduced. In order to solve the above problems, we propose an improved parallel network traffic anomaly detection method based on Bagging and GRU.

GRU is a type of recurrent neural network, which can learn the long-term dependence between input data, and find the representation of the features behind the data, and then construct a detection model. The proposed model uses the GRU network as a detector, and both the training and testing processes of the detector use Spark technology for parallel acceleration to improve the overall efficiency, as shown in Fig. 2. Moreover, The Bagging algorithm is used for parallel fitting of GRU detectors, and the model averaging method is used to reduce the mean square error between GRU training models, improve the generalization error, and improve the detection accuracy of the combined GRU detector.

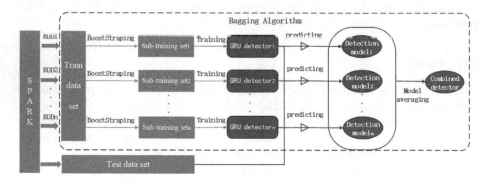

Fig. 2. PB-GRU model.

3.2 The PB-GRU Algorithm

The specific process of the PB-GRU algorithm is as follows.

1) Initialize the sample set size and the number of base detectors.
2) Use the Spark platform to create and execute tasks, each task is executed in the form of RDD, and use the BoostStraping method to sampling the dataset.
3) For each RDD task, the sub-training set obtained by sampling is used, and the Bagging algorithm and the GRU network are used for model training to obtain a GRU detector.
4) Collect all the GRU detectors, and then use the model averaging method to obtain the final integrator.

Algorithm 1 describes the pseudo code of the PB-GRU method.

Algorithm 1: $PB - GRU(S, T, M, n)$

Input: S-train data, T-test data, M-sample size, n-number of base classifiers.
Output: results-detection results
1: Initializes the size of M and n;
2: for i=1 to n do
3:     $S_i \leftarrow BoostStraping(S, M)$;
4:     $GRU_i \leftarrow GRU(S_i)$;
5:     $\{ GRU_i \} \leftarrow GRU_i$;
6: endfor
7:     $C \leftarrow Combine\{GRU_i\}$;
8: return results $\leftarrow C(T)$

---

4 Experiment Study

4.1 Experiment Environment

The Spark cluster used in the experiments has a total of 4 nodes, one as the master node and the rest as slave nodes. Each node comes with a CentOS 7 operating system, an Intel I7-8700 CPU, a 256G SSD hard disk, a 16G memory, and is equipped with Java 1.8, Spark 2.2.0, Python 3.6 and other environments.

4.2 Experiment Dataset

The dataset used in the experiment is UNSW-NB15 dataset [20, 21], which is the latest network intrusion detection data set used in academia. The dataset covers 9 types of modern attacks. Each record consists of 49 features and 1 label. It is divided into 4 csv files and a total of 2540044 records. Among them, the normal traffic data is network normal traffic data captured over time, and there are a total of 300,000 abnormal traffic data.

For the convenience of verification, the dataset is divided into sub-datasets of different sizes with 500,000 pieces of data as the step size. Among them, the smallest contains 500,000 pieces of data, and the largest contains 2.5 million pieces of data. In addition, to ensure the feasibility of the experiment, the ratio of abnormal traffic in each sub-data set was set to 12%.

4.3   Experiment Results

Precision Evaluation. Firstly, a comparative experiment is used for analysis. The experiments cited in [22] and [23] were used to conduct comparative experiments, which included deep learning methods and non-deep learning methods. The results of comparative experiments are shown in Fig. 3.

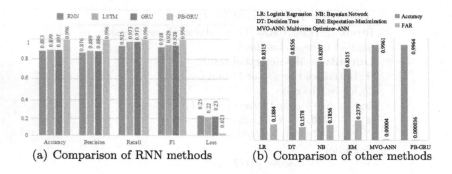

(a) Comparison of RNN methods   (b) Comparison of other methods

Fig. 3. Comparison of different methods in literature [22] and [23].

From Fig. 3, the performance of PB-GRU method on various indicators is superior to the RNN series algorithms used for comparison and some common algorithms. First of all, the loss value of the experiment is only 0.023, which shows that the GRU detector has been improved by the Bagging algorithm, and its discriminating ability of anomaly detection has been very close to the real level, and the detection accuracy has reached 99.6%. Moreover, the FAR of the proposed method is also comparable to the MVO-ANN method, only 0.0036%. In addition, through the experimental data recording, the mean square error of the GRU detection model was reduced to 0.0178, indicating that the PB-GRU method successfully reduced the mean square error and the generalization error of the model with the help of the Bagging algorithm, which greatly improved the detection ability.

Effectiveness Evaluation. In order to measure the efficiency improvement brought by Spark parallel detection, the experiment continued to use the Speedup ratio as the measurement index.

The Speedup ratio is defined by the following formula.

$$S_p = \frac{T_1}{T_p} \tag{13}$$

Among them, p refers to the number of computer nodes; T_1 refers to the execution time of the algorithm in a stand-alone environment; T_p refers to the execution time of the algorithm when there are p nodes calculating at the same time.

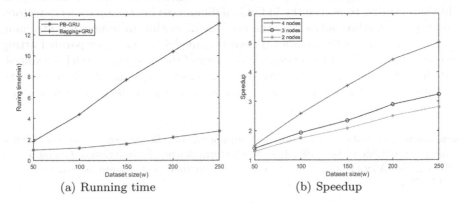

(a) Running time   (b) Speedup

Fig. 4. Running time and Speedup of different dataset

As shown in Fig. 4(a), the running time of the Bagging+GRU-based network traffic anomaly detection method in single-machine environment increases linearly with the increase in the amount of data, while the improved PB-GRU method only shows a slow growth trend and increases. And the growth trend and range of the PB-GRU method are far less than the detection method in a single machine environment. Because the Spark platform reads data from memory rather than disk when performing iterations, I/O operations that read data from local disks are avoided. Therefore, the calculation speed of the proposed method is faster. Experimental results show that the PB-GRU method is suitable for large-scale network traffic anomaly detection task scenarios.

Next, by substituting the running time of the method in the single-machine environment and Spark cluster environment into formula 13, the Speedup ratio curve of this experiment can be obtained. The results are shown in Fig. 4(b).

According to Fig. 4(b), when the size of the dataset is constant, the speedup ratio keeps increasing with the increase of the number of computer nodes; moreover, the larger the number of nodes, the more obvious the trend of increasing the Speedup ratio. Due to the parallel advantages of the Spark big data platform, when the number of computing nodes is larger, tasks can be distributed to more work nodes for execution at the same time. Therefore, the greater the number of parallel nodes on the Spark platform, the stronger the improvement in operating efficiency. The experimental results show that Spark big data processing technology can help the PB-GRU method to perform network traffic anomaly detection tasks more efficiently, and provide strong scalability for the PB-GRU method.

5   Conclusion

In this paper, we propose an improved parallel network traffic anomaly detection method based on Bagging and GRU. The proposed method makes use of the advantages of GRU to perform hierarchical feature representation on complex network traffic data, and learns the time-dependent characteristics therein to construct a high-quality detection model. Then use Spark to parallelize the training and testing process of the detector to improve the overall efficiency. In addition, in order to reduce the individual differences between parallel detectors, the proposed method introduces the Bagging algorithm to improve the training process, and obtains the combined detection model by means of parallel fitting and model averaging. The generalization error of the detection model is reduced, and the detection accuracy is improved. Extensive experiments show that the improved method has been greatly improved in both detection accuracy and detection efficiency.

Acknowledgements. This work was supported by the National Natural Science Foundation of China (No. 61962015), the Natural Science Foundation of Guangxi (No. 2016GXNSFAA380098) and the Science and Technology Program of Guangxi (No. AB17195045).

References

1. He, Z., Cai, Z., Yu, J.: Latent-data privacy preserving with customized data utility for social network data. IEEE Trans. Vehic. Technol. **67**(1), 665–673 (2018)
2. Yu, L., Shen, H.Y., Karan, S., Ye, L., Cai, Z.P.: CoRE: cooperative end-to-end traffic redundancy elimination for reducing cloud bandwidth cost. IEEE Trans. Parallel Distrib. Syst. **28**(2), 446–461 (2017). https://doi.org/10.1109/TPDS.2016.2578928
3. Lakhina, A., Papagiannaki, K., Crovella, M., et al.: Structural analysis of network traffic flows. ACM SIGMETRICS **32**(1), 61–72 (2004)
4. Holme, P.: Efficient local strategies for vaccination and network attack. EPL **68**(6), 908–914 (2004)
5. Mahoney, M.V.: Network traffic anomaly detection based on packet bytes. In: ACM Symposium on Applied Computing, SAC 2003, Melbourne, pp. 346–350. ACM (2003). https://doi.org/10.1145/952532.952601
6. Gu, Y., McCallum, A., Towsley, D.: Detecting anomalies in network traffic using maximum entropy estimation. In: 5th ACM SIGCOMM Conference on Internet Measurement, IMC 2005, p. 32. USENIX Association, Berkeley (2005). https://doi.org/10.1145/1330107.1330148
7. Zaidi, Z.R., Hakami, S., Moors, T., et al.: Detection and identification of anomalies in wireless mesh networks using Principal Component Analysis (PCA). J. Interconnect. Netw. **10**(04), 517–534 (2009)
8. Song, R.N., Liu, F.: Real-time anomaly traffic monitoring based on dynamic k-NN cumulative-distance abnormal detection algorithm. In: 3rd International Conference on Cloud Computing and Intelligence Systems, CCIS 2014, Shenzhen, pp. 187–192. IEEE (2014). https://doi.org/10.1109/CCIS.2014.7175727

9. Huang, C.T., Thareja, S., Shin, Y.J.: Wavelet-based real time detection of network traffic anomalies. Int. J. Netw. Secur. **6**(3), 309–320 (2008)
10. Han, J., Zhang, J.Z.: Network traffic anomaly detection using weighted self-similarity based on EMD. In: Proceedings of IEEE Southeastcon 2013, SECON, Jacksonville, pp. 1–5. IEEE (2013). https://doi.org/10.1109/SECON.2013.6567395
11. Ye, X.L., Lan, J.L., Huang, W.W.: Network traffic anomaly detection based on self-similarity using FRFT. In: 4th International Conference on Software Engineering and Service Science, ICSESS 2013, Beijing, pp. 837–840. IEEE (2013). https://doi.org/10.1109/ICSESS.2013.6615435
12. Pukkawanna, S., Hazeyama, H., Kadobayashi, Y., et al.: Detecting anomalies in massive traffic with sketches. In: Proceedings of the Ninth International Conference on Future Internet Technologies, CFI 2014, p. 14. ACM, New York (2014). https://doi.org/10.1145/2619287.2619301
13. Chen, Z., Yeo, C.K., Lee, B.S., et al.: Detection of network anomalies using Improved-MSPCA with sketches. Comput. Secur. **65**, 314–328 (2017)
14. Chen, Z., Yeo, C.K., Lee, B.S., et al.: A novel anomaly detection system using feature-based MSPCA with sketch. In: Wireless and Optical Communication Conference, WOCC 2017, Newark, pp. 1–6. IEEE (2017). https://doi.org/10.1109/WOCC.2017.7928975
15. Huang, S., Huang, Y.: Network traffic anomaly detection based on growing hierarchical SOM. In: 43rd Annual IEEE/IFIP International Conference on Dependable Systems and Networks, DSN 2013, Budapest, pp. 1–2. IEEE (2013). https://doi.org/10.1109/DSN.2013.6575338
16. Kim, T.Y., Cho, S.B.: Web traffic anomaly detection using C-LSTM neural networks. Expert Syst. Appl. **106**, 66–76 (2018)
17. Lu, X.L., Liu, P.J., Lin, J.Y.: Network traffic anomaly detection based on information gain and deep learning. In: 3rd International Conference on Information System and Data Mining, ICISDM 2019, pp. 11–15. ACM, New York (2019). https://doi.org/10.1145/3325917.3325946
18. Cho, K., Van Merrënboer, B., Gulcehre, C., et al.: Learning phrase representations using RNN encoder-decoder for statistical machine translation. Comput. Lang. 1724–1734 (2014). arXiv
19. Cho, K., Van Merriënboer, B., Bahdanau, D., et al.: On the properties of neural machine translation: encoder-decoder approaches. Comput. Lang. 103–111 (2014). arXiv
20. Moustafa, N., Slay, J.: UNSW-NB15: a comprehensive data set for network intrusion detection systems (UNSW-NB15 network data set). In: Military Communications and Information Systems Conference, MilCIS 2015, Canberra, pp. 1–6. IEEE (2015). https://doi.org/10.1109/MilCIS.2015.7348942
21. Moustafa, N., Slay, J.: The evaluation of Network Anomaly Detection Systems: statistical analysis of the UNSW-NB15 data set and the comparison with the KDD99 data set. Inf. Secur. J. Global Perspect. **25**(1), 18–31 (2016)
22. Vinayakumar, R., Soman, K.P., Poornachandran, P.: Evaluation of recurrent neural network and its variants for Intrusion Detection System (IDS). Int. J. Inf. Syst. Model. Des. **8**(3), 43–63 (2017)
23. Benmessahel, I., Xie, K., Chellal, M.: A new evolutionary neural networks based on intrusion detection systems using multiverse optimization. Appl. Intell. **48**(8), 2315–2327 (2017). https://doi.org/10.1007/s10489-017-1085-y

Joint Server Selection and SFC Routing for Anycast in NFV-enabled SDNs

Huaqing Tu, Hongli Xu[✉], Liusheng Huang, Xuwei Yang, and Da Yao

University of Science and Technology of China, Hefei, China
{thq527,issacyxw,yddzf}@mail.ustc.edu.cn, {xuhongli,lshuang}@ustc.edu.cn

Abstract. Anycast mechanism has been used as a fundamental technology in many fields, with multiple servers providing the same service. Each request does not care which server it is served by. For security and performance reasons, requests must meet the requirements of service function chain (SFC) in network function virtualization (NFV) enabled networks. Though the routing of SFC has been widely studied, most of these works focus on unicast, which does not involve server selection, and cannot be applied directly for anycast. If we simply combine the traditional anycast algorithms and SFC unicast routing algorithms, it will overload the links and servers. Since overloaded links and servers will reduce the quality of services, it is important to balance the load of links and servers. In this work, we focus on designing an SFC routing mechanism for anycast that takes server selection into account and achieves load balancing among servers as well as links with the help of software defined network (SDN). We first propose the problem of joint server selection and SFC routing for anycast in NFV-enabled SDNs (JSR). Then based on the method of random rounding, we design an algorithm called RBLB with approximate ratio guarantee that can solve the JSR problem. The extensive simulation results show that our algorithm can reduce the load of servers and links. For example, algorithm RBLB can reduce the server load by 41.4%–60.1% compared with the comparison algorithm, when the number of requests exceeds 20k.

Keywords: Software defined network · Network function virtualization · Anycast routing

1 Introduction

The software defined network (SDN) [12] technology is a new networking paradigm which is designed to separate the control logic from the data plane. It can explore a higher utilization of links and servers by scheduling flows smartly through logically centralized control [9]. With these advantages of SDN, operators can manage the network flexibly [10] and compute forwarding paths of network flows to achieve certain objectives in data-centers and WAN [6,11].

The network function virtualization (NFV) is another kind of network technology, which uses virtualization technology to implement network functions

© Springer Nature Switzerland AG 2020
D. Yu et al. (Eds.): WASA 2020, LNCS 12384, pp. 432–443, 2020.
https://doi.org/10.1007/978-3-030-59016-1_36

such as firewall and WAN load-balancers, which play an important role in enhancing performance and ensuring security [14,17]. Typically, network flows need to traverse multiple virtual network functions (VNF) in a certain order, which is called SFC [15]. With the help of SDN and the trend of NFV, it is easy for operators to manage the network flexibly [10] and design routing path to pursue certain objectives in managing the traffic flows [6,11].

There are many studies pointing out the importance of anycast routing, such as resource/service requirement. In the definition of anycast routing, it allows multiple servers in the network to provide the same services. Each request can be served by one of these servers and does not particularly care which server it is served by. For example, Content Distribution Network (CDN) deploys multiple proxy servers across the network. Users request resources from the server, but they do not care which server the resources come from. For security and performance reasons, requests must traverse some network functions before reaching the server, which increases the complexity of anycast algorithm and may lead to poor performance. Thus, it is necessary to design an efficient anycast mechanism with SFC requirements.

However, since the traditional anycast routing algorithms, such as SSPF [20], does not consider SFC requirements when determining the routing path, they can not be applied directly for requests with SFC requirements. The state of art research of SFC routing, such as SIMPLE [14] and PDA [7], mainly focus on unicast. Since these algorithms do not involve server selection, they can not be applied directly in anycast. One may think that it is feasible that first determine the closest server for each request, and then use SFC unicast routing algorithm, which converts anycast to unicast. However, this heuristic method separates server selection from SFC routing in anycast, which can not provide provable performance guarantee. At the same time, this method makes the actual path length longer than expected, which will increase the load on the links. According to the experiment in Sect. 4, this method also causes overloaded links and servers. Therefore, it is important to design an efficient anycast mechanism that takes the SFC requirements into consideration.

In an anycast system, when a large number of requests for resources are generated, it is important to design an effective routing algorithm to avoid link and server congestion. Take an anycast routing algorithm called SSPF as an example, in which each request will be directed to the closest server using shortest path algorithm for resource access. Even if some links and servers are overloaded, this routing method may still direct requests to the overloaded links and servers. Previous work in [18] studies high throughput anycast routing in SDN network, which does not concern SFC requirements. Different from this work, our proposed solution concentrates on anycast routing with SFC requirements and achieves load balancing among servers as well as links.

We summarize our contributions as follows. In this paper, we first present the problem of designing of anycast system with SFC requirements in NFV-enabled SDNs. Different from the previous anycast mechanism, this anycast system meet SFC requirement and provide an efficient anycast routing mechanism, which can achieve load balancing among servers as well as links. We propose the problem of joint server selection and SFC routing for anycast in NFV-enabled SDNs (JSR). We formulate this problem as an integer linear program, and design an algorithm called RBLB with approximation guarantee based on random rounding to solve JSR problem. We also verify the performance of our algorithm through simulation. Compared with the comparison algorithms, the algorithm can reduce the maximum load of servers by 41.4%–60.1%, when the number of requests exceeds 20k.

The rest of this paper mainly consists of the following sections. In Sect. 2, we analyze and define the problem of joint server selection and SFC routing for anycast in NFV-enabled SDNs. In Sect. 3, an algorithm called RBLB is proposed to deal with this problem. In Sect. 4, the simulation result are reported. Section 5 concludes the paper.

2   Preliminaries and Problem Definition

2.1   Network and Flow Models

An anycast system is composed of five different device sets: a host sets $H = \{h_1, ..., h_m\}$, with $m = |H|$; a server set $S = \{s_1, ..., s_n\}$, with $n = |S|$; an SDN switch set $V = \{v_1, ..., v_p\}$, with $p = |V|$; a VNF instance set $F = \{f_1, ..., f_q\}$, with $q = |F|$ and a cluster of controllers. Instances of all different network functions are included in VNF instance set F. In an SDN-enabled network, the controller only participates in selecting route paths for all flows and not be responsible for the packet forwarding. Thus, we model the NFV-enabled SDN network topology as $G = \{H \cup S \cup V \cup F, E\}$, where E is the set of link which connect these devices. Note that, the servers cannot be directly connected, but connected through SDN switches.

Each host can generate some requests which need to be served by only one of servers in S. The set of requests in the network is denoted by Γ. For simplicity and ease of flow management, we assume that all requests are unsplitted. For each request $\gamma \in \Gamma$, the information including the SFC requirement, the traffic size and the duration can be collected by controllers. With the help of flow statistics collection supported by OpenFlow protocol, controllers can get all information mentioned before.

2.2   Problem Definition

We will provides more precise description of the problem, which is joint server selection and SFC routing for load balancing (JSR). According to the definition of anycast routing, a request generated by a host $h \in H$ can be served by only one server, say s. We denote $P_{\gamma,s}$ as the path set of for request γ which will be served by server $s \in S$. Similar to the work in [7], each path $P_{\gamma,s}$ passes through VNF instances in a particular order required by its SFC requirement. The traffic intensity of request γ is denoted as $f(\gamma)$. For the ease of expression, we regard the

CPU usage as the main resource constraint of servers. Other types of resource (e.g., memory, bandwidth) can be handled similarly [8]. Since the computation power of each server is limited, we denote the computation capacity of server $s \in S$ as $c(s)$. Let $c(e)$ be the maximum bandwidth load of link $e \in E$. With the help of logically centralized control plane, the SDN controllers can get the information of the load on all the links and servers. We denote the network load ratio as $\lambda = \{\frac{l(e)}{c(e)}, \frac{l(s)}{c(s)}, e \in E, s \in S\}$, where $l(e)$ and $l(s)$ are the load of link e and server s, respectively. Note that, we do not include the load ratio of VNF instance in network load ratio, since the number and capacity of VNF instance can be changing with network load varying within the certain time [16]. We aim to reduce the maximum load of links and servers, that is, $\min \lambda$. The JSR problem is formulated as follows:

$$\min \quad \lambda$$

$$S.t. \begin{cases} \sum_{s \in S} x_\gamma^s = 1, & \forall \gamma \in \Gamma \\ \sum_{p \in P_{\gamma,s}} y_{\gamma,s}^p = x_\gamma^s, & \forall \gamma \in \Gamma, s \in S \\ \sum_{\gamma \in \Gamma} x_\gamma^s \cdot f(\gamma) \le \lambda \cdot c(s), & \forall s \in S \\ \sum_{\gamma \in \Gamma} \sum_{s \in S} \sum_{e \in p:p \in P_{\gamma,s}} y_{\gamma s}^p \cdot f(\gamma) \le \lambda \cdot c(e), & \forall e \in E \\ \sum_{\gamma \in \Gamma} \sum_{s \in S} \sum_{m \in p:p \in P_{\gamma,s}} y_{\gamma,s}^p \cdot f(\gamma) \le c(m), & \forall m \in M \\ x_\gamma^s \in \{0,1\}, & \forall \gamma, s \\ y_{\gamma,s}^p \in \{0,1\}, & \forall \gamma, s, p \end{cases} \quad (1)$$

Where x_γ^s denotes whether request γ will be served by server s or not, and $y_{\gamma,s}^p$ denotes whether the path $p \in P_{\gamma,s}$ will be selected for request γ or not when γ will be served by server s. The first set of equations represents that request γ can only choose at most one server to provide service. The second set of equations means that the path $p \in P_{\gamma,s}$ can be chosen if and only if this request will be served by server s. The third and forth sets of inequations denote the link and server capacity constraints, respectively. The fifth set of inequations denotes that the load on each VNF instance can not violate its limitation.

Theorem 1. *The load-balancing anycast routing and service function chaining problem (defined in Eq. (1)) is NP-hard.*

The proof is omitted here due to space limit.

3   Algorithm Design

3.1   Rounding-Based Algorithm for JSR

To solve JSR problem, we design an algorithm called RBLB based on random rounding. We first construct a relaxation of JSR problem as a linear program described in Eq. (2). Specifically, the variables $\{x_\gamma^s\}$ and $\{y_{\gamma,s}^p\}$ are relaxed to be fractional, which means that a request can be served by several servers and the traffic of each request can be arbitrarily splitted on more than one feasible path. The relaxed version linear program LP_1 is formulated as follows:

$$\min \quad \lambda$$

$$S.t. \begin{cases} \sum_{s \in S} x_\gamma^s = 1, & \forall \gamma \in \Gamma \\ \sum_{p \in P_{\gamma,s}} y_{\gamma,s}^p = x_\gamma^s, & \forall \gamma \in \Gamma, s \in S \\ \sum_{\gamma \in \Gamma} x_\gamma^s \cdot f(\gamma) \le \lambda \cdot c(s), & \forall s \in S \\ \sum_{\gamma \in \Gamma} \sum_{s \in S} \sum_{e \in p: p \in P_{\gamma,s}} y_{\gamma s}^p \cdot f(\gamma) \le \lambda \cdot c(e), & \forall e \in E \\ \sum_{\gamma \in \Gamma} \sum_{s \in S} \sum_{m \in p: p \in P_{\gamma,s}} y_{\gamma,s}^p \cdot f(\gamma) \le c(m), & \forall m \in M \\ x_\gamma^s \in [0,1], & \forall \gamma, s \\ y_{\gamma,s}^p \in [0,1], & \forall \gamma, s, p \end{cases} \quad (2)$$

The RBLB algorithm is comprised of two steps. We first solve the linear program described in Eq. (2) in the first step. Let $\{\tilde{x}_\gamma^s\}$ and $\{\tilde{y}_{\gamma,s}^p\}$ be the optimal solution. Since we have polynomial variables and constraints, this step can be finished in polynomial time. We assume that the optimal result is denoted as $\tilde{\lambda}$.

The second step determines how to select a proper server and a efficient SFC routing for each request. By using the randomized rounding method, we can get the integer solutions $\{\hat{x}_\gamma^s\}$ and $\{\hat{y}_{\gamma,s}^p\}$ with $\gamma \in \Gamma, s \in S$ and $p \in P_{\gamma,s}$. For each request, the algorithm sets $\hat{x}_{\gamma^s}$ to 1 with probability $\tilde{x}_\gamma^s$ independently. If $\hat{x}_\gamma^s = 1$, it suggests that request γ will be processed by server s. Otherwise, request γ will not be served by server s. After determining which server to serve the request γ, the algorithm selects an efficient SFC routing path. It sets $\hat{y}_{\gamma,s}^p$ to 1 with probability $\frac{\tilde{y}_{\gamma,s}^p}{\tilde{x}_\gamma^s}$, independently. If $\hat{y}_{\gamma,s}^p = 1$, it suggests that the path p is selected for request γ. If $\hat{y}_{\gamma,s}^p = 0$, it means that the path p will not be chosen. The RBLB algorithm is formally described in Algorithm 1.

Algorithm 1. RBLB: Rounding-Based Algorithm for JSR Problem

1: **Step 1: Solving the Relaxed JSR Problem**
2: Construct a linear program in Eq. (2)
3: Obtain the optimal solution $\{\tilde{x}_\gamma^s\}$ and $\{\tilde{y}_{\gamma,s}^p\}$
4: **Step 2: Determining Server and Anycast Routing**
5: Derive integer solutions $\{\hat{x}_\gamma^s\}$ and $\{\hat{y}_{\gamma,s}^p\}$ with $\gamma \in \Gamma$, $s \in S$ and $p \in P_{\gamma,s}$
6: **for** each request $\gamma \in \Gamma$ **do**
7:     Set $\hat{x}_\gamma^s$ to 1 with probability $\tilde{x}_\gamma^s$
8:     **for** each server $s \in S$ **do**
9:        **if** $\hat{x}_\gamma^s = 1$ **then**
10:           Set $\tilde{y}_{\gamma,s}^p$ to 1 with probability $\frac{\tilde{y}_{\gamma,s}^p}{\tilde{x}_\gamma^s}$
11:        **end if**
12:     **end for**
13: **end for**
14: Select server s for request γ if $\hat{x}_\gamma^s = 1$ and choose path p as its SFC routing if $\hat{y}_{\gamma,s}^p = 1$

3.2   Performance Analysis of RBLB Algorithm

We will present the performance analysis of the proposed RBLB algorithm in this section. Our proof process will use the following two famous theorems.

Theorem 2 (Union Bound). *Given a countable set of n events: $A_1, A_2, ...,$ A_n, each event A_i happens with possibility $\mathbf{Pr}(A_i)$. Then, $\mathbf{Pr}(A_1 \cup A_2 \cup ... \cup A_n) \leq \sum_{i=1}^{n} \mathbf{Pr}(A_i)$.*

Theorem 3 (Chernoff Bound). *Given n independent variables: $y_1, y_2, ..., y_n$, where $\forall z_i \in [0,1]$. Let $\mu = \mathbb{E}[\sum_{i=1}^{n} y_i]$. Then, $\mathbf{Pr}[\sum_{i=1}^{n} y_i \geq (1+\epsilon)\mu] \leq e^{\frac{-\epsilon^2 \mu}{2+\epsilon}}$, in which ϵ is an arbitrary value greater than 0.*

In the following, we first prove that, after randomizing the optimal solution, the algorithm still can guarantee that only one SFC routing path is selected for each request after determining which server will serve this request.

Lemma 1. *Only one SFC routing path is selected for each request after the randomized rounding process.*

Proof. On lines 4 to 14 of the algorithm, for each request γ, a server s is chosen with probability $\tilde{x}_\gamma^s$. After the server has been determined for this request, an SFC routing path $p \in P_{\gamma s}$ is selected by algorithm with probability $\frac{\tilde{y}_{\gamma,s}^p}{\tilde{x}_\gamma^s}$. If we can get that the total probability assigned for all feasible paths of each request is 1, it means that only one SFC routing path is selected.

According to the description of the proposed RBLB algorithm, the probability that SFC routing path p is selected is:

$$
\begin{aligned}
\mathbf{Pr}[\hat{y}_{\gamma,s}^p = 1] &= \mathbf{Pr}[\hat{y}_{\gamma,s}^p = 1 | \hat{x}_\gamma^s = 1] \cdot \mathbf{Pr}[\hat{x}_\gamma^s = 1] \\
&\quad + \mathbf{Pr}[\hat{y}_{\gamma,s}^p = 1 | \hat{x}_\gamma^s = 0] \cdot \mathbf{Pr}[\hat{x}_{\gamma s} = 0] \\
&= \frac{\tilde{y}_{\gamma,s}^p}{\tilde{x}_\gamma^s} \cdot \tilde{x}_\gamma^s = \tilde{y}_{\gamma,s}^p
\end{aligned}
\tag{3}
$$

Then, the total probability on all paths is:

$$
\begin{aligned}
\sum_{s \in S} \sum_{p \in P_{\gamma,s}} \mathbf{Pr}[\hat{y}_{\gamma,s}^p = 1] &= \sum_{s \in S} \sum_{p \in P_{\gamma s}} \tilde{y}_{\gamma,s}^p \\
&= \sum_{s \in S} \tilde{x}_\gamma^s = 1
\end{aligned}
\tag{4}
$$

Note that, the first, second and third equations hold according to Eq. (3) and equations described in Eq. (2). Equation (4) shows that a SFC routing path will be selected for each request after the randomized rounding process.

For the convenience of the following proof, we denote the minimum capacity of all servers, links and VNF instances as $c^{min}(s)$, $c^{min}(e)$ and $c^{min}(f)$, respectively. The whole request set is denoted as Γ. Variable α is defined as follows:

$$\alpha = \min\{\frac{c^{min}(s) \cdot \tilde{\lambda}}{f(\gamma)}, \frac{c^{min}(e) \cdot \tilde{\lambda}}{f(\gamma)}, \frac{c^{min}(m)}{f(\gamma)}, \gamma \in \Gamma\} \quad (5)$$

It can be observed that $\alpha \gg 1$ is true under many practical situations [2,19]. Even if the RBLB algorithm is a randomized rounding algorithm, we can still calculate the expected load on each server, link and VNF instance. Next, we give the performance analysis on server capacity constraints.

Theorem 4. *The proposed RBLB algorithm ensures that the total load on any server $s \in S$ is less than the load of the fractional solution by a factor of $\frac{3\log n}{\alpha} + 3$*

Proof. We express the load generated by request γ on server s as $\varphi_{\gamma,s}$, then the expectation of variable $\varphi_{\gamma,s}$ is:

$$\mathbb{E}[\varphi_{\gamma,s}] = \mathbf{Pr}[\hat{x}_\gamma^s = 1] \cdot f(\gamma) = \tilde{x}_\gamma^s \cdot f(\gamma) \quad (6)$$

Then, combining Eq. (6) and the third set of inequations in Eq. (2), we can get the total expected load on server s is:

$$\mathbb{E}\left[\sum_{\gamma \in \Gamma} \varphi_{\gamma,s}\right] = \sum_{\gamma \in \Gamma} \mathbb{E}[\varphi_{\gamma,s}] = \sum_{\gamma \in \Gamma} \tilde{x}_\gamma^s \cdot f(\gamma) \le \tilde{\lambda} \cdot c(s) \quad (7)$$

According to the definition of α in Eq. (5), we have:

$$\begin{cases} \frac{\varphi_{\gamma,s} \cdot \alpha}{\tilde{\lambda} \cdot c(s)} \in [0,1] \\ \mathbb{E}\left[\sum_{\gamma \in \Gamma} \frac{\varphi_{\gamma,s} \cdot \alpha}{\tilde{\lambda} \cdot c(s)}\right] \le \alpha \end{cases} \quad (8)$$

Then applying Theorem 3, we get the following formula:

$$\mathbf{Pr}\left[\sum_{\gamma \in \Gamma} \frac{\varphi_{\gamma,s} \cdot \alpha}{\tilde{\lambda} \cdot c(s)} \ge (1+\xi)\alpha\right] \le e^{\frac{-\xi^2 \alpha}{2+\xi}} \quad (9)$$

where ξ is an arbitrary positive value. Now, we assume that:

$$\mathbf{Pr}\left[\sum_{\gamma \in \Gamma} \frac{\alpha \cdot \varphi_{\gamma,s}}{\tilde{\lambda} \cdot c(s)} \ge (1+\xi)\alpha\right] \le e^{\frac{-\xi^2 \alpha}{2+\xi}} \le \frac{\mathcal{P}}{n} \quad (10)$$

where $\mathcal{P}$ is a variable related to the size of the network. We can use the number of switches to indicate the size of the network. When the network scale increase, $\mathcal{P} \to 0$.

By solving the inequality in Eq. (10) and setting $\mathcal{P} = \frac{1}{n^2}$, we have:

$$\xi \ge \frac{\log \frac{n}{\mathcal{P}} + \sqrt{\log^2 \frac{n}{\mathcal{P}} + 8\alpha \log \frac{n}{\mathcal{P}}}}{2\alpha} \quad (11)$$

$$\Rightarrow \xi \ge \frac{3\log n}{\alpha} + 2, \quad n \ge 2$$

Then, applying Theorem 2 and following Eq. (10), we can get that:

$$\mathbf{Pr}\left[\bigvee_{s \in S} \sum_{\gamma \in \Gamma} \frac{\varphi_{\gamma,s}}{\tilde{\lambda} \cdot c(s)} \geq (1 + \xi)\right]$$

$$\leq \sum_{s \in S} \mathbf{Pr}\left[\sum_{\gamma \in \Gamma} \frac{\varphi_{\gamma,s}}{\tilde{\lambda} \cdot c(s)} \geq (1 + \xi)\right] \tag{12}$$

$$\leq |S| \cdot \frac{1}{n^3} \leq \frac{1}{n^2}, \quad \xi \geq \frac{3 \log n}{\alpha} + 2$$

Then, following Eq. (12), we can get $1 + \xi = \frac{3 \log n}{\alpha} + 3$, which means that the total load on server s is no more than the load of the fractional solution by a factor of $\frac{3 \log n}{\alpha} + 3$ after the randomized rounding process.

Theorem 5. *The RBLB algorithm ensures that the total traffic load on any link $e \in E$ is no more than the traffic of the fractional solution by a factor of $\frac{4 \log n}{\alpha} + 3$.*

Since the space is limited and the proof of Theorem 5 and Theorem 4 are similar, the proof of Theorem 5 is omitted here.

Theorem 6. *The RBLB algorithm ensures that the total load on any VNF instance $f \in F$ is no more than the capacity of this VNF instance a factor of $\frac{3 \log n}{\alpha} + 3$.*

Similar to Theorem 5, the proof of Theorem 6 is omitted.

4 Performance Evaluation

We compare the RBLB algorithm with the comparison algorithms to check the performance and correctness of the RBLB algorithm in this section. We first introduce the simulation settings (Sect. 4.1), then give the benchmarks (Sect. 4.2). After that, through extensive simulations, we evaluate the load balancing anycast routing algorithm with several comparison algorithms (Sect. 4.3).

4.1 Simulation Setting

To objectively evaluate the performance of RBLB algorithm, we choose two typical and practical topologies to verify the performance of the algorithm. The first topology is the fat-tree topology [1], denoted as (a), which contains 80 switches, 118 hosts and 10 servers. The fat-tree topology has been applied in many data center networks. The second topology is Monash campus network, denoted as (b), which contains 100 switches, 180 hosts and 10 servers. The capacity of each server is set as 1 Gbps. The request set is generated randomly. In detail, the source host of a request is randomly picked in the network, and is SFC requirement is also randomly picked in network function set. For the traffic size of request (or flow), the 20% of the top-ranked requests may produce more than 80% of the total traffic [3]. We allocate the size of each flow and each request according to this rule. The network function set contains 5 different kinks of VNFs, which is Firewall, IDS, Load-Balancer, Monitor, NAT. According to [13], the CPU cycles per packet of each VNF is 1348, 1348, 1348, 1676, 1631, respectively. We generate at most 32K requests in the network, and construct a layered graph to compute feasible path set for each request by using Dijkstras shortest path algorithm.

4.2 Benchmarks and Performance Metrics

In the simulations, different metrics are adopted to evaluate performance. The first one is the maximum server load, which is used to indicate the load balancing of servers. The second metric is maximum link load, which is used to indicate the load balancing of links. The last metric is maximum VNF load, which is used to reflect that the proposed algorithm can not only realize the load balancing of servers and links, but also reduce the maximum load of VNF instances. We compare it with two benchmarks to evaluate how well proposed algorithm performs. Since there are no previous solutions for the anycast routing with SFC requirement, the first benchmark, called nearest server routing (NSR), is modified on the basis of SSPF algorithm [20]. Specifically, for these requests, we first use SSPF algorithm to get the neatest server, then construct a layered graph and use Dijkstras shortest path algorithm [4,5] to get SFC paths. The second benchmark is called shortest SFC anycast routing (SAR). In detail, for each request, it uses algorithm in [5] to get the shortest path set of each server that meets SFC requirements, and then selects the shortest one as anycast routing.

4.3 Simulation Results

We observe the maximum server load by changing the number of requests from 8K to 32K in the network in the first set of simulations. Figure 1 and Fig. 2 show that the maximum traffic load on all servers increases with the growing number of requests in the network for all three algorithms on both topologies. The reason for this is that as the number of requests increases, so does the requests that need to be processed by the server. Thus, the resources consumed by each server will also increase. Specifically, in topology (a), when the number of requests is 20K, the maximum server load of RBLB, NSR and SAR is 251 Mbps, 664 Mbps and 708 Mbps, respectively. That is, RBLB can reduces the maximum server load ratio by 41.4% and 45.7% compared with NSR and SAR, respectively.

The second set of simulations applies three algorithms on two topologies. We observe changes in the maximum link load by altering the number of requests from 8K to 32K in the network. Figure 3 and Fig. 4 show the maximum link load on all links grows with the changing size of requests in the network for all three algorithms on both topologies. The reason for this is that when the number of requests grows, the total traffic load in the network also increases, and the load on each link also increases. Specifically, in topology (b), when the

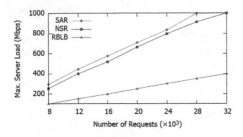
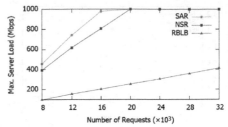

Fig. 1. Max. server load vs. number of requests for topology (a).

Fig. 2. Max. server load vs. number of requests for topology (b).

number of requests is 12K, the maximum link load of RBLB, NSR, SAR is 156 Mbps, 618 Mbps and 740 Mbps, respectively. That is, RBLB can cuts down the maximum load ratio of link by 46.2% and 58.4% compared with NSR and SAR, respectively.

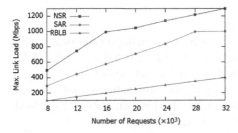
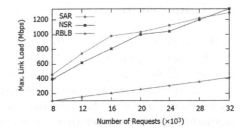

Fig. 3. Max. link load vs. number of requests for topology (a).

Fig. 4. Max. link load vs. number of requests for topology (b).

In third set of simulations, we observe the maximum load ratio of VNF instances by changing the number of requests from 8K to 32K in the network on two topologies. Figure 5 and Fig. 6 show the maximum load ratio on all VNF instances grows with the changing size of requests for all three algorithms on both topologies. The reason for this is that when the number of requests grows, each VNF instance needs to handle more requests, thus the maximum load ratio on VNF instances grows. Specifically, in topology (a), when the number of requests is 20K, the maximum load ratio of VNF instances for RBLB, NAR and SAR is 0.54, 1.02 and 0.82, respectively. That is, RBLB can reduces the maximum load ratio of all VNF instances by 48% and 32%, respectively.

Through the above three sets of simulation results, we can draw the following conclusions. First, RBLB algorithm achieve smaller maximum server load. For example, RBLB can reduces the maximum server load by 41.4% and 45.7% compared with NSR and SAR when there are 20K requests in topology (a). Second, RBLB can achieve smaller maximum link load. For example, given 12K requests in topology (b), the maximum link load is reduced by 46.2% and 58.4% compared with NSR and SAR. Third, in addition to reducing the maximum server

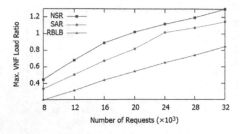

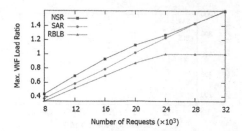

Fig. 5. Max. VNF load ratio vs. number of requests for topology (a).

Fig. 6. Max. VNF load ratio vs. number of requests for topology (b).

and link load, RBLB also reduces the maximum load ratio of VNF instances. For example, RBLB can reduces the maximum load ratio of all VNF instances by 48% and 32% compared with NSR and SAR when there are 20K requests in topology (a). These data reflect the advantages of the proposed algorithm.

5   Conclusion

In this work, we analysis how to implement an anycast routing mechanism which satisfies SFC requirements and achieves link and server load balancing in NFV-enabled SDNs. This problem is formulated as an integer linear program. To solve this problem, we propose an algorithm with approximation guarantee based on random rounding. Through simulation results, the performance of proposed algorithm RBLB is better than the comparison algorithms.

References

1. Al-Fares, M., Loukissas, A., Vahdat, A.: A scalable, commodity data center network architecture. ACM SIGCOMM Comput. Commun. Rev. **38**(4), 63–74 (2008)
2. Cohen, R., Lewin-Eytan, L., Naor, J.S., Raz, D.: On the effect of forwarding table size on SDN network utilization. In: IEEE Conference on Computer Communications, IEEE INFOCOM 2014, pp. 1734–1742. IEEE (2014)
3. Curtis, A.R., Mogul, J.C., Tourrilhes, J., Yalagandula, P., Sharma, P., Banerjee, S.: Devoflow: scaling flow management for high-performance networks. In: Proceedings of the ACM SIGCOMM 2011 Conference, pp. 254–265 (2011)
4. Dijkstra, E.W., et al.: A note on two problems in connexion with graphs. Numer. Math. **1**(1), 269–271 (1959)
5. Dwaraki, A., Wolf, T.: Adaptive service-chain routing for virtual network functions in software-defined networks. In: Proceedings of the 2016 Workshop on Hot Topics in Middleboxes and Network Function Virtualization, pp. 32–37 (2016)
6. Gember-Jacobson, A., et al.: OpenNF: enabling innovation in network function control. ACM SIGCOMM Comput. Commun. Rev. **44**(4), 163–174 (2014)
7. Guo, L., Pang, J., Walid, A.: Dynamic service function chaining in SDN-enabled networks with middleboxes. In: 2016 IEEE 24th International Conference on Network Protocols (ICNP), pp. 1–10. IEEE (2016)

8. Guo, L., Pang, J., Walid, A.: Joint placement and routing of network function chains in data centers. In: IEEE Conference on Computer Communications, IEEE INFOCOM 2018, pp. 612–620. IEEE (2018)

9. Hong, C.Y., et al.: Achieving high utilization with software-driven WAN. In: Proceedings of the ACM SIGCOMM 2013 Conference on SIGCOMM, pp. 15–26 (2013)

10. Li, B., et al.: ClickNP: highly flexible and high performance network processing with reconfigurable hardware. In: Proceedings of the 2016 ACM SIGCOMM Conference, pp. 1–14 (2016)

11. Li, Y., Phan, L.T.X., Loo, B.T.: Network functions virtualization with soft real-time guarantees. In: The 35th Annual IEEE International Conference on Computer Communications, IEEE INFOCOM 2016, pp. 1–9. IEEE (2016)

12. Malboubi, M., Wang, L., Chuah, C.N., Sharma, P.: Intelligent SDN based traffic (de)aggregation and measurement paradigm (ISTAMP). In: IEEE Conference on Computer Communications, IEEE INFOCOM 2014, pp. 934–942. IEEE (2014)

13. Martins, J., et al.: ClickOS and the art of network function virtualization. In: 11th USENIX Symposium on Networked Systems Design and Implementation (NSDI 2014), pp. 459–473 (2014)

14. Qazi, Z.A., Tu, C.C., Chiang, L., Miao, R., Sekar, V., Yu, M.: SIMPLE-fying middlebox policy enforcement using SDN. In: Proceedings of the ACM SIGCOMM 2013 Conference on SIGCOMM, pp. 27–38 (2013)

15. Quinn, P., Nadeau, T.: Problem statement for service function chaining. In: RFC 7498. RFC Editor (2015)

16. Rajagopalan, S., Williams, D., Jamjoom, H., Warfield, A.: Split/merge: system support for elastic execution in virtual middleboxes. In: Presented as Part of the 10th USENIX Symposium on Networked Systems Design and Implementation (NSDI 2013), pp. 227–240 (2013)

17. Sherry, J., Hasan, S., Scott, C., Krishnamurthy, A., Ratnasamy, S., Sekar, V.: Making middleboxes someone else's problem: network processing as a cloud service. ACM SIGCOMM Comput. Commun. Rev. **42**(4), 13–24 (2012)

18. Xu, H., Li, X., Huang, L., Wang, J., Leng, B.: High-throughput anycast routing and congestion-free reconfiguration for SDNs. In: 2016 IEEE/ACM 24th International Symposium on Quality of Service (IWQoS), pp. 1–6. IEEE (2016)

19. Xu, H., Yu, Z., Li, X.Y., Qian, C., Huang, L., Jung, T.: Real-time update with joint optimization of route selection and update scheduling for SDNs. In: 2016 IEEE 24th International Conference on Network Protocols (ICNP), pp. 1–10. IEEE (2016)

20. Xuan, D., Jia, W., Zhao, W.: Routing algorithms for anycast messages. In: Proceedings of 1998 International Conference on Parallel Processing (Cat. No. 98EX205), pp. 122–130. IEEE (1998)

Blockchain-Based Privacy-Preserving Dynamic Spectrum Sharing

Zhitian Tu[1]($\boxtimes$), Kun Zhu[1,2], Changyan Yi[1,2], and Ran Wang[1,2]

[1] College of Computer Science and Technology,
Nanjing University of Aeronautics and Astronautics, Nanjing, China
{tzt,zhukun,changyan.yi,wangran}@nuaa.edu.cn
[2] Collaborative Innovation Center of Novel Software
Technology and Industrialization, Nanjing, China

Abstract. For improving the utilization and alleviating the shortage of spectrum resources, centralized database-based dynamic spectrum sharing system has been proposed. However, the centralized architecture is often considered to be nontransparent and more vulnerable to be attacked. To address the above issues, in this work, we propose a blockchain-based dynamic spectrum sharing framework. The distributed architecture based on blockchain technology can bring advantages including decentralization, openness, transparency, immutability and auditability. Considering that the introduction of blockchain technology in spectrum sharing will also bring privacy issues, we design a differential privacy-based privacy-preserving double auction mechanism. The auction can be implemented in smart contracts running on the blockchain. The proposed double auction mechanism is proved to satisfy differential privacy, individual rationality, computational efficiency, and truthfulness. The extensive experiments demonstrate the effectiveness of the proposed dynamic spectrum sharing scheme.

Keywords: Dynamic spectrum sharing · Blockchain · Privacy preservation · Double auction

1 Introduction

The International Telecommunication Union has predicted that the international mobile communication spectrum demand will reach 1340 MHz–1960 MHz by 2020. The contradiction between supply and demand of future spectrum resources will be extremely prominent. To get out of this dilemma, spectrum sharing has been proposed to improve spectrum utilization and alleviate shortage of spectrum resources by sharing idle resources. Such spectrum management method can be divided into two categories: static spectrum sharing and dynamic spectrum sharing [1]. Since the spectrum utilization of the static spectrum sharing is limited, dynamic spectrum sharing has gradually become the major trend in the academia and industry so as to further improve the spectrum utilization [2].

© Springer Nature Switzerland AG 2020
D. Yu et al. (Eds.): WASA 2020, LNCS 12384, pp. 444–456, 2020.
https://doi.org/10.1007/978-3-030-59016-1_37

A database-based spectrum access system can reduce the management cost of the system, improve the spectrum utilization, and further increase access levels among users. In such a system, users or devices do not need to sense the surrounding wireless environment to opportunistically access spectrum resources. Federal Communications Commission (FCC) promotes dynamic spectrum sharing in 2015 and launches Citizens Broadband Radio Services (CBRS) at 3.5 GHz [3]. CBRS dynamically manages different types of wireless traffic through a centralized spectrum access database system to improve spectrum efficiency [4]. However, a centralized database is often considered costly and more vulnerable to be attacked.

Recently, blockchain technology has attracted great interest of the academic community for its potential capability to overcome the shortcomings of the centralized architecture. Blockchain is viewed as a digital ledger designed to keep a traceable, transparent, accessible, verifiable and auditable distributed record [5]. And this digital ledger can be safely updated without a central intermediary [6]. Blockchain can be viewed as a low-cost alternative for database system to dynamically allocate spectrum resources. Blockchain-enabled dynamic spectrum sharing has attracted the attention of some researchers from both academia and industry. In [7], the blockchain technology is regarded as a distributed database to record the history of shared spectrum access by individual users. And secondary users decide how to opportunistically access spectrum referring to the historical information stored in the blockchain. In [8], blockchain is deployed as a distributed database and a trading platform to decide on resources allocation for sharing and record every spectrum resource transaction and access information of PUs and SUs. In [9], the author discussed the operation process of the blockchain-based dynamic spectrum sharing system in detail from the perspective of cryptography and designed a series of mechanisms to protect the privacy of SUs.

However, these schemes mainly focus on the concept of bringing blockchain for dynamic spectrum sharing, while not providing specific mechanism design for spectrum sharing in blockchain. Moreover, users' transaction information is recorded in the form of blocks in blockchain-based spectrum resource trading platform. The transaction information contains the users' information. Users' private information may be recorded in these transactions. And any node in the blockchain can easily obtain the information recorded in the block. Thus, users' privacy cannot be guaranteed. And few existing works consider are discussing in depth how to take advantage of tools provided by blockchain technology, likely smart contracts, to achieve a privacy-preserving spectrum resource sharing in an untrust environment.

In this paper, we first propose a blockchain-based dynamic spectrum sharing platform. Transactions are recorded in the blockchain in the form of blocks. And every node can monitor, verify all transaction information and run smart contracts. A privacy-preserving double auction mechanism is designed to run on blockchain network in the form of smart contract. And the mechanism can protect users' privacy, increase social welfare, and improve spectrum resource utilization in an untrusted environment of blockchain network. Then, we formulate a winner determination problem in the double auction mechanism as an integer linear programming (ILP) problem. We take advantage of Hungarian algorithm to solve this ILP problem. Based on the allocation results, the clearing price is calculated. In the scenario of blockchain application, we introduce asymmetric encryption and differential privacy during the bidding and transaction processes to protect the privacy of users. And the proposed double auction mechanism is proved to satisfy differential privacy, individual rationality, and truthfulness. We conduct extensive experiments and the experimental results demonstrate the effectiveness of our proposed blockchain-based dynamic spectrum sharing scheme.

The rest of the paper is organized as follows: we first provide a detail description of our proposed framework of dynamic spectrum sharing based on blockchain in Sect. 2. In Sect. 3, we introduce our system model and preliminaries of spectrum trading and privacy preservation. In Sect. 4, we theoretically prove that the proposed double auction mechanism satisfies differential privacy, individual rationality, computational efficiency, and truthfulness. In Sect. 5, we present our performance evolution results. Finally, we draw a conclusion in Sect. 6.

2   The Proposed Blockchain-Based Framework for Dynamic Spectrum Sharing

In this section, we describe the operation of the blockchain-based spectrum sharing system we proposed in detail. This system is built on consortium blockchain. Consortium blockchain can achieve partial decentralization and high efficiency [10]. Each node on consortium blockchain usually has a corresponding physical institution or organization. Participants are authorized to join the blockchain network and form a stakeholder consortium to jointly maintain the operation of the blockchain. The system architecture based on the consortium blockchain can effectively reduce latency and improve system throughput.

2.1   Architecture Components

This system is composed of three entities, as is depicted in Fig. 1. We divide users into two types, spectrum providers (SPs) and spectrum demanders (SDs). SPs obtain resources from some official institutions, like FCC, by competing with other PUs or acquire resources from PUs by competing with other SUs through cooperation sharing or non-cooperative sharing as mentioned in [7]. Due to changes in SP's spectrum requirements or usage scenarios, some of their spectrum resources become idle. In order to increase spectrum utilization and users' revenue, SPs desire to share their idle spectrum resources. The other entity is SD that dying for spectrum resources. For more efficient allocation, we introduce local aggregators (LAGs) as the third entity to be the smart contract manager

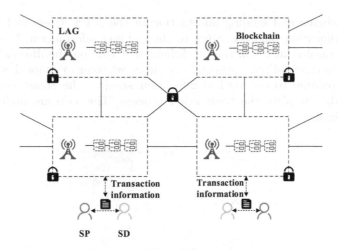

Fig. 1. Structure of our proposed blockchain-based spectrum sharing system

and auctioneer in this system. Since lots of users may not have sufficient computing power to support resource allocation, we select local aggregators to match resources and maintain the operations of the smart contract and blockchain.

2.2 Smart Contracts Designed for Privacy Preservation and Spectrum Sharing

We are using the truffle framework to develop a decentralized application (Dapp) for SDs, SPs, and LAGs. Every transaction slot, a LAG is selected as the auctioneer, establishes a smart contract and records a public key for RSA encryption in the smart contract. After being verified by the CA, users that have paid a certain amount of deposit is allowed to join this blockchain. Once a fraud occurs, the deposit of the node incurred will be fined.

SPs store the specific information of their idle spectrum resources in the Inter Planetary File System (IPFS) and create the corresponding hash addresses to record these addresses in smart contract. SUs can consult these information to get their valuation. Users obtain the encrypted public key stored in the smart contract to encrypt their real bids and send them to the smart contract. After a certain time, the smart contract decrypts the encrypted information stored in the blockchain and calculates the parameters to operate the differential privacy mechanism. Users obtain these parameters from smart contract to generate encrypted bids and send their encrypted bids as well as tokens to the smart contract. After reaching the final deadline of the transaction, the LAG that initiated the contract obtains the bidding information of all users.

And the LAG calls computing resources to get the final resource allocation result. The LAG stores the bid information and allocation plan in the IFPS and stores the hash address from IPFS in the blockchain. Users and other LAGs can obtain the hash address by interacting with smart contract and obtain the allocation scheme and bidding information in the IFPS. Users and LAGs can verify the allocation plan according to the bidding information. Based on the verification results, nodes in the blockchain will vote on the distribution plan. The smart contract collects votes and determine whether to adopt this allocation scheme. According to the verified allocation scheme, the smart contract will automatically complete the transaction process. The software architecture is shown in Fig. 2.

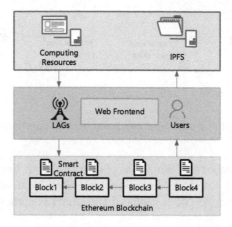

Fig. 2. The software architecture of our proposed spectrum sharing system

3   Privacy-Preserving Double Auction

3.1   System Model

We assume that SPs and SDs share resources that will take effect in the future within a fixed time period T through transactions. We assume that each SP has one idle channel during time period T. SPs will rent their idle spectrum resource for benefits. Meanwhile SDs desire one channel to meet their needs for data transmission in T period. The market can reflect changes in supply and demand in a timely and flexible manner, transmit information on supply and demand, and achieve a reasonable allocation of resources. Thus, we decide to take advantage of double auction to allocate and price resources. In order to protect the privacy of SPs and SDs during the auction, we have proposed privacy-preserving double auction mechanism.

3.2   Proposed Privacy-Preserving Double Auction Mechanism

In this double auction mechanism, we assume that the utility of SD j is the difference between the valuation and the payment of the spectrum resource he obtains.

Definition 1 *(An SD's Utility): The utility of SD j that participating in spectrum trading is:*

$$U_j = \sum_{i \in M} v_{j,i} x_{j,i} - \sum_{i \in M} p x_{j,i}, \tag{1}$$

where $x_{j,i}$ means SD j successfully obtain SP i's idle spectrum resource and M is the collection of SPs.

Similarly, the utility of SP i can be defined in this way.

Definition 2 *(An SP's Utility): The profit of SP i that participating in spectrum trading is defined as:*

$$L_i = p \sum_{j \in N} x_{i,j} - s_i \sum_{j \in N} x_{i,j}. \tag{2}$$

N is the collection of SDs.

Social welfare is defined as the difference between SDs' utility and SPs' utility.

Definition 3 *(Social welfare): The social welfare of this trading platform is defined as:*

$$SW = \sum_{j \in N} U_j - \sum_{i \in M} L_i \tag{3}$$

$$= \sum_{j \in N} \sum_{i \in M} v_{j,i} x_{j,i} - s_i \sum_{i \in M} \sum_{j \in N} x_{i,j} \tag{4}$$

$$= \sum_{j \in N} \sum_{i \in M} x_{j,i} \cdot (v_{j,i} - s_i). \tag{5}$$

Differential privacy is a method in cryptography that aims to provide a method to maximize the accuracy of data queries when querying from a statistical database while minimizing the chance of identifying its records.

Definition 4 *(ϵ-differential Privacy [11]). A randomized mechanism $\mathcal{M}$ gives ϵ- differential privacy if for all data sets $\boldsymbol{D}_1$ and $\boldsymbol{D}_2$ differing on a single user, and all $s \subseteq range(m)$,*

$$\Pr\left[\mathcal{M}\left(\boldsymbol{D}_1 \in \mathcal{S}\right)\right] \leq \exp(\epsilon) \times \Pr\left[\mathcal{M}\left(\boldsymbol{D}_2 \in \mathcal{S}\right)\right], \tag{6}$$

where $\epsilon \geq 0$ is a small constant.

Laplace mechanism and exponential mechanism are the most commonly used mechanisms that satisfy ϵ-differential privacy [12]. For Laplace mechanism, its main idea is to add noise that following Laplace distribution into the data set that is to be submitted. Exponential mechanism mainly deals with some algorithms whose output results are non-numeric. The bids submitted by SPs and SDs are continuous. Thus, the Laplace mechanism is chosen to protect users' privacy in the double auction scheme we proposed.

Definition 5 *(Laplace Mechanism [11]). Given a function* $f : \mathcal{D} \rightarrow \mathcal{R}^d$ *over a dataset* $\mathcal{D}$, *mechanism* $\mathcal{M}$ *provides the* ϵ-*differential privacy if it follows*

$$\mathcal{M}(D) = f(D) + \mathrm{Lap}(\Delta f/\epsilon), \tag{7}$$

where the noise $\mathrm{Lap}(\Delta f/\epsilon)$ *is drawn from a Laplace distribution with mean zero and scale* $\Delta f/\epsilon$.

Definition 6 *(l_1-sensitivity [11]). Let* $f : \mathcal{D} \rightarrow \mathcal{R}^d$ *be a deterministic function. The* l_1-*sensitivity of* f *is:*

$$\Delta f = \max_{x,y \in \mathcal{R}^d} \|f(x) - f(y)\|_1, \tag{8}$$

We use l_1-*sensitivity to represent the largest difference between the values of* f *of any two neighboring datasets.*

In the blockchain, each node can obtain information in blocks easily by querying its local blockchain copy. And these blocks include users' bids and other information. The bid information implies some hidden information of users. In order to protect the privacy of users in such an open and transparent environment in blockchain network, we decided to introduce a differential privacy mechanism. Let $\tilde{s}_i$ denote additive noise l_i that follow the Laplace distribution to spectrum provider SP_i's bid value s_i as:

$$\tilde{s}_i = s_i + l_i. \tag{9}$$

Similarly, $\tilde{b}_j$ denotes additive noise l_j to SD_j's bid value b_j.

4   Solution and Analysis

4.1   Winner Determination

We maximize social welfare, as the goal of the resource allocation problem. The social welfare is defined as follows:

$$\max_{\mathbf{X}} \quad \sum_{j=1}^{J} \sum_{i=1}^{I} x_{j,i} \cdot (v_{j,i} - s_i) \tag{10}$$

$$\text{s.t.} \quad x_{j,i} \in \{0,1\}, \tag{11}$$

$$\sum_{j=1}^{J} x_{j,i} \leq 1, \forall i \in \{1, 2, ...I\}, \tag{12}$$

$$\sum_{i=1}^{I} x_{j,i} \leq 1, \forall j \in \{1, 2, ...J\}. \tag{13}$$

I and J represent the total number of SPs and SDs respectively. The first constraint indicates that this problem is actually a decision problem, that is, whether to give the channel of SP i to SD j according to the contribution to social welfare based on this decision. Since we assume that the entire system is deployed in a smaller area, the spectrum resources of the same channel cannot be reused by geographical division. So we set the restriction that spectrum resources cannot be reused. And the winner determination problem is an linear programming problem (ILP). And ILP is well known as NP. Thus, the winner determination problem is also NP.

After SDs and SPs obtain the obfuscation function from execution result of smart contract from order blockchain, they add noise to their original bids according to the parameters in the obfuscation function. The winner determination problem in the spectrum sharing scheme we proposed can be regarded as an $0-1$ ILP problem. Thus, this WDP problem for the maximum social welfare can be thought as an assignment problem. So we express our WDP problem as a standard form of assignment problem as:

$$\min_{\mathbf{X}} \quad \sum_{j=1}^{J}\sum_{i=1}^{I}(\tilde{s}_i - \tilde{v}_{j,i})x_{j,i} \tag{14}$$

$$\text{s.t.} \quad \sum_{j=1}^{J}x_{j,i} \leq 1, \forall i \in \{1,2,...I\}, \tag{15}$$

$$\sum_{i=1}^{I}x_{j,i} \leq 1, \forall j \in \{1,2,...J\}, \tag{16}$$

$$x_{j,i} \in \{0,1\}. \tag{17}$$

With the standard form of the assignment problem, the Hungarian algorithm can be exploited to solve the problem and obtain the optimal solution efficiently. The computational cost is dominated by the Hungarian method with the complexity of $O\left(n^3\right)$.

4.2   Clearing Price Determination

After solving the optimization problem, a resource allocation scheme that meets the optimization objective we proposed can be obtained. We suggest a simple but reasonable pricing strategy in such a static double auction scheme running on the blockchain. We prosume that n SDs and m SPs are matched according to the execution result of the algorithm. In this allocation result, $\underline{b}_n$ is the lowest matched bid and $\bar{a}_m$ is the highest matched ask of channels. we take use of the k-double auction(k-DA)[13] to decide the clearing price as:

$$p_c = k\underline{b}_n + (1-k)\bar{a}_m. \tag{18}$$

And k is a parameter between 0 and 1. When the number of users participating in spectrum sharing increases, this auction is able to converge to being strategy-proof and truthful bidding [14].

4.3   Theoretical Analysis

In this section, we analyze the properties of the proposed privacy-preserving double auction scheme. We first show that the proposed mechanism can achieve individual rationality.

Theorem 1. *The privacy-preserving double auction scheme satisfies individual rationality.*

Proof: According to the policy of winner determination and pricing, the payment must less than or equal to the bid. The clearing price is $p_c = k\underline{b}_n + (1 - k)\bar{a}_m$. We assume that SP i and SD j are in the winner set. The utility of SP i is $L_i = s_i - p_c$. And the utility of SD j is $U_j = v_{j,i} - p_c$. And k is a parameter between 0 and 1. $U_j \geq 0$, $L_i \geq 0$ for all winners. Therefore, we prove that individual rationality is satisfied.

Next, we will prove that the auctioneer obtains non-negative utility.

Theorem 2. *The privacy-preserving double auction scheme satisfies budget balance.*

Proof: In our proposed scheme, an auctioneer also acts as a block manager. It can get its commission from the generation of the block as an auctioneer in the form of tokens, which is also recorded into a block. Thus, the auction scheme will keep a budget balance.

Then, we will show that the proposed mechanism has the property of truthfulness. No participant can obtain a higher utility by misreporting its true valuation.

Theorem 3. *The privacy-preserving double auction scheme satisfies truthfulness.*

Proof: The privacy-preserving double auction scheme we proposed has the property of truthfulness if any SP and SD can not obtain a better utility through misreporting their true valuation for spectrum resources. We focus on the SPs and envision four situations:

1. We consider the scenario where a SP is not selected in the winner set no matter whether he gives his true valuation. In this case, the SP will obtain zero utility. SPs can not obtain better utility by misreporting his true valuation.
2. We consider the scenario where a SP is selected as in the winner set only when he bids truthfully. If he gives a higher bid than his valuation, he is not selected as a winner seller and obtains zero utility. If he gives a lower bid than his valuation, he receives a negative utility. Consequently, SPs can not obtain better utility through misreporting his true valuation.
3. We consider the scenario where a SP is selected as in the winner set only when he bids untruthfully. In this case, his valuation equals the clearing price. If the SP gives a higher bid, he does not obtain the spectrum resource and finally receives a zero utility. If the SP gives a lower bid, he obtains a negative utility. Therefore, the SP's untruthful bidding can not achieve high utility.

4. We consider the scenario where a SP is selected in the winner set no matter whether he gives his true valuation. In this case, the SP is charged the same clearing price p_c when he bids truthfully and untruthfully. Thus, the SP can not obtain better utility through misreporting his true valuation.

Therefore, SPs can not achieve higher utility by misreporting their true valuation. Similarly, we can conclude that SDs can not obtain higher utility by misreporting their true valuation as well. Thus, the privacy-preserving double auction scheme satisfies truthfulness.

Differential privacy ensure that the change in any users bid will not bring a significant change to the result of the proposed mechanism to avoid the inference attack. We prove that the proposed mechanism satisfies ϵ-differential privacy.

Theorem 4 *(ϵ-differential Privacy). Our privacy ϵ-preserving double auction scheme satisfies ϵ-differential privacy.*

Proof: We present a Laplace-based winner determination and pricing policy as the main logic of smart contracts to protect the privacy of the valuation information of SPs and SDs in the blockchain-based dynamic spectrum sharing scheme. We add randomly distributed noise following Laplace distribution $\mathrm{Lap}(\Delta f/\epsilon)$ to each user's bid information. The proof of *Definition 6* can be found in [15].

5 Performance Evaluation

In this section, we evaluate the performance of the blockchain-based privacy-preserving mechanism on spectrum trading and bid privacy preservation.

5.1 Simulation Setup

We take advantage of the truffle framework to build this platform. The smart contract was written by the remix tool and deployed on the test chain. Web3.js is adopted to interact with the smart contract. The server built by python is started locally and the function of solving resource allocation problem is realized on the server. Related code implementation can be consulted on https://WWW.github.com/ZhitianTU-NUAA/Dapp.

In the resource allocation problem we introduced, the number of SPs is set to 30 while the number of SDs varies from 5 to 100 with a step of 5. We assume that each SP's resources can only be exploited exclusively by one SD due to the small geographic distance between each user for simplicity. The bids of users are random picked over $(5, 10]$. All the results are averaged over 100 times.

5.2 Performance on Spectrum Trading

To solve the problem of resource allocation, we introduced Hungarian Algorithm[16]. And we set one allocation scheme based on the Greedy algorithm

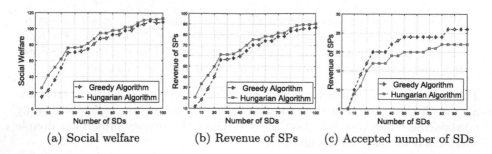

(a) Social welfare   (b) Revenue of SPs   (c) Accepted number of SDs

Fig. 3. Performance on spectrum trading

as a comparison. Figure 3a and Fig. 3b show that the Hungarian algorithm can be used to allocate spectrum resources to obtain the maximum social welfare and SPs' revenue, compared to Greedy algorithm under the same number of SDs. However, the utilization of spectrum resources cannot be taken into account at the same time. The Greedy algorithm considers from the perspective of SPs. And for each spectrum resource of SP, the corresponding SD who can provide the maximal social benefit is selected as the winner. So, the Greedy algorithm can obtain a higher spectrum resource utilization rate compared to Hungarian Algorithm, as is shown in Fig. 3c. Since there may be a situation during the transaction process that no SD can give a bid higher than the price a certain SP asks, some transactions will fail.

5.3   Performance on Bid Privacy Preservation

Figure 4 illustrates the social welfare and revenue of SPs as well as the accepted number of SDs under different differential privacy parameters respectively in our proposed auction scheme. With the increasing number of SDs, social welfare grows rapidly at the beginning and then gradually approaches a certain maximum. Revenue of SPs and the number of accepted SDs will gradually increase in a similar way, as is revealed in Fig. 4b and Fig. 4c. Adding noise to users' bids will cause some certain disturbance to the result of social welfare, revenue of SPs and the accepted number of SDs. When ϵ decreases, the disturbance becomes larger. ϵ indicates the degree of privacy protecting. When the parameter ϵ is small, it can largely guarantee users' privacy in differential privacy. But this also lead to a result that users have to add more noise to their bids which will result in less data availability.

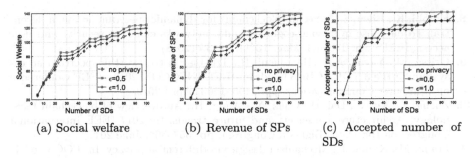

(a) Social welfare   (b) Revenue of SPs   (c) Accepted number of SDs

Fig. 4. Performance on bid privacy preservation

6   Conclusion

In this paper, we introduce blockchain technology in spectrum resource sharing and propose a blockchain-based spectrum resource sharing platform. A privacy-preserving double auction mechanism is designed to run on the blockchain network in the form of smart contracts to protect users' privacy, reach reasonable allocation of spectrum resources and improve spectrum resource utilization in an untrusted environment. And the proposed double auction mechanism is proved to satisfy differential privacy, individual rationality, computational efficiency and truthfulness. The experimental evaluations show that blockchain-based privacy-preserving dynamic spectrum sharing scheme has the ability to improve spectrum trading efficiency and protect users' privacy.

References

1. Peha, J.M.: Approaches to spectrum sharing. IEEE Commun. Mag. **43**(2), 10–12 (2005)
2. Zhao, Q., Sadler, B.M.: A survey of dynamic spectrum access. IEEE Sig. Process. Mag. **24**(3), 79–89 (2007)
3. Sohul, M.M., Yao, M., Yang, T., Reed, J.H.: Spectrum access system for the citizen broadband radio service. IEEE Commun. Mag. **53**(7), 18–25 (2015)
4. Yrjölä, S.: Analysis of blockchain use cases in the citizens broadband radio service spectrum sharing concept. In: Marques, P., Radwan, A., Mumtaz, S., Noguet, D., Rodriguez, J., Gundlach, M. (eds.) CrownCom 2017. LNICST, vol. 228, pp. 128–139. Springer, Cham (2018). https://doi.org/10.1007/978-3-319-76207-4_11
5. Dai, Y., Xu, D., Maharjan, S., Chen, Z., He, Q., Zhang, Y.: Blockchain and deep reinforcement learning empowered intelligent 5g beyond. IEEE Netw. **33**(3), 10–17 (2019)
6. Kumar, S.P., Yeon, M.S., Hyuk, P.J.: Block-VN: a distributed blockchain based vehicular network architecture in smart city. In: Annual Symposium on Foundations of Computer Science, vol. 13, no. 1, pp. 184–195 (2017)
7. Weiss, M.B.H., Werbach, K., Sicker, D.C., Bastidas, C.E.C.: On the application of blockchains to spectrum management. IEEE Trans. Cognit. Commun. Netw. **5**(2), 193–205 (2019)

8. Kotobi, K., Bilen, S.G.: Secure blockchains for dynamic spectrum access: a decentralized database in moving cognitive radio networks enhances security and user access. IEEE Veh. Technol. Mag. **13**(1), 32–39 (2018)
9. Grissa, M., Yavuz, A.A., Hamdaoui, B.: Trustsas: a trustworthy spectrum access system for the 3.5 GHZ CBRS band. In: IEEE INFOCOM 2019 - IEEE Conference on Computer Communications, pp. 1495–1503, April 2019
10. Zheng, Z., Xie, S., Dai, H., Chen, X., Wang, H.: An overview of blockchain technology: Architecture, consensus, and future trends. In: 2017 IEEE International Congress on Big Data (BigData Congress), pp. 557–564, June 2017
11. Frank, M., Kunal, T.: Mechanism design via differential privacy. In: FOCS vol. 7, pp. 94–103 (2007)
12. Wang, Z., Li, J., Hu, J., Ren, J., Li, Z., Li, Y.: Towards privacy-preserving incentive for mobile crowdsensing under an untrusted platform. In: IEEE INFOCOM 2019 - IEEE Conference on Computer Communications, pp. 2053–2061, April 2019
13. Mark, S., Steven, W.: Bilateral trade with the sealed bid k-double auction: existence and efficiency. J. Econ. Theory **48**(1), 107–133 (1989)
14. Kazuo, M.: Online double auction mechanism for perishable goods. Elsevier Electron. Commer. Res. Appl. **13**(5), 355–367 (2014)
15. Cynthia, D., Aaron, R., et al.: The algorithmic foundations of differential privacy. Found. Trends® Theoret. Comput. Sci. **9**(3–4), 211–407 (2014)
16. Harold, K.W.: The Hungarian method for the assignment problem. Naval Res. Logist. Q. **2**(1–2), 83–97 (1955)

A Survey: Applications of Blockchains in the Internet of Vehicles

Chao Wang, Xiaoman Cheng, Jitong Li, Yunhua He$^{(\boxtimes)}$, and Ke Xiao

North China University of Technology, Beijing 100144, China
wangchao.andy@gmail.com, amycxiaoman@163.com,
ljt_IT@163.com, {heyunhua,xiaoke}@ncut.edu.cn

Abstract. To enhance the performance of Internet of Vehicles (IoVs), it is essential to solve some security concerns such as distributed trust management among vehicles. Blockchain, a ledger technology with the characteristics of distributivity, immutability and security could be a way to overcome these security issues and to get better performance in the IoVs. Thus, the integration of the blockchain and the IoV is an important research direction currently. With the aim to provide directions for future work in the area of blockchain-based vehicular networks, this survey illustrates different applications of the blockchain in vehicular environment from different perspectives. Firstly, we compare and analyze the existing surveys about the blockchain-enabled IoV environment. Besides, several works with the aim to overcome vehicular security issues are presented from different aspects. Finally, the future research directions related to the integration of the blockchain in IoVs are discussed.

Keywords: Internet of Vehicles · Blockchain · Security · Survey

1 Introduction

Internet of Vehicles (IoVs) has attracted wide attentions from both research institutes and scholars in the past years. There are two communication modes [1] in IoVs, namely vehicle-to-vehicle (V2V) communications and vehicle-to-everything (V2X) communications, to provide services. In both communication modes, vehicles act as information collectors equipped with on-board units (OBUs) and followed the dedicated short-range communication (DSRC) or LTE-V protocol, and communicate with other entities [2]. Figure 1 depicts a set of complicated communication modes in the IoV environment. Unfortunately, IoV applications are still facing challenges. For example, in the process of collecting information, malicious vehicles can easily publish false information, modify or drop shared data which leads to a series of security problems as shown in paper [3]. What's worse, the privacy of vehicles may also be disclosed, such as vehicle trajectories.

This work was supported in part by the National Natural Science Foundation of China under Grant 61802004 and Grant 61802005.

© Springer Nature Switzerland AG 2020
D. Yu et al. (Eds.): WASA 2020, LNCS 12384, pp. 457–468, 2020.
https://doi.org/10.1007/978-3-030-59016-1_38

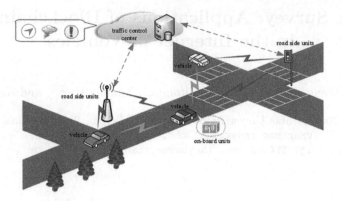

Fig. 1. Architecture of a vehicular network.

The blockchain [4], as a popular distribute ledger, could be considered as a powerful tool to deal with these challenges. It can provide a transparent, immutable and privacy preserving environment for the IoVs [5]. The blockchain is expected to provide credit support for the core information management in the IoVs at low cost. For example, the complete lifeline information of vehicles, such as vehicle certificate, car insurance and other information can be saved safely on the chain. Specifically, the incentive mechanisms can be utilized with the blockchain to improve vehicles' cooperation. The smart contract stored inside a blockchain is immutable and distributed to guarantee the executive process safe and efficient.

Several surveys have already explored the integration of blockchain technology with the IoTs, such as [6]. However, they don't describe the applications of blockchain in the IoVs in details. Some other papers focus on the applications of blockchain in the environment of IoVs, including security and privacy preserving problems. Compared with the existing surveys, our investigation focuses on the question that *"Applications of Blockchains in IoVs"*, and highlights several different aspects on how to implement the blockchain in IoVs. The main contributions of this survey are listed as follows.

– A comprehensive analysis of the existing surveys on integrating blockchains in IoVs is conducted.
– A comparison of implementing the blockchain in IoVs is analyzed from several aspects, such as security, privacy, etc.
– An analysis of the future directions in the field of blockchain-enabled IoVs is presented.

The organization of the survey is as follows. Section 2 offers a comprehensive analysis and comparison of existing blockchain-based IoV surveys. In Sect. 3, the advanced integrated implements (architecture, privacy, security, data management, and etc.) of blockchain and IoVs are presented and discussed. Some future directions of the blockchain used in IoVs are analyzed in Sect. 4. Finally, Sect. 5 concludes this survey.

2   Related Surveys

The existing surveys about blockchain-based vehicular networks are introduced first. Then the advantages and disadvantages of these surveys are also analyzed in this section. Papers [7–12] focus on the combination of the blockchain technology and the IoV and the applications based on the combination. However, some of them [7–9], focus much more on IoTs and the benefits of the blockchain within different challenges of IoTs. These papers don't illustrate how the blockchain technology could be implemented in the vehicular environments and what the main research points related to this integration are.

Paper [10] focuses on the trust management of social IoVs (SIoVs). However, the blockchain-based trust model introduced in this survey is not described and analyzed in details. Besides, this paper doesn't review the security and privacy preservation issues.

Paper [11] introduces the IoV, and the blockchain in details. A comprehensive comparison of different blockchain technologies applied to IoVs is conducted. The applications in IoVs based on the blockchain can be divided into four types by authors: security, trust establishment, incentive and privacy-preservation. Besides, existing applications are analyzed and discussed in this paper. Although vehicular networks can be improved in terms of privacy, security, etc., there are still many aspects of these applications that have not been considered, such as throughput and latency.

In paper [12], some example applications of blockchain applied to Vehicular Ad-hoc Networks (VANETs) are analyzed and presented. The main scenarios are preventing forged data, revocation of users in the network, vehicular announcement network and transportation as a service. The rationality behind the idea of using blockchain in VANETs is also given by the authors. However, according to the authors, the challenges such as limited storage, inadequate nodes and fast changing architecture still exist, and some approaches to solve those have been proposed. It is believed that a better way to improve the VANETs' performance is needed.

3   Integration of the Blockchain and the IoV

As shown in Sect. 2, more analysis is needed on the applications of blockchain in the environment of IoVs. This section analyzes the combination of the blockchain and the IoV from seven aspects. Table 1 categorizes and illustrates various proposed scenarios in recent researches.

3.1   Blockchain-Based IoV Security

Security problems in the IoVs come from the centralized IoV model and its dependence on the third party trust authority. Once the centralized authority failed, the overall system may not work properly which is threat to the system availability. In order to keep network security, the traditional IoV model should have the access control mechanisms and the operation of message validations.

Table 1. Integration of the blockchain and the IOV

Categories		Proposed	Implemented by
IoV security	Access control	[13]	BlockAPP
		[14]	Intelligent Vehicle Trust Point (IVTP)
	Message validation	[15]	Blockchain-based Traffic Event Validation(BTEV) framework
Trust management		[16]	Vehicular announcement protocol Echo-Announcement
		[17]	Anonymous cloaking region construction scheme
		[18]	Blockchain-based Trust management with Conditional Privacy-perserving Scheme(BTCPS)
Certificate management		[19]	Blockchain-based Privacy Preserving Authentication (BPPA) scheme
		[20]	Decentralized Key Management Mechanism (DB-KMM)
		[21]	A Blockchain-based Anonymous Reputation System (BARS)
Data management		[22]	Miner selection and Block verification solutions
		[23]	Mmobile Crowd Sensing (MCS) with blockchain
		[24]	A DQDA incentive mechanism
Data monetization		[25]	Blockchain-based data-trading and loaning system
		[26]	Consortium blockchain-based data trading framework
Privacy preserving		[27]	A hybrid blockchain-PermiDAG
Revised IoV architecture		[28]	Blockchain-based software-defined VANET (block-SDV) framework
		[29]	Blockchain-SDN-enabled architecture in 5G and fog computing systems

Access Control: The availability of the IoVs seriously affects the quality of service of all the transportation services. Two main aspects of robustness are considered in paper [13], which are authentication and privacy preservation. The authenticity of authorized access is reflected by adding a valid transaction to the blockchain. The registration server, service providers, blockchain and vehicles are the four major entities and compose the proposed three-phase system, namely the registration phase, authentication phase and authorization phase. These steps work together with their own function to maintain the robustness of the proposed system. Implementing the smart contract with Remix platform, the blockchain used in the authentication phase ensures the security and privacy preservation of the system.

Paper [14] utilizes the blockchain technology to solve the authentication problem of communications in VANETs. In this paper, there are two blockchains: a local dynamic blockchain and a main blockchain. The local blockchain is responsible of storing some summary information on vehicle movement and message transmitting. When unusual events happened, these events would be stored on the main blockchain. The authors split the local dynamic blockchain to multiple parallel blockchains, each of which is responsible of distinct regions or movement directions. To solve the problem of trust, the authors propose the conception of intelligent vehicle trust point(IVTP), which is used to evaluate the degree of trustiness of a vehicle.

Message Validation: Many applications can be implemented in ITSs with the maturity of communication technology, and more and more information is shared in the ITSs, which affects the road traffic, such as road status information. Therefore, message verification mechanism should be proposed on the shared messages. Encouraged by the advantages of blockchains, a Blockchain-based Traffic Event Validation(BTEV) framework is proposed in the paper [15]. In BTEV, a two-pass threshold-based event validation mechanism can help validate an event, and the submission of transactions can be accelerated based on a two-phase consecutive transaction. Besides, a proof-of-event(PoE) consensus mechanism is introduced, which is proposed for achieving the reliability of event occurrence. In addition, the Merkle Patricia Trie(MPT) structure is introduced to BTEV to make RSUs to submit the confirmed event to the blockchain more efficiently.

3.2   Trust Management in IoVs

With the consideration of security, it is assumed that the third party authority can be trusted absolutely. However, the assumption cannot always be satisfied due to the network instability or in-network attacks. Thus, a trust-less architecture is proposed to solve the above problems, where the trust value of each vehicle in the network is kept by other vehicles. Then the behavior of each vehicle can be evaluated with the help of vehicle trust. The details of trust management are described in the following papers.

An effective announcement network - CreditCoin is proposed in the paper [16] to solve two main problems of message forwarding in the IoVs. In detail, one is how to forward reliable announcements without exposing users' privacy; the other is how to motivate vehicle nodes to forward announcements. For the first problem, the vehicular announcement protocol Echo-Announcement is proposed, which can achieve efficiency and privacy-preserving while forwarding announcements. Then a blockchain-based incentive mechanism is proposed for the second problem. Each user can manage its reputation points while earning or spending coins which act as the incentive.

Paper [17] focuses on the issue of location privacy leakage. This paper proposes a distributed management mechanism of location privacy protection based on the blockchain and the distributed k-anonymity [1] mechanism. First, based on the characteristics of different participants, the authors design a trust management method based on Dirichlet distribution. Then, the blockchain acts as a distributed database to record the trust value in this mechanism, so that the initiating vehicles and the cooperating vehicles only cooperate with the vehicles they trust in the anonymous cloaking region.

Paper [18] targets to solve two issues in the network that whether messages are reliable and whether the privacy of vehicles is protected. For the first question, a conditional privacy-preserving announcement protocol(BTCPS) for secure vehicular communication is proposed. In BTCPS, message aggregation can achieve authentication effectively and reduce the network overhead. The reliability of message announcement can be improved by the threshold number of vehicles. For the second issue, a blockchain-based trust management model is implemented which contains two parts, the updating algorithm of reputation and the distributed consensus algorithm. The reputation data is stored in the blocks and its value will be evaluated by the direct trust value and the indirect trust value. Conditional Privacy, reliability and timeliness can be guaranteed with the method proposed in this paper.

3.3   Certificate Management in IoVs

The certificate issued to each vehicle is the communication identity of each vehicle in the IoVs. In the traditional IoVs, the work of certificate management is accomplished by the Public Key Infrastructure(PKI), including certificate issuing and revoking. However, this architecture suffers from the single point failure problem, which will reduce the reliability of the network. The following papers solve this problem from several aspects.

Paper [19] offers a blockchain-based privacy preserving authentication (BPPA) scheme for VANETs. Authors in this paper assume that the trusted authority (TA) is semi-trusted and will not maliciously track or reveal the linkage between the public key and the real identity of the target vehicle in case of dispute. In addition, semi-TAs are transparency and verifiable because all the certificates and transactions are recorded permanently and immutably in the blockchain. Finally, BPPA employs the Chronological Merkle Tree (CMT) and the Merkle Patricia Tree (MPT) to extend the conventional blockchain structure, which enhances efficiency and scalability.

To solve the certificate management problem, a decentralized key management mechanism(DB-KMM) is proposed in the paper [20], in which the lightweight authentication and the blockchain-based key agreement are integrated. DB-KMM is implemented with the blockchain and the smart contract. Based on the mechanism, some typical attacks such as resisting internal and external attacks, public key tampering, DoS attack and collusion attack can be defensed.

Paper [21] presents a blockchain-based anonymous reputation system to solve three problems in VANETs, which are the reputation management, certificate management and the privacy preservation between the certificate and the vehicle identity. In the blockchain-based anonymous reputation system, the authors propose three blockchains, including blockchain for messages, blockchain for certificates and blockchain for revoked public keys, to manage the process of certificate initialization, updating, revocation and authentication. Second, it presents a reputation evaluation algorithm to build the trust model in VANETs. This algorithm utilizes the reward mechanism to motivate honest and active nodes while utilizing the punishment mechanism to suppress misbehaviors such as distributing forged messages.

3.4   Data Management in IoVs

Data sharing in the IoVs involves online data storage and sharing, as well as offline query-processing and data analysis. Thus, data management systems are required to have live dual operations in communication as well as storage. Data management solutions based on the traditional infrastructure generally follow a trend that the data is tackled in a centralized fashion, with the problem that they do not simultaneously provide guarantees for data integrity and trust in handling heterogenous vehicle data,

Paper [22] proposes an blockchain based platform in the scenario of IoVs to keep the data sharing records. In this paper, two problems are solved. One is how to select proper miners to add blocks to the platform. The other is how to motivate all the miners to participate the process of block verification and defend from the internal collusion in candidates. For the first problem, authors design a reputation based policy to select the miners. The reputations of candidates are calculated from the historical interactions with other vehicles and recommended opinions from other vehicles. Candidates with high reputations are selected to be the active miners and standby miners. In terms of the block verification problem, the authors utilize the contract theory to design an incentive mechanism to motivate the standby miners to participate the verification process and to protect from internal collusion.

Mobile crowdsensing (MSC) is a promising way to solve the issue of huge data collecting in the scenarios such as IoVs. Paper [23] presents a blockchain-based efficient collaboration and incentive mechanism for IoVs with security information exchange. An incentive mechanism is designed for the general sensing task to encourage the vehicles to contribute their targets. Besides, a blockchain based framework has been proposed so that security information exchange can be handled among participated vehicles in the MCS network. In the proposed scenario, the blockchain serves as a medium for security information exchange between devices and the IoT center.

The paper [24] presents an auction incentive mechanism, which is based on the quality of the consortium blockchain drive to ensure the data trust for both the on-chain and the off-chain data. For off-chain data, authors propose the data quality estimation based on an expectation maximization (EM) algorithm to evaluate the actual task data and the quality of data. For on-chain data, authors import a consortium blockchain mechanism to address the security issue of on-chain data; moreover, a smart contract for automatic data sharing and cost computing is designed. Moreover, this paper formulates the process of filtering messages as a reverse auction in which the server acts as an auctioneer that purchases data from users. Finally, the incentive mechanism is based on the data quality-driven auction (DQDA) model with blockchain to maximize welfare at a low cost.

3.5   Monetization of IoV Data

With the development of various devices in the IoVs, the collected data is explosive increasing and becoming of great importance resources. Cloud-based centralized framework is far from meeting the requirements of protecting users' privacy and fast data exchange. However, blockchain-based trading system still face many challenges, such as instability of connections, large trading time gap and "cold-start" problem. Blockchain-based data markets are still not effective enough.

An auxiliary debt-credit mechanism for the blockchain-based IoV data-trading system is proposed in paper [25] to address the efficiency challenges. The proposed data-trading and debt-credit system lets multi-interface-based stations be aggregators so that high-speed communication and ledge storage service for vehicles can be provided. Moreover, a consortium blockchain for secure P2P data-trading and loan services is exploited. Based on the five layered legacy architecture, a two stage Stackelberg game used to solve the pricing problem in the debt-credit process is formulated, in which the borrower vehicle acts as the leader and sets its loan rate for each lender.

A realistic and general P2P data trading framework based on consortium blockchain is proposed to solve the problems in the paper [26]. The verification of transactions is executed without relying on a trusted third party by letting local aggregators gathering data trading information be the authorized nodes. A broker is also introduced to manage the data trading market in the framework. About the problem of commercialization, a budget balanced double auction is proposed to achieve the desired economic benefits and protect the privacy of buyers and sellers.

3.6   Privacy Preserving Through Blockchain in IoVs

The development of IoV has generated a lot of data, such as trajectories and camera data [30], which can improve the driving experience and service quality if they can be mined and analyzed well. Data sharing is a way of improving the quality of IoV applications. However, the security and privacy issues make trouble to the data providers.

An architecture named blockchain empowered asynchronous federated learning architecture for machine learning is proposed in this paper [27]. The hybrid permissioned blockchain scheme-PermiDAG is proposed to improve data security and reliability of model parameters, with consideration of the privacy preserving. The permissioned blockchain and the local Directed Acyclic Graph(DAG) are the two main components of PermiDAG. Highly efficient consensus protocol DPoS is adopted in the permissioned blockchain, wich the reputation of vehicles considered. Besides, Deep Reinforcement Learning(DRL) is utilized for proposing an asynchronous federated learning scheme for node selection, in order to minimize the execution time and maximize the accuracy of the aggregated model.

Some other works [16,19,21] also concern the privacy preserving problem. In these papers, privacy preserving is not the main purpose, but an important condition for other targets. However, all of them protect the privacy of network entities with kinds of methods. Authors in the paper [19] assume that the trusted authority (TA) is semi-trusted and will not maliciously track or reveal the linkage between the public key and the real identity of the target vehicle in case of dispute. In paper [21], the third party – law enforcement authority – is used to keep the privacy on vehicle identities.

3.7   Blockchain-Based Revised IoV Architecture

Distributed software-defined networking(SDN) is considered a promising network to process the large volume of real-time, high-speed and uninterrupted data stream generated in the IoVs. Some architectures are proposed to be used in IoVs, such as software-defined network and fog computing. With these new architectures, some traditional problems in IoVs can be solve, with some other problems imported. Therefore, we classify these class of implementations as revised architectures of IoVs.

A blockchain-based distributed software-defined VANETs framework(block-SDV) is proposed in this paper [28], in which the permissioned blockchain system is used. In order to ensure all the consensus nodes perform relevant operations which include executing and writing transactions correctly, consensus mechanism is proposed, named redundant Byzantine fault tolerance (RBFT). Compared to traditional consensus algorithm, block-SDV is a permissioned blockchain system and has better performance.

Paper [29] brings blockchain, SDN, fog computing and 5G communication system to the standardized vehicular communication architecture. The combination of them can efficiently and effectively manage and control the network. The system incorporates blockchain and SDN into the IoVs for sharing management, which not only ensures the need of trust among the connected peers, but also guarantees the effective network management and the control process. In addition, the fog computing solves the handover problems of SDN when lots of vehicles are connected to the RSUs. 5G provides services on low-latency communication to enhance network performance.

4   Future Direction

As shown in the previous section, different aspects of blockchain based IoV applications, have been designed and discussed. The major benefit of these integrations is that they could contribute to improve vehicular network environment. Nevertheless, future research directions in this field should be highlighted.

4.1   Trust of Off-chain Data

Blockchain can only solve the issue of data trust or creditability on the chain in IoVs. However, the trust of off-chain data for blockchains is still an open issue. In addition, in the context of the requirement for privacy and security of IoV, off-chain data should be more protected. For example, paper [24] proposes a scheme to guarantee the data trust both on-chain data and off-chain data by consortium blockchain and DQDA model. Therefore, in the case of ensuring the security and non-disclosure of the data on the chain, the privacy of the data off the chain also deserves attention.

4.2   Evaluation Criteria

Although many proposed systems have been tested to evaluate their security and availability, most of the studies are based on independent evaluation and simulation, and there is no comparative evaluation experiment as a benchmark. In fact, these independent assessments have no practical significance. As a result, the feasibility of these solutions cannot be evaluated. Therefore, the evaluation criteria are needed to compare and evaluate these solutions.

4.3   Integration of Future Architectures

To fully utilize the advantages of different technologies in IoVs, they should be integrated in IoVs. Blockchain could complete and improve these technologies with better performance. For example, paper [29] utilized different technologies into IoVs: SDN, fog computing and 5G, etc. In this architecture, blockchain is a way to securely manage the SDN enabled IoVs as its immutability and transparency. Thus, the applications of combining blockchain and other technologies could be interesting research directions in vehicular networks.

5   Conclusion

In this paper, we provide an extensive discussion and comparison of the existing surveys about applications of blockchain, with a specific focus on the integration of the blockchain technology with the IoVs. Then we analyze and compare the combination of blockchain and IoVs in seven aspects, including architecture, security, trust management and privacy protection and so on. Specifically, we propose different comments and improvements for each blockchain-based vehicular application. Finally, by analyzing the improvement of these applications, several open issues help us reveal directions that have the potential to yield major outcomes in the near future.

References

1. Wang, J., Cai, Z., Yu, J.: Achieving personalized k-anonymity-based content privacy for autonomous vehicles in CPS. IEEE Trans. Ind. Inform. **16**(6), 4242–4251 (2020)
2. Wang, C., Li, J., He, Y., Xiao, K., Zhang, H.: Destination prediction-based scheduling algorithms for message delivery in IoVS. IEEE Access **8**, 14965–14976 (2020)
3. Cai, Z., Zheng, X., Yu, J.: A differential-private framework for urban traffic flows estimation via taxi companies. IEEE Trans. Ind. Inform. **15**(12), 6492–6499 (2019)
4. Zhu, S., Cai, Z., Hu, H., Li, Y., Li, W.: zkCrowd: a hybrid blockchain-based crowdsourcing platform. IEEE Trans. Ind. Inform. **16**(6), 4196–4205 (2020)
5. Pu, Y., Xiang, T., Hu, C., Alrawais, A., Yan, H.: An efficient blockchain-based privacy preserving scheme for vehicular social networks. Inf. Sci. **540**, 308–324 (2020)
6. Zhu, S., Li, W., Li, H., Tian, L., Luo, G., Cai, Z.: Coin hopping attack in blockchain-based IoT. IEEE Internet Things J. **6**(3), 4614–4626 (2019)
7. Dorri, A., Kanhere, S.S., Jurdak, R.: Blockchain in Internet of Things: challenges and solutions (2016)
8. Ferrag, M.A., Derdour, M., Mukherjee, M., Derhab, A., Maglaras, L., Janicke, H.: Blockchain technologies for the internet of things: research issues and challenges. IEEE Internet Things J. **6**(2), 2188–2204 (2019)
9. Ali, M.S., Vecchio, M., Pincheira, M., Dolui, K., Antonelli, F., Rehmani, M.H.: Applications of blockchains in the Internet of Things: a comprehensive survey. IEEE Commun. Surv. Tutor. **21**(2), 1676–1717 (2019)
10. Iqbal, R., Butt, T.A., Afzaal, M., Salah, K.: Trust management in social internet of vehicles: factors, challenges, blockchain, and fog solutions. Int. J. Distrib. Sensor Netw. **15**(1), 1550147719825820 (2019)
11. Mendiboure, L., Chalouf, M.A., Krief, F.: Survey on blockchain-based applications in internet of vehicles. Comput. Electr. Eng. **84**, 106646 (2020). http://www.sciencedirect.com/science/article/pii/S0045790620305012
12. Majumder, S., Mathur, A., Javaid, A.Y.: A study on recent applications of blockchain technology in vehicular adhoc network (VANET). In: Choo, K.-K.R., Morris, T.H., Peterson, G.L. (eds.) NCS 2019. AISC, vol. 1055, pp. 293–308. Springer, Cham (2020). https://doi.org/10.1007/978-3-030-31239-8_22
13. Sharma, R., Chakraborty, S.: Blockapp: using blockchain for authentication and privacy preservation in IoV, pp. 1–6 (2018)
14. Singh, M., Kim, S.: Branch based blockchain technology in intelligent vehicle. Comput. Netw. **145**, 219–231 (2018). http://www.sciencedirect.com/science/article/pii/S1389128618308399
15. Yang, Y.T., Chou, L.D., Tseng, C.W., Tseng, F.H., Liu, C.C.: Blockchain-based traffic event validation and trust verification for VANETs. IEEE Access **7**, 30868–30877 (2019)

16. Li, L., et al.: Creditcoin: a privacy-preserving blockchain-based incentive announce-ment network for communications of smart vehicles. IEEE Trans. Intell. Transp. Syst. **19**(7), 2204–2220 (2018)
17. Luo, B., Li, X., Weng, J., Guo, J., Ma, J.: Blockchain enabled trust-based location privacy protection scheme in vanet. IEEE Trans. Veh. Technol. **69**(2), 2034–2048 (2020)
18. Liu, X., Huang, H., Xiao, F., Ma, Z.: A blockchain-based trust management with conditional privacy-preserving announcement scheme for VANETs. IEEE Internet Things J. **7**(5), 4101–4112 (2020)
19. Lu, Z., Wang, Q., Qu, G., Zhang, H., Liu, Z.: A blockchain-based privacy-preserving authentication scheme for VANETs. IEEE Trans. Very Large Scale Integr. (VLSI) Syst. 27(12), 2792–2801 (2019)
20. Ma, Z., Zhang, J., Guo, Y., Liu, Y., Liu, X., He, W.: An efficient decentralized key management mechanism for VANET with blockchain. IEEE Trans. Veh. Technol. **69**(6), 1 (2020)
21. Lu, Z., Liu, W., Wang, Q., Qu, G., Liu, Z.: A privacy-preserving trust model based on blockchain for VANETs. IEEE Access **6**, 45655–45664 (2018)
22. Kang, J., Xiong, Z., Niyato, D., Ye, D., Kim, D.I., Zhao, J.: Toward secure blockchain-enabled internet of vehicles: optimizing consensus management using reputation and contract theory. IEEE Trans. Veh. Technol. **68**(3), 2906–2920 (2019)
23. Yin, B., Wu, Y., Hu, T., Dong, J., Jiang, Z.: An efficient collaboration and incentive mechanism for internet of vehicles (IoV) with secured information exchange based on blockchains. IEEE Internet Things J. **7**(3), 1582–1593 (2020)
24. Chen, W., Chen, Y., Chen, X., Zheng, Z.: Toward secure data sharing for the iov: a quality-driven incentive mechanism with on-chain and off-chain guarantees. IEEE Internet Things J. **7**(3), 1625–1640 (2020)
25. Liu, K., Chen, W., Zheng, Z., Li, Z., Liang, W.: A novel debt-credit mechanism for blockchain-based data-trading in internet of vehicles. IEEE Internet Things J. **6**(5), 9098 9111 (2019)
26. Chen, C., Wu, J., Lin, H., Chen, W., Zheng, Z.: A secure and efficient blockchain-based data trading approach for Internet of vehicles. IEEE Trans. Veh. Technol. **68**(9), 9110–9121 (2019)
27. Lu, Y., Huang, X., Zhang, K., Maharjan, S., Zhang, Y.: Blockchain empowered asynchronous federated learning for secure data sharing in internet of vehicles. IEEE Trans. Veh. Technol. **69**(4), 4298–4311 (2020)
28. Zhang, D., Yu, F.R., Yang, R.: Blockchain-based distributed software-defined vehicular networks: a dueling deep Q-learning approach. IEEE Trans. Cognit. Commun. Netw. **5**(4), 1086–1100 (2019)
29. Gao, J.: A blockchain-SDN-enabled internet of vehicles environment for fog com-puting and 5G networks. IEEE Internet Things J. **7**(5), 4278–4291 (2020)
30. Xiong, Z., Li, W., Han, Q., Cai, Z.: Privacy-preserving auto-driving: a GAN-based approach to protect vehicular camera data. In: IEEE International Conference on Data Mining (ICDM) 2019, pp. 668–677 (2019)

A Secure Topology Control Mechanism for SDWSNs Using Identity-Based Cryptography

Rui Wang[1(✉)], Donglan Liu[1], Jianfei Chen[2], Lei Ma[1], Xin Liu[1], and Hao Zhang[1]

[1] State Grid Shandong Electric Power Research Institute, Jinan, China
wangrui_dky@163.com
[2] State Grid Shandong Electric Power Company, Jinan, China

Abstract. As one of the most critical procedures of Software-Defined Wireless Sensor Networks (SDWSNs), topology control is used to maintain the global view of the network. However, the security issues of SDWSNs are still in infancy. Due to the open wireless channels, the malicious node could tamper, steal or insert the information of topology messages and then cause huge damage on the network operations. Compared with the traditional cryptography, Identity-based Cryptography (IBC) may be more suitable for SDWSNs with its ability to derive the public key from node identity directly. Specifically, an Identity-based Combined Encryption and Signature Cryptography (IBCES) can use the same identity to encrypt and sign the message. Based on IBCES, we design a neighbor discovery and secure communication mechanism using a mutual authentication scheme. And then we propose a secure topology control mechanism to protect data confidentiality, integrity and authentication during the topology collection and management processes. Finally, the security analysis indicates that our scheme meets the basic security requirements of topology messages and resists multiple attacks. The performance analysis and experiment results support that our approach is suitable for SDWSNs.

Keywords: SDWSNs · IBC · IBCES · Topology control · Authentication · Secure communication

1 Introduction

The topology control is one of the most critical procedures of Software-Defined Wireless Sensor Networks (SDWSNs) [12]. To formulate a graph representing an abstract view of the nodes and the wireless links between them, the Controller needs to collect the underlying topology information periodically and also pushes topology rules to manage the sensor network. Unlike the wired SDN which has a dedicated control channel, both data and control packets in SDWSNs share the same wireless link [1]. It makes the transmission of topology messages vulnerable

© Springer Nature Switzerland AG 2020
D. Yu et al. (Eds.): WASA 2020, LNCS 12384, pp. 469–481, 2020.
https://doi.org/10.1007/978-3-030-59016-1_39

to eavesdropping, tampering and forgery attacks. For instance, the Sybil attacker could use multiple identities and advertise it to neighboring nodes [8]. This would cripple the neighborhood detection and topology maintenance processes and then lead to significant degradation of routing performance [5]. However, most studies of SDWSNs tended to design the architecture and application scenarios. Security within SDWSNs is still in infancy and few studies have been focused on the security of SDWSN topology control [7].

Cryptography owns the ability to protect communication in open networks and effectively defends against the external attackers. Symmetric cryptography is advantage in speed and low energy cost. However, it suffers the key management and scalability drawback in the large-scale network [2]. Asymmetric cryptography could establish secure communication via easy key agreement algorithms. Whereas it usually uses Public Key Infrastructure (PKI) and certificates to ensure the authentication of public key, the complexity and computation overhead of certificate operations make it unfeasible to WSNs. Recently, Identity-based Cryptography (IBC) has attracted much attention. IBC requires less resource regarding process power, storage and communication bandwidth [3]. Instead of using a certificate to bind the identity to its public key, the identity of an entity (e.g. IP address, name) can be used as a public key. It enables message encryption without the need to previously distribute keys or verify certificates [6]. Such a facility is attractive in WSN use-cases and lots of IBC security schemes have been designed for WSNs and Internet of Things (IoT).

IBC is also fit for SDWSNs. The Controller is trusted by all the network nodes and could act as the Private Key Generator (PKG) of IBC which is in charge of generating nodes' private keys. IBC cryptosystem could reduce the communication between nodes and Controller, and make the system scalable. Especially, by combining Identity-based Encryption (IBE) with Identity-based Signature (IBS), an Identity-based Combined Encryption and Signature (IBCES) scheme can be constructed. IBCES utilizes the same identity for both signature and encryption, which greatly lessens the amount of identities and saves the storage space. On account of IBC and IBCES, we put forward a secure topology control scheme to verify the validity of nodes, establish secure communication, build a correct topology view and authenticate the control messages. To the best of our knowledge, we are among the first to study the IBC-based secure topology control mechanism for SDWSNs. The main contributions of this paper are summarized as follows:

1. Based on IBE, we present a secure neighbor node discovery and secure communication mechanism for SDWSNs using a mutual authentication with key agreement scheme.
2. Based on IBE and IBS, we propose a secure topology control scheme to protect the data confidentiality, integrity and authentication of topology messages during the topology collection and management processes.
3. The security analysis indicates our mechanism meets the basic security requirements of topology messages and resists multiple attacks, including man-in-the-middle attack, Sybil attack and so on. The performance analysis

and experiments on the middle-class WSN devices, such as Raspberry Pi, support that our approach is fit for SDWSNs.

The remainder of this paper is organized as below. Section 2 discusses the related works. Section 3 presents the basic concept of IBCES and the motivation of this paper. Sections 4 describes the secure neighbor node discovery and topology control mechanisms in detail. Sections 5 and 6 provide the security analysis and experimental results, respectively. Finally, Sect. 7 concludes our work and indicates the directions for future research.

2   Related Work

2.1   Topology Control in SDWSNs

As a key factor in WSNs, topology control is responsible for the seamless and efficient operation of the network [12]. The topology control strategies usually contain topology construction and topology maintenance. Galluccio et al. introduced a **S**oftware **D**efined **N**etworking solution for **WI**reless **SE**nsor networks (SDN-WISE). SDN-WISE presents a state-of-art Topology Discovery (TD) protocol for SDWSNs [4]. By running the TD protocol, all the nodes maintain information about the next hop towards the Controller and its current neighbors. To improve WSN management, control and operation, Theodorou et al. put forward a Software-Defined topology control strategy for the IoT and the strategy reduces time and control overhead [12]. However, the above studies do not integrate security into their deign. The malicious attackers could join the network and tamper the topology packets to disrupt the normal operation of the network. Wang et al. [15] demonstrated an energy-efficient topology aggregating collection mechanism and designed a centralized trust management scheme to detect and isolate the malicious nodes. However, they are based on the assumption that secure communications between the nodes have been already established. The topology control in SDWSNs is still at an initial stage and related security problems need more special concerns [12].

2.2   Communication Security in SDWSNs

The communication in SDWSNs is mostly carried out through wireless links that are prone to eavesdropping and man-in-the-middle attacks [2]. However, the security issues in SDWSNs have not received enough attention [10] and fewer studies are focused on node authentication and communication security [1]. In the existing cryptography methods for SDWSNs, Pritchard et al. investigated the AES and RSA algorithms within SDWSNs and figured out that the centralized control would benefit the resource-intense cryptographic solutions implemented on the control plane [10]. Alves et al. designed a wireless secure SDN-based communication for sensor networks W^{3}SN [1]. W^{3}SN supports secure node admission and end-to-end key distribution in TinySDN. However, they do not take the threats on the transmission of topology messages into consideration, such as the Sybil nodes between the node and Controller.

In the last decade, many IBC-based security approaches have been applied to WSNs and IoT. Oliveira et al. proposed TinyPBC, an efficient implementation of IBC primitives for 8, 16, and 32-bit processors commonly found in WSN nodes [9]. Karantaidou et al. conducted feasibility tests of IBC for middle-class IoT devices, such as the Raspberry Pi 3 platform [6]. The study results above show that IBC could be adopted by the WSN resource-constrained devices. Some researchers have applied IBC to strengthen the network security of software defined networks. Wang et al. developed an IBC-based solution to authenticate the validity of flow rules in SDN [14]. The fake flow rules generated by unregistered applications can be efficiently identified and rejected. Salman et al. presented an identity-based identification and authentication scheme for heterogeneous IoT networks [11]. However, they do not test in an SDN environment and present performance analysis for memory or communication overheads. Although the above research could not be directly adapted to the WSNs, their schemes are still beneficial for applying IBC to SDWSN scenarios [1].

3   Identity-Based Cryptography: An Overview

In this section, we briefly introduce the Identity-based Combined Encryption and Signature (IBCES) and describe the motivation of this paper.

3.1   Identity-Based Combined Encryption and Signature (IBCES)

In 2019, Li et al. have proved that **B**oneh and **F**ranklin's Identity-based Encryption (BF-IBE) and **C**ha and **C**heon's Identity-based Signature (CC-IBS) could be simultaneously used, and constructed an Identity-based Combined Encryption and Signature (IBCES) scheme [17]. By using the same key pair for both the signature and encryption operations, the task of key management and storage space could be reduced. In order to aid understanding of later sections, we list a brief introduction of IBCES including six algorithms as follows.

- **Setup**: The system setup algorithm is performed by PKG. The PKG takes a security parameter k as input and then outputs a master key s and the system public parameters $params$. s is kept by PKG secretly.
- **Extract**: The extract algorithm is also performed by PKG. The PKG takes as input $params$, s, an node's identity ID_U, and then outputs a private key S_U. PKG will send S_U to the user via a secure way.
- **Encrypt**: The encryption algorithm takes as input $params$, the receiver's identity ID_U and a plaintext m, and outputs a ciphertext c. Here we represent it as $c = E_{ID_U}(m)$.
- **Decrypt**: The decryption algorithm takes as input $params$, a ciphertext c, the receiver's identity ID_U and private key S_U, and then outputs the plaintext m. Here we represent it as $m = D_{S_U}(c)$.

- **Sign**: The signature algorithm takes as input the plaintext m, the signer's identity ID_U and private key S_U, and then outputs the signture σ. Here we represent it as $\sigma = S_{S_U}(m)$.
- **Verify**: The verification algorithm takes as input $params$, the message m, the signature σ and the signer's identity ID_U, and then outputs a correct symbol ($\top$) or an error symbol ($\bot$). Here we represent it as $\top$ or $\bot = V_{ID_U}(m, \sigma)$.

3.2 Motivation

To achieve centralized network control, the SDWSNs need to collect the underlying topology information generated by nodes periodically. However, open wireless channel makes the transmission vulnerable to eavesdropping, tampering, man-in-the-middle attacks. The malicious nodes could fake other nodes' identities, and disrupt the normal topology control of SDWSNs. For instance, the Sybil attacker could use multiple identities, fake near path close to the sink and advertises it to neighboring nodes. This will cripple the neighborhood detection and topology maintenance processes [5]. In SDWSNs, the node authentication, data integrity and confidentiality need to be guaranteed during the topology control procedure.

Particularly, we use the IBCES scheme to guarantee data privacy and communication security in topology control. The same identity can be applied to execute encryption and signature operations, which could reduce the number of node identity and the private key generation cost. We propose a secure topology control mechanism that contains the secure neighbor discovery, topology collection, and topology management schemes based on IBCES. The BF-IBE is used to realize the mutual authentication between the two nodes and conduct a shared symmetric key. Therefore, the confidentiality of topology report messages could be guaranteed. We apply CC-IBS to protect the integrity and authentication of important topology control messages. Finally, the Controller could effectively maintain a correct topology view and manage the underlying nodes.

4 Design of the Secure Topology Control Mechanism

In this section, we give the assumptions on the secure topology control mechanism and then present the secure neighbor node discovery, topology collection, and topology management mechanisms, respectively.

4.1 Assumptions

We make the following assumptions to make our analysis clear and simple.

1. The network is static and randomly deployed.
2. All the nodes are homogeneous and possess enough capabilities to run IBCES cryptosystem.
3. The sink and Controller are connected through Ethernet and the communication between them is secure. They are always trusted.

4.2   Neighbor Node Discovery Phase

After deployment, all the nodes start the neighbor discovery process. Identity authentication is used to verify the validity of neighbor nodes. Here we adopt an IBE-based mutual authentication with key agreement scheme designed by Han et al. [16] and make some modification to suit the SDWSN scenario.

To begin with, each node broadcasts a hello packet which contains its identity. When receiving the broadcast packets, every neighbor node adds these identities to its unauthenticated neighbor list. Before connecting and exchanging data with each other, node A N_A and node B N_B (note that N_B can be a sink) need to authenticate each other. The details of the mutual authentication mechanism are explained as follows:

1. N_A randomly chooses $a \in \mathbb{Z}_q^*$ and calculates aP where P is the generator of cyclic additive group $\mathbb{G}_1$. Using N_B's identity ID_B, N_A encrypts the message $C_1 = E_{ID_B}(aP||ID_A||ID_B||T_1)$. Here the timestamp T is used to prevent the replay attack. Then N_A sends the neighbor authentication request $R_1 = Request||C_1$ to N_B.
2. Upon receiving the request R_1, N_B will reject this request if ID_A is not in its unauthenticated neighbor list. Otherwise, it decrypts C_1 using its private key S_B and checks whether ID_B is equal to its identity. If matches, N_B randomly chooses $b \in \mathbb{Z}_q^*$ and calculates bP. Using ID_A, N_B encrypts the aP together with bP getting the ciphertext $C_2 = E_{ID_A}(aP||bP||ID_B||ID_A||T_2)$. Then N_B sends the response $R_2 = Reponse||C_2$ to N_A.
3. After R_2 is received, N_A decrypts C_2 using its private key S_A. If aP is consistent with the one it sends, N_A could ensure it really authenticates with N_B. The shared symmetric key $K_{AB} = a(bP)$ can be generated from a and bP. Based on a symmetry cryptography algorithm AES, N_A uses the K_{AB} to encrypt bP together with a secret message $C_3 = AES_{K_{AB}}(bP||T_2||Message_A)$. N_A sends the reply $R_3 = Reply||C_3$ to N_B.
4. Likewise, N_B can get $K_{AB} = b(aP)$. After obtaining R_3 from N_A, N_B could decrypt C_3 using K_{AB}. If bP is consistent with the sent one, N_A could be verified by N_B. N_B also ensures it achieves a key agreement with N_A.

Because the encrypted messages can only be decrypted by the other party's private key, the man-in-the-middle attacker could not intercept or modify aP or bP, which achieves the **mutual authentication** between N_A and N_B. A Key Derivation Function (KDF) could be applied to K_{AB} in order to generate a series of keys appropriate for symmetry cryptosystems [9]. This establishes a secure communication between N_A and N_B. After all the authentications have been completed, N_A adds the authenticated neighbor nodes to the legal neighbor list, i.e., $LN_A = \{ID_B, ID_E\}$ as well as the failed nodes to the illegal neighbor list, i.e., $IN_A = \{ID_F, ID_G\}$.

4.3   Topology Collection Phase

To build an abstract view of the current network status, the Controller needs to start the topology collection process periodically. Considering the forgery identity attackers in the network, we propose a secure topology collection mechanism to guarantee the authentication, data integrity and confidentiality of the local topology information. Here the mutual authentication mechanism is used to achieve the authentication and communication security between two remote nodes, such as the node and sink.

Topology Discovery. The Controller periodically broadcasts a Topology Discovery (TD) packet via the sinks. The TD packet contains the **identity** of the sink which has generated it and the current hop from the sink which is initially set to 0 [4]. When receiving a TD packet from N_B (note that B can also be a sink), N_A executes the following operations as SDN-WISE's TD process.

1. Firstly it checks whether N_B and its identity are in its LN_A. If not, it will discard this packet. Otherwise, N_A updates N_B along with the current RSSI.
2. If this TD packet has a lower value of the current hop from the sink, N_A sets its next hop towards the Controller equal to N_B.
3. N_A adds one to the current hop value and transmits the updated TD packet over the broadcast wireless channel.

N_A only forwards the TD packet from the authenticated neighbor nodes which ensures the reliable forwarding of topology discovery. The node may receive multiple TD packets from different sinks and it just selects the nearest one. After finishing the TD process, all the nodes establish the path towards the Controller.

Topology Report. At the end of each topology discovery process, N_A sends a Topology Report (TR) packet to the Controller. The TR packet contains its current state, legal neighbor list LN_A, and illegal neighbor list IN_A. If N_A has already authenticated with the sink, they would get K_{AB}. To ensure the integrity and confidentiality of the data, N_A encrypts TR packet as follows.

- $TR_A = current\_state_A || LN_A || IN_A || T$
- $Digest_A = HMAC_{K_{AB}}(TR_A)$
- $Message_A = AES_{K_{AB}}(TR_A) || Digest_A$

Otherwise, N_A requires a mutual authentication with the sink. If success, the reply R_3 could directly carry the TR packet to reduce the number of transmissions. N_A inserts the sink into its legal sink list and the sink adds N_A to its legal node list. The authentication verifies the validity of the sink and also avoids the unauthorized node sending the forged topology information.

Topology Aggregation. After receiving the encrypted messages, the sink decrypts them using the corresponding K_{AB} to obtain the TR packets. The sink verifies $Digest_A$ to ensure the integrity of the received message and sends the aggregated topology information to the Controller. The Controller could maintain the global topology view and nodes' connectivity based on the underlying topology information.

4.4   Topology Management Phase

The topology management maintains the integrity of network connectivity during network operations [12]. Based on the topology view, the Controller could remove the malicious nodes from the network and add new nodes into the network. To defend against the tamper attack, we propose an IBS-based message authentication mechanism to protect the integrity of topology management messages.

Node Removal. Some nodes may be captured and compromised at the runtime. They may launch malicious behaviors, such as blackhole and greyhole attacks. These internal attackers could be detected by trust management solutions [15]. To report these malicious nodes safely, N_A firstly signs the digest of the alarm message m_A using its private key S_A. And then N_A encrypts the alarm message along with its signature σ_A using the PKG's identity ID_{PKG}.

- $m_A = ID_E || Behavior\_Description || T$
- $\sigma_A = S_{S_A}(Hash(m_A))$
- $ID_A \rightarrow ID_{PKG} : E_{ID_{PKG}}(m_A || \sigma_A)$

After decrypting and verifying the alarm messages, the Controller could maintain a list of malicious nodes and generate the node removal messages. The identities of the malicious nodes, together with a timestamp, are signed by the Controller. The topology management messages are broadcasted by sinks.

$$ID_{S_i} \rightarrow broadcast : ID_E || ID_G || T || (S_{S_{PKG}}(ID_E || ID_G || T))$$

Upon the broadcast is received, N_A will verify the signature to ensure the control information is not modified.

$$ID_A : \top \text{ or } \bot = V_{ID_{PKG}}(ID_E || ID_G || T, S_{S_{PKG}}(ID_E || ID_G || T))$$

Later, it will add the nodes ID_E and ID_G to its blacklist. The flow rules related to these nodes will also be removed.

Node Addition. As the system runs, some nodes may exhaust their battery and some extra nodes need to be added into the SDWSNs. Meanwhile, certain sinks may be deployed when the network gets congested. To reduce the topology discovery and communication overhead, the Controller could sign the identities of these nodes and promote the sinks broadcast the node addition message to the whole network.

$$ID_{S_i} \rightarrow broadcast : ID_H || ID_{S_j} || T || (S_{S_{PKG}}(ID_H || ID_{S_j} || T))$$

Similarly, every node will verify the signature and add these identities into its legal node list or legal sink list.

$$ID_A : \top \text{ or } \bot = V_{ID_{PKG}}(ID_H || ID_{S_j} || T, S_{S_{PKG}}(ID_H || ID_{S_j} || T))$$

5 Security Analysis

In this section, we analyze the security of the proposed scheme from two aspects, including data security and attack defense.

5.1 Topology Message Security

Our security mechanism can ensure the data security of topology messages.

Data Confidentiality. The topology report message is encrypted by the shared symmetric key K_{AB} between the node and sink. It is transmitted in the form of ciphertext which can keep the data secretly from malicious nodes.

Data Integrity. The MAC derived from shared symmetric key K_{AB} is appended to the topology report message. The message digest of the topology alarm message is signed by the reporting node. These methods can ensure the messages are transmitted without any modification by the unauthorized nodes.

Authentication. The topology management messages are signed by the Controller. The receiving nodes only accept the management messages verified correctly. This ensures that the source of messages is really from the Controller.

5.2 Attack Defense

Man-in-the-Middle Attack. Without the knowledge of the corresponding private keys, the man-in-the-middle attacker could not tamper, steal, or modify the information in the messages without the receiver's attention. Although the plaintext of the message may be changed by the attacker, the modified message will be discarded due to the failure of matching with the decrypted message. The communication scheme can resist against the man-in-the-middle attack.

Replay Attack. The replay attack can be prevented by the timestamp T. Because T is encrypted in the message by the sender, the attacker could not be able to decrypt and change the value of T. The receiver will check T and ignore the messages whose T stays at the same time.

Sybil Attack. The malicious nodes could present multiple identities to launch the Sybil attack. The mutual authentication scheme does not allow the Sybil attacker to join the network. By verifying the identity of each node and sink, the node only communicate the entity in its legal node and sink lists. Therefore, this attack is not feasible anymore.

Controller DoS Attack. The attacker could send lots of illegal packets to exhaust the resource of Controller and crash the whole network. In our scheme, the sinks only accept the packets from the authenticated nodes and also check the timestamp to defend the relay packets. The flooding packets from malicious nodes will be discarded at the sinks. As a consequence, our scheme can weaken the Controller DoS attack to a certain extent.

Compromised Attack. Our mechanism can defend against the external attackers. The captured node may be compromised and launch internal attacks, such as select forwarding attack. The internal attackers would be detected by the trust management schemes [15] but they are out of our work scope. However, every node communicates with the sink and the Controller separately and the compromised nodes do not affect the communication of other nodes. Our scheme also provides an alarm reporting mechanism to help the Controller detect and isolate the attacker from the network.

6   Performance Analysis

6.1   Computation and Communication Cost

In the whole IBC scheme, the most expensive operations includes the addition operation C_a, exponent operation C_e, pairing operation C_p and point multiplication C_m. For the sake of simplicity, the costs of the hash functions, random number generations, bitwise XOR, and AES algorithm are omitted because their cost is much lower than that of bilinear pairing. $|\mathbb{G}_1|$ is the number of bits of an element in group $\mathbb{G}_1$ and $|m|$ is the number of bits of message m. So in our topology control mechanism, the total computation and communication cost of node authentication and message authentication processes are listed in Table 1.

Table 1. Computation and communication cost for each party

Scheme	Computation cost		Communication cost
	Sender	Receiver	
Node authentication	$3C_m + C_e + 2C_p$	$3C_m + C_e + 2C_p$	$2|\mathbb{G}_1| + 4|m|$
Message authentication	$2C_m$	$C_a + C_m + 2C_p$	$2|\mathbb{G}_1|$

In node authentication process, the computation cost of the sender is the same as the receiver. The identity authentication usually occurs during the deployment phase without causing much overhead to the node. In message authentication process, the computation cost of the versifier is higher than that of the signer. However, the message authentication often happens when the malicious nodes are detected or some new nodes join the network, which would also not increase the burden on the nodes. Indeed, the cryptosystem produces a certain communication overhead and the communication cost of node authentication is higher than that of message authentication.

6.2   Performance Test

We have implemented our scheme using the Paring-based Cryptography (PBC) Library [13]. The SDWSN node is simulated by a medium-class WSN device – Raspberry Pi 4B with 1.5-GHz Cortex-A72 CPU and 2GB RAM. The operating system is Ubuntu 18.04. Our study employs Type A pairings of PBC which are constructed from the curve $y^2 = x^3 + x$ over the field $\mathbb{F}_q$ for some $q = 3 \mod 4$. The group order is set as 160-bit and the base field size is set as 512-bit.

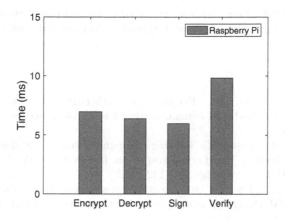

Fig. 1. The running time of cryptographic operations.

The average running time of four basic cryptographic operations on the node is displayed in Fig. 1. The verification takes the longest 9.82 ms due to the two necessary pairing operations which are the most time-consuming. However, because the pairing operation of Type A is the fastest in PBC, all the cryptographic running time is acceptable. We assume the message length is 128 Bytes. In node authentication process, the communication cost of encryption and decryption is 384 Bytes. In message authentication process, the communication cost of signature and verification is 256 Bytes, which is also acceptable. The performance results suggest that our topology control scheme is suitable for SDWSNs.

7   Conclusion

Based on IBCES cryptosystem, we propose a secure topology control scheme to guarantee the data privacy of topology messages. Using a mutual authentication with key agreement scheme, we achieve the authentication and secure communication between the neighbor nodes. During the topology collection and management processes, the basic data security requirements are satisfied by IBE and IBS, respectively. The security analysis indicates that our scheme satisfies the security requirements of topology packets and resists multiple attacks. The performance analysis and experiments on the middle-class WSN devices reveal that our approach is appropriate to SDWSNs.

In future work, we will conduct an in-depth study of IBC cryptosystem. Signcryption can achieve the signature and encryption simultaneously. To get a lower cost, we intend to introduce signcryption into our topology control mechanism. Moreover, we plan to investigate a lightweight IBC framework and carry out the feasibility tests on the low-class WSN platforms, e.g., MICAz motes, which are more resource-constrained.

Acknowledgement. This work was sponsored by the project of State Grid Shandong Electric Power Company Science and Technology Program No. 520615200006.

References

1. Alves, R.C., Oliveira, D.A., Pereira, G.C., Albertini, B.C., Margi, C.B.: WS³N: wireless secure SDN-based communication for sensor networks. Secur. Commun. Netw. (2018)
2. Anggorojati, B., Prasad, R.: Securing communication in inter domains Internet of Things using identity-based cryptography. In: International Workshop on Big Data and Information Security, pp. 137–142 (2017)
3. Chen, S., Ma, M., Luo, Z.: An authentication scheme with Identity-based cryptography for M2M security in cyber-physical systems. Secur. Commun. Netw. **9**(10), 1146–1157 (2016)
4. Galluccio, L., Milardo, S., Morabito, G., Palazzo, S.: SDN-WISE: design, prototyping and experimentation of a stateful SDN solution for WIreless SEnsor networks. In: IEEE Conference on Computer Communications (INFOCOM), pp. 513–521 (2015)
5. Ishmanov, F., Bin Zikria, Y.: Trust mechanisms to secure routing in wireless sensor networks: current state of the research and open research issues. J. Sensors (2017)
6. Karantaidou, I., Halkidis, S.T., Petridou, S., Mamatas, L., Stephanides, G.: Pairing-based cryptography on the Internet of Things: a feasibility study. In: Chowdhury, K.R., Di Felice, M., Matta, I., Sheng, B. (eds.) WWIC 2018. LNCS, vol. 10866, pp. 219–230. Springer, Cham (2018). https://doi.org/10.1007/978-3-030-02931-9_18
7. Kobo, H.I., Abu-Mahfouz, A.M., Hancke, G.P.: A survey on software-defined wireless sensor networks: challenges and design requirements. IEEE Access **5**, 1872–1899 (2017)
8. McCusker, K., O'Connor, N.E.: Low-energy symmetric key distribution in wireless sensor networks. IEEE Trans. Dependable Secure Comput. **8**(3), 363–376 (2010)
9. Oliveira, L.B.: TinyPBC: pairings for authenticated identity-based non-interactive key distribution in sensor networks. Comput. Commun. **34**(3), 485–493 (2011)
10. Pritchard, S.W., Hancke, G.P., Abu-Mahfouz, A.M.: Cryptography methods for software-defined wireless sensor networks. In: IEEE 27th International Symposium on Industrial Electronics, pp. 1257–1262 (2018)
11. Salman, O., Abdallah, S., Elhajj, I.H., Chehab, A., Kayssi, A.: Identity-based authentication scheme for the Internet of Things. In: IEEE Symposium on Computers and Communication, pp. 1109–1111 (2016)

12. Theodorou, T., Mamatas, L.: Software defined topology control strategies for the Internet of Things. In: IEEE Conference on Network Function Virtualization and Software Defined Networks, pp. 236–241 (2017)
13. Stanford University. PBC Library (2013). https://crypto.stanford.edu/pbc/
14. Wang, M., Liu, J., Chen, J., Liu, X., Mao, J.: Perm-guard: authenticating the validity of flow rules in software defined networking. J. Signal Process. Syst. **86**(2–3), 157–173 (2017)
15. Wang, R., Zhang, Z., Zhang, Z., Jia, Z.: ETMRM: an energy-efficient trust management and routing mechanism for SDWSNs. Comput. Netw. **139**, 119–135 (2018)
16. Han Yanan and Li fagen: Research on combined public key cryptographic scheme for smart grid. J. Cryptol. Res. **3**(4), 340–351 (2016)
17. Zhou, Y., Li, Z., Hu, F., Li, F.: Identity-based combined public key schemes for signature, encryption, and signcryption. In: Chandra, P., Giri, D., Li, F., Kar, S., Jana, D.K. (eds.) Inf. Technol. Appl. Math. AISC, vol. 699, pp. 3–22. Springer, Singapore (2019). https://doi.org/10.1007/978-981-10-7590-2_1

A Blockchain-Based Decentralized Public Auditing Scheme for Cloud Storage

Ying Wang[1,2], Conghao Ruan[1,2(✉)], and Chunqiang Hu[1,2(✉)]

[1] School of Big Data and Software Engineering, Chongqing University,
Chongqing, China
{wang,rch963,chu}@cqu.edu.cn
[2] Key Laboratory of Dependable Service Computing in Cyber Physical Society,
Ministry of Education (Chongqing University), Chongqing, China

Abstract. Cloud computing has attracted wide attention because that it can provide the data storage and computation to us. However, when the users outsource the data to the cloud server, the users lost the control over the data, so the data auditing is very important to protect users' data. To reduce computation and communication costs of the users, the existing schemes utilized a trusted third party (TPA) to conduct verification on behalf of users. However, TPA is a centralized party, which is vulnerable to external attacks and internal faults. In this paper, we present a decentralized public auditing scheme for cloud storage based on blockchain, which improves the reliability and stability of auditing result. In the proposed scheme, the cloud service providers works together to perform data verification without TPA. Finally, the security analysis shows that the scheme can resist a variety of attacks, and the experimental results demonstrate that proposed scheme has enhanced security and reliability.

Keywords: Cloud storage · Security · Public auditing · Blockchain · E-voting

1 Introduction

Cloud computing is one of the most influential innovations, which provides high quality data outsourcing services for customers. Because it has on-demand self-service, convenient network access, huge storage resources, and high flexibility, more and more organizations and individuals preferring to outsource data to cloud service provider (CSP), so that they can save storage and computation resources. There are already many corporations to provide cloud computing services, such as Alibaba Cloud, Amazon AWS. Besides, cloud computing is widely used in the Internet of vehicles [8], medical care [2] and many other fields.

Cloud computing brings us convenience [11], while the users are also facing security and privacy disclosure issues [6]. The data transmission process face the problem of data leakage. What's worse, once the users outsourced data to CSP, the data is lost the control, so the users cannot verify the integrity and correctness of outsourced data through the traditional way. Moreover, CSP is not entirely trusted. When encountering hardware or software problems, CSP may conceal the data errors from the users.

© Springer Nature Switzerland AG 2020
D. Yu et al. (Eds.): WASA 2020, LNCS 12384, pp. 482–493, 2020.
https://doi.org/10.1007/978-3-030-59016-1_40

And even worse, in order to reduce the storage resource, CSP may deliberately delete ordinary users' data which has not been or rarely accessed. Therefore, considering limited storage and computing power of the user, how to design an efficient and reliable data auditing scheme to perform remote data verification? It is an important problem.

To solve the problem, many researchers have proposed various schemes under different application scenario. The existing schemes can be divided into two categories: private auditing and public auditing. For private auditing scheme, the verification operation is performed by user and CSP. Although there are some advantages, frequent audit operations consume computing and network resources on the users side and CSP. To reduce the computation cost for users, public auditing is proposed called Third Party Auditor (TPA) on the basis of private auditing [1], in which TPA performs all the audit tasks and interchange audit results with users. Comparison to private auditing, public auditing is more practical and more widely used [12]. However, the employment of TPA may also causes some problems. In existing schemes, TPA is a trusted entity that performs verification operations honestly. In practice applications, TPA's credibility may not meet customers' expectation. TPA may collude with CSP to hide the fact that outsourced data are corrupted or lost.

In this paper, we propose a decentralized data auditing scheme for cloud storage. We employ multiple CSPS to independently audit the same data, and we obtain final audit result through statistics of blockchain-enabled e-voting, the content of each vote is the audit result of a single CSP. Our contributions are summarized as follows:

- We propose a novel data auditing scheme, which improves the credibility of auditing result by using multiples CSPs to audit the same data.
- We propose a simplified blockchain-enabled e-voting protocol to collect and publish all CSP audit results, which performs these operations without the third-party. The presented auditing scheme and e-voting protocol are supported by blockchain technology, which guarantees the traceability and transparency of auditing process and voting results.
- We prove the security of the proposed scheme, and justify the performance of our scheme via theoretical analysis and experimental results.

The rest of this paper is organized as follows: Sect. 2 present related work about cloud auditing. In Sect. 3, we define the system model, threat model, and our design goals. Section 4 gives related technologies contained in our scheme. The detailed description of proposed scheme is presented in Sect. 5, Sect. 6 and 7 give the security analysis and performance evaluation, respectively. Finally, we conclude in Sect. 8.

2   Related Works

Recent years, the existing schemes presented cloud storage auditing. Juels et al. [5] defined proofs of retrievability (PoR), which is employing error correcting code and spot-checking to guarantees possession and retrievability of outsourced data in cloud. Ateniese et al. [1] firstly proposed the model of "provable data possession" (PDP), PDP could check if remote server possesses original files correctly without retrieving it. They utilize homomorphic verifiable tags (HVTs) to realize public auditability, which adopts

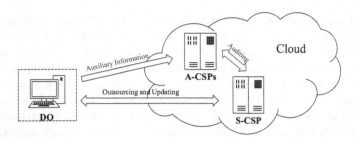

Fig. 1. System model

random sample sets to realize efficient validation. Shacham et al. [9] presented a compact PoR model. They demonstrates PoR protocol with full proofs of security against arbitrary adversaries, which is public verification scheme based on BLS signature. In order to realize dynamic data operation, Erway et al. [3] proposed a fully dynamic auditing scheme. They introduced rank-based authenticated skip list to implement block level dynamic data operation. Their dynamic auditing framework has been widely used.

Considering the security problems that may be caused by TPA, some researchers took blockchain into consideration. Xue et al. [10] proposed an identity-based public auditing (IBPA) scheme, they made use of the nonces in a blockchain to construct challenge message, thereby preventing TPA from forging auditing results.

3   System Model, Security Model, and Design Goal

3.1   System Model

As depicted in Fig. 1, there are two types of entities in our scheme: Data Owner (DO) and Cloud Service Providers (CSP). For the sake of simplicity, we will only describe proposed scheme for one DO. The details are as follows:

- DO: DO has large amount of files and limited capacity of storage and computing. In order to save cost and improve efficiency, DO outsources files to CSP and rely on CSP to maintain the integrity and correctness of the data. Besides, DO will update the data not on a regular basis.
- CSP: CSP is responsible for storing DO's data, generating proof after receiving auditing challenge, launching auditing challenge and verifying proof. For a DO, there are two types of CSP in our system, one stores data and responds to audit requests, which is named S-CSP. The other stores auxiliary message for data auditing and perform auditing, which is called A-CSP. Before the system starts, DO randomly selects one CSP as S-CSP, and the others automatically become A-CSP.

In our proposed scheme, DO can save a large amount of storage and computing resources by outsourcing data to CSP. As DO does not physically possess data, the correctness and integrity of data is of vital importance. In this paper, we consider a decentralized cloud data auditing scheme, in which the auditing task is performed by A-CSPs. An audit is considered successful only if more than half of all A-CSPS have passed the auditing, otherwise it indicates a problem with the data.

3.2 Security Model and Design Goal

In this paper, we assume that CSP is semi-trustable. That is to say, CSP performs the store and proof generating reliably, while it may hide the fact that part of the data being corrupted. S-CSP may want to pass the auditing by providing false data proof, or collude with A-CSP to effect auditing result. In order to achieve efficient and secure auditing scheme for cloud storage, our design goal can be summarized as follows:

1. Privacy preserving: Nobody can derive any concrete information of others data from auditing information in the blockchain.
2. Public auditing: Any data owner or blockchain user is able to verify the correctness of outsourced data in CSP while it does not need to retrieve any original data.
3. Decentralization: Auditing history are recorded in blockchain and stored by multiple nodes, all DO and CSP can access it.

4 Preliminaries

In this section, we introduce the preliminaries such as Dynamic Hash Table, Blockchain and Ethereum, and E-Voting System as follows.

4.1 Dynamic Hash Table (DHT)

DHT is a two dimensional data structure to achieve dynamic auditing. As shown in Fig. 2, it records data owners' file identifier and corresponding block version and timestamp. Block search is to locate the required element by visiting the order of the first node while inserting a block after (before) into an existing block is to first track a given (before) node, and then insert a new node after it. When a block is deleted, first track the required node and delete it from the current linked list. The search for the file is to locate the file element according to the index of the file element, and other file operations will involve operations on file elements and block elements.

DHT can be used by data owner to generate data block tag for verification and supports file level operation and block level operation. Based on DHT, the verification time can be greatly reduced.

4.2 Blockchain and Ethereum

Blockchain is the underlying technology of bitcoin, which is first proposed by Satoshi [7]. It is a linear collection of a series of data blocks, and blocks are connected through hash values. Each block contains a hash pointer to point to previous block, a timestamp, its own hash value and transactions data. The blockchain is stored and managed by multiple nodes, the addition of blocks can only be realized after all of nodes reach consensus through consensus algorithm without trusting each other. That is to say, if adversary wants to tamper with blockchain data or add an illegal block, it have to coordinate at least half of the nodes. It is this mechanism that ensures the security of blockchain.

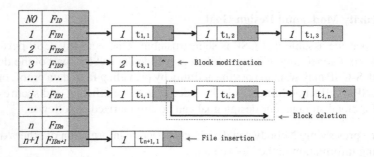

Fig. 2. Dynamic Hash Table (DHT)

Ethereum is a blockchain platform with smart contracts. There are two types of accounts in Ethereum: 1) external account: Like other blockchain systems, such accounts are created and controlled by user; 2) contract account: It is a smart contract, which is controlled by its code. In ethereum, programs can be written into blocks as smart contract, external account invokes program by interacting with contract account, and the proper execution of smart contracts is enforced through node networks, which means the contract caller must follow contract logic.

4.3   E-Voting System

E-voting is the application of electronic technology to cast and count votes in an election, which is a more convenient and less expensive forms of voting [4]. Typically, constituents cast their vote from computer, then trusted authority, such as government or company, counts the votes and announces the results.

5   The Proposed Scheme

Our scheme can be described in three parts:

1. Setup: DO will preprocess files and generate other keying materials, then outsource the data to S-CSP and data information to A-CSPs.
2. Dynamic data operation: According to DO's data updating request, S-CSP updates stored data and A-CSPs update corresponding data information.
3. Integrity Verification: A-CSPs verify the data outsourced in S-CSP, the audit results are then sent to the smart contract account via transactions in the form of votes. The smart contract account counts votes and announces the final audit result (Fig. 3).

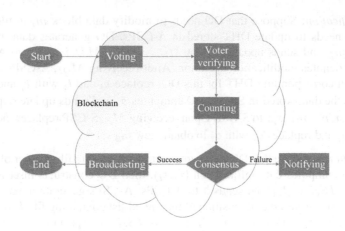

Fig. 3. Auditing process

5.1 Setup

Let $\mathbb{G}_1$ and $\mathbb{G}_2$ be two multiplicative cyclic groups of large prime order p, e be a bilinear map $\mathbb{G}_1 \times \mathbb{G}_1 \to \mathbb{G}_2$. H is a hash function $\{0,1\}^* \to \mathbb{G}_1$. We assume that DO's data file F (probably preprocessed by encryption algorithm) is divided into n blocks, like $F = \{m_1, m_2, ..., m_n\}$. And the setup phase involves following three parts:

KeyGen: DO selects two random elements g and u from $\mathbb{G}_1$, a random exponents $\alpha \in \mathbb{Z}_p$ and computes $\beta = g^\alpha$. Then Do generates a random key pair (sk, pk) for signature on the basis of a designed provably signature scheme. DO's secret key is $SK = (sk, \alpha)$, public key is $PK = (pk, \beta, g, u)$.

DIGen: DO randomly selects a CSP from CSPs as S-CSP, the other as A-CSPs. For A-CSPs, DO constructs $DI = \{F_{ID}, \Phi = \{(v_i, t_i) | 1 \le i \le n\}\}$, in which F_{ID} is the unique identifier of file F, $\Phi = \{(v_i, t_i) | 1 \le i \le n\}$ is the set of all blocks' version and timestamp records. DO sends DI to A-CSPs, after receiving it, A-CSPs add it into corresponding DHT.

TagGen: For $F = \{m_1, m_2, ..., m_n\}$, DO computes signature for each block $m_i (i = 1, 2, ..., n)$: $\sigma_i = (H(v_i||t_i) \cdot u^{m_i})^\alpha$. Let the set of all tags be $\theta = \{\sigma_i | 1 \le i \le n\}$. Then DO computes file tag for F under private key sk as $T = F_{ID}||sig_{sk}(F_{ID})$. DO sends $\{F, T, \theta\}$ to S-CSP and deletes $\{F, T, \theta\}$ from local database. S-CSP will stores verification data $\{T, \theta\}$ and file F together.

5.2 Dynamic Data Operation

Besides outsourcing, DO will also performs dynamic operations on the data, such as modification, insertion and deletion. For dynamic data manipulation, proposed scheme supports file level operations and block level operations. The file level operation is similar to block level operation but simpler, because file insertion and deletion are more straightforward. The block level operation is as follows:

Block Modification: Suppose that DO needs to modify data block m_i in file F to m_i'. Firstly, DO needs to update DHT stored in A-CSPs. DO generates data information (v_i', t_i') for m_i', and sends update request $M_{DI} : \{F_{ID}, MD, i, v_i', t_i'\}$ to A-CSPs, in which MD denotes modification operation. After receiving M_{DI}, A-CSPs find the ith node of F in corresponding DHT for this DO, replace v_i and t_i with v_i' and t_i'. Then, DO updates the data stored in S-CSP. DO computes σ_i' and sends update request $M_F : \{F_{ID}, MD, i, m_i, m_i', \sigma_i'\}$ to S-CSP. Upon receiving M_F, S-CSP replaces the block m_i in F with m_i' and replaces σ_i with σ_i' to obtain new tag set θ'.

Block Insertion: Suppose that DO needs to insert block m_i into file F after block m_{i-1}. At first, DO computes data information (v_i, t_i), then DO constructs insertion request $I_{DI} : \{F_{ID}, IS, i, v_i, t_i\}$ and sends it to A-CSPs. A-CSPs generate a new node with (v_i, t_i) and insert it into the ith position of the linked list containing file F information. After generating I_{DI}, DO generates $I_F : \{F_{ID}, IS, i, m_i, \sigma_i\}$ and sends it to S-CSP. Upon receiving it, S-CSP insert m_i and σ_i into F and θ.

5.3 Integrity Verification

The verification process is a combination of cloud auditing and blockchain-enabled e-voting. We supposed that S-CSP and A-CSPs are nodes of blockchain, and each has a blockchain account, DO has a blockchain user account too. Besides, there is a smart contract account for ballot counting and result broadcasting, denoted as SC. This phase can be completed by follows parts:

Challenge: All of A-CSPs can verify the integrity of outsourced data. In one verification, One of A-CSPs, denoted as A_1, launches a challenge to S-CSP. Before challenging, A_1 retrieves file tag T from S-CSP, verifies the signature $sig_{sk}(F_{ID})$ under DO's public key pk. If validation fails, A_1 ends the verification by returning $FALSE$, else A_1 recovers file identifier F_{ID}. Then A_1 generates challenge information $chal = \{F_{ID}, i, s_i, R\}_{i \in I}$, where I is a randomly selected subset of $[1, n]$ with c elements, representing the index of blocks to be checked, $\{s_i \subseteq \mathbb{Z}_p\}_{i \in I}$ are c randomly chosen coefficients. R is a random masking : $R = \beta^r$, in which r is a random element in $\mathbb{Z}_p$. Then, A_1 creates a transaction Tx_{A_1}, which is shown in Fig. 4, to send $chal$ to S-CSP.

Response: S-CSP extracts transaction from blockchain and acquires $chal$, then S-CSP computes tag proof and data proof for subsequent verification. The tag proof is the aggregated authenticator of blocks' tag being checked: $\Theta = \prod_{i \in I} \sigma_i^{s_i}$. The data proof is: $M = \sum_{i \in I} s_i \cdot m_i$. Then, S-CSP creates a transaction Tx_S with SC. As illustrated in Fig. 5, the data value of the transaction is $\{pr = (\Theta, M), FT\}$, in which FT indicates the time when the poll end.

Verification: We assumed that a whitelist of all CSP accounts was contained in smart contract code before it was deployed, so that SC knows how many accounts will vote and whether the voter is eligible. The voting process can be completed as follows:

1. Preparation: After sending $\{pr, FT\}$ to SC, S-CSP notifies A-CSPs on the whitelist to begin voting.

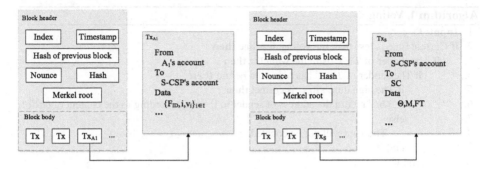

Fig. 4. A-CSP's transaction with S-CSP   **Fig. 5.** S-CSP's transaction with SC

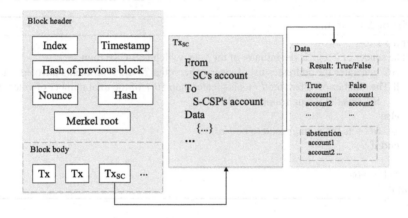

Fig. 6. SC's transaction with S-CSP

2. Verification: All A-CSPs acquire $chal$ and pr from extracted transactions Tx_{A_1} and Tx_S. Next, for all challenged blocks, A-CSPs compute $H = \sum_{i \in I} H(v_i \| t_i)^{s_i}$. Then, A-CSPs verify the equation: $e(\Theta, g)^r = e(H \cdot u^M, R)$. If the equation holds, let $ballot = True$, else let $ballot = False$. Finally, A-CSPs sign their own ballot by their own secret key, and calls the Algorithm 1 in the smart contract code to vote. The call of the function is expressed in the form of transaction Tx_{A_i}, the receiver of the transaction is SC, the data value of the transaction is $\{ballot, sig_{A_i}\}$.

3. Counting and broadcasting: When the deadline is up, S-CSP can call the Algorithm 2 in the smart contract code to obtain the voting result, the call of the function is also expressed in the form of transaction. SC sends the voting result to S-CSP in the form of a transaction Tx_{SC}. Tx_{SC} is shown in Fig. 6, which contains voting result, the addresses of accounts that vote $True$, $False$, and did not vote. If the voting result is $False$, it implies that there were A-CSPs' misoperations during voting or the challenged data has been modified.

Algorithm 1. Voting

1: **Input:** Tx_{A_i}
2: **if** Current time is less than the voting deadline **then**
3:     **if** The sender of Tx_{A_i} is in the whitelist **then**
4:         **if** The sender of Tx_{A_i} has not voted before **then**
5:             **if** The signature sig_{A_i} is correct **then**
6:                 SC record the address of sender in the list according to the content of *ballot*.
7:             **else**
8:                 The vote will not be counted.
9:             **end if**
10:         **end if**
11:     **end if**
12: **end if**

Algorithm 2. Counting

1: **Input:** Tx_{S_o}
2: **if** The sender of Tx_{S_o} is the initiator of the vote, which is S-CSP **then**
3:     SC generates the addresses list of voters who voted $True$, $False$, and unvoted voters.
4:     **if** The number of voters for $True$ is greater than 50% of the total number of voters **then**
5:         SC sets the voting result to be $True$.
6:     **else**
7:         SC sets the voting result to be $False$.
8:     **end if**
9: **else**
10:     Failed vote
11: **end if**

---

6 Security Analysis

In this section, we discuss the security performance of proposed scheme in theory.

6.1 Resisting Collusion Attack

In our scheme, CSPs perform both storage and audit functions. For one DO's data verification, there are multiple A-CSPs calculate independently to get their own audit result. After that, A-CSPs generate ballot and send signed ballot to smart contract account for statistic. If S-CSP collude with a A-CSP to modify individual audit result so that S-CSP can hide the fact of some data being corrupted, the final result reached by smart contract account will hardly be affected. Therefore, it is more effective to prevent S-CSP from corrupting the data by auditing the same data with multiple A-CSPs. Further more, the votes are counted by smart contract account and the results are announced by smart contract account. Smart contract cannot be tampred once deployed on blockchain, and anyone can verify that it is performing correctly or not, which ensures the traceability of auditing process.

6.2 Resistant to Attacks

Our scheme is capable of resisting forge attack, modification attack, and Counterfeiting attack, the details are as follows:

- *Forge attack*: The malicious cloud service provider cannot forge outsourced data. Before outsourcing, DO computes tags for each blocks based on DU's public key and data information. Due to the security of bilinear map and hash algorithm, the malicious cloud service provider cannot forge valid data.
- *Modification attack*: In our scheme, all the challenge messages, auditing proofs and corresponding results are recorded in the blockchain. Only if the attacker can modify the data in each block of each node can the modification attack be implemented, which is an impossible mission as long as the attacker cannot violating blockchain security rules.

7 Performance Evaluation

In this section, we evaluate the performance of our scheme in terms of property comparison and computation cost experiment.

The computation cost in different phase of proposed scheme is shown in Table 1, where n denotes the number of data blocks in a file, c is the number of challenged blocks when auditing a file. Let M and E be the multiplication operation and the exponentiation operation on the group respectively. BP represents the bilinear pairing operation.

Table 1. The computation costs in different phase.

Phase	Computation costs
KeyGen	E
TagGen	$n(M + 2E)$
Response	$(2c - 1)M + cE$
Verification	$cM + (c + 2)E + 2BP$
Announce voting results	0

In the setup phase, the computation cost is mainly concentrated upon the DO, DO needs to perform key generation and tag generation. For key generation, the cost is E. For tag generation, DO needs to generates tags for all data blocks, thus the cost is $n(M + 2E)$. In the integrity verification phase, computation cost mainly contain two parts: response and verification. For response, S-CSP performs $(2c - 1)M + cE$ to generate the proof information. For verification, every A-CSP needs $cM + (c + 2)E + 2BP$ to perform data proof verification. In the announcing phase, all of the statistics and calculations are done after all A-CSPs vote or after the deadline, that is, the computation overhead at this phase has been completed by blockchain network.

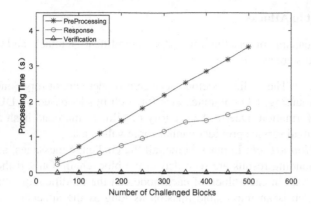

Fig. 7. Performance of proposed scheme

We validate the computation cost of our scheme by conducting experiments on a laptop running Windows 7 with a 2.4 GHz Intel Core i7-4500U CPU and 4 GB of memory. We implement all the algorithms by using the Pairing-Based-Cryptography(PBC) library version 0.5.14. The experiments employ type A pairing parameters which has a 160-bit group order. In addition, we set the block size as 10 KB, all running time statistics were averaged over 20 trials.

Figure 7 shows the computation time of three phase with different numbers of data blocks. We can see that the time consuming of verification phase is very small and basically stable, the reason is the cohesiveness of BLS signature. When generating data proof and tag proof, S-CSP has aggregated the signatures and contents of a challenged blocks, A-CSP only needs to verify the integrity and correctness of the data through an equation. The computation of file process grows linearly as the number of blocks increases, but the time consumption of file process is acceptable because the block tags need to be generated only once before outsourcing. The computation cost of response phase is also increasing, but the total cost is lower.

8 Conclusion

In this paper, we proposed a blockchain-based public auditing scheme for cloud storage, which improves the reliability of audit results. The proposed scheme achieves reliable collaborative auditing based on blockchain, and all auditing history can be traced so that any data owner or data user can verify it at any time. Further, our scheme can be easily applied to other decentralized data auditing scheme by incorporating blockchain. Theoretical analysis and experimental results demonstrated that our scheme is secure and protect the data privacy.

Acknowledgment. This research was supported partially by the Fundamental Research Funds for the Central Universities (2019CDQYRJ006), the National Natural Science Foundation of China(61702062), the Chongqing Research Program of Basic Research and Frontier Technology with Grant (cstc2018jcyjAX0334), Key Project of Technology Innovation and Application Development of Chongqing (cstc2019jscx-mbdxX0044), and Overseas Returnees Innovation and Entrepreneurship Support Program of Chongqing (cx2018015).

References

1. Ateniese, G., et al.: Provable data possession at untrusted stores. In: Proceedings of the 14th ACM Conference on Computer and Communications Security, pp. 598–609 (2007)
2. Cao, S., Zhang, G., Liu, P., Zhang, X., Neri, F.: Cloud-assisted secure ehealth systems for tamper-proofing EHR via blockchain. Inf. Sci. **485**, 427–440 (2019)
3. Erway, C.C., Küpçü, A., Papamanthou, C., Tamassia, R.: Dynamic provable data possession. ACM Trans. Inf. Syst. Secur. (TISSEC) **17**(4), 1–29 (2015)
4. Gritzalis, D.A.: Principles and requirements for a secure e-voting system. Comput. Secur. **21**(6), 539–556 (2002)
5. Juels, A., Kaliski Jr, B.S.: Pors: proofs of retrievability for large files. In: Proceedings of the 14th ACM Conference on Computer and Communications Security, pp. 584–597 (2007)
6. Markandey, A., Dhamdhere, P., Gajmal, Y.: Data access security in cloud computing: a review. In: 2018 International Conference on Computing, Power and Communication Technologies (GUCON), pp. 633–636. IEEE (2018)
7. Nakamoto, S.: Bitcoin a peer-to-peer electronic cash system (2008). https://bitcoin.org/bitcoin.pdf
8. Qureshi, K.N., Bashir, F., Iqbal, S.: Cloud computing model for vehicular ad hoc networks. In: 2018 IEEE 7th International Conference on Cloud Networking (CloudNet), pp. 1–3. IEEE (2018)
9. Shacham, H., Waters, B.: Compact proofs of retrievability. In: Pieprzyk, J. (ed.) ASIACRYPT 2008. LNCS, vol. 5350, pp. 90–107. Springer, Heidelberg (2008). https://doi.org/10.1007/978-3-540-89255-7_7
10. Xue, J., Xu, C., Zhao, J., Ma, J.: Identity-based public auditing for cloud storage systems against malicious auditors via blockchain. Sci. China Inf. Sci. **62**(3), 1–16 (2019). https://doi.org/10.1007/s11432-018-9462-0
11. Yu, L., Cai, Z.: Dynamic scaling of virtual clusters with bandwidth guarantee in cloud datacenters. In: IEEE INFOCOM 2016-The 35th Annual IEEE International Conference on Computer Communications, pp. 1–9. IEEE (2016)
12. Yu, L., Shen, H., Cai, Z., Liu, L., Pu, C.: Towards bandwidth guarantee for virtual clusters under demand uncertainty in multi-tenant clouds. IEEE Trans. Parallel Distrib. Syst. **29**(2), 450–465 (2017)

A New Fully Homomorphic Signatures from Standard Lattices

Yukun Wang and Mingqiang Wang[✉]

School of Mathematics, Shandong University, Jinan, China
wangyukun@mail.sdu.edu.cn, wangmingqiang@sdu.edu.cn

Abstract. Recently, Gorbunov, Vaikuntanathan and Wichs [6] propose a new powerful (fully) homomorphic trapdoor function (HTDF) based on *small integer solution* (SIS) problem in standard lattices, and construct the first fully homomorphic signature (FHS) schemes. Later Wang et al. [10] extend the notion of HTDF to identity-based setting with strongly security and construct the first identity based fully homomorphic signature (IBFHS) schemes.

In this paper, we provide a new IBHTDF which satisfies *claw-free* and *collision-resistant*. Moreover, we find a homomorphic algorithm for our new IBHTDF where the noise level of multiplication gate is the same as that of addition gate. So, the noise level of IBHTDF for evaluating a circuit of depth d is reduced from $O(4^d m\beta)$ to $O(2^d \beta)$. Finally, we construct a new leveled strongly-unforgeable identity-based fully homomorphic signature (IBFHS) schemes based on our IBHTDF.

Keywords: Identity-based homomorphic trapdoor function · Small integer solution · Strong unforgeability

1 Introduction

In recent years, with the rapid development of cloud computing, a large number of researchers pay more attention to the cryptographic scheme with homomorphic property. The property allows a client to upload his/her encrypted/signed data to a remote server securely. Then, the client could use the computation ability of the server to help him process data but doesn't worry about data leakage. The study of fully homomorphic encryption (FHE) [5], demonstrates how to perform homomorphic computation over encrypted data without the knowledge of secret key, has a far-reaching influence on the latter research. The recent works [1,4,5] of (leveled) fully homomorphic signatures show that how to do homomorphic computation on signed data.

In this work, we focus on the latter question: the public authenticity of the result of homomorphic computation over signed data. In a homomorphic signature scheme, a client signs a message $\mathbf{x} = (x_1, \dots, x_N)$ using his secret key. After

Supported by organization x.

© Springer Nature Switzerland AG 2020
D. Yu et al. (Eds.): WASA 2020, LNCS 12384, pp. 494–506, 2020.
https://doi.org/10.1007/978-3-030-59016-1_41

that, the client upload the signed data $\sigma = (\sigma_1, \ldots, \sigma_N)$ to a remote server. At any later point, the server obtains an admissible circuit g that $y = g(\mathbf{x})$ and do some homomorphic computation over the signed data σ. In particular, the server produce a short signature σ_g on y which is a correct output of the operation g over the data $\mathbf{x}$. Anyone can verify the tuple (g, y, σ_g) using the client public verification key and accept this fact without the knowledge of the underlying data $\mathbf{x}$.

Leveled FHS. Gorbunov, Vaikuntanathan and Wichs [6] proposed the first leveled FHS schemes based on SIS problem in standard lattices. They put forward a new primitive: HTDF. They required that HTDF functions have *claw-freeness* property, which is necessary for the security of their FHS schemes. Their FHS schemes are existentially unforgeable in the static chosen-message-attack (EU-sCMA) model. Additionally, they showed that one can transform an EU-sCMA secure FHS to an existentially unforgeable under adaptive chosen-message-attack(EU-aCMA) secure FHS via homomorphic chameleon hash function. Recently, Boyen, Fan and Shi also brought up a EU-aCMA secure FHS schemes using vanishing trapdoor technique [3]. In the meantime, Xie and Xue [9] showed that leveled FHS schemes can be constructed if indistinguishability obfuscation and injective one way function exist.

Leveled IBFHS. Wang et al. [10] proposed the first leveled strongly-unforgeable IBFHS schemes. They construct an IBHTDF which is not only *claw-free*, but also *collision-resistant*. They use Barrington's theorem to reduce the parameters as done in field of FHE [2]. The maximum noise-level comparing to Gorbunov, Vaikuntanathan and Wichs' FHS roughly reduces from $O(m^d\beta)$ to $O(4^d m\beta)$, which will result in polynomial modulus $q = \text{poly}(\lambda)$ when $d = O(\log\lambda)$, where λ is the security parameter and d is the maximum depth of admissible circuit.

1.1 Results and Techniques

In this paper, we provide a new IBHTDF and construct a leveled IBFHS based on our IBHTDF. Our new IBFHS scheme is existentially unforgeable in the static chosen-message-attack (EU-sCMA).

For integers n, q and $\ell = \lceil \log q \rceil$, let $\mathbf{G} = \mathbf{I}_n \otimes \mathbf{g}^T \in \mathbb{Z}_q^{n \times n\ell}$, where $\mathbf{g}^T = (1, 2, 2^2, \ldots, 2^{\ell-1})$ and $\mathbf{I}_n$ denotes the n-dimensional identity matrix. The HTDF in [6] is constructed by the function $f_{pk,x} = \mathbf{A} \cdot \mathbf{U} + x \cdot \mathbf{G}$, where $\mathbf{A}$ is a matrix with a trapdoor for invert, and $\mathbf{U}$ is a matrix with small norm. Homomorphic operation relies on the invertibility property of the matrix $\mathbf{G}$. Notice that, if the matrix $\mathbf{G}$ in $f_{pk,x}$ is replaced by the matrix $\mathbf{A}$, one still can evaluate the new function homomorphic. Therefore, the function $f_{pk,x} = \mathbf{A} \cdot \mathbf{U} + x \cdot \mathbf{A}$ is a new HTDF. The homomorphic operation algorithm of our new HTDF is as following.

Homomorphic Operations. Let $\mathbf{U}_1, \mathbf{U}_2 \in \mathbb{Z}_q^{m \times m}$ be "short" matrices and

$$\mathbf{V}_1 = f_{pk,x_1}(\mathbf{U}_1) = \mathbf{A}\mathbf{U}_1 + x_1 \cdot \mathbf{A} \ , \ \mathbf{V}_2 = f_{pk,x_2}(\mathbf{U}_2) = \mathbf{A}\mathbf{U}_2 + x_2 \cdot \mathbf{A}.$$

Addition. We can simply set $\mathbf{U}^* := \mathbf{U}_1 + \mathbf{U}_2$, $\mathbf{V}^* := \mathbf{V}_1 + \mathbf{V}_2$ and get

$$f_{pk,x_1+x_2}(\mathbf{U}^*) = \mathbf{A}\mathbf{U}^* + (x_1 + x_2)\mathbf{A} = \mathbf{V}^*.$$

Multiplication. Homomorphic multiplication is slightly more complex. We set

$$\mathbf{U}^* := \mathbf{U}_1 + x_1 \cdot \mathbf{U}_2, \quad \mathbf{V}^* := \mathbf{V}_1 - x_1 \cdot \mathbf{A} + x_1 \cdot \mathbf{V}_2.$$

It is easy to verify

$$f_{pk,x_1 \cdot x_2}(\mathbf{U}^*) = \mathbf{A}\mathbf{U}^* + (x_1 \cdot x_2)\mathbf{A} = \mathbf{V}^*.$$

To evaluate a circuit g of depth d for our new HTDF, the maximum noise level of our algorithm is $O(2^d\beta)$. The homomorphic operation algorithm for the original HTDF require the invert operation of $\mathbf{G}$ which makes the the nose level increasing m multiples. A permutation branching program is used in [10] for evaluating a circuit g of depth d for a new HTDF, that reduce the maximum noise level from $O(m^d\beta)$ to $O(4^d m\beta)$. While, the multiplication operation for our new HTDF does not need invert operation of any matrix. The noise level for our new HTDF of multiplication gate is the same as that of addition gate. So, our noise level should be optimal.

Gorbunov's pioneering work shows that any HTDF must satisfy *claw-free* for security. Later Wang extend the notion of HTDF to IBHTDF with stronger security. The stronger security requires that IBHTDF is not only *claw-free* but also *collision-resistant*. We use a special trapdoor generator which can generates a public matrix with trapdoor for any identity and the function f to construct a new IBHTDF. Because of the new function f, we improve the proving method in [10] to make sure that the new IBHTDF could satisfy *claw-free* and *collision-resistant*.

Finally, we construct a new leveled strongly-unforgeable identity-based fully homomorphic signature (IBFHS) schemes based on our IBHTDF. The maximum noise-level comparing to Wang's FHS [10] roughly reduces from $O(4^d m\beta)$ to $O(2^d\beta)$.

1.2   Paper Organization

In Sect. 2, we give some backgrounds on lattices and related tools used in this paper. We propose the new IBHTDF function in Sect. 3 and demonstrate the homomorphic evaluation algorithm in Sect.4. In Sect. 5 we recall the leveled strongly-unforgeable IBFHS. Finally, we conclude in Sect. 6.

2   Preliminaries

We use the hold upper-case letters (e.g.,$\mathbf{A},\mathbf{B}$) to represent matrices and bold lower-case letters (e.g.,$\mathbf{a},\mathbf{b}$) to represent column vectors. Let $\|\mathbf{A}\|_\infty = \max_{i,j}\{|a_{i,j}|\}$ denote the infinite norm and a_i or $\mathbf{a}[i]$ represent the i-entry of $\mathbf{a}$. Let $[\mathbf{A}\|\mathbf{B}]$ denote the concatenation of two matrices and $(\mathbf{A}, \mathbf{B}) = [\mathbf{A}^T\|\mathbf{B}^T]^T$. We use λ to denote the *security parameter* and $\mathrm{negl}(\lambda)$ to denote a negligible function that grows slower than λ^{-c} for any constant $c > 0$ and any large enough value of λ. For an integer N, we let $[N] \overset{def}{=} \{1,\ldots,N\}$.

2.1   Entropy and Statistical Distance

For discrete random variables $X \leftarrow \mathcal{X}, Y \leftarrow \mathcal{Y}$, we define the *statistical distance*

$$\triangle(X, Y) \triangleq \frac{1}{2} \sum_{w \in \mathcal{X} \cup \mathcal{Y}} |Pr[X = w] - Pr[Y = w]|.$$

We say that two random variables X, Y are statistically indistinguishable, denoted by $X \overset{stat}{\approx} Y$, if $\triangle(X, Y) = \mathrm{negl}(\lambda)$. The *min-entropy* of a random variable X, denoted by $\mathbf{H}_\infty(X)$, is defined as $\mathbf{H}_\infty(X) \triangleq -\log(max_x Pr[X = x])$. The *average min-entropy* of X conditioned on Y, denoted by $\mathbf{H}_\infty(X|Y)$, is defined as

$$\mathbf{H}_\infty(X|Y) \triangleq -\log(\mathbf{E}_{y \leftarrow \mathcal{Y}}[max_x Pr[X = x|Y = y]]) = -\log(\mathbf{E}_{y \leftarrow \mathcal{Y}}[2^{-\mathbf{H}_\infty(X|Y=y)}]).$$

The optimal probability of an unbounded adversary guessing X given the correlated value Y is $2^{-\mathbf{H}_\infty(X|Y)}$.

Lemma 1. *Let $X \leftarrow \mathcal{X}, Y \leftarrow \mathcal{Y}$ be arbitrarily random variables where the support of Y lies in $\mathcal{Y}$. Then $\mathbf{H}_\infty(X|Y) \le \mathbf{H}_\infty(X) - \log(|\mathcal{Y}|)$.*

2.2   Background on Lattices and Hard Problems

Lattices. Lattices-based cryptography usually use so-called q-ary integer lattices, which contain $q\mathbb{Z}^m$ as a sublattice for some modulus q. Let n, m, q be positive integers. For a matrix $\mathbf{A} \in \mathbb{Z}_q^{n \times m}$ we define following q-ary integer lattice

$$\Lambda^\perp(\mathbf{A}) = \{\mathbf{u} \in \mathbb{Z}^m : \mathbf{A}\mathbf{u} = 0 \mod q\}.$$

For a vector $\mathbf{v} \in \mathbb{Z}_q^n$, we define the coset:

$$\Lambda_{\mathbf{v}}^\perp(\mathbf{A}) = \{\mathbf{u} \in \mathbb{Z}^m : \mathbf{A}\mathbf{u} = \mathbf{v} \mod q\}.$$

SIS. Let n, m, q, β be integers. The short integer solution ($\mathrm{SIS}_{n,m,q,\beta}$) problem is that given a uniformly random matrix $\mathbf{A} \xleftarrow{\$} \mathbb{Z}_q^{n \times m}$, to find a nonzero vector $\mathbf{u} \in \mathbb{Z}_q^n$ with $\|\mathbf{u}\|_\infty \le \beta$ such that $\mathbf{A}\mathbf{u} = 0 \mod q$ (i.e. $\mathbf{u} \in \Lambda^\perp(\mathbf{A})$). For $q \ge \beta \cdot (\sqrt{n \log n})$, the $\mathrm{SIS}_{n,m,q,\beta}$ problem in average case is as hard as solving $\mathrm{GapSVP}_{\widetilde{O}(\beta \cdot \sqrt{n})}$ in the worse case in standard lattices [7,11].

Discrete Gaussian Distribution. Let $\mathcal{D}_{\mathbb{Z}^m, r}$ be the truncated discrete Gaussian distribution over $\mathbb{Z}^m$ with parameter r. That means $\|\mathbf{u}\|_\infty \le r \cdot \sqrt{m}$ with probability 1 if $\mathbf{u} \leftarrow \mathcal{D}_{\mathbb{Z}^m, r}$. If $\|\mathbf{u}\|_\infty$ is larger than $r \cdot \sqrt{m}$, then the output is replaced by $\mathbf{0}$.

Lattices Trapdoor. Here we recall the trapdoor generation algorithm and Gaussian sampling algorithm in [8]. We ignore all details of implementation which are not strictly necessary in this work.

For integers n, q and $\ell = \lceil \log q \rceil$, let $\mathbf{G} = \mathbf{I}_n \otimes \mathbf{g}^T \in \mathbb{Z}_q^{n \times n\ell}$, where $\mathbf{g}^T = (1, 2, 2^2, \dots, 2^{\ell-1})$ and $\mathbf{I}_n$ denotes the n-dimensional identity matrix.

Lemma 2. *Let n, q, ℓ, m_0, m_1 be integers such that $n=poly(\lambda)$, $q = q(n)$, $\ell = \lceil \log q \rceil$, $m_0 = n(\ell + O(1))$, $m_1 = n\ell$. For $\mathbf{A}_0 \xleftarrow{\$} \mathbb{Z}_q^{n \times m_0}$ and $\mathbf{H} \in \mathbb{Z}_q^{n \times n}$, there exists a randomized algorithm $\mathbf{TrapGen}(\mathbf{A}_0, \mathbf{H})$ to generate a matrix $\mathbf{A} = [\mathbf{A}_0 \| \mathbf{HG} - \mathbf{A}_0\mathbf{R}] \in \mathbb{Z}_q^{n \times (m_0+m_1)}$ with trapdooor $\mathbf{R}$ such that $\mathbf{R} \leftarrow \mathcal{D}_{\mathbb{Z}^{m_0 \times m_1}, r}$ for large enough $r (\geq \omega(\sqrt{\log n}))$ and $\mathbf{A}$ is negl(λ)-far from $(\mathbf{V}_0, \mathbf{V}_1) \xleftarrow{\$} \mathbb{Z}_q^{n \times m_0} \times \mathbb{Z}_q^{n \times m_1}$. Here, $\mathbf{R}$ is called $\mathbf{G}$-trapdoor of $\mathbf{A}$ with tag $\mathbf{H}$. Furthermore, for any non-zero $\mathbf{u} = (\mathbf{u}_0, \mathbf{u}_1) \in \mathbb{Z}_q^{m_0+m_1}$, the average min-entropy of $\mathbf{Ru}_1$ given $\mathbf{A}_0$ and $\mathbf{A}_0\mathbf{R}$ is at least $\Omega(n)$.*

Lemma 3. *Given parameters in above lemma and an uniformly random vector $\mathbf{v} \in \mathbb{Z}_q^n$, for some $s (\geq O(\sqrt{n \log q})) \in \mathbb{R}$ and a fixed function $\omega(\sqrt{\log n})$ growing asymptotically faster than $\sqrt{\log n}$, if the tag $\mathbf{H}$ is invertiable, then there exists an efficient algorithm $\mathbf{SamPre}(\mathbf{A}_0, \mathbf{R}, \mathbf{H}, \mathbf{v}, s)$ that samples a vector $\mathbf{u}$ from $\mathcal{D}_{\Lambda_v^\perp(\mathbf{A}), s \cdot \omega(\sqrt{\log n})}$ such that $\mathbf{A} \cdot \mathbf{u} = \mathbf{v}$. Note that $\|\mathbf{u}\|_\infty \leq s\sqrt{m_0 + m_1} \cdot \omega(\sqrt{\log n})$ with probability 1. Furthermore, for $\mathbf{u}' \leftarrow \mathcal{D}_{\mathbb{Z}^m, s \cdot \omega(\sqrt{\log n})}$ and $\mathbf{v}' = \mathbf{Au}'$, we have $(\mathbf{A}, \mathbf{R}, \mathbf{u}, \mathbf{v}) \stackrel{stat}{\approx} (\mathbf{A}, \mathbf{R}, \mathbf{u}', \mathbf{v}')$.*

3 Identity-Based Homomorphic Signature

In this section, we come up with the definition of IBHTDF and construct a new function f. Based on f, we design a new IBHTDF which satisfy *claw free* and *collision-resistance*. Our IBHTDF is selective-identity secure under the SIS assumption.

3.1 Definition Identity-Based Trapdoor Functions

An *identity-based homomorphic trapdoor function* (IBHTDF) consists of six polynomial algorithms(**IBHTDF.Setup**, **IBHTDF.Extract**, f, **Invert**, **IBHTDF.Eval^{in}**, **IBHTDF.Eval^{out}**) with syntax as follows:

- $(mpk, msk) \leftarrow$ **IBHTDF.Setup**(1^λ): Master key setup procedure. The security parameter λ defines the identity space $\mathcal{I}$, the index spacce $\mathcal{X}$, the input space $\mathcal{U}$, the output space $\mathcal{V}$ and some efficiently samplable input distribution $\mathcal{D}_\mathcal{U}$ over $\mathcal{U}$. We require that elements of $\mathcal{I}, \mathcal{U}, \mathcal{V}$, or $\mathcal{X}$ can be efficiently certified and we can efficiently sample elements from $\mathcal{V}$ uniformly at random.
- $(pk_{id}, sk_{id}) \leftarrow$ **IBHTDF.Extract**(mpk, msk, id): An identity-key extraction procedure. We require that pk_{id} can be extracted deterministically from mpk and $id \in \mathcal{I}$ without using the knowledge of msk.
- $f_{pk_{id},x}: \mathcal{U} \to \mathcal{V}$: A deterministic function indexed by pk_{id} and $x \in \mathcal{X}$.
- **Invert**$_{sk_{id},x} : \mathcal{V} \to \mathcal{U}$: A probability inversion algorithm indexed by sk_{id} and $x \in \mathcal{X}$.
- $u_g =$ **IBHTDF.Eval**$^{in}(g, (x_1, u_1, v_1), \ldots, (x_\ell, u_\ell, v_\ell))$: A deterministic *input* homomorphic evaluation algorithm. It takes as input some function $g : \mathcal{X}^\ell \to \mathcal{X}$ and values $\{x_i \in \mathcal{X}, u_i \in \mathcal{U}, v_i \in \mathcal{V}\}_{i \in [\ell]}$ and output $u_g \in \mathcal{U}$.

- $v_g = \textbf{IBHTDF.Eval}^{out}(g, v_1, \ldots, v_\ell)$: A deterministic *output* homomorphic evaluation algorithm. It takes as input some function $g : \mathcal{X}^\ell \to \mathcal{X}$ and values $\{v_i \in \mathcal{V}\}_{i \in [\ell]}$ and output $v_g \in \mathcal{V}$.

Correctness of Homomorphic Computation. Let algorithm $(pk_{id}, sk_{id}) \leftarrow$ **IBHTDF.Extract**(mpk, msk, id) extracts the identity-key for id. Let $g : \mathcal{X}^\ell \to \mathcal{X}$ be a function on $x_1, \ldots, x_\ell \in \mathcal{X}$ and $y = g(x_1, \ldots, x_\ell)$. Let $u_1, \ldots, u_\ell \in \mathcal{U}$ and set $v_i = f_{pk_{id}, x_i}(u_i)$ for $i \in [\ell]$. Set $u_g = \textbf{IBHTDF.Eval}^{in}(g, (x_1, u_1, v_1), \ldots, (x_\ell, u_\ell, v_\ell))$, $v_g = \textbf{IBHTDF.Eval}^{out}(g, v_1, \ldots, v_\ell)$. We require that $u_g \in \mathcal{U}$ and $v_g = f_{pk_{id}, y}(u_g)$.

Distributional Equivalence of Inversion. For the security of our construction IBFHS in next section, we require the following statistical indistinguishability:

$$(pk_{id}, sk_{id}, x, u, v) \stackrel{stat}{\approx} (pk_{id}, sk_{id}, x, u', v')$$

Where $(pk_{id}, sk_{id}) \leftarrow \textbf{IBHTDF.Extract}$, $x \in \mathcal{X}$, $u \leftarrow \mathcal{D}_\mathcal{U}$, $v = f_{pk_{id}, x}(u)$, $v' \xleftarrow{\$} \mathcal{V}$, $u' \leftarrow \textbf{Invert}_{sk_{id}, x}(v')$.

IBHTDF Security. We require not only *claw-freenesss* but also *collision-resistance* for **IBHTDF** security to guarantee *strong-unforgeability* for **IBFHS**.

The experiment $\textbf{Exp}^{sID}_{\mathcal{A}, \textbf{IBHTDF}}(1^\lambda)$ describe the selective-*identiy* security, where the adversary has to appoint a target identity id^* to attack before seeing the public key. Moreover, the adversary can query identity-key for all identity except id^*. Then he is required to find $u \neq u' \in \mathcal{U}$, $x, x' \in \mathcal{X}$ such that $f_{pk_{id^*}, x}(u) = f_{pk_{id^*}, x'}(u')$. It's easy to see that if $x = x'$, then (u, u') is a collision, a claw otherwise.

$$\textbf{Exp}^{sID}_{\mathcal{A}, \textbf{IBHTDF}}(1^\lambda)$$

- $(id^*, state) \leftarrow \mathcal{A}(1^\lambda)$.
- $(mpk, msk) \leftarrow \textbf{IBHTDF.Setup}(1^\lambda)$.
- $(u, u', x, x') \leftarrow \mathcal{A}^{\textbf{IBHTDF.Extract}(mpk, msk) \setminus id^*}(mpk, state)$.
- $\mathcal{A}$ wins if $u \neq u' \in \mathcal{U}, x, x' \in \mathcal{X}$ are such that $f_{pk_{id^*}, x}(u) = f_{pk_{id^*}, x'}(u')$.

We say that an identity-based homomorphic trapdoor function is *selective-identity* secure if $\Pr[\textbf{Exp}^{sID}_{\mathcal{A}, \textbf{IBHTDF}}(1^\lambda)] \leq \text{negl}(\lambda)$.

3.2 Construction: Basic Algorithms and Security

To describe the **IBHTDF** functions, we give some public parameters as follows.

- Let flexible d be the circuit depth such that $d \leq poly(\lambda)$ and λ be a security parameter.
- Choose an integer $n = \text{poly}(\lambda)$ and a sufficiently large prime $q = q(n)$. Let $\ell = \lceil \log q \rceil$, $m_0 = n(\ell + O(1))$, $m_1 = n\ell$ and $m = m_0 + 2m_1$. Set $\beta_0 = O((n \log q)^{3/2})$, $\beta_{max} = O(2^d \beta_0)$, $\beta_{SIS} = O(m_1 \beta_0)\beta_{max} < q$.
- $\mathbf{G} = \mathbf{I_n} \otimes \mathbf{g}^T \in \mathbb{Z}_q^{n \times n\ell}$ is the primitive matrix, where $\mathbf{g}^T = (1, 2, 2^2, \ldots, 2^{\ell-1})$.

- We assume that identities are elements in $GF(q^n)$, and say $\mathbf{H} : GF(q^n) \rightarrow \mathbb{Z}_q^{n \times n}$ is an invertible difference, if $\mathbf{H}(id_1) - \mathbf{H}(id_2)$ is invertible for any two different identities id_1, id_2 and $\mathbf{H}$ is computable in polynomial time in $n\ell$.
- Set $\mathcal{X} = \mathbb{Z}_2$, $\mathcal{I} = \mathbb{Z}_q^n$, $\mathcal{V} = \mathbb{Z}_q^{n \times m}$ and $\mathcal{U} = \{\mathbf{U} \in \mathbb{Z}_q^{m \times m} : \|\mathbf{U}\|_\infty \leq \beta_{\max}\}$. Define the distribution $\mathcal{D}_\mathcal{U}$ is a truncated discrete Gaussian distribution over $\mathcal{U}$, so that $\|\mathbf{U}\|_\infty \leq \beta_0$ if $\mathbf{U} \leftarrow \mathcal{D}_\mathcal{U}$.

Now we describe the basic algorithms of **IBHTDF** function $\mathcal{F}$.

- **IBHTDF.Setup**(1^λ): On input a security parameter λ, set d, n, m_0, m_1, m, q, β_0, β_{max}, β_{SIS} as specified above. Then do
  1. Choose $\mathbf{A_0} \xleftarrow{\$} \mathbb{Z}_q^{n \times m_0}$ and run $\mathbf{TrapGen}(\mathbf{A_0}, \mathbf{0})$ to generate a matrix $\mathbf{A} = [\mathbf{A_0}\|\mathbf{A_1}] = [\mathbf{A_0}\|-\mathbf{A_0R}]$ and a trapdoor R such that $\mathbf{R} \leftarrow \mathcal{D}_{\mathbb{Z}^{m_0 \times m_1}, \omega(\sqrt{\log n})}$ and $\mathbf{A}$ is negl(λ)-far from uniform. Set the master secret key as $msk = \mathbf{R}$. Note that $\mathbf{A} \cdot (\mathbf{R}, \mathbf{I}_{m_1}) = \mathbf{0}$, namely $\mathbf{R}$ is a G-trapdoor of $\mathbf{A}$ with tag $\mathbf{0}$.
  2. Choose $\mathbf{A_2} \xleftarrow{\$} \mathbb{Z}_q^{n \times m_1}$ and set public key as $mpk = \{\mathbf{A}, \mathbf{A_2}\}$.
- **IBHTDF.Extract**$(mpk, \mathbf{R}, id)$: On input a master public key mpk, a master secret key $\mathbf{R}$ and an identity $id \in \mathcal{I}$, do
  1. Compute $\mathbf{H}_{id}$ for $id \in \mathcal{I}$ and let $\mathbf{A}'_{id} = [\mathbf{A_0}\|\mathbf{H}_{id} \cdot \mathbf{G} + \mathbf{A_1}]$. Then $\mathbf{R}$ is a G-trapdoor of $\mathbf{A}'_{id}$ with tag $\mathbf{H}_{id}$. Set user's public key $pk_{id} = \mathbf{A}_{id} = [\mathbf{A}'_{id}\|\mathbf{A_2}]$.
  2. Run $\mathbf{SamPre}(\mathbf{A_0}, \mathbf{R}, \mathbf{H}(id), \mathbf{G} - \mathbf{A_2}, O(\sqrt{n \log q}))$ to output $\mathbf{R}_{id} \in \mathbb{Z}^{(m_0 + m_1) \times m_1}$ such that $\mathbf{A}'_{id} \cdot \mathbf{R}_{id} = \mathbf{G} - \mathbf{A_2}$. Then $\mathbf{R}_{id}$ is a G-trapdoor of $\mathbf{A}_{id}$ with tag $\mathbf{I}_n$. Set secret key $sk_{id} = \mathbf{R}_{id}$.
- $f_{pk_{id}, x}(\mathbf{U})$: On input $mpk, id \in \mathcal{I}, x \in \mathcal{X}$ and $\mathbf{U} \in \mathcal{U}$, do
  1. Compute $pk_{id} = \mathbf{A}_{id} = [\mathbf{A_0}\|\mathbf{H}_{id} \cdot \mathbf{G} + \mathbf{A_1}\|\mathbf{A_2}]$ as above.
  2. For $id \in \mathcal{I}$, $x \in \mathcal{X}$ and $\mathbf{U} \in \mathcal{U}$, define $f_{pk_{id}, x}(\mathbf{U}) \overset{\triangle}{=} \mathbf{A}_{id} \cdot \mathbf{U} + x \cdot \mathbf{A}_{id}$.
- **Invert**$_{sk_{id}, x}(\mathbf{V})$: On input identity $id \in \mathcal{I}$, an identity-key $\mathbf{R}_{id}$, an index $x \in \mathcal{X}$ and $\mathbf{V} \in \mathcal{V}$, run $\mathbf{SamPre}(\mathbf{A}'_{id}, \mathbf{R}_{id}, \mathbf{I}_n, \mathbf{V} - x \cdot \mathbf{A}_{id}, O(n \log q))$ to output $\mathbf{U}$ (such that $\mathbf{A}_{id} \cdot \mathbf{U} = \mathbf{V} - x \cdot \mathbf{A}_{id}$).

Distributional Equivalence of Inversion. Let $x \in \mathcal{X}$ and $(pk_{id} = \mathbf{A}_{id}, sk_{id} = \mathbf{R}_{id}) \leftarrow$ **IBHTDF.Extract** $(mpk, \mathbf{R}, id)$. $\mathbf{U} \in \mathcal{U}$, $\mathbf{V} = f_{pk_{id}, x}(\mathbf{U}) = \mathbf{A}_{id} \cdot \mathbf{U} + x \cdot \mathbf{A}_{id}$, $\mathbf{V}' \xleftarrow{\$} \mathcal{V}$, $\mathbf{U}' \leftarrow \mathbf{SamPre}(\mathbf{A}'_{id}, \mathbf{R}_{id}, \mathbf{I}_n, \mathbf{V}' - x \cdot \mathbf{A}_{id}, O(n \log q))$. By Lemma3 and the fact that $(\mathbf{V}' - x\mathbf{A}_{id})$ is uniformly random, we have

$$(\mathbf{A}_{id}, \mathbf{R}_{id}, \mathbf{U}, \mathbf{A}_{id} \cdot \mathbf{U}) \overset{stat}{\approx} (\mathbf{A}_{id}, \mathbf{R}_{id}, \mathbf{U}', \mathbf{V}' - x\mathbf{A}_{id}).$$

Then, we have

$$(\mathbf{A}_{id}, \mathbf{R}_{id}, x, \mathbf{U}, \mathbf{V} = \mathbf{A}_{id} \cdot \mathbf{U} + x \cdot \mathbf{A}_{id}) \overset{stat}{\approx} (\mathbf{A}_{id}, \mathbf{R}_{id}, x, \mathbf{U}', \mathbf{V}').$$

IBHTDF Security. We now show that the **IBHTDF** function $\mathcal{F}$ is selective-identity secure assuming the SIS assumption.

Theorem 1. *The function $\mathcal{F}$ constructed above is a selective-secure* **IBHTDF** *assuming the* $\mathbf{SIS}_{n, m_0, q, \beta_{SIS}}$.

Because of space limitations, we put the proof of the theorem in the full version.

4 Homomorphic Evaluation and Noise Analysis

In this section, we give a new construction of homomorphic evaluation algorithm. Our construction could do better in homomorphic evaluation based on the fact that the noise growth is slower.

4.1 Basic Homomorphic Evaluation

We now define the basic homomorphic addition and multiplication algorithms that will be used in IBHTDFs. These algorithms for IBHTDFs are simple and faster than that in [10]. But the parameters used in this section are same as that in [10] because of the similar structure. Recall that $\mathbf{V}_i = \mathbf{A}\mathbf{U}_i + x_i\mathbf{A}$ $(i = 1, 2)$, where we set $\mathbf{A} = \mathbf{A}_{id}$ for simplicity throughout Sect. 5. Let $\|\mathbf{U}_i\|_\infty \leq \beta_i$ and $x_i \in \{0, 1\}$.

4.2 Construction: Homomorphic Evaluation and Noise Growth

Now we define the algorithms $\mathbf{Eval}^{in}, \mathbf{Eval}^{out}$ with the syntax

$$\mathbf{U}^* := \mathbf{IBHTDF}.\mathbf{Eval}_{pk}^{in}(g, (x_1, \mathbf{U}_1), \dots, (x_\ell, \mathbf{U}_\ell)),$$

$$\mathbf{V}^* := \mathbf{IBHTDF}.\mathbf{Eval}_{pk}^{out}(g, \mathbf{V}_1, \dots, \mathbf{V}_\ell).$$

We consider the function g as basic gates in an arithmetic circuit: *addition, multiplication, addition-with-constant* and *multiplication-by-constant*. These functions are complete and can be composed to evaluate arbitrary arithmetic circuit. Let the matrice $\mathbf{U}_i$ have noise-levels bounded by β_i.

– Let $g(x_1, x_2) = x_1 + x_2$ be an *addition* gate. The algorithms $\mathbf{IBHTDF}.\mathbf{Eval}^{in}$, $\mathbf{IBHTDF}.\mathbf{Eval}^{out}$ respectively compute

$$\mathbf{U}^* := \mathbf{U}_1 + \mathbf{U}_2, \quad \mathbf{V}^* := \mathbf{V}_1 + \mathbf{V}_2.$$

The matrix $\mathbf{U}^*$ has noise level $\beta^* \leq \beta_1 + \beta_2$. The correctness follows by $(\mathbf{V}_1 + \mathbf{V}_2) = \mathbf{A}(\mathbf{U}_1 + \mathbf{U}_2) + (x_1 + x_2)\mathbf{A}$.

– Let $g(x_1, x_2) = x_1 \cdot x_2$ be a *multiplication* gate. The algorithms $\mathbf{Eval}^{in}, \mathbf{Eval}^{out}$ respectively compute

$$\mathbf{U}^* := \mathbf{U}_1 + x_1 \cdot \mathbf{U}_2, \quad \mathbf{V}^* := \mathbf{V}_1 - x_1 \cdot \mathbf{A} + x_1 \cdot \mathbf{V}_2.$$

The matrix $\mathbf{U}^*$ has noise level $\beta^* \leq \beta_1 + |x_1|\beta_2 = \beta_1 + \beta_2$. The correctness follows by a simple computation assuming $\mathbf{V}_i = \mathbf{A}\mathbf{U}_i + x_i\mathbf{G}$.

– Let $g(x) = x + a$ be *addition-with constant* gate, for the constant $a \in \mathbb{Z}_q$. The algorithms $\mathbf{IBHTDF}.\mathbf{Eval}^{in}$, $\mathbf{IBHTDF}.\mathbf{Eval}^{out}$ respectively compute

$$\mathbf{U}^* := \mathbf{U}, \quad \mathbf{V}^* := \mathbf{V} - a \cdot \mathbf{A}.$$

The matrix $\mathbf{U}^*$ have the same noise level as $\mathbf{U}$.

– Let $g(x) = a \cdot x$ be a *multiplication-by-constant* gate for the constant $a \in \mathbb{Z}_q$. The algorithms **IBHTDF.Eval**^{in}, **IBHTDF.Eval**^{out} respectively compute

$$\mathbf{U}^* := a \cdot \mathbf{U}, \quad \mathbf{V}^* := a \cdot \mathbf{V}.$$

The matrix $\mathbf{U}^*$ have the same noise level as $a \cdot \beta$.

Bounded-Depth Circuits. In Wang's IBHTDF, a depth-d ($d \le \operatorname{poly}(\lambda)$) circuit can be transformed to a length $L = 4^d$ permutation branching program. The maximum noise comparing to Gorbunov-Vaikuntanathan-Wich's HTDF reduces roughly from $O(m^d\beta)$ to $O(4^d m\beta)$. Then in our HTDF we do not use permutation branching program and reduces roughly from $O(m^d\beta)$ to $O(2^d\beta)$. In particular, we can set polynomial modulus $q = \operatorname{poly} > O(2^d\beta)$ when $d = O(\log \lambda)$ which will result in better security based on GapSVP with polynomial approximation factors.

5   Strongly-Unforgeable Identity-Based Fully Homomorphic Signatures

In this section, we give a strongly-unforgeable identity-based fully homomorphic signature scheme. The scheme will take advantage of IBHTDF in Sect. 3 and homomorphic evaluation in Sect. 4.

5.1   Definition of IBFHS

A single data-set identity-based homomorphic signature scheme consists of following algorithms (**PrmsGen, Setup, Extract, Sign, SignEval, Process, Verify**) with syntax:

– $prms \leftarrow$ **PrmsGen**$(1^\lambda, 1^\ell)$: Take the security parameter λ and the maximum data-size N. Output public parameters $prms$. The message space $\mathcal{X}$ is defined by security parameter λ.
– $(mpk, msk) \leftarrow$ **Setup**(1^λ): Take the security parameter λ. Output a master key pair (mpk, msk).
– $(pk_{id}, sk_{id}) \leftarrow$ **Extract**(mpk, msk, id): An identity-key extraction procedure.
– $(\sigma_1, \ldots, \sigma_N) \leftarrow$ **Sign**$_{sk_{id}}(prms, x_1, \ldots, x_N)$: Sign message data $(x_1, \ldots, x_N) \in \mathcal{X}^N$ for ID.
– $\sigma_g =$ **SignEval**$_{prms}(g, (x_1, \sigma_1), \ldots, (x_\ell, \sigma_\ell))$: A deterministic homomorphic signature algorithm output a signature σ_g for some function g over$(x_1, \ldots, x_\ell) \in \mathcal{X}^\ell$.
– $v_g =$ **Process**$_{prms}(g)$: Deterministically and homomorphically evaluate a *certificate* v_g for the function g from the public parameters $prms$.
– **Verify**$_{pk_{id}}(v_g, y, \sigma_g)$: Verify that y is the correct output of g by proving σ_g corresponding to v_g.

Correctness. For $prms \leftarrow \mathbf{PrmsGen}(1^\lambda, 1^\ell)$, $(pk_{id}, sk_{id}) \leftarrow \mathbf{Extract}(mmpk, msk, id)$, $(x_1, \ldots, x_N) \in \mathcal{X}^N$, $(\sigma_1, \ldots, \sigma_N) \leftarrow \mathbf{Sign}_{sk_{id}}(prms, x_1, \ldots, x_N)$ and $g : \mathcal{X}^\ell \rightarrow \mathcal{X}$, we require following equation

$$\mathbf{Verify}_{pk_{id}}(v_g, y = g(x_1, \ldots, x_\ell), \sigma_g) = \mathrm{accept}$$

holds, where $v_g = \mathbf{Process}_{prms}(g)$ and $\sigma_g = \mathbf{Process}_{prms}(g, (x_1, \sigma_1), \ldots, (x_\ell, \sigma_\ell))$.

Correctness of Leveled IBFHS. The correctness of leveled IBFHS follows from that of leveled IBHTDF and hence is omitted.

Security Experiment. The experiment $\mathbf{Exp}_{\mathcal{A}, \mathrm{IBFHS}}^{\mathrm{SU-sID-sCMA}}(1^\lambda)$ defined in following describes the *strongly-unforgeable selective-identity static chosen-message-attack* security game, where the adversary has to fix a target identity id^* to attack before obtaining the master public-key and public parameters. Moreover the adversary can query identity-keys for all identity except id^*. Then the adversary is forced to find (g, y', σ') such that the **Verify** algorithm output accept. If $y = y'$ then σ' is a strongly-forgeable signature, otherwise is a existentially-forgeable signature.

$$\mathbf{Exp}_{\mathcal{A}, \mathrm{IBFHS}}^{\mathrm{SU-sID-sCMA}}(1^\lambda)$$

- $(id^*, \{x_i\}_{i \in [N]}, state) \leftarrow \mathcal{A}(1^\lambda)$.
- $prms \leftarrow \mathbf{PrmsGen}(1^\lambda, 1^N), (mpk, msk) \leftarrow \mathbf{Setup}(1^\lambda)$.
- $(g, y', \sigma') \leftarrow \mathcal{A}^{\mathbf{Extract}(mpk, msk, \cdot) \backslash \{id^*\}, \mathbf{Sign}(id^*, \{x_i\}_{i \in [N]})}(prms, mpk, state)$.
- $\mathcal{A}$ wins if all of the following hold:
  1. g is a admissible circuit on the messages $x_1, \ldots, x_N$;
  2. $\sigma' \neq \sigma_g$, where $\sigma_g = \mathbf{SignEval}_{prms}(g, (x_1, \sigma_1), \ldots, (x_\ell, \sigma_\ell))$;
  3. $\mathbf{Verify}_{pk_{id^*}}(v_g, y', \sigma')$ accept, where $v_g = \mathbf{Process}_{prms}(g)$.

We say that an IBFHS is *strongly-unforgeable selective-identity static chosen-message-attack* (SU-sID-sCMA) secure if $\Pr[\mathbf{Exp}_{\mathcal{A}, \mathrm{IBFHS}}^{\mathrm{SU-sID-sCMA}}(1^\lambda)] \leq \mathrm{negl}(\lambda)$.

5.2 Construction

We use the IBHTDF and homomorphic evaluation given in Sect. 3 and Sect. 4 to construct a leveled IBFHS.

Let $\mathcal{F} = (\mathbf{IBHTDF.Setup}, \mathbf{IBHTDF.Extract}, f, \mathbf{Invert}, \mathbf{IBHTDF.Eval}^{\mathrm{in}}, \mathbf{IBHTDF.Eval}^{\mathrm{out}})$ be an IBHTDF with identity space $\mathcal{I}$, index space $\mathcal{X}$, input space $\mathcal{U}$, output space $\mathcal{V}$ and some efficiently samplable input distribution $\mathcal{D}_{\mathcal{U}}$ over $\mathcal{U}$. We construct an IBFHS scheme $\mathcal{S} = (\mathbf{PrmsGen}, \mathbf{Setup}, \mathbf{Extract}, \mathbf{Sign}, \mathbf{SignEval}, \mathbf{Process}, \mathbf{Verify})$ with message space $\mathcal{X}$ as follows.

- $prms \leftarrow \mathbf{PrmsGen}(1^\lambda, 1^\ell)$: Sample $v_i \xleftarrow{\$} \mathcal{V}$, $i \in [N]$ and set public parameters $prms = (v_1, \ldots, v_N)$.

- $(mpk, msk) \leftarrow$ **Setup**(1^λ): Select$(mpk', msk') \leftarrow$ **IBHTDF.Setup**(1^λ) and set master-key pair $(mpk = mpk',\ msk = msk')$.
- $(pk_{id}, sk_{id}) \leftarrow$ **Extract**(mpk, msk, id): Run **IBHTDF.Extract**(mpk', msk', id) to get (pk'_{id}, sk'_{id}) and set $pk_{id} = pk'_{id}, sk_{id} = sk'_{id}$ for $id \in \mathcal{I}$.
- $(\sigma_1, \ldots, \sigma_N) \leftarrow$ **Sign**$_{sk_{id}}(prms, x_1, \ldots, x_N)$: Sample $u_i \leftarrow$ **Invert**$_{sk'_{id}, x_i}(v_i)$ and set $\sigma_i = u_i, i \in [N]$.
- $\sigma_g =$ **SignEval**$_{prms}(g, (x_1, \sigma_1), \ldots, (x_\ell, \sigma_\ell))$: perform deterministic algorithm **IBHTDF.Eval**^{in} $(g, (x_1, u_1, v_1), \ldots, (x_\ell, u_\ell, v_\ell))$ to get u_g and set $\sigma_g = u_g$.
- $v_g =$ **Process**$_{prms}(g)$: Perform **IBHTDF.Eval**$^{out}(g, v_1, \ldots, v_\ell)$ and output the result v_g.
- **Verify**$_{pk_{id}}(v_g, y, \sigma_g)$: If $f_{pk'_{id}, y}(\sigma_g) = v_g$ accept, else reject.

Security. We now show the SU-sID-sCMA security of the leveled IBFHS.

Lemma 4. *The leveled* IBFHS *scheme* $\mathcal{S}$ *constructed above is SU-sID-sCMA secure assuming that* $\mathcal{F}$ *is a leveled selective-identity secure IBHTDF.*

Proof. Assume that there exist a PPT adversary $\mathcal{A}$ that wins the security experiment $\mathbf{Exp}_{\mathcal{A}, \text{IBFHS}}^{\text{SU-sID-sCMA}}(1^\lambda)$ of IBFHS with non-negligible probability δ. We can construct a PPT reduction $\mathcal{B}$ that breaks the selective-identity security of $\mathcal{F}$.

Let id^* be the identity that $\mathcal{A}$ intends to attack. $\mathcal{B}$ will run the changed algorithms(**PrmsGen***, **Setup***, **Extract***, **Sign***).

- **Setup**$^*(1^\lambda)$: Run $(mpk', msk') \leftarrow$ **IBHTDF.Setup**$^*(1^\lambda)$ and set $mpk = mpk', msk = msk'$.
- **Extract**$^*(mpk, msk, id)$: Run **IBHTDF.Extract**$^*(mpk, \mathbf{R}, id)$ to get (pk'_{id}, sk'_{id}). When $id \neq id^*$ and set $pk_{id} = pk'_{id}, sk_{id} = sk'_{id}$. However, if $id = id^*$, then the trapdoor disappears and $\mathcal{B}$ can not generate the identity key for id^*.
- **PrmsGen**$^*(1^\lambda, 1^N)$: Choose $u_i \leftarrow \mathcal{D}_{\mathcal{U}}$ and compute $v_i = f_{pk_{id^*}, x_i}(u_i)$. Output $prms = (v_1, \ldots, v_N)$.
- **Sign**$^*(x_1, \ldots, x_N)$: Set $\sigma_i = u_i$ and output $(\sigma_1, \ldots, \sigma_N)$.

As the *Distributional Equivalence of Inversion* property underlying **IBHTDF** discussed above, the views of adversary $\mathcal{A}$ between the original experiment and the changed experiment are distinguishable. In particular, the winning probability of $\mathcal{A}$ attacking the changed experiment is at least $\delta - \text{negl}(\lambda)$.

For any PPT adversary $\mathcal{A}$ which can win the changed experiment with nonnegligible probability $\delta - \text{negl}(\lambda)$, we now show that there exists a PPT reduction $\mathcal{B}$ can break the security of $\mathcal{F}$ with probability $\delta - \text{negl}(\lambda)$ by access to $\mathcal{A}$.

The reduction $\mathcal{B}$ receives the challenge identity id^* and message data-set $(x_1, \ldots, x_N)$, generates $(mpk, msk, \{\sigma_i = u_i, v_i\}_{i \in [N]})$ and send $(mpk, \{\sigma_i, v_i\}_{i \in [N]})$ to $\mathcal{A}$. If $id \neq id^*$ then $\mathcal{B}$ can respond to any identity-key query for id by msk. But, if $id = id^*$, then the trapdoor disappears, $\mathcal{B}$ doesn't have ability to generate identity-key for id^*.

Assume the adversary $\mathcal{A}$ wins the $\mathbf{Exp}_{\mathcal{A},\mathrm{IBFHS}}^{\mathrm{SU-sID-sCMA}}(1^{\lambda})$ that means $\mathcal{A}$ outputs value (g, y', σ'). $g : \mathcal{X}^{\ell} \to \mathcal{X}$ on $(x_1, \ldots, x_{\ell})$ is an admissible function and $\sigma' = u'$. Let $y = g(x_1, \ldots, x_{\ell}), u_g = \sigma_g = \mathbf{SignEval}_{prms}(g, (x_1, \sigma_1), \ldots, (x_{\ell}, \sigma_{\ell}))$, $v_g = \mathbf{Process}_{prms}(g)$. On the one hand, since σ' could verify, $f_{pk_{id^*}, y'}(u') = v_g$ holds. On the other hand, $f_{pk_{id^*}, y}(u_g) = v_g$ must hold because of the correctness of homomorphic computation. Then we have $u_g \neq u' \in \mathcal{U}$ and $y, y' \in \mathcal{X}$ satisfying $f_{pk_{id^*}, y}(u_g) = f_{pk_{id^*}, y'}(u')$, that allow $\mathcal{B}$ break the $\mathbf{Exp}_{\mathcal{A},\mathrm{IBHTDF}}^{\mathrm{sID}}(1^{\lambda})$ security of $\mathcal{F}$ with probability $\delta-\mathrm{negl}(\lambda)$ whenever $\mathcal{A}$ wins the changed experiment with probability $\delta-\mathrm{negl}(\lambda)$. This complete the proof of this lemma.

6 Conclusions

In this work, we construct a new leveled strongly-unforgeable IBFHS scheme which is based on our new IBHTDF. The maximum noise level of addition gate and multiplication gate are exactly the same in our IBHTDF. That means that the maximum noise level of our IBHTDF is optimal. It remains open to decrease the leveled aspect and ideally come up with a signature scheme where there is no priori bound on the depth of the circuits that can be efficiently evaluated with short public parameters. What's more, the existence of any other schemes, e.g. homomorphic encryption or ABE, could use our trapdoor generation technique is still a puzzle.

References

1. Agrawal, S., Boneh, D., Boyen, X.: Efficient lattice (H)IBE in the standard model. In: Gilbert, H. (ed.) EUROCRYPT 2010. LNCS, vol. 6110, pp. 553–572. Springer, Heidelberg (2010). https://doi.org/10.1007/978-3-642-13190-5_28
2. Brakerski, Z., Vaikuntanathan, V.: Lattice-based FHE as secure as PKE. In: ITCS, pp. 1–12 (2014)
3. Boyen, X., Fan, X., Shi, E.: Adaptively secure fully gomomorphic signatures based on lattices. Cryptology ePrint Archive, Report 2014/916. http://eprint.iacr.org/2014/916
4. Gentry, C., Peikert, C., Vaikuntanathan, V.: Trapdoors for hard lattices and new cryptographic constructions. In: STOC, pp. 197–206. ACM, New York (2008)
5. Gentry, C.: Fully homomorphic encryption using ideal lattices. In: STOC 2009, pp. 169–178. ACM (2009)
6. Gorbunov, S., Vaikuntanathan, V., Wichs, D.: Leveled fully homomorphic signatures from standard lattices. In: STOC 2015, pp. 469–477. ACM (2015)
7. Micciancio, D., Peikert, C.: Hardness of SIS and LWE with small parameters. In: Canetti, R., Garay, J.A. (eds.) CRYPTO 2013. LNCS, vol. 8042, pp. 21–39. Springer, Heidelberg (2013). https://doi.org/10.1007/978-3-642-40041-4_2
8. Micciancio, D., Peikert, C.: Trapdoors for lattices: simpler, tighter, faster, smaller. In: Pointcheval, D., Johansson, T. (eds.) EUROCRYPT 2012. LNCS, vol. 7237, pp. 700–718. Springer, Heidelberg (2012). https://doi.org/10.1007/978-3-642-29011-4_41
9. Xie, X., Xue, R.: Bounded Fully Homomorphic Signature Schemes. IACR Cryptology ePrint Archive, p. 420 (2014)

10. Wang, F., Wang, K., Li, B., Gao, Y.: Leveled strongly-unforgeable identity-based fully homomorphic signatures. In: Lopez, J., Mitchell, C.J. (eds.) ISC 2015. LNCS, vol. 9290, pp. 42–60. Springer, Cham (2015). https://doi.org/10.1007/978-3-319-23318-5_3

11. Micciancio, D., Regev, O.: Worst-case to average-case reductions based on gaussian measures. SIAM J. Comput. **37**, 267–302 (2007)

An Efficient Malicious User Detection Mechanism for Crowdsensing System

Xiaocan Wu[1], Yu-E Sun[2(✉)], Yang Du[1], Xiaoshuang Xing[3(✉)], Guoju Gao[1], and He Huang[1]

[1] School of Computer Science and Technology, Soochow University, Suzhou, China
[2] School of Rail Transportation, Soochow University, Suzhou, China
sunye12@suda.edu.cn
[3] School of Computer Science and Engineering, Changshu Institute of Technology, Changshu, China
xing@cslg.edu.cn

Abstract. Although crowdsensing has emerged as a promising data collection paradigm by applying embedded sensors in mobile devices to monitor the real world, the data quality problem is still a big issue for the existence of malicious users in the crowdsensing system. There have been many mechanisms proposed to improve the quality of submitted observations. However, they are not cost-efficient enough to be widely applied or only compatible with limited applications. Therefore, we propose an efficient malicious user detection method by developing a Hidden Markov Model, which can distinguish malicious users from normal users. We also provide a malicious user pre-detection method by using a Gradient Boosting Decision Tree model, which is targeted at the crowdsensing system in long-term operation and has new participation constantly. The experimental results based on real-world datasets reveal that the proposed method has good accuracy of the user distinguishment and shows significant changes in improving the existing truth discovery methods.

Keywords: Crowdsensing · Malicious user detection · Hidden Markov model

1 Introduction

With the prevalence of mobile devices and the rapid development of wireless technology, mobile crowdsensing (MCS) has become a promising paradigm. Unlike traditional data collection methods by arranging various sensors at targeted places, MCS applies embedded sensors such as gyroscopes, accelerometers and global positioning systems (GPS) in mobile devices and utilizes a large group of mobile device users to monitor the real world in real-time, which is more efficient. Thus, various kinds of crowdsensing-based applications have been developed currently, including urban traffic monitoring, environment monitoring, public safety, and emergency preparedness [7].

© Springer Nature Switzerland AG 2020
D. Yu et al. (Eds.): WASA 2020, LNCS 12384, pp. 507–519, 2020.
https://doi.org/10.1007/978-3-030-59016-1_42

However, the involvement of mobile device users in sensing tasks can also lead to some data quality problems. While the monetary incentives offered by MCS attract more participating users, they also invite the participation of malicious users, some of whom try to fool the platform by submitting false data without actually executing the assigned task in order to quickly obtain monetary gains. Besides, other malicious users may even come from competing parts of requesters and keep submitting false data to destroy released tasks [1,2]. Since false observations damage the operation of the entire crowdsensing system, it is necessary to design an efficient approach to identify the malicious users in the system, which helps the platform provide a high-quality sensing dataset. Some of the related researches evaluate the submitted data based on location verification. For example, Talasila *et al.* discussed location reliability, based on the GPS location and Bluetooth scan of the device, as a step toward data reliability and detected false location claims from malicious users [10]. Some studies use reputation/trust as an indicator to identify adversaries in the system according to users' behavior. For instance, Kantarci *et al.* proposed a distributed voting solution for detecting adversaries who manipulate sensor readings to spread disinformation in mobile crowdsensing systems [3]. Wang *et al.* and Xuan *et al.* trained machine learning models for detecting malicious users based on massive labeled datasets [13,14]. However, existing studies on identifying malicious users in the crowdsensing system are still limited, as none of them are cost-efficient and general enough to be applied in most crowdsensing systems.

Therefore, we propose a malicious detection method for crowdsensing system, which can distinguish malicious users (*i.e.*, users who keep submitting false observations) from the normal users (*i.e.*, users who submit low-quality observations or high-quality observations) in order to improve the quality of the sensing dataset. The proposed method identifies malicious users in the system by evaluating users' performance in the past allocation periods. It contains three parts: observation reliability calculation, user reliability calculation and user classification. We first calculate the observation reliability based on existing truth discovery algorithms [6]. After that, we apply a Hidden Markov Model (HMM) and use the calculated reliabilities of all submitted observations in past allocation periods as input to compute reliabilities of all participating users in the system. Finally, we classify the type of users by clustering the calculated reliability of all users in the system. In addition, as new participating users in the system are always accompanied by some new malicious users, we also provide a method for malicious user pre-detection by training a classifier based on Gradient Boosting Decision Tree (GBDT) with the behavior features of the labeled users in constructed malicious user set and high-quality user set as the training dataset.

The main contributions of this article are summarized as follows:

- We propose a malicious detection method for crowdsensing system, which can distinguish malicious users from the normal ones. Since the method only uses all the observations submitted by users in various task allocation periods as input without requiring any other additional information, we are convinced

that the method is cost-efficient and general enough for most crowdsensing system.
- We also provide a malicious user pre-detection method by adopting a GBDT model, which allows the system to constantly review new participating users.
- We evaluate experimental results on the accuracy of the malicious user detection method and its performance in improving existing truth discovery methods. The malicious user pre-detection method is also evaluated in experiments.

2 Problem Formulation

As is shown in Fig. 1, the studied mobile crowdsensing system model consists of requesters, the platform and users. In order for users to obtain specific information about their tasks and to perform tasks more efficiently, requesters usually divide their requirements into multiple simple tasks, which require users to provide observations for different entities, and then publish their divided tasks on the platform. In addition, as requesters release tasks on the platform from time to time, the task assignment is usually carried out on a periodic basis. In each task allocation period, requesters first publish several tasks on the platform, and then the platform assigns the published tasks to users. Once users finish their allocated tasks, their submitted observations are collected by the platform and a truth discovery method is applied on the collected observations for the purpose of inferring the truth of the requesters' targeted entities. After that, the platform submits the estimated truths as the result in this period to requesters, and rewards users based on the usefulness of the observations they provide.

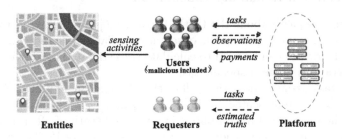

Fig. 1. Mobile crowdsensing system model.

Assume a set of N_L tasks released by requesters in the L-th task allocation period, denoted by $T_L = \{t_1, t_2, \ldots, t_{N_L}\}$, and a set of M users $\mathbf{U} = \{u_1, u_2, \ldots, u_M\}$. In order to be allocated in each allocation period and earn profit continuously, users have to make interaction with the platform, and then the platform is able to accumulate users' behavior features, such as the interval of accessing the system, refresh rate, response time after receiving tasks, and historic locations. Thus, each user u_i has a vector $\mathbf{p}_i$ to record u_i's behavior features. After the task t_j is allocated to the user u_i, the user performs the tasks according to the instruction with the mobile device and obtains the observation. The obtained observation is denoted by v_{i,t_j}, and the notation d_{t_j} represents the estimated truth of the assigned task t_j.

All of the tasks published by requesters and the observations submitted by users are recorded by the platform in each task allocation period, and the notation $\mathbf{T} = \{T_1, T_2, \ldots, T_L\}$ is used to represent all of the tasks released in each past period. We use the notation $\mathbf{D} = \{D_1, D_2, \ldots, D_L\}$ to represent the estimated truth of all tasks released in each past period, where $D_l = \{d_{t_j}\}_{t_j \in T_l}$ is the estimated truth of all tasks released in the l-th allocation period. In addition, all of the observations submitted by the participating users in the l-th allocation period are represented by the symbol $\{v_{i,t_j}\}_{i \in U, t_j \in T_l}$.

As there are always some malicious users who keep submitting false data with the intention of destroying released tasks or quickly obtaining monetary gains, given the description of the mobile crowdsensing system and notations above, this paper is proposed to design a malicious detection method for crowdsensing system, which can distinguish malicious users from normal users.

The definition of the malicious detection problem is as follows.

Definition. Given all the tasks $\mathbf{T} = \{T_l\}_{l=1}^L$ released in past periods and all the observations $\mathbf{V} = \{V_l\}_{l=1}^L$ in the past periods submitted by all the users $\mathbf{U} = \{u_i\}_{i=1}^M$ in the system, the goal of malicious user detection is to find the existing malicious users in the system.

3   Malicious User Detection Method

3.1   Observation Reliability Calculation

Since existing research about the truth discovery [6] is quite extensive and efficient, in this part of calculating the observation reliability, several existing truth discovery algorithms can be used to calculate the estimated truth with the input of all observations about a specific task.

In each task assignment period, all of the observation submitted by the participating users is represented by $V_l = \{v_{i,t_j}\}_{i \in U, t_j \in T_l}$. An existing truth discovery method is applied to compute the estimated truth of all tasks $\{d_{t_j}\}_{t_j \in T_l}$ released in the current allocation period with the input of V_l. The reliability of each submitted observation can now be calculated as:

$$w_{i,t_j} = \begin{cases} 0 & , \text{ if } |v_{i,t_j} - d_{t_j}| \geq Th \\ 1 - \frac{|v_{i,t_j} - d_{t_j}|}{Th} & , \text{ otherwise} \end{cases} \tag{1}$$

Therefore, all of the observation reliabilities submitted by the participating users in this allocation period can be denoted by $W_l = \{w_{i,t_j}\}_{i \in U, t_j \in T_l}$.

3.2 User Reliability Calculation

Although the platform receives all the reliability of observations submitted by the participating users in each task allocation period, it can still be difficult to judge if a user is malicious. This is mainly because of the misjudgment between the malicious users and the low-quality users (*i.e.*, users who are malicious also are likely to provide high-quality judged observations. More specifically, as low-quality users are always casual in performing the allocated task or even are ignorant of the task instructions, their submitted observations may already be in low-quality, let alone some factors will reduce the quality of observations further, such as environmental changes in sensing regions or defects in mobile devices. Therefore, we apply the Hidden Markov Model [8] to calculate user reliability, which uses all of the observation reliabilities submitted by the participating users in past allocation periods as input. Moreover, the applied HMM is composed of five parts $\{Q, A, O, B, \pi\}$, and the descriptions of notations are as follows:

Symbol Q represents the hidden states of the Markov chain in the model, there are three hidden states: false observations submitted without executing (*"malicious"* state), low-quality observations submitted (*"low-quality"* state), and high-quality observations submitted (*"high-quality"* state), more in detail $Q = \{$ *"malicious"*, *"low-quality"*, *"high-quality"*$\}$. The notation A is a transition probability matrix that describes the transition probabilities of the hidden states. The notation $O = \{o_t\}$ is a set that records all the possible observation reliabilities of an observation; o_t is regarded as a possibly existing reliability of a submitted observation. The symbol $B = \{b_i(o_t)|i \in Q, o_t \in O\}$ denotes the observation probability distribution in each state, and $b_i(o_t)$ is the probability that a user in the i state attains the observation reliability o_t for the submitted observation of the user. The notation π is the initial state distribution, which can be viewed as the proportion of users in the three types, *i.e.*, *"malicious"*, *"low-quality"* and *"high-quality"*.

Apparently, high-quality users and malicious users separately have a high proportion of *"high-quality"* states and *"malicious"* states in their hidden state sequence. Therefore, determining the proportion of three different states in a user's hidden state sequence is helpful to determine the type of user later on. The symbol $\psi_{i,l}$ denotes the reliability features of all observation reliabilities belonging to the participating user u_i in the l-th allocation period, and the notation $\psi_i = \{\psi_{i,1}, \psi_{i,2}, \ldots, \psi_{i,L}\}$ represents the reliability features of all participating user u_i in the past L allocation periods. In order to train the contemplated HMM model, $\psi = \{\psi_1, \psi_2, \ldots, \psi_M\}$ is used as the training set of the targeted model. Since the number of the allocated tasks for a user varies by task allocation period, for the purpose of avoiding the inconsistent dimension of the training data, it is impossible to set the reliability features $\psi_{i,l}$ of the user u_i as $[w_{i,t_j}]_{t_j \in T_l}$. The reliability features $\psi_{i,l}$ of a user u_i is set as:

$$\psi_{i,l} = [mean(W_{i,l}), median(W_{i,l}), std(W_{i,l})], W_{i,l} = \{w_{i,t_j}\}_{t_j \in T_l}. \quad (2)$$

Then, the Baum-Welch algorithm is applied to establish the targeted model, which uses the constructed training set ψ as input. After that, either the Viterbi algorithm or the Beam Search algorithm is executed with the input of $\boldsymbol{\psi}_i = \{\psi_{i,1}, \psi_{i,2}, \ldots, \psi_{i,L}\}$ to find the hidden state sequence $S_i = \{s_{i,l}\}$ of the user u_i. Finally, we use notations n_{high}, n_{low} and $n_{malicious}$ to represent the quantity of "*high-quality*" states, "*low-quality*" states and "*malicious*" states in the hidden state sequence S_i, and we have equations $n_{high} = |\{s_i'\}_{s_i' = "high-quality", s_i' \in S_i}|$, $n_{low} = |\{s_i'\}_{s_i' = "low-quality", s_i' \in S_i}|$ and $n_{malicious} = |\{s_i'\}_{s_i' = "malicious", s_i' \in S_i}|$. The reliability of the user u_i is computed by figuring out the proportion of the three states in user's hidden state sequence, and the equation is obtained in the following:

$$\mathbf{r}_i = [n_{high}/|S_i|, n_{low}/|S_i|, n_{malicious}/|S_i|]. \tag{3}$$

3.3   User Classification

High-quality users are likely to have a higher proportion of "*high-quality*" states in their hidden state sequences than the other two states, which reflects in the reliability $\mathbf{r}_i$ of the high-quality user u_i that the value of the first feature is greater than the other two features. Besides, in the extreme case of a typical high-quality user u_i, the user reliability $\mathbf{r}_i$ equals $[1, 0, 0]$. Similarly, if the reliability $\mathbf{r}_i$ of a user u_i equals $[0, 0, 1]$, he is no doubt a malicious user. Therefore, by clustering the reliabilities of all users in the system into three clusters, the obtained corresponding three cluster centers can be labeled according to the two cases mentioned above. More specifically, the closest cluster center to $[1, 0, 0]$ is the center of the cluster where user reliabilities of high-quality users are gathered, and the closest cluster center to $[0, 0, 1]$ is the center of the cluster where user reliabilities of malicious users are gathered. Furthermore, the type of the user is judged by determining the closest labeled center to the reliability of user u_i. This part of classifying users in the system employs the reliabilities of all users in the system $\mathbf{r} = \{\mathbf{r}_1, \mathbf{r}_2, \ldots, \mathbf{r}_M\}$ as input to determine high-quality users and malicious users, and the high-quality user set $\mathbf{U}_{high-quality}$ and malicious user set $\mathbf{U}_{malicious}$ are the output of this part.

3.4   Algorithm Flow

Details about the malicious user detection algorithm are shown in the Algorithm 1. The proposed algorithm uses all of the observations $\mathbf{V} = \{V_l\}_{l=1}^L$ in the past periods as input, and outputs the high-quality users and the malicious users in the system. The execution of the algorithm is divided into several parts. First, the truth of entities in each allocation period is computed based on the existing truth discovery method, and the reliability of each observation is calculated according to Eq. (1), along with the estimated truth. Then, all reliability features of all participating users in the past allocation periods are used as the training set of the targeted HMM model, and the hidden state sequence $S_i = \{s_{i,l}\}$ of each user u_i is estimated in order to compute the reliability of the user u_i by determining the proportion of the three states in the user's hidden state sequence. After that, the type of each user is determined by clustering the reliabilities of all participating users.

Algorithm 1. Malicious user detection algorithm

Require:
   all the observations $\{V_l\}_{l=1}^{L}$ in the past periods and user set in the system $\mathbf{U}$
Ensure:
   a high-quality user set $\mathbf{U}_{high\text{-}quality}$ and a malicious user set $\mathbf{U}_{malicious}$
1: Set $\mathbf{U}_{high\text{-}quality} = \phi$, $\mathbf{U}_{malicious} = \phi$;
2: **for** each l in $[1, L]$ **do**
3:    Get all estimated truth $D_l = \{d_{t_j}\}_{t_j \in T_l}$ based on a existing truth discovery method;
4:    **for** each v_{i,t_j} in V_l **do**
5:       Calculate the reliability w_{i,t_j} according to Eq. (1), and add w_{i,t_j} into W_l;
6: **for** each l in $[1, L]$ **do**
7:    **for** each user u_i in $\mathbf{U}$ **do**
8:       Calculate the reliability features of u_i in the l-th allocation period $\psi_{i,l}$ according to the Eq. (2), and add $\psi_{i,l}$ into ψ_i;
9: Use $\{\psi_i\}_{i=1}^{M}$ as training set to obtain an established HMM model;
10: **for** each user u_i in $\mathbf{U}$ **do**
11:    Find the hidden state sequence $S_i = \{s_{i,l}\}$ of the user u_i with the input of ψ_i;
12:    Compute reliability $\mathbf{r}_i$ of user u_i by figuring out the proportion of different states in S_i;
13: Uses the reliabilities of all users $\mathbf{r}$ as input to obtain the high-quality user set and malicious user set, based on the proposed user classification method;
14: **return** $\mathbf{U}_{high\text{-}quality}$ and $\mathbf{U}_{malicious}$;

3.5 Malicious User Pre-detection Method

For the purpose of serving requesters more efficiently and in higher quality, the platform tends to attract the participation of more users, which also entails the participation of some new malicious users. Since the former operation has already accumulated some labeled users (the recorded high-quality user set and malicious user set), based on the behavior features of the labeled users in the system as a training set, a classifier is constructed to determine the malicious users in the new participating users. In this part of pre-detecting malicious users, a GBDT model is adopted to obtain an efficient classifier with the behavior features of the labeled users as the training data.

Before training the GBDT model, a training data set denoted by D is constructed. Based on the recorded high-quality user set and malicious user set, the training data set $D = \{(x_i, y_i)_{u_i \in \mathbf{U}}\}$ is constructed as:

$$(x_i, y_i) = \begin{cases} (\mathbf{p}_i, -1), & \text{if } u_i \in \mathbf{U}_{malicious} \\ (\mathbf{p}_i, 1), & \text{if } u_i \in \mathbf{U}_{high\text{-}quality} \\ null, & \text{otherwise} \end{cases}.$$

After that, a negative binomial log-likelihood is proposed as the loss function of a GBDT model for two-category classification $\Psi(y, F) = \log(1 + \exp(-2yF))$, $y \in \{-1, 1\}$, where $F(x) = \frac{1}{2} \log\left[\frac{Pr(y=1|\mathbf{x})}{Pr(y=-1|\mathbf{x})}\right]$. The process for training a logistic GBDT model is as follows:

Step 1 : Initialize $F_0(\mathbf{x}) = \frac{1}{2} \log \frac{1+\bar{y}}{1-\bar{y}}$, $m = 1$ and set the iteration for training model at M.

Step 2 : In the m-th iteration, calculate the residual according to the loss function $\tilde{y}_i = 2y_i / (1 + \exp(-2y_i F_{m-1}(x_i)))$, $i = 1, 2, \ldots, |D|$.

Step 3 : Construct a regression tree $h_m(\mathbf{x})$ with the training data set $\{(x_i, \tilde{y}_i)\}_{i=1}^{|D|}$.

Step 4 : Calculate the weight of the new constructed tree
$\gamma_m = \sum_{i=1}^{|D|} \tilde{y}_i / \sum_{i=1}^{|D|} |\tilde{y}_i|(2 - |\tilde{y}_i|)$.

Step 5 : Update the targeted model $F_m(\mathbf{x}) = F_{m-1}(\mathbf{x}) + \gamma_m h_m(\mathbf{x})$.

Step 6 : $m = m + 1$, go to Step 2 if $m \leq M$.

Finally, we use the constructed GBDT model to judge a new user according to the behavior features of the user. Choose a new user u_i from the user set $\mathbf{U}$, and user's behavior features $\mathbf{p}_i$ is the input of the constructed model $F_m(\mathbf{x})$. If $F_m(\mathbf{p}_i) < 0$, remove the user u_i from the user set $\mathbf{U}$ and add the user into the malicious user set $\mathbf{U}_{malicious}$. Then choose another new user u_i from the user set $\mathbf{U}$ iteratively until all users are detected.

4   Experiment

4.1   Experimental Setup

A. Data Preparation: The data used in this experiment is divided into two parts: observations submitted by participating users and the dataset of users' behavior features. Shi *et al.* published an observation dataset submitted by 10 participating users which includes ground truths [9]. Users could choose different ways to execute the allocated tasks, and are labeled as high-quality or low-quality users based on their performance in the task execution. Besides, for the malicious users in the system, we follow the methods in [12] to generate malicious users' observations by adding a random deviation to the truth of entities. With regard to the dataset of users' behavior features, the relevant dataset is always related to user privacy, which makes it difficult to find appropriate datasets. We eventually decide to make use of a dataset that contains 1782 labeled websites with application layer and network characteristics recorded [11], and employ the obtained features of benign/malicious websites to simulate features of normal/malicious users in the system.

Although the observation dataset provides a large number of observations, the number of participating users is far from enough for our experiment. Thus, we try to simulate the observations submitted by a user of a specific type by summarizing the bias distributions of the observation from users in different types. Then, the experiment simulates the observations from an arbitrary user through the summarized bias distributions of the different types. For the observations submitted by high-quality users, the bias of the submitted observation is subject to the normal distribution $\mathcal{N}(\mu, \sigma)$, where the mean value of the bias μ ranges from 5 to 15, and the variance of the bias σ ranges from 1 to 15. Besides, for the observations submitted by low-quality users, the bias of the submitted observation is subject to the normal distribution $\mathcal{N}(\mu', \sigma')$, where the mean value of the bias μ' is in the range of $[20, 30]$, and the variance of the bias σ' changes within the range of $[20, 35]$.

B. Performance Metrics: The accuracy of the proposed malicious user detection and pre-detection method is emphasized in conducting our experiment. Thus, we use the metric of **Accuracy** to evaluate the performance of the malicious user detection method and pre-detection method. **Accuracy** is the fraction of the correctly judged users.

The experiment is also devoted to evaluating the performance of the proposed method in improving the existing truth discovery methods. More specifically, after determining the malicious users in the system, we remove the observations submitted by the determined malicious users from the originally submitted observations and calculate the estimated truth with the filtered observations as input. The performance of the proposed method is validated by comparing the bias of the original estimated truth and the bias of the filtered estimated truth, which are inferred from the original observations and the filtered observations, respectively. Therefore, we use the mean of absolute error (**MAE**) and the root of mean squared error (**RMSE**) to show the improvement of the proposed method to the existing truth discovery methods. MAE is used to measure the average absolute error between the estimated truth and ground truth, and RMSE is the square root of the average squared error between the estimated truth and ground truth.

C. Applied Truth Discovery Methods: The experiment applies several existing truth discovery methods to the proposed malicious user detection, including TruthFinder [15], CATD [4], CRH [5] and GTM [16]. TruthFinder is a truth discovery method based on the EM algorithm. CATD is a multi-source data truth discovery method based on user reliability. CRH estimates truth from multiple sources of heterogeneous data types. GTM is a multi-source data truth discovery method based on a Bayesian probability model.

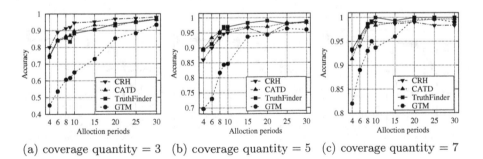

(a) coverage quantity = 3   (b) coverage quantity = 5   (c) coverage quantity = 7

Fig. 2. Performance of the proposed method under different truth discovery methods and user quantity = 300.

4.2 Experimental Analysis

A. Performance of the Proposed Method Under Different Truth Discovery Methods. From the experimental results, we can see that the accuracy of the method is improved compared to the previous accuracies when the task allocation period goes on. Synthesizing the experimental results from Figs. 2(b), 3(b) and 4(b), the experiment reflects the relationship between the user quantity and the accuracy of the proposed method by changing the number of users in the system and keeping other factors constant, and we can see that the increasing user quantity improves the accuracy of the proposed method. The experimental results in Fig. 3 reflect the influence that the coverage quantity has on accuracy. The ***coverage quantity*** is defined as the number of submitted observations in each task allocation period. In regard to those systems with high coverage quantity, the detection method can still achieve satisfactory accuracy even if the duration of the allocation period is relatively short.

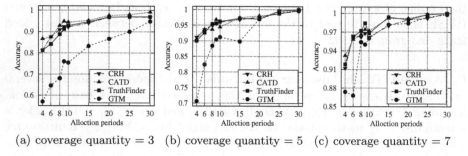

(a) coverage quantity = 3   (b) coverage quantity = 5   (c) coverage quantity = 7

Fig. 3. Performance of the proposed method under different truth discovery methods and user quantity = 500.

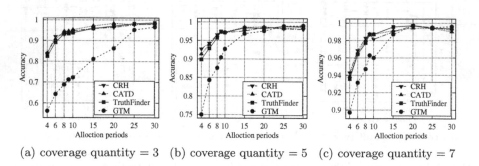

(a) coverage quantity = 3   (b) coverage quantity = 5   (c) coverage quantity = 7

Fig. 4. Performance of the proposed method under different truth discovery methods and user quantity = 1000.

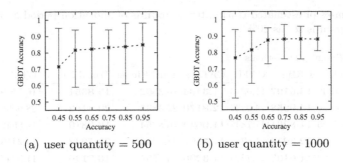

(a) user quantity = 500   (b) user quantity = 1000

Fig. 5. Performance of malicious user pre-detection method.

As illustrated by the cases of Figs. 2(a), 3(a) and 4(a) where the coverage quantity equals 3, the accuracies of the different malicious user detection methods, which apply different truth discovery methods, are all around 0.9 when the duration of the allocation period equals 20. Thus, in the experimental part of evaluating the performance of the proposed method in improving the existing truth discovery methods, the allocation period is always kept at 20.

Table 1 and 2 both reflect the influence on the biases of original estimated truth and filtered estimated truth when the proportion of malicious users and the applied truth discovery method are changed. The experiment shows that the bias of the estimated truth inferred from observations will reduce obviously after executing the proposed malicious user detection method. Regarding the system with different proportions of malicious users, the bias of the estimated truth still can be stable within a satisfactory range by executing the proposed method to filter out malicious observations.

Table 1. Biases of estimated truth after 20 rounds of allocation period and the malicious proportion is set as 40%.

		Different TD Methods							
		CRH	CRH+	CATD	CATD+	TruthFinder	TruthFinder+	GTM	GTM+
3	MAE	20.3764	12.9825	14.8957	12.2107	18.9256	16.7323	31.9381	13.9507
	RMSE	26.7751	**14.5259**	23.9603	**13.9703**	28.7998	**22.6928**	65.5056	**17.6523**
5	MAE	15.4814	**11.9990**	11.9789	**10.8766**	19.2718	**17.3560**	23.7787	**12.3196**
	RMSE	17.0464	**12.6741**	15.7452	**11.6551**	29.0262	**23.2905**	52.6088	**15.1848**
7	MAE	13.7792	**11.4463**	10.9736	**10.7041**	16.8717	**16.5800**	14.7437	**12.0385**
	RMSE	14.3761	**11.8167**	11.2653	**10.9918**	24.1855	**23.1517**	26.2336	**14.3751**

B. Performance of Malicious User Pre-detection Method. The experimental results in Fig. 5 reflect the influence of the user quantity and the accuracy of the malicious user detection method on the accuracy of the pre-detection method. We can see that the rising accuracy of the malicious user detection

Table 2. Biases of estimated truth after 20 rounds of allocation period and the malicious proportion is set as 20%.

		Different TD Methods							
		CRH	CRH+	CATD	CATD+	TruthFinder	TruthFinder+	GTM	GTM+
3	MAE	15.1830	**13.0197**	11.6813	**11.3404**	16.3562	**15.8351**	16.5129	**13.6615**
	RMSE	16.5670	**13.9958**	14.0232	**12.8170**	22.4335	**20.8162**	28.9596	**17.3767**
5	MAE	13.3595	**11.8261**	11.1842	**11.0642**	16.8354	**16.2810**	12.8549	**12.0277**
	RMSE	13.9358	**12.3013**	11.6781	**11.5591**	23.3938	**21.7948**	19.2419	**14.2240**
7	MAE	12.9389	**11.6107**	11.4295	**11.3286**	16.8864	**16.7149**	11.0347	**11.0346**
	RMSE	13.2446	**11.8513**	11.6387	**11.5425**	23.0948	**22.6286**	12.3781	**12.3781**

method and the increasing user quantity improve the accuracy of the pre-detection method. Especially when the accuracy of the malicious user detection method is around 0.95, and the user quantity is respectively set as 500 and 1000, the accuracies of the pre-detection method are around 0.85 and 0.9. This is because the improved accuracy of the malicious user detection method results in a more accurate training dataset, and the increasing user quantity provides a larger training dataset. Furthermore, the increasing user quantity enhances the accuracy of the pre-detection method and shortens the scope of probable accuracies, particularly when the accuracy of the malicious user detection method is around 0.95, and the user quantity is set as 500 and 1000 respectively, the scope of probable accuracies of the pre-detection method are $[0.62, 0.98]$ and $[0.81, 0.96]$.

5 Conclusion

In this article, we studied the problem of distinguish malicious users from the normal users in a general crowdsensing system. The proposed malicious user detection method, which uses all observations submitted by users in various task allocation periods as input, can be applied in most crowdsensing systems without any additional requirements. In addition, the malicious user pre-detection method by using a GBDT model is proposed to help systems identify malicious users from other new participating users. We conducted extensive experiments to validate the performance of our proposed methods, and results show the efficiency of the malicious user detection method and its improvement to the existing truth discovery methods. Furthermore, the experimental results show that the accuracies of the pre-detection method are around 0.85 and 0.9 when the user quantity is respectively set as 500 and 1000, the feasibility of the malicious user pre-detection method is also validated.

Acknowledgment. The research of authors is supported by the National Natural Science Foundation of China (NSFC) under Grant Grant No. 61672369, No. 61873177.

References

1. Du, Y., et al.: Bayesian co-clustering truth discovery for mobile crowd sensing systems. IEEE Trans. Ind. Inform. **16**(2), 1045–1057 (2020)
2. Ipeirotis, P.G., Provost, F., Wang, J.: Quality management on Amazon mechanical turk. In: Proceedings of ACM HCOMP, pp. 64–67 (2010)
3. Kantarci, B., Carr, K.G., Pearsall, C.D.: SONATA: social network assisted trustworthiness assurance in smart city crowdsensing. Int. J. Distrib. Syst. Technol. **7**(1), 59–78 (2016)
4. Li, Q., et al.: A confidence-aware approach for truth discovery on long-tail data. Proc. VLDB Endow. **8**(4), 425–436 (2014)
5. Li, Q., Li, Y., Gao, J., Zhao, B., Fan, W., Han, J.: Resolving conflicts in heterogeneous data by truth discovery and source reliability estimation. In: Proceedings of ACM SIGMOD, pp. 1187–1198 (2014)
6. Li, Y., et al.: A survey on truth discovery. ACM SIGKDD Explor. Newsl. **17**(2), 1–16 (2016)
7. Liu, Y., Kong, L., Chen, G.: Data-oriented mobile crowdsensing: a comprehensive survey. IEEE Commun. Surv. Tutorials **21**(3), 2849–2885 (2019)
8. Rabiner, L.R.: A tutorial on hidden Markov models and selected applications in speech recognition. Proc. IEEE **77**(2), 257–286 (1989)
9. Shi, F., Qin, Z., Wu, D., McCann, J.A.: Effective truth discovery and fair reward distribution for mobile crowdsensing. Perv. Mob. Comput. **51**, 88–103 (2018)
10. Talasila, M., Curtmola, R., Borcea, C.: Mobile crowd sensing. In: CRC Press Handbook of Sensor Networking: Advanced Technologies and Applications (2015)
11. Urcuqui, C., Navarro, A., Osorio, J., García, M.: Machine learning classifiers to detect malicious websites. CEUR Workshop Proc. **1950**, 14–17 (2017)
12. Wang, B., Kong, L., He, L., Wu, F., Yu, J., Chen, G.: I(TS, CS): detecting faulty location data in mobile crowdsensing. In: Proceedings of IEEE ICDCS, pp. 808–817 (2018)
13. Wang, G., Wang, T., Zheng, H., Zhao, B.Y.: Man vs. machine: practical adversarial detection of malicious crowdsourcing workers. In: Proceedings of USENIX Security, pp. 239–254 (2014)
14. Xuan, Y., Chen, Y., Li, H., Hui, P., Shi, L.: LBSNShield: malicious account detection in location-based social networks. In: Proceedings of ACM CSCW, pp. 437–440 (2016)
15. Yin, X., Han, J., Yu, P.S.: Truth discovery with multiple conflicting information providers on the web. IEEE Trans. Knowl. Data Eng. **20**(6), 796–808 (2008)
16. Zhao, B., Han, J.: A probabilistic model for estimating real-valued truth from conflicting sources. In: Proceedings of VLDB-QDB (2012)

Implementation of Video Transmission over Maritime Ad Hoc Network

Hua Xiao, Ying Wang$^{(\boxtimes)}$, Shulong Peng, and Bin Lin

College of Information and Science Technology, Dalian Maritime University,
Dalian 116026, China
wangying@dlmu.edu.cn

Abstract. Video data plays an important role in ship safety monitoring. However, the traditional maritime communication systems cannot meet the requirements of the video data transmission. Wireless Ad Hoc networks are considered as an important component of the heterogeneous maritime communication networks, and can provide a feasible solution to support broadband data transmission over the sea. This paper proposes a design of video transmission software for ship safety monitoring based on a maritime broadband wireless Ad Hoc network system. The hardware and protocol stack structures of the maritime broadband wireless Ad Hoc network system are introduced. Furthermore, the design principle and implementation method of the video transmission software are presented. The experiment results show that the implemented software can support multi-hop video transmission over the maritime Ad Hoc network.

Keywords: Maritime ad hoc networks · Video transmission · Embedded software design · Multithreading

1 Introduction

With the rapid development of maritime economy, the maritime activities become more and more frequent, and at the same time, the video communication over the sea has become an urgent requirement. The video communication plays an important role in many kinds of maritime applications [1]. For examples, the video monitoring on ships can provide strong evidence for maritime accident investigation, and the video monitoring of ships in key areas and engine rooms are conducive to the control of the maritime situation by the maritime administrations. However, most of the current maritime wireless communication systems are based on high frequency (HF), very high frequency (VHF) or satellite communications [2], such as fishery radio, ship Automatic Identification System (AIS), VHF Data Exchange System (VDES), and the Very Small Aperture Terminal (VSAT) communication system. The HF and VHF maritime communication systems are characterized by narrow bandwidth, low transmission rate, and are often used for broadcasting security-related information. While satellite communication systems can provide wide area coverage, and support voice, video, and Internet access services. Nevertheless, the high cost of satellite communication will limit its wide application in video transmission in the maritime communication

© Springer Nature Switzerland AG 2020
D. Yu et al. (Eds.): WASA 2020, LNCS 12384, pp. 520–528, 2020.
https://doi.org/10.1007/978-3-030-59016-1_43

networks. As a result, it is necessary to develop low cost, flexible wireless broadband communication networks for the maritime applications.

In recent years, some wireless broadband communication systems have been proposed for maritime applications. In [3, 4], a WiMAX-based maritime wireless mesh network is presented, that can operate on busy shipping lanes close to the coast. The wireless mesh network extends the terrestrial broadband network to the coastal waters by forming a wireless multi-hop network with fixed on shore stations, ships, ocean lighthouses and buoys. [5] introduces the BLUECOM+ project, which supports cost-effective broadband wireless communications at offshore areas by means of the communication technologies of GPRS/UMTS/LTE and Wi-Fi. The BLUECOM + system can perform multi-hop relaying communications based on the tethered balloons. [6] proposes a long-term evolution for maritime, i.e., LTE-Maritime, which is aimed to construct a maritime communication system to support the data rates in the order of megabits per second with a communication coverage of 100 km. A testbed is also introduced in [6] which is comprised of LTE-Maritime routers installed on ships, based stations located along the coast, and an operation center. However, in order to achieve a communication coverage of 100 km, the LTE-Maritime system needs to set up many base stations at high altitude mountains, which will make it difficult to maintain.

Wireless ad-hoc networks are independent of fixed infrastructure, and the corresponding wireless mobile devices can be dynamically organized into multi-hop networks by means of self-organizing network protocols. Wireless ad-hoc network technology provides a practical solution for low-cost and flexible broadband ship-to-shore and ship-to-ship data communication. Wireless ad-hoc network based maritime communication systems have been proposed in [7, 8]. [7] introduces the concept of Maritime ad-hoc network (MANET) for communications among ships or buoys, where the communication devices can form a network based on ad hoc network technology. [8] analyzed the multiple access and duplexing schemes for its proposed nautical ad-hoc network. It should be noted that both networks proposed in [7] and [8] are narrowband communication systems. In this paper, a video transmission software is designed for a maritime broadband ad-hoc network. The key equipment of the broadband maritime ad-hoc network is the wireless broadband router which is developed using a software defined radio platform, and the video transmission software is developed using Java language. The functions of the designed video transmission software are validated through extensive laboratory testing.

The structure of this paper is as follows. Section 2 briefly discusses the maritime broadband wireless ad-hoc network system. Section 3 gives the design principle and implementation method of the video transmission software. In Sect. 4, the function of video transmission software is verified by experiments. Section 5 concludes of this paper.

2 MANET Router

With the consideration of the mobility and independence of ships, the maritime broadband ad-hoc network system is built to support high-speed and high-reliable data transmission among ships. The maritime broadband ad-hoc network consists of ships equipped with the MANET routers. The core processor of the MANET router is the XC7Z020 chip of ZYNQ series, which has a dual-core structure integrated with programmable logic and CortexA9. The RF front-end system adopts the high performance, highly integrated radio frequency chip AD9361, which supports 70 MHz to 6 GHz full band communication.

The physical layer of the MANET router is based on the OFDM communication technology, and the corresponding physical layer software is implemented in the programmable logic part of the XC7Z020 chip to meet the low latency requirement. The main modulation modes include BPSK, QPSK, 16QAM, 64QAM, and the supported data rate are 6, 9, 12, 24, 36, 48, 54Mbps. Furthermore, the carrier frequency is set to be 1.4 GHz and the physical layer communication bandwidth can be selected as 5, 10, or 20 MHz according to the channel conditions.

The medium access control (MAC) protocol is the IEEE 802.11 distributed coordination function (DCF) which is a contention-based protocol and suitable for wireless multi-hop network communication scenarios. The IEEE 802.11 DCF is based on the Carrier Sense Access with Collision Avoidance (CSMA/CA) algorithm [9], and the MAC protocol software is implemented in the CortexA9 part of the XC7Z020 chip.

The network layer is responsible for finding an effective route to the destination node in the network. For the wireless broadband router, the Ad-hoc On Demand Distance Vector (AODV) routing protocol [10] is used at the network layer. The AODV is a kind of on demand routing protocol, and its routing discovery process is carried out only when there is no routing information for the destination in the routing table. As a result, AODV protocol is very suitable for the dynamic topology maritime networks. The software of ADOV protocol is implemented in the CortexA9 part of the XC7Z020 chip as well.

3   Design of Video Transmission Software

The video transmission software is developed by using Java language under the Eclipse developing environment, and runs on the user's device which may be a personal computer or an Android tablet. The user's device can connect to the MANET router via the Ethernet interface, and communicate with the desired destination user through the maritime ad-hoc network constructed by the MANET router. On the one hand, the mobility of the ships equipped with the wireless broadband routers will result in a time-varying network topology, which may lead to an increasing end-to-end transmission delay. On the other hand, the video applications are sensitive to transmission delay and jitter, and it is very important to consider the effect of queuing state of video data. With the consideration of the above challenges in video transmission over the maritime ad-hoc network, the video transmission software adopts a multi-thread synchronous design, which makes the receiving and sending states change in an orderly way, and sets up a corresponding signal flag bit to deal with the processing priority of different messages and received data. In addition, the circular queues are used to cache different types of data, such as video data, control information, to increase the real time performance of the software.

The function of the video transmission software is mainly divided into three modules, namely, man-machine interface module, text data communication module and video data communication module. These three function modules are further implemented by using five threads which include mainThread, txtServerThread, txtClientThead, videoServerThread and videoClientThead. The mainThread is used to construct the man-machine interface. The txtServerThread and txtClientThead are respectively the receiving and sending threads of the text information. The video-ServerThread and videoClientThead are the receiving and sending threads of the video data, respectively.

3.1 Man-Machine Interface Module

The man-machine interface module provides methods for users to access the video transmission system and control the operation of the video transmission system, and the flowchart of the man-machine interface module is shown in Fig. 1. First, the layout of the man-machine interface and component variables are initialized. Then, the required multithreads are created by implementing the runnable interface, and the txtServerThread, txtClientThead, videoServerThread and videoClientThead are realized by rewriting the run() method. Finally, the event listeners of the txtServerThread, txtClientThead, videoServerThread and videoClientThead are initialized and started to monitor the user's operation instructions so that the appropriate actions can be performed.

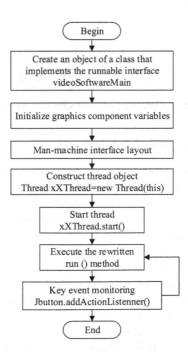

Fig. 1. Flow chart of man-machine interface module

The implemented man-machine interface of the software is shown in Fig. 2. The man-machine interface can be roughly divided into four display areas. The IP address of the corresponding MANET router, the address of the destination MANET router, routing information, and emergency information are displayed in the top left area. The lower left area is the text chat box. The right side area is used to display video, including video form the source node and the destination node, respectively. Through the graphical interface, users can setup the destination node and choose the type of communications which include audio and video communication, data text communication, and emergency information broadcast.

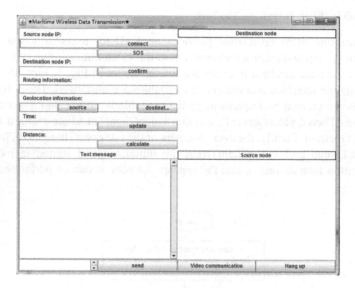

Fig. 2. Graphical interface of the video transmission software

3.2   Text Data Communication Module

The text data communication module is supported by the text data sending thread and receiving thread, which is used to exchange text information and control instructions between ship users.

At the source node, if the text data sending thread acquires any text message entered by the user via the graphical interface, then, it packages the input text message into packets, creates a Socket to bind the IP address and port number of the MANET router. Consequently, it sends the generated packets to the MANET router via a TCP connection established between the user device and the MANET router. If the TCP connection is interrupted, the Socket will be closed. The flowchart of the text message sending thread is shown in Fig. 3(a).

At the destination node, the text data receiving thread creates a ServerSocket and listens for connection request. If the MANET router wants to pass a received text packet to the video transmission software, it first establishes a TCP connection to the text data receiving thread, then passes the received text packet to the text data receiving

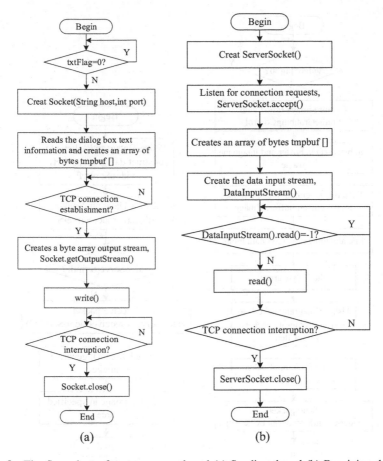

Fig. 3. The flow chart of text message thread (a) Sending thread (b) Receiving thread

thread through the read function. Then the text data receiving thread will process the text information and forward these text to the man-machine interface module for display. If the TCP connection is interrupted, the ServerSocket will be closed. The flowchart of the text data receiving thread is shown in Fig. 3(b).

3.3 Video Data Communication Module

The Java Media Framework (JMF) is utilized in the video data communication module. JMF is a Java class package which can be used to support multimedia applications, such as media capture, compression coding, playback and so on. The JPEG compression coding is used to reduce the amount of video data and improve the transmission efficiency. The JPEG compression coding technology can effectively compress the high frequency information, has been widely used in various Internet applications.

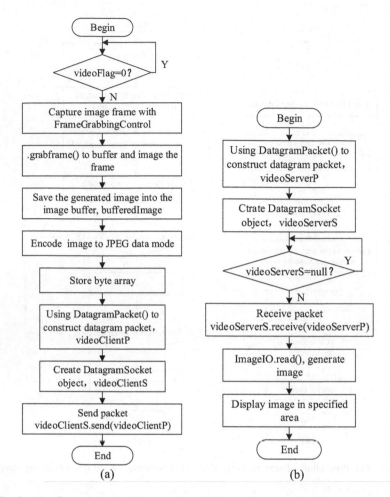

Fig. 4. The flow chart of video data thread (a) Sending thread (b) Receiving thread

The function of the video data communications is based on the video sending and receiving threads. The video sending and receiving threads can be used to realize the video data collection and process, and the video data exchange between user's device and the MANET router. At the source node, the video sending thread can control the camera to obtain the user's video data, and compress the collected video data into JPEG type data. Consequently, the video sending thread packages the compressed video data into packets for transmission. Finally, the data packet is sent to the MANET router based on the user datagram protocol (UDP) through the created DatagramSocket. The flowchart of the video data sending thread is shown in Fig. 4(a).

At the destination node, if the MANET router receives any video packet, it will pass the received video packet to the video receiving thread of the video transmission software via the UDP communication. The video receiving thread first decompresses and catches the video data, then, forwards the video data stored in the catch to the man-machine interface module for display in the graphical interface with a constant data rate. The video data receiving thread is shown in Fig. 4(b).

4   Experiment

In order to verify the function of the developed video transmission software, a two hop network communication system is set up as shown in Fig. 5. First, the executable configuration files for the data link layer and network layer software of the MANET router are generated under the Linux Xilinx SDK environment. Then, the configuration file for the physical layer parameters of the MANET router is created so that the MANET router can be set to operate with sampling frequency of 40 MHz, carrier frequency of 1.4 GHz, and time division duplex mode. The configuration files of the MANET router are copied to a TF card under the Linux operating system to control the operation of the MANET router.

Running the video transmission software on the PC, a connection between the PC and the MANET router can be established via the socket communication. Consequently, the text information and video data transmission experiments are conducted to verify the communication function of the video transmission software. The experiment results are shown in Fig. 5. In the experiment, the text data is reliably exchanged between the end users based the TCP protocol, and the video data can be transmitted with low latency based on the UDP protocol. The experiment results demonstrate that the developed video transmission software in this paper can achieve text and video data communications over the ad-hoc network constructed by the MANET routers.

Fig. 5. Schematic diagram of the function verification experiment

5   Conclusion

To meet the requirement for low-cost video transmissions in shore-to-ship and ship-to-ship communications, this paper implements a video transmission software for the MANET. Firstly, the hardware and network protocol structures of the MANET router are introduced. Then, the details of the implemented video transmission software are presented, including the design of the man-machine interface, text data communication and video data communication. The experiments for verifying the functions of the implemented video transmission software is carried out, and the experimental results demonstrate that the video transmission software developed in this paper is capable of supporting text and video communication based the MANET.

Acknowledgments. The work was supported by National Natural Science Foundation of China under 61971083 and 51939001 and Dalian Science and Technology Innovation Fund under 2019J11CY015.

References

1. Duan, R., Wang, J., Zhang, H., et al.: Joint multicast beamforming and relay design for maritime communication systems. In: IEEE Transactions on Green Communications and Networking, pp. 139–151. IEEE (2020)
2. Bekkadal, F.: Emerging maritime communications technologies. In: 2009 9th International Conference on Intelligent Transport Systems Telecommunications (ITST), pp. 358–363. IEEE (2009)
3. Zhou, M.T., Hoang, V.D., Harada, H., et al.: TRITON: high-speed maritime wireless mesh network. IEEE Wirel. Commun. **20**(5), 134–142 (2013)
4. Zhou, M.T., Harada, H., Wang, H.G., et al.: Multi-channel WiMAX mesh networking and its practice in sea. In: 2008 8th International Conference on ITS Telecommunications, pp. i–vi. IEEE (2008)
5. Campos, R., Oliveira, T., Cruz, N., et al.: BLUECOM+: cost-effective broadband communications at remote ocean areas. In: OCEANS 2016 - Shanghai, pp. 1–6. IEEE (2016)
6. Jo, S., Shim, W.: LTE-maritime: high-speed maritime wireless communication based on LTE technology. IEEE Access **7**, 53172–53181 (2019)
7. Laarhuis, J.H.: MaritimeManet: mobile ad-hoc networking at sea. In: 2010 International WaterSide Security Conference, pp. 1–6. IEEE (2010)
8. Kim, Y., Kim, J., Wang, Y., et al.: Application scenarios of nautical Ad-Hoc network for maritime communications. In: OCEANS 2009, pp. 1–4. IEEE (2009)
9. Santhameena, S., Adappa, S.A., Kumar, K.D., et al.: Implementation of unslotted and slotted CSMA/CA for 802.11 and 802.15.4 protocol. In: 2019 Global Conference for Advancement in Technology (GCAT), pp. 1–7. IEEE (2019)
10. Dorathy, P.E.I., Chandrasekaran, M.: Distance based dual path ad hoc on demand distance vector routing protocol for mobile ad hoc networks. In: 2017 4th International Conference on Advanced Computing and Communication Systems (ICACCS), pp. 1–6. IEEE (2017)

A Reliable Multi-task Allocation Based on Reverse Auction for Mobile Crowdsensing

Junlei Xiao[1,2], Peng Li[1,2(✉)], and Lei Nie[1,2]

[1] College of Computer Science and Technology,
Wuhan University of Science and Technology, Wuhan, Hubei, China
lipeng@wust.edu.cn
[2] Hubei Province Key Laboratory of Intelligent Information Processing
and Real-time Industrial System, Wuhan, Hubei, China

Abstract. Mobile crowdsensing (MCS) has been widely studied with the popularization of mobile intelligent devices, while a large number of sensing data can be obtained by using existing mobile devices. Multi-task allocation is an important problem for MCS. In this paper, we propose a highly reliable multi-task allocation (RMA) framework that considers the offline stage and online stage. In the offline stage, we propose a network flow model based on reverse auction, while adding the bid price compensation (BPC) strategy to ensure workers we recruit are reliable. In the online stage, we propose the asynchronous k-secretary strategy to achieve dynamic real-time recruitment of workers and prove the competitive ratio is $1/e^k$. Experimental results over the Rome taxi track data set show that our two-stage framework has better coverage and budget consumption, as well as good computational efficiency.

Keywords: Mobile crowdsensing · Multi-task allocation · Reverse auction · Asynchronous k-secretary

1 Introduction

With the emergence of sensor technology and mobile computing technology, people begin to study a new sensing paradigm: Mobile crowdsensing (MCS). Task assignment, as one of the key fields of mobile crowdsensing, has attracted wide attention. In this paper, we study a reliable assignment problem with a large number of tasks and workers in MCS. We divide the task assignment into offline and online stages to balance computing efficiency and coverage, as shown in Fig. 1. There are two main challenges: how to efficiently work out the selection problem for a large number of workers in the offline stage and how to solve the real-time recruitment problem in the online stage.

To deal with the two challenges above, we put forward a reliable multi-task allocation (RMA) framework that considers the offline and online stages. In the offline

P. Li—This work is partially supported by the NSF of China (No. 61802286), the Hubei Provincial Natural Science Foundation of China (No. 2018CFB424).

© Springer Nature Switzerland AG 2020
D. Yu et al. (Eds.): WASA 2020, LNCS 12384, pp. 529–541, 2020.
https://doi.org/10.1007/978-3-030-59016-1_44

stage, we first propose a reverse auction to obtain available bids from workers. Then, we construct a network flow model to match workers and tasks to minimize cost and maximize coverage. This achieves the simultaneous optimization of two objectives, which is another non-trivial challenge. Finally, we propose a bid price compensation (BPC) strategy to improve the selection priority of high-quality workers and reduce the selection priority of inferior workers, which will ensure that the workers we recruit are reliable. In the online stage, we assume that the distribution of all workers participation time is cyclic and can be obtained from historical data. Thus, we first estimate the number of all participating workers according to the time constraint. In this way, we can transform the online recruitment problem into a classic secretarial problem. In the task-centric assignment problem, the assignment of each task does not affect each other, so we propose a variant of the secretary problem: the asynchronous k-secretary problem, with the characteristics of fewer workers and fewer tasks in the online stage.

In summary, our contributions are summarized in the following:

- We consider two objective optimizations, minimizing platform payments and maximizing task coverage. We combine the reverse auction mechanism with the network flow model to effectively minimize cost and maximize coverage.
- We propose a reliable multi-task allocation (RMA) framework, which solves the problem of selecting suitable workers from a large number of bids in offline scenario and real-time recruitment of workers in online scenario. The bid price compensation (BPC) strategy is proposed to improve task completion in the offline stage. The asynchronous k-secretary strategy is proposed and the competitive ratio is proved to be $1/e^k$ in the online stage.
- We conduct extensive experiments on real data set to demonstrate the performance of our proposed algorithms.

2   Related Work

MCS is a new sensing paradigm, which uses mobile devices embedded with abundant sensors to complete various sensing tasks [4]. The task assignment

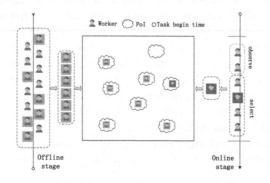

Fig. 1. An example of two stage task assignment in MCS.

is an important part of MCS. Tao *et al.* [7] proposed a genetic algorithm to maximize data quality, and then proposed a detection algorithm to maximize the benefits of workers. Gong *et al.* [3] studied online task allocation and path planning under the constraint of moving distance to maximize the total task quality. However, most of the existing task assignment problems focused on single-object optimization. In practice, it is often necessary to optimize more than one goal, such as quality, coverage, cost, and so on. In [6,10], they proposed the network flow model to achieve dual-objective simultaneous optimization. But they listed all possible task sets to get all the possible task sets, in which the combination explosion would occur when the number of tasks increases. We combine the reverse auction with network flow to achieve dual objectives simultaneously optimized and efficient computation.

In [5,8,9], they proposed a user recruitment algorithm based on the semi-Markov model. They solved the task assignment problem in the offline stage. In [11,12], they predicted the probability of users reaching each task by the inhomogeneous Poisson process model to achieve the offline phase of user recruitment. In [2,13], they studied the online incentive mechanism and worker selection under budget constraints. However, these works focus on online or offline for MCS. For the offline prediction mode, task coverage is often lower than the online stage. Furthermore, online real-time recruitment requires timely recruitment decisions, so computational efficiency is a major challenge. To balance task coverage and computational efficiency, we propose a reliable task allocation framework, considering the offline stage and the online stage. The offline stage deals with the allocation of most tasks and workers, while the online stage deals with the allocation of a small number of remaining workers and tasks.

3   System Description and Problem Definition

3.1   System Description

In the MCS system, there are some tasks in each point of interest (PoI), defined as $P = \{p_1, p_2, ..., p_n\}$, where p_i denotes the i-th task. We assume all possible workers have registered as candidate workers, denoted by the set $W = \{w_1, w_2, ..., w_m\}$, where w_j denotes the j-th worker. These workers are willing to receive task push from the platform and participate in sensing tasks according to their actual conditions. In this paper, the two-stage task assignment model is proposed, which considers the task assignment of online scenario and offline scenario, respectively.

In the offline scenario, we assume that there are sufficient time and workers. Then, we combine the reverse auction mechanism with the network flow model. In this strategy, we recruit as many qualified workers as possible and assign corresponding tasks. Due to the high mobility of these workers, to ensure the completion of the task, we set q workers to be recruited for each task. In the online scenario, recruitment between tasks does not affect each other. We propose an asynchronous k-secretary strategy, which needs to know the number of workers who participate in advance, and we only need to know the probability of workers arriving at each task, not the specific moving behavior. Therefore, we can use the inhomogeneous Poisson process model to predict the vector M of the number of workers connecting each task in the online scenario.

3.2   Reverse Auction Model

Based on the reverse auction mechanism, we use the network flow model to select the winner. The specific implementation steps are as follows:

1) Task distribution: The platform publishes tasks to all candidate workers.
2) Bid submission: Each candidate worker w_j submits the bid pair $B_j = (b_j, P_j)$ according to his/her mobile trajectory, where $P_j(P_j \subseteq P)$ is the subset of tasks reported by worker w_j, and b_j is the set of bid prices. That is the price at which worker w_j is willing to participate in the sensing service.
3) Bid price compensation: We propose the BPC strategy to improve the probability of reliable workers who are selected based on the worker's reputation. The BCP is not a reward to the worker but rather represents the priority of workers to be selected. The network flow model greedily selects the least expensive augmented path in each round of selection. The higher the worker's credit is, the higher the priority is. And the lower the cost is, the higher the priority is. So we set a lower compensation to the worker with a higher reputation. Conversely, we set a higher compensation to the worker with a lower reputation. BPC and reputation are inversely proportional. We next employ the bid price update function as follows:

$$b'_{i,j} = b_{i,j} + \rho/R_j, \tag{1}$$

where $b_{i,j}$ is the bid price submitted by worker w_j for task p_i, $b'_{i,j}$ is a new bid price after BPC, which represents the cost of the edge between the worker node and the task node in the network flow, ρ is the inverse proportional coefficient, R represents the set of workers' reputation and R_j is the reputation of worker w_j.

4) Winner selection: We select the optimal user in each round of the network flow.
5) Upload data: The winner uploads the sensing data to the platform.
6) Payment: The platform pays workers who complete tasks.

3.3   Problem Formulation

The problem of platform-centered task allocation is to maximize the utility of the platform in MCS. We define the utility of the platform as formula 2.

$$U = \sum_{p_i \in P} V_i - C_i \tag{2}$$

Where V_i and C_i represent the task value and cost of task P_i, respectively. We assume the value of each task after being completed is a fixed value of η, and if it is not completed, the value is 0. Therefore, this paper focuses on how to maximize coverage and minimize cost. We divide the task assignment problem into two stages.

Offline Stage: Since the offline phase has sufficient time and workers, there is enough time to get more users' bids. Then, the objective is to maximize the coverage and minimize the cost. We denote $\mathbb{W}$ and $\mathbb{P}$ as the worker set and the task set that has been assigned. $C(\mathbb{W}, \mathbb{P})$ represents the cost of completing the allocation of worker set $\mathbb{W}$ and task set $\mathbb{P}$, respectively. So, the offline stage of the optimization problem can be formalized as follows:

$$\begin{cases} maximize & |\mathbb{P}| \\ minimize & C(\mathbb{W}, \mathbb{P}) \end{cases} \tag{3}$$

Subject to: $\mathbb{W} \subseteq W, C(\mathbb{W}, p_i) < \eta$.

Where $C(\mathbb{W}, p_i) < \eta$ describes the cost of each task must not exceed its value η.

Online Stage: In the actual situation, the offline phase cannot complete the assignment of all tasks, so we propose the task assignment problem in the online scenario as a compliment. Then, the objective of the online stage can be formalized as follows:

$$minimize \quad |P \backslash \mathbb{P}| \tag{4}$$

subject to: $T^b < t < T^e$.

Where $P \backslash \mathbb{P}$ is the set of tasks that have not been assigned during the offline stage. T^b and T^e represent beginning time and end time, respectively.

4   Offline Task Allocation

4.1   RA-MCMF Algorithm

The flow network is a directed graph, where each edge has the cost, capacity, and flow. The capacity of an edge represents the maximum flow allowed by the edge. In the construction of network flow, it plays a crucial role to determine which tasks that workers can complete. We use the reverse auction to get these task sets. The network flow model based on reverse auction is composed of four layers of nodes: the original node, worker nodes, task nodes, and the sink node, as shown in Fig. 2. The original node and sink node represent the start and end of the flow network, respectively. For the edge between the original node and the worker node, the capacity of each edge is set as n, indicating the worker can complete all tasks, and the cost is 0. There is an edge between the worker node and the task node, which means that the worker can complete the task in the corresponding task. Note that the capacity of this edge is 1, and the cost is the new bid price $b'_{i,j}$ of the worker w_j for task p_i after BPC. For the edge between the worker node and the sink node, the capacity of each edge is q, indicating that each task needs to recruit q workers to ensure the quality of task completion, and the cost is 0. The pseudocode is presented in Algorithm 1.

Algorithm 1. RA-MCMF algorithm

Input: $W, P, B = \cup_{w_j \in W} B_j, R$
Output: $\mathbb{W}, \mathbb{P}$

1: Initialize $B' \leftarrow \emptyset$
2: **for** each bid $B_j \in B$ **do**
3:    **for** each bid price $b_{i,j} \in b_j$ **do**
4:        $b'_{i,j} = b_{i,j} + \rho/R_j$
5:    $B'_j \leftarrow (b'_j, P_j)$
6: Construct the flow network $G = (E, N, F, C)$;
7: Initialize flow f to 0
8: **while** the residual network exists an augmenting path **do**
9:    Choose the augmenting path $p*$ with minimum cost by BFS ;
10:    Add worker and the corresponding set of task in the path $p*$ to $\mathbb{W}$ and $\mathbb{P}$, respectively;
11:    $cf(p^*) = 1$;
12:    Update the residual network with $cf(p^*)$;
13: **return** $\mathbb{W}, \mathbb{P}$

The RA-MCMF algorithm consists of two stages: the first stage is to build a reverse auction-based network flow model (see line 1–6). The second stage is to find the optimal task assignment scheme in the network (see line 7–12). The platform broadcasts information about the tasks to all candidate workers, who bid to the platform based on their next stage of movement and their equipment consumption. Then, the bid price of workers is updated by the BPC strategy as the cost of the edge between the worker nodes and the task nodes in the network flow model. Based on the results obtained from the reverse auction and the updated results, we build a flow network $G = (E, N, F, C)$, where E represents the set of edges, N represents the set of nodes, F represents the capacity of each edge and C represents the cost of each edge. We greedily select the augmenting path p^* with the minimum cost in the residual network. Then, we add the worker and the corresponding set of tasks in the path p^* to $\mathbb{W}$ and $\mathbb{P}$, respectively. Finally, we update the residual network with $cf(p*)$. Repeating these operations until the residual network does not have an augmenting path.

4.2   Algorithm Complexity Analysis

We first analyze the time complexity of the proposed algorithm and then compare it with the previous method. The bid submitted by each worker contains a maximum of n tasks, that is, all tasks. So the time complexity of the BPC stage is $o(mn)$. And the time complexity of finding the least expensive augmented path by BFS is $o((m + n + 2)^2)$. Therefore, the overall time complexity of RA-MCMF is $o(mn) + o((m + n + 2)^2)$. The time complexity of the network flow algorithm proposed by Liu et al. [6] is $o(mC_n^q q^3) + o(mq(m + n + C_n^q))$, where q is defined as the number of tasks that each worker can complete. Usually, $q \ll n$ and $q > 1$. So $C_q^n = \frac{n!}{(n-q)! * q}$ will explode as n grows. In general, n and m

are larger numbers, so the time complexity of our algorithm is better, namely:
$o(mn) + o((m + n + 2)^2) < o(mC_n^q q^3) + o(mq(m + n + C_n^q))$.

4.3   Performance Analysis

Theorem 1. *The reverse auction-based offline task allocation mechanism is individually rational.*

Proof. For every worker who bids, if he is not selected, his utility to the platform is zero, and the platform pays him zero. If a worker is selected, then $b_{i,j} < \eta(\forall b_{i,j} \in b_j)$. And each worker's bid is based on his actual situation to ensure the compensation he receives can cover his losses. Therefore, the offline task allocation mechanism based on the reverse auction satisfies individual rationality.

Theorem 2. *The reverse auction-based offline task allocation mechanism is truthful.*

Proof. We first show that the task allocation mechanism is monotone. We suppose that the worker w_j becomes the winner in iteration and the winning price is $b_{i,j}$ for task P_i. While the worker w_j gives a lower price $\widehat{b_{i,j}}$, where $\widehat{b_{i,j}} < b_{i,j}$, so $\widehat{b_{i,j}} + \frac{\rho}{R_j} < b_{i,j} + \frac{\rho}{R_j}$. It means our task allocation mechanism will choose a lower bid, so the offline task allocation mechanism satisfies monotony. Then, we prove that the bid price of the winner in each round is critical. The worker w_j wins the bid $b_{i,j}$. If his bid price is higher than this price, it means the platform will pay a higher price, so the worker who bids higher than this price will not win. So the winner's bid price is critical. Therefore, the offline scenario task allocation mechanism based on reverse auctions is truthful.

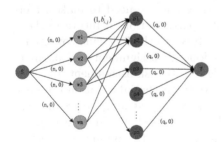

Fig. 2. Network flow model.

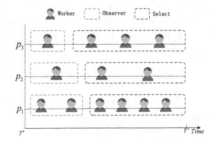

Fig. 3. Asynchronous k-secretary strategy.

5 Online Task Allocation

5.1 Mobility Prediction Model

The historical track of workers is used to predict the distribution of workers at the online stage. Similar to [10,11], we assume the probability of users reaching tasks obeys the inhomogeneous Poisson process. By this model, we can ignore the workers' historical moving process and focus on what tasks that workers have accomplished. We count the average number of connections by each worker w_j at each task p_i, where $p_i \in P \backslash \mathbb{P}$, which is denoted as $\lambda_{i,j}$. For example, setting the sensing period as one day. The probability of worker w_j connecting to task p_i for h times during a specific day can be modeled as:

$$\varphi_{i,j}(h) = \lambda_{i,j}^h * e^{-\lambda_{i,j}} / h! \tag{5}$$

Hence, the probability of worker w_j connecting task p_i at least once during a day can be estimated as follows:

$$Q_{i,j} = \sum_{h=1}^{\infty} \varphi_{i,j}(h) = 1 - e^{-\lambda_{i,j}} \tag{6}$$

Thus, we predict the probability of a worker w_j completing task p_i as follows:

$$Pr_{i,j} = 1 - e^{-\lambda_{i,j}} \tag{7}$$

Then, we can predict the number of workers arriving at each task $p_i (p_i \in P \backslash \mathbb{P})$ vector $M = [m_1, m_2, \cdots, m_v]$, where $v = |P \backslash \mathbb{P}|$.

5.2 Online Algorithm

In an online scenario, workers arrive in real-time and we need to make timely decisions (choose/reject) without knowing the participation of future workers. The task assignment in online stage shall be subject to the following conditions: 1) once the task is assigned, it cannot be undone; 2) assignment and payment decisions must be made before the workers leave; 3) task assignment and payments must be calculated online and depend only on the information obtained so far. Then, we propose the asynchronous k-secretary strategy to realize the online multi-task assignment. The detailed algorithm is shown in Algorithm 2.

We model the task assignment for task-centric in the online scenario, in which each task is independent. Workers choose tasks according to their travel paths, and they will not change or delay their journey because of the execution of tasks. Therefore, when a worker is assigned to a task, his/her subsequent journey will not be affected. The assignment of each task is done simultaneously and independently, so we can consider the assignment of each task problem separately, which we call the asynchronous assignment of multiple tasks. Then we propose the asynchronous k-secretary strategy, as shown in Fig. 3. This strategy recruits an optimal worker for each task. Then, we turn each task assignment problem into a single secretary recruitment problem. Therefore, an observation area is set for each task, and we recruit workers outside the observation area. Once the worker who is better than the optimal worker in the observation area shows up, we recruit him/her, immediately.

5.3   Performance Analysis

Theorem 3. *Online task allocation problem under time constraint is NP-hard.*

Proof. The purpose of the task assignment is to ensure that each task in the task set $P'(\cup_{\forall p_i \in P'} p_i \in P\backslash\mathbb{P})$ is covered by one worker. We need to choose a group of workers who can cover the task set $S = \{P^{w_1}, P^{w_2}, ..., P^{w_k}\}$ from the candidate worker set $W'(\cup_{\forall w_j \in W'} w_j \in W\backslash\mathbb{W})$ to make sure it can cover the task set P', where P^{w_j} is the set that the worker w_j can cover. This is a classic NP-hard problem, Max-k-cover [1]: there is a set S, and F is a subset of the set S. The problem of selecting k subsets of F to ensure that the elements in S are selected at least once is NP-hard. Therefore, the online task assignment problem under the time constraint is a special NP-hard problem.

Theorem 4. *The asynchronous k-secretary strategy can be implemented approximately by $1/e^k$.*

Algorithm 2. Asynchronous k-secretary algorithm

Input: P, W, $\mathbb{W}$, $\mathbb{P}$
Output: $\mathbb{P}$, $\mathbb{W}$
1: Initialize $r = [0], \varepsilon = [0], W' = W\backslash\mathbb{W}, P' = P\backslash\mathbb{P}$
2: Estimate for the probability of each worker completing each task;
3: Estimate vector M for the number of workers arriving in each task;
4: **while** $P' \neq \emptyset$ **do**
5:     **if** $currentTime \geq T^e$ **then**
6:         break;
7:     Waiting for the next user w_j coming for p_i, $w_j \in W'$, $p_i \in P'$;
8:     Calculate the credit R_j of worker w_j;
9:     $r[i] + +$;
10:    **if** $r[i] \leq M[i]/e$ **then**
11:        $\varepsilon[i] = min\{\varepsilon[i], R_j\}$;
12:    **else if** $R_j > \varepsilon[i]$ **then**
13:        $\mathbb{P} \leftarrow \mathbb{P} \cup p_i$, $\mathbb{W} \leftarrow \mathbb{W} \cup w_j$
14:        $P' \leftarrow P' \setminus p_i$
15: **return** $\mathbb{P}$, $\mathbb{W}$

Proof. The asynchronous k-secretary problem proposed in the online stage divides the task allocation process into k separate threads. Threads do not interact with each other. In other words, the worker is allocated at a certain time, and the worker can be recruited by other tasks in the following time. In [1], they have proven that the approximate ratio of single secretary recruitment is $1/e$, so the approximate ratio of the optimal workers assigned to k tasks is $1/e^k$.

6   Performance Evaluation

6.1   Data Sets and Setting

Based on the real data set of Rome taxi trace, we evaluate the performance of our algorithms. The trace contains the tracks of 320 taxis in February 2014, as shown in Fig. 4. We set February 28 as the sensing cycle. For the offline algorithm, task assignment results should be obtained before February 28. For the prediction algorithm, the trajectory from February 1 to February 27 is taken as the historical data to predict the probability of workers connecting tasks online. The radius of tasks is set at r. We suppose that once workers reach the area of the task, they can complete the corresponding tasks. Ignoring the time it takes to execute the task. We assume all of these taxis are candidates for the MCS platform.

Fig. 4. The taxi trace of Rome.

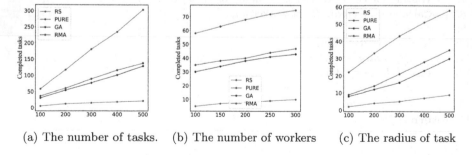

(a) The number of tasks.   (b) The number of workers   (c) The radius of task

Fig. 5. The completion of the task under the circumstances of different number of tasks, number of workers and radius of task, respectively.

6.2   Comparison Algorithms and Metrics

We evaluate the performance of our solution by the metrics of the number of tasks completed, the cost paid, and the running time. We compare the performance of our proposed algorithms with the following algorithms:

RS, Randomly Selects (RS) workers as recruiters until the budget is used up.
PURE, Prediction-based User Recruitment for mobile crowdsEnsing (PURE) [8]. Complete the assignment in the offline phase according to the workers historical movement.
GA, Genetic Algorithm (GA) [7] is an evolutionary computing technique inspired by natural selection in biological evolution. The GA evolves iteratively from the initial generation to the optimal solution.

6.3   Evaluation Results

The task coverage is an important indicator of the task assignment algorithm in MCS. We compare the task coverage of algorithms mentioned above under different numbers of tasks, the number of workers, and the radius of the task, as shown in Fig. 5. We change the number of tasks from 100 to 500, the number of workers from 100 to 300, and the radius of task from 100 to 500, while keeping other parameters fixed. It can be seen from the experimental results that our proposed algorithms have a better performance than others. Specifically, with the increase in the number of tasks, the number of workers, and the radius of tasks, the number of tasks completed is also increasing. RMA and PURE outperform GA since the RMA not only employs a reverse auction mechanism with high authenticity in offline but also uses the asynchronous k-secretary strategy with a high approximation ratio in online. Furthermore, we can get that the growth rate of task completion over task number and task radius is greater than workers. This is because different task number and task radius directly affect whether workers can participate in the task. However, tasks that have already been assigned are not affected by new workers, so more workers do not have a significant improvement for task completion.

Budget consumption is another important indicator of the algorithm. We set the budget from 500 to 2000 and compare the budget consumption of four algorithms under different budgets, as shown in Fig. 6. The budget consumption of four algorithms is almost exhausted at 500 and 1000, owing to the budget having been used up, but the tasks and workers still have a surplus. After the budget exceeds 1500, all possible matches have been completed by the RMA algorithm. And the GA reaches the maximum generations. The deadline is budget used up for the PURE and RA. Obviously, the budget consumption of our algorithm is at a better level.

We further compare the running time of the algorithms, as shown in Fig. 7. Note that the MT-MCMF algorithm is based on the network flow model in [6]. We compare the running time when the number of tasks increases (from 10 to 18). The results of RA-MCMF, PURE, and GA are obtained in a short time.

And the running time of MT-MCMF increases sharply with tasks increased. The computational efficiency of our improved algorithms is greatly improved compared with MT-MCMF. Note that we don't take bidding time into account within running time.

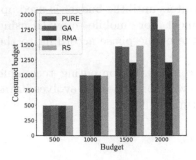
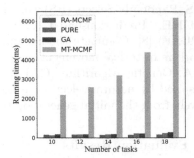

Fig. 6. Consumed budget under different budget.

Fig. 7. Performance comparison under different number of tasks.

7 Conclusion

In this paper, we propose a reliable task allocation framework, considering the offline and online stages of MCS, to balance computing efficiency and coverage. In the offline stage, the network flow model is combined with the reverse auction to reduce the computational complexity and achieve the simultaneous optimization of two objectives. Then, we come up with a BPC strategy to ensure that the worker recruited is reliable. In the online stage, workers participate in real-time, and we make timely decisions. We use the inhomogeneous Poisson process to predict the number of workers connected to tasks, then the asynchronous k-secretary strategy is used to recruit an optimal worker for each task. Furthermore, we prove the problem is NP-hard and our proposed strategy can achieve an approximate ratio of $1/e^k$. Finally, the experimental results based on the Rome taxi track data set show that our experiment has better performance.

References

1. Feige, U.: A threshold of ln n for approximating set cover. J. ACM **45**(4), 634–652 (1998)
2. Gao, H., Liu, C.H., Tang, J., Yang, D., Hui, P., Wang, W.: Online quality-aware incentive mechanism for mobile crowd sensing with extra bonus. IEEE Trans. Mob. Comput. **18**(11), 2589–2603 (2018)
3. Li, C., Zhang, B., Gong, W.: Location-based online task assignment and path planning for mobile crowdsensing. IEEE Trans. Veh. Technol. **68**(2), 1772–1783 (2018)

4. Liu, J., Shen, H., Narman, H.S., Chung, W., Lin, Z.: A survey of mobile crowd-sensing techniques: a critical component for the Internet of Things. ACM Trans. Cyber.-Phys. Syst. **2**(3), 1–26 (2018). Article no. 18

5. Liu, W., Yang, Y., Wang, E., Wu, J.: User recruitment for enhancing data inference accuracy in sparse mobile crowdsensing. IEEE Internet Things J. **7**(3), 1802–1814 (2020)

6. Liu, Y., Guo, B., Wang, Y., Wu, W., Yu, Z., Zhang, D.: TaskMe: multi-task allocation in mobile crowd sensing. In: Proceedings of the 2016 ACM International Joint Conference on Pervasive and Ubiquitous Computing, UbiComp 2016, pp. 403–414. Association for Computing Machinery, New York (2016)

7. Tao, X., Song, W.: Location-dependent task allocation for mobile crowdsensing with clustering effect. IEEE Internet Things J. **6**(1), 1029–1045 (2019)

8. Wang, E., Yang, Y., Jie, W., Liu, W., Wang, X.: An efficient prediction-based user recruitment for mobile crowdsensing. IEEE Trans. Mob. Comput. **17**(1), 16–28 (2018)

9. Wang, E., Yang, Y., Wu, J., Lou, K., Luan, D., Wang, H.: User recruitment system for efficient photo collection in mobile crowdsensing. IEEE Trans. Hum.-Mach. Syst. **50**(1), 1–12 (2020)

10. Wang, J., et al.: HyTasker: hybrid task allocation in mobile crowd sensing. IEEE Trans. Mob. Comput. **19**(3), 598–611 (2020)

11. Wang, J., Wang, F., Wang, Y., Zhang, D., Wang, L., Qiu, Z.: Social-network-assisted worker recruitment in mobile crowd sensing. IEEE Trans. Mob. Comput. **18**(7), 1661–1673 (2019)

12. Wang, L., Yu, Z., Zhang, D., Guo, B., Liu, C.H.: Heterogeneous multi-task assignment in mobile crowdsensing using spatiotemporal correlation. IEEE Trans. Mob. Comput. **18**(1), 84–97 (2019)

13. Zhou, R., Li, Z., Wu, C.: A truthful online mechanism for location-aware tasks in mobile crowd sensing. IEEE Trans. Mob. Comput. **17**(8), 1737–1749 (2018)

A Blockchain Based Privacy-Preserving Cloud Service Level Agreement Auditing Scheme

Ke Xiao[1,2], Ziye Geng[1], Yunhua He[1(✉)], Gang Xu[1], Chao Wang[1], and Wei Cheng[2]

[1] North China University of Technology, Beijing 100144, China
heyunhua@ncut.edu.cn
[2] University of Washington, Tacoma 98402, USA

Abstract. Cloud computing can provide on-demand resource services for customers, but also faces server downtime and security issues. The cloud Service Level Agreement (SLA), as a compensation agreement between customers and service providers, has some problems such as non active execution, disputes and infringement. Existing SLA monitoring solutions either lack multi-party trust, have weak audit ability, or have privacy issue. To address the above problems, a blockchain-based cloud SLA violation monitoring and auditing model is proposed. This model provides multi-party trust through blockchain, ensures data authenticity by a dual monitoring method and keeps monitoring result securely stored on the blockchain by appling trapdoor order revealing encryption algorithm (TORE). Besides, a smart contract is designed to automatically perform auditing tasks to ensure credible violation judgment and privacy preserving. At last, some punishment strategies for violations are introduced, which can distribute compensation or change user's reputation with smart contracts. With experiments, we exam the cost of the blockchain-based system and demonstrate the feasibility of our proposed model.

Keywords: SLA · Cloud service · Blockchain · Violation auditing · Privacy-preserving

1 Introduction

Cloud computing, as the representative technology of the third information wave, has brought profound industrial changes. Customer can easily obtain scalable and on-demand cloud services offered by cloud service provider which can economize time and other resources. However, the cloud service model may face server downtime and security issues. The disruption of AWS cloud service affected the service quality of Spotify, Dropbox and Trello in 2017 and the operation of Atlassian, Twilio and Slack which were relying on AWS in 2018. The downtime of Alibaba cloud servers led to the unavailability of core business. The failure of Tencent cloud services caused the loss of stored data can not to be recovered.

© Springer Nature Switzerland AG 2020
D. Yu et al. (Eds.): WASA 2020, LNCS 12384, pp. 542–554, 2020.
https://doi.org/10.1007/978-3-030-59016-1_45

The cloud Service Level Agreements (SLA) has been proposed to solve this problem. The cloud SLA is an agreement between customers and providers, which includes a description of the negotiated service, the requirements of service quality and the compensation for violations. However, SLA may not perform automatically by cloud servers, which may require customers to submit compensation claims within one month. In addition, there are a lot of compensation disputes. In 2018, Frontier CNC company disagreed with the compensation solution of Tencent cloud, and it proposed compensation amount of 11.016 million which was nearly 81 times of Tencent's. In 2015, Alibaba was sued to the court by Locojoy company for constituting a joint infringement. Thus, it is necessity to design SLA monitoring and auditing scheme to ensure SLA enforcement.

In traditional SLA monitoring scheme, the SLA monitoring tasks are completed by service providers [4]. Customers can only trust the violation report provided by service providers, however, the providers may tamper with the report. Then, some researchers introduced a trusted platform module (TPM) [12] or a third party auditors (TPA) [15] to monitor service and prevent service provider from cheating. However, the fully trusted third party doesn't exist in practice and it may cheat for benefits. Some multi-party monitoring schemes based on reputation mechanism [6] or reasoning techniques [10] are proposed to improve SLA monitoring by collecting and inferring information from different SLA parameters. However, it is difficult to establish a trust relationship between multiple parties, and either party may provide false data. Blockchain brings new opportunities, it is a distributed ledger [7] which can establish trust relationship between multiple parties and provide a trustful platform for SLA monitoring and auditing [8,13]. In the blockchain based SLA auditing scheme, all witnesses which are selected from the blockchain network nodes can detect violation and report credible feedback cooperatively [14]. However, the ability of witness is limited and user's privacy may be disclosed due to the openness and transparency of blockchain.

Since order preserving encryption(OPE) [1] can ensure that the sort order of ciphertexts is consistent with the corresponding plaintext sorting order, it is considered as one of the feasible solutions to solve the privacy leakage problem in SLA monitoring and audit. However, Naveed et al. [9] proved that databases encrypted by OPE are extremely vulnerable to "inference attacks". The order-revealing encryption (ORE) as an improved OPE has been proposed [2]. The plaintext comparison result can be judged by ciphertext and corresponding indexes in the ORE scheme [3]. However, the indexes of the first bit of two encrypted data are different which may leak information in this scheme. Lewi et al. [5] proposed a trapdoor order-revealing encryption scheme (TORE) which disclosures less sequential information and provide stronger data security.

We propose a blockchain-based cloud SLA violation monitoring and auditing model. In this model, a dual monitoring method is used to ensure data authenticity by comparing the parameters of services collected by customers and service providers. All the monitoring data will be recorded on the blockchain to ensure that the data cannot be tampered. A SLA audit smart contract is also designed to record the requirements of service quality under negotiations between customers and service providers. It can also automatically execute audit task, such as comparing monitoring parameters and distributing compensation. In addition, as the data recorded on the blockchain is public and transparent, TORE algorithm is applied to encrypt monitored data, which ensures that the query and comparison operations involving data can be carried out efficiently in ciphertext space to protect the privacy and data security of customers. At last, some punishment strategies are designed to punish the offending party in order to reduce violations. The contributions of this paper are summarized as follows:

- We present a blockchain-based cloud SLA monitoring and auditing model, which adopts the dual monitoring method to ensure the authenticity of the various customized monitoring data and the blockchain to ensure the immutability of the stored data.
- We introduce the TORE algorithm to audit task and design a SLA audit smart contract to perform audit tasks automatically, which realizes the ciphertext comparison on the blockchain and ensures data security during the whole auditing process.
- We evaluate the cost of SLA audit smart contract and TORE based privacy protection mechanism which demonstrates the feasibility of our proposed model.

The remainder of the paper is organized as the follows. Section 2 presents the cloud SLA violations monitoring and auditing model, with Sect. 3 detailing the key techniques of the model. Section 4 conducts the performance evaluation of the proposed model. At last, the paper is concluded in Sect. 5.

2   Smart Contract Based Cloud SLA Violations Monitoring and Auditing Model

In this section, we elaborate the details of the blockchain-based system model, the audit model and the corresponding threat model. Figure 1 illustrates the overall blockchain system architecture for cloud SLA violations monitoring and auditing.

In order to keep the authenticity of data, our system adopts the dual monitoring method provided by consumers and service providers. Both sides monitor the services in real time, and the monitoring parameters will be recorded in the blockchain after encryptions. We define a new data format called *ServPara* to ensure that the monitoring parameters have the same specification and format. Our scheme can monitor multiple parameters, and all the fields in the data structure of *ServPara* can be customized or extended according to users' service requirements, as shown in Table 1. A SLA audit smart contract is implemented to execute audit tasks. Once violations happen, the SLA audit smart contract will be triggered to compare the monitoring data and audit data. Then the smart contract automatically distributes rewards or gives compensation to customers, with the reputations of customers updated.

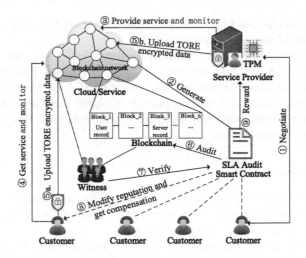

Fig. 1. System architecture for cloud SLA audit model

Table 1. *ServPara* description

Parameter notation	Description
Service Provider ID	The ID of the cloud service provider
CPU Capacity	CPU utilization
Network Capacity	Throughput, latency times
Storage Capacity	Disk space size
System Availability	SLA execution times, service times
Number of VMs	Number of provided virtual machines
Performance	Percentage of uptime

2.1 Blockchain-Based System

This cloud SLA violation monitoring and auditing system is based on blockchain which is regarded as a trustful platform. The blockchain network is used to record the monitoring data from customers and service providers. The cloud network is composed of cloud nodes, any cloud node who has own wallet address can be registered as a node in the blockchain. These nodes consist the blockchain network and can interact with customers and service providers.

Any transaction initiated by users in the blockchain network will be broadcasted and verified by miners in the blockchain network. The consensus protocol of blockchain can guarantee the security and consistency of transactions. Once the transaction passes verifications, it will be permanently recorded into the blockchain and spread throughout the network which cannot be tampered. In order to monitor and verify the transaction on the blockchain, some miners in the blockchain will be selected as witnesses to finish verification tasks. The selection of witness can be executed by a witness smart contract to ensure unbiasedness and randomness of the selection process [14].

In this system, when the monitoring data has been uploaded to the blockchain, the SLA audit smart contract will be triggered to finish auditing tasks. This smart contract is designed according to SLA requirements and it can interact with customers and service providers. After auditing, the SLA audit smart contract will automatically generate a transaction to distribute rewards and update users' reputations.

2.2   Audit Model

The core of the model is violations audit by comparing the monitoring data from customers and service providers. Therefore, the audit model is one of the most important part, which is described as follows.

On the side of service providers, we install a TPM (Trusted Platform Module) to prevent service providers from submitting a fake violation report. The service parameters are monitored by TPM instead of service providers himself to provide relatively reliable monitoring data $ServPara\_p$. In order to keep security of the monitoring parameters, $ServPara\_p$ will be encrypted by TORE. Then, the ciphertext will be uploaded to the blockchain, and the service provider's data will be finally recorded into a block. In the monitoring phase, the credibility of data can be achieved by TPM. The security of data is guaranteed by TORE algorithm in the transmission phase. The data recorded on the blockchain is also credible, since the blockchain can record provider's behaviors and data, which cannot be tampered.

However, the data monitored by TPM is not entirely credible, and it may be out of order. Therefore, customers also keep monitoring service parameters. Similar to the service provider side, $ServPara\_c$ monitored by customers is also encrypted by TORE, and then the corresponding ciphertexts are uploaded to the blockchain. In order to maintain the credibility of the whole auditing process, the SLA audit smart contract extracts ciphertexts of the two sides first, and then compares them by decrypting. If the monitoring data of both sides are equal, it proves that the true monitoring data is recorded. Then, actual monitoring data will be compared with the standard values of service parameters, to determine whether the service conforms to the SLA standard. During this process, the smart contract will judge the fault party, and some punishments will be implemented.

2.3   Threat Model

We assume that attackers can monitor the network and obtain the uploaded data of customers or service providers. A basic inference attack can be launched by attackers who utilize the information of comparison results of both two sides and obtain the real monitoring information. In addition, attackers in the blockchain network may also launch linking attacks, with the assumption that the adversary can successfully find the corresponding block and acquire customer cloud service records. Then, attackers can discover the associations between IP addresses and usage records of customers. In this situation, more privacy of customers will be leaked. Our scheme aims to defend the inference attack and the linking attack.

3   Privacy-Preserving SLA Auditing

In this section, we show the privacy auditing process of the SLA audit smart contract in details. In order to protect monitored data security and make ciphertexts comparison feasible, the TORE encryption scheme is applied in the auditing task. Figure 2 illustrates the privacy auditing process. When a secret key is received from the SLA audit smart contract, both the customer and service provider sides will encrypt their monitored data by TORE and upload the ciphertext to the blockchain. Since the standard parameters of the service are included by the plaintext, the SLA audit smart contract will use the corresponding key to calculate the ciphertexts with TORE. Then, the smart contract will be triggered to compare the ciphertexts and then the comparison results can be obtained. We can fix whether the monitored data from two sides is consistent and whether it achieves the standard level of the service, and some punishments will be executed according to different situations.

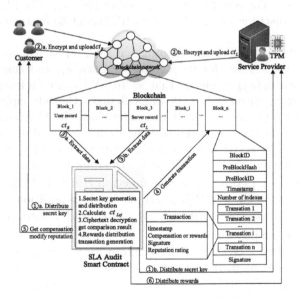

Fig. 2. Privacy auditing process of SLA audit smart contract

3.1   TORE Based Privacy Protection Mechanism

In the proposed system, each service attribute parameter in $ServPara$ has a specific plaintext space which has individual domain. A customer and a service provider share the same plaintext space of each service attribute, and all their monitored data and the standard values of the service parameters in SLA are included in the plaintext space. If data $ServPara$ has k service attributes, the corresponding plaintext space is recorded as $[N_1]$, $[N_2]$, ..., $[N_k]$ individually. In addition, the number of elements in $[N_j]$ is represented by n which can be set according to SLA protocol and each element $x_{ji} \in [N_j]$ associated with an encryption key k_{ji}. Our scheme can monitor multiple parameters and customize $ServPara$ according to users' requirements on cloud services.

All the monitoring data will be encrypted by the TORE algorithm before uploading to blockchain in order to protect data security while comparing ciphertexts. The TORE encryption algorithm includes a left $Encrypt_L$ algorithm and a right $Encrypt_R$ algorithm, with the corresponding ciphertext consisting of a left component ct_L and a right component ct_R [5]. The whole TORE execution process includes four steps: $Setup$, $Encrypt_L$, $Encrypt_R$, and $Compare$. The encryption scheme is defined as follows:

- $Setup\left(1^\lambda\right)$: First, input a security parameter λ. The SLA audit smart contract generates key $k_{ji} \xleftarrow{R} \{0,1\}^\lambda$ of a secure pseudo-random function $F : \{0,1\}^\lambda \times \{0,1\}^\lambda \to \{0,1\}^\lambda$ for each element in plaintext spaces. Next, sample a uniformly random permutation π on each plaintext space domain $\pi : [N_j] \to [N_j]$. The pair (k_{ji}, π) is the secret key sk_{ji}. The SLA audit smart contract will distribute secret key of each element to customers and service providers.

- $Encrypt_L\left(sk, x_j\right)$: In the service provider side, TPM will select the corresponding secret key sk_j for its monitoring data x_j, and compute the permuted position $\pi\left(x_j\right)$ to ensure that x_j in $[N_j]$ can't be learned from others during comparison. Then, it will calculate the left ciphertext for x_j, $ct_{Lj} = \left(F\left(sk, \pi\left(x_j\right)\right), \pi\left(x_j\right)\right)$. At the same time, the SLA audit smart contract will extract the negotiated standard parameters of attributes and use the corresponding secret key to calculate the standard left ciphertext ct_{Lsj} for each parameter. The ct_{Lsj} will be recorded into a block.

- $Encrypt_R\left(sk, y_j\right)$: In this step, a hash function $H : \{0,1\}^\lambda \times \{0,1\}^\lambda \to \mathbb{Z}_3$ and a comparison function $CMP\left(m_i, m_j\right)$ are used. In addition, $CMP\left(m_i, m_j\right)$ outputs -1 with $m_i > m_j$, 0 with $m_i = m_j$, and 1 with $m_i < m_j$. First, the customers samples a random nonce $r \xleftarrow{R} \{0,1\}^\lambda$. Next, the customer uses the corresponding secret key and the monitoring parameter from customer which is recorded as y_j to compute the index $v_{jz} \leftarrow CMP\left(\pi^{-1}\left(z\right), y_j\right) + H\left(F\left(k, z\right), r\right) \pmod 3$ for each $z \in [N_j]$, and a group of index v_{j1}, v_{j2}, ..., v_{jn} is obtained. Finally, the customer uses a corresponding tuple $ct_{Rj} = \left(r, v_{j1}, v_{j2}, \cdots, v_{jn}\right)$ as the right ciphertext.

After the left and right encryption are completed, ct_{Lj} and ct_{Rj} will be uploaded to the blockchain, and these ciphertexts will be recorded in different blocks. Once audit tasks start, the SLA audit contract will be triggered to extract ct_{Lj}, ct_{Rj}, and then the $Compare$ algorithm is executed automatically to obtain the comparison result between customers and service providers. The *Compare* algorithm is defined as follow:

- *Compare* (ct_{Lj}, ct_{Rj}): Input ct_{Lj} and ct_{Rj}, and the smart contract will parse $ct_{Lj} = (k', h)$ and $ct_{Rj} = (r, v_{j1}, v_{j2}, \cdots, v_{jn})$. Then, it computes the index $I_j = v_j - H(k', r) \pmod{3}$ for comparison between x_j and y_j. I_j is 0 if $x_j = y_j$; I_j is 1, if $x_j < y_j$; otherwise I_j is 2.

We set $z = Compare(ct_L, ct_R)$, and the correctness of this algorithm is shown as follows:

$$
\begin{aligned}
z &= v_{jh} - H(k', r) \\
&= CMP\left(\pi^{-1}(h), y_j\right) + H(F(k, h), r) - H(k', r) \\
&= CMP\left(\pi^{-1}(\pi(x_j)), y_j\right) + H(F(k, \pi(x_j)), r) - H(F(k, \pi(x_j)), r) \\
&= CMP(x_j, y_j) \in \mathbb{Z}_3
\end{aligned}
\tag{1}
$$

3.2 Punishment Strategies for Violations

Once receiving comparison for each service attribute in $ServPara_j$, there will be two cases of results. First, for $\forall j$, $I_j = 0$, which means all the monitored parameters of consumers and providers are equal and there is no malicious party to report false data. Then, the SLA audit smart contract will judge whether the service parameters meet the SLA standard values. It is triggered to extract ct_{Lsj} and execute $Compare(ct_{Lsj}, ct_{Rj})$ algorithm. After that, the comparison index I_{sj} between the monitoring data and the standard value of service parameters will be obtained. If $I_{sj} = 0$ or 2, it is proved that the quality of service provided is not lower than the negotiated standard in SLA agreement, and there is no service violation. The SLA audit contract will automatically distribute service fees F_s to the service provider. Otherwise, the service provider will be punished for providing unsatisfied service, that the deposit F_d will be distributed to miners as a reward rather than returning to the service provider and the SLA audit smart contract will give compensation F_c to the customer.

Second, there exists at least one value that $I_j \neq 0$, which means the monitored parameters from the two sides are not absolutely equal. Then, the SLA audit contract is triggered to check the comparison information which is recorded in the block, and to fix the value of num_{dif} that how many times the comparison results are not equal between different consumers and the same TPM during the time slice t_s. num_{all} is the time of comparison for TPM during the time slice t_s. In order to prevent the malicious customer from cheating and reporting fake data for many times, the mismatching comparison result of the same customer will be only recorded once. If $num_{dif} > \lfloor num_{all}/2 \rfloor$, the monitored data of the TPM is inaccurate and abnormal, and the TPM needs to be checked. Otherwise, the TPM is normal, and the consumer cheats in the monitored task. Then, the SLA audit contract will reduce the reputation of the consumer as a punishment according to the following formula.

$$
T_x(i, t) = T_x(i, t_s) - \left(\frac{F_{deposit} - F_{min}}{F_{max} - F_{min}}\right) \times (1 - T_x(i, t_s))
\tag{2}
$$

$T_x(i,t)$ is the reputation value of customer x who requests service i in time t and $T_x(i,t_s)$ is the reputation value of x during time slice t_s. $T_x(i,t_s)$ integrates users' rating as a subjective source and service quality monitoring information as an objective source, and it can change dynamically with service preferences of customers [11]. The punishment degree is determined by the compensation ratio of negotiated compensation F_c, the minimum compensation F_{min} and the maximum compensation F_{max}. We use punishment degree to measure the importance of this service task and multiply it by the customer's unreliability value as the reputation reduction value. At the same time, the customer's deposit F_d will be distributed to miners and the payment F_s for the service will be automatically sent to the service provider. When a consumer reputation value is lower than 0, it will not be able to apply for the cloud service. This reputation can be used to regulate user behaviors.

4   Experiment

In this section, we first compare our scheme with other different SLA monitoring and auditing scheme, and the comparison results are summarized in Table 2. In the SLA-BPPM centralized scheme, all monitoring and violation reporting is performed by a third party. However, the fully trusted third party may cheat for benefits. Our distributed scheme based on blockchain can ensures the credibility of data. SLA-ICM [13] scheme and Sec-rSLA [14] scheme are all blockchain based SLA audit scheme, and they do not pay attention to the privacy leakage of data stored on blockchain. Our scheme introduce TROE algorithm to keep monitoring result securely stored on the blockchain and ensure privacy security. In addition, our scheme has better scalability which can customize and monitor multiple parameters. After comparing these schemes, we also evaluate the cost of SLA audit smart contract and TORE algorithm in detail as follows.

Table 2. Comparison of SLA monitoring and auditing schemes

Scheme	Distributed model	Multiple parameters	Security	Privacy protection
SLA-BPPM [15]		✓		✓
SLA-ICM [13]	✓		✓	
Sec-rSLA [14]	✓		✓	
Our scheme	✓	✓	✓	✓

4.1   Overheads of SLA Audit Smart Contract

According to the SLA monitoring and auditing model, we implement our system based on smart contract of Ethereum and use solidity programming language to implement the SLA audit smart contract. Since the smart contract is triggered by its interfaces' states transition and the miners in Ethereum will execute the program defined in these interfaces, the execution of smart contract needs to consume electricity or other resources. The gas is a unit to measure the miner's workload of executing the transaction in the Ethereum. We deploy the SLA audit smart contract on the test net of Ethereum blockchain named Rinkeby on which we can debug the smart contract. Figure 3 shows the main gas consumption of the SLA audit smart contract. The audit task involves more complex interface, so this process needs much gas. The end process of SLA will check whether all roles in the service have been withdrawn, and whether the compensation distribution has been completed, so there will be corresponding high gas cost. Overall, the total gas consumption of the SLA smart contract is acceptable.

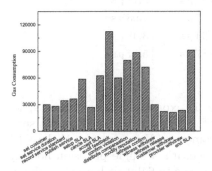

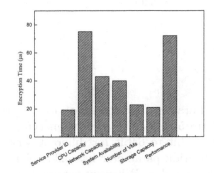

Fig. 3. The main gas consumption of SLA audit smart contract

Fig. 4. The encryption time cost of each parameter

4.2 Overheads of TORE Encryption

In our scheme, the encryption of monitoring service parameters by TORE is the foundation of privacy auditing, and ciphertexts comparison is an important part. However, any encryption algorithm has overheads, so we test the cost of TORE in main phases of our model including *encrypt* phase and *compare* phase respectively. We set $\lambda = 128$, which operates at 128-bits of security. F is instantiated with AES-128, and AES is modeled as a random oracle to generate a random permutation or cipher. The program runs on a laptop in an Intel Core i7 with 2.2 GHz CPU, 8 GB of RAM.

We firstly test the time cost of the main TORE phases including *Encrypt* and *Compare*. Since parameters in *ServPara* can be customized or extended in our model, we set the number of parameters to 1, 3, 5, 7 in turn, select several random parameters in Table 1 correspondingly, and set 32-bit plaintext space for each parameter. Table 3 shows that the time cost of comparison is much lower than that of encryption, so the main overheads is the encryption process in our system. And the time cost of both encryption and comparison is small, so it will not affect the system execution. In addition, less monitoring service parameters take less time, thus it is worth sacrificing little time to set more parameters for stronger violation auditing.

Since the main time cost is encryption, we set 7 service parameters in *ServPara* and test the encryption time of each parameter. Various parameters may have different-sized plaintext spaces, we set the plaintext space size of service provider ID, CPU capacity, network capacity, system availability, number of VMs, storage capacity and performance to 8bit, 32bit, 16bit, 16bit, 8bit, 8bit and 32bit respectively. Figure 4 shows the encryption time of each parameter.

Table 3. The time cost of encrypt and compare phase

Plaintext space	Number of n	Encrypt time	Compare time
32bit	1	58.62 μs	0.71 μs
	3	169.57 μs	1.98 μs
	5	291.24 μs	3.48 μs
	7	396.87 μs	5.17 μs

Parameter can be expanded its precision by expanding the plaintext space. Figure 5 shows the average encryption time for different size of plaintext space from 8bit to 64bit for different service parameters. For example, if the CPU utilization parameter has 32bit plaintext space, it's a single precision floating-point number. When we extend its plaintext space to 64bit, it becomes a double precision floating point parameter and can be used to more accurate parameter auditing. In addition, the larger the plaintext space is, the wider the service range can be represented by this parameter. Besides, it can be illustrated from Fig. 5 that the larger the size of plaintext space is, the much encryption time costs. Which is because that the more comparison elements in plaintext space, the much index of each elements will be generated in process of right encryption. Although the above overheads of encryption time is under the acceptable range, the relatively small plaintext space will perform better.

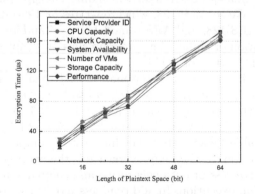

Fig. 5. Encryption time cost of multiple parameters in different size of plaintext space

5   Conclusion

In this paper, a blockchain based privacy-preserving cloud SLA violation monitoring and auditing model is proposed. We adopt the dual monitoring method and introduce TORE algorithm to ensure the credibility and security of the monitoring data. In addition, a SLA audit smart contract is designed to automatically execute ciphertexts comparison and violation auditing, which can ensure credible violation judgment and privacy preserving. Experiments on our blockchain based system have been carried out to demonstrate the feasibility of our scheme. In future work, we plan to introduce reasoning technology to analyze information from different SLA monitoring parameters and infer violation behavior on the premise of ensuring the security of users' privacy.

References

1. Agrawal, R., Kiernan, J., Srikant, R., Xu, Y.: Order preserving encryption for numeric data. In: ACM SIGMOD, pp. 563–574 (2004)
2. Boneh, D., Lewi, K., Raykova, M., Sahai, A., Zhandry, M., Zimmerman, J.: Semantically secure order-revealing encryption: multi-input functional encryption without obfuscation. In: Oswald, E., Fischlin, M. (eds.) EUROCRYPT 2015. LNCS, vol. 9057, pp. 563–594. Springer, Heidelberg (2015). https://doi.org/10.1007/978-3-662-46803-6_19
3. Chenette, N., Lewi, K., Weis, S.A., Wu, D.J.: Practical order-revealing encryption with limited leakage. In: Peyrin, T. (ed.) FSE 2016. LNCS, vol. 9783, pp. 474–493. Springer, Heidelberg (2016). https://doi.org/10.1007/978-3-662-52993-5_24
4. Kaaniche, N., Mohamed, M., Laurent, M., Ludwig, H.: Security SLA based monitoring in clouds. In: IEEE EDGE, pp. 90–97. IEEE (2017)
5. Lewi, K., Wu, D.J.: Order-revealing encryption: new constructions, applications, and lower bounds. In: ACM SIGSAC, pp. 1167–1178 (2016)
6. Macías, M., Guitart, J.: Analysis of a trust model for SLA negotiation and enforcement in cloud markets. Future Gener. Comput. Syst. **55**, 460–472 (2016)
7. Nakamoto, S., Bitcoin, A.: A peer-to-peer electronic cash system. Bitcoin (2008). https://bitcoin.org/bitcoin.pdf
8. Nakashima, H., Aoyama, M.: An automation method of SLA contract of web APIs and its platform based on blockchain concept. In: IEEE ICCC, pp. 32–39. IEEE (2017)
9. Naveed, M., Kamara, S., Wright, C.V.: Inference attacks on property-preserving encrypted databases. In: ACM SIGSAC, pp. 644–655 (2015)
10. Nawaz, F., Hussain, O., Hussain, F.K., Janjua, N.K., Saberi, M., Chang, E.: Proactive management of SLA violations by capturing relevant external events in a cloud of things environment. Future Gener. Comput. Syst. **95**, 26–44 (2019)
11. Nguyen, H.T., Zhao, W., Yang, J.: A trust and reputation model based on Bayesian network for web services. In: IEEE ICWS, pp. 251–258. IEEE (2010)
12. Park, K.-W., Han, J., Chung, J. and Park, K.H.: Themis: a mutually verifiable billing system for the cloud computing environment. IEEE Trans. Serv. Comput. **6**(3), 300–313 (2013)
13. Wonjiga, A.T., Peisert, S., Rilling, L., Morin, C.: Blockchain as a trusted component in cloud SLA verification. In: ACM International Conference on Utility and Cloud Computing Companion, pp. 93–100 (2019)

14. Zhou, H., Ouyang, X., Ren, Z., Su, J., de Laat, C., Zhao, Z.: A blockchain based witness model for trustworthy cloud service level agreement enforcement. In: IEEE INFOCOM, pp. 1567–1575. IEEE (2019)
15. Zhou, S., Wu, L., Jin, C.: A privacy-based SLA violation detection model for the security of cloud computing. China Commun. 14(9), 155–165 (2017)

CPBA: An Efficient Conditional Privacy-Preserving Batch Authentication Scheme for VANETs

Jieyao Xu, Dongmei Zhang$^{(\boxtimes)}$, Gaoyuan Xiong, and Han Zhang

School of Computer Science, Beijing University of Posts and Telecommunications,
Beijing 100876, China
{xujieyao,zhangdm,xionggy,zhanghan0608}@bupt.edu.cn

Abstract. The vehicular ad-hoc networks (VANETs) are the products
of close integration of wireless communication technologies and modern automotive technologies, from which real-time traffic information
and effective safety protections can be provided to managers and drivers
respectively. Two major problems in VANETs are privacy protection
and certificate revocation list management. With the exiting signature
schemes, certificates provided by management center should be stored
in vehicles and these vehicles need to check certificate revocation lists
(CRLs) prior to message authentication. To realize the security and efficient authentication of information transmission between vehicle nodes
in VANETs, we propose a new certificateless aggregate signature scheme
(CLAS) that addresses the key escrow problem, supports batch verification and conditional privacy preservation. By using Chinese remainder
theorem (CRT), the trusted authority (TA) generates and broadcasts
new domain keys to the vehicles in the network dynamically, which means
that vehicles can prevent false security information attacks from malicious vehicles without storing CRLs. The results show that the scheme
can not just achieve these security properties, including anonymity, revocability, anti-forgery, and traceability, but can meet the requirements of
real-time and efficiency for VANETs as well.

Keywords: VANETs · CRLs · Pseudonym · CLAS · CRT

1 Introduction

The vehicular ad-hoc networks (VANETs) are the products of close integration
of wireless communication technologies and modern automotive technologies,
from which real-time traffic information and effective safety protections can be
provided to managers and drivers respectively. The performance of safety application of VANETs mainly depends on the authenticity and accuracy of vehicle
sharing road traffic information. Moreover, from the perspective of vehicles, it
is unacceptable that the verification process of security messages may disclose
personal privacy including identity and location. In order to solve the problem of

© Springer Nature Switzerland AG 2020
D. Yu et al. (Eds.): WASA 2020, LNCS 12384, pp. 555–567, 2020.
https://doi.org/10.1007/978-3-030-59016-1_46

security authentication and conditional privacy protection of vehicle communication applications, a variety of conditional privacy authentication mechanisms are introduced into the vehicle network.

In a traditional public key infrastructure (PKI-based) authentication scheme [1–3], a vehicle is equipped with a public/private key pair for pseudonymous communication. The vehicle-generated signature carries a corresponding certificate with the public key pair and short-term pseudonym of the signer of the message. In ID-based schemes [4–7], RSUs and vehicles use pseudo-identity information as public keys, and their private keys are generated by semi-trusted third parties called Private Key Generator Centers (KGC). In 2016, Jiang et al. [9] proposed a batch authentication scheme named ABAH, which calculates a hashed message authentication code. However, ABAH uses a bilinear pairing-based signature scheme, which takes longer to encrypt and decrypt. In 2018, P. Kumar et al. [8] proposed a certificateless signature (CLS) authentication scheme and a certificateless aggregate signature (CLAS) scheme designed for VANETs using bilinear pairings. Yang et al. [10] proposed a certificateless signature authentication scheme based on elliptic curve encryption (ECC), named PCPA, which does not require bilinear pairing and hash operations mapped to points, and has low computation and communication costs. Jiang et al. [14] proposed RAU protocol based on Homomorphic encryption, which can generate any number of authentication identities. However, every time a new communication is established, authentication is required through the VS server.

Any security authentication scheme must provide a way to revoke users from the system. Certificate revocation list (CRL) is a digital list issued by an authority that stores all certificate information that has been revoked and not expired yet. Once a revoked certificate expires, it is cleared from the CRLs. Most signature schemes require the vehicle to store a certificate generated by a trusted authority, and before verifying the received message, the vehicle has to query the CRLs to check if the sender is authentic or not. In most of the certificateless signature schemes that have been proposed already in VANET, revocation list query and storage problems still exist. Considering the limited computing power and storage space of the vehicle, storage and inspection of CRLs can result in excessive computational overhead and storage space occupied.

To realize the security and efficient authentication of information transmission between vehicle nodes in VANETs, we propose an efficient conditional privacy-preserving batch authentication (CPBA) scheme. In the proposed CPBA scheme, TA implements regional management to ensure vehicle legitimacy, eliminating the need of vehicles' storage and inspection of the CRLs. TA can revoke malicious vehicles in the domain by updating the domain key dynamically, because only using the key can domain member sign the massage. By using Chinese Remainder Theorem (CRT) [13], only the legal vehicles can calculate the new domain key from the broadcast updating message of the TA by performing one module division operation. The proposed CPBA scheme combines dynamical domain key management with a certificateless aggregate signature scheme, considered that the certificateless signature scheme can solve high cost of certificate management of PKI-based schemes and the key escrow problem of the ID-based schemes.

The contributions of this paper can be summarized in to three points:

- **Secure certificateless aggregate signature scheme without bilinear pairing:** Considering that the computational energy consumption of the bilinear pairing operation is more than 20 times that of the elliptic curve point multiplication operation, we propose a CLAS scheme based on ECC, which improves the efficiency of the signature and verification phases.
- **Domain key distribution dynamically:** TA manages VANET by region, and implements the broadcast distribution and update of the domain key through the CRT, ensuring that legitimate vehicles can acquire the domain key, thereby achieving the efficiency of vehicle revocation, and solving the problem that the vehicle must store and query the CRL.
- **Relatively higher efficiency while security is guaranteed:** The security analysis is conducted to prove that the CPBA scheme meets the security and privacy requirements. By analyzing the computation cost and transmission overhead, it is concluded that the proposed CPBA scheme performs better than [9,10] in terms of efficiency.

Section 2 gives a brief description of our model. The proposed CPBA scheme is described in Sect. 3. The security analysis and efficiency of the scheme is carried out in Sect. 4 and 5. Section 6 is the conclusion of this work.

2   Our Model

2.1   System Model

Figure 1 shows the relationship of the four entities in our proposed scheme: TA, KGC, RSU and OBU.

(1) **TA:** TA is a trusted center, generates the system parameters, and in charge of storing real identities of vehicles. At the same time, TA is also responsible registering RSUs and OBUs. The utilization of the concept of domain management improves the efficiency of CRLs. In our scheme, each city of the country is assigned a dedicated TA, which performs the generation and update of the domain key. All TAs in the same country has the same functionalities and databases. Only the TA can uncover the real identity of the malicious vehicle from false messages.

(2) **KGC:** KGC is a semi-trusted third party, which is in charge of generating the partial secret key of vehicles.

(3) **RSU:** RSU is the intermediary point of transmission between TA, KGC and OBUs, which is located along the roadside. The main function of RSU is message transmission. Communication between RSU and TA relies on laying of wired channels, and sends messages to the vehicle over the wireless network.

(4) **OBU:** Each vehicle, equipped with an OBU, is responsible to collect vehicle's driving information. The vehicles communicate with other vehicles through the Dedicated Short-Range Communication (DSRC) protocol.

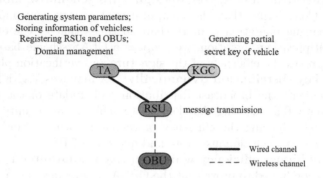

Fig. 1. Relationship of four entities.

2.2 Security Requirements

In order to communicate securely in VANET, security requirements that must be satisfied are as follows:

Message Integrity and Authentication: The receiver needs to verify the legality of the sender and ascertain any changes to the message received.

Anonymity: The real identity of the vehicle cannot be identified or be traced by any adversary other than the TA through analyzing the message received.

Traceability and Revocability: TA need to be able to detect the real identity of the malicious vehicle from fake messages and revoke it from the VANETs.

Role Separation: TA takes charge of generating the pseudo identity of the vehicle as well as updating the domain key, while KGC takes responsibility for the generation of the vehicle's partial private key.

Resistance Against Different Types of Attacks: VANETs are susceptible to numerous kinds of security attacks, such as replay attack, impersonation attack and conclusion attack. Thus, schemes should have the ability to against various attacks.

3   The Proposed Scheme

3.1   System Initialization

After selecting two large prime number p and q, where $p > q$ and $q < \lceil p/4 \rceil$, the system chooses an elliptic curve E as: $y^2 = (x^3 + ax + b)(mod\ p)$ and chooses a group G from E.TA outputs the system parameter by the steps as follows:

(1) KGC randomly selects the master secret key $s \in Z_q^*$ for partial key generation and calculates $P_{pub} = s \cdot P$.
(2) TA randomly selects the master secret key $t \in Z_q^*$ for identity traceability and computes $T_{pub} = t \cdot P$.
(3) TA selects four one-way hash functions: $h_i : \{0,1\}^* \to Z_q^* (1 \leq i \leq 4)$.

From the steps above, the parameters of the system are $\{p, q, P, T_{pub}, P_{pub}, h_1, h_2, h_3, h_4\}$. There are notations used in this paper as shown in Table 1.

Table 1. Notations and definitions

Notations	Definitions
p, q	Large prime number
G, P	The additive group, and the generator of it
V_i	The i-th vehicle
RID_i	Real identity of V_i
PID_i, T_i	Pseudo identity of V_i, and the valid time of it
PSK_i, SK_i	Partial secret key and secret key of V_i
m_i	Message sent by V_i
tm_i	Current timestamp of the message m_i
h_1, h_2, h_3, h_4	Four secure one-way hash functions
$\oplus$	Exclusive-or
$\|$	The message concatenation

3.2 Domain Initialization

TA selects secret member keys sk_i from the multiplicative group Z_q^*, which will be distributed to 'n' number of vehicle drivers when they join the multicast group. TA compute $\partial_g = sk_1 sk_2 \cdots sk_n = \prod_{i=1}^n sk_i$, and $x_i = \frac{\partial_g}{sk_i}$ where $i = 1, 2, \cdots, n$. Then TA compute y_i that $x_i y_i \equiv 1 \ mod \ sk_i$. TA multiply all drivers x_i and y_i values as $var_i = x_i \times y_i$, and compute the value $\mu = \sum_i^n var_i$.

3.3 Domain Key Generation

Each TA manages the corresponding domain by domain key distribution. When a new vehicle enters the domain, TA first verifies the identity of the vehicle and the timeliness of the pseudo identity. If successful, TA sends a secret key sk_i to the vehicle in secure. TA computes the new domain key and broadcasts it to the vehicles of the domain in the following way.

(1) TA randomly choose a new element $k_d \in Z_q^*$ as domain key and computes $\gamma = k_d \times \mu$.
(2) The TA broadcasts $\{\gamma, K_{pub}, SIG_{sk_{TA}}(\gamma\|t_d)\}$ to all the domain members, where K_{pub} is the domain public key and t_d is the valid time of it. An authorized vehicle can obtain the domain key k_d by just one mod operation $\gamma \ mod \ sk_i = k_d$.

The result k_d is equal to the value of k_d chosen by TA. When 'i' reaches to 'n', TA excuses the Domain Initialization to compute ∂_g, var_i and μ for 'm' vehicles, in which $m = n \times \delta$. δ is constant and $\delta < 5$.

3.4   Pseudo Identity Generation and Partial-Secret-Key Generation

As introduced above, TA needs to produce the pseudo identity of the vehicle and updating the domain key.

(1) The real identity RID_i of V_i is sent to TA in secure.
(2) TA randomly chooses $w_i \in Z_q^*$ and computes $PID_{i,1} = w_iP$, $PID_{i,2} = RID_i \oplus h_1(w_iT_{pub}, T_i)$. The pseudo identity of the vehicle $\{PID_{i,1}, PID_{i,2}, T_i\}$ is delivered to the KGC in a secure channel, where T_i is the time validity.
(3) KGC randomly chooses $r_i \in Z_q^*$ and then computes $R_i = r_i \cdot P$, $h_{2i} = h_2(PID_i, P_{pub}, T_{pub}, R_i)$, $\alpha_i = r_i + h_{2i} \cdot s$ and $PSK_i = (R_i, \alpha_i)$.
(4) KGC sends (PID_i, PSK_i) to the vehicle in a secure channel.

3.5   Secret-Key-Gen and Message Signature

The vehicle receives the message from KGC and perform the following steps:

(1) The vehicle V_i can verify PSK_i by checking $\alpha_i \cdot P = R_i + h_{2i} \cdot P_{pub}$.
(2) The vehicle V_i randomly selects $\beta_i, x_i \in Z_q^*$ and calculates $h_{3i} = h_3(PID_i, x_i, R_i)$, $\mu_i = \beta_i \cdot h_{3i}$, $X_i = x_i \cdot P$ and $U_i = \mu_i \cdot P$. Then the private key of the vehicle SK_i is (x_i, μ_i) and public key of the vehicle is U_i.
(3) The vehicle V_i randomly selects $b_i \in Z_q^*$, calculates $B_i = b_i \cdot X_i + R_i$ and $h_{4i} = h_4(m_i, PID_i, B_i, U_i, P_{pub}, tm_i)$, where tm_i is the current timestamp to avoid replay attack.
(4) The domain key k_d can be calculated from the broadcast message $\{\gamma, K_{pub}, SIG_{sk_{TA}}(\gamma\|t_d)\}$ by the operation $\gamma \ mod \ sk_i = k_d$. Then the vehicle computes $\delta_i = b_i \cdot x_i + h_{4i} \cdot \mu_i + \alpha_i + k_d$. The signature of the message m_i is $\sigma_i = (B_i, \delta_i)$.

3.6   Message Authentication

The receiver verifies the message $\{PID_i, m_i \parallel tm_i, U_i, \sigma_i\}$ through the following steps:

(1) First checks times $tm_i : T_{tmp} - tm_i \leq \triangle T$, where T_{tmp} is the received time and $\triangle T$ is the transmission delay.
(2) Calculates $h_{4i} = h_4(m_i, PID_i, B_i, U_i, P_{pub}, tm_i)$ and $h_{2i} = h_2(PID_i, P_{pub}, T_{pub}, R_i)$.
(3) Then the receiver checks whether the following equation holds.

$$\delta_i \cdot P = B_i + h_{4i} \cdot U_i + h_{2i} \cdot P_{pub} + K_{pub} \qquad (1)$$

(4) The receiver can verify a batch of messages $\{PID_1, m_1 \parallel tm_1, U_1, \sigma_1\}$, $\{PID_2, m_2 \parallel tm_2, U_2, \sigma_2\}, \cdots, \{PID_n, m_n \parallel tm_n, U_n, \sigma_n\}$ by checking:

$$(\sum_{i=1}^{n} \delta_i) \cdot P = \sum_{i=1}^{n} B_i + \sum_{i=1}^{n}(h_{4i} \cdot U_i) + \sum_{i=1}^{n}(h_{2i}) \cdot P_{pub} + n \cdot K_{pub} \quad (2)$$

3.7   Aggregate and Aggregate-Verify

Aggregate Signature can reduce the bandwidth and storage overheads. The aggregator, such as RSUs or vehicles, can aggregate n messages $\{PID_i, m_i \parallel tm_i, U_i, \sigma_i\}_{1 \leq i \leq n}$ received in a time slot T. For $1 < i < n$, the aggregator computes $B = \sum_{i=1}^{n} B_i$ and $\delta = \sum_{i=1}^{n} \delta_i$ and outputs $\sigma = (B, \delta)$ as certificateless aggregate signature.

Received the signature $\sigma = (B, \delta)$, the receiver checks the freshness of the timestamp tm_i firstly. If tm_i is valid, the verifier performs the following steps:

(1) Computes $h_{4i} = h_4(m_i, PID_i, B_i, U_i, P_{pub}, tm_i)$ and $h_{2i} = h_2(PID_i, P_{pub}, T_{pub}, R_i)$, and then calculates $U = \sum_{i=1}^{n}(h_{4i} \cdot U_i)$.
(2) Then checks whether the equation $\delta \cdot P = B + U + (\sum_{i=1}^{n} h_{2i}) \cdot P_{pub} + n \cdot K_{pub}$ is hold. The verifier will accept the signature only when the equation holds.

3.8   Domain Key Updating

When the vehicles in the domain change, the domain manager, TA needs to generate a new domain key. In addition, the domain key needs to change regularly.

– **user leave**
  When a vehicle V_i leaves, TA subtract var_i from $\mu : \mu - var_i$.
– **batch leave**
  When a batch of vehicles wants to leave, TA has to update the domain key. For example, if the vehicle V_3, V_5, V_7 and V_9 want to leave the domain, TA subtract $var_3, var_5, var_7, var_9$ from μ: $\mu' = \mu - var_3 - var_5 - var_7 - var_9$.
– **batch join**
  When a batch of vehicles wants to join the domain, TA has to distribute the domain key. For example, if the vehicle V_3, V_5, V_7 and V_9 want to join the domain, TA subtract $var_3, var_5, var_7, var_9$ from μ: $\mu' = \mu + var_3 + var_5 + var_7 + var_9$.

In above three cases, TA selects $k_d' \in Z_q^*$, and multiplied it with μ' as follows: $\gamma' = k_d' \times \mu'$. To update the domain key, message γ' is broadcast. All the legitimate vehicles can acquire domain key k_d' by only one modulo operation since their var_i values are included in μ'.

On the whole, if 'n' vehicles want to join or leave the domain, TA needs to perform 'n' additions for updating the domain key, which cause $O(1)$ computation complexity for TA. In addition, the computation complexity of the domain member is also minimized, since the vehicle only needs to perform one module division operation. What's more, TA can broadcast the updating message to the vehicles in this domain.

4   Security Analysis

4.1   Correctness Proof

The proof of consistency of the proposed scheme CPBA is as follows:

Verification. Having received the message $\{PID_i, m_i \parallel tm_i, U_i, \sigma_i\}$, the receiver verify the signature $\sigma_i = (B_i, \delta_i)$ by checking if $\delta_i \cdot P = B_i + h_{4i} \cdot U_i + h_{2i} \cdot P_{pub} + K_{pub}$. That is,

$$
\begin{aligned}
\delta_i \cdot P &= (b_i \cdot x_i + h_{4i} \cdot \mu_i + \alpha_i + k_d) \cdot P \\
&= (b_i \cdot x_i + h_{4i} \cdot \mu_i + r_i + h_{2i} \cdot s + k_d) \cdot P \\
&= b_i \cdot x_i \cdot P + h_{4i} \cdot \mu_i \cdot P + r_i \cdot P + h_{2i} \cdot s \cdot P + k_d \cdot P \\
&= b_i \cdot X_i + h_{4i} \cdot U_i + R_i + h_{2i} \cdot P_{pub} + K_{pub} \\
&= B_i + h_{4i} \cdot U_i + h_{2i} \cdot P_{pub} + K_{pub}
\end{aligned}
$$

Therefore, the correctness of the verification algorithm is verified.

Aggregate Verification. Having received the message $\{PID_i, m_i \parallel tm_i, U_i, \sigma_i\}_{1 \leq i \leq n}$, the receiver verify the signature $\sigma = (B, \delta)$ by checking the equation $(\sum_{i=1}^{n} \delta_i) \cdot P = \sum_{i=1}^{n} B_i + \sum_{i=1}^{n}(h_{4i} \cdot U_i) + \sum_{i=1}^{n}(h_{2i}) \cdot P_{pub} + n \cdot K_{pub}$. That is,

$$
\begin{aligned}
\delta \cdot P &= \left(\sum_{i=1}^{n} \delta_i\right) \cdot P \\
&= \sum_{i=1}^{n} b_i x_i \cdot P + \sum_{i=1}^{n} h_{4i}\mu_i \cdot P + \sum_{i=1}^{n} \alpha_i \cdot P + \sum_{i=1}^{n} k_d \cdot P \\
&= \sum_{i=1}^{n} (b_i X_i + h_{2i} \cdot P_{pub}) + \sum_{i=1}^{n} h_{4i} \cdot U_i + R + n K_{pub} \\
&= B + U + \sum_{i=1}^{n}(h_{2i} \cdot P_{pub}) + n \cdot K_{pub}
\end{aligned}
$$

Therefore, The correctness of the aggregate verification algorithm is verified.

4.2   Security Analysis

In this part, we present a process to analyse the security requirements satisfaction of the CPBA scheme proposed.

Message Integrity and Authentication: The message receiver needs to verify the legality of the sender and check if the received message has been modified. The receivers verify the legality of the sender by checking the equation $\delta_i \cdot P = B_i + h_{4i} \cdot U_i + h_{2i} \cdot P_{pub} + K_{pub}$ and $(\sum_{i=1}^{n} \delta_i) \cdot P = \sum_{i=1}^{n} B_i + \sum_{i=1}^{n}(h_{4i} \cdot U_i) + \sum_{i=1}^{n}(h_{2i}) \cdot P_{pub} + n \cdot K_{pub}$. Therefore, the CPBA scheme proposed meets the requirements of message integrity and authentication.

Anonymity: The real identity of vehicle RID_i is hidden in the pseudo identity $PID_i = \{PID_{i,1}, PID_{i,2}, T_i\}$, where $PID_{i,1} = w_iP$, $PID_{i,2} = RID_i \oplus h_1(w_iT_{pub}, T_i)$ and $T_{pub} = t \cdot P$. To find out the identity RID_i of a vehicle, the adversary has to calculate $RID_i = PID_{i,2} \oplus h_1(w_iT_{pub}, T_i) = PID_{i,2} \oplus h_1(t \cdot PID_{i,1}, T_i)$. However, t is the secret master key of TA and w_i is chosen by TA in random, both of them are stored in TA. The adversary cannot extract RID_i without the value of t and w_i. The vehicle cannot be identified or be traced by any adversary other than the TA through analyzing the message received. Thus, the CPBA scheme proposed meets the requirements of identity privacy protection.

Traceability and Revocability: TA can calculate the vehicle's RID_i from the pseudo-identity $PID_i = \{PID_{i,1}, PID_{i,2}, T_i\}$ involved in the broadcast message. Therefore, TA can detect the real identity of the malicious vehicle from fake messages and revoke it from the VANETs. Then TA will to remove the malicious vehicle from the domain by updating the domain key. Thus, the proposed CPBA scheme meets the requirements of traceability and revocability.

Role Separation: TA is a trusted center, producing the vehicle's pseudo identity and updating the domain key. It can uncover malicious vehicle's real identity from by using the master key t. KGC takes responsibility for the generation of the vehicle's partial private key. However, adversaries can only output a valid signature if they have the secret key of the vehicle.

Resistance Against Different Types of Attacks: VANETs are susceptible to suffer multiple security attacks, such as replay attack, impersonation attack and conclusion attack. The CPBA scheme can resist these attacks securely. Prove as follows:

Replay Attack: The timestamp tm_i in the broadcast message $\{PID_i, m_i \parallel tm_i, U_i, \sigma_i\}$ is used to ensure the message freshness. Forgery of a timestamp would fail the signature validation. Thus, the CPBA scheme is secure from replay attacks.

Impersonation Attack: The ECDLP problem can be described as: Given two random points $P, Y = yP \in G$, find a integer s, such that $Y = sP$, where $s \in Z_q^*$. It has been proved that it is infeasible to calculate s from P, Y. Considering the ECDLP is hard, no polynormal adversary is able to forge a legal message $\{PID_i, m_i \parallel tm_i, U_i, \sigma_i\}$ satisfying the equation $\delta_i \cdot P = B_i + h_{4i} \cdot U_i + h_{2i} \cdot P_{pub} + K_{pub}$. Therefore, the CPBA scheme can resist impersonation attacks.

Conclusion Attack: Conclusion attack means that several attackers work together to obtain the secret key. Once a malicious vehicle has been identified, the CRL list containing all the pseudonyms it use would prevent it from regaining a domain key upon its join. Several revoked adversaries cooperate with each other to infer the updated domain key. Multiple existing vehicles cannot conspire to get the current domain key k_d, since the value of var_i is subtracted from μ and the paired relative primes used are sufficiently large. Thus, the CPBA scheme can resist conclusion attacks.

5 Performance Analysis and Comparison

5.1 Computation Analysis

In this part, we analysis the computation overheads with its related work: ABAH [9] and PCPA [10]. Utilizing the MIRACL library [11], duration of executing basic cryptographic operations can be obtained. We adopt the execution duration in the PCPA as shown in Table 2, to reduce the comparative phase and more intuitively represent the advantage of CPBA scheme in terms of computational efficiency. we will not take point addition and one-way hash function into consideration due to their negligible impact in complexity comparison.

We set the bilinear pairing on 80 bits security level, as $\bar{e} : G_1 \times G_1 \rightarrow G_T$, where G_1 is an additive group which is generated by a point $\bar{p}$ with the order $\bar{q}$ on a super singular elliptic curve $\bar{E} : y^2 = x^3 + x \bmod \bar{p}$ with embedding degree 2. The length of the prime $\bar{q}$ and $\bar{p}$ is 160-bit and 512-bit, respectively. For the proposed scheme CPBA, we use a generator P to construct an additive group G on a non-singular elliptic curve $E : y^2 = x^3 + ax + b \bmod p$, where p, q are 160 bits, and $a, b \in Z_q^*$.

Table 2. Execution time of cryptographic operation

Cryptographic operation	Time (ms)
The bilinear pairing T_p	9.0791
The scale multiplication in bilinear pairing T_{m-bp}	3.7770
The scale multiplication in ECC T_{m-ecc}	0.8310

As shown in Table 3 and Fig. 2, the proposed CPBA scheme has a lower computation costs than ABAH and PCPA, ignoring the time cost of CRL distribution and query. According to [12], the time of inserting all of the certificates from a revoked vehicle to CRL is 10–100 ms, while the search operation costs half of time.

Table 3. Execution time of cryptographic operation.

Scheme	Sign	Batch verification
ABAH	15.108 ms	3.777n+31.0143 ms
PCPA	0.8310 ms	3.324n ms
Proposed	0.8310 ms	0.8310n+1.662 ms

In the Sign phases of ABAH, the signer takes four scalar multiplications in bilinear pairing during the Sign phases of ABAH, and the signing time of ABAH is $4T_{m-bp} = 15.108$ ms. Batch verification of ABAH requires (n + 1) scalar multiplications in bilinear pairing and three bilinear pairings. Thus, the total verification time of ABAH is $(n + 1)T_{m-bp} + 3T_p = 3.777n + 31.0143$ ms. The signing time of PCPA is $T_{m-ecc} = 0.8310$ ms and the verification time of PCPA is $4nT_{m-ecc} = 3.324n$ ms. The signing time of the proposed CPBA scheme is $T_{m-ecc} = 0.8310$ ms and the verification time is $(n + 2)T_{m-ecc} = 0.8310n + 1.662$ ms.

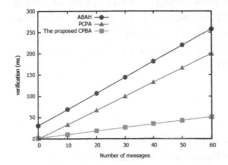

Fig. 2. Batch verification cost.   **Fig. 3.** Communication Cost.

5.2   Communication Analysis

We analysis the communication cost of ABAH, PCPA and the proposed CPBA scheme. According to the previous section, the length of $\overline{P}$ is 64 bytes and the length of p is 20 bytes. Therefore, the length of elements in G and G_1 are 40 bytes and 128 bytes respectively. The length of timestamp and a hash function's output is 4 bytes and 20 bytes, respectively.

Table 4. Comparison of communication cost.

Scheme	Send a message	Send n messages
ABAH	408 bytes	408n bytes
PCPA	188 bytes	188n bytes
Proposed	168 bytes	168n bytes

In ABAH, the structure of message is $\{M, tt, PID, Y\}$, where $PID = H_3(S_{1,j} \oplus S_{2,C-j+1})$, which denotes the pseudo-identity of , and $Y = (T, U, W)$ is the signature of the message, $T, U, W \in G_1$. Therefore, the additional communication cost of PCPA is $|tt| + |PID| + |T| + |U| + |W| = 4 + 20 + 3 \times 128 = 408$ bytes.

In PCPA, the structure of message is $\{M_i, PID_i, PK_i, ct_i, u_i, v_i\}$, where $PID_i = \{PID_{i,1}, PID_{i,2}, T_i\}$, $PID_{i,1} \in G$ and $PID_{i,2} \in Z_q^*$. T_i denotes the validity time. Therefore, the additional communication cost of PCPA is $|PID_i| + |PK_i| + |ct_i| + |u_i| + |v_i| = 64 + 80 + 4 + 20 + 20 = 188$ bytes.

In the proposed CPBA scheme, the structure of message is $\{PID_i, m_i\|tm_i, U_i, \sigma_i\}$, where $PID_i = \{PID_{i,1}, PID_{i,2}, T_i\}$, $PID_{i,1} \in G$ and $PID_{i,2} \in Z_q^*$. The timestamp of the message tm_i can avoid replay attack and $\sigma_i = (B_i, \delta_i)$. Therefore, the additional communication cost of CPBA is $|PID_i| + |tm_i| + |U_i| + |B_i| + |\delta_i| = 64 + 4 + 40 + 40 + 20 = 168$ bytes.

As shown in Table 4 and Fig. 3, we make comparisons on the communication cost between sending one message and multiple messages. In all those schemes, the communication cost grows in logarithmic in the number of the messages. The proposed CPBA scheme has a lower communication costs than ABAH and PCPA, ignoring the storage overhead of CRLs.

6 Conclusion

An efficient authentication scheme is proposed in this paper for VANET, namely CPBA, with the purpose of solving the problem of inadequate CRLs checking overhead. Our CPBA scheme proposed is able to realize conditional privacy preservation through vehicle pseudo identity, and support batch verification while not having to broadcast CRLs to each vehicle, avoiding excessive computational overhead and storage space occupied in vehicles. In addition, we can solve the key escrow. Moreover, the security analysis indicates that CPBA complies with VANET security and privacy needs; the performance analysis indicates that compared with other schemes, the CPBA scheme proposed is more efficient from the aspect of communication efficiency and computational overhead. Overall, CPBA achieves better security and performance.

Acknowledgment. This paper was supported by the National Key R&D Program of China under Grant No. 2017YFB0802703 and the National Natural Science Foundation of China under Grant No. 61602052.

References

1. Liu, X., Fang, Z., Shi, L.: Securing vehicular ad hoc networks. In: 2007 2nd International Conference on Pervasive Computing and Applications, pp. 424–429 (2007)
2. Lin, X., Sun, X., Ho, P., Shen, X.: GSIS: a secure and privacy-preserving protocol for vehicular communications. IEEE Trans. Veh. Technol. **56**(6), 3442–3456 (2007)
3. Sun, Y., Lu, R., Lin, X., Shen, X., Su, J.: An efficient pseudonymous authentication scheme with strong privacy preservation for vehicular communications. IEEE Trans. Veh. Technol. **59**(7), 3589–3603 (2010)
4. Sun, J., Zhang, C., Zhang, Y., Fang, Y.: An identity-based security system for user privacy in vehicular ad hoc networks. IEEE Trans. Parallel Distrib. Syst. **21**(9), 1227–1239 (2010)

5. Lee, C., Lai, Y.: Toward a secure batch verification with group testing for VANET. Wirel. Netw. **19**(6), 1441–1449 (2013). https://doi.org/10.1007/s11276-013-0543-7

6. Lo, N., Tsai, J.: An efficient conditional privacy-preserving authentication scheme for vehicular sensor networks without pairings. IEEE Trans. Intell. Transp. Syst. **17**(5), 1319–1328 (2015)

7. Li, J., Lu, H., Guizani, M.: ACPN: a novel authentication framework with conditional privacy-preservation and non-repudiation for VANETs. IEEE Trans. Parallel Distrib. Syst. **26**(4), 938–948 (2014)

8. Kumar, P., Kumari, S., Sharma, V., Li, X., Sangaiah, A.K., Islam, S.K.H.: Secure CLS and CL-AS schemes designed for VANETs. J. Supercomput. **75**(6), 3076–3098 (2018). https://doi.org/10.1007/s11227-018-2312-y

9. Jiang, S., Zhu, X., Wang, L.: An efficient anonymous batch authentication scheme based on HMAC for VANETs. IEEE Trans. Intell. Transp. Syst. **17**(8), 2193–2204 (2016)

10. Ming, Y., Shen, X.: PCPA: a practical certificateless conditional privacy preserving authentication scheme for vehicular ad hoc networks. Sensors **18**(5), 1573 (2018)

11. Wenger, E., Werner, M.: Evaluating 16-bit processors for elliptic curve cryptography. In: Prouff, E. (ed.) CARDIS 2011. LNCS, vol. 7079, pp. 166–181. Springer, Heidelberg (2011). https://doi.org/10.1007/978-3-642-27257-8_11

12. Haas, J., Hu, Y., Laberteaux, K.: Efficient certificate revocation list organization and distribution. IEEE J. Sel. Areas Commun. **29**(3), 595–604 (2011)

13. Vijayakumar, P., Bose, S., Kannan, A.: Chinese remainder theorem based centralised group key management for secure multicast communication. IET Inf. Secur. **8**(3), 179–187 (2014)

14. Jiang, W., Li, F., Lin, D.: No one can track you: randomized authentication in vehicular ad-hoc networks. In: 2017 IEEE International Conference on Pervasive Computing and Communications (PerCom), pp. 197–206 (2017)

Consensus in Wireless Blockchain System

Qiang Xu[1], Yifei Zou[2,3], Dongxiao Yu[1(✉)], Minghui Xu[4], Shikun Shen[5],
and Feng Li[1(✉)]

[1] School of Computer Science and Technology, Shandong University,
Qingdao, People's Republic of China
2018148410mail.sdu.edu.cn, {dxyu,fli}@sdu.edu.cn
[2] Shenzhen Institutes of Advanced Technology, Chinese Academy of Sciences,
Shenzhen, People's Republic of China
yf.zou@siat.ac.cn
[3] Department of Computer Science, The University of Hong Kong,
Hong Kong, People's Republic of China
[4] Department of Computer Science, The George Washington University,
Washington DC, USA
mhxu@gwu.edu
[5] School of Computer Science, Wuhan University, Wuhan, People's Republic of China
whussk@qq.com

Abstract. In recent years, blockchain system has attracted more and
more attention from people around the world, not only due to its popular
application: Bitcoin [8], but also because it is an important building block
in city Internet-of-Things. In this paper, we study the consensus problem
in wireless blockchain system. As the first one considering the challenges
of message transmission in wireless blockchain system, we propose an
optimal consensus protocol for the devices in wireless blockchain system,
by executed which all devices can achieve a consensus within $O(\log n)$
time steps with high probability. We believe that this consensus protocol can facilitate many fundamental operations in wireless blockchain
system, and make the smart city system more efficient and robust.

Keywords: Consensus protocol · Wireless blockchain system ·
Internet-of-Things

1 Introduction

In the past decades, with the exponential implementation of large-scale wireless networks, the **Internet-of-Things** (IoT) technology has become an integral part of the real world [3,4,6,14,17,19], especially in the scenarios of data
sensing/gathering from environment in smart city systems. As one of the most

This work is partially supported by National Key R & D Program of China with grant
No. 2019YFB2102600, and NSFC (No. 61971269, 61702304), Shandong Provincial Nat-
ural Science Foundation (Grant No. ZR2017QF005), Industrial Internet Innovation and
Development Project in 2019 of China.

© Springer Nature Switzerland AG 2020
D. Yu et al. (Eds.): WASA 2020, LNCS 12384, pp. 568–579, 2020.
https://doi.org/10.1007/978-3-030-59016-1_47

appropriate technologies to support IoT [7,9,20,21], **blockchain** technology has also come into people's sight in both of the academic research and the industrial application. Briefly, the implementation of a blockchain system consists of several fundamental technologies, including cryptographic hash, digital signature and distributed consensus protocol. The cryptographic hash technology help to construct Merkle tree, design PoW puzzle and so on. The digital signature makes sure that the identity of the node sending the message is unique. The distributed consensus protocol is executed by each node in blockchain network to exchange message and make local decision, which guarantees the consistency of the distributed ledgers. Thus, all nodes in blockchain network can maintain a same and common transaction ledger. Among all technologies above, the distributed consensus protocol is the key technology that enables blockchain's decentralization, which can greatly affect the performance of a blockchain network, including its throughput, scalability, and fault tolerance. Obviously, an efficient fault-tolerant consensus protocol can greatly facilitate the fundamental operations in Internet of Things, also satisfy the high-confidence demands in city IoT, which directly motivate our work in this paper.

Generally in the previous works, two main kinds of consensus protocols are widely used in blockchain. The first one is Proof-of-X (PoX) consensus protocols, e.g.., Proof-of-Work (PoW), Proof-of-Stake (PoS) [1], which requires the nodes in blockchain to prove that they are more qualified than the others to do the appending work. The other one is Byzantine Fault Tolerant (BFT)-based consensus protocols, e.g.., Practical Byzantine Fault Tolerance (PBFT) [2] and HotStuff [10], which requires nodes in the blockchain network to exchange their results of verifying a new block or transaction, before voting for the final decision. Each of them has its own trade-offs. For example, most of PoX consensus protocols are highly scalable but inefficient, which are mainly used in pubic blockchain. Whereas, BFT-based consensus protocols are efficient but are not scalable in terms of number of nodes in the blockchain network. Thus, they are more suitable in consortium and private blockchain.

Main Challenges. To design an efficient consensus protocol in IoT, there are three main challenges considering the edge device and environment of IoT. Firstly, due to the low-powered mobile devices in the IoT, the consensus protocol is required to be high throughput, energy efficiency, and insensitive to the mobility of device. Second, because multi-devices can get access to a same wireless channel, the transmissions between nodes influence with each other. The uncertainty (i.e., transmission of a message may fail) and instability (i.e., an efficient transmission of information over long periods of time is not guaranteed) of message transmission in wireless network contribute to the difficulty of achieving consensus in wireless environment. The third challenge is taken by the notorious state fork problem, which happens when more than one valid block appear simultaneously. It deserves to note that the state fork problem also reduces the scalability and energy efficiency in consensus protocol. And the situation even gets worse in a multi-hop wireless network because of the inherent latency in message transmission.

To solve the challenges mentioned above, a new Proof-of-Communication (PoC) consensus protocol in wireless blockchain system is proposed in our work. Specifically, all miners, i.e., edge devices in IoT participate in a leader competition process via communication. The miner who is elected as the leader can broadcast the verified block to other miners. An efficient leader competition scheme, which fully makes use of the received signal in channel to elect one and only one leader to write the block in the blockchain, is adopted to solve the fork problem.

Our Contributions. In this paper, we present an efficient and fair distributed consensus protocol in wireless blockchain network, by executing which all miners can achieve a consensus within $O(\log n)$ time-steps w.h.p.(with high probability for short). Specifically, we highlight our contributions in the following:

(a). In our work, the proposed PoC consensus protocol has the time complexity of $O(\log n)$, which is asymptotically optimal considering a well known lower bound $\Omega(\log n)$ [11].

(b). We are the first one considering the blockchain consensus protocol in the context of wireless network. Thus, our wireless blockchain consensus protocol makes the wireless research in blockchain system more completed.

(c). In this paper, we show how to design a PoC based scheme in wireless environment to achieve the consensus in blockchain, and how to solve the fork problem by a wireless competition scheme, which may take a new sight for the following wireless protocol design in blockchain system.

2   Model and Problem Definition

We model a wireless blockchain network in a 2-dimensional Euclidean space. The devices of IoT in the network are called miners[1]. We consider the blockchain network as a peer-to-peer overlay network, where every miners are directly reachable by all others. Every miner is equipped with a half-duplex transceiver, i.e., each miner can transmit or listen in each slot but cannot do both. The time is divided into synchronized slot, which is a time unit for transmitting a message.

The realistic SINR model, which has been widely considered in [12,13,15,16, 18,22] recently, is adopted to depict the message reception in this work. For a miner v, let $Signal(v)$ be the strength of the signal received by v, and $SINR(u,v)$ be the SINR ratio of miner v for the transmission from u. Then, we have

$$Signal(v) = \sum_{w \in S} P_w \cdot d(w,v)^{-\alpha} + \mathcal{N},$$

$$SINR(u,v) = \frac{P_u \cdot d(u,v)^{-\alpha}}{\sum_{w \in S \setminus \{u\}} P_w \cdot d(w,v)^{-\alpha} + \mathcal{N}}$$

---

[1] (Although the IoT edge devices in wireless blockchain network can be categorized as lightweight node and full node, for the sake of simplification, we briefly use miners to denote the devices in our protocol).

In the above equations, S is the set of transmitters in current slot, $d(w, v)$ denotes the Euclidean distance between miners w and v, P_w is the transmission power of miner w, $\alpha \in (2, 6]$ is the path-loss exponent, $\mathcal{N}$ is the ambient noise. When $SINR(u, v) \geq \beta$, the message from u can be successfully decoded by v, where β is a threshold determined by hardware and larger than 1 in usual.

Here, we take N as a close upper bound of ambient noise $\mathcal{N}$. N is so close to ambient noise $\mathcal{N}$ that when there are transmissions in network, the accumulation of signals from transmissions and ambient noise on any miner is larger than N. Thus, at this moment, for any listening miner v with a non-empty set S, the received signal has the strength $Signal(v)$ larger than N. Also, physical carrier sensing, which is a part of the IEEE 802.11 standard in medium access control (MAC) layer, is equipped on each miner. Considering the permissionless blockchain network with loose control on the synchronization and behaviors of the miners, asynchronous wake-up mode is adopted(i.e., each miner can wake up at the beginning of any round at will) to make our model closer to the reality.

Problem Definition. There are n miners deployed on a 2-dimensional Euclidean space, which can transmit with each other via the multiple access wireless channel. n can be sufficient large and miners only have a rough estimation on n. In each interval which consists of sufficient slots, by executing the designed blockchain consensus protocol, a group of miners are required to elect a miner as the leader, who will record transactions of the network occurred in current interval into a block and write the block in the blockchain. Finally, all miners make a consensus on the recorded block.

3   PoC Consensus Protocol

3.1   Framework of Consensus Protocol

We follow the general framework of blockchain consensus to design our protocol. Specifically, there are four phases in the consensus process: leader election, block proposal, block validation, and chain update. The input of the consensus process is trading data generated and validated by miners; while the output is encapsulated blocks and the updated blockchain. Our consensus protocol follows the four phases above completely. In leader election phase, only one leader will be elected w.h.p. by means of an efficient wireless competition scheme. In the next phase, the leader proposes a new block and transmits the block to all the other miners. In the third phase, all other miners feed back their validation results to the leader. And in the final phase, the leader decides whether to update the block in the blockchain according to the received feedback. It deserves to note that in our protocol, only one valid block will be accepted by all miners eventually in each time of the consensus process, which helps to avoid the state fork problem in traditional blockchain consensus design.

Goal of Consensus. The classical consensus in a distributed system is a state that all nodes in system agree on same data values, which satisfies the termination (i.e., all nodes terminate in finite time), validity (i.e., the decision value must be the input value of a node) and agreement (i.e., all nodes agree on a same value) [5].

3.2 Detail Description for PoC Consensus

In our protocol, the executed time is divided into rounds, each of which contains 5 slots. Four functions are given in our protocol: Leader Election( ), Block Proposal( ), Block Validation( ) and Chain Update( ). In each round, each miner will execute the four functions one by one. The pseudocode is given in Fig. 1.

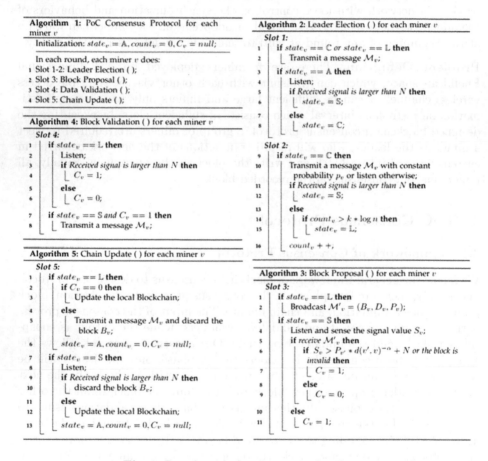

Fig. 1. Pseudo code for consensus algorihtms

Four states are used to help the execution for each miners: $\mathbb{A}$ is the mining state, in which miners wake up and try to compete for the leadership to propose a new block; $\mathbb{C}$ is the candidate state, in which miners are in the leader competition; $\mathbb{S}$ is the silence state, in which miners have already given up the leader election; and $\mathbb{L}$ is the leader state, in which the miner succeeded in leader competition and becomes the leader to propose a new block.

For each miner v, it is firstly in state $\mathbb{A}$ when waking up. Then, it starts to execute the four functions in each of the following rounds as is given in Algorithm 1.

In slot 1, miners v in state $\mathbb{C}$ or $\mathbb{L}$ would transmit a message $\mathcal{M}_v$ in order to stop other mining miners from leader competition. Meanwhile, miners u in state $\mathbb{A}$ listen and sense the channel. If the received signal of u has the strength larger than N, which means that there are already some miners in $\mathbb{C}$ or $\mathbb{L}$, u gives up the leader election and move in state $\mathbb{S}$. Otherwise, u move to state $\mathbb{C}$ at the end of slot 1. Slot 1 makes sure that only the group of miners that firstly wake up in current interval become the candidates in the following leader election in slot 2. With this manner, the number of miners competing for leader can be reduced to some extent.

In slot 2, miners v in state $\mathbb{C}$ transmit with a constant probability. If a miner v listens and the received signal has its strength larger than N, v moves to state $\mathbb{S}$, which means that v gives up the leader competition. If v keeps in state $\mathbb{C}$ in at least $k * \log n$ rounds, in which k is a sufficient large constant, v moves to state $\mathbb{L}$, i.e., v becomes the leader. Via actions in slot 2, one and only one miner is elected out as the leader w.h.p, the proof of which is given in the next section. The function Block Proposal( ) is given in Algorithm 3, which is executed by each miner in slot 3. The leader v packs up the newly proposed block B_v, its location information D_v and transmission power P_v into message $\mathcal{M}'_v$, and then disseminates message $\mathcal{M}'_v$ to all other miners in the blockchain network. If the message $\mathcal{M}'_v$ is received by the miners in state $\mathbb{S}$, the miners would confirm the uniqueness of the leader v and verify the validity of the block B_v. Specially, this is to make sure that there is only one leader elected, and only one valid block proposed in each time of the consensus process. and we call a leader that meeting the above condition as legitimate leader. It deserves to note that the location information and transmission power of leader v in message $\mathcal{M}'_v$ is used by other miners to calculate the theoretical maximum of signal strength $P_{v'} * d(v', v)^{-\alpha} + N$ to judge whether there is only one leader elected in the blockchain network.

The fourth slot of a round is used for Block Validation( ) as given in Algorithm 4. As described in the algorithm, the dissenting miner in state $\mathbb{S}$ who has sensed that there are multiple leaders in the wireless blockchain network or verified the block as an invalid one would transmit a message $\mathcal{M}_v$. The leader v would decide whether to accept the new block B_v in the following phase according to the strength of received signal.

The last slot of each round is for the function Chain Update( ) as shown in Algorithm 5. If there are multiple leaders in the blockchain network or the new block is regarded as invalid, the leader v would transmit a message $\mathcal{M}_v$ and discard block B_v, meanwhile other miners in state $\mathbb{S}$ would discard block

B_v according to the leader's decision. Otherwise, every miner in the wireless blockchain network will write the new block B_v on its local blockchain.

4   Protocol Analysis

In this section, we analyze the correctness, efficiency and security of our PoC consensus protocol.

Theorem 1. *It takes at most $O(\log n)$ rounds to make all miners in blockchain network achieve consensus w.h.p.*

We prove Theorem 1 from three aspects, termination, validity and agreement by the subsequent Lemma 1 and Lemma 3, respectively.

Lemma 1. *After at most $O(\log n)$ rounds from the time when there are miners waking up, all miners terminate the consensus process, w.h.p.*

Obviously, when exactly only one leader is elected out, an extra round is enough for the leader to propose a new block and the other nodes to make a consensus on the block. Thus, it is the leader election process matters for the termination of our consensus protocol, which is analysis and proved by the following Lemma 2.

Lemma 2. *It takes at most $O(\log n)$ rounds to exactly elect one leader from the time when there are miners waking up, w.h.p.*

We first show that only those miners who firstly wake up and participate in the consensus process can become the candidates in the leader competition. Then, it is proved that exactly only one leader is elected out among the candidates within $O(\log n)$ rounds w.h.p.

Claim 1. *Only the miners firstly waking up and participating in the consensus process can become the candidates in the leader competition.*

Proof. From the algorithm 2, it is easy to see that the miners first waking up and participating in the consensus process can become the candidates. Hence, we in the next consider that miners that waking up later will not become the candidate. Consider a miner u that waking up later. By thepf algorithm description, there have been some miners becoming the candidates or the leader, and transmitting in Slot 1 of every round. So the signal strength sensed by u is larger than N in Slot 1 of the first round when it wakes up. Hence, u will change its state to $\mathbb{S}$ and stop competing.

Claim 1 indicates that the number of miners in state $\mathbb{C}$ will not increase after there are miners joining in state $\mathbb{C}$. We next consider the reduction of the candidates. By the algorithm, we only need to show that after $k * \log n$ rounds, there is exactly one candidate left w.h.p, which will become the leader.

Let's assume that at round t, the first group of miners become the candidates for leader election, denoted by set C. The following analysis for candidates' reduction in the slot 1 is divided into three cases: (1) $|C| = 1$; (2) $|C|$ is a constant larger than 1; (3) $|C|$ is sufficiently large, not a constant any more. If $|C| = 1$, the leader election is already finished. For the other two cases, assume that $\{v_1, v_2, \ldots, v_{|C|}\}$ are the candidates in C. In slot 2, each candidate v transmits $\mathcal{M}_v$ with a same constant probability p by setting $p_v = p$.

Claim 2. *When $|C|$ is a constant larger than 1, it takes $O(\log n)$ rounds to exactly elect one leader w.h.p.*

Proof. It is easy to prove that at least one miner in set C gives up the leader election in each round with at least a constant probability. Thus, by applying a Chernoff bound, this claim can be proved.

We next consider the case that $|C|$ is sufficiently large.

Claim 3. *If $|C|$ is sufficiently large, it takes $O(\log n)$ rounds to elect a leader w.h.p.*

Proof. We prove this claim by two steps. Firstly, we show that in each round, at least a constant fraction of candidates stop the leader competition with a constant probability. Then, by applying a Chernoff bound, we prove this claim.

Thus, only one leader will be elected out within $O(\log n)$ rounds after the first group of miners waking up w.h.p. Then, all miners will get a consensus in the next round with the help of the leader. Combining the three Claims above, we prove that the protocol satisfies termination requirement and has an efficient time complexity. Although the situation that more than one leader are elected occurs with a negligible probability, we still take into account it. This problem is fully solved by the Block Proposal phase and Block Validation phase, the proof of which is given in Lemma 3.

Lemma 3. *The protocol satisfies the validity and agreement requirement.*

The following three claims are used to prove the validity and agreement of our consensus algorithm.

Claim 4. *If and only if the new block B_v generated by the only one leader v is valid and approved by the other miners in the current round, B_v will be updated to the local blockchain as the next block for each miner in the blockchain network.*

Proof. The following analysis is divided into two cases: (1) There is only one leader in the current round in the blockchain network. Then, every miner u in state $\mathbb{S}$ will verify the validity of the block proposed by leader. (2) There are multiple leaders v_is elected in current round. Then, every miner u in state $\mathbb{S}$ will receive a message $\mathcal{M}'_{v_i}$, or receive nothing. If the received message is $\mathcal{M}'_{v_i}$, each miner u will confirm the uniqueness of the leader v_i by comparing $S(u)$ with the theoretical maximum value $S'_u = P_{v_i} * d(v_i, u)^{-\alpha} + N$. If there are multiple leaders, $S(u) > S'_u$. Then, u set $C_u = 1$ to indicate a multiple leader situation. Also, if nothing is received, u set $C_u = 1$.

Claim 5. *Whether the new block B_v proposed by the only one leader v is valid or not, all miners of the blockchain network will have the same decision on either accept or discard B_v.*

Proof. From the proof of Claim 4 we can get the following facts: (1) If the new block B_v proposed by the leader v is valid, B_v will accept by all miners; (2) Conversely, if the new block B_v proposed by the leader v is invalid, B_v will discard by all miners. Therefore, for any miner the latest block of its local blockchain is the same.

Claim 6. *For any pair of miners v and u in blockchain network, if the block B_v^i and B_u^i is the i'th block in local blockchain of u and v, B_v^i and B_u^i are the same.*

Proof. If one of the miner v and u becomes the leader in round l. Without loss of generality assume that v is the leader, and propose the i'th valid block B_v^i. According to Claim 4, v will write the new block B_v^i into its local blockchain, and the miner u will update its local blockchain by B_v^i simultaneously.

If neither of the miner v and u becomes the leader in round l, assume that the i'th valid block B_w^i is generated by leader w. Similarly according to Claim 4, the leader w will write the new block B_w^i into its local blockchain, the miner v and u will update their local blockchain B_w^i simultaneously. Therefore, B_v^i and B_u^i are same anyway.

5   Simulation Result

In this section, we present the empirical performance of our PoC consensus protocol in simulation. Specifically, we focus on the time used for achieving consensus in the wireless blockchain network with different network sizes in case of (i) only one leader elected, and (ii) multiple leaders elected, which is in usual caused by faults or adversary attacks. Meanwhile, the reduction of candidates and the fairness of the protocol presented in simulation can further verify our theoretical analysis.

Parameter Setting. In the simulation, n miners are randomly and uniformly distributed in a wireless blockchain network with size of $100m \times 100m$, the minimum distance between miners is $1m$. The ambient noise upper bound N is

Table 1. Parameters in simulation

Parameters	Value	Parameters	Value
N	1.0	β	1.5
λ	1.0	η	$\in \{1, 3, 5, 7, 9\} * 10^{-1}$
p_v	0.2	n	$\in \{0.01, 0.1, 0.5, 1, 2, 4, 6, 8, 10\} * 10^3$
α	3.0	P_v	$\in [(100\sqrt{2})^\alpha * \beta N, 200^\alpha * \beta N]$

normalized as 1.0. The constant η is used to depict the proportion of miners, who firstly wake up and participate in the consensus process. Specifically, it is assumed that η fraction of miners firstly wake up and participate in the consensus process. Considering some redundant leaders elected because of faults or adversary attack, we assume that the number of redundant leaders in each consensus period follows an exponential distribution with expected value $\lambda = 1.0$. The transmission probability is set to $p_v = 0.2$. P_v is the transmission power of each miner, which is randomly selected from an interval and makes sure any pair of miners could receive a message from each other in the wireless network. Table 1 summarizes the parameters given above.

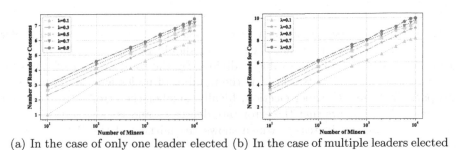

(a) In the case of only one leader elected (b) In the case of multiple leaders elected

Fig. 2. Rounds used for achieving consensus

Protocol Performance. The correctness and efficiency of our protocol used for achieving consensus in wireless blockchain network is given in Fig. 2, in which the x-axes and y-axes represent the blockchain network size n and rounds used for achieving consensus respectively. From Fig. 2 (a), which depicts the scenario in a wireless blockchain network with $\alpha = 3.0$ and $\beta = 1.5$, we can see that when n is fixed and λ gets larger or λ is fixed and n gets larger, the round used for achieving consensus increases. This phenomenon indicates that it is the number of miners that firstly wakes up and participates PoC consensus process in blockchain network determines the running time of our consensus protocol. Even in the case of $n = 10000$ and $\lambda = 0.9$, which means that 9000 miners initially waking up simultaneously, our protocol can achieve consensus within 10 rounds, which confirms the efficiency of our protocol. Figure 2 (b) shows the redundant leaders caused by faults and adversary attacks does not gain too much difficulty for our consensus protocol. It just takes several more rounds for miners to achieve a consensus when facing redundant leaders problem.

In our protocol, only the miners firstly waking up and participating in the consensus process can become the candidates in the leader competition. To illustrate the leader competition process in details, fixing $n = 10000$, we show the number of candidates in each round in Fig. 3. We get that a constant fraction of candidates are reduced in each round, which further verifies our previous analysis. We use the concept of error rate to present the fairness of the PoC consensus

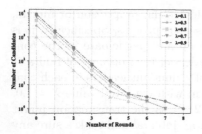
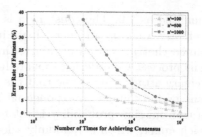
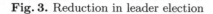

Fig. 3. Reduction in leader election   **Fig. 4.** Fairness in consensus

protocol. We first take the number of times that each miners became a leader minus the number of times that each miners should become a leader in expectation, and then the absolute value is divided by the total number of times for achieving consensus in network. n' is the number of nodes who firstly wake up and participate in the leader election. Ideally, smaller the error rate, fairer our protocol is Fig. 4 shows that the error rate decreases and is close to 0 when the number of consensus increases, which shows the fairness of the PoC consensus protocol.

6   Conclusion

In this paper, we are the first one considering the blockchain consensus protocol in the context of wireless network, which makes blockchain technology more suited to edge devices in IoT. Specifically, a Proof-of-Communication consensus protocol with the time complexity of $O(\log n)$ is proposed, with the performance of efficiency and security guaranteed. Also, it deserves to note that our way of implementing blockchain consensus protocol in wireless network can take some new sight for the following wireless protocol design in the blockchain system. The wireless research in blockchain system with jamming or even byzantine fault tolerance will become our future direction, since jamming and byzantine failure are the common phenomena in the IoT networks.

References

1. Bitcoinwiki. Proof of stake (2014). https://en.bitcoin.it/wiki/Proof_of_Stake
2. Castro, M., Liskov, B.: Practical byzantine fault tolerance. In: OSDI (1999)
3. Cheng, S., Cai, Z., Li, J.: Curve query processing in wireless sensor networks. IEEE Trans. Veh. Technol. **64**(11), 5198–5209 (2015)
4. Cheng, S., Cai, Z., Li, J., Fang, X.: Drawing dominant dataset from big sensory data in wireless sensor networks. In: INFOCOM (2015)
5. Dwork, C., Lynch, N.A., Stockmeyer, L.J.: Consensus in the presence of partial synchrony (preliminary version). In: PODC (1984)

6. He, Z., Cai, Z., Cheng, S., Wang, X.: Approximate aggregation for tracking quantiles and range countings in wireless sensor networks. Theor. Comput. Sci. **607**(3), 381–390 (2015)
7. Huckle, S., Bhattacharya, R., White, M., Beloff, N.: Internet of things, blockchain and shared economy applications. In: EUSPN/ICTH (2016)
8. Nakamoto, S.: Bitcoin: a peer-to-peer electronic cash system (2008). https://bitcoin.org/bitcoin.pdf
9. Novo, O.: Blockchain meets IoT: an architecture for scalable access management in IoT. IEEE Internet Things J. **5**(2), 1184–1195 (2018)
10. Yin, M., Malkhi, D., Reiter, M.K., Golan-Gueta, G., Abraham, I.: Hotstuff: BFT consensus with linearity and responsiveness. In: PODC (2019)
11. Yu, D., Hua, Q., Wang, Y., Lau, F.C.M.: An o(log n) distributed approximation algorithm for local broadcasting in unstructured wireless networks. In: DCOSS (2012)
12. Yu, D., Ning, L., Zou, Y., Yu, J., Cheng, X., Lau, F.C.M.: Distributed spanner construction with physical interference: constant stretch and linear sparseness. IEEE/ACM Trans. Netw. **25**(4), 2138–2151 (2017)
13. Yu, D., Wang, Y., Halldórsson, M.M., Tonoyan, T.: Dynamic adaptation in wireless networks under comprehensive interference via carrier sense. In: IPDPS (2017)
14. Yu, J., et al.: Efficient link scheduling in wireless networks under Rayleigh-fading and multiuser interference. IEEE Trans. Wirel. Commun. (2020). https://doi.org/10.1109/TWC.2020.2994998
15. Yu, D., Zhang, Y., Huang, Y., Jin, H., Yu, J., Hua, Q.: Exact implementation of abstract MAC layer via carrier sensing. In: INFOCOM (2018)
16. Yu, D., et al.: Stable local broadcast in multihop wireless networks under SINR. IEEE/ACM Trans. Netw. **26**(3), 1278–1291 (2018)
17. Yu, D., et al.: Implementing abstract MAC layer in dynamic networks. IEEE Trans. Mob. Comput. (2020). https://doi.org/10.1109/TMC.2020.2971599
18. Yu, D., et al.: Distributed dominating set and connected dominating set construction under the dynamic SINR model. In: IPDPS (2019)
19. Zanella, A., Bui, N., Castellani, A.P., Vangelista, L., Zorzi, M.: Internet of things for smart cities. IEEE Internet Things J. **1**(1), 22–32 (2014)
20. Zhu, S., Cai, Z., Hu, H., Li, Y., Li, W.: zkCrowd: a hybrid blockchain-based crowdsourcing platform. IEEE Trans. Ind. Inform. **16**(6), 4196–4205 (2020)
21. Zhu, S., Li, W., Li, H., Tian, L., Luo, G., Cai, Z.: Coin hopping attack in blockchain-based IoT. IEEE Internet Things J. **6**(3), 4614–4626 (2019)
22. Zou, Y., et al.: Fast distributed backbone construction despite strong adversarial jamming. In: INFOCOM (2019)

Blockchain-Based Service Recommendation Supporting Data Sharing

Biwei Yan[1], Jiguo Yu[2,3,4(✉)], Yue Wang[2], Qiang Guo[1], Baobao Chai[2], and Suhui Liu[1]

[1] Qufu Normal University, Qufu 273165, Shandong, People's Republic of China
for_yanbiwei@163.com, 18265888368@163.com, suhliu@126.com
[2] School of Computer Science and Technology, Qilu University of Technology
(Shandong Academy of Sciences),
Jinan 250353, Shandong, People's Republic of China
jiguoyu@sina.com, wyjn@outlook.com, bbchai94@163.com
[3] Shandong Computer Science Center (National Supercomputer Center in Jinan),
Jinan 250014, Shandong, People's Republic of China
[4] Shandong Key Laboratory of Computer Networks, Jinan 250014, China

Abstract. With the rapid development of cloud computing, massive web services have appeared quickly with a heavy burden for user to choose services that they preferred. To cope with the stress, many recommendation algorithms have been proposed. Nonetheless, the recommendation effects were not ideal due to the insufficient data in a cloud platform. For this situation, it is necessary for cloud platforms to cooperate with each other to share data. However, the cloud platforms generally do not intend share the data because of the uses' privacy. Meanwhile, the traditional recommendation exist a series of challenges such as security and privacy, data tampering and so on. In order to address the above problems, we propose a blockchain-based service recommendation scheme (BPDS–SR) which can achieve a higher accuracy and lower cost with more profits.

Keywords: Blockchain · Service recommendation · Data sharing · Locality-sensitive hashing

1 Introduction

With the rapid development of the Internet and cloud computing, a large number of web services have appeared quickly, providing users with more conveniences. People can access web services to buy favorite commodities. However, due to the rapid growth of Internet users, the service information generated based on user activities has also exploded, increasing the burden for users to choose the services. In order to relieve the burden on users, many recommendation algorithms have been proposed. The early collaborative filtering recommendation

© Springer Nature Switzerland AG 2020
D. Yu et al. (Eds.): WASA 2020, LNCS 12384, pp. 580–589, 2020.
https://doi.org/10.1007/978-3-030-59016-1_48

algorithm was the user-based collaborative filtering recommendation algorithm [1]. Subsequently, in [2], Chung et al. proposed an item-based collaborative filtering recommendation algorithm. But, the algorithm does not consider the difference between users. Thus, in [3], Jiang et al. proposed a hybrid recommendation method. In order to preserve the users' privacy, in [4], Yan et al. proposed a novel distributed social Internet of Things (IoT) service recommendation scheme using LSH forest to protect the user's privacy. In [5] and [6], Frey et al. used blockchain to solve the problem of users' privacy, but in the scheme, the original data can only be accessed by the owner, meanwhile, they did not simulate relevant experiments on the accuracy. In [11], Zhu et al. proposed a hybrid blockchain crowdsourcing platform to secure communications, verify transactions, and preserve privacy. In [7], Yu et al. proposed a lightweight hybrid attribute-based signcryption scheme for cloud-fog assisted IoT to achieve the data confidentiality. In [10], Zheng et al. proposed a data sharing scheme among multiple parties in IIoTs to share data. In [8], Liu et al. proposed a blockchain-aided searchable attribute-based encryption for cloud-IoT to realize the data sharing. Besides, Wang et al. used blockchain to share information in [9], but they do not consider the security of shared data.

From the above analysis, it can be seen that the current recommendation algorithms based on the centralized data which exist many problems such as security and privacy of data, data tampering and so on. It is noted that a blockchain is a distributed ledger, which can prevent data from being tampered with and guarantee the quality of shared data in data sharing. Therefore, in this paper, we propose a blockchain-based data sharing recommendation scheme to effectively improve the distributed recommendation accuracy and protect users' privacy.

The main contribution can be summarized as follows:

- To the best of our knowledge, the current work rarely considers the service recommendation of multiple platforms for secure data sharing. In this paper, we introduce the blockchain into the recommendation system, which supports data sharing among the cloud platforms and guarantees the security of data provenance.
- A series of experiments are performed based on the dataset WS-DREAM. Through RMSE (Root Mean Square Error), MAE (Mean Absolute Error), and the usage of gas, the proposed scheme realizes a high accuracy and it can obtain more profits for cloud platforms.

The rest of the paper is organized as follows. Section 2 introduces the preliminaries of our scheme. Section 3 proposes blockchain-based service recommendation scheme in detail. Section 4 elaborates security analysis and performance evaluation based on WS-DREAM dataset. Section 5 summarizes the paper.

2   Preliminaries

2.1   Blockchain

Blockchain is the underlying technology of Bitcoin, which was originally proposed by Nakamoto in 2008 [12]. It is a distributed ledger and an effective method to solve distributed problems. Currently, blockchains are divided into three types: the public blockchain, the private blockchain, and the consortium blockchain. The public blockchain is completely decentralized, and any node can join the blockchain network and access all the data on the blockchain. The private blockchain is constructed by an institution or an organization, and only nodes belonged to the institution or the organization can join and access. The consortium blockchain allows authorized nodes to join the blockchain network. Nodes in the network access data according to their admissions. It is usually applied to several institutions or organizations.

The consortium blockchain integrates the advantages of private blockchain and public blockchain. Therefore, it has the characteristics of privacy and the decentralization belonged to the private blockchain and public blockchain, respectively. Nodes need to be authenticated before they join the consortium blockchain. Combined with the advantages of fast transaction processing, flexible transactions, multi-centralization, and high scalability, the application scope is wider. Therefore, we use the consortium blockchain to build our scheme.

2.2   Modern Encryption Algorithm

There are two main types of modern encryption algorithms, one is the symmetric encryption algorithm, and the other is the asymmetric encryption algorithm. In the symmetric encryption algorithm, the encryption key and decryption key are identical, and the efficiency is relatively high. While in an asymmetric encryption algorithm, it has different keys for encryption and decryption. Thus, it is more secure than the symmetric encryption algorithm. The asymmetric encryption algorithm generates a pair of keys, which are a public key and a private key, respectively. Generally, the public key is used for encryption and the private key is used for decryption. In addition, the public and private keys can also be used in the digital signature. The private key is used to sign the data, and the public key is used to verify the integrity of data. However, whether it is a symmetric encryption algorithm or an asymmetric encryption algorithm, malicious users cannot obtain real data as long as the key is not leaked.

3   Blockchain-Based Service Recommendation Scheme

3.1   Overview

In this section, a blockchain-based recommendation scheme which supports data sharing is proposed to solve distributed service recommendation. We use the consortium blockchain to construct our service recommendation scheme. Figure 1

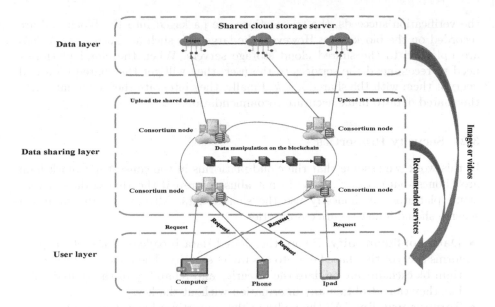

Fig. 1. The model of service recommendation using blockchain

shows our system model. This model is mainly divided into three layers: User layer, Data sharing layer, and Data layer.

1) User layer: This layer is mainly users who will access the web services by various devices. Thereby, they generate massive data in the cloud platforms. These users come from different platforms.
2) Data sharing layer: In this layer, we establish the consortium blockchain. These cloud platforms intend to share their data and record the digest of the shared on the blockchain. Then, they can get more profits through the shared data. Moreover, they also maintain a public ledger that is stored at each cloud platform.
3) Data layer: This layer includes shared cloud storage servers. Since the blockchain cannot store large amounts of data, we store large files such as images on the cloud.

As shown in Fig. 1, users send a request to the cloud platforms, and they choose a number of services they preferred. Meanwhile, they generate lots of data and store these data on the blockchain. To provide a better quality of experience (QoE) and gain maximize profits, cooperation among cloud platforms is essential. Thus, they cooperate and construct the consortium blockchain, in which they share their data. Firstly, they perform the symmetric encryption algorithm to generate the shared key k, which is assigned by the smart contract. Next, the shared data is encrypted with the shared key k, and then it is uploaded to the blockchain in the form of transaction i. After that, our system broadcasts all the transactions on the consortium blockchain, and the nodes on the consortium blockchain receive broadcasts. Then, the miners verify the shared data. If the verification succeeds, the transactions are packaged into the block and are recorded on the blockchain. However, the large files such as images and videos are uploaded to the shared cloud storage servers. When the cloud platforms need to recommend the services to the user, they will get the shared data and decrypt them with the shared key k. Finally, they integrate their own data with the shared data to make accurate recommendation.

3.2 Security Properties

In this work, we assume that the cloud platforms in the consortium blockchain are "honest-but-curious", they do not abuse or reveal the shared data. Every cloud platform can honestly use the shared data. Meanwhile, the proposed scheme should follow security properties.

- **Data confidentiality.** Before the shared data broadcasts, the cloud platforms encrypt the shared data to ensure its security. The nodes in the consortium blockchain can validate the integrity and reliability of the shared data, but they cannot obtain any information without the key.
- **Tamper-proofing.** All the nodes in the consortium blockchain cannot tamper the shared data. Once they try to tamper the shared data, they will be detected.

3.3 BPDS–SR Construction

In this section, we introduce our scheme in detail. We regard the cloud platforms which intend to share their data as the nodes on the consortium blockchain. Moreover, we use the technology of [13] for recommendation. Our scheme mainly include the following six phases (Table 1):

(1) **Key generation.** The cloud platforms execute a symmetric encryption algorithm. They input the secure parameter 1^λ and output the shared key k. Then, they record it in the smart contract.
(2) **Share the data.** The cloud platform encrypts the shared data d with key k. Then, the cloud platform sends the shared data in the form of transactions i and broadcast it to the blockchain. Meanwhile, the transactions will cost the gas. Next, the blockchain validates the shared data, and records them on the blockchain when the verification succeeds.
(3) **Decrypt the shared data.** The cloud platforms which want to use the shared data, they can get them on the blockchain. And, the smart contract will assign the shared key k to the cloud platforms which intend to use the shared data. Then, they decrypt the shared data using the key k.
(4) **Build indices for each service.** We integrate the shared data with the shared data and recommend the services and utilize the vector $\boldsymbol{I}$ to denote the web service I in the platform cp_i. The quality dimension of I is denoted by q. The vector is denoted as $\boldsymbol{I}(i) = (I_{i,1}^q, ..., I_{i,n}^q)$. Here, if $I_i^q = 0$, the user has never invoked the service I_i. Then, with the technology LSH, we

calculate the hash of $I(i)$ by the following equation in (1). Where $v = (v_1, ..., v_n)$ is an u-dimensional vector and v_i is chosen randomly from $[-1,1]$; the symbol $\circ$ denotes the dot product of two vectors.

$$h(I(i)) = \begin{cases} 1 & \text{If } I(i) \circ v > 0 \\ 0 & \text{If } I(i) \circ v \leq 0 \end{cases} \tag{1}$$

Repeat the above steps l times with different vector v, then the sub-index of the user in the platform cp_i can be gained, which is represented as $H_i(I) = \{h_{i,1}(I(i)), ..., h_{i,l}(I(i))\}$

(5) **Get the final service index by integrating indexes offline.** Using the obtained web service I's sub-index, we construct the final service index $H(I) = \{H_1(I), ..., H_m(I)\}$. Next, there is a mapping relationships of "$I \rightarrow H(I)$" and we record it in the hash table.

(6) **Service recommendation.** For the targeted web service I_q, according to the LSH, We can get the similar web services I_x with the targeted service I_q if the following condition (2) holds.

$$H(I_x) = H(I_q) \tag{2}$$

However, due to the fact that LSH is a probability-based neighbor search technology, we cannot conclude I_x is not similar to the targeted service I_q. Therefore, we create L hash tables to make the recommendation accurately. Then, when the following condition (3) holds, we say that service I_x is similar to I_q.

$$\exists \, Table_t \ (t \in \{1, ..., L\}), satisfies \ H(I_x)_t = H(I_q)_t \tag{3}$$

Table 1. Notations

Symbol	Semantics
u	The number of users in each cloud platform
I_j	The j-th service
$I_{i,j}^q$	The j-th quality dimension q of I_j in platform cp_i
l	The number of the hash functions
cp_i	The i-th cloud platform
m	The number of cloud platforms
n	The number of web services
L	The number of hash tables
c	The ciphertext of the service data
d	The plaintext of the service data
k	The key of shared data
λ	The security parameter of the system
t	The t-th hash table

Then, we put the similar service I_x that has never called by the targeted user into the set *sim_web*. We will repeat (1)–(3) to choose the optimal service and put them into the set *sim_web* if the targeted user has several targeted services. Next, by the following Eq. (4), we recommend the optimal service I_x to the targeted user.

$$I_x^q = optimal(I_k^q | I_x \in sim\_web) \tag{4}$$

4 Security Analysis and Performance Evaluation

4.1 Security Analysis

In this section, we present a brief security analysis of our scheme.

Data Confidentiality. BPDS-SR can guarantee the confidentiality of the shared data. Before sharing the data, we use the symmetric encryption algorithm to generate the encrypted key so that malicious attackers cannot get any information without the key, guaranteeing the confidentiality of the shared data.

Tamper-Proofing. In BPDS-SR, if an adversary intends to tamper the shared data in the consortium blockchain, he/she needs to control at least 51% nodes on the blockchain. Assume that ϵ is the probability that the adversary controls a node and there are m nodes on the consortium blockchain. Then, we assume that the adversary has controlled w nodes and the current block height is h. Meanwhile, we construct a random oracle and the adversary can make q queries. If the adversary tamper k blocks, he needs to make $(k-h)(m/2+1)q$ queries. The probability p of successfully tampering with the shared data is $p > 1\backslash(\epsilon^{m/2+1}(k-h)\backslash(m\backslash2+1)q)$. We can conclude that it is non-negligible for adversaries to tamper the data if m is large.

4.2 Performance Evaluation

In this section, we validate the performance of BPDS–SR through a series of experiments based on the WS–DREAM dataset. WS–DREAM is a large-scale web service QoS dataset that is a common dataset for recommendation. In BPDS–SR, the cloud platforms share the user's data on the blockchain. And they will cost the gas. In our experiments, we send a user's data as a transaction, namely, we regard 5825 web services of a user as a transaction.

In the experiments, we calculate the gas usage and compare BPDS–SR with three existing approaches: P–UIPCC, P–UPCC, P–IMEAN in [14]. We use gas usage , RMSE and MAE as the metrics to measure BPDS–SR. The experiments were run on linux virtual machine with Ubuntu 16.04 operating system. We use python 3.5, web3.py and Ethereum to simulate experiments. We use four nodes in Ethereum to simulate the four cloud platform. When the cloud platform uploads the shared data to Ethereum, it will cost gas.

Algorithm 1. Upload the shared data to the consortium blockchain

---

Input: input *Data*: the service data in quality dimension q of the u users
Output: *gasUsage*: Gas usage of Users

1   $gasUsage = []$
2   $failureTransaction = []$
3   **for** j *to* u **do**
4     $c_j = encrypt(Data[j])$ //encrypt the service of each user
     $uploadedData[j] = b2a\_hex(c_j)$ //convert the ciphertext to 16-ary that is required by the blockchain
5     $transaction[j] = buildTransaction(uploadedData[j])$
6     $gasUsage.append(w3.eth.estimateGas(transaction[j]))$ // estimate the Gas that the transaction[j] cost
7     $tx\_hash = w3.eth.sendTransaction(transaction[j])$ //send the transaction to blockchain
8     $receipt = w3.eth.waitForTransactionReceipt(tx\_hash, 15)$ // obtain the receipt from the blockchain
9   **if** *receipt* **then**
10   continue
11   **else**
12       $failureTransaction.append(transaction[j])$
13   return $transaction[j]$ *send failure*
14   **end**
15   **end**
16   return $gasUsage$

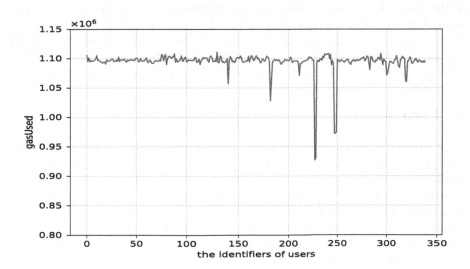

Fig. 2. The Gas usage of each user

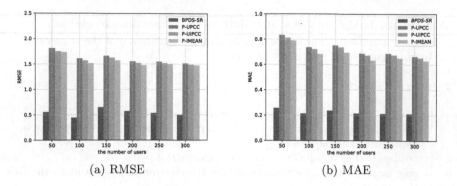

(a) RMSE   (b) MAE

Fig. 3. The accuracy of service recommendation

Gas Usage of BPDS–SR. As shown in Fig. 2, it is gas usage of each user. When the cloud platforms share the user's data on the consortium blockchain in form of each transaction which contain 5825 services. And it will consume gas. Through the algorithm 1, the maximum consumption of gas is about 1105352 gas and the minimum consumption of gas is about 927048 gas. In February 20, 2020, 1 $ether \approx 248$ USD, 1 $gas \approx 1wei$ (0.000000001 eth). Therefore, it will cost at most 1105352 $gas \approx 0.27$ USD for sharing a piece of user's data. It is worthy for cloud platform to share data with other cooperation platforms because they will obtain more profits.

Recommendation Accuracy Among Four Schemes. We test the accuracy of the four schemes with respect to the RMSE and MAE. We set the experimental parameters as below: $L = 4, l = 10$ and u is varied from 50 to 300. The experiment results show in Fig. 3, in which $n = 5825$ holds. The RMSE and MAE (the smaller the better) of BPDS–SR is the lowest among the four schemes. Namely, the accuracy of our scheme is the highest as m grows.

5   Conclusion

In this paper, we propose a service recommendation scheme which supports the data sharing based on the consortium blockchain. In order to guarantee data security, we encrypt the shared data before sharing by using the shared key that generated by the symmetric encryption algorithm. Based on the blockchain, the cloud platforms can easily get the shared data and use it to maximize the profits. Finally, we evaluate our scheme based on WS–DREAM and verify the experimental performance. The experimental results show that BPDS–SR achieves a high accuracy. Meanwhile, its cost is low so it can obtain more profits.

Acknowledgment. This work was supported in part by National Key R&D Program of China under Grant 2019YFB2102600, the National Natural Science Foundation of

China (NSFC) under Grants 61832012, 61672321 and 61771289 and the Key Research and Development Program of Shandong Province under Grant 2019JZZY020124.

References

1. Rong, H., Huo, S., Hu, C., Mo, J.: User similarity-based collaborative filtering recommendation algorithm. J. Commun. **35**(2), 16–24 (2014)
2. Chung, K.-Y., Lee, D., Kim, K.J.: Categorization for grouping associative items using data mining in item-based collaborative filtering. Multimedia Tool Appl. **71**(2), 889–904 (2011). https://doi.org/10.1007/s11042-011-0885-z
3. Jiang, C., Duan, R., Jain, H., Liu, S., Liang, K.: Hybrid collaborative filtering for high-involvement products: A solution to opinion sparsity and dynamics. Decis. Support Syst. **79**, 195–208 (2015)
4. Yan, B., Yu, J., Yang, M., Jiang, H., Wan, Z., Ni, L.: A novel distributed social internet of things service recommendation scheme based on LSH forest. Pers. Ubiquit. Comput , 1–14 (2019). https://doi.org/10.1007/s00779-019-01283-4
5. Frey, R., Vuckovac, D., Ilic, A. : A secure shopping experience based on blockchain and beacon technology. In: Proceedings of the 22nd American Conference Information System, pp. 1–5 (2016)
6. Frey, R., Vuckovac, D., Ilic, A.: A secure shopping experience based on blockchain and beacon technology. In: Poster Proceedings of the 10th ACM Conference Recommender System (2016)
7. Yu, J., Liu, S., Wang, S., Xiao, Y., Yan, B.: LH-ABSC: a lightweight hybrid attribute-based signcryption scheme for cloud-fog assisted IoT. IEEE Internet Things J. (2020). https://doi.org/10.1109/JIOT.2020.2992288
8. Liu, S., Yu, J., Xiao, Y., Wan, Z., Wang, S., Yan, B.: BC-SABE: blockchain-aided searchable attribute-based encryption for cloud-IoT. IEEE Internet Things J. (2020). https://doi.org/10.1109/JIOT.2020.2993231
9. Wang, Y., Yu, J., Yan, B., Wang, G., Shan, Z.: BSV-PAGS: Blockchain-based special vehicles priority access guarantee scheme. Comput. Commun. (2020). https://doi.org/10.1016/j.comcom.2020.07.012
10. Zheng, X., Cai, Z.: Privacy-preserved data sharing towards multiple parties in industrial IoTs. IEEE J. Sel. Areas Commun. **38**(5), 968–979 (2020)
11. Zhu, S., Cai, Z., Hu, H., Li, S., Li, W.: zkCrowd: a hybrid blockchain-based crowdsourcing platform. IEEE Trans. Ind. Inf. **16**(6), 4196–4205 (2019)
12. Nakamoto, S.: Bitcoin: a peer-to-peer electronic cash system (2008). https://bitcoin.org/bitcoin.pdf
13. Yan, C., Cui, X., Qi, L., Xu, X., Zhang, X.: Privacy-aware data publishing and integration for collaborative service recommendation. IEEE Access **6**, 43021–43028 (2018)
14. Zhu, J., He, P., Zheng, Z., Lyu, M.R.: A Privacy-preserving QoS prediction framework for web service recommendation. In: Proceeding of the 2015 IEEE International Conference on Web Services, pp. 241–248. IEEE (2015). https://doi.org/10.1109/ICWS.2015.41

Multi-objective Disaster Backup in Inter-datacenter Using Reinforcement Learning

Jiaxin Yan[1], Hua Wang[1(✉)], Xiaole Li[2], Shanwen Yi[3], and Yao Qin[3]

[1] School of Software, Shandong University, Jinan 250101, China
wanghua@sdu.edu.cn
[2] School of Information Science and Engineering, Linyi University,
Linyi 276005, China
[3] School of Computer Science and Technology, Shandong University,
Jinan 250101, China

Abstract. With rapid growth of data centers and great rising concern on data security in recent years, disaster backup has attracted the attention of many researchers. Most researchers focus on reducing the backup bandwidth cost by using multicast routing, but pay less attention to load balance. The local link congestion will seriously affect the user's experience interacting with the data center. To optimize bandwidth cost and load balance simultaneously, we use multicast routing and store-and-forward mechanism to build multiple disaster-backup multicast trees, and forward data at appropriate time slots to reduce link congestion. To solve the weight selection problem between cost and load balance, we propose the multicasting backup multi-objective reinforcement learning algorithm based on Chebyshev scalarization function, which significantly improve the hypervolume of solution set. Simulation results show that our algorithm outperforms existing algorithms in terms of bandwidth cost, maximal link congestion and the hypervolume of solution set.

Keywords: Disaster backup · Inter-datacenter · Load balance · Reinforcement learning · Multi-objective optimization

1 Introduction

In recent years, many large enterprises such as Amazon, Google, Microsoft deploy large-scale datacenters (DCs) at multiple geographical locations to provide various services for millions of users all over the global [1,2]. Due to natural disasters and human-made destruction, data security has also attracted more and more attention. Data redundancy is the most common method of ensuring data security. To achieve data redundancy, terabytes or petabytes amount of data produced during a period are regularly replicated in inter-DC WAN and assigned to three or more other remote DCs, which is called disaster backup [3].

Bulk data transfer is a significant feature of disaster backup [4]. Its huge practical value has attracted the attention of many researchers, among which reducing bandwidth cost by leveraging multicast routing is a research hotspot in

© Springer Nature Switzerland AG 2020
D. Yu et al. (Eds.): WASA 2020, LNCS 12384, pp. 590–601, 2020.
https://doi.org/10.1007/978-3-030-59016-1_49

recent years. The author of [5] used multiple multicast forwarding trees in each data transfer to reduce bandwidth cost. The author of [6] optimized multicast routing from the perspective of DC's limited capacity, thereby reducing the total bandwidth consumption. However, these work did not consider the load balance of network. When some links are severely congested, DC's daily service will be difficult to guarantee, and the user's experience interacting with DC will also be seriously affected, so the above work are not applicable to disaster backup. How to achieve load balance while reducing bandwidth cost is the focus of this paper.

Forwarding data in some free time slots to reduce link congestion is a classic method to achieve load balance [7]. The natural storage function of DCs can temporarily store data and forward data when the link is free, and the emergence of software defined network (SDN) allows us to be more flexible in traffic management and congestion control. Therefore, we use time-expanded network (TEN) and store and forward mechanism to alleviate local link congestion in SDN. Wang Y et al. [8] constructed the elastic TEN to reduce network congestion in less computation time. The author of [9] used VTEN to schedule traffic better, thereby quickly evacuating data before disaster coming. However, the above work used unicast routing, which caused a huge bandwidth waste with redundant backup, while the multicast routing that delivers the same data to a group of DC is more suitable for redundant backup. In our work, we implement multicast routing in TEN and build multiple multicast trees based on shared degree, so that both bandwidth cost and load balance can be optimized.

Multi-objective optimization of DC's disaster backup is more in line with actual needs [4,10]. Among them, reducing bandwidth cost [5,6,9] and load balance [6–8] are the two most valuable optimization goals. In multi-objective optimization, Determining weight is a recognized problem [11]. If the weights are inappropriate, the quality of the solutions will be reduced. As a new algorithm framework, reinforcement learning (RL) based on Chebyshev scalarization function can achieve good results in most weight tuples, which effectively solves the weight selection problem [12]. We leverage it in our multicast backup model, and design our multicast backup multi-objective algorithm.

Our Solution: We use RL in TEN to find the multicast routing tree, and use the store-and-forward mechanism to send backup data in relatively free time slots, and finally optimize bandwidth cost and load balance at the same time. During optimization, we leverage RL based on Chebyshev scalarization function to solve the weight selection problem, so as to obtain the solution set with the highest quality. Finally, we compare our algorithm with other three algorithms, namely MB-ACO [6,8] and inexact ADMM-based algorithm [9]. Simulation results show that our algorithm outperforms above algorithms in terms of bandwidth cost, load balance and the hypervolume of solution set.

The main contributions of this paper can be summarized as follows:

Model: We use multicast routing and store-and-forward mechanism in TEN for backup data transfer to achieve the minimum total bandwidth cost and load balance, then we formulate the Load Balanced-Multiple Steiner Trees (LB-MST) problem.

Algorithm: We propose the Multicasting Backup Multi-Objective RL (MB-MORL) algorithm based on the Chebyshev scalarization function, which solves the weight selection problem between cost and load balance, and significantly improves the quality of solution set.

The rest of this paper is organized as follows. In Sect. 2 we construct the network model and formulate LB-MST problem. In Sect. 3 we present MB-MORL algorithm in detail. Section 4 illustrates our simulation results, and Sect. 5 concludes the paper.

2   System Model and Problem Formulation

In this section, we use the store-and-forward mechanism and multicast routing in TEN to optimize both backup bandwidth cost and load balance. Finally, we formulate the LB-MST problem.

2.1   Time-Expanded Network

The Time-Expanded Network (TEN) is introduced by Ford and Fulkerson in [13]. It transforms the flow over time problem as a static flow problem by copying the network status at each time slot. We use a directed graph $G = (V, E)$ with $n := |V|$ nodes and $m := |E|$ edges to represent a network. Each node $v \in V$ denotes a DC, and each edge $e = (u, v) \in E$ denotes an inter-DC link from u to v. A T-time-expanded network $G^T = (V^T, E^T)$ is composed of T copies of the node set in G for each time slot. We use $v_t \in V^T$ to denotes node v at time slot t. While the edge set E^T is consisted of two parts: transit edges E_t^T and holdover edges E_h^T. The transit edges is T copies of the edge set in G which denoted as $e_t = (u_t, v_t)$ and the holdover edge $e_h = (v_t, v_{t+1})$ represent the edge between node v at time slot t and v at time slot $t + 1$.

Due to SDN, we can schedule the data more flexibly in TEN. For disaster backup, we can temporarily store the data in DC, and forward data when the link is free. Store-and-forward mechanism can significantly reduce the congestion of the network and achieve load balance.

2.2   Multicasting Backup

Here, we address disaster backup for n application DCs and each of them tries to distribute the new data to be backed up to $k_{rp}(e.g.k_{rp} \geq 3)$ other geo-distributed backup DCs for data redundancy.

In a T-time-expanded network G^T, each node $v_t \in V^T$ denotes a data-center v at time slot t. Each backup request is specified as a 5-tuple $r_i = \{s(T_{r_i}^s), d(T_{r_i}^d), dem_i, T_{r_i}^s, T_{r_i}^d\}$, where $s(T_{r_i}^s)$ and $d(T_{r_i}^d) = \{d_{i1}, d_{i2}, \ldots, d_{ik_{rp}}\}$ denote the source and destinations of request, dem_i denotes the backup data's volume, $T_{r_i}^s$ and $T_{r_i}^d$ denote the request's start time and deadline time, respectively. For each backup request $r_i \in R$, we build a corresponding disaster-backup

Table 1. Key notations

Notation	Meaning
b_{eh}	The available storage capacity at DC v at time slot t
b_{et}	The available bandwidth of link e at time slot t
f_{et}	The flow on link e at time slot t
$\mu_e = f_{et}/b_{et}$	The link congestion factor of link e at time slot t
V_{src}	The set of source nodes of all requests r_i
V_{dest}	The set of all possible destinations nodes of all requests r_i
$R = \{r_1, r_2, \ldots r_k\}$	The set of all backup requests r_i
$T = \{t_1, t_2, \ldots, t_k\}$	The set of all DBMTs

multicast tree (DBMT) t_i. Table 1 summarizes some key notations used in the paper.

We use multicast tree shared degree $tsd(t_i, e)$ to represent the number of paths through the link e, which effectively reduces the duplication of the same backup data during transmission, thereby reducing bandwidth cost and link congestion factor. $tsd(t_i, e)$ is defined as follows:

$$tsd\,(t_i, e) = \sum_{d_{ij} \in d(T_{r_i}^d)} x_e^{i,j} \tag{1}$$

where $x_e^{i,j}$ denotes if the path, which from the source node of request r_i to destination nodes d_{ij}, passes through the link e.

We use $\mu(T)$ to represent the link congestion factor of the multicast group trees T, which is the link congestion factor of the most congested link in T. $\mu(T)$ is defined as follows:

$$\mu(T) = \max\{\mu_e\}, \forall e \in t_i \cap E_t^T, \forall t_i \in T \tag{2}$$

We use uc_e and binary variable $\delta_{i,e}$ to denote the unit bandwidth cost and whether link e is in t_i, respectively. The total cost of the multicast group trees T is defined as follows:

$$c(T) = \sum_{t_i \in T} \sum_{e \in E_t^T} \delta_{i,e} \cdot uc_e \cdot dem_i \tag{3}$$

We use $fitness(t_i, e)$ to evaluate the fitness of link e, where the function values of cost and multicast tree shared degree can be used as the criteria. The function is defined as follows:

$$fitness\,(t_i, e) = \alpha_1 \cdot e^{-uc_e/avgcost} + \alpha_2 \cdot e^{tsd(t_i,e)/avgtsd} \tag{4}$$

The parameters α_1 and α_2 are the weight values of the unit bandwidth cost and multicast tree shared degree function of link e. The variables $avgcost$ and $avgtsd$ represent the average unit bandwidth cost and average multicast tree shared degree of the links in t_i, respectively.

2.3 Mathematical Formulation

In the following, we first formally define LB-MST, and then we present the integer programming formulation for LB-MST.

For network $G^T = (V^T, E^T)$ and multicast group T, LB-MST is to define the routing of every $t_i \in T$ for each request $r_i \in R$, and assign k_{rp} disaster backup data replicas in every t_i. Our goal is to minimize the total bandwidth cost and maximal link congestion of T. Based on Eqs. (2) and (3), the LB-MST problem is formulated as follow:

Goals:

$$\min c(T) \ and \ \min \mu(T) \tag{5}$$

Constraints:

$$f_e^{r_i} \geq 0, 0 \leq \mu_e \leq 1, \forall e \in E^T \tag{6}$$

$$\sum_{r_i \in R} f_e^{r_i} \leq \mu_e \cdot b_e, \forall e \in E_t^T \tag{7}$$

$$\sum_{r_i \in R} f_e^{r_i} \leq b_e, \forall e \in E_h^T \tag{8}$$

$$\sum_{e \in \delta^+(v)} f_e^{r_i} - \sum_{e \in \delta^-(v)} f_e^{r_i} = 0, \forall r_i \in R, \forall v \notin \left(V_{src}^T \cup V_{dest}^T \right) \tag{9}$$

$$\sum_{e \in \delta^+(v)} f_e^{r_i} - \sum_{e \in \delta^-(v)} f_e^{r_i} = \begin{cases} dem_i, v = d_{ij}\left(T_{r_i}^d\right) \\ -dem_i, v = s_i\left(T_{r_i}^s\right) \end{cases} \tag{10}$$

$$\forall r_i \in R, d_{ij}\left(T_{r_i}^d\right) \in d_i\left(T_{r_i}^d\right) \subseteq V_{dest}^D, s_i\left(T_{r_i}^s\right) \in V_{srcc}^D$$

$$\sum_{d_{ij}\left(T_{r_i}^d\right)} \sum_{e \in t_i \cap E_l^T} x_e^{i,j} \geq k_{rp} \tag{11}$$

$$x_e^{i,j} \in \{0,1\}, \forall r_i \in R, \forall d_{ij} \in d\left(T_{r_i}^d\right), \forall e \in E^T \tag{12}$$

The constraint (6) ensures that the flow value and the congestion value are feasible. The constraint (7) and (8) ensures that the aggregate traffic along any transit edge and any holdover edge cannot exceed the link capacity and storage capacity, respectively. The constraint (9) ensures that no flows at any node other than source nodes or destination nodes. The constraint (10) ensures that each transfer receives the specified volume of data within its deadline time. The constraint (11) ensures that redundant backups are sufficient. The constraint (12) defines the decision variables.

The LB-MST problem is an extension of the Steiner Trees problem. However, the LB-MST problem is more challenging due to optimizing multi objectives. Since Steiner Trees problem has been proved to be NP-hard [14], the LB-MST problem is also NP-hard. In order to solve LB-MST problem in polynomial time, we will apply the multi-objective RL algorithm based on the Chebyshev scalarization function in the next section.

3   MB-MORL Algorithm

In this section, we first give a brief overview of RL based on Chebyshev scalarization function, then introduce how we use it to determine the weights, and finally describe the MB-MORL algorithm.

3.1   RL Based on Chebyshev Scalarization Function

Multi-objective RL algorithm aims to find a Pareto approximate set that can approximate the Pareto optimal set. In a famous RL algorithm called Q-learning. $\widehat{Q}(s, a)$ is proposed to iteratively approximate Q^*. The $\widehat{Q}(s, a)$ value is updated accordingly to following update rule:

$$\widehat{Q}(s, a) = (1 - \alpha_i)\,\widehat{Q}(s, a) + \alpha_i \left(\overrightarrow{r} + \gamma \max_{a'} \widehat{Q}\left(s', a'\right)\right) \tag{13}$$

where $\alpha_i \in (0, 1]$ denotes the learning rate at time step i, $\overrightarrow{r}$ is the reward vector of taking action a in state s and $\gamma \in (0, 1]$ is the discount factor.

In multi-objective RL, The Chebyshev scalarization function evaluates actions using the metric $\widehat{SQ}(s, a)$. Then, the $\widehat{SQ}$ value, which is the scalarized $\widehat{Q}$ value, of a state-action pair (s, a) can be calculated as follows:

$$\widehat{SQ}(s, a) = \max_{i=1\cdots m} w_i \left|\widehat{Q}_i(s, a) - z_i^*\right| \tag{14}$$

where $0 \le w_i \le 1$ denotes the weight of each objective i, which satisfies the equation $\sum_{i=1}^{m} w_i = 1$. $\widehat{Q}_i(s, a)$ denotes the $\widehat{Q}$ value for each objective i. z^* is the utopian point which denotes the best value for each objective.

The action corresponding to the smallest $\widehat{SQ}$ value will be chosen as the greedy action in state s. The greedy strategy can be expressed as follows:

$$greedy_a(s) = \arg \min_{a \in A} \widehat{SQ}_i(s, a) \tag{15}$$

where A is the available action set in state s.

3.2   Determination of Weight

Hypervolume is often used as the metric to measure the quality of Pareto approximate set. As a nonlinear scalarization method, the Chebyshev scalarization function is not particularly dependent on the actual weights used, which means most weight tuples can achieve good results [12].

In our algorithm, we use Chebyshev scalarization function to replace the action selection strategy in Q-learing. Algorithm 1 shows the scalarized ϵ-greedy strategy for a multi-objective RL algorithm, where $\overrightarrow{w}$ is the vector of weights for multiple objectives.

With Algorithm 1, we randomly generated 15 tuples of weights in our simulation. Except for the 4th and 13th tuple, the hypervolume of other tuples are stable at a higher level.

Algorithm 1. scal-ϵ-greedy()

Input: the current state s
Output: the action a choosed form available action set A
1: Initialize the list of SQ-values $List_{sq}$ to $\varnothing$
2: Figure out the available action set A in current state s
3: **for** each action $a \in A$ **do**
4:     $\overrightarrow{o} = \{\widehat{Q}_1(s, a), \cdots, \widehat{Q}_m(s, a)\}$
5:     $\widehat{SQ}(s, a) = scalarize(\overrightarrow{o}, \overrightarrow{w})$ % According to Eq. (14)
6:     Append $\widehat{SQ}(s, a)$ to $List_{sq}$
7: **end for**
8: $a = \epsilon$-greedy($List_{sq}$)
9: **return** a

3.3   The Description of MB-MORL

In the following, we first introduce the learning agent of MB-MORL in terms of the state space, the available action set, and the reward vector. Then we present the description of MB-MORL.

State Space: We use $S = \{s_1, s_2, \ldots, s_q\}$ to represent the state space. For the current state s_i, we select the next routing node v from the available action set, then add v to the current multicast routing path to get the next state s_{i+1}.

Available Action Set: We use $A = \{a_1, a_2, \ldots, a_p\}$ to denote the set of available actions in the current state. Selecting the action a_i means selecting the next node for routing.

Reward Vector: We use $fitness(t_i, e)$ and μ_e as optimization metrics for minimum cost and load balance, respectively. It is worth noting that we use $fitness(t_i, e)$ instead of directly using the link unit cost uc_e to minimize cost, which is an important manifestation of multicast routing. Specifically, it is to use the public link as much as possible to copy the backup data as late as possible, which is the key to reduce the total cost.

The Description of MB-MORL: The final solution obtained by our algorithm is a Pareto approximate set S_p, each of which is a set of DBMT $t_i \in T$. Each t_i corresponds to a multicast tree path for a backup request, and T corresponds to all backup requests. We store a t_i in an adjacency matrix. In order to avoid the mutual influence among multiple trees, we separately assign a Q_i to each t_i, which satisfies the requirement of forest spanning [6].

Algorithm 2 shows the pseudocode of the MB-MORL algorithm. This algorithm can also be described in the following four steps.

The pseudocode of MB-MORL algorithm is as follows.

4   Performance Evaluation

4.1   Implementation and Settings

We implemented and ran our MB-MORL algorithm on a PC equipped with i7-4790 CPU and 8 GB RAM. We performed simulation evaluation of our algorithm in the US-Backbone topology [9]. Each node in network represents a DC and each link is a bidirectional link, while the link capacity in both directions is the same. We randomly select 5 nodes and 8 nodes as application DC and backup DC, respectively. The multicast size is 3. Table 2 summarizes the remaining main parameters.

In Sect. 3.2, the hypervolume of the 7th tuple is the highest, so we chose the 7th tuple's weight for subsequent experimental comparison. We set the cost of the total backup data across all links and maximal link congestion factor as the upper

---

Algorithm 2. Pseudocode of MB-MORL

Input: $G^T = (v^T, e^T), R = \{r_1, r_2, ... r_k\}$
Output: Pareto approximate set S_p
 1: Initialize the Pareto approximate set S_p to $\varnothing$
 2: Initialize the value of k $\widehat{Q_i}$ tables for each objective to 0
 3: **repeat**
 4:    Initialize the remaining bandwidth of each link $e \in e^T$
 5:    **for** each backup request $r_i \in R$ **do**
 6:        Initialize the adjacency matrix m_i
 7:        **while** the number of $d_{ij} \in d\left(T_{r_i}^d\right) < k_{rp}$ **do**
 8:            **repeat**
 9:                Initialize the current state s and the available action set A
10:                $a = $ scal-ϵ-greedy(s) % According to Algorithm 1
11:                Get the next node and update the adjacency matrix m_i
12:                Figure out the next state s'
13:                Update the remaining bandwidth of each link $e \in e^T$
14:                Update the available action set A
15:                $a' = greedy(s')$ % According to Eq. (15)
16:                Calculate the reward vector consisting of $fitness(t_i, e)$ and μ_e
17:                Update $\widehat{Q_i}(s, a)$ % According to Eq. (13)
18:                $s \leftarrow s'$
19:            **until**   reach a feasible destination node d_{ij}
20:            **if** constraint (10) and (11) are met **then**
21:                Add feasible destination node d_{ij} to $d\left(T_{r_i}^d\right)$
22:            **end if**
23:        **end while**
24:    **end for**
25:    **if** The solution is not dominated by any other solutions in S_p **then**
26:        Add this solution to S_p
27:    **end if**
28: **until** The maximal number of iterations is reached
29: **return** Pareto approximate set S_p

Table 2. Main parameter setting

Parameter	Value	Parameter	Value
Limit duration	5 h	Number of time slots	30
Storage of a DC	[1000, 3000] TB	Bandwidth of each link	[500, 1500] Gb/s
Unit bandwidth cost	[5, 40] units/TB	Number of backup requests	50
Amount of a requests	[10, 80] TB	Amount of a requests	2000 TB

limit of minimizing the total bandwidth cost and load balance, respectively. We select the solution point with the largest Euclidean distance from the reference point as the final solution to be compared with other algorithms.

We compared our MB-MORL algorithm with SnF-LexMin [8], MB-ACO [6] and the inexact ADMM-based algorithm [9]. The SnF-LexMin algorithm expands the network to an elastic TEN, and lexicographically minimize the congestion of all links among DCs to achieve load balance. The MB-ACO algorithm leverages the ant colony algorithm to optimize the generation of multicast trees, and finally constructs multi Steiner Trees to minimize the bandwidth cost. We added time slots to MB-ACO for subsequent comparison. The inexact ADMM-based algorithm expands the network to VTEN, and calculate the near-optimal backup benefit in the short time before the disaster coming.

4.2   Simulation Results

We compared the MB-MORL algorithm with SnF-LexMin [8], MB-ACO [6] and the inexact ADMM-based algorithm [9] in terms of total bandwidth cost, maximal link congestion and hypervolume of Pareto approximate set in the following.

Since the amount of backup data directly affects the performance of algorithms, we first test the performance of each algorithm under the conditions of different amount of backup data. Keeping other parameters unchanged, we set the total backup data ranging from 1000 to 3000 TB. In Fig. 1, when the amount of backup data continued to increase, the total bandwidth cost calculated by all algorithms are all increasing. Due to the unicast routing, SnF-LexMin and ADMM generated more transmission paths while the amount of backup data increases, and the cost is increasing faster and faster. The MB-ACO and MB-MORL, because of the shared path in the multicast backup trees, the rate of cost growth gradually slowed down. With the help of Chebyshev scalarization functions, MB-MORL has a greater probability of choosing a better action, which makes its cost lower than MB-ACO.

In order to reflect the impact of the number of backups on bandwidth cost more clearly, we set the multicast size from 2 to 5, while other parameters remained unchanged. It can be seen from Fig. 2 that MB-ACO and MB-MORL have obvious advantages than other two algorithms, and they both reduced many unnecessary repeated traffic in unicast algorithms. Since the MB-MORL algorithm builds a unique Q table for each multicast backup tree, the total bandwidth cost is lower than MB-ACO.

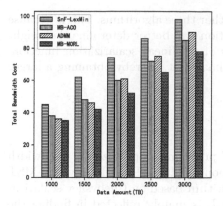

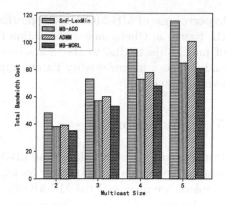

Fig. 1. Comparison of total bandwidth cost with increase in data amount

Fig. 2. Comparison of total bandwidth cost with increase in multicast size

In terms of the maximal link congestion, the division of time slots plays an important role. Therefore, in our simulation, we set the number of time slots from 10 to 50, and other parameters remained unchanged. Figure 3 shows that SnF-LexMin and MB-MORL have lower congestion. This is because the finer time granularity can generate more accurate traffic scheduling, which can better achieve load balance. However, the increase of time slots will greatly increase the difficulty of calculation, and the effect of reducing congestion will gradually decrease, so there is no need to divide too many time slots. The ADMM algorithm has always been very congested due to its rapid evacuation. Due to its rapid evacuation, the ADMM algorithm's solution always had a higher maximal link congestion than other algorithms.

Finally, we compared the quality of the Pareto approximate set generated by each algorithm through hypervolume. It can be seen from Fig. 4 that the

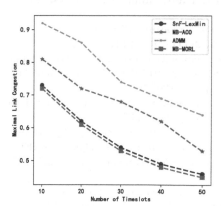

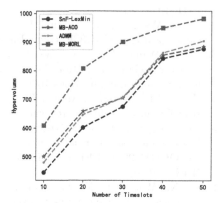

Fig. 3. Comparison of maximal link congestion with increase in time slots

Fig. 4. Comparison of Hypervolume with increase in time slots

hypervolume of MB-MORL is larger than other three algorithms. This is because RL based on Chebyshev scalarization function can better determine the weight of multi-objects due to the characteristics of nonlinear scalarization function, and obtain a higher quality Pareto approximate set, thereby obtaining a larger hypervolume.

5 Conclusion

In this article, we formulated the LB-MST problem to optimize the bandwidth cost and load balance of disaster backup among multiple DCs. To solve LB-MST problem, we proposed the MB-MORL algorithm based on Chebyshev scalarization function. The innovation of MB-MORL is mainly reflected in finding the routing tree and free time slots in TEN to forward backup data by leveraging multicast routing and store-and-forward mechanism, and solving the weight selection problem by leveraging RL based on Chebyshev scalarization function. Simulation results showed that our algorithm outperforms other three comparison algorithms in terms of bandwidth cost, load balance and the hypervolume of solution set. In future work, we will choose the backup DCs for each backup request, which is more in line with the actual needs of the data centers, to make our work more practical.

Acknowledgments. The study was supported by the National Natural Science Foundation of China (NSFC No. 61972228), the Natural Science Foundation of Shandong Province (Grant No. ZR2019MF072), and the Key Research and Development Program of Shandong Province (2017GGX10122, 2017GGX10142).

References

1. Xia, Q., Xu, Z., Liang, W., Zomaya, A.Y.: Collaboration-and fairness-aware big data management in distributed clouds. IEEE Trans. Parallel Distrib. Syst. **27**(7), 1941–1953 (2015)
2. Li, X., Wang, H., Yi, S., Zhai, L.: Progressive forwarding disaster backup among cloud datacenters. IEICE Trans. Inf. Syst. **102**(11), 2135–2147 (2019)
3. Li, X., Wang, H., Yi, S., Yao, X.: Receiving-capacity-constrained rapid and fair disaster backup for multiple datacenters in SDN. In: 2017 IEEE International Conference on Communications (ICC), pp. 1–6. IEEE (2017)
4. Wang, J.H., Wang, J., An, C., Zhang, Q.: A survey on resource scheduling for data transfers in inter-datacenter wans. Comput. Netw. **161**, 115–137 (2019)
5. Noormohammadpour, M., Raghavendra, C.S., Kandula, S., Rao, S.: QuickCast: fast and efficient inter-datacenter transfers using forwarding tree cohorts. In: IEEE INFOCOM 2018-IEEE Conference on Computer Communications, pp. 225–233. IEEE (2018)
6. Li, X., Wang, H., Yi, S., Zhai, L.: Cost-efficient disaster backup for multiple data centers using capacity-constrained multicast. Concurr. Comput.: Pract. Expe. **31**(17), e5266 (2019)

7. Lin, X., Sun, W., Wang, X., Yue, S., Veeraraghavan, M., Hu, W.: Time-space decoupled SNF scheduling of bulk transfers across inter-datacenter optical networks. IEEE Access **8**, 24829–24846 (2020)
8. Wang, Y., Su, S., Liu, A.X., Zhang, Z.: Multiple bulk data transfers scheduling among datacenters. Comput. Netw. **68**, 123–137 (2014)
9. Xie, X., Ling, Q., Lu, P., Xu, W., Zhu, Z.: Evacuate before too late: distributed backup in inter-DC networks with progressive disasters. IEEE Trans. Parallel Distrib. Syst. **29**(5), 1058–1074 (2017)
10. Noormohammadpour, M., Kandula, S., Raghavendra, C.S., Rao, S.: Efficient inter-datacenter bulk transfers with mixed completion time objectives. Comput. Netw. **164**, 106903 (2019)
11. Qin, Y., Wang, H., Yi, S., Li, X., Zhai, L.: An energy-aware scheduling algorithm for budget-constrained scientific workflows based on multi-objective reinforcement learning. J. Supercomput. **76**(1), 455–480 (2019). https://doi.org/10.1007/s11227-019-03033-y
12. Van Moffaert, K., Drugan, M.M., Nowé, A.: Scalarized multi-objective reinforcement learning: novel design techniques. In: 2013 IEEE Symposium on Adaptive Dynamic Programming and Reinforcement Learning (ADPRL), pp. 191–199. IEEE (2013)
13. Ford Jr., L.R., Fulkerson, D.R.: Constructing maximal dynamic flows from static flows. Oper. Res. **6**(3), 419–433 (1958)
14. Garey, M.R., Graham, R.L., Johnson, D.S.: The complexity of computing Steiner minimal trees. SIAM J. Appl. Math. **32**(4), 835–859 (1977)

Detecting Internet-Scale NATs for IoT Devices Based on Tri-Net

Zhaoteng Yan[1,2], Nan Yu[2(⊠)], Hui Wen[2], Zhi Li[2], Hongsong Zhu[2], and Limin Sun[2]

[1] School of Cyber Security, University of Chinese Academy of Sciences, Beijing, China
[2] Institute of Information Engineering, Chinese Academy of Sciences, Beijing, China
{yanzhaoteng,yunan,wenhui,lizhi,zhuhongsong,sunlimin}@iie.ac.cn

Abstract. Due to the lack of available labeled Network Address Translation (NAT) samples, it is still difficult to actively detect the large-scale NATs on the Internet. In this paper, we propose an novel method to identify NATs for online Internet of Things (IoT) devices based on Tri-net (a semi-supervised deep neural network). By learning the features on three layers (network, transport and application layer) in the small labeled data set (with thousands of instances), the Tri-net can automatically identify millions of online NATs. We evaluate this approach on the real-world dataset with more than 8 million online IoT devices, and the performance shows the precision and recall can be both up to 92%. Moreover, we found 2,511,499 IoT devices connecting to the Internet via NAT, which account for one-third of the total. To our knowledge, this is the first successful attempt to automatically identify Internet-scale NATs.

Keywords: NAT detecting · IoT devices · Tri-net

1 Introduction

The number of online IoT devices (e.g., IP camera, wireless router, etc.) has grown explosively. Meanwhile, limited public IPv4 addresses can not meet the needs of those devices connecting on the Internet. NAT has become the ideal solution that allows multiple devices sharing one public IP address or providing Internet-wide services via port mapping. However, NAT also undoubtedly bring some security issues to the online IoT devices: (1) NAT prevents the empirical investigation into counting the actual number of vulnerable devices in cyberspace. (2) Unauthorized NAT devices provide the convenience for the malicious code infection. Therefore, it is necessary to actively detect NAT behaviours of IoT devices in the cyberspace.

Consequently, NAT detection has become a typical and valuable research issue. Most studies focused on passive approaches on traffic traces [2,8,11,13]. That is because the performance evaluation of active detecting NAT devices

© Springer Nature Switzerland AG 2020
D. Yu et al. (Eds.): WASA 2020, LNCS 12384, pp. 602–614, 2020.
https://doi.org/10.1007/978-3-030-59016-1_50

is more uncontrollable and uncertain than passive measurement. As a result, the current research on active NAT detection approaches have been slightly fewer [9,11]. Moreover, there are still no usable approaches to identify NAT for the large-scale targets, especially for the online IoT devices in the complex cyberspace.

Motivation: In this paper, we aim to quantify the above assumption, and conduct an comprehensive Internet-scale study on active NAT detection toward online IoT devices with multiple features on network, transport, and application layers based on Deep Neural Network (DNN). Specifically, we try to answer the following questions: (1) *How many NATs are used by online IoT devices across IPv4 address space?* (2) *How many IoT devices connected to the Internet via their public IP addresses?* (3) *What is the distribution of geography, type, and protocol of those NATs?*

Challenges: To achieve this end, we need to address the three main challenges. One the unstable features for active detecting NATs has its limitation. For instance, IP identification (IP ID) and time-to-live (TTL) can be modified or forged. More importantly, due to the large heterogeneity in IoT devices, not all features on each layer can be obtained on the Internet. Besides, inadequacy features cause the lackness of labeled NAT samples for training the applicable machine learning modules. These main reasons make the active NAT detection seems to be impossible in the real world.

Method: To address these challenges, we design and implement an approach to identify NATs for online IoT devices in IPv4 space automatically. The workflow of our approach consists of three steps. First, we pre-label a small part of the dataset and extract the relatively features on network, transport, and application layers. Second, we train the modules of Tri-net by automatically feature learning and three pseudo-labels on diverse layers predicting. Third, we determine whether it is a NAT or straight-connecting device based on the trained Tri-net and the enlarged labeled dataset.

Results: To evaluate the performance, we implement our approach to the real Internet-wide public data. The data set contains 8,644,288 online IoT devices with four categories (routing, monitor, printing, and industrial control). Among which, we identified 2,511,499 IoT devices using NAT for Internet access, which occupy 29.1% of the total experimental data set.

Contributions: Overall, we make the following desirable contributions:

- *First available online NAT detecting approach:* Combined five new features we introduced on the application layer and six typical features on the transport and network layer, our work is the first to conduct an automatic approach that can be used to identify Internet-wide NATs of the online IoT devices.
- *High precision and recall in the real experiment:* According to the real evaluation in the cyberspace, our novel approach present that the average precision and recall can both be up to 92%.

– *First investigation of NAT usage status which do not require cooperation:* We
identified 2,511,499 Internet-wide IoT devices using NAT, which occupy one-
third of the total number. Moreover, we analyzed the distribution from four
dimensions: protocol, type, vendor, and geography.

The remainder of the paper is structured as follows. In Sect. 2, we discuss the
related works. In Sect. 3 and 4, we present the features and detailed approach,
followed by the experimental results in Sect. 5. We discuss the future work and
conclude the paper in Sect. 6.

2   Related Work

Previous studies on of detecting NAT devices or identify behavior mainly focused
on passive measurement [1,2,8,10,12–14,17]. Features (*e.g.*, IP ID [2], TTL [3],
the HTTP user-agent strings [14], *etc.*) for passive NAT detection can be easily
obtain from the collecting traffic traces of the internal network. Thus, machine
learning (ML) algorithm for passive NAT detection has not been complex. Support Vector Machine (SVM), *C4.5* and Naive Bayes has been commonly used
as the classifiers [1,13]. Khatouni *et al.* comprehensively employed ten kinds of
ML-based classifiers to achieve higher accuracy [10]. Sun *et al.* proposed a novel
density-based clustering algorithm (*DBSCAN*) and proved its efficiency [17].

However, these aforementioned ML algorithms made unavailable for active
measurement. On one hand, it is hard to receive the traditional features from
active probe data from the uncoordinated network. On the other hand, the target
scale of active NAT detection is relatively larger than passive measurement.
Murakami *et al.* and Ishikawa *et al.* both proposed the limited approach in their
specific applications [9,14]. In summary, in order to actively identify the NAT-
like IoT devices in the cyberspace, new features and method need be employed.

3   Preliminary Knowledge

3.1   Features of Network Layer

All packets traveling over the network layer contain the IP header with twenty
fixed bytes. Among which, some classic fields are used as features for fingerprinting OS, device types [19], brands and models [18]. In order to actively identify
NAT devices based on the <request, response> packets, we choose three features on the network layer as follows: *Time to Live (ttl)*, *IP identification (id)*
and *ICMP type and code IDs (icmp)*.

The initial value TTL_{init} is set to range from 32 to 255, which is distinct
from the diverse device type or OS. For instance, the TTL_{init} of D-Link IP
Camera and ZyXEL wireless router are both 64 because they are using the
same embedded Linux OS, and the TTL_{init} of Siemens PLC is 30 with its unique
OS. Moreover, the TTL value is decremented by one as the IP datagram packet
is transported at every hop. That means if the online device is directly connected

to the Internet, the value of TTL is $TTL_{init} - 1$. For instance, Table 1 shows the TTL value of `Dell Printer` is 254, which means it can be concluded a non-NAT device. However, there are still some limitations of the TTL as a feature [8].

IP ID field also is useful but limited as a feature of NAT detection because it can be modified by a gateway. The unreachable message (Type: 3, Code: 3) or host unreachable message (Type: 3, Code: 1) can be used as a feature vector for NAT detection. And the feature has been proved effective for Internet-scale scan on unreachable hosts [16].

Table 1. Ten features of three layer among IoT devices.

Feature	Example 1	Example 2	Example 3	Example 4
ttl	60	47	254	30
id	61275	61930	0	730
icmp	{3, 1}	{0, 0}	{3 ,1}	{3 ,3}
sn & an	-	-	-	-
ws	4128	5840	2920	2048
protocol	HTTP	RTSP	PJL Raw	Ethernet/IP
port	80	554	9100	44818
banner	Non-null	Non-null	Non-null	Non-null
category	Routing	Monitor	Printing	Industial
device-type	Router	IPcam	Printer	PLC
vendor	ZyXEL	D-Link	Dell	Siemens
product	P-330W	DCS-930	b2360dn	S7-200

3.2 Features of Transport Layer

To ensure monotonically-increasing, a NAT may rewrite the sequence number, acknowledgement number, and window size of TCP packets being forwarded into the internal realm. *TCP sequence number (sn), TCP acknowledgment number (an)* and *TCP window size (ws)*. As shown in Table 1, the window size value of `D-Link IP camera` is 5840 and the different value of `Dell Printer` is 2920. But only a part of features of transport layer can be extracted due to the inconspicuous differences between various device types. Thus, *sn, an* and *ws* can not be independently used for NAT detection.

3.3 Features of Application Layer

Researchers proposed Internet-wide fingerprinting device type, vendor, and product based on the banners of application protocols of IoT devices such as firewalls,

SCADA and webcam [7,19], which improved the basic conditions for fingerprinting NAT devices on the Internet. Thus, we employ the following features of banners of eight general protocols, and ten particular protocols which including two monitor protocols (MP), three printing protocols (PP) and five industrial control protocols (ICP):

- *Diverse protocol categories:* Once more than two different types of particular protocols are opened on one host, we can determine that these various protocol services sharing one IP address by NAT device. For instance, Modbus and RTSP respectively belong to ICP and MP, which can not be simultaneously implemented on one network device. In this case, this feature is not suitable between general protocols and particular protocols because most IoT device products support multiple general protocols.
- *Standard service on well-known ports:* Some well-known ports have the official numbers for their corresponding protocol services that are assigned by IANA. However, there are still quite a number of online hosts opening their services on these well-known ports. For instance, there 660 K hosts that open HTTP services on port 23 (the official port for Telnet) on the Internet according to our statistics. That is one kind of typical NAT behavior that is supported by port mapping. Similarly, a part of unofficial ports are generally designed for designative services by the IoT Manufactures.
- *Multiple standard services on unknown ports:* Part of IoT devices allow the users to open various services on any ports with one IP address by port forwarding. For instance, Network Video Recorder (NVR) can be configured to simultaneously open RTSP services for several IP cameras on 515 (designated for a Line Printer Daemon (LPD) official port) or 1515 of an unknown port.
- *NAT Devices:* Many IoT devices have all series or parts of products offering native NAT functions, including wireless routers, Digital Video Recorder(DVR), etc. Their dimensional features can be learnt by the neural network.
- *Multiple different device types, vendors or products:* Generally, an independent device connects to the Internet and exposes its only TVP (type, vendor, product). Hence, if there are two or more device types, vendors or products are identified simultaneously on one IP address, it can be detected as a NAT device sharing the IP by multiple devices. Undoubtedly, this feature depends on the high accuracy of TVP fingerprinting identification.

Although features on the application layer behave more obvious than other layers, there is still a key limitation: features on the application layer mainly depend on multiple dimensional fields on two ports or more. However, these are about two-thirds of online devices in our experimental data set, that have the only open one port on the Internet, features on the application layer can not be effective in the single banner. Hence, we still need to employ other features on the network or transport layer to detect these single-port devices are whether NAT or not.

4   Methodology

In this section, we introduce our architecture and the deep learning algorithm for detecting NAT devices base on Tri-net.

4.1   Overview

As illustrated in Fig. 1, the workflow of our approach has three steps: pre-labeling, label learning, and detection. After labeled a part of instances, the training data set can be extracted features on three layers. Along with the label learning process, training data set can be enlarged and the modules of Tri-net can be trained for NAT detection as the last step. First of all, the features which are depicted in detail as follows.

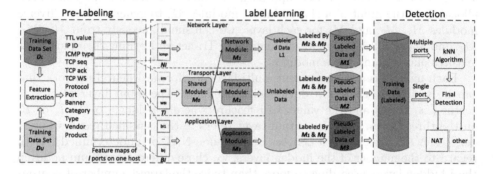

Fig. 1. The main system architecture.

4.2   Pre-labeling

As the first step of our approach, we need to conduct a part of the original data set as the training data $D_L = \{(H_{li}, y_l) | l = 1, 2, ..., L\}$ with L labeled instances in advance.

Features Extraction. An active IoT device H_{li} ($l = 1, 2, ..., L$) may open i ($1 \leq i$) ports on the Internet, we define a group of feature values on one port of H_{li} as an instance. Among which, the values of the referring features are divided into $N_i = [ttl_i, id_i, icmp_i]$ on network layer, $T_i = [sn_i, an_i, ws_i]$ on transport layer, and $B_i = [b_{i1}, b_{i2}, b_{i3}, ..., b_{ij}]$ where $b_{ij}(1 \leq j \leq 7)$ on application layer.

And y_i is defined for the detection result where $y_i = 1$ if the current host is connecting on the Internet via NAT, otherwise $y_l = 0$ means it is directly connecting on the Internet via the real public IP address or unable to determine. Based on the limit and effective features N_i, T_i or B_i on the three layers that we have discussed in Sect. 3, we can respectively label three small data set D_N, D_T, and D_B. Then the data set $D_L = D_N \bigcup D_T \bigcup D_B$ can be the input of the

NAT detection training neural network which automatically learns the respective features from each other layers to label the unlabeled instances. We denote the remaining unlabeled data set $D_U = ((H_{ui})|u = 1, 2, ..., U$ with U unlabeled online IoT devices.

4.3   Label Learning

In the second step, the unlabeled instances in D_U need be automatically labeled as NAT or *other* and added into D_L by synchronized training Tri-net through learning features.

Modules. Considering the faults of traditional NAT detecting algorithm and the weak crossing of the features on three independent layers, we employ the Tri-net as our semi-supervised approach [4]. Since the feature map has been allocated as the input of a shared initial modules M_0 to generate three diverse modules M_1, M_2, and M_3 for each layer, we can simultaneously train M_0, M_1, M_2, and M_3 modules. Then, we explore to use Tri-net for learning their particular features and training these modules.

Each module is an independent multi-layer feedforward neural network that can be trained to classify a device with one port. The input layer receives a vector (x_1 to x_i) and the values of i feature where x belongs to N_i, T_i or B_i on the three layers. And the output layer refers to the classified result where 1 denotes NAT device and 0 denotes *other* (non-NAT or undetermined). With regard to the number of the hidden layers, we chose different optimum nodes in the i hidden layers according to more than twice the largest number of neurons in the input layer. Then, the neural network can be initialized for simultaneously training each module.

With the training process in multiple rounds with the increasing labeled data set, three modules M_1, M_2, and M_3 become more and more similar. Considering the logical regression two-category classifier of our neural network, we define the probability $p_j \in [0, 1]$ calculating function of the three modules M_v ($v = 1, 2, 3$) as follows:

$$p_j = \frac{e^{z_j}}{\sum_{k=1}^{2} e^{z_k}}, \tag{1}$$

where e^{z_j} is an exponent of network output for category j. And the cross-entropy loss function $Loss$ is:

$$Loss = \frac{1}{L} \sum_{1}^{L} \sum_{i=1}^{2} y_j \cdot \log(p_j), \tag{2}$$

where L denotes the total number of samples in training dataset D_L and $y_j \in \{0, 1\}$ denotes the labeling result.

Pseudo-label Editing. The three modules M_v $(v = 1, 2, 3)$ may generate different labeling results of one instance H_{li} based on their local features. For solving the divergence, we introduced the $pseudo - label$ strategy to denote the intermediate results which are produced by the independent modules. If one instance x is simultaneously predicted as the same pseudo-labels of the other two modules, that the same result of x will be voted as the final label. If x is differently predicted as NAT and $other$ by the other two modules, it will not be labeled for continuous training in the next ground. For one instance x in M_1, if it has been both determined as a NAT device by M_2 and M_3, that x will be as NAT by our algorithm. Then the new labeled instance will be added into the training data set for the renewed training of M_1. With regard to the unseen instance M_1 which has been denoted as $other$ by both M_2 and M_3 after three rounds, it will be dropped from the training data set to avoid degenerating the performance.

For determining the final label for H_i with its single port with three diverse pseudo-labels $M_v(M_0(H_i))$ and posterior probability p_j, we employ the Maximum posterior probability (MAP) as follows:

$$y_j = arg \max_{y_j \in \{0,1\}} \{p(M_1(M_0(H_i)) = y_j|H_i) \\ + p(M_2(M_0(H_i)) = y_j|H_i) + p(M_3(M_0(H_i)) = y_j|H_i)\} \tag{3}$$

4.4   Detection

After the training process, we got the steady modules M_v $(v = 1, 2, 3)$ and the stable labeled training dataset D_L. With regard to the host H_l in D_L may open $i(1 \leq i \leq 65,535)$ ports on the Internet. That means i multiple diverse labels can be produced in the training process. Hence, we employ k-Nearest Neighbors (kNN) to identify the final result infers the brand and model of a host H_l. In detail, we first calculate the distance between H_{li} its labels y_{ij} on each port every port H_{lj}. The final NAT detection result is determined by the closest distance in the trained dataset D_L.

5   Experiments and Result

In this section, we implemented the experiment to perform the actual validity and accuracy of our approach with real data on the Internet.

5.1   Experimental Data

Original Data Set. Considering the adversarial behavior of active port scan on the Internet and ethical guidelines which we must be followed [5], we employed three open data sets [6, 15, 16]. While there are no existing NAT labels in the three original data set. Thus, we need to label parts of the hosts as NAT or not by our pre-labeling algorithm and the above-mentioned feature fields.

With regard to the banners in three data set, device type, vendor and product can be identified by using the fingerprinting method [7,19]. After data processing and device fingerprinting, we take advantage of 7,197,713 public IP addresses with the identified IoT devices as our experimental data set. Due to multiple devices may share the same IP by NAT or a device may simultaneously open multiple ports on one IP address, we denote one port on one IP as one instance. As illustrated in Table 2, 8,644,288 instances have been classified 4 device categories, including 41 device types, 1,598 vendors, and 11,253 products. Among which, the routing or switching category devices are only identified based on the general protocol banners. And the other category devices may be identified based on the general or special protocols. For one instance, a `Dell Printer` can be identified as its device type and vendor on both HTTP and PJL Raw services.

Table 2. Experimental data set and identification result.

Category	Protocol	Port	IoTs	NATs	Type	IoTs	NATs
General	FTP	21	300,858	156,974	Router	1,193,270	238,252
	SSH	22	310,538	35,649	Gateway	502,021	312,893
	Telnet	23	468,732	84,522	UTM	431,806	33,218
	HTTP	80	3,295,851	916,489	Switch	153,539	18,647
	SNMP	161	520,363	175,276	Modem	136,479	64,864
	HTTPs	443	2,780,104	860,725	VPN	37,332	12,509
	UPnP	1900	89,453	16,978	Firewall	16,122	11,550
Monitor	RTSP	554	498,917	146,956	NVR	802,201	260,146
	ONVIF	3702	308,249	70,413	DVR	764,100	156,875
Printing	LPD	515	63,721	11,718	IPcam	763,963	172,482
	IPP	631	17,177	4,936	Printer	438,421	156,449
	PJL Raw	9100	26,233	10,560	Scanner	4,675	1,633
Industrial control	Siemens S7	102	826	411	PLC	11,742	6,754
	Modbus	502	19,730	10,945	HMI	1,799	778
	PCworx	1962	676	293	RTU	647	432
	Ethernet/IP	44818	6,720	3,243	SCADA	442	262
	BACnet	47808	9,847	5,431	DCS	364	243
Total	-	-	8,644,288	2,511,499	Other	3,385,980	1,063,512

Pre-labeling. Based on the features on the network, transport, application layer which has been discussed above, we separately labeled three labels N_1, N_2, and N_3 of the devices. Due to not all features on the three layers that can be covered for some devices, only part of the devices can be labeled, and three labels N_1, N_2 and N_3 may can not be all labeled for these devices. In essence, there also exist conflicts among three labels of N_1, N_2, and N_3 on one port or multiple ports of some hosts. This condition does not affect the training process because these labels are only pseudo-labels for the neural network model to determine the devices are NAT or not finally. After the pre-labeling process, we got a D_L labeled data set with $50k$ instances and the remaining unlabeled data set D_U with more than 8 million instances. In this case, the labeled instances only occupy the low rate of 6.2% of the total instances.

Training Process. In order to label the unlabeled instances in D_U to be labeled and added into D_L, we have programmed our aforementioned Tri-net method of the training neural network in Python. For semi-supervised training the shared initial modules M_0 to generate three diverse modules M_1, M_2, and M_3 for each layer, we fine-tuned different structures and depths for M_1, M_2, and M_3 to adjust their diverse input feature maps. Then, we denote N_4 for the synthesize labeling result which is determined by the stable pseudo-labels N_1, N_2, and N_3 of three layers.

We implemented the training program on a Lenovo server with two Intel Xeon CPU E5-2650 v4, 256 GB 2400 Mhz memory chips and two NVIDIA Tesla K80 graphics cards. It has taken about 49 h until the training process ended and the stable data set D_L with 6,318,165 instances were labeled. Eventually, 1,704,833 instances are dropped out because they can not be judged whether NAT or not.

Table 3. Experimental result of detecting NATs performance.

Category	Precision	Recall	F1 score
Routing	0.924	0.911	0.917
Monitor	0.943	0.937	0.939
Printing	0.953	0.968	0.960
Industrial control	0.967	0.944	0.955
Average	0.930	0.922	0.926

Identification. As shown in Table 2, 2,511,499 instances are determined as NATs, that account for 29.1% percent of total 8,644,288 instances. With regard to the IoT devices which only open one port on the Internet, 5,845,382 instances in our experimental data belong to the single-port class. Among which, $1,692,384$ instances are identified as NATs.

According to our statistics, 1,352,331 IP addresses were shared by more than two ports. Based on the kNN identification algorithm, 538,596 IPs are recognized as NATs. Overall, 2,130,980 IPs can be detected as NAT, which nearly rating one-third of the total 7,197,713 IPs of experimental data set.

5.2   Evaluation

Measurement. To evaluate the performance of our approach, we introduce two evaluation indexes: `precision` and `recall`. Precision reflects the rating of NAT devices correctly classified, which is calculated using Eq. (4):

$$Precision = \frac{TP}{TP + FP} \tag{4}$$

where True Positive (TP) denotes the number of NAT devices correctly classified as `NAT`, False Positive denotes the number of non-NAT devices incorrectly classified as `NAT` and False Negative (FN) reflects the number of NAT devices incorrectly classified as `Other` (i.e. non-NAT devices). On the other hand, recall reflects the number of `Other` devices incorrectly classified as NATs using Eq. (5):

$$Recall = \frac{TP}{TP + FN} \tag{5}$$

Naturally, high precision and recall are the desirable outcomes. And the harmonic means of precision and recall `F1` is calculated using Eq. (6):

$$F1 = \frac{2 * Precision * Recall}{Precision + Recall} \tag{6}$$

Verification Result. The detailed performance is revealed in Table 3. We observe that the precision of monitor devices is lower than the other categories because of the NAT functional components of themselves. Experimental results show that it is efficient and robust for detecting NATs of online IoT devices based on the features of three layers and the Tri-net method with high precision and recall rate.

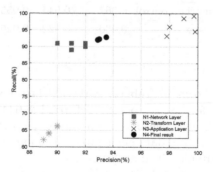

Fig. 2. The precision and recall of features on three layers.

Feature Effectiveness on Three Layers. As shown in Fig. 2, X-axis and Y-axis separately indicate the precision and recall of the diverse features on network, transport and application layers. That obviously indicates that features on the application layer have the highest precision and recall, and the transport layer has the lowest performance. The difference depends on the feature effectiveness of three layers. For example, the variation of TCP sequence and acknowledgment number between NAT and non-NAT is not obvious.

6 Conclusion

In this paper, we presented a new approach based on Tri-net for active NAT detecting with eight features on three layers. Through experimenting on real Internet open data, we found almost one-third of online IoT devices using NATs to connect to the IPv4 space. Among the four IoT categories, industrial control devices are more using NAT than routing, printing, and monitor. The final evaluation of our measurement revealed the precision and recall both can be up to 92%. With the wide deployment of IPv6, a further test would be to identify NAT on intelligent devices which are connected to Internet via IPv6.

Acknowledgments. This work was supported by National Key R&D Program of China (Grant 2017YFC0820701), National Natural Science Foundation of China (Grant U1766215, 61702504).

References

1. Abt, S., Dietz, C., Baier, H., Petrović, S.: Passive remote source NAT detection using behavior statistics derived from NetFlow. In: Doyen, G., Waldburger, M., Čeleda, P., Sperotto, A., Stiller, B. (eds.) AIMS 2013. LNCS, vol. 7943, pp. 148–159. Springer, Heidelberg (2013). https://doi.org/10.1007/978-3-642-38998-6_18
2. Bellovin, S.M.: A technique for counting Natted hosts. In: Proceedings of ACM SIGCOMM Workshop on Internet Measurment (2002)
3. Beverly, R.: A robust classifier for passive TCP/IP fingerprinting. In: Barakat, C., Pratt, I. (eds.) PAM 2004. LNCS, vol. 3015, pp. 158–167. Springer, Heidelberg (2004). https://doi.org/10.1007/978-3-540-24668-8_16
4. Chen, D., Wang, W., Gao, W., Zhou, Z.: Tri-net for semi-supervised deep learning. In: Proceedings of International Joint Conference on Artificial Intelligence (2018)
5. Dittrich, D., Kenneally, E.: The Menlo Report: Ethical Principles Guiding Information and Communication Technology Research. Technical report, U.S. Department of Homeland Security (2012)
6. Durumeric, Z., Adrian, D., Mirian, A., Bailey, M., Halderman, J.A.: A search engine backed by Internet-wide scanning. In: Proceedings of 22nd Computer and Communications Security (2015)
7. Feng, X., Li, Q., Wang, H., Sun, L.: Acquisitional rule-based engine for discovering Internet-of-Thing devices. In: Proceedings of 27th USENIX Security Symposium (2018)
8. Gokcen, Y., Foroushani, V.A., Heywood, A.N.Z.: Can we identify NAT behavior by analyzing traffic flows. In: Proceedings of IEEE Symposium on Security and Privacy (2014)
9. Ishikawa, Y., Yamai, N., Okayama, K., Nakamura, M.: An identification method of PCs behind NAT router with proxy authentication on HTTP communication. In: Proceedings of Symposium on Applications and the Internet (2011)

10. Khatouni, A.S., Zhang, L., Aziz, K., Zincir, I., Zincirheywood, N.: Exploring NAT detection and host identification using machine learning. In: Proceedings of Conference on Network and Service Management (2019)
11. Kohno, T., Broido, A., Claffy, K.C.: Remote physical device fingerprinting. IEEE Trans. Dependable Secur. Comput. **2**(2), 93–108 (2005)
12. Komarek, T., Grill, M., Pevny, T.: Passive NAT detection using HTTP access logs. In: Proceedings of International Workshop on Information Forensics and Security (2016)
13. Li, R., Zhu, H., Xin, Y., Yang, Y., Wang, C.: Remote NAT detect algorithm based on support vector machine. In: Proceedings of Information Engineering and Computer Science (2009)
14. Maier, G., Schneider, F., Feldmann, A.: NAT usage in residential Broadband networks. In: Spring, N., Riley, G.F. (eds.) PAM 2011. LNCS, vol. 6579, pp. 32–41. Springer, Heidelberg (2011). https://doi.org/10.1007/978-3-642-19260-9_4
15. Rapid7: Open data. https://opendata.rapid7.com/
16. Rüth, J., Zimmermann, T., Hohlfeld, O.: Hidden treasures – recycling large-scale Internet measurements to study the Internet's control plane. In: Choffnes, D., Barcellos, M. (eds.) PAM 2019. LNCS, vol. 11419, pp. 51–67. Springer, Cham (2019). https://doi.org/10.1007/978-3-030-15986-3_4
17. Sun, W., Zhang, H., Cai, L., Yu, A., Shi, J., Jiang, J.: A novel device identification method based on passive measurement. Secur. Commun. Netw. 1–11 (2019)
18. Yan, Z., Lv, S., Zhang, Y., Zhu, H., Sun, L.: Remote fingerprinting on Internet-Wide printers based on neural network (2019)
19. Yang, K., Li, Q., Sun, L.: Towards automatic fingerprinting of IoT devices in the cyberspace. Comput. Netw. **148**, 318–327 (2019)

Data Integrity Checking Supporting Reliable Data Migration in Cloud Storage

Changsong Yang[1,2,3](✉), Xiaoling Tao[1,2], Sufang Wang[1], and Feng Zhao[2]

[1] Guangxi Colleges and Universities Key Laboratory of Cloud Computing
and Complex Systems, Guilin University of Electronic Technology,
Guilin 541004, China
{csyang,txl}@guet.edu.cn, wang_susu20@163.com

[2] Guangxi Cooperative Innovation Center of Cloud Computing and Big Data,
Guilin University of Electronic Technology, Guilin 541004, China
fengzhao@guet.edu.cn

[3] Shanghai Key Laboratory of Integrated Administration Technologies
for Information Security, Shanghai 200240, China

Abstract. With the rapid development of cloud computing, more and more users are willing to employ cloud storage. As a result, an increasing number of companies invest cloud storage thus provide users with data storage services, which equipped with distinct quality, e.g., storage capacity, access speed, security, prices and reliability. To enjoy more suitable data storage service, the user may change the cloud service providers. As a result, outourced data migration between two different cloud servers has become a fundamental requirement. Therefore, how to securely migrate outsourced data from one semi-trusted cloud to another becomes a primary concern of user. To solve this problem, we construct a blockchain-based publicly verifiable outsourced data migration scheme supporting integrity verification. In the proposed scheme, the user can migrate outsourced data blocks from the original cloud to the target cloud without retrieving them from the original cloud. Meanwhile, the target cloud can check the data integrity to guarantee that the data blocks are migrated integrally. Moreover, by making use of the decentration of blockcahin, the proposed scheme can achieve public verifiability without requiring any third party auditor. Finally, we provide the security analysis and efficiency evaluation, which can respectively demonstrate the security and practicality of the novel proposed scheme.

Keywords: Cloud computing · Blockchain · Data integrity · Data migration · Public verification

1 Introduction

Cloud computing is a newly-developing and promising computing paradigm, which connects a number of distributed resources together through network and establishes a computing resource pool to provide tenants with plenty of on-demand services, such as data sharing service, data storage service [2]. As one of

© Springer Nature Switzerland AG 2020
D. Yu et al. (Eds.): WASA 2020, LNCS 12384, pp. 615–626, 2020.
https://doi.org/10.1007/978-3-030-59016-1_51

the most attractive services, cloud storage can provide convenient data storage service in the manner of pay-as-you-go [14, 19]. As a result, an increasing number of users are willing to embrace cloud storage service to greatly reduce local storage overhead. Thus, more and more companies, e.g., Microsoft, Google, Dropbox and Alibaba offer cloud storage services characterized by different prices, access speed, reliability, security, etc [10, 21].

Due to the various features of different cloud storage services, the users might change their cloud service providers for more suitable data storage services. Moreover, the users can change the cloud service providers for some uncontrollable factors, such as a civil servant is transferred to another department, a patient is diverted to another hospital, etc. In these cases, the users need to migrate their outsourced data from the original cloud server to the target cloud server, which makes outsourced data migration become more and more common. According to the investigation of Cisco [3], 95% of the total traffic will be the cloud traffic by the end of 2021, and almost 14% of the total cloud traffic is expected to be the traffic between different cloud data centers. Therefore, how to securely and efficiently achieve outsourced data migration will attract more and more attentions [23, 24].

To achieve outsourced data migration between two different cloud servers, an application called *Cloudsfer* has been designed, which adopted encryption technique to protect the transferred outsourced data during migration process. However, *Cloudsfer* cannot guarantee transferred outsourced data integrity against the semi-honest cloud servers. On the one hand, the original cloud server might maliciously delete some data blocks that are rarely accessed for saving storage cost and computation overhead, or hide some data accidents. On the other hand, outsourced data migration may take up plenty of network bandwidths, which will lower the access speed of other users. Hence, the original cloud server might only send part of the data, or even deliver some unrelated data to the target cloud server. In order to solve the above problems, a few solutions have already been proposed.

However, there are still some security challenges in processing the problem of outsourced data migration. Firstly, in order to guarantee the transferred outsourced data integrity, the existing solutions have to contain some complex protocols, such as provable data possession (PDP) protocol, vector commitment (VC) scheme and so on. That will lead to heavy computation cost and communication overhead. Secondly, most of the existing solutions have to introduce a third party auditor (TPA) to manage key or verify migration result. However, the TPA might refuse to serve due to the increasing computation overhead, resulting in service interruption. Moreover, the privacy information (such as key) might be leaked because of the hardware/software failures of TPA. As a result, TPA would become the bottleneck that impedes the development of outsourced data migration system. Blockchain is a decentralized system, which provides a solution to achieve outsourced data migration without TPA. To the best of our knowledge, there is no research work on data integrity verification supporting reliable data migration based on blockchain.

1.1 Our Contributions

In this paper, we utilize blockchain to construct a novel scheme, which can simultaneously achieve secure outsourced data migration and efficient transferred data integrity verification. As a result, the main contributions of this paper are as follows:

- We propose a blockchain-based scheme, which can simultaneously achieve outsourced data migration and data integrity verification. Specifically, the user can migrate outsourced data blocks from original cloud to target cloud without downloading them. Then, the target cloud can check the received data blocks integrity, which can guarantee that the data blocks are integrally migrated. Hence, if the original cloud does not migrate the data blocks honestly, or the data blocks are polluted during the migration process, the malicious behaviors will be detected with an overwhelming probability.
- The proposed scheme can achieve (private/public) verifiability without requiring any third party auditor, which is much better than most of the existing solutions. Meanwhile, the theoretical computational complexity analysis shows that the proposed scheme does not contain any complex calculations and protocols. Moreover, we provide the detailed security analysis, which can demonstrate the security of the proposed scheme.

1.2 Related Work

In cloud storage, the outsourced data security, especially for data privacy preserving [1,4] and data integrity verification [5] have been widely studied. To protect outsourced data privacy, Kamara and Lauter [6] studied the application of cryptographic techniques in cloud storage. Then, they described some architectures which combine non-standard and recent cryptographic primitives. Morales-Sandoval et al. [11] designed a pairing-based cryptographic scheme to protect data privacy, which uses attribute-based encryption (ABE) and short signatures (SSign) as building blocks. To guarantee data integrity, Li et al. [7] proposed a fuzzy identity-based data integrity auditing scheme. In their scheme, they solved the problem of complex key management. Meanwhile, they proved the security and practicality of their proposal. Yan et al. [18] adopted lattice and Bloom filter to design a dynamic cloud data integrity verification scheme, which not only can improve the utilization of cloud storage space ultimately, but also can resist the quantum computer attacks. However, the above protocols do not consider the problem of secure data migration.

Secure outsourced data migration is a new hot topic of cloud data security in recent years. Yu et al. [25] presented a provable data possession scheme which also supports verifiable data migration. After migration, the user can check the transferred data integrity on the target cloud server through provable data possession (PDP) protocol. To the best of our knowledge, their proposed scheme is the first solution to achieve efficient data migration. Wang et al. [16] proposed a novel concept called provable data possession with outsourced data migration (DT-PDP). Then, they designed a concrete DT-PDP scheme based on bilinear pairings. In 2016, Ni et al. [12] proposed a secure outsourced data transfer (SODT) scheme. In their scheme, they adopted the improved BCP encryption scheme and polynomial-based authenticators to guarantee data confidentiality and data integrity on the target cloud server. However, the above schemes [12,16,25] are not workable for clear data. To overcome this deficiency, Xue et al. [17] designed a new scheme, which is suitable for both plaintext and ciphertext. Moreover, their proposed scheme is more efficient and practical compared with schemes [12,16,25].

However, Liu et al. [8] pointed out that there is a security flaw in Xue et al.'s scheme [17]. That is, the malicious cloud server is able to modify a data block and then forge a corresponding block tag that can pass verification successfully. To overcome this security flaw, they proposed an improved data migration scheme. Moreover, they adopted a new protocol to verify data integrity, which can greatly improve the efficiency in data integrity checking process [9]. However, the above solutions need to introduce a TPA, which could become the bottleneck that impedes the development of outsourced data migration system. To remove the TPA, Yang et al. [22] proposed a vector-commitment-based solution, which allows the user to migrate outsourced data from one cloud to another one. In 2018, Wang et al. [15] also designed a two-party secure outsourced data migration protocol. In their proposed scheme, they adopted homomorphic encryption and homomorphic authenticators to achieve data integrity checking. Although schemes [15,22] can achieve secure data migration without TPA, their efficiency is not appealing since they both need to pay expensive computation overhead, such as modular exponential operation, bilinear pairings calculation, homomorphic computation and so on.

1.3 Organization

The organization of this paper is as follows. In Sect. 2, the preliminary of blockchain is described. Subsequently, the problem statement is presented in Sect. 3, including the system model, the security threats and the security goals. In Sect. 4, we proposed the concrete scheme in detail, which can simultaneously achieve data confidentiality, data integrity and secure data migration. After that, we provide the scheme analysis in Sect. 5, including the security analysis and the oretical efficiency evaluation. Finally, we briefly conclude this paper in Sect. 6.

2   Preliminaries

As a decentralized system, Blockchain network was first proposed by Nakamoto in 2008 and implemented in 2009, which is proposed as the underlying technology of Bitcoin [13]. Blockchain network composed of distributed data storage technology, point-to-point network communication technology and modern cryptographical technology. Generally speaking, blockchain network can be divided into three major categories: public blockchain network, private blockchain network and consortium blockchain network. The construction of these three categories are same, and they all satisfy the properties of decentration, persistency, anonymity and auditability. A blockchain network consists of many blocks, as illustrated in Fig. 1. Every block utilizes a Merkle hash tree (MHT) to maintain plenty of data items, such as transaction. After that, a hash chain is computed to connect all the root nodes of the MHT. In the hash chain, the inputs of the current hash value are the concatenation of the previous hash value, the timestamping and the current root node of the MHT. That is, when the hash chain is extended, the current hash value is fed into the next hash function to compute the new hash value, which makes it be impossible to tamper the hash chain maliciously [20].

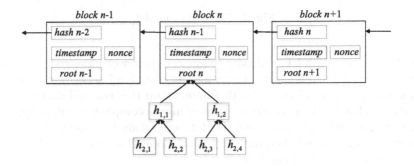

Fig. 1. The structure of blockchain

3   Problem Statement

In this following section, we will firstly formalize the system model. Then, we describe the main security threats. Finally, we identify the design goals that the proposed scheme should achieve.

3.1   System Model

In our system model, there are two cloud servers and an user, as illustrated in Fig. 2. The user outsources his personal data to the cloud server to greatly reduce local storage overhead. Later, the user might change the cloud service providers and migrate the outsourced data to another cloud server. In our system model, we assume that cloud A is the original cloud server, which might migrate some data blocks, or even the whole file to another cloud according to user. Moreover, we assume that cloud B is the target cloud server, which receives the transferred data blocks from the cloud A. Meanwhile, the cloud B checks transferred data blocks integrity. Then, the cloud B informs the user the result of data migration.

Note that, due to the competitive relationship, we can assume that cloud A and cloud B will not maliciously collude together to cheat the user. It means

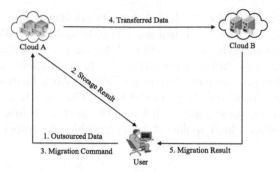

Fig. 2. The system model

that cloud A and cloud B will both follow our protocol independently. Otherwise, the two cloud servers can be viewed as one cloud server and outsourced data migration is meaningless. Furthermore, cloud B is rational during the data migration. That is, cloud B tries to successfully accomplish the data migration, rather than maliciously corrupting the data migration to slander cloud A. This assumption is reasonable because the goal of cloud B is to provide data storage service for the user and benefit from it.

3.2   Security Threats

In the proposed scheme, we should consider the following security threats. Firstly, the outsourced file usually contains some sensitive information, which should be kept secret from the user's point of view. However, the attackers might try to access the outsourced file to dig the privacy information. Hence, data confidentiality is a challenge that we should consider. Secondly, the cloud A may delete some data blocks that are rarely accessed. Moreover, the data blocks might be polluted during the migration process. Thus, data integrity is one concern of the user. Thirdly, the data migration might cost plenty of bandwidths, which is unexpected from the cloud A's point of view. As a result, the cloud A may not honestly migrate data blocks.

3.3   Design Goals

In the proposed scheme, we should achieve the following design goals.

- **Data confidentiality.** The adversary cannot obtain any plaintext information from the ciphertext without the corresponding data decryption key.
- **Data integrity.** If the cloud A does not deliver the data blocks honestly, or the data blocks are polluted during the migration process, the user and the cloud B can detect the dishonest behaviors.
- **Public verifiability.** If given the migration evidence, any verifier can check the data migration result without any private information.

4 Our Scheme

In this part, we introduce the proposed scheme in detail. As we know, the user must be authenticated by the cloud server before enjoying data storage service. For simplicity, we assume that the user has passed the authentication and become a legal client of cloud A and cloud B.

Initialization. Firstly, the PKI generates ECDSA public/private key pairs (PK_X, SK_X), where $X \in \{U, A, B\}$. Meanwhile, let $Cert_X$ denote the public key certificate of participant X and $Sign_Y(M)$ the ECDSA signature generated by signing message M with the private key Y. After that, the user chooses two secure one-way collision-resistant hash functions $H_1(\cdot)$ and $H_2(\cdot)$. Meanwhile, the user denotes by n_f the name of outsourced file F, where file name n_f is unique in the storage system.

Data Oursourcing. The user must encrypt the outsourced file before uploading, which can protect the sensitive information. Specifically, the user first computes a data encryption key $K = H_1(SK_U \| n_f)$ and utilizes it to encrypt the outsourced file $C = Enc_K(F)$, where Enc is an IND-CPA secure symmetric encryption algorithm. Secondly, the user divides the ciphertext C into n data blocks $C_1, C_2, \cdots, C_n$. Finally, the user outsources the data set $D = (n_f, C_1, C_2, \cdots, C_n)$ to the cloud A and the timestamping server of the blockchain network.

Data Storage. The cloud A maintains outsourced data set D for the user, and the timestamping server adds a new block to the blockchain network, where the new block stores the outsourced data set.

- Upon receiving data set D from the user, the cloud A constructs a Merkle hash tree MHT_A to maintain the received data set D. After that, the cloud A sends $CT = (D, R_A, Sig_{R_A}, Cert_A)$ to the timestamping server, where R_A is the root node of the Merkle hash tree MHT_A and Sig_{R_A} is the signature on the root node R_A, ie., $Sig_{R_A} = Sign_{SK_A}(R_A)$.
- The timestamping server checks whether the public key certificate $Cerr_A$ is valid and MHT_A is correct. Meanwhile, the timestamping server verifies the validity of signature Sig_{R_A}. Only if all the verifications are successful will the timestamping server add a new block to the blockchain network. Then, the timestamping server sends a storage proof $\lambda = (R_A, Sign_{R_A}, h_k)$ to the user, where h_k is the current hash of the blockchain.
- On receipt of λ, the user randomly chooses a data block to check the correctness of the root node R_A. Then, the user verifies whether the signature Sig_{R_A} is valid and the hash value h_k is correct. Only if all the verifications are successful will the user believe that the data set D is maintained honestly and delete the local back.

Data Migration. The user might migrate some data blocks from cloud A to cloud B for more suitable service or some uncontrollable factors.

- The user first generates a set of data block indices φ, which represents the data blocks that need to be migrated to cloud B. After that, the user computes a signature $Sig_t = Sign_{SK_U}(n_f||\varphi||T_t)$, where T_t is the timestamping. Further, the user generates a migration command $TR = (n_f, \varphi, T_t, Sig_t)$. Then, the user sends command TR and certificate $Cert_U$ to the cloud A and the cloud B.
- After receiving TR and $Cert_U$ from the user, the cloud A checks the validity of signature Sig_t and certificate $Cert_U$. Meanwhile, the cloud A checks whether the timestamp T_t has expired. If not all of the verifications are successful, the cloud A aborts and returns failure. Otherwise, the cloud A sends data blocks $\{C_i\}_{i\in\varphi}$, signature Sig_{R_A} and auxiliary authentication information[1] $\{\eta_i\}_{i\in\varphi}$ to the cloud B.

Migration Checking. The cloud B can check the transferred data blocks integrity to guarantee that the data blocks are migrated integrally.

- On receipt of TR, $Cert_U$ and $\{C_i, \eta_i\}_{i\in\varphi}$, the cloud B checks the integrity of received data blocks. Specifically, the cloud B verifies the validity of $Cert_U$ and TR. Then, the cloud B utilizes $\{C_i, \eta_i\}_{i\in\varphi}$ to construct a new root node R'_A and compares it with R_A. Meanwhile, the cloud B checks the validity of signature Sig_{R_A} and the correctness of the hash values on the blockchain. Only if all the verifications are successful, the cloud B believes that the received data blocks are intact.
- The cloud B maintains $\{C_i\}_{i\in\varphi}$, and computes $Sig_B = Sign_{SK_B}(n_f||\varphi||T_t)$. After that, the cloud B returns the migration evidence $\tau = (Sig_B, Cert_B)$ to the user. As a result, the user can check the migration result by verifying the validity of Sig_B and $Cert_B$. Only both the verifications are successful, the user trusts that the data blocks are migrated honestly.

5   Scheme Analysis

Lemma 1. *Assume that $(\mathcal{K}, E, D)$ is an IND-CPA secure symmetric encryption scheme, $\mathcal{F}$ is a pseudo-random function, where $\mathcal{K} = \{0,1\}^m$, $E : \mathcal{K} \times \mathcal{K} \to \mathcal{Y}$, $\mathcal{K}^F = \{0,1\}^n$. Then, $(\mathcal{K}', E')$ is IND-CPA secure, where $E'_k(x) = E_{F'_k(s)}(x)$.*

Proof: $(\mathcal{K}', E')$ is IND-CPA secure means that for any messages x, y and TTP attacker $\mathcal{A}$, there always exists a polynomial $p(n)$ and integer N, if $n > N$, $AdvA_{xy}^{E'_{k'}} = |Pr[\mathcal{A}^{E'_{k'}}(E_{F_{k'}(x)}(x)) = 1] - Pr[\mathcal{A}^{E'_{k'}}(E_{F_{k'}(y)}(y)) = 1]| < \frac{1}{p(n)}$. Then, we first define some games.

---

[1] In a Merkle hash tree, the auxiliary authentication information is a data set which contains all of the sibling nodes on the path from the desired leaf node to the root node.

Game 0:
1. Challenger $\mathcal{C}$ runs $Gen(1^n)$ to generate key k'.
2. Input 1^n, the attacker $\mathcal{A}$ asks random predictor $Enc_{F_{k'}}(\cdot)$, outputs messages m_0 and m_1 with the same length.
3. Challenger $\mathcal{C}$ chooses $b \in_R \{0,1\}$ randomly, computes $c = Enc_{F_{k'}}(m_b)$ and sends it to attacker $\mathcal{A}$
4. Attacker $\mathcal{A}$ asks random predictor $Enc_{F_{k'}}(\cdot)$, outputs b' as a guess at b.
5. If $b = b'$, output 1; otherwise, output 0.

Game 1:
The Game 1 is very similar to the Game 0. The only difference between the Game 0 and the Game 1 is that attacker $\mathcal{A}$ asks random predictor $Enc_\phi.(\cdot)$. Hence, we do not describe Game 1 in detail.

Game 2:
Game 2 is similar to Game 1. The difference is that the encrypted message is independent of the key.

Based on the indistinguishability of pseudo-random function and the IND-CPA security of $(\mathcal{K}', E')$, we can prove that the Game 0 and the Game 1 are indistinguishable. That is, for any message x and any PPT attacker $\mathcal{A}$, there exists a polynomial time algorithm $p(n)$ and an integer N_1, when $n > N_1$, the following equation holds:

$AdvA_1 = |Pr[\mathcal{A}^{E'_{k'}}(E_{F_{k'}(x)}(x)) = 1] - Pr[\mathcal{A}^{E_\phi}(E_{\phi(x)}(x)) = 1]| < \frac{1}{4p(n)}$.

Similarly, for any message y and any PPT attacker $\mathcal{A}$, there always exists a polynomial $p(n)$ and an integer N_4, if $n > N_1$, the following equation holds:

$AdvA_4 = |Pr[\mathcal{A}^{E'_{k'}}(E_{F_{k'}(y)}(y)) = 1] - Pr[\mathcal{A}^{E_\phi}(E_{\phi(y)}(y)) = 1]| < \frac{1}{4p(n)}$. As a result, we can say that Game 0 and Game 1 are indistinguishable.

Moreover, we can prove that Game 1 and Game 2 are indistinguishable. Since the proof is similar, so we do not describe it here in detail.

Theorem 1. *The proposed scheme can satisfy data confidentiality.*

Proof: Data confidentiality can guarantee that only the user can correctly decrypt the ciphertext. Even if the adversaries collude with the cloud server maliciously, they cannot obtain any plaintext information from the ciphertext. In the proposed scheme, the user utilizes a symmetric encryption algorithm to encrypt the file before uploading. Based on the Lemma 1, we can find that the security of outsourced file is guaranteed by the chosen symmetric encryption algorithm so that without the data decryption key, the encrypted data is IND-CPA secure. Hence, our proposed scheme can ensure that only the user can decrypt the ciphertext correctly. That is, the proposed scheme can satisfy the outsourced data confidentiality.

Theorem 2. *The proposed scheme can satisfy transferred data integrity.*

Proof: Data integrity means that the transferred data blocks cannot be destroyed. Otherwise, the cloud B can detect the data tampering. In the proposed scheme, the cloud A migrates the data blocks $\{C_i\}_{i \in \varphi}$, the signature Sig_{R_A} and the auxiliary authentication information $\{\eta_i\}_{i \in \varphi}$ to the cloud B. The cloud B utilizes $\{C_i, \eta_i\}_{i \in \varphi}$ to construct the root node R'_A and compares it with R_A. Meanwhile, the cloud B checks the validity of signature Sig_{R_A} and the correctness of the hash values on the blockchain. Blockchain characterised by decentration, persistency, anonymity and auditability. As a result, once a block is added into the blockchain network, nobody can tamper it. Thus, if the transferred data blocks are tampered, the data blocks cannot pass the verification. That is, if the cloud A does not migrate the data blocks honestly, or the data blocks are polluted during the migration process, the cloud B can detect the data pollution with an overwhelming probability. Hence, the proposed scheme can guarantee the transferred data blocks integrity.

5.1   Computational Complexity Comparison

In this section, we analyze the theoretical computational complexity of the proposed scheme and the existing scheme [22]. Then, the computation overhead is analyzed by presenting the numeric results. For simplicity, we ignore the multiplication calculation and the communication overhead.

We first introduce some symbols that will be used in the comparison. We respectively use symbols $\mathcal{E}$ and Exp to represent a data encryption operation and an exponentiation computation. Moreover, we denote by $\mathcal{S}$ a signature generation calculation, $\mathcal{V}$ a signature verification, $\mathcal{H}$ a hash computation, $\mathcal{P}$ an operation of computing a bilinear pairing, n the number of outsourced data blocks, l the number of transferred data blocks, and the least hash value on the blockchain is II_{k+q}. Then, the results are shown in Table 1.

Table 1. Theoretical computational complexity between two schemes

Scheme	Scheme [22]	Our scheme
Data outsourcing	$1\mathcal{E} + (2n+1)\mathcal{H} + nExp$	$1\mathcal{E} + 1\mathcal{H}$
Data Storage	$n^2 Exp + 2n\mathcal{P}$	$1\mathcal{S} + 2\mathcal{V} + 2(\log_2 n + n + 1)\mathcal{H}$
Data migration	$2\mathcal{S} + 1\mathcal{V}$	$1\mathcal{S} + 1\mathcal{V}$
Migration checking	$1\mathcal{V} + (n+l)Exp + 2l\mathcal{P}$	$1\mathcal{S} + 3\mathcal{V} + (\log_2 n + q)\mathcal{H}$

From Table 1 we can have the following three findings. Firstly, to encrypt the outsourced file, our scheme's overhead increases with the size of plaintext, while the overhead of scheme [22] increases with the size of plaintext and the number of outsourced data blocks. Secondly, in data storage and migration checking processes, scheme [22] contains some complex computations, such as exponentiation computation and bilinear pairing calculation. Thirdly, in the data migration phase, the difference of computation overhead between the two schemes is very small. Therefore, we can say that our proposed scheme is more efficient than the existing scheme [22].

6 Conclusion

In this paper, we investigate the problem of reliable outsourced data migration between two different cloud servers, which is a very challenging problem in cloud computing. To solve this issue, we design a data integrity verification scheme that also supports reliable data migration. In the proposed scheme, the user can migrate the outsourced data blocks from one cloud to another without downloading them. Meanwhile, the target cloud can check the received data blocks integrity before accepting them. Moreover, by making use of blockchain, the proposed scheme can achieve private/public verifiability without any TPA. Finally, we provide the security analysis and computational complexity comparison, which can demonstrate the security and practicability of the proposal.

Acknowledgement. This work was supported by the Opening Project of Shanghai Key Laboratory of Integrated Administration Technologies for Information Security, the National Natural Science Foundation of China (No. 61962015), the Science and Technology Program of Guangxi (No. AB17195045) and the Natural Science Foundation of Guangxi (No. 2016GXNSFAA380098).

References

1. Zhang, S., Sun, W., Liu, J., Kato, N.: Physical layer security in large-scale probabilistic caching: analysis and optimization. IEEE Commun. Lett. **23**(9), 1484–1487 (2019)
2. Cui, Y., Lai, Z., Wang, X., Dai, N., Miao, C.: QuickSync: improving synchronization efficiency for mobile cloud storage services. IEEE Trans. Mob. Comput. **16**(12), 3513–3526 (2017)
3. C. V. Networking, Cisco global cloud index: forecast and methodology, 2016–2021, White paper. Cisco Public, San Jose
4. Du, M., Wang, Q., He, M., Weng, J.: Privacy-preserving indexing and query processing for secure dynamic cloud storage. IEEE Trans. Inf. Forensics Secur. **13**(9), 2320–2332 (2018)
5. Garg, N., Bawa, S.: RITS-MHT: relative indexed and time stamped Merkle hash tree based data auditing protocol for cloud computing. J. Netw. Comput. Appl. **84**, 1–13 (2017)
6. Kamara, S., Lauter, K.: Cryptographic cloud storage. In: Sion, R., Curtmola, R., Dietrich, S., Kiayias, A., Miret, J.M., Sako, K., Sebé, F. (eds.) FC 2010. LNCS, vol. 6054, pp. 136–149. Springer, Heidelberg (2010). https://doi.org/10.1007/978-3-642-14992-4_13
7. Li, Y., Yu, Y., Min, G., Susilo, W., Ni, J., Choo, K.: Fuzzy identity-based data integrity auditing for reliable cloud storage systems. IEEE Trans. Dependable Secur. Comput. **16**(1), 72–83 (2019)

8. Liu, Y., Xiao, S., Wang, H., Wang, X.: New provable data transfer from provable data possession and deletion for secure cloud storage. Int. J. Distrib. Sens. Netw. **15**(4), 1–12 (2019)
9. Liu, Y., Wang, X.A., Cao, Y., Tang, D., Yang, X.: Improved provable data transfer from provable data possession and deletion in cloud storage. In: Xhafa, F., Barolli, L., Greguš, M. (eds.) INCoS 2018. LNDECT, vol. 23, pp. 445–452. Springer, Cham (2019). https://doi.org/10.1007/978-3-319-98557-2_40
10. Mohtasebi, S., Dehghantanha, A., Choo, K.: Cloud storage forensics : analysis of data remnants on SpiderOak, JustCloud, and pCloud. arXiv: Cryptography and Security
11. Morales-Sandoval, M., Gonzalez-Compean, J.L., Diaz-Perez, A., Sosa-Sosa, V.J.: A pairing-based cryptographic approach for data security in the cloud. Int. J. Inf. Secur. **17**(4), 441–461 (2017). https://doi.org/10.1007/s10207-017-0375-z
12. Ni, J., Lin, X., Zhang, K., Yu, Y., Shen, X.: Secure outsourced data transfer with integrity verification in cloud storage. In: Proceedings of the 2016 IEEE/CIC International Conference on Communications in China, ICCC 2016, pp. 1–6. IEEE Computer Society, Washington, DC (2016)
13. Nakamoto, S., et al.: Bitcoin: A Peer-to-Peer Electronic Cash System
14. Wang, C., Wang, Q., Ren, K., Cao, N., Lou, W.: Toward secure and dependable storage services in cloud computing. IEEE Trans. Serv. Comput. **5**(2), 220–232 (2012)
15. Wang, Y., Tao, X., Ni, J., Yu, Y.: Data integrity checking with reliable data transfer for secure cloud storage. Int. J. Web Grid Serv. **14**(1), 106–121 (2018)
16. Wang. H., He. D., Fu. A, Li. Q., Wang. Q: Provable data possession with outsourced data transfer. IEEE Trans. Serv. Comput. 1–12 (2019)
17. Xue, L., Ni, J., Li, Y., Shen, J.: Provable data transfer from provable data possession and deletion in cloud storage. Comput. Stand. Interfaces **54**, 46–54 (2017)
18. Yan, Y., Wu, L., Gao, G., Wang, H., Xu, W.: A dynamic integrity verification scheme of cloud storage data based on lattice and bloom filter. J. Inf. Secur. Appl. **39**, 10–18 (2018)
19. Yu, L., Shen, H., Cai, Z., Liu, L., Calton, P.: Towards bandwidth guarantee for virtual clusters under demand uncertainty in multi-tenant clouds. IEEE Trans. Parallel Distrib. Syst. **29**(2), 450–465 (2018)
20. Yang, C., Chen, X., Xiang, Y.: Blockchain-based publicly verifiable data deletion scheme for cloud storage. J. Netw. Comput. Appl. **103**, 185–193 (2018)
21. Yu, L., Shen, H., Karan, S., Ye, L., Cai, Z.: CoRE: cooperative end-to-end traffic redundancy elimination for reducing cloud bandwidth cost. IEEE Trans. Parallel Distrib. Syst. **28**(2), 446–461 (2017)
22. Yang, C., Wang, J., Tao, X., Chen, X.: Publicly verifiable data transfer and deletion scheme for cloud storage. In: Naccache, D., Xu, S., Qing, S., Samarati, P., Blanc, G., Lu, R., Zhang, Z., Meddahi, A. (eds.) ICICS 2018. LNCS, vol. 11149, pp. 445–458. Springer, Cham (2018). https://doi.org/10.1007/978-3-030-01950-1_26
23. Yang, C., Tao, X., Zhao, F., Wang, Y.: Secure data transfer and deletion from counting Bloom filter in cloud computing. Chin. J. Electron. **29**(2), 273–280 (2020)
24. Yang, C., Tao, X., Zhao, F.: Publicly verifiable data transfer and deletion scheme for cloud storage. Int. J. Distrib. Sens. Netw. **15**, 1–12 (2019)
25. Yu, Y., Ni, J., Wu, W., Wang, Y.: Provable data possession supporting secure data transfer for cloud storage. In: Proceedings of the 10th International Conference on Broadband and Wireless Computing, Communication and Applications, BWCCA 2015, pp. 38–42. IEEE Computer Society, Washington (2015)

A Blockchain-Based Privacy-Preserving Mechanism for Attribute Matching in Social Networks

Feihong Yang[1,2], Yuwen Pu[1,2], Chunqiang Hu[1,2(✉)], and Yan Zhou[3]

[1] School of Big Data and Software Engineering, Chongqing University,
Chongqing, China
{yfh,yw.pu,chu}@cqu.edu.cn
[2] Key Laboratory of Dependable Service Computing in Cyber Physical Society,
Ministry of Education (Chongqing University), Chongqing, China
[3] School of Computer Science, Chongqing Electric Power College, Chongqing, China
157201915@qq.com

Abstract. Online social network has become an indispensable part of people's life, and people are willing to make friends in social network. However, semi-honest social network platforms may reveal users' private information, which will cause great losses to users. Existing schemes either are based on Secure Multi-party Computation (SMC), which have a lot of resource consumption, or are based on vector dot product calculation, which are vulnerable to statistical attacks. In this paper, we propose an attribute matching scheme based on hierarchical blockchain and Ciphertext Policy Attribute-based Encryption (CP-ABE), which can realize attribute matching in semi-honest servers and offer fine-grained attributes selection for users to get more precise matching. Additionally, a novel blockchain architecture is proposed in our scheme, which reduces the storage consumption and improve running efficiency. Finally, we present the security analysis that the scheme can resist a variety of attacks, and the experiment results demonstrate the feasibility of the scheme.

Keywords: Attribute matching · CP-ABE · Hierarchical blockchain · Social network · Friend discovery

1 Introduction

Online social network provides a platform for people to establish the friend relationship. The server implements users' personal attributes matching (such as gender, age, occupation, hobbies, etc) to determine whether the attributes between users meet certain conditions to become friends [1,2]. However, it may lead to the leakage of private information. Oukemeni et al. [3] shows that social network platforms may sell users' attribute information to third parties for advertisement or statistical purposes. If the user's privacy information is disclosed,

© Springer Nature Switzerland AG 2020
D. Yu et al. (Eds.): WASA 2020, LNCS 12384, pp. 627–639, 2020.
https://doi.org/10.1007/978-3-030-59016-1_52

it will do great harm to their lives [4]. For example, more than 25 gigabytes users' information of an extramarital affair platform named Ashley Madison was leaked such as real name, home address and other information [5]. Furthermore, adversaries can predict sensitive information that users are unwilling to publish through inference attacks [6]. And attackers may use information stolen from social networks to blackmail victims [7].

The basic mechanism for making friends in social networks is through private attribute matching. The main idea is to compare users' attribute similarity without disclosing user information. Researchers have made great efforts to address the problem. There are three traditional solutions. The first category considers the user information as a set of attributes and achieves attribute matching based on Private Set Intersection (PSI) or Private Set Intersection Cardinality (PSI-CA) [5,8,9]. The second category considers user information as a vector and calculate the vector distance by dot product calculation to measure social distance [10–12]. The third category uses Ciphertext Policy Attribute-based Encryption (CP-ABE) to achieve friend discovery [1,13–15]. However, the following problems remain to be resolved:

1) Most of the category mechanisms are implemented based on Secure Multiparty Computing (SMC) or homomorphic encryption, which consume a lot of computing resources, or based on vector dot product calculation, which is vulnerable to statistical analysis attacks.
2) Online social network platforms may collude with some users to steal and disclose other users' privacy information.

Based on the above considerations, we propose a novel privacy-preserving scheme based on CP-ABE and hierarchical blockchain for making friends in online social networks. The basic idea of our scheme is as follows. We define the user's profile as a set of attributes $S = \{s_1, ..., s_n\}$. Users shares symmetric keys based on CP-ABE, and then encrypt S with symmetric keys. Besides, hierarchical blockchain replaces the server to compare similarity of users' attributes. The contributions of the paper are summarized as follows:

- We propose a novel attribute matching scheme based on CP-ABE and hierarchical blockchain technology, which can realize the attribute matching in semi-honest social network platforms.
- A new blockchain architecture is proposed to realize the decentralization, traceability and transparency of attribute matching. Additionally, this architecture can reduce the storage load of blockchain and improve efficiency.
- We theoretically prove that our scheme can resist many kinds of attacks and demonstrate its effectiveness in simulation experiments.

The rest of this paper is organized as follows: Sect. 2 describes the related work. The preliminaries are presented in Sect. 3. Section 4 discusses our system model, new blockchain architecture and attack model. Section 5 elaborates the proposed scheme. We present the security analysis and performance evaluation of our scheme in Sect. 6 and 7. Finally, we summarize the paper in Sect. 8.

2 Related Works

Many researchers represent users' attributes as a set to compute the attribute intersection. Li et al. [8] first proposed an improved Private Set Intersection (PSI) technique based on Secure Multi-party Computing (SMC) to achieve private attribute matching. Yi et al. [5] gave a privacy-preserving user profile matching scheme using homomorphic encryption and mutiple servers. Users encrypt their attribute sets with homomorphic encryption and the server calculates whether the dissimilarity is less than the threshold given by users.

Another popular approach considers users' attributes as a vector to calculate the vector distance. Gao et al. [11] defined the user's proximity as the dot product of two vectors and proposed a profile-matching scheme under multiple keys based on additive homomorphism. Luo et al. [10] and Li et al. [12] presented dot product calculation without homomorphic encryption to reduce the consumption. Luo et al. [10] designed a lightweight confusion matrix transformation algorithm, and Li et al. [12] mixed the private attributes with random noise.

The popular approach is based on CP-ABE. Luo et al. [13] proposed a friend discovery scheme based on CP-ABE, which focused on the management of master key in the system using Shamirs scheme. Cui et al. [1] designed a privacy-preserving user attribute matching scheme based on CP-ABE, which uses pre-matching to filter out some users to improve the matching efficiency. Besides, it provides the verifiability of matching results and create a secure communication channel for matched users. Qi et al. [14] designed a friend discovery protocol with hidden keywords and fine-grained access control based on searchable encryption and CP-ABE.

Moreover, in view of the unreliability of centralized servers, researchers pay attention to the blockchain technology. Jiang et al. [16] and Gu et al. [17] proposed novel social network architectures which use blockchain and smart contracts instead of centralized servers to provide online social network services.

3 Preliminaries

3.1 Ciphertext Policy Attribute-Based Encryption

Attribute-Based Encryption (ABE) is a one-to-many encryption technology that can achieve access control [18], which includes ciphertext policy ABE (CP-ABE) and key policy ABE (KP-ABE). There is a master key MK and a public key PK in CP-ABE. User's secret key SK can be generated by MK based on attribute sets specified by the user. Besides, users can generate ciphertext CT by using PK and access structure Γ, so that only those who possess these attributes can decrypt the CT.

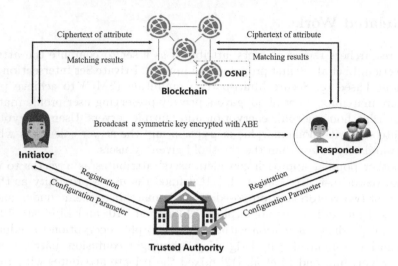

Fig. 1. System model

3.2 Blockchain

Blockchain technology is summarized from Bitcoin [19]. The blockchain can be regarded as some nodes maintaining a common database. There are four important concepts in blockchain:

- Transaction: It is an operation that changes the state of the blockchain.
- Block: It records multiple transactions over a period of time and it is a consensus on the recent changes in the state of the blockchain.
- Consensus: Transaction is validated by all nodes before it is stored in a block.
- Chain: Each block records the hash value of the previous block, and then hashes the current block. Each block is connected to the previous block to form a chain.

Blockchain is divided into public blockchain, consortium blockchain and private blockchain. This paper is based on the consortium blockchain. And it is partially decentralized.

3.3 Smart Contract

Smart contract is a program running on the blockchain. Once successfully deployed, it can be called through unique address, and the correctness of execution results can be verified by consensus nodes. It is not controlled by anyone and remains visible to everyone. Hence, smart contracts can replace centralized servers.

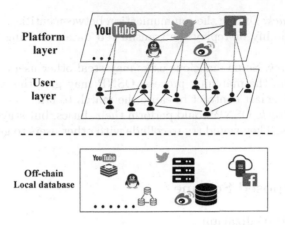

Fig. 2. Consortium blockchain model

4 System Model, Blockchain Architecture and Attacker Model

4.1 System Model

The system model is illustrated in Fig.1. It consists of four entities as follows.

- *User:* User would like to make friends who meet certain attributes requirements. The initiator and the responder are considered as exemplary users.
- *OSNP:* It is a provider of online social networking services with local database and computing capabilities. In blockchain, they are consensus nodes responsible for generating new blocks, also known as miners in some blockchain networks.
- *BC:* Blockchain is mainly responsible for calculating the similarity of users' attributes and judging whether the matching is successful.
- *TA:* Trusted third party is only responsible for key generation.

4.2 Hierarchical Blockchain Architecture

The hierarchical design can obviously improve performance of blockchain system [20]. We design the consortium blockchain architecture as demonstrated in Fig. 2.

The platform layer consists of many OSNPs that perform smart contracts to match friends and be consensus on execution results. The user layer consists of social network platform users who can communicate casually and match friends through the platform layer. Off-chain is a private database for each platform that stores ciphertext of users' information.

4.3 Attacker Model

In our paper, we emphasize protecting users' attribute information. We propose and analyze the following attacker models.

1) *External Attack:* During the communication between entities, adversaries may eavesdrop, modify or replay the transmitted data, resulting in user privacy leakage.
2) *Internal Attack:* Some malicious users may steal other users' attribute information during the matching process. OSNP may give the wrong execution results of the smart contract to cause the match to fail.
3) *Colluding Attack:* OSNP would perform their duties, but stays curious about users' privacy. They would try to collude with other users to get users' private information.

5   The Proposed Scheme

5.1   System Initialization

In this phase, all secret keys are transmitted to the corresponding entities via secure channels. TA first generates the asymmetrical key (PU_{bc}, PR_{bc}) for blockchain to communicate with users. Then it initializes the master key MK and the public key PK, and generates the secret key for each user. We construct the CP-ABE based on the classic CP-ABE scheme [18]. The details are as follows.

ABE Initialization. TA selects a bilinear group $\mathbb{G}_0$ of prime order p with generator g, then selects two random exponent $\alpha, \beta \in \mathbb{Z}_p$. The public key is published as:

$$PK = \mathbb{G}_0, g, h = g^\beta, e(g,g)^\alpha \tag{1}$$

and the master key MK is (β, g^α). PK is visible to all nodes of blockchain and social network users. MK is stored secretly by TA.

User Registration. When new online social network users sign up in the system, they should upload their personal attribute set S to TA for secret key SK. Attribute set $S = \{s_1, ..., s_n\}$ contains user's personal information, such as age, gender, hobbies, educational background, etc. TA first select a random $r \in \mathbb{Z}_p$ and a random $r_j \in \mathbb{Z}_p$ for each attribute $j \in S$. Then TA computes the SK as:

$$SK = (D = g^{(\alpha+r)/\beta}, \forall j \in S : D_j = g^r \cdot H(j)^{r_j}, D'_j = g^{r_j}) \tag{2}$$

If the attributes of user are changed, the SK has to be regenerated.

5.2   Users Communication

As depicted in Fig. 3, when an initiator wants to make new friends, it executes the following three steps: attribute set encryption, smart contract initialization and broadcasting message. The responder executes two steps: ABE decryption and smart contract interaction.

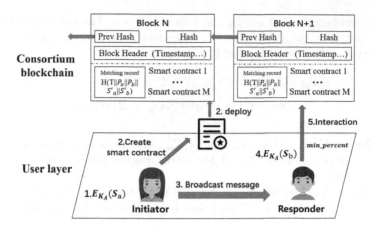

Fig. 3. User communication

Attribute Set Encryption. The initiator chooses symmetric encryption algorithms such as AES, and generates the corresponding symmetric key K_a. Then it encrypts each attribute of its attribute set S_a with K_a to obtain a ciphertext attribute set S'_a.

$$S'_a = \{s'_1, ..., s'_n \mid \forall s_i \in S_a, s'_i = E_{K_a}(s_i)\} \tag{3}$$

Smart Contract Initialization. The initiator submits a transaction on the blockchain to create smart contract. The content of the smart contract is visible to everyone. The main purpose of the smart contract is to calculate the similarity percentage between the attributes of initiators and users on the ciphertext. It will obtain a unique address P_{sc} after successful deployment. The initiator needs to upload S'_a, maximum number of friends she wants to make max_num and social platform contact address P_a to the smart contract. Therefore, the data transmitted to smart contract as:

$$CT_{asc} = E_{PU_{bc}}(T\|S'_a\|P_a\|max\_num\|H(T\|S'_a\|P_a\|max\_num)) \tag{4}$$

It should be noted that the smart contract is only generated and deployed here but not executed. Hence, the detailed analysis of smart contract is elaborated in Sect. 5.3.

Message Broadcasting. The information that the responder needs to use is $M = K_a\|P_{sc}$. To defend against external attacks and enable data integrity verification, the initiator needs to add time stamp T and hash value of M. Therefore, the message to be broadcast is: $M' = T\|K_a\|P_{sc}\|H(T\|K_a\|P_{sc})$.

Then, the initiator formulates the access structure Γ. The root node of Γ is R, each node x has a polynomial q_x, and Y is a set of leaf nodes. The degree d_x of each node's polynomial q_x is one less than the threshold k_x. Then initiator chooses a random number $s \in \mathbb{Z}_p$ and sets $q_x(R) = s$. The values of other nodes $q_x(0)$ are set as $q_{parent}(x)(index(x))$. After that, the initiator can use PK and Γ to encrypt M' to get CT_{ab} and broadcast it:

$$CT_{ab} = (\Gamma, \tilde{C} = M'e(g,g)^{\alpha s}, C = h^s,$$
$$\forall y \in Y : C_y = g^{q_y(0)}, C'_y = H(att(y))^{q_y(0)}) \tag{5}$$

ABE Decryption. After receiving CT_{ab}, the responder first uses SK_b to decrypt it to get message M'. If his attributes do not satisfy Γ, decryption is unsuccessful.

Firstly, we define an algorithm $DecryptNode(CT_{ab}, SK, x)$. Let x be the leaf node of the access structure Γ, and then let $i = att(x)$, if $i \in S_b$, then:

$$DecryptNode(CT_{ab}, SK, x) = \frac{e(D_i, C_x)}{e(D'_i, C'_x)} = e(g,g)^{rq_x(0)} \tag{6}$$

If $i \notin S_b$, $DecryptNode(CT_{ab}, SK, x) = \perp$. $DecryptNode(CT_{ab}, SK, z)$ is executed on all child nodes of x in the access structure Γ to get the result F_z. And let S_x be an arbitrary k_x-sized set of child nodes z and $F_z \neq \perp$. Then F_x can be calculated as follows:

$$F_x = \prod_{z \in S_x} F_z^{\Delta_{i,S'_x}(0)}, where\ i = index(z), S'_x = \{index(z) : z \in S_x\}$$
$$= e(g,g)^{r \cdot q_x(0)} \tag{7}$$

Then the responder can get the message M' by computing:

$$\tilde{C}/(e(C,D)/e(g,g)^{r\ q_x(0)}) = \tilde{C}/(e(h^s, g^{(\alpha+r)/\beta})/e(g,g)^{rs}) = M' \tag{8}$$

Smart Contract Interaction. If the responder gets M', it proves that he meets initiator's requirements for friends. And the responder gets T, K_a, P_{sc}, then he calculates their hash values to verify whether these values have been modified or replayed. If these data are not attacked, the responder uses K_a to encrypt his attribute set S_b to get S'_b.

$$S'_b = \{s'_1, ..., s'_n \mid \forall s_i \in S_b, s'_i = E_{K_a}(s_i)\} \tag{9}$$

Moreover, the responder sets the minimum similarity percentage $min\_percent$ between his attributes and initiator's. If the similarity reaches $min\_percent$, he will accept initiator as his friend. At last, he encrypts timestamp T, S'_b, social network contact address P_b, $min\_percent$ as:

$$CT_{bsc} = E_{PU_{bc}}(T\|S'_b\|P_b\|min\_percent\|H(T\|S'_b\|P_b\|min\_percent)) \tag{10}$$

The responder initiates a transaction and transmits CT_{bsc} to the smart contract at address P_{sc}.

5.3   Attribute Matching

After the blockchain node receives responder's transaction, blockchain node uses secret key PR_{bc} to decrypt CT_{bsc}, and checks whether the data has been modified or replayed. After that, the node executes the smart contract. It compares the similarity between the attributes of initiator and responder's on the ciphertext.

The matching algorithm is illustrated in Algorithm 1. The responder and the initiator become friends if their attribute similarity exceeds $min\_percent$, and the initiator makes at most max_num friends who satisfy her access structure Γ.

The execution results of the smart contract will be consensus by all nodes, and final results will be stored in the blockchain. It should be noted that what we store is the hash value of input parameters instead of the original data. It is to achieve auditability while avoiding the initiator or responder, using K_a to obtain attributes of other party. After that, the records will never be modified or deleted, which is convenient for viewing, auditing and tracing. Besides, if the matching result is success, a communication channel between the initiator and the responder will be established.

6   Security Analysis

6.1   Resisting External Attack

The scheme can resist the eavesdropping attack, replay attack and modification attack, the details are as follows:

- *Eavesdropping Attack:* The data transmission of the scheme adopts CP-ABE encryption or blockchain public key encryption. Therefore, attackers cannot obtain the plaintext of the transmitted data by eavesdropping the message.
- *Replay Attack:* Each transmitted data contains timestamp T and its own hash value, so the receiver can verify the validity of T to judge whether the data is replayed.
- *Modification Attack:* Each transmitted data contains a hash value of the data. The receiver executes hash operation on the received data and compares it with received hash value to judge whether the data has been modified.

6.2   Resisting Internal Attack

For internal attack, we mainly focus on three entities: initiator, responder and OSNP. We assume they are curious about users' privacy.

- *Initiator*: In the whole process, the initiator can get nothing except for the matching result. Hence, the initiator cannot get the attributes of other users.
- *Responder*: When the responder receives CT_{ab} from the initiator, if his attributes do not meet the access structure, he cannot get K_a and P_{sc}, nor can he know anything about the initiator. If the responder meets the access structure and becomes a friend with initiator, he only knows the similarity between initiator's attributes and his, but cannot get initiator's attributes.

Algorithm 1. Attribute Matching Algorithm

Input: The social network contact addresses of initiator and responder, P_a, P_b
    The ciphertexts of initiator's and responder's attribute set, S'_a, S'_b
    The maximum number of friends initiator wants, max_num
    The minimum attribute similarity percentage responder wants, $min\_percent$
1: num_now represents the number of friends that initiator has matched
2: **if** $num\_now \geq max\_num$ **then**
3:    **return** $False$
4: **end if**
5: Combine attribute sets S'_a and S'_b to get S
6: Quicksort for S to get S'
7: $num\_same = 0$
8: **for** $(i = 0; i < len(S'); i++)$ **do**
9:    **if** $S'[i] == S'[i+1]$ **then**
10:      $num\_same\ += 1$
11:    **end if**
12: **end for**
13: Calculate the number of attributes in S'_b as num_b
14: $same\_percent = num\_same/num\_b$
15: **if** $same\_percent < min\_percent$ **then**
16:    **return** $False$
17: **else**
18:    $num\_now = num\_now + 1$
19:    Establish a communication channel for contact addresses P_a and P_b
20:    Store this matching record and the hash values of input parameters
21:    **return** $True$
22: **end if**

- *OSNP*: OSNP compares the similarity of attributes on the ciphertext, so it cannot obtain user attributes. In addition, malicious nodes cannot give wrong execution results causing matching failure, because its execution results will be consensus by all nodes.

6.3 Resisting Collusion Attack

In the traditional scheme, the server may collude with some users to obtain other users' information. That is, the server uses K_a provided by users to decrypt the ciphertext of attributes. In our scheme, the server is replaced by hierarchical blockchain. Users have no idea about who executes the smart contract, and execution results will be verified by all nodes. If blockchain nodes find the data contains K_a, the uploader will be punished. In addition, K_a cannot be used to get initiator's attributes after matching, because the hash value of S'_a is stored in the blockchain instead of S'_a.

7 Performance Evaluation

The simulation experiments were completed on the Ubuntu 16.04 virtual machine under Windows 10 with Inter (R) Core (TM) i5-7500 CPU @ 3.40GHz. We used C language to implement the AES with 128-bit key. The CP-ABE was implemented based on Pairing Based Cryptograph (PBC) library and the capble toolkit provided by [18]. Moreover, we deployed a consortium blockchain on Hyperledger Fabric which was constructed based on Go and Docker. And the smart contract which is called 'chain code' in Fabric was coded by Go language. The reason why we chose Hyperledger Fabric instead of Ethereum is that Ethereum is a public chain which has low execution efficiency and requires additional fees for each transaction.

We mainly analyze the relationship between the number of attributes and time consumption, so we assumed that the initiator and the responder both have n attributes and $n = \{5, 10..., 95, 100\}$, so we got 20 sets of data. To facilitate the experiment, we set these attributes to $\{attr1, ..., attr100\}$. And we completed 20 experiments for each set of attributes to calculate average values to reduce errors.

The experimental results are depicted in Fig. 4. Figure 4(a) shows the time consumption of AES to encrypt different number of attributes. Figure 4(b) illustrates the performance of CP-ABE. Figure 4(c) presents the performance of blockchain, including smart contract initialization and attribute matching.

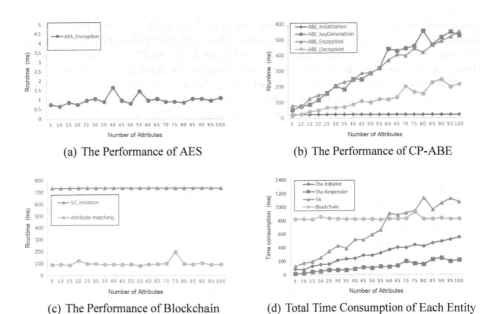

(a) The Performance of AES

(b) The Performance of CP-ABE

(c) The Performance of Blockchain

(d) Total Time Consumption of Each Entity

Fig. 4. Performance evaluation of our scheme

The total time consumption of each entity is presented in Fig. 4(d). TA needs to perform ABE initialization once and ABE key generation twice. For the initiator, it performs ABE encryption and AES encryption one time, separately. For the responder, it implements ABE decryption once and AES encryption for n attributes. For the blockchain, it executes the smart contract initialization and attribute matching. Experimental results show that our scheme is efficient and feasible.

8   Conclusion

In this paper, we propose a privacy-preserving attribute matching scheme by the combined use of hierarchical blockchain and CP-ABE. The scheme supports attribute matching in semi-honest online social network without revealing user information. Furthermore, the proposed hierarchical blockchain architecture can be applied in more fields, such as medical data sharing. Theoretical analysis have proved that our scheme can resist external attack, internal attack and colluding attack. And the effectiveness of the scheme is demonstrated by simulation experiments.

In the future, we plan to add the Proxy Cloud Server (PCS) into the system, which can outsource ABE encryption and decryption operations to reduce users computation cost. In addition, we consider using blockchain instead of TA to initialize ABE.

Acknowledgments. This research was supported partially by the Fundamental Research Funds for the Central Universities (No. 2019CDQYRJ006), the National Natural Science Foundation of China (No. 61702062, No. 61932006), the Chongqing Research Program of Basic Research and Frontier Technology with Grant (No. cstc2018jcyjAX0334), Key Project of Technology Innovation and Application Development of Chongqing (cstc2019jscx-mbdxX0044), and Overseas Returnees Innovation and Entrepreneurship Support Program of Chongqing (cx2018015).

References

1. Cui, W., Du, C., Chen, J.: CP-ABE based privacy-preserving user profile matching in mobile social networks. PLoS ONE **11**(6), e0157933 (2016)
2. Zheng, X., Cai, Z., Yu, J., Wang, C., Li, Y.: Follow but no track: privacy preserved profile publishing in cyber-physical social systems. IEEE Internet Things J. **4**(6), 1868–1878 (2017)
3. Oukemeni, S., Rifà-Pous, H., Puig, J.M.M.: Privacy analysis on microblogging online social networks: a survey. ACM Comput. Surv. (CSUR) **52**(3), 1–36 (2019)
4. Cai, Z., He, Z., Guan, X., Li, Y.: Collective data-sanitization for preventing sensitive information inference attacks in social networks. IEEE Trans. Dependable Secur. Comput. **15**(4), 577–590 (2018)
5. Yi, X., Bertino, E., Rao, F.-Y., Bouguettaya, A.: Practical privacy-preserving user profile matching in social networks. In: 2016 IEEE 32nd International Conference on Data Engineering (ICDE), pp. 373–384. IEEE (2016)

6. He, Z., Cai, Z., Yu, J.: Latent-data privacy preserving with customized data utility for social network data. IEEE Trans. Veh. Technol. **67**(1), 665–673 (2018)
7. Chaudhary, P., Gupta, B.B.: A novel framework to alleviate dissemination of XSS worms in online social network (OSN) using view segregation. Neural Netw. World **27**(1), 5 (2017)
8. Li, M., Cao, N., Yu, S., Lou, W.: FindU: privacy-preserving personal profile matching in mobile social networks. In: 2011 Proceedings IEEE INFOCOM, pp. 2435–2443. IEEE (2011)
9. Yang, J., Ouyang, C., Pan, M., Yu, Y., ter Hofstede, A.H.M.: Finding the "Liberos": discover organizational models with overlaps. In: Weske, M., Montali, M., Weber, I., vom Brocke, J. (eds.) BPM 2018. LNCS, vol. 11080, pp. 339–355. Springer, Cham (2018). https://doi.org/10.1007/978-3-319-98648-7_20
10. Luo, E., Liu, Q., Abawajy, J.H., Wang, G.: Privacy-preserving multi-hop profile-matching protocol for proximity mobile social networks. Future Gener. Comput. Syst. **68**, 222–233 (2017)
11. Gao, C., Cheng, Q., Li, X., Xia, S.: Cloud-assisted privacy-preserving profile-matching scheme under multiple keys in mobile social network. Cluster Comput. **22**(1), 1655–1663 (2018). https://doi.org/10.1007/s10586-017-1649-y
12. Li, R., et al.: Perturbation-based private profile matching in social networks. IEEE Access **5**, 19720–19732 (2017)
13. Luo, E., Liu, Q., Wang, G.: Hierarchical multi-authority and attribute-based encryption friend discovery scheme in mobile social networks. IEEE Commun. Lett. **20**(9), 1772–1775 (2016)
14. Qi, F., Chang, X., Tang, Z., Wang, W.: Searchable attribute-based encryption protocol with hidden keywords in cloud. In: Wang, G., Bhuiyan, M.Z.A., De Capitani di Vimercati, S., Ren, Y. (eds.) DependSys 2019. CCIS, vol. 1123, pp. 80–92. Springer, Singapore (2019). https://doi.org/10.1007/978-981-15-1304-6_7
15. Chandrasekaran, B., Nogami, Y., Balakrishnan, R.: An efficient hierarchical multi-authority attribute based encryption scheme for profile matching using a fast ate pairing in cloud environment. J. Commun. Softw. Syst. **14**(2), 151–156 (2018)
16. Jiang, L., Zhang, X.: BCOSN: a blockchain-based decentralized online social network. IEEE Trans. Comput. Soc. Syst. **6**(6), 1454–1466 (2019)
17. Ke, G., Wang, L., Jia, W.: Autonomous resource request transaction framework based on blockchain in social network. IEEE Access **7**, 43666–43678 (2019)
18. Bethencourt J., Sahai, A., Waters, B.: Ciphertext-policy attribute-based encryption. In: 2007 IEEE Symposium on Security and Privacy (SP 2007), pp. 321–334. IEEE (2007)
19. Crosby, M., Pattanayak, P., Verma, S., Kalyanaraman, V., et al.: Blockchain technology: beyond bitcoin. Appl. Innov. **2**(6–10), 71 (2016)
20. Liu, C., Xiao, Y., Javangula, V., Qin, H., Wang, S., Cheng, X.: NormaChain: a blockchain-based normalized autonomous transaction settlement system for IoT-based e-commerce. IEEE Internet Things J. **6**(3), 4680–4693 (2018)

A Real-Time Recommendation Algorithm
for Task Allocation in Mobile Crowd Sensing

Guisong Yang[1,2], Yanting Li[1], Yan Song[1], Jun Li[3(✉)], Xingyu He[1],
Linghe Kong[4], and Ming Liu[5]

[1] Department of Computer Science and Engineering,
Shanghai Key Lab of Modern Optical System, University of Shanghai
for Science and Technology, Shanghai, China
[2] Department of Electrical and Computer Engineering,
Michigan State University, East Lansing, USA
[3] China Industrial Control Systems Cyber Emergency Response Team,
Beijing, China
lijun@cics-cert.org.cn
[4] Department of Computer Science and Engineering,
Shanghai Jiao Tong University, Shanghai, China
[5] Department of Electrical and Computer Engineering,
Hong Kong University of Science and Technology, Hong Kong, China

Abstract. In mobile crowd sensing, whether or not the results of task allocation
are consistent with the user's preferences will greatly affect the efficiency of task
execution. Hence, recent studies have begun to focus on the user's preference
and, based on it, provide a task recommendation list to users. However, these
studies can neither accurately mine users' preferences nor consider the dynamic
updating of users' preferences. In this work, firstly, a matrix factorization
method is employed to mine users' preferences for tasks in mobile crowd
sensing system. Secondly, a method of generating a task recommendation list is
designed to provide task recommendations to users according to their preferences for tasks. Finally, a real-time update algorithm is proposed to make the
task recommendation list adapt to the users' preferences changed in real time, so
that the user's task recommendation list can be updated rapidly each time the
user's performance data changes, and the real-time task recommendation can be
realized. Extended evaluations based on real world mobility traces show that,
compared with the existing models, our model has significant advantages in
accuracy and the time cost.

Keywords: Mobile crowd sensing · Task allocation · Matrix factorization ·
Real-time recommendation algorithm

1 Introduction

Mobile crowd sensing (MCS) takes the intelligent device as the basic sensing unit. It is
composed of three parts: the platform, the task requester and the sensing user. In most
existing MCS applications, the tasks are combined into a task list for users to select and
execute. The specific process is as follows: (1) the task requester first uploads task

© Springer Nature Switzerland AG 2020
D. Yu et al. (Eds.): WASA 2020, LNCS 12384, pp. 640–652, 2020.
https://doi.org/10.1007/978-3-030-59016-1_53

requests to the platform. (2) The platform establishes a task list for all users according to the received task requests, which includes all tasks. Usually, the tasks are sorted according to the task's payment provided to the user and time emergency. (3) The user selects tasks from the list and uploads the sensing data to the platform after execution. (4) The platform finally feeds back the sensing data to the task requester.

In this process, the user's willingness to execute tasks are greatly influenced by the user's preferences. And there is evidence that, if a task that the user may like to execute is placed at the rear of the task list, according to psychological analysis, users are usually reluctant to search the entire task list to select this task [1]. The user may select a task that he is not familiar with but is at the front of the list and try to complete the task to get a reward. Since the task he then selects may not his preferred one, it therefore has an adverse impact on the user's willingness and ability to execute the task, resulting in a decrease in task execution efficiency. Thus, the platform needs to mine users' preferences for tasks, provide users with a personalized task recommendation list, and put the tasks that users are most interested in at the front of the list, so that users can execute tasks according to the task recommendation list successfully. Thus, approaches for mining users' preferences and based on which establishing the task recommendation list are needed for MCS systems.

In addition, in MCS system, tasks are executed continuously, so the user's historical performance data of executing tasks changes with time consecutively, and the real time updating of users' performance data while executing tasks will also affect the results of mining users' preferences. If these data are not taken into account, the accuracy of the inferred user preferences will be affected to some extent, thereby reducing the performance of task recommendation. Therefore, in order to improve the accuracy of task recommendation list, users' preferences need to be updated in time according to the updating of their performance data while executing tasks, so that the final task recommendation list can adapt to the changes of user preferences in time.

Consequently, in this paper, we present a real-time recommendation algorithm for task allocation in mobile crowd sensing (RRA), aiming to address two challenges: (1) how to mine user's preference accurately and based on which establish the task recommendation list, and (2) how to update the task recommendation list according to the updating of users' performance data in real time.

For the first challenge, we propose to use the matrix factorization method in the recommendation system to mine users' preference. In the MCS system, it is difficult to generalize users' preferences comprehensively by common methods. While the matrix factorization method in the recommendation system can learn useful patterns from the users' historical performance data of executing tasks and use active learning methods to mine users' preferences. Therefore, we propose to apply matrix factorization to the MCS system to mine users' preferences for tasks, so as to provide users with personalized task recommendation list based on their preferences, help users find more interested tasks faster and improve task allocation efficiency.

For the second challenge, we propose the idea of one update at a time to realize the real-time updating of task recommendation list, so as to achieve the purpose of real-time task recommendation. Many existing technologies in recommendation systems update the recommendation lists based on batch processing, that is, using all the user's performance data of executing tasks in the database to update the user's preferences.

However, since the number of users and tasks in the MCS system may be very large, updating the recommendation list based on the data of all users will be very expensive in terms of time cost and calculation costs. In order to reduce the delay of updating the recommendation list and save the calculation cost, a lightweight updating algorithm needs to be designed. Therefore, we propose the idea of one update at a time, which is only based on those directly affected data instead of all data, thus reducing the cost and realizing the real-time update of task recommendation list. And according to the idea of one update at a time, we proposed a real-time recommendation algorithm (RRA). When the data of the user performing the task is updated, only one row vector in the latent factor matrix corresponding to the data is updated instead of the entire latent factor matrix. Thus, the time cost and calculation consumption for updating the task recommendation list are greatly reduced, and the requirement for real-time updating of the task recommendation list can be satisfied.

The main contributions of this paper are as follows:

- A matrix factorization method is employed to mine users' preference and realize personalized task recommendation for users.
- In order to reduce the time cost and calculation cost, the RRA is proposed to realize the real-time update of the task recommendation list.

The remainder of this paper is organized as follows. In Sect. 2, the related works of tasks allocation and recommendation systems are introduced. The real-time updating algorithm is designed in Sect. 3. In Sect. 4, performance evaluation is given. Finally, conclusions are drawn in Sect. 5.

2 Related Work

More attention has been paid to real-time update technology in recent years. The online task allocation problem has been widely studied. [2] proposed an average makespan sensitive online task assignment (AOTA) algorithm and a largest makespan sensitive online task assignment (LOTA) algorithm, which viewed online task assignment as multiple rounds of virtual offline task assignments. [3] proposed a local Voronoi decomposition (LVD) algorithm, which can perform robust online task allocation operations based entirely on local information. A flexible two-sided online task assignment (FTOA) strategy is proposed in [4], which aims to guide idle workers based on the prediction of tasks and workers to increase the total number of worker-task pairs. However, these studies are based on historical data to perform task allocation, so that the results of task allocation cannot adapt to the users' preferences changed in real time, thereby reducing the efficiency of task execution.

The recommendation system originated from the situation of information overload, which consists of three parts: users, items and corresponding rating. The recommendation system can improve the personalized service, which has a broad application prospect. In the recommendation system, in order to discover important information from historical data, many models have been proposed over the years, such as trace-norm regularization-based models [5], multidimensional probabilistic models [6] and latent factor (LF) models [7]. Compared with other models, LF models have proved to have excellent performance in collaborative filtering, achieving the required performance while reducing the computation and storage costs; therefore, LF models have received extensive attention [8–11]. Among the LF models, the matrix factorization method (MF) is the most widely used. MF has the advantages of high precision and scalability, so it has been commonly used to process various data analysis tasks [12, 13]. Therefore, this paper considers applying matrix factorization to the task allocation process of mobile crowd sensing.

There are a few studies in the recommendation system that take the need of real-time updates into account; for example, [14] proposed a hybrid real-time incremental stochastic gradient descent updating technique (RI-SGD) for matrix factorization recommendation systems. However, the accuracy of the RI-SGD continues to decline with the increase of update times, which greatly reduces the efficiency of recommendation list update.

Although these aforementioned techniques have shown superior performance in some respects, to the best of our knowledge, no other works have applied the matrix factorization to the field of task allocation in MCS. Therefore, based on this technique, how to update the task recommendation list in real-time is of great research value.

3   Real-Time Updating Algorithm

In order to provide users with a personalized task recommendation list in real time, in this work, a real-time recommendation algorithm (RRA) is proposed. It can be divided into the following steps, as shown in Fig. 1. (1) The platform needs to collect the users' historical performance data of executing tasks, and establish the user-task rating matrix with missing values. (2) The platform uses the matrix factorization method to decompose the user-task rating matrix obtained in step (1), and generate the initial user latent factor matrix and task latent factor matrix. (3) The predicted user-task rating matrix without missing values can be obtained by the product of two latent factor matrices. The values of the row vectors in the predicted user-task matrix are sorted, and the sorted results can be used as the initial task recommendation list for each user. (4) The personalized task recommendation list should be updated in real time with the updating of the user's performance data while executing tasks.

To indicate the aforementioned process more clearly, we present the detailed symbols and descriptions utilized in this paper as follows:

In this paper, we focus on predicting the user's ratings of tasks in real time to provide users with an appropriate task recommendation list. There are a set of users $U = \{u_1, u_2, \cdots, u_m\}$ and a set of tasks $T = \{t_1, t_2, \cdots, t_n\}$ in the MCS system. Users' historical performance data of executing tasks are given in a rating matrix $R = \left[r_{u,i} \right]_{m \times n}$. In this matrix, $r_{u,i}$ is characterized by the number of times the user u_u has executed the task t_i. The binary matrix $P = \left[p_{u,i} \right]_{m \times n}$ is a matrix formed according to the rating matrix, which is used to indicate whether the user is interested in the task.

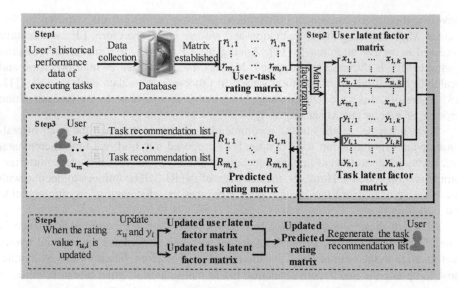

Fig. 1. The model of real-time updating algorithm.

The attenuation matrix $C = [c_{u,i}]_{m \times n}$ is used to indicate the reliability of using the binary matrix P to indicate the user's interest in tasks. $c_{u,i} = 1 + \alpha p_{u,i}$, α is the attenuation parameter. $X_{m \times k}$ denotes the user latent matrix, and $Y_{n \times k}$ denotes the task latent matrix (Table 1).

Table 1. Symbols and descriptions.

Symbol	Description	Symbol	Description
U	The set of users	$R_{m \times n}$	The rating matrix
T	The set of tasks	$P_{xm \times n}$	The binary matrix
m	The number of users	$C_{m \times n}$	The attenuation matrix
n	The number of tasks	$X_{m \times k}$	The user latent matrix
k	The dimension of the latent space	$Y_{n \times k}$	The task latent matrix
α	The attenuation parameter		

3.1 Step1: User-Task Rating Matrix Established

In MCS, the user's historical performance data of executing tasks need to be collected to mine the user's preference. However, on the one hand, the vast majority of applications in MCS do not require users to rate the tasks they have executed, which makes it difficult to obtain the explicit feedback data of users on tasks. On the other hand, the number of times users have executed tasks can indicate their preferences to some extent. As a result, we consider using the implicit data of the user's execution times for task recommendation, and establish a user-task rating matrix based on the historical data. The rating value $r_{u,i}$ in the matrix is the times user u_u has executed task t_i.

3.2   Step2: Generation of Initial Latent Factor Matrix

In order to mine the user's preference, the matrix factorization method is used to decompose the user-task rank matrix to generate the initial latent factor matrix describing the user's preference. Since the user-task matrix in this paper is an implicit feedback matrix, in order to obtain the initial latent factor matrix, Formula (1) needs to be solved.

$$\underset{X,Y}{argmin}\, d(X,Y) = \frac{1}{2}\sum_{u,i} c_{u,i}\left(p_{u,i}-x_u^T y_i\right)^2 + \left(\frac{\lambda_u}{2}\sum_u \|x_u\|^2 + \frac{\lambda_i}{2}\sum_i \|y_i\|^2\right), \quad (1)$$

where $p_{u,i} = \begin{cases} 0, & \text{if } r_{u,i} > 0 \\ 1, & \text{if } r_{u,i} = 0 \end{cases}$, and $r_{u,i}$ is the value of user-task rating matrix established in Sect. 3.1. $p_{u,i}$ is used to indicate whether user u_u is interested in task t_i. If $p_{u,i} = 1$, that is, user u_u has executed task t_i, we assume that user u_u is interested in task t_i. Otherwise user u_u has no interest in item t_i. Furthermore, consider the fact that if the user does not execute the task in the historical data, it may be because the user is really not interested in the task. However, it cannot be excluded that the user has not been exposed to the task. Therefore, the attenuation degree $c_{u,i} = 1 + \alpha p_{u,i}$ is introduced to indicate the degree of interest of user u_u in task t_i, and α is the attenuation parameter.

For formula (1), we use ALSWR to solve to obtain the initial latent factor matrix. The formula for the vector update using ALSWR is

$$x_u = \left(\lambda_u I + Y^T C^u Y\right)^{-1} Y^T C^u P(u) \quad (2)$$

and

$$y_i = \left(\lambda_i I + X^T C^i X\right)^{-1} X^T C^i P(i), \quad (3)$$

where X is the user latent matrix and Y is the task latent matrix, x_u and y_i are the row vectors of X and Y, respectively. $C^u \in R^{n\times n}$ and $C^i \in R^{m\times m}$ are the diagonal matrix with $C_{i,i}^u = c_{u,i}$ for user u_u and that with $C_{u,u}^i = c_{u,i}$ for task t_i. $P(u) \in R^n$ and $P(i) \in R^m$ respectively represent the vector of P for user u_u and that for task t_i.

3.3   Step3: Generation of Initial Personalized Task Recommendation List

After the initial latent factor matrix X and Y are obtained, the predicted user-task rating matrix can be generated by $X \cdot Y$, and then the initial personalized task recommendation list can be obtained by sorting the values of the row vectors in the predicted user-task matrix, that is, the predicted ratings of users for all tasks, and the sorted results can be used as a task recommendation list for each user.

3.4   Step4: Update of the Personalized Task Recommendation List in Real Time

In an MCS system, with the real time updating of the user's performance data while executing tasks, the user's preferences will change accordingly. In order to adapt the recommendation list to the changes of the updating of the user's performance data, it is necessary to update the task recommendation list in real time.

When the user u_u has executed the task t_i, the corresponding rating value $r_{u,i}$ in the rating matrix R will change, and this change will cause the data in the latent factor matrix to change. Therefore, in order to adapt to the update of the user's performance data, the latent factor matrix needs to be updated. Since each update of the rating value is usually mainly related to one element in the matrix, it mainly affects one vector in the latent factor matrix, i.e. one row in the user latent factor matrix and the task latent factor matrix. Therefore, we propose the idea of one update at a time. When the value of the rating matrix changes, only the corresponding user latent factor vector and task latent factor vector are updated, corresponding to the vectors in the red box in Fig. 1, and based on it, the updated latent factor matrix can be obtained.

Based on the updated latent factor matrix, we can get the updated predicted rating matrix by the method in Sect. 3.3, and further can regenerate the new task recommendation list. Since the amount of data of the latent factor vector is much smaller than that of the latent factor matrix, the time cost and resource consumption for updating the latent factor matrix are greatly reduced, and the requirement for real-time updating of the task recommendation list can be satisfied. The specific process is shown in Fig. 2.

In conclusion, this paper proposes to use the matrix factorization method to mine user preferences and build personalized task recommendation list for each user. This paper also proposes a lightweight updated real-time task recommendation algorithm (RRA) to update the task recommendation list in real time. However, we can see that although our algorithm RRA can greatly reduce the time cost of updating, because we only update a few vectors at a time, the performance of RRA may decline over time compared with the re-trained ALSWR. Therefore, in the practical application of MCS, in order to ensure the accuracy of the recommended results, it may be necessary to run re-trained ALSWR from time to time to eliminate the deviation.

4   Performance Evaluation

4.1   General Settings

Data Sets. In order to further illustrate the advantages of the proposed model and algorithm, we conduct experiments on two Cambridge trajectory datasets *Cambridge Haggle Trace* [14], both of which are trajectory data collected by Cambridge students using iMote, and the nodes are divided into two categories: internal nodes and external nodes. We use these internal nodes as users and let external nodes be tasks. The first 10% of the data in the data set is selected as offline data, and the last 90% of the data is input as stream data. Table 2 presents the information about the dataset we use.

Algorithm 1 A Real-time recommendation Algorithm
Input: $R_{m \times n}$, λ_u, λ_i, α, k, $\mathcal{T}$, *Train.*
Output: Users' task recommendation list
1 **Initialize** $X_{m \times k}$, $Y_{n \times k}$, $P_{m \times n}$, $C_{m \times n}$
2 **Initialize** $t = 1$
3 //generate the initial latent factor matrix
4 **while** not converge and $t \leq \mathcal{T}$ **do**
5   **for** $i = 1$ *to* m **do**
6     $X[i] = (\lambda_u I + Y^T C^u Y)^{-1} Y^T C^u P(u)$ //update row vector of user latent factor matrix
7   **end for**
8   **for** $j = 1$ *to* n **do**
9     $Y[j] = (\lambda_i I + X^T C^i X)^{-1} X^T C^i P(i)$ //update row vector of task latent factor matrix
10   **end for**
11 **end while**
12 // generate the initial task recommendation list
13 $\widehat{R} = X \cdot Y$
14 **for** $g = 1$ *to* m **do**
15   Sort $R[g]$ as Participant u_g's task recommendation list
16 **end for**
17 //update the task recommendation list
18 **while** rating value $r_{u,i}$ changes **do**
19   update the corresponding value $P_{u,i}$, $C_{u,i}$
20   use ALSWR to update $X[u]$, $Y[i]$ respectively //one update at a time
21   repeat line 13–16
22 **end while**

Fig. 2. The real-time recommendation algorithm.

Table 2. Data sets.

Data sets	The number of users	The number of tasks	The entries density
$\mathcal{D}1$	41	233	60.1%
$\mathcal{D}2$	54	11367	5.3%

Model Settings. In order to compare the results of several models, we use 10-fold cross validation to select the same coefficient for each model. Figure 3 describes the effect of different dimensions of the latent factor space on accuracy. We can see that accuracy increases with an increasing k value. For the two data sets D1 and D2, when k values are greater than 10 and 12, the increase in accuracy begins to slow down. And with the increase of the latent space dimensions, the time cost and resources cost will increase accordingly. Therefore, in order to save costs while improving accuracy as much as possible, we set the k value of the two data sets as 10 and 12, separately. In addition, we use 10-fold cross validation to set α as 0.2, $\lambda_u = \lambda_i = 0.01$ in two data sets separately.

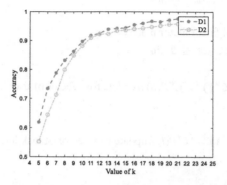

Fig. 3. Difference in accuracy due to different dimensions of the latent space on two datasets.

Compared Models. In order to emphasize the advantages of the proposed real-time model and algorithm, we compare it with the following vector update methods:

- *ALSWR.* The initial latent factor matrix is obtained by using the ALSWR. When the rating value changes, the model is retrained by the method of ALSWR.
- *SGD.* The initial latent factor matrix is obtained by using the SGD. When the rating value changes, the model is retrained by the method of SGD.
- *RI-SGD.* The initial latent factor matrix is obtained by using the ALSWR. When the rating value changes, the corresponding vectors are updated using the SGD.
- *NoIter.* The initial latent factor matrix is obtained by using the ALSWR. When the rating value changes, the latent factor matrix is not updated.

Evaluation Metrics

- *Accuracy.*

$$Accuracy = \frac{\sum_{i=1}^{m} \frac{hitcount_i}{Total\,Recommend\,Number_i}}{m}. \tag{4}$$

Where $hitcount_i$ represents the number of tasks executed by user u_i in the recommendation list, $Total\,Recommend\,Number_i$ represents the number of tasks recommended to user u_i, and m represents the number of users. Accuracy is characterized by the proportion of tasks executed by users to tasks recommended to users, which is used to evaluate whether the recommended tasks have been executed by users.

- *Ranking metrics normalized discounted cumulative gain (NDCG).*

$$NDCG = \frac{DCG}{IDCG}.\qquad(5)$$

Where DCG is the discounted cumulative gain, and IDCG is the maximum DCG value under ideal conditions. NDCG is used to measure whether or not the order of tasks in the task recommendation list is consistent with the user's preferences.

4.2 Results and Discussion

To illustrate the effectiveness and the superiority of the proposed models, we will show their results on addressed metrics compared with previous methods.

Accuracy. Figure 4 presents the accuracy results of our model RRA, ALSWR, RI-SGD, NoIter, and SGD. As can be seen from Fig. 4, as RRA updates the task recommendation list with the real time updating of the user's performance data, it can accurately adapt to user's preferences, so its accuracy is much higher than that of NoIter which does not update the task recommendation list. Secondly, due to the advantages of ALSWR in stability, the accuracy of RRA is also larger than that of the SGD and the RI-SGD. In addition, the accuracy of RRA is slightly lower than the re-trained ALSWR model. This shows that the updated task recommendation list obtained according to RRA has advantages in accuracy in MCS system, users are more likely to execute the tasks in the recommendation list obtained by RRA.

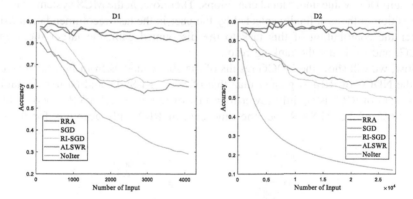

Fig. 4. Difference in accuracy due to different vector update methods on two datasets.

Time Cost. Figure 5 describes the time cost results of RRA, ALSWR, RI-SGD, NoIter, and SGD. As can be seen from Fig. 5, although the accuracy of RRA in Fig. 4 is slightly lower than that of ALSWR, since RRA only needs to update a couple of latent factor vectors at a time, and the amount of data to be updated by RRA is much smaller than the amount of data to be updated by ALSWR, the running time in RRA on the two data sets is much less than that in ALSWR, and the time spent on all data update is only about 0.03% of that in ALSWR, which meets the requirement of real-time update.

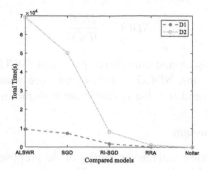

Fig. 5. Difference in time cost due to different vector update methods on two datasets.

NDCG. In order to use NDCG to evaluate the ranking performance of the model, we first need to calculate the discounted cumulative gain DCG:

$$DCG = \sum_{i=1}^{b} \frac{2^{rel_i} - 1}{log_2 i + 1}, \tag{6}$$

where b is the number of tasks in the recommendation list. In this paper, set $b = n$, where n is the number of tasks in the MCS system. rel_i is the gain of the i-th task. If the user has executed the task i, rel_i is set to 1, otherwise it is set to 0. IDCG is the maximum DCG value under ideal conditions. Therefore, in the MCS system, the higher the position of the task finally selected by the user in the task recommendation list, the greater the contribution of this task to the discounted gain, the larger the value of NDCG, and the better the ranking result.

Now, we will show the NDCG results of the above models from Fig. 6. We can see that the NDCG of RRA is greater than that of SGD, RI-SGD, and NoIter. In addition, the NDCG of RRA is slightly lower than that of re-trained ALSWR model, which is about 96% of the ALSWR, but the time cost of RRA only accounts for 0.03% of

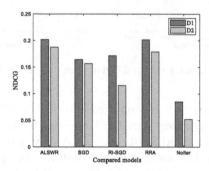

Fig. 6. Difference in NDCG due to different vector update methods on two datasets.

ALSWR. That is, in the MCS system, the ranking results of tasks in the task recommendation list updated by RRA are more suitable according to user preferences.

5 Conclusion

In this paper, we consider mining user preferences and focus on task allocation based on matrix factorization to provide users with a recommended list of tasks consistent with their preferences. To solve this problem, the matrix factorization is used to mine the user's preference for the task. Then, the prediction rating of users on tasks obtained by matrix factorization is used to provide a task recommendation list for users. Finally, a lightweight updated real-time task recommendation algorithm (RRA) is proposed to ensure that the task recommendation list can adapt to the change of user preferences in time. Extensive evaluations based on real-world mobility traces demonstrate that our algorithm outperforms the baseline methods under various settings. In future work, we will consider other factors that may affect task allocation in MCS systems. More sophisticated optimization methods and theoretical foundations will also be explored.

References

1. Chilton, LB., Horton, J.J., Miller, R.C., et al.: Task search in a human computation market. In: Proceedings of the ACM SIGKDD Workshop on Human Computation, vol. 1, no. 9 (2010)
2. Xiao, M., Wu, J., Huang, L., et al.: Online task assignment for crowdsensing in predictable mobile social networks. IEEE Trans. Mob. Comput. 1(1) (2016)
3. Fu, J.G.M., Bandyopadhyay, T., Ang, M.H.J.: Local voronoi decomposition for multi-agent task allocation. In: IEEE International Conference on Robotics & Automation (2009)
4. Tong, Y., Wang, L., Zimu, Z., et al.: Flexible online task assignment in real-time spatial data. Proc. VLDB Endow. 10(11), 1334–1345 (2017)
5. Srebro, N., Salakhutdinov, R.R.: Collaborative filtering in a non-uniform world: learning with the weighted trace norm. In: Advances in Neural Information Processing Systems, pp. 2056–2064 (2010)
6. Chu, W., Ghahramani, Z.: Probabilistic models for incomplete multi-dimensional arrays. In: Artificial Intelligence and Statistics, pp. 89–96 (2009)
7. Chatzis, S.: Nonparametric Bayesian multitask collaborative filtering. In: Proceedings of the 22nd ACM international conference on Information & Knowledge Management, pp. 2149–2158 (2013)
8. Adomavicius, G., Tuzhilin, A.: Toward the next generation of recommender systems: a survey of the state-of-the-art and possible extensions. IEEE Trans. Knowl. Data Eng. 17(6), 734–749 (2015)
9. Huang, K., Sidiropoulos, N.D., Swami, A.: Non-negative matrix factorization revisited: uniqueness and algorithm for symmetric decomposition. IEEE Trans. Signal Process. 62(1), 211–224 (2014)
10. Piao, X., Hu, Y., Sun, Y., et al.: Correlated spatio-temporal data collection in wireless sensor networks based on low rank matrix approximation and optimized node sampling. Sensors 14 (12), 23137–23158 (2014)

11. Luo, X., Wu, H., Yuan, H., et al.: Temporal pattern-aware QoS prediction via biased non-negative latent factorization of tensors. IEEE Trans. Cybern. **1**(12), 99 (2019)
12. Luo, X., Zhou, M., Li, S., et al.: A nonnegative latent factor model for large-scale sparse matrices in recommender systems via alternating direction method. IEEE Trans. Neural Netw. Learn. Syst. **1**(1), (2015)
13. Févotte, C., Idier, J.: Algorithms for nonnegative matrix factorization with the beta-divergence. Neural Comput. **23**(9), 2421–2456 (2010)
14. Lin, C., Wang, L., Tsai, K.: Hybrid real-time matrix factorization for implicit feedback recommendation systems. IEEE Access **1**(1), 99 (2018)
15. Scott, J., et al.: http://crawdad.cs.dartmouth.edu/cambridge/haggle

A Dual Scale Matching Model
for Long-Term Association

Zhen Ye[1,2], Yubin Wu[1,3], Shuai Wang[1,3], Yang Zhang[1,2], Yanbing Chen[4],
Wei Ke[4], and Hao Sheng[1,2(✉)]

[1] State Key Laboratory of Software Development Environment, School of Computer
Science and Engineering, Beihang University,
Beijing 100191, People's Republic of China
{yezhen4320,yubin.wu,shuaiwang,yang.zhang,shenghao}@buaa.edu.cn
[2] Beijing Advanced Innovation Center for Big Data and Brain Computing,
Beihang University, Beijing 100191, People's Republic of China
[3] Beihang Hangzhou Institute for Innovation at Yuhang, Beihang University,
Hangzhou 311121, People's Republic of China
[4] School of Applied Sciences, Macao Polytechnic Institute,
Macao SAR 999078, People's Republic of China
{yanbing.chen,wke}@ipm.edu.mo

Abstract. Multi-object tracking can be characterized as a data association problem. The advantage of RNN in processing temporal dependence makes it an ideal selection in data association. When factors such
as scene congestion and weak illumination cause detection failure especially long intervals, association is often very difficult and eventually
leads to tracking failure. To solve this problem, Dual Scale Matching
model (DSM) containing a Motion Trend Match Network (MTMNet)
and an Appearance History Memory Network (AHMNet) is proposed.
DSM is a long-term optimization method based on multiple hypothesis
tracking. MTMNet aims to learn a similarity metric matching function
between tracklets leveraging the motion feature. AHMNet is designed
to provide optimal pruning strategies leveraging long period appearance
feature. Our method is effective on MOT17 benchmark and it shows that
we achieve considerable competitive results with current state-of-the-art
trackers.

Keywords: Multi-object tracking · Dual Scale Matching · Motion
Trend Match Net · Appearance History Memory Net · Data association

1 Introduction

Multi-object tracking (MOT) is a significant problem in computer vision, which
is widely used in robot navigation, intelligent surveillance, industrial inspection
[23,24], etc. The main task of MOT is to give the integrated trajectory of different
targets in image sequence, and correspond to the objects in different frames one
by one, finally. Multiple Hypothesis Tracking (MHT) [17] is one of the successful

© Springer Nature Switzerland AG 2020
D. Yu et al. (Eds.): WASA 2020, LNCS 12384, pp. 653–665, 2020.
https://doi.org/10.1007/978-3-030-59016-1_54

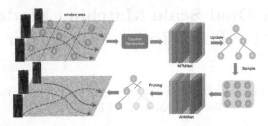

Fig. 1. The architectures of our proposed Dual Scale Matching Model based consisting two sub-networks: MTMNet and AHMNet. The dashed gray arrows represent the undetermined sequences, and the orange solid arrow represents the determined sequence. (Color figure online)

algorithms for MOT. It establishes a potential trajectory hypothesis tree for each target, thus providing a solution to the problem of data association. It needs to calculate the probability of each trajectory in MHT to select the most likely combination of tracks. Therefore, MHT assumes that the size of hypothesis tree is as small as possible while ensuring the correct recall rate, so as to prevent the efficiency problems caused by the explosion of calculation time and memory.

Traditional multi-object tracking methods do the associassion referring to time and space information [1], such as Meanshift algorithm based on color modeling and Kalman Filter algorithm to model target motion model [6]. Recently learning-based tracking methods are being studied, and their results prove the potential of learning-based methods in tracking [10,19]. The learning-based tracking methods usually learn cues including appearance in spatial dimension and motion in temporal dimension [9].

Traditional multi-target tracking methods often loss the historical feature information of the target gradually over time, and eventually resulting in tracking failure. Learning-based multi-target tracking methods can handle this issue by learning the long-term dependence of trajectory features. The advantage of LSTM in learning time series features has caused a lot of attention in learning-based methods. The method like Bilinear LSTM [13] jointly uses appearance and motion LSTM gating networks in an MHT framework, handing the scoring task of the association part of MHT to Bilinear LSTM. This method gives the target's trajectory sequence to the LSTM network, predict the feature of the next frame, and then calculate the similarity by comparing with the observations. However, the above method inevitably leads to higher rate of the estimated fault tolerance in crowded scenes, and predictive failure in long intervals.

In this paper, the proposed Dual Scale Matching Model based on multiple hypothesis tracking architecture to address the tracking failure of long intervals. Our model integrates the features of sequences and abstract the deep features of tracklets. DSM contains two sub-networks. First, Motion Trend Match Network (MTMNet), a sub-network exploiting motion feature to learn metric functions between tracklets helps achieve the best match between tracklets. Then, Appearance History Memory Network (AHMNet), a trajectory confidence network which exploits appearance feature to further determine the optimal hypothesis branches during pruning.

Our main contributions in this paper can be summarized as follows:

(1) To overcome tracking failure caused by long intervals, Dual Scale Matching model (DSM) is proposed. DSM is designed to enhance long-term association in multiple hypothesis tracking (MHT), including two sub-networks, providing solutions for tree update and pruning in MHT.
(2) To enhance the robustness of data association in crowded scenes, Motion Trend Match Network (MTMNet) is proposed. MTMNet is designed for accurate feature match by modelling short-term movement in crowded scenes.
(3) To improve the robustness of data association in long time intervals, Appearance History Memory Network (AHMNet) is proposed which is designed to learn reliable dependencies of appearance in long period.

2 Related Work

2.1 Overview of MHT

In recent years, as the accuracy of the detector has improved, tracking-by-detection becomes the mainstream multi-target tracking method [11,22]. The multi-target tracking can be solved through data association that a set of tracks can be generated by assigning a track label to each detection. While MHT benefits from it since the establishment of the hypothesis tree depends on the detection or detection sequence. MHT provides a hypothetical range for each target's trajectory sequence and solve the data association problem by generating multiple tracking proposals explicitly and then selects the most promising ones. In recent years MHT has proved feasible in the current visual tracking environment [12]. MHT proposes to arrange all the trajectories in a tree. The root node of the tree is the detection of the target in the first frame, and its child nodes represent the detection of subsequent frames, thus detections at the same depth are in the same frame.The detection sequences from the root node to all leaf nodes represent all trajectory proposals. Obviously, MHT can be roughly divided into two stages: update hypothesis tree and pruning. MHT's job is to iterate continuously in these two stages until the last frame is completed.

In the stage of updating hypothesis tree, new object observations are assigned to existing tracklet hypothesis which are within gating, usually referring to appearance and motion. Powerful appearance features can help reduce the data association ambiguity [20]. With the galloping progresses of deep learning technology, more abundant features can be obtained through Convolutional Neural Networks (CNNs) [8,27]. XianHui [5] added the appearance features extracted from Faster-RCNN to the MHT framework, which makes the data association ambiguity reduced surprisingly. Kim [13]replaced the gating of mht with a bilinear LSTM-based gating, and integrated motion and appearance information in a learning-based way to obtain a similarity evaluation score. Different from this method, instead of predicting the detection state of the next frame, we predict the change trend of the target's future trajectory, to a certain extent, reducing the number of hypothesis of child nodes in a crowded scene.

In the stage of pruning, screen out the most likely hypothetical trajectories and prun the rest. After scoring all trajectory proposals, the task of selecting the optimal proposals can be formulated as a Maximum Weighted Independent Set (MWIS) [3] problem. Kevin [4] uses a new K-track, List-Viterbi algorithm to help pruning to make sure hypotheses to be a manageable level. Williams [28] proposes a structured cost-functionbased approach to the hypothesis control problem. However, for these methods, there is a high probability that the same target will be pruned after crossing non-adjacent windows when a long occlusion occurs. We propose to use the learning-based method to solve this problem by modeling dependence of long-term historical appearance and scoring the confidence of the appearance of each trajectory to select the best proposal.

2.2 LSTM-Based Tracking Methods

In recent years, Recurrent Neural Network (RNN) has proven its potential in the field of tracking [22]. Long Short-Term Memory (LSTM) also attracts attention in the field of visual tracking due to its outstanding achievements in dealing with long sequence dependencies [16]. These methods can be categorized into two classes: generative and discriminative models [7, 14]. In generative methods, feature representation is learned by minimizing reconstruction error. While discriminative methods often learn the intrinsic connection of features to obtain a similarity score which is an important basis for the association phase.

For generative models, LSTM helps predict the generation of trajectories. Anton Milan [15] first employed end-to-end training for multi-target tracking, which proved the excellent strength of an LSTM network in learning a globally optimal assignment. Different from the conventional LSTM approaches, Kim [13] proposed the Bilinear LSTM, scoring prediction detection and observations, which improved the learning ability to appearance feature especially in terms of multiple past appearance feature memory.

For discriminant models, LSTM directly scores existing trajectories and candidate detections. Amir Sadeghian [18] found an online method to encode dependencies across multiple cues including motion, appearance and even interaction cues. His model uses three network structures to learn the representation of these three cues, all of which will be used to calculate the similarity scores between targets and the observations. Xingyu [26] merged the relevant features of the trajectory into an LSTM, interpreted the time and space components in a non-linear manner, and output similarity scores simultaneously. Although LSTM-based trackers have shown surprising performance in the past, there is still a lot of potential for improvement in performance.

3   Dual Scale Matching Model

The overall architecture of our proposed approach is shown in Fig. 1 which is based on MHT. To deal with the long-term occlusion, our proposed approach

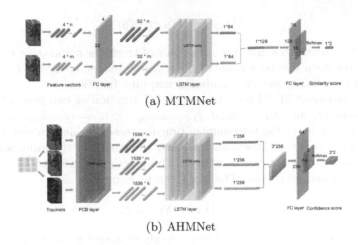

(a) MTMNet

(b) AHMNet

Fig. 2. Structure of MTMNet and AHMNet.

includes two subnetworks: 1) Motion Trend Match Network (MTMNet), which is for tracklets atching based on motion deep feature in the update stage of MHT; 2) Appearance History Memory Network (AHMNet), which exploits the appearance feature of tracklets to determine the best matching branches when pruning. In order to learn the information of the target's feature change trend, tracklet is used as the tree node in MHT. The video sequences are divided into multiple non-overlapping small windows in 5 frames and then the tracklets are matched in each unit window. The details of the tracklets generation are elaborated in Sect. 4.1. Given the tracklets, our remaining tracking task is to associate the tracklets across different windows.

During the tracking process, motion feature sequences of two tracklets are first fed into MTMNet. The similarity score of these two tracklets can be estimated according to the short-term movement trend of these two. Through the pairwise matching between a target tracklet and the tracklets to be selected, the possible target hypothesis are chosen by searching the similarity scores which are above the threshold. Then, AHMNet takes all trajectory generation hypothesis as input. For each hypothesis, the historical appearance feature of each trajectory can be captured and the confidence level of this trajectory from the same target is obtained after the overall AHMNet. Finally, the globally optimal association hypothesis can be found according to the highest confidence score.

3.1 MTMNet for Tracklet Association

The video sequence is denoted as $S = D_1, ..., D_t, ..., D_T$, T is the maximum number of frames for this video. The set of all detections in frame t can be denoted as $D_t = d_{t_1}, ..., d_{t_n}, ..., d_{t_N}$, where d_{t_n} is nth detection in tth frame of this video. As shown in Fig. 2 (a), a Long Short-Term Memory (LSTM) layer is adopted as the extractor of tracklet motion deep feature. Our aim is to learn a matching decision equation:

$$f(x, y) = g(\psi(x), \psi(y)) \tag{1}$$

where $f(x, y)$ refers to similarity of the pair of tracklets x and y, $\psi(x)$ and $\psi(y)$ represent the deep motion feature of the tracklets extracted by the LSTM layer. while g is a similarity metric calculation mapping function.

In our proposed MTMNet, the motion information of two tracklets τ_m, τ_n is took as input, and $\tau_m = (d_\nu, d_{\nu+1}, ..., d_{\nu+m-1})$, $\tau_n = (d_\upsilon, d_{\upsilon+1}, ..., d_{\upsilon+n-1})$, where ν and υ refer to the beginning of time for these tracklets, n and m indicate the length of these two. Based on tracklets, the length of the input sequence is usually 3 to 5 frames at the beginning. The length increases with time, but it should not exceed 40 frames. The input can be expressed as:

$$X = [\chi_1, ..., \chi_t, ..., \chi_n] \tag{2}$$

where $\chi_t = (x, y, w, h)^T$, x, y, w, h respectively represent x, y coordinates, width, and height of the bounding box of a detection. First the fully connected layer which contains 32 output units is fed X as input, enriching these original motion features. Then the LSTM layer containing 64 hidden units further extracts the sequence-dependent information of these preprocessed features. As time goes by, this LSTM layer gradually updates its internal memory storage units as well as external storage units, and extracts deep movement features of the tracklet finally. To obtain the similarity score, these two extracted deep features are stitched together. It is further processed through two fully connected layers which finally contain 2 output units. MTMNet gets a similarity score according to the values of these two units in a softmax layer.

The similarity score is a key factor for the hypothetical tree generation, and the following constraints need to be considered simultaneously:

$$Score_{(\tau_i, \tau_j)} \geq Score_{thr} \tag{3}$$

$$Win_{\tau_i} \cap Win_{\tau_j} = \emptyset \tag{4}$$

$$abs(min(f_{\tau_i}) - min(f_{\tau_j}))/windowsize \leq 5 \tag{5}$$

$$max(N_{\tau_i}) = 4 \tag{6}$$

where $Score_{(\tau_i, \tau_j)}$ refers to the similarity score between τ_i and τ_j, and $Score_{thr}$ represents the lowest threshold value judged as the same target. Equation 4 and Eq.5 limit the two tracklets to different windows and the interval between the two tracklets does not exceed 5 windows. Finally, Eq.6 indicates that the number of candidate child nodes of τ_i is at most 4.

3.2   Pruning with AHMNet

Accurate tracklets matching results in MTMNet help improve the recall rate in MHT. In addition, effective pruning is beneficial to enhance the robustness of the hypothesis tree.

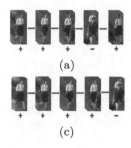

(a)

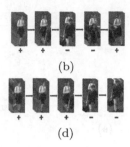

(b)

(c)

(d)

Fig. 3. (a) and (b) are positive samples containing occlusion and recovery processes. (c) and (d) are negative samples, where the target of (c) is occluded but not recovered at the end, and the first few nodes of (d) are tracking correctly but the ID switch happen at the end.

AMHNet is proposed to makes full use of the appearance feature of tracklets to realize a new pruning strategy. The architecture of AHMNet consists of following layers: pre-trained Part-based Convolutional Baseline (PCB) [25] layer, LSTM layer, fully connected layer and binary classification layer with softmax cross-entropy loss.

For the recovery process after a long-term occlusion of the target, the appearance feature is usually an important reference factor. AMHNet takes each branch of the hypothetical tree as an input sample, as Fig. 2(b) indicates. The pre-trained PCB layer cuts each detection of a tracklet into 6 pieces vertically, and calculates the appearance features of each piece separately. Each piece gets a 256-dimensional feature for a total of 1536 dimensions. That means there is a feature sequence with dimension 1536*n should be generated following the PCB layer where n is determined by the number of detections of all tracklet nodes. The LSTM layer contains 256 hidden units and outputs the last element of the sequence. After the LSTM layer, the deep appearance features of the trajectory hypothesis should become the same dimension. The LSTM layer abstracts higher-level features according to the changing trend of the appearance of the tracklets. Then, two fully connected layers containing 2 output units and a softmax layer help calculate the confidence score of each sample which represents the probability that a trajectory is the same target. Finally, the hypothetical branches with the highest total confidence score can be selected as the optimal association result, and the remaining hypothetical branches should be pruned.

4 Experiment

Dataset. For two sub-networks' training, we use ground truth data of MOT17 and CVPR2019 datasets. Then we test our approach on the MOT17 benchmark which contains a total of seven training sequences and seven test sequences for static and moving cameras. We use the public detection set given by MOT17 as our input to maintain a fair comparison.

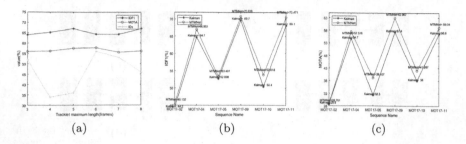

(a)   (b)   (c)

Fig. 4. (a) shows IDF1, MOTA, ID switch indicators in diffrent tracklet maximum lengthes in MOT17-04 which is the longest one among all videos. (b) shows the IDF1 indicator of six video sequences on two methods based on MHT, including Kalman and MTMNet. (c) shows the MOTA indicator of six video sequences on these two methods.

Evaluation Metric. We evaluate our tracking performance following the standard CLEAR MOT metrics [2]. The metrics include multiple tracking accuracy (MOTA↑), which influenced by ID switches (IDs↓), false positives (FP↓), and false negatives (FN↓). In addition, we also report mostly tracked (MT↑), mostly lost (ML↓), fragmentation (FM↓) and the ratio of correctly identified detections (IDF1↑).

4.1   Implementation Details

Tracklet Generation. The videos are divided into multiple non-overlapping small windows. In each window, the tracklet's feature change trend information is fully utilized. The correlation information of detections is also utilized to obtain the optimal tracklets matching according to Linear programming. The impact of different tracklet maximum lengthes on several important indicators is shown in Fig. 4(a). The ID switch indicator is optimal when the tracklet maxmum length is 4 or 5, while referring to IDF1 and MOTA, 5 frames is slightly better. Here our window size is set to 5 and the length of the tracklet is a minimum of 3 frames and no more than 5 frames.

MTMNet Training. The training task is defined as a binary classification problem. If the two tracklets are the same person, the label is set to 1, otherwise it is set to 0. During the training process, the ratio of our training sample to positive and negative samples is 1:9, and the time interval between the two tracklets of each training sample is in the range of 1 to 5 frames. The total time length of the two tracklets that make up a sample does not exceed 20 frames.

AHMNet Training. The training task of AHMNet is defined as a binary classification problem, where the label set to 1 If the sample comes from the same person while set to 0 when the sample contains features from different targets. In addition to the common positive sample design of the unoccluded training set, some special case of training sets are also designed as shown in Fig. 3. A sample consists of multiple tracklets, the number of which is between 5 and 7.

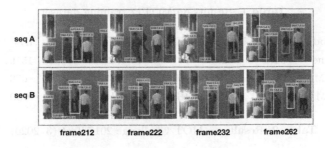

Fig. 5. The results of baseline method and our DSM model in a long interval case. The picture sequence Seq A in the first row shows the results of the baseline, and the picture sequence Seq B in the second row shows our results.

The first node (tracklet) in the sequence is default to the object that needs to be tracked. If the last node is also the target's tracklet, the sample is determined to be a positive sample, otherwise it is determined to be a negative sample.

4.2 Effectiveness Analysis of MTMNet and AHMNet

Our approach is verified on MOT17 training sequences. The results of three experiments are recorded separately including one baseline approach, one intermediate result with only MTMNet and one final result of adding AHMNet as shown in Table 1. The baseline method is a published tracklet-level association method [21] based on MHT and Kalman framework. To verify the robustness of our approach in dealing with tracklets associations, MTMNet is first added. As the results shown, compared with the baseline, our MOTA indicator has increased by 3.8 % points and IDF1 indicator has increased by 4 % points. It is worth mentioning that the IDs indicator has dropped by 55.8% directly which strongly proves that MTMNet has great potential in optimizing data associations. More specifically, Fig. 4.(b) and (c) show the comparison results of multiple videos on the IDF1 and MOTA indicators on the baseline of the Kalman method and the MTMNet method based on learning. It can be seen that whether it is a moving camera including MOT17-05, MOT17-10 and MOT17-11 or other still cameras, the MTMNet method is always slightly better than most.

Then AHMNet is added to verify the ability to handle long time intervals of our method. Compared with previous results, the final result shows its power. Although the FP and FM indicators have increased slightly, while the MOTA still increased by 0.1%, the IDF1 increased by 0.3%, and the IDs decreased from 679 to 600. Intuitive results are shown in Fig. 5. All detections are generated by the DPM detector. The red arrows represent the pedestrian tracked. He started to be blocked at 222 frames. The detector could not capture him. After a long interval of 40 frames, the target was recaptured at 262 frame . In seq A based on the baseline method, the target was not detected during the long-term occlusion, but another id was recognized when it was captured again, resulting in tracking errors. In seq B based on our method, two trajectories with a long interval are

Table 1. Results on MOT17 training dataset

Method	MOTA↑	IDF1↑	MT↑	ML↓	FP↓	FN↓	IDs↓	FM↓
baseline	52.6	62.8	431	554	**7655**	150529	1519	1505
+MTMNet	56.4	66.8	460	575	8072	138076	679	**1219**
+AHMNet	**56.5**	**67.1**	**465**	**571**	8105	**137790**	**600**	1222

Table 2. Results on MOT Challenge 2017 Test (3/2020)

Method	MOTA↑	IDF1↑	MT↑	ML↓	FP↓	FN↓	IDs↓	FM↓
FWT [11]	51.3	47.6	21.4%	35.2%	24101	247921	2648	4279
AFN17 [19]	51.5	46.9	20.6%	35.5%	22391	248420	2593	4308
eHAF17 [22]	51.8	54.7	23.4%	37.9%	33212	236772	1834	2739
eTC17 [27]	51.9	58.1	23.1%	35.5%	36164	232783	2288	3071
FAMNet [8]	52.0	48.7	19.1%	**33.4%**	14138	253616	3072	5318
Tracktor17 [1]	53.5	52.3	19.5%	36.6%	**12201**	248047	2072	4611
LSST17 [9]	**54.7**	62.3	20.4%	40.1%	26091	**228434**	1243	3726
ours(MCLT17)	54.2	**63.5**	**24.0%**	38.1%	23602	233783	**1208**	**2394**

successfully correlated , and to a certain extent, the problem of missed detection due to the inaccuracy of the detector is alleviated. These results prove that our method can still track the target well when there are long intervals. Compared with the original baseline method, most of our results are better, which proves the effectiveness of our method.

4.3 Benchmark Comparison

Our proposed tracking method is tested on MOT17 benchmark. The comparison is shown in Table 2. The comparison can also be found in the MOT Challenge website, and our tracker is named MCLT17. Our tracker has proven to be very competitive comparing with the published state-of-art trackers. MOTA and IDF1 are the two most comprehensive indicators in evaluating tracker performance. Among trackers that have already published articles, our proposed tracker ranks second on the MOTA score (54.2), 0.5 % points away from the first, and takes the first place sorted by IDF1 score (63.5). In addition, our IDs and FM scores are ranked first, which shows that our proposed tracker has shown good performance in handling long-term interval problems.

5   Conclusion

This paper proposes a Dual Scale Matching model (DSM) for long-term association based on multiple hypothsis tracking in crowded scenes. It contains two sub-networks: MTMNet and AHMNet. MTMNet models the short-term movement trend of the tracklets to match tracklets with high similarity in crowded scences which helps optimize the update of hypothesis trees. AHMNet exploits appearance of tracklets to learn reliable dependencies of appearance in long period, dealing with the tracking failure caused by long time intervals when pruning. Although frequent scoring increases the amount of calculation and reduces the efficiency slightly, the tracking result of DSM is indeed convincing. Experiments have shown that MTMNet has great potential in solving short-term dependent data associations, and AHMNet has a significant effect on the problems of tracking failure caused by long intervals. Demonstrated on the MOT17 benchmark, the DSM model shows superior results than most existing learning-based methods which proves that our method is competitive.

Acknowledgement. This study is partially supported by the National Key R&D Program of China(No.2018YFB2100800), the National Natural Science Foundation of China(No. 61861166002, 61872025, 61635002) , the Science and Technology Development Fund, Macau SAR (File no. 0001/2018/AFJ), the Fundamental Research Funds for the Central Universities and the Open Fund of the State Key Laboratory of Software Development Environment(No. SKLSDE2019ZX-04). Thank you for the support from HAWKEYE Group.

References

1. Bergmann, P., Meinhardt, T., Leal-Taixe, L.: Tracking without bells and whistles. In: Proceedings of the IEEE International Conference on Computer Vision, pp. 941–951 (2019)
2. Bernardin, K., Stiefelhagen, R.: Evaluating multiple object tracking performance: the clear mot metrics. EURASIP J. Image Video Process. **2008**, 1–10 (2008)
3. Brendel, W., Amer, M., Todorovic, S.: Multiobject tracking as maximum weight independent set. In: CVPR 2011, pp. 1273–1280. IEEE (2011)
4. Buckley, K., Vaddiraju, A., Perry, R.: A new pruning/merging algorithm for MHT multitarget tracking. In: IEEE International Radar Conference, pp. 71–75. Citeseer (2000)
5. Chen, L., Peng, X., Ren, M.: Recurrent metric networks and batch multiple hypothesis for multi-object tracking. IEEE Access **7**, 3093–3105 (2018)
6. Cheng, S., Cai, Z., Li, J.: Curve query processing in wireless sensor networks. IEEE Trans. Veh. Technol. **64**(11), 5198–5209 (2014)
7. Cheng, S., Cai, Z., Li, J., Fang, X.: Drawing dominant dataset from big sensory data in wireless sensor networks. In: 2015 IEEE conference on Computer communications (INFOCOM), pp. 531–539. IEEE (2015)
8. Chu, P., Ling, H.: Famnet: joint learning of feature, affinity and multi-dimensional assignment for online multiple object tracking. In: Proceedings of the IEEE International Conference on Computer Vision, pp. 6172–6181 (2019)
9. Feng, W., Hu, Z., Wu, W., Yan, J., Ouyang, W.: Multi-object tracking with multiple cues and switcher-aware classification (2019). arXiv preprint arXiv:1901.06129
10. He, Z., Cai, Z., Cheng, S., Wang, X.: Approximate aggregation for tracking quantiles and range countings in wireless sensor networks. Theor. Comput. Sci. **607**, 381–390 (2015)

11. Henschel, R., Leal-Taixé, L., Cremers, D., Rosenhahn, B.: Fusion of head and full-body detectors for multi-object tracking. In: Proceedings of the IEEE Conference on Computer Vision and Pattern Recognition Workshops, pp. 1428–1437 (2018)
12. Kim, C., Li, F., Ciptadi, A., Rehg, J.M.: Multiple hypothesis tracking revisited. In: Proceedings of the IEEE International Conference on Computer Vision, pp. 4696–4704 (2015)
13. Kim, C., Li, F., Rehg, J.M.: Multi-object tracking with neural gating using bilinear LSTM. In: Proceedings of the European Conference on Computer Vision (ECCV), pp. 200–215 (2018)
14. Kim, H.I., Park, R.H.: Residual LSTM attention network for object tracking. IEEE Sig. Process. Lett. **25**(7), 1029–1033 (2018)
15. Milan, A., Rezatofighi, S.H., Dick, A., Reid, I., Schindler, K.: Online multi-target tracking using recurrent neural networks. In: Thirty-First AAAI Conference on Artificial Intelligence (2017)
16. Ran, N., Kong, L., Wang, Y., Liu, Q.: A robust multi-athlete tracking algorithm by exploiting discriminant features and long-term dependencies. In: Kompatsiaris, I., Huet, B., Mezaris, V., Gurrin, C., Cheng, W.-H., Vrochidis, S. (eds.) MMM 2019. LNCS, vol. 11295, pp. 411–423. Springer, Cham (2019). https://doi.org/10.1007/978-3-030-05710-7_34
17. Reid, D.: An algorithm for tracking multiple targets. IEEE Trans. Autom. Control **24**(6), 843–854 (1979)
18. Sadeghian, A., Alahi, A., Savarese, S.: Tracking the untrackable: learning to track multiple cues with long-term dependencies. In: Proceedings of the IEEE International Conference on Computer Vision, pp. 300–311 (2017)
19. Shen, H., Huang, L., Huang, C., Xu, W.: Tracklet association tracker: an end-to-end learning-based association approach for multi-object tracking (2018). arXiv preprint arXiv:1808.01562
20. Sheng, H., Zheng, Y., Ke, W., Yu, D., Cheng, X., Lyu, W., Xiong, Z.: Mining hard samples globally and efficiently for person re-identification. IEEE Internet Things J. 1–1 (2020)
21. Sheng, H., Chen, J., Zhang, Y., Ke, W., Xiong, Z., Yu, J.: Iterative multiple hypothesis tracking with tracklet-level association. IEEE Trans. Circuits Syst. Video Technol. **29**(12), 3660–3672 (2018)
22. Sheng, H., Zhang, Y., Chen, J., Xiong, Z., Zhang, J.: Heterogeneous association graph fusion for target association in multiple object tracking. IEEE Trans. Circuits Syst. Video Technol. **29**(11), 3269–3280 (2018)
23. Shi, T., Cheng, S., Li, J., Gao, H., Cai, Z.: Dominating sets construction in RF-based battery-free sensor networks with full coverage guarantee. ACM Trans. Sens. Netw. (TOSN) **15**(4), 1–29 (2019)
24. Shi, T., Li, J., Gao, H., Cai, Z.: Coverage in battery-free wireless sensor networks. In: IEEE INFOCOM 2018-IEEE Conference on Computer Communications, pp. 108–116. IEEE (2018)
25. Sun, Y., Zheng, L., Yang, Y., Tian, Q., Wang, S.: Beyond part models: person retrieval with refined part pooling (and a strong convolutional baseline). In: Proceedings of the European Conference on Computer Vision (ECCV), pp. 480–496 (2018)
26. Wan, X., Wang, J., Zhou, S.: An online and flexible multi-object tracking framework using long short-term memory. In: Proceedings of the IEEE Conference on Computer Vision and Pattern Recognition Workshops, pp. 1230–1238 (2018)

27. Wang, G., Wang, Y., Zhang, H., Gu, R., Hwang, J.N.: Exploit the connectivity: multi-object tracking with trackletnet. In: Proceedings of the 27th ACM International Conference on Multimedia, pp. 482–490 (2019)
28. Williams, J.L., Maybeck, P.S.: Cost-function-based gaussian mixture reduction for target tracking. In: Proceedings of the Sixth International Conference of Information Fusion, vol. 2, pp. 1047–1054. IEEE Publishing, Piscataway (2003)

A Real-Time Vehicle Logo Detection Method Based on Improved YOLOv2

Kangning Yin, Shaoqi Hou, Ye Li, Chao Li, and Guangqiang Yin$^{(\boxtimes)}$

University of Electronic Science and Technology of China, Chengdu, China
{knyin,sqhou,liye}@std.uestc.edu.cn,
sjklaj313@163.com, yingq@uestc.edu.cn

Abstract. Confirming the vehicle information in the surveillance video is an important issue in the intelligent transportation system at present. As a key and fixed feature, the vehicle logo can play a role in assisting the discrimination. According to the characteristics of the vehicle logo image, we propose a high-efficiency logo detection method based on the improved YOLOv2, which adopts the strategies of separable convolution, multi-scale channel fusion and auto-mated multi-scale test, compared with the traditional vehicle identification method based on manual extraction features, so the method has the advantages of self-learning features, direct input of images, and the like, and can realize the dual functions of positioning and recognition of the vehicle logo. Experiments show that the model has excellent stability under low-resolution (very small target), illumination effects, angular rotation and noise pollution, and has high accuracy, recall and real-time. On the data set used, our model was trained on the NVIDIA GTX1070 GPU (8G memory) server, which achieved a recall rate of Recall = 0.997, an average accuracy of mAP = 0.990, and a test speed of approximately 21.3 FPS, far exceeding the performance of any other current vehicle logo detection method.

Keywords: Vehicle logo detection · Improved YOLOv2 · Separable convolution · Feature fusion · Multi-scale test

1 Introduction

With the development of the world economy, the number of social motor vehicles has also shown a rising trend. Traffic congestion and traffic accidents occur from time to time. For this reason, collecting vehicle information and identifying vehicles that have violated regulations have become an important part of intelligent transportation. However, in some intersection areas that are not equipped with high-definition cameras, the monitoring cannot accurately capture the vehicle license plate information. Areas with complicated background and environment also have a certain degree of influence on the recognition of license plate information. At this time, as a key feature, the vehicle logo can assist the identification in the monitoring and tracking of the vehicle.

With regard to vehicle logo recognition, some researchers have tried various methods and achieved certain results. Most of the early vehicle logo recognition methods mainly focused on feature extraction methods, and classification methods used

© Springer Nature Switzerland AG 2020
D. Yu et al. (Eds.): WASA 2020, LNCS 12384, pp. 666–677, 2020.
https://doi.org/10.1007/978-3-030-59016-1_55

support vector machine (SVM). For example, Luo Bin, Wang et al. used edge histograms as features [1, 2], Wang Mei et al. used principal component analysis (PCA) and invariant matrix to identify vehicle logo [3]. These methods are relatively simple, the running speed of it is fast, but the accuracy of the results is not high. Mo Shaoqing et al. increased the image quality analysis based on using only PCA [4].

YU et al. used Bag of Words (BoW) to count and match the features of the car logo. By clustering the features and generating a codebook, getting the representation of the vehicle logo images corresponding to the codebook was obtained [5]. Llorca. D. F et al. use HOG features [6], Kam-Tong Sam uses AdaBoost for classification [7], and some researchers use symmetry [8] or local feature description [9]. Although these methods enhance feature extraction, they are mainly based on artificial feature extraction. Apostolos P. Psyllos et al. [10] systematically introduced vehicle logo recognition with complete methods and experimental data. This literature has a high citation rate in the field of vehicle logo recognition, but it still does not depart from manual feature extraction, and cannot avoid the one-sidedness of using SIFT features alone. Guan et al. [11] set virtual ports (VP) served by stopping vehicle which is waiting for the traffic light in front of the intersection in urban-area. Xiong et al. [12] used Auto-Driving GAN (ADGAN) to offer an effective tradeoff between recognition utility and privacy protection for camera data. Cai et al. [13] proposed a novel framework for privacy-preserved traffic sharing among taxi companies. Wang et al. [13] proposed client-based personalized k-anonymity (CPkA) to achieve sufficient privacy preservation and satisfactory query utility for autonomous vehicles querying services. Geoffery Hinton first put forward the idea of "multi-hidden-layer artificial neural network has excellent feature learning ability" in 2006, in the following years, deep learning is used in image processing, speech recognition, search engines, etc. These fields have made breakthrough developments. In contrast to traditional neural networks, deep learning allows machines to learn features autonomously, thereby freeing tedious steps of manually selecting features.

1.1   Related Strategies and Methods

Convolutional neural networks (CNN) [14, 15] is a type of deep learning, CNN usually is composed of several feature extraction layers, downsampled layers, and a fully connected classifier. Its weight-sharing network structure makes it more similar to biological neural networks. It has lower model complexity and fewer weights, so that it can directly input the target images, eliminating the tedious features extraction process; the local parts of the images are used as the input of the lowest layer to obtain the most basic features of the input images, so it has better resistance to deformation and rotation of the target object or image.

Based on the characteristics of the vehicle logo photos, this paper selects the advanced YOLOv2 [16] target detection algorithm in the convolutional neural network for improvement. The main contributions are as follows:

(1) Investigate various local vehicle supervision sites, collect 4,400 vehicle pictures data sets, including 22 common vehicle brands (set of 200 pictures/type), and follow the data set PASCAL VOC format [17] for all dataset photos are manually tagged.

(2) Adjust the network structure and introduce a separable convolution strategy in YOLOv2's network model to split all large-scale convolution kernels into cascades of small-size convolution kernels.

(3) Introduce a multi-scale feature fusion strategy, combine the feature maps of different depths, and combine the inherent k-means clustering method of YOLOv2 to design different initialized anchor sizes, the logo images of different sizes can perform accurate detection, thereby improving the stability of the model.

(4) Design an automated multi-scale test method. The YOLOv2 algorithm can use the inherent multi-scale training to increase the training sample sets and improve the training effect, but this strategy is not considered in the test.

1.2   Introduction to Two Categories of Detectors

Object detection methods can be roughly divided into two categories. One is a traditional method based on manual selected features, and the other is a modern method based on deep convolutional neural networks. In addition, modern methods can be roughly divided into two categories. One is a single-stage detector, and the other is a multi-stage detector (such as SPP-Net [18]).

Two-Stage Detector. Recent methods, such as the R-CNN series [19–21], use region suggestion methods that first generate potential bounding boxes in the image and then run a classifier on these suggested boxes. After classification, the post-processing is used to refine the bounding boxes, eliminate duplicate detection, and re-check the bounding box based on other objects in the scene [22]. These complex pipelines are slow and difficult to optimize because each individual component must be trained separately.

One-Stage Detector. SSD [22] and YOLOv1 [23] introduce single-stage detection to general target detection for the first time. By using anchor boxes, the target position and target category can be predicted simultaneously on each fixed grid of the feature map. The most obvious advantages of this single-stage detector are that it is relatively faster, simpler in structure than two-stage and multi-stage detectors, and its speed is related to the number of objects in the image.

Our vehicle logo detector is also a one-stage detector, which detects the vehicle logo directly from the feature map obtained from the fusion convolution layer, unlike the regional suggestion network (RPN) commonly used in the RCNN series [24].

2   YOLOv2 Model and Improvements

2.1   Introduction of YOLOv2

The full name of YOLOv2's dissertation is YOLO9000: Better, Faster, Stronger, which won the CVPR 2017 Best Paper Honorable Mention. With the YOLO9000 model, it can detect more than 9,000 types of objects. Therefore, this article actually contains two models: YOLOv2 and YOLO9000, but the latter is proposed based on the former, and the main structure of the two models is the same.YOLOV2's network is darknet-19, which contains 19 convolutional layers and 5 max polling Layers. This is a network similar to VGG. The network uses a large number of convolution kernels and doubles the number of channels after each pooling operation.

2.2 Improvements of the Model

Separable Convolution. On the one hand, splitting a large convolution kernel into a cascade of two or more small convolution kernels can properly deepen the network, make the model's learning ability and learning effect better, on the other hand, it can reduce the calculation amount of model parameters. The idea is shown in Fig. 1, where the parameter quantity N * N < n1 * n1 + n2 * n2:

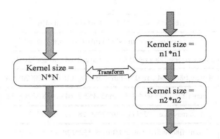

Fig. 1. Split an N * N convolution kernel into two convolution kernels n1 * n1 and n2 * n2.

Multi-scale Features Fusion. According to the difference in the size of the receptive field of different network layers and the adaptability to the detection of different size targets, the multi-scale features are fused to make the network more robust to the detection performance of different size targets (Fig. 2).

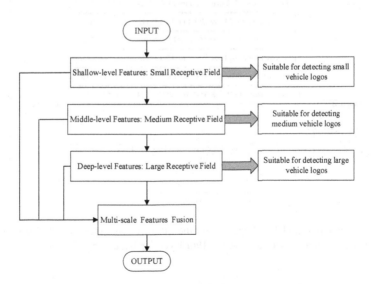

Fig. 2. Multi-scale feature fusion concept map.

Multi-scale Test. Within the range of 416 * 416 ∼ 1024 * 1024, step 32 is used to sequentially initialize the size of all vehicle photos in the test set to random resize initialization, and to test each set of vehicle photos after each resize. For a group of tests, a new picture size is randomly selected, and multiple tests are performed to achieve the best detection effect and prevent missed detection and false detection.

The Overall Model Framework. In summary, the improved model architecture is shown in Fig. 3.

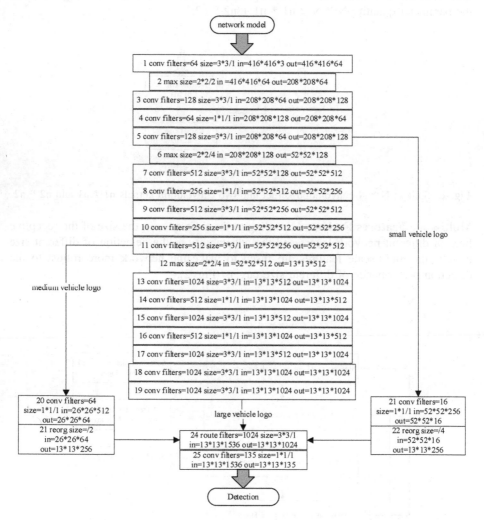

Fig. 3. The improved model architecture, on the 5th layer for small vehicle logo, on the 11th layer for medium vehicle logo, and on the 19th layer for large vehicle logo.

The network is divided into 4 blocks, the number of convolutional layers of each block is 1, 3, 5, 7, and the feature scales of the second, third, and fourth blocks are responsible for the detection of large, medium, and small vehicle logos, respectively. The sizes are uniformly cascaded using small sizes of 1 * 1 and 3 * 3.

The reorg represents the tensor dimensional transformation operation, and route represents the tensor merging operation (channel merging), which merges feature maps of different scales (depths) generated by the three branches.

3   Experiment and Analysis

3.1   Datasets

The vehicle pictures used in this article are from multiple traffic checkpoints and vehicle monitoring sites. There are a total of 4400 pictures of 22 kinds of vehicle logos (200 pictures of each vehicle logo). According to a 5: 1 ratio, 3665 pictures are randomly selected as the training set and 735 pictures are used as the test sets. The ratio of the number of each type of vehicle logo is the same. This experiment was performed on a Linux server with NVIDIA GTX1070 GPU and 8G memory (Table 1).

Table 1. The 22 kinds of vehicle logo.

class							
jac-truck	honda	ford	benz	kia	youyi-bus	iveco	suzuki
zhonghua	bmw	jac	buick	sgmw	mitsubishi	toyota	
changan-mpv	nissan	mg	audi	byd	jmc-truck	hyundai	

The LabelImg tool is used to make the vehicle logo datasets according to the deep learning standard VOC datasets format. The data file storage structure is shown in Fig. 4:

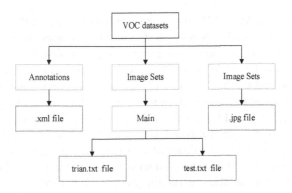

Fig. 4. VOC datasets storage structure.

3.2   Data Enhancement

In order to avoid overfitting the network and enhance the robustness of the model, in addition to the testing process, each training image sent to the network is sequentially subjected to the following data enhancement steps:

(1) Color and lighting: For each iteration training, the model can adjust the saturation, exposure, and hue of the picture, and generate new training samples according to the set values. This makes it possible to significantly improve the model's detection effect on vehicle logo images with different saturation, exposure, and hue while increasing the training set, and enhance the robustness of the model.

(2) Angle rotation: In each iteration of training, the horizontal or vertical rotation angle of the sample picture can be randomly set, and a new training sample can be generated according to the set value. This enables the model to adapt to the detection of multi-angle sample targets, and to better simulate the true state of vehicle photos in actual scenes.

(3) Noise interference: For each time iterative training, a certain degree of random noise can be added to the training set, and new training samples can be generated according to the set value. This makes the model better able to cope with interference from the external environment and prevents overfitting while enhancing the generalization ability of the model.

3.3   Loss Function Design

Using stochastic gradient descent (SGD) training methods, the loss function of the improved model is designed as follows:

$$
\begin{aligned}
loss_t = \sum_{i=0}^{W}\sum_{j=0}^{H}\sum_{k=0}^{A} & 1_{MaxIOU<Thresh}\lambda_{noobj} * (-b_{ijk}^{o})^2 \\
& + 1_{t<12800}\lambda_{prior} * \sum_{r\in(x,y,w,h)} (prior_k^r - b_{ijk}^r)^2 \\
& + 1_k^{truth}\left(\lambda_{coord} * \sum_{r\in(x,y,w,h)} *(truth^r - b_{ijk}^r)^2 + \lambda_{obj} * (IOU_{truth}^k - b_{ijk}^o)^2 + \lambda_{class} * \sum_{c=1}^{C} (truth^c - b_{ijk}^c)^2\right)
\end{aligned}
\tag{1}
$$

Among them, first, W and H refer to the width and height of the feature map (13 * 13, containing 13 * 13 cells), A refers to the number of prior frames (here is 5), and each λ value is each Loss partial weighting factor. The first loss is to calculate the confidence error of the background. You need to first calculate the IOU of each prediction box and all Ground Truth, and take the maximum value Max_IOU. If the value is less than a certain threshold (in this article is 0.6) Then this prediction box is marked as Background, and the confidence error of noobj needs to be calculated. The second term is to calculate the coordinate error between the a priori box and the prediction width, but it is only calculated between the first 12,800 iterations. Quickly learn the shape of the prior box. The third term calculates the Loss value of each part of the prediction box that matches a certain ground truth, including coordinate errors, confidence errors, and classification errors.

3.4 Parameter Setting

To adapt to the computing performance of the server and speed up network convergence, the model hyperparameters are set as follows:

(1) Set training Batch = 32 and Subdivisions = 8, that is, the number of samples sent in each training session is Batch/Subdivisions = 4, which effectively reduces GPU computing pressure and prevents memory overflow.
(2) Set the weight attenuation parameter Decay = 0.0005, adjust the impact of model complexity on the loss function, and prevent the model from overfitting.
(3) Set the step learning rate strategy, the initial learning rate to 0.001, when the network iterations iterate to the 100 and 130 epochs respectively, the learning rate is changed correspondingly to 0.1 times and 0.01 times in order to accelerate the network convergence to the global optimum. After training a total of 140 epochs, the training stop, the Loss drops to the decimal point and nearly no longer changes.

3.5 Multi-scale Training

In order to make the network model robust to sample pictures of different sizes, this is also taken into account during training. Unlike the method of fixing the input picture size of the network, a new one is randomly selected after every 10 batches of training picture. The downsampling parameter used by the network is 32, so multiples of 32 [320, 352, ..., 608] are used. This mechanism allows the network to better predict pictures of different sizes, and the same network can perform detection tasks with different resolutions.

3.6 Test and Compare

In order to test the performance of this network, the following experiments were performed: Experiment 1 tests the car standard test set; Experiment 2 compares the method in this paper with the method in [25]; Experiment 3 compares the improved YOLOv2 model with the original YOLOv2 network.

(1) Experiment 1

A total of 735 pictures in the test set, where the average accuracy rate is mAP = 99.0%, the recall is 99.73%, and the car with the worst detection accuracy is jmc-truck (0.930), and the detection accuracy of various vehicle logos is 100%. The specific test results are shown in the following table (Table 2):

Table 2. The accuracy of improved model.

class	AP	class	AP	class	AP	class	AP
jac-truck	0.997	buick	0.996	nissan	0.974	byd	1.000
mg	0.999	audi	0.999	ford	1.000	toyota	0.993
changan-mpv	0.971	kia	1.000	jac	0.997	hyundai	0.980
honda	0.984	sgmw	1.000	zhonghua	0.996	iveco	0.976
bmw	1.000	mitsubishi	0.999	benz	1.000	jmc-truck	0.930
youyi-bus	1.000	suzuki	1.000				
mAP				0.990			

The test results are shown in Fig. 5, 6, 7 and 8, experiments show that the model has excellent stability.

Fig. 5. Scene 1: Low resolution.

Fig. 6. Scene 2: Multiple objectives.

Fig. 7. Scene 3: Spin target.

Fig. 8. Scene 4: Small targets and big targets.

(2) Experiment 2

Table 3 shows the comparison results between the model method and the method in reference [22]. Reference [22] is also a method for vehicle logo recognition based on deep learning. As can be seen from Table 3, under certain conditions, the accuracy of the model in this paper has been greatly improved on the basis of [22].

Table 3. Detection effect comparisonl.

Serial number	Class	Accuracy of Literature [22]	Accuracy of this article
1	hyundai	0.900	0.980
2	honda	0.975	0.984
3	toyota	0.925	0.993
4	ford	0.950	1.000
5	nissan	0.967	0.974
6	audi	0.975	0.999
7	bmw	0.950	1.000
8	benz	0.950	1.000
9	buick	0.950	0.996
10	suzuki	0.967	1.000
	mAP	0.951	0.993

(3) Experiment 3

Under the same conditions, the YOLOv2 model before the training is used to train and test the vehicle logo data set. The average accuracy rate achieved is mAP = 96.2%, and the recall rate is 97.83%. The test performance of many vehicle standards is less than the improvement after the YOLOv2 model, we can see that the improved YOLOv2 model has a significant effect. The test results are shown in Table 4:

Table 4. Accuracy of the original model.

class	AP	class	AP	class	AP	class	AP
jac-truck	0.999	buick	0.998	nissan	0.924	byd	0.996
mg	0.995	audi	0.973	ford	0.998	toyota	0.997
changan-mpv	0.877	kia	0.996	jac	0.935	hyundai	0.866
honda	0.915	sgmw	1.000	zhonghua	0.976	iveco	0.964
bmw	0.894	mitsubishi	0.962	benz	1.000	jmc-truck	0.898
youyi-bus	0.821	suzuki	0.995				
mAP				0.954			

4 Conclusion

This paper proposes a real-time vehicle logo detection method based on improved YOLOv2. Compared with the traditional vehicle logo recognition method, it has the ability of self-learning and extraction of features, it can simultaneously locate and recognize targets and has higher accuracy, recall and good real-time performance; compared with other deep learning recognition method, its structure is simple, it is an end-to-end one-stage structure, and it has automatic sample expansion and data enhancement capabilities. With adaptive ability, higher stability and robustness, it can effectively improve the performance of vehicle logo positioning and recognition at this stage, and become a powerful means to achieve intelligent transportation.

References

1. Luo, B., You, Z., Cao, G.: Fast vehicle identification method based on edge histogram. J. Comput. Appl. **21**(6), 150–151 (2004)
2. Wang, Y., Liu, Z., Xiao, F.: A fast coarse-to-fine vehicle logo detection and recognition method. In: IEEE International Conference on Robotics & Biomimetics (2008)
3. Wang, M., Wang, G., Fang, P., Sun, S.: Method for vehicle-logo location and recognition based on PCA and invariant moment. Geomat. Inf. Sci. Wuhan Univ. **33**(1), 36–40 (2008)
4. Mu, S., Liu, Z., Zhang, J.: Vehicle identification method based on image quality and PCA subspace. J. Comput. Appl. **30**(8), 2244–2246 (2010)
5. Yu, S., Zheng, S., Hua, Y., et al.: Vehicle logo recognition based on Bag-of-Words. In: IEEE International Conference on Advanced Video & Signal Based Surveillance (2013)
6. Llorca, D.F., Arroyo, R., Sotelo, M.Á.: Vehicle logo recognition in traffic images using HOG features and SVM. In: IEEE Intelligent Transportation Systems Conference (ITSC). IEEE (2013)
7. Sam, K.T., Tian, X.L.: Vehicle logo recognition using modest AdaBoost and radial Tchebichef moments. In: International Proceedings of Computer Science & Information Tech (2012)
8. Wang, Y., Liu, Z., Xiao, F.: Real-time vehicle location and recognition method based on symmetry. J. Syst. Simul. **21**(4) (2009)

9. Wang, S.K., Liu, L., Xu, X.: Vehicle logo recognition based on local feature descriptor. Appl. Mech. Mater. **263–266**, 2418–2421 (2013)
10. Psyllos, A.P., Kayafas, E.: Vehicle logo recognition using a SIFT-based enhanced matching scheme. IEEE Trans. Intell. Transp. Syst. **11**(2), 322–328 (2010)
11. Guan, X., Huang, Y., Cai, Z., Ohtsuki, T.: Intersection-based forwarding protocol for vehicular ad hoc networks. Telecommun. Syst. J. **62**(1), 67–76 (2016)
12. Xiong, Z., Li, W., Han, Q., Cai, Z.: Privacy-preserving auto-driving: a GAN-based approach to protect vehicular camera data. In: 19th IEEE International Conference on Data Mining (ICDM 2019) (2019)
13. Wang, J., Cai, Z., Yu, J.: Achieving personalized k-anonymity based content privacy for autonomous vehicles in CPS. IEEE Trans. Ind. Inform. (TII) **16**(6), 4242–4251 (2020)
14. Fan, J., Xu, W., Wu, Y., et al.: Human tracking using convolutional neural networks. IEEE Trans. Neural Netw. **21**(10), 1610–1623 (2010)
15. Karpathy, A., Toderici, G., Shetty, S., et al.: Large-scale video classification with convolutional neural networks. In: 2014 IEEE Conference on Computer Vision and Pattern Recognition (CVPR). IEEE (2014)
16. Redmon, J., Farhadi, A.: YOLO9000: better, faster, stronger. In: IEEE Conference on Computer Vision & Pattern Recognition (2017)
17. Everingham, M., Winn, J.: The PASCAL visual object classes challenge 2007 (VOC 2007) development kit. Int. J. Comput. Vis. **111**(1), 98–136 (2006)
18. Purkait, P., Zhao, C., Zach, C.: SPP-Net: Deep Absolute Pose Regression with Synthetic Views (2017)
19. Girshick, R., Donahue, J., Darrell, T., Malik, J.: Rich feature hierarchies for accurate object detection and semantic segmentation. In: Computer Vision and Pattern Recognition (CVPR), pp. 580–587. IEEE (2014)
20. Ren, S., He, K., Girshick, R., et al.: Faster R-CNN: Towards Real-Time Object Detection with Region Proposal Networks (2015)
21. Girshick, R.: Fast R-CNN. In: IEEE International Conference on Computer Vision (2015)
22. Liu, W., et al.: SSD: single shot multibox detector. In: Leibe, B., Matas, J., Sebe, N., Welling, M. (eds.) ECCV 2016. LNCS, vol. 9905, pp. 21–37. Springer, Cham (2016). https://doi.org/10.1007/978-3-319-46448-0_2
23. Redmon, J., Divvala, S., Girshick, R., Farhadi, A.: You only look once: unified, real-time object detection. In: Proceedings of the IEEE Conference on Computer Vision and Pattern Recognition, pp. 779–788 (2016)
24. Ren, S., et al.: Faster R-CNN: towards real-time object detection with region proposal networks. In: Advances in Neural Information Processing Systems (2015)
25. Bo, P., Di, Y.: Research on vehicle identification method based on deep learning. Comput. Sci. **42**(4), 268–273 (2015)

SEM: APP Usage Prediction
with Session-Based Embedding

Zepeng Yu, Wenzhong Li[✉] ⓘ, Pinhao Wang, and Sanglu Lu[✉]

State Key Laboratory for Novel Software Technology,
Nanjing University, Nanjing 210023, China
{lwz,sanglu}@nju.edu.cn

Abstract. Nowadays smartphone users have installed dozens or even hundreds of APPs on their phones. Predicting APP usage not only helps the mobile phone system to speed up APP launching but also reduces the time for users to search them. In this paper, we focus on a novel session-based APP usage prediction problem that tends to predict a sequence of APPs to be used in a period. We propose a session-based embedding framework called *SEM* to solve the problem. To deal with the heterogeneity of APP sessions, we present a session embedding algorithm to form uniform feature representation, which alleviates the problem of user sparsity and obtains the vector representation of sessions. Based on session embedding, we train a two-layer GRU-based recursive neural network model for APP usage session prediction. Extensive experiments based on real datasets show that the proposed framework outperforms conventional APP recommendation approaches.

Keywords: APP usage prediction · Session-based embedding · Recurrent neural network (RNN) · Gated Recurrent Unit (GRU)

1 Introduction

Nowadays, smartphones have become an indispensable part of people's lives. A report[1] in 2019 showed that the number of APPs available for download on Google Play is 2.57 million and that on Apple APP Store is 1.84 million. Most smartphone users have installed dozens or even hundreds of APPs on their phones. When a smartphone user wants to use a particular APP, he needs to swipe the screen on the phone, searching for the APP, which is inconvenient and time-consuming. In addition, even with better smartphone hardware, it still takes a few seconds to lauch an APP. Therefore it is essential to predict the APP usage, which can decrease the time of searching for APPs and accelerate APP launching by prefetching content.

APP usage prediction has been widely studied in the past decade. Church et al. [4] summarized the challenges for mobile phone usage learning, such as

---

[1] https://www.statista.com/statistics/276623/number-of-apps-available-in-leading-app-stores/.

© Springer Nature Switzerland AG 2020
D. Yu et al. (Eds.): WASA 2020, LNCS 12384, pp. 678–690, 2020.
https://doi.org/10.1007/978-3-030-59016-1_56

launcher prediction and APP recommendation. Some works proposed the usage of contextual information to achieve that goal. As Verkasalo [19] found, time and location are two important contextual information for APP usage prediction. Shin et al. [16] adopted a personalized Naive Bayes model for individual user. Their study used sensor data on the smartphone as context information to improve prediction results. In addition, various algorithms and information types have been explored for prediction and recommendation in different domains.

Unlike conventional APP recommendation works that tend to predict the next APP to be used by the user, we focus on the *session-based APP usage prediction problem* that tends to predict a series of APPs that will be consecutively used by a user in a time interval. We propose a session-based embedding framework called *SEM* for APP usage session prediction. Given the fact that APP usage sessions have variable lengths and contain heterogeneous semantic and contextual information, we present a feature embedding learning method to embed the heterogeneous sessions to uniform feature representation. Based on the embedded feature vectors, we propose a two-layer recurrent neural network (RNN) with Gated Recurrent Unit (GRU) model to predict the next session.

The contributions of our paper are summarized as follows.

- We focus on a novel session-based APP usage prediction problem that tends to predict a set of APPs to be used in a period. The proposed research problem is challenging and has wide practical implications.
- To deal with the heterogeneity of APP sessions, we propose a session-based embedding method to form uniform feature representation, which alleviates the problem of user sparsity and obtains the vector representation of sessions.
- Based on session embedding, we train a two-layer GRU-based recurrent neural network model for APP usage session prediction.
- We evaluate the proposed model on two real-world dataset. Extensive experiments are conducted to verify the effectiveness of our model in APP usage prediction.

2   Related Work

In this section, we briefly summarize related works of APP usage prediction and feature representation with embedding technique.

2.1   APP Usage Prediction

A number of prior works has studied the problem of predicting smartphone APP usage. As Shin [16] found, sensor contexts that we can get from smartphone, were useful for APP prediction. They collected data from different sensors and built a naive Bayes based prediction model to get the probability of a specific APP with respect to a given context. What's more, time and location also play an important role in APP usage prediction [19]. According to the research of Parate et al. [14], an APP prediction algorithm called APPM that requires no prior training was proposed. Ye et al. [27] proposed a multi-faceted approach which utilized three key factors to understand and predict APP usage behavior. On the basis of the approach, they used contextual features to enhance the prediction results. To remedy slow APP launch, Yan et al. [26] designed and built a framework named FALCON to predict and prelaunch the APPs. They used temporal access patterns and user location as context information to do the prediction. Chen et al. [2] took the location and time as contextual information as well, and used attribution information in addition.

2.2   Feature Representation with Embedding

Since embedding technology has shown very good performance in natural language processing (NLP) [10,13,18], the concept of embedding has been extended to other domains. Perozzi et al. [15] first applied skip-gram model to graphs, and used random walks on graph to obtain node representations. Grover et al. [7] optimized the random walk process by balancing BFS and DFS strategy to equilibrate homophily and structural equivalence. Tang et al. [17] proposed an algorithm for graph embedding, trying to preserve both the first-order proximity and the second-order proximity. Dong et al. [5] studied the problem of representation learning in heterogeneous networks. Some deep learning models [20] used deep neural networks to improve the model's ability of capturing higher level information. Graph embedding had wide applications in recommendation systems [21] and mobile social networks [11,12], and it had been adopted in the products of many companies such as Alibaba [22], Facebook [23], and Airbnb [6].

3   Problem Description

In this paper, we study the problem of *session-based APP usage prediction* which is described as follows.

A *session* of APP usage is defined as a sequence of APPs that are continuously used by the user in a period of time, i.e., $s = (a_1, a_2, ..., a_n) \in S$, where a_i is the i-th APP used in session s and S is the set of all sessions. The usage interval between two APPs in a session should be less than a predefined threshold τ. If the access time interval of two APPs is larger than τ, they should belong to two different sessions. In our system, τ is set to 30 min in the experiments.

The objective of our work is to predict what APPs a user will use in the next session. Given the user's APP usage history represented by a number of sessions, we want to predict a session $s_p = (a_{p1}, a_{p2}, ..., a_{pn})$, that consists of a sequence of APPs will be used in the next time duration. Unlike the previous works on APP recommendation [1,8,24] that only predicts the next APP to be used, our prediction problem outputs a sequence of APPs in the next session, which is more challenging and has wider implications.

4   Session-Based APP Usage Prediction

4.1   SEM Framework

We propose a session-based APP prediction approach called SEM, whose framework is shown in Fig. 1. It consists of three parts.

1) *Data Preprocessing:* Given a real world dataset, the first step is to clean the data. We extract several important features from the original set of data and remove the noise data. Then we build session set S from the clean data.
2) *Session-based Embedding:* This module uses session set S as input and outputs a set of session vectors V. The information in the session can be mapped into a latent space based on co-occurrence relationship. A session-based learning method is designed to capture the contextual information of the session.
3) *Prediction Model:* This module predicts what APPs a user will use in the next session. We use historical session vectors to train a stacked neural network, and use the network to predict the next APP usage session.

The three modules are presented in detail below.

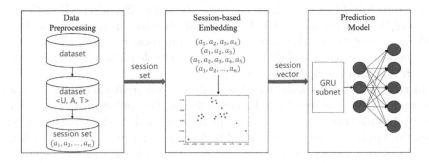

Fig. 1. Overview of the proposed model

4.2   Data Preprocessing

Data preprocessing module provides clean data for following operations. Given the raw data that contains the logs of user accessing to different APPs, we extract the user ID U, the APP ID A and the time stamp T from the original data. We remove some redundant data by checking the time stamp T. We also remove some APPs that are used almost by all users because they do not contain too much useful information like stopwords in natural language. Then each record in the dataset can be represented as $\langle U, A, T \rangle$. We use these records to construct APP usage sessions. A session s = $(a_1, a_2, ..., a_n) \in S$ is defined as a period of time during which the user has a continuous record of using APPs.

4.3   Session-Based Embedding

Since the sessions extracted from the dataset have variable lengths and contain heterogeneous semantic and contextual information, to form a uniform feature representation, we propose a session-based embedding method to map the heterogeneous sessions to fixed length feature vectors.

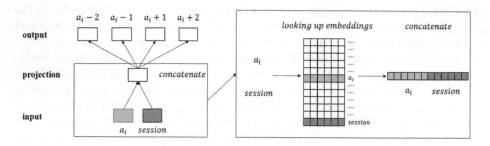

Fig. 2. Skip-gram model for session-based embeddings

The proposed session-based embedding method works similar to the idea of graph embedding [6,15,22]. Given a graph $G = (V, E)$, where V is the set of all nodes in the network, and E is the set of all edges in the network. For v $\in$ V, the aim is to learn a low dimension representation $r_v \in R^d$, where d $\ll |V|$. In other words, the goal of graph embedding is to learn a mapping function f: $V \rightarrow R^d$ to map the nodes into vectors.

In the problem of session-based embedding, we treat each APP as a node. Two nodes are connected by a directed edge if they occur in a session consecutively. In this way, we obtain the sequences needed in the embedding phase. Then, we apply the Skip-Gram model to learn the representation of each node. The Skip-Gram model for session-based embedding is illustrated in Fig. 2. The process of session-based embedding works as follows. We use a sliding window in the session to get the input and output of our model, with the central node of the current window as input and the rest as the output of context information. In addtion to the central node, we also add another node representing the session as input. The difference is that the central node changes as the window slides, but the session node remains the same. Therefore, the session node can be taken as another node that act as a globel context. Then the central node and the session node will be mapped to vectors. We concatenate them subsequently in the projection layer and use the concatenate vector to derive the output.

To preserve the structure information in the graph, the objective function of the Skip-Gram model is to maximize the average log probability:

$$\arg\max_{f} \sum_{s \in S} \sum_{a_i \in s} \sum_{c \in N(a_i)} \log P(c|f(a_i)), \tag{1}$$

where $N(a_i)$ is the neighborhood of node a_i, i.e., the context of a_i. $P(c|f(a_i))$ is the conditional probability of observing contextual neighborhood of the given node a_i, which is defined as follows:

$$P(c\,|f(a_i)) = \frac{\exp(v_{a_i}^\top v_c')}{\sum_{n=1}^{|V|}\exp(v_{a_i}^\top v_n')}, \tag{2}$$

where v_a and v_a' are the "input" and "output" vector representation of node a.

From Eq. (1) and Eq. (2) we can see that it is computationally expensive to compute the gradient, which is proportional to the size of $|V|$. It is impractical when facing large scale dataset. To reduce the cost of computing the gradient, we adopt a negative sample approach. When training a node a_i's vector, we use their context nodes $c \in N(a_i)$ as positive samples, and choose N other nodes randomly as negative samples, then the probability becomes

$$-\sum_{c\in N(a_i)} \log \sigma(-v_c'v_{a_i}) - \sum_{n=1}^{N} \log \sigma(v_c'v_{a_i}) \tag{3}$$

where σ is the sigmoid function. The stochastic gradient descent algorithm is used for optimization.

The benefits of session-based embedding are as follows: First, it preserves the direct occurrence of interactions between APP usage; Second, it helps to capture the higher order relationship propagated by the graph; Finally, it lowers the dimension to represent the data which reduces computation and storage cost.

4.4 Prediction Model

Given a user's historical sessions, we propose a neural network model to predict what APPs the user will use in his subsequent behavior. As shown in Fig. 3, we present a stacked recurrent neural network consisting of a Gated Recurrent Unit (GRU) [3] subnet and a fully connected output layer explained below.

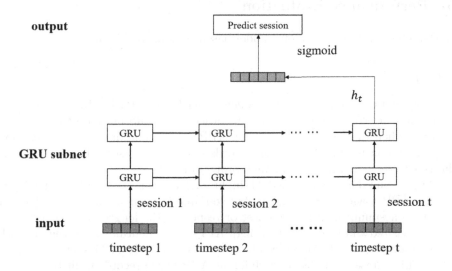

Fig. 3. Session usage prediction model.

We adopt a two-layer GRU model to transform the historical session vectors. GRU is a type of recurrent neural network. It can model long-term dependencies in a sequence and solves the vanishing gradient problem of conventional recurrent neural network. GRU transforms the input by reset gate r_t and update gate z_t.

$$r_t = \sigma(W_r x_t + U_r h_{t-1}) \tag{4}$$

$$z_t = \sigma(W_z x_t + U_z h_{t-1}) \tag{5}$$

where σ is the sigmoid function. x_t and h_{t-1} are the session vector and the previous hidden state. W and U are weight matrices which are learned. The reset gate r_t allows the hidden state to drop information and the update gate z_t determines how much information from the previous will keep around. Current hidden state h_t is computed by

$$h_t = z_t h_{t-1} + (1 - z_t)\overline{h_t} \tag{6}$$

where
$$\overline{h_t} = \tanh(W_h x_t + U_h(r_t \odot h_{t-1})) \tag{7}$$

The input of GRU should be a 3-dimensional tensor like (*samples, timesteps, input_dim*). In our module, *samples* is the number of instances, *timesteps* is the number of history sessions that we need, and *input_dim* is the dimension of session vector. We use dropout layer after each layer in order to prevent overfitting. We use the hidden state at the last timestep as the subnet output. It is further fed to a fully connected output layer which transforms the hidden state to our prediction session. We choose sigmoid function as the activation function to form the final result. We use binary_crossentropy as the loss function.

5   Performance Evaluation

In this section, we evaluate our model based on real world datasets.

5.1   Datasets

The first dataset called CTD was collected with Deep Packet Inspection appliances by a telecom operator [25]. It recorded some information of mobile subscribers when they access network for APP usage. The dataset includes more than 2 million mobile APP usage records from 31064 users. The users in the dataset were anonymized for privacy protection.

The second dataset is named "Tsinghua APP Usage Dataset" (TAUD) [28]. In this APP usage dataset, each entry contained an anonymized User identification, timestamps of HTTP request or response, the length of the packet, the domain visited and the user-agent field. APPs were identified from the networking metadata and APP category was crawled from Android Market and Google Play. This dataset included 1696 different APP usage records from 1000 users.

The statistics of the datasets are depicted in Table 1.

Table 1. Statistics of the two datasets

Dataset	# users	# usage	# APPs	Duration
CTD	31064	2041697	933	3 days
TAUD	1000	1696	2000	7 days

5.2 Baseline Algorithms

We compare our approach with the following baselines:

- **Statistics:** This method simply counts the users' history of mobile APP usage, and selects the most frequently used APPs as prediction results.
- **Modified graph-embedding (MGE)** [2]: It uses random walks on graph to obtain node samples and adopts skip-gram model [15] to get vector representations.
- **WMF** [9]: It is a weighted collaborative filtering method commonly used in recommendation system to find the top-k interested items.

5.3 Performance of Next APP Prediction

We first test the ability of SEM to predict the next used APP, which is a common task of the existing APP prediction works. For both datasets, we sorted the user's APP usage records by time. We use the first 80% of records as training data and the rest 20% of the records for test.

We use recall@N as a evaluation metric, which is defined as:

$$Recall@N = \frac{|Real(u) \cap Test(u)_N|}{|Real(u)|} \tag{8}$$

where $Test(u)_N$ represents the list of Top-N recommendations based on the model output, and $Real(u)$ represents the list of the user's actual behavior.

We also adopt mean reciprocal rank (MRR@N) as the second metric because recall does not take the order of APPs in the list into account. MRR@N is defined as:

$$MRR@N = \frac{1}{T} \sum_{i=1}^{T} \frac{1}{rank_i} \tag{9}$$

where T is the testing set and $rank_i$ is the rank of the prediction.

The comparison of different algorithms in predicting next APP is shown in Table 2, and the best results w.r.t each evaluation metric are marked in bold. From the table, we have the following observations:

- The proposed SEM approach achieve the best performance compared with all baselines on both datasets in term of all metrics, except that Statistics obtains a better result in term of MRR@5 on CTD dataset, and WMF obtains a better result on TAUD in term of MRR@5.

Table 2. Comparison of performance on next APP prediction

Dataset	Algorithm	Performance metric			
		Recall@5	Recall@10	MRR@5	MRR@10
CTD	Statistics	0.750	0.773	**0.514**	0.519
	MGE	0.742	0.783	0.498	0.505
	WMF	0.682	0.780	0.492	0.507
	SEM	**0.763**	**0.805**	0.511	**0.524**
TAUD	Statistics	0.279	0.317	0.183	0.188
	MGE	**0.371**	0.394	0.177	0.215
	WMF	0.361	0.406	**0.196**	0.215
	SEM	**0.371**	**0.411**	0.195	**0.218**

– MGE also achieves good performance on both datasets, which indicates using graph embedding based algorithm to cope with the recommendation problem is suitable. SEM performs better than MGE, which shows that using session information is effective.

5.4 Performance of APP Session Prediction

Next, we study the performance of the algorithms in predicting a sequence of APPs in the next session. Consistent with the above experiment, we use the first 80% sessions as training data and the rest 20% as test.

We adopt Jaccard coefficient to measure the similarity between the real session S_r and the predicted session S_p, which is defined as:

$$J(S_r, S_p) = \frac{|S_r \cap S_p|}{|S_r \cup S_p|} = \frac{|S_r \cap S_p|}{|S_r| + |S_p| - |S_r \cap S_p|} \tag{10}$$

We also adopt normalized discounted cumulative gain (NDCG) to measure the prediction quality of ordered sequence items. We make slight change on NDCG, which we called $\widehat{NDCG}$, which is defined as:

$$DCG_k = \sum_{i=1}^{k} \frac{2^{rel_i} - 1}{log_2(i + 1)} \tag{11}$$

$$\widehat{NDCG}_k = \frac{DCG_k \times |rel|}{IDCG_k \times k} \tag{12}$$

$$\widehat{NDCG} = \frac{1}{T} \sum_{1}^{T} \widehat{NDCG}_k \tag{13}$$

where k is the length of session; rel_i is the correlation coefficient of the i-th APP in the session; $|rel|$ denotes the number of relevant APPs in the session; T is the testing set; and $IDCG_k$ is the ideal DCG_k which is used for normalize.

Table 3. Comparison of performance on next APP session prediction.

Dataset	Algorithm	Performance metric	
		Jaccard	$\widehat{NDCG}$
CTD	Statistics	0.121	0.107
	MGE	0.324	0.292
	WMF	0.216	0.075
	SEM	**0.617**	**0.600**
TAUD	Statistics	0.130	0.096
	MGE	0.284	0.204
	WMF	0.411	0.347
	SEM	**0.496**	**0.437**

The results are compared in Table 3, and the best results are marked in bold. From the table, we can draw the following conclusions:

- The proposed SEM approach significantly outperforms all baselines on both datasets in term of the two metrics, which validates the effectiveness of the proposed model on predicting a series of APPs, which is much more superior than the existing approaches.
- Under the task of APP session prediction, the baseline algorithms have a large gap with our model probably due to accumulated errors.
- Noting that all algorithms perform better on CTD dataset than TAUD, probably due to that CTD has more data making the models learning better.

5.5   Parameter Sensitivity Analysis

There are two important parameters in our model: the dimension of session vector and the context window size in the Skip-gram model. In this section, we examine how the different choices of parameters affect the performance of our model. When testing a specific parameter, other parameters remain unchanged.

The influence of dimension can be seen in Fig. 4(a). It can be found that when the dimension is less than 32, increasing the dimension of session vector, the performance of SEM improves obviously. The performance decrease slightly as the parameter keeps increasing. Similarly, we can observe the influence of window size in Fig. 4(b). When the window size is less than 8, the performance of SEM continues to increase as the window size grows. After that, the performance drops slightly, which suggests a suitable window size 8.

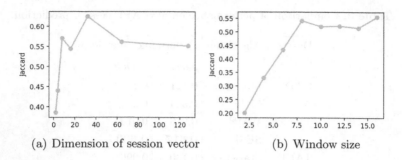

(a) Dimension of session vector   (b) Window size

Fig. 4. Performance of SEM under different hyperparameters.

6   Conclusion

In this paper, we proposed a session-based embedding framework called SEM to solve the problem of predicting a series of APPs that will be consecutively used by a user in a time interval. The proposed framework consists of three parts: a data preprocessing module to provide clean data for later processing; a session-based embedding method to map heterogeneous sessions into uniform feature representation; and a two-layer recurrent neural network (RNN) with Gated Recurrent Unit (GRU) model for APP usage session prediction. We evaluate the proposed model on two real-world dataset. Extensive experiments are conducted to verify the effectiveness of the proposed framework in APP usage prediction.

Acknowledgements. This work was partially supported by the National Key R&D Program of China (Grant No. 2018YFB1004704), the National Natural Science Foundation of China (Grant Nos. 61972196, 61672278, 61832008, 61832005), the Key R&D Program of Jiangsu Province, China (Grant No. BE2018116), the open Project from the State Key Laboratory of Smart Grid Protection and Operation Control "Research on Smart Integration of Terminal-Edge-Cloud Techniques for Pervasive Internet of Things".

References

1. Baeza-Yates, R., Di, J., Silvestri, F., Harrison, B.: Predicting the next app that you are going to use. In: Proceedings of the Eighth ACM International Conference (2015)
2. Chen, X., Wang, Y., He, J., Pan, S., Li, Y., Zhang, P.: CAP: context-aware app usage prediction with heterogeneous graph embedding. Proc. ACM Interact. Mobile Wearable Ubiquitous Technol. **3**(1), 1–25 (2019)
3. Cho, K., et al.: Learning phrase representations using RNN encoder-decoder for statistical machine translation (2014)
4. Church, K., et al.: Understanding the challenges of mobile phone usage data. ACM (2015)
5. Dong, Y., Chawla, N.V., Swami, A.: metapath2vec: scalable representation learning for heterogeneous networks. In: Proceedings of the 23rd ACM SIGKDD International Conference on Knowledge Discovery and Data Mining (2017)

6. Grbovic, M., Cheng, H.: Real-time personalization using embedding. In: Proceedings of the 24th ACM SIGKDD International Conference on Knowledge Discovery and Data Mining, pp. 311–320. ACM (2018)
7. Grover, A., Leskovec, J.: node2vec: scalable feature learning for networks. In: Proceedings of the 22th ACM SIGKDD International Conference on Knowledge Discovery and Data Mining (2016)
8. Han, D., Li, J., Li, W.: An app usage recommender system: improving prediction accuracy for both warm and cold start users. Multimed. Syst. **25**, 603–616 (2019)
9. Hu, Y., Koren, Y., Volinsky, C.: Collaborative filtering for implicit feedback datasets. In: IEEE International Conference on Data Mining (2008)
10. Kandola, E.J., Hofmann, T., Poggio, T., Shawe-Taylor, J.: A neural probabilistic language model. Studies in Fuzziness Soft Comput. **194**, 137–186 (2006)
11. Lin, Y., Cai, Z., Wang, X., Hao, F.: Incentive mechanisms for crowdblocking rumors in mobile social networks. IEEE Trans. Veh. Technol. **68**(9), 9220–9232 (2019)
12. Lin, Y., et al.: Dynamic control of fraud information spreading in mobile social networks. IEEE Trans. Syst. Man Cybern.: Syst., 1–14 (2019)
13. Mikolov, T., Sutskever, I., Chen, K., Corrado, G., Dean, J.: Distributed representations of words and phrases and their compositionality (2013)
14. Parate, A., Böhmer, M., Chu, D., Ganesan, D., Marlin, B.: Practical prediction and prefetch for faster access to applications on mobile phones (2013)
15. Perozzi, B., Al-Rfou, R., Skiena, S.: Deepwalk: Online learning of social representations. In: Proceedings of the 20th ACM SIGKDD International Conference on Knowledge Discovery and Data Mining, pp. 701–710 (2014)
16. Shin, C., Hong, J.H., Dey, A.K.: Understanding and prediction of mobile application usage for smart phones. In: Proceedings of the ACM Conference on Ubiquitous Computing, p. 173 (2012)
17. Tang, J., Qu, M., Wang, M., Zhang, M., Yan, J., Mei, Q.: Line: Large-scale information network embedding. In: International Conference on World Wide Web WWW (2015)
18. Turian, J.P., Ratinov, L.A., Bengio, Y.: Word representations: a simple and general method for semi-supervised learning. In: Proceedings of the 48th Annual Meeting of the Association for Computational Linguistics (2010)
19. Verkasalo, H.: Contextual patterns in mobile service usage. Personal Ubiquitous Comput. **13**(5), 331–342 (2009)
20. Wang, D., Peng, C., Zhu, W.: Structural deep network embedding. In: the 22nd ACM SIGKDD International Conference (2016)
21. Wang, D., Deng, S., Xin, Z., Xu, G.: Learning music embedding with metadata for context aware recommendation (2016)
22. Wang, J., Huang, P., Zhao, H., Zhang, Z., Zhao, B., Lee, D.L.: Billion-scale commodity embedding for e-commerce recommendation in alibaba (2018)
23. Wu, L., Fisch, A., Chopra, S., Adams, K., Bordes, A., Weston, J.: Starspace: embed all the things! (2017)
24. Xu, S., et al.: Predicting smartphone app usage with recurrent neural networks. In: Chellappan, S., Cheng, W., Li, W. (eds.) WASA 2018. LNCS, vol. 10874, pp. 532–544. Springer, Cham (2018). https://doi.org/10.1007/978-3-319-94268-1_44
25. Yan, F., Ding, Y., Li, W.: Mining mobile users' interests through cellular network browsing profiles. In: Chellappan, S., Cheng, W., Li, W. (eds.) WASA 2018. LNCS, vol. 10874, pp. 806–812. Springer, Cham (2018). https://doi.org/10.1007/978-3-319-94268-1_71

26. Yan, T., Chu, D., Ganesan, D., Kansal, A., Liu, J.: Fast app launching for mobile devices using predictive user context. In: ACM Mobisys (2012)
27. Ye, X., et al.: Preference, context and communities: a multi-faceted approach to predicting smartphone app usage patterns (2013)
28. Yu, D., Li, Y., Xu, F., Zhang, P., Kostakos, V.: Smartphone app usage prediction using points of interest. Proc. ACM Interact. Mobile Wearable Ubiquitous Technol. **1**(4), 174 (2018)

Intelligent Dynamic Spectrum Access for Uplink Underlay Cognitive Radio Networks Based on Q-Learning

Jingjing Zhang[1], Anming Dong[2] (iD), and Jiguo Yu[1,2,3](✉) (iD)

[1] School of Information Science and Engineering,
Qufu Normal University, Rizhao 276826, China
jingjingzhangsdwf@126.com, jiguoyu@sina.com
[2] School of Computer Science and Technology, Qilu University of Technology
(Shandong Academy of Sciences), Jinan 250353, China
anmingdong@qlu.edu.cn
[3] Shandong Provincial Key Laboratory of Computer Networks, Shandong Computer
Science Center (National Supercomputer Center in Jinan), Qilu University
of Technology (Shandong Academy of Sciences), Jinan 250014, China

Abstract. In this paper, the dynamic spectrum access (DSA) technique for an uplink underlay cognitive radio (CR) network is considered. The objective of the DSA scheme is to allow the secondary users (SUs) access the network on the premise of ensuring the quality of service of the primary user (PU). This DSA process is formulated as an optimization problem to maximize the sum rate of the SUs subject to the constraints of signal-to-interference-and-noise ratio (SINR) of both the PU and SUs, through adjusting the transmit powers and thus SINR thresholds of the SUs. Under the assumption of discrete feasible set, the formulated DSA problem is nonconvex and thus difficult to solve. We develop an intelligent solving method for this DSA problem based on Q-Learning. Numerical simulations show that the proposed algorithm can efficiently learn a solution that guarantees the link quality of the PU after allowing access of the SUs.

1 Introduction

With the rapid development of the mobile Internet and the continuous updating of smart terminal technologies, the number of wireless mobile users have been continuously increased in the past years. It is predicted that this trend will continue in the coming years [1]. As a consequence of the booming of users,

This work was supported in part by the National Key R&D Program of China under Grant 2019YFB2102600, the National Natural Science Foundation of China (NSFC) under Grants 61672321, 61701269, 61832012 and 61771289, the Key Research and Development Program of Shandong Province under Grants 2019JZZY020124 and 2019JZZY010313, and the Natural Science Foundation of Shandong Province under Grant ZR2017BF012.

© Springer Nature Switzerland AG 2020
D. Yu et al. (Eds.): WASA 2020, LNCS 12384, pp. 691–703, 2020.
https://doi.org/10.1007/978-3-030-59016-1_57

the mobile traffic of wireless network will also continuously increasing. In order to meet the future demand of mobile traffic, the network capacity should be consistently improved in the future.

An effective way to increase the capacity is to allocate more spectrum resource to the wireless communication systems. However, the spectrum resource is scare and it is unrealistic to allocate adequate bandwidth for any user in the networks due to the scarcity of the spectrum [2,3]. On the other hand, the spectrum resource that have been allocated is far from fully utilized due to the traditional spectrum management policy [4]. Under such background, it is expected that the efficiency of the spectrum usage should be improved through spectrum sharing. Such spectrum sharing mechanism can be realized through the cognitive radio (CR) technique in practice. CR offers the promise of intelligent radios that can learn from and adapt to their environment, which provides an effective solution for alleviating the conflict between spectrum shortage and spectrum under-utilization [5]. Based on the perceived information on the wireless environment, the devices in CR networks can access the available spectrum in a dynamical and opportunistic way.

The dynamic spectrum sharing in a CR network requires simultaneously adjusting a slew of parameters and policies, including transmit power, coding scheme, modulation scheme, sensing algorithm, communication protocol, sensing policy, etc [6]. This process is complex due to the complicated interactions among these factors and their impact on the environment [7]. This means that it is impossible to determine these setup parameters simultaneously by simple formulas.

The recent advantages of modern machine learning techniques shed new light on the realization of CR networks. By applying the machine learning methods, the CR networks are capable of adapting to their environments without the complete knowledge of the dependence among these parameters [8]. Among the variety of machine learning methods, reinforcement learning (RL) is preferred when little knowledge is known about the environment and a CR device needs to learn and adapt to its environment with significant uncertainty [9]. Currently, reinforcement learning has been applied in multiple area of CR networks, such as energy harvesting [10], spectrum sensing [11], and spectrum access [12,13], etc.

As an efficient model-free reinforcement learning, Q-Learning is the main method adopted in the above-mentioned works. The Q-Learning can identify an optimal policy for the finite Markov decision process (MDP), which is used to model decision making under uncertainty for the dynamic spectrum access problems. Recently, some novel dynamic spectrum resource allocation methods based on Q-learning were presented in [14–16]. In [14], a dynamic spectrum access (DSA) method base on mean opinion score (MOS) criterion was proposed. By extending the work of [14], papaer [15] proposed an QoE-drive DSA scheme based on deep Q-network. These methods were reviewed in the recent book chapter [16]. All these works show the power of Q-learning in resource management in CR networks.

Following these works, we further study DSA method for CR networks based on reinforce learning technique in this paper. In the considered DSA scheme, we aim at maximizing the sum rate of the secondary network (SN) subject to the SINR constraints of both the PU and SUs. By considering the situation of discrete set of SINR thresholds of SUs, the formulated DSA problem is nonconvex. After feasbility analysis, we develop a Q-learning based method to find the DSA solution intelligently. We demonstrates the effectiveness of the proposed intelligent DSA algorithm through numerical simulations.

2 System Model

2.1 System Model

In this paper, we consider an underlay spectrum sharing scenario consisting of an primary network (PN) and an secondary network (SN), as shown in Fig. 1. We assume that the PN shares the same channel spectrum with the SN in the up-link. The PN consists of a base station and a user, which are respectively referred as the primary base station (PBS) and the primary user (PU). The SN serves K secondary users (SUs) that are randomly located around a secondary base station (SBS). Under the underlay mode, interference links exist between SN and PU as shown in Fig. 1. The SUs are allowed to access the spectrum if the quality of signal-to-interference-plus-noise ratio (SINR) of the PU is not deteriorated lower than a predefined threshold after the access.

We assume the transmit power of the PU is constant during the transmission, considering that the PU is licensed and it has the privilege to access the channel. In order to satisfy the quality of service (QoS) of signal-to-interference-plus-noise ratio (SINR) requirement at the PBS, each SU needs to adapt its transmit parameters dynamically. We assume that the adaptive modulation and coding (AMC) technique is adopted on all the primary and secondary links, such that this dynamic parameter adjustment can be achieved by the CR systems.

We consider a Rayleigh quasi-static block-fading channel, where the channel state is constant over the transmission of a block, but independently and identically distributed from block to block. We assume that the global channel state information (CSI) can be obtained by users through feedback or learning and inferring. Denote SINR_0 as the SINR of the PU, and SINR_k as SINR of the k-th SU with $k = 1, 2, \ldots, K$. They can be written as

$$\text{SINR}_0 = \frac{G_0^P P_0}{\sigma^2 + \sum_{j=1}^{K} G_j^P P_j}, \tag{1}$$

$$\text{SINR}_k = \frac{G_k^S P_k}{\sigma^2 + G_0^S P_0 + \sum_{j=1\neq k}^{K} G_j^s P_j}, \tag{2}$$

where P_0 is the transmit power of the PU, P_j denotes the transmit power of the j-th SU, G_0^P denotes the channel gain between the PU and the

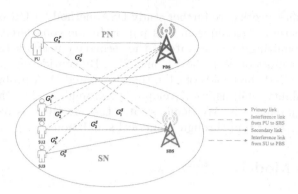

Fig. 1. System model

PBS, G_j^P denotes the channel gain between the j-th SU and the PBS, P_j denotes the transmit power of the j-th SU, G_j^S denotes the channel gain between the j-th SU and the SBS, and σ^2 denotes the noise power.

2.2   Problem Formulation of the Dynamic Spectrum Access

We aim to maximize the sum rate of all the users in the SU network while guaranteeing the SINR constraint of not only the PU but also the SUs. Let $\mathcal{K} = \{1, 2, \ldots, K\}$ denote the set of SUs in the CR network, this DSA process can be formulated as the following model

$$\max_{\{P_k, \beta_k, k \in \mathcal{K}\}} \sum_{k=1}^{K} r_k \tag{3}$$

$$\text{s.t.:} \quad \text{SINR}_0 \geq \beta_0,$$
$$\text{SINR}_k \geq \beta_i, \quad i \in \mathcal{K},$$

where β_0 is a predefined parameter by the PN, β_k is the SINR threshold for k-th SU, while the transmit powers and the SINR thresholds of SUs are to be determined. We have to adjust the SINR thresholds of the SUs to satisfying the SINR demand of the PU, meanwhile maximizing the sum rate.

In this work, in order to apply the machine learning technique, we assume the set of SINR thresholds is discrete. Since the feasible set is discrete, the formulated DSA problem is nonconvex. To find its optimal solution is generally NP-hard.

Before develop the algorithm, we first analyze the feasibility of the formulated problem, and reformulate it as an equivalent form, which is super to be optimized by reinforce learning method.

3   Feasibility Analysis and Problem Reformulation

In this section, we briefly analyze the feasibility of the DSA problem. Based on the analysis, the original problem is reformulated as an equivalent form.

3.1   Feasibility Analysis

The feasibility of problem (3) can be written as

$$\text{Find:} \quad \{P_k, \beta_k, \forall k\} \tag{4}$$
$$\text{s.t.:} \quad \text{SINR}_0 \geq \beta_0,$$
$$\text{SINR}_k \geq \beta_k, \ k \in \mathcal{K}.$$

A necessary condition for the feasibility of problem (4) can be established, when the SINR constraints are satisfied with equality, i.e.,

$$\text{Find:} \quad \{P_i, \beta_i, \forall i\} \tag{5}$$
$$\text{s.t.:} \quad \text{SINR}_0 = \beta_0,$$
$$\text{SINR}_k = \beta_k, \ k \in \mathcal{K}.$$

Then, a candidate solution for problem (5) can be derived as [14, 15, 17]

$$P_k = \frac{\psi_k(\sigma^2 + G_0^{(s)} P_0)}{G_k^{(s)}(1 - \sum_{j=1}^K \psi_j)}, \ k = 1, 2, \ldots, K, \tag{6}$$

where $\psi_j = (1 + \frac{1}{\beta_j})^{-1}$.

Obviously, to make the power allocation in (6) valid, it is necessary that

$$1 - \sum_{j=1}^K \psi_j > 0. \tag{7}$$

Recall that β_0 and P_0 are constants that determined by the PU, this condition can be satisfied by adjusting the values of β_j. Specifically, the condition (7) can always satisfied once the SINR targets are small enough.

Moreover, by substituting (6) into (4), the SINR constraints of (4) can be recast as

$$\sum_{j=1}^K \alpha_j \psi_j \leq 1, \tag{8}$$

where $\alpha_j \triangleq \dfrac{G_j^{(p)}(\sigma^2 + G_0^{(s)} P_0)}{G_j^{(s)}(G_0^{(p)} P_0/\beta_0 - \sigma^2)} + 1.$

3.2   Problem Reformulation

By combining the derivations on the SINR constraints (7) and (8), the sum rate maximization problem (3) can be reformulated as

$$\max_{\{\beta_k, k \in \mathcal{K}\}} \quad \sum_{k=1}^{K} \log_2(1 + c\beta_k) \tag{9a}$$

$$\text{s.t.} : \quad \sum_{j=1}^{K} \psi_j < 1 \,, \tag{9b}$$

$$\sum_{j=1}^{K} \alpha_j \psi_j \leq 1 \,, \tag{9c}$$

$$\alpha_j = \frac{G_j^{(p)}(\sigma^2 + G_0^{(s)} P_0)}{G_j^{(s)}(G_0^{(p)} P_0/\beta_0 - \sigma^2)} + 1 \,. \tag{9d}$$

Problem (9a, 9b, 9c, 9d) is still nonconvex with discrete feasible set. In the follow section, we develop a learning-based method to find the solution of this problem.

4   Dynamic Spectrum Allocation Based on Q-Learning

In the considered CR network, each SU plays the role of agent. An SU perceives the wireless environment characterized by the level of interference to the PU. The intelligence of RL turns the considered DSA problem (9a, 9b, 9c, 9d) into the MDP problem that the agents selects the SINR targets to maximize the expected reward.

4.1   Reinforcement Learning

Reinforcement learning (RL) is one of three branches in machine learning, together with the *supervised* and *unsupervised learning*. RL is focused on goal-directed learning from interaction [18]. In a typical RL setting, there is a learner and decision maker called *agent* interacts with the surrounding called *environment*. The problems of RL are associated with the *Markov decision process* (MDP). Specifically, let $\mathcal{S}$, $\mathcal{A}$ and $\mathcal{R}$ denote the *state* space, the *action* space and the *reward* space of the system, respectively. The *policy* of an agent is defined as a mapping from sates to probabilities of selecting each possible action, i.e., $\pi : \mathcal{S} \times \mathcal{A} \mapsto \mathbb{R}$. A separate Markov chain is associated to each policy. Based on this policy, the agent perceives a sate $S_t = s \in \mathcal{S}$ at a discrete time step t, and determines an action $A_t = a \in \mathcal{A}$ following the probability $\pi(a|s)$. At the following time step, the agent gains an *immediate reward* in the environment, which is denoted by $R_{t+1}(s, a) \in \mathcal{R}$.

The optimal policie that achieves the optimal action-value function is defined as

$$q_*(s, a) \triangleq \max_{\pi} q_\pi(s, a) \, , \forall s \in \mathcal{S}, a \in \mathcal{A}. \tag{10}$$

According to the *Bellman optimality equation*, the state-value under an optimal policy must equal the expected return for the best action, i.e.,

$$q_*(s, a) = \mathbb{E} \left[R_{t+1} + \gamma \max_{a'} q_*(s_{t+1}, a') | s_t = s, a_t = a \right] \tag{11}$$

4.2   Q-Learning

When the exact knowledge on the reward model and the complete probability distributions of all possible transitions is not completely known, the agent has to estimate the state-value through exploration in a step-by-step manner. The Q-learning algorithm belongs to the incremental dynamic programming (DP) [19], and can be constructed from the Temporal Differences (TD) method [20]. In specific, the learned action-value function (i.e., Q-value) of the Q-learning is updated based on

$$Q(s, a) \leftarrow Q(s, a) + \alpha[R(s, a) + \gamma \max_{a'} Q(s', a') - Q(s, a)] \, , \tag{12}$$

where $0 < \alpha < 1$ is the learning rate. Along with iterating, the Q-value approximates the optimal action-value function q_* in (11), independent of the policy being followed.

4.3   Definitions of Action and State Spaces

For the considered DSA model, we define the action as to select an SINR value for each user. The action space of SU k is defined as $\mathcal{A}^k = \{\beta_1^k, \dots, \beta_n^k\}$.

Similar with papers [14, 21], we define the state of the system at time step t as $s_t^k = (I_t, L_t)$, which indicates whether the interference constraints (9b) and (9c) are satisfied, where I_t and L_t are respectively defined as

$$I_t = \begin{cases} 0, & \text{if } \sum_{k=1}^{K} \psi_k(a_t^k) < 1, \\ 1, & \text{otherwise.} \end{cases} \tag{13}$$

$$L_t = \begin{cases} 0, & \text{if } \sum_{k=1}^{K} \alpha_k \psi_k(a_t^k) < 1, \\ 1, & \text{otherwise.} \end{cases} \tag{14}$$

Based on these definitions, the Q-table for the k-th user in the SN can be devised following Table 1.

Algorithm 1. Q-Learning based DSA Algorithm

Given: Channel state information $\{G_0^P, G_1^P, \ldots, G_K^P\}$ and $\{G_0^S, G_1^S, \ldots, G_K^S\}$, discount
  rate γ, learning rate α, reward function R, maximum episode number t_{max}, exploration probability ε;
Initialize: $Q_k(s, a) = 0, \forall s \in \mathcal{S}, a \in \mathcal{A}, k = 1, 2, \ldots, K; t = 0$;
Initialize: s_0;
1: **while** $t < t_{\max}$ **do**
2:     **if** rand$(1) < \varepsilon$ **then**
3:         Randomly select action $a_t^k, \forall k$;
4:     **else**
5:         Choose action $a_t^k = \arg\max_{a'} Q^k(s_t, a'), \forall k$;
6:     **end if**
7:     Observe state $s_{t+1} = (I, L)$ based on (13) and (14);
8:     **for** $k = 1 : K$ **do**
9:         Measure the reward $R_k(a_t)$ based on (15);
10:        Update Q-table: $Q_k(s_t, a_t) \leftarrow (1 - \alpha)Q_k(s_t, a_t) + \alpha[R_k(a_t) + \gamma\max_{a'} Q_k(s_{t+1}, a')]$;
11:    **end for**
12:    $t = t + 1$;
13: **end while**

Table 1. Q-table of the k-th SU.

(I, L)	a_1	a_2	$\cdots$	a_N
$s_1 = (00)$	$Q_k(s_1, a_1)$	$Q_k(s_1, a_2)$	$\cdots$	$Q_k(s_1, a_N)$
$s_2 = (01)$	$Q_k(s_2, a_1)$	$Q_k(s_2, a_2)$	$\cdots$	$Q_k(s_2, a_N)$
$s_3 = (10)$	$Q_k(s_3, a_1)$	$Q_k(s_3, a_2)$	$\cdots$	$Q_k(s_3, a_N)$
$s_4 = (11)$	$Q_k(s_4, a_1)$	$Q_k(s_4, a_2)$	$\cdots$	$Q_k(s_4, a_N)$

4.4   Reward Function

By observing the DSA problem (9a, 9b, 9c, 9d), the objective is to maximize the
sum rate of the SU. Therefore, the value of achievable rate can be straightforwardly used to design the immediate reward function. Specifically, for the k-th
user, the immediate reward function is constructed as

$$R_t^k = \begin{cases} \log_2(1 + a_t^k), & \text{if } s_t = s_1;, \\ -1, & \text{otherwise.} \end{cases} \tag{15}$$

When -1 is returned, it means that the actions taken are unsuccessful and the
interference constraints are violated. On the other hand, when the interference
constraints are satisfied, the achievable rate is used as the reward. This reward
function is simple and effective in achieving the goals of RL of the DSA problem.

4.5 The Q-Learning Algorithm for DSA

Based on the above analysis and definitions, the Q-learning algorithm can be applied for each SU. By collaborating with all the SUs in the SN, we finally propose the Q-learning based DSA method, which is summarized in Algorithm 1.

5 Simulation Results

In this section, we present the simulation results to validate the performance of the proposed Q-learning algorithm with modified reward function. The original algorithm proposed in [14] is used as the performance benchmark. The bandwidth is set as 10 MHz. The SINR of the PU is set to 10 dB. The Gaussian noise power is set to 1 nW. The transmission power of the PU is set to 10 mW. The channel gain follows a log-distance path loss model with a path loss exponent of 2.8. We assume that the PBS locates at the origin, and the PU locates randomly around the PBS within a circle with a radius of 50 m. The SBS locates around the PBS within the circle with a radius of 100 m. The SUs are located near the SBS within a circle of a radius of 30 m.

We first test the Q-learning base DSA algorithm for a network with $K = 4$ SUs. In this case, the SINR set (i.e., action set) is set as $\{-10 : 1 : 10\}$ dB. The parameters of Q-learning are set as $\alpha = 0.1$, $\gamma = 0.6$. For the ε-greedy policy, the parameter is set as $\varepsilon = e^{-\frac{t}{1000}}$. In Fig. 2, we plot the sum of the Q-tables versus iteration numbers. It is shown that the algorithm converges after about 5000 iterations.

The actions (SINR thresholds) determined by the algorithm are shown in Fig. 3 (a). It can be observed that SINR of PU is guaranteed since $SINR_0 > 10$ dB. The access SINR of the SUs are $\{-4, -6, -10, -9\}$, respectively. The rate achieved by each use is shown in Fig. 3 (b). The rate of the PU is about 36.3 Megabits per second (Mbps) and the sum rate of all the users in the SN is about 10.6 Mbps.

To further show the effectiveness of the Q-learning based DSA algorithm, we also provide experiments for a network with $K = 8$ SUs. The distribution of these users is shown in Fig. 4. In this case, the action space is set as $\{-20 : 1 : 10\}$ dB. The learning rate, discounting factor and ε are set the same as that in the above example. The convergence performance is shown in Fig. 5. It can be observed that the algorithm converges after about 15000 iterations. Compared with Fig. 2, the convergence speed becomes slow, since more users are need to be learn compare with the previous case.

In Fig. 6 (a), we show the SINR thresholds determined by the algorithm for the network with $K = 8$ SUs. Again, it is observed that SINR of PU is guaranteed, and the access SINRs of the SUs are $\{-19, -5, -18, -12, -7, -7, -12, -7\}$ dB, respectively. In Fig. 6 (b), the rates of the users are illustrated. It is shown that the rate of the PU is about 53.1 Mbps and the sum rate of all the users in the SN is about 13.4 Mbps. Therefore, the Q-learning based DSA algorithm can intelligently determine the SINR thresholds

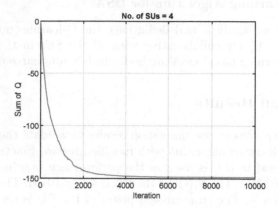

Fig. 2. Convergence of the Q-learning based DSA algorithm for a network with 4 SUs.

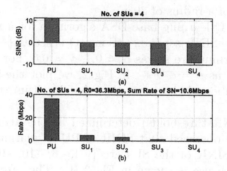

Fig. 3. SINR thresholds and rates determined by the Q-learning based DSA algorithm for a network with 4 SUs.

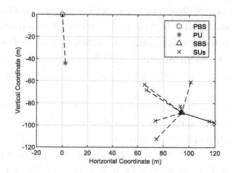

Fig. 4. Distribution of the users of a CR network with 8 SUs.

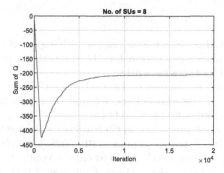

Fig. 5. Convergence of the Q-learning based DSA algorithm for a network with 8 SUs.

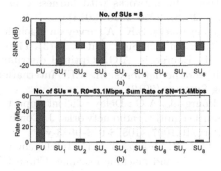

Fig. 6. SINR thresholds and rates determined by the Q-learning based DSA algorithm for a network with 8 SUs.

of the SUs in the secondary network. Under such SINR thresholds, the quality of service of the PU can be guaranteed.

6   Conclusion

This paper studied an intelligent dynamic spectrum allocation algorithm for uplink underlay cognitive networks based on reinforcement learning. The considered dynamic spectrum allocation scheme was to maximize the sum rate of the secondary network while satisfying the quality of services of not only the primary user but also the secondary users. This problem was formulated as a nonconvex SINR threshold optimization problem, which is challenging to solve. We resorted to the Q-learning method to develop an intelligent algorithm to find the solution automatically. The effectiveness of the proposed method was verified through numerical simulations.

References

1. Sun, S., Rappaport, T.S., Shafi, M., Tang, P., Zhang, J., Smith, P.J.: Propagation models and performance evaluation for 5G millimeter-wave bands. IEEE Trans. Veh. Technol. **67**(9), 8422–8439 (2018)
2. Lu, J., Cai, Z., Wang, X., Zhang, L., Li, P., He, Z.: User social activity-based routing for cognitive radio networks. Pers. Ubiquit. Comput. **22**(3), 471–487 (2018). https://doi.org/10.1007/s00779-018-1114-9
3. Wang, W., et al.: Joint precoding optimization for secure SWIPT in UAV-aided NOMA networks. IEEE Trans. Commun. **68**, 5028–5040 (2020)
4. Clancy, C., Hecker, J., Stuntebeck, E., O'Shea, T.: Applications of machine learning to cognitive radio networks. IEEE Wirel. Commun. **14**(4), 47–52 (2007)
5. Cai, Z., Ji, S., He, J., Wei, L., Bourgeois, A.G.: Distributed and asynchronous data collection in cognitive radio networks with fairness consideration. IEEE Trans. Parallel Distrib. Syst. **25**(8), 2020–2029 (2014)
6. Bkassiny, M., Li, Y., Jayaweera, S.K.: A survey on machine-learning techniques in cognitive radios. IEEE Commun. Surv. Tutor. **15**(3), 1136–1159 (2012)
7. Cai, Z., Ji, S., He, J., Bourgeois, A.G.: Optimal distributed data collection for asynchronous cognitive radio networks. In: IEEE International Conference on Distributed Computing Systems (2012)
8. Cai, Z., Duan, Y., Bourgeois, A.G.: Delay efficient opportunistic routing in asynchronous multi-channel cognitive radio networks. J. Comb. Optim. **29**(4), 815–835 (2013). https://doi.org/10.1007/s10878-013-9623-y
9. Zhou, X., Sun, M., Li, G.Y., Juang, B.-H.F.: Intelligent wireless communications enabled by cognitive radio and machine learning. China Commun. **15**(12), 16–48 (2018)
10. Aprem, A., Murthy, C.R., Mehta, N.B.: Transmit power control policies for energy harvesting sensors with retransmissions. IEEE J. Sel. Topics Signal Process. **7**(5), 895–906 (2013)
11. Reddy, Y.B., Detecting primary signals for efficient utilization of spectrum using Q-learning. In: Fifth International Conference on Information Technology: New Generations (ITNG 2008), pp. 360–365. IEEE (2008)
12. Venkatraman, P., Hamdaoui, B., Guizani, M.: Opportunistic bandwidth sharing through reinforcement learning. IEEE Trans. Veh. Technol. **59**(6), 3148–3153 (2010)
13. Galindo-Serrano, A., Giupponi, L.: Distributed Q-learning for aggregated interference control in cognitive radio networks. IEEE Trans. Veh. Technol. **59**(4), 1823–1834 (2010)
14. Mohammadi F.S., Kwasinski, A.: QoE-driven integrated heterogeneous traffic resource allocation based on cooperative learning for 5G cognitive radio networks. In: IEEE 5G World Forum (5GWF), pp. 244–249. IEEE (2018)
15. Shah-Mohammadi, F., Kwasinski, A.: Deep reinforcement learning approach to QoE-driven resource allocation for spectrum underlay in cognitive radio networks. In: IEEE International Conference on Communications Workshops (ICC Workshops), pp. 1–6. IEEE (2018)
16. Kwasinski, A., Wang, W., Mohammadi, F.S.: Reinforcement learning for resource allocation in cognitive radio networks. In: Machine Learning for Future Wireless Communications, pp. 27–44 (2020)
17. Pietrzyk, S., Janssen, G.J.M.: Radio resource allocation for cellular networks based on OFDMA with QoS guarantees. In: IEEE Global Telecommunications Conference GLOBECOM 2004, vol. 4, pp. 2694–2699. IEEE (2004)

18. Sutton, R.S., Barto, A.G.: Reinforcement Learning: An Introduction, 2nd edn. The MIT Press, Cambridge (2018)
19. Watkins, C.J.C.H., Dayan, P.: Q-learning. Mach. Learn. **8**(3–4), 279–292 (1992)
20. Sutton, R.S.: Learning to predict by the methods of temporal differences. Mach. Learn. **3**(1), 9–44 (1988)
21. Mendonca, M.R.F., Bernardino, H.S., Neto, R.F.: Reinforcement learning with optimized reward function for stealth applications. Entertainment Comput. **25**, 37–47 (2018)

A Trajectory-Privacy Protection Method Based on Location Similarity of Query Destinations in Continuous LBS Queries

Lu Zhang[1], Saide Zhu[2], Fengyin Li[1], Ruinian Li[3], Jing Meng[1]([✉]), and Wei Li[2]([✉])

[1] Qufu Normal University, Rizhao, China
qfmj@163.com
[2] Georgia State University, Atlanta, USA
wli28@gsu.edu
[3] Bowling Green State University, Bowling Green, USA

Abstract. In the continuous location-based service (LBS) queries, the trajectory k-anonymity method that incorporates user's moving trend is becoming popular because of its high quality of service (QoS). The existing works often apply user's moving direction to represent the user's moving trend. However, the query destinations of the users with closer moving directions are not necessarily closer. As a result, the users in a cloaked set may diverge with the proceeding of the continuous queries, leading to large cloaked areas as well as a reduction of QoS. Therefore, in this paper, a new concept named "location similarity of query destination (LS-QD)", is proposed to reflect user's global moving trend. By incorporating LS-QD, we develop a novel trajectory k-anonymity method for continuous LBS queries. Our system architecture utilizes a quadtree model with a pyramid structure to construct the user cloaked sets conveniently. Both theoretical analysis and simulation experiments are carried out to evaluate the robustness and security performance of our proposed method. Compared with other existing methods, our LS-QD based k-anonymity method can reduce the cloaking area and cloaking time while increasing the cloaking success ratio by about 40%–70%, which demonstrates its superiority in guaranteeing QoS for continuous LBS queries.

Keywords: Continuous LBS queries · Trajectory k-anonymity · User's moving trend · Trajectory privacy

1 Introduction

With the development of smart mobile devices and various applications established on mobile social networks [1–3], privacy-preserving issues in this field are attracted with much attention [4–12]. A number of privacy protection methods

---

L. Zhang and S. Zhu—Both authors contributed equally to this work.

© Springer Nature Switzerland AG 2020
D. Yu et al. (Eds.): WASA 2020, LNCS 12384, pp. 704–715, 2020.
https://doi.org/10.1007/978-3-030-59016-1_58

in social networks have been proposed in recent years [13–19]. In particular, location-based services (LBS) is one of the most popular applications for mobile users where users can use LBS to query some point of interests (POIs) nearby or provide information for some social activities [20–23]. Although LBS brings convenience to people's lives, it also yields severe risks of privacy leakage. Typically, mobile users are required to submit their location information to untrusted LBS providers (LSP) where the malicious LSP may use the users' location information in the queries to infer sensitive personal information such as religious activities and health/living habits. Especially, in the case of a continuous LBS query, the malicious LSP can track a user's route to the destination to infer the user's trajectory. By further analyzing the trajectory, the LSP can infer the user's workplace, home address, and lifestyle, etc, which may lead to some criminal activities. Therefore, it is essential to protect the user's trajectory in continuous LBS queries [24–26].

As is well known, trajectory k-anonymity is a popular method to preserve the user's trajectory-privacy in continuous LBS queries, in which k trajectories are stored in the same cloaked set such that LBS providers cannot distinguish a certain user's location from other $k - 1$ users [27, 28]. The earliest method of trajectory k-anonymity is implemented based on the user's initial query location [29, 30]. For example, Chow et al. proposed a k-sharing region scheme that requires each cloaking region contains k identical users in the whole continuous query process, so that the attacker cannot recognize the user's location [30]. Xiao et al. designed a δ_p-privacy model and a δ_q-distortion model considering the user's initial location and speed [31]. Y. Wang et al. proposed a velocity dynamic cloaking algorithm (VDCA), where the cloaked set is constructed of the users with similar speed and acceleration [32]. However, the cloaked set in above methods are constructed only based on the users' initial status, which may cause the users cloaked set diverge in the subsequent continuous query, leading to a decrease of QoS [33]. To construct more effective cloaked sets, several solutions based on the trajectory prediction have been developed. Shin et al. proposed the idea of trajectory partitioning, which divides the continuous request into multiple shorter trajectories [34]. Xu et al. used $k - 1$ historical trajectories to construct cloaking regions [35]. Hwang et al. proposed a time-obfuscation technique that randomizes the order of user query times to prevent malicious users from reconstructing trajectory [36]. Though these methods can construct more effective cloaked sets compared with previous introduced methods, they will result in large computational and storage overhead when predicting and processing trajectories. During recent years, researchers have developed another trajectory k-anonymity method considering the user's moving trend, where the cloaked set consists of users with similar moving trend. Shin et al. firstly proposed the idea of incorporating user's moving direction into the anonymous process [37]. Followed by this work, Yankson et al. introduced the direction speed dynamic cloaking algorithm (DSDCA), which collects users with similar moving direction, similar speed, and traveling with the same transport mode for cloaking [38]. Ma et al. proposed a cooperative k-anonymity method based on the prediction of user moving direction [39]. Recently, Al-Dhubhani *et al.* clearly pointed out that grouping users with similar moving trends can effectively reduce the impact of the cloaking area expansion in the continuous LBS queries [40]. Compared with other methods without incorporating the user's moving trend, this kind of methods achieve better QoS and provide higher level of privacy preservation. However, the user's moving trend is generally determined by their moving directions without considering the location information of query destinations. In fact, as shown in Fig. 1, the distances among query destinations of users with close moving directions may be large, which leads to the divergence of users in the cloaked set in later stage of continuous queries due to the different query destinations. As a result, the cloaking area may become large or need to be rebuilt, which will reduce QoS and increase the system overhead.

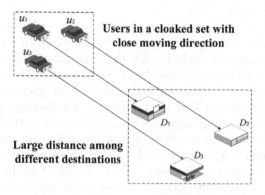

Fig. 1. The construction of cloaked set with user's moving direction

Based on the above analysis, we find that the location information of query destinations is an excellent indicator when representing user's global moving trend. Therefore, in this paper, we take the distances among the destinations into account and develop a trajectory-privacy protection method combining the location similarity of query destination (LS-QD) to protect the privacy of trajectory in the continuous LBS queries. The main contributions of this work are as follows:

- We propose the concept of "location similarity of query destination (LS-QD)" and establish a trajectory-privacy protection system architecture with incorporating the LS-QD for the continuous LBS queries.
- Based on our system model, the trajectory cloaking algorithms are designed to construct the cloaked sets for the new and subsequent active queries.
- Security analysis and simulation experiments are performed to evaluate the security of our proposed method and demonstrate its superiority on improving the QoS.

The rest of this paper is organized as follows. The concept of LS-QD and system architecture with a quadtree structure are introduced in Sect. 2. Section 3 details the design of the cloaking algorithms for new query and active query. The theoretical security analysis and the simulation experiments are shown in Sect. 4 and Sect. 5, respectively. At last, Sect. 6 includes the discussion and conclusions.

2 System Model

2.1 System Architecture

Our system contains three basic components: mobile user, trusted anonymizing server (AS), and LBS provider. In addition, a hash table in the Cloaked Repository located in AS is built to store the coordinates of interest places. By referring to this hash table, the cloaking algorithm with LS-QD can quickly find the coordinates of any query destination. When a mobile user needs the LBS service, he can send the query request to AS. The query request is formatted as:

$$Q = <uid, loc, T_{init}, T_{exp}, \ con, \ profile>, \tag{1}$$

where uid is the identifier of the user, loc represents the user's location (longitude, latitude), T_{init} represents the query initiation time, T_{exp} is the query expiration time, and con is the query content. The lifetime of this query can be defined by the difference between T_{init} and T_{exp}. After a user submits his new query request, the cloaking algorithm in AS will construct the cloaked set for the new query according to the destination information from the cloaked respiratory and the user's privacy-protection requirements. Then, AS submits the cloaking area covered by the cloaked set to the LSP, while saving the cloaked set to the Cloaked Repository for the subsequent usage. If an active query (existing query) is created, the user just needs to update his location loc using the uid, without resubmitting the query request Q. Once the user's location is updated, the cloaking algorithm will first extract the cloaked set of his new query from the Cloaked Repository to initialize the cloaked set for the active query. Then, the final cloaked set for the active query will be constructed by the corresponding cloaking algorithm. Finally, the final cloaking area is sent to the LSP.

When the LSP receives the cloaking area of a query, it will return the candidate results to the AS through the query processing. And then, the AS uses Results Refiner to refine the candidate results and returns the final query results to the mobile user. The goal of this work is to hide the trajectory information of mobile query users. The query processing technology used by LSP is beyond the scope of this paper.

2.2 Definition

Three definitions related to LS-QD were introduced in this section.

Definition 1. *Trajectory. A trajectory is a sequence of time-ordered geographic locations of a moving object. It is represented by:*

$$T = \{uid, (x_1, y_1, t_1), (x_2, y_2, t_2), ..., (x_n, y_n, t_n)\}(t_1 < t_2 < ... < t_n), \tag{2}$$

where uid represents the unique identity of a mobile user, and (x_i, y_i, t_i) indicates the location (x_i, y_i) of the mobile user at time t_i.

Definition 2. *Trajectory set S. The trajectory set is represented by $S = \{T_1, T_2, ..., T_r\}$, where each $T_i, i \in \{1, ..., r\}$ is a trajectory defined by Eq. 2. A trajectory k-anonymity set consists of k trajectories respectively from the querying user and other $k - 1$ users.*

Definition 3. *Location similarity of the query destination (LS-QD). Given two users u_i and u_j, their query destination coordinates are (x_i, y_i) and (x_j, y_j), respectively. Here, the Euclidean distance is used to represent the LS-QD between the two users:*

$$L(u_i, u_j) = \sqrt{(x_i - x_j)^2 + (y_i - y_j)^2}. \tag{3}$$

The smaller L indicates higher location-similarity between two query destinations. For example, if given $L_1 = 1\,\text{km}$ and $L_2 = 5\,\text{km}$, we say that the destination with $L_1 = 1\,\text{km}$ has a higher location similarity of query destinations than the two with $L_2 = 5\,\text{km}$.

2.3   Quadtree Model

To construct the cloaked set considering the LS-QD for a query, an improved Casper model was developed, illustrated in Fig. 2. Here, the improved model is called a quadtree structure. The geospatial region used for constructing a cloaked set is designed as a large rectangle, which is the 0th layer of the quadtree, i.e. root. This area is recursively divided into multiple layers, and each layer consists of 4 separate cells with the same size as shown in the spatial region of Fig. 2. In other words, each parent node is split into 4 children nodes to form a quadtree structure. Each cell in a geographic region is a node in a quadtree, represented by (cid, N), where cid is the unique identifier of the cell, and N is the number of users in this cell. To construct a cloaked set of the query user, a cell list $L(cid, uidlink)$ is established, in which the pointer $uidlink$ links to a set C formed by all users that have not been anonymized in the user's current cell and obviously $|C| \leq N$. In addition, we use a hash table $H(uid, cid)$ to establish the relationship between the users and the cells they are located. Moreover, the user's privacy profile is also tracked according to the query, which contains two data items of k and A_{min}: k represents k-anonymity, A_{min} is the predefined smallest cloaking area for the user.

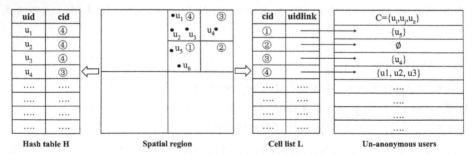

Fig. 2. The quadtree structure

3 Algorithm Design

Based on the developed system architecture and the improved quadtree model introduced above, the cloaking algorithm with LS-QD for the continuous LBS query is detailly designed. The flowchart of this algorithm is shown in Fig. 3.

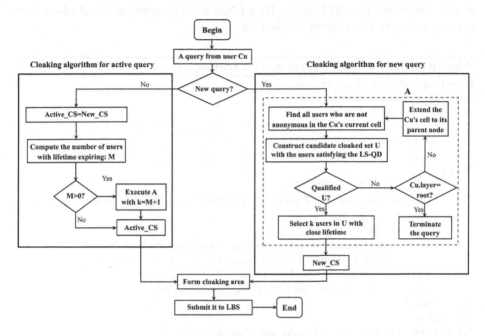

Fig. 3. Flowchart of cloaking algorithm with LS-QD

Initially, when a user Cu initiates a query, he first submits the query contents to the AS. As the AS receives the query, it then makes a judgment on whether the query is a new one. If the query is new, part A (shown in Fig. 3) of the algorithm for new queries will be executed. Firstly, the algorithm finds all users who are not anonymous in the Cu's current cell by checking the information in the cell list, and construct the candidate cloaked set U with users who satisfying the LS-QD. If the set U is satisfied, i.e. it collects enough users, then the algorithm selects k users with a similar lifetime from it to form the cloaked set for the new query, called New_CS. Otherwise, the Cu's cell is extended to its parent node for finding the required users in a larger spatial region. This process will be continuously executed until the New_CS is achieved or some query failure happens (i.e. not finding enough users even in the root layer).

If the initiating query is an active query, the cloaking algorithm for the active query will be executed. The cloaked set of the new query for user Cu is extracted from the cloaked repository firstly and was used to initialize the cloaked set Active_CS for the active query. If the Active_CS is not qualified, i.e. the query exceeds its expire time T_{exp}, then part A in Fig. 3 will be executed to find more qualified users for new queries. No matter for the new query or the active query, as the cloaked set is finally generated, the corresponding cloaking area is computed and submitted to the LSP.

The pseudo-codes of the cloaking algorithm with LS-QD is listed in Algorithm 1. In this algorithm: *BuildCandidateCloakSet()* is used to construct the candidate cloaked set U in the user's current cell; *SelectKUser()* is used to select k users satisfying LS-QD from U. *FormCloakArea()* computes the cloaking area corresponding to the current cloaked set.

Algorithm 1. Cloaking algorithm with LS-QD

Input: $quadtree, k, A_{min}, cid, uid$
Output: Cloaking Area C_area
 1: **if** query is new **then**
 2:     $U = BuildCandidateCloakSet(quadtree, k, A_{min}, cid, uid)$
 3:     $New\_CS = SelectKUser(U, k, uid)$
 4:     $C\_area \leftarrow FormCloakArea(cid, k, New\_CS)$
 5: **else**
 6:     $Active\_CS = New\_CS$
 7:     Compute the number of users with lifetime expiring: M, then $Active\_CS = Active\_CS - Musers$
 8:     **if** $M \neq 0$ **then**
 9:         $cid \leftarrow$ Obtain the cid corresponding to uid from hash table $H()$
10:         $U = BuildCandidateCloakSet(quadtree, M + 1, A_{min}, cid, uid)$
11:         $UK \leftarrow SelectKUser(U, M + 1, uid)$
12:         $Active\_CS \leftarrow FormCloakArea(cid, k, Active\_CS)$
13:     **end if**
14: **end if**
15: **return** The area of the cloaked set C_area

---

4   Security Analysis

The trajectory privacy protection method proposed in this paper should be built with a fully trusted AS. Therefore, the security analysis in this section focuses on the query tracking attack that occurred on LSP. Here, we assume the attackers know the background information of the user's locations and its cloaked sets during his query lifetime.

In continuous queries, users continuously report their locations to LSP. Query tracking attacks can link consecutive time snapshots together to identify a query issuer among all users in its cloaked set. Let K_g represent the number of common users found in all intersection of cloaked sets for consecutive snapshots in a continuous query, the probability of the attacker identifying the user is $\frac{1}{K_g}$. Based on the theoretical analysis of our proposed trajectory k-anonymity method with LS-QD in Sect. 1, the users in a cloaked set have a similar moving trajectory in their query lifetime (which will also be verified by the simulation experiments in the next section). As a result, the probability of most users in the current cloaked set that will be replaced in the subsequent snapshots is small, leading to a small value of $\frac{1}{K_g}$. Further, we can set a threshold τ to determine the number of users with expiring lifetime in our algorithm. If the total number of users to be replaced in the cloaked set is greater than τ, the current query will be terminated. Therefore, because of the incorporation of LS-QD in our proposed k-anonymous method, the probability of most users in the cloaked set that will be updated in the subsequent active queries is small, thus preventing the query tracking attack. Through the above analysis, our proposed method has strong security on fighting against the query tracking attack in the continuous LBS queries due to the incorporation of LS-QD in our proposed k-anonymous construction strategy.

5   Experiments and Results

To evaluate our proposed LS-QD based trajectory-privacy protection method in continuous LBS queries, a series of simulation experiments were performed. Specifically, Thomas Brinkhoff Network-based Generator of Moving Objects was used to generate mobile users with the medium speed in 1000 unit time, which is a common speed used in experiments [41]. The input of the generator is the road map of Oldenburg, Germany, with an area of about $16 * 16\,\text{km}^2$. In our work, we make comparisons between our proposed method, robust spatial cloaked algorithm (RSCA) [26] and K^{LD_ϵ} [42]. RSCA is a typical k-anonymity method without considering the user's moving direction, its main idea is to group a set of mobile users together such that the cloaked query region for each mobile user in a group G is the spatial region that includes all users in G. K^{LD_ϵ} takes the user's moving direction into account during the anonymity process. In this method, it uses a normal distribution to indicate the matching probability of moving direction among users, and thus estimating the parameters in the normal distribution. The algorithms selects 500 random samples and computed the variance by maximum likelihood estimation. In our following experiments, we discussed the optimal range of LS-QD by performing a series of tests.

5.1   The Optimal Range of LS-QD

In our method, the Euler distance L between the query destinations of the current user and other users are defined to evaluate the LS-QD among users. Generally, smaller L indicates a larger similarity. However, too small L cannot provide enough users to construct the cloaked set, resulting in a query failure, and too large L causes a large average cloaking area with the processing of queries because users in the cloaked set constructed with weak LS-QD will become dispersed over time. As a result, we tested the range of L from 1 km to 5.5 km and found that when L lies in [2 km, 4 km], the cloaking areas are relatively small and stable for all snapshots. Therefore, an optimal range [2 km, 4 km] of L is determined by our observations, which is adopted in the following experiments.

5.2   Effects of K-Anonymity of LS-QD

In this section, we verify the k-anonymity performance of our proposed LS-QD based trajectory-privacy protection method under different values of k, and the comparisons with RSCA and K^{LD_ϵ} were also performed. Figure 4(a) and 4(b)

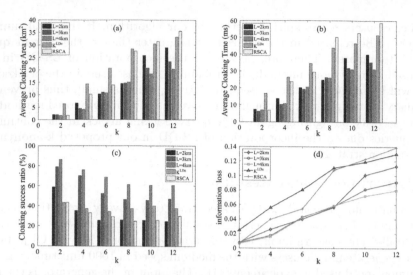

Fig. 4. K-anonymity evaluations. (a) Average cloaking areas; (b) Average cloaking times; (c) Cloaking success ratios; (d) Information loss ratios.

show the bar graphs of the average cloaking area and average cloaking time of different methods. Compared with the RSCA and the K^{LD_ϵ}, our proposed LS-QD based method has the smallest average cloaking areas which is about 52–71% of K^{LD_ϵ} and RSCA, and the least average cloaking time is about 57–65% of K^{LD_ϵ} and RSCA. These results demonstrated that the LS-QD based method can provide better QoS. Noticeably, the cloaking areas generated by our method generally become larger with the increasing of k value. This phenomenon is reasonable because larger k can enhance the privacy-protection level, thereby larger area will be required to form a cloaked set satisfying the query demands. This also increases the user's cloaking time, as can be seen from Fig. 4(b). Figure 4(c) shows the histogram of the cloaking success ratio (CSR) using different methods, which is the ratio of the number of successfully anonymized trajectories to all transmitted trajectories. CSR can reflect the ability of a cloaking algorithm satisfying the anonymous requests. From this subfigure, it can be seen that the cloaking success ratio of our proposed method was improved dramatically: approximately 1.7 times the RSCA and 1.4 times of the K^{LD_ϵ}. The results verify the advantages of our method in the continuous LBS query from mobile users. It can be also seen that with the increasing of k, the success rates of anonymity of all methods are decreasing, due to the higher requirements of larger k.

Data utility is the availability of location information for publishing, and it is inversely proportional to the information loss. Here, it is measured by the information loss rate, which is defined by the ratio between the area of the trajectory k-anonymity and the area of the entire space. Figure 4(d) shows the curves of information loss ratios under different k with different methods. As can be seen, our proposed method has lower information loss ratios for all k values than the RSCA and K^{LD_e}. Moreover, the information loss rate increases with the increasing of k value, which is because larger k typically requires a larger cloaking area. Fortunately, when k is small than 8 (which is enough generally), the information loss rate of our method keeps at a low level (<0.06), satisfying the user requirements completely. This experiment demonstrates that our proposed method can provide higher data utility. Generally speaking, the larger cloaking area for k-anonymity requires the LSP to spend more time to retrieve the result set, resulting in a long response time for users to obtain the service. Our method can achieve user anonymity in a large range of k with less cloaking area and cloaking time, and thus providing a better QoS.

6 Conclusions

In this paper, a trajectory-privacy protection method based on LS-QD is proposed. A system model is also developed with an improved quadtree structure incorporating the LS-QD. Our simulation experiments on different datasets demonstrate the effectiveness and feasibility of our proposed method and it is clear that our proposed method achieves higher QoS for trajectory-privacy protection in the continuous LBS queries than the state-of-art research. Security analysis is also conducted to show the strong resistance against the query tracking attack. In our future work, we will consider more attributes of destination such as the semantic similarity of query destination. Moreover, we will consider improving our method by removing the assumption of fully trusting the anonymous server.

References

1. Yan, B., Yu, J., Yang, M., Jiang, H., Wan, Z., Ni, L.: A novel distributed social internet of things service recommendation scheme based on LSH forest. Pers. Ubiquit. Comput. 1–14 (2019). https://doi.org/10.1007/s00779-019-01283-4
2. Song, T., Li, R., Mei, B., Yu, J., Xing, X., Cheng, X.: A privacy preserving communication protocol for IoT applications in smart homes. IEEE Internet Things J. **4**(6), 1844–1852 (2017)
3. Xing, K., Hu, C., Yu, J., Cheng, X., Zhang, F.: Mutual privacy preserving k-means clustering in social participatory sensing. IEEE Trans. Ind. Inform. **13**(4), 2066–2076 (2017)
4. Pu, Y., et al.: Two secure privacy-preserving data aggregation schemes for IoT. Wirel. Commun. Mob. Comput. **2019**, 3 985 232:1–3 985 232:11 (2019)
5. Ni, L., Li, C., Wang, X., Jiang, H., Yu, J.: DP-MCDBSCAN: differential privacy preserving multi-core DBSCAN clustering for network user data. IEEE Access **6**, 21053–21063 (2018)
6. He, Z., Cai, Z., Yu, J.: Latent-data privacy preserving with customized data utility for social network data. IEEE Trans. Veh. Technol. **67**(1), 665–673 (2018)
7. Cai, Z., Zheng, X., Yu, J.: A differential-private framework for urban traffic flows estimation via taxi companies. IEEE Trans. Ind. Inform. **15**(12), 6492–6499 (2019)
8. Cai, Z., Zheng, X.: A private and efficient mechanism for data uploading in smart cyber-physical systems. IEEE Trans. Netw. Sci. Eng. **7**(2), 766–775 (2018)

9. Liang, Y., Cai, Z., Han, Q., Li, Y.: Location privacy leakage through sensory data. Secur. Commun. Netw. **2017**, 7 576 307:1–7 576 307:12 (2017)
10. Zhu, S., Cai, Z., Hu, H., Li, Y., Li, W.: zkCrowd: a hybrid blockchain-based crowdsourcing platform. IEEE Trans. Ind. Inform. **16**(6), 4196–4205 (2019)
11. Li, K., Tian, L., Li, W., Luo, G., Cai, Z.: Incorporating social interaction into three-party game towards privacy protection in IoT. Comput. Netw. **150**, 90–101 (2019)
12. Zheng, X., Cai, Z.: Privacy-preserved data sharing towards multiple parties in industrial IoTs. IEEE J. Sel. Areas Commun. **38**(5), 968–979 (2020)
13. Cai, Z., He, Z., Guan, X., Li, Y.: Collective data-sanitization for preventing sensitive information inference attacks in social networks. IEEE Trans. Dependable Secure Comput. **15**(4), 577–590 (2018)
14. Zheng, X., Cai, Z., Li, Y.: Data linkage in smart Internet of Things systems: a consideration from a privacy perspective. IEEE Commun. Mag. **56**(9), 55–61 (2018)
15. Liang, Y., Cai, Z., Yu, J., Han, Q., Li, Y.: Deep learning based inference of private information using embedded sensors in smart devices. IEEE Netw. **32**(4), 8–14 (2018)
16. Zheng, X., Cai, Z., Li, J., Gao, H.: Location-privacy-aware review publication mechanism for local business service systems. In: 2017 IEEE Conference on Computer Communications, INFOCOM 2017, Atlanta, GA, USA, 1–4 May 2017, pp. 1–9 (2017)
17. Zheng, X., Cai, Z., Yu, J., Wang, C., Li, Y.: Follow but no track: privacy preserved profile publishing in cyber-physical social systems. IEEE Internet Things J. **4**(6), 1868–1878 (2017)
18. Li, W., Hu, C., Song, T., Yu, J., Xing, X., Cai, Z.: Privacy-preserving data collection in context-aware applications. In: 2018 IEEE Symposium on Privacy-Aware Computing, PAC 2018, Washington, DC, USA, 26–28 September 2018, pp. 75–85 (2018)
19. Li, W., Song, T., Li, Y., Ma, L., Yu, J., Cheng, X.: A hierarchical game framework for data privacy preservation in context-aware IoT applications. In: IEEE Symposium on Privacy-Aware Computing, PAC 2017, Washington, DC, USA, 1–4 August 2017, pp. 176–177 (2017)
20. Wang, Y., Xia, Y., Hou, J., Gao, S., Nie, X., Wang, Q.: A fast privacy-preserving framework for continuous location-based queries in road networks. J. Netw. Comput. Appl. **53**, 57–73 (2015)
21. Yi, X., Paulet, R., Bertino, E., Varadharajan, V.: Practical approximate k nearest neighbor queries with location and query privacy. IEEE Trans. Knowl. Data Eng. **28**(6), 1546–1559 (2016)
22. Zhang, J., Yuan, Y., Wang, X., Ni, L., Yu, J., Zhang, M.: RPAR: location privacy preserving via repartitioning anonymous region in mobile social network. Secur. Commun. Netw. **2018**, 6 829 326:1–6 829 326:10 (2018)
23. Cai, Z., He, Z.: Trading private range counting over big IoT data. In: 39th IEEE International Conference on Distributed Computing Systems, ICDCS 2019, Dallas, TX, USA, 7–10 July 2019, pp. 144–153 (2019)
24. Zhang, J., Wang, X., Yuan, Y., Ni, L.: RcDT: privacy preservation based on r-constrained dummy trajectory in mobile social networks. IEEE Access **7**, 90 476–90 486 (2019)
25. Zhang, S., Wang, G., Liu, Q., Abawajy, J.H.: A trajectory privacy-preserving scheme based on query exchange in mobile social networks. Soft Comput. **22**(18), 6121–6133 (2017). https://doi.org/10.1007/s00500-017-2676-6

26. Zhang, L., Jin, C., Huang, H., Fu, X., Wang, R.: A trajectory privacy preserving scheme in the CANNQ service for IoT. Sensors **19**(9), 2190 (2019)
27. Palanisamy, B., Liu, L.: Attack-resilient mix-zones over road networks: architecture and algorithms. IEEE Trans. Mob. Comput. **14**(3), 495–508 (2015)
28. Yang, Z., Yang, M., Ning, B.: User relationship privacy protection on trajectory data. In: Liang, Q., Liu, X., Na, Z., Wang, W., Mu, J., Zhang, B. (eds.) CSPS 2018. LNEE, vol. 517, pp. 1038–1045. Springer, Singapore (2020). https://doi.org/10.1007/978-981-13-6508-9_126
29. Chow, C., Mokbel, M.F.: Trajectory privacy in location-based services and data publication. SIGKDD Explor. **13**(1), 19–29 (2011)
30. Chow, C.-Y., Mokbel, M.F.: Enabling private continuous queries for revealed user locations. In: Papadias, D., Zhang, D., Kollios, G. (eds.) SSTD 2007. LNCS, vol. 4605, pp. 258–275. Springer, Heidelberg (2007). https://doi.org/10.1007/978-3-540-73540-3_15
31. Pan, X., Meng, X., Xu, J.: Distortion-based anonymity for continuous queries in location-based mobile services. In: 17th ACM SIGSPATIAL International Symposium on Advances in Geographic Information Systems, ACM-GIS 2009, Seattle, Washington, USA, Proceedings, November, vol. 2009, pp. 256–265 (2009). pp. 4–6
32. Wang, Y., He, L.P., Peng, J., Zhang, T.T., Li, H.Z.: Privacy preserving for continuous query in location based services. In: 18th IEEE International Conference on Parallel and Distributed Systems, ICPADS 2012, Singapore, 17–19 December 2012, pp. 213–220 (2012)
33. Ye, A., Li, Y., Xu, L.: A novel location privacy-preserving scheme based on l-queries for continuous LBS. Comput. Commun. **98**, 1–10 (2017)
34. Shin, H., Vaidya, J., Atluri, V., Choi, S.: Ensuring privacy and security for LBS through trajectory partitioning. In: Eleventh International Conference on Mobile Data Management, MDM 2010, Kanas City, Missouri, USA, 23–26 May 2010, pp. 224–226 (2010)
35. Xu, T., Cai, Y.: Exploring historical location data for anonymity preservation in location-based services. In: INFOCOM 2008. 27th IEEE International Conference on Computer Communications, Joint Conference of the IEEE Computer and Communications Societies, Phoenix, AZ, USA, 13–18 April 2008, pp. 547–555 (2008)
36. Hwang, R., Hsueh, Y., Chung, H.: A novel time-obfuscated algorithm for trajectory privacy protection. IEEE Trans. Serv. Comput. **7**(2), 126–139 (2014)
37. Shin, H., Vaidya, J., Atluri, V.: Anonymization models for directional location based service environments. Comput. Secur. **29**(1), 59–73 (2010)
38. Gustav, Y.H., Wang, Y., Domenic, M.K., Zhang, F., Memon, I.: Velocity similarity anonymization for continuous query location based services. In: 2013 International conference on Computational Problem-Solving (ICCP), pp. 433–436. IEEE (2013)
39. Ma, C., Zhou, C., Yang, S.: A voronoi-based location privacy-preserving method for continuous query in LBS. IJDSN **11**, 326 953:1–326 953:17 (2015)
40. Al-Dhubhani, R., Cazalas, J.M.: An adaptive geo-indistinguishability mechanism for continuous LBSqueries. Wirel. Netw. **24**(8), 3221–3239 (2018)
41. Brinkhoff, T.: A framework for generating network-based moving objects. Geo Inform. **6**(2), 153–180 (2002)
42. Al-Hussaeni, K., Fung, B.C.M., Cheung, W.K.: Privacy-preserving trajectory stream publishing. Data Knowl. Eng. **94**, 89–109 (2014)

Reliable Potential Friends Identification Based on Trust Circuit for Social Recommendation

Shuo Zhang and Jinghua Zhu$^{(\boxtimes)}$

Heilongjiang University, Harbin 150080, Heilongjiang, China
zhujinghua@hit.edu.cn

Abstract. Direct trust links among users may be unreliable due to noise. Simple use of these direct trust links may lead to inferior recommend effects, and most of the existed methods don't consider the difference in trust strength. We propose a novel model called TrustE which combines the trust relationships and users similarity. Specifically, we design a new method called Trust Circuit in TrustE to model trust relationships which calculates trust values by taking into account the asymmetry, transitivity, attenuation, and multiplicity-paths of trusts. Then we calculate user similarity through meta-paths guided embedded representation learning in the heterogeneous information network. Finally, we combine trust value and users similarity to get the personalized numbers of reliable potential friends for each user and make recommendation for target user according to his friends' preferences. The experimental results on Epinions and Douban datasets verify that TrustE is superior to other existing recommendation methods and it also has high accuracy for cold-start users' recommendation.

Keywords: Recommender systems · Social networks · Reliable potential friends · Trust Circuit

1 Introduction

Collaborative filtering is the most widely used method in recommender systems, but there are some problems such as data sparse and cold start users. One way to solve these problems is to refer to social relationships [1,2]. When they are shopping, they often adapt their friends' recommendations [3,4]. Researches on recommender systems based on trust relationships have increased in recent years [5,6], but most of them have the following shortcomings: (1) only explicit trust relationships are used and these explicit social relationships may be unreliable (e.g., spammers, bots, or accidental click). (2) they ignore the strength of trust and only consider trust or distrust among users.

The user-item bipartite graph has been widely used in previous recommender systems [7], but these models ignore the trust relationships between

© Springer Nature Switzerland AG 2020
D. Yu et al. (Eds.): WASA 2020, LNCS 12384, pp. 716–729, 2020.
https://doi.org/10.1007/978-3-030-59016-1_59

users. Although user-item bipartite graph and user social network are two different networks, we can concatenate them into a heterogeneous network by user nodes to get rich information [8]. But they don't realize that the explicit trust links are not always reliable and simply classifying social relationships into trust or distrust can't accurately describe the strength of trust. Therefore, in this paper, we design a novel model called TrustE to solve the above problems. First, inspired by the circuit, we design a novel trust calculation method called Trust Circuit. We can transform social networks into circuits, quantify the strength of trust between users, and obtain different numbers of trusted friends for each user. Then we can obtain the similarity between users through random walk and skip-gram on the heterogeneous information network guided by meta-paths. Finally, we combine trusted friends and user similarity to obtain different numbers of reliable potential friends for each user. We also treat positive and negative ratings differently and recommend to users based on the preferences of different types of reliable potential friends.

2   Related Work

Nowadays many researches begin to focus on social recommender systems. Jamali et al. [9] proposed a Trust Walker algorithm for random walk on user-item rating networks and user-user social networks. Then they proposed a new method SocialMF [2], which combined social networks and matrix factorization to obtain higher recommendation accuracy. No difference in the strength of trust was considered in these researches. Pan et al. [10] proposed a social recommendation algorithm based on the implicit similarity of trust relationships. The TrustMF model proposed by Yang et al. [11] made mixed recommendations from two different aspects of trust or distrust. Ma et al. [12] believed that trust strength and user similarity were related and combined both of these to acquire more accurate results. Chaney et al. [13] proposed a probability model that introduced social relationships into traditional factorization methods. However, all these methods only consider the direct trust relationship.

With the data increases rapidly in recommender systems, some researches begin to focus on personalized recommendation. Rendle et al. [14] first proposed a Bayesian personalized ranking recommendation model BPR based on matrix decomposition that could process implicit feedback. Next, Rendle et al. [15] extended the BPR framework from matrix factorization to tensor factorization for better recommendation results. Krohn-Grimberghe et al. [16] extended the BPR model by incorporating user feedback and social relationships into their model. Zhao et al. [17] proposed a new model called SBPR which considered trust relationships in social networks. Yu et al. [18] proposed an adaptive recommendation algorithm IF-BPR that could identify different numbers of potential friends for each user. Among the above methods, IF-BPR is the most similar to our TrustE. However, there are the following differences between them: our model considers trust propagation over longer paths. Then we combine trust

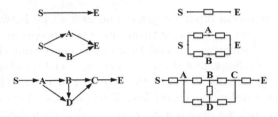

Fig. 1. A simple example of a trust relationship transformed into a circuit diagram.

values and user similarity to identify more trustworthy friends for each user. We treat one-way trust and bidirectional trust differently. And we also believe that a trusted friend has a greater impact on users.

3   Our Model

In this part, we design a new trust calculation method that takes into account the asymmetry, indirection, attenuation, and multiplicity-paths of trust relationships. We first combine trust value and similarity between users to identify different numbers of reliable potential friends for each user. Then we add these friends to BPR and rank items based on different types of friends.

3.1   Trust Calculation in Social Networks

Inspired by the circuit, we find that the circuit has similar properties to trust relationships, then we set users as nodes in circuits and set trust links as the resistances between two nodes. In this way, we can generate circuit diagrams between different users, and the circuits transformed from trust relationships are defined as Trust Circuit. Figure 1 illustrates the transformation of trust links into Trust Circuits. The left of Fig. 1 represents the trust links and the right side represents the Trust Circuits. It is worth noting that trust links are asymmetric, the Trust Circuit from user S to user E is probably different from E to S.

After obtaining Trust Circuit, we can easily imagine that when we add a voltage between two nodes, the current value depends on resistance value. The current value can approximately represent the trust value. In addition, we also refer to the idea of previous research that users who trust each other will have higher information transmission efficiency than users who trust on one-way, so we treat bidirectional trust and one-way trust differently. Through these settings, we can find: (1) If two users are connected in series, the longer path between two users is, the more resistances are, and the resistance value increases accordingly. (2) If two users are connected in parallel, the more paths between two users are and the smaller resistance value tends to be. (3) Because trust links are asymmetric, the Trust Circuit generated from user S to user E is likely to be different from user E to user S. (4) If there are enough paths between two indirectly connected users, their trust value is likely to exceed the directly connected users.

In fact, we find that the obtained Trust Circuits are likely to be very complicated. Therefore, we adopt the Node Voltage Method [19] commonly used in circuit science to solve this problem. Given the beginning node user u, all users within k steps can be obtained and be denoted as N_u^k, for each user $v \in N_u^k$, we can obtain all paths from u to v and denote as $P(u \sim v)$. Then we can compute the trust value with a method based on the Node Voltage Method. We first construct a Node Admittance Matrix M based on the number of nodes in $P(u \sim v)$, if the number of nodes in $P(u \sim v)$ is m, the size of matrix M is $m \times m$. Afterwards, we decompose all paths in $P(u \sim v)$ to the links, such as a path $(u \to v_1 \to v_2 \to v_3 \to v)$ in $P(u \sim v)$ (where $\to$ present a one-way trust link), v_1, v_2, and v_3 are nodes in the path from u to v. Moreover, we decompose this path as $(u \to v_1)$, $(v_1 \to v_2)$, $(v_2 \to v_3)$, $(v_3 \to v)$ and denote as $P'(u \sim v)$. Next, we fill the matrix M by each element in $P'(u \sim v)$. In this process, we distinguish the links is one-way trust or bidirectional trust and add different negative conductance values X to the matrix M (X is the reciprocal of the resistance). Then we fill in the negative numbers of the sum of the rows (or columns) into the diagonal of the matrix M. For calculation convenience, we set node u as the first row and column of the matrix M, while set node v as the last row and column of the matrix M. Afterwards, we regard node v as an earthing node and delete the last rows and columns in the matrix M, by this way we can obtain the matrix M'. We set a node current vector $Q = (q, 0, 0 \cdots 0)$ with length $m-1$. According to $M' \times A = Q$, we can calculate the node voltage vector $A = (a_1, a_2, a_3 \cdots a_{m-1})$ and get the element a_1 from A, then we set a voltage a_0 and a fixed value resistor r_0, and put them in series between node u and v, so we can calculate the voltage difference $\triangle a = a_1 - a_0$. Finally, we can compute the current value by calculating $Q(u,v) = \triangle a / r_0$, where $q = a_0 / r_0$. For calculation convenience, we can set al.l the value of q, a_0 and r_0 to 1. The current value $Q(u,v)$ can represent the trust value between users u and v to some extent. The specific calculation process is shown in Algorithm 1 and Algorithm 2.

For different users, the size of trusted users set can be varied greatly after k-step and the trust value also changes dramatically. Therefore, we map the $Q(u,v)$ to $T(u,v)$ through sigmoid function and the value of $T(u,v)$ is between 0 to 1, then we define $T(u,v)$ as the trust value from u to v. Next, we rank these users by the trust values, we define the top 80% of users as trusted friends of user u, and the remaining 20% are distrusted friends. Finally, we can get different numbers of trusted friends for user u.

Algorithm 1. Trust value calculation
___
Input: $G_t = (V_t, E_t)$, N_u^k
Output: $Q_{(u,N_u^k)}$ for all $u \in V_t$
1: **for** all $u \in V_t$ **do**
2:     **for** all $v \in N_u^k$ **do**
3:         Get $P(u \sim v)$
4:         Compute $Q_{(u,v)}$ according to Algorithm 2
5:     **end for**
6: **end for**

Algorithm 2. Node Voltage Method
___
Input: $v \in N_u^k$, X_1, X_2, Q, a_0, r_0
Output: $Q_{(u,v)}$
1: Initialization matrix M
2: Get $P(u \sim v)$ from $P'(u \sim v)$
3: **for** each $P'_{xy} \in P'(u \sim v)$ **do**
4:     **if** P'_{xy} is one-way trust **then**
5:         $M(x,y) = M(x,y) - X_1$
6:     **else**
7:         $M(x,y) = M(x,y) - X_2$
8:     **end if**
9: **end for**
10: **for** i from i to m **do**
11:     $M(i,i) = - \sum_{j=1}^{m} M(i,j)$
12: **end for**
13: Delete rows and columns according to the position of v
14: Set Q
15: Compute A by $A = M^{-1}Q$
16: Get a_1 in A
17: Compute $\triangle a$ by $\triangle a = a_1 - a_0$
18: Compute $Q_{(u,v)}$ by $Q(u,v) = \triangle a / r_0$

3.2   Identification of Potential Friends in Heterogeneous Information Network

In social networks, explicit trust relationships are always very sparse and fragile. So our model uses potential friends to enrich user's information. Potential friends refer to users with similar tastes, but such users may not be directly connected in social networks. Previous researches have proved that potential friends can improve the accuracy of recommendation effect to a certain extent [18].

Heterogeneous Information Network. We denote U as the user set and I as the item set. $G_p = (V_p, E_p)$ is used to denote the user-items interaction networks while $G_t = (V_t, E_t)$ is used to denote the social networks between users. There are two types of nodes in the G_p (user and item). One type of links

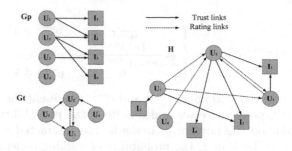

Fig. 2. User social network and user-item interaction network can form heterogeneous information network for more information

Table 1. Five kinds of meta-paths and their descriptions

Path	Schema	Description
P1	$U \rightarrow I \leftarrow U$	User may be similar to the user who consumed the same item
P2	$U \leftarrow U \rightarrow U$	A user's friends may be similar to each other
P3	$U \rightarrow U \leftarrow U$	Users with the same friends may be similar to each other
P4	$U \rightarrow U \rightarrow U$	Friends' friends can be trusted
P5	$U \rightarrow U \rightarrow I \leftarrow U$	A user may be similar to a friend of a user who has the same interaction history

(ratings), where $(u, i) \in Ep$ represents that user u has rated item i. In G_t, there is only one type of nodes (user) and one type of links (trust), where $(u_1, u_2) \in E_t$ represents that user u_1 trusts user u_2. It is worth noting that it doesn't mean that user u_2 also trusts user u_1. After obtaining G_p and G_t, we concatenate the two different types of networks as a heterogeneous information network (HIN), which is denoted as $H = (V, E)$, where V represents the set of nodes that is composed of two different types of nodes: user U and item I, and E represents the set of links that is composed of ratings and trust links. By this way, we can get more information (as shown in Fig. 2). For example, user U_1 has rated item I_1 and I_2, and after two steps U_1 can reach item I_3 and I_4; user U_4 has never rated any item, after two steps he can reach item I_2, I_3 and I_4. The rating links can also be divided into positive ratings and negative ratings, we defined the ratings of 4 and 5 as positive, and the ratings of 1 and 2 as negative.

User Similarity Calculation. In this part, we design five meta-paths to match the model(show as Table 1). Random walk and skip-gram were widely used on recommender systems [20]. At first, we need to conduct random walk on the meta-paths to obtain the sequences of nodes. For different types of links, we set different transition probability, the transition probability is defined as follows:

$$p\left(v^{n+1}|v^{n}, p\right) = \begin{cases} \frac{1}{|v^{n+1}|} & v^{n+1} \in I \\ \frac{t(v^{n}, v^{n+1})}{\sum_{v^{m+1} \in U} t(v^{n}, v^{m+1})} & v^{n+1} \in U \\ 0 & v^{n+1} \notin V \end{cases} \tag{1}$$

where v^{n} represents the seed node, v^{n+1} and v^{m+1} represent the neighborhoods of v^{n}. When the type of successor nodes is item, the probability of walking to this node depends on the number of items he has interacted with. When the type of successor nodes is user, the probability of walking depends on the trust value of two users. Obviously, for two users v^{n} and v^{n+1}, the higher the trust value between them, the higher the probability of walking from v^{n} to v^{n+1}.

In our model, we generate positive and negative two different corpus by positive and negative feedbacks. Then we learn the embedding $Y \in R^{|V| \times d}(d \ll |V|)$ in the heterogeneous skip-gram. Given the sequences of nodes guided by the meta-paths and node v^{n}, the objective function is defined as follows:

$$\max_{\theta} \sum_{v \in V} \sum_{v_n^m \in C(v^n)} \log p\left(v_n^m | v^n; \theta\right) \tag{2}$$

where $C(v^n)$ represents the context nodes of v^n (with window size w), $p(v_n^m|v^n; \theta)$ is commonly defined as the SoftMax function as follows:

$$p\left(v_n^m | v^n; \theta\right) = \frac{e^{y_{v_n^m} \cdot y_{v^n}}}{\sum_{v \in V_n} e^{y_v \cdot y_{v^n}}} \tag{3}$$

where y^v is the vth row of Y, representing the embedding vector of node v, and V_n represents the node of type n in heterogeneous information network. However, the size of corpus may be very large in actual work, in order to reduce the time cost, we adopt negative samples in learning task [20]. Then we update Eq. (2) by maximizing the following objective function:

$$O(Y) = \log \sigma\left(y_{v_v^m} \cdot y_{v^n}\right) + \sum_{i=1}^{B} E_{v_n^i \sim P_n(v_n)}\left[\log \sigma\left(-y_{v_n^i} \cdot y_{v^n}\right)\right] \tag{4}$$

where $\sigma(y) = \frac{1}{1+e^{-y}}$ and $P_n(v_n)$ denotes the sampling distribution which is determined by the dimension of the node. Through stochastic gradient ascent on Eq. (4), we can achieve the representation of each node. Then, we can compute the similarity among these users through cosine similarity, and identify the same number of Top-K positive and negative potential friends for each user.

3.3   Reliable Potential Friends Identification

Some users have a rich history of behavior, while others are sparse. We can easily imagine that identification the same number of potential friends for each user may have a negative effect for recommendation. We define the overlapping part of potential friends and trust friends for each user's as reliable potential friends. The reliable potential friends are not only similar to the target users but also are trust friends to the target users. In order to avoid a few number of reliable potential friends (even the number is 0), we decide if the number of a user's reliable potential friends is less than $k/2$, it will be filled with the most similar users of the target users until it's number reaches $k/2$.

3.4 TrustE Recommendation

In fact, we find that sometimes the positive friends and negative friends are partially overlap, and the users in the overlapped part have similar performance with the target users in both positive and negative ratings. We defined this part of users as fair friends. Therefore, we can classified items that have not been interacted with by target users. The proposed classification is shown as Table 2.

Table 2. Six different types of items

Items name	Description
General items: GEu	Items purchased by target users
Perfect item: PEu	Items purchased by fair friends and rated positively
Positive item: POu	Items purchased and rated positively by positive friends
Negative item: NEu	Items purchased and rated negatively by negative friends
Worst item: WOu	Items purchased by fair friends and given negative ratings
Unknown item: UNu	The items in addition to the above 5 kinds of items

It is obvious that $GE_u \cup PE_u \cup PO_u \cup NE_u \cup WO_u \cup UN_u = I$. Different from previous researches, we believe that a trustworthy friend plays a more important role and the classification of items is not detailed. For example, IF-BPR ranks the purchase probability of different types of items as follows:

$$f: \quad x_{ui} \geqslant x_{uj} \geqslant x_{uk} \geqslant x_{uc} \geqslant x_{un}$$
$$i \in GE_u, j \in PE_u, k \in PO_u, c \in UN_u, n \in NE_u \tag{5}$$

where x_{ui} denotes the preference score of user u for item i, while the remaining items in Eq. (5) also respectively represent the preference of user u for different types of items. In our model, we believe that reliable potential friends should be more important for a user, the above assumption is further expanded as Eq. (6):

$$f: \quad x_{ui} \geqslant x_{uj} \geqslant x_{uk} \geqslant x_{uc} \geqslant x_{un} \geqslant x_{uo}$$
$$i \in GE_u, j \in PE_u, k \in PO_u, c \in UN_u, n \in NE_u, o \in WO_u \tag{6}$$

The above assumption can be easily understood: users are more likely to purchase items that fair friends purchased and give positive ratings than purchased by themselves. Then they will consider positive friends' recommendations, and the probability of purchasing items that negative friends have purchased is lower than purchasing items that have never been purchased. The last of the list is the items which fair friends have purchased with negative ratings. Therefore we can use the following function to optimize likelihood for each user u:

$$\prod_{i \in GE_u, j \in PE_u} P\left(x_{ui} \geq x_{uj}|\psi\right) \quad \prod_{j \in PE_u, k \in PO_u} P\left(x_{uj} \geq x_{uk}|\psi\right) \quad \prod_{k \in PO_u, c \in UN_u} P\left(x_{uk} \geq x_{uc}|\psi\right)$$

$$\prod_{c \in UN_u, n \in NE_u} P\left(x_{uc} \geq x_{un}|\psi\right) \quad \prod_{n \in NE_u, o \in WO_u} P\left(x_{un} \geq x_{uo}|\psi\right)$$

(7)

where ψ represents the potential feature vectors of users and items, and $\psi \equiv (O, D)$. User preferences for items are calculated by matrix factorization, for example the preference of user u to item i is represented by $x_{ui} = O_u^T D_i$, $P(x_{ui} \geq x_{uj}|\psi)$ is represented by $\sigma(x_{ui} - x_{uj})$. By log-form the posterior probability, our model maximizes the following objective function that is composed of order modeling and regularization terms:

$$
\begin{aligned}
L = \sum_u \Bigg[& \sum_{i \in GE_u} \sum_{j \in PE_u} \ln\left(\sigma\left(x_{ui} - x_{uj}\right)\right) \\
& + \sum_{j \in PE_u} \sum_{k \in PO_u} \ln(\sigma\left(x_{uj} - x_{uk}\right)) + \sum_{k \in PO_u} \sum_{c \in UN_u} \ln(\sigma\left(x_{uk} - x_{uc}\right)) \\
& + \sum_{c \in UN_u} \sum_{n \in NE_u} \ln(\sigma\left(x_{uc} - x_{un}\right)) + \sum_{n \in NE_u} \sum_{o \in WO_u} \ln(\sigma\left(x_{un} - x_{uo}\right)) \Bigg] - Rt
\end{aligned}
$$

(8)

where Rt is the regularization term used to avoid overfitting in the learning process. Then we can use stochastic gradient descent to deal with Eq. (8).

4   Experiments and Results

4.1   Experimental Setup

Datasets. In our paper, the commonly used Epinions and Douban datasets are adopted for experimental evaluation. Both datasets include the user's ratings and trust relationships. Moreover, the rating interval is 1–5. Douban dataset contains 2848 users, 39,586 items, 984,887 ratings and 35,570 trust links, and the ratings and trusts of density were 0.793% and 0.441%, respectively. Epinions dataset included 49289 users, 139738 items, 664823 ratings and 487183 trust links, and the ratings and trusts density were 0.0097% and 0.0201%, respectively.

Baseline Methods. We select BPR, SBPR, TBPR [21], CUNE [22] and IF-BPR as comparative experiments. BPR is a classical personalized ranking algorithm. Only explicit feedbacks are used in SBPR and implicit feedbacks are not considered. TBPR considers the strength of explicit feedback. CUNE uses homogeneous network on their model and makes recommendations based on Top-K potential friends. IF-BPR uses heterogeneous information network in their model that considers the interactive relationships between users and selects Top-K potential friends for recommendation adaptively.

Evaluation Metrics and Parameter Settings. In this paper, we adopt $Prec@k$, $Rec@k$ and $MAP@k$ as the evaluation criteria for experimental effects. The number of step k and the maximum path length are set as 3 according to the experimental results, and the number of potential friends is set as 150. The dimension of the potential feature is 20, the number and length of the walk are both 20, the size of the context window is 5, and the embedded dimension is 25.

4.2   Recommendation Performance

The experimental results of different methods is shown in Table 3. We can see that our method has a high improvement in Douban dataset. $Prec@10$ and $Prec@20$ have an improvement of 15.28% and 9.14% respectively; $Rec@10$ and $Rec@20$ also increase by 17.83% and 6.96%; similarly, there is a certain improvement in average accuracy: $MAP@10$ and $MAP@20$ are improved by 13.76% and 11.63% respectively. There are also improved in Epinions dataset. $Prec@10$ and $Prec@20$ increased by 28.93% and 26.52%, respectively; $Rec@10$ and $Rec@20$ also increase by 3.3% and 7.32%; $MAP@10$ and $MAP@20$ show relatively little improvement, with 3.27% and 0.85%, respectively.

Table 3. The comparison of the performance of different methods

Dataset	Metric	BPR	SBPR	TBPR	CUNE	IFBPR+	TrustE	Improv
Douban	$Prec@10$	10.37%	8.81%	9.58%	11.44%	16.36%	18.86%	15.28%
	$Prec@20$	8.10%	6.91%	7.19%	8.38%	14.77%	16.12%	9.14%
	$Rec@10$	3.55%	2.71%	3.35%	3.87%	4.43%	5.22%	17.83%
	$Rec@20$	5.30%	4.23%	4.86%	5.50%	6.47%	6.92%	6.96%
	$Map@10$	0.05636	0.04517	0.05115	0.06455	0.10545	0.1199	13.76%
	$Map@20$	0.03921	0.03062	0.03413	0.04263	0.08102	0.09044	11.63%
Epinions	$Prec@10$	1.73%	1.83%	1.96%	2.04%	2.20%	2.83%	28.93%
	$Prec@20$	1.38%	1.28%	1.38%	1.42%	1.48%	1.88%	26.52%
	$Rec@10$	4.03%	3.98%	4.00%	3.92%	4.54%	4.69%	3.3%
	$Rec@20$	5.43%	5.52%	5.42%	5.30%	5.96%	6.39%	7.32%
	$Map@10$	0.01877	0.0182	0.01942	0.01937	0.02264	0.02338	3.27%
	$Map@20$	0.01883	0.01837	0.01953	0.01944	0.02244	0.02263	0.85%

4.3   Effect of Step k on Experiment

During our experiments we find the value of k has a significant influence on the experimental results. Then we set the value of k as 1–5 to observe the influence of k on the experimental results. The experimental results are shown in Fig. 3.

We use $Prec@10$ and $Prec@20$ as evaluation indicators. From Fig. 3, we can see when k is 3, we can get the best experimental results on both Douban and

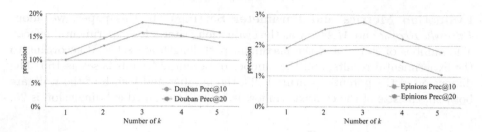

Fig. 3. Experimental performance with different number of k.

Epinions datasets. We consider that if the value of k is too small, we cannot find enough trust relations for users, while if the value of k is too large, we may identify too many friends who are not helpful to the target users. In a special case, some users can cover almost the whole users after many steps. It is obviously impossible for a user to have so many friends in a dataset.

4.4 Experimental Results of Cold Start Users

In our experiment, we define the users with less than 10 interactive items as cold start users. Then use $Prec@10$, $Rec@10$ and $MAP@10$ to measure the recommendation performance. The experimental results are shown in Fig. 4. We can see that our method is effective for alleviating the cold start problem.

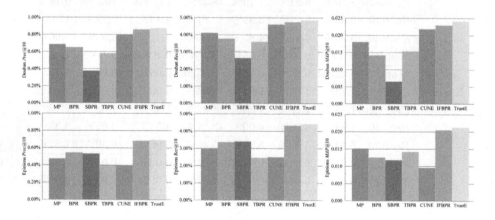

Fig. 4. Evaluation on cold-start users.

4.5 Are Reliable Potential Friends Really Reliable?

In order to prove that the reliable potential friends identified by our method are really reliable, we design a comparative experiment called $TrustE^-$, the differents from TrustE is TrustE$^-$ can only identify the same number of potential friends for each user. When step k is set as 3, $Prec@10$ and $Rec@10$ are adopted as experimental evaluation. The experimental results are shown in Table 4, we can see that the reliable potential friends are more reliable than Top-K similar users.

Table 4. TrustE vs. TrustE$^-$.

	Douban Prec@10	Epinion Prec@10	Douban Rec@10	Epinion Rec@10
TrustE	18.86%	2.83%	5.22%	4.69%
TrustE$^-$	17.67%	2.45%	4.79%	4.46%

5 Conclusion and Future Work

In this paper, we design a personalized recommendation algorithm called TrustE and convert the trust relationships into circuits to calculate the trust value between users. TrustE can identify different numbers of reliable potential friends and make recommendations to target users based on their friends' preferences. Experiments on Epinions and Douban datasets have proved that our method can have a better performance in the accuracy of recommendation and the problem of cold-start users can also be alleviated. This paper focuses on the trust relationship between users, but does not consider the dynamic of trust, we will explore this in future work.

References

1. Ma, H., Yang, H., Lyu, M.R., King, I.: SoRec: social recommendation using probabilistic matrix factorization. In: Proceedings of the 17th ACM Conference on Information and Knowledge Management, pp. 931–940. ACM (2008)
2. Jamali, M., Ester, M.: A matrix factorization technique with trust propagation for recommendation in social networks. In: Proceedings of the Fourth ACM Conference on Recommender Systems, pp. 135–142. ACM (2010)
3. Sinha, R.R., Swearingen, K., et al.: Comparing recommendations made by online systems and friends. In: DELOS (2001)
4. Yin, H., Zhou, X., Cui, B., Wang, H., Zheng, K., Nguyen, Q.V.H.: Adapting to user interest drift for poi recommendation. IEEE Trans. Knowl. Data Eng. **28**(10), 2566–2581 (2016)
5. Wu, H., Zeng, C., Ma, Y., He, P.: Truser: an approach to service recommendation based on trusted users. Chin. J. Comput. **42**(4), 851–863 (2019)
6. X. Y., Ziyi, Z., Hengru, Z., et al.: Recommendation algorithm combining user's asymmetric trust relationships. Comput. Sci. **10**(45), 37–42 (2018)
7. Chen, L.-J., Gao, J.: A trust-based recommendation method using network diffusion processes. Phys. A **506**, 679–691 (2018)

8. Yin, H., Chen, H., Sun, X., Wang, H., et al.: SPTF: a scalable probabilistic tensor factorization model for semantic-aware behavior prediction. In: 2017 IEEE International Conference on Data Mining (ICDM), pp. 585–594. IEEE (2017)
9. Jamali, M., Ester, M.: TrustWalker: a random walk model for combining trust-based and item-based recommendation. In: Proceedings of the 15th ACM SIGKDD International Conference on Knowledge Discovery and Data Mining, pp. 397–406. ACM (2009)
10. Pan, Y., He, F., Yu, H.: Social recommendation algorithm using implicit similarity in trust. Chin. J. Comput. **41**(1), 65–81 (2018)
11. Yang, B., Lei, Y.: Social collaborative filtering by trust. IEEE Trans. Pattern Anal. Mach. Intell. **39**(8), 1633–1647 (2016)
12. Ma, H., Zhou, D., Liu, C., Lyu, M.R., King, I.: Recommender systems with social regularization. In: Proceedings of the Fourth ACM International Conference on Web Search and Data Mining, pp. 287–296. ACM (2011)
13. Chaney, A.J., Blei, D.M., Eliassi-Rad, T.: A probabilistic model for using social networks in personalized item recommendation. In: Proceedings of the 9th ACM Conference on Recommender Systems, pp. 43–50. ACM (2015)
14. Rendle, S., Freudenthaler, C., Gantner, Z.: BPR: Bayesian personalized ranking from implicit feedback. In: Proceedings of the Twenty-Fifth Conference on Uncertainty in Artificial Intelligence, pp. 452–461. AUAI Press (2009)
15. Rendle, S., Schmidt-Thieme, L.: Pairwise interaction tensor factorization for personalized tag recommendation. In: Proceedings of the Third ACM International Conference on Web Search and Data Mining, pp. 81–90. ACM (2010)
16. Krohn-Grimberghe, A., Drumond, L., Freudenthaler, C., Schmidt-Thieme, L.: Multi-relational matrix factorization using Bayesian personalized ranking for social network data. In: Proceedings of the Fifth ACM International Conference on Web Search and Data Mining, pp. 173–182. ACM (2012)
17. Zhao, T., McAuley, J., King, I.: Leveraging social connections to improve personalized ranking for collaborative filtering. In: Proceedings of the 23rd ACM International Conference on Conference on Information and Knowledge Management, pp. 261–270. ACM (2014)
18. Yu, J., Gao, M., Li, J., Yin, H., Liu, H.: Adaptive implicit friends identification over heterogeneous network for social recommendation. In: Proceedings of the 27th ACM International Conference on Information and Knowledge Management, pp. 357–366. ACM (2018)
19. GuanYuan, Q., et al.: Electric Circuit. Higher Education Press (1982)
20. Mikolov, T., Sutskever, I., Chen, K., Corrado, G.S., Dean, J.: Distributed representations of words and phrases and their compositionality. In: Advances in Neural Information Processing Systems, pp. 3111–3119 (2013)
21. Wang, X., Lu, W., Ester, M., Wang, C., Chen, C.: Social recommendation with strong and weak ties. In: Proceedings of the 25th ACM International on Conference on Information and Knowledge Management, pp. 5–14. ACM (2016)
22. Zhang, C., Yu, L., Wang, Y., Shah, C., Zhang, X.: Collaborative user network embedding for social recommender systems. In: 17th SIAM International Conference on Data Mining, SDM 2017, pp. 381–389. Society for Industrial and Applied Mathematics Publications (2017)
23. Wang, Y., Yin, G., Cai, Z., Dong, Y., Dong, H.: A trust-based probabilistic recommendation model for social networks. J. Netw. Comput. Appl. **55**, 59–67 (2015)
24. Wang, Y., Cai, Z., Yin, G., Gao, Y., Tong, X., Wu, G.: An incentive mechanism with privacy protection in mobile crowdsourcing systems. Comput. Netw. **102**, 157–171 (2016)

25. Wang, Y., Cai, Z., Tong, X., Gao, Y., Yin, G.: Truthful incentive mechanism with location privacy-preserving for mobile crowdsourcing systems. Comput. Netw. **135**, 32–43 (2018)
26. Wang, Y., Gao, Y., Li, Y., Tong, X.: A worker-selection incentive mechanism for optimizing platform-centric mobile crowdsourcing systems. Comput. Netw. **171**, 107144 (2020)

GaitID: Robust Wi-Fi Based Gait Recognition

Yi Zhang[1], Yue Zheng[1], Guidong Zhang[1], Kun Qian[2], Chen Qian[1], and Zheng Yang[1(✉)]

[1] Tsinghua University, Beijing, China
zhangyithss@gmail.com, cczhengy@gmail.com, zhanggd18@gmail.com,
chen.cronus.qian@gmail.com, hmilyyz@gmail.com
[2] University of California San Diego, San Diego, CA, USA
qiank10@gmail.com

Abstract. Gait, the walking manner of a person, has been perceived as a physical and behavioral trait for human identification. Compared with cameras and wearable sensors, Wi-Fi based gait recognition is more attractive because Wi-Fi infrastructure is almost available everywhere and is able to sense passively without the requirement of on-body devices. However, existing Wi-Fi sensing approaches impose strong assumptions of fixed user walking trajectory and sufficient training data. In this paper, we present *GaitID*, a Wi-Fi based human identification system, to overcome above unrealistic assumptions. To deal with various walking trajectories and speeds, *GaitID* first extracts target specific features that best characterize gait patterns and applies novel normalization algorithms to eliminate gait irrelevant perturbation in signals. On this basis, *GaitID* reduces the training efforts in new deployment scenarios by transfer learning. Extensive experiments have been conducted on the implementation and the outcomes are satisfying. To the best of our knowledge, *GaitID* is the first gait-based identification approach without any restriction on walking trajectory and speed.

Keywords: Gait recognition · Channel state information · Wi-Fi

1 Introduction

Various sensor modalities, e.g., cameras [3], inertial sensors on wearables [19] and Wi-Fi signals [14] emitted by wireless devices [12], have been certificated to be able to extract gait of a user for person identification. Among these sensors, video has the risk of privacy leakage and inertial sensors require users to actively carry mobile devices. In contrast, Wi-Fi signal becomes a more attractive carrier for gait-based person identification since Wi-Fi infrastructure is ubiquitously available [13] and able to work without user's perception.

Current state of Wi-Fi based gait identification approaches [12,17,18], however, rely on extensive training efforts for *every* target person in *each* monitoring area. Such cumbersomeness stems from three limitations of the existing

© Springer Nature Switzerland AG 2020
D. Yu et al. (Eds.): WASA 2020, LNCS 12384, pp. 730–742, 2020.
https://doi.org/10.1007/978-3-030-59016-1_60

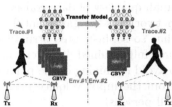
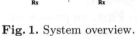

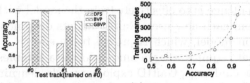

(a) Cross-track perfor- (b) Dataset scale de-
mance. manded by DNN.

Fig. 1. System overview.   **Fig. 2.** Challenges of Wi-Fi based gait identification.

approaches. First, Wi-Fi signals reflected by a target person not only possess the
gait signature of the person, but also are distorted by the surrounding multi-
path environment. Thus, the recognition model directly trained with raw Wi-Fi
features or their statistics, as WiWho [17], may overfit the environment where
the data is collected and cannot be generalized to new environments without
retraining. Second, besides the effect of environment factors, features related to
the gait of the person in Wi-Fi signals still depend on how the person moves relative to the Wi-Fi devices. WiFiU [12] derives parameters of gaits from Doppler
Frequency Spectrum (DFS). However, it requires that the target person walks
right towards or away from the Wi-Fi devices on fixed trajectories to ensure the
consistency of the DFS, which limits the practicality of the approach. Third, as
the learning model becomes more and more sophisticated, e.g., in terms of the
number of parameters that need to be trained, a sufficiently large amount of
training data is required when each new person is added.

In this paper, we present GaitID, an ubiquitous Wi-Fi based person identification framework, which is robust to walking manners and environment variance, and reduces training efforts significantly as Fig. 1 shows. GaitID has two
key characteristics that enhance the robustness of this system with limited training samples. On one hand, GaitID is immune to environmental variations and
motion status (e.g., location and velocity) of target persons, and retains prominent generalizability between environments and trajectories. On the other hand,
GaitID is able to transfer the learning model of existing persons to newcomers
with only a small amount of training data collected from the person. To support
these features, we overcome two critical challenges.

The first challenge is to overcome the negative impact of environmental variations and motion status of target person during walking. GaitID borrows the
idea of body-coordinate velocity profile (BVP) in [20], which represents the velocities of body parts during walking, and proposes a dedicated feature GBVP
for gait characterization. The GBVP is resilient to scenario factors, including
environmental changes, and the location and orientation of walking trajectories. To adapt GBVP to realtime gait identification, we propose a bunch of agile
extraction and normalization algorithms to boost its robustness to gait-irrelevant
factors. The designed feature GBVP is theoretically both environment and trajectory independent, which mitigates gait-irrelevant components. The second

challenge is to effectively train the model with a small quantity of data collected from each new user. GaitID adopts deep neural networks as the gait identification model, which is proved to be effective but has so sophisticated structure that requires a large amount of data samples to get fully trained. To overcome the challenge, GaitID exploits transfer learning to avoid retraining of the partial network which extracts high-level gait features from the input velocity profile and has the same network parameters shared by all persons.

In summary, we make the following contributions. First, we propose an agile algorithm to extract gait-specific feature GBVP that is resilient to environment and trajectory change, and thus relieves restrictions on walking manners. Second, the proposed gait identification approach requires little training efforts for various scenarios and persons, and thus can be easily deployed and extended. Third, we implement GaitID on COTS Wi-Fi devices and extensive experiments have demonstrated the effectiveness and robustness of the proposed system.

2   Related Work and Motivation

GaitID attempts to tackle two main challenges in Wi-Fi based gait identification.

Immune to Trajectory and Speed Variance. Both WiWho [17] and WiFiU [12] try to preserve human-specific information in their extracted features, e.g., Doppler frequency shifts, from Wi-Fi signals. Such features, however, are highly correlated with users' relative movements to Wi-Fi devices, thus impose stringent restrictions on their monitoring tracks. Widar3.0 [20] proposes a domain-independent feature BVP, which is mainly designed for in-place activities and sensitive to the moving speed of the target. As a brief example in Fig. 2(a), gait samples are collected from two users with different walking manners and a classifier based on CNN and RNN is trained and tested on datasets from different walking tracks. While DFS and BVP perform better for the same track, they fail to hold performance for testing on different tracks. Whereas, GBVP is robust to track and speed variance.

Reducing Training Data for Newcomers. To fully exploit the spatial and temporal property of motion features, existing works [2] leverage sophisticated deep neural networks to achieve high accuracy. However, a more complex structure usually means more parameters need to be trained, which leads to the requirement of a massive amount of training data. This problem becomes increasingly conspicuous when new users are added and the network should be retrained. Figure 2(b) illustrates the exponential growing trend of required training samples needed to reach specific accuracy for a typical DNN network.

Lessons Learned. The deficiency of existing gait identification works demand to be relieved before practical usage is achieved. GaitID is designed to address these issues.

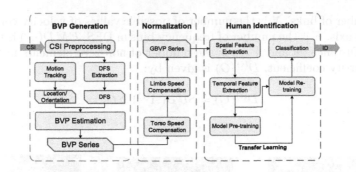

Fig. 3. Work flow of GaitID.

3 System Design

Figure 3 shows the work flow of our system.

3.1 GBVP Extraction

Widar3.0 [20] proposed an environment-independent motion feature BVP to portray human activities, which is resilient to location, orientation and environment changes. However, BVP can not be directly used for gait recognition and the reasons are two-fold. 1) BVP are modeled with in-place activities where movements of the reflection objects can be ignored, while gait activity involves meters of torso movements. 2) The complexity of BVP extraction algorithm is especially high and can hardly be applied into realtime systems. Therefor, GaitID designed a rigorous and agile feature extraction algorithm to acquire environment-independent and gait-specific feature GBVP (gait-BVP). In the following formulations, we establish the coordinates whose origin is the location of the person and positive x-axis aligns with his/her face orientation.

GBVP Formulation. To formulate GBVP, we first define an operator $\otimes$:

$$\mathcal{A} \otimes \mathcal{B} \triangleq \sum_{i=1}^{M} \sum_{j=1}^{N} \mathcal{A}_{(i,j,*)} \cdot \mathcal{B}_{(i,j)}, \qquad (1)$$

Where $\mathcal{A} \in R^{M \times N \times P}$ and $\mathcal{B} \in R^{M \times N}$. Hence, the operation result $\mathcal{A} \otimes \mathcal{B} \in R^{P}$ is equivalent to multiply each element of $\mathcal{B}$ with corresponding vector in the third dimension of $\mathcal{A}$ and then sum them up. Using the defined operator, we formulate GBVP as follows:

$$[GBVP] = \min_{G} \sum_{i=1}^{L} |\text{EMD}(D^{(i)}(G), [DFS]^{(i)})| + \eta \|G\|_0, \qquad (2)$$

Where $G \in R^{N \times N}$ is GBVP. $D^{(i)}(G) \in R^{N \times N \times F}$ is the reconstructed DFS from GBVP for i^{th} Wi-Fi link. $[DFS]^{(i)}$ is the observed DFS on i^{th} link. L is the total number of links. N is the number of possible values of velocity components along x/y axis. F is the number of frequency bins in DFS. $EMD(\cdot, \cdot)$ is the Earth Mover's Distance [8] and $|| \cdot ||_0$ is the number of non-zero elements in GBVP. η is the sparsity coefficient. $D^{(i)}(G)$ is given by:

$$D^{(i)}(G) = SUB(A^{(i)}) \otimes G, \tag{3}$$

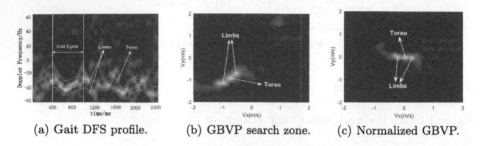

(a) Gait DFS profile.   (b) GBVP search zone.   (c) Normalized GBVP.

Fig. 4. GBVP extraction and normalization

Where $A^{(i)} \in R^{(N \times N \times F)}$ is the coefficient matrix to map GBVP into DFS on i^{th} link. The $SUB(\cdot)$ is the operator to cherry-pick the most relevant elements in the coefficient matrix to reduce the search space of GBVP and eventually reduce algorithm complexity. We will shortly introduce the algorithm on how to do that reduction in the **Accelerating GBVP extraction** part. Each element in the coefficient matrix can be determined by:

$$A^{(i)}_{(j,k,m)} = \begin{cases} 1 & f_m = f^{(i)}(<v_j, v_k>) \\ 0 & \text{else} \end{cases}, \tag{4}$$

Where $<v_j, v_k>$ is the corresponding velocity of the $<i,j>^{th}$ element in GBVP matrix. f_m is the mth frequency sampling point in the DFS profile. $f^{(i)}(\cdot)$ is a mapping function to convert target velocity into DFS observation for i^{th} link with $f^{(i)}(<v_x, v_y>) = a_x v_x + a_y v_y$. Specifically:

$$a_x = \frac{1}{\lambda}(\frac{x_t}{\|(x_t, y_t)\|_2} + \frac{x_r}{\|(x_r, y_r)\|_2}), a_y = \frac{1}{\lambda}(\frac{y_t}{\|(x_t, y_t)\|_2} + \frac{y_r}{\|(x_r, y_r)\|_2}) \tag{5}$$

Where (x_t, y_t) and (x_r, y_r) are the locations of transmitter and receiver and should be updated whenever the target position changes during walking. We sanitize CSI with existing works [7] and acquire target user's torso position and orientation by existing passive tracking system, e.g., IndoTrack [4] and Widar2.0 [6].

Accelerating GBVP Extraction. For activity recognition tasks with Wi-Fi, only a few major reflection paths are considered and Widar3.0 [20] leveraged this sparsity by adding a regular term in target function to recover BVP. However, this sparsity is not fully exploit and the algorithm is still too cumbersome to be applicable. Our key insight is that, the spatial correlation embodied in human motion could potentially be used to reduce the complexity of GBVP extraction algorithm.

We observe that, during gait activity, the limbs would swing to opposite sides of the torso with limited speeds and the velocity of all the reflection paths would cluster around the velocity of torso. This observation can be confirmed by Fig. 4(a). This profile is constructed with CSI for 4 continuous cycles from one user. The red curve demonstrates the major energy corresponding to torso motion and the white curves demonstrate the residual energy corresponding to limbs motion. It is clearly shown that both sparsity and spatial clustering phenomenon exist in the reflected signal. Hence, if we can pinpoint the velocity of torso on GBVP matrix, then the whole body GBVP components can be searched within a small area centered on torso component.

Based on the above observations, GaitID first identifies the maximum frequency bins in DFS from each Wi-Fi link and formulates the relationship between frequency bins and velocity with the methods provided in [6]. Solving the equations from multiple links, GaitID pinpoints the torso velocity on GBVP matrix. On top of that, GaitID crops the adjacent elements of torso component in the coefficient matrix described in Eq. 3. The subtracted coefficient matrix is then used for GBVP recover with Eq. 2. After the above process, the GBVP search space is hereby reduced. In our experiments, the crop window's size is empirically selected and a smaller window would results in shorter running time but deteriorative accuracy, vice versa. The torso and limbs components as well as the search zone in GBVP is visualized in Fig. 4(b).

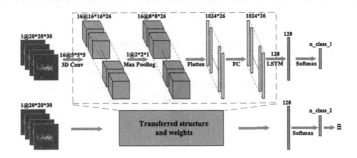

Fig. 5. Gait recognition model.

GBVP Normalization. While GBVP is theoretically only related to the gait of the target, it requires extra normalization to increase the stability as gait indicator. The reasons are three-fold. First, literature [16] has proven that the torso movement contains little information of gait patterns and need to be removed. Second, the reflected signal power is correlated with torso position relative to transceivers. Third, different walking speeds correspond to different limbs swing speeds, which results in variation of the number of GBVP frames and value floating within each GBVP matrix.

Thereafter, GaitID first compensates the torso speed by applying translation and rotation on GBVP. The translation displacement is $\|v_{torso}\|_2$ and the rotation angle is $\angle v_{torso} - \angle v_{ref}$ where v_{ref} is the manually selected reference orientation. This transformation procedure is similar to moving the target human to a treadmill, on which the target performs fixed-speed walking.

GaitID then normalizes the sum of all elements in each GBVP to 1. It is based on the observation that the absolute reflection power contains environment information while the relative power distribution over physical velocities doesn't. Lastly, GaitID scales each single GBVP with a scaling ratio $\frac{v_{ob}}{v_{tg}}$, where v_{ob} is the observed walking speed and v_{tg} is the target walking speed. GaitID then resamples GBVP series over time with a resampling ratio of $\frac{v_{tg}}{v_{ob}}$, which is based on the hypothesis that the total displacement of the limbs relative to the torso is analogous across different walking speeds.

After normalization, only human identity information is retained while gait-irrelevant factors are removed. The normalized GBVP is visualized in Fig. 4(c), where torso speed is compensated and walking direction is normalized to a fixed direction.

3.2   Recognition Mechanism

Fundamental Model. Generally speaking, each single GBVP captures limbs' velocity distribution relative to the torso, and GBVP series exhibit how the distribution varies over time. As shown in the upper half of Fig. 5, we adopt a deep neural network (DNN) to best depict the characteristics of GBVP.

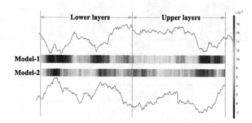

Fig. 6. Network weights trained from two datasets (lower layers share commonalities).

The input of the fundamental DNN model is of size $20 \times 20 \times 30$, as velocity is quantized into 20 bins along the axis of the body-coordinate system, and GBVP series is adjusted to 30 snapshots after normalization. GaitID first applies 3D CNN onto the GBVP series for spatial feature compression and time redundancy reduction. Convolution operations along the time domain also alleviate single GBVP estimation error. 16 convolutional filters of size $5 \times 5 \times 5$ output 16 3D matrices of size $16 \times 16 \times 26$. Then the max-pooling layer is applied to down-sample feature maps to the size of $8 \times 8 \times 26$. By flattening the feature maps except for the time dimension, we obtain a vector series of size 1024×26. And a fully connected (FC) layer is appended.

Recurrent layers are also incorporated into the model to model the temporal dynamics of the vector series. Considering the long-term characteristics of GBVP as a gait cycle always lasts for a duration of more than one second [5], regular RNN suffers from the vanishing gradient problem [9], which hinders them from being used for long-term information extraction. Thus, instead of regular RNN, we adopt a better variation of RNNs: Long Short Term Networks (LSTM) [10]. The output of LSTM is then encoded with the softmax layer to do multiclass classification.

Transfer Learning for Reducing Training Efforts. Despite the fact that the structure of the fundamental model is not that sophisticated, the DNN model still demands enormous training data to converge. And when a new user is added into the human identification system, he/she must perform massive gait activities. Evaluation results in Sect. 4 shows that there will be a rapid reduction in recognition accuracy even if the amount of training data decreases slightly.

Our solution was inspired by the observation that neural networks trained on similar datasets often share commonalities, i.e., the model trained on similar datasets undergo analogous convergence procedure to some extent [11,15]. This characteristic is exploited in a well-known research realm called *Transfer Learning*.

To testify the validity of Transfer Learning in gait recognition, we tune the fundamental model from scratch on two independent datasets separately, each of which is composed of GBVP series from two different users. We visualize and compare the network weights from the two converged models. As can be seen from Fig. 6, the lower layers of the neural network have an analogous distribution of weights while the upper layers vary a lot. This phenomenon paves the way to transfer the information learned from different datasets and alleviate data collection effort.

To leverage this generalizability between datasets, GaitID first trains a model on the pre-collected large-scale dataset, which consists of GBVP from n_class_1 persons. Then GaitID replaces the softmax layer in the fundamental model with a different shape of n_class_2 and initiates it randomly. The remaining weights of the model are initialized with the weights copied from the pre-trained model. The lower half of Fig. 5 shows how transfer learning is applied in GaitID. We will demonstrate that starting from the transferred structure and weights, our model can converge on the new dataset with significantly fewer data instances in Sect. 4.

4   Evaluation

4.1   Experimental Methodology

GaitID is implemented on one Wi-Fi sender and six Wi-Fi receivers, each of which is equipped with Intel 5300 wireless NIC and Linux CSI Tool [1]. We conduct experiments under two different indoor environments illustrated in Fig. 7(a). We designed four linear tracks, including two perpendicular lines to both axes and two diagonal lines shown in Fig. 7(b). Each of these tracks has enough length for five steps and users can walk on both ways.

We recruited 11 volunteers(4 females and 7 males) to participate in our experiments, covering the height 155 cm to 186 cm and weight 44 kg to 75 kg and age from 20 to 28 years old. These volunteers were asked to walk normally with different speeds on those tracks and each data sample contains five steps. Specifically, 10 of the volunteers were asked to walk on each direction of four tracks 50 times in Hall, contributing 10 users × 4 tracks × 2 directions × 50 instances for datasets. 3 of the volunteers in the Discussion Room contributed 3 users × 4 tracks × 2 directions × 25 instances in the dataset. All experiments were approved by our IRB.

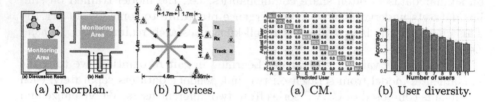

(a) Floorplan.   (b) Devices.   (a) CM.   (b) User diversity.

Fig. 7. Experiment setup.   **Fig. 8.** Overall accuracy.

4.2   Overall Performance

Figure 8(a) shows the confusion matrix (CM) for all of the 11 users. The overall identification accuracy is 76.2%. From the confusion matrix, most users experience an accuracy over 75% except for user E, H and J, which may be attributed to their walking manner of putting hands in pockets, leading to infrequent motion on arms and induce less features in GBVP. User J and F are likely to be confused, which may be caused by their similarities in body shape.

Figure 8(b) further shows the identification accuracy for different user numbers. Basically, the identification accuracy declines with more users involved, which is intuitive because more categories would lead to more crowded feature clusters in feature space. The accuracy for two users is above 99%, meaning that the extracted gait features are distinct for identification. It's notable that GaitID holds its accuracy above 93.2% for about 5 users, demonstrating its potential for smart home applications where there are only a few users in indoor scenarios.

4.3   Generalizability Evaluation

Accelerating Performance. The process of GBVP extraction is accelerated by the novel acceleration algorithm. To validate the efficiency and effectiveness of GBVP over BVP, we collect 400 samples of CSI from three volunteers and each corresponds to 4 steps. We then extract BVP as well as GBVP with different accelerating windows sizes (as described in Sect. 3.1). The system is running on a server with 32 cores of Intel Xeon CPU E5-2620 v4 @ 2.10 GHz and Matlab2016b installed. The system running delay and recognition accuracy are demonstrated in Fig. 9(a). As can be seen, even with 2 s of CSI as input, the BVP extraction would last for unbearably 78 s. However, with our proposed accelerating algorithm, the feature extraction speed can be accelerated 156 times while maintaining the recognition accuracy to some extent. The GBVP extraction delay is 0.5 s with a window size of 5×5 and the accuracy holds above 83%, which enables the system responds in real-time. We believe the proposed accelerating algorithm would push the BVP to a broader application prospect on other motion recognition scenarios.

Normalization Performance. For walking tracks independence, we randomly select two users' data from all the datasets, using one track as test and the remaining three tracks to train our model, ignoring their walking speed. As is shown in Fig. 9(b), the overall accuracy with normalized GBVP is significantly above that without normalization. The second track benefits least from normalization because we selected its direction as the reference direction and the GBVP from other tracks are rotated to match this orientation. For walking speed independence, we classify all the collected data into 6 categories, each with quantized speed. We then select one category as test and the others to train the model. Figure 9(c) demonstrates the remarkable improvements with normalization. The fifth category benefits the least from normalization because we selected its speed as the reference speed and GBVP with other speeds are normalized to this case.

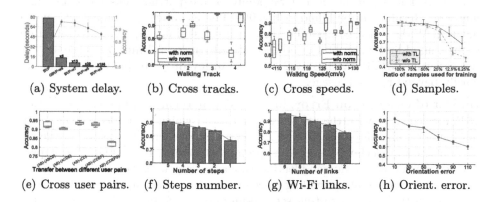

(a) System delay.   (b) Cross tracks.   (c) Cross speeds.   (d) Samples.

(e) Cross user pairs.   (f) Steps number.   (g) Wi-Fi links.   (h) Orient. error.

Fig. 9. Experimental results of GaitID.

Transfer Learning Performance. Transfer learning needs fewer data to retrain the model. To verify the number of samples needed for convergence, we randomly selected four([A,B,C,D]) users' data with 4×400 samples containing all the tracks and speeds. These samples are feed into a pre-trained model that has already been tuned on users [A,E]. Results can be found in Fig. 9(d). With transferred model structure and weights, only 12.5% of the data samples are needed to keep accuracy above 80%. But when training from scratch, accuracy can hardly exceed above 60%. We also evaluated the transformation between different user pairs. Figure 9(e) exhibits a consistency in generalizability between different user set pairs. The slight degradation of accuracy for user pair (A,B)-(C,D,E,F,G) may attributes to user G's great similarities in gait patterns with the other users.

4.4   Parameter Study

Impact of Gait Instances. To evaluate the impact of gait instances on identification accuracy, we randomly select four users and let them to perform 5 steps of walk. We then manually split steps into different numbers by DFS peaks and valleys. Results can be found in Fig. 9(f). The performance falls slightly from 5 steps to 2 steps but tumbles to below 78% with a single step. The reason is that a full gait cycle contains 2 consecutive steps, each of which is insufficient for representations of identity. Meanwhile, gait is a periodic motion and the repetition of gait cycles introduces trivial extra information for gait characteristics. Result from temporal memorability of LSTM in our model, GaitID is capable of retaining distinctions from single gait cycles. Hence, we claim that 2 consecutive steps are sufficient for human identification. In practice, we suggest to use four steps for a more robust performance.

Impact of Link Numbers. In the formulation of extracting GBVP for gait, we adopted 6 Wi-Fi links, which potentially contains redundancy. In this section, we evaluate the impact of link numbers to the performance. We randomly selected four users for classification and randomly prune partial links to reduce link numbers. Results can be found in Fig. 9(g). The accuracy gradually slides when involved Wi-Fi links reduced. This is because less links captures less reflection paths caused by human body, and theoretically at least 3 links are necessary to recover valid GBVP. With only 2 links, accuracy drops to below 80% and are hardly beyond research usage.

Impact of Orientation Error. In the GBVP normalization process, we rotate GBVP to identify with the reference orientation, which demands a precise estimation of walking direction. However, orientation extracted from state-of-the-art motion tracking techniques contains prominent errors. To evaluate the impact of orientation error on human identification accuracy, we generated training and testing set by manually providing trace orientation, and added controllable orientation disturbance to testing set. Results can be found in Fig. 9(h). As the illustration shown, an orientation error within $50°$ doesn't noticeably deteriorate accuracy, while an orientation error above $50°$ witnesses an unacceptable dilution in identification accuracy. Hence, the four tracks with eight orientations designed in our evaluation implementation are sufficient to represent more complicated walking traces.

5 Conclusion

In this paper, we present GaitID, a Wi-Fi based person identification framework which is robust to walking trajectory with few training efforts. GaitID first proposes an enhanced gait-specific feature, which is theoretically environment, trajectory and speed independent, and then reduces the training efforts for new users by transfer learning technique.

Acknowledgments. This work is supported in part by the National Key Research Plan under grant No. 2016YFC0700100.

References

1. Halperin, D., Hu, W., Sheth, A., Wetherall, D.: Tool release: gathering 802.11n traces with channel state information. In: SIGCOMM CCR, p. 53, January 2011
2. Jiang, W., et al.: Towards environment independent device free human activity recognition. In: Proceedings of ACM MobiCom, pp. 289–304 (2018)
3. Han, J., Bhanu, B.: Statistical feature fusion for gait-based human recognition. In: Proceedings of IEEE CVPR, p. II (2004)
4. Li, X., et al.: Indotrack: device-free indoor human tracking with commodity WI-FI. In: Proceedings of ACM IMWUT, pp. 72:1–72:22, September 2017
5. Murray, M.P., Drought, A.B., Kory, R.C.: Walking patterns of normal men, March 1964
6. Qian, K., Wu, C., Zhang, Y., Zhang, G., Yang, Z., Liu, Y.: Widar2.0: passive human tracking with a single Wi-Fi link. In: Proceedings of ACM MobiSys, pp. 350–361 (2018)
7. Qian, K., Wu, C., Zhou, Z., Zheng, Y., Yang, Z., Liu, Y.: Inferring motion direction using commodity Wi-Fi for interactive exergames. In: Proceedings of ACM CHI (2017)
8. Rubner, Y., Tomasi, C., Guibas, L.J.: The earth mover's distance as a metric for image retrieval. Int. J. Comput. Vis. **40**, 99–121 (2000). https://doi.org/10.1023/A:1026543900054
9. Sak, H., Senior, A.W., Beaufays, F.: Long short-term memory based recurrent neural network architectures for large vocabulary speech recognition. CoRR abs/1402.1128 (2014)
10. Sherstinsky, A.: Fundamentals of recurrent neural network (RNN) and long short-term memory (LSTM) network. CoRR abs/1808.03314 (2018)
11. Taylor, M.E., Stone, P.: Transfer learning for reinforcement learning domains: a survey. J. Mach. Learn. Res. **10**, 1633–1685 (2009)
12. Wang, W., Liu, A.X., Shahzad, M.: Gait recognition using WiFi signals. In: Proceedings of ACM IMWUT, pp. 363–373 (2016)
13. Yang, Z., Wu, C., Liu, Y.: Locating in fingerprint space: wireless indoor localization with little human intervention. In: Proceedings of ACM MobiCom, pp. 269–280 (2012)

14. Yang, Z., Zhou, Z., Liu, Y.: From RSSI to CSI: indoor localization via channel response. ACM Comput. Surv. **46**, 25:1–25:32 (2013)
15. Yosinski, J., Clune, J., Bengio, Y., Lipson, H.: How transferable are features in deep neural networks? CoRR abs/1411.1792 (2014)
16. Zatsiorky, V., Werner, S., Kaimin, M.: Basic kinematics of walking: step length and step frequency: a review. J. Sports Med. Phys. Fitness **34**, 109–134 (1994)
17. Zeng, Y., Pathak, P.H., Mohapatra, P.: WiWho: WiFi-based person identification in smart spaces. In: Proceedings of ACM/IEEE IPSN, pp. 1–12 (2016)
18. Zhang, J., Wei, B., Hu, W., Kanhere, S.S.: WiFi-id: Human identification using WiFi signal. In: Proceedings of DCOSS, pp. 75–82 (2016)
19. Zhang, Y., Pan, G., Jia, K., Lu, M., Wang, Y., Wu, Z.: Accelerometer-based gait recognition by sparse representation of signature points with clusters. IEEE Trans. Cybern. **45**, 1864–1875 (2015)
20. Zheng, Y., et al.: Zero-effort cross-domain gesture recognition with Wi-Fi. In: Proceedings of ACM MobiSys, pp. 313–325 (2019)

Optimal Node Placement for Magnetic Relay and MIMO Wireless Power Transfer Network

Yubin Zhao[1], Junjian Huang[1(✉)], Xiaofan Li[2], and Cheng-Zhong Xu[3]

[1] Shenzhen Institutes of Advanced Technology, Chinese Academy of Sciences, Shenzhen 518055, China
{zhaoyb,huangjj}@siat.ac.cn
[2] School of Intelligent System Science and Engineering, Jinan Unniversity, Zhuhai 519070, China
lixiaofan0511@126.com
[3] State Key Laboratory of IoTSC and Department of Computer and Information Science, University of Macau, Macau 999078, China
czxu@um.edu.mo

Abstract. In this paper, we investigate a hybrid architecture of magnetic resonance multi-input multi-output (MIMO) and relay for wireless power transfer (WPT) network which both extend the power transfer distance and increases received power efficiency. We formulate the system model and derive the closed-form optimal beamforming solution. Then, we propose a hybrid transmitter (Tx) and relay coil placement algorithm, which is a linear searching scheme to find the optimal positions to provide the maximum uniform power distribution. The simulation results demonstrate that using the placement and beamforming algorithms can attain 2 to 5 times received power efficiency improvement, which is compared with equally assigned power on each Tx coil.

Keywords: Wireless power transfer · Magnetic MIMO · Node placement · Relay · Beamforming

1 Introduction

Wireless power transfer (WPT) is considered as a promising alternative for charging portable devices in the near future [2,10,13]. There are three main WPT technologies nowadays: inductive coupling, magnetic resonance and microwave

This work was partially supported by National Key R&D Program of China (No. 2019YFB2102100), National Nature Science Foundation of China (No. 61801306), Shenzhen Fundamental Research (No. JCYJ20180302145755311), Guangdong Special Fund for Science and Technology Development (No. 2019A050503001), Science and Technology Development Fund of Macao S.A.R (FDCT) under number 0015/2019/AKP, Shenzhen Discipline Construction Project for Urban Computing and Data Intelligence.

© Springer Nature Switzerland AG 2020
D. Yu et al. (Eds.): WASA 2020, LNCS 12384, pp. 743–754, 2020.
https://doi.org/10.1007/978-3-030-59016-1_61

radiation [1]. Among them, magnetic resonance (MR) has the advantages of having relatively long power transfer distance and high power transmission efficiency [5]. However, the power transfer efficiency quickly drops down if the coils are beyond the effective distance, which is bounded by the geometric parameters and topologies [12].

Recently, multiple transmitter coils are proposed to supply several devices simultaneously with a limited transmitted power [16]. Multiple transmitter coils can provide more degrees of freedom of the primary field or current distribution [9]. Motivated by the MIMO beamforming techniques, multiple coils can power up multiple devices using proper scheme, which is called Magnetic MIMO [14]. Lang proposed a maximum power transfer efficiency scheme with multiple transmitters using convex optimization [6]. Jadidian proposed MagMIMO technique in a real prototype, which employs a simple beamforming method to charge a single device with two transmitters [4]. Later, Shi et al. proposed the beamforming method to charge multiple devices with multiple transmitters, and implemented in the same prototype [15]. Moghadam et al. studied the node placement and distributed beamforming problem of the magnetic WPT system, and provided a close form formulation for 1D and 2D region [11]. However, the beamforming schemes mainly focus on increasing the power transfer efficiency, the distance is actually not effectively improved due to its near field nature.

Another improvement method is to add relay (or intermediate) coils to extend the charging distance. G. Dumphart et al. found frequency selective fading effect, which is similar to the wireless communications, and proposed a frequency tuning method [3]. Y. Zhang et al. constructed the equivalent circuit model (ECM) and analyzed the load matching problem of multiple relay coils [17]. K. Lee et al. investigated the relay coil placement with fixed Tx and Rx coils, and also analyze the key factors of power transfer efficiency [7,8]. W. X. Zhong et al. demonstrated an architecture with 2 Tx coils and 1 relay coil is more efficient than only 2 Tx coils, which is a simple magnetic MIMO and relay architecture [18].

In this paper, we investigate a hybrid architecture which combines the magnetic MIMO and relay coils to both extend the charging distance and power transfer efficiency. The first contribution is that we derive the optimal energy beamforming method of the hybrid architecture. The maximum power transfer efficiency is achieved with a given positions of Tx, relay and Rx coils. As a near-field power transfer technique, the power transfer efficiency of magnetic resonance also relies on the relative positions of the coils. Thus, the second contribution is that we investigate the placement strategy for Tx and relay coils to ensure the Rx coils can attain sufficient power in a certain charging area. A linear searching method for optimal placement is proposed. The beamforming algorithm and placement method are evaluated via simulations. The results demonstrate the improvements of the power efficiency and transmission distance of the proposed hybrid architecture.

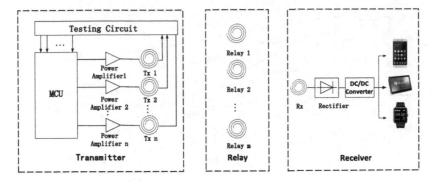

Fig. 1. The architecture of hybrid magnetic relay and MIMO WPT system.

2   Hybrid Magnetic Relay and MIMO Network

The hybrid architecture of magnetic resonance WPT system is depicted in Fig. 1, which mainly consists of the magnetic MIMO transmitter, the relay coils and the receivers. On the transmitter side, there are 4 components: the microcontroller unit (MCU), the testing circuit, the power amplifiers, and the transmitter coils. The central frequency is working at 6.78 MHz which follows the standards of AirFuel. The MCU is used to control the power amplifiers and the testing circuit is to detect the phase and amplitude of the coils, and sends the results to the MCU. On the relay side, a capacitor is embedded in the electric circuits with a coil so as to work on the same resonance frequency to the transmitter. The relay coil is a pure passive coil, which contains no battery, no load or communication module. On the receiver side, a single coil with a capacitor is embedded in the circuit together with a rectifier and a DC/DC converter.

3   Equivalent Circuit Model

Based on the hybrid architecture, we build the equivalent circuit in Fig. 2. We assume there are N_T transmitter coils, N_L relay coils and N_R receiver coils. In each transmitter coil, $V_{Tx(n)}$ indicates the input voltage for transmitter n, and $n \in N_T$; and $R_{Tx(n)}$, $I_{Tx(n)}$, $L_{Tx(n)}$ and $C_{Tx(n)}$ are the residence, current, self-inductance and capacitance for transmitter n. On the relay side, $R_{Rel(m)}$, $I_{Rel(m)}$, $L_{Rel(m)}$ and $C_{Rel(m)}$ are the parasitic residence, current, self-inductance and capacitance for relay m, where $m \in N_L$. Note that $R_{Rel(m)}$ can be very small. On the receiver side, $R_{Rx(k)}$, $I_{Rx(k)}$, $L_{Rx(k)}$ and $C_{Rx(k)}$ are the parasitic residence, current, self-inductance and capacitance for receiver k, where $k \in N_R$.

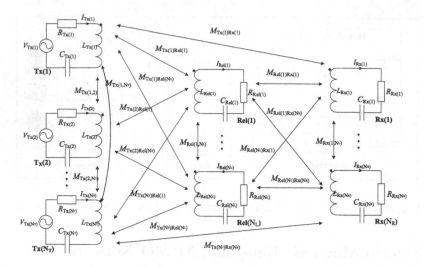

Fig. 2. Equivalent Circuit Model.

Then, we define the transmitter impedance and mutual inductance in the matrix form as follows:

$$\mathbf{Z}_T = \begin{pmatrix} Z_{Tx(1)} & j\omega M_{Tx1,2} & \cdots & j\omega M_{Tx1,N_T} \\ j\omega M_{Tx1,2} & Z_{Tx(2)} & \cdots & j\omega M_{Tx2,N_T} \\ \vdots & \vdots & \ddots & \vdots \\ j\omega M_{TxN_T,1} & j\omega M_{TxN_T,2} & \cdots & Z_{TxN_T} \end{pmatrix} \quad (1)$$

where $M_{Txn,u}$ indicates the mutual inductance between transmitter n and u. If the currents of the transmitter coils are working at resonance frequency, $L_{Tx(n)}$ and $C_{Tx(n)}$ can be eliminated and $Z_{Tx(n)} = R_{Tx(n)}$.

Since both of the relay coils and receiver coils are attaining the energy from the transmitter, we put the mutual inductance and impedance of these coils together. Thus, the mutual inductance matrix to the transmitter side is expressed as follows:

$$\mathbf{M} = \begin{pmatrix} M_{Rx(1)Tx(1)} & \cdots & M_{Rx(1)Tx(N_T)} \\ \vdots & \ddots & \vdots \\ M_{Rx(N_R)Tx(1)} & \cdots & M_{Rx(N_R)Tx(N_T)} \\ M_{Rel(1)Tx(1)} & \cdots & M_{Rel(1)Tx(N_T)} \\ \vdots & \ddots & \vdots \\ M_{Rel(N_L)Tx(1)} & \cdots & M_{Rel(N_L)Tx(N_T)} \end{pmatrix} \quad (2)$$

If we use $\mathbf{M}_{RxTx}$ and $\mathbf{M}_{RelTx}$ to indicate the mutual inductance matrix from receiver side and relay side to the transmitter side respectively, $\mathbf{M}$ is written as:

$$\mathbf{M} = \begin{pmatrix} \mathbf{M}_{RxTx} \\ \mathbf{M}_{RelTx} \end{pmatrix} \quad (3)$$

Then, we define the equivalent receiver impedance matrix, which consists of the impedances of receiver load and relay parasitic residence, mutual inductances among relay and receiver coils as shown in:

$$\mathbf{Z}_R = \begin{pmatrix} \mathbf{Z}_{Rx} & j\omega\mathbf{M}_{RxRel} \\ j\omega\mathbf{M}_{RxRel}^H & \mathbf{Z}_{Rel} \end{pmatrix} \tag{4}$$

where:

$$\mathbf{Z}_{Rx} = \begin{pmatrix} Z_{Rx(1)} & \cdots & j\omega M_{Rx(1,N_R)} \\ \vdots & \ddots & \vdots \\ \omega M_{Rx(N_R,1)} & \cdots & Z_{Rx(N_R)} \end{pmatrix} \tag{5}$$

and:

$$\mathbf{M}_{RxRel} = \begin{pmatrix} M_{Rx(1)Rel(1)} & \cdots & M_{Rx(1)Rel(N_L)} \\ \vdots & \ddots & \vdots \\ M_{Rx(N_R)Rel(1)} & \cdots & M_{Rx(N_R)Rel(N_L)} \end{pmatrix} \tag{6}$$

and:

$$\mathbf{Z}_{Rel} = \begin{pmatrix} Z_{Rel(1)} & \cdots & j\omega M_{Rel(1,N_L)} \\ \vdots & \ddots & \vdots \\ j\omega M_{Rel(N_L,1)} & \cdots & Z_{Rel(N_L)} \end{pmatrix} \tag{7}$$

According to Kirchhoffs voltage law (KVL) and Kirchhoffs current law (KCL), we attain the following equations:

$$i_R = j\omega\mathbf{Z}_R^{-1}\mathbf{M}i_T \tag{8}$$

$$V_T = (\mathbf{Z}_T + \omega^2\mathbf{M}^T\mathbf{Z}_R^{-1}\mathbf{M})i_T \tag{9}$$

where $i_R = [i_{Rx}^T, i_{Rel}^T]^T$ is the receiver current vector $i_{Rx} = [I_{Rx(1)}, \ldots, I_{Rx(N_R)}]^T$ and relay current vector $i_{Rel} = [I_{Rel(1)}, \ldots, I_{Rel(N_L)}]^T$ respectively; the transmitter current vector is $i_T = [I_{Tx(1)}, \ldots, I_{Tx(N_T)}]^T$; and $V_T = [V_{Tx(1)}, \ldots, V_{Tx(1)}]^T$ is the transmitter voltage vector.

4   Optimal Beamforming

Considering (8), we define the magnetic channel $\mathbf{H} = j\omega\mathbf{Z}_R^{-1}\mathbf{M}$. Then, we can separate $\mathbf{H}$ into 2 independent channel: $\mathbf{H} = [\mathbf{H}_{Rx}^T, \mathbf{H}_{Rel}^T]^T$, where $\mathbf{H}_{Rx}$ is the equivalent channel from Tx to the Rx coils, and $\mathbf{H}_{Rel}$ is the equivalent channel from Tx to the relay coils. Substituting $\mathbf{H}$ into (8), we have:

$$\begin{pmatrix} i_{Rx} \\ i_{Rel} \end{pmatrix} = \begin{pmatrix} \mathbf{H}_{Rx} \\ \mathbf{H}_{Rel} \end{pmatrix} i_T \tag{10}$$

The total power consumption is the sum of transmitters, relay coils and the receivers, which is $P = P_{Rx} + P_{Rel} + P_{Tx}$. Consider $P_{Rx} = i_{Rx}^*\mathbf{R}_{Rx}i_{Rx}$, $P_{Rel} = i_{Rel}^*\mathbf{R}_{Rel}i_{Rel}$, and $P_{Tx} = i_{Tx}^*\mathbf{R}_{Tx}i_{Tx}$. Then, the total power consumption is the sum of power consumptions on transmitters, receivers, and relays, in which we obtain:

$$P = i_{Rx}^* \mathbf{R}_{Rx} i_{Rx} + i_{Rel}^* \mathbf{R}_{Rel} i_{Rel} + i_T^* \mathbf{R}_{Tx} i_T \tag{11}$$

Substituting (10) into P, we have:

$$P = i_T^* (\mathbf{H}_{Rx}^* \mathbf{R}_{Rx} \mathbf{H}_{Rx} + \mathbf{H}_{Rel}^* \mathbf{R}_{Rel} \mathbf{H}_{Rel} + \mathbf{R}_{Tx}) i_T \tag{12}$$

We assume that the maximum total power is a constant value and our goal is to maximize the received power efficiency by controlling the transmitter coil currents, which is:

$$
\begin{aligned}
i_T^{bf} &= \arg\min_{i_T} \frac{P_{Rx}}{P} \\
&= \arg\min_{i_T} \frac{i_{Rx}^* \mathbf{R}_{Rx} i_{Rx}}{i_{Rx}^* \mathbf{R}_{Rx} i_{Rx} + i_{Rel}^* \mathbf{R}_{Rel} i_{Rel} + i_T^* \mathbf{R}_{Tx} i_T} \\
&= \arg\min_{i_T} \frac{i_T^* \mathbf{H}_{Rx}^* \mathbf{R}_{Rx} \mathbf{H}_{Rx} i_T}{i_T^* (\mathbf{H}_{Rx}^* \mathbf{R}_{Rx} \mathbf{H}_{Rx} + \mathbf{H}_{Rel}^* \mathbf{R}_{Rel} \mathbf{H}_{Rel} + \mathbf{R}_{Tx}) i_T}
\end{aligned}
\tag{13}
$$

with subject to $P \leq P_c$.

The objective is a non-convex quadratical constraint quadratic programming (QCQP) problems. A feasible solution is to use Lagrangian relaxation and Lagrangian multiplier method to approximate the optimal value. Here, we define the multiplier λ for the total power consumption constrain. Then, we obtain:

$$
\begin{aligned}
F(i_T, \lambda) = {}& i_T^* \mathbf{H}_{Rx}^* \mathbf{R}_{Rx} \mathbf{H}_{Rx} i_T \\
& + \lambda (i_T^* \mathbf{R}_{Tx} i_T + i_T^* \mathbf{H}_{Rel}^* \mathbf{R}_{Rel} \mathbf{H}_{Rel} i_T + i_T^* \mathbf{H}_{Rx}^* \mathbf{R}_{Rx} \mathbf{H}_{Rx} i_T - P_c)
\end{aligned}
\tag{14}
$$

and further attain the partial derivative to i_T as expressed:

$$\frac{\partial F(i_T, \lambda)}{\partial i_T} = \mathbf{H}_{Rx}^* \mathbf{R}_{Rx} \mathbf{H}_{Rx} i_T + \lambda (\mathbf{R}_T + \mathbf{H}_{Rel}^* \mathbf{R}_{Rel} \mathbf{H}_{Rel} + \mathbf{H}_{Rx}^* \mathbf{R}_{Rx} \mathbf{H}_{Rx}) i_T = 0 \tag{15}$$

Since $\lambda \neq 0$, we attain:

$$\lambda i_T = -(\mathbf{R}_T + \mathbf{H}_{Rel}^* \mathbf{R}_{Rel} \mathbf{H}_{Rel} + \mathbf{H}_{Rx}^* \mathbf{R}_{Rx} \mathbf{H}_{Rx})^{-1} \mathbf{H}_{Rx}^* \mathbf{R}_{Rx} \mathbf{H}_{Rx} i_T \tag{16}$$

Here, we define $\mathbf{Y} = -(\mathbf{R}_T + \mathbf{H}_{Rel}^* \mathbf{R}_{Rel} \mathbf{H}_{Rel} + \mathbf{H}_{Rx}^* \mathbf{R}_{Rx} \mathbf{H}_{Rx})^{-1} \mathbf{H}_{Rx}^* \mathbf{R}_{Rx} \mathbf{H}_{Rx}$, then, $\lambda i_T = \mathbf{Y} i_T$. According to the definition of matrix eigenvalue, it is obviously that λ is one of the eigenvalues for matrix $\mathbf{Y}$. Suppose $\mathbf{Y}$ has L_Y non-zero eigenvalues, where $L_Y \leq N_T$. Let λ_s denote the s-th eigenvalue of $\mathbf{Y}$, and x_s denote the corresponding unit eigenvector. Then, the corresponding vector i_T can be expressed as $\alpha_s x_s$, where α_s is a scale factor. Here, we define $\mathbf{X}_1 = \mathbf{R}_T + \mathbf{H}_{Rel}^* \mathbf{R}_{Rel} \mathbf{H}_{Rel} + \mathbf{H}_{Rx}^* \mathbf{R}_{Rx} \mathbf{H}_{Rx}$, and $\mathbf{X}_2 = \mathbf{H}_{Rx}^* \mathbf{R}_{Rx} \mathbf{H}_{Rx}$. Thus, the total power P can be formulated as:

$$P = \alpha_s{}^2 x_s^* \mathbf{X}_1 x_s \tag{17}$$

Then, we obtain:

$$\alpha_s = \sqrt{P(x_s^* \mathbf{X}_1 x_s)^{-1}} \tag{18}$$

Then, the received power efficiency is defined as $\phi_s = (x_s^* X_1 x_s)^{-1} x_s^* X_2 x_s$. It is obviously that $\phi_s = -\lambda_s$. Thus, we define $Z = -Y$, then, $\phi_s = \mu_s = -\lambda_s$, where μ_s is the eigenvalue of Z. Finally, we attain the maximum received power efficiency, which is the maximum eigenvalue of Z.

5 Node Placement

Since the magnetic channel (or mutual inductance) which relies on the relative positions of the coils determines the beamforming and received power efficiency performance, the coil placement is an essential aspect for magnetic relay and MIMO network. Due to the page limits, we only discuss the network node placement in 2D scenario.

5.1 2D Deployment

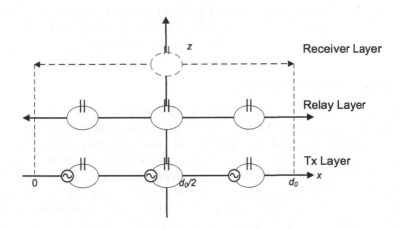

Fig. 3. The magnetic MIMO and relay coils deployment.

We consider deploying the Tx and relay coils in fixed positions horizontally, and the receiver can move around over the Tx and relay coils at a fixed height. Thus, as shown in Fig. 3, we divide the charging space into 3 layers, which is Tx layer, relay layer and Rx layer. The bottom is the Tx layer, where the Tx coils are placed horizontally along a line in parallel. The relay layer is in the middle between the Tx layer and Rx layer, in which the relay coils are also deployed along a line and above the Tx coils. And the Rx layer is above relay layer. Node that, all the coils can be moved horizontally. However, when the system is charging the receiver, Tx and relay coils are assumed to be fixed and Rx coil can still move along the Rx layer.

We also assume that the moving area of a receiver is limited, since magnetic resonance WPT is still a near-field wireless charging technique. Accordingly, the placing areas of Tx and relay coils are also limited, otherwise the transmitted power cannot be concentrated on the receiver. As illustrated in Fig. 3, the charging area is bound from 0 to d_0 for all the coils and vertical height for each layer is fixed. Then, the main objective for Tx and relay coil deployment is to maximize the received power around the effective moving area. However, the received power depends on the geometric relationship among the coils. Even if the Tx and relay coils are fixed, the receiver can also move along the Rx layer. We just ensure the minimum received power is maximized, and then all the positions along the Rx layer can attain sufficient power. In addition to beamforming, another kind of parameters can be adapted is the positions of Tx and relay coils. Consider the symmetric feature of magnetic MIMO topology, we just need to adapt the interval among the coils, which simplify the problem. Thus, the placement problem is formulated as:

$$\{\triangle d_{Tx}, \triangle d_{Rel}\} = \arg \max\{\min\{P_{Rx}(x_{Rx})\|x_{Rx} \in (0, d_0)\}\} \tag{19}$$

where $\triangle d_{Tx}$ and $\triangle d_{Rel}$ indicate the intervals of Tx coils and relay coils respectively, x_{Rx} is the receiver's position. Define $x_{Tx}(i)$ as the position of Tx coil, where $i \in N_T$, then $x_{Tx}(i) = \frac{d_0}{2} + (i - \frac{N_T+1}{2})\triangle d_{Tx}$. Similarly, define $x_{Rel}(j)$ as the position of relay coil, where $j \in N_{Rel}$, then $x_{Rel}(j) = \frac{d_0}{2} + (j - \frac{N_{Rel}+1}{2})\triangle d_{Rel}$.

5.2 Placement Optimization

To find the optimal placement of the Tx and relay coils, we propose a linear search scheme. Given a fixed number of Tx and relay coils, the maximum intervals are defined as d_{Tx} and d_{Rel} for Tx and relay coils respectively. Then, we have $0 < \triangle d_{Tx} \le d_{Tx}$ and $0 < \triangle d_{Rel} \le d_{Rel}$. We set a fixed step β, and increase $\triangle d_{Tx}$ and $\triangle d_{Rel}$ gradually with it. With given $\triangle d_{Tx}$ and $\triangle d_{Rel}$, we can construct placement topology of the Tx and relay coils, and calculate the optimal beamforming results of every position on the Rx layer according to μ_s. Then, the system will record the minimum received power and repeat the calculation with another $\triangle d_{Tx}$ and $\triangle d_{Rel}$. The algorithm is illustrated in Algorithm 1. To simplified the algorithm, we just need half of the Rx layer to find the minimum received power according to the symmetric feature of the magnetic resonance system.

6 Simulations

The beamforming and placement schemes are evaluated on a magnetic MIMO WPT simulation platform. On the transmitter side, several transmitter (Tx) coils with a serial of capacitors are connected with power amplifiers. An MCU is used to control the output voltages of the power amplifier and a testing circuit monitors the currents of the Tx coils. On the receiver side, an Rx coil and a serial capacitor are connect to a device. We assume that the device can measure the received power. The feedback information is transmitted from Rx to Tx via

---

Algorithm 1. Linear Searching Scheme for Optimal Placement

---
while $\triangle d_{Tx} > 0$ **do**
    for beamforming vectors $i = 1 : N_T$ **do**
        $x_{Tx}(i) = \frac{d_0}{2} + (i - \frac{N_T+1}{2})\triangle d_{Tx};$
    end for
    while $\triangle d_{Rel} > 0$ **do**
        for beamforming vectors $j = 1 : N_{Rel}$ **do**
            $x_{Rel}(j) = \frac{d_0}{2} + (j - \frac{N_{Rel}+1}{2})\triangle d_{Rel};$
        end for
        for All the Rx positions **do**
            Calculate according to μ_s and (12)
        end for
        Record minimum $\hat{P}_r$
        $\triangle d_{Rel} = \triangle d_{Rel} + \beta$
    end while
    $\triangle d_{Tx} = \triangle d_{Tx} + \beta$
end while
Find $\triangle d_{Tx}$ and $\triangle d_{Rel}$ with maximum $\hat{P}_r$

---

outband communication module. In our simulation, the resonance frequency is 6.78 MHz, which follows the AirFuel Standard. The radius of the Tx coil is 0.1 m, and the radius of the Rx coil is 0.05 m. Every coil has 10 turns. The inductance of the Tx coil is 20.4 μHz, and the series capacitor is 27 Pf for resonance. On the Rx side, the inductance of the Rx coil is 11.9 μHz and the series capacitor is 46 Pf. The total equivalent resistance for each single circuit is 10 Ω, considering the equivalent circuit resistance and the parasitic resistance. And the total power consumption of the whole system should not exceed 20 W.

6.1 Beamforming Performance

We firstly evaluate the improvements of the received power using relay coils. Three Tx coils and two relay coils are deployed. The vertical distance between the Tx and relay layers is 10 cm. One Rx coil is deployed above the relay layer, and we increase the vertical distance between the Rx and relay layers to observe the beamforming performance. As a comparison simulation, we only deploy three Tx coils with the same parameters and one Rx coil which is above the Tx layer. We also increase the vertical distance between the Tx and Rx layers to see the performance changes. As illustrated in Fig. 4, when the Rx coil is quite close to the Tx or relay coils, the received power efficiencies are similar and approach nearly 100%. However, when the vertical charging distance is increased, the received power efficiency drops dramatically using only magnetic MIMO, especially it is below 20% with 20 cm vertical charging distance. The hybrid architecture can significantly improve the beamforming performance, where the received power efficiency is still above 40% with a 30 cm charging distance.

6.2   Optimal Placement Evaluation

In the next simulation, we evaluate the optimal placement of the Tx and relay coils. We firstly deploy 2 Tx coils and 3 relay coils to extend the effective charging area. We compare the power transfer efficiency with the magnetic MIMO without relay coils. When the optimal placement are attained, the beamforming results are depicted in Fig. 5. Note that, the charging distance between Tx layer and Rx layer in Fig. reffigspstx2a is the same distance in Fig. 5b from relay layer to Rx layer. It can be observed that without the relay coils, the power transfer efficiency varies significantly from the boundary to the center in Fig. 5a. The lowest efficiency can achieve below 10%. With the improvement of relay coils in Fig. 5b, the efficiency is between 95% and 98.5%, which is greatly increased and the variations are reduced.

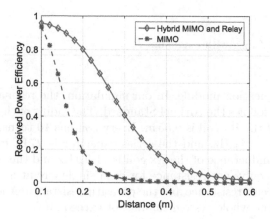

Fig. 4. The beamforming performance comparison. We compare the architecture of hybrid magnetic MIMO and relay topology with only magnetic MIMO.

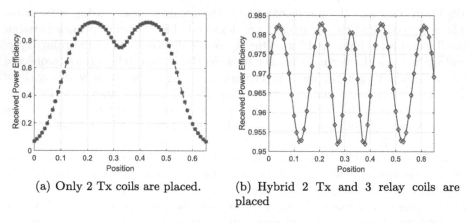

(a) Only 2 Tx coils are placed.   (b) Hybrid 2 Tx and 3 relay coils are placed

Fig. 5. The beamformed received power distributions for 2 Tx coils with and without relay coils.

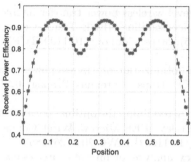

(a) Only 3 Tx coils are placed.

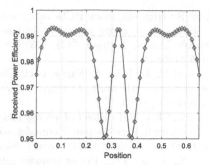

(b) Hybrid 3 Tx and 3 relay coils are placed

Fig. 6. The beamformed received power distributions for 3 Tx coils with and without relay coils.

Then, we employ 3 Tx and 3 relay coils for placement and evaluate the power transfer efficiency through all the charging area. The charging distance is the same in Fig. 5. The efficiencies are drawn in Fig. 6. It can be observed that even with 3 Tx coils, the variations are still high in Fig. 6a. However, when the relay coils are deployed, the efficiencies can be above 95% and even higher than 99% in some places.

7 Conclusion

The hybrid architecture of magnetic MIMO and relay can both extend the wireless power transfer distance and efficiency. In this paper, we investigate the beamforming method in such scenario. Further, we develop the placement algorithm for Tx and relay coils to effectively increase the power transfer efficiency in the whole charging area. Simulation results indicate that with our schemes, the power efficiency can be kept above 90% in the whole playing field.

References

1. Europe and the future for WPT: European contributions to wireless power transfer technology. IEEE Microwave Mag. **18**(4), 56–87 (2017). https://doi.org/10.1109/MMM.2017.2680078
2. Barzegaran, M.R., Zargarzadeh, H., Mohammed, O.A.: Wireless power transfer for electric vehicle using an adaptive robot. IEEE Trans. Magn. **53**(6), 1–4 (2017). https://doi.org/10.1109/TMAG.2017.2664800
3. Dumphart, G., Slottke, E., Wittneben, A.: Magneto-inductive passive relaying in arbitrarily arranged networks. In: 2017 IEEE International Conference on Communications (ICC), pp. 1–6 (2017). https://doi.org/10.1109/ICC.2017.7997344
4. Jadidian, J., Katabi, D.: Magnetic MIMO: how to charge your phone in your pocket. In: International Conference on Mobile Computing and NETWORKING, pp. 495–506 (2014)

5. Kim, S.: High-efficiency PCB- and package-level wireless power transfer interconnection scheme using magnetic field resonance coupling. IEEE Trans. Compon. Packag. Manuf. Technol. **5**(7), 863–878 (2015). https://doi.org/10.1109/TCPMT.2015.2446613

6. Lang, H.D., Ludwig, A., Sarris, C.D.: Convex optimization of wireless power transfer systems with multiple transmitters. IEEE Trans. Antennas Propag. **62**(9), 4623–4636 (2014)

7. Lee, K., Chae, S.H.: Effect of quality factor on determining the optimal position of a transmitter in wireless power transfer using a relay. IEEE Microw. Wirel. Compon. Lett. **27**(5), 521–523 (2017). https://doi.org/10.1109/LMWC.2017.2690853

8. Lee, K., Chae, S.H.: Power transfer efficiency analysis of intermediate-resonator for wireless power transfer. IEEE Trans. Power Electron. **33**(3), 2484–2493 (2018). https://doi.org/10.1109/TPEL.2017.2698638

9. Lee, S.B., Lee, C., Jang, I.G.: Precise determination of the optimal coil for wireless power transfer systems through postprocessing in the smooth boundary representation. IEEE Trans. Magn. **53**(6), 1–4 (2017). https://doi.org/10.1109/TMAG.2017.2654679

10. Li, Z., Zhu, C., Jiang, J., Song, K., Wei, G.: A 3-kw wireless power transfer system for sightseeing car supercapacitor charge. IEEE Trans. Power Electron. **32**(5), 3301–3316 (2017). https://doi.org/10.1109/TPEL.2016.2584701

11. Moghadam, M.R.V., Zhang, R.: Node placement and distributed magnetic beamforming optimization for wireless power transfer. IEEE Trans. Sig. Inf. Process. Netw. **4**, 264–279 (2017)

12. Moon, J., Hwang, H., Jo, B., Kwon, C.K., Kim, T.G., Kim, S.W.: Design and implementation of a high-efficiency 6.78 MHz resonant wireless power transfer system with a 5 W fully integrated power receiver. IET Power Electron. **10**(5), 577–587 (2017). https://doi.org/10.1049/iet-pel.2016.0107

13. Moon, J., Hwang, H., Jo, B., Shin, H.A., Kim, S.W.: Design of a 5 W power receiver for 6.78 MHZ resonant wireless power transfer system with power supply switching circuit. IEEE Trans. Consum. Electron. **62**(4), 349–354 (2016). https://doi.org/10.1109/TCE.2016.7838086

14. Sandoval, F.S., Delgado, S.M.T., Moazenzadeh, A., Wallrabe, U.: Nulls-free wireless power transfer with straightforward control of magnetoinductive waves. IEEE Trans. Microw. Theory Tech. **65**(4), 1087–1093 (2017). https://doi.org/10.1109/TMTT.2017.2672546

15. Shi, L., Kabelac, Z., Katabi, D., Perreault, D.: Wireless power hotspot that charges all of your devices. In: Proceedings of the 21st Annual International Conference on Mobile Computing and Networking, pp. 2–13. ACM (2015)

16. Sun, H., Lin, H., Zhu, F., Gao, F.: Magnetic resonant beamforming for secured wireless power transfer. IEEE Sig. Process. Lett. **24**(8), 1173–1177 (2017). https://doi.org/10.1109/LSP.2017.2703105

17. Zhang, Y., Lu, T., Zhao, Z., Chen, K., He, F., Yuan, L.: Wireless power transfer to multiple loads over various distances using relay resonators. IEEE Microw. Wirel. Compon. Lett. **25**(5), 337–339 (2015). https://doi.org/10.1109/LMWC.2015.2409776

18. Zhong, W.X., Zhang, C., Liu, X., Hui, S.Y.R.: A methodology for making a three-coil wireless power transfer system more energy efficient than a two-coil counterpart for extended transfer distance. IEEE Trans. Power Electron. **30**(2), 933–942 (2015). https://doi.org/10.1109/TPEL.2014.2312020

EdgeCC: An Authentication Framework for the Fast Migration of Edge Services Under Mobile Clients

Zhihui Zhao[1,2], Weizhong Wang[3(✉)], Hongsong Zhu[1,2], Hong Li[1,2], Limin Sun[1,2], Sen Zhao[1,2], and Yan Hu[4]

[1] School of Cyber Security, University of Chinese Academy of Sciences, Beijing, China
{zhaozhihui0820, zhuhongsong, lihong, sunlimin, Zhaosen}@iie.ac.cn
[2] Institute of Information Engineering, Chinese Academy of Sciences, Beijing, China
[3] China Academy of Industrial Internet, Beijing, China
wangweizhong@china-aii.com
[4] School of Computer and Communication Engineering, University of Science and Technology, Beijing, China
huyan@ustb.edu.cn

Abstract. Nowadays edge computing has been widely recognized. It is a location sensitive service, which is suitable for mobile clients to get local real-time services. In order to ensure the service's reliability and continuity during moving, clients need to switch service edges and data of clients need to be migrated between different edges. This process is different from mobile communication, in which clients cannot decide when to switch by judging the state of the network, edge need to perform the action actively and seamlessly. To solve the problem, we base on the advantages of three-level architecture of edge computing and propose EdgeCC, a client-edge-cloud collaborative authentication framework. By theoretical analysis and simulation with NS3, we compare EdgeCC with two existed frameworks in terms of processing and transmission delay, client's energy consumption and participation, migration frequency, proving the superiority of EdgeCC. Meanwhile, we analyze security issues for mobile clients, edges and cloud in migration authentication of edge computing, and provide some security settings to solve them.

Keywords: Edge computing · Mobile client · Service migration authentication · Client-edge-cloud collaboration

1 Introduction

In the context of growing data on IoT (Internet of Things) devices, cloud computing is increasingly difficult to provide great services because of high latency and high bandwidth consumption. With the rise of edge computing [1], the IoT has entered the era of client-edge-cloud collaboration, and the edge will play a more important role in

© Springer Nature Switzerland AG 2020
D. Yu et al. (Eds.): WASA 2020, LNCS 12384, pp. 755–767, 2020.
https://doi.org/10.1007/978-3-030-59016-1_62

the open service of IoT. The basic idea of edge computing is that the location where tasks are computed is close to data source, therefore edge computing is a typical location sensitive service (LSS). At present, some computing paradigms are similar with edge computing, such as fog computing [2], Cloudlet [3], sea-cloud computing [4], etc. Their architecture has different special characteristics. Here we mainly consider the three-level client-edge-cloud architecture for edge computing. The definitions of client, edge and cloud are as follows: **1) Client.** Devices, such as mobile phones, intelligent household appliances, various sensors, cameras, etc. **2) Edge.** An edge usually serves a specific area, such as a district, county, etc. And it is deployed 10 to 30 km from the target service area to provide computing, storage and network services. It has a special line or backbone network to connect with cloud. **3) Cloud.** It is the center of traditional cloud computing, which is rich in resources to serve multiple regions. Meanwhile, the cloud is the controller for edge computing.

Motivation and Challenge

In some application scenarios where mobile clients obtain services from edge computing, clients need to aware context of edge services. For example, under the Internet of Vehicles, users enjoy the real-time voice services from edges through mobile clients. When the user is away from the original service edge in an intelligent voice dialogue scenario, the new service edge needs to obtain the existed relative data of original edge. Therefore, it is necessary to analyze users' expression comprehensively to ensure the correctness and rationality of the reply. This procedure focuses on the migration of service data between different edges. Mobile clients need to achieve switching edge seamlessly when access service from different edges, and service data should migrate between different edges as well. Liu et al. [5] proposed that client's mobility support is a key research issue in edge computing. The process for mobile clients to obtain services between different edges involves communication among client, edge and cloud, which need to implement strict identity authentication and permission verification mechanisms. Xiao et al. [6] reviewed existed authentication mechanisms of edge computing and acknowledged their importance. Therefore, a fast and secure migration authentication framework of edge services for mobile clients is an urgent issue.

The process of cross-region service migration of edge computing is different from mobile communication [7] services in the following three aspects: 1) Mobile clients cannot naturally perceive edge's service efficiency. Switching base stations does not necessarily require switching of edge service access points; 2) In edge computing, deploying applications and access networks in base stations belong to different service providers, resulting in data heterogeneity and increasing difficulty of migration; 3) Edge computing service is a LSS. It is easy to leak the user's location privacy during communication, and link the user's real identity with anonymous identity.

Our Contribution

To solve these problems and achieve the goal of low latency, low overhead and high security, we make full use of the three-level architecture of edge computing to propose the EdgeCC, a client-edge-cloud collaborative service migration authentication framework for mobile clients. During service migration authentication, we prove the EdgeCC's advantage by comparing with existed works. The main results and contributions of this paper are as follows:

- EdgeCC solves the shortcomings of existed works without compromising security. Compared existed frameworks, EdgeCC saves about 40% of the service migration authentication delays in a single authentication. At the same client's moving path and speed, EdgeCC can reduce the frequency of service migration and client's energy consumption with low and medium client's moving speeds, the savings can reach 50%.
- We analyze the possible security issues of clients, edges and clouds during service migration authentication, and use asymmetric cryptography, ring signature and timestamp to realize the security and anonymity. EdgeCC weakens the participation of clients with low security protection levels.

The rest of the paper is organized as follows. We first discuss related work in Sect. 2. We describe the problem and EdgeCC in Sect. 3. The theoretical analysis and simulation with NS3 [8] are in Sect. 4 and Sect. 5 respectively. We analyze the security of EdgeCC in Sect. 6. Finally, we introduce the possible future research directions and conclusion in Sect. 7.

2   Related Work

Wang et al. [9] used the Markov decision process (MDP) to analyze the threshold conditions in the case of a random walk in one dimension, and judged whether the edge data was stored at the original edge or migrated to the new edge. Meanwhile, to decide whether or not to migrate service data between edges, Wang et al. [10] also use MDP to analyze the migration strategy in the case of a random walk in two dimensions. Further, they applied theoretical results to practical verification [11]. For specific migration schemes, some scholars have proposed using VM agents [12] and mobile agents [13], where mobile agents are better [14]. We think that mobile agents and VM agents focus on the movement of computing data between edges, they do not address the issue of service migration authentication.

Existing researches have studied some fast authentication for edge computing. Huang et al. [15] proposed a physical non-updatable function (PUF) authentication scheme for edge devices with limited resources. Wu et al. [12] proposed an identity-based lightweight message authentication scheme using elliptic curve cryptography. It reduces the overhead of signing and authentication and provides conditional privacy protection. Zhang et al. [16] proposed a roadside base station unit-assisted authentication scheme in a connected vehicle scenario using k-anonymity mechanism. They are detailed mechanisms and not applicable to the problem in this paper. Cloudlet [3] and CloudPath [17] obtain new services by terminating existed tasks and starting new VMs at the new edge, avoiding the edge service migration. Xie et al. [18] propose two migration frameworks: **1) Edge dominated migration:** The edge is connected to certain mobile base stations (BS). When clients switch the BS during moving, if the BS doesn't connect to the original edge, clients will request service from new edges, the request information provides the location of the original edge. New edge uses it to establish connection and migration service data with the original edge. For location information from clients, the new edge need query the cloud to obtain the original edge's location, the accuracy of this method is poor. **2) Client assisting migration:** the client's storage capacity is used to transfer the data for service migration. When the client leaves the service area of original edge, the edge sends application and status data to client for storage. When the client enters a service area of new edge and requests service, it sends the stored relevant data to the new edge for reconstructing state, and then the new edge provides service. It has very obvious disadvantages: a large amount of application and status data is translated between edge and client will consume much bandwidth, and it will occupy a large amount of memory resources of clients, their memory resources are limited.

Therefore, current academic researches about migration authentication for edge computing service do not solve problem for mobile clients well. At the same time, because edge computing is a new thing, a large number of applications are gradually landed. According to our investigation, our research problem has not been well considered and resolved in the industry.

3   Overview Design

In this chapter, we first describe the problem intuitively. Based on taking advantage of three-level architecture of edge computing, we propose EdgeCC, a client-edge-cloud collaborative authentication framework for the fast migration of edge-services under mobile clients, and analyze its unique features and advantages.

Problem Description
When a mobile client accesses different edges to obtain services, its service switching capability should be similar to mobile communication. Here, we simplified the edge computing to a three-level logical architecture with client, edge and cloud, as shown in Fig. 1. The client obtains services from edge 1 currently, but due to it is moving, there will be the situation where the client location exceeds the reliable service range provided by edge 1, resulting that it is unable to enjoy high-quality services. Because edges have obvious local characteristics, client needs to request service from the edge 2 which is closer. The edge 1 migrates client's data to edge 2 to ensure service reliability and continuity. Our work focus on achieving fast identity authentication when data migrates from edge 1 to edge 2 under mobile clients, and ensuring the security.

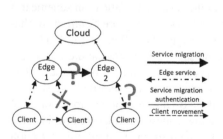

Fig. 1. The migration problem for Edge computing

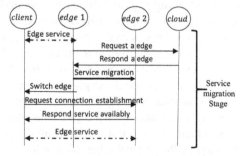

Fig. 2. The process of EdgeCC

EdgeCC

We propose EdgeCC, an authentication framework for the fast migration of edge services for mobile clients. In the EdgeCC, the original edge will participate in the entire migration authentication process as the main body. It is responsible for sensing the QoS and requesting or notifying the cloud or client for the new serviceable edge. The client only receives service and new edge information passively. The basic process of EdgeCC is as follows. When the original edge perceives that the client's QoS cannot be guaranteed, without client's knowledge, it requests cloud for a new edge that can provide service subsequently, then original edge migrates service data to new edge, and notifies the client to request service from the new edge. After client establishes a connection with the new edge, the edge service migration ends. We find that in EdgeCC, the edges with rich resource take the main part in the entire process. The total times of communication and the times of communication of client participates in are reduced significantly, and greatly reduces participation of client in migration authentication. The process of EdgeCC is shown in Fig. 2. It should be noted that the new edge obtained all data about the mobile client from the original edge, including service data and identity data. Therefore, the new edge does not need to verify the client's identity to cloud, and can directly provide service to the client, saving time for performing verification again.

In summary, we have implemented the EdgeCC that is a client-edge-cloud collaborative service migration authentication framework for mobile clients. Intuitively, it takes full advantage of the three-level architecture of edge computing and greatly reduces the migration authentication cost.

4 Theoretical Analysis

We compare EdgeCC with Edge dominated migration and Client assisting migration by theoretical analyzing. Because mobile clients have limited computing power, battery and other resources, edges' and cloud's resource are abundant relatively, we take the mobile client as the main research object, and take the delay, energy consumption, and frequency of service migration authentication as evaluation indicators. In completing a service migration authentication, we compare three frameworks, proving the superiority of EdgeCC. We assume when an edge fails to provide service for clients nearly, cloud can quickly detect and respond to schedule the optimal edge that can provide services for clients. We assume that times of mobile client, edge and cloud send or receive messages are t_1, t_2, t_3 respectively, the energy consumption are e_1, e_2, e_3, and the communication times of client-cloud, client-edge, edge-edge and edge-cloud are $\tau_1, \tau_2, \tau_3, \tau_4$.

Edge Dominated Migration. During the service migration phase, the client, edge and cloud are all involved in receiving or sending messages. The times of operations are 2, 8 and 2. Their total delays and energy consumption are $2t_1$, $8t_2$, $2t_3$ and $2e_1$, $8e_2$, $2e_3$. Throughout the process, the times of client-cloud, client-edge, edge-edge and edge-cloud communication are 0, 2, 2 and 2 respectively.

We find that the total times of communications is 6, and the total delay of the client, edge and cloud processing sending or receiving messages is $t_{total} = 2t_1 + 8t_2 + 2t_3$, the total transmission delay is $\tau_{total} = 2\tau_2 + 2\tau_3 + 2\tau_4$, the total energy consumption of client is $E_{client} = 2e_1$.

Client Assisting Migration. During the service migration phase, the client, edge and cloud are all involved in receiving or sending messages. The times of operations are 5, 5 and 4. Their total delays and energy consumption are $5t_1$, $5t_2$, $4t_3$ and $5e_1$, $5e_2$, $4e_3$. Throughout the process, the times of client-cloud, client-edge, edge-edge and edge-cloud communication are 2, 3, 0 and 2 respectively.

We find that the times of communications is 7, and the total delay of the client, edge and cloud processing sending or receiving messages is $t'_{total} = 5t_1 + 5t_2 + 4t_3$, the total transmission delay is $\tau'_{total} = 2\tau_1 + 3\tau_2 + 2\tau_4$, the total energy consumption of client is $E'_{client} = 5e_1$. Noting that the total energy consumption of client only includes the authentication process.

EdgeCC. In the service migration phase of EdgeCC, the operations times of receiving or sending messages for client, edge and cloud are 3, 5 and 2 respectively, so their total delays and energy consumption are $3t_1$, $5t_2$, $2t_3$ and $3e_1$, $5e_2$, $2e_3$. Throughout the process, the times of client-cloud, client-edge, edge-edge and edge-cloud communication are 0, 3, 0 and 2, respectively.

We find that the total times of communications is 5, and the total delay of client, edge and cloud processing sending or receiving messages is $t''_{total} = 3t_1 + 5t_2 + 2t_3$, the total transmission delay is $\tau''_{total} = 3\tau_2 + 2\tau_4$, the total energy consumption of mobile client is $E''_{client} = 3e_1$.

Migration Authentication Delay
According to formalization of indicators for service migration authentication, we find that the message processing delays for three frameworks are as follows:
$$t_{total} = 2t_1 + 8t_2 + 2t_3, \; t'_{total} = 5t_1 + 5t_2 + 4t_3 \; \text{and} \; t''_{total} = 3t_1 + 5t_2 + 2t_3$$

Apparently, EdgeCC's message processing delay is lower than Client assisting migration's. When EdgeCC compares with edge-dominated migration, the result isn't very clear.

For transmission delay, the delay of three frameworks are as follows:
$$\tau_{total} = 2\tau_2 + 2\tau_3 + 2\tau_4, \; \tau'_{total} = 2\tau_1 + 3\tau_2 + 2\tau_4 \; \text{and} \; \tau''_{total} = 3\tau_2 + 2\tau_4$$

Apparently, EdgeCC's transmission delay is lower than Client assisting migration's. Different edges were connected by wired network, mobile clients and edges were connected by wireless network. When EdgeCC compares with edge-dominated migration, EdgeCC has a smaller transmission delay intuitively.

Migration Energy Consumption
The energy consumption of sending or receiving for client is the main source. For three frameworks are as $E_{client} = 2e_1$, $E'_{client} = 5e_1$ and $E''_{client} = 3e_1$. In once migration authentication, EdgeCC has less client's energy consumption than edge dominated migration, and EdgeCC has more client's energy consumption than edge dominated migration.

Above, we assume that client's location is same at any time for three migration authentication frameworks, and the locations of the edge and cloud are fixed, so we do not consider that QoS is varying with client moving. Then the three migration frameworks only have the difference of migration authentication framework.

Service Migration Frequency

Here, we analyze the case that QoS is varying with client moving. considering the maximum service radius of edges to provide reliable service, we analyze the service migration frequency of three frameworks on same paths. It is assumed that the coverage area of edges diverges outward in a circle, and the QoS changes the most in the radial direction.

In Client assisting migration, edge-dominated migration and EdgeCC, the service migration authentication delays are $t_{total} + \tau_{total}$ $t'_{total} + \tau'_{total}$ and $t''_{total} + \tau''_{total}$ respectively. During this period, the maximum distances that client can move in the radial direction can calculate by $d = t_{total} \times v$ where v is client's moving speed. The guaranteed QoS coverage radius is d_b, then there is a threshold for the client-edge migration distance: $d_{c-ed} \leq d_b - (t_{total} + \tau_{total})v.d_{ch-e}$ has a negative linear relationship with $t_{total} + \tau_{total}$ under v. $t''_{total} + \tau''_{total}$ is the smallest intuitively, so EdgeCC's d_{c-ed} is the biggest. Therefore, EdgeCC has a larger migration distance threshold for the client-edge. Edges can provide reliable QoS with a larger service radius, and mobile clients maintain same service connection for longer time. At the same edge distribution density and moving path, mobile clients can have smaller migration frequency with EdgeCC, so it reduces the energy consumption and service delay caused by frequent migration.

5 Simulation Analysis

At present, edge computing is emerging. Many Internet companies, telecom operators, etc. are rapidly joining the field and actively deploying it to earn. However, applications of edge computing are appearing gradually, and suitable experimental platforms and environments are lacking extremely. Therefore, we will simulate by NS3 to verify the theoretical result. We set 1 node to act the cloud and 25 nodes to act edges and AP nodes simultaneously, edges are evenly distributed in a mesh network, and are connected to the cloud with one hop. Meanwhile we set 1 node to act the mobile client.

Migration Authentication Delay

For the message processing delay, we set the processing capabilities of clients, edges and cloud are same. Since the processing time of one data packet is short extremely, so we statistic the time for sending 1000 data packets and repeat 10 times. As shown in Fig. 3, the blue and orange lines are the time for accepter and sender to process a message respectively, and they are same basically, it also proves that our assumption is reasonable that the time of sending or receiving message is equal in theoretical analysis. The red and yellow lines are the ratio of processing time once migration authentication for EdgeCC, Edge dominated migration and client assisting migration respectively. When EdgeCC compare with Client assisting migration and edge-dominated migration, the simulation results show that EdgeCC can reduce message processing delay by about 40% and 20%.

For the message transmission delay, it is affected by the actual deployment of clients, edges and cloud. Due to the lack of large-scale applications of edge computing and relevant public data about delay, so we test the delay on actual cloud servers. Here, we search for "keyword: cloud server, country: China, city: Beijing" through Shodan [19], and obtain 222 valid server IPs. We randomly selected 10 pingable server IPs from the China Unicom Cloud. A mobile client performs 1000 times ping operations, the internet is provided by China Unicom. The client-cloud average delay is 13 ms. Meanwhile, we set up the edge in the path of client and cloud. Similarly, the client performs ping operations to edge, the client-edge average delay is 2 ms, so the edge-cloud average delay is 11 ms. According to [20], the edge-edge average delay is 10 ms.

Based on the above data, we can get in the actual transmission delay of edge computing for edge-dominated migration, Client assisting migration and EdgeCC respectively

$$\tau_{total} = 46\,ms,\ \tau'_{total} = 54\,ms\ \text{and}\ \tau''_{total} = 28\,ms$$

$$\text{So}\quad \omega_1 = \frac{\tau''_{total}}{\tau_{total}} \approx 0.61\ \text{and}\ \omega_2 = \frac{\tau''_{total}}{\tau'_{total}} \approx 0.52$$

As a result, under current internet condition, EdgeCC has a significant effect on some delay-sensitive scenarios. EdgeCC Compare with Client assisting migration and edge-dominated migration, EdgeCC's transmission delay can reduce about 50% and 40% respectively, the absolute value is about 20 ms or more. For some application scenarios with high real-time requirements and frequent service migration (such as high-speed vehicles), EdgeCC is great.

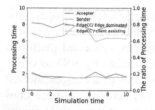
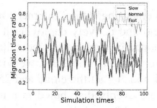
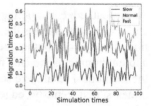

Fig. 3. The processing time for sending and receiving messages (Color figure online)

Fig. 4. EdgeCC compares with edge dominated migration (Color figure online)

Fig. 5. EdgeCC compares with client assisting migration (Color figure online)

Service Migration Frequency

Under same paths, the mobile client starts random walk from the network's center. We set the mobile client's number of steps to 500 and perform 100 simulation experiments.

The ratio of service migration times for mobile clients with EdgeCC and edge-dominated migration and Client assisting migration show in Fig. 4 and Fig. 5 respectively. Where the moving speed of blue line, red line and green line increases sequentially in proportion. In the same movement path, because EdgeCC has a smaller migration authentication delay, at the same client's moving speed, EdgeCC edge has a larger maximum service radius that can provide reliable QoS. Meanwhile EdgeCC's migration authentication times is the smallest under low, medium and high-speed for the mobile client. Because edge-dominated migration is obviously better than Client assisting migration, so we will only compare EdgeCC with edge-dominated migration.

As Fig. 4, under low, medium and high-speed for the mobile client, the ratios of migration times for EdgeCC and edge-dominated migration are about 0.3, 0.5 and 0.8 respectively. At lower speed, the migration times of EdgeCC differs from edge-dominated migration significantly. However, as the moving speed increasing, the gap of migration times will decrease. Therefore, under the same path and service case, EdgeCC's migration times are reduced by about 70%, 50% and 20%.

Migration Energy Consumption

Since only mobile clients have limited energy and storage, so we analyze mobile clients' energy consumption here. Mobile client's energy consumption in EdgeCC is 1.5 times of edge-dominated migration in a service migration authentication.

When the client moves in the same path, the migration times of the two frameworks are different, so the energy consumption is different. EdgeCC reduces mobile client's energy consumption about 55% and 25% under low and medium speed respectively, and energy consumption increases about 20% under high-speed, this loss is acceptable given the advantage of migrating authentication delay. As show in Table 1, we summarized the advantages of EdgeCC.

Table 1. The advantages of EdgeCC

EdgeCC's superiority	Migration authentication delay		Mobile client's energy consumption			Service Migration Frequency			Improvement
	processing delay	transmission delay	Low speed	Medium speed	High speed	Low speed	Medium speed	High speed	
Compared with edge dominated migration	about 20% ↓	about 40% ↓	about 55% ↓	about 25% ↓	about 20% ↑	about 70% ↓	about 50% ↓	about 20% ↓	1) The original edge can be located accurately. 2) BSs needn't bound to certain edge server.
Compared with client assisting migration	about 40% ↓	about 50% ↓	at least 40% ↓			about 90% ↓	about 70% ↓	about 50% ↓	1) the network bandwidth consumption is saved. 2) EdgeCC saves the client's limited storage resources.

6   Security Settings and Analysis

Edge computing is an LSS, edge servers need to obtain the location information of clients to provide service. Malicious users may attack the communication by intercepting, viewing and tampering with message to seek improper benefits. EdgeCC's main communication is concentrated among clients, edges and cloud. It is possible to link the user's real identity with an anonymous identity, therefore there is a risk of revealing the user's true identity and geographic trajectory. We analyze security issues for mobile clients, edges and cloud, clients may suffer man-in-the middle attack and privacy leakage, edges and cloud may suffer man-in-the middle attack and replay attack. To ensure the security and anonymity of edge service migration authentication for mobile clients, we propose the following security settings:

1) Before mobile clients request a service, they need to register with cloud server to obtain their unique identity. The cloud keeps all identity information of clients that have access to enjoy edge service; 2) In order to guarantee the freshness of messages, we insert a timestamp T_s in messages; 3) In order to ensure security and anonymity, we adopt the asymmetric cryptography and ring signature in communication among client, edge and cloud, where sender executes the ring signature.

We prove that client, edge and cloud can solve these security issues by security settings.

Mobile client

1) Weakening of man-in-the-middle Attack

The sender digitally signs the message $s_k(M_i)$ with his private key. Because the user's private key is private and unique, it can guarantee that the sender has undeniable behavior. At the same time, the sender uses the encryption function negotiated by the sender and receiver, such as an asymmetric cryptography, to encrypt the message $p'_k(M_i)$, and the receiver uses a specific way to view the message $M'_i = s'_k(p'_k(M_i))$, it keeps the message confidential. To ensure message integrity, the sender sends $\{y_m, p'_k(M_i)\}$ to the receiver, the receiver uses sender's public key to verify the signature. If $H(M'_i) = H(M_i)$ is true, the signature is correct, so the message $M'_i = M_i$. Otherwise, the message is discarded. To some degree, they weaken man-in-the-middle attack.

2) Protecting User's Anonymity

Edge computing is an LSS, it has the risk of revealing the users' real identity and geographic trajectory during the communication. The ring signature protects the user's anonymity to a certain extent.

We statistic the time of signing and verifying signature for sending 1000 packets, where the size of ring signature group is different. As well as we calculate the probability of anonymity failure. As shown in Fig. 6, the size of ring signature group m affects the anonymity. The anonymity and the size of signature group is nonlinear relationship. When m is small, the ring signature's computational overhead is slightly increased, but the anonymity has obvious improvement. The user is able to choose the size of ring signature group, according to the need of anonymity and efficiency. If the ring signature group are constructed randomly, the probability is less than $\frac{1}{m}$ which malicious users can obtain the user's true identity. However, the operation needs to use other users' public keys, it may meet malicious users and expose privacy. If the identity of public keys that is related the ring signature group is public, malicious users can obtain sender's real identity through backstepping. For example, if q public keys are controlled by malicious users, The probability of anonymization failure will increase from $\frac{1}{m}$ to $\frac{1}{m-q}$. In the case where m is small, even if q is small, it is easy to destroy anonymity.

Because clients are lack of resource, we are unable to enlarge ring signature group limitlessly. So we assume that a client has a public key set $(p_1, p_2, \ldots, p_n)$, it randomly selects a public key p_i for migration authentication in each communication. The probability of anonymization failure is $\frac{1}{n(m-q)}$. The n is bigger, the probability is smaller. As shown in Fig. 7, When q is const, although q is very big, with n increasing, the probability of anonymity failure will decrease rapidly. By expanding user's public key set, it is possible to further weaken the link between the user's public key and real identity. Meanwhile, the overhead of enlarging ring signature group is excessive. As shown in Fig. 8, we find that even m is small, increasing n can also improve the anonymity, it avoid the high delay and client's energy consumption of ring signature.

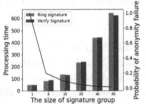 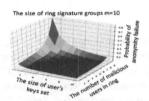 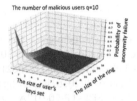

Fig. 6. The relationships between processing time, anonymity and the size of signature group respectively

Fig. 7. When the size of ring signature group is const, the relationships among the size of user's keys set, the number of malicious users and the probability of anonymity failure

Fig. 8. When the number of malicious users is const, the relationships among the size of user's keys set, the size of ring signature group and the probability of anonymity failure

Edge and Cloud

We use timestamps to mitigate replay attack. When senders sent messages, they add a timestamp T_s to messages, which indicates messages' freshness. The communication delay in edge computing cases is relatively small, we are able to refer the real transmission time to set the delay threshold T_t, the T is receiver's system time. According to the T_t, if $|T - T_s| < T_t$ is true, so the message is fresh, otherwise the message is considered abnormal and discarded. For man-in-the-middle Attack, the solution is same with mobile clients.

Additionally, clients have inherent shortcomings, such as the limited computing power, energy, storage and weak safety protection capability. EdgeCC weakens client's participation and improves the security of service migration authentication.

7   Conclusion

In the future, we will continue our research from the following three directions: **1) Path prediction.** Cloud needs to predict clients' movement trajectory to provide serviceable edges. **2) Queueing models.** Many mobile clients are in the service migration stage simultaneously, queueing model is important. **3) Lightweight cryptography.** We will look for secure and efficient ways to achieve light migration authentication scheme.

In this paper, we take advantage of characteristics of edge computing to propose the EdgeCC, a client, edge and cloud cooperative authentication framework for the fast migration of edge services under mobile clients. By comparing, we proved EdgeCC is better than existed frameworks in areas like message processing delay, transmission delay, mobile client's energy consumption and service migration frequency through theoretical analysis and simulation with NS3. When the edge distribution density and QoS are same, EdgeCC improve the efficiency of service migration authentication to certain extent. we analyze security issues for mobile clients, edges and cloud in migration authentication, and provide some security settings to achieve security. Finally, we analyze our shortcomings and introduce reasonable future research directions.

Acknowledgements. This work was supported in part by the key R&D Program of Guangdong, China under Grant 2019B010137004, in part by the National Natural Science Foundation of China under Grant U1766215, in part by the National Natural Science Foundation of China under Grant 61802016, in part by the Fundamental Research Funds for the Central Universities under Grant FRF-TP-20-012A2, in part by the National Social Science Foundation of China under Grant 17ZDA331, and in part by the Information Engineering Institute Program under Grant Y7Z0451104.

References

1. Ning, Z., Zhang, F., Shi, W.: A study of using TEE on edge computing. J. Comput. Res. Dev. **56**(7), 1441–1453 (2019)
2. Yi, S., Li, C., Li, Q.: A survey of fog computing: concepts, applications and issues. In: Proceedings of the 2015 Workshop on Mobile Big Data, pp. 37–42. ACM (2015)
3. Satyanarayanan, M., Bahl, V., Caceres, R., et al.: The case for VM-based cloudlets in mobile computing. IEEE Pervasive Comput. **8**(4), 14–23 (2009)
4. Xu, Z.W.: Cloud-sea computing systems: towards thousand-fold improvement in performance per watt for the coming zettabyte era. J. Comput. Sci. Technol. **29**(2), 177–181 (2014). https://doi.org/10.1007/s11390-014-1420-2
5. Liu, F., Tang, G., Li, Y., et al.: A survey on edge computing systems and tools. PIEEE **107**(8), 1537–1562 (2019)
6. Xiao, Y., Jia, Y., et al.: Edge computing security: state of the art and challenges. PIEEE **107**(8), 1608–1631 (2019)
7. Nie, H., Su, K., et al.: The study on the technology of over region switching in mobile communication system. Commun. Technol. **41**(8), 33–35 (2008)
8. NS3. https://www.nsnam.org/
9. Wang, S., Urgaonkar, R., He, T., et al.: Mobility-induced service migration in mobile micro-clouds. In: IEEE Military Communications Conference, pp. 835–840 (2014)
10. Wang, S., Urgaonkar, R., et al.: Dynamic service migration in mobile edge-clouds. In: IFIP Networking, pp. 1–9 (2015)
11. Wang, S., Chan, K., Urgaonkar, R., et al.: Emulation-based study of dynamic service placement in mobile micro-clouds. In: MILCOM, pp. 1046–1051 (2015)

12. Wu, L., Xie, Y., Zhang, Y.: Efficient and secure message authentication framework for VANET. J. Commun. **37**(11), 1–10 (2016)
13. Ha, K., Abe, Y., et al.: Adaptive VM handoff across cloudlets. Technical report CMU-CS-15-113 (2015)
14. Leppänen, T., et al.: Mobile agents for integration of Internet of Things and wireless sensor networks. In: IEEE International Conference on Systems, Man, and Cybernetics, pp. 14–21 (2013)
15. Huang, B., Cheng, X., et al.: Lightweight hardware based secure authentication framework for fog computing. In: IEEE/ACM Symposium on Edge Computing (SEC), pp. 433–439 (2018)
16. Zhang, C., Lin, X., Lu, R., et al.: RAISE: an efficient RSU-aided message authentication framework in vehicular communication networks. In: IEEE International Conference on Communications, pp. 1451–1457 (2008)
17. Mortazavi, S.H., Salehe, M., Gomes, C.S., et al.: CloudPath: a multi-tier cloud computing framework. In: IEEE/ACM Symposium on Edge Computing (SEC) (2017). Article no. 20
18. Xie, R., Huang, T., Yang, F., Liu, Y.: Principle and Practice of Edge Computing. Posts & Telecom Press, Beijing (2019)
19. Shodan. https://www.shodan.io
20. China Unicom edge business platform architecture and industrial ecology white paper. https://connect.intel.com/COS-ChinaUnicomEdge

Attention-Based Dynamic Preference Model for Next Point-of-Interest Recommendation

Chenwang Zheng and Dan Tao[(✉)]

School of Electronic and Information Engineering, Beijing Jiaotong University,
Beijing 100044, China
dtao@bjtu.edu.cn

Abstract. Next Point-of-Interest (POI) recommendation is a core task for various location-based intelligent services. It aims to predict the POI a user tends to visit next given the user's check-in history. However, this task is not trivial because of two challenges: 1) complicated sequential patterns of user mobility and 2) dynamic evolution of user preferences. In this paper, we propose a novel model called Attention-based Dynamic Preference Model (ADPM) for next POI recommendation, which can capture dynamic long- and short-term preferences of users. In particular, we design a spatio-temporal self-attention network to explore complicated POI-POI transition relationships and capture short-term sequential patterns of users. Moreover, we utilize a user-specific attention to learn evolving long-term preferences of users based on their constantly updated check-ins. Finally, a feature gating fusion module is introduced to adaptively combine long- and short-term preferences. We conduct extensive experiments on two real-world datasets, and the results demonstrate the effectiveness of our model.

Keywords: POI recommendation · Attention mechanism · Sequential pattern · Dynamic preference · Location-based social networks

1 Introduction

With the rapid development of mobile Internet, location-based social networks (LBSNs) like Foursquare and Gowalla are becoming prevalent in our daily lives. In LBSNs, users can share their physical locations and experiences on Point-of-Interests (POIs), e.g., restaurants and tourist attractions. The availability of abundant check-in data spawns a promising application called POI recommendation, which recommends unvisited POIs for a user based on his/her personal preferences and various contextual information [2].

In this work, we focus on the task of next POI recommendation. Besides users' general preferences, the next POI recommendation additionally considers the sequential patterns of users' geo-tagged and time-stamped check-ins [14].

© Springer Nature Switzerland AG 2020
D. Yu et al. (Eds.): WASA 2020, LNCS 12384, pp. 768–780, 2020.
https://doi.org/10.1007/978-3-030-59016-1_63

Increasing research efforts have been devoted to this task. Previous works proposed Markov Chains (MCs) based methods [3,6] to capture transition relationships between POIs, but they rely on a strong assumption that a user's next destination is only conditioned on the last check-in activity [9]. Recently, recurrent neural networks (RNNs) have shown great power in various sequential learning problems, many studies [4,10,14] extended classic RNNs with multiple contextual information to characterize higher order sequential patterns.

Existing methods have achieved encouraging results in modeling sequential patterns of user mobility. However, they often just model the overall sequence dependency and indiscriminately encode all the check-in records into a fixed hidden vector [1,7]. This fails to explicitly model complicated and fine-grained POI-POI transition relationships within the check-in sequences, which is essential for understanding sequential behaviors of users. We believe that there are some potential associations between any pair of checked POIs. On the other hand, existing methods often directly learn a static embedding vector to represent a user's general interests [3,11], which neglects the dynamic characteristics of long-term preferences.

In this paper, we propose a novel model called Attention-based Dynamic Preference Model (ADPM) for next POI recommendation. ADPM can jointly model both dynamic long- and short-term preferences by effectively employing the attention mechanisms. Specifically, to model the check-in sequences, we design a spatio-temporal self-attention network by improving the standard self-attention with temporal interval and geographical distance information among check-ins. This captures subtle POI-POI transition relationships, i.e., semantic, temporal, and spatial relations, which can hardly be learnt via existing methods. Then a target POI-guided attention is used to dynamically extract short-term interest tendencies of users. We further utilize a user-specific attention to construct evolving long-term preferences of users based on their up-dated historical check-in records. Finally, a feature gating fusion module is introduced for learning nonlinear combination of long- and short-term preferences. In the prediction stage, we accomplish POI recommendation by taking user preference and time influence into consideration. Our contributions are summarized as follows:

- We propose a hybrid neural model named ADPM for next POI recommendation. Our model can fully leverage the attention mechanisms to learn the dynamic evolution of long- and short-term preferences.
- We design a spatio-temporal self-attention network that incorporates spatial and temporal contextual information associated with check-ins. It well models complicated and subtle transition dependencies among POIs.
- Comprehensive experiments are conducted on two public-available LBSN datasets. The results demonstrate that ADPM consistently outperforms the comparative state-of-the-art methods in different evaluation metrics.

2   Related Work

Different to general POI recommendation that only learn users' general preferences from their historical check-in records [2,15], researches on next POI recommendation mainly focus on modeling users' sequential transition patterns and dynamic preferences. Early studies often employed Markov Chains (MCs) to capture sequential influence. For example, Cheng et al. [3] combined matrix factorization (MF) and first-order Markov Chain to jointly learn user general preferences and short-term POI-POI transitions. Motivated by the success of word2vec in natural language processing (NLP), Feng et al. [5] captured POI-POI transition dependencies by learning embedding representations for POIs.

Recently, RNNs were widely applied in next POI recommendation to effectively incorporate contextual information and model complicated sequential patterns [4,10,14]. For example, Liu et al. [10] extended RNN with time- and distance-special transition metrics to better model spatio-temporal contexts. Wu et al. [14] employed two parallel LSTM models to learn location-level and category-level sequential preferences of users, respectively. However, these RNN-based models often directly follow the temporal order to glance over the check-in sequence, which fails to fully explore complicated and subtle internal correlations of the sequence.

More recently, the neural attention mechanism has been successfully applied in recommendations [1,7,9]. It is introduced to augment existing models and strengthen their ability in selectively focusing on important information of the sequence. For example, Ying et al. [16] designed a hierarchical attention network that integrated long- and short-term preferences to recommend next items. Huang et al. [8] used the attention mechanism to enhance the LSTM framework and automatically select relevant historical check-ins for prediction.

3   Problem Formulation

Let $\mathcal{U} = \{u_1, u_2, \cdots, u_{|\mathcal{U}|}\}$ be a set of users and $\mathcal{L} = \{l_1, l_2, \cdots, l_{|\mathcal{L}|}\}$ be a set of POIs. Each POI $l_{id} \in \mathcal{L}$ has unique latitude and longitude coordinates, i.e., $<lat_{id}, lon_{id}>$. Each user $u \in \mathcal{U}$ is associated with a check-in sequence, which is denoted by his/her historical check-ins in temporal order: $C^u = \{r_1^u, r_2^u, \cdots, r_{|C^u|}^u\}$, where the check-in record $r_i^u = \langle u, l_i, t_i \rangle$ means user u visited POI l_i at time t_i. For a user u, given a specific time t, we take the most recent k check-ins before t from C^u as the short-term sequence: $S_{t-1}^u = \{r_{t-k}^u, r_{t-k+1}^u, ..., r_{t-1}^u\}$, which can reflect short-term preferences of users. We set the whole check-in records before t as the long-term sequence: $L_{t-1}^u = \{r_1^u, r_2^u, ..., r_{t-1}^u\}$.

Problem Statement (Next POI recommendation). Given the check-in sequence C^u and the prediction time t_q, the task of next POI recommendation is to predict the most likely POI $l_{t_q} \in \mathcal{L}/C^u$ that user u will visit at time t_q.

4   The Proposed Model

In this section, the proposed ADPM model is introduced. Figure 1 depicts the architecture of ADPM. We first embed sparse user, POI and time inputs into low-dimensional dense vectors. Then, we separately learn long- and short-term preferences of users from L_{t-1}^u and S_{t-1}^u. Finally, we combine these two types of preferences for prediction.

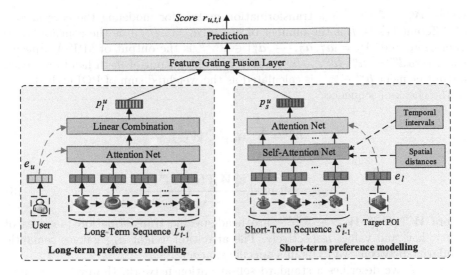

Fig. 1. Overall architecture of the proposed ADPM model

4.1 Embedding Layer

The embedding layer aims to produce precise semantic representations for users, POIs, and time. Formally, We create three embedding metrics $U \in \mathbb{R}^{|\mathcal{U}| \times d}$, $L \in \mathbb{R}^{|\mathcal{L}| \times d}$, and $T \in \mathbb{R}^{|\mathcal{T}| \times d}$, which consist of the user, POI, and timeslot embeddings, respectively, where d is the dimensionality of the embedding spaces, $|\mathcal{T}|$ is the number of timesolts. Specially, the original time information of each check-in record is a timestamp, and it is not feasible to directly embed the continuous timestamp. We thus split one week into 48 timeslots by considering two types of temporal granularities, i.e., hour-of-the-day and day-of-the-week. Each timestamp is transformed into the corresponding timeslot. Let $e_u \in \mathbb{R}^d$, $e_l \in \mathbb{R}^d$, and $e_t \in \mathbb{R}^d$ be the embeddings of user u, POI l, and time t.

4.2 Short-Term Preference Modeling

In the short-term module, we first design a spatio-temporal self-attention network to model the check-in sequence, and then use a target-guided attention network to further extract short-term preferences of users.

Taking the short-term sequence S_{t-1}^u as input, we first retrieve the embedding vectors of POIs in S_{t-1}^u and stack them together getting a sequence embedding matrix: $\boldsymbol{E}_s^u = [\boldsymbol{e}_1^u, \boldsymbol{e}_2^u, \cdots, \boldsymbol{e}_k^u] \in \mathbb{R}^{k \times d}$. To model the check-in sequence, we perform a multi-head self-attention (MHSA) introduced in [13] as follows:

$$\boldsymbol{A}_s^u = \mathrm{MHSA}(\boldsymbol{E}_s^u) = [\boldsymbol{head}^1 \oplus \boldsymbol{head}^2 \oplus \cdots \oplus \boldsymbol{head}^h]\boldsymbol{W}_o, \qquad (1)$$

where $\boldsymbol{W}_o \in \mathbb{R}^{hd_v \times d}$ is a transformation matrix for modeling the correlations of different heads, h is the number of heads, $d_v = d/h$, $\oplus$ is the concatenation operation, and $\boldsymbol{A}_s^u = [\boldsymbol{a}_1^u, \boldsymbol{a}_2^u, \cdots, \boldsymbol{a}_k^u] \in \mathbb{R}^{k \times d}$ is the output of MHSA. Specifically, $\boldsymbol{head}^m = [\boldsymbol{h}_1^m, \boldsymbol{h}_2^m, ..., \boldsymbol{h}_k^m] \in \mathbb{R}^{k \times d_v}$ is the output of m-th head, and each output element $\boldsymbol{h}_i^m \in \mathbb{R}^{d_v}$ is calculated as the weighted sum of POI embeddings in the check-in sequence:

$$\boldsymbol{h}_i^m = \sum_{j=1}^{k} \alpha_{i,j} (\boldsymbol{e}_j^u \boldsymbol{W}_V^m), \qquad (2)$$

$$\alpha_{i,j} = \mathrm{softmax}\left(\frac{\boldsymbol{e}_i^u \boldsymbol{W}_Q^m (\boldsymbol{e}_j^u \boldsymbol{W}_K^m)^T}{\sqrt{d_v}} \right), \qquad (3)$$

where $\boldsymbol{W}_Q^m, \boldsymbol{W}_K^m, \boldsymbol{W}_V^m \in \mathbb{R}^{d \times d_v}$ are head-specific transformation matrices of query, key, and value, respectively. The attention weight $\alpha_{i,j}$ gauges semantic similarity between two POIs in a specific space.

The above describes a standard self-attention network. However, it cannot be effectively applied to the check-in sequence. Since it neglects complicated spatio-temporal correlations among visited POIs, as follows:

$$\boldsymbol{T} = \begin{bmatrix} t_{1,1} & t_{1,2} & \cdots & t_{1,k} \\ t_{2,1} & t_{2,2} & \cdots & t_{2,k} \\ \vdots & \vdots & \ddots & \vdots \\ t_{k,1} & t_{k,2} & \cdots & t_{k,k} \end{bmatrix}, \quad \boldsymbol{D} = \begin{bmatrix} d_{1,1} & d_{1,2} & \cdots & d_{1,k} \\ d_{2,1} & d_{2,2} & \cdots & d_{2,k} \\ \vdots & \vdots & \ddots & \vdots \\ d_{k,1} & d_{k,2} & \cdots & d_{k,k} \end{bmatrix}, \qquad (4)$$

where $\boldsymbol{T} \in \mathbb{R}^{k \times k}$ and $\boldsymbol{D} \in \mathbb{R}^{k \times k}$ are temporal and spatial relationship metrics of the check-in sequence, $t_{i,j} = t_j - t_i$ and $d_{i,j} = \sqrt{(lat_i - lat_j)^2 + (lon_i - lon_j)^2}$ are the temporal interval and spatial distance between two check-ins, respectively. Intuitively, relatively short time and distance intervals often indicate a strong transition dependency between two check-in activities. Therefore, we improve the vanilla self-attention with these contextual information to capture more complex sequential patterns of user movements.

For matrix $\boldsymbol{T}$, we discretize the time interval $t_{i,j}$ by day and clip the maximize time interval to a maximum absolute value of w. Inspired by [12], we add $2w + 1$ learnable embedding vectors to represent the relative temporal relationships among check-ins: $\boldsymbol{r} = [\boldsymbol{r}_{-w}, ..., \boldsymbol{r}_w]$, s.t. $1 < w < k$. Every time interval $t_{i,j}$ is converted into an embedding vector $\boldsymbol{\tau}_{i,j} = \boldsymbol{r}_{t_{i,j}} \in \mathbb{R}^d$. With the relative temporal representations, we update the calculation of self-attention in Eq. (2) as:

$$\boldsymbol{h}_i^m = \sum_{j=1}^{k} \alpha_{i,j} (\boldsymbol{e}_j^u \boldsymbol{W}_{V,E}^m + \boldsymbol{\tau}_{i,j} \boldsymbol{W}_{V,T}^m), \qquad (5)$$

$$\alpha_{i,j} = \text{softmax}(\frac{e_i^u \boldsymbol{W}_Q^m (e_j^u \boldsymbol{W}_{K,E}^m + \tau_{i,j} \boldsymbol{W}_{K,T}^m)^T}{\sqrt{d_v}}), \tag{6}$$

where $\boldsymbol{W}_{V,E}^m, \boldsymbol{W}_{V,T}^m, \boldsymbol{W}_{K,E}^m$, and $\boldsymbol{W}_{K,E}^m \in \mathbb{R}^{d \times d_v}$ are head-specific projection matrices. In this way, we can incorporate temporal order information of the sequence for constructing dynamic sequential dependencies.

According to the First Law of Geography, everything is related to everything else, but near things are more related than distant things [7]. That is geographically adjacent POIs have stronger dependencies. We adopt the Gaussian radial basis function (RBF) kernel to measure spatial relationships of POIs. The RBF is defined as: $g_{i,j} = exp(-\gamma \parallel d_{i,j} \parallel^2)$, where γ is a scaling parameter. Considering the spatial relationships, the attention weight in Eq. (6) is modified as:

$$\alpha_{i,j} = \text{softmax}(\frac{e_i^u \boldsymbol{W}_Q^m (e_j^u \boldsymbol{W}_{K,E}^m + \tau_{i,j} \boldsymbol{W}_{K,T}^m)^T}{\sqrt{d_v}} + \eta \cdot g_{i,j}), \tag{7}$$

where η is a weight coefficient. With the spatio-temporal enhanced self-attention, we can fully explore semantic, temporal, and spatial transition relationships among POIs. This also reflects complex sequential patterns of user mobility.

Users interests that are more relevant to the target POI may impose greater impacts on whether the user will visit this POI. Therefore, we dynamically assign higher weights for informative POIs in S_{t-1}^u according to the target POI. The short-term preferences $\boldsymbol{p}_s^u \in \mathbb{R}^d$ is calculated as:

$$\alpha_i = \frac{exp(e_l^T \boldsymbol{W}_l a_i^u)}{\sum_{j=1}^{k} exp(e_l^T \boldsymbol{W}_l a_j^u)}, \tag{8}$$

$$\boldsymbol{p}_s^u = \sum_{i=1}^{k} \alpha_i a_i^u. \tag{9}$$

4.3   Long-Term Preference Modeling

Existing methods [3,10] often explicitly learn a latent vector $\boldsymbol{e}_u$ (named as *user intrinsic embedding*) to represent general preferences of users. However, users' historical check-ins usually changes over time, learning such a static embedding cannot fully express evolving long-term preferences of users. Following [1], we attentively compress users' historical check-ins to obtain another preference representation (named as *user memory embedding*), which can be dynamically reconstructed based on users' up-dated check-in records. To model more fine-grained personalized information, we employ a user-specific attention, which use $\boldsymbol{e}_u$ as the query vector attending to the long-term sequence L_t^u. The long-term memory preference $\boldsymbol{p}_m^u \in \mathbb{R}^d$ is calculated as follows:

$$\beta_i = \frac{exp(e_u^T \boldsymbol{W}_u e_{l_i})}{\sum_{l_j \in L_{t-1}^u} exp(e_u^T \boldsymbol{W}_u e_{l_j})}, \tag{10}$$

$$p_m^u = \sum_{l_i \in L_{t-1}^u} \beta_i e_{l_i}, \tag{11}$$

where $W_u \in \mathbb{R}^{d \times d}$ is the weight matrix. Since users' actual check-ins are limited, we use a linear combination to merge p_m^u with e_u and get a well-rounded long-term preference representation: $p_l^u = \sum_{l_i \in L_{t-1}^u} \beta_i e_{l_i} + e_u$.

4.4 Preference Fusion and Prediction

To effectively combine long- and short-term preferences, we employ a feature gating fusion module like various gates in LSTM. This gating fusion method can precisely model nonlinear preference correlations and balance contribution percentages of long- and short-term preferences for POI prediction:

$$g^u = \sigma(p_l^u W_g^{(1)} + p_s^u W_g^{(2)} + b_g), \tag{12}$$

$$p^u = g^u \odot p_l^u + (1 - g^u) \odot p_s^u, \tag{13}$$

where $W_g^{(1)}, W_g^{(2)} \in \mathbb{R}^{d \times d}$ are the weight matrices, $b_g \in \mathbb{R}^d$ is a bias vector, $\odot$ denotes the element-wise multiplication, $\sigma(x) = 1/(1 + e^{-x})$ is the sigmoid function. $p^u \in \mathbb{R}^d$ is final representation of user preference.

For each prediction request $<u, t, l_i>$, which considers user u visiting POI l_i at time t, the prediction score is calculated through the following equation:

$$r_{u,t,i} = p^u \cdot e_{l_i}^T + e_t \cdot e_{l_i}^T. \tag{14}$$

In the prediction function, the first term models user's preferences on POI, while the second term measures the relevance between time pattern and POI.

4.5 Model Training

In this paper, the task of next POI recommendation is regarded as a binary classification problem. Thus, we adopt the binary cross entropy as the loss function for model training, the objective function is defined as:

$$
\begin{aligned}
\mathcal{J}(\Theta) &= -\log \prod_{u \in \mathcal{U}} \prod_{l_i \in C^u} \sigma(r_{u,t,i}) \prod_{l_j \in \mathcal{L}/C^u} (1 - \sigma(r_{u,t,j})) + \frac{\lambda}{2} \|\Theta\|^2 \\
&= -\sum_{u \in \mathcal{U}} \Big(\sum_{l_i \in C^u} \log(\sigma(r_{u,t,i})) + \sum_{l_j \in \mathcal{L}/C^u} (1 - \sigma(r_{u,t,j})) \Big) + \frac{\lambda}{2} \|\Theta\|^2,
\end{aligned} \tag{15}
$$

where λ is the regularization parameter, $\Theta = \{U, L, T, r, W, b\}$ is a set of model parameters, which are learned by maximizing the objective function $\mathcal{J}(\Theta)$ on the training data. Following previous works [7,9], for each target POI l_i, we randomly sample a POI l_j from unvisited POIs as the negative instance, i.e., $l_j \in \mathcal{L}/C^u$. We adopt the Adaptive Moment Estimation (Adam) optimizer to train the model and employ the Dropout technique to avoid over-fitting problem.

5 Experiments

5.1 Experimental Setup

Datasets. We conduct the evaluation experiments on two publicly available datasets, i.e., Foursquare[1] and Gowalla[2]. Each check-in record in the datasets contains a user ID, a POI ID, a timestamp and the latitude and longitude of POI. For both datasets, we filter out users with fewer than 10 check-ins and POIs with fewer than 10 visitors. The statistics of two processed datasets are summarized in Table 1. We use the leave-one-out evaluation. For each user's check-in sequence, we hold out the most recent check-in for testing the model's performance, and the remaining check-ins are left for training the model.

Table 1. The statistics of datasets

Datasets	#Users	#POIs	#Check-ins	Density	Time span
Foursquare	23,686	27,055	1,121,315	0.17%	04/2012–09/2013
Gowalla	20,364	28,776	1,700,250	0.29%	01/2011–08/2011

Compared Methods. We compare ADPM with the following competitive baseline methods: (1) **POP**: This is a non-personalized method that makes recommendations based on the popularity of POIs. (2) **BPRMF** [11]: It enhances basic matrix factorization with bayesian personalized ranking to learn pairwise rankings from implicit feedback. (3) **FPMC-LR** [3]: This method combines matrix factorization and personalized Markov chains for next POI recommendation. (4) **POI2Vec** [5]: It integrates geographical relations of POIs in learning POI embeddings. Besides, it jointly models POI sequential transition and user preference. (5) **ST-RNN** [10]: It is a RNN-based next POI recommendation model, which extends classic RNN with time interval and geographical distance information of successive check-ins. (6) **SASRec** [9]: It is a self-attention based sequential recommendation model, which uses self-attention network to model the check-in sequences and attentively identifies relevant behaviors for prediction. (7) **SHAN** [16]: It employs two-layer hierarchical attention network to capture user dynamic preferences. The first attention layer learns long-term preferences, while the second one combines long- and short-term preferences.

Evaluation Metrics and Implementation Details. To evaluate the recommendation performance, we adopt two widely-used metrics, i.e., Acc@N and NDCG@N. Specifically, Acc@N is a ranking based accuracy, this metric is defined

---

[1] http://spatialkeyword.sce.ntu.edu.sg/eval-vldb17.
[2] http://www.yongliu.org/datasets/index.html.

as the fraction of ground-truth POIs which can emerge in the top-N recommended lists. We calculate Acc@N as introduced in [7]. NDCG@N is the normalized discounted cumulative gain, which evaluates the ranking performance by considering the positions of correctly recommended POIs. In this paper, we choose N = {5, 10, 20} for evaluation.

In the experiments, the initial learning rate is set to 0.001, the regularization coefficient is 5×10^{-5}, and the dropout rate is 0.5. The embedding size d is set to 50 for all models. In the short-term module, we set the scaling parameter $\gamma = 10$ and the weighing coefficient $\eta = 0.6$. The length of short-term sequence k is tuned from $\{1, 2, ..., 10\}$, while $k = 6$ and $k = 4$ give the best performances for Foursquare and Gowalla. Besides, we set the maximize time interval w to 5 day and 3 day for Foursquare and Gowalla, respectively. The number of heads h is chose from $\{1, 2, 5, 10\}$ and we set $h = 2$ for both datasets.

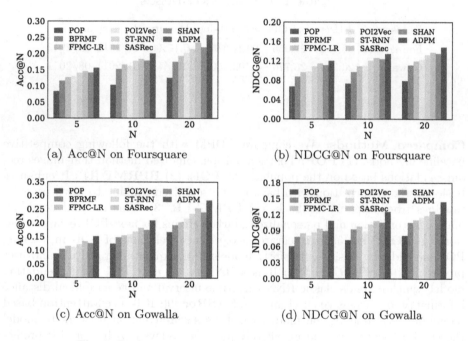

(a) Acc@N on Foursquare   (b) NDCG@N on Foursquare

(c) Acc@N on Gowalla   (d) NDCG@N on Gowalla

Fig. 2. Performance comparison of models on two datasets

5.2 Performance Comparison

The performance comparison of different models on two datasets are presented in Fig. 2. It can be observed that the proposed ADPM model significantly outperforms all the baselines on two datasets in terms of all evaluation metrics. For example, on the Foursquare dataset, ADPM improves 9.2% and 6.3% compared with the best baseline, i.e., SASRec, in Acc@10 and NDCG@10, respectively, while the improvements on the Gowalla dataset are 14.5% and 15.8% in the same metrics. This empirically verifies the effectiveness and superiority of our proposed model for next POI recommendation. Additionally, we make several observations on the baselines. FPMC-LR outperforms BPRMF, this validates the necessity of considering sequential information in next POI recommendation. ST-RNN performs better than FRCM-LR and POI2Vec. This is mainly because it can model the overall check-in sequence and capture more high-level transition patterns. SASRec outperforms other baselines in all cases, which demonstrates the advantage of self-attention network in modeling users' sequential behaviors. SHAN can perform better than other methods except SASRec in most cases. This verifies that combining long- and short-term preferences is essential for enhancing the recommendation performance.

Table 2. Performance comparison of ADPM and three variants

Dataset	Variants	Acc@5	Acc@10	Acc@20	NDCG@5	NDCG@10	NDCG@20
Foursquare	ADPM-L	0.1363	0.1656	0.2183	0.1034	0.1182	0.1320
	ADPM-S	0.1455	0.1863	0.2359	0.1147	0.1278	0.1415
	ADPM-NF	0.1539	0.1981	0.2496	0.1181	0.1332	0.1474
	ADPM	**0.1558**	**0.2010**	**0.2584**	**0.1202**	**0.1347**	**0.1487**
Gowalla	ADPM-L	0.1230	0.1672	0.2316	0.0873	0.1018	0.1195
	ADPM-S	0.1389	0.1882	0.2594	0.1018	0.1192	0.1375
	ADPM-NF	0.1449	0.2016	0.2701	0.1076	0.1243	0.1426
	ADPM	**0.1509**	**0.2091**	**0.2831**	**0.1083**	**0.1256**	**0.1443**

5.3 Influence of Components

To evaluate the contribution of each component for the overall performance gain, we further implement three variants of ADPM. ADPM-L and ADPM-S mean that only the long-term module and the short-term module are retained, respectively. ADPM-NF denotes the gating fusion module is removed. The experimental results are shown in Table 2. Obviously, the complete model ADPM achieves the best performance on both datasets, which validates that each component has positive impacts on modeling user preferences. Specially, compared with BPRMF, ADPM-L gives better performance since it can model users' general preferences in a dynamic way. ADPM-S always performs better than ADPM-L, which indicates that capturing complicated sequential patterns is more conducive to next POI recommendation. ADPM performs better than ADPM-NF, suggesting the gating fusion method indeed augments our model in adaptively combining these two kinds of preferences. Finally, both ADPM-NF and ADPM outperforms other variants, which verifies that it is essential to jointly model long- and short-term preferences.

5.4 Influence of Hyper-Parameters

There are two key hyper-parameters in the proposed ADPM model: the short-term sequence length k and the embedding size d. We investigate their in?uence by holding others parameters at the optimal settings. Due to space limit, we only present the results in Acc@10 and NDCG@10. The influence of sequence length is shown in Fig. 3. We observe that our model achieves the best results at $k = 6$ and $k = 4$ for Foursquare and Gowalla, respectively, while larger k leads to the degradation of performance to some extent. The reason may be that users' sequential patterns often involve a short sequence and a longer sequence tends to introduce more noises to the model. Figure 4 illustrates the performance of ADPM under different embedding sizes d. With the increasing of embedding size d, the performance of ADPM gradually improves first and then becomes relatively stable. Besides, a larger embedding size does not necessarily lead to better performance. The reason is that the larger d has strong expressive ability, but it may increase the complexity of the model and cause the overfitting issues. Considering the trade-off between the computation cost and the recommendation performance, we set $d = 50$ for both datasets.

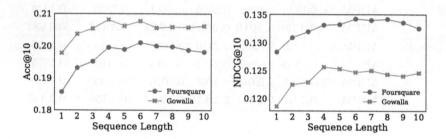

Fig. 3. The influence of sequence length k

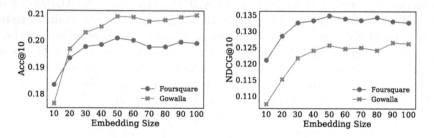

Fig. 4. The influence of embedding size d

6 Conclusion

In this paper, we propose a novel model named ADPM for the next POI recommendation problem considering the dynamic changing of users long- and short-term preferences. To model the check-in sequence, we improve the standard self-attention with spatio-temporal contextual information to effectively capture complicated transition patterns of user mobility. We further employ a user-guided attention to learn the long-term preferences of users from their up-dated check-ins. Extensive experiments are conducted on two real-world datasets, and the results demonstrate that ADPM significantly outperforms the state-of-the-art methods. Besides, every component of ADPM complements each other to enhance the overall recommendation performance.

Acknowledgments. This work was partly supported by the National Natural Science Foundation of China under Grant No. 61872027.

References

1. Chen, X., et al.: Sequential recommendation with user memory networks. In: Proceedings of the 11th ACM International Conference on Web Search and Data Mining, pp. 108–116 (2018)
2. Cheng, C., Yang, H., King, I., Lyu, M.R.: Fused matrix factorization with geographical and social influence in location-based social networks. In: Proceedings of the 26th AAAI Conference on Artificial Intelligence, pp. 17–23 (2012)
3. Cheng, C., Yang, H., Lyu, M.R., King, I.: Where you like to go next: successive point-of-interest recommendation. In: Proceedings of the 23rd International Joint Conference on Artificial Intelligence, pp. 2605–2611 (2013)
4. Cui, Q., Tang, Y., Wu, S., Wang, L.: Distance2Pre: personalized spatial preference for next point-of-interest prediction. In: Yang, Q., Zhou, Z.-H., Gong, Z., Zhang, M.-L., Huang, S.-J. (eds.) PAKDD 2019. LNCS (LNAI), vol. 11441, pp. 289–301. Springer, Cham (2019). https://doi.org/10.1007/978-3-030-16142-2_23
5. Feng, S., Cong, G., An, B., Chee, Y.M.: POI2Vec: geographical latent representation for predicting future visitors. In: Proceedings of the 31st AAAI Conference on Artificial Intelligence, pp. 102–108 (2017)
6. Feng, S., Li, X., Zeng, Y., Cong, G., Chee, Y.M., Yuan, Q.: Personalized ranking metric embedding for next new POI recommendation. In: Proceedings of the 24th International Joint Conference on Artificial Intelligence, pp. 2069–2075 (2015)
7. Huang, J., Zhao, W.X., Dou, H., Wen, J., Chang, E.Y.: A geographical-temporal awareness hierarchical attention network for next point-of-interest recommendation. In: Proceedings of the 2019 ACM International Conference on Multimedia Retrieval, pp. 7–15 (2019)
8. Huang, L., Ma, Y., Wang, S., Liu, Y.: An attention-based spatiotemporal LSTM network for next POI recommendation. IEEE Trans. Serv. Comput. **12**, 1 (2019)
9. Kang, W., McAuley, J.: Self-attentive sequential recommendation. In: Proceedings of 2018 IEEE International Conference on Data Mining, pp. 197–206 (2018)
10. Liu, Q., Wu, S., Wang, L., Tan, T.: Predicting the next location: a recurrent model with spatial and temporal contexts. In: Proceedings of the 30th AAAI Conference on Artificial Intelligence, pp. 194–200 (2016)

11. Rendle, S., Freudenthaler, C., Gantner, Z., Schmidt-Thieme, L.: BPR: Bayesian personalized ranking from implicit feedback. In: Proceedings of the 25th Conference on Uncertainty in Artificial Intelligence, pp. 452–461 (2009)
12. Shaw, P., Uszkoreit, J., Vaswani, A.: Self-attention with relative position representations. In: Proceedings of NAACL-HLT, pp. 464–468 (2018)
13. Vaswani, A., et al.: Attention is all you need. In: Proceedings of the 31st International Conference on Neural Information Processing Systems, pp. 5998–6008 (2017)
14. Wu, Y., Li, K., Zhao, G., Qian, X.: Long- and short-term preference learning for next POI recommendation. In: Proceedings of the 28th ACM International Conference on Information and Knowledge Management, pp. 2301–2304 (2019)
15. Yang, C., Bai, L., Zhang, C., Yuan, Q., Han, J.: Bridging collaborative filtering and semi-supervised learning: a neural approach for POI recommendation. In: Proceedings of the 25th ACM SIGKDD International Conference on Knowledge Discovery and Data Mining, pp. 1245–1254 (2017)
16. Ying, H., et al.: Sequential recommender system based on hierarchical attention network. In: Proceedings of the 27th International Joint Conference on Artificial Intelligence, pp. 3926–3932 (2018)

From When to Where: A Multi-task Learning Approach for Next Point-of-Interest Recommendation

Jinwen Zhong[1,2], Can Ma[1], Jiang Zhou[1(✉)], and Weiping Wang[1]

[1] Institute of Information Engineering, Chinese Academy of Sciences, Beijing, China
{zhongjinwen,macan,zhoujiang,wangweiping}@iie.ac.cn
[2] School of Cyber Security, University of Chinese Academy of Sciences,
Beijing, China

Abstract. Temporal information plays a crucial role in analyzing user behaviors in Location-Based Social Networks (LSBNs). Different from existing methods such as Matrix Factorization (MF) and Recurrent Neural Networks (RNNs) methodologies that only make use of historical temporal information, we try to explore the prediction of the user's future check-in time to help POI recommendation in this paper. We propose a new multi-task neural network recommendation model, namely MTNR, which jointly learns when and where users are likely to go next. To learn the user's next POI preference based on the next check-in time prediction, we introduce two kinds of time-decay POI transition tensors to calculate the user's common and personal POI transition probability, respectively. By combining the POI preference learned in POI and time prediction tasks, MTNR can get better recommendation accuracy in POI recommendation. We conducted experiments on three real-world datasets. The result shows that our model significantly outperforms well-known methods.

Keywords: Multi-task learning · Point-of-interest recommendation · Recurrent Neural Network

1 Introduction

Spatial and temporal information are essential factors for next POI recommendation, i.e., where the user visit and when the user arrives. There is a strong dependency between transitions of two arbitrary locations and the time required to transfer in LBSNs data. Many existing works have studied this law and used time information to build models to learn the user's next POI preference in different ways. Matrix Factorization (MF) methods [5,11,18] consider the user's time-varying behavioral trends and construct time-aware high order tensor to

W. Wang—This work was supported by Beijing Municipal Science and Technology Project (Grant No. Z191100007119002).

© Springer Nature Switzerland AG 2020
D. Yu et al. (Eds.): WASA 2020, LNCS 12384, pp. 781–793, 2020.
https://doi.org/10.1007/978-3-030-59016-1_64

recommend users their interested locations by dividing the check-in time into hourly time-slots. However, due to the high-order tensor design, they often suffer from the problems of data sparsity and cold start, thus different decomposition methods have been proposed to alleviate these problems. Other neural network approaches, such as recurrent neural networks (RNNs) [4,6,15–17], treat the temporal information as auxiliary input data and mostly take the accuracy of the POI recommendation as the only optimization goal. It is difficult for these end-to-end models to fully mine the complex correlation between temporal information and POI transition from sparse data without any explicit supervision, which is essential for making POI recommendation.

Different from existing approaches that only use historical temporal information, we try to predict **when** the user's will check-in next, which is never considered in previous work. We propose a new multi-task learning approach (MTNR) which jointly learns when and where users are likely to go next. From the prediction of **when** the user might check in next and modeling the correlation between time and POI transitions, we can learn **where** the user is most likely to go more accurately. The contribution of this study includes:

- We propose a multi-task learning neural model (MTNR) to jointly learn when and where that users are likely to go next. To the best of our knowledge, MTNR is the first study to explore the user's next check-in time prediction to achieve the next POI recommendation based on multi-task learning.
- We introduce two kinds of time-decay POI transition tensors in MTNR and operations on the tensors to infer the influence of user's different check-in times on POI preference, through which we can learn user's next POI preference based on the next check-in time prediction.
- We conducted experiments on three real-world datasets to demonstrate the effectiveness of MTNR. The results show that our model significantly outperforms the well-known methodologies.

2   Related Work

We discuss existing work in this section and compare them with our work.

2.1   POI Recommendation

Plenty of approaches have been proposed to work on POI recommendation within the last decade. Markov Chain (MC) methods, such as Mobility Markov Chain (MMC) [3] employs the properties of a Markov Chain to model the sequential influence, but seldom take into count the temporal information in modeling. Other collaborative filtering based models, such as Matrix Factorization (MF) [5], Factorizing Personalized Markov Chains (FPMC) [7] and Tensor Factorization (TF) [11], are widely used in POI recommendation. They attempt to capture the user's common preferences through decomposition methods while retaining the ability to learn personal preferences. However, these works divide user check-in time into time slots, which result in data sparsity and cold start problems. Recently, Recurrent Neural Networks (RNNs) have been widely used in sequential item recommendation [4,6,15–17]. ATST-LSTM [4] leverages the attention mechanism to focus on relevant historical check-in records in a check-in sequence by selectively using the spatio-temporal contextual information. However, these neural network approaches mostly treat the temporal feature as auxiliary input information, and cannot fully mine and explore potential regularity of temporal information and POI preference due to the sparsity of LBSNs data.

2.2 Multi-task Learning

Multi-task learning (MTL) is an approach to jointly train all tasks that share the parameters, so that it can improve performance compared to learn these tasks individually [2]. MTL has been used successfully across all applications of machine learning in recent years. However, there is a prerequisite that it should have sufficient training data relative to the target space of the task if a model want to benefit from MTL. The reason is that the sparse data makes it difficult for auxiliary tasks to extract useful information for the main task. On the contrary, the LBSN data of each user is sparse while the number of check-in venues is quite large. If directly applying the MTL framework to make the POI recommendation, we will achieve minimal improvement which is verified in our experiments (see Sect. 5.5). Therefore, we consider introducing additional knowledge and model structures to fully explore the potential of auxiliary tasks.

3   Research Problem

The next POI recommendation problem is to predict the next POI based on user's historical trajectories. Let $U = \{u_1, \ldots, u_m\}$ denote the user set and $P = \{p_1, \ldots, p_j\}$ denote the POI set, where $|U|$ and $|P|$ are the total numbers of users and POIs, respectively. Each POI p_k is associated with a geographic location $l_k = (l_a, l_o)$, where l_a and l_o mean the latitude and longitude of the POI location. For a user $u \in U$, a check-in behavior means u_i visits a POI p_k at time t_k, which is denoted as a tuple (u, p_k, t_k). Any check-in sequence with time intervals of successive check-ins less than a threshold value T_{delta} is called a trajectory. In this way, a user's historical check-ins will be divided into many trajectories. We denote $S_i^u = \{(u, p_1, t_1), \ldots, (u, p_n, t_n)\}$ as the i-th trajectory of the user u, and all the historical trajectories of the user u are described as S^u. Formally, given a user u and S^u, the problem of making the next POI recommendation is to predict the next POI p_{n+1} that the user is most likely to visit.

4   Model Description

In this section, we introduce the framework and the detailed design of each module of the MTNR model.

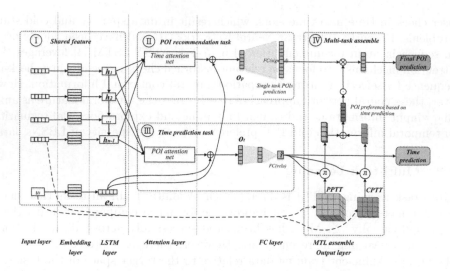

Fig. 1. The architecture of MTNR model.

4.1 Basic Framework

In order to make better use of time information for POI recommendation, we need to estimate the time and location of the next check-in at the same time. Inspired by the work in [2], we design a multi-task neural network model, which builds time and position prediction tasks on shared feature modules, and then uses an integration layer to correlate time prediction results with POI prediction. Figure 1 shows the architecture of our proposed model MTNR. It consists of four intelligent, correlated modules to achieve the POI prediction.

(I) **Shared Feature Module.** This module aims to learn the spatio-temporal sequences features from the user's historical trajectories. It receives the trajectories and user identifiers and generate the rough features of the trajectories.

(II) **POI Prediction Task Module.** The goal of this module is to make a preliminary prediction of the user's next POI tendency based on the shared spatio-temporal sequence features captured previously.

(III) **Time Prediction Task Module.** This model receives the share feature and predicts the time of the user's next check-in behavior.

(IV) **Multi-task Assemble Module.** The core problem to be solved in this module is to infer the user's POI preference from time prediction task results, and output a more accurate final POI prediction. We propose two kinds of POI transition tensors and design a time-decay operation on the tensors, which enables us to learn the next POI preference from the next check-in time prediction.

4.2   Shared Feature Module

As the foundation of all the modules, the shared feature module receives the user trajectory S_i and user identifier as the input, and learns rough spatial-temporal sequential feature, which is used by successive POI and time prediction task. It contains an input layer, an embedding layer, and an LSTM (Long-Short Memory Mechanism) layer.

Input and Embedding Layer. The input and embedding layer receives the input and encodes it into appropriate representation. Consider the trajectory $S_i^u = \{(u, p_1, t_1), \ldots, (u, p_n, t_n)\}$ for a given user u_j. The encoding representation capacity of the input is essential to the training effect of the model. Instead of large one-hot encoded vectors, we employ a fully connected layer to embed the original POI identifier p_k and the user identifier u_j into a distributed vector representation, which has greater representation capacity and reflects the similarities and differences between POIs and users.

$$e_k^p = \delta(W_p \cdot p_k + b_p) \tag{1}$$

$$e_j^u = \delta(W_u \cdot u_j + b_u) \tag{2}$$

where $W_p \in \mathbf{R}^{|P| \times d_p}, W_u \in \mathbf{R}^{|P| \times d_u}$ are the weight parameters and $b_p \in \mathbf{R}^{|d_p| \times 1}, b_u \in \mathbf{R}^{|d_u| \times 1}$ are the bias parameters.

We convert each check-in record of the trajectory into a concatenated vector, including POI embedding, longitude lo and latitude la of POI location, time interval Δs, and geographic distance Δt of consecutive check-ins of the trajectory. The transformed input check-in I_k is described as follows:

$$I_k = [(e_k^p; la_k; lo_k; \Delta s_k; \Delta t_k)] \tag{3}$$

where the distance Δs_k between the successive POIs could be calculated by haversine formula, subscript $k \in [2, |S^u|]$

LSTM Layer. We adopt the Long-Short Memory Mechanism (LSTM) in the recurrent layer to capture the sequential feature of trajectory data. The LSTM unit consists of an input gate i_k, an input gate f_k, and an output gate o_k, the detail of these parameters are introduced as follows:

$$f_k = \delta(W_f \cdot [h_{k-1}; I_k] + b_f) \qquad i_k = \delta(W_i \cdot [h_{k-1}; I_k] + b_i) \tag{4}$$

$$\widetilde{c}_k = \delta(W_c \cdot [h_{k-1}; I_k] + b_c) \qquad c_k = f_k \odot c_{k-1} + i_c \odot \widetilde{c}_k \tag{5}$$

$$o_k = \delta(W_o \cdot [h_{k-1}; I_k] + b_o) \qquad h_k = o_k \odot tanh(c_k) \tag{6}$$

The hidden state size of the LSTM recurrent unit is d_k. The output states $(h_1, h_2, \ldots, h_n)$ are obtained as the input of the successive modules.

4.3 POI Prediction Task Module

The goal of the POI prediction task is to make a preliminary prediction of the user's next POI tendency based on the shared spatio-temporal sequence features captured previously. This module consists of a task-scope attention layer and a fully connected layer.

Attention Layer. The attention mechanism is a critical progress in deep learning, which shows promising performance improvement on RNNs [1,9,14]. We choose dot-product attention to capture the weight of all hidden states of the trajectory sequence in the POI prediction task. Following the work of [12], we introduce Z_u as the user context, which can be learned in the training process. The weight of each hidden state β_i is calculated with the softmax function:

$$\beta_i = \frac{exp(h_i \cdot Z_u)}{\sum_{j=1}^{n} exp(h_j \cdot Z_u)} \tag{7}$$

After obtaining the normalized attention scores, we can get the overall trajectory latent state output O_n with all weighted state sequence as follows:

$$O_n = \sum_{i=1}^{n} \beta_i \odot h_i \tag{8}$$

Fully Connected Output Layer. We apply a fully connected network with softmax function to transform the prediction problem into a POI classification problem. In addition to the dynamic states of trajectory, the user's static personal preference is also essential for POI recommendation. Hence we fuse these two factors by summing the latent state output O_n and the user embedding e_u:

$$Q_n = W_o \cdot O_n + W_u \cdot e_u \tag{9}$$

where parameters $W_o, W_u \in \mathbf{R}^{d_k \times d_k}$.

Then, we put the sum Q_n into a fully connected layer, which uses softmax function to calculate the probability of each POI:

$$\hat{y}_n = softmax(sigmoid(W_s \cdot Q_n + b_s)) \tag{10}$$

where $W_s \in \mathbf{R}^{|P| \times d_k}$ and $b_s \in \mathbf{R}^{|P| \times 1}$ is the bias parameter.

The output $y_n \in \mathbf{R}^{|P| \times 1}$ is the preliminary prediction probability vector of every POI that use is likely to visit next in the POI prediction task.

4.4 Time Prediction Task Module

Temporal information is considered as a critical factor in POI recommendation [10]. Different from previous methods, we estimate when the user may check-in next to infer the user's POI preference. It contains a task scope attention layer and two fully connected layers.

Attention Layer. The attention Layer in time prediction task is similar to the POI prediction task, but keeps its own parameters.

Fully Connected Output Layer. First, we add the user embedding e_u to the dynamic state output O_n^t and get the overall state Q_n^t:

$$Q_n^t = W_o t \cdot O_n^t + W_u \cdot e_u \tag{11}$$

To better capture the complex regularity, we design a two-layer fully connected network and feed Q_n^t into it. Unlike to POI prediction task, the output of this module is a continuous value. To better adapt the input and the output, we set ReLU (Rectified Linear Unit) instead of sigmoid as the activation function in fully connected layers. The output time prediction t_n is computed as:

$$\hat{t}_n = ReLU(W_2 \cdot ReLU(W_1 \cdot Q_n + b_1) + b_2) \tag{12}$$

where parameters $W_1 \in \mathbf{R}^{d_k \times d_t}, W_2 \in \mathbf{R}^{d_t \times 1}$ and $b_1 \in \mathbf{R}^{d_t \times 1}, b_2 \in \mathbf{R}^{1 \times 1}$.

4.5   Multi-task Assemble Module

The core issue we try to solve in this module is to infer the POI preference from the time prediction results, and make a more accurate final POI prediction.

We establish a user's personal POI transition tensor (**PPTT**) from the user's historical trajectories to describe the user's personal spatio-temporal regularity of transitions of POIs. **PPTT** is a three-order tensor with dimensions $|P| \times |P| \times |U|$, with each value of the tensor $v_{ijk} = (\bar{t}_{ijk}, prb_{ijk})$ represents the average time interval and the probability of transition from P_i to P_j of user u_k in history.

However, due to the users' check-in behavior is limited and restricted within a local area, which makes the PPTT tensor extremely sparse and has a limited help on POI recommendations. On the other hand, common preferences have a significant impact on a user's short-term behavior decisions [7]. To this end, we construct the user's common POI transition tensor (**CPTT**) to describe user's common spatio-temporal regularity of transitions of POIs. As shown in Fig. 2, **CPTT** is built by **rolling-up** (a concept from on-line analytical processing) the **PPTT** along the user dimension. Each value $v_{ij} = (\bar{t}_{ij}, prb_{ij})$ in tensor **CPTT** represents the average time interval and the probability of transition from P_i to P_j of all users.

Suppose a user is now at position p_i and will check in after a certain time $\hat{t}$, the probability that the user will appear at p_j is opposite to the difference between $\hat{t}$ and the average time $\bar{t}_{ij}$ from p_i to p_j. The greater the time difference, the smaller the probability is. To this end, we define a time-decay operation π on **PPTT** and **CPTT**, which calculates the probability vector of POI transition from p_i to all POIs of the user u_k. The formula operation of π is as follows:

$$\pi_{pptt}(u_k, p_i, \hat{t}) = [v_1, \cdots, v_{|P|}], v_j = exp(|\mu(\bar{t}_{ijk} - \hat{t})|) \cdot prb_{ijk} \tag{13}$$

$$\pi_{cptt}(p_i, \hat{t}) = [v_1, \cdots, v_{|P|}], v_j = exp(\mu(\bar{t}_{ij} - \hat{t})) \cdot prb_{ij} \tag{14}$$

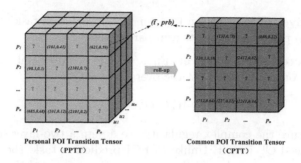

Fig. 2. The POI transmit tensors.

We use a compressed storage method to store these two sparse tensors and convert the involved part into a common vector representation during calculation for efficiency.

Given the location of the last occurrence $\hat{p}_{n-1}$ and the predicted time $\hat{t}_n$ of user u_k, combined with the spatio-temporal transfer tensor, we can know a user's POI transition preference based on time prediction.

$$w = \alpha_p \cdot \pi_{pptt}(u_k, p_{n-1}, \hat{t}) + \alpha_c \cdot \pi_{cptt}(p_{n-1}, \hat{t}) \qquad (15)$$

where $\alpha_p, \alpha_c \in \mathbf{R}$ are the hyper-parameters.

Finally, we multiply the correction weight based on time prediction and preliminary POI prediction results of task prediction, and get the user's final next POI correction prediction result as follows:

$$\hat{y}_t = y_t \odot w \qquad (16)$$

4.6 Loss Function

To guide the training of the model, we use the weighted sum of final POI result cross-entropy loss, time prediction error, and L2 regularization to measure the whole loss in this module. We use the relative error of $\hat{t}_n$ and target time t to evaluate the time prediction error, and use a tanh function to smooth the large error value to avoid affecting the stability of the model.

$$L_t = tanh(|\hat{t}_n - t + \varepsilon|)/(t + \varepsilon) \qquad (17)$$

where ε is the smoothing parameter and is set to 1×10^{-5}.

We adopt the cross-entropy loss between the ground truth POI y_t and the predicted POI $\hat{y}_t$. The POI prediction loss function can be calculated as follows:

$$L_p = -\frac{1}{N} \sum_{n=1}^{N} y_t log(\hat{y}_t) + (1 - y_t)log(1 - \hat{y}_t) \qquad (18)$$

The complete loss function of MTNR is as follows:

$$L = L_p + \alpha \cdot L_t + \frac{\lambda}{2} \left\| \Theta^2 \right\| \qquad (19)$$

where α and λ are hyper-parameters, and Θ denotes the parameter set of MTNR. We use L2 regularization term to avoid overfitting. To optimize the above loss function, we use Stochastic Gradient Descent to train the model.

Table 1. The statistics of datasets.

Dataset	#Users	#check-ins	#location	#trajectories
LA	1,083	22,7428	38,333	31,941
TKY	2,293	57,3703	61,858	66,663
CA	4,163	48,3805	2,9529	47,276

5   Experiments

5.1   Datasets

We conducted experiments on three publicly available LBSN datasets, NYC, TKY and CA. NYC and TKY [13] are two datasets collected from the Foursquare website in New York and Tokyo, respectively. CA is a subset of a Foursquare dataset [12], which includes global-scale check-in data. We chose the check-ins of users in California for the CA dataset. The check-in times of above datasets range from 2012 Apr. to 2013 Sep. To alleviate the problem of data sparsity, we expand the set of trajectories by adding the sub-trajectories of original trajectories. The sub-trajectories are generated by intercepting the original trajectories of a certain length range. The basic statistics of both datasets are summarized in Table 1. For each individual user in the datasets, we randomly mark off 90% of each user's trajectories as the training set and the remaining 10% as testing data.

5.2   Baseline Methods

We compare MTNR with several representative methods for location prediction:

- **MC** [3]: This is a basic method for POI prediction, which employ the properties of a Markov Chain to model the sequential influence for POI prediction.
- **FPMC** [7]: This method utilizes Matrix Factorization (MF) method to capture the user's common preferences through decomposition methods while retaining the ability to learn personal preferences.
- **LSTM** [8]: This is a variant of the RNN model, which contains a memory cell and three multiplicative gates to allow long-term dependency learning.
- **ATST-LSTM** [4]: This is a state-of-the-art method for POI prediction, which applies an attention mechanism to a LSTM network.
- **MTNR:** This is our approach, which learns user personal dynamic preference base on current spatial and temporal context.

5.3   Experiment Setup

For the key hyper parameters in MNTR model, we set $d_u = d_p = d_h = 200$. For the regularization parameter λ, we tried values in $\{1, 0.1, 0.01, 0.001\}$ and $\lambda = 0.01$ turns out to have the best performance.

To evaluate the performance of all methods for POI recommendation, we employ commonly used metrics recall@N and Mean Average Precision (MAP) used in [6]. We choose N = $\{1, 5, 10, 20\}$ to illustrate different results of recall@N.

Table 2. Performance comparison on three dataset.

Dataset	Method	Recall@1	Recall@5	Recall@10	Recall@20	MAP
LA	MC	0.0111	0.0683	0.0831	0.0988	0.0381
	FPMC	0.0342	0.2281	0.2752	0.3084	0.1239
	LSTM	0.0455	0.1518	0.2357	0.3395	0.1037
	ATST-LSTM	0.0873	0.2723	0.3946	0.5230	0.1787
	MTNR	**0.1883**	**0.3489**	**0.4540**	**0.5554**	**0.2693**
TKY	MC	0.0052	0.0567	0.0837	0.1125	0.0321
	FPMC	0.0222	0.1295	0.1792	0.2268	0.0773
	LSTM	0.0261	0.0734	0.1011	0.1371	0.0531
	ATST-LSTM	0.0564	0.1972	0.2878	0.3684	0.1262
	MTNR	**0.1636**	**0.2825**	**0.3528**	**0.4315**	**0.2257**
CA	MC	0.0045	0.0182	0.0235	0.0317	0.0124
	FPMC	0.0180	0.0697	0.0895	0.1064	0.0350
	LSTM	0.0503	0.1115	0.1580	0.2064	0.0841
	ATST-LSTM	0.0679	0.1760	0.2388	0.3012	0.1210
	MTNR	**0.1309**	**0.2498**	**0.3067**	**0.3771**	**0.1907**

5.4   Evaluation of Models

The performance comparison of different methods on three datasets is illustrated in Table 2. FPMC improves the performance greatly by 2-4x over MC on all three datasets, which shows that effect of Matrix Factorization method. LSTM outperforms FPMC on CA dataset because of its memory and forgot gate design on RNN network, but fails on some of the metrics for the LA and TKY datasets. ATST-LSTM turns out to be the best baseline and shows significant improvement over other baseline methods. It shows that attention mechanism is an effective supplement to LSTM model.

MTNR outperforms all above baseline methods in all metrics. Compared with ATST-LSTM, MTNR obtains 2 times improvements of recall@1 on LA and CA, and nearly three times improvements of recall@1 on TKY. Moreover, compared with ATST-LSTM, the MAP of MTNR on LA, TKY, and CA are improved by **50.7%**, **78.84%**, and **57.6%**, respectively. These results show that our proposed MTNR can well model user's next POI preference. The main reason is that the time prediction result helps to filter the unreasonable POIs recommended by sequential or geographical law from the time dimension, and improves the ranking of POIs with high correlation with the time prediction.

5.5 Impact of Multi-task Learning and Assemble Layer

In order to study the influence of multi-task learning and assembly layer design on the prediction effect, we adjusted the structure of the model to produce the following two new contrast models:

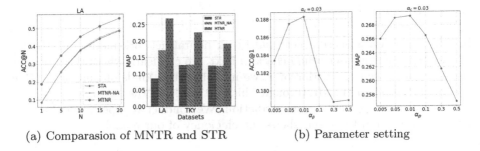

(a) Comparasion of MNTR and STR   (b) Parameter setting

Fig. 3. Comparison of MNTR and STR and parameter setting of α_p and α_c.

– **STR** (Single Task Recommendation): STR has no multi-task learning and the assemble layer design. It only keeps the shared feature layer and POI prediction task of the MTNR, and the output of the POI prediction.
– **MTNR-NA** (Multi-task Neural Recommendation with No Assemble layer): MTNR-NA removes the assemble layer, and directly take the outputs of time prediction task and POI prediction task as the final result.

We carried out experiments to compare the performance of STR, MTNR-NA, and MTNR on the LA dataset. As shown in Fig. 3(a), MTNR-NA works better than STR on the MAP metric for the LA dataset, but obtains minimal improvement on TOP accuracy metrics on all datasets. The reason is the user's check-in data is relatively sparse compare to all POI and time slots, so that it is hard to automatically capture the implicit spatial-temporal transition regularity by directly incorporating the auxiliary time prediction task. MTNR, by contrast, greatly outperforms MTNR-NA and MTNR on three datasets. MTNR has 2-3x improvement on the ACC@1 metric and 50% improvement on MAP metric for all three datasets, which shows the efficiency of the assemble Layer design.

5.6 Impact of Parameters

The α_p and α_c are key parameters which determine the weight of the user's personal preference and general preference in the model. We conducted experiments on the LA dataset to investigate the effect of parameter α_p and α_c on recommendation accuracy. We first fix the value of the parameter α_p, and study the effect of α_c on the accuracy of the model and find the best value. Then we fix the α_c in reverse and determine the best value of α_p.

As shown in Fig. 3(b), the performance of the model is not monotonically increasing or decreasing with the change of α_p or α_c, and the performance reaches the best level at a balance point: $\alpha_p = 0.01, \alpha_c = 0.03$ in our experiment, which indicates that common preferences have a more significant impact on users' behavior compared with personal preferences.

6 Conclusion

In this paper, we propose a new multi-task neural network model MTNR. By predicting when the user would check in next, we can learn where the user may check-in more accurately. Moreover, we introduce two kinds of time-decay POI transition tensors in MTNR, through which we can learn the next POI preference based on the next check-in time prediction. We conducted experiments on real-world datasets and the result shows the efficiency of our model.

References

1. Bahdanau, D., Cho, K., Bengio, Y.: Neural machine translation by jointly learning to align and translate. ArXiv arXiv:1409.0473, September 2014
2. Caruana, R.: Multitask learning. Mach. Learn. **28**(1), 41–75 (1997). https://doi.org/10.1023/A:1007379606734
3. Gambs, S., Killijian, M.O., del Prado Cortez, M.N.: Next place prediction using mobility Markov chains. In: Proceedings of the First Workshop on Measurement, Privacy, and Mobility, MPM 2012 (2012)
4. Huang, L., Ma, Y., Wang, S., Liu, Y.: An attention-based spatiotemporal LSTM network for next poi recommendation. IEEE Trans. Serv. Comput. 1 (2019)
5. Koren, Y., Bell, R., Volinsky, C.: Matrix factorization techniques for recommender systems. Computer **42**(8), 30–37 (2009)
6. Liu, Q., Wu, S., Wang, L., Tan, T.: Predicting the next location: a recurrent model with spatial and temporal contexts. In: Proceedings of the Thirtieth AAAI Conference on Artificial Intelligence, AAAI 2016, pp. 194–200. AAAI Press (2016)
7. Rendle, S., Freudenthaler, C., Schmidt-Thieme, L.: Factorizing personalized Markov chains for next-basket recommendation. In: WWW 2010, pp. 811–820 (2010)
8. Schuster, M., Paliwal, K.: Bidirectional recurrent neural networks. IEEE Trans. Sig. Process. **45**, 2673–2681 (1997)
9. Vaswani, A., et al.: Attention is all you need, June 2017
10. Xie, M., Yin, H., Wang, H., Xu, F., Chen, W., Wang, S.: Learning graph-based POI embedding for location-based recommendation. In: CIKM 2016, pp. 15–24 (2016)

11. Xiong, L., Chen, X., Huang, T.K., Schneider, J.G., Carbonell, J.G.: Temporal collaborative filtering with Bayesian probabilistic tensor factorization. In: SDM, pp. 211–222. SIAM (2010)
12. Yang, D., Zhang, D., Qu, B.: Participatory cultural mapping based on collective behavior data in location-based social networks. ACM Trans. Intell. Syst. Technol. **7**(3), 1–23 (2016)
13. Yang, D., Zhang, D., Zheng, V., Yu, Z.: Modeling user activity preference by leveraging user spatial temporal characteristics in LBSNs. IEEE Trans. Syst. Man Cybern. Syst. **45**, 129–142 (2015)
14. Yang, Z., Yang, D., Dyer, C., He, X., Smola, A., Hovy, E.: Hierarchical attention networks for document classification, pp. 1480–1489, January 2016
15. Yao, D., Zhang, C., Huang, J., Bi, J.: SERM: a recurrent model for next location prediction in semantic trajectories, pp. 2411–2414, November 2017
16. Zhang, Y., et al.: Sequential click prediction for sponsored search with recurrent neural networks. In: Proceedings of AAAI 2014, pp. 1369–1375 (2014)
17. Zhao, P., et al.: Where to go next: a spatio-temporal gated network for next POI recommendation. In: Proceedings of the AAAI Conference on Artificial Intelligence, vol. 33, pp. 5877–5884, July 2019
18. Zheng, V.W., Cao, B., Zheng, Y., Xie, X., Yang, Q.: Collaborative filtering meets mobile recommendation: a user-centered approach. In: AAAI 2010, July 2010

An Adversarial Learning Model for Intrusion Detection in Real Complex Network Environments

Ying Zhong[1], Yiran Zhu[2], Zhiliang Wang[1,4(✉)], Xia Yin[3,4], Xingang Shi[1,4], and Keqin Li[5]

[1] Institute for Network Sciences and Cyberspace at Tsinghua University, Beijing, China
zhongy18@mails.tsinghua.edu.cn, wzl@cernet.edu.cn
[2] Beijing Normal University, Beijing, China
[3] Department of Computer Science and Technology at Tsinghua University, Beijing, China
[4] Beijing National Research Center for Information Science and Technology, Beijing, China
[5] Department of Computer Science, State University of New York, New Paltz, USA

Abstract. Network intrusion detection plays an important role in network security. With the deepening of machine learning research, especially the generative adversarial networks (GAN) proposal, the stability of the anomaly detector is put forward for higher requirements. The main focus of this paper is on the security of machine learning based anomaly detectors. In order to detect the robustness of the existing advanced anomaly detection algorithm, we propose an anomaly detector attack framework MACGAN (maintain attack features based on the generative adversarial networks). The MACGAN framework consists of two parts. The first part is used to analyze the attack fields manually. Then, the learning function of GAN in the second part is used to bypass the anomaly detection. Our framework is tested on the latest Kitsune2018 and CICIDS2017 data sets. Experimental results demonstrate the ability to bypass the state-of-the-art machine learning algorithms. This greatly helps the network security researchers to improve the stability of the detector.

Keywords: Generative adversarial networks · Traffic anomaly detection · Machine learning security

1 Introduction

Intrusion detection system (IDS) is a key component in securing computing infrastructure. The purpose of this component is to prevent violations of the defense mechanism. In fact, IDS itself is part of the computing infrastructure, so they may also be attacked by adversaries [1]. In [2], skilled attacker can

© Springer Nature Switzerland AG 2020
D. Yu et al. (Eds.): WASA 2020, LNCS 12384, pp. 794–806, 2020.
https://doi.org/10.1007/978-3-030-59016-1_65

use ambiguity in the traffic flow seen by the monitor to evade detection. Many evasion techniques are proposed in [3], but they are all limited to botnet traffic evasion. And, many of the anomaly detection algorithms used for experiments are now outdated.

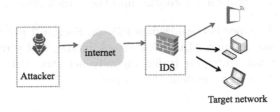

Fig. 1. Network attacks in the presence of IDS.

Because of the development of machine learning, the accuracy of network traffic anomaly detection algorithms continues to increase, but the stability of the algorithm itself faces enormous challenges [4–6]. Attackers can carefully design adversarial samples that are not too different from normal samples, and make machine learning algorithms make completely different decisions. Aiming at the lack of research on adversarial learning in the existing network IDS, this paper proposes adversarial sample generation algorithms to reveal potential security problems in the existing IDS. In order to explore the robustness of machine learning-based IDS, as shown in Fig. 1, we will attack wireless devices in the presence of IDS.

In summary, we propose a new attack method based on GAN. The reason for choosing GAN is that we need the characteristics of GAN to generate adversarial samples [25]. The generator of GAN modifies some of the fields that can be disturbed so that its data features are close to those of benign data packets. Therefore, the adversarial sample can deceive the anomaly detector well while maintaining the attack features of the traffic. We call it the MACGAN model. To the best of our knowledge, this paper is the first work to bypass network intrusion detection in real network traffic.

The main contributions of this paper are summarized below.

- For the network IDS, we design the MACGAN attack model. This model can bypass anomaly detectors by modifying meaningless fields. The main reason is that we add the target anomaly detector to the model so that it can be fitted by the discriminator of GAN. We attack before the anomaly detector extracts traffic features, which has practical application significance.
- We propose to divide the fields of network packets into perturbable and non-perturbable parts. We perturb the fields that can be perturbed so that the current network packets will not be detected by the anomaly detector after the perturbation.

- We design a series of experiments for the MACGAN model. We first explore the effects of parameters in GAN on the experiment, and then test the impact of the number of iterations on the attack effect. Finally, experiments on the latest Kitsune2018 and CICIDS2017 datasets prove the effectiveness of our attack model. In order to further explain the practicality of the attack, we attack other classification algorithms, and the attack effect is significant.

The rest of this paper is organized as follows. Section 2 presents the related work. In Sect. 3, we design a MACGAN attack model, and provides a detailed description about how to bypass traffic anomaly detector. Performance evaluation is in Sect. 4. Section 5 concludes the paper.

2   Related Work

We analyze the application of the adversarial samples in anomaly detection [1]. [7] investigated the performances of the state-of-the-art attack algorithms against deep learning-based intrusion detection on the NSL-KDD data set. The roles of individual features in generating adversarial examples were explored. [8] showed that by modifying on average as little as 1.38 of the input features, an adversary could generate malicious inputs which effectively fooled a deep learning based NIDS. Therefore, when designing such systems, it was crucial to consider the performance from not only the conventional network security perspective but also the adversarial machine learning domain. [9] presented an approach to generate explanations for incorrect classifications made by the data-driven IDS. An adversarial approach was used to find the minimum modifications (of the input features) required to correctly classify a given set of misclassified samples. The magnitude of such modifications was used to visualize the most relevant features that could explain the reason for the misclassification. [10] proposed the use of GANs for generating network traffic in order to mimic other types of traffic. In particular, they modified the network behavior of a real malware in order to mimic the traffic of a legitimate application, and therefore avoided detection. [11] investigated how adversarial examples affect the performance of deep neural network (DNN) trained to detect abnormal behaviors in the black-box model. They demonstrated that adversary could generate effective adversarial examples against DNN classifier trained for NIDS even when the internal information of the target model was isolated from the adversary. In [12], a framework of the GAN, IDSGAN, was proposed to generate the adversarial attacks, which could deceive and evade the IDS. The internal structure of the detection system was unknown to attackers, thus adversarial attack examples performed the black-box attacks against the detection system.

Among the adversarial sample generation algorithms mentioned in the above literature, some of them were not used for traffic anomaly detection, but were used for other aspects [10]. Some algorithms used data sets that were too ideal and not representative, such as NSLKDD [7,9,12]. The others could completely bypass the anomaly detector, but the corresponding samples had lost the features of the attack [8,9,12]. Therefore, we need to design an algorithm that can attack the latest cyber attack data without losing the significance of the sample itself.

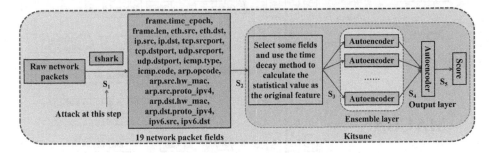

Fig. 2. Internal structure of Kitsune [1].

3   MACGAN Model: An Adversarial Learning Model for Intrusion Detection

The existing mainstream network traffic anomaly detection algorithms are based on machine learning methods. These methods require extraction of features. The establishment of these features is inseparable from the choice of fields. Our general idea is to first ensure that the fields necessary for the attack cannot be modified. For the remaining fields called non-attack field, we bypass the anomaly detector through the sample generation function of GAN.

3.1   Analysis of Advanced Anomaly Detection Algorithm

Figure 2 depicts the advanced anomaly detection algorithm Kitsune. In order to make the attack algorithm more versatile, we put the attack step on S_1, because many anomaly detectors are modeled based on network packet fields. Thus, if the abnormal detection algorithm are based on field modeling, our attack mode also applicable. The details of the specific Kitsune algorithm can be found in [13].

3.2   MACGAN Attack Model

There are many versions of GANs, which are selected according to different design requirements. In order to prevent the non-convergence and instability of GAN, we design MACGAN based on the Wasserstein GAN structure [14]. It is an improved model of GAN, for the evasion attacks against IDS. The framework of MACGAN is described in Fig. 3, where the noun of the input and output data represents the sample set, and the letter represents each sample. For example, in

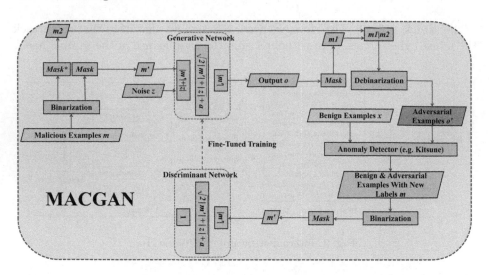

Fig. 3. The framework of MACGAN.

"Malicious Examples m", "Malicious Examples" represents a malicious data set, and "m" represents each malicious sample. Algorithm 1 illustrates the training process of MACGAN.

Generation Module: The generation network G is a three-layer feed forward neural network. The malicious sample m (traffic packet labeled abnormal) is first binarized, and then the non-attack field is reserved by $mask$ to obtain m'. m' is connected to the noise vector z as an input of G. The input layer size of the generation network is $|m'| + |z|$, and hidden layer size is $\sqrt{2|m'| + |z|} + a$, a is the adjustment constant between $[1, 9]$, and the output layer size is $|m'|$. The output of the generated network is o. To ensure the enforceability and aggression against the sample, o and $mask$ are operated together, and only the generation data of the non-attack field is retained, and $m1$ is obtained. At the same time, $mask$ is reversed to get $mask*$, and all the bits except the non-attack field can be reserved by $mask*$. The original malicious data m is done with $mask*$ and gets $m2$. After $m1$ and $m2$ are superimposed, they are debinarized to obtain a new sample o'.

Discriminating Module: The discriminating module is composed of an abnormality detector K (Kitsune) that is expected to be deceived and a discriminating network D. The benign sample x and the new sample o' retain the binary vector of the non-attack field as the input of D. Before the input, the two samples need to be discriminated by the anomaly detector, and the sample attributes are re-marked according to the discriminating result (benign or malicious). The input layer size of the discriminant network is $|m'|$, the hidden layer size is $\sqrt{2|m'| + |z|} + a$, a is the adjustment constant between $[1, 9]$, and the output layer size is 1. The sample data after updating the label passes through the discriminant network, and the discriminating result is output. Then, the loss function is calculated based on the discriminating result. When the input sample is o', if K discriminates o' as a malicious sample, that is, $K(o') = 0$, then $D(o')$ is made as 0 as possible; if K discriminates o' as a benign sample, That is, $K(o') = 1$, so that $D(o')$ tends to be as large as 1. When the input sample is x, if K discriminates x as a benign sample, that is, $K(x) = 1$, $D(x)$ is made as close as possible to 1. After the loss is calculated, the gradient backward propagation is performed, and the parameters of the discriminant model are updated, so that the degree of fitting of D to K is continuously improved.

Algorithm 1 The training process of MACGAN

Input:

Malicious traffic examples M, the vector $mask$ for protecting the non-attack field, benign traffic examples X, the learning rate α, the clipping parameter c, the batch size n, the number of iterations of the critic per generator iteration n_{critic}, the noise Z for the adversarial generation, initial discriminator parameters ω_0, initial generator parameters θ_0.

Output:

The trained generator g_θ and the trained discriminator f_ω.

1: Step 1: Merging 19 fields (after the tag) in Kitsune with other perturbed ficlds (such as optional fields in the network packet) to form a malicious traffic.
2: Step 2: Vectorize malicious samples and add perturbations to marked fields.
3: //Step 3
4: **while** θ has not converged **do**
5:    **while** n_{critic}-- **do**
6:      Sample $\{M^{(i)}\}_{i=1}^n \sim P_r$ a batch from the malicious traffic examples.
7:      Sample $\{X^{(i)}\}_{i=1}^n \sim P_g$ a batch from the benign traffic examples.
8:      Sample $\{Z^{(i)}\}_{i=1}^n \sim P_z$ a batch of prior samples.
9:      $f_\omega \leftarrow \nabla_\omega [\frac{1}{n}\sum_{i=1}^n f_\omega(X^{(i)} * mask) - \frac{1}{n}\sum_{i=1}^n f_\omega(g_\theta(M^{(i)} * mask + Z^{(i)}))]$ //* - Hadamard Product
10:      $\omega \leftarrow \omega + \alpha \cdot RMSProp(\omega, g_\omega)$ //$RMSProp$ - An optimization algorithm: Root Mean Square Prop
11:      $\omega \leftarrow clip(\omega, -c, c)$
12:    **end while**
13:    $g_\theta \leftarrow -\nabla_\theta \frac{1}{n}\sum_{i=1}^n f_\omega(g_\theta(M^{(i)} * mask + Z^{(i)}))$
14:    $\theta \leftarrow \theta - \alpha \cdot RMSProp(\theta, g_\theta)$
15: **end while**
16: Step 4: Inverse vectorization, the meaningless fields after the disturbance are mapped to meaningful fields by hashing.
17: **return** g_θ, f_ω.

With the increase of the number of trainings, the discriminative ability of D tends to be consistent with the anomaly detector. At the same time, the ability to generate forged samples is continuously strengthened. Finally, D cannot effectively distinguish the generated adversarial examples and the original real samples generated by G. The adversarial examples generated at this time are not only discriminated by the anomaly detector as benign classification, but also use the mask to preserve the aggressiveness of the sample, and realize the deception of the anomaly detector.

4   Experiments and Evaluation

This section covers our experimental results. Our codes are available at the open-source code repository[1]. In order to systematically evaluate our method, we want to check the following two points: (1) How about our attack model's performance based on Kitsune anomaly detection algorithm. (2) How about our attack model's performance based on multiple anomaly detection algorithms.

4.1   Metrics for Evaluating Anomaly Detection Algorithm

We use the following metrics to evaluate the effectiveness of our MACGAN model. Attack Effect Rate $(AER)1 - \frac{TPR_{After\_attack}}{TPR_{Before\_attack}}$: It measures the extent to which an attack method reduces the accuracy of anomaly detection. True Positive Rate $(TPR)\frac{TP}{TP+FN}$: It measures the proportion of outliers that are correctly identified. Among them, True Negative (TN): a measure of the number of normal events rightly classified normal. True Positive (TP): a measure of the number of abnormal events rightly classified abnormal. False Positive (FP): a measure of normal events misclassified as attacks. False Negative (FN): a measure of attacks misclassified as normal. Higher AER means better attack performance and higher TPR means better detection performance.

4.2   Datasets and Experimental Settings

Datasets. We investigate DARPA, KDD99, NSL_KDD, UNSW_NB and other data sets, and find that some of these data sets are not real traffic, and some are real traffic but are outdated and cannot represent changing attack behavior. Thus, two data sets, Kitsune2018[2] [13] and CICIDS2017[3], are used in this paper to evaluate the performance of our scheme.

The Kitsune dataset comes from two parts. The first part is to attack in a real IP camera video surveillance network. For example, an attack can affect the availability and integrity of the video uplink. In order to establish a more noisy network attack environment, the second part of the attack data comes from the attack environment of 9 IoT devices and 3 PCs, including wireless network equipment. There are 9 data sets used to evaluate Kitsune: OS Scan, Fuzzing, Video Injection, ARP MitM, Active Wiretap, SSDP Flood, SYN DoS, SSL Renegotiation and Mirai. See [13] for detailed description.

CICIDS2017 contains benign and the most up-to-date common attacks, which resembles the true real-world data (PCAPs). It also includes the results

---

[1] https://github.com/zyyrrr/MACGAN.

[2] https://goo.gl/iShM7E.

[3] https://www.unb.ca/cic/datasets/ids-2017.html.

of the network traffic analysis using CICFlowMeter with labeled flows based on the time stamp, source and destination IPs, source and destination ports, protocols and attack (CSV files). The implemented attacks include Brute Force FTP, Brute Force SSH, DoS, Heartbleed, Web Attack, Infiltration, Botnet and DDoS. We use the original label from CICIDS2017.

Experiment Environment. In the experiment, PyTorch [15] is adopted as the deep learning framework to implement MACGAN. The purposed model is run and evaluated on a Linux PC with Intel Core i7-5500 and 1080Ti GPU.

Table 1. Identify data sets that require further attack. TPR measures the proportion of abnormaly that are correctly identified. 926554.8557720063 is expressed in the form of 9e5. *no* represents a range of dataset sizes we choose that do not require further attack anomaly detection algorithms. Because TPR itself is very low. *yes* stands for the need to use the MACGAN algorithm for further attacks.

Attack Name	Benign + Malicious	train + test	Threshold	TPR	Need attack
OS Scan	65845 + 34155	14000 + 86000	12.194	0.441	No
Fuzzing	77206 + 22794	50000 + 50000	0.348	0.004	No
Video Injection	80395 + 19605	40000 + 60000	1.713	0.002	No
ARP MitM	61995 + 38005	50000 + 50000	9e5	0.001	No
Active Wiretap	62285 + 37715	50000 + 50000	4e10	5e − 05	No
SSDP Flood	62295 + 37705	50000 + 50000	27.571	0.994	Yes
SYN Flood	92962 + 7038	10000 + 90000	1e3	0.004	No
SSL Renegotiation	89468 + 10532	40000 + 60000	33.151	0.005	No
Mirai	69999 + 30001	55000 + 45000	1.595	0.818	Yes
CICIDS2017	71860 + 28140	35000 + 65000	4.958	0.659	Yes

Table 2. Analysis of fields that can be disturbed based on three data sets. The numbers here are the numbers of the 19 network packet fields in Fig. 2.

Data set	Non-attack field number	Reserved	Modified
Mirai	0, 2–5, 14, 16–18	0, 3 ,5, 7, 9, 18	2, 4, 14, 16, 17
SSDP Flood	1–7, 9, 14, 16–18	0, 3, 5, 7, 9, 11, 13–16, 18	1, 2, 4, 6, 17
CICIDS2017	1–5, 14, 16–18	0, 1, 3, 5, 7, 9, 11, 18	2, 4, 14, 16, 17

4.3 Experimental Results and Implications

Attack Based on Kitsune Anomaly Detection Algorithm. This section illustrates a group of experiments to verify the effectiveness of our MACGAN attack model. We first sample the original data set of this algorithm. There are 100,000 benign samples along with malicious samples. The current TPR is tested in the case of $FPR = 0.001$. We decide whether to further use our attack algorithm based on the value of TPR. Table 1 describes which data sets can be used for further attacks. Among them, TPR of Kitsune on the SSDP data set can reach 0.994. The training set and test set size are both 50000. In order to ensure the robustness of our attack algorithm, we also use the CICIDS2017 data set to conduct experiments.

According to Table 1, we further attack Kitsune on the three data sets Mirai, SSDP Flood, and CICIDS2017 when we specify the size of the training sample. In order to maintain the aggressiveness of these attack methods, we not only retain the fields that these attacks must retain. The details are shown in Table 2.

From the previous section, we have been able to determine which fields can be attacked. Figure 4 shows the experiment on the CICIDS2017 data set. It can be seen from Fig. 4(a) that when the algorithm is iterated to the tenth times, Kitsune's TPR is already zero, which proves the effectiveness of our attacks. At the same time, in order to analyze the influence of the hidden layer parameter a on the convergence of the algorithm, we supplemented the experiment. As shown in Fig. 4(b), when a is greater than 2, the attack effect can be best. Figure 5 and 6 are similar to the attack effect in Fig. 4. The difference is that the value of convergence point a of Mirai data set in Fig. 5 is 3 and 9, and the value of convergence point a of SSDP Flood data set in Fig. 6 is greater than 6.

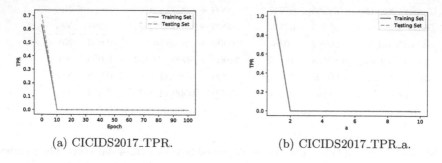

(a) CICIDS2017_TPR.   (b) CICIDS2017_TPR_a.

Fig. 4. Changes in TPR under the Mirai data set.

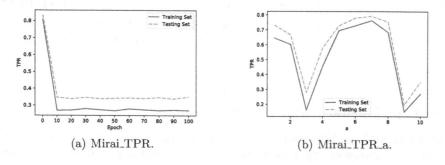

(a) Mirai_TPR.   (b) Mirai_TPR_a.

Fig. 5. Changes in TPR under the SSDP_Flood data set.

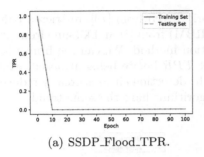

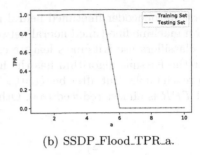

(a) SSDP_Flood_TPR.   (b) SSDP_Flood_TPR_a.

Fig. 6. Changes in TPR under the SSDP_Flood data set.

Table 3. AER under different parameters a. The larger AER, the better the attack effect. TPR_{before} is abbreviated as T_b. Negative number indicates a side effect of the attack. Hidden layer size is $\sqrt{2|m'| + |z| + a}$.

a	Mirai (T_b=0.818)	SSDP Flood (T_b=0.994)	CICIDS2017 (T_b=0.659)
$a = 1$	0.106	−0.006	−0.517
$a = 2$	0.187	−0.006	1
$a = 3$	0.658	−0.006	1
$a = 4$	0.293	−0.006	1
$a = 5$	0.111	−0.006	1
$a = 6$	0.047	1	1
$a = 7$	0.968	1	1
$a = 8$	0.079	1	1
$a = 9$	0.762	1	1
$a = 10$	0.572	1	1

Next, we introduce the concept of AER. As shown in Table 3, this is an assessment of the attack effect under different parameters a of different data sets. We can see that when a is 7, our attack effect can be best on different data sets. In short, as long as we can satisfy the detection part of the anomaly detector and change the undiscovered part by disturbance, our attack effect will be better. For example, the increase in the number of network addresses and the spread of timestamps will reduce the likelihood that a real attacker will be discovered.

Attacks Based on Multiple Anomaly Detection Algorithms. In order to further verify the effectiveness of our attack, we select another 300,000 data packets from the CICIDS2017 dataset for experiments. We use Isolation Forests (IF) [16] and Gaussian Mixture Models (GMM) [17]. IF is an ensemble based method of outlier detection, and GMM is a statistical method based on the expectation maximization algorithm. Then we use support vector machine (SVM) from [18],

sparse autoencoder finetuned neural network (SAE) from [19], restricted boltzmann machine fine-tuned neural network (RBM) from [1] and kitsune from [20].
All classifiers use Kitsune's feature extraction method. We can see from Fig. 7
that the Kitsune algorithm has the highest TPR before being attacked, which
can reach 0.998. But after being attacked, the detection effect is greatly reduced,
and TPR is almost reduced to 0. Other algorithms have the same trend.

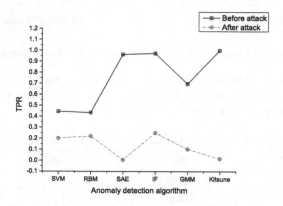

Fig. 7. Attack effects of different algorithms based on the 300,000 CICIDS2017 dataset.

5   Conclusion

The development of machine learning has facilitated network anomaly detection. However, attacks on machine learning methods are also needed to consider. This paper proposes an anomaly detector attack framework MACGAN
based on GAN. Our attack effect is better, indicating that the robustness of the
machine based anomaly detector needs to be further improved. Inspired by the
works [21–24], we will defense our MACGAN attack model in our future work.
For example, we can design a defense GAN to let it play a dynamic game with
MACGAN.

Acknowledgment. This work is supported by the National Key Research and Development Program of China under Grant No. 2018YFB1800204.

References

1. Corona, I., Giacinto, G., Roli, F.: Adversarial attacks against intrusion detection
   systems: taxonomy, solutions and open issues. Inf. Sci. **239**, 201–225 (2013)
2. Handley, M., Paxson, V., Kreibich, C.: Network intrusion detection: evasion, traffic
   normalization, and end-to-end protocol semantics. In: USENIX Security Symposium (2001)

3. Stinson, E., Mitchell, J.C.: Towards systematic evaluation of the evadability of bot/botnet detection methods. In: WOOT (2008)
4. Barreno, M., Nelson, B., Joseph, A.D., Tygar, J.D.: The security of machine learning. Mach. Learn. **81**(2), 121–148 (2010). https://doi.org/10.1007/s10994-010-5188-5
5. Barreno, M., Nelson, B., Sears, R., Joseph, A.D., Tygar, J.D.: Can machine learning be secure?. In: AsiaCCS (2006)
6. Moosavi-Dezfooli, S.-M., Fawzi, A., Frossard, P.: DeepFool: a simple and accurate method to fool deep neural networks. In: IEEE Conference on Computer Vision and Pattern Recognition (CVPR), pp. 2574–2582 (2016)
7. Wang, Z.: Deep learning-based intrusion detection with adversaries. IEEE Access **6**, 38367–38384. IEEE (2018)
8. Clements, J.H., Yang, Y., Sharma, A., Hu, H., Lao, Y.: Rallying Adversarial Techniques against Deep Learning for Network Security. CoRR, vol. abs/1903.11688 (2019)
9. Marino, D.L., Wickramasinghe, C.S., Manic, M.: An adversarial approach for explainable AI in intrusion detection systems. In: IECON 2018–44th Annual Conference of the IEEE Industrial Electronics Society, pp. 3237–3243 (2018)
10. Rigaki, M., Garcia, S.: Bringing a GAN to a knife-fight: adapting malware communication to avoid detection. In: IEEE Security and Privacy Workshops (SPW), pp. 70–75. IEEE (2018)
11. Yang, K., Liu, J., Zhang, V.C., Fang, Y.: Adversarial examples against the deep learning based network intrusion detection systems. In: IEEE Military Communications Conference (MILCOM), pp. 559–564. IEEE (2018)
12. Lin, Z., Shi, Y., Xue, Z.: IDSGAN: Generative adversarial networks for attack generation against intrusion detection. arXiv preprint arXiv:1809.02077 (2018)
13. Mirsky, Y., Doitshman, T., Elovici, Y., Shabtai, A.: Kitsune: an ensemble of autoencoders for online network intrusion detection. In: NDSS (2018)
14. Arjovsky, M., Chintala, S., Bottou, L.: Wasserstein generative adversarial networks. In: International Conference on Machine Learning, pp. 214–223 (2017)
15. Paszke, A., Gross, S., Chintala, S., Chanan, G.: Automatic differentiation in pytorch. In: NIPS 2017 Autodiff Workshop: The Future of Gradient-based Machine Learning Software and Techniques (2017)
16. Liu, F.T., Ting, K.M., Zhou, Z.-H.: Isolation forest. In: IEEE International Conference On Data Mining, pp. 413–422 (2008)
17. Reynolds, D.: Gaussian mixture models. Encyclopedia Biometrics, pp. 827–832 (2015)
18. Sahu, S.K., Jena, S.K.: A multiclass SVM classification approach for intrusion detection. In: Bjørner, N., Prasad, S., Parida, L. (eds.) ICDCIT 2016. LNCS, vol. 9581, pp. 175–181. Springer, Cham (2016). https://doi.org/10.1007/978-3-319-28034-9_23
19. Yan, B., Han, G.: Effective feature extraction via stacked sparse autoencoder to improve intrusion detection system. IEEE Access 41238–41248 (2018)
20. Fiore, U., Palmieri, F., Castiglione, A., Santis, A.D.: Network anomaly detection with the restricted Boltzmann machine. Neurocomputing 13–23 (2013)
21. Madani, P., Vlajic, N.: Robustness of deep autoencoder in intrusion detection under adversarial contamination. In: Proceedings of the 5th Annual Symposium and Bootcamp on Hot Topics in the Science of Security. ACM (2018)
22. Carlini, N., Wagner, D.A.: Towards evaluating the robustness of neural networks. In: IEEE Symposium on Security and Privacy (SP), pp. 39–57 (2017)

23. Ma, S., Liu, Y., Tao, G., Lee, W.C., Zhang, X.: NIC: detecting adversarial samples with neural network invariant checking. In: NDSS (2019)
24. Papernot, N., McDaniel, P., Wu, X., Jha, S., Swami, A.: Distillation as a defense to adversarial perturbations against deep neural networks. In: IEEE Symposium on Security and Privacy (SP), pp. 582–597. IEEE (2016)
25. Goodfellow, I., et al.: Generative adversarial nets. In: Advances in Neural Information Processing Systems, pp. 2672–2680 (2014)

HotDAG: Hybrid Consensus via Sharding in the Permissionless Model

Chun-Xuan Zhou, Qiang-Sheng Hua$^{(\boxtimes)}$, and Hai Jin

National Engineering Research Center for Big Data Technology and System,
Services Computing Technology and System Lab, Cluster and Grid Computing Lab,
School of Computer Science and Technology,
Huazhong University of Science and Technology, Wuhan 430074, China
{chxzhou,qshua,hjin}@hust.edu.cn

Abstract. A major design to improve scalability and performance of blockchain is sharding, which maintains a distributed ledger by running classical Byzantine Fault Tolerance (BFT) protocols through several relatively small committees. However, there are several drawbacks with the existing sharding protocols. First, the sharding mechanism which ensures that each committee is strongly bias-resistant either weakens the decentralization or reduces the performance of the protocol. Second, BFT protocols are either unresponsive or take quadratic communication complexities under a byzantine leader. Third, they cannot defend against transaction censorship attacks. Finally, nodes do not have enough motivation to follow the protocol and selfish nodes can obtain more rewards through collusive behaviors. A recent study proposes HotStuff – a BFT protocol that achieves linear view-change and optimistic responsiveness. In this paper, we present HotDAG, a hybrid consensus protocol based on HotStuff via sharding in the permissionless model. By employing the parallel Nakamoto consensus protocol, we present a decentralized and bias-resistant sharding mechanism. HotDAG has a linear communication complexity on transaction confirmation by introducing a scalable BFT protocol and an inter-committee consensus mechanism based on blockDAG. By achieving an unpredictable leader rotation, HotDAG prevents the censorship attacks. At the same time, HotDAG provides an incentive mechanism that is compatible with the scalable BFT protocol to encourage nodes to actively participate in the protocol. Finally, we formally prove the security and analyze the performance of HotDAG.

Keywords: Blockchain · Consensus · Byzantine fault tolerance · Scalability · Sharding · blockDAG

1 Introduction

Since the advent of Bitcoin [1] in 2008, cryptocurrency and the underlying technology behind Bitcoin (blockchain) have attracted widespread attention in the finance and academia. The blockchain is essentially a distributed database system that provides a decentralized, open, and Byzantine fault-tolerant protocol.

© Springer Nature Switzerland AG 2020
D. Yu et al. (Eds.): WASA 2020, LNCS 12384, pp. 807–821, 2020.
https://doi.org/10.1007/978-3-030-59016-1_66

Each participant maintains a distributed ledger which provides the total order of transactions and runs a distributed consensus protocol (Nakamoto consensus) to ensure the consistency of the distributed ledger. Although the blockchain is a fully decentralized and securely designed protocol, it still faces scalability barriers such as low transaction throughput and high latency. Bitcoin and Ethereum process at most 7 transactions per second (tx/s) and 25 tx/s respectively, which is far from meeting the actual market demand. Therefore, many recent research efforts such as [2–6] have been devoted to scaling the Nakamoto consensus.

Variants of Nakamoto consensus still suffer from low throughput and high latency due to the probabilistic consistency and decentralization. It is an inherently tradeoff between security and performance. In contrast, classical BFT protocols have deterministic consistency and the period of blocks is much shorter. Thereby they obtain higher transaction throughput and lower latency. However, these protocols work in a permissioned setting where the set of participants is fixed and the identity of each participant is known (we define the participant as the validator, and the set of validators as a committee). It is easy to be broken in a permissionless setting when suffering from the sybil-attack [7] and it can't run in the dynamic network [9,10]. Therefore, several hybrid protocols that combine the classical BFT protocol with Proof-of-Work (PoW) [8] or other proof-based protocols have been proposed [11–15]. However, BFT protocols have poor scalability, that is, an increase in the size of committee reduces transaction throughput. It motivated a design of protocols based on multiple committees so that transaction throughput scales linearly as the network size increases [16–19]. These protocols are also known as sharding-based protocols.

Unfortunately, there are some limitations in previous sharding-based protocols. First, to ensure that committees are bias-resistant, these protocols need to run a distributed randomness generation protocol to generate a seed for sharding securely (assign validators to committees). It causes additional communication overhead. In addition, it will cause temporary inoperability of the system for sharding protocols that use threshold signature schemes. Second, these protocols usually remain a fixed leader unless it fails. It makes them more vulnerable to transaction censorship (transactions are suppressed by the malicious leader) and the cost for the leader replacement to take a quadratic communication complexity. Other protocols [18–20] follow the leader rotation regime. However, they might be risky to deploy over the Internet because of the synchronous network assumption, and they forego the optimistic responsiveness. Responsiveness requires that an honest leader can drive the protocol to consensus in time depending only on the actual delay of the network. Third, cross-shard transactions rely on honest clients or leaders and require multiple committees to run the BFT protocol to resist the double-spend attack. Finally, previous work does not give incentive for nodes to participate in the protocol very well or causes serious resource monopoly problems.

To solve the above issues, we introduce HotDAG. It is a novel sharding protocol that ensures security in the perminssionless model. At the same time, HotDAG is scalable and strongly censorship-resistant. First, by introducing a parallel Nakamoto consensus protocol that is proposed by OHIE [6], HotDAG chooses a set of representative validators periodically via Proof-of-Work. Then HotDAG automatically and securely assigns validators to committees without any distributed randomness generation protocol or any honest third party. Second, HotDAG builds on the HotStuff [21] and provides an unpredictable leader rotation to guarantee censorship-resistance. Then, HotDAG extends the blockchain to the directed acyclic graph(blockDAG) and provides a safe total-ordering protocol that all honest nodes are agreed upon the total order of transactions. Finally, we introduce an incentive mechanism that is based on the epoch reputation to provide validators with enough motivation to participate in consensus. The rewards are distributed through the current committee's dynamic block reward coefficient and the node's contribution to processing transactions. It solves the problems of collusive behaviors and resource monopoly. Assume that any node outputs a total ordering of transactions at any time, we define it as a *LOG*. HotDAG achieves the following properties:

- **Decentralization**: Our protocol runs in a permissionless setting and does not rely on any trusted third party.
- **Consistency**: Suppose that an honest node p_i outputs *LOG* at time t and an honest node p_j outputs LOG' at time t' (i may equals to j and t may equals t'). Then with high probability, either LOG is prefix of LOG' or LOG' is prefix of *LOG*. We use $\prec$ to represent the relationship of the prefix.
- **Scalability**: The throughput increases linearly with the number of committees.
- **Strongly censorship-resistance**: The probability that a malicious validator is selected as the leader is equal to the percentage of malicious validators in a committee.
- **Incentive**: Rational nodes have incentive to follow the protocol and selfish nodes will not get more rewards through collusion.

The remainder of this paper is organized as follows. In Sect. 2, we review the related work. In Sect. 3, we give the system, the network and the adversary models. The protocol details are present in Sect. 4. Then, we formally prove the security of HotDAG in Sect. 5. In Sect. 6, we analyze the theoretical performance and incentive. Finally, we conclude the paper in Sect. 7.

2   Related Work

In this section, we will review hybrid consensus protocols and sharding-based protocols.

Due to the strong consistency of BFT protocols, several hybrid consensus protocols [11,13] have been proposed to scale up the throughput. Usually, hybrid consensus protocols select committees by PoW and transactions are confirmed by the PBFT protocol. In addition, there are other hybrid consensus protocols based on Proof-of-Stake (PoS), including Tendermint [20], Alogorand [14].

Although hybrid consensus protocols significantly improve performance over Nakamoto consensus, there still exists a major limitation: the size of committee is not scalable. It inspires protocols based on multiple committees that allow multiple committees to process transactions in parallel. Elastico [16] is the first permissionless blockchain protocol based on transaction sharding. Elastico has a hierarchical committee topology where normal committees propose blocks, and the final committee combines blocks received from normal committees. Based on this work, some protocols that adopt the state sharding have been proposed, such as [17] and [18]. They have a flat committee topology that all committees are at the same level. However, these protocols need to deal with cross-shard transactions. [17] depends on the assumption that honest clients participate actively when handling cross-shard transactions. And [18] relies on honest leaders, which is an unrealistic assumption in practice. CycLedger [19] is the reputation-based sharding protocol. Unfortunately, they both face serious reputation monopoly issues. We present a comparison of HotDAG with previous sharding blockchain protocols in Table 1.

Table 1. Comparison between HOTDAG and the existing works

	Elastico	OmniLedger	RapidChain	CycLedger	HotDAG
Resiliency	1/4	1/4	1/3	1/3	1/4
Responsive	✓	✓	×	×	✓
Decentralizaton[a]	✓	×	×	×	✓
Anti-censorship	×	×	×	×	✓
Incentive	×	×	×	✓	✓
Operability[b]	×	×	×	×	✓

[a] There are no always honest parties in Elastico and HotDAG. OmniLedger, RapidChain and CycLedger rely on honest clients, the honest reference committee and honest leaders, respectively.

[b] The system can process transactions during the transition phase when the threshold signature scheme is used.

3   System Overview

3.1   System Model

HotDAG adopts the UTXO (unspent transaction outputs) model which is similar to Bitcoin. Our system has a public key infrastructure (PKI) and each node holds a public/private key pair. We adopt a double-layer architecture that consists of the identity chain and the transaction chain. And multiple transaction chains form a blockDAG. At a high level, HotDAG has a flat committee topology. All blocks generated by a committee constitute a transaction chain. Blocks on all transaction chains and references between blocks together form a blockDAG.

Consider that each committee adds transactions to the corresponding transaction chain, we will use the transaction chain to illustrate our protocol in subsequent sections, instead of using the blockDAG.

3.2   Network Model

We assume a δ-partially synchronous network model as in HotStuff. After an unknown Global Stabilization Time (GST), any message broadcast by an honest node at time t will arrive at all honest nodes at time $t + \delta$ (δ is known). In addition, we assume a priori loose upper bound Δ of network delay. The confirmation time of a block only depends on the network's actual delay δ.

3.3   Adversary Model

We adopt the adversary model which is the same as [13]. We regard Byzantine nodes as being controlled by an *adversary*, denoted as $\mathcal{A}$. Honest nodes strictly follow the protocol while $\mathcal{A}$ can run away from protocol, such as reordering messages and delaying up to the maximal network delay δ. We stress that $\mathcal{A}$ cannot drop or modify messages by honest nodes. Honest nodes may be corrupted due to the adversary's attack. We adopt a τ-corruption model [13] where it takes τ time for honest nodes to be corrupted after the attack. We assume that $\mathcal{A}$ can have up to 25% of the total hashpower at any given moment.

3.4   Cryptographic Primitives

Our protocol makes use of a threshold signature scheme [22–24]. The (n, k)-threshold signature scheme can tolerate up to $n - k$ malicious nodes when there are n nodes. The node can generate a partial signature by using the private key and can combine a signature of the message m with k partial signatures on m. The signature can be verified by the single public key. It is computationally infeasible to forge a signature or to modify a signature to match a modified message.

4   Main Protocol

4.1   Identity Establishment and Committee Configuration

To ensure a negligible probability that any committee is compromised, committees need to be re-formed periodically (we assume that committees are re-formed per epoch). To reduce the communication overhead and to make committees re-form in an independent epoch, we aim to extend the identity chain in [17] to parallel identity chains. In this way, validators are automatically assigned to committees while identities are established. To securely assign validators to committees, we need to ensure that $\mathcal{A}$ gains no significant advantage in trying to bias its computational power towards any identity chain. We adopt a parallel

Nakamoto consensus model to force $\mathcal{A}$ to evenly split its power across all identity chains and to guarantee the safety of each committee.

In (λ, p, T)-Nakamoto consensus, there is a security parameter λ and a mining hardness parameter p which is the probability of successful execution of a random oracle query. All blocks on blockchain except the last T blocks are confirmed. Nodes iterate through a nonce which makes the hash digest of a block to include a certain number of leading zeros, and the length of the hash is λ. In HotDAG, we assume that there are k identity chains corresponding to k committees. And we define that the hash of a block is $\mathcal{H}(preHash|nonce|PK)$ where $\mathcal{H}$ is a cryptographic hash function ($\mathcal{H}$ is modeled as random oracles in the analysis), $preHash$ is the hash of the last block that is determined by the Merkle Tree, $nonce$ is a random number and PK is the public key. It inputs hashes of the last blocks on k identify chains as leaves, and outputs the root's hash as $preHash$. The hash of a valid block should have $log_2 \frac{1}{kp}$ leading zeros. We use the last log_2^k bits of the block hash to specify the id of the identify chain. As shown in Fig. 1a, the last blocks on all identity chains are A, B, C, D. When a node mines the block E and we assume that the last log_2^k bits of $E.hash$ is 0, then the block E is added to i-$chain_0$. For any identity chain, the probability of successful execution of a random oracle query is the same as in Nakamoto consensus ($log_2 \frac{1}{p} = log_2 \frac{1}{kp} + log_2^k$) [6].

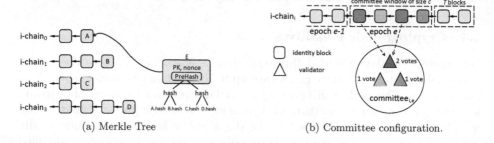

(a) Merkle Tree   (b) Committee configuration.

Fig. 1. Structure of identity chains.

From *Lemma* 3 in [6], the existing properties on (λ, p, T)-Nakomato consensus can directly carry over to each identity chain. Therefore, it guarantees that the proportion of malicious validators in each committee is less than $\frac{1}{3}$ with high probability. The committee reconfiguration is triggered when the identity chain grows by c blocks (c is the committee size), as shown in Fig. 1b. We define i-$chain_i[:-T]$ to denote the chain that removes the last T blocks on the i-$chain_i$. Let's take the switch from $committee_{i,e-1}$ to $committee_{i,e}$ as an example. When the height of i-$chain_i[:-T]$ is $(e+1)*c$, miners in the committee window form a new committee to take place of $committee_{i,e-1}$. Validators in $committee_{i,e}$ send *stop* messages to validators in $committee_{i,e-1}$. The color of the identity block indicates different miners. Validators' shares or voting power are directly proportional to their commitment to hashpower in the *committee window*. When the epoch $e - 1$ is terminated, $committee_{i,e}$ starts processing transactions by running the intra-committee consensus protocol.

4.2 Intra-committee Consensus

In HotStuff, the leader commits a block by collecting $2f + 1$ votes in three phases: *pre-commit*, *commit* and *decide*. The leader generates a QC(quorum certificate) through the threshold signature scheme. The Chained-HotStuff [21] pipelines these phases and works in a succession of rounds. The leader collects votes for a block b and proposes a new block b', and the work of collecting votes for b' will be handed over to the next leader. Votes for the block b' also serve as votes for the second phase of b. Its chain structure is similar to Bitcoin, as shown in Fig. 2. $QC.block$ means that QC is generated by enough votes for $block$ and the round of QC is the same as the round of $QC.block$. Each validator keeps track of the following state variables: (1) qc_{high}: the QC with the highest round, and the validator updates it when it receives a new block(or QC); (2) b_{lock}: the latest block that finished the second phase; (3) b_{commit}: the lastest block that finished all voting phases. (4) v: the round of last voted block. For example in Fig. 2, $B_0.round = r_0$, $B_1.round = r_1$, $B_2.round = r_2$. We have $qc_{high} = B.QC$, $b_{lock} = B_1$, $b_{commit} = B_0$.

The intra-committee consensus protocol is based on the Chained-HotStuff. We extend the chain structure of Chained-HotStuff to k chains and each validator maintains k sets of state variables. We define $t\text{-}chain_i$ as the i-th transaction chain. We consider a committee consisting of $c = 3f + 1$ validators where f is the number of Byzantine validators and each round has a unique dedicated leader. We add the termination condition for timely termination [13] to ensure that the current committee will not generate any valid block upon all honest validators reach a consensus on entering the next epoch.

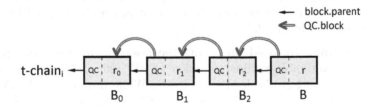

Fig. 2. Structure of Chained-HotStuff.

Protocol Specification. The intra-committee consensus protocol has four phases:

1. Startup phase: At the beginning, the validator sends a *new-view* message to the leader, including its qc_{high}. Then the committee enters the normal phase.

2. Normal phase: Upon receiving enough votes or *new-view* messages, the leader generates a QC. The leader selects transactions according to the transaction hash and proposes a new block b. Then it sends b to validators in the committee (including itself). At the same time, the leader also broadcasts QC and the block in QC to other committees. Upon receiving b and b is valid, the validator sends a vote (with qc_{high}) to the next leader and enters the next round.

3. Timeout phase: To guarantee the liveness, honest validators cannot keep the same round all the time. The validator starts a timer T_1 when it enters a new round. When T_1 expires, it sends a *new-view* message with qc_{high} to a new leader and enters the next round. We make use of an exponential back-off mechanism. The timer doubles value every time it expires [25].

4. Stop phase: When the leader receives enough *stop* messages from the next committee, it proposes a *stop* block and the current committee enters the stop phase. When the *stop* block finishes all voting phases, the current epoch is terminated and the next committee enters the startup phase.

Voting Rules. In the normal phase, validators check the validity of a block according to the following rules:

1. The current epoch is not terminated.
2. Each transaction is valid: the sum of outputs is less than the sum of inputs and all inputs are outputs of some transactions on transaction chains.
3. The round of b is greater than the round of the last voted block, that is $b.round > v$.
4. $b.parent.round \geqslant b_{lock}.round$.

Partially-Committed Rule. Consider four blocks B, B_0, B_1 and B_2 such that $B_2 = B.parent, B_1 = B_2.parent$ and $B_0 = B_1.parent$. If $B_2.round = B_1.round + 1$ and $B_1.round = B_0.round + 1$, we consider the branch led by B_0 is partially-committed. For example, blocks that on the branch led by B_0 are partially-committed in Fig. 2.

Leader Selection. To avoid predicting the leader in advance, our protocol makes use of a verifiable random function (VRF) [26] and a pseudo-random function (PRF) to select the leader randomly. While proposing a block b, the leader also generates a seed $s = VRF_{sk}('leader'||e||r)$ and a proof π where sk is the private key of the leader, e is the current epoch and r is the round of $b.QC$. Anyone can verify the seed using the leader's public key and the proof π. Each validator keeps track of the latest seed s and calculates the leader'id of round n by $id = PRF(s, n) \bmod c$. In order to ensure that validators will not keep different seeds for a long time (it will cause validators' views on the next leader to be different), we need to setup a timeout T_2 that is used by the validator to synchronize the latest seed. The first block on the transaction chain contains the initial seed.

4.3   Inter-committee Consensus

In intra-committee consensus, transactions are partitioned to different committees and multiple committees process transactions in parallel. To detect conflicting transactions in partially-committed blocks to prevent the double-spend attack, each validator needs to output a total-ordering of all blocks. A simple approach to order all blocks is to include the first block of each chain into LOG, and then the second block, etc. That is, $LOG = \{b_{0,0}...b_{k-1,0}, b_{0,1}...b_{k-1,1}...\}$. However, OHIE points out that the difference in the block growth rate among the k transaction chains will cause that some blocks may not be confirmed for a long time. Our protocol is different from OHIE where the block in OHIE is in a random manner to extend the transaction chain, but this difference still exists in HotDAG due to malicious leaders and the committee reconfiguration.

OHIE provides a total-ordering protocol to solve this issue. However, OHIE may violate happen-before relationships between transactions. For example in Fig. 3, the total order is B00, B10, B01, B11, B12, B13, B14 according to [6]. Therefore, $Tx2$ is before $Tx1$ which makes $Tx2$ invalid. (A more detailed explanation can be found in the full version [27].) To ensure that each non-conflicting transaction can be successfully confirmed, we extend parallel blockchains to a directed acyclic graph (DAG) where blocks specify the happen-before relationships among transactions. Each block b contains three fields $<height, nextHeight, references>$ where $height$ is the height of b and $nextHeight$ represents the $height$ of the next block to compensate for the gap between the current transaction chain and the longest transaction chain, that is, $nextHeight$ is the largest $nextHeight$ of the lastest blocks on transaction chains. $references$ is a set of block hashes and it represents the happen-before relationships among transactions. The height of b should be greater than all reference block, that is, $b.height = max(b.parent.nextHeight, \{r \in b.references | r.height + 1\})$. It should be noted that the cyclic dependencies between blocks do not occur. For example, we define that the transaction $Tx1$ depends on $Tx2$ and the transaction $Tx3$ depends on $Tx4$. $Tx1$ and $Tx4$ are included in block A, and $Tx2$, $Tx3$ are included in block B. Without loss of generality, we assume that A is proposed first, $Tx3$ has not been on the transaction chain at this time. Honest validators will consider the block A to be invalid because the input of $Tx4$ is invalid.

Eventually-Committed Rule. We define that blocks that meet eventually-committed rule can be included in LOG: Consider an honest node and a blockDAG $\mathcal{G}$ consisting of k transaction chains at time t, we define B is a set of b_{commit} of k transaction chains. Let $Height_{confirm} = min(\{b \in B | b.nextHeight\})$, then blocks in the set $\{b \in \mathcal{G} | b.height < Height_{confirm}\}$ are *eventually-committed*. *Eventually-committed* blocks are ordered by the $height$, with tie-breaking favoring smaller transaction chain ids.

As shown in Fig. 4, each block has a tuple $<round, height, nextHeight>$. There are three transaction chains and the lastest *partially-committed* blocks on each chain are A6, B8 and C6 according to the partially-committed rule.

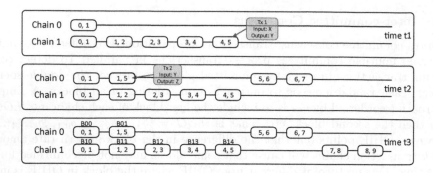

Fig. 3. The transaction $Tx1$ is proposed at time t_1, and the transaction $Tx2$ which spends the output in $Tx1$ is proposed at time t_2.

Then, $Height_{confirm} = 7$. If there are two conflicting transactions in A_1 and B_2, then the transaction in B_2 is invalid. The pseudo-code of the ordering protocol can be found in [27].

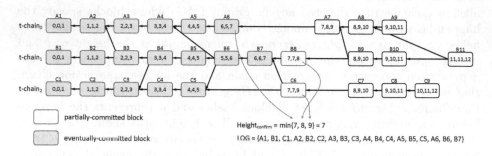

Fig. 4. Structure of transaction chains.

4.4   Incentive Mechanism

The key to our design is to use the *epoch reputation* to represent the performance of validators in committees, including the resources and behaviors. Our incentive mechanism includes three parts: malicious behaviors, epoch reputation and rewards allocation.

Malicious Behaviors. HotDAG can detect three malicious behaviors: malicious votes, conflicting blocks and double-spending transactions. We can judge whether a validator is malicious through the first two behaviors. If a leader receives a vote that violates the voting rules, it can conclude that the validator who sends the vote is malicious. If a node receives two different blocks with the same round that are proposed by the same validator, it can conclude that this validator proposes conflicting blocks. The leader can propose a block with the evidence of malicious behaviors. Finally, double-spending transactions can be easily detected in LOG: transactions in LOG that cost the same input. For nodes who have sent double-spending transactions, we can increase the cost of malicious behaviors by increasing its transaction fee.

Epoch Reputation. Inspired by Accountable-Subgroup Multisignatures Scheme [28], we assume that a quorum certificate(QC) contains the identity information of $2f + 1$ voters. [28] guarantees that leaders cannot forge the identity information. After the epoch ends for a period of time, any node can calculate the epoch reputation because the proposer and voters of a block are recorded on the transaction chains. The epoch reputation of the validator i is calculated according to *Algorithm* 1 and notations are defined in Table 2 . It is worth noting that $Y \in \{0, 1\}$ represents the honesty of the validator. It is '1' for each new validator and it is set to '0' if the validator has misbehaved[1]. For the validator i, x_i is the standard score (z-score) and r_i is the epoch reputation. It should be noted that the epoch reputation will not be accumulated, that is, the epoch reputation previously obtained by the validator will not have any impact on rewards allocation of the current epoch (unless malicious behaviors of the node has been detected).

Block Rewards and Transaction Fees. Similar to Bitcoin, there are two kinds of rewards in HotDAG: block rewards and transaction fees. We assume that a committee confirmed L blocks in epoch e, and LOG grew S blocks during this period. The basic block rewards is R_b and the total transaction fees in epoch e are F. We assume that A $(A > 1)$ is the rewards parameter and the rewards for the validator i is:

$$R_i = F * \frac{r_i}{\Sigma_{i=1}^c r_i} + (1 + \frac{L}{S} * A) * R_b * l_i \tag{1}$$

Table 2. Notations of incentive mechanism

Notation	Explanation
γ	Epoch reputation parameter
c	The size of committee
L	The length of the *t-chain* generated in the current epoch
v_i	The number of the i-th validator's votes[a]
l_i	The number of blocks that are proposed by the i-th validator
Y	Whether the validator is honest("1") or not ("0")

[a] The vote is not included when it is the leader.

---

[1] It includes sending malicious votes and proposing conflicting blocks.

Algorithm 1. Epoch reputation

Require: $c, L, \{v_i\}_{i=1}^c, \{l_i\}_{i=1}^c, \{Y_i\}_{i=1}^c, \gamma.$

1: $mean_v = \frac{\Sigma_{i=1}^c v_i}{c}$

2: $mean_l = \frac{\Sigma_{i=1}^c l_i}{c}$

3: $s_v = \sqrt{\frac{\Sigma_{i=1}^c (v_i - mean_v)^2}{c}}$

4: $s_l = \sqrt{\frac{\Sigma_{i=1}^c (l_i - mean_l)^2}{c}}$

5: $mean_v = mean_v - \gamma * L$

6: $x_i = \frac{l_i - mean_l}{s_l} + \frac{v_i - mean_v}{s_v}$

7: $r_i = Y_i * \frac{1}{1+e^{-x_i}}$

8: **return** r_i;

5 Security Analysis

Due to the page limit, the analysis (the security on committee configuration and the security on committee consensus) can be found in [27].

6 Performance Analysis and Incentive Analysis

6.1 Performance Analysis

We use n to denote the total number of nodes, c to denote the committee size and b to denote the block size. We summarize a comparison of theoretical performance analysis with previous sharding blockchain protocols in Table 3, and the detailed analysis can be found in [27].

Table 3. A comparison of theoretical performance analysis

Communication complexity	OmniLedger	RapidChain	CycLedger	HotDAG
Identity establishment[a]	$\mathcal{O}(n^2)$	$\mathcal{O}(nc)$	$\mathcal{O}(nc)$	$\mathcal{O}(n^2)$
Committee configuration	$\mathcal{O}(n^2 + nc^2)$	$\mathcal{O}(nc)$	$\mathcal{O}(nc)$	$-^b$
Intra-committee consensus[c]	$\mathcal{O}(nc/b)$	$\mathcal{O}(nc/b)$	$\mathcal{O}(nc/b)$	$\mathcal{O}(c/b)$
Inter-committee consensus	$\mathcal{O}(n)$	$\mathcal{O}(c \log n)$	$\mathcal{O}(nc/b)$	$\mathcal{O}(n/b)$

[a]RapidChain and CycLedger achieve the lower communication complexity at the cost of weakening decentralization.

[b]There is no communication overhead.

[c] We assume that a cross-shard transaction is relative with all committees.

6.2 Incentive Analysis

To avoid the serious monopoly problem, HotDAG decouples the reputation from consensus and focuses on designing a fair incentive mechanism for the protocol that uses a threshold signature scheme. The goal of HotDAG's incentive mechanism is that the epoch reputation can correctly reflect the resources (including computing resources and network resources) of honest validators, which means that the proportion of rewards obtained by honest validators is close to the proportion of their resources. We analyze two attack strategies: the free-riding attack and the aggregation attack. Due to the page limit, the detailed analysis can be found in [27].

7 Conclusion

We present HotDAG, a hybrid consensus protocol via sharding in the permissionless model. HotDAG achieves security and scalability through a novel method consisting of four parts. First, we present a decentralized and bias-resistant committee formation protocol for sharding securely. Second, each transaction requires only one committee to run the BFT protocol and the inter-committee consensus has linear communication complexity. Third, HotDAG is strongly censorship-resistant due to the unpredictable leader rotation. Finally, we design an incentive mechanism that is compatible with the scalable BFT protocol and all rational nodes are motivated to honestly follow the protocol. In the future, we will implement and evaluate HotDAG in the real network.

Acknowledgement. This work is supported in part by the National Natural Science Foundation of China Grant No. 61972447.

References

1. Nakamoto, S.: Bitcoin: A peer-to-peer electronic cash system (2009). http://www.bitcoin.org
2. Sompolinsky, Y., Zohar, A.: Secure high-rate transaction processing in bitcoin. In: Böhme, R., Okamoto, T. (eds.) FC 2015. LNCS, vol. 8975, pp. 507–527. Springer, Heidelberg (2015). https://doi.org/10.1007/978-3-662-47854-7_32
3. Eyal, I., Gencer, A.E., Sirer, E.G., van Renesse, R.: Bitcoin-NG: a scalable blockchain protocol. In: 13th USENIX Symposium on Operating Systems Design and Implementation, pp. 45–59 (2016)
4. Sompolinsky, Y., Zohar, A.: Phantom: A scalable blockdag protocol. Cryptology ePrint Archive 2018, 104 (2018)
5. Li, C., Li, P., Xu, W., Long, F., Yao, A.C.C.: Scaling nakamoto consensus to thousands of transactions per second. CoRR, abs/1805.03870 (2018)
6. Yu, H., Nikolic, I., Hou, R., Saxena, P.: OHIE: blockchain scaling made simple. In: Proceedings of the 41st IEEE Symposium on Security and Privacy, pp. 112–127
7. Douceur, J.R.: The sybil attack. In: Druschel, P., Kaashoek, F., Rowstron, A. (eds.) IPTPS 2002. LNCS, vol. 2429, pp. 251–260. Springer, Heidelberg (2002). https://doi.org/10.1007/3-540-45748-8_24
8. Dwork, C., Naor, M.: Pricing via processing or combatting junk mail. In: Brickell, E.F. (ed.) CRYPTO 1992. LNCS, vol. 740. Springer, Heidelberg (1992). https://doi.org/10.1007/3-540-48071-4_10

9. Yu, D., Zou, Y., Yu, J., et al.: Implementing abstract MAC layer in dynamic networks. IEEE Trans. Mob. Comput. (2020). https://doi.org/10.1109/TMC.2020.2971599

10. Hua, Q.S., Shi, Y., Yu, D., et al.: Faster parallel core maintenance algorithms in dynamic graphs. IEEE Trans. Parallel Distrib. Syst. **31**(6), 1287–1300 (2020)

11. Kokoris, E., Jovanovic, P., Gailly, N., Khoffi, I., Gasser, L., Ford, B.: Enhancing bitcoin security and performance with strong consistency via collective signing. In: 25th USENIX Security Symposium, pp. 279–296 (2016)

12. Abraham, I., Malkhi, D., Nayak, K., Ren, L., Spiegelman, A.: Solida: a blockchain protocol based on reconfigurable byzantine consensus. In: 21st International Conference on Principles of Distributed Systems, pp. 25:1–25:19 (2016)

13. Pass, R., Shi, E.: Hybrid consensus: efficient consensus in the permissionless model. In: 31st International Symposium on Distributed Computing (DISC 2017), pp. 39:1–39:16. Leibniz International Proceedings in Informatics (LIPIcs) (2017)

14. Gilad, Y., Hemo, R., Micali, S., Vlachos, G., Zeldovich, N.: Algorand: Scaling byzantine agreements for cryptocurrencies. In: Proceedings of the 26th Symposium on Operating Systems Principles, pp. 51–68 (2017)

15. Zhu, S., Cai, Z., Hu, H., et al.: zkCrowd: a hybrid blockchain-based crowdsourcing platform. IEEE Trans. Ind. Inform. (TII) **16**(6), 4196–4205 (2020)

16. Luu, L., Narayanan, V., Zheng, C., Baweja, K., Gilbert, S., Saxena, P.: A secure sharding protocol for open blockchains. In: Proceedings of the 2016 ACM SIGSAC Conference on Computer and Communications Security, pp. 17–30 (2016)

17. Kokoris-Kogias, E., Jovanovic, P., Gasser, L., Gailly, N., Syta, E., Ford, B.: Omniledger: A secure, scale-out, decentralized ledger via sharding. Cryptology ePrint Archive, Report 2017/406 (2017)

18. Zamani, M., Movahedi, M., Raykova, M.: Rapidchain: scaling blockchain via full sharding. In: Proceedings of the 2018 ACM SIGSAC Conference on Computer and Communications Security, pp. 931–948 (2018)

19. Zhang, M., Li, J., Chen, Z., Chen, H., Deng, X.: Cycledger: a scalable and secure parallel protocol for distributed ledger via sharding. In: Proceedings of the 34th IEEE International Parallel and Distributed Processing Symposium (2020)

20. Buchman, E.: Tendermint: Byzantine fault tolerance in the age of blockchains. Ph.D. thesis, The University of Guelph, Guelph, Ontario, Canada, June 2016

21. Yin, M., Malkhi, D., Reiter, M.K., Gueta, G.G., Abraham, I.: Hotstuff: Bft consensus with linearity and responsiveness. In: Proceedings of the 2019 ACM Symposium on Principles of Distributed Computing (2019)

22. Desmedt, Y., Frankel, Y.: Threshold cryptosystems. In: Brassard, G. (ed.) CRYPTO 1989. LNCS, vol. 435, pp. 307–315. Springer, New York (1990). https://doi.org/10.1007/0-387-34805-0_28

23. Shoup, V.: Practical threshold signatures. In: Preneel, B. (ed.) EUROCRYPT 2000. LNCS, vol. 1807, pp. 207–220. Springer, Heidelberg (2000). https://doi.org/10.1007/3-540-45539-6_15

24. Boneh, D., Lynn, B., Shacham, H.: Short signatures from the Weil pairing. In: Boyd, C. (ed.) ASIACRYPT 2001. LNCS, vol. 2248, pp. 514–532. Springer, Heidelberg (2001). https://doi.org/10.1007/3-540-45682-1_30

25. Castro, M., Liskov, B.: Practical byzantine fault tolerance. In: Proceedings of the Third USENIX Symposium on Operating Systems Design and Implementation, pp. 173–186 (1999)

26. Micali, S., Rabin, M., Vadhan, S.: Verifiable random functions. In: 40th Annual Symposium on Foundations of Computer Science (Cat. No. 99CB37039) (1999)

27. Zhou, C.X., Hua, Q.S., Jin, H.: HotDAG: Hybrid consensus via sharding in the permissionless model. https://qiangshenghua.github.io/papers/hotdag.pdf
28. Boneh, D., Drijvers, M., Neven, G.: Compact multi-signatures for smaller blockchains. In: Peyrin, T., Galbraith, S. (eds.) ASIACRYPT 2018. LNCS, vol. 11273, pp. 435–464. Springer, Cham (2018). https://doi.org/10.1007/978-3-030-03329-3_15
29. Archetti, M., Scheuring, I.: Review: game theory of public goods in one-shot social dilemmas without assortment. J. Theoret. Biol. **299**, 9–20 (2012)

Distributed Data Aggregation in Dynamic Sensor Networks

Yifei Zou[1,2], Minghui Xu[3], Yicheng Xu[1], Yong Zhang[1], Bei Gong[4],
and Xiaoshuang Xing[5(✉)]

[1] Shenzhen Institutes of Advanced Technology, Chinese Academy of Sciences,
Shenzhen, People's Republic of China
{yf.zou,yc.xu,zhangyong}@siat.ac.cn
[2] Department of Computer Science, The University of Hong Kong,
Hong Kong, People's Republic of China
yfzou@cs.hku.hk
[3] Department of Computer Science, The George Washington University,
Washington DC, USA
mhxu@gwu.edu
[4] Faculty of Information Technology, Beijing University of Technology, Beijing, China
gongbei@bjut.edu.cn
[5] Department of Computer Science and Engineering, Changshu Institute
of Technology, Changshu, People's Republic of China
xing@cslg.edu.cn

Abstract. In the past decades, dynamic sensor networks have played a
conspicuously more important role in many real-life areas, including disaster relief, environment monitoring, public safety and so on, to rapidly
collect information from the environment and help people to make the
decision. Meanwhile, due to the widespread implementation of dynamic
sensor networks, there exists an enormous demand on designing suitable
models and efficient algorithms for fundamental operations in dynamic
sensor networks, such as the data aggregation from mobile sensors to the
base station. In this paper, we firstly present a general dynamic model
to comprehensively depict most of the dynamic phenomena in sensor
networks. Then, based on the proposed dynamic model, an efficient distributed data aggregation algorithm is proposed to aggregate k messages
from sensors to the base station within $O(k)$ time steps in expectation
and $O(k + \log n)$ time steps with high probability. Rigid theoretical analysis and extensive simulations are presented to verify the efficacy of our
proposed algorithm.

Keywords: Data aggregation · Distributed algorithms · Dynamic
sensor networks

This work is partially supported by National Key R&D Program of China with grant
No. 2019YFB2102303 and NSFC (No. 61971014, No. 11675199).

© Springer Nature Switzerland AG 2020
D. Yu et al. (Eds.): WASA 2020, LNCS 12384, pp. 822–833, 2020.
https://doi.org/10.1007/978-3-030-59016-1_67

1   Introduction

In recent years, with the dynamic sensor networks extensively exploited for many environment monitoring scenarios, there exists an enormous demand on designing realistic models and efficient algorithms for dynamic sensor networks. In reality, the dynamicity in dynamic sensor networks mainly comes from the unpredictable mobility and churns of sensor nodes. Specifically, when sensor nodes are collecting information from the environment or do the monitoring, they can move at will in the network area, which is termed as the mobility of sensors. Compared with the sensor networks in which nodes are fixed in their specific locations, the mobility of sensor nodes makes it possible for collecting more useful information from the environment with less sensor nodes. Thus, it can greatly facilitate the efficiency of sensor networks. The churns of sensor nodes include the sleeping/waking up, breaking down/recovering, and arriving/leaving behaviours of nodes, which is nearly impossible to avoid especially for some large scale sensor networks. Obviously, the mobility and churns of nodes can lead to dramatic changes on the topology of networks, the local contention and global interference for transmissions in channel. Thus, for the research on dynamic sensor networks, a general dynamic model to comprehensively depict the mobility and churns of nodes is always the first step, and an efficient design on the data aggregation from sensor nodes to the base station in dynamic sensor networks will be a good starting point.

In this paper, we propose a new dynamic model to cover most of the dynamic behaviours of nodes in dynamic sensor networks. Based on the dynamic model, a realistic data aggregation problem is considered. Specifically, only the location of the base station is fixed. All sensor nodes can move at will in network area to collect the information from the environment or do the monitoring[1]. Churns may occurs at any node at any moment. When sensor nodes are within the transmission range of the base station, they try to send their collected information to the base station.

Contribution. In this work, we firstly propose a comprehensive dynamic model to depict most of the dynamic behaviours in dynamic sensor networks. Then, an efficient data aggregation algorithm is presented, which can aggregate k messages from sensor nodes to the base station within $O(k)$ time steps in expectation and $O(k + \log n)$ time steps with high probability, i.e., with probability $1 - n^{-c}$ for some constant $c > 0$, also termed as w.h.p. for short. Obviously, the performance of our algorithm in terms of time complexity is already asymptotically optimal considering that the base station can only receive one message in each time step because of the contention in transmission and the lower bound $\Omega(\log n)$ to guanrantee that a randomized transmission succeeds w.h.p., which has already been proved in [23,33]. The beauty of our work lies in that, even under a general dynamic model without any severe restriction on the dynamicity of nodes, we still design an asymptotically optimal algorithm in terms of time complexity for the data aggregation from sensor nodes to the base station. Also, the skills of

---

[1] In usual, the movements of nodes are decided by their collection/monitoring tasks.

fully making use of physical carrier sensing presented in this paper shed some new sights on researches about wireless communications.

Related Work. In the past decades, the research in wireless sensor networks focuses on many hot topics [1,2,8,19,20,26,29,30], one of which is the dynamic sensor networks. Due to the popularity of dynamic sensor networks, many dynamic models have been proposed to reflect the dynamicity in wireless networks. To depict the insertions of nodes in network, a series of unstructured models are proposed in [7,12,18] under the SINR model, the unit disk graph model, and the bounded independence graph model, respectively. Another model was proposed in [3] to consider the node crash failures. Also, some dynamic models are proposed to consider the impact of unreliable links with the assumption of static nodes, including the dual graph model in [4,10], the T-interval connectivity model in [11], and the pairing model in [5,6]. The dual graph model defines two graphs on the same node set, and separates the links into two graphs according to the reliability of them. The T-interval connectivity model has a constraint that there is a stable connected spanning subgraph in network during each interval of T rounds. The pairing model requires that the links in the network constitute a matching at each round. Obviously, those models on dynamic links ignore the dynamicity of nodes and some of them have severe assumptions, which makes them unrealistic. More recently, Yu *et al.* in [27,31] proposed a dynamic model that considers both dynamic nodes and links, under the SINR model. However, this model is a very theoretical one and can not directly map to the dynamic behaviours in reality. A survey on dynamic network models was given in [13].

In the past dacades, there has already been some distributed researches on data aggregation problem based on graph model [9,14,21,22,24] and SINR model [15–17,32]. The paper in [9] is the first work achieves the $O(\Delta + R)$ aggregation time complexity lower bound, in which Δ is the maximal node degree and R is the network radius in hops. In the following years, works in [14,22], reach the time complexity of $O(\Delta + R')$ and $\Delta + 16R - 14$ for data aggregation, where $R/2 \leq R' \leq R$ is the inferior network radius. Also, in [24], the data aggregation problem was extended to the cases with multiple sinks with time complexity of $O(\Delta + kR)$, in which k is the number of sinks. Recently, the data aggregation problem is also considered under the more realistic SINR interference model with the time complexity of $O(\Delta + R)$ in [17] and $O(K)$ in [15], in which K is the logarithm of the ratio between he length of the longest link and that of the shortest link. It deserve to note that with the help of successive interference cancellation technique, the work in [16] reaches the time complexity of $O(D)$, where D is the diameter of the network. However, none of them considered the data aggregation problem in dynamic networks. Whether the above works can still reach a well performance in a dynamic environment is unknown.

2   Model

We model our dynamic sensor network in a 2-dimensional Euclidean space. All n nodes in sensor network are initially arbitrarily deployed in the transmission range of the base station. The time in our algorithm execution is divided into rounds, each of which contains constant slots. A slot is the time unit for base station/nodes to send or receive a message. Also, it is assumed that the transmissions between base station and sensor nodes in a slot are synchronized.

Communication Model. The SINR model is adopted here to depict the contention and interference generated by simultaneous transmissions between base station and nodes in the multiple access channel. Specifically, in each slot, let's use the transmitters/receivers to denote the base station and nodes who transmit/listen in current slot, respectively. For any receiver v, let $Signal(v)$ be the value of the signal at v. Then, each transmitter in current slot contributes to the strength of the signal at v, as is illustrated by SINR equation 1. v can receive the message from transmitter u if v's SINR rate $SINR(u,v)$ is no smaller than β, the detail of which is given in SINR equation 2.

$$Signal(v) = \sum_{w \in S} P_w \cdot d(w,v)^{-\alpha} + N, \tag{1}$$

$$SINR(u,v) = \frac{P_u \cdot d(u,v)^{-\alpha}}{\sum_{w \in S \setminus \{u\}} P_w \cdot d(w,v)^{-\alpha} + N}. \tag{2}$$

In the above SINR equations, S is the set of transmitters in current slot; for each transmitter w, P_w is the transmission power, and $d(w,v)$ is the Euclidean distance between w and v; Path-loss exponent α and ambient noise N are constants determined by the environment. When $SINR(u,v) \geq \beta$, v can decode the message from u, where β is a threshold determined by hardware. In usual, $\alpha \in (2,6]$ and $\beta > 1$, and we also have this assumption in our work.

The base station and all nodes has a maximum transmission power P in transmission, and they can choose a transmission power no larger than P to transmit a message in each slot. The transmission range R of a receiver v is defined as the maximum distance at which v can receive a message from a transmitter u. Then, according to the SINR equations, $R = (P/\beta N)^{1/\alpha}$.

Dynamic Model. A very general dynamic model is proposed here to depict various dynamic behaviours in dynamic sensor networks. It is assumed that sensor nodes can move at will in sensor networks to collect data from the environment. And churns may occur at any node. The only fixed point in our model is that location of the base station is unchanged. Roundly-based dynamicity is assumed in our model, i.e., all dynamic behaviours of sensor nodes occur at the end of each round, before the starting of the next round.

Capability and Knowledge of Nodes. Asynchronous wakeup mode is assumed for nodes, which means that the sleeping nodes can wake up at the end of any round. When initially waking up, nodes know nothing about the network and the environment. All the necessary parameters a node needed in algorithm execution are gradually learnt by itself from the signals received in the channel. All nodes and the base station are equipped with a half-duplex transceiver with physical carrier sensing. Thus, each node and the base station can transmit or listen on each slot but cannot do both.

3 Algorithm Description

As is mentioned above, all nodes initially asynchronous wakeup in the transmission range a base station. Then, nodes can move at will, maybe out of the transmission range of the base station to collect the data from the environment, and then back later to report the data to the base station. When a waked up node is within the transmission range of the base station, we term it as an *active node*. Otherwise, we say it is an inactive node. In each round, the active nodes always try to send the collected data to the base station; and the base station always prepare to receive the data from the active nodes. The main challenge in our algorithm is how to estimate the number of active nodes, and then properly handle the contention of the active nodes under a dynamic setting by a distributed scheme. In the previous works without considering the dynamic scenarios, there are two classical solutions. One is to collect the ID of the active nodes one by one, (e.g. [25]) and the other is to estimate the number of active nodes according to the history information of the transmissions in channel (e.g. [28,29]), both of which at least cost $\Omega(\Delta + \log n)$ time steps w.h.p. considering the worst cases. However, in our general dynamic model, the number of active nodes can dramatically change at the end of each round. The number of active nodes estimated by the classical solutions is out-of-date or even wrong. Fortunately, by a good tuning on the transmission power and fully making use of the accumulated signals from all active nodes, we propose a real-time scheme to estimate the number of active nodes, which helps to handle the contention of the transmissions within the transmission range of the base station. The pseudo-codes for the base station and all the nodes are given in Algorithms 1 and 2, specifically.

Algorithm 1: Data aggregation algorithm for base station

In each round, base station v does:

Initialization: $N_1(v) = N_2(v) = 0$;
Slot 1: Transmit a message with transmission power P;
Slot 2: Listen; $N_1(v) = signal(v)$;
Slot 3: Listen; $N_2(v) = signal(v)$; $X = \frac{N_2(v)}{N_1(v)} - 1$;
Slot 4: Transmit the value of X with transmission power P;
Slot 5: Listen; **if** received a data from sensor nodes, **then** store it;

The base station v and all active nodes u cooperate together in slots 1–3 to achieve the real-time estimation on the number of active nodes. Specifically, v transmits a message with the transmission power P in slot 1. As is proved in the next section, all active nodes and only active nodes can receive the message from the base station v in slot 1. Thus, when receiving a message from v, a sensor node u knows that it is an active node within the transmission range of v and sets it state to $\mathbb{A}$, i.e., $state_u = \mathbb{A}$. Otherwise, u is not an active node and $state_u = \mathbb{I}$. Only active nodes execute the following algorithms in slot 2–5 and inactive nodes do nothing in the remaining slots of current round. In slot 2, both the base station and the active nodes listen in channel, and record the value of ambient noise N by parameter N_1. In slot 3, by a good tuning on the transmission power, each active node u transmits a message to make sure that the signal from u has the strength of N at the base station v according to the SINR Eq. 1. So, if there are totally X active nodes in current round, the strength of the signal received by base station v is $(X + 1)N$ because of the feature of accumulation for wireless signal. Meanwhile in slot 3, v listens and senses the value of received signal N_2 by physical carrier sensing. So, v can estimate the number of active nodes by letting $X = \frac{N_2}{N_1} - 1$. In slot 4, base station v broadcasts the value of X to all active nodes. In slot 5, each active node transmits its data with transmission power $\frac{PN_1}{N_2-N_1}$ and with probability $1/X$. Thus, in each round, we can see that the contention of active nodes in data aggregation is a constant in expectation even under a dynamic setting, and the base station successfully receives a message from the active nodes at least with a constant probability.

Algorithm 2: Data aggregation algorithm for sensor nodes

In each round, sensor node u does:

Initialization: $state_u = \mathbb{I}$; $N_1(u) = N_2(u) = 0$;

Slot 1: Listen; $N_2(u) = signal(u)$; **if** received a message from the base station, **then** $state_u = \mathbb{A}$;

Slot 2: **if** $state_u == \mathbb{A}$, **then** listen, and $N_1(u) = signal(v)$;

Slot 3: **if** $state_u == \mathbb{A}$, **then** transmit with transmission power $\frac{PN_1(u)}{N_2(u)-N_1(u)}$;

Slot 4: Listen; **if** $state_u == \mathbb{A}$ and received a message with the value of X, **then** $p_u = 1/X$;

Slot 5: **if** $state_u == \mathbb{A}$, **then** transmit with transmission power $\frac{PN_1(u)}{N_2(u)-N_1(u)}$ with probability p_u;

---

4   Algorithm Analysis

In this section, we analyze the correctness and efficiency of our algorithm.

Lemma 1. *In slot 1, when the base station v transmits with transmission power P, all active nodes and only active nodes receive the message from v.*

Proof. Note that a node is called an active node if it is within the transmission range of the base station. Otherwise, it is an inactive node. For any active node u, inactive node w, and the base station v, we have $d(u, v) \leq R$ and $d(w, v) > R$. Then, according to the SINR equation 2, when only v transmits with transmission power P in slot 1, $SINR(v, u) \geq \beta$ and $SINR(v, w) < \beta$, which directly proves the lemma.

According to our algorithm, in slot 1, an active node u senses the channel to get the strength of the received signal in channel, and stores it in parameter $N_2(u)$. If it successfully receives the message from base station in slot 1, it sets $state_u = \mathbb{A}$, and execute the algorithms in slots 2–5.

In slot 2, both of the base station v and active nodes u sense the channel to get the value of the ambient noise in current round, which is stored in the parameter $N_1(v)$, $N_1(u)$.

Lemma 2. *If there are Y active nodes transmitting in slot 3, equation $Y = \frac{N_2(v)}{N_1(v)} - 1$ holds.*

Proof. In slot 3, each active node u transmits with the transmission power $\frac{PN_1(u)}{N_2(u)-N_1(u)}$. The base station sense the channel and store the strength of the received signal in parameter $N_2(v)$. Obviously, $N_1(v) = N_1(u) = N$, which is the ambient noise in the environment. $N_2(u) = \frac{P}{d(u,v)^\alpha} + N$. Let S be the set of active nodes in slot 3, then, we have

$$N_2(v) = \sum_{u \in S} P_u \cdot d(u,v)^{-\alpha} + N = \sum_{u \in S} \frac{PN_1(u)}{N_2(u) - N_1(u)} \cdot d(u,v)^{-\alpha} + N$$

$$= \sum_{u \in S} \frac{PN_1(u)}{P \cdot d(u,v)^{-\alpha} + N - N_1(u)} \cdot d(u,v)^{-\alpha} + N$$

$$= \sum_{u \in S} \frac{PN}{P \cdot d(u,v)^{-\alpha}} \cdot d(u,v)^{-\alpha} + N = (Y+1)N$$

According to the value of $N_1(v)$, $N_2(v)$, $N_1(u)$, and $N_2(u)$, the equation $Y = \frac{N_2(v)}{N_1(v)} - 1$ holds.

Thus, by setting $X = \frac{N_2(v)}{N_1(v)} - 1$, the base station v can exactly estimate the number of active nodes in current round.

Lemma 3. *In slot 4, when the base station transmits with transmission power P, all active nodes receive the message from the base station.*

The proof of Lemma 3 is similar with that of Lemma 1. With Lemma 3, we can see that each active node knows the number of active nodes in current round.

Lemma 4. *In slot 5, when the base station transmits with transmission power $\frac{PN_1(u)}{N_2(u)-N_1(u)}$ with probability $p_u = 1/X$, the base station v receive a message from the active nodes at least with a constant probability.*

Proof. Let event $\mathcal{E}_0$ be the event that base station v receives a message from the active nodes, and $Pr(\mathcal{E}_0)$ be the probability event $\mathcal{E}_0$ occurs in slot 5. According to our SINR model, a sufficient condition for event $\mathcal{E}_0$ to occur is that there is only one active node u transmitted in slot 5. Thus,

$$Pr(\mathcal{E}_0) \geq \sum_{u \in S} p_u \cdot \Pi_{w \in S \setminus \{u\}} (1 - p_w) \geq \sum_{u \in S} p_u \cdot (1/4)^{\sum_{w \in S \setminus \{u\}} p_w}$$

$$\geq \sum_{u \in S} \frac{1}{X} \cdot (1/4)^{1-1/X} \geq 1/4,$$

in which S is the set of active nodes in slot 5.

Theorem 1. *For any given positive integer* k, *our algorithm aggregates* k *messages from the active nodes within* $O(k)$ *round in expectation and within* $O(k + \log n)$ *rounds with high probability.*

Proof. From Lemma 4, we can directly get the result that the expectation time to aggregate k message is no larger than $4k$ rounds.

Also, consider a interval T with length of I. Define variable $x(t)$ as follows

$$x(t) = \begin{cases} 0 & \text{the base station receives nothing in slot 5 of round t} \\ 1 & \text{the base station receives data from nodes in slot 5 of round t} \end{cases}$$

Let μ be the expectation of $\sum_{t \in T} x(t)$. We can get that $\mu = \mathbb{E}\left[\sum_{t \in T} x(t)\right] = \sum_{t \in T} Pr(\mathcal{E}_0) \geq I/4$. Applying the Chernoff bound with a constant $\delta \in (0, 1)$:

$$Pr(\sum_{t \in T} x(t) \leq (1 - \delta)I/4) \leq Pr(\sum_{t \in T} x(t) \leq (1 - \delta)\mu) \leq e^{-\frac{\delta^2 \mu}{3}}.$$

By setting $I = \frac{4k + \log n}{1 - \delta}$, we get that

$$Pr(\sum_{t \in T} x(t) \leq k) \leq Pr(\sum_{t \in T} x(t) \leq k + \log n/4) \leq e^{-\frac{\delta^2 \mu}{3}} \leq e^{-\frac{\delta^2 (4k + \log n)}{12(1 - \delta)}}$$

$$\leq e^{-\frac{\delta^2}{12(1 - \delta)} \log n} = (1/n)^{\frac{\delta^2}{12(1 - \delta)}}.$$

So, we prove that within $O(k + \log n)$ rounds, k messages are aggregated to the base station with high probability.

5   Simulation Result

In this section, empirical performances of our data aggregation algorithm are presented. Specifically, we focus on the number of rounds used to aggregate k messages from sensor nodes when the network size, the number of aggregated messages and the dynamic level of the sensor network vary.

Table 1. Parameters in simulation

Parameter	Value	Parameter	Value
N	1.0	P	$R^\alpha \beta N$
α	3.0	n	$\in [1000, 10000]$
β	2.0	k	$\in [1000, 10000]$
R	$30m$	λ	$\in \{0.2, 0.4, 0.6, 0.8\}$

Dynamic Pattern. To depict the various dynamic behaviours including movements and churns of sensor nodes, two state $\mathcal{S}_0$ and $\mathcal{S}_1$ are set for the nodes in our simulation. When a node is working in the network, it is in state S_1. When a node in S_1 sleeps, breaks down, or leaves the network, it changes its state to S_0. When a node in state S_0 wakes up, recovers from the breaking down, or joins the network, it changes its state to S_1. Dynamic parameter λ is used to depict the dynamic level of sensor network. At the end of each round, each node in state S_0 or S_1 has the probability of λ to change to another state. And all nodes have the probability λ to move to another random position.

Parameter Setting. In the simulation, we randomly and uniformly implement n nodes and a base station into a network with the area of $300\,\mathrm{m} \times 300\,\mathrm{m}$. All nodes are initially in state S_0 (sleeping) and asynchronous wake up with probability λ. The ambient noise N is normalized as 1.0. The value of SINR parameters α, β and some other parameters are given in Table 1

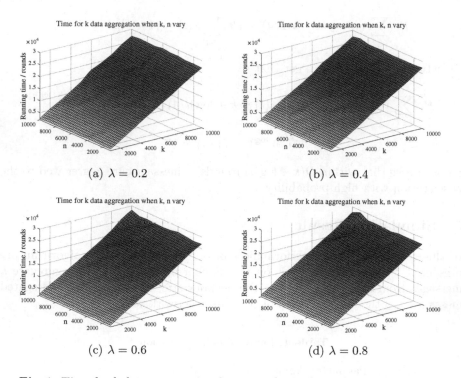

(a) $\lambda = 0.2$

(b) $\lambda = 0.4$

(c) $\lambda = 0.6$

(d) $\lambda = 0.8$

Fig. 1. Time for k data aggregation from n nodes in dynamic sensor networks

Algorithm Performance. The time our algorithm used for k data aggregation from n nodes in dynamic networks with various dynamic levels is given in Fig. 1 (a)–(d), in which the x-axis, y-axis, and z-axis represent the number of aggregated date k, the number of nodes in network n, and the number of rounds used for k data aggregation, respectively. From Fig. 1, two conclusions can be drawn:

(I). The time for k data aggregation linearly increases when k gets larger, n and λ unchanged, which validates our theoretical results of $O(k)$ rounds in expectation and $O(k + \log n)$ rounds w.h.p. for k data aggregation. Also, those curves indicates that the constant hides behind the O in our theoretical results is no larger than 3;

(II). The performance of our algorithm is insensitive to the number of nodes and the dynamic levels in networks. Obviously, when n and λ vary in cases with a same value of k, the time for k data aggregation is similar. Thus, it is believed that even when the number of nodes and the dynamic level of the sensor network dramatically change, the performance of our algorithm can still be guaranteed;

6   Conclusion

In this paper, we present a general dynamic model to comprehensively depict the various dynamic behaviours of sensor nodes in dynamic sensor networks. Based on the proposed model, a distributed data aggregation algorithm is proposed to collect k messages from n nodes to the base station within $O(k)$ time steps in expectation and $O(k + \log n)$ time steps w.h.p., which is asymptotically optimal in terms of time complexity. Also, it deserves to note that no priori knowledge is required for sensor nodes in our algorithm and nodes can get all the necessary information to execute the algorithm by sensing the channel. Thus, our algorithm can be applied in a very widely scenarios.

In this paper, we fully make use of the accumulative signals from multiple sensor nodes to estimate the number of nodes within the transmission range of the base station. It is very likely that this skill can be combined with NOMA technique to facilitate some primitives in wireless network, such as leader election, local broadcast and backbone construction, which can be an interesting future research direction.

References

1. Cheng, S., Cai, Z., Li, J.: Curve query processing in wireless sensor networks. IEEE Trans. Veh. Technol. **64**(11), 5198–5209 (2015)
2. Cheng, S., Cai, Z., Li, J., Fang, X.: Drawing dominant dataset from big sensory data in wireless sensor networks. In: INFOCOM (2015)
3. Chlebus, B.S., Kowalski, D.R., Strojnowski, M.: Fast scalable deterministic consensus for crash failures. In: PODC (2009)
4. Clementi, A.E.F., Monti, A., Silvestri, R.: Round robin is optimal for fault-tolerant broadcasting on wireless networks. J. Parallel Distrib. Comput. **64**(1), 89–96 (2004)
5. Cornejo, A., Gilbert, S., Newport, C.: Aggregation in dynamic networks. In: PODC (2012)
6. Dinitz, M., Fineman, J.T., Gilbert, S., Newport, C.: Smoothed analysis of dynamic networks. Distrib. Comput. **31**(4), 273–287 (2017). https://doi.org/10.1007/s00446-017-0300-8
7. Goussevskaia, O., Moscibroda, T., Wattenhofer, R.: Local broadcasting in the physical interference model. In: DIALM-POMC (2008)

8. He, Z., Cai, Z., Cheng, S., Wang, X.: Approximate aggregation for tracking quantiles and range countings in wireless sensor networks. Theor. Comput. Sci. **607**(3), 381–390 (2015)

9. Huang, S.C.H., Wan, P.J., Vu, C.T., Li, Y., Yao, F.: Nearly constant approximation for data aggregation scheduling in wireless sensor networks. In: INFOCOM (2007)

10. Kuhn, F., Lynch, N.A., Newport, C.C.: Brief announcement: hardness of broadcasting in wireless networks with unreliable communication. In: PODC (2009)

11. Kuhn, F., Lynch, N.A., Oshman, R.: Distributed computation in dynamic networks. In: STOC (2010)

12. Kuhn, F., Moscibroda, T., Wattenhofer, R.: Initializing newly deployed ad hoc and sensor networks. In: MOBICOM (2004)

13. Kuhn, F., Oshman, R.: Dynamic networks: models and algorithms. SUGACT **42**(1), 82–96 (2011)

14. Li, Y., Guo, L., Prasad, S.K.: An energy-efficient distributed algorithm for minimum-latency aggregation scheduling in wireless sensor networks. In: ICDCS (2010)

15. Li, H., Hua, Q.-S., Wu, C., Lau, F.C.M.: Minimum-latency aggregation scheduling in wireless sensor networks under physical interference model. In: MSWiM (2010)

16. Li, H., Wu, C., Yu, D., Hua, Q.-S., Lau, F.C.M.: Aggregation latency-energy tradeoff in wireless sensor networks with successive interference cancellation. IEEE Trans. Parallel Distrib. Syst. **24**(11), 2160–2170 (2013)

17. Li, X.Y., et al.: Efficient data aggregation in multi-hop wireless sensor networks under physical interference model. In: MASS (2009)

18. Schneider, J., Wattenhofer, R.: Coloring unstructured wireless multihop networks. In: PODC (2009)

19. Shi, T., Li, J., Gao, H., Cai, Z.: Coverage in battery-free wireless sensor networks. In: INFOCOM (2018)

20. Shi, T., Cheng, S., Li, J., Gao, H., Cai, Z.: Dominating sets construction in RF-based battery-free sensor networks with full coverage guarantee. ACM Trans. Sens. Netw. **15**(4), 43:1–43:29 (2019)

21. Wan, P.J., Huang, S.C.H., Wang, L.X., Wan, Z.Y., Jia, X.H.: Minimum-latency aggregation scheduling in multihop wireless networks. In: MOBIHOC (2009)

22. Xu, X., Li, X.-Y., Mao, X., Tang, S., Wang, S.: A delay-efficient algorithm for data aggregation in multihop wireless sensor networks. IEEE Trans. Parallel Distrib. Syst. **22**(1), 163–175 (2011)

23. Yu, D., Hua, Q., Wang, Y., Lau, F.C.M.: An O(log n) distributed approximation algorithm for local broadcasting in unstructured wireless networks. In: DCOSS 2012 (2012)

24. Yu, B., Li, J.: Minimum-time aggregation scheduling in multi-sink sensor networks. In: SECON (2011)

25. Yu, D., Ning, L., Zou, Y., Yu, J., Cheng, X., Lau, F.C.M.: Distributed spanner construction with physical interference: constant stretch and linear sparseness. IEEE/ACM Trans. Netw. **25**(4), 2138–2151 (2017)

26. Yu, J., Yu, K., Yu, D., Lv, W., Cheng, X., Chen, H., Cheng, W.: Efficient link scheduling in wireless networks under Rayleigh-fading and multiuser interference. IEEE Trans. Wirel. Commun. (2020). https://doi.org/10.1109/TWC.2020.2994998

27. Yu, D., Wang, Y., Halldórsson, M.M., Tonoyan, T.: Dynamic adaptation in wireless networks under comprehensive interference via carrier sense. In: IPDPS (2017)

28. Yu, D., Zhang, Y., Huang, Y., Jin, H., Yu, J., Hua, Q.: Exact implementation of abstract MAC layer via carrier sensing. In: INFOCOM (2018)

29. Yu, D., et al.: Stable local broadcast in multihop wireless networks under SINR. IEEE/ACM Trans. Netw. **26**(3), 1278–1291 (2018)
30. Yu, D., et al.: Implementing abstract MAC layer in dynamic networks. IEEE Trans. Mob. Comput. (2020). https://doi.org/10.1109/TMC.2020.2971599
31. Yu, D., et al.: Distributed dominating set and connected dominating set construction under the dynamic SINR Model. In: IPDPS (2019)
32. Zhang, S., Zhang, H., Di, B., Song, L.: Joint trajectory and power optimization for UAV sensing over cellular networks. IEEE Commun. Lett. **22**(11), 2382–2385 (2018)
33. Zou, Y., et al.: Fast distributed backbone construction despite strong adversarial jamming. In: INFOCOM (2019)

39. Su, L., et al.: Whole body and localized in additions selected network, under SDN. IEEE/ACM Trans. Netw. 2016, 1794-1794 (2016).
40. Yang, et al.: In place topic abstract DNA flow in top place network for IEEE/Trans. Mob. Comput. 15(5) https://doi.org/10.1109/TMC.2045.02.1558
41. Xu, B., et al.: Distributed domain big-sex and optimal design in net consumer flow under-line system. SNPS 2 vol. No. 3(2)-453439).
42. Zhang, P., Zhang, B., Li, et al., Feng, L.: Sensor networks and power optimization. In: VAN exchange or ceiling interaction. DEL Commun. LXR 32(11)-8189-7562 (2016).
43. Qian, Y., et al.: User distribution rank cooperation flow them decode Mong. refer virtual. See http://doi.org/10.1109/DNPD.XDV.(2)0.2.

Author Index

Printed in the United States
By Bookmasters

Printed in the United States
By Bookmasters